| PRESCHOOL PERIOD (3 to 6 years) | MIDDLE CHILDHOOD (6 to 12 years) |
|---|---|
| • Height and weight continue to increase rapidly.<br>• The body becomes less rounded and more muscular.<br>• The brain grows larger, neural interconnections continue to develop, and lateralization emerges.<br>• Gross and fine motor skills advance quickly. Children can throw and catch balls, run, use forks and spoons, and tie shoelaces.<br>• Children begin to develop handedness. | • Growth becomes slow and steady. Muscles develop, and "baby fat" is lost.<br>• Gross motor skills (biking, swimming, skating, ball handling) and fine motor skills (writing, typing, fastening buttons) continue to improve.<br>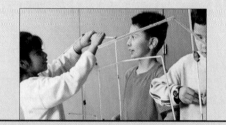 |
| • Children show egocentric thinking (viewing world from their own perspective) and "centration," a focus on only one aspect of a stimulus.<br>• Memory, attention span, and symbolic thinking improve, and intuitive thought begins.<br>• Language (sentence length, vocabulary, syntax, and grammar) improves rapidly.<br> | • Children apply logical operations to problems.<br>• Understanding of conservation (that changes in shape do not necessarily affect quantity) and transformation (that objects can go through many states without changing) emerge.<br>• Children can "decenter"—take multiple perspectives into account.<br>• Memory encoding, storage, and retrieval improve, and control strategies (meta-memory) develop.<br>• Language pragmatics (social conventions) and metalinguistic awareness (self-monitoring) improve. |
| • Children develop self-concepts, which may be exaggerated.<br>• A sense of gender and racial identity emerges.<br>• Children begin to see peers as individuals and form friendships based on trust and shared interests.<br>• Morality is rule-based and focused on rewards and punishments.<br>• Play becomes more constructive and cooperative, and social skills become important. | • Children refer to psychological traits to define themselves. Sense of self becomes differentiated.<br>• Social comparison is used to understand one's standing and identity.<br>• Self-esteem grows differentiated, and a sense of self-efficacy (an appraisal of what one can and cannot do) develops.<br>• Children approach moral problems intent on maintaining social respect and accepting what society defines as right.<br>• Friendship patterns of boys and girls differ. Boys mostly interact with boys in groups, and girls tend to interact singly or in pairs with other girls. |
| Preoperational stage | Concrete operational stage |
| Initiative-versus-guilt stage | Industry-versus-inferiority stage |
| Phallic stage | Latency period |
| Preconventional morality level | Conventional morality level |

|  | **ADOLESCENCE**<br>(12 to 20 years) | **YOUNG ADULTHOOD**<br>(20 to 40 years) |
|---|---|---|
| **PHYSICAL DEVELOPMENT** | • Girls begin the adolescent growth spurt around age 10, boys around age 12.<br>• Girls reach puberty around age 11 or 12, boys around age 13 or 14.<br>• Primary sexual characteristics develop (affecting the reproductive organs), as do secondary sexual characteristics (pubic and underarm hair in both sexes, breasts in girls, deep voices in boys). | • Physical capabilities peak in the 20's, including strength, senses, coordination, and reaction time.<br>• Growth is mostly complete, although some organs, including the brain, continue to grow.<br>• For many young adults, obesity becomes a threat for the first time, as body fat increases.<br>• Stress can become a significant health threat.<br>• In the mid-30's, disease replaces accidents as the leading cause of death. |
| **COGNITIVE DEVELOPMENT** | • Abstract thought prevails. Adolescents use formal logic to consider problems in the abstract.<br>• Relative, not absolute, thinking is typical.<br>• Verbal, mathematical, and spatial skills improve.<br>• Adolescents are able to think hypothetically, divide attention, and monitor thought through meta-cognition.<br>• Egocentrism develops, with a sense that one is always being observed. Self-consciousness and introspection are typical.<br>• A sense of invulnerability can lead adolescents to ignore danger. | • As world experience increases, thought becomes more flexible and subjective, geared to adept problem solving.<br>• Intelligence is applied to long-term goals involving career, family, and society.<br>• Significant life events of young adulthood may shape cognitive development. |
| **SOCIAL/ PERSONALITY DEVELOPMENT** | • Self-concept becomes organized and accurate and reflects others' perceptions. Self-esteem grows differentiated.<br>• Defining identity is a key task. Peer relationships provide social comparison and help define acceptable roles. Popularity issues become acute; peer pressure can enforce conformity.<br>• Adolescents' quest for autonomy can bring conflict with parents as family roles are renegotiated.<br>• Sexuality assumes importance in identity formation. Dating begins. | • Forming intimate relationships becomes highly important. Commitment may be partly determined by the attachment style developed in infancy.<br>• Marriage and children bring developmental changes, often stressful. Divorce may result, with new stresses.<br>• Identity is largely defined in terms of work, as young adults consolidate their careers. |

**THEORIES & THEORISTS**

| | | | |
|---|---|---|---|
| Jean Piaget | Formal operations stage | |
| Erik Erikson | Identity-versus-confusion stage | Intimacy-versus-isolation stage |
| Sigmund Freud | Genital stage | |
| Lawrence Kohlberg | Postconventional morality level may be reached | |

**Editorial Director:** Craig Campanella
**Editor in Chief:** Jessica Mosher
**Executive Editor:** Jeff Marshall
**Editorial Project Manager:** LeeAnn Doherty
**Editorial Assistant:** Michael Rosen
**Director of Marketing:** Brandy Dawson
**Senior Marketing Manager:** Nicole Kunzmann
**Marketing Assistant:** Jessica Warren
**Managing Editor:** Maureen Richardson
**Project Manager:** Marianne Peters-Riordan
**Senior Operations Specialist:** Sherry Lewis
**Senior Art Director:** John Christiana
**Text and Cover Designer:** Mary Siener
**Cover Art:** Shutterstock
**Media Director:** Brian Hyland
**Senior Digital Media Editor:** Beth Stoner
**Supplements Editor:** LeeAnn Doherty
**Full-Service Project Management:** Priya Sundaram
**Composition:** S4Carlisle Publishing Services
**Printer/Binder:** Courier Kendallville
**Cover Printer:** Lehigh-Phoenix Color/Hagerstown
**Text Font:** Minion Pro 10/12

To Jon, Leigh, Josh, Julie, and Sarah

Credits and acknowledgments borrowed from other sources and reproduced, with permission, in this textbook appear on appropriate page within text, on pages xiii-xiv, or on page C-1.

**Library of Congress Cataloging-in-Publication Data**
Feldman, Robert S. (Robert Stephen), (date)
    Discovering the life span / Robert S. Feldman.—2nd ed.
        p. cm.
    Includes bibliographical references and index.
    ISBN-13: 978-0-205-23388-5
    ISBN-10: 0-205-23388-0
    1. Developmental psychology—Textbooks.    2. Life cycle, Human—Textbooks.
3. Human growth—Textbooks. I. Title.
BF713.F46 2011
155—dc23

                                    2011017327

9 8 7 6 5 4 3

                                                        student edition
                                            ISBN 10: 0-205-23388-0
                                            ISBN 13: 978-0-205-23388-5

                                        instructor's review edition
                                            ISBN 10: 0-205-06355-1
                                            ISBN 13: 978-0-205-06355-0

                                                    à la carte edition
                                            ISBN 10: 0-205-06352-7
                                            ISBN 13: 978-0-205-06352-9

PEARSON

www.pearsonhighered.com

| MIDDLE ADULTHOOD (40 to 65 years) | LATE ADULTHOOD (65 years to death) |
| --- | --- |
| • Physical changes become evident. Vision declines noticeably, as does hearing, but less obviously.<br>• Height reaches a peak and declines slowly. Osteoporosis speeds this process in women. Weight increases, and strength decreases.<br>• Reaction time slows, but performance of complex tasks is mostly unchanged due to lifelong practice.<br>• Women experience menopause, with unpredictable effects. The male climacteric brings gradual changes in men's reproductive systems. | • Wrinkles and gray or thinning hair are marks of late adulthood. Height declines as backbone disk cartilage thins. Women are especially susceptible to osteoporosis.<br>• The brain shrinks, and the heart pumps less blood through the body. Reactions slow, and the senses become less acute. Cataracts and glaucoma may affect the eyes, and hearing loss is common.<br>• Chronic diseases, especially heart disease, grow more common. Mental disorders, such as depression and Alzheimer's disease, may occur. |
| • Some loss of cognitive functioning may begin in middle adulthood, but overall cognitive competence holds steady because adults use life experience and effective strategies to compensate.<br>• Slight declines occur in the efficiency of retrieval from long-term memory. | • Cognitive declines are minimal until the 80's. Cognitive abilities can be maintained with training and practice, and learning remains possible throughout the life span.<br>• Short-term memory and memory of specific life episodes may decline, but other types of memory are largely unaffected.  |
| • People in middle adulthood take stock, appraising accomplishments against a "social clock" and developing a consciousness of mortality.<br>• Middle adulthood, despite the supposed "midlife crisis," usually is tranquil and satisfying. Individuals' personality traits are generally stable over time.<br>• While marital satisfaction is usually high, family relationships can present challenges.<br>• The view of one's career shifts from outward ambition to inner satisfaction or, in some cases, dissatisfaction. Career changes are increasingly common. | • Basic personality traits remain stable, but changes are possible. "Life review," a feature of this period, can bring either fulfillment or dissatisfaction.<br>• Retirement is a major event of late adulthood, causing adjustments to self-concept and self-esteem.<br>• A healthy lifestyle and continuing activity in areas of interest can bring satisfaction in late adulthood.<br>• Typical circumstances of late adulthood (reduced income, the aging or death of a spouse, a change in living arrangements) cause stress. |
| Generativity-versus-stagnation stage | Ego-integrity-versus-despair stage |

# DISCOVERING THE LIFE SP

## SECOND EDITION

**ROBERT**
University of M

Boston  Columbus  Indianapolis  New York  San F
Cape Town  Dubai  London  Madrid  Milan  Mu
Mexico City  São Paulo  Sydney  Hong Kong

# Brief Contents

# Contents

# Text Credits

**Chapter 1** Page 8, Morrelli et al. (1992) Cultural variation in infants' sleeping arrangements: Questions of independence (Special Issue: Cross-Cultural Studies of Development). Developmental Psychological, 28, 604-613. Copyright © 1992 the American Psychological Association. Adapted with permission; p. 4, Moreton, "World's first test tube baby, Louise Brown, has a child of her own" Independent, January 14, 2007 Copyright © 2007 Reprinted by permission of the Independent. www.independent.co.uk; p. 15, Watson, BEHAVIORISM Copyright © New York, NY: 1925 W.W. Norton and Company.; p. 25, From THE STORY OF PSYCHOLOGY by Morton Hunt, copyright © 1993 by Morton Hunt. Used by permission of Anchor Books, a division of Random House, Inc.; p. 31, figure 1-3, Based on an experiment by Leyens et al. (1975) Effects of movie violence on aggression in a field setting as a function of group dominance and cohesion. Journal of Personality and Social Psychology, 32, 346-360. American Psychological Association.

**Chapter 2** Page 42, Naik. "Parents agonize over treatments in the womb" THE WALL STREET JOURNAL by Dow Jones & Company. Copyright © 2009 Reproduced with permission of DOW JONES & COMPANY INC in the formats Textbook and Other Book via Copyright Clearance Center.; p. 57, Bennett. "Lori Schiller emerges from the torments of schizophrenia" The Wall Street Journal by Dow Jones & Company. Copyright © 2009. Reproduced with permission of DOW JONES & COMPANY, INC. in the formats Textbook and Other Book via Copyright Clearance Center.; p. 57, Bennett. "Lori Schiller emerges from the torments of schizophrenia" The Wall Street Journal by Dow Jones & Company. Copyright © 2009. Reproduced with permission of DOW JONES & COMPANY, INC. in the formats Textbook and Other Book via Copyright Clearance Center.; p. 44, figure 2-2, Martin et al., National Vital Statistic Reports, 54, Table J, page 21 (2010); p. 47, figure 2-5, Celera Genomics: International Human Genome Sequencing Consortium, 2001.; p. 54, figure 2-6, Bourchard and McGue, et al. Sources of Human Psychological Differences: The Minnesota Study of Twins Reared Apart SCIENCE, 250, 233-228 Copyright 1990 Reprinted with permission.; p. 56, figure 2-7, Adapted from Tellegen et al. (1988) Personality similarity in twins reared apart and together. Journal of Personality and Social Psychology, 54, 1031-1039. American Psychological Association.; p.57, figure 2-8, Irwin I. Gottesman, excerpt from Schizophrenia Genesis: The Origins of Madness (New York: W.H. Freeman) Copyright © 1991 Reprinted by permission of the author.; p. 67, Excerpt from Miller and Underwood "Not always the Happiest Time" Newsweek, May 2006. Copyright © 2006 Reprinted with permission of The Newsweek/Daily Beast Company, LLC.; p. 59, Figure 2-9, Reprinted from Moore, K.L. Before We Were Born: Basic Embryology and Birth Defects (FL: W.B. Saunders) Copyright 1998 Reprinted with permission of Elsevier; p. 62, Figure 2-11, Adapted from Munne and Cohen (1998) Chromosome abnormalities in human embryos. Human Reproduction Update, 4, 842-855. Copyright © 1998 Reprinted by permission of Oxford University Press.; p. 65, Figure 2-12, Reprinted from Moore, K.L. Before We Were Born: Basic Embryology and Birth Defects (FL: W.B. Saunders) Copyright 1998 Reprinted with permission of Elsevier.; p. 71, Adapted from INFANTS AND MOTHERS: DIFFERENCES IN DEVELOPMENT by T. Berry Brazelton, M.D., copyright © 1969, 1983 by T. Berry Brazelton, M.D. Used by permission of Delacorte Press, an imprint of The Random House Publishing Group, a division of Random House, Inc.; p. 77, Thomas. "Washington's infant mortality rate, more than twice the national average, reflects urban woes" The Wall Street Journal by Dow Jones & Co., Copyright © 1994 Reproduced with permission of DOW JONES & COMPANY, INC in the formats Textbook and Other Book via Copyright Clearance Center.; p. 81, Figure2-16, Based on material by the International Cesarean Awareness Network; p. 82, figure 2-17, Child Health, USA (2005); p. 47, table 2-1, Adapted from McGuffin et al (2001) toward behavioral genomics, SCIENCE, 291, 1232-49 Copyright © 2001. Reprinted by permission of AAAS.; p. 73, table 2-3, Adapted from V. Apgar (1953) A proposal for a new method of evaluation in the newborn infant. Current Research in Anesthesia and Analgesia, 32, 1953. Copyright © 1953 Reprinted with permission of Wolters Kluwer Health, a division of Lippincott Williams & Wilkins.; p. 80, table 2-4, Adapted from Committee to Study the Prevention of Low Birth Weight, 1985.; p. 88, table 2-6, Adapted from Carol O. Eckerman et al (1992) Very low birth weight newborns and parents as early as social partners. In S.L. Friedman and M.D. Seligman (eds) the Psychological Development of Low-Birth Weight Children. Copyright (c) 1992 Reprinted with permission.

**Chapter 3** Page 100, table 3-2, Evelyn B. Thoman and Mary P. Whitney. "Sleep states of infants monitored in the home: Individual differences, developmental trends, and origins of diurnal cyclicity" Infant Behavior and Development. Copyright 1989 Reprinted by permission of Elsevier; p. 122, Excerpt from Sandra Blakeslee "In brain's early growth, timetable may be crucial" New York Times, August 29, 1995. Copyright © 1995. Reprinted with permission of The New York Times Company. All rights reserved.; p. 124, table 3-7, Bayley Scales of Infant Development (BSID). Copyright ©) 1969 by NCS Pearson, Inc.; p. 125, Excerpt from Tamar Lewin. "See baby touch screen. But does baby get it?" New York Times, December 15, 2005 Copyright © 2005 New York Times Company. Reprinted with permission. All rights reserved.; p. 134, Excerpt from Daniel Goleman. "'Expert' babies found to each each other" New York Times, July 21, 1993. Copyright © 1993 New York Times Company. Reprinted by permission. All rights reserved.; p. 139, Adapted from INFANTS AND MOTHERS: DIFFERENCES IN DEVELOPMENT by T. Berry Brazelton, M.D., copyright © 1969, 1983 by T. Berry Brazelton, M.D. Used by permission of Delacorte Press, an imprint of The Random House Publishing Group, a division of Random House, Inc.; p. 148, Schellenberger (2003) Natural Musical Intervals: Evidence from infant listeners Psychological Science. Copyright © 2003 Association for Psychological Science. Adapted with permission.; p. 95, figure 3-1, CRATTY, BRYANT, PERPETUAL AND MOTOR DEVELOPMENT IN INFANTS AND CHILDREN., 2nd © 1979. Printed and Electronically reproduced by permission of Pearson Education, Inc., Upper Saddle River, New Jersey.; p. 97, figure 3-3, Adapted from Van De Graaff. Human anatomy, 2/e Copyright © 1988 Reprinted by permission of The McGraw-Hill Companies, inc.; p. 97, figure 3-4, Reprinted by permission of the publisher from THE POSTNATAL DEVELOPMENT OF THE HUMAN CEREBRAL CORTEX, VOLUMES I-VIII, by J. LeRoy Conel, Cambridge, Mass: Harvard University Press, Copyright © 1939, 1941, 1947,1951,1955,1959, 1963,1967 by the President and Fellows of Harvard College, Copyright © renewed 1967,1969,1975,1979,1983,1987,1991.; p. 101, figure 3-5, Dr. Howard P. Roffwarg et al REM sleep through the lifespan. Ontogenic development of the human sleep-dream cycle. Science, April, 1966, 29,152, 604-619. Copyright © 1966 Reprinted with permission.; p. 105, Adapted from William Frankenburg et al. The Denver II: A major revision and re-standardization of the Denver Screening Test, PEDIATRICS 89, Copyright 1992 Reprinted by permission.; p. 111, figure 3-9, R.L. Fantz. "The origin of form perception" Scientific American, Copyright © 1961. Adapted by permission.; p. 128, figure 3-13, Bornstein, Marc and Lamb, Michael. Development in Infancy: An Introduction, 3/e Copyright © 1992 Reprinted with permission of The McGraw-Hill Companies, Inc.; p. 132, figure 3-14, Ghislaine Dehaene-Lambertz, Lucie Hertz-Pannier, and Jessica Dubois. "Nature and nurture in language acquisition: anatomical and functional brain-imaging studies in infants" Trends in neuroscience, Copyright © 2006 Reprinted by permission of Elsevier.; p. 137, figure 3-16, Reprinted by permission of the publisher from INFANCY: ITS PLACE IN HUMAN DEVELOPMENT by Jerome Kagan, Richard B. Kearsley, and Philip R. Zelazo, p. 107, Cambridge, Mass: Harvard University Press, Copyright © 1978 by the President and Fellows of Harvard College.

**Chapter 4** Page 162, table 4-1, Corbin. A Textbook of Motor Development. Copyright © 1973. Reprinted with permission of The McGraw-Hill Companies.; p. 169, Ceci & Brick (1993) The suggestability of the child witness: A historical review and synthesis Psychological Bulletin, 113 Copyright © 1993 American Psychological Association. Adapted with permission.; p. 170, Tharp (1989) Psychocultural variables and constants: Effects on teaching and learning in schools: Special Issue: Children and Their development: knowledge base, research agenda, and social policy application. American Psychologist, 44, Copyright © 1989 American Psychological Association. Adapted with permission.; p. 173, A Toddler's Life: Becoming a Person by Marilyn Shatz (1994), p. 179 approx. 118 words. By permission of Oxford University Press, Inc.; p. 174, table 4-2, Growing speech Capabilities from THE LANGUAGE INSTINCT by STEVEN PINKER Copyright © 1994 by STEVEN PINKER. Reprinted by permission of HarperCollins Publishers.; p. 192, Excerpt from "Beginner's Ethics" by Katz Parent's Magazine Copyright © 1989 Reprinted by permission.; p. 160, figure 4-3, From Fischer & Rose (1995) Concurrent cycles in the dynamic development of brain and behavior. Newsletter of the Society for Research in Development Copyright © 1995 Reprinted with permission.; p. 173, figure 4-6, Jean Berko Gleason. "Appropriate Formationof Words" Adapted from Jean Berko, 1958, "The Child's Learning of English Morphology" Word, vol. 14, p. 154. Copyright 1958 Reprinted by permission of Jean Berko Gleason.; p. 190, figure 4-9, Reprinted by permission of the illustrator, Carol Lescoulie Donner.

**Chapter 5** Page 210, Excerpt from Pat Wingert and Barbara Kantrowitz, "Why Andy Couldn't Read" Newsweek, October 27, 1997 Copyright © 1997 Reprinted with permission of The Newsweek/Daily Beast Company, LLC.; p. 211, Claudia Wallis, "Life in Overdrive" TIME, July 18, 1994 Copyright © 1994 Reprinted by permisson.; p. 213, Segal and Segal, "No More Couch Potatoes" PARENTS Copyright © 1992 Reprinted by permission.; p. 213, Steinberg (1997) Intelligence and lifelong learning: What's new and how can we use it? American Psychologist, 52, 1152-1159. Copyright © 1997 American Psychological Association. Adapted with permission.; p. 219, Leslie, "Classroom of Babel" NEWSWEEK, February 11, 1991 Copyright © 1991 Reprinted by permission.; p. 233, Diana Jean Schemo, "Schools Facing Tight Budgets Leave Gifted Programs Behind" NEW YORK TIMES, Copyright © 2004 Reprinted by permission.; p. 235, Margaret Renkl, "Five Facts About Kids' Social Lives" www.parenting.com Copyright © 2005 Reprinted by permission.; p. 240, table 5-1, Kohlberg. Handbook of Socialization Theory and Research. Copyright © 1969 Reprinted with permission of Rand McNally via Copyright Clearance Center in the format Text.; p. 240, table 5-1, Kohlberg. Handbook of Socialization Theory and Research. Copyright © 1969 Reprinted with permission of Rand McNally via Copyright Clearance Center in the format of Other Book.; p. 243, Damon, Social and Personality Development. Copyright © 1983 New York: W.W. Norton and Company.; p. 245, Cullen, "Too Little Too Late Against Bully Tactics" BOSTON GLOBE Copyright © 2010 Reprinted by permission.; p. 246, Goodwin, "Tactical use of stories: Participation frameworks within girls' and boys' disputes" DISCOURSE PROCESSES, 13, Copyright 1990 Taylor & Francis, Ltd. Reprinted with permission.; p. 248, Katrowitz and Wingert, "Step by Step" NEWSWEEK Special Edition, Copyright © 1990 Reprinted by permission of The Newsweek/Daily Beast Company, LLC.; p. 207, figure 5-2, CRATTY, PERPETUAL AND MOTOR DEVELOPMENT IN INFANTS AND CHILDREN, 3rd, © 1986. Printed and Electronically reproduced by permission of Pearson Education, Inc., Upper Saddle River, New Jersey.; p. 212, figure 5-3, Shaw et al. ADHD is characterized by a delay in control maturation. Proceedings of the national Academy of Sciences, 104, 19649-19654. Copyright © 2007 National Academy of Sciences, USA.; p. 216, figure 5-4, Adapted from Dasen et al (1979) Cross-cultural training studies of concrete operations. In L.H. Edenberger et al Cross Cultural Contributions to Psychology. Copyright © 1979 Taylor & Francis. Adapted with permission.; p. 229, figure 5-8, Gardner's Eight intelligences. In Walters & Gardiner (1986) The theory of multiple intelligences: some issues and answers. In R.J. Sternberg and R. Wagner Practical Intelligence. Copyright © 1986 Reprinted with permission of Howard Gardner.; p. 245, figure 5-9, Adapted from K.A. Dodge Educational Psychology Copyright 1985 Reprinted by permission of the author.

**Chapter 6** Page 258, Mohler, "So Much Homework, So Little Time" PARENTS website, November 23, 2009. Copyright © 2009 Reprinted by permission.; p. 263, Sandler, "First Denial then a near-suicidal plea, "Mom, I need help" People Weekly, Copyright 1994. Reprinted by permission.; p. 266, Raeburn, "Too Young fr the Death Penalty?" NEW YORK TIMES Magazine, Copyright © 1994 Reprinted with permission.; p. 270, Ecenbarger, "America's New Merchants of Death" THE READER'S DIGEST, copyright © 1993. Reprinted by permission.; p. 273, Excerpted from Randy Kennedy "Six Whose Path to Excellence Was on the Mean Streets of Adversity" New York Times, March 3, 1999 Copyright © 1999 New York Times Company. Reprinted with permission. All rights reserved.; p. 283, Excerpted from Tamara Lewin "A Growing Number of video viewers Watch From the Crib" New York Times October 29, 2003 Copyright © 2003 The New York Times Company. Reprinted with permission.; p. 284, Excerpted from McGrath "Being 13: Riding the Rails" New York Times magazine May 17, 1998 Copyright © 1998 The New York Times

# Preface

I've never met an instructor of a lifespan development course who didn't feel that he or she was fortunate to teach the course. The subject matter is inherently fascinating, and there is a wealth of information to convey that is at once fascinating and practical. Students come to the course with anticipation, motivated to learn about a topic that, at base, is about their own lives and the lives of every other human being.

At the same time, the course presents unique challenges. For one thing, the breadth of lifespan development is so vast that it is difficult to cover the entire field within the confines of a traditional college term. In addition, many instructors find traditional lifespan development texts too long. Students are concerned about the length of the texts and have trouble completing the entire book. As a result, instructors are often reluctant to assign the complete text and are forced to drop material, often arbitrarily.

Finally, instructors often wish to incorporate into their classes computer-based electronic media that promote understanding of key concepts and take advantage of students' capabilities using electronic media. Yet traditional lifespan development textbooks do little to integrate the electronic media with the book. Consequently, in most courses, the book and accompanying electronic media stand largely in isolation to one another. This lack of integration diminishes the potential impact of both traditional and electronic media and the advantages that an integration of the two could produce in terms of helping students engage with and learn the subject matter.

*Discovering the Life Span,* **second edition,** directly addresses these challenges. The book, which is based on the highly popular *Development Across the Life Span,* is some 25 percent shorter than traditional lifespan books. At the same time, it maintains the student friendliness that has been the hallmark of the original. It is rich in examples and illustrates the applications that can be derived from the research and theory of lifespan developmentalists.

The book uses a modular approach to optimize student learning. Each chapter is divided into three modules, and in turn each module is divided into several smaller sections. Consequently, rather than facing long, potentially daunting chapters, students encounter material that is divided into smaller, more manageable chunks. Of course, presenting material in small chunks represents a structure that psychological research long ago found to be optimum for promoting learning.

The modular approach has another advantage: It allows instructors to customize instruction by assigning only those modules that fit their course. Each of the book's chapters focuses on a particular period of the life span, and within each chapter separate modules address the three main conceptual approaches to the period: physical development, cognitive development, and social and personality development. Because of the flexibility of this structure, instructors who wish to highlight a particular theoretical or topical approach to lifespan development can do so easily.

Finally, *Discovering the Life Span,* **second edition,** provides complete integration between the book and a huge array of electronic media in **MyDevelopmentLab,** including online electronic exercises, videos, sample tests, and literally hundreds of activities that extend the text and make concepts come alive. **MyVirtualChild** is included within MyDevelopmentLab. This interactive simulation allows students to raise a child and monitor the effects of their parenting decisions over time. MyDevelopmentLab and MyVirtualChild are referenced throughout the book in an engaging way, enticing students to go online to make use of the electronic materials that will help them understand the material in the book more deeply.

## An Introduction to *Discovering the Life Span,* Second Edition

*Discovering the Life Span,* **second edition**—like its predecessor—provides a broad overview of the field of human development. It covers the entire range of the human life, from the moment of conception through death. The text furnishes a broad, comprehensive introduction to the field, covering basic theories and research findings, as well as highlighting current applications outside the laboratory. It covers the life span chronologically, encompassing the prenatal period, infancy and toddlerhood, the preschool years, middle childhood,

adolescence, early and middle adulthood, and late adulthood. Within these periods, it focuses on physical, cognitive, and social and personality development.

In a unique departure from traditional lifespan development texts, each chapter integrates the physical, cognitive, and social and personality domains within each chronological period. Chapters begin with a compelling story about an individual representing the age period covered by the chapter, and the chapter ends by refocusing on that individual and integrating the three domains. At the same time, chapters drive students to **MyDevelopmentLab** through marginal queries and reminders about the rich media content available to them.

The book also blends and integrates theory, research, and applications, focusing on the breadth of human development. Furthermore, rather than attempting to provide a detailed historical record of the field, it focuses on the here-and-now, drawing on the past where appropriate, but with a view toward delineating the field as it now stands and the directions toward which it is evolving. Similarly, while providing descriptions of classic studies, the emphasis is more on current research findings and trends.

The book strives to be user friendly. Written in a direct, conversational voice, it replicates as much as possible a dialogue between author and student. The text is meant to be understood and mastered on its own by students of every level of interest and motivation. To that end, it includes a variety of pedagogical features that promote mastery of the material and encourage critical thinking. These features include:

- **Chapter-Opening Prologues.** Each of the chapters starts with an attention-grabbing account of an individual who is at the developmental stage covered by the chapter. The material in the Prologue sets the stage for the chapter, and the material is addressed in the end of the chapter when the physical, cognitive, and social and personality aspects are integrated.

- **Module-Opening Vignette and Looking Ahead.** Modules (which are nestled within chapters) begin with short vignettes, describing an individual or situation that is relevant to the basic developmental issues being addressed in the module. In addition, "Looking Ahead" sections provide learning objectives in the form of engaging questions.

- **From Research to Practice.** Each chapter includes a box that describes current developmental research or research issues, applied to everyday problems.

- **Cultural Dimensions.** Every chapter includes several "Cultural Dimensions" sections incorporated into the text. These sections highlight issues relevant to today's multicultural society. Examples of these sections include discussions about preschools around the world, gay and lesbian relationships, the marketing of cigarettes to the less advantaged, and race, gender, and ethnic differences in life expectancy.

- **Becoming an Informed Consumer of Development.** Every chapter includes information on specific uses that can be derived from research conducted by developmental investigators. For instance, the text provides concrete information on how to encourage children to become more physically active, help troubled adolescents who might be contemplating suicide, and plan and live a good retirement.

- **Review, Check, and Apply Sections.** Each module is divided into several subsections. At the end of each section is a series of questions on the chapter content (questions that are also found in MyDevelopmentLab), short recaps of the chapter's main points, and a question oriented to apply the chapter content to the real world. In addition, students are encouraged to use the online resources associated with the chapter.

- **"From the Perspective of . . ." Questions.** Students will encounter frequent questions throughout the text designed to show the applicability of the material to a variety of professions, including education, nursing, social work, and health care providers.

- **Running Glossary.** Key terms are defined along the top margins of the page on which the term is presented.

- **End-of-Chapter Integrative Material.** At the end of each chapter, the chapter-opening prologue is recapped and addressed from the three domains of physical, cognitive, and social and personality development. In addition, questions address the prologue from the perspective of people such as parents, professional caregivers, nurses, and educators.

# What's New in the Second Edition?

The second edition of *Discovering the Life Span* has been extensively revised in response to the comments of dozens of reviewers. Among the major changes are the following:

- **Addition of Learning Objectives.** The new edition includes specific, numbered learning objectives. These learning objectives, which are posed as questions, permit students to clearly understand what they are expected to learn in a given section of the book. The learning objectives are tied to review summaries at the end of every section of the book, and they are also keyed to testbank items.

- **Reorganization of the First Chapter.** Chapter 1 of the first edition covered introductory material, theories, research methods, the prenatal period, and birth. In order to make the material more manageable for students, the chapter has been divided into two chapters in this new edition.

- **Reordering of End-of-section Material.** The end-of-section material now begins with a review, followed by several objective questions (called "Check Yourself"), and ends with an "Applying Lifespan Development" critical thinking question.

- **Additions of New and Updated Material.** The revision incorporates a significant amount of new and updated information. For instance, advances in such areas as neuroscience and brain scanning, behavioral genetics, brain development, and cross-cultural approaches to development receive expanded and new coverage. Overall, hundreds of new citations have been added, with most of those from articles and books published in the last two years.

The following sample of new and revised topics featured in this edition provides a good indication of the currency of the revision:

## Chapter 1 Introduction

Qualitative research
Graphical representation of experiment
Clarification of critical vs. sensitive periods

## Chapter 2 The Start of Life

Maternal depression during pregnancy
In vitro fertilization success rates
Infant mortality rates
Circumcision statistics
Bradley method specifics
Personal values and philosophy
Intracervical insemination (ICI)
Intrauterine insemination (IUI)
Psychological issues in infertility
Risks to children of depressed mothers
Grief following miscarriage

## Chapter 3 Infancy

Nonhuman numeric skill
Malnutrition in underdeveloped countries
Effects of touch and massage
"Wave" views of the progression of cognitive development
Lack of value of formal education for infants
Association of reading to infants and later literacy skills
Use of deception by infants
Reactive attachment disorder
Multiple attachment relationships
Causes of SIDS
Co-sleeping

## Chapter 4 The Preschool Years

Preschoolers' numeric abilities
Preschool entry competition
Brain development through play
Additional toilet training guidelines
Evolutionary explanations of aggression
Incidence of televisions in preschoolers' bedrooms

## Chapter 5 Middle Childhood

Media and body image
Web safety and social network sites
Brain activity in monolinguals and bilinguals
Phoebe Prince bullying case
Turiel moral domain theory
Children with gay and lesbian parents
Poverty, stress, and susceptibility to disease
Challenges of children of immigrants
Brain development in children with ADHD
Accident statistics

## Chapter 6 Adolescence

Causes of obesity
Cultural factors and anorexia
Sleep deprivation
Social networking sites
U.S. student achievement compared to international students
*No Child Left Behind* act
Adolescent media use
Religion
Spirituality

Racial and ethnic differences in timing of first intercourse
Addiction treatment challenges
Safer sex and use of dental dams

### Chapter 7 Early Adulthood

Emerging adulthood
Gambling in college
Obesity statistics and causes
Acute and chronic stressors
Social support and web use
First generation college student challenges
Marriage gradient and race
Homicide statistics
Relationship stability in homosexual couples

### Chapter 8 Middle Adulthood

Hormone therapy (HT)
Type A, B, & D personalities
Mammogram frequency
Personality changes through adulthood
Marital satisfaction
Infidelity
Boredom and marital dissatisfaction
Stability of happiness set points

### Chapter 9 Late Adulthood

Brain size and cognitive declines
Ageism and stereotyping
Updated figures on aging
Alzheimer's disease statistics
Genetic preprogramming
Social networks for older adults
Rising health care costs in late adulthood
Lack of support for disengagement theory
Decision making and use of information
Complicated grief
Happiness during late adulthood
Technology and learning in late adulthood
Health care costs

### Chapter 10 Death and Dying

Social networking sites and death
Reincarnation
Resiliency after death
Complicated grief
Prolonged grief disorder

# A Final Note

I am very excited about the new edition of **Discovering the Life Span**. I believe its length, structure, and media and text integration will help students learn the material in a highly effective way. Just as important, I hope it will spark and nurture their interest in the field of lifespan development, drawing them into its way of looking at the world, building their understanding of developmental issues, and showing them how the field can have a significant impact on their own and others' lives.

# Teaching and Learning Resources

**Discovering the Life Span** is accompanied by a superb set of teaching and learning materials.

- **Instructor's Resource Manual (0205063470).** Designed to make your lectures more effective and save you preparation time, this extensive resource gathers together the most effective activities and strategies for teaching your course. The Instructor's Resource Manual includes learning objectives, key terms and concepts, self-contained lecture suggestions and class activities for each chapter with handouts, supplemental reading suggestions, and an annotated list of additional multimedia resources. The Instructor's Resource Manual can be downloaded via the Instructor's Resource Center at www.pearsonhighered.com/IRC or the MyDevelopmentLab® platform.

- **PowerPoint Lecture Slides (0205063497).** The PowerPoints provide an active format for presenting concepts from each chapter and feature relevant figures and tables from the text. Available for download via the Instructor's Resource Center at www.pearsonhighered.com/IRC or the MyDevelopmentLab® platform.

- **Classroom Response System PowerPoint Slides (0205225365).** The Classroom Response System (CRS) facilitates class participation in lectures as well as provides a method of measurement of student comprehension. CRS also enables student polling and in-class quizzes. CRS is highly effective in engaging students with class lectures, in addition to adding an element of excitement to the classroom. Simply, CRS is a technology that allows professors to ask questions to their students through text-specific PowerPoints provided by Pearson. Student reply using handheld transmitters called "clickers," which capture and immediately display student responses. These responses are saved in the system gradebook and/or can later be downloaded to either a Blackboard or WebCT gradebook for assessment purposes. It is available for download via the Instructor's Resource Center at www.pearsonhighered.com/IRC or the MyDevelopmentLab® platform.

- **Test Item File (0205063705).** The test bank contains multiple choice, true/false, and essay questions. Each question has been accuracy checked to ensure that the correct answer was marked and the page reference was accurate. An additional feature for the test bank is the identification of each question as factual, conceptual, or applied. This allows professors to customize their tests and to ensure a balance of questions types. Each chapter of the test item file begins with the Total Assessment Guide: an easy-to-reference grid that makes creating tests easier by organizing the test questions by text section, question type, and whether it is factual, conceptual, or applied. It is available for download via the Instructor's Resource Center at www.pearsonhighered.com/IRC or the MyDevelopmentLab® platform.

- **MyTest Test Bank (0205063489).** This powerful assessment generation program helps instructors easily create and print quizzes and exams. Questions and tests can be authored online, allowing instructors ultimate flexibility and the ability to efficiently manage assessments any time, anywhere! Instructors can easily access existing questions, edit, create, and store using simple drag-and-drop techniques and Word-like controls. Data on each question provide information on difficulty level and page number of the corresponding text discussion. In addition, each question maps to the text's major section and learning objective. For more information, go to www.PearsonMyTest.com/IRC or the MyDevelopmentLab® platform.

- **MyDevelopmentLab.** The new MyDevelopmentLab combines proven learning applications with powerful assessment to engage students, assess their learning, and help them succeed.

  - **An individualized study plan for each student,** based on performance on chapter pretests, helps students focus on the specific topics where they need the most support. The personalized study plan arranges content from less complex thinking—like remembering and understanding—to more complex critical thinking skills—like applying and analyzing—and is based on Bloom's taxonomy. Every level of the study plan provides a formative assessment quiz.
  - **MyVirtualChild,** an interactive simulation, allows students to raise a child from birth to age 18 and monitor the effects of their parenting decisions over time.
  - **Media assignments** for each chapter—including videos with assignable questions—feed directly into the gradebook, enabling instructors to track student progress automatically.
  - **The Pearson eText** lets students access their textbook any time and anywhere, and any way they want, including listening online.

With assessment tied to every video, application, and chapter, students get immediate feedback, and instructors can see what their students know with just a few clicks. Instructors can also personalize MyDevelopmentLab to meet the needs of their students.

- **MyVirtualChild,** included within MyDevelopmentLab or sold as a stand-alone product, is an interactive simulation that allows students to act as a parent and raise their own virtual child. By making decisions about specific scenarios, students can raise their children from birth to age 18 and learn firsthand how their own decisions and other parenting actions affect their child over time. At each age, students are given feedback about the various milestones their child has attained; key stages of the child's development will include personalized feedback. As in real life, certain "unplanned" events may occur randomly. Students take a personality test at the beginning of the program, the results of which will have an impact on the temperament of their child. Observational videos are included throughout the program to help illustrate key concepts. Critical thinking questions within the program help students to apply what they are learning about in class and in their textbook to their own virtual child. These questions can be assigned or used as the basis for in-class discussion.

- **Observations in Developmental Psychology videos** bring to life more than 30 key concepts discussed in the narrative of the text. They are indicated by a marginal icon, and offer additional extended videos that coincide with each part in the text to allow students to see real children in action. Students get to view each video twice: once with an introduction to the concept being illustrated and again with commentary describing what is taking place at crucial points in the video. Whether your course has an observation component or not, these videos provide your students the opportunity to see children in action. The videos can be accessed through MyDevelopmentLab.

- **CourseSmart Online Textbooks** are an exciting choice for students looking to save money. As an alternative to purchasing the print textbook, students can subscribe to the same content online and save up to 60 percent off the suggested list price of the print text. With a CourseSmart eTextbook, students can search the text, make notes online, print out reading assignments that incorporate lecture notes, and bookmark important passages for later review. For more information, or to subscribe to the CourseSmart eTextbook, visit www.coursesmart.com.

# Supplementary Texts

Contact your Pearson representative to package any of these supplementary texts with **Discovering the Life Span, second edition**.

- **Current Directions in Developmental Psychology (0205597505).** Readings from the American Psychological Society. This exciting reader includes over 20 articles that have been carefully selected for the undergraduate audience, and taken from the very accessible *Current Directions in Psychological Science* journal. These timely, cutting-edge articles allow instructors to bring their students real-world perspective about today's most current and pressing issues in psychology. Available in print or within MyDevelopmentLab.

- **Twenty Studies That Revolutionized Child Psychology (0130415723).** This brief text by Wallace E. Dixon, Jr., presents the seminal research studies that have shaped modern developmental psychology, and provides an overview of the environment that gave rise to each study, its experimental design, its findings, and its impact on current thinking in the discipline.

- **Human Development in Multicultural Context: A Book of Readings (0130195235).** Written by Michele A. Paludi, this compilation of readings highlights cultural influences in developmental psychology.

- **The Psychology Major: Careers and Strategies for Success (0205684688).** Written by Eric Landrum (Idaho State University) and Stephen Davis (Emporia State University), this 160-page paperback provides valuable information on career options available to psychology majors, tips for improving academic performance, and a guide to the APA style of research reporting.

## Acknowledgments

I am grateful to the following reviewers of the first and second editions who provided a wealth of comments, constructive criticism, and encouragement.

Lola Aagaard, Morehead State University

Glen Adams, Harding University

Sharron Adams, Wesleyan College

Leslie Adams Lariviere, Assumption

Carolyn Adams-Price, Mississippi State University

Judi Addelston, Valencia Community College

Bill Anderson, Illinois State University

Carrie Andreoletti, Central Connecticut State University

Harold Andrews, Miami Dade College–Wolfson

Ivan Applebaum, Valencia Community College

Sally Archer, The College of New Jersey

Janet Arndt, Gordon College

Christine Bachman, University of Houston–Downtown

Harriet Bachner, Pittsburg State University

Nannette Bagstad, Mayville State University

Mary Ballard, Appalachian State University

Michelle Bannoura, Hudson Valley Community College

Daniel Barajas, Community Collge of Denver

Ted Barker, Okaloosa-Walton College

Catherine Barnard, Kalamazoo Valley Community College

Gena Barnhill, Lynchburg College

Sue Barrientos, Butler Community College

Sandra Barrueco, The Catholic University of America

Carolyn Barry, Loyola College in Maryland

Chris Barry, University of Southern Mississippi

Robin Bartlett, Northern Kentucky University

Kellie Bassell, Palm Beach Community College

Shirley Bass-Wright, St. Philip's College

Bette Beane, The University of North Carolina at Greensboro

Dan Bellack, Trident Technical College

Amy Bender, University of Milwaukee

Marshelle Bergstrom, University of Wisconsin–Oshkosh

Doreen Berman, Queens College

Debra Berrett, Solano Community College

Irene Bersola-Nguyen, Sacramento State University

Wendy Bianchini, Montana State University

John Bicknell, Temple College

Robert Birkey, Goshen College

Carol Bishop, Solano Community College

Angela Blankenship, Nash Community College

Cheryl Bluestone, Queensborough Community (CUNY)

Tracie Blumentritt, University of Wisconsin–La Crosse

Kathy Bobula, Clark College

Denise Ann Bodman, Arizona State University

Kathleen Bonnelle, Lansing Community College

Janet Boseovski, The University of North Carolina at Greensboro

Teri Bourdeau, University of Tulsa

Sarah Boysen, The Ohio State University

Nicole Bragg, Mt. Hood Community College

Gregory Braswell, Illinois State University

Judith Breen, College of DuPage

Alaina Brenick, University of Maryland

Jennifer Brennom, Kirkwood Community College

Barbara Briscoe, Kapiolani Community College

Caralee Bromme, San Joaquin Delta Community College

Betty Cecile Brookover, Xavier University of Louisiana

Veda Brown, Prairie View A&M University

Janine Buckner, Seton Hall University

Sharon Burson, Temple College

Cathy Bush, Carson-Newman College

Jean Cahoon, Pitt Community College

Cheryl Camenzuli, Molloy College

Angela Campbell, Harrisburg Area Community College

Debb Campbell, College of the Sequoias

Diane Caulfield, Honolulu Community College

Rick Caulfield, University of Hawaii at Manoa

Lisa Caya, University of Wisconsin–La Crosse

Laura Chapin, Colorado State University

Jing Chen, Grand Valley State University

John Childers, East Carolina University

Saundra Ciccarelli, Gulf Coast Community College

Diana Ciesko, Valencia Community College

Wanda Clark, South Plains College

Cherie Clark, Queens University of Charlotte

J. B. Clement, Daytona College

Kimberly Cobb, Edgecombe Community College

Margaret Coberly, University of Hawaii–Windward

Lawrence Cohn, University of Texas at El Paso

Barbara Connolly, University of Tennessee Heath Sciences Center

Deborah Copeland, Palm Beach Community College

Ellen Cotter, Georgia Southwestern State University

Jodi Crane, Lindsey Wilson College

Pat Crane, Santa Ana College

Amanda Creel, Sowela Technical Community College

Jeanne Cremeans, Hillsborough Community College

Don Crews, Southwest Georgia Technical College

Geraldine Curley, Bunker Hill Community College

Gregory Cutler, Bay de Noc Community College

Chris Daddis, The Ohio State University at Marion

Anne Dailey, Community College of Allegheny County

Billy Daley, Fort Hays State University

Dianne Daniels, UNC Charlotte

Karen Davis, Southwest Georgia Technical College

Dora Davison, Southern State Community College

Paul Dawson, Weber State University

Tara Dekkers, Northwestern College

Barbara DeFilippo, Lansing Community College

A. J. DeSimone, William Paterson University

Michael Devoley, Montgomery College

David Devonis, Graceland University

Ginger Dickson, The University of Texas at El Paso

Trina Diehl, Northwest Vista College

Darryl Dietrich, The College of St. Scholastica

Jennie Dilworth, Georgia Southern University

Stephanie Ding, Del Mar College

Betsy Diver, Lake Superior College

Delores Doench, Southwestern Community College

Margaret Dombrowski, Harrisburg Area Community College–Lancaster

Heather Dore, Florida Community College at Jacksonville

Jackie Driskill, Texas Tech University

Victor Duarte, North Idaho College

Susan Dubitsky, Florida International University

Shelley Dubkin-Lee, Oregon State University

Beryl Dunsmoir, Concordia University at Austin

Paula Dupuy, The University of Toledo

Kathleen Dwinnells, Kent State University–Trumbull Campus

Linda EagleHeart Thomas, The University of Montana–COT

Darlene Earley-Hereford, Southern Union State Community College

Mary B. Eberly Lewis, Oakland University

David Edgerly, Quincy University

Jean Egan, Asnuntuck Community College

Trish Ellerson, Miami University

Kelley Eltzroth, Mid-Michigan Community College

Laurel End, Mount Mary College

Dale Epstein, University of Maryland

Diana E. Espinoza, Laredo Community College

Melissa Essman, California State University, Fullerton

Jenni Fauchier, Metropolitan Community College

Nancy Feehan, University of San Francisco

Jef Feldman, Los Angeles Pierce College

Pamela Fergus, MCTC and IHCC

Ric Ferraro, University of North Dakota

Donna Fletcher, Florida State University

Christine Floether, Centenary College

June Foley, Clinton Community College

Jeanene Ford, Holmes Community College

Lee Fournet, Central Arizona College

Jody Fournier, Capital University

Tony Fowler, Florence-Darlington Technical College

James Francis, San Jacinto College

Inoke Funaki, Brigham Young University Hawaii

Sonia Gaiane, Grossmont College

Donna Gainer, Mississippi State University

Teresa Galyean, Wytheville Community College

Mary Garcia-Lemus, California Polytechnic State University, San Luis Obispo

Laura Garofoli, Fitchburg State College

Andy Gauler, Florida Community College at Jacksonville

C. Ray Gentry, Lenior-Rhyne College

Jarilyn Gess, Minnesota State University Moorhead

Sharon Ghazarian, The University of North Carolina–Greensboro

Pam Gingold, Merced College

Shery Ginn, Rowan Cabarrus Community College

Drusilla Glascoe, Salt Lake Community College

Donna Goetz, Elmhurst College

Rob Goralewicz, Dabney Lancaster Community College

Christina Gotowka, Tunxis Community College

Thomas Grady, Neosho County Community College

Donna Gray, Irvine Valley College

Troianne Grayson, Florida Community College at Jacksonville–South Campus

Jo Greathouse, Brazosport College

Jerry Green, Tarrant County College

Janelle Grellner, University of Central Oklahoma

Kristi Guest, University of Alabama at Birmingham

James Guinee, University of Central Arkansas

Jill Haasch, Glenville State College

Sharon Habermann, Providence Theological Seminary

Helen Hagens, Central Michigan University

Lisa Hager, Spring Hill College

Carolyn Halliburton, Dallas Baptist University

Sam Hardy, Brigham Young University

Mark Harmon, Reedley College–North Centers

Dyan W. Harper, University of Missouri–St. Louis

Melody Harrington, St. Gregory's University

Nancy Hartshorne, Central Michigan University

Loretta Hauxwell, McCook Community College

Christina Hawkey, Arizona Western College

Lora Haynes, University of Louisville

Sam Heastie, Fayetteville State University

Patti Heer, Clarke College

Steve Hendrix, James Sprunt Community College

Sarah Herald, Arizona State University

Mary Hetland, Minnesota State Community and Tech College

Carolyn Hildebrandt, University of Northern Iowa

Pamela Hill, San Antonio College

Sharon Hogan, Cuyahoga Community College

Frank Holiwski, South Georgia College

Debra Hollister, Valencia Community College

Sachi Horback, Baltimore City Community College

Scott Horton, Mitchell College

Herman Huber, College of Saint Elizabeth

Julie Howard, Vanguard University

Martha Hubertz, Florida Atlantic University

Mary Hughes Stone, San Francisco State University

Heidi Humm, Mercy College

Bob Humphries, Walsh University

David Hurford, Pittsburg State University

MaryLu Hutchins, West Liberty State College

Cynthia Ingle, Bluegrass Community and Technical College

Nicolle Ionascu, Queen's University

Jessica Jablonski, Richard Stockton College of New Jersey

Alisha Janowsky, University of Central Florida

Debbra Jennings, Richland College

Sybillyn Jennings, Russell Sage College

Daphne Johnson, Sam Houston State University

Margaret Johnson, Bridgewater State College

Stephanie Johnson, Southeast Community College

Deborah Jones, Florida Community College at Jacksonville

Katherine Jones, Mississippi College

Linda G. Jordan, Skagit Valley College

James Jordan, Lorain County Community College

Terri Joseph, Kent State University East Liverpool

Diana Joy, Community College of Denver

Carl Jylland-Halverson, University of Saint Francis

Louise Kahn, University of New Mexico

Susan Kamphaus, Tulsa Community College West Campus

Richard Kandus, Mt. San Jacinto College

Paul Kaplan, SUNY at Stony Brook

Michele Karpathian, Waynesburg College

Mark Kavanaugh, Kennebec Valley Community College

Henry Keith, Delaware Technical & Community College

Debbie Keller, College of the Ozarks

Jeffrey Kellogg, Marian College

Colleen Kennedy, Roosevelt University

Rosalie Kern, Michigan Tech University

Lisa Kiang, Wake Forest

Tim Killian, University of Arkansas

William Kimberlin, Lorain County Community College

Michalene King, Kent State Tuscarawas

Jennifer King-Cooper, Sinclair Community College

Kenyon Knapp, Troy University, Montgomery Campus

Don Knox, Midwestern State University

Larry Kollman, North Iowa Area Community College

Leslee Koritzke, Los Angeles Trade Tech College

Nicole Korzetz, Lee College

Holly Krogh, Mississippi University for Women

August Lageman, Virginia Intermont College

Carol Laman, Houston Community College

Warren Lambert, Somerset Community College

Jonathan Lang, Borough of Manhattan C. College

Yvonne Larrier, Indiana University South Bend

Rich Lanthier, George Washington University

Richard Lazere, Portland Community College

Jennifer Leaver, Eastern Arizona College

Maria LeBaron, Randolph Community College

Gary Leka, University of Texas–Pan American

Diane Lemay, University of Maine at Augusta

Elizabeth Lemerise, Western Kentucky University

Cynthia Lepley, Thomas College

Norma Lestikow, Highland Community College

Bud Levin, Blue Ridge Community College

Lawrence Lewis, Loyola University New Orleans

Linda McIntosh Liptok, Kent State University–Tuscarawas

Nancey Lobb, Alvin Community College

R. Martin Lobdell, Pierce College

Janet Lohan, Washington State University

Don Lucas, Northwest Vista College

Joe Lund, Taylor University

Salvador Macias, University of South Carolina Sumter

Grace Malonai, Saint Mary's College of California

Donna Mantooth, Georgia Highlands College

Rebecca Marcon, University of North Florida

T. Darin Matthews, The Citadel

Kelly McCabe, University of Mary Hardin Baylor

William McCracken, Delaware Technical & Community College

Jim McDonald, California State University, Fresno

Cathy Mcelderry, University of Alabama at Birmingham

Jim McElhone, The University of Texas of the Permian Basin

Cathy McEvoy, University of South Florida

Annie McManus, Parkland College

Beth McNulty, Lake Sumter Community College

Marcia McQuitty, Southwestern Theological Seminary

Dixie Cranmer McReynolds, St. Vincent's College

Joan Means, Solano Community College

Omar Mendez, William Paterson University of New Jersey

K. Mentink, Chippewa Valley Technical College

Peter Metzner, Vance Granville Community College

LeeAnn Miner, Mount Vernon Nazarene University

Ellen Mink, Elizabethtown Community and Technical College

Michael Miranda, Kingsborough Community College/CUNY

Steve Mitchell, Somerset Community College

Yvonne Montgomery, Langston University

Beverly Moore, Sullivan County Community College

Brad Morris, Grand Valley State University

Dolly Morris, University Alaska Fairbanks, TVC Campus

AudreyAnn C. Moses, Hampton University

Jean Mosley, Oral Roberts University

Carol Mulling, Des Moines Area Community College

Jeannette Murphey, Meridian Community College

Sylvia Murray, University of South Carolina Upstate

Ron Naramore, Angelina College

Lisa Newell, Indiana University of Pennsylvania

Glenda Nichols, Tarrant County College–South

David Nitzschke, Western Iowa Tech Community College

Harriett Nordstrom, University of Michigan–Flint

Meghan Novy, Palomar College

Elleen O'Brien, UMBC

Shirley Ogletree, Texas State–San Marcos

Valerie O'Krent, California State University–Fullerton

Jennifer Oliver, Rockhurst University

Leanne Olson, Wisconsin Lutheran College

Rose Olver, Amherst College

Sharon Ota, Honolulu Community College

John Otey, Southern Arkansas University

Karl Oyster, Tidewater Community College

Gwynne Pacheco, Hawaii Community College

Roger Page, Ohio State University–Lima

Joseph Panza, Southern Connecticut State University

Jennifer Parker, University of South Carolina Upstate

Brian Parry, San Juan College

Joan Paterna, Manchester Community College

Julie Patrick, West Virginia University

Sue Pazynski, Glen Oaks Community College

Carola Pedreschi, Miami Dade College

Colleen Peltz, Iowa Lakes Community College

John Phelan, Western Oklahoma State College

Peter Phipps, Dutchess Community College

Laura Pirazzi, San Jose State University

Michelle Pilati, Rio Hondo College

Diane Pisacreta, St. Louis Community College

Deanna Pledge, Stephens College

Leslee Pollina, Southeast Missouri State University

Yuly Pomares, Miami Dade College

Jean Poppei, The Sage Colleges/Russell Sage College

Lydia Powell, Vance-Granville Community College

Elizabeth Rellinger Zettler, Illinois College

Sherri Restauri, Jacksonville State University

Kate Rhodes, Dona Ana Community College

Shannon Rich, Texas Woman's University

Cynthia Riedi, Morrisville State College, Norwich Campus

Laura Rieves, Tidewater Community College

Jane Roda, Penn State–Hazleton Campus

Keith Rosenbaum, Dallas Baptist University

Karl Rosengren, University of Illinois at Urbana-Champaign

Renda Ross, Capital University

Willow Rossmiller, Montana State University–Great Falls College of Technology

Melinda Rouse, Alamance Community College

Marlo Rouse-Arnett, Georgia Southern

Lisa Routh, Pikes Peak Community College

Loretta Rudd, Texas Tech University

Robert Rycek, University of Nebraska at Kearney

Brooke Saathoff, Labette Community College

James Sapp, Kentucky Christian University

Marie Saracino, Stephen F. Austin State University

Al Sarno, Hannibal-LaGrange College

Patricia Sawyer, Middlesex Community College

Linda Schaefer, Minot State University

Troy Schiedenhelm, Rowan Cabarrus Community College

Celeste Schneider, Saint Mary's College

Pamela Schuetze, Buffalo State College

Joe Schuh, Northern Kentucky University

Candace Schulenburg, Cape Cod Community College

Eric Seemann, University of Alabama in Huntsville

Nancy Segal, California State University–Fullerton

Sandy Sego, American International College

Zewelanji Serpell, James Madison University

Nitya Sethuraman, Indiana University

Virginia Shipman, University of New Mexico

Beth Sigmon, Robeson Community College

Denise Simonsen, Fort Lewis College

Julie Singer, University of Nevada, Reno

Peggy Skinner, South Plains College

Tara Smith, Elizabethtown College

Todd Smith, Lake Superior State University

Jerry Snead, Coastal Carolina Community College

James Snowden, Midwestern State University

Le'Ann Solmonson, Stephen F. Austin State University

Brooke Spatta, Lynn University

Tracy Spinrad, School of Social and Family Dynamics

Melinda Spohn, Spokane Falls Community College

Jill Steinberg, University of Wisconsin–Madison

Robby Stewart, Oakland University

Nancy Stinnett, University of Alabama

Deborah Stipp Evans, Ivy Tech Community College

Julia Stork, Jefferson State Community College

Amy Strimling, Sacramento City College

Rose Suggett, Southeast Community College

Terre Sullivan, Chippewa Valley Technical College

Cyril Svoboda, University of Maryland University College

Peter Talty, Keuka College

Amber Tatnall, SUNY Delhi

Becky Taylor, Texas Christian University

Marianne Taylor, Pacific Lutheran University

Luis Terrazas, California State University–San Marcos

Thomas Thieman, College of St. Catherine

Mojisola Tiamiyu, University of Toledo

Vicki Tinsley, Brescia University

Ed Titus, Troy University

Ivonne Tjoefat, Rochester Community & Technical College

Adrian Tomer, Shippensburg University

Barbara Townsend, Gannon University

Jeannine Turner, Florida State University

Jeffrey Turner, Mitchell College

Dave Urso, Lord Fairfax Community College

Cecelia Valrie, East Carolina University

Y. van Ecke, College of Marin

Deborah Van Marche, Glendale Community College

Michael Vandehey, Midwestern State University

Marina Vera, Southwestern College

Monica Vines, Central Oregon Community College

Steven Voss, Moberly Area Community College

John Wakefield, University of North Alabama

Rebecca Walker-Sands, Central Oregon Community College

James Wallace, St. Lawrence University

Todd Walter, D'Youville College

Mark Wasicsko, Northern Kentucky University

Sheree Watson, University of Southern Mississippi

Debbie Watson, Shawnee State University

Nancy Wedeen, Los Angeles Valley College

Glenn Weisfeld, Wayne State University

Orville Weiszhaar, Minneapolis Community and Technical College

Lori Werdenschlag, Lyndon State College

Laurie Westcott, New Hampshire Community Technical College

Linda Whitney, Houston Community College Northwest

Robert Wiater, Bergen Community College

Sharon Wiederstein, Blinn College

Jacqueline Williams, Moorpark College

June Williams, Southeastern Louisiana University

Kay Williams, Tidewater Community College

Patti Williams, Tidewater Community College

Lois Willoughby, Miami Dade College

Stephen Wills, Mercer University

Cynthia Wilson, University of South Alabama–Baldwin County

Christy Wolfe, University of Louisville

Peter Wooldridge, Durham Technical Community College

Shelly Wooldridge, University of Arkansas Community College at Batesville

Bonnie Wright, Gardner-Webb University

Kent Yamauchi, Pasadena City College

Robin Yaure, Penn State Mont Alto

Ani Yazedjian, Texas State University–San Marcos

Mahbobeh Yektaparast, Central Piedmont Community College

Susan Zandrow, Bridgewater State College

Rowan Zeiss, Blue Ridge Community College

Laura Zettel-Watson, California State University–Fullerton

Ginny Zhan, Kennesaw State University

Ling-Yi Zhou, University of St. Francis

Renee' Zucchero, Xavier University

Many others deserve a great deal of thanks. I am indebted to the numerous people who provided me with a superb education, first at Wesleyan University and later at the University of Wisconsin. Specifically, Karl Scheibe played a pivotal role in my undergraduate education, and the late Vernon Allen acted as mentor and guide through my graduate years. It was in graduate school that I learned about development, being exposed to such experts as Ross Parke, John Balling, Joel Levin, Herb Klausmeier, and many others. My education continued when I became a professor. I am especially grateful to my colleagues at the University of Massachusetts, who make the university such a wonderful place in which to teach and do research.

Several people played important roles in the development of this book. Edward Murphy, Amy Henry, and Christopher Poirier provided significant research and editorial support. In addition, John Graiff was essential in juggling and coordinating the multiple aspects of writing a book. I am very grateful for his help.

I am also thankful to the superb Pearson team that was instrumental in the inception and development of this book. Jeff Marshall, Executive Editor, conceived of the format of this book, and he has brought creativity and a wealth of good ideas to the project. Apart from being a relentless taskmaster, Jeff is a fantastic editor, and I count myself lucky to work with him. I'm also extremely grateful to LeeAnn Doherty, Associate Editor, who stayed on top of every aspect of the project and brought inventiveness and imagination to the book. I can't thank her enough for her way-beyond-the-call-of duty efforts and patience with me.

Editorial Director Craig Campanella and Editor in Chief Jessica Mosher stood behind the project, and I'm very grateful for their support. On the production end of things, Marianne Peters-Riordan, the Production Supervisor, and Mary Siener, Designer, helped in giving the book its distinctive look. Finally, I'd like to thank (in advance) Marketing Manager Nicole Kunzmann, on whose skills I'm counting.

I also wish to acknowledge the members of my family, who play such an essential role in my life. My brother, Michael, my sisters-in-law and brother-in-law, and my nieces and nephews all make up an important part of my life. In addition, I am always indebted to the older generation of my family, who led the way in a manner I can only hope to emulate. I will always be obligated to Harry Brochstein, Mary Vorwerk, and Ethel Radler. Most of all, the list is headed by my father, the late Saul Feldman, and my mother, Leah Brochstein.

In the end, it is my immediate family who deserve the greatest thanks. My son, Jon, his wife, Leigh, and my grandson, Alex; my son, Josh, and his wife, Julie; and my daughter, Sarah, are not only nice, smart, and good-looking, but my pride and joy. And ultimately my wife, Katherine Vorwerk, provides the love and grounding that makes everything worthwhile. I thank them, with all my love.

Robert S. Feldman
University of Massachusetts at Amherst

# About the Author

*Robert S. Feldman* is Professor of Psychology and Dean of the College of Social and Behavioral Sciences at the University of Massachusetts Amherst. A recipient of the College Distinguished Teacher Award, he teaches psychology classes ranging in size from 15 to nearly 500 students. During the course of more than two decades as a college instructor, he has taught both undergraduate and graduate courses at Mount Holyoke College, Wesleyan University, and Virginia Commonwealth University, in addition to the University of Massachusetts.

Feldman, who initiated the Minority Mentoring Program at the University of Massachusetts, also has served as a Hewlett Teaching Fellow and Senior Online Teaching Fellow. He initiated distance learning courses in psychology at the University of Massachusetts.

Feldman also is actively involved in promoting the field of psychology. He is on the Board of Directors of the Federation of Associations in Behavioral and Brain Sciences (FABBS), and he also is on the Board of the FABBS Foundation.

A Fellow of both the American Psychological Association and the Association for Psychological Science, Professor Feldman received a B.A. with High Honors from Wesleyan University and an M.S. and Ph.D. from the University of Wisconsin–Madison.

Feldman is a winner of a Fulbright Senior Research Scholar and Lecturer award, and he has written more than 150 books, book chapters, and scientific articles. He has edited *Development of Nonverbal Behavior in Children* (Springer-Verlag), *Applications of Nonverbal Behavioral Theory and Research* (Erlbaum), and co-edited *Fundamentals of Nonverbal Behavior* (Cambridge University Press). He is also author of *Child Development, Understanding Psychology,* and *P.O.W.E.R. Learning: Strategies for Success in College and Life*. His books have been translated into a number of languages, including Spanish, French, Portuguese, Dutch, Chinese, and Japanese.

His research interests include honesty and deception in everyday life and the use of nonverbal behavior in impression management, and his research has been supported by grants from the National Institute of Mental Health and the National Institute on Disabilities and Rehabilitation Research.

Feldman loves music, is an enthusiastic—if not-exactly-expert—pianist, and he enjoys cooking and traveling. He has three children, and he and his wife, a psychologist, live in western Massachusetts, in a home overlooking the Holyoke mountain range.

# CHAPTER 1

# Introduction

As David Furek looked around the Thanksgiving table, he felt content. This had nothing to do with the array of food on the table; the bounty he was thankful for was his large family.

David's three youngest children (Louise, Brad, and his "surprise present," baby Glenn) lived at home with David and his wife, Carla. For the past five years, David's widowed mother also lived with them. And just last year his eldest child, Erin, had been laid off from her job and moved in temporarily with her family. This added to the household Erin; her husband Peter, who was a graduate student; and their baby, Peter—just a year younger than David's youngest son.

David's two other children, Marco and Ted, were out of the house and making a living on their own, but they shared an apartment in the same neighborhood and visited the family just about every day.

David looked around the table. When he came to his youngest child, baby Glenn, who was hard at work becoming a complete person, he recalled the worries he'd had about the effects on the baby of Carla's bearing him at age 48. So far so good. Now he wondered what it must feel like to grow up surrounded by two parents,

## MODULE **1.1** Beginnings

## Nature vs. Nurture: Which has the greater influence? see page 4.

## MODULE **1.2** Theoretical Perspectives on Lifespan Development

## Is one right and one wrong?

see page 12.

a grandparent, a slew of brothers and sisters, a brother-in-law, and now, oddly, a nephew. So many people to watch, interpret, learn from, and be influenced by.

David knew he had his father's stubbornness and his mother's patience. He could see that little Glenn had Carla's eyes and his smile. But what about the less visible things? Where would Glenn's personality come from? His intelligence? His emotionality? Would he have his brother Marco's sense of humor or Ted's dogged seriousness? Would he be musical like Brad or athletic like Louise? Or would he be unlike anyone else in the family, drawing his habits and behaviors by observing and interacting with his family or the larger society outside the house?

As David watched the varied, noisy, entertaining show around the Thanksgiving table, he smiled and thought: *He'll certainly have a variety of traits to draw on.*

Lifespan development is a diverse and growing field with a broad focus and wide applicability. It covers the entire lifespan of the individual from birth to death as it examines the ways in which people develop physically, intellectually, and socially. It asks and attempts to answer questions about the ways in which people change and remain the same over their years of life.

Many of the questions that developmentalists ask are, in essence, the scientist's version of the questions that parents ask about their children and themselves: How the genetic legacy of parents plays out in their children; how children learn; why they make the choices they make; whether personality

## MODULE 1.3 Research Methods

# What kind of research could you conduct using David's four-generation household?

see page 25.

## My Virtual Child

How much of your child's personality is inherited through genetics and how much comes from the environment he or she is brought up in? How will your parenting decisions affect your child's development? What decisions would you make when it comes to raising a newborn?

Log onto *My Virtual Child* through MyDevelopmentLab.com and start making those choices.

characteristics are inherited and whether they change or are stable over time; how a stimulating environment affects development; and many others. To pursue their answers, of course, developmentalists use the highly structured, formal scientific method, while parents mostly use the informal strategy of waiting, observing, engaging with, and loving their kids.

In this chapter, we will introduce the field of lifespan development. We first discuss the breadth of the field, both in the range of years it covers and in the topics it addresses, and we look at the major theoretical perspectives that have examined those topics. We also describe the key features of the scientific method, the main approach that scientists take to answering questions of interest.

## MODULE 1.1 Beginnings

# New Conceptions

*What if for your entire life, the image that others held of you was colored by the way in which you were conceived?*

*In some ways, that's what it has been like for Louise Brown, who was the world's first "test tube baby," born by in vitro fertilization (IVF), a procedure in which fertilization of a mother's egg by a father's sperm takes place outside the mother's body.*

*Louise was a preschooler when her parents told her how she was conceived, and throughout her childhood she was bombarded with questions. It became routine to explain to her classmates that she in fact was not born in a laboratory.*

*As a child, Louise sometimes felt completely alone. But as she grew older, her isolation declined as more and more children were born in the same manner.*

*In fact, today Louise is hardly isolated. More than 1.5 million babies have been born using the procedure, which has become almost routine. And at the age of 28, Louise became a mother herself, giving birth to a baby boy named Cameron—conceived, by the way, in the old-fashioned way. (Moreton, 2007)*

Louise Brown's conception may have been novel, but her development since then has followed a predictable pattern. While the specifics of our development vary, the broad strokes set in motion in that test tube more than three decades ago are remarkably similar for all of us. Shaquille O'Neal, Donald Trump, the Queen of England—all are traversing the territory known as lifespan development.

Louise Brown's conception is just one of the brave new worlds of the day. Issues that affect human development range from cloning to poverty to the prevention of AIDS. Underlying these are even more fundamental issues: How do we develop physically? How does our understanding of the world change throughout our lives? And how do our personalities and social relationships develop as we move through the life span?

These questions and many others are central to lifespan development. The field encompasses a broad span of time and a wide range of areas. Consider the range of interests that different specialists might focus on when considering Louise Brown:

- Lifespan development researchers who investigate behavior at the biological level might ask if Louise's functioning before birth was affected by her conception outside the womb.
- Specialists in lifespan development who study genetics might examine how the genetic endowment from Louise's parents affects her later behavior.
- Lifespan development specialists who investigate thinking processes might examine how Louise's understanding of the circumstances of her conception changed as she grew older.

- Other researchers in lifespan development, who focus on physical growth, might consider whether her growth rate differed from children conceived more traditionally.
- Lifespan development experts who specialize in the social world and social relationships might look at the ways that Louise interacted with others and the kinds of friendships she developed.

Although their interests take many forms, these specialists share one concern: understanding the growth and change that occur during life. Taking many different approaches, developmentalists study how both our biological inheritance from our parents and the environment in which we live jointly affect our future behavior, personality, and potential as human beings.

Whether they focus on heredity or environment, all developmental specialists acknowledge that neither one alone can account for the full range of human development. Instead, we must look at the interaction of heredity and environment, attempting to grasp how both underlie human behavior.

In this module, we orient ourselves to the field of lifespan development. We begin with a discussion of the scope of the discipline, illustrating the wide array of topics it covers and the full range of ages it examines. We also survey the key issues and controversies of the field and consider the broad perspectives that developmentalists take. Finally, we discuss the ways developmentalists use research to ask and answer questions.

# An Orientation to Lifespan Development

**LO1**  What is the scope of the field of lifespan development?

**LO2**  What are cohorts, and how do they influence development?

Have you ever wondered at the way an infant tightly grips your finger with tiny, perfectly formed hands? Or marveled at how a preschooler methodically draws a picture? Or at the way an adolescent can make involved decisions about whom to invite to a party or the ethics of downloading music files? Or the way a middle-aged politician can deliver a long, flawless speech from memory? Or what makes a grandfather at 80 so similar to the father he was at 40?

If you've ever wondered about such things, you are asking the kinds of questions that scientists in the field of lifespan development pose. **Lifespan development** is the field of study that examines patterns of growth, change, and stability in behavior that occur throughout the life span.

In its study of growth, change, and stability, lifespan development takes a *scientific* approach. Like members of other scientific disciplines, researchers in lifespan development test their assumptions by applying scientific methods. They develop theories about development and use methodical, scientific techniques to validate the accuracy of their assumptions systematically.

Lifespan development focuses on *human* development. Although there are developmentalists who study nonhuman species, the vast majority study people. Some seek to understand universal principles of development, while others focus on how cultural, racial, and ethnic differences affect development. Still others aim to understand the traits and characteristics that differentiate one person from another. Regardless of approach, however, all developmentalists view development as a continuing process throughout the life span.

As developmental specialists focus on change during the life span, they also consider stability. They ask in which areas, and in what periods, people show change and growth, and when and how their behavior reveals consistency and continuity with prior behavior.

Finally, developmentalists assume that the process of development persists from the moment of conception to the day of death, with people changing in some ways right up to the end of their lives and in other ways exhibiting remarkable stability. They believe that no single period governs all development, but instead that people maintain the capacity for substantial growth and change throughout their lives.

**lifespan development** the field of study that examines patterns of growth, change, and stability in behavior that occur throughout the entire life span

**physical development** development involving the body's physical makeup, including the brain, nervous system, muscles, and senses, and the need for food, drink, and sleep

**cognitive development** development involving the ways that growth and change in intellectual capabilities influence a person's behavior

**personality development** development involving the ways that the enduring characteristics that differentiate one person from another change over the lifes pan

**social development** the way in which individuals' interactions with others and their social relationships grow, change, and remain stable over the course of life

## Characterizing Lifespan Development: The Scope of the Field

Clearly, the definition of lifespan development is broad and the scope of the field extensive. Typically, lifespan development specialists cover several diverse areas, choosing to specialize in both a topical area and an age range.

***Topical Areas in Lifespan Development.*** Some developmentalists focus on **physical development,** examining the ways in which the body's makeup—the brain, nervous system, muscles, and senses, and the need for food, drink, and sleep—helps determine behavior. For example, one specialist in physical development might examine the effects of malnutrition on the pace of growth in children, while another might look at how athletes' physical performance declines during adulthood (Fell & Williams, 2008).

Other developmental specialists examine **cognitive development,** seeking to understand how growth and change in intellectual capabilities influence a person's behavior. Cognitive developmentalists examine learning, memory, problem-solving, and intelligence. For example, specialists in cognitive development might want to see how problem-solving skills change over the course of life, or if cultural differences exist in the way people explain their academic successes and failures, or how traumatic events experienced early in life are remembered later in life (Alibali, Phillips, & Fischer, 2009; Dumka et al., 2009).

Finally, some developmental specialists focus on personality and social development. **Personality development** is the study of stability and change in the characteristics that differentiate one person from another over the life span. **Social development** is the way in which individuals' interactions and relationships with others grow, change, and remain stable over the course of life. A developmentalist interested in personality development might ask whether there are stable, enduring personality traits throughout the life span, while a specialist in social development might examine the effects of racism or poverty or divorce on development. These four major topic areas—physical, cognitive, social, and personality development—are summarized in Table 1-1.

***Age Ranges and Individual Differences.*** In addition to choosing a particular topical area, developmentalists also typically look at a particular age range. The life span is usually divided into broad age ranges: the prenatal period (from conception to birth); infancy and toddlerhood (birth to 3); the preschool period (3 to 6); middle childhood (6 to 12); adolescence (12 to 20); young adulthood (20 to 40); middle adulthood (40 to 60); and late adulthood (60 to death).

It's important to keep in mind that these periods are social constructions. A *social construction* is a shared notion of reality that is widely accepted but is a function of society and culture at a given time. Thus, the age ranges within a period—and even the periods themselves—are in many ways arbitrary and culturally derived. For example, we'll see how the concept of childhood as a special period did not even exist during the seventeenth century—children were seen then simply as miniature adults. Furthermore, while some periods have a clear-cut boundary (infancy begins with birth, the preschool period ends with entry into public school, and adolescence starts with sexual maturity), others don't.

For instance, consider the period of young adulthood, which at least in Western cultures is typically assumed to begin at age 20. That age, however, is notable only because it marks the end of the teenage period. In fact, for many people, such as those enrolled in higher education, the age change from 19 to 20 has little special significance, coming as it does in the middle of college. For them, more substantial changes are likely to occur when they leave college around age 22. Furthermore, in some cultures adulthood starts much earlier, as soon as a child can begin full-time work.

In short, there are substantial *individual differences* in the timing of events in people's lives. In part, this is a biological fact of life: People mature at different rates and reach developmental milestones at different points. However, environmental factors also play a significant role; for example, the typical age of marriage varies from one culture to another, depending in part on the functions that marriage plays.

***The Links Between Topics and Ages.*** Each of the broad topical areas of lifespan development—physical, cognitive, social, and personality development—plays a role throughout the life span. Consequently, some developmental experts may focus on physical

## TABLE 1-1 APPROACHES TO LIFESPAN DEVELOPMENT

| Orientation | Defining Characteristics | Examples of Questions Asked* |
|---|---|---|
| Physical development | Emphasizes how brain, nervous system, muscles, sensory capabilities, and needs for food, drink, and sleep affect behavior | • What determines the sex of a child? (2.1)<br>• What are the long-term results of premature birth? (2.3)<br>• What are the benefits of breast milk? (3.1)<br>• What are the consequences of early or late sexual maturation? (6.1)<br>• What leads to obesity in adulthood? (7.1)<br>• How do adults cope with stress? (8.1)<br>• What are the outward and internal signs of aging? (9.1)<br>• How do we define death? (10.1) |
| Cognitive development | Emphasizes intellectual abilities, including learning, memory, problem solving, and intelligence | • What are the earliest memories that can be recalled from infancy? (3.2)<br>• What are the intellectual consequences of watching television? (4.2)<br>• Do spatial reasoning skills relate to music practice? (4.2)<br>• Are there benefits to bilingualism? (5.2)<br>• How does an adolescent's egocentrism affect his or her view of the world? (6.2)<br>• Are there ethnic and racial differences in intelligence? (5.2)<br>• How does creativity relate to intelligence? (7.2)<br>• Does intelligence decline in late adulthood? (9.2) |
| Personality and social development | Emphasizes enduring characteristics that differentiate one person from another, and how interactions with others and social relationships grow and change over the lifetime | • Do newborns respond differently to their mothers than to others? (2.3)<br>• What is the best procedure for disciplining children? (4.3)<br>• When does a sense of gender identity develop? (4.3)<br>• How can we promote cross-race friendships? (5.3)<br>• What are the causes of adolescent suicide? (6.3)<br>• How do we choose a romantic partner? (7.3)<br>• Do the effects of parental divorce last into old age? (9.3)<br>• Do people withdraw from others in late adulthood? (9.3)<br>• What are the emotions involved in confronting death? (10.1) |

*Numbers in parentheses indicate in which chapter and module the question is addressed.

development during the prenatal period, and others during adolescence. Some might specialize in social development during the preschool years, while others look at social relationships in late adulthood. And still others might take a broader approach, looking at cognitive development through every period of life.

In this book, we'll take a comprehensive approach, proceeding chronologically from the prenatal period through late adulthood and death. Within each period, we'll look at physical, cognitive, social, and personality development.

## Cohort and Other Influences on Development: Developing with Others in a Social World

Bob, born in 1947, is a baby boomer; he was born soon after the end of World War II, when returning soldiers caused an enormous bulge in the birth rate. He was an adolescent at the height of the Civil Rights movement and protested against the Vietnam War. His mother, Leah, was born in 1922; her generation passed its childhood and teenage years in the shadow of the Depression. Bob's son, Jon, was born in 1975. Now building a career

This wedding of two children in India is an example of how environmental factors can play a significant role in determining the age when a particular event is likely to occur.

## *Cultural Dimensions*

### How Culture, Ethnicity, and Race Influence Development

*Mayan mothers in Central America are certain that almost constant contact between themselves and their infant children is necessary for good parenting, and they are physically upset if contact is not possible. They are shocked when they see a North American mother lay her infant down, and they attribute the baby's crying to the poor parenting of the North American.* (Morelli et al., 1992)

What are we to make of the two views of parenting depicted in this passage? Is one right and the other wrong? Probably not, if we take cultural context into consideration. Different cultures and subcultures have their own views of appropriate and inappropriate childrearing, just as they have different developmental goals for children (Tolchinsky, 2003; Feldman & Masalha, 2007; Huijbregts et al., 2009).

Clearly, to understand development, developmentalists must take into consideration broad cultural factors, such as an orientation toward individualism or collectivism, as well as finer ethnic, racial, socioeconomic, and gender differences. If they succeed in doing this, not only can they achieve a better understanding of human development, but they may be able to derive more precise applications for improving the human social condition.

To complicate the study of diverse populations, the terms *race* and *ethnic group* are often used inappropriately. *Race* is a biological concept, which should refer to classifications based on physical and structural characteristics of species. In contrast, *ethnic group* and *ethnicity* are broader, referring to cultural background, nationality, religion, and language.

The concept of race has proven particularly problematic. It has inappropriately taken on nonbiological meanings ranging from skin color to religion to culture. Moreover, as a concept it is exceedingly imprecise; depending on how it is defined, there are between 3 and 300 races, and no race is genetically distinct. The fact that 99.9 percent of humans' genetic makeup is identical in all humans makes the question of race seem insignificant (Jernigan & Mascher, 2005; Smedley & Smedley, 2005; Alfred & Chlup, 2010).

In addition, there is little agreement about which names best reflect different races and ethnic groups. Should the term *African American*—which has geographical and cultural implications—be preferred over *black,* which focuses primarily on race and skin color? Is *Native American* preferable to *Indian*? Is *Hispanic* more appropriate than *Latino*? And how can researchers accurately categorize people with multiracial backgrounds?

In order to fully understand development, then, we need to take the complex issues associated with human diversity into account. In fact, it is only by looking for similarities and differences among various ethnic, cultural, and racial groups that developmental researchers can distinguish principles of development that are universal from ones that are culturally determined. In the years ahead, then, it is likely that lifespan development will move from a discipline that primarily focuses on North American and European development to one that encompasses development around the globe (Fowers & Davidov, 2006; Matsumoto & Yoo, 2006; Kloep et al., 2009).

and starting a family, he is a member of what has been called Generation X. Jon's younger sister, Sarah, who was born in 1982, is part of the next generation, which sociologists have called the Millennial Generation.

These people are in part products of the social times in which they live. Each belongs to a particular **cohort,** a group of people born at around the same time in the same place. Such major social events as wars, economic upturns and depressions, famines, and epidemics (like the one due to the AIDS virus) work similar influences on members of a particular cohort (Mitchell, 2002; Dittmann, 2005).

*Cohort effects* are an example of *history-graded influences,* biological and environmental influences associated with a particular historical moment. For instance, people who lived in New York City during the 9/11 terrorist attack on the World Trade Center experienced shared biological and environmental challenges due to the attack. In fact, the specter of terrorism is a history-graded influence that is common to people living in the United States today (Bonanno, Galea, & Bucciarelli, 2006; Laugharne, Janca, & Widiger, 2007; Breslau, Bohnert, & Koenen, 2010).

⊙ **From an educator's perspective:** How would a student's cohort membership affect his or her readiness for school? For example, what would be the benefits and drawbacks of coming from a cohort in which Internet use was routine, compared with earlier cohorts before the appearance of the Internet?

In contrast, *age-graded influences* are biological and environmental influences that are similar for individuals in a particular age group, regardless of when or where they are raised. For example, biological events such as puberty and menopause are universal events that occur at about the same time in all societies. Similarly, a sociocultural event such as entry into formal education can be considered an age-graded influence because it occurs in most cultures around age 6.

**cohort** a group of people born at around the same time in the same place

Development is also affected by *sociocultural-graded influences,* the social and cultural factors present at a particular time for a particular individual, depending on such variables as ethnicity, social class, and subcultural membership. For example, sociocultural-graded influences will be considerably different for white and nonwhite children, especially if one lives in poverty and the other in affluence (Rose et al., 2003).

Finally, *non-normative life events* are specific, atypical events that occur in a particular person's life at a time when such events do not happen to most people. For example, a child whose parents die in an automobile accident when she is 6 has experienced a significant non-normative life event.

## REVIEW, CHECK, AND APPLY

### REVIEW

**L01** What is the scope of the field of lifespan development?

- Lifespan development is a scientific approach to understanding human growth and change throughout life.
- The field covers a broad range of ages and topical areas. Its chief aim is to examine the links between human age groups and the areas of physical, cognitive, social, and personality development.

**L02** What are cohorts, and how do they influence development?

- Membership in a cohort, based on age and place of birth, subjects people to influences based on historical events (history-graded influences).
- People are also subject to age-graded influences, sociocultural-graded influences, and non-normative life events.

### CHECK YOURSELF

1. Three assumptions made by lifespan developmentalists are: 1) a focus on human development, 2) an understanding of stability in addition to growth and change, and 3) _____.
   a. the perception that development persists throughout our entire lives
   b. the perception that childhood developmental changes are the only changes worth studying
   c. the idea that some periods of the life span are more important than others
   d. the perception that development is a stagnant process

2. Stages of the life span such as adolescence and middle age are universal across cultures and stable across history.
   - True
   - False

3. The time when children utter their first complete sentence is an example of:
   a. a history-graded influence.
   b. an age-graded influence.
   c. a sociocultural-graded influence.
   d. a non-normative life event.

### APPLYING LIFESPAN DEVELOPMENT

- What are some examples in your life of events and experiences that have affected your age cohort differently from other cohorts?

✓—┤**Study** and **Review** on **MyDevelopmentLab.com**

Answers: 1) a; 2) False; 3) b

# Key Issues and Questions: Determining the Nature—and Nurture—of Lifespan Development

**L03**   **What are the key issues in the field of development?**
**L04**   **How have developmental researchers resolved these issues?**

Lifespan development is a decades-long journey through shared milestones, with many individual routes along the way. For developmentalists, the variations in lifespan development raise many questions. What are the best ways to think about the enormous changes that a person undergoes from before birth to death? How important is chronological age? Is there a clear timetable for development? How can one begin to find common threads and patterns?

These questions have been debated since lifespan development became established as a separate field in the late nineteenth and early twentieth centuries, though a fascination with the nature and course of humans' development can be traced back to the ancient Egyptians and Greeks.

**continuous change** gradual development in which achievements at one level build on those of previous levels

**discontinuous change** development that occurs in distinct steps or stages, with each stage bringing about behavior that is assumed to be qualitatively different from behavior at earlier stages

**critical period** a specific time during development when a particular event has its greatest consequences and the presence of certain kinds of environmental stimuli are necessary for development to proceed normally

**sensitive period** a point in development when organisms are particularly susceptible to certain kinds of stimuli in their environments, but the absence of those stimuli does not always produce irreversible consequences

In this section we examine four of the most important—and continuously argued—issues in the field of lifespan development. We also consider the resolutions to which researchers have come regarding these issues.

## Continuous Change versus Discontinuous Change

One of the primary issues challenging developmentalists is whether development proceeds in a continuous or discontinuous fashion. In **continuous change,** development is gradual, with achievements at one level building on those of previous levels. Continuous change is quantitative; the underlying developmental processes remain the same over the life span. In this view changes are a matter of degree, not of kind—like changes in a person's height. Some theorists suggest that changes in people's thinking abilities are also continuous, building on gradual improvements rather than developing entirely new processing capabilities.

In contrast, others see development as primarily a matter of **discontinuous change,** occurring in distinct stages. Each stage brings about behavior that is assumed to be qualitatively different from behavior at earlier stages. Consider cognitive development again. Some cognitive developmentalists suggest that our thinking changes in fundamental ways as we develop, not just quantitatively but qualitatively.

Most developmentalists agree that it makes little sense to take an either/or position on this issue. While many types of developmental change are continuous, others are clearly discontinuous (Flavell, 1994; Heimann, 2003; Gumz et al., 2010).

## Critical and Sensitive Periods: Gauging the Impact of Environmental Events

If a woman comes down with a case of rubella (German measles) in the 11th week of pregnancy, the consequences for the child she is carrying—possible blindness, deafness, and heart defects—can be devastating. However, if she comes down with the same strain of rubella in the 30th week of pregnancy, damage to the child is unlikely.

The differing outcomes demonstrate the concept of critical periods. A **critical period** is a specific time during development when a particular event has its greatest consequences. Critical periods occur when the presence of certain kinds of environmental stimuli are necessary for development to proceed normally (Uylings, 2006).

Although early specialists in lifespan development placed great emphasis on critical periods, recent thinking suggests that individuals are more malleable, particularly in the domain of personality and social development. For instance, rather than suffering permanent damage from a lack of certain early social experiences, there is increasing evidence that people can use later experiences to help overcome earlier deficits.

Consequently, developmentalists are now more likely to speak of **sensitive periods** rather than critical periods. In a sensitive period, organisms are particularly susceptible to certain kinds of stimuli in their environments. In contrast to a critical period, however, the absence of those stimuli during a sensitive period does not always produce irreversible consequences.

It is important to understand the difference between the concepts of critical periods and sensitive periods: In critical periods, it is assumed that the absence of certain kinds of environmental influences is likely to produce permanent, irreversible consequences for the developing individual. In contrast, although the absence of particular environmental influences during a sensitive period may hinder development, it is possible for later experiences to overcome the earlier deficits. In other words, the concept of sensitive period recognizes the plasticity of developing humans (Konig, 2005; Armstrong et al., 2006; Hooks & Chen, 2008).

## Lifespan Approaches versus a Focus on Particular Periods

Early developmentalists tended to focus their attention on infancy and adolescence, largely to the exclusion of other parts of the life span. Today, however, developmentalists believe the entire life span is important, largely because developmental growth and change continue during every part of life—as we'll discuss throughout this book.

Furthermore, to fully understand the social influences on a person of a given age, we need to understand the person's social environment—the people who in large measure provide those influences. For instance, to understand development in infants, we need to unravel the effects of their parents' ages on their social environments. A 15-year-old first-time mother and an experienced 37-year-old mother will provide parental influences of very different sorts. Consequently, infant development is in part an outgrowth of adult development.

Additionally, as lifespan developmentalist Paul Baltes points out, development across the life span involves both gains and losses. With age, certain capabilities become more refined and sophisticated, while others decline. For example, vocabulary tends to grow throughout childhood and continue through most of adulthood, but certain physical abilities, like reaction time, improve until early and middle adulthood, and then begin to decline (Baltes, Staudinger, & Lindenberger, 1999; Baltes, 2003; Ghisletta et al., 2010).

## The Relative Influence of Nature and Nurture on Development

One of the enduring questions of development involves how much of people's behavior is due to genetics (nature) and how much to the physical and social environment (nurture) (Wexler, 2006).

*Nature* refers to traits, abilities, and capacities that are inherited from one's parents. It encompasses any factor that is produced by the predetermined unfolding of genetic information—a process known as **maturation.** These genetic, inherited influences are at work as we move from the one-cell organism created at conception to the billions of cells that make up a fully formed human. Nature influences whether our eyes are blue or brown, whether we have thick hair throughout life or eventually go bald, and how good we are at athletics. Nature allows our brains to develop in such a way that we can read the words on this page.

In contrast, *nurture* refers to the environmental influences that shape behavior. Some influences may be biological, such as the impact of a pregnant mother's use of cocaine on her unborn child or the amount and kind of food available to children. Other influences are more social, such as the ways parents discipline their children and the effects of peer pressure on an adolescent. Finally, some influences are a result of societal factors, such as the socioeconomic circumstances in which people find themselves.

Although developmentalists reject the notion that behavior is the sole result of either nature or nurture, the nature–nurture question can cause heated debate. Take, for instance, intelligence. If intelligence is primarily determined by heredity and is largely fixed at birth, then efforts to improve intellectual performance later in life may be doomed to failure. In contrast, if intelligence is primarily a result of environmental factors, such as the amount and quality of schooling and home stimulation, then an improvement in social conditions could cause intelligence to increase.

Clearly, neither nature nor nurture stands alone in most developmental matters. The interaction of genetic and environmental factors is complex, in part because certain genetically determined traits have not only a direct influence on children's behavior, but an indirect influence in shaping children's *environments*. For example, children who cry a great deal—a trait that may be produced by genetic factors—may influence their environment by making their parents rush to comfort them whenever they cry. The parents' responsivity to their children's genetically determined behavior becomes an environmental influence on the children's subsequent development.

Similarly, although our genetic background orients us toward particular behaviors, those behaviors will not necessarily occur without an appropriate environment. People with similar genetic backgrounds (such as identical twins) may behave in very different ways; and people with highly dissimilar genetic backgrounds can behave quite similarly to one another in certain areas (Garcia, Bearer, & Lerner, 2004; Kato & Pedersen, 2005; Gangestad, 2010).

In sum, the nature–nurture question is challenging. Ultimately, we should consider the two sides of the issue as ends of a continuum, with particular behaviors falling somewhere between the ends. The same can be said of the other controversies that we have considered. For instance, continuous versus discontinuous development is not an either/or proposition; some forms of development fall toward the continuous end of the continuum, while others lie closer to the discontinuous end. In short, few statements about development involve either/or absolutes (Deater-Deckard & Cahill, 2006; Rutter, 2006).

**maturation** the predetermined unfolding of genetic information

## REVIEW, CHECK, AND APPLY

### REVIEW

**L03** What are the key issues in the field of development?

- Four important issues in lifespan development are continuity versus discontinuity in development, the importance of critical periods, whether to focus on certain periods or on the entire life span, and the nature–nurture controversy.

- These issues have been the subject of research and discussions since the field of development began.

**L04** How have developmental researchers resolved these issues?

- Research and discussions on these issues have led to the conclusion that for three of them, no either–or answer makes sense.

- For the "focus on certain periods" issue, however, there is general agreement that development is not limited to childhood and adolescence, but continues through the life span.

### CHECK YOURSELF

1. Grady believes that human development occurs in small, measurable amounts. His sister Andrea disagrees and suggests that human development is more distinct and steplike. Their argument is most reflective of the _____ issue.

   a. critical and sensitive period
   b. nature and nurture
   c. continuous and discontinuous
   d. lifespan approach and particular period

2. A _____ is a specific time during development when a particular event has its greatest consequence.

3. Nurture refers to traits, abilities, and capacities that are inherited from one's parents.

   - True
   - False

### APPLYING LIFESPAN DEVELOPMENT

- What are some examples of the ways culture (either broad culture or aspects of culture) affects human development?

✓—**Study** and **Review** on **MyDevelopmentLab.com**

Answers: 1) c; 2) critical period; 3) False

---

## MODULE 1.2 Theoretical Perspectives on Lifespan Development

Society's view of childhood, and what is appropriate to ask of children, has changed through the ages. These children worked full-time in mines in the early 1900s.

*In Europe, there was no concept of "childhood" until the seventeenth century. Instead, children were simply thought of as miniature adults. They were assumed to be subject to the same needs and desires as adults, to have the same vices and virtues, and to warrant no more privileges. They were dressed the same as adults, and their work hours were the same. Children also received the same punishments for misdeeds. If they stole, they were hanged; if they did well, they could achieve prosperity, at least so far as their station in life or social class would allow.*

This view of childhood seems wrong-headed now, but at the time it was society's understanding of lifespan development. From this perspective, there were no differences due to age; except for size, people were assumed to be virtually unchanging, at least on a psychological level, throughout most of the life span (Aries, 1962; Acocella, 2003; Hutton, 2004; Wines, 2006).

It is easy to reject the medieval view but less clear how to formulate a contemporary substitute. Should our view of development focus on the biological aspects of change, growth, and stability over the life span? The cognitive or social aspects? Or some other factors?

In fact, people who study lifespan development approach the field from different perspectives. Each perspective encompasses one or more **theories:** broad, organized explanations and predictions concerning phenomena of interest. A theory provides a framework for understanding the relationships among a seemingly unorganized set of facts or principles.

We all develop theories about development, based on our experience, folklore, and stories in the media. However, theories in lifespan development are different. Whereas our own personal theories are haphazardly built on unverified observations, developmentalists' theories are more formal, based on a systematic integration of prior findings and theorizing. Theories allow developmentalists to summarize and organize prior observations, and they allow them to move beyond existing observations to draw deductions that may not be immediately apparent. In addition, theories are subject to rigorous testing through research. By contrast, the developmental theories of individuals are not subject to testing and may never be questioned at all (Thomas, 2001).

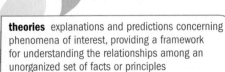

**theories** explanations and predictions concerning phenomena of interest, providing a framework for understanding the relationships among an unorganized set of facts or principles

We'll consider the six major theoretical perspectives used in lifespan development—the psychodynamic, behavioral, cognitive, humanistic, contextual, and evolutionary perspectives—and discuss them in greater detail in later chapters. Each perspective emphasizes somewhat different aspects of development and steers developmentalists in particular directions. Furthermore, each continues to evolve, as befits a dynamic discipline.

# The Psychodynamic, Behavioral, and Cognitive Perspectives

**LO5**  Which theoretical perspectives have guided lifespan development?

**LO6**  What are the main characteristics of the psychodynamic, behavioral, and cognitive perspectives?

## The Psychodynamic Perspective: Focusing on the Inner Person

When Marisol was 6 months old, she was involved in a bloody automobile accident—or so her parents tell her, since she has no recollection of it. Now, however, at age 24, she is having difficulty maintaining relationships, and her therapist is seeking to determine whether her current problems are a result of the earlier accident.

Looking for such a link might seem a bit far-fetched—but not to proponents of the **psychodynamic perspective.** Advocates believe that much behavior is motivated by inner forces, memories, and conflicts of which a person has little awareness or control. The inner forces, which may stem from childhood, influence behavior throughout the life span.

**Freud's Psychoanalytic Theory.** The psychodynamic perspective is most closely associated with Sigmund Freud. Freud, who lived from 1856 to 1939, was a Viennese physician whose revolutionary ideas had a profound effect not only on psychology and psychiatry, but on Western thought in general (Masling & Bornstein, 1996).

Freud's **psychoanalytic theory** suggests that unconscious forces act to determine personality and behavior. To Freud, the *unconscious* is a part of the personality about which a person is unaware. It contains infantile wishes, desires, demands, and needs that are hidden, because of their disturbing nature, from conscious awareness. Freud suggested that the unconscious is responsible for a good part of our everyday behavior.

According to Freud, everyone's personality has three aspects: id, ego, and superego. The *id* is the raw, unorganized, inborn part of personality that is present at birth. It represents primitive drives related to hunger, sex, aggression, and irrational impulses. The id operates according to the *pleasure principle,* in which the goal is to maximize satisfaction and reduce tension.

The *ego* is the part of personality that is rational and reasonable. The ego acts as a buffer between the external world and the primitive id. The ego operates on the *reality principle,* in which instinctual energy is restrained in order to maintain the safety of the individual and help integrate the person into society.

Finally, Freud proposed that the *superego* represents a person's conscience, incorporating distinctions between right and wrong. It begins to develop around age 5 or 6 and is learned from an individual's parents, teachers, and other significant figures.

Freud also addressed personality development during childhood. He argued that **psychosexual development** occurs as children pass through distinct stages in which pleasure, or gratification, is focused on a particular biological function and body part. As illustrated in Table 1-2, he suggested that pleasure shifts from the mouth (the *oral stage*) to the anus (the *anal stage*) and eventually to the genitals (the *phallic stage* and the *genital stage*).

According to Freud, if children are unable to gratify themselves sufficiently during a particular stage, or if they receive too much gratification, fixation may occur. *Fixation* is behavior reflecting an earlier stage of development due to an unresolved conflict. For instance, fixation at the oral stage might produce an adult unusually absorbed in oral activities—eating, talking, or chewing gum. Freud also argued that fixation is represented through symbolic oral activities, such as the use of "biting" sarcasm.

Sigmund Freud

**psychodynamic perspective** the approach that states behavior is motivated by inner forces, memories, and conflicts that are generally beyond people's awareness and control

**psychoanalytic theory** the theory proposed by Freud that suggests that unconscious forces act to determine personality and behavior

**psychosexual development** according to Freud, a series of stages that children pass through in which pleasure, or gratification, is focused on a particular biological function and body part

**TABLE 1-2** FREUD'S AND ERIKSON'S THEORIES

| Approximate Age | Freud's Stages of Psychosexual Development | Major Characteristics of Freud's Stages | Erikson's Stages of Psychosocial Development | Positive and Negative Outcomes of Erikson's Stages |
|---|---|---|---|---|
| Birth to 12–18 months | Oral | Interest in oral gratification from sucking, eating, mouthing, biting | Trust vs. mistrust | *Positive:* Feelings of trust from environmental support<br><br>*Negative:* Fear and concern regarding others |
| 12–18 months to 3 years | Anal | Gratification from expelling and withholding feces; coming to terms with society's controls relating to toilet training | Autonomy vs. shame and doubt | *Positive:* Self-sufficiency if exploration is encouraged<br><br>*Negative:* Doubts about self, lack of independence |
| 3 to 5–6 years | Phallic | Interest in the genitals; coming to terms with Oedipal conflict, leading to identification with same-sex parent | Initiative vs. guilt | *Positive:* Discovery of ways to initiate actions<br><br>*Negative:* Guilt from actions and thoughts |
| 5–6 years to adolescence | Latency | Sexual concerns largely unimportant | Industry vs. inferiority | *Positive:* Development of sense of competence<br><br>*Negative:* Feelings of inferiority, no sense of mastery |
| Adolescence to adulthood (Freud) Adolescence (Erikson) | Genital | Reemergence of sexual interests and establishment of mature sexual relationships | Identity vs. role diffusion | *Positive:* Awareness of uniqueness of self, knowledge of role to be followed<br><br>*Negative:* Inability to identify appropriate roles in life |
| Early adulthood (Erikson) | | | Intimacy vs. isolation | *Positive:* Development of loving, sexual relationships and close friendships<br><br>*Negative:* Fear of relationships with others |
| Middle adulthood (Erikson) | | | Generativity vs. stagnation | *Positive:* Sense of contribution to continuity of life<br><br>*Negative:* Trivialization of one's activities |
| Late adulthood (Erikson) | | | Ego-integrity vs. despair | *Positive:* Sense of unity in life's accomplishments<br><br>*Negative:* Regret over lost opportunities of life |

**psychosocial development** the approach that encompasses changes in our interactions with and understandings of one another, as well as in our knowledge and understanding of ourselves as members of society

**Erikson's Psychosocial Theory.** Psychoanalyst Erik Erikson, who lived from 1902 to 1994, provided an alternative psychodynamic view, emphasizing our social interaction with other people. In Erikson's view, society and culture both challenge and shape us. **Psychosocial development** encompasses changes in our interactions with and understandings of one another as well as in our knowledge and understanding of us as members of society (Erikson, 1963).

Erikson's theory suggests that development proceeds throughout our lives in eight stages (see Table 1-2), which emerge in a fixed pattern and are similar for all people. Each stage presents a crisis or conflict that the individual must resolve. Although no crisis is ever fully resolved, the individual must at least address the crisis of each stage sufficiently to deal with demands made during the next stage of development. Unlike Freud, who regarded development as relatively complete by adolescence, Erikson suggested that growth and change continue throughout the life span (de St. Aubin, McAdams, & Kim, 2004).

***Assessing the Psychodynamic Perspective.*** Freud's insight that unconscious influences affect behavior was a monumental accomplishment, and the fact that it seems at all reasonable to us shows how extensively the idea of the unconscious has pervaded thinking in Western cultures. In fact, work by contemporary researchers studying memory and learning suggests that we unconsciously carry with us memories that have a significant impact on our behavior.

Some of the most basic principles of Freud's psychoanalytic theory have been questioned, however, because they have not been validated by research. In particular, the notion that childhood stages determine adult personalities has little research support. In addition, because much of Freud's theory was based on a limited population of upper-middle-class Austrians living during a strict, puritanical era, its application to broad, multicultural populations is questionable. Finally, because Freud's theory focuses primarily on male development, it has been criticized as sexist and interpreted as devaluing women (Messer & McWilliams, 2003; Schachter, 2005; Gillham, Law, & Hickey, 2010).

Erikson's view that development continues throughout the life span is highly important—and has received considerable support. However, the theory also has its drawbacks. Like Freud's theory, it focuses more on men than women. Further, its vagueness makes it difficult to test rigorously. And, as with psychodynamic theories in general, it is difficult to make definitive predictions about a given individual's behavior using the theory (Whitbourne et al., 1992; Zauszniewski & Martin, 1999; De St. Aubin & McAdams, 2004).

Erik Erikson

## The Behavioral Perspective: Focusing on Observable Behavior

When Elissa Sheehan was 3, a large brown dog bit her, and she needed dozens of stitches and several operations. From the time she was bitten, she broke into a sweat whenever she saw a dog, and in fact never enjoyed being around any pet.

To a lifespan development specialist using the behavioral perspective, the explanation for Elissa's behavior is straightforward: She has a learned fear of dogs. Rather than looking inside the organism at unconscious processes, the **behavioral perspective** suggests that the keys to understanding development are observable behavior and environmental stimuli. If we know the stimuli, we can predict the behavior. In this respect, the behavioral perspective reflects the view that nurture is more important to development than nature.

Behavioral theories reject the notion that people universally pass through a series of stages. Instead, people are affected by the environmental stimuli to which they happen to be exposed. Developmental patterns, then, are personal, reflecting a particular set of environmental stimuli, and behavior is the result of continuing exposure to specific factors in the environment. Furthermore, developmental change is viewed in quantitative, rather than qualitative, terms. For instance, behavioral theories hold that advances in problem-solving capabilities as children age are largely a result of greater mental *capacities,* rather than changes in the *kind* of thinking that children can bring to bear on a problem.

### *Classical Conditioning: Stimulus Substitution.*

*Give me a dozen healthy infants, well-formed, and my own specified world to bring them up in and I'll guarantee to take any one at random and train him to become any type of specialist I might select—doctor, lawyer, artist, merchant-chief, and yes, even beggar-man and thief, regardless of his talents, penchants, tendencies, abilities. . . .* (Watson, 1925)

With these words, John B. Watson, one of the first American psychologists to advocate a behavioral approach, summed up the behavioral perspective. Watson, who lived from 1878 to 1958, believed strongly that we could gain a full understanding of development by carefully studying the stimuli that composed the environment. In fact, he argued that by effectively controlling—or *conditioning*—a person's environment, it was possible to produce virtually any behavior.

**behavioral perspective** the approach that suggests that the keys to understanding development are observable behavior and outside stimuli in the environment

John B. Watson

**Classical conditioning** occurs when an organism learns to respond in a particular way to a neutral stimulus. For instance, if the sound of a bell is paired with the arrival of meat, a dog will learn to react to the bell alone in the same way it reacts to the meat—by salivating and wagging its tail. The behavior is a result of conditioning, a form of learning in which the response associated with one stimulus (food) comes to be connected to another—in this case, the bell.

The same process of classical conditioning explains how we learn emotional responses. In the case of dog-bite victim Elissa Sheehan, for instance, Watson would say that one stimulus has been substituted for another: Elissa's unpleasant experience with a particular dog (the initial stimulus) has been transferred to other dogs and to pets in general.

*Operant Conditioning.* In addition to classical conditioning, the behavioral perspective accounts for other types of learning, especially what behavioralists call operant conditioning. **Operant conditioning** is a form of learning in which a voluntary response is strengthened or weakened by its association with positive or negative consequences. It differs from classical conditioning in that the response being conditioned is voluntary and purposeful rather than automatic (such as salivating). In operant conditioning, formulated and championed by psychologist B. F. Skinner (1904–1990), individuals learn to *operate* on their environments in order to bring about desired consequences (Skinner, 1975).

Whether or not children and adults will seek to repeat a behavior depends on whether it is followed by reinforcement. *Reinforcement* is the process by which a behavior is followed by a stimulus that increases the probability that the behavior will be repeated. Hence, a student is apt to work harder if he or she receives good grades; workers are likely to labor harder if their efforts are tied to pay increases; and people are more apt to buy lottery tickets if they are reinforced by winning occasionally. In addition, *punishment,* the introduction of an unpleasant or painful stimulus or the removal of a desirable stimulus, will decrease the probability that a preceding behavior will occur in the future.

Behavior that is reinforced, then, is more likely to be repeated, while behavior that receives no reinforcement or is punished is likely to be *extinguished* in the language of operant conditioning. Principles of operant conditioning are used in **behavior modification,** a formal technique for promoting the frequency of desirable behaviors and decreasing the incidence of unwanted ones. Behavior modification has been used in situations ranging from teaching people with severe retardation basic language to helping people with self-control problems stick to diets (Christophersen & Mortweet, 2003; Hoek & Gendall, 2006; Matson & LoVullo, 2008).

*Social-Cognitive Learning Theory: Learning through Imitation.* A 5-year-old boy seriously injures his 22-month-old cousin while imitating a violent wrestling move he has seen on television. Although the baby sustained spinal cord injuries, he improved and was discharged 5 weeks after his hospital admission (Reuters Health eLine, 2002).

Cause and effect? We can't know for sure, but it certainly seems possible, especially to social-cognitive learning theorists. According to developmental psychologist Albert Bandura and colleagues, a significant amount of learning is explained by **social-cognitive learning theory,** an approach that emphasizes learning by observing the behavior of another person, called a *model* (Bandura, 1994, 2002).

⟶ **From a social worker's perspective:** How do the concepts of social learning and modeling relate to the mass media, and how might exposure to mass media influence a child's family life?

According to social-cognitive learning theory, behavior is learned primarily through observation and not through trial and error, as it is with operant conditioning. We don't need to experience the consequences of a behavior ourselves to learn it. Social-cognitive learning theory holds that when we see the behavior of a model being rewarded, we are likely to imitate that behavior. For instance, in one classic experiment, children who were afraid of dogs were exposed to a model, nicknamed the "Fearless Peer," who was seen playing happily with a dog (Bandura, Grusec, & Menlove, 1967). After exposure, the children who previously had been afraid were more likely to approach a strange dog than children who had not seen the model.

**classical conditioning** a type of learning in which an organism responds in a particular way to a neutral stimulus that normally does not bring about that type of response

**operant conditioning** a form of learning in which a voluntary response is strengthened or weakened by its association with positive or negative consequences

**behavior modification** a formal technique for promoting the frequency of desirable behaviors and decreasing the incidence of unwanted ones

**social-cognitive learning theory** learning by observing the behavior of another person, called a model

***Assessing the Behavioral Perspective.*** Research using the behavioral perspective has made significant contributions, ranging from the education of children with severe mental retardation to the development of procedures for curbing aggression. At the same time, the perspective has experienced internal disagreements. For example, although part of the same behavioral perspective, classical and operant conditioning and social learning theory disagree in some basic ways. Classical and operant conditioning consider learning in terms of external stimuli and responses, in which the only important factors are the observable features of the environment. People and other organisms are like inanimate "black boxes"; nothing that occurs inside the box is understood—nor much cared about, for that matter.

To social learning theorists, such an analysis is an oversimplification. They argue that what makes people different from rats and pigeons is the mental activity, in the form of thoughts and expectations. We cannot derive a full understanding of people's development without moving beyond external stimuli and responses.

In many ways, social learning theory has won this argument in recent decades. In fact, another perspective that focuses explicitly on internal mental activity—the cognitive perspective—has become enormously influential.

## The Cognitive Perspective: Examining the Roots of Understanding

On the reality show *Survivor*, contestants often must learn new survival skills in order to be successful. What form of learning is prevalent?

When 3-year-old Jake is asked why it sometimes rains, he answers "so the flowers can grow." When his 11-year-old sister Lila is asked the same question, she responds "because of evaporation from the surface of the Earth." And when their cousin Ajima, who is studying meteorology in graduate school, considers the same question, her extended answer includes a discussion of cumulo-nimbus clouds, the Coriolis Effect, and synoptic charts.

To a developmental theorist using the cognitive perspective, the difference in the sophistication of the answers is evidence of a different degree of knowledge and understanding, or cognition. The **cognitive perspective** focuses on the processes that allow people to know, understand, and think about the world.

The cognitive perspective emphasizes how people internally represent and think about the world. By using this perspective, developmental researchers hope to understand how children and adults process information and how their ways of thinking and understanding affect their behavior. They also seek to learn how cognitive abilities change as people develop, the degree to which cognitive development represents quantitative and qualitative growth in intellectual abilities, and how different cognitive abilities are related to one another.

***Piaget's Theory of Cognitive Development.*** No one has had a greater impact on the study of cognitive development than Jean Piaget, a Swiss psychologist who lived from 1896 to 1980. Piaget proposed that all people pass through a fixed sequence of universal stages of cognitive development—and not only does the *quantity* of information increase in each stage, but the *quality* of knowledge and understanding changes as well. His focus was on the change in cognition that occurs as children move from one stage to the next (Piaget, 1952, 1962, 1983). Broadly speaking, Piaget suggested that human thinking is arranged into *schemes,* organized mental patterns that represent behaviors and actions. In infants, schemes represent concrete behavior—a scheme for sucking, for reaching, and for each separate behavior. In older children, the schemes become more sophisticated and abstract, such as the skills involved in riding a bike or playing an interactive video game. Schemes are like intellectual computer software programs that direct and determine how data from the world are looked at and handled (Parker, 2005).

Piaget suggested that the growth in children's understanding of the world could be explained by two basic principles: assimilation and accommodation. *Assimilation* is the process in which people understand a new experience in terms of their current stage of cognitive development and existing ways of thinking. In contrast, *accommodation* refers to changes in existing ways of thinking in response to encounters with new stimuli or events. Assimilation and accommodation work in tandem to bring about cognitive development.

***Assessing Piaget's Theory.*** Piaget has profoundly influenced our understanding of cognitive development and is one of the towering figures in lifespan development. He provided masterly descriptions of intellectual growth during childhood—descriptions that have stood

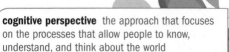

**cognitive perspective** the approach that focuses on the processes that allow people to know, understand, and think about the world

**information processing approaches** the model that seeks to identify the ways individuals take in, use, and store information

**cognitive neuroscience approaches** the approach that examines cognitive development through the lens of brain processes

the test of literally thousands of investigations. Broadly, then, Piaget's view of cognitive development is accurate.

However, the specifics of the theory have been questioned. For instance, some cognitive skills clearly emerge earlier than Piaget suggested. Furthermore, the universality of Piaget's stages has been disputed. Growing evidence suggests that particular cognitive skills emerge on a different timetable in non-Western cultures. And in every culture, some people never seem to reach Piaget's highest level of cognitive sophistication: formal, logical thought (McDonald & Stuart-Hamilton, 2003; Genovese, 2006: Kesselring & Müller, 2010).

Ultimately, the greatest criticism is that cognitive development is not necessarily as discontinuous as Piaget's stage theory suggests. Many developmental researchers argue that growth is considerably more continuous. These critics have suggested an alternative perspective, known as the information processing approach, that focuses on the processes that underlie learning, memory, and thinking throughout the life span.

**Information Processing Approaches.** Information processing approaches have become an important alternative to Piagetian approaches. **Information processing approaches** to cognitive development seek to identify the ways individuals take in, use, and store information.

Information processing approaches grew out of developments in computers. They assume that even complex behavior such as learning, remembering, categorizing, and thinking can be broken down into a series of individual, specific steps.

Like computers, children are assumed by information processing approaches to have limited capacity for processing information. As they develop, though, they employ increasingly sophisticated strategies that allow them to process information more efficiently.

In stark contrast to Piaget's view, information processing approaches assume that development is marked more by quantitative advances than qualitative ones. Our capacity to handle information changes with age, as does our processing speed and efficiency. Furthermore, information processing approaches suggest that as we age, we are better able to control the nature of processing and the strategies we choose to process information.

An information processing approach that builds on Piaget's research is known as neo-Piagetian theory. In contrast to Piaget's original work, which viewed cognition as a single system of increasingly sophisticated general cognitive abilities, *neo-Piagetian theory* considers cognition as made up of different types of individual skills. Using the terminology of information processing approaches, neo-Piagetian theory suggests that cognitive development proceeds quickly in certain areas and more slowly in others. For example, reading ability and the skills needed to recall stories may progress sooner than the abstract computational abilities used in algebra or trigonometry. Furthermore, neo-Piagetian theorists believe that experience plays a greater role in advancing cognitive development than traditional Piagetian approaches claim (Case, Demetriou, & Platsidou, 2001; Yan & Fischer, 2002; Loewen, 2006).

**Assessing Information Processing Approaches.** As we'll see in future chapters, information processing approaches have become a central part of our understanding of development. At the same time, they do not offer a complete explanation of behavior. For example, they have paid little attention to behavior such as creativity, in which the most profound ideas often are developed in a seemingly nonlogical, nonlinear manner. In addition, they do not take into account the social context in which development takes place—and theories that do this have become increasingly popular.

**Cognitive Neuroscience Approaches.** One of the most recent additions to the array of approaches are **cognitive neuroscience approaches,** which look at cognitive development at the level of brain processes. Like other cognitive perspectives, cognitive neuroscience approaches consider internal, mental processes, but they focus specifically on the neurological activity that underlies thinking, problem solving, and other cognitive behavior.

Cognitive neuroscientists seek to identify actual locations and functions within the brain that are related to different types of cognitive activity. For example, using sophisticated brain scanning techniques, cognitive neuroscientists have demonstrated that thinking about the meaning of a word activates different areas of the brain than thinking about how the word sounds when spoken.

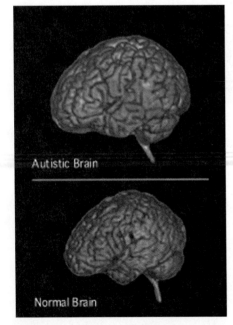

**FIGURE 1-1 The Autistic Brain**
Neuroscientists found in one study that brains of individuals with autism were larger than those without autism. This finding can help determine the disorder early so proper health care can be provided.
Source: Courchesne website at http://www.courchesneautismlab.org/mri.html.

Cognitive neuroscientists are also providing clues to the cause of *autism*, a major developmental disability that can produce profound language deficits and self-injurious behavior in young children. For example, neuroscientists have found that the brains of children with the disorder show explosive, dramatic growth in the first year of life, making their heads significantly larger than those of children without the disorder (see Figure 1-1). By identifying children with the disorder very early in their lives, health care providers can provide crucial early intervention (Akshoomoff, 2006; Nadel & Poss, 2007; Lewis & Elman, 2008; Bal et al., 2010).

Cognitive neuroscience approaches are also on the forefront of cutting edge research that has identified genes associated with disorders ranging from physical problems such as breast cancer to psychological disorders such as schizophrenia. Identifying the genes that make one vulnerable to such disorders is the first step in genetic engineering in which gene therapy can reduce or even prevent the disorder from occurring (DeLisi & Fleischhaker, 2007; Strobel et al., 2007; Ranganath, Minzenberg, & Ragland, 2008).

## REVIEW, CHECK, AND APPLY

### REVIEW

**LO5** Which theoretical perspectives have guided lifespan development?

- Lifespan development has been viewed from six major theoretical perspectives: the psychodynamic, behavioral, cognitive, humanistic, contextual, and evolutionary perspectives. Each emphasizes somewhat different aspects of development and steers developmentalists in particular directions.

**LO6** What are the main characteristics of the psychodynamic, behavioral, and cognitive perspectives?

- The psychodynamic perspective looks primarily at the influence of internal, unconscious forces on development.
- In contrast, the behavioral perspective focuses on external, observable behaviors as the key to development.
- The cognitive perspective focuses on mental activity, holding that individuals pass through stages in which their ways of thinking change both qualitatively and quantitatively.

### CHECK YOURSELF

1. _____ are organized explanations and predictions concerning phenomena of interest and provide frameworks for understanding the relationships across variables.
   a. Evaluations
   b. Constitutions
   d. Intuitions
   d. Theories

2. The _____ perspective suggests that the key to understanding one's actions involves observation of those actions and the outside stimuli in the environment.

3. Which of the following is NOT a concern with Piaget's cognitive perspective?
   a. Everyone reaches Piaget's highest level of thought, suggesting that it isn't much of an achievement.
   b. Some cognitive skills appear much earlier than Piaget originally thought.

c. The timing of cognitive skills differs as a function of culture.

d. Cognitive development does not appear to be as discontinuous as Piaget suggested.

### APPLYING LIFESPAN DEVELOPMENT

- Can you think of examples of human behavior that may have been inherited from our ancestors because they helped survival and adaptation? Explain why you think this.

✔—Study and Review on
MyDevelopmentLab.com

Answers: 1) d; 2) behavioral; 3) a

# The Humanistic, Contextual, and Evolutionary Perspectives

**LO7** What are the main characteristics of the humanistic, contextual, and evolutionary perspectives?

**LO8** Why is there no "right" approach to development?

LEARNING OBJECTIVES

## The Humanistic Perspective: Concentrating on Uniquely Human Qualities

The unique qualities of humans are the central focus of the humanistic perspective, the fourth of the major theories used by lifespan developmentalists. Rejecting the notion that behavior is largely determined by unconscious processes, the environment, or cognitive processing, the **humanistic perspective** contends that people have a natural capacity to make decisions about their lives and to control their behavior. According to this approach, each individual has the ability and motivation to reach more advanced levels of maturity, and people naturally seek to reach their full potential.

The humanistic perspective emphasizes *free will*, the ability of humans to make choices and come to decisions about their lives. Instead of relying on societal standards, then, people are assumed to be motivated to make their own decisions about what they do with their lives.

Carl Rogers, one of the major proponents of the humanistic perspective, suggests that people need positive regard, which results from an underlying wish to be loved and respected. Because positive regard comes from other people, we become dependent on them. Consequently, our view of ourselves and our self-worth is a reflection of how we think others view us (Rogers, 1971; Motschnig & Nykl, 2003; Cornforth, 2010).

Rogers, along with another key figure in the humanistic perspective, Abraham Maslow, suggests that self-actualization is a primary goal in life. *Self-actualization* is a state of self-fulfillment in which people achieve their highest potential in their own unique way (Maslow, 1970; Jones & Crandall, 1991; Sheldon, Joiner, & Pettit, 2003).

***Assessing the Humanistic Perspective.*** Despite its emphasis on important and unique human qualities, the humanistic perspective has not had a major impact on the field of lifespan development. This is primarily due to its inability to identify any sort of broad developmental change that is the result of increasing age or experience. Still, some of the concepts drawn from the humanistic perspective, such as self-actualization, have helped describe important aspects of human behavior and are widely discussed in areas ranging from health care to business (Laas, 2006; Zalenski & Raspa, 2006; Elkins, 2009).

## The Contextual Perspective: Taking a Broad Approach to Development

Although lifespan developmentalists often consider physical, cognitive, personality, and social factors separately, such a categorization has one serious drawback: In the real world, none of these broad influences occurs in isolation from any other. Instead, there is a constant, ongoing interaction between the different types of influence.

The **contextual perspective** considers the relationship between individuals and their physical, cognitive, personality, and social worlds. It suggests that a person's unique development cannot be properly viewed without seeing how that person is enmeshed within a rich social and cultural context. We'll consider two major theories that fall under this category, Bronfenbrenner's bioecological approach and Vygotsky's sociocultural theory.

***The Bioecological Approach to Development.*** In acknowledging the problem with traditional approaches to lifespan development, psychologist Urie Bronfenbrenner (1989; 2000; 2002) has proposed an alternative perspective, the bioecological approach. The **bioecological approach** suggests that there are five levels of the environment that simultaneously influence individuals. Bronfenbrenner suggests that we cannot fully understand development without considering how a person is influenced by each of these levels.

- The *microsystem* is the everyday, immediate environment of children's daily lives. Homes, caregivers, friends, and teachers all are influences, but the child is not just a passive recipient. Instead, children actively help construct the microsystem, shaping their immediate world. The microsystem is the level to which most traditional work in child development has been directed.

- The *mesosystem* connects the various aspects of the microsystem. The mesosystem binds children to parents, students to teachers, employees to bosses, friends to friends. It

**humanistic perspective** the theory that contends that people have a natural capacity to make decisions about their lives and control their behavior

**contextual perspective** the theory that considers the relationship between individuals and their physical, cognitive, personality, and social worlds

**bioecological approach** the perspective suggesting that levels of the environment simultaneously influence individuals

acknowledges the direct and indirect influences that bind us to one another, such as those that affect a mother who has a bad day at the office and then is short-tempered with her son or daughter at home.

- The *exosystem* represents broader influences: societal institutions such as local government, the community, schools, places of worship, and the local media. Each of these institutions can have an immediate and major impact on personal development, and each affects how the microsystem and mesosystem operate. For example, the quality of a school will affect a child's cognitive development and potentially can have long-term consequences.

- The *macrosystem* represents the larger cultural influences on an individual, including society in general, types of governments, religious and political value systems, and other broad, encompassing factors. For example, the value a culture places on education affects the values of the people who live in that culture. Children are part of both a broader culture (such as Western culture) and members of one or more subcultures (for instance, Mexican American subculture).

- Finally, the *chronosystem* underlies each of the previous systems. It involves the way the passage of time—including historical events (such as the terrorist attacks in September of 2001) and more gradual historical changes (such as changes in the number of women who work outside the home)—affects children's development.

The bioecological approach emphasizes the *interconnectedness of the influences on development*. Because the various levels are related to one another, a change in one part of the system affects other parts. For instance, a parent's loss of a job (involving the mesosystem) has an impact upon a child's microsystem.

Conversely, changes on one environmental level may make little difference if other levels are not also changed. For instance, improving the school environment may have a negligible effect on academic performance if children receive little support for academic success at home. Similarly, the influences among family members are multidirectional. Parents don't just influence their child's behavior—the child also influences the parents' behavior.

Finally, the bioecological approach stresses the importance of broad cultural factors that affect development. Researchers in lifespan development increasingly look at how membership in cultural groups influences behavior.

Consider, for instance, whether you agree that children should be taught that their classmates' assistance is essential to getting good grades in school, or that they should plan to continue their fathers' businesses, or that they should take their parents' advice in choosing a career. If you have been raised in the most widespread North American culture, you would likely disagree with all three statements, since they violate the premises of *individualism,* the dominant Western philosophy that emphasizes personal identity, uniqueness, freedom, and the worth of the individual.

On the other hand, if you were raised in a traditional Asian culture, your agreement with the three statements is considerably more likely because the statements reflect the value orientation known as collectivism. *Collectivism* is the notion that the well-being of the group is more important than that of the individual. People raised in collectivistic cultures sometimes emphasize the welfare of the group at the expense of their own personal well-being.

The individualism–collectivism spectrum is one of several dimensions along which cultures differ, and it illustrates differences in the cultural contexts in which people operate. Such broad cultural values play an important role in shaping the ways people view the world and behave (Garcia & Saewyc, 2007; Yu & Stiffman, 2007; Boles, Le, & Nguyen, 2010).

**Assessing the Bioecological Approach.**  Although Bronfenbrenner regards biological influences as an important component of the bioecological approach, ecological influences are central to the theory. In fact, some critics argue that the perspective pays insufficient attention to biological factors. Still, the bioecological approach is important because it suggests the multiple levels at which the environment affects children's development.

**Vygotsky's Sociocultural Theory.**  To Russian developmentalist Lev Semenovich Vygotsky, a full understanding of development is impossible without taking into account the culture in which

According to Vygotsky, children can develop cognitively in their understanding of the world, and learn what is important in society, through play and cooperation with others.

people develop. Vygotsky's **sociocultural theory** emphasizes how cognitive development proceeds as a result of social interactions between members of a culture (Vygotsky, 1979, 1926/1997; Beilin, 1996; Winsler, 2003; Edwards, 2005; Ferholt & Lecusay, 2010).

Vygotsky, who lived a brief life, from 1896 to 1934, argued that children's understanding of the world is acquired through their problem-solving interactions with adults and other children. As children play and cooperate with others, they learn what is important in their society and, at the same time, advance cognitively. Consequently, to understand development, we must consider what is meaningful to members of a given culture.

More than most other theories, sociocultural theory emphasizes that development is a *reciprocal transaction* between the people in a child's environment and the child. Vygotsky believed that people and settings influence the child, who in turn influences the people and settings. This pattern continues in an endless loop, with children being both recipients of socialization influences and sources of influence. For example, a child raised with his or her extended family nearby will grow up with a different sense of family life than a child whose relatives live far away. Those relatives, too, are affected by that situation and that child, depending upon how close and frequent their contact is with the child.

*Assessing Vygotsky's Theory.* Sociocultural theory has become increasingly influential, despite Vygotsky's death almost eight decades ago. The reason is the growing acknowledgment of the central importance of cultural factors in development. Children do not develop in a cultural vacuum. Instead, their attention is directed by society to certain areas, and as a consequence, they develop particular kinds of skills. Vygotsky was one of the first developmentalists to recognize and acknowledge the importance of the cultural environment, and—as today's society becomes increasingly multicultural—sociocultural theory helps us to understand the rich and varied influences that shape development (Fowers & Davidov, 2006; Koshmanova, 2007; Rogan, 2007).

Sociocultural theory is not without its critics, however. Some suggest that Vygotsky's strong emphasis on the role of culture and social experience led him to ignore the effects of biological factors on development. In addition, his perspective seems to minimize the role that individuals play in shaping their environment.

## Evolutionary Perspectives: Our Ancestors' Contributions to Behavior

One increasingly influential approach is the evolutionary perspective, the sixth and final developmental perspective that we will consider. The **evolutionary perspective** seeks to identify behavior that is the result of our genetic inheritance from our ancestors (Buss & Kern, 2003; Bjorklund, 2005; Goetz & Shackelford, 2006).

Evolutionary approaches grow out of the groundbreaking work of Charles Darwin. In 1859, Darwin argued in *On the Origin of Species* that a process of natural selection creates traits in a species that are adaptive to its environment. Using Darwin's arguments, evolutionary approaches contend that our genetic inheritance not only determines such physical traits as skin and eye color, but certain personality traits and social behaviors as well. For instance, some evolutionary developmentalists suggest that behaviors such as shyness and jealousy are produced in part by genetic causes, presumably because they helped in increasing survival rates of humans' ancient relatives (Easton, Schipper, & Shackelford, 2007; Buss, 2003, 2009).

The evolutionary perspective draws heavily on the field of *ethology,* which examines the ways in which our biological makeup influences our behavior. A primary proponent of ethology was Konrad Lorenz (1903–1989), who discovered that newborn geese are genetically preprogrammed to become attached to the first moving object they see after birth. His work, which demonstrated the importance of biological determinants in influencing behavior

**sociocultural theory** the approach that emphasizes how cognitive development proceeds as a result of social interactions between members of a culture

**evolutionary perspective** the theory that seeks to identify behavior that is a result of our genetic inheritance from our ancestors

patterns, led developmentalists to consider the ways in which human behavior might reflect inborn genetic patterns.

The evolutionary perspective encompasses one of the fastest growing areas within the field of lifespan development: behavioral genetics. *Behavioral genetics* studies the effects of heredity on behavior. Behavioral geneticists seek to understand how we might inherit certain behavioral traits and how the environment influences whether we actually display those traits. It also considers how genetic factors may produce psychological disorders such as schizophrenia (Li, 2003; Bjorklund & Ellis, 2005; Rembis, 2009).

***Assessing the Evolutionary Perspective.*** There is little argument among lifespan developmentalists that Darwin's evolutionary theory provides an accurate description of basic genetic processes, and the evolutionary perspective is increasingly visible in the field of lifespan development. However, applications of the evolutionary perspective have been subjected to considerable criticism.

Some developmentalists are concerned that because of its focus on genetic and biological aspects of behavior, the evolutionary perspective pays insufficient attention to the environmental and social factors involved in producing children's and adults' behavior. Other critics argue that there is no good way to experimentally test theories derived from this approach because humans evolved so long ago. For example, it is one thing to say that jealousy helped individuals to survive more effectively and another thing to prove it. Still, the evolutionary approach has stimulated research on how our biological inheritance influences at least partially our traits and behaviors (Buss & Reeve, 2003; Bjorklund, 2006; Baptista et al., 2008).

Konrad Lorenz, seen here with geese who from their birth have followed him, considered the ways in which behavior reflects inborn genetic patterns.

## Why "Which Approach Is Right?" Is the Wrong Question

We have considered the six major perspectives on development—psychodynamic, behavioral, cognitive, humanistic, contextual, and evolutionary—summarized in Table 1-3 and applied to a specific case. It would be natural to wonder which of the six provides the most accurate account of human development.

For several reasons, this is not an appropriate question. For one thing, each perspective emphasizes different aspects of development. For instance, the psychodynamic approach emphasizes unconscious determinants of behavior, while behavioral perspectives emphasize overt behavior. The cognitive and humanistic perspectives look more at what people *think* than at what they do. The contextual perspective examines social and cultural influences on development, and the evolutionary perspective focuses on how inherited biological factors underlie development.

For example, a developmentalist using the psychodynamic approach might consider how the 9/11 terrorist attacks on the World Trade Center and Pentagon might affect children, unconsciously, for their entire life span. A cognitive approach might focus on how children perceived and came to interpret and understand terrorism, while a contextual approach might consider what personality and social factors led the perpetrators to adopt terrorist tactics.

Clearly, each perspective is based on its own premises and focuses on different aspects of development. Furthermore, the same developmental phenomenon can be looked at from a number of perspectives simultaneously. In fact, some lifespan developmentalists use an *eclectic* approach, drawing on several perspectives simultaneously.

In the same way, the various theoretical perspectives provide different ways of looking at development. Considering them together paints a fuller portrait of the myriad ways human beings change and grow over the course of their lives. However, not all theories and claims derived from the various perspectives are accurate. How do we choose among competing explanations? The answer can be found through *research,* which we consider in the final part of this chapter.

## TABLE 1-3 MAJOR PERSPECTIVES ON LIFESPAN DEVELOPMENT

| Perspective | Key Ideas About Human Behavior and Development | Major Proponents | Example |
|---|---|---|---|
| Psychodynamic | Behavior throughout life is motivated by inner, unconscious forces, stemming from childhood, over which we have little control. | Sigmund Freud, Erik Erikson | This view might suggest that a young adult who is overweight has a fixation in the oral stage of development. |
| Behavioral | Development can be understood through studying observable behavior and environmental stimuli. | John B. Watson, B. F. Skinner, Albert Bandura | In this perspective, a young adult who is overweight might be seen as not being rewarded for good nutritional and exercise habits. |
| Cognitive | Emphasis on how changes or growth in the ways people know, understand, and think about the world affect behavior. | Jean Piaget | This view might suggest that a young adult who is overweight hasn't learned effective ways to stay at a healthy weight and doesn't value good nutrition. |
| Humanistic | Behavior is chosen through free *will* and motivated by our natural capacity to strive to reach our full potential. | Carl Rogers, Abraham Maslow | In this view, a young adult who is overweight may eventually choose to seek an optimal weight as part of an overall pattern of individual growth. |
| Contextual | Development should be viewed in terms of the interrelationship of a person's physical, cognitive, personality, and social worlds. | Urie Bronfenbrenner, Lev Vygotsky | In this perspective, being overweight is caused by a number of interrelated factors in that person's physical, cognitive, personality, and social worlds. |
| Evolutionary | Behavior is the result of genetic inheritance from our ancestors; traits and behavior that are adaptive for promoting the survival of our species have been inherited through natural selection. | Influenced by early work of Charles Darwin, Konrad Lorenz | This view might suggest that a young adult might have a genetic tendency toward obesity because extra fat helped his or her ancestors to survive in times of famine. |

## REVIEW, CHECK, AND APPLY

### REVIEW

**LO7** What are the main characteristics of the humanistic, contextual, and evolutionary perspectives?

- The humanistic perspective maintains that individuals have the ability and motivation to reach advanced levels of maturity and that people naturally seek to reach their full potential.

- The contextual perspective considers the relationship between individuals and their physical, cognitive, personality, and social worlds. Bronfenbrenner's bioecological approach and Vygotsky's sociocultural theory fall into this category.

- The evolutionary perspective attempts to identify behavior that is a result of our genetic inheritance.

**LO8** Why is there no "right" approach to development?

- The theoretical perspectives provide different ways of looking at development. Considering them together paints a fuller portrait of the myriad ways human beings change and grow over the course of their lives.

- However, not all theories and claims derived from the various perspectives are accurate.

### CHECK YOURSELF

1. According to the humanistic perspective, people reject the urge to seek love and respect from others and strive to achieve personal independence free of societal interconnections.
   - True
   - False

2. Bronfenbrenner's bioecological approach and Vygotsky's sociocultural theory fall under the category of the _____ perspective.
   a. humanistic
   b. ethnological
   c. contextual
   d. evolutionary

3. The researcher most closely associated with the evolutionary perspective is:
   a. Konrad Lorenz.
   b. Jean Piaget.
   c. Carl Rogers
   d. B. F. Skinner

### APPLYING LIFESPAN DEVELOPMENT

- Can you think of people you have known who exhibited distinct signs of being in a stage of psychosocial development discussed by Erikson? What stage were they in and what were the signs?

✓—[**Study** and **Review** on
**MyDevelopmentLab.com**

Answers: 1) False; 2) c; 3) a

## MODULE **1.3** Research Methods

*The Egyptians had long believed that they were the most ancient race on earth, and Psamtik [King of Egypt in the seventh century, B.C.], driven by intellectual curiosity, wanted to prove that flattering belief. Like a good researcher, he began with a hypothesis: If children had no opportunity to learn a language from older people around them, they would spontaneously speak the primal, inborn language of humankind—the natural language of its most ancient people—which, he expected to show, was Egyptian.*

*To test his hypothesis, Psamtik commandeered two infants of a lower-class mother and turned them over to a herdsman to bring up in a remote area. They were to be kept in a sequestered cottage, properly fed and cared for, but were never to hear anyone speak so much as a word. The Greek historian Herodotus, who tracked the story down and learned what he calls "the real facts" from priests of Hephaestus in Memphis, says that Psamtik's goal "was to know, after the indistinct babblings of infancy were over, what word they would first articulate."*

*The experiment, he tells us, worked. One day, when the children were two years old, they ran up to the herdsman as he opened the door of their cottage and cried out "Becos!" Since this meant nothing to him, he paid no attention, but when it happened repeatedly, he sent word to Psamtik, who at once ordered the children brought to him. When he too heard them say it, Psamtik made inquiries and learned that becos was the Phrygian word for bread. He concluded that, disappointingly, the Phrygians were an older race than the Egyptians. (Hunt, 1993, pp. 1–2)*

With the perspective of several thousand years, we can easily see the shortcomings—both scientific and ethical—in Psamtik's approach. Yet his procedure represents an improvement over mere speculation, and as such is sometimes looked upon as the first developmental experiment in recorded history (Hunt, 1993).

# Theories, Hypotheses, and Correlational Studies

**LO9** What roles do theories and hypotheses play in the study of development?

**LO10** What sorts of studies and methods are used in correlational research?

**LEARNING OBJECTIVES**

## Theories and Hypotheses: Posing Developmental Questions

Questions such as those raised by Psamtik drive the study of development. In fact, developmentalists are still studying how children learn language. Others are working on such questions as, What are the effects of malnutrition on intellectual performance? How do infants form relationships with their parents, and does day care disrupt such relationships? Why are adolescents particularly susceptible to peer pressure? Can mentally challenging activities reduce the declines in intellectual abilities related to aging? Do any mental faculties improve with age?

To answer such questions, developmentalists, like all psychologists and other scientists, rely on the scientific method. The **scientific method** is the process of posing and answering questions using careful, controlled techniques that include systematic, orderly observation and the collection of data. The scientific method involves three major steps: (1) identifying questions of interest, (2) formulating an explanation, and (3) carrying out research that either lends support to the explanation or refutes it.

The scientific method involves the formulation of **theories,** broad explanations, and predictions about phenomena of interest. For instance, the idea that there is a crucial bonding period between parent and child immediately after birth is a theory.

**scientific method** the process of posing and answering questions using careful, controlled techniques that include systematic, orderly observation and the collection of data

**theories** broad explanations, and predictions about phenomena of interest

Developmental researchers use theories to form hypotheses. A **hypothesis** is a prediction stated in a way that permits it to be tested. For instance, someone who subscribes to the general theory that bonding is crucial might derive the hypothesis that effective bonding occurs only if it lasts for a certain length of time.

## Choosing a Research Strategy: Answering Questions

Once researchers have formed a hypothesis, they must develop a research strategy to test its validity. There are two major categories of research: correlational research and experimental research. Correlational research seeks to identify whether an association or relationship between two factors exists. As we'll see, **correlational research** cannot determine whether one factor *causes* changes in the other. For instance, correlational research could tell us if there is an association between the number of minutes a mother and her newborn child are together immediately after birth and the quality of the mother–child relationship when the child reaches age 2. Such correlational research indicates whether the two factors are *associated* or *related* to one another, but not whether the initial contact caused the relationship to develop in a particular way (Schutt, 2001).

In contrast, **experimental research** is designed to discover *causal* relationships between various factors. In experimental research, researchers deliberately introduce a change in a carefully structured situation in order to see the consequences of that change. For instance, a researcher conducting an experiment might vary the number of minutes that mothers and children interact immediately following birth, in an attempt to see whether the bonding time affects the mother–child relationship.

Because experimental research is able to answer questions of causality, it is fundamental to finding answers to various developmental hypotheses. However, some research questions cannot be answered through experiments, for either technical or ethical reasons (for example, it would be unethical to design an experiment in which a group of infants was offered no chance to bond with a caregiver at all). In fact, a great deal of pioneering developmental research—such as that conducted by Piaget and Vygotsky—employed correlational techniques. Consequently, correlational research remains an important tool for developmental researchers.

## Correlational Studies

As we've noted, correlational research examines the relationship between two variables to determine whether they are associated, or *correlated*. For instance, researchers interested in the relationship between televised aggression and subsequent behavior have found that children who watch a good deal of aggression on television—murders, crime shows, shootings, and the like—tend to be more aggressive than those who watch only a little. In other words, viewing aggression and actual aggression are strongly associated, or correlated (Center for Communication & Social Policy, 1998; Singer & Singer, 2000; Feshbach & Tangney, 2008; Coyne et al., 2010).

But can we conclude that the viewing of televised aggression *causes* the more aggressive behavior? Not at all. Consider some of the other possibilities: It might be that being aggressive in the first place makes children more likely to choose to watch violent programs. In this case, the aggressive tendency causes the viewing behavior, not the other way around.

Or consider that there may be a *third* factor operating on both the viewing and the aggression. Suppose, for example, that children of lower socioeconomic status are more likely to behave aggressively *and* to watch higher levels of aggressive television than those raised in more affluent settings. In this case, the third variable—socioeconomic status—causes *both* the aggressive behavior and the television viewing. (The various possibilities are illustrated in Figure 1-2).

In short, finding that two variables are correlated proves nothing about causality. Although the variables may be linked causally, this is not necessarily the case.

Correlational studies do provide important information, however. For instance, as we'll see in later chapters, we know from correlational studies that the closer the genetic link between two people, the more highly associated is their intelligence. We have learned that the more parents speak to their young children, the more extensive are the children's vocabularies. And

---

**hypothesis** a prediction stated in a way that permits it to be tested

**correlational research** research that seeks to identify whether an association or relationship between two factors exists

**experimental research** research designed to discover causal relationships between various factors

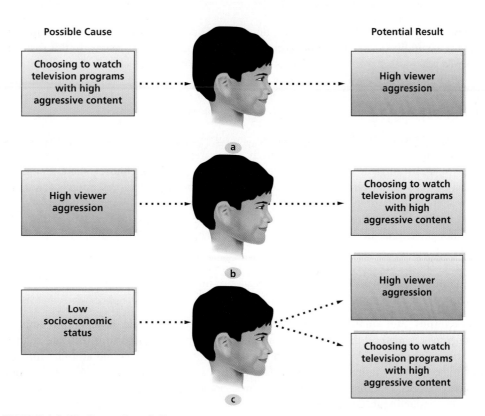

**Possible Cause**

**Potential Result**

**FIGURE 1-2 Finding a Correlation**

Finding a correlation between two factors does not imply that one factor *causes* the other factor to vary. For instance, suppose a study found that viewing television shows with high levels of aggression is correlated with actual aggression in children. The correlation may reflect at least three possibilities: (a) watching television programs containing high levels of aggression causes aggression in viewers; (b) children who behave aggressively choose to watch TV programs with high levels of aggression; or (c) some third factor, such as a child's socioeconomic status, leads both to high viewer aggression and to choosing to watch television programs with high viewer aggression. What other factors, besides socioeconomic status, might be plausible third factors?

we know from correlational studies that the better the nutrition that infants receive, the fewer the cognitive and social problems they experience later (Hart, 2004; Colom, Lluis-Font, & Andrés-Pueyo, 2005; Robb, Richert, & Wartella, 2009).

***The Correlation Coefficient.*** The strength and direction of a relationship between two factors is represented by a mathematical score, called a *correlation coefficient*, that ranges from +1.0 to −1.0. A *positive* correlation indicates that as the value of one factor increases, it can be predicted that the value of the other will also increase. For instance, if we administer a job satisfaction survey and find that the more money people make in their first job, the higher their job satisfaction, and the less money they make the lower their job satisfaction, we have found a positive correlation The correlation coefficient would be indicated by a positive number, and the stronger the association between salary and job satisfaction, the closer the number would be to +1.0.

In contrast, a correlation coefficient with a *negative* value informs us that as the value of one factor increases, the value of the other factor declines. For example, suppose we found that the more time adolescents spend using instant messaging on their computers, the worse their academic performance is. This would produce a negative correlation, a number between 0 and −1. More instant messaging would be associated with lower performance, and less instant messaging with higher performance. The stronger the association between instant messaging and school performance, the closer the correlation coefficient will be to −1.0.

**naturalistic observation** a type of correlational study in which some naturally occurring behavior is observed without intervention in the situation

**case studies** studies that involve extensive, in-depth interviews with a particular individual or small group of individuals

**survey research** a type of study where a group of people chosen to represent some larger population are asked questions about their attitudes, behavior, or thinking on a given topic

**psychophysiological methods** research that focuses on the relationship between physiological processes and behavior

Finally, it may be that two factors are unrelated to one another. For example, it is unlikely that we would find a correlation between school performance and shoe size. In this case, the lack of a relationship would be indicated by a correlation coefficient close to 0.

It is important to repeat that, even if a correlation coefficient is very strong, there is no way we can know whether one factor *causes* the other factor to vary. It simply means that the two factors are associated with one another in a predictable way.

*Types of Correlational Studies.* There are several types of correlational studies. **Naturalistic observation** is the observation of a naturally occurring behavior without intervention. For instance, an investigator who wishes to learn how often preschool children share toys might observe a classroom over a 3-week period, recording how often the preschoolers spontaneously share with one another. The key point is that the investigator observes without interfering (e.g., Beach, 2003; Prezbindowski & Lederberg, 2003; Mortensen & Cialdini, 2010).

Though naturalistic observation has the advantage of identifying what children do in their "natural habitat," there is an important drawback to the method: Researchers are unable to exert control over factors of interest. For instance, in some cases researchers might find so few naturally occurring instances of the behavior of interest that they are unable to draw any conclusions at all.

**Ethnography and qualitative research.** Increasingly, naturalistic observation employs *ethnography,* a method that borrows from anthropology and is used to investigate cultural questions. In ethnography, the goal is to understand a culture's values and attitudes through careful, extended examination. Typically, researchers act as participant observers, living for a period of weeks, months, or even years in another culture. By carefully observing everyday life and conducting in-depth interviews, researchers can obtain a deep understanding of life within another culture (Dyson, 2003).

Ethnographic studies are an example of a broader category of research known as qualitative research. In *qualitative research,* researchers choose particular settings of interest and seek to carefully describe, in narrative fashion, what is occurring, and why. Qualitative research can be used to generate hypotheses that can later be tested using more objective, quantitative methods.

Although ethnographic and qualitative studies provide a fine-grained view of behavior in particular settings, they suffer from several drawbacks. As mentioned, the presence of a participant observer may influence the behavior of the individuals being studied. Furthermore, because only a small number of individuals are studied, it may be hard to generalize the findings to other settings. Finally, ethnographers carrying out cross-cultural research may misinterpret and misconceive what they are observing, particularly in cultures that are very different from their own (Polkinghome, 2005).

**Case studies** involve extensive, in-depth interviews with a particular individual or small group of individuals. They often are used not just to learn about the individual being interviewed, but to derive broader principles or draw tentative conclusions that might apply to others. For example, case studies have been conducted on children who display unusual genius and on children who have spent their early years in the wild, apparently without human contact. These case studies have provided important information to researchers, and have suggested hypotheses for future investigation (Cohen & Cashon, 2003; Wilson, 2003; Ng & Nicholas, 2010).

Using *diaries,* participants are asked to keep a record of their behavior on a regular basis. For example, a group of adolescents may be asked to record each time they interact with friends for more than 5 minutes, thereby providing a way to track their social behavior.

Surveys represent another sort of correlational research. In **survey research,** a group of people chosen to represent some larger population are asked questions about their attitudes, behavior, or thinking on a given topic. For instance, surveys have been conducted about parents' use of punishment on their children and on attitudes toward breastfeeding. From the responses, inferences are drawn regarding the larger population represented by the individuals being surveyed.

*Psychophysiological Methods.* Some developmental researchers, particularly those using a cognitive neuroscience approach, make use of psychophysiological methods. **Psychophysiological methods** focus on the relationship between physiological processes and

This fMRI shows activity in different regions of the brain.

behavior. For instance, a researcher might examine the relationship between blood flow in the brain and problem-solving ability. Similarly, some studies use infants' heart rate as a measure of their interest in stimuli to which they are exposed (Santesso, Schmidt, & Trainor, 2007; Field, Diego, & Hernandez-Reif, 2009; Mazoyer et al., 2009).

Among the most frequently used psychophysiological measures:

- **Electroencephalogram (EEG).** The EEG uses electrodes placed on the skull to record electrical activity in the brain. The brain activity is transformed into a pictorial representation of brain wave patterns, permitting the diagnosis of disorders such as epilepsy and learning disabilities.
- **Computerized axial tomography (CAT) scan.** In a CAT scan, a computer constructs an image of the brain by combining thousands of individual x-rays taken at slightly different angles. Although it does not show brain activity, it does illuminate the structure of the brain.
- **Functional magnetic resonance imaging (fMRI) scan.** An fMRI provides a detailed, three-dimensional computer-generated image of brain activity by aiming a powerful magnetic field at the brain. It offers one of the best ways of learning about the operation of the brain, down to the level of individual nerves.

## REVIEW, CHECK, AND APPLY

### REVIEW

**LO9** What roles do theories and hypotheses play in the study of development?

- Theories are systematically derived explanations of facts or phenomena.
- Theories suggest hypotheses, which are predictions that can be tested.

**LO10** What sorts of studies and methods are used in correlational research?

- Correlational studies examine the relationship, or correlation, between two factors without demonstrating causality.
- Correlational methods include naturalistic observation, ethnography, case studies, survey research, and psychophysiological methods.

### CHECK YOURSELF

**1.** Consider the following steps of the scientific method and rank them from first to last.

_____ Formulating an explanation.

_____ Carrying out research that either lends support to the explanation or refutes it.

_____ Identifying questions of interest.

**2.** In order to make a prediction in such a way that permits it to be tested, one must make a(n)

_____.

a. theory
b. hypothesis
c. analysis
d. judgment

**3.** A researcher stands near an intersection and writes down the time it takes for the lead driver to start up after the light turns green. The researcher records the gender and approximate age of the driver. This researcher is most likely engaged in:

a. a case study.
b. naturalistic observation.
c. an ethnography.
d. survey research.

**4.** Researchers using correlational methods typically use a study group and a control group to isolate cause-and-effect relationships.

- True
- False

### APPLYING LIFESPAN DEVELOPMENT

- Formulate a theory about one aspect of human development and a hypothesis that relates to it.

✓•—[**Study** and **Review** on **MyDevelopmentLab.com**

Answers: 1) 2, 3, 1; 2) b; 3) b; 4) False

# Experiments: Determining Cause and Effect

**LO11** What are the characteristics of experimental research?

**LO12** Why is it important to think critically about "expert" advice?

In an **experiment,** an investigator or experimenter typically devises two different conditions (or *treatments*) and then compares how the behavior of the participants exposed to each condition is affected. One group, the *treatment* or *experimental group*, is exposed to the treatment variable being studied; the other, the *control group*, is not.

For instance, suppose you want to see if exposure to movie violence makes viewers more aggressive. You might show a group of adolescents a series of movies with a great deal of violent imagery. You would then measure their subsequent aggression. This group would constitute the treatment group. For the control group you might show a second group of adolescents movies that contain no violent imagery, and measure their subsequent aggression. By comparing the amount of aggression displayed by members of the treatment and control groups, you would be able to determine if exposure to violent imagery produces aggression in viewers. In fact, this describes an experiment conducted at the University of Louvain in Belgium. Psychologist Jacques-Philippe Leyens and colleagues found that the level of aggression rose significantly for the adolescents who had seen the movies containing violence (Leyens et al., 1975).

The central feature of this experiment—and all experiments—is the comparison of the consequences of different treatments. The use of both treatment and control groups allows researchers to rule out the possibility that something other than the experimental manipulation produced the results found in the experiment. For instance, if a control group was not used, experimenters could not be certain that some other factor, such as the time of day the movies were shown or even the mere passage of time, produced the observed changes. By using a control group, experimenters can draw accurate conclusions about causes and effects.

***Independent and Dependent Variables.*** The **independent variable** is the variable that researchers manipulate in the experiment (in our example, it is the type of movie participants saw—violent or non-violent). In contrast, the **dependent variable** is the variable that researchers measure to see if it changes as a result of the experimental manipulation. In our example, the degree of aggressive behavior shown by the participants after viewing violent or non-violent films is the dependent variable. (One way to remember the difference: A hypothesis predicts how a dependent variable *depends* on the manipulation of the independent variable.) Every experiment has an independent and dependent variable.

Experimenters must make sure their studies are not influenced by factors other than those they are manipulating. For this reason, they take great care to make sure that the participants in both the treatment and control groups are not aware of the purpose of the experiment (which could affect their responses or behavior) and that the experimenters do not influence who is chosen for the control and treatment groups. The procedure that is used for this is known as random assignment. In *random assignment*, participants are assigned to different experimental groups or "conditions" purely on the basis of chance. This way the laws of statistics ensure that personal characteristics that might affect the outcome of the experiment are divided proportionally among the participants in the different groups, making the groups equivalent. Equivalent groups achieved by random assignment allow an experimenter to draw conclusions with confidence.

Figure 1-3 illustrates the Belgian experiment on adolescents exposed to films containing violent or non-violent imagery, and the effects of such imagery on subsequent aggressive behavior. As you can see, it contains each of the elements of an experiment:

- An independent variable (the assignment to a violent or nonviolent film condition)
- A dependent variable (measurement of the adolescents' aggressive behavior)
- Random assignment to condition (viewing a film with violent imagery versus a film with nonviolent imagery)
- A hypothesis that predicts the effect the independent variable will have on the dependent variable (that viewing a film with violent imagery will produce subsequent aggression)

**experiment** a process in which an investigator, called an experimenter, devises two different experiences for participants

**independent variable** the variable that researchers manipulate in an experiment

**dependent variable** the variable that researchers measure to see if it changes as a result of the experimental manipulation

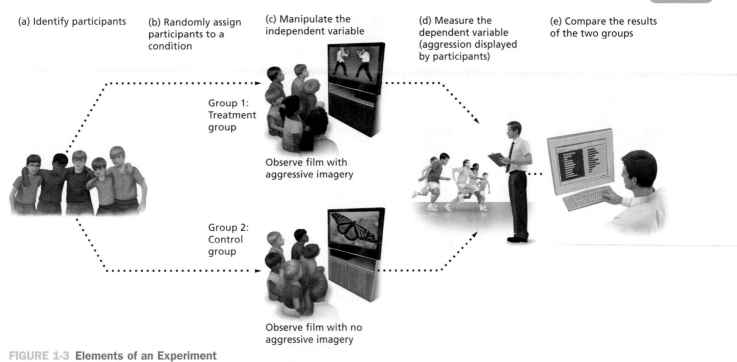

(a) Identify participants

(b) Randomly assign participants to a condition

(c) Manipulate the independent variable

(d) Measure the dependent variable (aggression displayed by participants)

(e) Compare the results of the two groups

Group 1: Treatment group

Observe film with aggressive imagery

Group 2: Control group

Observe film with no aggressive imagery

**FIGURE 1-3 Elements of an Experiment**
In this experiment, researchers randomly assigned a group of adolescents to one of two conditions: viewing a film that contained violent imagery, or viewing a film that lacked violent imagery (manipulation of the independent variable). Then participants were observed later to determine how much aggression they showed (the dependent variable). Analysis of the findings showed that adolescents exposed to aggressive imagery showed more aggression later. (Based on an experiment by Leyens et al., 1975)

Given the advantage of experiments—that they provide a means of determining causality—why aren't experiments always used? The answer is that there are some situations that a researcher, no matter how ingenious, simply cannot control. And there are some situations in which control would be unethical, even if it were possible. For instance, no researcher would be able to assign different groups of infants to parents of high and low socioeconomic status in order to learn the effects of such status on subsequent development. In situations in which experiments are logistically or ethically impossible, developmentalists employ correlational research.

Furthermore, keep in mind that a single experiment is insufficient to answer a research question definitively. Before complete confidence can be placed in a conclusion, research must be *replicated*, or repeated, sometimes using other procedures and techniques with other participants. Sometimes developmentalists use a procedure called *meta-analysis,* which permits the combination of results of many studies into one overall conclusion (Peterson & Brown, 2005; Le et al., 2010).

***Choosing a Research Setting.*** Deciding *where* to conduct a study may be as important as determining *what* to do. In the Belgian experiment on the influence of exposure to media aggression, the researchers used a real-world setting—a group home for boys who had been convicted of juvenile delinquency. They chose this **sample,** the group of participants chosen for the experiment, because it was useful to have adolescents whose normal level of aggression was relatively high, and because they could incorporate the films into the everyday life of the home with minimal disruption.

Using a real-world setting (as in the aggression experiment) is the hallmark of a field study. A **field study** is a research investigation carried out in a naturally occurring setting. Field studies capture behavior in real-life settings, where research participants may behave more naturally than in a laboratory.

Field studies may be used in both correlational studies and experiments. They typically employ naturalistic observation, the technique in which researchers observe a naturally occurring behavior without intervening or changing the situation. A researcher might

**sample** the group of participants chosen for the experiment

**field study** a research investigation carried out in a naturally occurring setting

In experimental research, developmentalists use controlled conditions to discover causal relationships between various factors.

examine behavior in a child-care center, view the groupings of adolescents in high school corridors, or observe elderly adults in a senior center.

Because it is often difficult to control the situation and environment enough to run an experiment in a real-world setting, field studies are more typical of correlational designs than experimental designs. Most developmental research experiments are conducted in laboratory settings. A **laboratory study** is a research investigation conducted in a controlled setting explicitly designed to hold events constant. The laboratory may be a room or building designed for research, as in a university psychology department. Their ability to control the settings in laboratory studies enables researchers to learn more clearly how their treatments affect participants.

## Theoretical and Applied Research: Complementary Approaches

Developmental researchers typically focus on either theoretical research or applied research. **Theoretical research** is designed to test some developmental explanation and expand scientific knowledge, while **applied research** is meant to provide practical solutions to immediate problems. For instance, if we were interested in the processes of cognitive change during childhood, we might carry out a study of how many digits children of various ages can remember after one exposure to multidigit numbers—a theoretical approach. Alternatively, we might focus on the more practical question of how teachers can help children to remember information more easily. Such a study would represent applied research, because the findings are applied to a particular setting and problem.

There is not always a clear distinction between theoretical and applied research. For instance, is a study that examines the consequences of ear infections in infancy on later hearing loss theoretical or applied? Because such a study may help illuminate the basic processes involved in hearing, it can be considered theoretical. But if it helps to prevent hearing loss, it may be considered applied (Lerner, Fisher, & Weinberg, 2000).

In fact, as we discuss in the accompanying "From Research to Practice" box, research of both a theoretical and applied nature has played a significant role in shaping and resolving a variety of public policy questions.

## Measuring Developmental Change

How people grow and change through the life span is central to the work of all developmental researchers. Consequently, one of the thorniest research issues they face concerns the measurement of change and differences over age and time. To solve this problem, researchers have developed three major research strategies: longitudinal research, cross-sectional research, and sequential research.

*Longitudinal Studies: Measuring Individual Change.* If you were interested in learning how a child develops morally between 3 and 5, the most direct approach would be to take a group of 3-year-olds and follow them until they were 5, testing them periodically.

This strategy illustrates longitudinal research. In **longitudinal research,** the behavior of one or more study participants is measured as they age. Longitudinal research measures change over time. By following many individuals over time, researchers can understand the general course of change across some period of life.

The granddaddy of longitudinal studies, which has become a classic, is a study of gifted children begun by Lewis Terman about 80 years ago. In the study—which has yet to be concluded—a group of 1,500 children with high IQs were tested about every 5 years. Now in their 80s, the participants—who call themselves "Termites"—have provided information on everything from intellectual accomplishment to personality and longevity (Feldhusen, 2003; McCullough, Tsang, & Brion, 2003; Subotnik, 2006).

Longitudinal research has also provided insight into language development. For instance, by tracing how children's vocabularies increase on a day-by-day basis, researchers have been

**laboratory study** a research investigation conducted in a controlled setting explicitly designed to hold events constant

**theoretical research** research designed specifically to test some developmental explanation and expand scientific knowledge

**applied research** research meant to provide practical solutions to immediate problems

**longitudinal research** research in which the behavior of one or more participants in a study is measured as they age

## From Research to Practice

### Using Developmental Research to Improve Public Policy

*Was national legislation designed to "leave no child behind" effective in improving the lives of children?*

*Does research support the legalization of marijuana?*

*What are the effects of gay marriage on children in such unions?*

*Should preschoolers diagnosed with attention deficit hyperactivity disorder receive drugs to treat their condition?*

*Is DARE—the national program designed to curb drug abuse in schoolchildren—effective?*

Each of these questions represents a national policy issue that can be answered only by considering the results of relevant research studies. By conducting controlled studies, developmental researchers have made a number of important contributions affecting education, family life, and health on a national scale. Consider, for instance, the variety of ways that public policy issues have been informed by various types of research findings (Brooks-Gunn, 2003; Maton et al., 2004; Mervis, 2004; Aber et al., 2007):

- **Research findings can provide policymakers a means of determining what questions to ask in the first place.** For example, studies of children's caregivers (some of which we'll consider in Chapter 3) have led policymakers to question whether the benefits of infant day care are outweighed by possible deterioration in parent–child bonds.

- **Research findings and the testimony of researchers are often part of the process by which laws are drafted.** A good deal of legislation has been passed based on findings from developmental researchers. For example, research revealed that children with developmental disabilities benefit from exposure to children without special needs, ultimately leading to passage of national legislation mandating that children with disabilities be placed in regular school classes as much as possible. Similarly, research on the benefits of foster care encouraged legislation extending eligibility for foster care to older children (Peters et al., 2008).

- **Policymakers and other professionals use research findings to determine how best to implement programs.** Research has shaped programs designed to reduce the incidence of unsafe sex among teenagers, to increase the level of prenatal care for pregnant mothers, to raise class attendance rates in school-age children, and to promote flu shots for older adults. The common thread among such programs is that many of the details of the programs are built upon basic research findings.

- **Research techniques are used to evaluate the effectiveness of existing programs and policies.** Once a public policy has been implemented, it is necessary to determine whether it has been effective and successful in accomplishing its goals. To do this, researchers employ formal evaluation techniques, developed from basic research procedures. For instance, researchers have continually scrutinized the Head Start preschool program, which has received massive federal funding, to ensure that it really does what it is supposed to do—improve children's academic performance.

Similarly, careful studies of DARE, a popular program meant to reduce children's use of drugs, began to find that it was ineffective. Using the research findings of developmentalists, DARE instigated new techniques, and preliminary findings suggest the revised program is more effective (Rhule, 2005; University of Akron, 2006).

By building upon research findings, developmentalists have worked hand-in-hand with policymakers, and research has a substantial impact on public policies that can benefit us all.

- *What are some policy issues affecting children and adolescents that are currently being debated nationally?*

- *Despite the existence of research data that might inform policy about development, politicians rarely discuss such data in their speeches. Why do you think that is the case?*

able to understand the processes that underlie the human ability to become competent in using language (Gershkoff-Stowe & Hahn, 2007; Oliver & Plomin, 2007; Childers, 2009; Fagan, 2009).

Longitudinal studies can provide a wealth of information about change over time, but they have drawbacks. For one thing, they require a tremendous investment of time, because researchers must wait for participants to become older. Furthermore, participants often drop out over the course of the research. Participants may drop out of a study, move away, or become ill or even die as the research proceeds.

Finally, participants who are observed or tested repeatedly may become "test-wise" and perform better each time they are assessed as they become more familiar with the procedure. Even if the observations of participants in a study are not terribly intrusive (such as simply recording, over a lengthy period of time, vocabulary increases in infants and preschoolers), experimental participants may be affected by the repeated presence of an experimenter or observer.

Consequently, despite the benefits of longitudinal research, particularly its ability to look at change within individuals, developmental researchers often turn to other methods. The alternative they choose most often is the cross-sectional study.

*Cross-Sectional Studies.* Suppose again that you want to consider how children's moral development, their sense of right and wrong, changes from ages 3 to 5. Instead of following the same children over several years, we might look simultaneously at three groups of children: 3 year olds, 4-year-olds, and 5-year-olds, perhaps presenting each group with the same problem and then seeing how they respond to it and explain their choices.

Such an approach typifies cross-sectional research. In **cross-sectional research,** people of different ages are compared at the same point in time. Cross-sectional studies provide information about differences in development between different age groups.

Cross-sectional research takes far less time than longitudinal research: Participants are tested at just one point in time. Terman's study might have been completed 75 years ago if Terman had simply looked at a group of gifted 15-year-olds, 20-year-olds, 25-year-olds, and so forth, up to 80-year-olds. Because the participants would not be periodically tested, there would be no chance that they would become test-wise, and problems of participant attrition would not occur. Why, then, would anyone choose to use a procedure other than cross-sectional research?

The answer is that cross-sectional research brings its own set of difficulties. Recall that every person belongs to a particular *cohort,* the group of people born at around the same time in the same place. If we find that people of different ages vary along some dimension, it may be due to differences in cohort membership, not age per se.

Consider a concrete example: If we find in a correlational study that people who are 25 perform better on a test of intelligence than those who are 75, there are several possible explanations other than that intelligence declines in old age. Instead, the finding may be attributable to cohort differences. The 75-year-olds may have had less formal education than the 15-year-olds because members of the older cohort were less likely to finish high school and attend college than members of the younger one. Or perhaps the older group received less adequate nutrition as infants than the younger group. In short, we cannot rule out the possibility that age-related differences in cross-sectional studies are actually cohort differences.

Cross-sectional studies may also suffer from *selective dropout,* in which participants in some age groups are more likely to stop participating than others. For example, suppose a study of cognitive development in preschoolers includes a long test of cognitive abilities, which young preschoolers find more difficult than older preschoolers. If more young children quit than the older preschoolers and if it is the least competent young preschoolers who drop out, then the remaining sample of that age group will consist of the more competent young preschoolers—together with a broader and more representative sample of older preschoolers. The results of such a study would be questionable (Miller, 1998).

Finally, cross-sectional studies have an additional, and more basic, disadvantage: They are unable to inform us about changes in individuals or groups. If longitudinal studies are like videos taken of a person at various ages, cross-sectional studies are like snapshots of entirely different groups. Although we can establish differences related to age, we cannot fully determine if such differences are related to change over time.

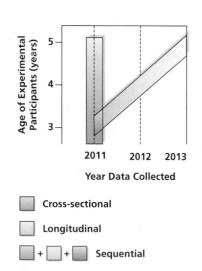

**FIGURE 1-4 Research Techniques for Studying Development**
In a *cross-sectional study,* 3-, 4-, and 5-year-olds are compared at a similar point in time (in 2011). In *longitudinal research,* a set of participants who are 3 years old in 2011 are studied when they are 4 years old (in 2012) and when they are 5 years old (in 2013). Finally, a *sequential study* combines cross-sectional and longitudinal techniques; here, a group of 3-year-olds would be compared initially in 2011 with 4- and 5-year-olds, but would also be studied 1 and 2 years later, when they themselves were 4 and 5 years old. Although the graph does not illustrate this, researchers carrying out this sequential study might also choose to retest the children who were 4 and 5 in 2011 for the next 2 years. What advantages do the three kinds of studies offer?

*Sequential Studies.* Because both longitudinal and cross-sectional studies have drawbacks, researchers have turned to some compromise techniques. Among the most frequently employed are sequential studies, which are essentially a combination of longitudinal and cross-sectional studies.

In **sequential studies,** researchers examine a number of different age groups at several points in time. For instance, an investigator interested in children's moral behavior might begin a sequential study by examining the behavior of three groups of children, who are either 3, 4, or 5 years old at the time the study begins.

The study continues for the next several years, with each participant tested annually. Thus, the 3-year-olds would be tested at ages 3, 4, and 5; the 4-year-olds at ages 4, 5, and 6; and the 5-year-olds at ages 5, 6, and 7. By combining the advantages of longitudinal and cross-sectional research, this approach permits developmental researchers to tease out the consequences of age *change* versus age *difference.* The major research techniques for studying development are summarized in Figure 1-4.

# Ethics and Research

In the "study" conducted by Egyptian King Psamtik, two children were removed from their mothers and held in isolation in an effort to learn about the roots of language. If you found yourself thinking this was extraordinarily cruel, you are in good company. Clearly, such an experiment raises blatant ethical concerns, and nothing like it would ever be done today.

But sometimes ethical issues are more subtle. For instance, U.S. government researchers proposed a conference to examine possible genetic roots of aggression. Some researchers had begun to raise the possibility that genetic markers might be found that would identify particularly violence-prone children. If so, it might be possible to track these children and provide interventions to reduce the likelihood of later violence.

Critics objected strenuously, however, arguing that identification might lead to a self-fulfilling prophecy. Children labeled as violence-prone might be treated in a way that would actually *cause* them to be more aggressive. Ultimately, under intense political pressure, the conference was canceled (Wright, 1995).

In order to help researchers deal with ethical problems, the major organizations of developmentalists, including the Society for Research in Child Development and the American Psychological Association, have developed ethical guidelines for researchers. Among the principles are those involving freedom from harm, informed consent, the use of deception, and maintenance of participants' privacy (Sales & Folkman, 2000; American Psychological Association, 2002; Fisher, 2003, 2004; 2005; Curlette & Kern, 2010):

- **Researchers must protect participants from physical and psychological harm.** Their welfare, interests, and rights come before those of researchers. In research, participants' rights always come first (Sieber, 2000; Fisher, 2004).

- **Researchers must obtain informed consent from participants before their involvement in a study.** If they are over the age of 7, participants must voluntarily agree to be in a study. If under 18, parents or guardians must also provide consent.

  Informed consent can be a sensitive requirement. Suppose, for instance, researchers want to study the psychological effects of abortion on adolescents. To obtain the consent of an adolescent minor who has had an abortion, the researchers would need to get her parents' permission as well. But if the adolescent hasn't told her parents about the abortion, the request for parental permission would violate her privacy—leading to a breach of ethics.

- **The use of deception in research must be justified and cause no harm.** Although deception to disguise the true purpose of an experiment is permissible, any experiment that uses deception must undergo careful scrutiny by an independent panel before it is conducted. Suppose, for example, we want to know the reaction of participants to success and failure. It is ethical to tell participants that they will be playing a game when the true purpose is actually to observe how they respond to doing well or poorly on the task. However, this is ethical only if it causes no harm to participants, has been approved by a review panel, and includes a full explanation for participants when the study is over (Underwood, 2005).

- **Participants' privacy must be maintained.** If participants are videotaped during a study, for example, they must give their permission for the videotapes to be viewed. Furthermore, access to the tapes must be carefully restricted.

⊙ **From the perspective of a health care provider:** Do you think there are some special circumstances involving adolescents, who are not legally adults, that would justify allowing them to participate in a study without obtaining their parents' permission? What might such circumstances involve?

## *Thinking Critically About "Expert" Advice*

### Becoming an Informed Consumer of Development

If you immediately comfort crying babies, you'll spoil them.

If you let babies cry without comforting them, they'll be untrusting and clingy as adults.

\*\*\*

Spanking is one of the best ways to discipline your child.

Never hit your child.

\*\*\*

If a marriage is unhappy, children are better off if their parents divorce than if they stay together.

No matter how difficult a marriage is, parents should avoid divorce for the sake of their children.

There is no lack of advice on the best way to raise a child or, more generally, to lead one's life. From bestsellers such as *Chicken Soup for the Soul: On Being a Parent,* to magazine and newspaper columns that provide advice on every imaginable topic, to a myriad of websites and blogs, each of us is exposed to tremendous amounts of information.

Yet not all advice is equally valid. The mere fact that something is in print, on television, or on the web does not make it legitimate or accurate. Fortunately, some guidelines can help distinguish when recommendations and suggestions are reasonable and when they are not:

- Consider the source of the advice. Information from established, respected organizations such as the American Medical Association, the American Psychological Association, and the American Academy of Pediatrics reflects years of study and is usually accurate. If you don't know the organization, investigate it further to find out more about its goals and philosophy.

- Evaluate the credentials of the person providing advice. Trustworthy information tends to come from established, acknowledged researchers and experts, not from persons with obscure credentials. Consider where the author is employed and whether he or she has a particular political or personal agenda.

- Understand the difference between anecdotal evidence and scientific evidence. Anecdotal evidence is based on one or two instances of a phenomenon, haphazardly discovered or encountered; scientific evidence is based on careful, systematic procedures. If an aunt tells you that all her children slept through the night by 2 months of age and therefore your child will too, that is quite different from reading a report that 75 percent of children sleep through the night by 9 months. Of course, even with such a report, it would be a good idea to find out how large the study was or how this number was arrived at.

- If advice is based on research findings, there should be a clear, transparent description of the studies on which the advice is based. Who were the participants? What methods were used? What do the results show? Think critically about the way the findings were obtained before accepting them.

- Don't overlook the cultural context of the information. An assertion may be valid in some contexts, but not in all. For example, it is typically assumed that providing infants the freedom to move about and exercise their limbs facilitates their muscular development and mobility. Yet in some cultures, infants spend most of their time closely bound to their mothers—with no apparent long-term damage (Kaplan & Dove, 1987; Tronick, 1995).

- Don't assume that because many people believe something, it is necessarily true. Scientific evaluation has often proved that some of the most basic presumptions about the effectiveness of various techniques are invalid.

In short, the key to evaluating information relating to human development is to maintain a healthy dose of skepticism. No source of information is invariably, unfailingly accurate. By keeping a critical eye on the statements you encounter, you'll be in a better position to determine the very real contributions made by developmentalists to understanding how humans develop over the course of the life span.

## REVIEW, CHECK, AND APPLY

### REVIEW

**L011**  What are the characteristics of experimental research?

- Experimental research seeks to discover cause-and-effect relationships.
- Experiments typically create two different conditions and use an experimental group and a control group.
- Researchers measure age-related change by longitudinal studies, cross-sectional studies, and sequential studies.

**L012**  Why is it important to think critically about "expert" advice?

- Scientific evaluation has shown that some practices supposedly based on developmental research are at best dubious and at worst invalid.
- The key to evaluating information relating to human development is to maintain a healthy dose of skepticism.

### CHECK YOURSELF

1. If a control group is not used in an experiment, the researcher cannot rule out the possibility that something other than the treatment produced the observed outcome.

   - True
   - False

2. In a(n) _____, an investigator devises two conditions (treatment or control) and compares the outcomes of the participants exposed to those two different conditions in order to see how behavior is affected.

   a. experiment
   b. correlational study
   c. interview
   d. naturalistic observation

3. In a _____ research study, researchers are interested in measuring change in a single group of subjects over time.

   a. correlational
   b. cross-sectional
   c. longitudinal
   d. sequential

### APPLYING LIFESPAN DEVELOPMENT

- High school students who routinely do their homework while writing text messages to friends, watching a program on television, and playing an electronic game in a window of their computer often claim that they are "multitasking" and are able to study more quickly and effectively this way. How might you design a basic experiment to test this claim?

✔•⌐**Study** and **Review** on
**MyDevelopmentLab.com**

Answers: 1) True; 2) a; 3) c

# Putting It All Together
## Introduction

**DAVID FUREK,** the head of the large, multigenerational household we met in the chapter opener, found himself pondering many of the questions that developmentalists study formally. In thinking back to the time before the birth of his youngest son, he remembered worrying that his wife's advanced age—and his own—might negatively affect the newborn baby. He speculated about how the traits of the members of the generations around his table might be expressed in his young son. He considered both potentially inherited characteristics and traits acquired from social and environmental interactions. David's "laboratory" (four generations of his family) gave him a lot to think about.

### MODULE 1.1 Beginnings

- David's consideration of his four-generation household mirrors the work of developmentalists with a wide range of interests, including those who focus on genetic versus environmental influences, cognitive changes across the life span, and social and personality development. **(pp. 4–5)**

- The age range of David's family mirrors the full range that developmentalists cover, from before birth to old age. **(pp. 5–7)**

- Each family member naturally experiences different cohort influences, which interact with their shared genetic heritage. **(pp. 7–9)**

- Key issues in development are reflected in David's thoughts, including the nature–nurture issue and continuity versus discontinuity. **(pp. 9–12)**

### MODULE 1.2 Theoretical Perspectives on Lifespan Development

- Developmentalists with different perspectives might guide David's musings. Erikson might help David interpret his family's changes in terms of stages along the life span, Piaget might illuminate baby Glenn's changing thought processes, and Vygotsky might underscore the importance of social interactions in cognitive, social, and physical development. **(pp. 13–23)**

- David seems to understand that it is best to avoid considering any particular theoretical perspective either all wrong or all right. **(pp. 23–24)**

✳ Explore on mydevelopmentlab.com

To read how real-life educators, social workers, and parents responded to these questions, log on to MyDevelopmentLab.com.

*Do you agree or disagree with their responses? Why? What concepts that you've read about back up their opinion?*

What kind of parent would you be? What decisions would you make?

*Log onto My Virtual Child through MyDevelopmentLab.com and start making those choices.*

## MODULE **1.3** Research Methods

- David reveals an instinctive knack for constructing theories about development and using informal hypotheses to test them. **(pp. 25–27)**

- David asks and answers questions about the development of his family members and himself through a combination of a sort of "life experiment" and naturalistic observation. **(pp. 28–29)**

- In a sense, David's curiosity about development contains elements of the case study (i.e., observing his family's life), longitudinal research (i.e., reflecting on and interpreting his whole life span thus far), and the cross-sectional study (i.e., his Thanksgiving table is a cross-section of development across the life span). **(pp. 30–36)**

### What would an EDUCATOR do?

- How could you prepare David and Carla for the changes in educational practice that may have occurred since their last experience with schooling?

- What might you tell them to look for in gauging young Glenn's cognitive, physical, and social readiness for school?

- What ideas could you give them to help Glenn prepare for school?

- Do you think David and Carla may need to be cautioned against taking Glenn's learning for granted, given their long, successful experience with putting kids through school?

  **HINT** Review page 11 and 17–18

  *What's your response?*

### What would a PARENT do?

- How would you help David and Carla understand what their daughter Erin, who has recently lost her job and taken on new responsibilities as a parent, may be going through?

- David is a parent who is also a son. How would you suggest he balance his "upward" responsibilities toward his mother with his "downward" responsibilities toward his children?

- David and Carla's children themselves represent a range of developmental stages and ages. How would you help them deal differently with the needs and potential sources of support that such a variety of children offers?

  **HINT** Review pages 12–24

  *What's your response?*

### What would a HEALTH CARE PROVIDER do?

- How would you help David and Carla understand the different stages of development, with all their varying states of physical, cognitive, and emotional health, represented in their family?

- How could you help them accept their power and limitations in perceiving and responding to their family's varied physical and emotional needs?

- How could you help David and Carla prepare for a death in their family (e.g., parent, spouse, children, grandson)?

  **HINT** Review pages 7–9 and 14–15

  *What's your response?*

### What would YOU do?

- How would you help David understand his varying roles as a father, son, and grandfather?

- What things would you suggest that David's own mother could help him with or advise him about? Has the role of grandmother and mother changed too much for cross-generational wisdom to be shared helpfully?

  **HINT** Review pages 12–24, *especially pages 14–15*

  *What's your response?*

# The Start of Life

As Rachel's delivery date approached, she and her husband Jack thought the usual thoughts that occupy parents-to-be. They wondered whether they would have a daughter or a second son. They discussed what another son might look like, and which of them a daughter would resemble. They speculated about their baby's disposition, intelligence, and even potential career, and they congratulated themselves for having moved to a pleasant community with good public schools, a wealth of stimulating activities, and lots of places for kids to play safely.

A few months later, when Rachel's contractions began at 4 in the morning, she woke Jack and they drove to the hospital. She was pleased with her decision to use a midwife instead of an obstetrician, as she had done for her first birth. That time, her labor had lasted 31 hours and had been indescribably painful. With a midwife in attendance, Rachel was sure that the labor and birth would proceed more smoothly.

Rachel was also happy that she had relatively few complications during her pregnancy. Her friend Janet, who was also pregnant, was having a tough time; her

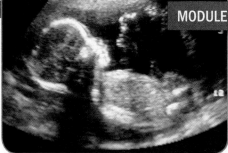

### MODULE **2.1** Prenatal Development

## What role is genetics playing in the prenatal development of Rachel and Jack's baby?

see page 42.

### MODULE **2.2** Prenatal Growth and Change

## What can Rachel and Jack do, or not do, to help their baby develop normally?

see page 58.

blood pressure was high, and she had to remain in bed for the last two months of her pregnancy.

At the hospital, Rachel walked through her contractions, stopping to lean against the wall as each one peaked, until the midwife arrived. Four hours after labor began, the midwife told her that the birth was imminent. Rather than lie flat, a position that had necessitated the use of oxygen for her first birth, Rachel chose to kneel and pushed her baby—a daughter, Eva—into the world. As the baby was cleaned up and placed in Jack's arms, Rachel asked a nurse for some water. At that moment, Eva turned her head toward her mother. Jack said, "Look, Rachel, she recognizes the sound of your voice."

In this chapter, we start our voyage through the life span at its logical beginning: conception. We discuss genetics and the ways in which genetic information is transmitted from parents to child. We then introduce a topic that receives a great deal of attention from developmentalists: the comparative roles of heredity and environment (or nature versus nurture) in forming the individual.

Next we discuss what happens inside the womb once an egg has been fertilized. We proceed through the stages of the prenatal period, from fertilization to the fetal stage. We look at factors that can affect the health and development of the fetus before birth.

MODULE **2.3** Birth

What can Rachel and Jack expect during each stage of labor? see page 70.

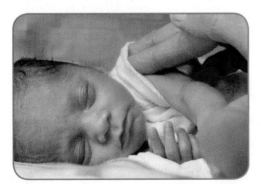

## My Virtual Child

What decisions would you make when it comes to birthing options and raising a newborn?

Log onto *My Virtual Child* through MyDevelopmentLab.com and start making those choices.

We finish the chapter with a discussion of the process of birth, including the ways women experience labor and the choices that parents have available for care before and during childbirth. We touch on some of the complications that can attend birth, including infants born significantly before or after their due date. We end with a discussion of the considerable abilities that a newborn possesses from the moment it enters the world.

## MODULE 2.1 Prenatal Development

## An Agonizing Choice

*When the Morrisons were expecting their second child, the young couple faced an anguishing dilemma.*

*Their first child, a girl born in 2002, had a condition known as congential adrenal hyperplasia, or CAH, which can sometimes result in male-like genitals in female newborns. So when Mrs. Morrison became pregnant again, the couple was well aware the baby had a 1-in-8 chance of being born with the same disorder.*

*There were choices. They could treat the fetus with a powerful steroid that would most likely avert the possibility of the genitals becoming malformed. But the couple worried about doing this. There was little research on the long-term effects of treating a fetus with steroids, and statistically, there was a much greater chance that the baby wouldn't have the genital problem at all . . . .*

*The couple decided to forgo the steroid treatment. "It was touch-and-go, but in the end I couldn't expose the baby to the drugs," says Mrs. Morrison. When the baby arrived, it was a girl and, like her older sister, was born with swollen genitalia.* (Naik, 2009, p. D1)

The Morrisons will never know if the steroid treatment would have prevented the problem afflicting their daughter. But their case illustrates the difficult decisions that parents sometimes face because of advances in the treatment of inherited disorders and our understanding of genetics.

In this chapter, we'll examine what developmental researchers and other scientists have learned about ways that heredity and the environment work in tandem to create and shape human beings, and how that knowledge is being used to improve people's lives. We begin with the basics of heredity, the genetic transmission of characteristics from biological parents to their children, by examining how we receive our genetic endowment. We'll consider an area of study, behavioral genetics, that specializes in the consequences of heredity on behavior. We'll also discuss what happens when genetic factors cause development to go off track, and how such problems are dealt with through genetic counseling and, in some cases, manipulation of a child's genes.

But genes are only one part of the story of prenatal development. We'll also consider the ways in which a child's genetic heritage interacts with the environment in which he or she grows up—how one's family, socioeconomic status, and life events can affect a variety of characteristics, including physical traits, intelligence, and even personality.

## Earliest Development

**LEARNING OBJECTIVES**

**LO1** What is our basic genetic endowment?

**LO2** What are the major genetic threats to normal development?

**LO3** What is the role of behavioral genetics?

We humans begin the course of our lives simply.

Like individuals from tens of thousands of other species, we start as a single tiny cell weighing no more than one 20-millionth of an ounce. But from this humble beginning, in a matter of a few months, a living, breathing individual infant is born. That first cell is created when a male reproductive cell, a *sperm*, pushes through the membrane of the *ovum*, the female reproductive cell. These *gametes,* as the male and female reproductive cells are also called, contain huge amounts of genetic information. About an hour or so after the sperm enters the ovum, the two gametes suddenly fuse, becoming one cell, a **zygote.** The resulting combination of their genetic instructions—over two billion chemically coded messages—is sufficient to begin creating a whole person. ⊙ Watch on **mydevelopmentlab.com**

## Genes and Chromosomes: The Code of Life

The blueprints for creating a person are stored and communicated in our **genes,** the basic units of genetic information. The roughly 25,000 human genes are the biological equivalent of "software" that programs the future development of all parts of the body's "hardware."

All genes are composed of specific sequences of **DNA (deoxyribonucleic acid) molecules.** The genes are arranged in specific locations and in a specific order along 46 **chromosomes,** rod-shaped portions of DNA that are organized in 23 pairs. Each of the sex cells—ovum and sperm—contains half this number, so that a child's mother and father each provide one of the

The moment of conception.

⊙ Watch on **mydevelopmentlab.com**

To watch the process you're reading about happening, check MyDevelopmentLab.com for an Observations Video on zygote development.

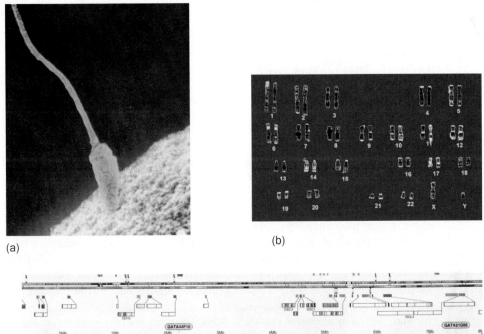

(a)

(b)

(c)

At the moment of conception (a), humans receive 23 pairs of chromosomes (b), half from the mother and half from the father. These chromosomes contain thousands of genes, shown in the computer-generated map (c).

**zygote** the new cell formed by the process of fertilization

**genes** the basic unit of genetic information

**DNA (deoxyribonucleic acid) molecules** the substance that genes are composed of that determines the nature of every cell in the body and how it will function

**chromosomes** rod-shaped portions of DNA that are organized in 23 pairs

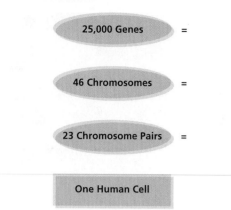

**FIGURE 2-1 The Contents of a Single Human Cell**
At the moment of conception, humans receive about 25,000 genes, contained on 46 chromosomes on 23 pairs.

two chromosomes in each of the 23 pairs. The 46 chromosomes (in 23 pairs) in the new zygote contain the genetic blueprint that will guide cell activity for the rest of the individual's life (Pennisi, 2000; International Human Genome Sequencing Consortium, 2001) (see Figure 2-1). Through a process called *mitosis,* which accounts for the replication of most types of cells, nearly all the cells of the body will contain the same 46 chromosomes as the zygote.

Genes determine the nature and function of every cell in the body. For instance, they determine which cells will become part of the heart and which will become part of the muscles of the leg. Genes also establish how different parts of the body will function: how rapidly the heart will beat, or how much strength a muscle will have.

If each parent provides just 23 chromosomes, where does the vast diversity of human beings come from? The answer resides primarily in the processes that underlie the cell division of the gametes. When gametes—the sex cells, sperm and ova—are formed in the adult body in a process called *meiosis,* each gamete receives one of the two chromosomes that make up each of the 23 pairs. Because for each pair the chromosome that is chosen is largely a matter of chance, there are $2^{23}$, or some eight million, different combinations possible. Furthermore, other processes, such as random transformations of particular genes, add to the variability of the genetic brew. The ultimate outcome: tens of *trillions* of possible genetic combinations.

With so many possible genetic mixtures, there is no likelihood that someday you'll bump into a genetic duplicate—with one exception: an identical twin.

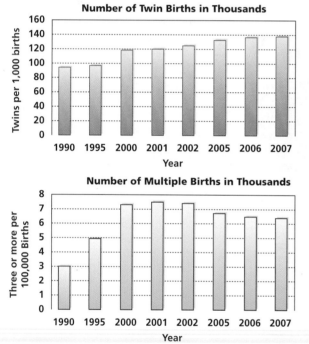

**FIGURE 2-2 Rising Multiples**
Multiple births have increased significantly over the last 25 years. What are some of the reasons for this phenomenon?
Source: Martin et al. 2010.

## Multiple Births: Two—or More—for the Genetic Price of One

Although it is routine for dogs and cats to give birth to several offspring at one time, in humans multiple births are cause for comment. They should be: Less than 3 percent of all pregnancies produce twins, and the odds are even slimmer for three or more children.

Why do multiple births occur? Some occur when a cluster of cells in the ovum splits off within the first two weeks after fertilization. The result is two genetically identical zygotes, which, because they come from the same original zygote, are called monozygotic. **Monozygotic twins** are twins who are genetically identical. Any differences in their future development can be attributed only to environmental factors.

However, multiple births are more commonly the result of two separate sperm fertilizing two separate ova at roughly the same time. Twins produced in this fashion are known as **dizygotic twins.** Because they are the result of two separate ovum–sperm combinations, they are no more genetically similar than two siblings born at different times. Triplets, quadruplets, and even more births are produced by either (or both) of the mechanisms that yield twins. Thus, triplets may be some combination of monozygotic, dizygotic, or trizygotic.

Of course, not all multiple births produce only two babies. Triplets, quadruplets, and even more births are produced by either (or both) of the mechanisms that yield twins. Thus, triplets may be some combination of monozygotic, dizygotic, or trizygotic.

Although the chances of having a multiple birth are typically slim, the odds rise considerably when fertility drugs are used before conception. Older women, too, are more likely to have multiple births, and multiple births are also more common in some families than in others. The increased use of fertility drugs and the rising average age of mothers giving birth means that multiple births have increased in the last 25 years (see Figure 2-2) (Martin et al., 2005, 2010).

There are also racial, ethnic, and national differences in the rate of multiple births, probably due to inherited differences in the likelihood that more than one ovum will be released at a time. For example, 1 out of 70 African American couples have dizygotic births, compared with 1 out of 86 white American couples (Vaughan, McKay, & Behrman, 1979; Wood, 1997).

***Boy or Girl? Establishing the Sex of the Child.*** In 22 of the 23 matched chromosome pairs, each chromosome is similar to the other member of its pair. The one exception is the 23rd pair—the one that determines the sex of the child. In females, the 23rd pair consists of two matching, relatively large X-shaped chromosomes, identified as XX. In males, on the other hand, one member of the pair is an X-shaped chromosome, but the other is a shorter, smaller Y-shaped chromosome. This pair is identified as XY.

**monozygotic twins** twins who are genetically identical

**dizygotic twins** twins who are produced when two separate ova are fertilized by two separate sperm at roughly the same time

Since a female's 23rd pair of chromosomes are both Xs, an ovum will always carry an X chromosome. A male's 23rd pair is XY, so each sperm could carry either an X or a Y chromosome. If the sperm contributes an X chromosome when it meets an ovum, the child will have an XX pairing on the 23rd chromosome—and will be a female. If the sperm contributes a Y chromosome, the result will be an XY pairing—a male (see Figure 2-3).

Since the father's sperm determines the gender of the child, new techniques are being developed to help specify in advance the gender of the child. In one new technique, lasers measure the DNA in sperm. Discarding sperm that harbor the unwanted sex chromosome dramatically increases the chances of having a child of the desired sex (Hayden, 1998; Belkin, 1999; Van Balen, 2005).

Sex selection raises ethical and practical issues. For example, in cultures that value one gender over the other, might there be a kind of gender discrimination before birth? And could there ultimately be a shortage of children of the less-preferred sex? Many questions of this type will have to be addressed before sex selection can ever become routine (Sharma, 2008; Sleeboom-Faulkner, 2010).

## The Basics of Genetics: The Mixing and Matching of Traits

What determined the color of your hair? Why are you tall or short? What made you susceptible to hay fever? And why do you have so many freckles? To answer these questions, we need to consider the basic mechanisms through which the genes we inherit from our parents transmit information.

We can start by examining the discoveries of an Austrian monk, Gregor Mendel, in the mid-1800s. In a series of simple yet convincing experiments, Mendel cross-pollinated pea plants that always produced yellow seeds with pea plants that always produced green seeds. The result was not, as one might guess, a plant with a combination of yellow and green seeds. Instead, all of the resulting plants had yellow seeds. At first it appeared that the green-seeded plants had had no influence.

However, additional research on Mendel's part proved this was not true. He bred together plants from the new, yellow-seeded generation that had resulted from his original cross-breeding of the green-seeded and yellow-seeded plants. The consistent result was a ratio of three-quarters yellow seeds to one-quarter green seeds.

It was Mendel's genius to figure out why this ratio appeared so consistently. Based on his experiments with pea plants, he argued that when two competing traits, such as green or yellow coloring, were both present, only one could be expressed. The one that was expressed was called a **dominant trait.** Meanwhile, the other trait remained present in the organism, although unexpressed (displayed). This was called a **recessive trait.** In the case of the pea plants, the offspring plants received genetic information from both the green-seeded and yellow-seeded parents. However, the yellow trait was dominant, and consequently the recessive green trait did not assert itself.

Keep in mind, though, that genetic material from both parent plants is present in the offspring, even if unexpressed. The genetic information is known as the organism's genotype. A **genotype** is the underlying combination of genetic material present (but outwardly invisible) in an organism. In contrast, a **phenotype** is the observable trait, the trait that actually is seen.

Although the offspring of the yellow-seeded and green-seeded pea plants all have yellow seeds (i.e., they have a yellow-seeded phenotype), the genotype consists of genetic information relating to both parents.

And what is the nature of the information in the genotype? To answer that question, let's turn from peas to people. In fact, the principles are the same not just for plants and humans, but for the majority of species.

Recall that parents transmit genetic information to their offspring via the chromosomes they contribute through the gamete they provide during fertilization. Some of the genes form pairs called *alleles,* genes governing traits that may take alternate forms, such as hair or eye color. For example, brown eye color is a dominant trait (B); blue eyes are recessive (b). A child's allele may contain similar or dissimilar genes from each parent. If the child receives similar genes, he or she is said to be **homozygous** for the trait. On the other hand, if the child receives different forms of the gene from its parents, he or she is said to be **heterozygous.** In the case of heterozygous alleles (Bb), the dominant characteristic (brown eyes) is expressed. However, if the child happens to receive a recessive allele from each of its parents, and therefore lacks a dominant characteristic (bb), it will display the recessive characteristic (in this case, blue eyes).

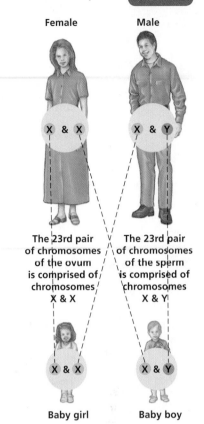

**FIGURE 2-3 Determining Sex**
When an ovum and sperm meet at the moment of fertilization, the ovum is certain to provide an X chromosome, while the sperm will provide either an X or a Y chromosome. If the sperm contributes its X chromosome, the child will have an XX pairing on the 23rd chromosome and will be a girl. If the sperm contributes a Y chromosome, the result will be an XY pairing—a boy. Does this mean that girls are more likely to be conceived than boys?

**dominant trait** the one trait that is expressed when two competing traits are present

**recessive trait** a trait within an organism that is present, but is not expressed

**genotype** the underlying combination of genetic material present (but not outwardly visible) in an organism

**phenotype** an observable trait; the trait that actually is seen

**homozygous** inheriting from parents similar genes for a given trait

**heterozygous** inheriting from parents different forms of a gene for a given trait

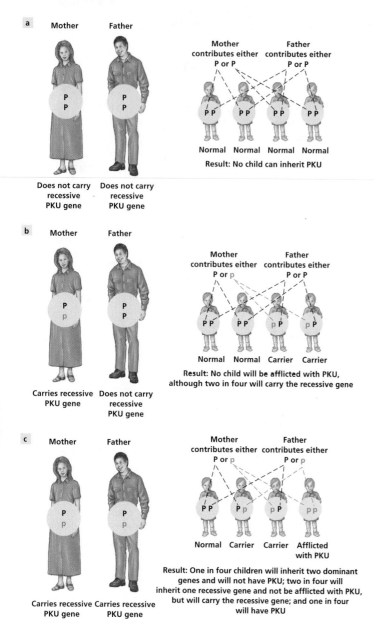

**FIGURE 2-4 PKU Probabilities**
PKU, a disease that causes brain damage and mental retardation, is produced by a single pair of genes inherited from one's mother and father. If neither parent carries a gene for the disease (a), a child cannot develop PKU. Even if one parent carries the recessive gene, but the other doesn't (b), the child cannot inherit the disease. However, if both parents carry the recessive gene (c), there is a one in four chance that the child will have PKU.

## Transmission of Genetic Information

One example of this process at work is the transmission of *phenylketon-uria (PKU),* an inherited disorder in which a child is unable to make use of phenylalanine, an essential amino acid present in proteins found in milk and other foods. If untreated, PKU allows phenylalanine to build to toxic levels, causing brain damage and mental retardation (Moyle et al., 2007; Widaman, 2009; McCabe & Shaw, 2010).

PKU is produced by a single allele, or pair of genes. As shown in Figure 2-4, we can label each gene of the pair with a *P* if it carries a dominant gene, which causes the normal production of phenylalanine, or a *p* if it carries the recessive gene that produces PKU. In cases in which neither parent is a PKU carrier, both the mother's and the father's pairs of genes are the dominant form, symbolized as *PP,* in which case the child's genes will be *PP,* and the child will not have PKU.

Imagine what happens if one parent has the recessive *p* gene. In this case, symbolized as *Pp,* the parent will not have PKU, since the normal *P* gene is dominant. But the recessive gene can be passed down to the child. This is not so bad: If the child has only one recessive gene, it will not suffer from PKU. But what if both parents carry a recessive *p* gene? In this case, although neither parent has the disorder, it is possible for the child to receive a recessive gene from both parents. The child will have the *pp* genotype for PKU and will have the disorder.

Remember, though, that even children whose parents both have the recessive gene for PKU have only a 25 percent chance of inheriting the disorder. Due to the laws of probability, 25 percent of children with *Pp* parents will receive the dominant gene from each parent (these children's genotype would be *PP*), and 50 percent will receive the dominant gene from one parent and the recessive gene from the other (their genotypes would be either *Pp* or *pP*). Only the unlucky 25 percent who receive the recessive gene from each parent and end up with the genotype *pp* will suffer from PKU.

***Polygenic Traits.*** PKU illustrates the basic principles of genetic transmission, although PKU transmission is simpler than most cases. Relatively few traits are governed by a single pair of genes. Instead, most traits are the result of polygenic inheritance. In **polygenic inheritance,** a combination of multiple gene pairs is responsible for the production of a particular trait.

Furthermore, some genes come in several alternate forms, and still others act to modify the way that particular genetic traits (produced by other alleles) are displayed. Genes also vary in terms of their *reaction range,* the potential degree of variability in the expression of a trait due to environmental conditions. And some traits, such as blood type, are produced by genes in which neither member of a pair of genes can be classified as purely dominant or recessive. Instead, the trait is expressed in terms of a combination of the two genes—such as type AB blood.

A number of recessive genes, called **X-linked genes,** are located only on the X chromosome. Recall that in females, the 23rd pair of chromosomes is an XX pair, while in males it is an XY pair. One result is that males have a higher risk for a variety of X-linked disorders, since males lack a second X chromosome that can counteract the genetic information that produces the disorder. For example, males are significantly more apt to have red-green color blindness, a disorder produced by a set of genes on the X chromosome. Similarly, *hemophilia,* a blood disorder, is produced by X-linked genes, a recurrent problem in the royal families of Europe.

***The Human Genome and Behavioral Genetics: Cracking the Genetic Code.*** Mendel's trailblazing achievements mark only the beginning of our understanding of genetics. The most recent milestone was reached in early 2001, when molecular geneticists succeeded in mapping the sequence of genes on each chromosome. This is one of the most important accomplishments in the history of genetics (International Human Genome Sequencing Consortium, 2001; Oksenberg & Hauser, 2010).

Already, the mapping of the gene sequence has significantly advanced our understanding of genetics. For instance, the number of human genes, long thought to be 100,000, has been revised downward to 25,000—not many more than organisms that are far less complex (see Figure 2-5). Furthermore, scientists have discovered that 99.9 percent of the gene sequence is shared by all humans—meaning that many of the differences that seemingly separate people—such as race—are, literally, only skin-deep. Genome mapping will also help in the identification of disorders to which a given individual is susceptible (Gee, 2004; DeLisi & Fleischhaker, 2007; Gupta & State, 2007).

The mapping of the human gene sequence is supporting the field of behavioral genetics. As the name implies, **behavioral genetics** studies the effects of heredity on behavior and psychological characteristics. Rather than simply examining stable, unchanging characteristics such as hair or eye color, behavioral genetics takes a broader approach, considering how our personality and behavioral habits are affected by genetic factors (Eley, Lichtenstein, & Moffitt, 2003, Li, 2003, McGue, 2010).

Personality traits such as shyness or sociability, moodiness, and assertiveness are among the areas being studied. Other behavior geneticists study psychological disorders, such as depression, attention deficit hyperactivity disorder, and schizophrenia, looking for possible genetic links (Baker, Mazzeo, & Kendler, 2007; DeYoung, Quilty, & Peterson, 2007; Haeffel et al., 2008) (see Table 2-1).

## Inherited and Genetic Disorders: When Development Deviates from the Norm

As we saw with PKU, a recessive gene responsible for a disorder may be passed on unknowingly from one generation to the next, revealing itself only when, by chance, it is paired with another recessive gene. When this happens, the gene will express itself and the unsuspected genetic disorder will be inherited.

Another way that genes are a source of concern is that they may become physically damaged. Genes may break down due to wear-and-tear or chance events occurring during the cell division processes of meiosis and mitosis. Sometimes genes, for no known reason, spontaneously change their form, a process called *spontaneous mutation*. Also, certain environmental factors, such as x-rays or even highly polluted air, may produce a malformation of genetic material. When damaged genes are passed on to a child, the results can be disastrous for physical and cognitive development (Samet, DeMarini, & Malling, 2004).

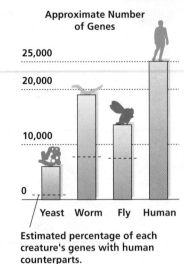

**Approximate Number of Genes**

25,000 · 20,000 · 10,000 · 0 · Yeast Worm Fly Human

**Estimated percentage of each creature's genes with human counterparts.**

FIGURE 2-5 **Uniquely Human?** Humans have about 25,000 genes, making them not much more genetically complex than some primitive species.
Source: Celera Genomics: International Human Genome Sequencing Consortium, 2001.

---

**TABLE 2-1**  CURRENT UNDERSTANDING OF THE GENETIC BASIS OF SELECTED BEHAVIORAL DISORDERS AND TRAITS

| Behavioral Trait | Current Ideas of Genetic Basis |
|---|---|
| Huntington's disease | Huntington gene identified. |
| Early onset (familial) Alzheimer's disease | Three distinct genes have been identified. |
| Fragile X mental retardation | Two genes have been identified. |
| Late-onset Alzheimer's disease | One set of genes has been associated with increased risk. |
| Attention deficit hyperactivity disorder | Three locations related to the genetics involved with the neurotransmitter dopamine may contribute. |
| Dyslexia | Relationships to two locations, on chromosomes 6 and 15, have been suggested. |
| Schizophrenia | There is no consensus, but links to numerous chromosomes, including 1, 5, 6, 10, 13, 15, and 22 have been reported. |

Source: From McGuffin, P., Riley, B., & Plomin (2001, Feb. 16). Toward behavioral genomics, *Science*, 291, 1232–1249. Reprinted with permission from AAAS.

**behavioral genetics** the study of the effects of heredity on behavior

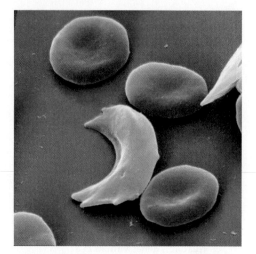

Sickle-cell anemia, named for the presence of misshapen red blood cells, is carried in the genes of 1 in 10 African Americans.

In addition to PKU, which occurs once in 10- to 20-thousand births, other inherited and genetic disorders include:

- **Down syndrome.** Instead of 46 chromosomes in 23 pairs, individuals with **Down syndrome** have an extra chromosome on the 21st pair. Once referred to as mongolism, Down syndrome is the most frequent cause of mental retardation. It occurs in about 1 out of 500 births, although the risk is much greater in mothers who are unusually young or old (Crane & Morris, 2006; Sherman et al., 2007; Davis, 2008).

- **Fragile X syndrome. Fragile X syndrome** occurs when a particular gene is injured on the X chromosome. The result is mild to moderate mental retardation (Cornish, Turk, & Hagerman, 2008).

- **Sickle-cell anemia.** Around one-tenth of people of African descent carry genes that produce sickle-cell anemia, and 1 individual in 400 actually has the disease. **Sickle-cell anemia** is a blood disorder named for the shape of the red blood cells in those who have it. Symptoms include poor appetite, stunted growth, swollen stomach, and yellowish eyes. People afflicted with the most severe form rarely live beyond childhood. However, for those with less severe cases, medical advances have produced significant increases in life expectancy (Ballas, 2010).

- **Tay-Sachs disease.** Occurring mainly in Jews of eastern European ancestry and in French-Canadians, **Tay-Sachs disease** usually causes death before its victims reach school age. There is no treatment for the disorder, which produces blindness and muscle degeneration prior to death.

- **Klinefelter's syndrome.** One male out of every 400 is born with **Klinefelter's syndrome,** the presence of an extra X chromosome. The resulting XXY complement produces underdeveloped genitals, extreme height, and enlarged breasts. Klinefelter's syndrome is one of a number of genetic abnormalities that result from receiving the improper number of sex chromosomes. For instance, there are disorders produced by an extra Y chromosome (XYY), a missing second chromosome (X0, called *Turner syndrome*), and three X chromosomes (XXX). Such disorders are typically characterized by problems relating to sexual characteristics and by intellectual deficits (Ross, Stefanatos, & Roeltgen, 2007; Murphy & Mazzocco, 2008; Murphy, 2009).

It is important to keep in mind that the mere fact a disorder has genetic roots does not mean that environmental factors do not also play a role. Consider sickle-cell anemia. Because the disease can be fatal in childhood, we'd expect that those who suffer from it would be unlikely to live long enough to pass it on. And this does seem to be true in the United States: Compared with parts of West Africa, the incidence in the United States is much lower.

But why the difference between the United States and West Africa? Ultimately, scientists determined that carrying the sickle-cell gene raises immunity to malaria, a common disease in West Africa. This heightened immunity meant that people with the sickle-cell gene had a genetic advantage (in terms of resistance to malaria) that offset, to some degree, the disadvantage of being a carrier of the gene.

## Genetic Counseling: Predicting the Future from the Genes of the Present

If you knew that your mother and grandmother had died of Huntington's disease—a devastating, always fatal inherited disorder marked by tremors and intellectual deterioration—how could you learn your own chances of getting the disease? The best way is a field that, just a few decades ago, was nonexistent: genetic counseling. **Genetic counseling** focuses on helping people deal with issues relating to inherited disorders.

Genetic counselors use a variety of data in their work. For instance, couples thinking about having a child may want to know the risks involved in a pregnancy. The counselor will take a thorough family history, looking for a familial incidence of birth defects that might indicate a pattern of recessive or X-linked genes. In addition, the counselor will take into account factors such as the age of the mother and father and any previous abnormalities in other children they may have already had (Fransen, Meertens, & Schrander-Stumpel, 2006; Resta et al., 2006).

Typically, genetic counselors suggest a thorough physical examination to identify physical abnormalities that the potential parents may be unaware of. In addition, samples of blood, skin, and urine may be used to isolate and examine specific chromosomes. Possible genetic

**Down syndrome** a disorder produced by the presence of an extra chromosome on the 21st pair; once referred to as mongolism

**fragile X syndrome** a disorder produced by injury to a gene on the X chromosome, producing mild to moderate mental retardation

**sickle-cell anemia** a blood disorder that gets its name from the shape of the red blood cells in those who have it

**Tay-Sachs disease** a disorder that produces blindness and muscle degeneration prior to death; there is no treatment

**Klinefelter's syndrome** a disorder resulting from the presence of an extra X chromosome that produces underdeveloped genitals, extreme height, and enlarged breasts

**genetic counseling** the discipline that focuses on helping people deal with issues relating to inherited disorders

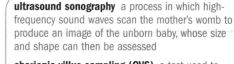

defects, such as the presence of an extra sex chromosome, can be identified by assembling a *karyotype,* a chart containing enlarged photos of each of the chromosomes.

***Prenatal Testing.*** If the woman is already pregnant, there are a variety of techniques to assess the health of her unborn child (see Table 2-2 for a list of currently available tests). The earliest is a *first-trimester screen,* which combines a blood test and ultrasound sonography in the 11th to 13th week of pregnancy and can identify chromosomal abnormalities and other disorders, such as heart problems. In **ultrasound sonography,** high-frequency sound waves bombard the mother's womb, producing an image of the unborn baby, whose size and shape can then be assessed. Repeated use of ultrasound sonography can reveal developmental patterns.

A more invasive test, **chorionic villus sampling (CVS),** can be employed in the 10th to 13th week of the first trimester if blood tests and ultrasound have identified a potential problem or if there is a family history of inherited disorders. CVS involves inserting a thin needle into the placenta and taking small samples of hairlike material that surrounds the embryo. The test can be done between the 8th and 11th week of pregnancy. However, it produces a risk of miscarriage of 1 in 100 to 1 in 200. Because of the risk, its use is relatively infrequent.

In **amniocentesis,** a small sample of fetal cells is drawn by a tiny needle inserted into the amniotic fluid surrounding the unborn fetus. Carried out 15 to 20 weeks into the pregnancy, amniocentesis allows the analysis of the fetal cells that can identify a variety of genetic defects with nearly 100 percent accuracy. In addition, the sex of the child can be determined. Although there is always a danger to the fetus in an invasive procedure such as amniocentesis, it is generally safe.

After the various tests are complete the couple will meet with the genetic counselor again. Typically, counselors avoid giving recommendations. Instead, they lay out the facts and present options for the parents, which typically range from doing nothing to taking more drastic steps, such as an abortion.

***Screening for Future Problems.*** The newest role of genetic counselors involves testing people to identify whether they themselves, rather than their children, are susceptible to future disorders because of genetic

> **ultrasound sonography** a process in which high-frequency sound waves scan the mother's womb to produce an image of the unborn baby, whose size and shape can then be assessed
>
> **chorionic villus sampling (CVS)** a test used to find genetic defects that involves taking samples of hairlike material that surrounds the embryo
>
> **amniocentesis** the process of identifying genetic defects by examining a small sample of fetal cells drawn by a needle inserted into the amniotic fluid surrounding the unborn fetus

In amniocentesis, a sample of fetal cells is withdrawn from the amniotic sac and used to identify a number of genetic defects.

## TABLE 2-2 FETAL DEVELOPMENT MONITORING TECHNIQUES

| Technique | Description |
| --- | --- |
| Amniocentesis | Done between the 15th and 20th week of pregnancy, this procedure examines a sample of the amniotic fluid, which contains fetal cells. Recommended if either parent carries Tay-Sachs, spina bifida, sickle-cell, Down syndrome, muscular dystrophy, or Rh disease. |
| Chorionic villus sampling (CVS) | Done at 8 to 11 weeks, either transabdominally or transcervically, depending on where the placenta is located. Involves inserting a needle (abdominally) or a catheter (cervically) into the substance of the placenta but staying outside the amniotic sac and removing 10 to 15 milligrams of tissue. This tissue is manually cleaned of maternal uterine tissue and then grown in culture, and a karyotype is made, as with amniocentesis. |
| Embryoscopy | Examines the embryo or fetus during the first 12 weeks of pregnancy by means of a fiber-optic endoscope inserted through the cervix. Can be performed as early as week 5. Access to the fetal circulation may be obtained through the instrument, and direct visualization of the embryo permits the diagnosis of malformations. |
| Fetal blood sampling (FBS) | Performed after 18 weeks of pregnancy by collecting a small amount of blood from the umbilical cord for testing. Used to detect Down syndrome and most other chromosome abnormalities in the fetuses of couples who are at increased risk of having an affected child. Many other diseases can be diagnosed using this technique. |
| Sonoembryology | Used to detect abnormalities in the first trimester of pregnancy. Involves high-frequency transvaginal probes and digital image processing. In combination with ultrasound, can detect more than 80 percent of all malformations during the second trimester. |
| Sonogram | Uses ultrasound to produce a visual image of the uterus, fetus, and placenta. |
| Ultrasound sonography | Uses very-high-frequency sound waves to detect structural abnormalities or multiple pregnancies, measure fetal growth, judge gestational age, and evaluate uterine abnormalities. Also used as an adjunct to other procedures such as amniocentesis. |

abnormalities. For instance, Huntington's disease typically does not appear until people reach their 40s. However, genetic testing can identify much earlier the flawed gene that produces Huntington's. Presumably, knowing that they carry the gene can help people prepare for the future (van't Spijker & ten Kroode, 1997; Ensenauer, Michels, & Reinke, 2005).

In addition to Huntington's disease, more than a thousand disorders can be predicted on the basis of genetic testing, ranging from cystic fibrosis to ovarian cancer. Negative results can bring welcome relief, but positive results may produce just the opposite effect. In fact, genetic testing raises difficult practical and ethical questions (Human Genome Project, 2006; Twomey, 2006; Wilfond & Ross, 2009).

Suppose, for instance, a woman is tested in her 20s for Huntington's and finds that she does not carry the defective gene. Obviously, she would be relieved. But suppose she finds that she does carry the flawed gene and will therefore get the disease. In this case, she might well experience depression and remorse. In fact, some studies show that 10 percent of people who find they have the flawed gene that leads to Huntington's disease never recover fully on an emotional level (Groopman, 1998; Hamilton, 1998; Myers, 2004; Wahlin, 2007).

Genetic testing is a complicated issue. It rarely provides a simple yes/no answer, typically presenting a range of probabilities instead. In some cases, the likelihood of becoming ill depends on the stressors in a person's environment. Personal differences also affect susceptibility to a disorder (Patenaude, Guttmacher, & Collins, 2002; Bonke et al., 2005; Martin, Greenwood, & Nisker, 2010).

⊙ **From the perspective of a health care provider:** What are some ethical and philosophical questions that surround the issue of genetic counseling? Might it sometimes be unwise to know ahead of time about possible disorders that might affect your child or yourself?

Today many researchers and medical practitioners have moved beyond testing and counseling to actually modifying flawed genes. For example, in *germ line therapy,* cells with defective genes are taken from an embryo, repaired, and replaced.

---

## REVIEW, CHECK, AND APPLY

### REVIEW

**LO1** What is our basic genetic endowment?

- In humans, the male sex cell (the sperm) and the female sex cell (the ovum) provide the developing baby with 23 chromosomes each, making up roughly 25,000 genes, the basic units of genetic information.

**LO2** What are the major genetic threats to normal development?

- A recessive gene responsible for a disorder may be passed on silently, revealing itself only when it is paired with another recessive gene.

- Another way that genes are a source of concern is that they may become physically damaged.

**LO3** What is the role of behavioral genetics?

- The field of behavioral genetics, a combination of psychology and genetics, studies the effects of heredity on personality and behavioral characteristics.

### CHECK YOURSELF

1. Sex cells (the ova and the sperm) are different from other cells because they:

   a. have twice the 46 chromosomes necessary so that when the cells combine and material is "spilled," the appropriate number of chromosomes will still be there.

   b. each have half of the 46 chromosomes so that when they combine, the new zygote will have all the genetic information necessary.

   c. are younger than all other cells in the developing human body.

   d. are the only cells with chromosomal information.

2. According to Mendel, when competing traits are both present, only one trait, also known as the _____ trait, can be expressed.

3. Just because a disorder has genetic roots does not mean that environmental factors do not also play a role.

   - True
   - False

### APPLYING LIFESPAN DEVELOPMENT

- How can the study of identical twins who were separated at birth help researchers determine the effects of genetic and environmental factors on human development?

✓─Study and Review on
**MyDevelopmentLab.com**

Answers: 1) b; 2) dominant; 3) True

# The Interaction of Heredity and Environment

**LO4** How do the environment and genetics work together?

**LO5** What is the role of genetics and the environment in determining specific major human characteristics?

*Like many other parents, Jared's mother, Leesha, and his father, Jamal, tried to figure out which of them their new baby resembled more. He seemed to have Leesha's big, wide eyes, and Jamal's generous smile. As he grew, they noticed that his hairline was just like Leesha's, and his teeth made his smile resemble Jamal's. He also seemed to act like his parents. For example, he was a charming little baby, always ready to smile at people who visited the house—just like his friendly, jovial dad. He seemed to sleep like his mom, which was lucky since Jamal was an extremely light sleeper who could do with as little as 4 hours a night, while Leesha liked a regular 7 or 8 hours.*

Were Jared's ready smile and regular sleeping habits something he just luckily inherited from his parents? Or did Jamal and Leesha provide a happy and stable home that encouraged these welcome traits? What causes our behavior? Nature or nurture? Is behavior produced by genetic influences or factors in the environment?

The simple answer is: There is no simple answer.

## The Role of the Environment in Determining the Expression of Genes: From Genotypes to Phenotypes

As developmental research accumulates, it is becoming increasingly clear that to view behavior as due to *either* genetic *or* environmental factors is inappropriate, since behavior is the product of some combination of the two.

For instance, consider **temperament,** patterns of arousal and emotionality that represent consistent and enduring characteristics in an individual. Suppose we found—as increasing evidence suggests—that a small percentage of children are born with an unusual degree of physiological reactivity—a tendency to shrink from anything unusual. Such infants react to novel stimuli with a rapid increase in heartbeat and unusual excitability of the limbic system of the brain. By age 4 or 5, children with heightened reactivity to stimuli are often considered shy by their parents and teachers. But not always: some of them behave indistinguishably from their peers at the same age (Kagan & Snidman, 1991; McCrae et al., 2000; Gerken, 2010).

What makes the difference? The answer seems to be the children's environment. Children whose parents encourage them to be outgoing by arranging new opportunities for them may overcome their shyness. In contrast, children raised in a stressful environment marked by marital discord or a prolonged illness may be more likely to retain their shyness later in life (Kagan, Arcus, & Snidman, 1993; Joseph, 1999; Propper & Moore, 2006). Jared, described earlier, may have been born with an easy temperament, which was easily reinforced by his caring parents.

*Interaction of Factors.*  Such findings illustrate that many traits reflect **multifactorial transmission,** meaning that they are determined by a combination of both genetic and environmental factors. In multifactorial transmission, a genotype provides a range within which a phenotype may be expressed. For instance, people with a genotype that permits them to gain weight easily may vary in their actual body weight. They may be *relatively* slim, given their genetic heritage, but never able to get beyond a certain degree of thinness (Faith, Johnson, & Allison, 1997). In many cases, then, the environment determines how a particular genotype will be expressed as a phenotype (Wachs, 1992, 1993, 1996; Plomin, 1994a).

On the other hand, certain genotypes are relatively unaffected by environmental factors. For instance, pregnant women who were severely malnourished during famines caused by World War II had children who were, on average, unaffected physically or intellectually as

**temperament** patterns of arousal and emotionality that represent consistent and enduring characteristics in an individual

**multifactorial transmission** the determination of traits by a combination of both genetic and environmental factors in which a genotype provides a range within which a phenotype may be expressed

adults (Stein et al., 1975). Similarly, people will never grow beyond certain genetically imposed limitations in height, no matter how well or how much they eat. And the environment had little to do with Jared's hairline.

Although we can't attribute specific behaviors exclusively to nature or nurture, we can ask how much of a behavior is caused by genetic factors and how much by environmental factors. We'll turn to this question next.

## Studying Development: How Much Is Nature? How Much Is Nurture?

Developmental researchers use several strategies to study the relative influence of genetic and environmental factors on traits, characteristics, and behavior. Their studies involve both nonhuman species and humans.

***Nonhuman Animal Studies: Controlling Both Genetics and Environment.*** It is relatively simple to develop breeds of animals with genetically similar traits. The Butterball people do it all the time, producing Thanksgiving turkeys that grow especially rapidly so that they can be brought to market inexpensively. Similarly, strains of laboratory animals can be bred to share similar genetic backgrounds.

By observing genetically similar animals in different environments, scientists can determine, with reasonable precision, the effects of specific kinds of environmental stimulation. For example, to examine the effects of different environmental settings, researchers can raise some of the genetically similar animals in unusually stimulating environments, with lots of items to climb over or through, and others in relatively barren environments. Conversely, by exposing groups of genetically *dissimilar* animals to *identical* environments, researchers can examine in a different way the role that genetic background plays.

Animal research offers substantial opportunities, but the drawback is that we can't be sure how well our findings can be generalized to people.

***Contrasting Relatedness and Behavior: Adoption, Twin, and Family Studies.*** Obviously, researchers can't control either the genetic backgrounds or the environments of humans as they can with nonhumans. However, nature conveniently has provided ideal subjects for carrying out various kinds of "natural experiments"—twins.

*New Yorker, August 18/25, 2003, p. 141*

*"The title of my science project is 'My Little Brother: Nature or Nurture.'"*

Recall that identical, monozygotic twins are *genetically* identical. Because their inherited backgrounds are precisely the same, any variations in their behavior must be due entirely to environmental factors.

Theoretically, identical twins would make great subjects for experiments about the roles of nature and nurture. For instance, by separating identical twins at birth and placing them in totally different environments, researchers could assess the impact of environment unambiguously. Of course, ethical considerations make this impossible.

What researchers can—and do—study, however, are cases in which identical twins have been put up for adoption at birth and are raised in substantially different environments. Such instances allow us to draw fairly confident conclusions about the relative contributions of genetics and environment (Bailey et al., 2000; Richardson & Norgate, 2007; Agrawal & Lynskey, 2008).

The data from such studies of identical twins raised in different environments are not always without bias. Adoption agencies typically take the characteristics (and wishes) of birth mothers into account when they place babies in adoptive homes. For instance, children tend to be placed with families of the same race and religion. Consequently, even when monozygotic twins are placed in different adoptive homes, there are often similarities between the two home environments. As a result, researchers can't always be certain that differences in behavior are due to differences in the environment.

Studies of nonidentical, dizygotic twins also present opportunities to learn about nature and nurture. Recall that dizygotic twins are genetically no more similar than siblings in a family born at different times. By comparing the behavior of dizygotic twins with that of monozygotic twins (who are genetically identical) researchers can determine if monozygotic twins tend to be more similar on a particular trait than dizygotic twins. If so, they can assume that genetics plays an important role in determining the expression of that trait.

Still another approach is to study people who are totally unrelated and therefore have dissimilar genetic backgrounds, but who share an environmental background. For instance, a family that adopts, at the same time, two very young unrelated children probably will provide them with similar environments. In this case, similarities in the children's characteristics and behavior can be attributed with some confidence to environmental influences (Segal, 1993, 2000).

Finally, developmental researchers have examined groups of people in light of their degree of genetic similarity. For instance, if we find a high association on a particular trait between biological parents and their children but a weaker association between adoptive parents and their children, we have evidence for the importance of genetics in determining the expression of that trait. On the other hand, if there is a stronger association on a trait between adoptive parents and their children than between biological parents and their children, we have evidence for the importance of the environment in determining that trait. If a particular trait tends to occur at similar levels among genetically similar individuals, but at different levels among genetically distant individuals, genetics probably plays a major role in the development of that trait.

Developmental researchers using all these approaches, and more, for decades have come to a general conclusion: Virtually all traits, characteristics, and behaviors result from the combination and interaction of nature and nurture (Robinson, 2004; Waterland & Jirtle, 2004; Jaworski & Accardo, 2010).

## Physical Traits: Family Resemblances

When patients entered the examining room of Dr. Cyril Marcus, they didn't realize that sometimes they were actually being treated by his identical twin brother, Dr. Stewart Marcus. So similar in appearance and manner were the twins that even long-time patients were fooled by this admittedly unethical behavior, which occurred in a bizarre case made famous in the film *Dead Ringers*.

Monozygotic twins are merely the most extreme example of the fact that the more genetically similar two people are, the more likely they are to share physical characteristics. Tall parents tend to have tall children and short parents short children. Obesity also has a strong genetic component. For example, in one study, pairs of identical twins were put on diets that contained an extra 1,000 calories a day—and ordered not to exercise. Over a three-month period, the twins gained almost identical amounts of weight. Moreover, different pairs of twins varied substantially in how much weight they gained, with some pairs gaining almost three times as much weight as other pairs (Bouchard et al., 1990).

Other, less obvious physical characteristics also show strong genetic influences. For instance, blood pressure, respiration rates, and even the age at which life ends are more similar in closely related individuals than in those who are less genetically alike (Price & Gottesman, 1991; Melzer, Hurst, & Frayling, 2007).

## Intelligence: More Research, More Controversy

No other nature–nurture issue has generated more research than intelligence. The reason is that intelligence, generally measured as an IQ score, is a central human characteristic that differentiates humans from other species. In addition, intelligence is strongly related to scholastic success and, somewhat less strongly, to other types of achievement.

Genetics plays a significant role in intelligence. In studies of both overall or general intelligence and of specific subcomponents of intelligence (such as spatial skills, verbal skills, and memory), as can be seen in Figure 2-6, the closer the genetic link between two individuals, the greater the correspondence of their overall IQ scores.

Not only is genetics an important influence on intelligence, but the impact increases with age. For instance, as fraternal (i.e., dizygotic) twins move from infancy to adolescence, their IQ scores become less similar. Not so with identical (monozygotic) twins, who become increasingly similar as they age (Brody, 1993; McGue et al., 1993; Chamorro-Premuzic et al., 2010).

Clearly, heredity plays an important role in intelligence, but to what degree is it inherited? Perhaps the most extreme view is held by psychologist Arthur Jensen (2003), who argues that as much as 80 percent of intelligence is a result of heredity. Others suggest more modest figures, ranging from 50 to 70 percent. It is critical to recall that these figures are averages across many people and say nothing about any individual's degree of inheritance (e.g., Herrnstein & Murray, 1994; Devlin, Daniels, & Roeder, 1997).

It is important to keep in mind that, whatever role heredity plays, environmental factors such as exposure to books, good educational experiences, and intelligent peers are profoundly influential. In fact, in terms of public policy, environmental influences are the focus of efforts geared toward maximizing people's intellectual success. As developmental psychologist Sandra Scarr suggests, we should be asking what can be done to maximize the intellectual development of each individual (Scarr & Carter-Saltzman, 1982; Storfer, 1990; Bouchard, 1997).

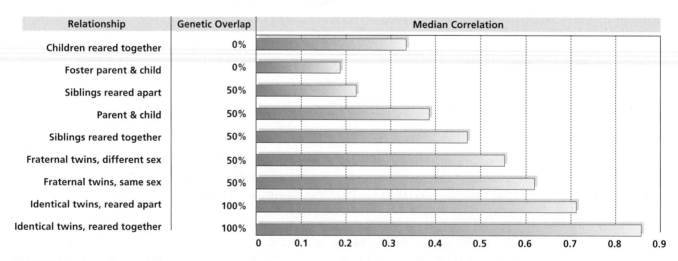

FIGURE 2-6 **Genetics and IQ**
The closer the genetic link between two individuals, the greater the correspondence between their IQ scores. Why do you think there is a sex difference in the fraternal twins' figures? Might there be other sex differences in other sets of twins or siblings, not shown on this chart?
Source: Bouchard & McGue, 1981.

➡ **From an educator's perspective:** Some people have used the proven genetic basis of intelligence to argue against strenuous educational efforts on behalf of individuals with below-average IQs. Does this viewpoint make sense based on what you have learned about heredity and environment? Why or why not?

## Genetic and Environmental Influences on Personality: Born to Be Outgoing?

Do we inherit our personality?

At least in part. Evidence suggests that some of our most basic personality traits have genetic roots. For example, two of the "Big Five" personality traits, neuroticism and extroversion, have been linked to genetic factors. *Neuroticism,* as used by personality researchers, is the degree of emotional stability an individual characteristically displays. *Extroversion* is the degree to which a person seeks to be with others, to behave in an outgoing manner, and generally to be sociable. For instance, Jared, the baby described earlier, may have inherited an outgoing personality from his extroverted father, Jamal (Benjamin, Ebstein, & Belmaker, 2002; Zuckerman, 2003; Horwitz, Luong, & Charles, 2008).

How do we know which personality traits reflect genetics? Some evidence comes from direct examination of genes themselves. For instance, it appears that a specific gene is very

Are some children born to be outgoing and extroverted? The answer seems to be "yes."

## *Cultural Dimensions*

### Cultural Differences in Physical Arousal: Might a Culture's Philosophical Outlook Be Determined by Genetics?

The Buddhist philosophy of many Asian cultures emphasizes harmony and peace. In contrast, many Western philosophies accentuate the control of anxiety, fear, and guilt, which are assumed to be basic parts of the human condition.

Could such philosophical approaches reflect, in part, genetic factors? That is the controversial suggestion made by developmental psychologist Jerome Kagan and his colleagues. They speculate that the underlying temperament of a given society, determined genetically, may predispose people in that society toward a particular philosophy (Kagan, Arcus, & Snidman, 1993; Kagan, 2003a, 2010).

Kagan bases his admittedly speculative suggestion on well-confirmed findings that show clear differences in temperament between Caucasian and Asian children. For instance, one study that compared 4-month-old infants in China, Ireland, and the United States found several relevant differences. In comparison to the Caucasian American babies and the Irish babies, the Chinese babies had significantly lower motor activity, irritability, and vocalization.

Kagan suggests that the Chinese, who enter the world temperamentally calmer, may find Buddhist notions of serenity more in tune with their nature. In contrast, Westerners, who are emotionally more volatile, tense, and prone to guilt, may be attracted to philosophies that focus on the control of unpleasant feelings, which are usual features of everyday experience (Kagan et al., 1994; Kagan, 2003, 2010).

Of course, neither philosophical approach is better or worse than the other; that's a matter of personal values. Also, any individual within a culture can be more or less temperamentally volatile and the range of temperaments even within a single culture is vast. Finally, environmental conditions can have a significant effect on the portion of a person's temperament that is not genetically determined. But

The Buddhist philosophy emphasizes harmony and peacefulness. Could this decidedly non-Western philosophy be a reflection, in part, of genetic causes?

what this speculation does reflect is the complex interaction between culture and temperament. Religion may help mold temperament; temperament may make certain religious ideals more attractive.

To validate this intriguing notion would require additional research to determine just how the unique interaction of heredity and environment within a given culture may produce a framework for viewing and understanding the world.

influential in determining risk-taking behavior. This novelty-seeking gene affects the production of the brain chemical dopamine, making some people more prone than others to seek out novel situations and to take risks (Gillespie et al., 2003; Serretti et al., 2007; Ray et al., 2009).

Other evidence comes from studies of twins. In one major study, researchers looked at the personality traits of hundreds of pairs of twins. Because a good number of the twins were genetically identical but had been raised apart, it was possible to determine with some confidence the influence of genetic factors (Tellegen et al., 1988). The researchers found that certain traits reflected the contribution of genetics considerably more than others. As you can see in Figure 2-7, social potency (the tendency to be a masterful, forceful leader who enjoys being the center of attention) and traditionalism (strict endorsement of rules and authority) are strongly associated with genetic factors (Harris, Vernon, & Jang, 2007).

Even less basic personality traits are linked to genetics. For example, political attitudes, religious interests and values, and even attitudes toward human sexuality have genetic components (Bouchard, 2004; Koenig et al., 2005; Bradshaw & Ellison, 2008).

Clearly, genetic factors play a role in determining personality—but so does the environment in which a child is raised. For example, some parents encourage high activity levels as a manifestation of independence and intelligence. Other parents may encourage lower levels of activity, feeling that more passive children will get along better in society. In part these parental attitudes are culturally determined: U.S. parents may encourage higher activity levels, while parents in Asian cultures may encourage greater passivity. In both cases, children's personalities will be shaped in part by their parents' attitudes (Cauce, 2008).

Because both genetic and environmental factors have consequences for a child's personality, personality development is a perfect example of the interplay between nature and nurture. Furthermore, it is not only individuals who reflect the interaction of nature and nurture, but even entire cultures, as we see next.

| Trait | Percentage |
|---|---|
| **Social potency** | **61%** |
| A person high in this trait is masterful, a forceful leader who likes to be the center of attention. | |
| **Traditionalism** | **60%** |
| Follows rules and authority, endorses high moral standards and strict discipline. | |
| **Stress reaction** | **55%** |
| Feels vulnerable and sensitive and is given to worries and is easily upset. | |
| **Absorption** | **55%** |
| Has a vivid imagination readily captured by rich experience; relinquishes sense of reality. | |
| **Alienation** | **55%** |
| Feels mistreated and used, that "the world is out to get me." | |
| **Well-being** | **54%** |
| Has a cheerful disposition, feels confident and optimistic. | |
| **Harm avoidance** | **50%** |
| Shuns the excitement of risk and danger, prefers the safe route even if it is tedious. | |
| **Aggression** | **48%** |
| Is physically aggressive and vindictive, has taste for violence and is "out to get the world." | |
| **Achievement** | **46%** |
| Works hard, strives for mastery, and puts work and accomplishment ahead of other things. | |
| **Control** | **43%** |
| Is cautious and plodding, rational and sensible, likes carefully planned events. | |
| **Social closeness** | **33%** |
| Prefers emotional intimacy and close ties, turns to others for comfort and help. | |

FIGURE 2-7 **Inheriting Traits**

These traits are among the personality factors that are related most closely to genetic factors. The higher the percentage, the greater the degree to which the trait reflects the influence of heredity. Do these figures mean that "leaders are born, not made"? Why or why not?
Source: Adapted from Tellegen et al., 1988.

# Psychological Disorders: The Role of Genetics and Environment

*Lori Schiller began to hear voices when she was a teenager in summer camp. Without warning, the voices screamed "You must die! Die! Die!" She ran from her bunk into the darkness, where she thought she could get away. Camp counselors found her screaming as she jumped wildly on a trampoline. "I thought I was possessed," she said later.* (Bennett, 1992)

In a sense, she *was* possessed: possessed with schizophrenia, one of the severest types of psychological disorder. Schiller's world, normal and happy through childhood, took a tumble during adolescence as she increasingly lost her hold on reality. For the next two decades, she would be in and out of institutions.

What was the cause of Schiller's mental disorder? Evidence suggests that schizophrenia is brought about by genetic factors and runs in families. Moreover, the closer the genetic links between family members, the more likely it is that if one person develops schizophrenia, the other will too. For instance, a monozygotic twin has close to a 50 percent risk of developing schizophrenia when the other twin develops the disorder (see Figure 2-8). On the other hand, a niece or nephew of a person with schizophrenia has less than a 5 percent chance of developing the disorder (Prescott & Gottesman, 1993; Hanson & Gottesman, 2005).

These data also illustrate that genetics alone does not influence the development of the disorder. If genetics were the sole cause, the risk for an identical twin would be 100 percent. Consequently, other factors account for the disorder, ranging from structural abnormalities in the brain to a biochemical imbalance (e.g., Lyons et al., 2002; Hietala, Cannon, & van Erp, 2003; Howes & Kapur, 2009).

It also seems that even if individuals harbor a genetic predisposition toward schizophrenia, they are not destined to develop the disorder. Instead, they may inherit an unusual sensitivity to stress in the environment. If stress is low, schizophrenia will not occur. But if stress is sufficiently strong, schizophrenia will result. On the other hand, for someone with a strong genetic predisposition toward the disorder, even relatively weak environmental stressors may lead to schizophrenia (Paris, 1999; Norman & Malla, 2001; Mittal, Ellman, & Cannon, 2008).

Several other psychological disorders have been shown to be related, at least in part, to genetic factors. For instance, major depression, alcoholism, autism, and attention-deficit hyperactivity disorder have significant inherited components (Dick, Rose, & Kaprio, 2006; Monastra, 2008; Burbach & van der Zwaag, 2009).

These disorders, which are genetic but far from preordained, illustrate a fundamental principle regarding the relationship between heredity and environment. Genetics often produces a tendency toward a future course of development, but when and whether the characteristic will be displayed depends on the environment. Thus, although a predisposition for schizophrenia may be present at birth, typically people do not show the disorder until adolescence—if at all.

Similarly, other traits are more likely to be displayed as the influence of parents and other socializing factors declines. For example, young adopted children may display traits that are relatively similar to those of their adoptive parents. As they get older and their parents' day-to-day influence declines, genetically influenced traits may begin to manifest themselves as unseen genetic factors (Caspi & Moffitt, 1993; Arsenault et al., 2003; Poulton & Caspi, 2005).

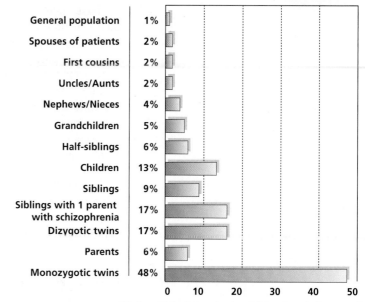

**FIGURE 2-8 The Genetics of Schizophrenia**
The psychological disorder of schizophrenia has clear genetic components. The closer the genetic links between someone with schizophrenia and another family member, the more likely it is that the other person will also develop schizophrenia.
Source: Gottesman, 1991.

## Can Genes Influence the Environment?

According to developmental psychologist Sandra Scarr (1993, 1998), the genetic endowment provided to children by their parents not only determines their genetic characteristics, but also actively influences their environment. Scarr suggests three ways a child's genetic predisposition might influence his or her environment.

First, children tend to focus on aspects of their environment that are most in tune with their genetic abilities. For example, an active, aggressive child may gravitate toward sports, while a reserved child may be more engaged by academics or solitary pursuits like computer games or drawing. Or, one girl reading the school bulletin board may notice the upcoming tryouts for Little League baseball, while her less coordinated but more musically endowed friend might spot a poster recruiting students for an after-school chorus. In these examples the children are attending to those aspects of the environment in which their genetically determined abilities can flourish.

Second, the gene–environment influence may be more passive and less direct. For example, a particularly sports-oriented parent, who has genes that promote good physical coordination, may provide many opportunities for a child to play sports.

Finally, the genetically driven temperament of a child may *evoke* certain environmental influences. For instance, an infant's demanding behavior may cause parents to be more attentive to the infant's needs than they would be otherwise. Or, a child who is genetically well coordinated may play ball with anything in the house so often that her parents notice and decide to give her some sports equipment.

In sum, determining whether behavior is primarily attributable to nature or nurture is like shooting at a moving target. Not only are behaviors and traits a joint outcome of genetic and environmental factors, but the relative influence of genes and environment for specific characteristics shifts over the life span. Although the genes we inherit at birth set the stage for our future development, the constantly shifting scenery and the other characters in our lives determine just how our development eventually plays out. The environment both influences our experiences and is molded by the choices we are temperamentally inclined to make.

## REVIEW, CHECK, AND APPLY

### REVIEW

**LO4** How do the environment and genetics work together?

- Using a variety of approaches, developmental researchers have come to the general conclusion that virtually all traits, characteristics, and behaviors result from a combination and interaction of nature and nurture.

**LO5** What is the role of genetics and the environment in determining specific major human characteristics?

- Genetic influences have been identified in physical characteristics, intelligence, personality traits and behaviors, and psychological disorders.

- There is speculation that entire cultures may be predisposed genetically toward certain types of philosophical viewpoints and attitudes.

### CHECK YOURSELF

1. Most behavioral traits are a product of genetic influence and environmental factors. This is also known as _____.

   a. systematic desensitization

   b. creative orientation

   c. genetic predetermination

   d. multifactorial transmission

2. Instead of asking if behavior is caused by genetic *or* environmental influence, we should be asking *how much* of the behavior is caused by genetic factors and *how much* is caused by environmental factors.

   - True

   - False

3. According to psychologist Jerome Kagan, differences in temperament between Chinese and American children suggest a culture's philosophical outlook may be related to _____ factors.

### APPLYING LIFESPAN DEVELOPMENT

- How might an environment different from the one you experienced have affected the development of personality characteristics that you believe you inherited from one or both of your parents?

✓⬤ **Study** and **Review** on
**MyDevelopmentLab.com**

Answers: 1) d; 2) True; 3) genetic

## MODULE 2.2 Prenatal Growth and Change

*At her first appointment with Robert and Lisa, the midwife checked the results of tests to confirm the couple's home pregnancy test. "Yep, you're going to have a baby," she said to Lisa. "You'll need to set up monthly visits for 6 months, then more frequently as your due date approaches. Get this prescription for prenatal vitamins filled at a pharmacy and read these guidelines about diet and exercise. You don't smoke, do you? Good." Then she turned to Robert. "How about you? Do you smoke?" After many more minutes of instructions and advice, she left the couple feeling slightly dazed, but ready to do whatever they could to have a healthy baby.*

From the moment of conception, development proceeds relentlessly. Much of it is guided by the complex set of genetic guidelines inherited from the parents, but much is also influenced from the start by environmental factors (Leavitt & Goldson, 1996). And both parents, like the bewildered Lisa and Robert, will have the chance to provide a good prenatal environment.

In this module, we trace the first stirrings of life, when the father's sperm meets the mother's egg. We consider the stages of prenatal development, as the fertilized egg rapidly grows and differentiates into the vast variety of cells that make up the human body. We also look at how pregnancy can go awry, and conclude with a discussion of the factors that present threats to normal development.

# The Prenatal Period

**L06**  What are the major milestones during the prenatal stages of development?

**L07**  What are some of the problems that can arise during a pregnancy?

When most of us think about the facts of life, we tend to focus on the events that cause a male's sperm cells to begin their journey toward a female's ovum. Yet the act of sex that brings about the potential for conception is both the consequence and the start of a long string of events that precede and follow conception.

## Fertilization: The Moment of Conception

**Fertilization**, or conception, is the joining of sperm and ovum to create the single-celled zygote from which all of us began our lives. Both the male's sperm and the female's ovum come with a history of their own. Females are born with around 400,000 ova located in the two ovaries (see Figure 2-9 for the basic anatomy of the female reproductive organs). However, the ova do not mature until the female reaches puberty. From that point until she reaches menopause, the female will ovulate about every 28 days. During ovulation, an egg is released from one of the ovaries and pushed by minute hair cells through the fallopian tube toward the uterus. If the ovum meets a sperm in the fallopian tube, fertilization takes place (Aitken, 1995).

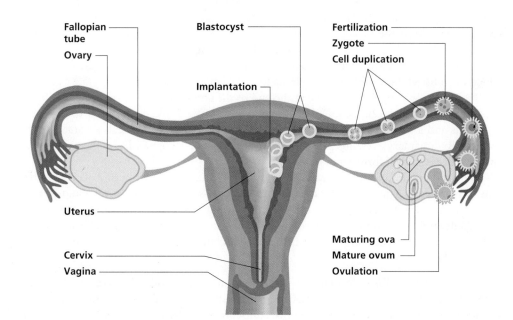

**FIGURE 2-9  Anatomy of the Female Reproductive Organs**
The basic anatomy of the female reproductive organs is illustrated in this cutaway view.
Source: Moore & Persaud, 2003.

**fertilization**  the process by which a sperm and an ovum—the male and female gametes, respectively—join to form a single new cell

Sperm, which look a little like microscopic tadpoles, have a shorter life span. They are created by the testicles at a rapid rate: An adult male typically produces several hundred million sperm a day. Consequently, the sperm ejaculated during sexual intercourse are of considerably more recent origin than the ovum to which they are heading.

When sperm enter the vagina, they begin a winding journey through the cervix—the opening into the uterus—and into the fallopian tube, where fertilization may take place. However, only a tiny fraction of the 300 million cells that are typically ejaculated during sexual intercourse ultimately survive the arduous journey. That's usually okay, though: It takes only one sperm to fertilize an ovum, and each sperm and ovum contains all the genetic data necessary to produce a new human.

## The Stages of the Prenatal Period: The Onset of Development

The prenatal period consists of three phases: the germinal, embryonic, and fetal stages.

**The Germinal Stage: Fertilization to 2 Weeks.** During the **germinal stage**, the first—and shortest—stage of the prenatal period, the zygote begins to divide and grow in complexity. The fertilized egg (now called a *blastocyst*) travels toward the *uterus,* where it becomes implanted in the uterus's wall, which is rich in nutrients. The germinal stage is characterized by methodical cell division, which gets off to a quick start: Three days after fertilization, the organism consists of some 32 cells, and by the next day the number doubles. Within a week, it comprises 100 to 150 cells, and the number rises with increasing rapidity.

The cells of the organism become not only more numerous, but also more specialized. For instance, some cells form a protective layer around the mass of cells, while others begin to establish the rudiments of a placenta and umbilical cord. When fully developed, the **placenta** serves as a conduit between the mother and fetus, providing nourishment and oxygen via the *umbilical cord*. In addition, waste materials from the developing child are removed through the umbilical cord.

**The Embryonic Stage: 2 Weeks to 8 Weeks.** By the end of the germinal period—just 2 weeks after conception—the organism is firmly secured to the wall of the mother's uterus. At this point, the child is called an *embryo*. The **embryonic stage** is the period from 2 to 8 weeks following fertilization. One of the highlights of this stage is the development of the major organs and basic anatomy.

At the beginning of this stage, the developing child has three distinct layers, each of which will form a different set of structures that eventually make up every part of the body. The outer layer of the embryo, the *ectoderm,* will form skin, hair, teeth, sense organs, and the brain and spinal cord. The *endoderm,* the inner layer, produces the digestive system, liver, pancreas, and respiratory system. Sandwiched between the ectoderm and endoderm is the *mesoderm,* from which the muscles, bones, blood, and circulatory system are forged.

If you were looking at an embryo at the end of the embryonic stage, you might be hard-pressed to identify it as human. Only an inch long, an 8-week-old embryo has what appear to be gills and a tail-like structure. On the other hand, a closer look reveals several familiar features. Rudimentary eyes, nose, lips, and even teeth can be recognized, and the embryo has stubby bulges that will form arms and legs.

The head and brain undergo rapid growth during the embryonic period. The head begins to represent a significant proportion of the embryo's size, encompassing about 50 percent of its total length. The growth of nerve cells, called *neurons,* is astonishing: as many as 100,000 neurons are produced every minute during the second month of life! The nervous system begins to function around the fifth week, emitting weak brain waves (Lauter, 1998; Nelson & Bosquet, 2000).

**The Fetal Stage: 8 Weeks to Birth.** It is not until the final period of prenatal development, the fetal stage, that the developing child becomes easily recognizable. The **fetal stage** starts about 8 weeks after conception and continues until birth. The fetal stage formally starts when the major organs have differentiated.

Now called a **fetus,** the developing child undergoes astoundingly rapid change. It increases in length some 20 times, and its proportions change dramatically. At 2 months, around half

---

**germinal stage** the first—and shortest—stage of the prenatal period, which takes place during the first 2 weeks following conception

**placenta** a conduit between the mother and fetus, providing nourishment and oxygen via the umbilical cord

**embryonic stage** the period from 2 to 8 weeks following fertilization during which significant growth occurs in the major organs and body systems

**fetal stage** the stage that begins at about 8 weeks after conception and continues until birth

**fetus** a developing child, from 8 weeks after conception until birth

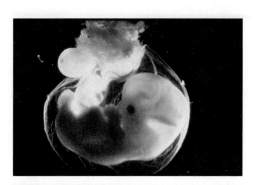

(a) Fetus at 5–6 weeks

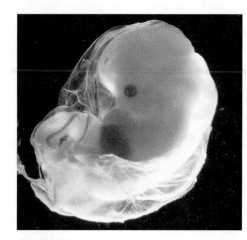

(b) Fetus at 8 weeks

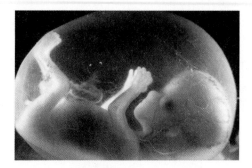

(c) Fetus at 14 weeks

the fetus is what will ultimately be its head; by 5 months, the head accounts for just over a quarter of its total size (see Figure 2-10). The fetus also substantially increases in weight. At 4 months, the fetus weighs an average of about 4 ounces; at 7 months, it weighs about 3 pounds; and at the time of birth the average child weighs just over 7 pounds.

At the same time, the developing child is rapidly becoming more complex. Organs become more differentiated and start to work. By 3 months, for example, the fetus swallows and urinates. In addition, the interconnections between the different parts of the body become more complex and integrated. Arms develop hands; hands develop fingers; fingers develop nails.

As this is happening, the fetus makes itself known to the outside world. In the earliest stages of pregnancy, mothers may be unaware that they are, in fact, pregnant. As the fetus becomes increasingly active, however, most mothers take notice. By 4 months, a mother can feel the movement of her child, and several months later others can feel the baby's kicks through the mother's skin. In addition, the fetus can turn, do somersaults, cry, hiccup, clench its fist, open and close its eyes, and suck its thumb.

The brain, too, becomes increasingly sophisticated. The symmetrical left and right halves of the brain, known as *hemispheres,* grow rapidly, and the interconnections between neurons become more complex. The neurons become coated with an insulating material called *myelin,* which helps speed the transmission of messages from the brain to the rest of the body.

By the end of the fetal period, brain waves indicate that the fetus passes through different stages of sleep and wakefulness. The fetus is able to hear (and feel the vibrations of) sounds to which it is exposed. Researchers Anthony DeCasper and Melanie Spence (1986) asked a group of pregnant mothers to read aloud the Dr. Seuss story *The Cat in the Hat* two times a day during the latter months of pregnancy. Three days after the babies were born, they appeared to recognize the story, responding more to it than to another story with a different rhythm.

In weeks 8 to 24 following conception, hormones are released that lead to the increasing differentiation of male and female fetuses. For example, high levels of androgen are produced in males that affect the size of brain cells and the growth of neural connections. Some scientists speculate that this may ultimately lead to differences in male and female brain structure and even to later variations in gender-related behavior (Berenbaum & Bailey, 2003; Reiner & Gearhart, 2004; Knickmeyer & Baron-Cohen, 2006; Burton et al., 2009).

Just as no two adults are alike, no two fetuses are the same. Some fetuses are exceedingly active (a trait that will probably remain with them after birth), while others are more sedentary. Some have relatively quick heart rates, while others have slower rates (DiPietro et al., 2002; Niederhofer, 2004; Tongsong et al., 2005). Such differences are due in part to genetic characteristics inherited at the moment of fertilization. Other differences, though, are caused by the nature of the environment in which the child spends its first 9 months. The prenatal environment can affect infants' development in many ways—for good or ill.

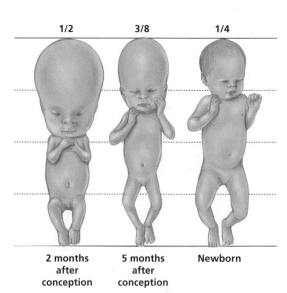

1/2    3/8    1/4

**2 months after conception**    **5 months after conception**    **Newborn**

**FIGURE 2-10 Body Proportions**
During the fetal period, the proportions of the body change dramatically. At 2 months, the head represents about half the fetus, but by the time of birth, it is one-quarter of its total size.

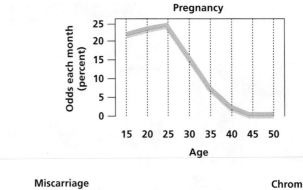

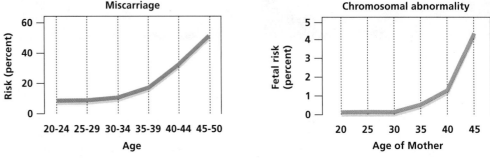

**FIGURE 2-11 Older Women and Risks of Pregnancy**
Not only does the rate of infertility increase as women get older, but the risk of chromosomal abnormality increases as well.
Source: Reproductive Medicine Associates of New Jersey, 2002.

## Pregnancy Problems

For some couples, conception presents challenges—both physical and ethical—that relate to pregnancy.

*Infertility.* Some 15 percent of couples suffer from **infertility,** the inability to conceive after 12 to 18 months of trying. Infertility is correlated with age: The older the parents, the more likely infertility will occur (see Figure 2-11). Regardless of when it occurs in the life span, the inability to conceive is a difficult problem for couples, who may feel a combination of sadness, frustration, and even guilt, particularly on the part of the individual who is infertile (Miles et al., 2009; Sexton, Byrd, & von Kluge, 2010).

In men, infertility most often results from producing too few sperm. Use of illicit drugs or cigarettes and previous bouts of sexually transmitted infections also increase infertility. For women, the most common cause is failure to release an egg through ovulation. This may occur because of a hormone imbalance, a damaged fallopian tube or uterus, stress, or abuse of alcohol or drugs (Lewis, Legato, & Fisch, 2006; Kelly-Weeder & Cox, 2007; Wilkes et al., 2009).

Several treatments for infertility exist. Some difficulties can be corrected through the use of drugs or surgery. Another option may be **artificial insemination,** a procedure in which a man's sperm is placed directly into a woman's reproductive tract by a physician. In some situations, the woman's husband provides the sperm, while in others the source is an anonymous donor from a sperm bank.

The most common type of artificial insemination is *intracervical insemination (ICI),* in which sperm is placed directly into a woman's cervix. In *intrauterine insemination (IUI),* sperm is deposited into the uterus after being "washed," a process that concentrates sperm in a small amount of fluid.

In other cases, fertilization takes place outside the mother's body. **In vitro fertilization (IVF)** is a procedure in which a woman's ova are removed from her ovaries, and a man's sperm is used to fertilize the ova in a laboratory. The fertilized egg is then implanted in the uterus. Similarly, *gamete intrafallopian transfer (GIFT)* and *zygote intrafallopian transfer (ZIFT)* are procedures involving the implantation of an egg and sperm or a fertilized egg in a woman's fallopian tubes.

**infertility** the inability to conceive after 12 to 18 months of trying to become pregnant

**artificial insemination** a process of fertilization in which a man's sperm is placed directly into a woman's reproductive tract by a physician

**in vitro fertilization (IVF)** a procedure in which a woman's ova are removed from her ovaries, and a man's sperm are used to fertilize the ova in a laboratory

*"I'm their real child, and you're just a frozen embryo thingy they bought from some laboratory."*

In IVF, GIFT, and ZIFT, implantation is usually done in the woman who provided the donor eggs. More rarely, a *surrogate mother* is used. The surrogate mother is artificially inseminated by the biological father or some other male, brings the baby to term, and gives up rights to it (Frazier et al., 2004; Kolata, 2004; Aydiner, Yetkin, & Seli, 2010).

Success rates for in vitro fertilization vary drastically, depending on the age of the woman, the cause of her infertility, and a host of other factors. Overall, about a third of in vitro fertilizations result in the birth of a child. Furthermore, reproductive technologies are becoming increasingly sophisticated, permitting parents to choose the sex of their baby. One technique is to separate sperm carrying the X and Y chromosome and implant the desired type into a woman's uterus. In another technique, eggs are removed from a woman and fertilized with sperm through in vitro fertilization. Three days after fertilization, the embryos are tested to determine their sex. If they are the desired gender, they are then implanted into the mother (Duenwald, 2003, 2004; Kalb, 2004).

The use of surrogate mothers, in vitro fertilization, and sex selection techniques presents a web of ethical and legal issues, as well as many emotional concerns. In some instances, surrogate mothers have refused to give up the child after its birth, while in others the surrogate mother has sought to have a role in the child's life. In such cases, the rights of the mother, the father, the surrogate mother, and ultimately the baby are in conflict. Even more troubling are concerns raised by sex selection techniques.

Although these ethical and legal questions are difficult to resolve, we can answer one question: How do children conceived through emerging reproductive technologies such as in vitro fertilization fare?

Research shows that they do quite well. In fact, some studies find that the quality of life for the children of families who have used such techniques may be superior to that of children in families who used natural conception. Furthermore, the later psychological adjustment of children conceived through in vitro fertilization and artificial insemination is no different from that of children conceived through natural techniques (DiPietro, Costigan, & Gurewitsch, 2005; Hjelmstedt, Widström, & Collins, 2006; Siegel, Dittrich, & Vollmann, 2008).

On the other hand, the increasing use of IVF techniques by older individuals (who might be quite elderly when their children reach adolescence) may change these positive findings. Because the use of IVF has only recently become widespread, we don't yet know what outcomes will be most common in families with aging parents (Colpin & Soenen, 2004).

## Miscarriage and Abortion

A *miscarriage*—known as a spontaneous abortion—occurs when the embryo detaches from the wall of the uterus and is expelled before the child can survive outside the womb. Some 15 to 20 percent of pregnancies end in miscarriage, usually in the first several months. Some sort of genetic abnormality accounts for most miscarriages.

Although many miscarriages occur so early that the mother doesn't know that she had one and may not even be aware she was pregnant, in many other cases parents are aware of the pregnancy. When they are aware, they often feel a deep sense of grief, having already formed a bond with their unborn child (Brier, 2008; Swanson et al., 2009).

In *abortion,* a mother chooses to terminate pregnancy. Abortion is a difficult choice for any woman in that it involves complex physical, psychological, legal, and ethical issues. A task force of the American Psychological Association found that, after an abortion, most women experienced a combination of relief and guilt, but in most cases the negative psychological effects were short-lived (APA Reproductive Choice Working Group, 2000). Still, abortion is always a difficult decision (Fergusson, Horwood, & Ridder, 2006; Warren, 2009).

## REVIEW, CHECK, AND APPLY

### REVIEW

**LO6** What are the major milestones during the prenatal stages of development?

- Fertilization joins the sperm and ovum to start prenatal development.
- The prenatal period consists of three stages: germinal, embryonic, and fetal.

**LO7** What are some of the problems that can arise during a pregnancy?

- In addition to difficulties in conceiving due to infertility, some 15 to 20 percent of all pregnancies end in miscarriage, usually in the first several months of pregnancy.

### CHECK YOURSELF

1. The fertility treatment in which fertilization is induced outside the mother's body is known as:
   a. artificial insemination.
   b. intracervical insemination.
   c. intrauterine insemination.
   d. in vitro fertilization.

2. A _____ occurs when the embryo is expelled from the uterus before the child can survive outside the womb.

### APPLYING LIFESPAN DEVELOPMENT

- In your opinion, is it wiser for a woman to ask a friend or a stranger to be the surrogate mother for her child? Why?

✓●─ **Study** and **Review** on
**MyDevelopmentLab.com**

Answers: 1) d; 2) miscarriage

# The Prenatal Environment: Threats to Development

**LEARNING OBJECTIVES**

**LO8** What are the major threats to the fetal environment and what can be done about them?

According to the Siriono people of South America, a pregnant woman who eats the meat of certain animals risks having a child who acts and looks like those animals. According to opinions on TV talk shows, a pregnant mother should never lose her temper or else her child may enter the world angry (Cole, 1992).

While these views are largely the stuff of folklore, there is some evidence that a mother's feelings and emotions may have an effect on her fetus. For example, a mother's anxiety during pregnancy may affect the sleeping patterns of the fetus prior to birth. There are even aspects of a mother's and father's behavior, both before and after conception, that can produce lifelong consequences for the child. Some effects show up immediately, but others don't appear until years later (Groome et al., 1995; Couzin, 2002). Among the most profound negative effects are those caused by teratogenic agents. A **teratogen** is an environmental agent such as a drug, chemical, virus, or other factor that produces a birth defect. Although the placenta is responsible for keeping teratogens from the fetus, it is not 100 percent successful and probably every fetus is exposed to some teratogens.

The timing and quantity of exposure to a teratogen are crucial. At some phases of prenatal development, a certain teratogen may have only a minimal impact, while at others the consequences may be profound. Generally, teratogens have their severest effects during periods of especially rapid prenatal development. Sensitivity to specific teratogens is also related to racial and cultural background. For example, Native American fetuses are more susceptible to the effects of alcohol than European American fetuses (Kinney et al., 2003; Winger & Woods, 2004).

Furthermore, different organ systems are vulnerable to teratogens at different times. For example, the brain is most susceptible 15 to 25 days after conception, while the heart is most vulnerable 20 to 40 days after conception (Needleman & Bellinger, 1994; Bookstein et al., 1996; Pajkrt et al., 2004) (see Figure 2-12).

## Mothers' Diet

A mother's diet clearly plays an important role in fetal development. A mother who eats a varied diet high in nutrients is apt to have fewer complications during pregnancy, an easier labor, and a generally healthier baby than a mother whose diet is restricted in nutrients (Kaiser & Allen, 2002; Guerrini, Thomson, & Gurling, 2007).

**teratogen**  a factor that produces a birth defect

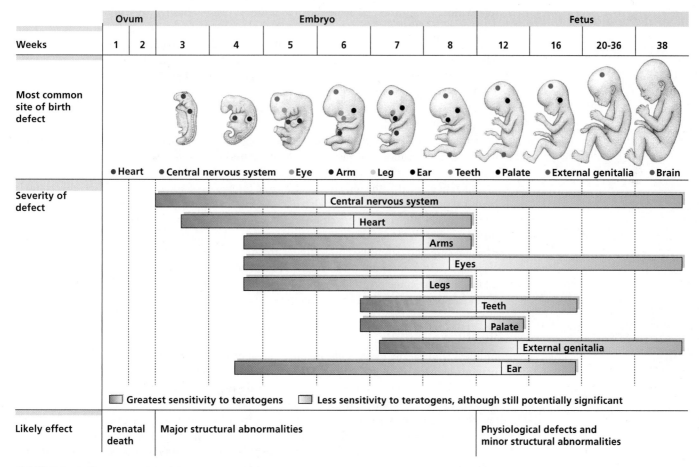

FIGURE 2-12 **Teratogen Sensitivity**
Depending on their state of development, some parts of the body vary in their sensitivity to teratogens.
Source: Moore, 1974.

Clearly, nutrient-poor diets are of immense global concern, since there are 800 million hungry people in the world and close to one *billion* people vulnerable to hunger. Hunger on such a massive scale inevitably affects millions of children (United Nations, 2004).

Fortunately, there are ways to counteract maternal malnutrition. Dietary supplements for mothers can reverse some of the problems produced by a poor diet. Furthermore, research shows that babies who were malnourished as fetuses, but who are subsequently raised in enriched environments, can overcome some of the effects of early malnutrition. However, the reality is that few of the world's children whose mothers were malnourished *before* their birth are apt to find themselves in enriched environments after birth (Grantham-McGregor, Ani, & Fernold, 1994; Kramer, 2003; Olness, 2003).

## Mothers' Age

More women are giving birth later in life than was true just two or three decades ago. This change is largely due to transformations in society, as more women choose to continue their education by seeking advanced degrees and to defer child rearing until they have started careers (Gibbs, 2002; Wildberger, 2003; Bornstein et al., 2006).

Consequently, the number of women in their 30s and 40s who give birth has grown considerably since the 1970s—a situation that may have consequences for both mothers' and children's health. Women over 30 who give birth are at greater risk for a variety of pregnancy and birth complications than younger women. They are more apt to give birth prematurely and to have children with low birthweights. This occurs in part because of a decline in the condition of a woman's eggs. By the time women reach age 42, 90 percent of their eggs are no longer normal (Cnattingius, Berendes, & Forman, 1993; Gibbs, 2002). Older mothers are also considerably more likely to give birth to children with Down syndrome, a form of mental retardation. About 1 in 100 babies born to mothers over 40 has Down syndrome; for mothers over 50, the incidence increases to 1 in 4 (Gaulden, 1992). On the other hand, some research shows that older mothers are not automatically at risk. For instance, one study found that when women in their 40s who have not experienced health difficulties are considered, they are no more likely to have prenatal problems than those in their 20s (Ales, Druzin, & Santini, 1990; Dildy et al., 1996).

The risks involved in pregnancy are greater not only for older mothers, but for atypically young women as well. Women who become pregnant during adolescence—and such pregnancies actually encompass 20 percent of all pregnancies—are more likely to have premature deliveries. Furthermore, the mortality rate of infants born to adolescent mothers is double that for mothers in their 20s (Kirchengast & Hartmann, 2003).

Keep in mind that the higher mortality rate for babies of adolescent mothers reflects more than just physiological problems related to the mothers' young age. Young mothers often face adverse social and economic factors that can affect infant health. Many teenage mothers do not have adequate financial or social support, a situation that prevents them from getting good prenatal care and parenting support after the baby is born. Poverty or social circumstances, such as a lack of parental involvement or supervision, may even have set the stage for the adolescent to become pregnant in the first place (Huizink, Mulder, & Buitelaar, 2004; Langille, 2007; Meade, Kershaw, & Ickovics, 2008).

## Mothers' Health

Mothers who eat the right foods, maintain an appropriate weight, and exercise appropriately maximize the chances of having a healthy baby. Furthermore, they can reduce the lifetime risk of obesity, high blood pressure, and heart disease in their children by maintaining a healthy lifestyle (Walker & Humphries, 2005, 2007).

Depending on when it strikes, an illness in a pregnant woman can have devastating consequences. For instance, the onset of *rubella* (German measles) before the 11th week of pregnancy can cause blindness, deafness, heart defects, or brain damage in the baby. In later stages of a pregnancy, however, rubella has less serious effects.

Several other diseases may affect a developing fetus, depending on when they are contracted. For instance, *chicken pox* may produce birth defects, while *mumps* may increase the risk of miscarriage.

## *From Research to Practice*

### From Joy to Sorrow: When Pregnant Mothers Become Depressed

*Imagine that you, like Lynne Walder from Nottingham, England, are a jet-setting executive who loves life. But then you get pregnant, and what was supposed to be the happiest time in your life triggers a flood of hormones and changes that make it feel like the worst thing that ever happened to you. Walder, 39 years old, felt her mood plummet six months after she conceived. Although she put on a brave face to her colleagues, her family, and her doctor, to her private journal she confided thoughts of suicide. "There's this collusion around motherhood and pregnancy," she says. "Everyone makes you believe it's fantastic and wonderful, but for some of us, it's destroyed us." (Miller & Underwood, 2006)*

It's a surprising fact: As many as 10 percent of pregnancies are complicated by maternal depression. And not only does such depression afflict the mother, there's increasing evidence that it affects her developing fetus too. For example, maternal depression is related to such harmful effects as low birthweight, premature birth, pregnancy complications, and decreased immune function (DiPietro, Costigan, & Gurewitsch, 2003; Mattes et al., 2009).

Maternal depression may have even more lasting effects on a child, extending beyond birth. Some research finds that maternal depression is related to poor motor control in infancy, inadequate behavior control in childhood, and even emotional problems in adulthood. But it's difficult to know what these studies really mean because they are always correlational. Factors such as environmental stressors that might tend to coincide with depression (such as financial problems or reduced social support) can't be ruled out as the real cause of these enduring postnatal problems. Furthermore, genetic factors might be at work in both the maternal depression and the emotional and behavioral problems in the child, independent of any specific effects of depression during pregnancy (Huizink, de Medina, & Mulder, 2002; Martini et al., 2010).

Concerns over the possible harmful effects of maternal depression make it tempting for physicians to prescribe antidepressant drugs to depressed pregnant patients. But it's unclear that this solution is any less of a concern than the original problem: While most research suggests that the effects of common antidepressant drugs on a developing fetus are minimal and temporary, there's just not enough research to be certain. Research on potential long-term effects is especially lacking (Boucher, Bairm, & Beaulac-Baillargeon, 2008; Miller et al., 2008; Ramos et al., 2008; Einarson et al., 2009).

Given this reality, the best option for women who experience depression during pregnancy may be to seek out non-drug-based psychotherapeutic interventions. Forms of talk therapy offer expectant mothers an option for treatment while posing no additional risk to the developing fetus (Oberlander & DiPietro, 2003; Cohen et al., 2010).

- *Suppose scientists found that there was a relationship between a mother's depression and her child's depression. How might both environmental factors and genetics explain such a relationship?*
- *Should mothers routinely be screened for depression during pregnancy? Why or why not?*

Some sexually transmitted infections (STIs) such as *syphilis* can be transmitted directly to the fetus, who will be born with the disease. Some STIs such as *gonorrhea* are communicated to the child as it passes through the birth canal to be born.

*AIDS (acquired immune deficiency syndrome)* is the newest of the diseases to affect a newborn. Mothers who have the disease or who merely are carriers of the virus may pass it on to their fetuses through the blood that reaches the placenta. However, if mothers with AIDS are treated with antiviral drugs such as AZT during pregnancy, less than 5 percent of infants are born with the disease. Those infants who are born with AIDS must remain on antiviral drugs their entire lives (Nesheim et al., 2004).

A mother's mental health status can also affect her children. For example, if the mother suffers from clinical depression while she is pregnant, the development of her children may be negatively affected, as we discuss in the "From Research to Practice" box.

## Mothers' Drug Use

The use of many kinds of drugs—both legal and illegal—poses serious risks to the unborn child. Even over-the-counter remedies for common ailments can have surprisingly injurious consequences. For instance, aspirin taken for a headache can lead to fetal bleeding and growth impairments (Griffith, Azuma, & Chasnoff, 1994).

Some drugs taken by mothers cause problems for their children decades after they were taken. As recently as the 1970s, the artificial hormone *DES (diethylstilbestrol)* was frequently prescribed to prevent miscarriage. Only later was it found that the daughters of mothers who took DES stood a much higher than normal chance of developing a rare form of vaginal or cervical cancer and had more difficulties during their pregnancies. Sons of the mothers who had taken DES had their own problems, including a higher than average rate of reproductive difficulties (Adams Hillard, 2001; Schecter, Finkelstein, & Koren, 2005).

Birth control or fertility pills taken by pregnant women before they are aware of their pregnancy can also cause fetal damage. Such medicines contain sex hormones which, when produced naturally, are related to sexual differentiation in the fetus and gender differences after birth. These medicines can cause significant damage to developing brain structures (Miller, 1998; Brown, Hines, & Fane, 2002).

Illicit drugs may pose equally great, and sometimes even greater, risks for the environments of prenatal children. For one thing, the purity of drugs purchased illegally varies significantly, so drug users can never be quite sure what specifically they are ingesting. Furthermore, the effects of some commonly used illicit drugs can be particularly devastating.

Consider, for instance, the use of *marijuana*. Certainly one of the most commonly used illegal drugs—millions of people in the United States have admitted trying it—marijuana used during pregnancy can restrict the oxygen that reaches the fetus. Its use can lead to infants who are irritable, nervous, and easily disturbed. Children exposed to marijuana prenatally show learning and memory deficits at the age of 10 (Mayes et al., 2007; Williams & Ross, 2007; Goldschmidt et al., 2008).

During the early 1990s, *cocaine* use by pregnant women led to the birth of thousands of so-called "crack babies." Cocaine restricts the arteries leading to the fetus, significantly reducing the flow of blood and oxygen and increasing the risk of fetal death, birth defects, and disabilities (Schuetze, Eiden, & Coles, 2007).

Children whose mothers were addicted to cocaine may themselves be born addicted and have to undergo painful withdrawal. Even if not addicted, they are often shorter and weigh less than average, and they may have serious respiratory problems, visible birth defects, or seizures. They behave quite differently from other infants: Their reactions to stimulation are muted, but once they start to cry, they may be hard to soothe (Singer et al., 2000; Eiden, Foote, & Schuetze, 2007; Richardson, Goldschmidt, & Willford, 2009).

It is difficult to determine the long-term effects of mothers' cocaine use in isolation, because such drug use is often accompanied by poor prenatal care and impaired nurturing after birth. In many cases it is neglectful caregiving by mothers who use cocaine that causes the children's problems, and not exposure to the drug. Treatment of such children requires not only that the mother stop using the drug, but that she or other caregivers provide improved care to the infant (Brown et al., 2004; Jones, 2006).

## Mothers' Use of Alcohol and Tobacco

Evidence strongly suggests that pregnant women who take even small amounts of alcohol or nicotine can disrupt the development of the fetus.

The children of alcoholics, who consume substantial quantities of alcohol during pregnancy, are at the greatest risk. Approximately 1 out of every 750 infants is born with **fetal alcohol syndrome (FAS),** a disorder that may include below-average intelligence and sometimes mental retardation, delayed growth, and facial deformities. FAS is now the primary preventable cause of mental retardation (Steinhausen & Spohr, 1998; Burd et al., 2003; Calhoun & Warren, 2007).

Even mothers who use smaller amounts of alcohol during pregnancy place their child at risk. **Fetal alcohol effects (FAE)** is a condition in which children display some, but not all, of the problems of FAS due to their mother's consumption of alcohol during pregnancy (Streissguth, 1997; Baer, Sampson, & Barr, 2003; Molina et al., 2007).

Children who do not have FAE may still be affected by their mothers' use of alcohol. Studies have found that maternal consumption of an average of just two alcoholic drinks a day during pregnancy is associated with lower intelligence in their offspring at age 7. Other research concurs, suggesting that relatively small quantities of alcohol taken during pregnancy can have future adverse effects on children's behavior and psychological functioning. Furthermore, the consequences of alcohol ingestion during pregnancy are long-lasting. For example, one study found that the success of 14-year-olds on a test involving spatial and visual reasoning was related to their mothers' alcohol consumption during pregnancy. The more the mothers reported drinking, the less accurately their children responded (Lynch et al., 2003; Mattson, Calarco, & Lang, 2006; Streissguth, 2007).

Because of these risks, physicians today counsel pregnant women and women who are trying to become pregnant to stop drinking alcohol entirely. They also caution against another practice proven to have an adverse effect on an unborn child: smoking.

**fetal alcohol syndrome (FAS)** a disorder caused by the pregnant mother consuming substantial quantities of alcohol during pregnancy, potentially resulting in mental retardation and delayed growth in the child

**fetal alcohol effects (FAE)** a condition in which children display some, although not all, of the problems of fetal alcohol syndrome due to the mother's consumption of alcohol during pregnancy

Like alcohol consumption, smoking has many consequences, none good. For starters, it reduces the oxygen content and increases the carbon monoxide of the mother's blood, which quickly restricts the oxygen available to the fetus. In addition, the nicotine and other toxins in cigarettes slow the respiration rate of the fetus and speed up its heart.

The ultimate result is an increased possibility of miscarriage and a higher likelihood of death during infancy. In fact, estimates suggest that smoking by pregnant women leads to more than 100,000 miscarriages and the deaths of 5,600 babies in the United States alone each year (Haslam & Lawrence, 2004; Triche & Hossain, 2007).

Smokers are two times as likely as nonsmokers to have babies with an abnormally low birthweight, and smokers' babies are shorter, on average, than those of nonsmokers. Furthermore, women who smoke during pregnancy are 50 percent more likely to have mentally retarded children. Finally, mothers who smoke are more likely to have children who exhibit disruptive behavior during childhood (Wakschlag et al., 2006; McCowan et al., 2009).

## Do Fathers Affect the Prenatal Environment?

It would be easy to believe that fathers, having done their part to cause conception, have no further effect on the *prenatal* environment of the fetus, but it turns out that a father's behavior may well have an influence. In fact, health practitioners are applying new research to suggest ways fathers can support healthy prenatal development.

For instance, fathers-to-be should avoid smoking. Secondhand smoke may affect the health of the mother and her unborn child. The more the father smokes, the lower the birthweight of his children (Hyssaelae, Rautava, & Helenius, 1995; Tomblin, Hammer, & Zhang, 1998).

Similarly, alcohol and drug use by a father can have significant effects on the fetus. Alcohol and drugs impair sperm and may lead to chromosomal damage, which may affect the fetus at conception. In addition, alcohol and drug use may create stress in the mother and generally produce an unhealthy environment. In addition, workplace toxins such as lead or mercury may bind to sperm and cause birth defects (Wakefield et al., 1998; Dare et al., 2002; Choy et al., 2002).

Finally, fathers who are physically or emotionally abusive to their pregnant wives can harm their unborn children by increasing maternal stress or causing actual physical damage. In

Pregnant women who use tobacco place their unborn children at significant risk.

## *Optimizing the Prenatal Environment*

### Becoming an Informed Consumer of Development

If you are contemplating ever having a child, you may be overwhelmed, at this point in the chapter, by the number of things that can go wrong. Don't be. Although both genetics and the environment pose their share of risks, in the vast majority of cases, pregnancy and birth proceed without mishap. Moreover, there are several things that women can do—both before and during pregnancy—to optimize the probability that pregnancy will progress smoothly (Massaro, Rothbaum, & Aly, 2006). Among them:

- For women who are planning to become pregnant, several precautions are in order. First, schedule any necessary nonemergency x-rays only during the first 2 weeks after your menstrual periods. Second, be sure you are vaccinated against rubella (German measles) at least 3, and preferably 6, months before getting pregnant. Finally, discontinue birth control pills, which disrupt hormone production, at least 3 months before trying to conceive.

- Eat well before and during pregnancy. As the saying goes, pregnant mothers are eating for two. It is more essential than ever to eat regular, well-balanced meals. In addition, take prenatal vitamins, including folic acid, which can decrease the likelihood of birth defects (Amitai et al., 2004).

- Don't use alcohol or other drugs. The evidence is clear that many drugs pass directly to the fetus and may cause birth defects. It is also clear that the more one drinks, the greater the risk to the fetus. The best advice: Don't use *any* drug unless directed by a physician. If you are planning to get pregnant, encourage your partner to avoid using alcohol or other drugs too (O'Connor & Whaley, 2006).

- Monitor caffeine intake. Although it is not clear that caffeine produces birth defects, it is known that the caffeine in coffee, tea, and chocolate can pass to the fetus, acting as a stimulant. Because of this, you probably shouldn't drink more than a few cups of coffee a day (Wisborg et al., 2003; Diego et al., 2007).

- Whether pregnant or not, don't smoke. This holds true for mothers, fathers, and anyone else in the vicinity of the pregnant mother, since research suggests that smoke in the fetal environment can affect birthweight.

- Exercise regularly. In most cases, pregnant women can continue with low-impact exercise, but should avoid extreme exercise, especially on very hot or cold days. "No pain, no gain" isn't applicable during pregnancy (O'Toole & Sawicki, 2003; Paisley, Joy, & Price, 2003; Schmidt et al., 2006).

fact, 4 to 8 percent of women face physical abuse during pregnancy (Gilliland & Verny, 1999; Gazmarian et al., 2000; Bacchus, Mezey, & Bewley, 2006; Martin et al., 2006).

**From the perspective of a health care provider:** In addition to avoiding smoking, what other sorts of things might fathers-to-be do to help their unborn children develop normally in the womb?

## REVIEW, CHECK, AND APPLY

### REVIEW

**LO8** What are the major threats to the fetal environment and what can be done about them?

- The prenatal environment significantly influences the development of the baby. The diet, age, prenatal support, and illnesses of mothers can affect their babies' health and growth.

- Mothers' use of drugs, alcohol, tobacco, and caffeine can adversely affect the health and development of the unborn child. The behavior of fathers and others can also affect the child.

- Eating well and nutritiously, exercising regularly, avoiding alcohol and tobacco, and controlling caffeine intake are sound strategies for averting threats to the fetal environment.

### CHECK YOURSELF

1. Match the following descriptions of prenatal development to their appropriate labels: germinal, embryonic, and fetal.

   a. This stage lasts from 8 weeks until birth and involves the differentiation of major organs. _____

   b. From 2 to 8 weeks following fertilization, when the major organs and basic anatomy begin developing. _____

   c. The first and shortest stage, where the zygote begins to divide and grow in complexity during the first 2 weeks following conception. _____

2. A _____ is an environmental agent such as a drug, chemical, virus, or other factor that produces a birth defect.

### APPLYING LIFESPAN DEVELOPMENT

- Studies show that "crack babies" who are now entering school have significant difficulty dealing with multiple stimuli and forming close attachments. How might both genetic and environmental influences have combined to produce these results?

✓• Study and Review on MyDevelopmentLab.com

Answers: 1) a—fetal, b—embryonic, c—germinal; 2) teratogen

## MODULE 2.3 Birth and the Newborn Infant

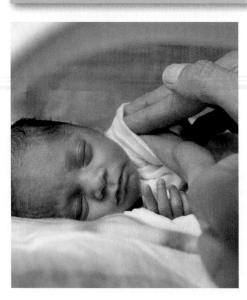

*Doctors gave infant Tamera Dixon at best a 15 percent chance of survival. The tiny girl entered the world after only 25 weeks of gestation, months earlier than normal. When she was born, she was 10 inches long, and weighed a mere 11 ounces—less than a can of soda.*

*Tamera was born by Caesarean section after her mother, Andrea Haws, experienced health problems during the pregnancy. "To see an 11-ounce baby, you wouldn't believe what it looked like," Andrea Haws said. "It was just skin and bones."*

*But Tamera beat the odds. She gained weight, and began to breathe on her own. After nearly four months in the hospital, she was released to the care of her parents. At the time she went home, she weighed over four pounds. She would have been about a week old had she been carried to term.*

*"It is a miracle," Andrea Haws said. "She is a miracle."*

Infants were not meant to be born as early as Tamera. Yet, for a variety of reasons, more than 10 percent of all babies today are born early, and the odds of their leading a normal life are improving dramatically.

All births, even those that reach full term, are a combination of excitement and anxiety. In the vast majority of cases delivery goes smoothly, and it is an amazing and joyous moment when a new being enters the world. The excitement of birth is soon replaced by wonder at the extraordinary nature of newborns themselves. Babies enter the world with a surprising array of abilities, ready from the first moments of life outside the womb to respond to the world and the people in it.

In this module we'll examine the events that lead to the delivery and birth of a child, and take an initial look at the newborn. We first consider labor and delivery, exploring how the process usually proceeds, as well as several alternative approaches.

We next examine some of the possible complications of birth. Problems that can occur range from premature births to infant mortality. Finally, we consider the extraordinary range of capabilities of newborns. We'll look not only at their physical and perceptual abilities, but at the way they enter the world with the ability to learn and with skills that help form the foundations of their future relationships with others.

# Birth

**L09    What is the normal process of labor?**

*Her head was cone-shaped. Although I knew this was due to the normal movement of the head bones as she came through the birth canal and would change in a few days, I was still startled. She also had some blood on the top of her head and was damp, a result of the amniotic fluid in which she had spent the last nine months. There was some white, cheesy substance over her body, which the nurse wiped off just before she placed her in my arms. I could see a bit of downy hair on her ears, but I knew this, too, would disappear before long. Her nose looked a little as if she had been on the losing end of a fistfight: It was squashed into her face, flattened by its trip through the birth canal. But as she seemed to fix her eyes on me and grasped my finger, it was clear that she was nothing short of perfect.* (Adapted from Brazelton, 1969)

For those of us accustomed to thinking of newborns in the images of baby food commercials, this portrait of a typical newborn may be surprising. Yet most **neonates**—the term used for newborns—resemble this one. Make no mistake, however: Babies are a welcome sight to their parents from the moment of birth.

The neonate gains its odd appearance during its journey from the uterus, down the birth canal, and into the world. We can trace this journey, beginning with the release of the chemicals that initiate labor.

## Labor: The Process of Birth Begins

About 266 days after conception, a protein called *corticotropin-releasing hormone (CRH)* triggers the release of various hormones, and the process that leads to birth begins. One critical hormone is *oxytocin,* from the mother's pituitary gland. When the concentration of oxytocin becomes high enough, the uterus begins periodic contractions (Heterelendy & Zakar, 2004; Terzidou, 2007).

During the prenatal period, the uterus, which is composed of muscle tissue, slowly expands as the fetus grows. For most of the pregnancy it is inactive, but after the fourth month it occasionally contracts to ready itself for the delivery. These *Braxton-Hicks contractions* are sometimes called "false labor" because they can fool eager and anxious parents.

When birth is imminent, the uterus begins to contract intermittently. The increasingly intense contractions force the head of the fetus against the *cervix,* the neck of the uterus that separates it from the vagina. Eventually, the contractions become strong enough to propel the fetus slowly down the birth canal until it enters the world (Mittendorf et al., 1990). This exertion and the narrow birth passageway often give newborns a battered, conehead appearance.

Labor proceeds in three stages (see Figure 2-13). In the *first stage of labor,* the uterine contractions initially occur around every 8 to 10 minutes and last about 30 seconds. As labor proceeds, the contractions occur more frequently and last longer. Toward the end of labor, the contractions may occur every 2 minutes and last almost 2 minutes. As the first stage of labor ends, the contractions reach their greatest intensity, a period known as *transition.* The mother's cervix fully opens, eventually expanding enough (usually to around 10 cm) to allow the baby's head to pass through.

This first stage of labor is the longest. Its duration varies depending on the mother's age, race, ethnicity, number of prior pregnancies, and other factors. Typically, labor takes 16 to

**neonates** the term used for newborns

| Stage 1 | Stage 2 | Stage 3 |
|---|---|---|

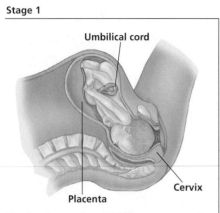

Umbilical cord

Cervix

Placenta

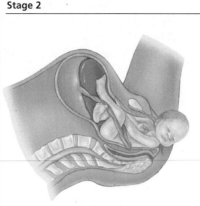

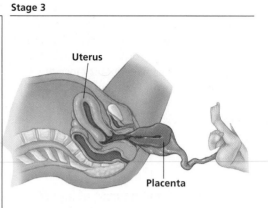

Uterus

Placenta

Uterine contractions initially occur every 8 to 10 minutes and last 30 seconds. Toward the end of labor, contractions may occur every 2 minutes and last as long as 2 minutes. As the contractions increase, the cervix, which separates the uterus from the vagina, becomes wider, eventually expanding to allow the baby's head to pass through.

The baby's head starts to move through the cervix and birth canal. Typically lasting around 90 minutes, the second stage ends when the baby has completely left the mother's body.

The child's umbilical cord (still attached to the neonate) and the placenta are expelled from the mother. This stage is the quickest and easiest, taking just a few minutes.

FIGURE 2-13 **The Three Stages of Labor**

24 hours for firstborn children, but there are wide variations. Labor becomes shorter for subsequent children.

During the *second stage of labor,* which typically lasts around 90 minutes, the baby's head proceeds further with each contraction, increasing the size of the vaginal opening. Because the area between the vagina and rectum must stretch, an incision called an **episiotomy** is sometimes made to increase the size of the opening of the vagina. However, this practice is now seen as potentially harmful, and the number of episiotomies has fallen drastically in the last decade (Goldberg et al., 2002; Graham et al, 2005; Dudding, Vaizey, & Kamm, 2008).

The second stage of labor ends when the baby has completely left the mother's body. Finally, in the *third stage of labor* the child's umbilical cord (still attached to the neonate) and the placenta are expelled from the mother. This stage is the quickest and easiest, taking just a few minutes.

The nature of a woman's reactions to labor reflects, in part, cultural factors. Although there is no evidence that the physiological aspects of labor differ among women of different cultures, expectations about labor and interpretations of its pain do vary significantly from one culture to another (Callister et al., 2003; Fisher, Hauck, & Fenwick, 2006). For instance, there is a kernel of truth to popular stories of women in some societies putting down their tools, giving birth, and immediately returning to work with their neonates on their backs. Accounts of the !Kung people in Africa describe women giving birth without much ado—or assistance—and quickly recovering. On the other hand, many societies regard childbirth as dangerous or even as essentially an illness.

## Birth: From Fetus to Neonate

Birth occurs when the fetus emerges fully from its mother's body. In most cases, babies automatically make the transition for their oxygen needs from the placenta to their lungs. Consequently, most newborns spontaneously cry, which helps them clear their lungs and breathe on their own.

What happens next varies widely. In Western cultures, health care workers are almost always on hand for the birth. In the United States, they attend 99 percent of births, but worldwide they are present for only about 50 percent (United Nations, 1990).

**episiotomy** an incision sometimes made to increase the size of the opening of the vagina to allow the baby to pass

***The Apgar Scale.*** In most cases, the newborn undergoes a quick visual inspection. While parents lovingly count fingers and toes, health care workers use the **Apgar scale,** a standard measurement system that looks for a variety of indications of good health (see Table 2-3). Developed by physician Virginia Apgar, the scale directs attention to five basic qualities, recalled most easily by using Apgar's name as a guide: *a*ppearance (color), *p*ulse (heart rate), *g*rimace (reflex irritability), *a*ctivity (muscle tone), and *r*espiration (respiratory effort).

The newborn receives a score ranging from 0 to 2 on each of the five qualities, for an overall score between 0 and 10. Most score 7 or above; the 10 percent who score under 7 require help to start breathing. Newborns who score under 4 need immediate, life-saving intervention.

In addition to problems or defects already present in the fetus, the process of birth itself may sometimes cause difficulties. Oxygen deprivation is one of the most profound. At times during labor, the umbilical cord may get wrapped around the neck or pinched during a prolonged contraction, thereby cutting off the supply of oxygen. Lack of oxygen for a few seconds is not harmful, but if it lasts longer it may cause serious harm. A restriction of oxygen, or **anoxia,** lasting a few minutes can produce cognitive deficits such as language delays and even mental retardation due to brain cell death (Hopkins-Golightly, Raz, & Sander, 2003).

***Physical Appearance and Initial Encounters.*** After assessing the newborn's health, health care workers deal with the remnants of the child's passage through the birth canal. They clean away the *vernix,* the thick, greasy substance (like cottage cheese) that covers the newborn and smoothes the passage through the birth canal. The fine, dark fuzz known as *lanugo* that covers the newborn's body soon disappears. The newborn's eyelids may be puffy from fluids that accumulated during labor, and blood or other fluids may remain on parts of his or her body.

The clean newborn is then handed to the parent or parents for their first, miraculous encounter with their child. The importance of this initial encounter has become a matter of controversy. Some psychologists and physicians argued in the 1970s that **bonding,** the close physical and emotional contact between parent and child during the period immediately following birth, was crucial for lasting parent–child relationships. More recent research suggests otherwise, however: Although it does appear that mothers who have early physical contact with their babies are more responsive to them than those who don't have such contact, the difference lasts only a few days. Such news is reassuring to parents whose children must receive immediate, intensive medical attention just after birth (Else-Quest, Hyde, & Clark, 2003; Weinberg, 2004; Miles et al., 2006).

> **Apgar scale** a standard measurement system that looks for a variety of indications of good health in newborns
>
> **anoxia** a restriction of oxygen to the baby, lasting a few minutes during the birth process, which can produce cognitive defects
>
> **bonding** close physical and emotional contact between parent and child during the period immediately following birth

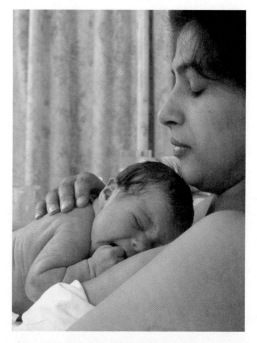

Although observation of nonhuman animals highlights the importance of contact between mother and offspring following birth, research on humans suggests that immediate physical contact is less critical.

## TABLE 2-3 APGAR SCALE

A score is given for each sign at 1 minute and 5 minutes after the birth. If there are problems with the baby, an additional score is given at 10 minutes. A score of 7–10 is considered normal, whereas 4–7 might require some resuscitative measures, and a baby with an Apgar score under 4 requires immediate resuscitation.

|   | Sign | 0 Points | 1 Point | 2 Points |
|---|------|----------|---------|----------|
| A | Appearance (skin color) | Blue-gray, pale all over | Normal, except for extremities | Normal over entire body |
| P | Pulse | Absent | Below 100 bpm | Above 100 bpm |
| G | Grimace (reflex irritability) | No response | Grimace | Sneezes, coughs, pulls away |
| A | Activity (muscle tone) | Absent | Arms and legs flexed | Active movement |
| R | Respiration | Absent | Slow, irregular | Good, crying |

Source: From Apgar, V., A proposal for a new method of evaluation in the newborn infant, *Current Research in Anesthesia and Analgesia,* 32, 1953, p. 260. Copyright © 1953 Lippincott Williams & Wilkins. Reprinted by permission.

## Approaches to Childbirth: Where Medicine and Attitudes Meet

*Ester Iverem knew herself well enough to know that she didn't like the interaction she had with medical doctors. So she opted for a nurse–midwife at Manhattan's Maternity Center where she was free to use a birthing stool and to have her husband, Nick Chiles, by her side. When contractions began, Iverem and Chiles went for a walk, stopping periodically to rock—a motion, she says, "similar to the way children dance when they first learn how, shifting from foot to foot." That helped her work through the really powerful contractions.*

> *"I sat on the birthing chair [a Western version of the traditional African stool, which lies low to the ground and has an opening in the middle for the baby to come through] and Nick was sitting right behind me. When the midwife said 'Push!' the baby's head just went 'pop!,' and out he came." Their son, Mazi (which means "Sir" in Ibo) Iverem Chiles, was placed on Ester's breast while the midwives went to prepare for his routine examination. (Knight, 1994, p. 122)*

Parents in the Western world have developed a variety of strategies—and some very strong opinions—to help them deal with something as natural as giving birth, which occurs apparently without much thought throughout the nonhuman animal world. Today parents need to decide, should the birth take place in a hospital or in the home? Should a physician, a nurse, or a midwife assist? Is the father's presence desirable? Should siblings and other family members be on hand to participate in the birth?

Most of these questions, of course, are matters not of fact but of values and opinions. No single approach will be effective for everyone, and no conclusive research indicates that one procedure is significantly more effective than another. And not only are personal preferences involved, culture also plays a role in the choice of birthing procedures.

The abundance of choices is largely due to a reaction to traditional medical practices that had been common in the United States until the early 1970s. Before that time, the typical birth went something like this: A woman in labor was placed in a room with many other women, all of whom were in various stages of childbirth, and some of whom were screaming in pain. Fathers and other family members were not allowed to be present. Just before delivery, the woman was rolled into a delivery room, where the birth took place. Often she was so drugged that she was not aware of the birth at all.

***Alternative Birthing Procedures.*** Now not all mothers give birth in hospitals, and not all births follow the traditional course. Among the alternatives:

- **Lamaze birthing techniques.** Based on the writings of Dr. Fernand Lamaze, this popular method uses breathing techniques and relaxation training (Lamaze, 1970). Typically, mothers-to-be attend weekly training sessions to learn to relax various parts of the body on command. A "coach," typically the father, is trained at the same time. Through the training, women learn how to deal positively with pain and to relax at the onset of a contraction.

  Does it work? Most mothers, as well as fathers, report that a Lamaze birth is a very positive experience. They enjoy the sense of mastery that they gain over the process of labor, a feeling of being able to exert some control over what can be a formidable experience. On the other hand, we can't be sure that parents who choose the Lamaze method aren't already more highly motivated about the experience of childbirth than parents who do not choose the technique. It is therefore possible that the accolades they express after Lamaze births are due to their initial enthusiasm, and not to the Lamaze procedures themselves (Larsen et al., 2001; Zwelling, 2006).

  Participation in Lamaze and other natural childbirth techniques is relatively rare among members of lower income groups, including many members of ethnic minorities. This may be merely a cultural preference, or it may be that parents in these groups lack the time or resources to attend classes of this type. Research shows that women in lower income groups tend to be less prepared for labor and may suffer more pain during childbirth (Brueggemann, 1999; Lu et al., 2003).

- **Bradley Method.** The Bradley Method, which is sometimes known as "husband-coached childbirth," is based on the principle that childbirth should be natural, without medication or medical interventions. To prepare for childbirth, mothers-to-be are taught muscle relaxation, breathing techniques, techniques for "trusting their bodies," and practices to promote good nutrition and exercise. Parents are urged to take responsibility for childbirth and the use of physicians is viewed as unnecessary and sometimes even dangerous. As you might expect, the discouragement of traditional medical interventions is quite controversial (McCutcheon-Rosegg, Ingraham, & Bradley, 1996; Reed, 2005).

- **Hypnobirthing.** Hypnobirthing is a new, but increasingly popular, technique. It involves a form of self-hypnosis during delivery that produces a sense of peace and calm, thereby reducing pain. The basic concept is to produce a state of focused concentration in which a mother relaxes her body while focusing inward. Increasing research evidence shows the technique can be effective in reducing pain (Olson, 2006; White, 2007; Alexander, Turnball, & Cyna, 2009).

*Childbirth Attendants: Who Delivers?* Traditionally, *obstetricians,* physicians who specialize in delivering babies, have been the childbirth attendants of choice. Recently, more mothers have chosen to use a *midwife,* who stays with the mother through labor and delivery. Midwives—most often nurses specializing in childbirth—are used primarily for pregnancies with no expected complications. They are now used in 10 percent of births in the United States. In other parts of the world, midwives help deliver some 80 percent of babies, often at home. Home birth is common in countries at all levels of economic development. For instance, a third of all births in the Netherlands occur at home (Ayoub, 2005).

The newest trend is also one of the oldest: the doula (pronounced *doo-lah*). A *doula* provides emotional, psychological, and educational support during birth. A doula does not replace an obstetrician or midwife, and does not do medical exams. Instead, doulas provide the mother with support and suggest consideration of birthing alternatives. This represents a return to a centuries-old tradition in which supportive, experienced older women serve as birthing assistants and guides.

A growing body of research indicates that the presence of a doula is beneficial to the birth process, speeding deliveries and reducing reliance on drugs. Yet concerns remain about their use. Unlike certified midwives, who are nurses and receive an additional year or two of training, doulas do not need to be certified or have any particular level of education (Ballen & Fulcher, 2006; Campbell et al., 2007; Mottl-Santiago et al., 2008).

**From the perspective of a health care provider:** While 99 percent of U.S. births are attended by professional medical workers or birthing attendants, this is the case in only about half of births worldwide. What do you think are some reasons for this, and what are the implications of this statistic?

*Use of Anesthesia and Pain-Reducing Drugs.* Certainly the ongoing discovery of pain-reducing drugs is one of the greatest advances of modern medicine, but the use of medication during childbirth has both benefits and pitfalls. About a third of women who choose anesthesia receive *epidural anesthesia,* which produces numbness from the waist down. Traditional epidurals immobilize women and can prevent them from helping to push the baby. A newer form—a *walking epidural* or *dual spinal-epidural*—uses smaller needles and administers doses continuously. This permits women to move more freely and has fewer side effects (Simmons et al., 2007).

It is important to remember that pain reduction comes at a cost. Drugs reach not just the mother but the fetus as well, and the stronger the drug, the greater its effects on the fetus and neonate. For example, anesthetics may temporarily depress the flow of oxygen to the fetus and slow labor. In addition, newborns whose mothers have been anesthetized are less physiologically responsive, show poorer motor control during the first days after birth, cry more, and may have more difficulty breastfeeding. Further, because of the size difference, doses that might have a minimal effect on the mother can have a magnified effect on the fetus (Ransjö-Arvidson, 2001; Torvaldsen et al., 2006; Irland, 2010).

In Lamaze classes, parents are taught relaxation techniques to prepare for childbirth and to reduce the need for anesthetics.

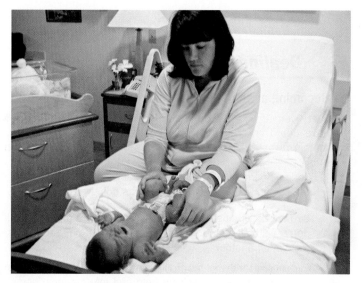

Mothers who spend more time in the hospital following the birth of a child do better than those discharged after a shorter period.

However, most research suggests that drugs as currently used produce only minimal risks. The American College of Obstetricians and Gynecologists suggests that a woman's request for pain relief at any stage of labor should be honored, and that the proper use of minimal amounts of drugs for pain relief is reasonable and has no significant effect on a child's later well-being (Shute, 1997; ACOG, 2002; Alberst et al., 2007).

***Postdelivery Hospital Stay: Deliver, Then Depart?***  When Diane Mensch was sent home from the hospital just a day after the birth of her third child, she still felt exhausted. But her insurance company insisted that 24 hours was sufficient time to recover, and it refused to pay for more. Three days later, her newborn was back in the hospital with jaundice. Mensch is convinced the problem would have been discovered and treated sooner had she and her newborn been allowed to remain in the hospital longer (Begley, 1995).

Mensch's experience is not unusual. In the 1970s the average hospital stay for a normal birth was 3.9 days. By the 1990s, it was 2 days. The change was prompted in large part by medical insurance companies focused on reducing costs.

Medical providers have fought this trend, citing definite risks for mothers and newborns. For instance, mothers may experience bleeding from tissues torn during childbirth, and newborns may require the intensive medical care that hospitals uniquely provide. Furthermore, mothers are better rested and more satisfied with their care when they stay longer (Finkelstein, Harper, & Rosenthal, 1998).

Accordingly, the American Academy of Pediatrics states that women should stay in the hospital no less than 48 hours after giving birth, and the U.S. Congress passed legislation mandating a minimum insurance coverage of 48 hours for childbirth (American Academy of Pediatrics Committee on Fetus and Newborn, 2004).

## Newborn Medical Screening

Just after birth, newborns typically are tested for a variety of diseases and genetic conditions. The American College of Medical Genetics recommends that all newborns be screened for 29 disorders, ranging from hearing difficulties and sickle-cell anemia to extremely rare conditions such as isovaleric acidemia (IVA), a disorder that interferes with the normal metabolism of leucine, an important amino acid. IVA and other disorders can be detected from a tiny quantity of blood drawn from an infant's heel (American College of Medical Genetics, 2006).

The advantage of newborn screening is that it permits early treatment of problems that might go undetected for years. In some cases, devastating conditions can be prevented through early treatment of the disorder, such as the implementation of a particular kind of diet (Goldfarb, 2005; Kayton, 2007).

## *Dealing with Labor*

### Becoming an Informed Consumer of Development

Every woman who is soon to give birth has some fear of labor. Most have heard gripping tales of extended, 48-hour labors. Still, few mothers would deny that the rewards of giving birth are worth the effort.

There is no right or wrong way to deal with labor. However, several strategies can help make the process as positive as possible:

- **Be flexible.** Although you may have carefully planned your labor, don't feel obliged to follow through exactly. If one strategy is ineffective, try another.

- **Communicate with your health care providers.** Let them know what you are experiencing and ask for help and information. They should be able to give you an indication of how much longer you will be in labor, which may help you feel you can handle it.

- **Remember that labor is . . . laborious.** Expect to become fatigued, but realize that toward the end you may well get a second wind.

- **Accept your partner's support.** If a spouse or other partner is present, allow that person to make you comfortable and provide support. Research has shown that women who are supported by a spouse or partner have a more comfortable birth experience (Bader, 1995; Kennell, 2002).

- **Be realistic and honest about your reactions to pain.** Even if you had planned an unmedicated delivery, realize that you may find the pain hard to bear. At that point, consider drugs. Asking for pain medication is not a sign of failure.

- **Focus on the big picture.** Keep in mind that labor is part of a process that leads to an event unmatched in the joy it can bring.

The exact number of tests that a newborn experiences varies drastically from state to state. In some states, only three tests are mandated, while in others over 30 are required. In jurisdictions with only a few tests, many disorders go undiagnosed. In fact, each year around 1,000 infants in the United States suffer from disorders that could have been detected at birth if appropriate screening had been conducted (American Academy of Pediatrics, 2005).

## REVIEW, CHECK, AND APPLY

### REVIEW

**LO9**  What is the normal process of labor?

- Labor proceeds through three stages.

- Immediately after birth, birthing attendants usually examine the neonate using a measurement system such as the Apgar scale.

- Birthing options include the use of anesthetics during birth and alternatives to traditional hospital birthing, such as the Lamaze method, the use of a birthing center, and the use of a midwife.

### CHECK YOURSELF

1. Labor proceeds in three stages. The longest stage of labor is _____.

   **a.** the first stage

   **b.** the second stage

   **c.** the third stage

   **d.** hard to determine

2. Women appear to respond differently to labor as a function of culture.

   - True

   - False

3. The _____ scale measures infant health by assessing appearance (color), pulse (heart rate), grimace (reflex irritability), activity (muscle tone), and respiration (respiratory effort).

   **a.** Bronfenbrenner

   **b.** Brazelton

   **c.** Anoxia

   **d.** Apgar

4. Which of the following factors influence a woman's delivery? (Check all that apply.)

   **a.** her preparation for childbirth

   **b.** the support she has before and during delivery

   **c.** her culture's view of pregnancy and delivery

   **d.** the specific nature of the delivery itself

   **e.** the weather on the day of delivery

### APPLYING LIFESPAN DEVELOPMENT

- Why might cultural differences exist in expectations and interpretations of labor?

✓● **Study** and **Review** on
**MyDevelopmentLab.com**

Answers: 1) a; 2) True; 3) d; 4) a–d

# Birth Complications

**LO10** **What complications can occur at birth, and what are their causes, effects, and treatments?**

**LO11** **How can infant mortality rates be lowered?**

LEARNING OBJECTIVES

*In addition to the usual complimentary baby supplies that most hospitals bestow on new mothers, the maternity nurses at Greater Southeast Hospital have become practiced in handing out "grief baskets."*

*Inside are items memorializing one of [Washington, D.C.'s] grimmest statistics—an infant mortality rate that's more than twice the national average. The baskets contain a photograph of the dead newborn, a snip of its hair, the tiny cap it wore, and a yellow rose.* (Thomas, 1994, p. A14)

The infant mortality rate in Washington, D.C., capital of the richest country in the world, is 13.7 deaths per 1,000 births, exceeding the rate of countries such as Hungary, Cuba, Kuwait, and Costa Rica. Overall, 44 countries have better birth rates than the United States, which has 6.26 deaths for every 1,000 live births (US DHHS, 2009; The World Factbook, 2009) (see Figure 2-14).

Why do infants have less chance of survival in the United States than in other, less developed countries? To answer this question, we need to consider the problems that can occur during labor and delivery.

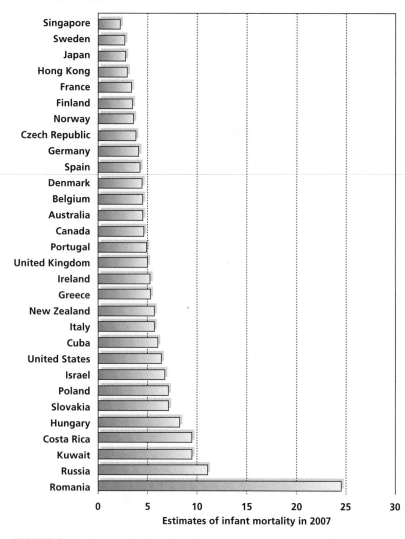

**FIGURE 2-14 International Infant Mortality**
Infant mortality rates in selected countries. While the United States has greatly reduced its infant mortality rate in the past 25 years, it ranks only 22nd among industrialized countries as of 2007. What are some of the reasons for this?
Source: The World Factbook, 2007.

## Preterm Infants: Too Soon, Too Small

Like Tamera Dixon, whose birth was described in the module prologue, 11 percent of infants are born early. **Preterm infants,** or premature infants, are born prior to 38 weeks after conception. Because they have not had time to develop fully, preterm infants are at high risk for illness and death.

The extent of danger faced by preterm babies largely depends on the child's weight at birth, which has great significance as an indicator of the extent of the baby's development. Although the average newborn weighs around 3,400 grams (about 7 1/2 pounds), **low-birthweight infants** weigh less than 2,500 grams (around 5 1/2 pounds). Although only 7 percent of U.S. newborns are in the low-birthweight category, they account for most newborn deaths (Gross, Spiker, & Haynes, 1997; DeVader et al., 2007).

Although most low-birthweight infants are preterm, some are small-for-gestational-age babies. **Small-for-gestational-age infants** are infants who, because of delayed fetal growth, weigh 90 percent (or less) of the average weight of infants of the same gestational age. Small-for-gestational-age infants are sometimes also preterm, but may not be. The syndrome may be caused by inadequate nutrition during pregnancy (Bergmann, Bergmann, & Dudenhausen, 2008; Karagianni et al., 2010).

If the baby is not very premature and the weight at birth is not extremely low, the threat is relatively minor. In such cases, the best treatment may be to keep the baby in the hospital to gain weight. Additional weight is critical because fat layers help prevent chilling in neonates, who are not very efficient at regulating body temperature.

Newborns who are born more prematurely and who have birthweights significantly below average face a tougher road. They are highly vulnerable to infection and, because their lungs are not fully developed, they have problems taking in oxygen. As a consequence, they may experience *respiratory distress syndrome (RDS)*, with potentially fatal consequences.

To deal with respiratory distress syndrome, low-birthweight infants are often placed in incubators, enclosures in which temperature and oxygen content are carefully monitored. Too low a concentration of oxygen will not provide relief, and too high a concentration can damage the delicate retinas of the eyes, leading to permanent blindness.

Preterm neonates are unusually sensitive to the sights, sounds, and sensations they experience, and their breathing may be interrupted or their heart rates may slow. They are often unable to move smoothly, with uncoordinated arm and leg movements that can be disconcerting to parents (Doussard-Roosevelt et al., 1997; Miles et al., 2006).

Despite the difficulties they experience at birth, the majority of preterm infants eventually develop normally. However, they develop more slowly and may be susceptible to subtle problems later. For example, by the age of 6 approximately 38 percent need special educational interventions. For instance, some show learning disabilities, behavior disorders, or lower-than-average IQ scores. Others have difficulties with physical coordination. Still, around 60 percent of preterm infants are free of even minor problems (Arseneault, Moffit, & Caspi, 2003; Dombrowski, Noonan, & Martin, 2007; Hall et al., 2008).

***Very-Low-Birthweight Infants: The Smallest of the Small.*** The story is less positive for the most extreme cases of prematurity. **Very-low-birthweight infants** weigh less than 1,250 grams (around 2 1/4 pounds) or, regardless of weight, have been in the womb less than 30 weeks.

Very-low-birthweight infants not only are tiny—some fitting easily in the palm of the hand at birth—they hardly seem to belong to the same species as full-term newborns. Their eyes may

**preterm infants** infants who are born prior to 38 weeks after conception (also known as premature infants)

**low-birthweight infants** infants who weigh less than 2,500 grams (around 5 1/2 pounds) at birth

**small-for-gestational-age infants** infants who, because of delayed fetal growth, weigh 90 percent (or less) of the average weight of infants of the same gestational age

**very-low-birthweight infants** infants who weigh less than 1,250 grams (around 2.25 pounds) or, regardless of weight, have been in the womb less than 30 weeks

be fused shut and their earlobes may look like flaps of skin on the sides of their heads. Their skin is a darkened red color, whatever their race.

Very-low-birthweight babies are in grave danger from the moment they are born because their organ systems are immature. Before the mid-1980s, these babies would not have survived; recent medical advances have pushed the *age of viability,* the point at which an infant can survive prematurely, to about 22 weeks—some four months earlier than the normal term. Of course, the longer the baby develops after conception, the higher the chance of survival. A baby born earlier than 25 weeks has less than a 50–50 chance of survival (see Figure 2-15).

If a very-low-birthweight preterm infant survives, the medical costs can be astonishing—between 3 and 50 times higher than the medical costs for a full-term child during the first 3 years of life. This fact has engendered ethical debates about the expenditure of substantial financial and human resources in cases in which a positive outcome may be unlikely (Prince, 2000; Doyle, 2004; Petrou, 2006). Still, emerging evidence suggests that high-quality care can provide protection from some of the risks of prematurity, and that by the time they reach adulthood, premature babies may be little different from other adults (Hack, 2002).

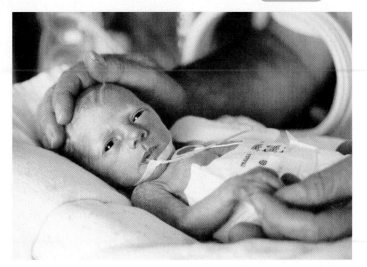

Preterm infants stand a much greater chance of survival today than they did even a decade ago.

Research also shows that preterm infants who receive more responsive, stimulating, and organized care are apt to show more positive outcomes than those children whose care is not as good. Some of these interventions are quite simple. For example, "Kangaroo Care," in which infants are held skin-to-skin against their parents' chests, appears to be effective in helping preterm infants develop. Massaging preterm infants several times a day triggers the release of hormones that promote weight gain, muscle development, and abilities to cope with stress (Tallandini & Scalembra, 2006; Erlandsson et al., 2007; Field et al., 2008).

***What Causes Preterm and Low-Birthweight Deliveries?*** About half of preterm and low-birthweight births are unexplained, but several known causes account for the remainder. In some cases, the cause arises from difficulties in the mother's reproductive system. For instance, twins place unusual stress on their mothers, which can lead to early labor. In fact, most multiple births are preterm to some degree (Tan et al., 2004; Luke & Brown, 2008).

In other cases, preterm and low-birthweight babies are a result of the immaturity of the mother's reproductive system. Young mothers—under age 15—are more prone to deliver prematurely than older ones. In addition, a woman who becomes pregnant within six months of her previous delivery is more likely to have a preterm or low-birthweight infant than a

| Selected Countries | 22–23 weeks[1] | 24–27 weeks | 28–31 weeks | 32–36 weeks | 37 weeks or more |
|---|---|---|---|---|---|
| United States | 707.7 | 236.9 | 45.0 | 8.6 | 2.4 |
| Austria | 888.9 | 319.6 | 43.8 | 5.8 | 1.5 |
| Denmark | 947.4 | 301.2 | 42.2 | 10.3 | 2.3 |
| England and Wales[2] | 880.5 | 298.2 | 52.2 | 10.6 | 1.8 |
| Finland | 900.0 | 315.8 | 58.5 | 9.7 | 1.4 |
| Northern Ireland | 1,000.0 | 268.3 | 54.5 | 13.1 | 1.6 |
| Norway | 555.6 | 220.2 | 56.4 | 7.2 | 1.5 |
| Poland | 921.1 | 530.6 | 147.7 | 23.1 | 2.3 |
| Scotland | 1,000.0 | 377.0 | 60.8 | 8.8 | 1.7 |
| Sweden | 515.2 | 197.7 | 41.3 | 12.8 | 1.5 |

FIGURE 2-15 **Survival and Gestational Age**
Chances of a fetus surviving greatly improve after 28 to 32 weeks. Rates shown are deaths per 1,000 live births.
Source: National Center for Health Statistics, 1997.

## TABLE 2-4 FACTORS ASSOCIATED WITH INCREASED RISK OF LOW BIRTHWEIGHT

**I. Demographic Risks**

  A. Age (less than 17; over 34)
  B. Race (minority)
  C. Low socioeconomic status
  D. Unmarried
  E. Low level of education

**II. Medical Risks Predating Pregnancy**

  A. Number of previous pregnancies (0 or more than 4)
  B. Low weight for height
  C. Genitourinary anomalies/surgery
  D. Selected diseases such as diabetes, chronic hypertension
  E. Nonimmune status for selected infections such as rubella
  F. Poor obstetric history, including previous low-birthweight infant, multiple spontaneous abortions
  G. Maternal genetic factors (such as low maternal weight at own birth)

**III. Medical Risks in Current Pregnancy**

  A. Multiple pregnancy
  B. Poor weight gain
  C. Short interpregnancy interval
  D. Low blood pressure
  E. Hypertension/preeclampsia/toxemia
  F. Selected infections such as asymptomatic bacteriuria, rubella, and cytomegalovirus
  G. First- or second-trimester bleeding

  H. Placental problems such as placenta previa, abruptio placentae
  I. Severe morning sickness
  K. Anemia/abnormal hemoglobin
  L. Severe anemia in a developing baby
  M. Fetal anomalies
  N. Incompetent cervix
  O. Spontaneous premature rupture of membrane

**IV. Behavioral and Environmental Risks**

  A. Smoking
  B. Poor nutritional status
  C. Alcohol and other substance abuse
  D. DES exposure and other toxic exposure, including occupational hazards
  E. High altitude

**V. Health-Care Risks**

  A. Absent or inadequate prenatal care
  B. Iatrogenic prematurity

**VI. Evolving Concepts of Risks**

  A. Stress, physical and psychosocial
  B. Uterine irritability
  C. Events triggering uterine contractions
  D. Cervical changes detected before onset of labor
  E. Selected infections such as mycoplasma and chlamydia trachomatis
  F. Inadequate plasma volume expansion
  G. Progesterone deficiency

woman whose reproductive system has had a chance to recover. The father's age matters, too: wives of older fathers are more likely to have preterm deliveries (Zhu, 2005; Branum, 2006; Chen et al., 2010).

Finally, factors that affect the general health of the mother, such as nutrition, level of medical care, amount of stress in the environment, and economic support, are all related to prematurity and low birthweight. Rates of preterm births differ between racial groups, not because of race per se, but because members of racial minorities have disproportionately lower incomes and higher stress as a result. For instance, the percentage of low-birthweight infants born to African American mothers is double that for Caucasian American mothers. (A summary of the factors associated with increased risk of low birthweight is shown in Table 2-4; Field, Diego, & Hernandez-Reif, 2006, 2008; Bergmann et al., 2008.)

## Postmature Babies: Later, Larger

One might imagine that a baby who spends extra time in the womb might have some advantages, given the opportunity to continue growth undisturbed by the outside world. Yet **postmature infants**—those still unborn 2 weeks after the mother's due date—face several risks.

For example, the blood supply from the placenta may become insufficient to nourish the still-growing fetus. A decrease in blood to the brain may lead to brain damage. Similarly, labor is riskier (for both mother and child) if a fetus nearly the size of a 1-month-old infant has to make its way through the birth canal (Shea, Wilcox, & Little, 1998; Fok, 2006).

Postmature infants are less of a problem than preterm babies because medical practitioners can induce labor artificially through drugs or a Cesarean delivery.

## Cesarean Delivery: Intervening in the Process of Birth

*As Elena entered her 18th hour of labor, her obstetrician began to look concerned. She told Elena and her husband, Pablo, that the fetus's heart rate had begun to fall after each contraction. After trying some simple remedies, such as repositioning Elena on her side, the obstetrician came to the conclusion that the fetus was in distress. She told them that the baby should be delivered immediately by Cesarean delivery.*

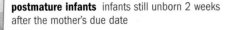

**postmature infants** infants still unborn 2 weeks after the mother's due date

Elena became one of the more than one million mothers in the United States who have a cesarean delivery each year. In a **cesarean delivery** (sometimes known as a *c-section*), the baby is surgically removed from the uterus, rather than traveling through the birth canal.

Cesarean deliveries are most often called for when the fetus shows distress of some sort (e.g., by a sudden rise in heart rate or if blood flows from the mother's vagina during labor). In addition, mothers over age 40 are more likely to have cesarean deliveries than younger ones (Gilbert, Nesbitt, & Danielsen, 1999; Tang et al., 2006).

Cesarean deliveries are sometimes used when the baby is in *breech position,* feet first in the birth canal. Breech position births, which occur in about 1 of 25 births, place the baby at risk because the umbilical cord is more likely to be compressed, depriving the baby of oxygen. Cesarean deliveries are also more likely in *transverse position* births, in which the baby lies crosswise in the uterus, or when the baby's head is so large it has trouble moving through the birth canal.

The routine use of **fetal monitors,** which measure the baby's heartbeat during labor, has contributed to a soaring rate of cesarean deliveries. Some 25 percent of children in the United States are born in this way, up some 500 percent from the early 1970s (U.S. Center for Health Statistics, 2003).

Are cesareans an effective medical intervention? Other countries have substantially lower rates of cesarean deliveries (see Figure 2-16), and there is no association between successful birth consequences and the rate of cesarean deliveries. In addition, cesarean deliveries are major surgeries that carry dangers. The mother's recovery can be relatively lengthy, particularly when compared to a normal delivery. In addition, the risk of maternal infection is higher with cesarean deliveries (Koroukian, Trisel, & Rimm, 1998; Miesnik & Reale, 2007).

Finally, a cesarean delivery presents some risks for the baby. Because cesarean babies are spared the stresses of passing through the birth canal, their relatively easy passage into the world may deter the normal release of certain stress-related hormones, such as catecholamines, into the newborn's bloodstream. These hormones help prepare the neonate to deal with the stress of the world outside the womb, and their absence may be detrimental to the newborn child. In fact, research indicates that babies born by cesarean delivery who have not experienced labor are more likely to experience breathing problems upon birth than those who experience at least some labor prior to being born via a cesarean delivery. Finally, mothers who deliver by cesarean are less satisfied with the birth experience, although their dissatisfaction does not influence the quality of mother–child interactions (Lobel & DeLuca, 2007; Porter et al., 2007; MacDorman et al., 2008).

Because the increase in cesarean deliveries is, as we have said, connected to the use of fetal monitors, medical authorities now recommend that they not be used routinely. There is evidence that outcomes are no better for newborns who have been monitored than for those who have not been monitored. In addition, monitors tend to indicate fetal distress when there is none—false alarms—with disquieting regularity. Monitors do, however, play a critical role in high-risk pregnancies and in cases of preterm and postmature babies (Albers & Krulewitch, 1993; Freeman, 2007).

## Mortality and Stillbirth: The Tragedy of Premature Death

Sometimes a child does not live to pass through the birth canal. **Stillbirth,** the delivery of a child who is not alive, occurs in less than 1 delivery out of 100. If the death is detected before labor begins, labor is typically induced, or physicians may perform a cesarean to remove the

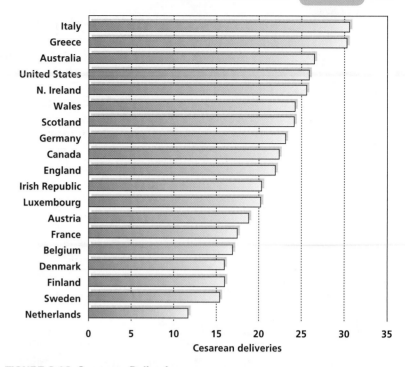

**FIGURE 2-16  Cesarean Deliveries**
The rate at which cesarean deliveries are performed varies substantially from one country to another. Why do you think the United States has one of the highest rates?
Source: International Cesarean Awareness Network, 2004.

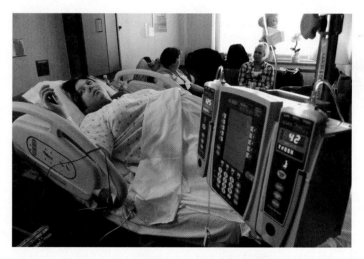

The use of fetal monitoring has contributed to a sharp increase of cesarean deliveries in spite of evidence showing few benefits from the procedure.

**cesarean delivery** a birth in which the baby is surgically removed from the uterus, rather than traveling through the birth canal

**fetal monitor** a device that measures the baby's heartbeat during labor

**stillbirth** the delivery of a child who is not alive, occurring in fewer than 1 delivery in 100

**infant mortality** death within the first year of life

body as soon as possible. In other cases of stillbirth, the baby dies during its travels through the birth canal.

The overall rate of **infant mortality** (defined as death within the first year of life) is 7.0 deaths per 1,000 live births. Infant mortality generally has been declining since the 1960s (MacDorman et al., 2005).

Whether the death is a stillbirth or occurs after the child is born, the loss of a baby is tragic, and the impact on parents is enormous. The loss and grief parents feel, and their passage through it, is similar to that experienced when an older loved one dies (discussed in Chapter 10). In fact, the juxtaposition of the first dawning of life and an unnaturally early death may make the death particularly difficult to accept and deal with. Depression is common, and it is often intensified due to a lack of support. Some parents even experience posttraumatic stress disorder (Badenhorst et al., 2006; Cacciatore & Bushfield, 2007; Turton, Evans, & Hughes, 2009).

**From an educator's perspective:** Why do you think the United States has for so long lacked national educational and health care policies that could reduce infant mortality rates overall and among poorer people? What arguments would you make to change this situation?

## Cultural Dimensions

### Overcoming Racial and Cultural Differences in Infant Mortality

Even though the overall U.S. infant mortality rate has declined over the past decades, African American babies are more than twice as likely to die before age 1 than white babies. This difference is largely socioeconomic: African American women are more likely to be living in poverty than Caucasian women and to receive less prenatal care. As a result, they are more likely to have low-birthweight babies—the factor most closely linked to infant mortality—than mothers of other racial groups (Duncan & Brooks-Gunn, 2000) (see Figure 2-17).

But members of particular racial groups in the United States are not alone in experiencing poor mortality rates. The overall rate in the United States is higher than in many other countries. For example, the U.S. mortality rate is almost double that of Japan.

Why? One answer is that the United States has a higher rate of low-birthweight and preterm deliveries than many other countries. In fact, when U.S. infants are compared to infants of the same weight who are born in other countries, the mortality rate differences disappear (Paneth, 1995; Wilcox et al., 1995).

Another reason relates to economic diversity. Compared to many other countries, the United States has a higher proportion of people living in poverty, who are less likely to have adequate medical care and to be healthy. This has an impact on the overall mortality rate (Terry, 2000; Bremner & Fogel, 2004; MacDorman et al., 2005).

Also, many countries do a much better job in providing prenatal care. For instance, low-cost and even free care, both before and after delivery, is often available. Paid maternity leave is frequently provided, lasting in some cases as long as 51 weeks. The opportunity to take an extended maternity leave can lead to better mental health for mothers and higher quality interactions with their infants (Clark et al., 1997; Waldfogel, 2001; Ayoola et al., 2010).

Better health care is only part of the story. In certain European countries, pregnant women receive many additional privileges, such as transportation benefits for medical visits. In Norway, pregnant women may be given living expenses for up to 10 days so they can be close to a hospital when it is time to give birth. And

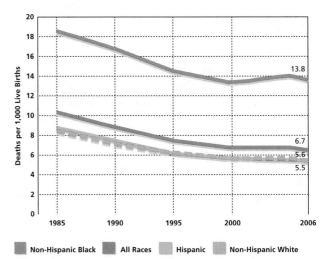

**FIGURE 2-17 Race and Infant Mortality**
Although infant mortality is dropping for both African American and white children, the death rate is still more than twice as high for African American children. These figures show the number of deaths in the first year of life for every 1,000 live births.
Source: Child Health USA 2009.

when their babies are born, new mothers receive, for just a small payment, the assistance of trained home helpers (Morice, 1998; DeVries, 2005).

In the United States, the story is different. The lack of a uniform national health policy and, until recently, universal health care means that prenatal care is often haphazard. About 1 out of every 6 pregnant women has insufficient prenatal care. Some 20 percent of white women and close to 40 percent of African American women receive no prenatal care early in their pregnancies. Five percent of white mothers and 11 percent of African American mothers do not see a health care provider until the last three months of pregnancy; some never see a health care provider at all (Johnson, Primas, & Coe, 1994; Mikhail, 2000; Laditka, Laditka, & Probst, 2006).

# Postpartum Depression: Moving from the Heights of Joy to the Depths of Despair

*Renata had been overjoyed when she found out that she was pregnant and had spent the months of her pregnancy happily preparing for her baby's arrival. The birth was routine, the baby a healthy, pink-cheeked boy. But a few days after her son's birth, she sank into the depths of depression. Constantly crying, confused, feeling incapable of caring for her child, she was experiencing unshakable despair.*

The diagnosis: postpartum depression. *Postpartum depression,* a period of deep depression following the birth of a child, affects some 10 percent of new mothers. The deep sadness that is its main symptom may last for months or even years. In about 1 in 500 cases, the symptoms evolve into a total break with reality. In extremely rare instances, postpartum depression may turn deadly. For example, Andrea Yates, a mother in Texas who was charged with drowning all five of her children in a bathtub, said that postpartum depression led to her actions (Yardley, 2001; Oretti et al., 2003; Misri, 2007).

The onset of depression usually comes as a complete surprise. Certain mothers seem more likely to become depressed, such as those who have been clinically depressed at some point in the past or who have depressed family members. Furthermore, women who are unprepared for the range of emotions that follow birth—some positive, some negative—may be more prone to depression (Kim et al., 2008; Howell et al., 2010).

Finally, postpartum depression may be triggered by the pronounced swings in hormone production that occur after birth. During pregnancy, the production of estrogen and progesterone increases significantly. However, 24 hours after birth they plunge to normal levels. This rapid change may result in depression (Verkerk, Pop, & Van Son, 2003; Klier et al., 2007; Yim et al., 2009).

Whatever the cause, maternal depression leaves its marks on the infant. As we'll see later in the chapter, babies are born with impressive social capacities, and they are highly attuned to the moods of their mothers. When depressed mothers interact with their infants, they are likely to display little emotion and to act detached and withdrawn. This lack of responsiveness leads infants to display fewer positive emotions and to withdraw from contact not only with their mothers but with other adults as well. In addition, children of depressed mothers are at risk for depression and other negative emotional and cognitive outcomes continuing into adulthood (Nylen et al., 2006; Goodman et al., 2008; Tompson et al., 2010).

## REVIEW, CHECK, AND APPLY

### REVIEW

**LO10** What complications can occur at birth, and what are their causes, effects, and treatments?

- Preterm infants may have substantial difficulties after birth and later in life.
- Preterm and low-birthweight deliveries can be caused by health, age, and pregnancy-related factors in the mother. Income (and, because of its relationship with income, race) is also an important factor.

**LO11** How can infant mortality rates be lowered?

- Infant mortality rates can be lowered by the availability of inexpensive health care and good education programs for mothers-to-be.

### CHECK YOURSELF

1. The amount of danger facing preterm infants largely depends on the child's _____ at birth.

2. The point at which an infant can survive prematurely is also known as the age of survivability.
   - True
   - False

3. _____, defined as death within the first year of life, has been declining since the 1960s.
   a. Infant decline
   b. Infant mortality
   c. Life expectancy
   d. Age of viability

### APPLYING LIFESPAN DEVELOPMENT

- What are some ethical considerations relating to providing intensive medical care to very-low-birth-weight babies? Do you think such interventions should be routine practice? Why or why not?

✓• **Study** and **Review** on
**MyDevelopmentLab.com**

Answers: 1) weight; 2) False; 3) d

# The Competent Newborn

**LO12** What capabilities does the newborn have?

*Relatives gathered around the infant car seat and its occupant, Kaita Castro, born just two days ago. This is Kaita's first day home from the hospital. Kaita's nearest cousin, 4-year-old Tabor, seems uninterested in the new arrival. "Babies can't do anything fun. They can't even do anything at all," he says.*

Kaita's cousin Tabor is partly right. There are many things babies cannot do. Neonates arrive in the world quite incapable of successfully caring for themselves, for example. Why are human infants born so dependent, while members of other species seem to arrive much better equipped for their lives?

One reason is that, in a sense, humans are born too soon. The brain of the average newborn is just one-quarter what it will be at adulthood. In comparison, the brain of the macaque monkey, which is born after just 24 weeks of gestation, is 65 percent of its adult size. Because of the relative puniness of the infant human brain, some have suggested that we emerge from the womb 6 to 12 months early.

In reality, evolution knew what it was doing: If we stayed inside our mothers' bodies an additional half-year to a year, our heads would be so large that we'd never manage to get through the birth canal (Schultz, 1969; Gould, 1977; Kotre & Hall, 1990).

The relatively underdeveloped brain of the human newborn helps explain the infant's apparent helplessness. But developmental researchers are coming to realize that infants enter this world with an astounding array of capabilities in all domains of development: physical, cognitive, and social.

## Physical Competence: Meeting the Demands of a New Environment

The world the neonate faces is markedly different from the "womb world." Consider, for instance, the significant changes that Kaita Castro encountered as she began the first moments of life in her new environment.

Kaita's first task was to bring air into her body. Inside her mother, the umbilical cord delivered air and removed carbon dioxide. The outside world was different: Once the umbilical cord was cut, Kaita's respiratory system had to start its lifetime's work.

For Kaita, the task was automatic. Most newborn babies begin to breathe on their own as soon as they are exposed to air. The ability to breathe immediately indicates that the respiratory system is reasonably well developed, despite its lack of rehearsal in the womb.

Neonates emerge from the uterus more practiced in other types of physical activities. For example, newborns such as Kaita have **reflexes**—unlearned, organized involuntary responses that occur automatically in the presence of certain stimuli. Some reflexes have been rehearsed for several months before birth. The *sucking reflex* and the *swallowing reflex* permit Kaita to ingest food right away. The *rooting reflex,* which involves turning in the direction of a stimulus (such as a light touch) near the mouth, is also related to eating. It guides Kaita toward nearby sources of food, such as a mother's nipple.  ⊙ Watch on **mydevelopmentlab.com**

Other reflexes that present themselves at birth—such as coughing, sneezing, and blinking—help the infant avoid stimuli that are potentially bothersome or hazardous. Kaita's sucking and swallowing reflexes, which help her to consume her mother's milk, are coupled with the newfound ability to digest nutriments. The newborn's digestive system initially produces feces in the form of *meconium,* a greenish-black material that is a remnant of the neonate's days as a fetus.

Because the liver, a critical component of the digestive system, does not always work effectively at first, almost half of newborns develop a yellowish tinge to their bodies and eyes. This *neonatal jaundice* is most prevalent in preterm and low-weight neonates and is typically not dangerous. Treatment involves placing the baby under fluorescent lights or administering medicine.

## Sensory Capabilities: Experiencing the World

Just after Kaita was born, her father was certain that she looked directly at him. Did she, in fact, see him?

⊙ Watch on **mydevelopmentlab.com**

To watch infants demonstrate the reflexes you have been reading about, log onto MyDevelopmentLab.com.

**reflexes**  unlearned, organized involuntary responses that occur automatically in the presence of certain stimuli

This is a hard question to answer. When sensory experts talk of "seeing," they mean both a sensory reaction to stimulation and an interpretation of that stimulation (the distinction between sensation and perception). Furthermore, it is tricky to pinpoint the specific sensory skills of newborns who can't explain what they are experiencing.

Still, it is clear that neonates such as Kaita can see to some extent. Although their visual acuity is not fully developed, newborns actively pay attention to certain types of information in their environment.

For instance, they attend to high-information elements in their field of vision, such as objects that sharply contrast with the rest of the environment. Furthermore, they can discriminate levels of brightness. There is even evidence that they may have a sense of size constancy—the awareness that objects stay the same size even though the size of the image on the retina varies with distance (Slater, Mattock, & Brown, 1990; Slater & Johnson, 1998; Chien et al., 2006).

In addition, not only can newborn babies distinguish different colors, they seem to prefer particular ones. For example, they can distinguish between red, green, yellow, and blue, and they take more time staring at blue and green objects (Dobson, 2000; Alexander & Hines, 2002; Zemach, Chang, & Teller, 2007).

Starting at birth, infants are able to distinguish colors and even show preferences for particular ones.

Newborns also clearly can hear. They react to certain sounds, showing startle reactions to loud, sudden noises, for instance. They also recognize sounds. For example, a crying newborn, hearing other newborns crying, will continue to cry. But on hearing a recording of its own crying, the newborn is more likely to stop crying, as if recognizing a familiar sound (Dondi, Simion, & Caltran, 1999; Fernald, 2001).

The auditory system is not completely developed, however, and auditory acuity is not as great as it will be. Moreover, amniotic fluid, which is initially trapped in the middle ear, must drain before the newborn can fully hear.

In addition to sight and hearing, the other senses also function quite adequately in the newborn. It is obvious that newborns are sensitive to touch. For instance, they respond to stimuli such as the hairs of a brush, and they are aware of puffs of air so weak that adults cannot notice them.

The senses of smell and taste are also well developed. Newborns suck and increase other physical activity when the odor of peppermint is placed near the nose. They also pucker their lips when a sour taste is placed on them, and respond with suitable facial expressions to other tastes as well. Such findings clearly indicate that the senses of touch, smell, and taste are not only present at birth, but are reasonably sophisticated (Cohen & Cashon, 2003; Armstrong et al., 2007).

In one sense, the sophistication of the sensory systems of newborns such as Kaita is not surprising. After all, the typical neonate has had 9 months to prepare for his or her encounter with the outside world. Human sensory systems begin their development well before birth. Furthermore, the passage through the birth canal may place babies in a state of heightened sensory awareness, preparing them for the world that they are about to encounter for the first time.

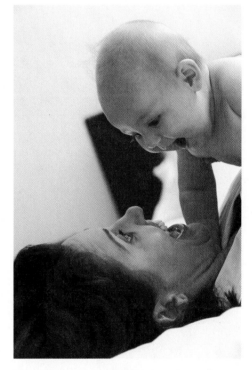

This infant is imitating the happy expressions of the adult. Why is this important?

## Circumcision of Newborn Male Infants: The Unkindest Cut?

An estimated three-quarters of males in the United States are circumcised, and worldwide the prevalence is around 30 percent. *Circumcision* is the surgical removal of part or all of the foreskin from the penis, most commonly performed shortly after birth (National Center for Health Statistics, 2006; World Health Organization, 2007).

Parents usually choose circumcision for a combination of health, religious, cultural, and traditional reasons. But although it is one of the most common surgical procedures in the United States, the American Medical Association, the American Academy of Pediatrics, and the American Academy of Family Physicians have long denied that it is medically necessary and recommended against its routine use (American Academy of Pediatrics, 1999; American Academy of Family Physicians, 2002).

But new research has added a twist: Circumcision provides protection against sexually transmitted diseases. A number of studies in Africa have found that circumcised men are less likely to become infected with HIV, even when other factors such as hygiene are controlled. In fact, when large experimental studies in Kenya and Uganda found compelling evidence that circumcision cut the risk of HIV infection nearly in half, researchers stopped the studies early to allow the uncircumcised men in the control groups to be circumcised and gain the same protective benefits (American Academy of Family Physicians, 2002; Mills & Siegfried, 2006; National Institutes of Health, 2006; Castro et al., 2010).

Circumcision may produce other medical benefits. The risk of urinary tract infections is reduced in circumcised males, especially during the first year of life, and the risk of penile cancer is about three times higher in uncircumcised men than in men who were circumcised at birth (Frisch et al., 1995; American Academy of Pediatrics, 1999).

On the other hand, circumcision is not without complications. The most common are bleeding and infection, both of which are easily treated. The procedure is also painful and stressful to the infant, as it is typically done without general anesthesia. Further, some experts believe that circumcision reduces sensation and sexual pleasure later in life, while others argue that it is unethical to remove a healthy body part without a person's consent when there is no medical need to do so (American Academy of Pediatrics, 1999; American Academy of Family Physicians, 2002).

One thing is clear: circumcision is highly controversial and evokes strong emotions. The decision ultimately comes down to the parents' personal preferences and values (Goldman, 2004).

## Early Learning Capabilities

*One-month-old Michael Samedi was on a car ride with his family when a violent thunderstorm suddenly began. Flashes of lightning were quickly followed by loud thunderclaps. Michael, clearly disturbed, began to sob. With each new thunderclap, the pitch and fervor of his crying increased. Unfortunately, before very long it wasn't just the thunder that would raise Michael's anxiety; the lightning alone was enough to make him cry out. In fact, even as an adult, Michael feels his chest tighten and his stomach churn at the mere sight of lightning.*

***Classical Conditioning.*** The source of Michael's fear is classical conditioning, a type of learning first identified by Ivan Pavlov, a Russian scientist. In **classical conditioning** an organism learns to respond in a particular way to a neutral stimulus that normally does not bring about that type of response.

Pavlov discovered that by repeatedly pairing two stimuli, such as the sound of a bell and the arrival of meat, he could make hungry dogs learn to respond (in this case by salivating) not only when the meat was presented, but even when the bell was sounded without the meat (Pavlov, 1927).

The key feature of classical conditioning is stimulus substitution, in which a stimulus that doesn't naturally bring about a particular response is paired with a stimulus that does evoke that response. Repeatedly presenting the two stimuli together results in the second stimulus taking on the properties of the first. In effect, the second stimulus is substituted for the first.

One of the earliest examples of classical conditioning shaping human emotions was the case of 11-month-old "Little Albert" (Watson & Rayner, 1920). Although he initially adored furry animals and showed no fear of rats, Little Albert learned to fear them when, during a laboratory demonstration, a loud noise was sounded every time he played with a cute and harmless white rat. In fact, the fear generalized to other furry objects, including rabbits and even a Santa Claus mask. (By the way, this demonstration would be considered unethical today and would never be conducted.)

Clearly, classical conditioning is in operation from the time of birth. One- and two-day-old newborns who are stroked on the head just before receiving a drop of sweet-tasting liquid soon learn to turn their heads and suck at the head-stroking alone (Blass, Ganchrow, & Steiner, 1984; Dominguez, Lopez, & Molina, 1999).

***Operant Conditioning.*** Infants also respond to operant conditioning. **Operant conditioning** is a form of learning in which a *voluntary* response is strengthened or weakened, depending on its association with positive or negative consequences. In operant conditioning, infants learn to act deliberately on their environments in order to bring about a desired consequence.

**classical conditioning** a type of learning in which an organism responds in a particular way to a neutral stimulus that normally does not bring about that type of response

**operant conditioning** a form of learning in which a voluntary response is strengthened or weakened, depending on its association with positive or negative consequences

An infant who learns that crying in a certain way attracts her parents' attention is displaying operant conditioning.

Like classical conditioning, operant conditioning functions from the earliest days of life. For instance, researchers have found that even newborns readily learn through operant conditioning to keep sucking on a nipple when it permits them to continue hearing their mothers read a story or to listen to music (DeCasper & Fifer, 1980; Lipsitt, 1986).

*Habituation.* Probably the most primitive form of learning is habituation. **Habituation** is the decrease in the response to a stimulus that occurs after repeated presentations of the same stimulus. 👁 Watch on mydevelopmentlab.com

Habituation in infants relies on the fact that when newborns are presented with a new stimulus, they produce an *orienting response,* in which they become quiet and attentive and experience a slowed heart rate as they take in the novel stimulus. When the novelty wears off, the infant no longer reacts. If a new and different stimulus is presented, the infant once again reacts with an orienting response. When this happens, we can say that the infant recognizes the original stimulus and can distinguish it from others.

Habituation occurs in every sensory system, and researchers have studied it in several ways. One is to examine changes in sucking, which stops temporarily when a new stimulus is presented. This reaction is not unlike that of an adult who temporarily puts down her knife and fork when a dinner companion makes an interesting statement to which she wishes to pay particular attention. Other measures of habituation include changes in heart rate, respiration rate, and the length of time an infant looks at a particular stimulus (Farroni et al., 2007; Colombo & Mitchell, 2009; Domsch, Thomas, & Hoben, 2010).

The development of habituation is linked to physical and cognitive maturation. It is present at birth and becomes more pronounced over the first 12 weeks of infancy. Difficulties involving habituation represent a signal of developmental problems such as mental retardation (Moon, 2002). The three basic processes of learning that we've considered—classical conditioning, operant conditioning, and habituation—are summarized in Table 2-5.

## Social Competence: Responding to Others

Soon after Kaita was born, her older brother looked into her crib and opened his mouth wide, pretending to be surprised. Kaita's mother was amazed when Kaita imitated his expression, opening her mouth as if *she* were surprised.

Researchers registered surprise of their own when they found that newborns could apparently imitate others' behavior. Although infants have all the facial muscles needed to express basic emotions, the appearance of such expressions was assumed to be random.

However, research beginning in the late 1970s began to suggest a different conclusion. For instance, developmental researchers found that, when exposed to an adult modeling a behavior that the infant already performed spontaneously, such as opening the mouth or sticking out the tongue, the newborn appeared to imitate the behavior (Meltzoff & Moore, 1977, 2002; Nagy, 2006).

**habituation** the decrease in the response to a stimulus that occurs after repeated presentations of the same stimulus

👁 Watch on mydevelopmentlab.com

*Do you understand habituation?* To learn more about it, check MyDevelopmentLab.com for an Observations Video.

### TABLE 2-5 THREE BASIC PROCESSES OF LEARNING

| Type | Description | Example |
|---|---|---|
| Classical conditioning | A situation in which an organism learns to respond in a particular way to a neutral stimulus that normally does not bring about that type of response. | A hungry baby stops crying when her mother picks her up because she has learned to associate being picked up with subsequent feeding. |
| Operant conditioning | A form of learning in which a voluntary response is strengthened or weakened, depending on its positive or negative consequences. | An infant who learns that smiling at his or her parents brings positive attention may smile more often. |
| Habituation | The decrease in the response to a stimulus that occurs after repeated presentations of the same stimulus. | A baby who showed interest and surprise at first seeing a novel toy may show no interest after seeing the same toy several times. |

**states of arousal** different degrees of sleep and wakefulness through which newborns cycle, ranging from deep sleep to great agitation

**TABLE 2-6** FACTORS THAT ENCOURAGE SOCIAL INTERACTION BETWEEN FULL-TERM NEWBORNS AND THEIR PARENTS

| Full-Term Newborn | Parent |
| --- | --- |
| Has organized states | Helps regulate infant's states |
| Attends selectively to certain stimuli | Provides these stimuli |
| Behaves in ways interpretable as specific communicative intent | Searches for communicative intent |
| Responds systematically to parent's acts | Wants to influence newborn, feel effective |
| Acts in temporally predictable ways | Adjusts actions to newborn's temporal rhythms |
| Learns from, and adapts to, parent's behavior | Acts repetitively and predictably |

Source: Eckerman & Oehler, 1992.

Even more exciting were findings from studies conducted by developmental psychologist Tiffany Field and her colleagues. They first showed that infants could discriminate between such basic facial expressions as happiness, sadness, and surprise. They then exposed newborns to an adult model with a happy, sad, or surprised facial expression. The results suggested that newborns produced a reasonably accurate imitation of the adult's expression (Field & Walden, 1982; Field et al., 1984; Field, 2010).

This result was questioned, however, when subsequent research found consistent evidence for only one movement: sticking out the tongue. And even that seemed to disappear around the age of 2 months. Since it seems unlikely that imitation would be limited to a single gesture of only a few months' duration, researchers began to question the earlier findings. In fact, some researchers suggested that sticking out the tongue was not imitation, but merely an exploratory behavior (Anisfeld, 1996; Bjorklund, 1997; Jones, 2006, 2007; Tissaw, 2007).

The jury is still out on exactly when true imitation begins, although it seems clear that some forms of imitation begin early. Imitative skills are important because effective social interactions rely in part on the ability to react to other people in an appropriate way and to understand the meaning of others' emotional states (Heimann, 2001; Meltzoff, 2002; Rogers & Williams, 2006; Zeedyk & Heimann, 2006; Legerstee & Markova, 2008).

Several other aspects of newborns' behavior also act as forerunners for more formal types of social interaction that develop later. As shown in Table 2-6, certain characteristics of neonates mesh with parental behavior to help produce a social relationship between child and parent, as well as relationships with others (Eckerman & Oehler, 1992).

For example, newborns cycle through various **states of arousal,** different degrees of sleep and wakefulness, that range from deep sleep to great agitation. Caregivers become involved in easing the baby through transitions from one state to another. For instance, a father who rhythmically rocks his crying daughter to calm her is engaged with her in a joint activity that is a prelude to future social interactions of different sorts. Similarly, newborns pay particular attention to their mothers' voices, in part because they have become familiar with them after months in the womb. In turn, parents and others modify their speech when talking to infants to gain their attention and encourage interaction, using a different pitch and tempo than they use with older children and adults (DeCasper & Fifer, 1980; Trainor, Austin, & Desjardins, 2000; Kisilevsky et al., 2003; Newman & Hussain, 2006; Smith & Trainor, 2008).

The ultimate outcome of the social interactive capabilities of the newborn infant, and the responses from parents, is a paved path for future social interactions. In sum, then, neonates display remarkable physical, perceptual, *and* social capabilities.

**From a child care worker's perspective:** Developmental researchers no longer view the neonate as a helpless, incompetent creature, but rather as a remarkably competent, developing human being. What do you think are some implications of this change in viewpoint for methods of child rearing and child care?

## REVIEW, CHECK, AND APPLY

### REVIEW

**L012** What capabilities does the newborn have?

- Newborns' respiratory and digestive systems begin to function at birth. They have an array of reflexes to help them eat, swallow, find food, and avoid unpleasant stimuli.

- Newborns' sensory competence includes the ability to distinguish objects in the visual field and to see color differences; the ability to hear and to discern familiar sounds; and sensitivity to touch, odors, and tastes.

- The processes of classical conditioning, operant conditioning, and habituation demonstrate infants' learning capabilities.

### CHECK YOURSELF

1. In order to survive the first few minutes or even days, infants are born with _____, or unlearned, organized, involuntary responses that occur automatically in the presence of certain stimuli.

2. Evidence suggests that infants have size constancy, meaning that they are aware that objects stay the same size even though the size of the image on the retina varies with distance.

   - True
   - False

3. An infant learning through _____ learns to respond in a particular way to a neutral stimulus that normally does not bring about that type of response.

   a. reward

   b. classical conditioning

   c. operant conditioning

   d. social learning

### APPLYING LIFESPAN DEVELOPMENT

- Can you think of examples of the use of classical conditioning on adults in everyday life, in such areas as entertainment, advertising, or politics?

✓●─[**Study** and **Review** on
**MyDevelopmentLab.com**

Answers: 1) reflexes; 2) True; 3) b

# *Putting It Together*
# Beginnings

**RACHEL AND JACK,** the parents we met in the chapter opener, looked forward to the birth of their second child. They speculated—just as lifespan developmentalists do—about the role of genetics and environment in their children's development, considering issues like intelligence, resemblance, personality, schooling, and neighborhood. For the birth itself, they had many options available. Rachel and Jack chose to use a midwife rather than an obstetrician and to give birth at a traditional hospital, but in a nontraditional way. And when their baby was born, both felt pride and happiness as Baby Eva reacted to the sound of her mother's voice, which she had heard from her intimate perch inside Rachel's body.

## MODULE 2.1 Prenatal Development

- Like all parents, Rachel and Jack contributed 23 chromosomes each at conception. Their baby's sex was determined from the particular mix of one pair of chromosomes. **(pp. 43–44)**

- Even before their baby's birth, Rachel and Jack had a range of options for checking for gender, possible genetic defects, and fetal growth. Measures available to them included such procedures as ultrasound sonography, amniocentesis, and fetal blood sampling. **(pp. 48–50)**

- Many of Eva's characteristics will have a strong genetic component, but virtually all will represent some combination of genetics and environment. **(pp. 51–58)**

## MODULE 2.2 Prenatal Growth and Change

- In the prenatal period, Rachel's baby showed a multistage pattern of development, starting with the germinal stage, progressing to the embryonic stage, and completing the prenatal period in the fetal stage. **(pp. 60–61)**

- Rachel was comparatively young, watched her diet, exercised regularly, and relied on strong family support. Consequently, there were few potential threats to her baby's health and development. **(pp. 65–67)**

- Since neither Rachel nor Jack smoked and Rachel abstained from alcohol during the pregnancy, she and her husband had relatively few worries about teratogenic agents harming the fetus. **(pp. 68–70)**

- Rachel's labor was intense and painful, although others experience labor in different ways due to individual and cultural differences. **(pp. 71–76)**

- Rachel chose to use a midwife, one of several alternative birthing methods. **(p. 75)**

- Like the vast majority of births, Rachel's was completely normal and successful. **(p. 76)**

- Although Baby Eva seemed utterly helpless and dependent, she actually possessed from birth an array of useful capabilities and skills. **(pp. 84–85)**

## What would a PARENT do?

- What strategies would you use to prepare yourself for the birth of your child?

- How would you evaluate the different options for prenatal care and delivery?

- How would you prepare your older child for the birth of a new baby?

  **HINT** Review pages 74–77.

## What would a HEALTH CARE PROVIDER do?

- How would you prepare Rachel and Jack for the birth of their baby?

- How would you respond to their concerns and anxieties?

- What would you tell them about the different options they have for giving birth?

  **HINT** Review pages 74–76.

## What would an EDUCATOR do?

- What strategies might you use to teach Rachel and Jack about the stages of pregnancy and the process of birth?

- What might you tell them about infancy to prepare them for caring for their child?

  **HINT** Review pages 60–64.

## What would YOU do?

- What would you say to Rachel and Jack about the impending birth of their child?

- What advice would you give to Rachel and Jack about prenatal care and their decision about the use of a midwife?

  **HINT** Review pages 74–76.

**✳ Explore on mydevelopmentlab.com**

To read how real-life educators, social workers, and parents responded to these questions, log onto MyDevelopmentLab.com.

*Do you agree or disagree with their responses? Why? What concepts that you've read about back up their opinion?*

The first few months of Alex's infancy went by in a blur. Although everyone had warned her parents that their lives would change with her birth, they weren't prepared for the sheer amount of work infancy would require. Not only were they physically exhausted from a lack of sleep, but the many decisions they had to make were daunting.

How should they respond when Alex began to cry in the middle of the night? Should Leigh only breastfeed Alex or supplement breastfeeding with a bottle? Should they use cloth or disposable diapers? Should they call their pediatrician when Alex, who was occasionally fussy after meals, got diarrhea? What kind of mobile should hang over Alex's crib? How should they try to encourage Alex's physical and intellectual development?

Yet there was not a moment when they questioned their decision to have a child. Alex was good looking, strong, and growing rapidly. She generally had a wonderful disposition. The best time of day was the morning, right after she woke up, when she showered her parents with huge, toothless smiles. Her smiles could melt anyone's heart, and her parents were entranced. Alex was the best!

## MODULE 3.1  Physical Development in Infancy

## What basic reflexes are we born with? see page 94.

## MODULE 3.2  Cognitive Development in Infancy

## Do infants have a memory?

see page 114.

All infants, whether they have good dispositions like Alex or are fussy and demanding, are engaging, energetic, and challenging. And they are constantly changing as they develop physically, cognitively, socially, and in terms of developing their own unique personality.

In this chapter, we examine infancy, the period of the life span that starts at birth and continues through the first two years of life. We'll first discuss the ways in which infants grow physically, examining their remarkably rapid progress from largely instinctual beings to individuals with a range of complex physical abilities.

Turning to infants' cognitive development, we'll discuss the notion of stages of development, as well as some alternative views. We'll consider the amazing growth in learning, memory, and language that infants experience—and adults witness with awe.

Finally we will examine social and personality development. We will look at personality and temperament and observe how gender differences are a matter of both genes and environment. We'll see how infants begin to develop as social beings, moving from interactions with their parents to relations with other adults and children.

Above all, we'll marvel at the rate of infants' progress, and we will get a preview of the ways in which characteristics that date from infancy continue to influence the individual into adulthood. As we proceed, keep in mind how the seeds of our futures appear in our earliest beginnings.

## MODULE 3.3 Social and Personality Development in Infancy

# Do infants know who they are?

see page 134.

## My Virtual Child

What decisions would you make while raising a child? What would the consequences of those decisions be?

Find out by logging onto *My Virtual Child* and raising your child from birth to 18 years.

## MODULE 3.1 Physical Development in Infancy

# First Steps

*Allan's parents were starting to get anxious. After 13 months, their son had yet to take his first steps. Clearly, he was getting close. Allan was able to stand still for several moments unaided. Clutching chairs and the sides of tables, he could shuffle his way around rooms. But as for taking those first, momentous, solo steps—Allan just wasn't there yet.*

*Allan's older brother, Todd, had walked at 10 months. Allan's parents read stories online of children walking at 9, 8, even 6 months old! Why, then, wasn't Allan walking on his own yet, they wondered.*

*The anticipation was building. Allan's father kept his digital camera at the ready whenever he was with his son, hoping to record Allan's milestone. Allan's mother frequently updated the family blog, keeping friends and extended family alert to Allan's progress.*

*Finally, the moment came. One afternoon, Allan lurched away from a chair, took a tottering step—then another, and then another. He made it all the way across the room to the opposite wall, laughing happily as he went. Allan's parents, who had been lucky enough to witness the event, were overjoyed.*

The reactions of Allan's parents in the lead-up to their son's first steps, and their elation at the steps themselves, were typical. Modern parents frequently scrutinize their children's behavior, worrying over what they see as potential abnormalities (for the record, walking at 13 months is entirely consistent with healthy childhood development) and celebrating important milestones. In this module, we consider the nature of the astonishing physical development that occurs during infancy, a period that starts at birth and continues until the second birthday. We begin by discussing the pace of growth during infancy, noting obvious changes in height and weight as well as less apparent changes in the nervous system. We also consider how infants quickly develop increasingly stable patterns in such basic activities as sleeping, eating, and attending to the world.

Our discussion then turns to infants' thrilling gains in motor development as skills emerge that eventually will allow an infant to roll over, take the first step, and pick up a cookie crumb from the floor—skills that ultimately form the basis of later, even more complex behaviors. We start with basic, genetically determined reflexes and consider how even these may be modified through experience. We also discuss the nature and timing of the development of particular physical skills, look at whether their emergence can be speeded up, and consider the importance of early nutrition to their development.

Finally, we explore how infants' senses develop. We investigate how sensory systems like hearing and vision operate, and how infants sort through the raw data from their sense organs and transform it into meaningful information.

# Growth and Stability

**LO1**   **How does physical growth in the body and nervous system proceed during infancy?**

**LO2**   **How are the bodily systems integrated during infancy?**

**LO3**   **What are the sleep patterns of infants?**

The average newborn weighs just over 7 pounds, which is less than the weight of the average Thanksgiving turkey. Its length is about 20 inches, shorter than a loaf of French bread. It is helpless; if left to fend for itself, it could not survive.

Yet after just a few years, the story is very different. Babies become much larger, they are mobile, and they become increasingly independent. How does this growth happen? We can answer this question first by describing the changes in weight and height that occur over the first two years of life, and then by examining some of the principles that underlie and direct that growth.

# Physical Growth: The Rapid Advances of Infancy

Infants grow at a rapid pace over the first two years of their lives (see Figure 3-1). By the age of 5 months, the average infant's birthweight has doubled to around 15 pounds. By the first birthday, the baby's weight has tripled to about 22 pounds. Although the pace of weight gain slows during the second year, it still continues to increase. By the end of his or her second year, the average child weighs around four times as much as he or she did at birth. Of course, there is a good deal of variation among infants. Height and weight measurements, which are taken regularly during physical exams in a baby's first year, provide a way to spot problems in development.

The weight gains of infancy are matched by increased length. By the end of the first year, the typical baby grows almost a foot and is about 30 inches tall. By their second birthdays, children average a height of 3 feet.

Not all parts of an infant's body grow at the same rate. For instance, at birth the head accounts for one-quarter of the newborn's entire body size. During the first two years of life, the rest of the body begins to catch up. By the age of 2, the baby's head is only one-fifth of its body length, and by adulthood it is only one-eighth (see Figure 3-2).

There also are gender and ethnic differences in weight and length. Girls generally are slightly shorter and weigh slightly less than boys, and these differences remain throughout childhood (and, as we will see later in the book, the disparities become considerably greater during adolescence). Furthermore, Asian infants tend to be slightly smaller than North American Caucasian infants, and African American infants tend to be slightly bigger than North American Caucasian infants.

***Four Principles of Growth.***   The disproportionately large size of infants' heads at birth is an example of one of four major principles (summarized in Table 3-1) that govern growth.

- The **cephalocaudal principle** states that growth follows a direction and pattern that begins with the head and upper body parts and then proceeds to the rest of the body. The cephalocaudal growth principle means that we develop visual abilities (located in the head) well before we master the ability to walk (closer to the end of the body).

- The **proximodistal principle** states that development proceeds from the center of the body outward. The proximodistal principle means that the trunk of the body grows before the extremities of the arms and legs. Furthermore, the development of the ability to use

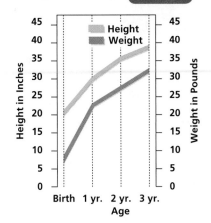

**FIGURE 3-1  Height and Weight Growth**
Although the greatest increase in height and weight occurs during the first year of life, children continue to grow throughout infancy and toddlerhood.
Source: Adapted from Cratty, B. J. (1979). PERCEPTUAL AND MOTOR DEVELOPMENT IN INFANTS AND CHILDREN, 2e, pg. 222. © Copyright © 1979 Pearson Education, Inc. Reprinted with permission of Pearson Education, Inc.

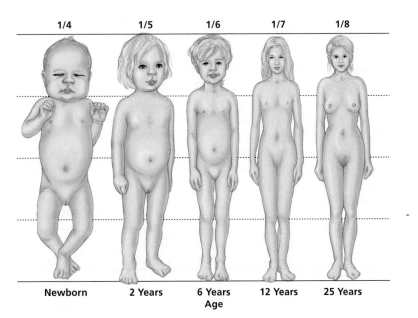

**FIGURE 3-2  Decreasing Proportions**
At birth, the head represents one-quarter of the neonate's body. By adulthood, the head is only one-eighth the size of the body. Why is the neonate's head so large?

**cephalocaudal principle**  the principle that growth follows a pattern that begins with the head and upper body parts and then proceeds down to the rest of the body

**proximodistal principle**  the principle that development proceeds from the center of the body outward

## TABLE 3-1 THE MAJOR PRINCIPLES GOVERNING GROWTH

| Cephalocaudal Principle | Proximodistal Principle | Principle of Hierarchical Integration | Principle of the Independence of Systems |
|---|---|---|---|
| Growth follows a pattern that begins with the head and upper body parts and then proceeds to the rest of the body. Based on Greek and Latin roots meaning "head-to-tail." | Development proceeds from the center of the body outward. Based on the Latin words for "near" and "far." | Simple skills typically develop separately and independently. Later they are integrated into more complex skills. | Different body systems grow at different rates. |

various parts of the body also follows the proximodistal principle. For instance, effective use of the arms precedes the ability to use the hands.

- The **principle of hierarchical integration** states that simple skills typically develop separately and independently, but that these simple skills are integrated into more complex ones. Thus, the relatively complex skill of grasping something in the hand cannot be mastered until the developing infant learns how to control—and integrate—the movements of the individual fingers.

- Finally, the **principle of the independence of systems** suggests that different body systems grow at different rates. For instance, the patterns of growth for body size, the nervous system, and sexual maturation are quite different. ◉ Watch on **mydevelopmentlab.com**

## The Nervous System and Brain: The Foundations of Development

When Rina was born, she was the first baby among her parents' circle of friends. These young adults marveled at the infant, oohing and aahing at every sneeze and smile and whimper, trying to guess at their meaning. Whatever feelings, movements, and thoughts Rina was experiencing, they were all brought about by the same complex network: the infant's nervous system. The *nervous system* comprises the brain and the nerves that extend throughout the body.

**Neurons** are the basic cells of the nervous system. Figure 3-3 shows the structure of an adult neuron. Like all cells in the body, neurons have a cell body containing a nucleus. But unlike other cells, neurons have a distinctive ability: They can communicate with other cells, using a cluster of fibers called *dendrites* at one end. Dendrites receive messages from other cells. At their opposite end, neurons have a long extension called an *axon*, the part of the neuron that carries messages destined for other neurons. Neurons do not actually touch one another. Rather, they communicate with other neurons by means of chemical messengers, *neurotransmitters*, that travel across the small gaps, known as **synapses**, between neurons.

Although estimates vary, infants are born with between 100 and 200 billion neurons. In order to reach this number, neurons multiply at an amazing rate prior to birth. In fact, at some points in prenatal development, cell division creates some 250,000 additional neurons every minute.

At birth, most neurons in an infant's brain have relatively few connections to other neurons. During the first two years of life, however, a baby's brain will establish billions of new connections between neurons. Furthermore, the network of neurons becomes increasingly complex, as illustrated in Figure 3-4. The intricacy of neural connections continues to increase throughout life. In fact, in adulthood a single neuron is likely to have a minimum of 5,000 connections to other neurons or other body parts.

*Synaptic Pruning.* Babies are actually born with many more neurons than they need. In addition, although synapses are formed throughout life, based on our changing experiences, the billions of new synapses infants form during the first two years are more numerous than necessary. What happens to the extra neurons and synaptic connections?

**principle of hierarchical integration** the principle that simple skills typically develop separately and independently but are later integrated into more complex skills

**principle of the independence of systems** the principle that different body systems grow at different rates

**neuron** the basic nerve cell of the nervous system

**synapse** the gap at the connection between neurons, through which neurons chemically communicate with one another

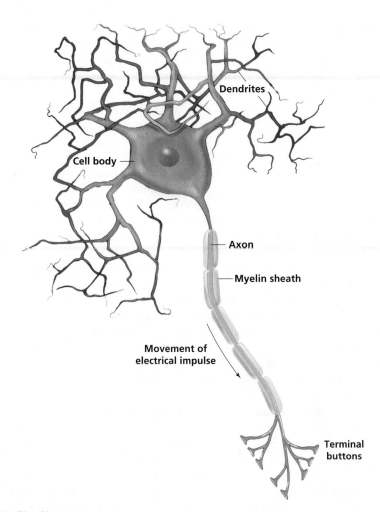

**FIGURE 3-3  The Neuron**
The basic element of the nervous system, the neuron is comprised of a number
of components.
Source: From Kent Van De Graff, *Human Anatomy,* 5e. Copyright © 1998 The McGraw-Hill Companies. Reprinted
with permission.

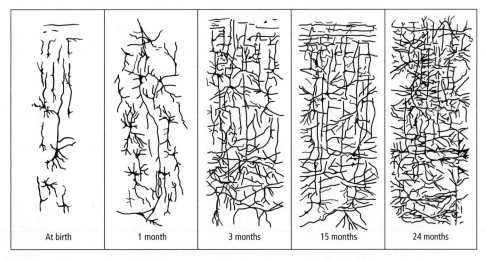

**FIGURE 3-4  Neuron Networks**
Over the first two years of life, networks of neurons become increasingly complex and
interconnected. Why are these connections important?
Source: From THE POSTNATAL DEVELOPMENT OF THE HUMAN CEREBRAL CORTEX, Vol I–VIII by Jesse LeRoy Conel,
Cambridge, Mass.: Harvard University Press, Copyright © 1939, 1975 by the President and Fellows of Harvard College.

**synaptic pruning** the elimination of neurons as the result of nonuse or lack of stimulation

**myelin** a fatty substance that helps insulate neurons and speeds the transmission of nerve impulses

**cerebral cortex** the upper layer of the brain

**plasticity** the degree to which a developing structure or behavior is modifiable due to experience

**sensitive period** a specific, but limited, time, usually early in an organism's life, during which the organism is particularly susceptible to environmental influences relating to some particular facet of development

◉—Watch on **mydevelopmentlab.com**

To watch an animation of the synaptic development process you just read about, log onto MyDevelopmentLab.com.

Like a farmer who, in order to strengthen the vitality of a fruit tree, prunes away unnecessary branches, brain development enhances certain capabilities in part by a "pruning down" of unnecessary neurons. Neurons that do not become interconnected with other neurons as the infant's experience of the world increases become unnecessary. They eventually die out, increasing the efficiency of the nervous system.

As unnecessary neurons are being reduced, connections between remaining neurons are expanded or eliminated as a result of their use or disuse during the baby's experiences. If a baby's experiences do not stimulate certain nerve connections, these, like unused neurons, are eliminated—a process called **synaptic pruning.** The result of synaptic pruning is to allow established neurons to build more elaborate communication networks with other neurons. Unlike most other aspects of growth, then, the development of the nervous system proceeds most effectively through the loss of cells (Johnson, 1998; Mimura, Kimoto, & Okada, 2003; Iglesias et al., 2005). ◉—Watch on **mydevelopmentlab.com**

After birth, neurons continue to increase in size. In addition to growth in dendrites, the axons of neurons become coated with **myelin,** a fatty substance that, like the insulation on an electric wire, provides protection and speeds the transmission of nerve impulses. So, even though many neurons are lost, the increasing size and complexity of the remaining ones contribute to impressive brain growth. A baby's brain triples its weight during his or her first two years of life, and it reaches more than three-quarters of its adult weight and size by the age of 2.

As they grow, the neurons also reposition themselves, becoming arranged by function. Some move into the **cerebral cortex,** the upper layer of the brain, while others move to *subcortical levels,* which are below the cerebral cortex. The subcortical levels, which regulate such fundamental activities as breathing and heart rate, are the most fully developed at birth. As time passes, however, the cells in the cerebral cortex, which are responsible for higher-order processes such as thinking and reasoning, become more developed and interconnected.

Although the brain is protected by the bones of the skull, it is highly sensitive to some forms of injury. One particularly devastating injury comes from a form of child abuse called *shaken baby syndrome,* in which an infant is shaken by a caretaker, usually out of frustration or anger due to a baby's crying. Shaking can lead the brain to rotate within the skull, causing blood vessels to tear and destroying the intricate connections between neurons, producing severe medical problems, long-term physical and learning disabilities, and often death (Jayawant & Parr, 2007; Runyan, 2008; Ashton, 2010).

***Environmental Influences on Brain Development.*** Brain development, much of which unfolds automatically because of genetically predetermined patterns, is also strongly susceptible to environmental influences. In fact, the brain's **plasticity,** the degree to which a developing structure or behavior is modifiable due to experience, is relatively great.

The brain's plasticity is greatest during the first several years of life. Because many areas of the brain are not yet devoted to specific tasks, if one area is injured, other areas can take over for the injured area. As a result, infants who suffer brain injuries typically are less affected and recover more fully than adults who have experienced similar types of brain injuries, showing a high degree of plasticity (Stiles, Moses, & Paul, 2006; Vanlierde, Renier, & DeVolder, 2008; Mercado, 2009).

Furthermore, infants' sensory experience affects both the size of individual neurons and the structure of their interconnections. Consequently, compared with those brought up in more enriched environments, infants raised in severely restricted settings are likely to show differences in brain structure and weight (Cicchetti, 2003; Cirulli, Berry, & Alleva, 2003; Couperus & Nelson, 2006).

Furthermore, researchers have found that there are particular sensitive periods during the course of development. A **sensitive period** is a specific but limited time, usually early in an organism's life, during which the organism is particularly susceptible to environmental influences relating to some particular facet of development. A sensitive period may be associated with a behavior—such as the development of vision—or with the development of a structure of the body, such as the configuration of the brain (Uylings, 2006).

The existence of sensitive periods raises several important issues. For one thing, it suggests that unless an infant receives a certain level of early environmental stimulation during a sensitive period, the infant may suffer damage or fail to develop capabilities that can never be fully remedied. If this is true, providing successful later intervention for such children may prove to be particularly challenging (Gottlieb & Blair, 2004; Zeanah, 2009).

The opposite question also arises: Does an unusually high level of stimulation during sensitive periods produce developmental gains beyond what a more commonplace level of stimulation would provide?

Such questions have no simple answers. Determining how unusually impoverished or enriched environments affect later development is one of the major questions addressed by developmental researchers as they try to find ways to maximize opportunities for developing children.

In the meantime, many developmentalists suggest that there are many simple ways parents and caregivers can provide a stimulating environment that will encourage healthy brain growth. Cuddling, talking and singing to, and playing with babies all help enrich their environment (Lafuente et al., 1997; Garlick, 2003).

⮕ **From a social worker's perspective:** What are some cultural or subcultural influences that might affect parents' childrearing practices?

## Integrating the Bodily Systems: The Life Cycles of Infancy

If you happen to overhear new parents discuss their newborns, chances are one or several bodily functions will be the subject. In the first days of life, infants' body rhythms—waking, eating, sleeping, and eliminating waste—govern the infant's behavior, often at seemingly random times.

These most basic activities are controlled by a variety of bodily systems. Although each of these individual behavioral patterns probably is functioning quite effectively, it takes some time and effort for infants to integrate the separate behaviors. In fact, one of the neonate's major missions is to make its individual behaviors work in harmony, helping it, for example, to sleep through the night (Ingersoll & Thoman, 1999; Waterhouse & DeCoursey, 2004).

***Rhythms and States.*** One of the most important ways that behavior becomes integrated is through the development of various **rhythms,** which are repetitive, cyclical patterns of behavior. Some rhythms are immediately obvious, such as the change from wakefulness to sleep. Others are more subtle, but still easily noticeable, such as breathing and sucking patterns. Still other rhythms may require careful observation to be noticed. For instance, newborns may go through periods in which they jerk their legs in a regular pattern every minute or so. Although some of these rhythms are apparent just after birth, others emerge slowly over the first year as the neurons of the nervous system become increasingly integrated (Thelen & Bates, 2003).

One of the major body rhythms is that of an infant's **state,** the degree of awareness he or she displays to both internal and external stimulation. As can be seen in Table 3-2, such states include various levels of wakeful behaviors, such as alertness, fussing, and crying, and different levels of sleep as well. Each change in state brings about an alteration in the amount of stimulation required to get the infant's attention (Diambra & Menna-Barreto, 2004).

***Sleep: Perchance to Dream?*** At the beginning of infancy, the major state that occupies a baby's time is sleep—much to the relief of exhausted parents, who often regard sleep as a welcome respite from caregiving responsibilities. On average, newborn infants sleep some 16 to 17 hours a day. However, there are wide variations. Some sleep more than 20 hours, while others sleep as little as 10 hours a day (Peirano, Algarin, & Uauy, 2003; Buysse, 2005; Tikotzky & Sadeh, 2009).

Infants sleep a lot, but you shouldn't wish to "sleep like a baby." The sleep of infants comes in fits and starts. Rather than covering one long stretch, sleep initially comes in spurts of around 2 hours, followed by periods of wakefulness. Because of this, infants—and their sleep-deprived parents—are "out of sync" with the rest of the world, for whom sleep comes at night and wakefulness during the day (Groome et al., 1997; Burnham et al., 2002). Most babies do not sleep through the night for

**rhythms** repetitive, cyclical patterns of behavior

**state** the degree of awareness an infant displays to both internal and external stimulation

Infants sleep in spurts, often making them out of sync with the rest of the world.

**TABLE 3-2** PRIMARY BEHAVIORAL STATES

| States | Characteristics | Percentage of Time When Alone in State |
|---|---|---|
| **Awake States** | | |
| Alert | Attentive or scanning, the infant's eyes are open, bright, and shining. | 6.7 |
| Nonalert waking | Eyes are usually open, but dull and unfocused. Varied, but typically high motor activity. | 2.8 |
| Fuss | Fussing is continuous or intermittent, at low levels. | 1.8 |
| Cry | Intense vocalizations occurring singly or in succession. | 1.7 |
| **Transition States Between Sleep and Waking** | | |
| Drowse | Infant's eyes are heavy-lidded, but opening and closing slowly. Low level of motor activity. | 4.4 |
| Daze | Open, but glassy and immobile eyes. State occurs between episodes of alert and drowse. Low level of activity. | 1.0 |
| Sleep–wake transition | Behaviors of both wakefulness and sleep are evident. Generalized motor activity; eyes may be closed, or they open and close rapidly. State occurs when baby is awakening. | 1.3 |
| **Sleep States** | | |
| Active sleep | Eyes closed; uneven respiration; intermittent rapid eye movements. Other behaviors: smiles, frowns, grimaces, mouthing, sucking, sighs, and sigh sobs. | 50.3 |
| Quiet sleep | Eyes are closed and respiration is slow and regular. Motor activity limited to occasional startles, sighs, sobs, or rhythmic mouthing. | 28.1 |
| **Transitional Sleep States** | | |
| Active-quiet transition sleep | During this state, which occurs between periods of active sleep and quiet sleep, the eyes are closed and there is little motor activity. Infant shows mixed behavioral signs of active sleep and quiet sleep. | 1.9 |

Source: Adapted from Thoman & Whitney, 1990.

several months. Parents' sleep is interrupted, sometimes several times a night, by the infant's cries for food and physical contact.

Luckily for their parents, infants gradually settle into a more adultlike pattern. After a week, babies sleep a bit more at night and are awake for slightly longer periods during the day. Typically, by the age of 16 weeks infants begin to sleep as much as six continuous hours at night, and daytime sleep falls into regular naplike patterns. Most infants sleep through the night by the end of the first year, and the total amount of sleep they need each day is down to about 15 hours (Mao, 2004).

Hidden beneath the supposedly tranquil sleep of infants is another cyclic pattern. During periods of sleep, infants' heart rates increase and become irregular, their blood pressure rises, and they begin to breathe more rapidly (Montgomery-Downs & Thomas, 1998). Sometimes, although not always, their closed eyes begin to move in a back-and-forth pattern, as if they were viewing an action-packed scene. This period of active sleep is similar, although not identical, to the **rapid eye movement (REM) sleep** that is found in older children and adults and is associated with dreaming.

At first, this active, REM-like sleep takes up around one-half of an infant's sleep, compared with just 20 percent of an adult's sleep (see Figure 3-5). However, the quantity of active sleep quickly declines, and by the age of 6 months, amounts to just one-third of total sleep time (Burnham et al., 2002; Staunton, 2005).

The appearance of active sleep periods that are similar to REM sleep in adults raises the intriguing question of whether infants dream during those periods. No one knows the answer, although it seems unlikely. First of all, young infants do not have much to dream about, given their relatively limited experiences. Furthermore, the brain waves of sleeping infants appear to be qualitatively different from those of adults who are dreaming. It is not until the baby reaches 3 or 4 months of age that the wave patterns become similar to those of dreaming adults, suggesting that young infants are not dreaming during active sleep—or at least are not

**rapid eye movement (REM) sleep** the period of sleep that is found in older children and adults and is associated with dreaming

doing so in the same way as adults do (McCall, 1979; Parmalee & Sigman, 1983; Zampi et al., 2002).

Then what is the function of REM sleep in infants? Although we don't know for certain, some researchers think it provides a means for the brain to stimulate itself—a process called *autostimulation* (Roffwarg, Muzio, & Dement, 1966). Stimulation of the nervous system would be particularly important in infants, who spend so much time sleeping and relatively little in alert states.

Infants' sleep cycles seem largely preprogrammed by genetic factors, but environmental influences also play a part. For instance, cultural practices affect infants' sleep patterns. For example, among the Kipsigis of Africa, infants sleep with their mothers at night, a practice known as *co-sleeping* that is typical in most non-Western cultures. Infants are allowed to nurse whenever they wake. In the daytime, they accompany their mothers during daily chores, often napping while strapped to their mothers' backs. Because they are often out and on the go, Kipsigis infants do not sleep through the night until much later than babies in Western societies, and for the first 8 months of life, they seldom sleep longer than 3 hours at a stretch. In comparison, 8-month-old infants in the United States may sleep as long as 8 hours at a time (Super & Harkness, 1982; Anders & Taylor, 1994; Gerard, Harris, & Thach, 2002).

## SIDS: The Unanticipated Killer

For a tiny percentage of infants, the rhythm of sleep is interrupted by a deadly affliction: sudden infant death syndrome, or SIDS. **Sudden infant death syndrome (SIDS)** is a disorder in which seemingly healthy infants die in their sleep. Put to bed for a nap or for the night, an infant simply never wakes up.

SIDS strikes about 1 in 1,000 infants in the United States each year. Although it seems to occur when the normal patterns of breathing during sleep are interrupted, scientists have been unable to discover why that might happen. It is clear that infants don't smother or choke; they die a peaceful death, simply ceasing to breathe.

While no reliable means for preventing the syndrome has been found, the American Academy of Pediatrics now suggests that babies sleep on their backs rather than on their sides or stomachs—called the *back-to-sleep* guideline. In addition, they suggest that parents consider giving their babies a pacifier during naps and bedtime (Task Force on Sudden Infant Death Syndrome, 2005).

The number of deaths from SIDS has decreased significantly since these guidelines were developed (see Figure 3-6). Still, SIDS is the leading cause of death in children under the age of 1 year (Daley, 2004; Blair et al., 2006).

Many hypotheses have been suggested to explain why infants die from SIDS. These include such problems as undiagnosed sleep disorders, suffocation, nutritional deficiencies, problems with reflexes, brainstem abnormalities, and undiagnosed illness. Still, the actual cause of SIDS remains elusive (Lipsitt, 2003; Machaalani & Waters, 2008; Kinney & Thach, 2009; Mitchell, 2009; Duncan et al., 2010).

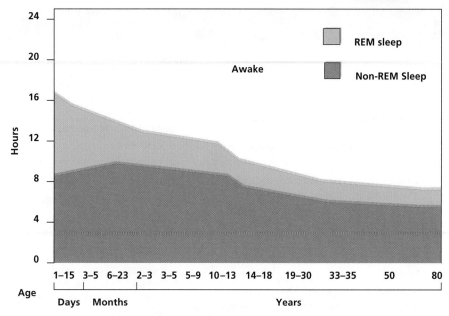

**FIGURE 3-5 Sleep Through the Life Span**
REM sleep is abundant in infancy but then declines in quantity. Non-REM sleep and total sleep continue to fall as we age, but the proportion of REM sleep stabilizes after our early twenties.
Source: Adapted from Roffwarg, Muzio, & Dement, 1966.

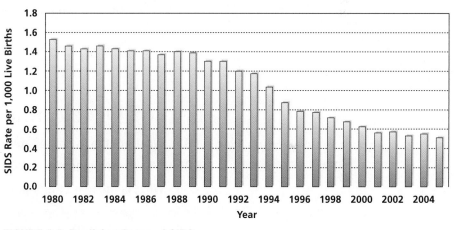

**FIGURE 3-6 Declining Rates of SIDS**
In the United States, SIDS rates have dropped dramatically as parents have become more informed and put babies to sleep on their backs instead of their stomachs.
Source: American SIDS Institute, based on data from the Center for Disease Control and the National Center for Health Statistics, 2004.

**sudden infant death syndrome (SIDS)** the unexplained death of a seemingly healthy baby

## REVIEW, CHECK, AND APPLY

### REVIEW

**LO1**  How does physical growth in the body and nervous system proceed during infancy?

- The major principles of growth are the cephalocaudal principle, the proximodistal principle, the principle of hierarchical integration, and the principle of the independence of systems.

- The development of the nervous system first entails the development of billions of neurons and interconnections among them. Later, the numbers of both neurons and connections decrease as a result of the infant's experiences.

**LO2**  How are the bodily systems integrated during infancy?

- Infants integrate their individual behaviors by developing rhythms, which are repetitive, cyclical patterns of behavior.

**LO3**  What are the sleep patterns of infants?

- The sleep of infants comes in fits and starts initially coming in spurts of around 2 hours, followed by periods of wakefulness. Because of this infants are "out of sync" with the rest of the world, for whom sleep comes at night and wakefulness during the day.

### CHECK YOURSELF

1. The _____ principle states that growth begins with the head and proceeds down to the rest of the body; the _____ principle states that development proceeds from the center of the body outward.

   **a.** cephalocaudal; proximodistal

   **b.** proximodistal; cephalocaudal

   **c.** hierarchical integration; independence of systems

   **d.** independence of systems; hierarchical integration

2. The process of synaptic pruning allows established neurons to build stronger networks and reduces unnecessary neurons during the first 2 years of life.

   - True

   - False

3. Although brain development is largely genetically predetermined, it is also susceptible to environmental experiences; the ability of the brain to be modifiable by the environment is called (a)

   _____.

   a. plasticity

   b. synaptic pruning

   c. sensitive period

   d. critical period

### APPLYING LIFESPAN DEVELOPMENT

- What evolutionary advantage could there be for infants to be born with more nerve cells than they actually need or use? How might our understanding of synaptic "pruning" affect the way we treat infants?

✓•⌐**Study** and **Review** on
**MyDevelopmentLab.com**

Answers: 1) a; 2) True; 3) a

# Motor Development

LEARNING OBJECTIVES

**LO4**  What are the major reflexes?

**LO5**  What developmental tasks must be accomplished during infancy?

**LO6**  What is the role of nutrition in physical development?

Suppose you were hired by a genetic engineering firm to redesign newborns and were charged with replacing the current version with a new, more mobile one. The first change you'd probably consider in carrying out this (luckily fictitious) job would be in the conformation and composition of the baby's body.

The shape and proportions of newborn babies are simply not conducive to easy mobility. Their heads are so large and heavy that young infants lack the strength to raise them. Because their limbs are short in relation to the rest of the body, their movements are further impeded. Furthermore, their bodies are mainly fat, with a limited amount of muscle; the result is that they lack strength.

Fortunately, it doesn't take too long before infants begin to develop a remarkable amount of mobility. In fact, even at birth they have an extensive repertoire of behavioral possibilities brought about by innate reflexes, and their range of motor skills grows rapidly during the first two years of life.

## Reflexes: Our Inborn Physical Skills

When her father pressed 3-day-old Christina's palm with his finger, she responded by tightly winding her small fist around his finger and grasping it. When he moved his finger upward, she held on so tightly that it seemed he might be able to lift her completely off her crib floor.

## TABLE 3-3 SOME BASIC REFLEXES IN INFANTS

| Reflex | Approximate Age of Disappearance | Description | Possible Function |
|---|---|---|---|
| Rooting reflex | 3 weeks | Neonate's tendency to turn its head toward things that touch its cheek. | Food intake |
| Stepping reflex | 2 months | Movement of legs when held upright with feet touching the floor. | Prepares infants for independent locomotion |
| Swimming reflex | 4–6 months | Infant's tendency to paddle and kick in a sort of swimming motion when lying face down in a body of water. | Avoidance of danger |
| Moro reflex | 6 months | Activated when support for the neck and head is suddenly removed. The arms of the infant are thrust outward and then appear to grasp onto something. | Similar to primate's protection from falling |
| Babinski reflex | 8–12 months | An infant fans out its toes in response to a stroke on the outside of its foot. | Unknown |
| Startle reflex | Remains in different form | An infant, in response to a sudden noise, flings out arms, arches its back, and spreads its fingers. | Protection |
| Eye-blink reflex | Remains | Rapid shutting and opening of eye on exposure to direct light. | Protection of eye from direct light |
| Sucking reflex | Remains | Infant's tendency to suck at things that touch its lips. | Food intake |
| Gag reflex | Remains | An infant's reflex to clear its throat. | Prevents choking |

***The Basic Reflexes.*** In fact, her father was right: Christina probably could have been lifted in this way. The reason for her resolute grip was activation of one of the dozens of reflexes with which infants are born. **Reflexes** are unlearned, organized, involuntary responses that occur automatically in the presence of certain stimuli. Newborns enter the world with a repertoire of reflexive behavioral patterns that help them adapt to their new surroundings and serve to protect them.   Watch on mydevelopmentlab.com

As we can see from the list of reflexes in Table 3-3, many reflexes clearly represent behavior that has survival value, helping to ensure the well-being of the infant. For instance, the *swimming reflex* makes a baby who is lying face down in a body of water paddle and kick in a sort of swimming motion. The obvious consequence of such behavior is to help the baby move from danger and survive until a caregiver can come to its rescue. Similarly, the *eye-blink reflex* seems designed to protect the eye from too much direct light, which might damage the retina.

Given the protective value of many reflexes, it might seem beneficial for them to remain with us for our entire lives. In fact, some do: The eye-blink reflex remains functional throughout the full life span. On the other hand, quite a few reflexes, such as the swimming reflex, disappear after a few months. Why should this be the case?

Researchers who focus on evolutionary explanations of development attribute the gradual disappearance of reflexes to the increase in voluntary control over behavior that occurs as infants become more able to control their muscles. In addition, it may be that reflexes form the foundation for future, more complex behaviors. As these more intricate behaviors become well learned, they encompass the earlier reflexes. Finally, it is possible that reflexes stimulate parts of the brain responsible for more complex behaviors, helping them develop (Myklebust & Gottlieb, 1993; Zelazo, 1998; Lipsitt, 2003).

***Ethnic and Cultural Differences and Similarities in Reflexes.*** Although reflexes are, by definition, genetically determined and universal throughout all infants, there are actually some cultural variations in the ways they are displayed. For instance, consider the *Moro reflex* which is activated when support for the neck and head is suddenly removed. The Moro reflex consists of the infant's arms thrusting outward and then appearing to seek to grasp onto something. Most scientists feel that the Moro reflex represents a leftover response that we humans have inherited from our nonhuman ancestors. The Moro reflex is an extremely

 Watch on **mydevelopmentlab.com**

To watch infants demonstrate the reflexes you have been reading about, log onto MyDevelopmentLab.com.

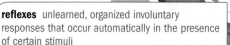

**reflexes** unlearned, organized involuntary responses that occur automatically in the presence of certain stimuli

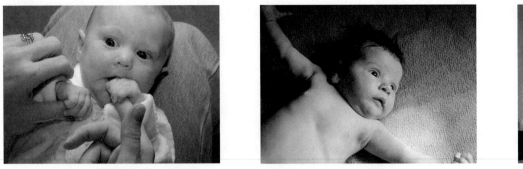 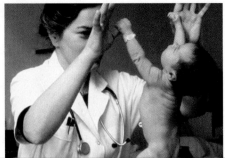

(a)                                        (b)                                        (c)

Infants showing (a) the rooting reflex, (b) the startle reflex, and (c) the Babinski reflex.

useful behavior for monkey babies, who travel about by clinging to their mothers' backs. If they lose their grip, they fall down unless they are able to grasp quickly onto their mother's fur—using a Moro-like reflex (Prechtl, 1982; Zafeiriou, 2004).

The Moro reflex is found in all humans, but it appears with significantly different vigor in different children. Some differences reflect cultural and ethnic variations (Freedman, 1979). For instance, Caucasian infants show a pronounced response to situations that produce the Moro reflex. Not only do they fling out their arms, but they also cry and respond in a generally agitated manner. In contrast, Navajo babies react to the same situation much more calmly. Their arms do not flail out as much, and they cry only rarely.

## Motor Development in Infancy: Landmarks of Physical Achievement

Probably no physical changes are more obvious—and more eagerly anticipated—than the increasing array of motor skills that babies acquire during infancy. Most parents can remember their child's first steps with a sense of pride and awe at how quickly she or he changed from a helpless infant, unable even to roll over, into a person who could navigate quite effectively in the world.

***Gross Motor Skills.*** Even though the motor skills of newborn infants are not terribly sophisticated, at least compared with attainments that will soon appear, young infants still are able to accomplish some kinds of movement. For instance, when placed on their stomachs they wiggle their arms and legs and may try to lift their heavy heads. As their strength increases, they are able to push hard enough against the surface on which they are resting to propel their bodies in different directions. They often end up moving backwards rather than forwards, but by the age of 6 months they become rather accomplished at moving themselves in particular directions. These initial efforts are the forerunners of crawling, in which babies coordinate the motions of their arms and legs and propel themselves forward. Crawling appears typically between 8 and 10 months. (Figure 3-7 provides a summary of some of the milestones of normal motor development.)

Walking comes later. At around the age of 9 months, most infants are able to walk by supporting themselves on furniture, and half of all infants can walk well by the end of their first year of life.

At the same time infants are learning to move around, they are perfecting the ability to remain in a stationary sitting position. At first, babies cannot remain seated upright without support. But they quickly master this ability, and most are able to sit without support by the age of 6 months.

***Fine Motor Skills.*** As infants are perfecting their gross motor skills, such as sitting upright and walking, they are also making advances in their fine motor skills (see Table 3-4). For instance, by the age of 3 months, infants show some ability to coordinate the movements of their limbs.

Furthermore, although infants are born with a rudimentary ability to reach toward an object, this ability is neither very sophisticated nor very accurate, and it disappears around

| TABLE 3-4 | MILESTONES OF FINE MOTOR DEVELOPMENT |
|---|---|

| Age (months) | Skill |
|---|---|
| 3 | Opens hand prominently |
| 3 | Grasps rattle |
| 8 | Grasps with thumb and finger |
| 11 | Holds crayon adaptively |
| 14 | Builds tower of two cubes |
| 16 | Places pegs in board |
| 24 | Imitates strokes on paper |
| 33 | Copies circle |

Source: From Frankenburg, W. K., Dodds, J., Archer, P., Shapiro, H., and Brunsneck, B., The Denver II: A Major Revision and Restandardization of the Denver Developmental Screening Test, *Pediatrics*, 89, pp. 91–97, 1992. Reprinted with permission from Dr. William K. Frankenburg.

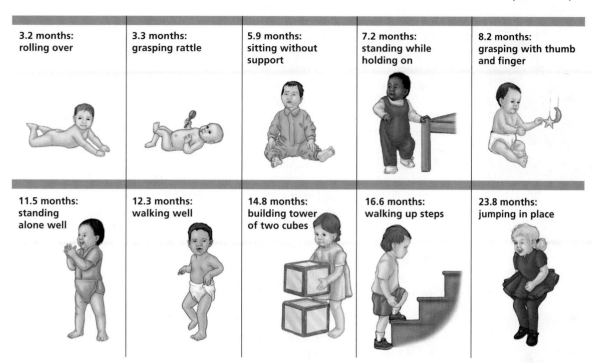

| 3.2 months: rolling over | 3.3 months: grasping rattle | 5.9 months: sitting without support | 7.2 months: standing while holding on | 8.2 months: grasping with thumb and finger |
| 11.5 months: standing alone well | 12.3 months: walking well | 14.8 months: building tower of two cubes | 16.6 months: walking up steps | 23.8 months: jumping in place |

**FIGURE 3-7 Milestones of Motor Development**
Fifty percent of children are able to perform each skill at the month indicated in the figure. However, the specific timing at which each skill appears varies widely. For example, one-quarter of children are able to walk well at 11.1 months; by 14.9 months, 90 percent of children are walking well. Is knowledge of such average benchmarks helpful or harmful to parents?
Source: Adapted from Frankenburg et al., 1992.

the age of 4 weeks. A different, more precise, form of reaching reappears at 4 months. It takes some time for infants to coordinate successful grasping after they reach out, but in fairly short order they are able to reach out and hold onto an object of interest (Claxton, Keen, & McCarty, 2003; Claxton, McCarty, & Keen, 2009; Grissmer et al., 2010).

The sophistication of fine motor skills continues to grow. By the age of 11 months, infants are able to pick up off the ground objects as small as marbles—something caregivers need to be concerned about, since the next place such objects often go is the mouth. By the time they are 2 years old, children can carefully hold a cup, bring it to their lips, and take a drink without spilling a drop.

Grasping, like other motor advances, follows a sequential developmental pattern in which simple skills are combined into more sophisticated ones. For example, infants first begin picking things up with their whole hand. As they get older, they use a *pincer grasp,* where thumb and index finger meet to form a circle. The pincer grasp allows for considerably more precise motor control (Barrett & Needham, 2008).

***Developmental Norms: Comparing the Individual to the Group.*** Keep in mind that the timing of the milestones in motor development that we have been discussing is based on norms. **Norms** represent the average performance of a large sample of children of a given age. They permit comparisons between a particular child's performance on a particular behavior and the average performance of the children in the norm sample.

For instance, one of the most widely used techniques to determine infants' normative standing is the **Brazelton Neonatal Behavioral Assessment Scale (NBAS),** a measure designed to determine infants' neurological and behavioral responses to their environment.

Taking about 30 minutes to administer, the NBAS includes 27 separate categories of responses that constitute four general aspects of infants' behavior: interactions with others (such as alertness and cuddliness), motor behavior, physiological control (such as the ability to be soothed after being upset), and responses to stress (Brazelton, 1973, 1990; Davis & Emory, 1995; Canals et al., 2003).

**norms** the average performance of a large sample of children of a given age

**Brazelton Neonatal Behavioral Assessment Scale (NBAS)** a measure designed to determine infants' neurological and behavioral responses to their environment

Cultural influences affect the rate of the development of motor skills.

Although the norms provided by scales such as the NBAS are useful in making broad generalizations about the timing of various behaviors and skills, they must be interpreted with caution. Because norms are averages, they mask substantial individual differences in the times when children attain various achievements.

Norms are useful only to the extent that they are based on data from a large, heterogeneous, culturally diverse sample of children. Unfortunately, many of the norms on which developmental researchers have traditionally relied have been based on groups of infants who are predominantly Caucasian and from the middle and upper socioeconomic strata (e.g., Gesell, 1946). The reason: Much of the research was conducted on college campuses, using the children of graduate students and faculty.

This limitation would not be critical if no differences existed in the timing of development in children from different cultural, racial, and social groups. But they do. For example, as a group, African American babies show more rapid motor development than Caucasian babies throughout infancy. Moreover, there are significant variations related to cultural factors, as we discuss next (Werner, 1972; Keefer et al., 1991; Gartstein et al., 2003; de Onis et al., 2007).

## Nutrition in Infancy: Fueling Motor Development

*Rosa sighed as she sat down to nurse the baby—again. She had fed 4-week-old Juan about every hour today, and he still seemed hungry. Some days, it seemed like all she did was breastfeed her baby. "Well, he must be going through a growth spurt," she decided, as she settled into her favorite rocking chair and put the baby to her nipple.*

The rapid physical growth that occurs during infancy is fueled by the nutrients that infants receive. Without proper nutrition, infants cannot reach their physical potential, and they may suffer cognitive and social consequences as well (Tanner & Finn-Stevenson, 2002; Costello et al., 2003; Gregory, 2005).

## *Cultural Dimensions*

### Motor Development Across Cultures

*Among the Ache people, who live in the rain forest of South America, infants face an early life of physical restriction. Because the Ache lead a nomadic existence, living in a series of tiny camps in the rain forest, open space is at a premium. Consequently, for the first few years of life, infants spend nearly all their time in direct physical contact with their mothers. Even when they are not physically touching their mothers, they are permitted to venture no more than a few feet away.*

*Infants among the Kipsigis people, who live in a more open environment in rural Kenya, Africa, lead quite a different existence. Their lives are filled with activity and exercise. Parents seek to teach their children to sit up, stand, and walk from the earliest days of infancy. For example, very young infants are placed in shallow holes in the ground designed to keep them in an upright position. Parents begin to teach their children to walk starting at the eighth week of life. The infants are held with their feet touching the ground, and they are pushed forward.*

Clearly, the infants in these two societies lead very different lives (Super, 1976; Kaplan & Dove, 1987). But do the relative lack of early motor stimulation for Ache infants and the efforts of the Kipsigis to encourage motor development really make a difference?

The answer is both yes and no. It's yes, in that Ache infants tend to show delayed motor development, relative both to Kipsigis infants and to children raised in Western societies. Although their social abilities are no different, Ache children tend to begin walking at around 23 months, about a year later than the typical child in the United States. In contrast, Kipsigis children, who are encouraged in their motor development, learn to sit up and walk several weeks earlier, on average, than U.S. children.

In the long run, however, the differences between Ache, Kipsigis, and Western children disappear. By late childhood, about age 6, there is no evidence of differences in general, overall motor skills among Ache, Kipsigis, and Western children.

As we see with the Ache and Kipsigis babies, variations in the timing of motor skills seem to depend in part on parental expectations of what is the "appropriate" schedule for the emergence of specific skills. For instance, one study examined the motor skills of infants who lived in a single city in England, but whose mothers varied in ethnic origin. In the research, English, Jamaican, and Indian mothers' expectations were first assessed regarding several markers of their infants' motor skills. The Jamaican mothers expected their infants to sit and walk significantly earlier than the English and Indian mothers, and the actual emergence of these activities was in line with their expectations. The source of the Jamaican infants' earlier mastery seemed to lie in the treatment of the children by their parents. For instance, Jamaican mothers gave their children practice in stepping quite early in infancy (Hopkins & Westra, 1989, 1990).

In sum, cultural factors help determine the time at which specific motor skills appear. Activities that are an intrinsic part of a culture are more apt to be purposely taught to infants in that culture, leading to the potential of their earlier emergence (Nugent, Lester, & Brazelton, 1989).

Although there are vast individual differences in what constitutes appropriate nutrition—infants differ in terms of growth rates, body composition, metabolism, and activity levels—some broad guidelines do hold. In general, infants should consume about 50 calories per day for each pound they weigh—an allotment that is twice the suggested caloric intake for adults (Dietz & Stern, 1999; Skinner et al., 2004).

Typically, though, it's not necessary to count calories for infants. Most infants regulate their caloric intake quite effectively on their own. If they are allowed to consume as much they seem to want, and not pressured to eat more, they will do fine.

*Malnutrition.*   *Malnutrition,* the condition of having an improper amount and balance of nutrients, produces several results, none good. For instance, malnutrition is more common among children living in many developing countries than among children who live in more industrialized, affluent countries. Malnourished children in these countries begin to show a slower growth rate by the age of 6 months. By the time they reach the age of 2 years, their height and weight are only 95 percent the height and weight of children in more industrialized countries.

Children who have been chronically malnourished during infancy later score lower on IQ tests and tend to do less well in school. These effects may linger even after the children's diet has improved substantially (Grantham-McGregor, Ani, & Fernald, 2001; Ratanachu-Ek, 2003).

The problem of malnutrition is greatest in underdeveloped countries, where overall 10 percent of infants are severely malnourished. In some countries the problem is especially severe. For example, 37 percent of North Korean children are chronically malnourished, suffering moderate to severe malnutrition (Gabriele & Schettino, 2008; United Nations World Food Programme, 2008).

Severe malnutrition during infancy may lead to several disorders. Malnutrition during the first year can produce *marasmus,* a disease in which infants stop growing. Marasmus, attributable to a severe deficiency in proteins and calories, causes the body to waste away and ultimately results in death. Older children are susceptible to *kwashiorkor,* a disease in which a child's stomach, limbs, and face swell with water. To a casual observer, it appears that a child with kwashiorkor is actually chubby. However, this is an illusion: The child's body is in fact struggling to make use of the few nutrients that are available (Douglass & McGadney-Douglass, 2008; Galler et al., 2010).

**From an educator's perspective:** What might be some of the reasons that malnourishment, which slows physical growth, harms IQ scores and school performance? How might malnourishment affect education in third-world countries?

In some cases, infants who receive sufficient nutrition act as though they have been deprived of food. Looking as though they suffer from marasmus, they are underdeveloped, listless, and apathetic. The real cause, though, is emotional: They lack sufficient love and emotional support. In such cases, known as **nonorganic failure to thrive,** children stop growing not for biological reasons but due to a lack of stimulation and attention from their parents. Usually occurring by the age of 18 months, nonorganic failure to thrive can be reversed through intensive parent training or by placing children in a foster home where they can receive emotional support.

*Obesity.*   It is clear that malnourishment during infancy has potentially disastrous consequences for an infant. Less clear, however, are the effects of *obesity,* defined as weight greater than 20 percent above the average for a given height. While there is no clear correlation between obesity during infancy and obesity at the age of 16 years, some research suggests that overfeeding during infancy may lead to the creation of an excess of fat cells, which remain in the body throughout life and may predispose a person to be overweight. In fact, weight gains during infancy are associated with weight at age 6. Other research shows an association between obesity after the age of 6 and adult obesity, suggesting that obesity in babies ultimately may be found to be associated with adult weight problems. A clear link between overweight babies and overweight adults, however, has not yet been found (Toschke et al., 2004; Dennison et al., 2006; Stettler, 2007; Adair, 2008).

Although the evidence linking infant obesity to adult obesity is inconclusive, it's plain that the societal view that "a fat baby is a healthy baby" is not necessarily correct. Parents should

**nonorganic failure to thrive** a disorder in which infants stop growing due to a lack of stimulation and attention as the result of inadequate parenting

concentrate less on their baby's weight and more on providing appropriate nutrition. But just what constitutes proper nutrition? Probably the biggest question revolves around whether infants should be breastfed or given a formula of commercially processed cow's milk with vitamin additives, as we consider next.

## Breast or Bottle?

Fifty years ago, if a mother asked her pediatrician whether breastfeeding or bottlefeeding was better, she would have received a simple and clear-cut answer: Bottle-feeding was the preferred method. Starting around the 1940s, the general belief among child-care experts was that breastfeeding was an obsolete method that put children unnecessarily at risk.

With bottle-feeding, the argument went, parents could keep track of the amount of milk their baby was receiving and could thereby ensure that the child was taking in sufficient nutrients. In contrast, mothers who breastfed their babies could never be certain just how much milk their infants were getting. Use of the bottle was also supposed to help mothers keep their feedings to a rigid schedule of one bottle every 4 hours, the recommended procedure at that time.

Today, however, a mother would get a very different answer to the same question. Child-care authorities agree: For the first 12 months of life, there is no better food for an infant than breast milk. Breast milk not only contains all the nutrients necessary for growth, but it also seems to offer some degree of immunity to a variety of childhood diseases, such as respiratory illnesses, ear infections, diarrhea, and allergies. Breast milk is more easily digested than cow's milk or formula, and it is sterile, warm, and convenient for the mother to dispense. There is even some evidence that breast milk may enhance cognitive growth, leading to high adult intelligence (American Academy of Pediatrics, 2005; Ferguson & Molfese, 2007; Kramer et al., 2008; Tanaka et al., 2009).

Breastfeeding is not a cure-all for infant nutrition and health, and the millions of mothers who must use formula (either because they are physically unable to produce milk or because of social factors such as work schedules) should not be concerned that their children are suffering significant harm. (In fact, recent research suggests that infants fed enriched formula show better cognitive development than those using traditional formula.) But it does continue to be clear that the popular slogan used by groups advocating the use of breastfeeding is right on target: "Breast Is Best" (Austad et al., 2003; Rabin, 2006; Sloan, Stewart, & Dunne, 2010).

*"I forgot to say I was breast-fed."*

## Introducing Solid Foods: When and What?

Although pediatricians agree that breast milk is the ideal initial food, at some point infants require more nutriments than breast milk alone can provide. The American Academy of Pediatrics and the American Academy of Family Physicians suggest that babies can start solids at around 6 months, although they aren't needed until 9 to 12 months of age (American Academy of Family Physicians, 1997; American Academy of Pediatrics, 1997).

Solid foods are introduced into an infant's diet gradually, one at a time, in order to be able to be aware of preferences and allergies. Most often cereal comes first, followed by strained fruits. Vegetables and other foods typically are introduced next, although the order varies significantly from one infant to another.

The timing of *weaning*, the gradual cessation of breast- or bottle-feeding, varies greatly. In developed countries such as the United States, weaning frequently occurs as early as 3 or 4 months. On the other hand, some mothers continue breastfeeding for 2 or 3 years or beyond. The American Academy of Pediatrics recommends that infants be fed breast milk for the first 12 months (American Academy of Pediatrics, 1997; Sloan et al., 2008).

---

## REVIEW, CHECK, AND APPLY

### REVIEW

**LO4** What are the major reflexes?

- Reflexes are universal, genetically determined physical behaviors.

- Among the major reflexes are the rooting reflex, the Moro reflex, and the startle reflex.

**LO5** What developmental tasks must be accomplished during infancy?

- During infancy, children reach a series of milestones in their physical development on a fairly consistent schedule, with some individual and cultural variations.

- Gross motor skills include rolling over, sitting, and walking. Later, fine motor skills appear, such as grasping.

**LO6** What is the role of nutrition in physical development?

- Nutrition strongly affects physical development.

- Without proper nutrition infants cannot reach their physical potential, and may suffer cognitive and social consequences as well.

- Breastfeeding has numerous advantages.

### CHECK YOURSELF

1. _____ are unlearned, organized, involuntary responses that occur automatically in the presence of certain stimuli.

2. Which of the following is NOT one of the consequences of malnutrition during infancy?

   a. Malnourished children sleep, on average, 6 to 8 hours less than nonmalnourished children of the same age.

   b. Malnourished children show a slower growth rate by the age of 6 months.

   c. Malnourished children score lower on IQ tests later in life.

   d. Malnourished children have a lower height and weight by age 2 than nonmalnourished children.

3. Breastfeeding has been associated with enhanced cognitive growth.

   - True

   - False

### APPLYING LIFESPAN DEVELOPMENT

- What advice might you give a friend who is concerned that her infant is still not walking at 14 months, when every other baby she knows started walking by the first birthday?

✓•—Study and Review on
**MyDevelopmentLab.com**

Answers: 1) Reflexes; 2) a; 3) True

---

# The Development of the Senses

**LO7** What sensory capabilities do infants possess?

**LO8** How does multisensory perception function?

LEARNING OBJECTIVES

William James, one of the founding fathers of psychology, believed the world of the infant is a "blooming, buzzing confusion" (James, 1890/1950). Was he right?

In this case, James's wisdom failed him. The newborn's sensory world does lack the clarity and stability that we can distinguish as adults, but day by day the world grows increasingly

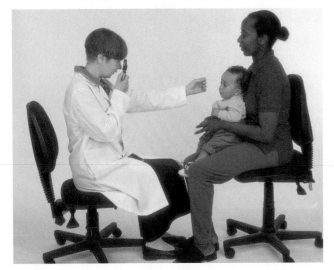

While an infant's distant vision is 10 to 30 times poorer than the average adult's, the vision of newborns provides the same degree of distance acuity as the uncorrected vision of many adults who wear eyeglasses or contact lenses.

**sensation** the physical stimulation of the sense organs

**perception** the sorting out, interpretation, analysis, and integration of stimuli involving the sense organs and brain

comprehensible as the infant's ability to sense and perceive the environment develops. In fact, babies appear to thrive in an environment enriched by pleasing sensations.

The processes that underlie infants' understanding of the world around them are sensation and perception. **Sensation** is the physical stimulation of the sense organs, and **perception** is the mental process of sorting out, interpreting, analyzing, and integrating stimuli from the sense organs and brain.

The study of infants' capabilities in the realm of sensation and perception challenges the ingenuity of investigators. As we'll see, researchers have developed a number of procedures for understanding sensation and perception in different realms.

## Visual Perception: Seeing the World

From the time of Lee Eng's birth, everyone who met him felt that he gazed at them intently. His eyes seemed to meet those of visitors. They seemed to bore deeply and knowingly into the faces of people who looked at him.

How good, in fact, was Lee's vision, and what, precisely, could he make out of his environment? Quite a bit, at least up close. According to some estimates, a newborn's distance vision ranges from 20/200 to 20/600, which means that an infant can only see with accuracy visual material up to 20 feet that an adult with normal vision is able to see with similar accuracy from a distance of between 200 and 600 feet (Haith, 1991).

These figures indicate that infants' distance vision is one-tenth to one-third that of the average adult's. This isn't so bad, actually: The vision of newborns provides the same degree of distance acuity as the uncorrected vision of many adults who wear eyeglasses or contact lenses. Furthermore, infants' distance vision grows increasingly acute. By 6 months of age, the average infant's vision is already 20/20—in other words, identical to that of adults (Aslin, 1987; Cavallini et al., 2002).

Depth perception is a particularly useful ability, helping babies acknowledge heights and avoid falls. In a classic study, developmental psychologists Eleanor Gibson and Richard Walk (1960) placed infants on a sheet of heavy glass. A checkered pattern appeared under one-half of the glass sheet, making it seem that the infant was on a stable floor. However, in the middle of the glass sheet, the pattern dropped down several feet, forming an apparent "visual cliff." The question Gibson and Walk asked was whether infants would willingly crawl across the cliff when called by their mothers (see Figure 3-8).

The results were clear: Most of the infants in the study, who ranged in age from 6 to 14 months, could not be coaxed over the apparent cliff. Clearly most of them had already developed the ability to perceive depth by that age (Campos, Langer, & Krowitz, 1970).

Infants also show clear visual preferences, preferences that are present from birth. Given a choice, infants reliably prefer to look at stimuli that include patterns than to look at simpler stimuli (see Figure 3-9). How do we know? Developmental psychologist Robert Fantz (1963) created a classic test. He built a chamber in which babies could lie on their backs and see pairs of visual stimuli above them. Fantz could determine which of the stimuli the infants were looking at by observing the reflections of the stimuli in their eyes.

Fantz's work was the impetus for a great deal of research on the preferences of infants, most of which points to a critical conclusion: Infants are genetically preprogrammed to prefer particular kinds of stimuli. For instance, just minutes after birth they show preferences for certain colors, shapes, and configurations of various stimuli. They prefer curved over straight lines, three-dimensional figures to two-dimensional ones, and human faces to nonfaces. Such capabilities may be a reflection of the existence of highly specialized cells in the brain that react to stimuli of a particular pattern, orientation, shape, and direction of movement (Hubel & Wiesel, 1979, 2004; Gliga et al., 2009; Soska, Adolph, & Johnson, 2010).

**FIGURE 3-8 Visual Cliff**
The "visual cliff" experiment examines the depth perception of infants. Most infants in the age range of 6 to 14 months cannot be coaxed to cross the cliff, apparently responding to the fact that the patterned area drops several feet.

However, genetics is not the sole determinant of infant visual preferences. Just a few hours after birth, infants have already learned to prefer their own mother's face to other faces. Similarly, between the ages of 6 and 9 months, infants become more adept at distinguishing between the faces of humans, while they become less able to distinguish faces of members of other species. They also distinguish between male and female faces. Such findings provide another clear piece of evidence of how heredity and environmental experiences are woven together to determine an infant's capabilities (Ramsey-Rennels & Langlois, 2006; Valenti, 2006; Quinn et al., 2008).

## Auditory Perception: The World of Sound

What is it about a mother's lullaby that helps soothe crying babies, like Alex, who we discussed in the chapter opener? Some clues emerge when we look at the capabilities of infants in the realm of auditory sensation and perception.

Infants hear from the time of birth—and even before, as the ability to hear begins prenatally. Even in the womb, the fetus responds to sounds outside of its mother. Furthermore, infants are born with preferences for particular sound combinations (Schellenberg & Trehub, 1996; Trehub, 2003).

Because they have had some practice in hearing before birth, it is not surprising that infants have reasonably good auditory perception after they are born. In fact, infants actually are more sensitive to certain very high and very low frequencies than adults—a sensitivity that seems to increase during the first two years of life. On the other hand, infants are initially less sensitive than adults to middle-range frequencies. Eventually, however, their capabilities within the middle range improve (Fenwick & Morongiello, 1991; Werner & Marean, 1996; Frenald, 2001).

In addition to the ability to detect sound, infants need several other abilities in order to hear effectively. For instance, *sound localization* permits us to pinpoint the direction from which a sound is emanating. Compared to adults, infants have a slight handicap in this task because effective sound localization requires the use of the slight difference in the times at which a sound reaches our two ears. Sound that we hear first in the right ear tells us that the source of the sound is to our right. Because infants' heads are smaller than those of adults, the difference in timing of the arrival of sound at the two ears is less than it is in adults, so they have difficulty determining from which direction sound is coming.

Despite the potential limitation brought about by their smaller heads, infants' sound localization abilities are actually fairly good even at birth, and they reach adult levels of success by the age of 1 year. Furthermore, young infants are capable of making the fine discriminations that their future understanding of language will require (Bijeljac-Babic, Bertoncini, & Mehler, 1993; Fenwick, Kimberley, & Morrongiello, 1998; van Heugten, & Johnson, 2010).

## Smell and Taste

What do infants do when they smell a rotten egg? Pretty much what adults do—crinkle their noses and generally look unhappy. On the other hand, the scents of bananas and butter produce a pleasant reaction on the part of infants (Steiner, 1979; Pomares, Schirrer, & Abadie, 2002).

The sense of smell is so well developed, even among very young infants, that at least some 12- to 18-day-old babies can distinguish their mothers on the basis of smell alone. For instance, in one experiment infants were exposed to the smell of gauze pads worn under the arms of adults the previous evening. Infants who were being breastfed were able to distinguish their mothers' scent from those of other adults. However, not all infants could do this: Those who were being bottle-fed were unable to make the distinction. Moreover, both breastfed and bottle-fed infants were unable to distinguish their fathers on the basis of odor (Porter, Bologh, & Malkin, 1988; Mizuno & Ueda, 2004; Allam, Marlier, & Schaal, 2006).

Infants seem to have an innate sweet tooth (even before they have teeth!), and they show facial expressions of disgust when they taste something bitter. Very young infants smile when a sweet-tasting liquid is placed on their tongues. They also suck harder at a bottle if it is sweetened. Since breast milk has a sweet taste, it is possible that this preference may be part of our evolutionary heritage, retained because it offered a survival advantage (Porges, Lipsitt, & Lewis, 1993; Liem & Mennella, 2002; Silveira et al., 2007).

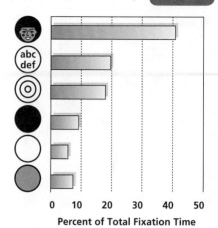

**Percent of Total Fixation Time**

FIGURE 3-9 **Preferring Complexity**
In a classic experiment, researcher Robert Fantz found that 2- and 3-month-old infants preferred to look at more complex stimuli than simple ones.
Source: Adapted from Fantz, 1961.

Infants' sense of smell is so well developed they can distinguish their mothers on the basis of smell alone.

By the age of 4 months infants are able to discriminate their own names from other, similar sounding words. What are some ways an infant is able to discriminate his or her name from other words?

## Sensitivity to Pain and Touch

Infants are born with the capacity to experience pain. Obviously, no one can be sure if the experience of pain in children is identical to that in adults, any more than we can tell if an adult friend who complains of a headache is experiencing pain that is more or less severe than our own pain when we have a headache.

What we do know is that pain produces distress in infants. Their heartbeat increases, they sweat, show facial expressions of discomfort, and change the intensity and tone of crying when they are hurt (Simons et al., 2003; Warnock & Sandrin, 2004; Kohut & Riddell, 2009).

There appears to be a developmental progression in reactions to pain. For example, a newborn infant who has her heel pricked for a blood test responds with distress, but it takes her several seconds to show the response. In contrast, only a few months later, the same procedure brings a much more immediate response. It is possible that the delayed reaction in infants is produced by the relatively slower transmission of information within the newborn's less-developed nervous system (Anand & Hickey, 1992; Axia, Bonichini, & Benini, 1995; Puchalsi & Hummel, 2002).

***Responding to Touch.*** Touch is one of the most highly developed sensory systems in a newborn. It is also one of the first to develop; there is evidence that by 32 weeks after conception, the entire body is sensitive to touch. Furthermore, several of the basic reflexes present at birth, such as the rooting reflex, require touch sensitivity to operate: An infant must sense a touch near the mouth in order to seek automatically a nipple to suck (Haith, 1986).

Infants' abilities in the realm of touch are particularly helpful in their efforts to explore the world. Several theorists have suggested that one of the ways children gain information about the world is through touching. As mentioned earlier, at the age of 6 months, infants are apt to place almost any object in their mouths, apparently taking in data about its configuration from their sensory responses to the feel of it in their mouths (Ruff, 1989).

Touch also plays an important role in an organism's future development, for it triggers a complex chemical reaction that assists infants in their efforts to survive. For example, gentle massage stimulates the production of certain chemicals in an infant's brain that instigate growth (Field, Hernandez-Reif, & Diego, 2006; Diego, Field, & Hernandez-Reif, 2008, 2009).

## Multimodal Perception: Combining Individual Sensory Inputs

*When Eric Pettigrew was 7 months old, his grandparents presented him with a squeaky rubber doll. As soon as he saw it, he reached out for it, grasped it in his hand, and listened as it squeaked. He seemed delighted with the gift.*

One way of considering Eric's sensory reaction to the doll is to focus on each of the senses individually: what the doll looked like to Eric, how it felt in his hand, and what it sounded like. In fact, this approach has dominated the study of sensation and perception in infancy.

However, let's consider another approach: We might examine how the various sensory responses are integrated with one another. Instead of looking at each individual sensory response, we could consider how the responses work together and are combined to produce Eric's ultimate reaction. The **multimodal approach to perception** considers how information that is collected by various individual sensory systems is integrated and coordinated (Farzin, Charles, & Rivera, 2009).

 **From a health care worker's perspective:** Persons who are born without the use of one sense often develop unusual abilities in one or more other senses. What can health care professionals do to help infants who are lacking in a particular sense?

Although the multimodal approach is a relatively recent innovation in the study of how infants understand their sensory world, it raises some fundamental issues about the development of sensation and perception. For instance, some researchers argue that sensations are initially integrated with one another in the infant, while others maintain that the infant's sensory systems are initially separate and that brain development leads to increasing integration (Lickliter & Bahrick, 2000; Lewkowicz, 2002; Flom & Bahrick, 2007).

We do not know yet which view is correct. However, it does appear that by an early age infants are able to relate what they have learned about an object through one sensory channel to

**multimodal approach to perception** the approach that considers how information that is collected by various individual sensory systems is integrated and coordinated

**affordances** the action possibilities that a given situation or stimulus provides

# Exercising Your Infant's Body and Senses

## Becoming an Informed Consumer of Development

Recall how cultural expectations and environments affect the age at which various physical milestones, such as the first step, occur. While most experts feel attempts to accelerate physical and sensory-perceptual development yield little advantage, parents should ensure that their infants receive sufficient physical and sensory stimulation. There are several specific ways to accomplish this goal:

- Carry a baby in different positions—in a backpack, in a frontpack, or in a football hold with the infant's head in the palm of your hand and its feet lying on your arm. This lets the infant view the world from several perspectives.

- Let infants explore their environment. Don't contain them too long in a barren environment. Let them crawl or wander around—after

first making the environment "childproof" by removing dangerous objects.

- Engage in "rough-and-tumble" play. Wrestling, dancing, and rolling around on the floor—if not violent—are activities that are fun and that stimulate older infants' motor and sensory systems.

- Let babies touch their food and even play with it. Infancy is too early to start teaching table manners.

- Provide toys that stimulate the senses, particularly toys that can stimulate more than one sense at a time. For example, brightly colored, textured toys with movable parts are enjoyable and help sharpen infants' senses.

what they have learned about it through another. For instance, even 1-month-old infants are able to recognize by sight objects that they have previously held in their mouths but never seen (Meltzoff, 1981; Steri & Spelke, 1988). Clearly, some cross-talk between various sensory channels is already possible a month after birth.

Infants' abilities in multimodal perception showcase the sophisticated perceptual abilities of infants, which continue to grow throughout the period of infancy. Such perceptual growth is aided by infants' discovery of **affordances,** the options that a given situation or stimulus provides. For example, infants learn that they might potentially fall when walking down a steep ramp—that is, the ramp *affords* the possibility of falling. Such knowledge is crucial as infants make the transition from crawling to walking. Similarly, infants learn that an object shaped in a certain way can slip out of their hands if not grasped correctly. For example, Eric is learning that his toy has several affordances: He can grab it and squeeze it, listen to it squeak, and even chew comfortably on it if he is teething (Flom & Bahrick, 2007; Wilcox et al., 2007).

The senses of sight and touch are integrated by infants through multimodal perception.

---

### REVIEW

**LO7**  What sensory capabilities do infants possess?

- Infants' sensory abilities are surprisingly well developed at or shortly after birth. Their perceptions help them explore and begin to make sense of the world.

- Very early on, infants can see depth and motion, distinguish colors and patterns, localize and discriminate sounds, and recognize the sound and smell of their mothers.

- Infants are sensitive to pain and touch, and most medical authorities now advocate for procedures, including anesthesia, that minimize infants' pain.

**LO8**  How does multisensory perception function?

- The multimodal approach to perception considers how information that is collected by individual sensory systems is integrated and coordinated.

### CHECK YOURSELF

**1.** _____ is the physical stimulation of the sense organs, and _____ is the mental process of interpreting and integrating stimuli from the brain.

**2.** We know that infants experience pain because their heartbeat increases, they sweat, they show discomfort, and their crying changes tone.

- True
- False

**3.** The _____ considers how information that is collected by various individual sensory systems is integrated and coordinated.

  a. multimodal approach to perception

  b. affordance theory

  c. multidisciplinary motor development cycle

  d. macrosystem

### APPLYING LIFESPAN DEVELOPMENT

- If you were selecting a mobile as a gift for a young infant, what features would you look for to make the mobile as interesting as possible to the baby?

✓•—**Study** and **Review** on **MyDevelopmentLab.com**

# MODULE 3.2 Cognitive Development in Infancy

## Prologue: Get Smart TV?

*In important ways, Anika Schwartz, who is 2 years old, and her 11-month-old brother, Tim, are like most kids. Anika usually spends a couple of hours watching TV, while Tim watches for an hour—close to the national average for children their age. And what are they watching most of the time? BabyFirstTV, an entire network devoted to children aged 6 months to 3 years old.*

*Tanya Schwartz could not be more pleased with her children's preference. The network features programs such as "Numbers Time" and "Shapes & Sizes" that teach the basics of numbers and language through colorful characters and animation that children respond to. Tanya believes it's never too early to start learning. Not only do her kids love watching, but she can do chores around the house, knowing that they're getting a head start on math and reading.*

## Looking Ahead

Can infants really become miniature Einsteins by watching educational media? What concepts are babies as young as 10-month-old Tim Schwartz actually grasping, and what intellectual abilities remain undeveloped at that age? Can an infant's cognitive development really be accelerated through intellectual stimulation, or does the process unfold on its own timetable despite the best efforts of parents to hasten it?

We address these questions in this module as we consider cognitive development during the first years of life, focusing on how infants develop their knowledge and understanding of the world. We first discuss the work of Swiss psychologist Jean Piaget, whose theory of developmental stages served as a highly influential impetus for a considerable amount of work on cognitive development.

We then cover more contemporary views of cognitive development, examining information processing approaches that seek to explain how cognitive growth occurs. We also examine memory in infants and address individual differences in intelligence.

Finally, we consider language, the cognitive skill that permits infants to communicate with others. We look at the roots of language in prelinguistic speech and trace the milestones indicating the development of language skills in the progression from the baby's first words to phrases and sentences.

## Piaget's Approach to Cognitive Development

**LEARNING OBJECTIVES**

**LO9** What are the fundamental features of Piaget's theories of cognitive development?

**LO10** How has Piaget's theory been supported and challenged?

*Olivia's dad is wiping up the mess around the base of her high chair—for the third time today! It seems to him that 14-month-old Olivia takes great delight in dropping food from the high chair. She also drops toys, spoons, anything it seems, just to watch how it hits the floor. She almost appears to be experimenting to see what kind of noise or what size of splatter is created by each different thing she drops.*

Swiss psychologist Jean Piaget (1896–1980) probably would have said that Olivia's dad is right in theorizing that Olivia is conducting her own series of experiments to learn more about the workings of her world. Piaget's views of the ways infants learn could be summed in a simple equation: *Action = Knowledge.*

Piaget argued that infants do not acquire knowledge from facts communicated by others, nor through sensation and perception. Instead, Piaget suggested that knowledge is the product of direct motor behavior. Although many of his basic explanations and propositions have been challenged by subsequent research, as we'll discuss later, the view that in significant ways infants learn by doing remains unquestioned (Piaget, 1952, 1962, 1983; Bullinger, 1997).

## Key Elements of Piaget's Theory

As we first noted in Module 1.1, Piaget's theory is based on a stage approach to development. He assumed that all children pass through a series of four universal stages in a fixed order from birth through adolescence: sensorimotor, preoperational, concrete operational, and formal operational. He also suggested that movement from one stage to the next occurs when a child reaches an appropriate level of physical maturation *and* is exposed to relevant experiences. Without such experience, children are assumed to be incapable of reaching their cognitive potential. Some approaches to cognition focus on changes in the *content* of children's knowledge about the world, but Piaget argued that it was critical to also consider the changes in the *quality* of children's knowledge and understanding as they move from one stage to another.

Swiss psychologist Jean Piaget.

For instance, as they develop cognitively, infants experience changes in their understanding about what can and cannot occur in the world. Consider a baby who participates in an experiment during which she is exposed to three identical versions of her mother all at the same time, thanks to some well-placed mirrors. A 3-month-old infant will interact happily with each of these images of mother. However, by 5 months of age, the child becomes quite agitated at the sight of multiple mothers. Apparently by this time the child has figured out that she has but one mother, and viewing three at a time is thoroughly alarming (Bower, 1977). To Piaget, such reactions indicate that a baby is beginning to master principles regarding the way the world operates, indicating that she has begun to construct a mental sense of the world that she didn't have two months earlier.

Piaget believed that the basic building blocks of the way we understand the world are mental structures called **schemes,** *organized patterns of functioning, that adapt and change with mental development*. At first, schemes are related to physical, or sensorimotor, activity, such as picking up or reaching for toys. As children develop, their schemes move to a mental level, reflecting thought. Schemes are similar to computer software: They direct and determine how data from the world, such as new events or objects, are considered and dealt with (Achenbach, 1992; Rakison & Oakes, 2003).

If you give a baby a new cloth book, for example, he or she will touch it, mouth it, perhaps try to tear it or bang it on the floor. To Piaget, each of these actions represents a scheme, and they are the infant's way of gaining knowledge and understanding of this new object.

Piaget suggested that two principles underlie the growth in children's schemes: assimilation and accommodation. **Assimilation** *is the process by which people understand an experience in terms of their current stage of cognitive development and way of thinking*. Assimilation occurs, then, when a stimulus or event is acted upon, perceived, and understood in accordance with existing patterns of thought. For example, an infant who tries to suck on any toy in the same way is assimilating the objects to her existing sucking scheme. Similarly, a child who encounters a flying squirrel at a zoo and calls it a "bird" is assimilating the squirrel to his existing scheme of bird.

In contrast, when we change our existing ways of thinking, understanding, or behaving in response to encounters with new stimuli or events, **accommodation** takes place. For instance, when a child sees a flying squirrel and calls it "a bird with a tail," he is beginning to *accommodate* new knowledge, modifying his scheme of bird.

Piaget believed that the earliest schemes are primarily limited to the reflexes with which we are all born, such as sucking and rooting. Infants start to modify these simple early schemes almost immediately, through the processes of assimilation and accommodation, in response to their exploration of the environment. Schemes quickly become more sophisticated as infants become more advanced in their motor capabilities—to Piaget, a signal of the

**scheme** an organized patterns of functioning that adapt and change with mental functioning

**assimilation** the process in which people understand an experience in terms of their current stage of cognitive development and way of thinking

**accommodation** changes in existing ways of thinking that occur in response to encounters with new stimuli or events

potential for more advanced cognitive development. Because Piaget's sensorimotor stage of development begins at birth and continues until the child is about 2 years old, we consider it here in detail.

## The Sensorimotor Period: The Earliest Stage of Cognitive Growth

Piaget suggests that the **sensorimotor stage,** the initial major stage of cognitive development, can be broken down into six substages. These are summarized in Table 3-5. It is important to keep in mind that although the specific substages of the sensorimotor period may at first appear to unfold with great regularity, as though infants reach a particular age and smoothly proceed into the next substage, the reality of cognitive development is somewhat different. First, the ages at which infants actually reach a particular stage vary a good deal among different children. The exact timing of a stage reflects an interaction between the infant's level of physical maturation and the nature of the social environment in which the child is being raised. Consequently, although Piaget contended that the order of the substages does not change from one child to the next, he admitted that the timing can and does vary to some degree.

Piaget viewed development as a more gradual process than the notion of different stages might seem to imply. Infants do not go to sleep one night in one substage and wake up the next morning in the next one. Instead, there is a rather steady shifting of behavior as a child moves toward the next stage of cognitive development. Infants also pass through periods of transition, in which some aspects of their behavior reflect the next higher stage, while other aspects indicate their current stage (see Figure 3-10).

**sensorimotor stage** (of cognitive development) Piaget's initial major stage of cognitive development, which can be broken down into six substages

### TABLE 3-5  PIAGET'S SIX SUBSTAGES OF THE SENSORIMOTOR STAGE

| Substage | Age | Description | Example |
|---|---|---|---|
| Substage 1: Simple reflexes | First month of life | During this period, the various reflexes that determine the infant's interactions with the world are at the center of its cognitive life. | The sucking reflex causes the infant to suck at anything placed in his lips. |
| Substage 2: First habits and primary circular reactions | From 1 to 4 months | At this age infants begin to coordinate what were separate actions into single, integrated activities. | An infant might combine grasping an object with sucking on it, or staring at something with touching it. |
| Substage 3: Secondary circular reactions | From 4 to 8 months | During this period, infants take major strides in shifting their cognitive horizons beyond themselves and begin to act on the outside world. | A child who repeatedly picks up a rattle in her crib and shakes it in different ways to see how the sound changes is demonstrating her ability to modify her cognitive scheme about shaking rattles. |
| Substage 4: Coordination of secondary circular reactions | From 8 to 12 months | In this stage infants begin to use more calculated approaches to producing events, coordinating several schemes to generate a single act. They achieve object permanence during this stage. | An infant will push one toy out of the way to reach another toy that is lying, partially exposed, under it. |
| Substage 5: Tertiary circular reactions | From 12 to 18 months | At this age infants develop what Piaget regards as the deliberate variation of actions that bring desirable consequences. Rather than just repeating enjoyable activities, infants appear to carry out miniature experiments to observe the consequences. | A child will drop a toy repeatedly, varying the position from which he drops it, carefully observing each time to see where it falls. |
| Substage 6: Beginnings of thought | From 18 months to 2 years | The major achievement of Substage 6 is the capacity for mental representation or symbolic thought. Piaget argued that only at this stage can infants imagine where objects that they cannot see might be. | Children can even plot in their heads unseen trajectories of objects, so that if a ball rolls under a piece of furniture, they can figure out where it is likely to emerge on the other side. |

**Substage 1: Simple Reflexes.** The first substage of the sensorimotor period is *Substage 1: Simple reflexes,* encompassing the first month of life. During this time, the various inborn reflexes, described in Module 3.1, are at the center of a baby's physical and cognitive life, determining the nature of his or her interactions with the world. At the same time, some of the reflexes begin to accommodate the infant's experience with the nature of the world. For instance, an infant who is being breastfed but who also receives supplemental bottles may start to change the way he or she sucks, depending on whether a nipple is on a breast or a bottle.

**Substage 2: First Habits and Primary Circular Reactions.** *Substage 2: First habits and primary circular reactions,* the second substage of the sensorimotor period, occurs from 1 to 4 months of age. In this period, infants begin to coordinate what were separate actions into single, integrated activities. For instance, an infant might combine grasping an object with sucking on it, or staring at something while touching it.

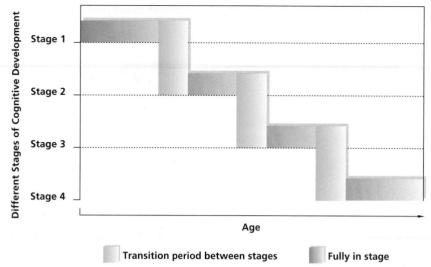

**FIGURE 3-10  Transitions**

Infants do not suddenly shift from one stage of cognitive development to the next. Instead, Piaget argues that there is a period of transition in which some behavior reflects one stage, while other behavior reflects the more advanced stage. Does this gradualism argue against Piaget's interpretation of stages?

If an activity engages a baby's interests, he or she may repeat it over and over, simply for the sake of continuing to experience it. This repetition of a chance motor event helps the baby start building cognitive schemes through a process known as a *circular reaction. Primary circular reactions* are schemes reflecting an infant's repetition of interesting or enjoyable actions, just for the enjoyment of doing them, which focus on the infant's own body.

**Substage 3: Secondary Circular Reactions.** *Substage 3: Secondary circular reactions* are more purposeful. According to Piaget, this third stage of cognitive development in infancy occurs from 4 to 8 months of age. During this period, a child begins to act upon the outside world. For instance, infants now seek to repeat enjoyable events in their environments if they happen to produce them through chance activities. A child who repeatedly picks up a rattle in her crib and shakes it in different ways to see how the sound changes is demonstrating her ability to modify her cognitive scheme about shaking rattles. She is engaging in what Piaget calls *secondary circular reactions,* which are schemes regarding repeated actions that bring about a desirable consequence.

**Substage 4: Coordination of Secondary Circular Reactions.** Some major leaps forward occur in *Substage 4: Coordination of secondary circular reactions,* which lasts from around 8 months to 12 months. In Substage 4, infants begin to employ *goal-directed behavior,* in which several schemes are combined and coordinated to generate a single act to solve a problem. For instance, they will push one toy out of the way to reach another toy that is lying, partially exposed, under it.

Infants' newfound purposefulness, their ability to use means to attain particular ends, and their skill in anticipating future circumstances owe their appearance in part to the developmental achievement of object permanence that emerges in Substage 4. **Object permanence** is the realization that people and objects exist even when they cannot be seen. It is a simple principle, but its mastery has profound consequences. **⊙⊢**Watch on **mydevelopmentlab.com**

Consider, for instance, 7-month-old Chu, who has yet to learn the idea of object permanence. Chu's mother shakes a rattle in front of him, then takes the rattle and places it under a blanket. To Chu, who has not mastered the concept of object permanence, the rattle no longer exists. He will make no effort to look for it.

Several months later, when he reaches Substage 4, the story is quite different (see Figure 3-11). This time, as soon as his mother places the rattle under the blanket, Chu tries to toss the cover aside, eagerly searching for the rattle. Chu clearly has learned that the object continues to exist even when it cannot be seen. For the infant who achieves an understanding of object permanence, then, out of sight is decidedly not out of mind.

**⊙⊢**Watch on **mydevelopmentlab.com**

To see a video of an infant demonstrating the principle of object permanence that you've been reading about, log onto MyDevelopmentLab.com.

**object permanence** the realization that people and objects exist even when they cannot be seen

**Before Object Permanence**

**After Object Permanence**

FIGURE 3-11 **Object Permanence**
Before an infant has understood the idea of object permanence, he will not search for an object that has been hidden right before his eyes. But several months later, he will search for it, illustrating that he has attained object permanence. Why is the concept of object permanence important?

The attainment of object permanence extends not only to inanimate objects, but to people, too. It gives Chu the security that his father and mother still exist even when they have left the room.

***Substage 5: Tertiary Circular Reactions.*** *Substage 5: Tertiary circular reactions* is reached at around the age of 12 months and extends to 18 months. As the name of the stage indicates, during this period infants develop these reactions, which are schemes regarding the deliberate variation of actions that bring desirable consequences. Rather than just repeating enjoyable activities, as they do with secondary circular reactions, infants appear to carry out miniature experiments to observe the consequences.

For example, Piaget observed his son Laurent dropping a toy swan repeatedly, varying the position from which he dropped it, carefully observing each time to see where it fell. Instead of just repeating the action each time, Laurent made modifications in the situation to learn about their consequences. As you may recall from our discussion of research methods in Module 1.1, this behavior represents the essence of the scientific method: An experimenter varies a situation in a laboratory to learn the effects of the variation. To infants in Substage 5, the world is their laboratory, and they spend their days leisurely carrying out one miniature experiment after another.

***Substage 6: Beginnings of Thought.*** The final stage of the sensorimotor period is *Substage 6: Beginnings of thought,* which lasts from around 18 months to 2 years. The major achievement of Substage 6 is the capacity for mental representation, or symbolic thought. A *mental representation* is an internal image of a past event or object. Piaget argued that by this stage infants can imagine where objects might be that they cannot see. They can even plot in their heads unseen trajectories of objects, so if a ball rolls under a piece of furniture, they can figure out where it is likely to emerge on the other side.

**From a caregiver's perspective:** What are some implications for childrearing practices of Piaget's observations about the ways children gain an understanding of the world? Would you use the same approaches in childrearing for a child growing up in a non-Western culture?

## Appraising Piaget: Support and Challenges

Most developmental researchers would probably agree that in many significant ways, Piaget's descriptions of how cognitive development proceeds during infancy are quite accurate (Harris, 1987; Marcovitch, Zelazo, & Schmuckler, 2003). Yet, there is substantial disagreement over the validity of the theory and many of its specific predictions.

Let's start with what is clearly accurate about the Piagetian approach. Piaget was a masterful reporter of children's behavior, and his descriptions of growth during infancy remain a monument to his powers of observation. Furthermore, literally thousands of studies have supported Piaget's view that children learn much about the world by acting on objects in their environment. Finally, the broad outlines sketched out by Piaget of the sequence of cognitive development and the increasing cognitive accomplishments that occur during infancy are generally accurate (Gratch & Schatz, 1987; Kail, 2004).

On the other hand, specific aspects of the theory have come under increasing scrutiny—and criticism—in the decades since Piaget carried out his pioneering work. For example, some researchers question the stage conception that forms the basis of Piaget's theory. Although, as we noted earlier, even Piaget acknowledged that children's transitions between stages are gradual, critics contend that development proceeds in a much more continuous fashion. Rather than showing major leaps of competence at the end of one stage and the beginning of the next, improvement comes in more gradual increments, growing step by step in a skill-by-skill manner.

For instance, developmental researcher Robert Siegler suggests that cognitive development proceeds not in stages but in "waves." According to Siegler, children don't one day drop a mode of thinking and the next take up a new form. Instead, there is an ebb and flow of cognitive approaches that children use to understand the world (Siegler, 2003, 2007; Opfer & Siegler, 2007; Siegler, & Lin, 2010).

Other critics dispute Piaget's notion that cognitive development is grounded in motor activities. They charge that Piaget overlooked the importance of the sensory and perceptual systems that are present from a very early age in infancy—systems about which Piaget knew little, since so much of the research illustrating how sophisticated they are even in infancy was done relatively recently (Decarrie, 1969; Butterworth, 1994).

With the attainment of the cognitive skill of deferred imitation, children are able to imitate people and scenes they have witnessed in the past.

To bolster their views, Piaget's critics also point to more recent studies that cast doubt on Piaget's view that infants are incapable of mastering the concept of object permanence until they are close to a year old. For instance, some work suggests that younger infants did not appear to understand object permanence because the techniques used to test their abilities were not sensitive enough to their true capabilities (Krojgaard, 2005; Walden et al., 2007; Baillargeon, 2004, 2008).

It may be that a 4-month-old doesn't search for a rattle hidden under a blanket because she hasn't learned the motor skills necessary to do the searching—not because she doesn't understand that the rattle still exists. Similarly, the apparent inability of young infants to comprehend object permanence may reflect more about their memory deficits than their lack of understanding of the concept: The memories of young infants may be poor enough that they simply do not recall the earlier concealment of the toy. In fact, when more age-appropriate tasks are employed, some researchers have found indications of object permanence in children as young as 3 1/2 months (Wang, Baillargeon, & Paterson, 2005; Ruffman, Slade, & Redman, 2006; Luo, Kaufman, & Baillargeon, 2009).

Piaget's work also seems to describe children from developed, Western countries better than those in non-Western cultures. For instance, some evidence suggests that cognitive skills emerge on a different timetable for children in non-Western cultures than for children living in Europe and the United States. Infants raised in the Ivory Coast of Africa, for example, reach the various substages of the sensorimotor period at an earlier age than infants reared in France (Dasen et al., 1978; Rogoff & Chavajay, 1995; Mistry & Saraswathi, 2003).

Appraising Piaget: Research on babies in non-Western cultures suggests that Piaget's stages are not universal, but are to some degree culturally derived.

However, even Piaget's most passionate critics concede that he has provided us with a masterful description of the broad outlines of cognitive development during infancy. His failings seem to be in underestimating the capabilities of younger infants and in his claims that sensorimotor skills develop in a consistent, fixed pattern. Still, his influence has been enormous and, although the focus of many contemporary developmental researchers has shifted to newer information processing approaches that we discuss next, Piaget remains a towering and pioneering figure in the field of development (Fischer & Hencke, 1996; Roth, Slone, & Dar, 2000; Kail, 2004; Maynard, 2008).

## REVIEW, CHECK, AND APPLY

### REVIEW

**LO9** What are the fundamental features of Piaget's theories of cognitive development?

- Piaget's theory of human cognitive development involves a succession of stages through which children progress from birth to adolescence.
- As infants move from one stage to another, the way they understand the world changes.
- The sensorimotor stage has six substages. The sensorimotor stage, from birth to about 2 years, involves a gradual progression through simple reflexes, single coordinated activities, interest in the outside world, purposeful combinations of activities, manipulation of actions to produce desired outcomes, and symbolic thought.

**LO10** How has Piaget's theory been supported and challenged?

- Although Piaget's theory accurately describes cognitive development in a broad sense, many specifics of the theory, particularly the age at which various skills develop, has been challenged.

### CHECK YOURSELF

1. According to Piaget, children can move from one cognitive stage to another only when a child _____ and is exposed to relative experiences.
   a. is adequately nourished
   b. is born with an adequate genetic predisposition for learning
   c. has remembered his or her goal of learning
   d. reaches an appropriate level of physical maturation

2. Infants' schemes for understanding the world usually involve their physical or sensorimotor activities.
   - True
   - False

3. In general, when it comes to infant cognitive development, it appears that Piaget:
   a. overestimated infants and what they could do.
   b. underestimated infants and what they could do.
   c. was more accurate about adolescent cognitive development.
   d. overestimated the role of culture.

### APPLYING LIFESPAN DEVELOPMENT

- Think of a common young children's toy with which you are familiar. How might its use be affected by the principles of assimilation and accommodation?

✔ **Study** and **Review** on **MyDevelopmentLab.com**

Answers: 1) d; 2) True; 3) b

# Information Processing Approaches to Cognitive Development

**LEARNING OBJECTIVES**

**LO11** How do infants process information?
**LO12** How is infant intelligence measured?

*Amber Nordstrom, 3 months old, breaks into a smile as her brother Marcus stands over her crib, picks up a doll, and makes a whistling noise through his teeth. In fact, Amber never seems to tire of Marcus's efforts at making her smile and, soon, whenever Marcus appears and simply picks up the doll, her lips begin to curl into a smile.*

Clearly, Amber remembers Marcus and his humorous ways. But how does she remember him? And how much else can Amber remember?

To answer questions such as these, we need to diverge from the road that Piaget laid out for us. Rather than seeking to identify the universal, broad milestones in cognitive development through which all infants pass, as Piaget tried to do, we must consider the specific processes by which individual babies acquire and use the information to which they are exposed. We need, then, to focus less on the qualitative changes in infants' mental lives and consider more closely their quantitative capabilities.

**Information processing approaches** to cognitive development seek to identify the way that individuals take in, use, and store information. According to this approach, the quantitative changes in infants' abilities to organize and manipulate information represent the hallmarks of cognitive development.

Taking this perspective, cognitive growth is characterized by increasing sophistication, speed, and capacity in information processing. Earlier, we compared Piaget's idea of schemes to computer software, which directs the computer in how to deal with data from the world. We might compare the information processing perspective on cognitive growth to the improvements that come from the use of more efficient programs that lead to increased speed and sophistication in the processing of information. Information processing approaches, then, focus on the types of "mental programs" that people use when they seek to solve problems (Siegler, 1998; Cohen & Cashon, 2003; Hugdahl & Westerhausen, 2010).

## Encoding, Storage, and Retrieval: The Foundations of Information Processing

Information processing has three basic aspects: encoding, storage, and retrieval (see Figure 3-12). *Encoding* is the process by which information is initially recorded in a form usable to memory. Infants and children—indeed, all people—are exposed to a massive amount of information; if they tried to process it all, they would be overwhelmed. Consequently, they encode selectively, picking and choosing the information to which they will pay attention.

Even if someone has been exposed to the information initially and has encoded it in an appropriate way, there is still no guarantee that he or she will be able to use it in the future. Information must also have been stored in memory adequately. *Storage* refers to the placement of material into memory. Finally, success in using the material in the future depends on retrieval processes. *Retrieval* is the process by which material in memory storage is located, brought into awareness, and used.

We can use our comparison to computers again here. Information processing approaches suggest that the processes of encoding, storage, and retrieval are analogous to different parts of a computer. Encoding can be thought of as a computer's keyboard, through which one inputs information; storage is the computer's hard drive, where information is stored; and retrieval is analogous to software that accesses the information for display on the screen. Only when all three processes are operating—encoding, storage, and retrieval—can information be processed.

***Automatization.*** In some cases, encoding, storage, and retrieval are relatively automatic, while in other cases they are deliberate. *Automatization* is the degree to which an activity requires attention. Processes that require relatively little attention are automatic; processes that require relatively large amounts of attention are controlled. For example, some activities such as walking, eating with a fork, or reading may be automatic for you, but at first they required your full attention.

Automatic mental processes help children in their initial encounters with the world by enabling them to easily and "automatically" process information in particular ways. For instance, by the age of 5, children automatically encode information in terms of frequency. Without a lot of attention to counting or tallying, they become aware, for example, of how often they have encountered various people, permitting them to differentiate familiar from unfamiliar people (Hasher & Zacks, 1984).

Some of the things we learn automatically are unexpectedly complex. For example, infants have the ability to learn subtle statistical patterns and relationships. The existence of basic mathematical skills in infants has been supported by findings that nonhumans are born with some basic numeric proficiency. Even newly hatched chicks show some counting abilities (Rugani, 2009).

The result of this growing body of research suggests that infants have an innate grasp of certain basic mathematical functions and statistical patterns. This inborn proficiency is likely to form the basis for learning more complex mathematics and statistical relationships later in life (Gelman & Gallistel, 2004; McCrink & Wynn, 2004, 2007, 2009; van Marle & Wynn, 2006, 2009).

**FIGURE 3-12 Information Processing**
The process by which information is encoded, stored, and retrieved.

**memory** the process by which information is initially recorded, stored, and retrieved

**infantile amnesia** the lack of memory for experiences that occurred prior to 3 years of age

# Memory During Infancy: They Must Remember This . . .

*Simona Young spent her infancy with virtually no human contact. For up to 20 hours each day, she was left alone in a crib in a squalid Romanian orphanage. Cold bottles of milk were propped above her small body, which she clutched to get nourishment. She rocked back and forth, rarely feeling any soothing touch or hearing words of comfort. Alone in her bleak surroundings, she rocked back and forth for hours on end.*

*Simona's story, however, has a happy ending. After being adopted by a Canadian couple when she was 2, Simona's life is now filled with the usual activities of childhood involving friends, class-mates, and above all, a loving family. In fact, now, at age 6, she can remember almost nothing of her miserable life in the orphanage. It is as if she has entirely forgotten the past.* (Blakeslee, 1995, p. C1)

How likely is it that Simona truly remembers nothing of her infancy? And if she ever does recall her first two years of life, how accurate will her memories be? To answer these questions, we need to consider the qualities of memory that exist during infancy.

***Memory Capabilities in Infancy.*** Certainly, infants have **memory** capabilities, defined as the process by which information is initially recorded, stored, and retrieved. As we've seen, infants can distinguish new stimuli from old, and this implies that some memory of the old must be present. Unless the infants had some memory of an original stimulus, it would be impossible for them to recognize that a new stimulus differed from the earlier one.

Infants' capability to recognize new stimuli from old tells us little about how age brings about changes in the capacities of memory and in its fundamental nature. Do infants' memory capabilities increase as they get older? The answer is clearly affirmative. In one study, infants were taught that they could move a mobile hanging over the crib by kicking their legs. It took only a few days for 2-month-old infants to forget their training, but 6-month-old infants still remembered for as long as three weeks (Rovee-Collier, 1993, 1999; Haley et al., 2010).

Furthermore, infants who were later prompted to recall the association between kicking and moving the mobile showed evidence that the memory continued to exist even longer. Infants who had received just two training sessions lasting 9 minutes each still recalled about a week later, as illustrated by the fact that they began to kick when placed in the crib with the mobile. Two weeks later, however, they made no effort to kick, suggesting that they had forgotten entirely.

But they hadn't forgotten: When the babies saw a reminder—a moving mobile—their memories were apparently reactivated. In fact, the infants could remember the association, following prompting, for as long as an additional month. Other evidence confirms these re-sults, suggesting that hints can reactivate memories that at first seem lost, and that the older the infant, the more effective such prompting is (Sullivan, Rovee-Collier, & Tynes, 1979; Bearce & Rovee-Collier, 2006; DeFrancisco & Rovee-Collier, 2008).

***The Duration of Memories.*** Although the processes that underlie memory retention and recall seem similar throughout the life span, the quantity of information stored and recalled does differ markedly as infants develop. Older infants can retrieve information more rapidly and they can remember it longer. But just how long? Can memories from infancy be recalled, for example, after babies grow up?

Researchers disagree on the age from which memories can be retrieved. Although early research supported the notion of **infantile amnesia,** the lack of memory for experiences occur-ring prior to 3 years of age, more recent research shows that infants do retain memories. For example, 6-month-old children exposed to an unusual series of events, such as intermittent periods of light and dark and unusual sounds, have some memories of their participation in the earlier experience two years later (Howe, Courage, & Edison, 2004; Neisser, 2004).

Still, although it is at least theoretically possible for memories to remain intact from a very young age—if subsequent experiences do not interfere with their recollection—in most cases memories of personal experiences in infancy do not last into adulthood. Memories of personal experience seem not to become accurate before age 18 to 24 months (Howe, 2003; Howe, Courage, & Edison, 2004; Bauer, 2007).

***The Cognitive Neuroscience of Memory.*** Some of the most exciting research on the development of memory is coming from studies of the neurological basis of memory.

Advances in brain scan technology, as well as studies of adults with brain damage, suggest that there are two separate systems involved with long-term memory. These two systems, called explicit memory and implicit memory, retain different sorts of information.

*Explicit memory* is memory that is conscious and that can be recalled intentionally. When we try to recall a name or phone number, we're using explicit memory. In comparison, *implicit memory* consists of memories of which we are not consciously aware, but that affect performance and behavior. Implicit memory consists of motor skills, habits, and activities that can be remembered without conscious cognitive effort, such as how to ride a bike or climb a stairway.

Explicit and implicit memories emerge at different rates and involve different parts of the brain. The earliest memories seem to be implicit, and they involve the cerebellum and brain stem. The forerunner of explicit memory involves the hippocampus, but true explicit memory doesn't emerge until the second half of the first year. When explicit memory does emerge, it involves an increasing number of areas of the cortex of the brain (Bauer, 2004; Squire & Knowlton, 2005; Bauer, 2007).

## Individual Differences in Intelligence: Is One Infant Smarter than Another?

*Maddy Rodriguez is a bundle of curiosity and energy. At 6 months of age, she cries heartily if she can't reach a toy, and when she sees a reflection of herself in a mirror, she gurgles and seems, in general, to find the situation quite amusing.*

Jared Lynch, at 6 months, is a good deal more inhibited than Maddy. He doesn't seem to care much when a ball rolls out of his reach, losing interest in it rapidly. And, unlike Maddy, when he sees himself in a mirror, he pretty much ignores the reflection.

As anyone who has spent any time at all observing more than one baby can tell you, not all infants are alike. Some are full of energy and life, apparently displaying a natural-born curiosity, while others seem, by comparison, somewhat less interested in the world around them. Does this mean that such infants differ in intelligence?

Answering questions about how and to what degree infants vary in their underlying intelligence is not easy. Although it is clear that different infants show significant variations in their behavior, the issue of just what types of behavior may be related to cognitive ability is complicated. Interestingly, the examination of individual differences between infants was the initial approach taken by developmental specialists to understand cognitive development, and such issues still represent an important focus within the field.

***What Is Infant Intelligence?*** Developmental specialists have devised several approaches (summarized in Table 3-6) to illuminate the nature of individual differences in intelligence during infancy.

***Developmental Scales.*** Developmental psychologist Arnold Gesell formulated the earliest measure of infant development, which was designed to distinguish between normally developing and atypically developing babies (Gesell, 1946). Gesell based his scale on examinations of hundreds of babies. He compared their performance at different ages to learn what behaviors were most common at a particular age. If an infant varied significantly from the norms of a given age, he or she was considered to be developmentally delayed or advanced.

Following the lead of researchers who sought to quantify intelligence through a specific score (known as an intelligence quotient, or IQ, score), Gesell developed a developmental quotient, or DQ. The **developmental quotient** is an overall developmental score that relates to performance in four domains: motor skills (for example, balance and sitting), language use, adaptive behavior (such as alertness and exploration), and personal–social (for example, adequately feeding and dressing oneself).

Later researchers have created other developmental scales. For instance, Nancy Bayley developed one of the most widely used measures for infants. The **Bayley Scales of Infant Development** evaluate an infant's development from 2 to 42 months. The Bayley Scales focus on two areas: mental and motor

> **developmental quotient** an overall developmental score that relates to performance in four domains: motor skills, language use, adaptive behavior, and personal-social
>
> **Bayley Scales of Infant Development** a measure that evaluates an infant's development from 2 to 42 months

A developmental quotient provides a measure of infant intelligence.

## TABLE 3-6 APPROACHES USED TO DETECT DIFFERENCES IN INTELLIGENCE DURING INFANCY

| | |
|---|---|
| Developmental quotient | Formulated by Arnold Gesell, the developmental quotient is an overall development score that relates to performance in four domains: motor skills (balance and sitting), language use, adaptive behavior (alertness and exploration), and personal–social behavior. |
| Bayley Scales of Infant Development | Developed by Nancy Bayley, the Bayley Scales of Infant Development evaluate an infant's development from 2 to 42 months. The Bayley Scales focus on two areas: mental (senses, perception, memory, learning, problem solving, and language) and motor abilities (fine and gross motor skills). |
| Visual-recognition memory measurement | Measures of visual-recognition memory, the memory of and recognition of a stimulus that has been previously seen, also relate to intelligence. The more quickly an infant can retrieve a representation of a stimulus from memory, the more efficient, presumably, is that infant's information processing. |

abilities. The mental scale focuses on the senses, perception, memory, learning, problem solving, and language, while the motor scale evaluates fine and gross motor skills (see Table 3-7). Like Gesell's approach, the Bayley yields a developmental quotient (DQ). A child who scores at an average level—meaning average performance for other children at the same age—receives a score of 100 (Bayley, 1969; Black & Matula, 1999; Gagnon & Nagle, 2000; Lynn, 2009).

The virtue of approaches such as those taken by Gesell and Bayley is that they provide a good snapshot of an infant's current developmental level. Using these scales, we can tell in an objective manner whether a particular infant falls behind or is ahead of his or her same-age peers. They are particularly useful in identifying infants who are substantially behind their peers, and who therefore need immediate special attention (Culbertson & Gyurke, 1990; Aylward & Verhulst, 2000).

What such scales are *not* useful for is predicting a child's future course of development. A child whose development is identified by these measures as relatively slow at the age of 1 year will not necessarily display slow development at age 5, or 12, or 25. The association between most measures of behavior during infancy and adult intelligence, then, is minimal (Molese & Acheson, 1997; Murray et al., 2007).

## TABLE 3-7 SAMPLE ITEMS FROM THE BAYLEY SCALES OF INFANT DEVELOPMENT

| Age | Mental Scale | Motor Scale |
|---|---|---|
| 2 months | Turns head to sound<br>Reacts to disappearance of face | Holds head erect/steady for 15 seconds<br>Sits with support |
| 6 months | Lifts cup by handle<br>Looks at pictures in book | Sits alone for 30 seconds<br>Grasps foot with hands |
| 12 months | Builds tower of 2 cubes<br>Turns pages of book | Walks with help<br>Grasps pencil in middle |
| 17–19 months | Imitates crayon stroke<br>Identifies objects in photo | Stands alone on right foot<br>Walks up stairs with help |
| 23–25 months | Matches pictures<br>Imitates a 2-word sentence | Laces 3 beads<br>Jumps distance of 4 inches |
| 38–42 months | Names 4 colors<br>Uses past tense<br>Identifies gender | Copies circle<br>Hops twice on 1 foot<br>Walks down stairs, alternating feet |

**From a nurse's perspective:** In what ways is the use of such developmental scales as Gesell's or Bayley's helpful? In what ways is it dangerous? How would you maximize the helpfulness and minimize the danger if you were advising a parent?

*Information Processing Approaches to Individual Differences in Intelligence.* Contemporary approaches to infant intelligence suggest that the speed with which infants process information may correlate most strongly with later intelligence, as measured by IQ tests administered during adulthood (Rose & Feldman, 1997; Sigman, Cohen, & Beckwith, 1997).

How can we tell if a baby is processing information quickly or not? Most researchers use habituation tests. Infants who process information efficiently ought to be able to learn about stimuli more quickly. Consequently, we would expect that they would turn their attention away from a given stimulus more rapidly than those who are less efficient at information processing, leading to the phenomenon of habituation. Similarly, measures of *visual-recognition memory*, the memory and recognition of a stimulus that has been previously seen, also relate to IQ. The more quickly an infant can retrieve a representation of a stimulus from memory, the more efficient, presumably, is that infant's information processing (Rose, Jankowski, & Feldman, 2002; Robinson & Pascalis, 2005; Karmiloff-Smith et al., 2010).

## From Research to Practice

### Why Formal Education Is Lost on Infants

*Jetta is 11 months old, with big eyes, a few pearly teeth—and a tiny index finger that can already operate electronic entertainment devices.*

*"We own everything electronic that's educational—LeapFrog, Baby Einstein, everything," said her mother, Naira Soibatian. "She has an HP laptop, bigger than mine. I know one leading baby book says, very simply, it's a waste of money. But there's only one thing better than having a baby, and that's having a smart baby. And at the end of the day, what can it hurt? She learns things, and she loves them."* (Lewin, 2005, p. A1)

Naira Soibatian's philosophy captures the sentiments of many parents who believe that exposing infants to educational toys and media may be beneficial to their infants' cognitive growth. Parents who want to give their infant children a leg up on learning quickly find that there is no shortage of products and services that claim to do exactly that. Educational videos such as "Baby Einstein" and "Brainy Baby" promise to stimulate young minds. A wide variety of infant toys are marketed with claims that they can enhance cognitive development. And parents sometimes try implementing structured learning activities of their own design, such as flash cards, to make their babies smarter (Interlandi, 2007).

But do any of these strategies really work? The evidence suggests that they don't, and that in some cases their use may even backfire and impede learning. The problem stems from the faulty assumption that infants learn the way older children do—that they can benefit from structured activities that have specific learning goals. Research suggests that this approach is at odds with the way that infants make sense of their world. Whereas older children and adults take in information in a goal-directed way, looking for solutions to defined problems, infants merely explore their surroundings in an unplanned way. Structured learning experiences fail to account for this unique infant perspective (Zimmerman, Christakis, & Meltzoff, 2007).

This is not to say that well-conceived toys do not encourage learning. For example, in one study, infants were presented with a new toy that consisted of two levers and two pop-up dolls. The researchers demonstrated the operation of the toy to two groups of infants in two different ways. One group saw the researcher press the two levers one at a time, such that each lever caused one of two different dolls to pop up. The other group saw the researcher press both levers at once, causing both dolls to pop up at once. The first group was therefore given a more complete understanding of how the toy worked, whereas the second group was left with the mystery of what happens when each lever is pressed independently of the other (Schulz & Bonawitz, 2007).

When they were allowed to play with the toy for themselves, the second group spent much more time playing with it than did the first group. The second group had an incomplete understanding of how the toy worked, and so they explored further to uncover the relationship between the levers and the dolls.

One researcher summarized the implications of this area of research this way: "Babies aren't trying to learn one particular skill or set of facts; instead, they are drawn to anything new, unexpected or informative." In other words, infants don't need a planned program of study—they learn by merely following their own curiosity in exploring the world around them (Interlandi, 2007, p. 14).

The message of the research findings is moving beyond the laboratory. In a surprising move, the Walt Disney Company, which distributes the Baby Einstein videos, offered refunds to millions of parents who had purchased Baby Einstein videos, based on studies showing that educational media not only were ineffective in promoting cognitive development, but actually may harm it. For example, one study showed the children who watched educational videos and DVDs between the ages of 7 and 16 months actually showed poorer language development, knowing fewer words and phrases, than those who did not watch such media (Zimmerman & Christakis, 2007; Zimmerman, Christakis, & Meltzoff, 2007; Lewin, 2009; Robb, Richert, & Wartella, 2009; Roseberry et al., 2009).

- Do you think that purchasing educational toys and media for infants is worth a try, despite the lack of scientific research supporting its use? Why? Under what conditions might its use actually have undesirable consequences?

- Why do you think parents generally do not seem to be concerned about the lack of scientific evidence for the effectiveness of educational toys and media for infants?

Research using an information processing framework clearly suggests a relationship between information processing efficiency and cognitive abilities: Measures of how quickly infants lose interest in stimuli that they have previously seen, as well as their responsiveness to new stimuli, correlate moderately well with later measures of intelligence. Infants who are more efficient information processors during the six months following birth tend to have higher intelligence scores between 2 and 12 years of age, as well as higher scores on other measures of cognitive competence (Fagan, Holland, & Wheeler, 2007; Domsch, Lohaus, & Thomas, 2009; Rose, Feldman, & Jankowski, 2004, 2009).

Although information processing efficiency during infancy relates moderately well to later IQ scores, we need to keep in mind two qualifications. Even though there is an association between early information processing capabilities and later measures of IQ, the correlation is only moderate in strength. Consequently, we should not assume that intelligence is somehow permanently fixed in infancy.

*Assessing Information Processing Approaches.* The information processing perspective on cognitive development during infancy is very different from Piaget's. Rather than focusing on broad explanations of the *qualitative* changes that occur in infants' capabilities, as Piaget does, information processing looks at *quantitative* change. Piaget sees cognitive growth occurring in fairly sudden spurts; information processing sees more gradual, step-by-step growth. (Think of the difference between a track-and-field runner leaping hurdles versus a slow-but-steady marathon racer.)

Because information processing researchers consider cognitive development in terms of a collection of individual skills, they are often able to use more precise measures of cognitive ability, such as processing speed and memory recall, than proponents of Piaget's approach. Still, the very precision of these individual measures makes it harder to get an overall sense of the nature of cognitive development, something at which Piaget was a master. It's as if information processing approaches focus more on the individual pieces of the puzzle of cognitive development, while Piagetian approaches focus more on the whole puzzle (Kagan, 2008; Quinn, 2008).

Ultimately, both Piagetian and information processing approaches provide an account of cognitive development in infancy. Coupled with advances in understanding the biochemistry of the brain and theories that consider the effects of social factors on learning and cognition, the two help us paint a full picture of cognitive development. (Also see the "From Research to Practice" box on page 125.)

## REVIEW, CHECK, AND APPLY

### REVIEW

**LO11** How do infants process information?

- Information processing approaches consider quantitative changes in children's abilities to organize and use information. Cognitive growth is regarded as the increasing sophistication of encoding, storage, and retrieval.

- Infants clearly have memory capabilities from a very early age, although the duration and accuracy of such memories are unresolved questions.

**LO12** How is infant intelligence measured?

- Traditional measures of infant intelligence focus on behavioral attainments, which can help identify developmental delays or advances.

### CHECK YOURSELF

**1.** The information processing approach to cognitive development emphasizes the increased sophistication, speed, and _____ associated with cognitive growth.

a. capacity

b. circular reactions

c. categorization

d. analysis

**2.** Infants have memory capabilities from a very early age, although the duration and accuracy of such memories are unresolved questions.

- True

- False

**3.** When Justin first learned to drive a stick shift he had a difficult time coordinating the movements associated with the clutch, the gas, and the gear shift. After much practice the motions became more fluid and each component of the process required less attention. According to the information processing model, this would be an example of _____.

### APPLYING LIFESPAN DEVELOPMENT

- What information from this module could you use to refute the claims of books or educational programs that promise to help parents increase their babies' intelligence or instill advanced intellectual skills in infants? Based on valid research, what approaches would you use for intellectual development of infants?

✓● **Study** and **Review** on
**MyDevelopmentLab.com**

Answers: 1) a; 2) True; 3) automatization

# The Roots of Language

*Vicki and Dominic were engaged in a friendly competition over whose name would be the first word their baby, Maura, said. "Say 'mama,'" Vicki would coo before handing Maura over to Dominic for a diaper change. Grinning, he would take her and coax, "No, say 'daddy.'" Both parents ended up losing—and winning—when Maura's first word sounded more like "baba," and seemed to refer to her bottle.*

*Mama. No. Cookie. Dad. Jo.* Most parents can remember their baby's first word, and no wonder. It's an exciting moment, this emergence of a skill that is, arguably, unique to human beings.

But those initial words are just the first and most obvious manifestations of language. Many months earlier, infants began to understand the language used by others to make sense of the world around them. How does this linguistic ability develop? What is the pattern and sequence of language development? And how does the use of language transform the cognitive world of infants and their parents? We consider these questions, and others, as we address the development of language during the first years of life.

## The Fundamentals of Language: From Sounds to Symbols

**Language,** the systematic, meaningful arrangement of symbols, provides the basis for communication. But it does more than this: It is closely tied to the way we think and understand the world. It enables us to reflect on people and objects and to convey our thoughts to others.

Language has several formal characteristics that must be mastered as linguistic competence is developed. They include:

- **Phonology.** Phonology refers to the basic sounds of language, called *phonemes,* that can be combined to produce words and sentences. For instance, the "a" in "mat" and the "a" in "mate" represent two different phonemes in English. Although English employs just 40 phonemes to create every word in the language, other languages have as many as 85 phonemes—and some as few as 15 (Akmajian, Demers, & Harnish, 1984).

- **Morphemes.** A morpheme is the smallest language unit that has meaning. Some morphemes are complete words, while others add information necessary for interpreting a word, such as the endings "-s" for plural and "-ed" for past tense.

- **Semantics.** Semantics are the rules that govern the meaning of words and sentences. As their knowledge of semantics develops, children are able to understand the subtle distinction between "Ellie was hit by a ball" (an answer to the question of why Ellie doesn't want to play catch) and "A ball hit Ellie" (used to announce the current situation).

In considering the development of language, we need to distinguish between linguistic *comprehension,* the understanding of speech, and linguistic *production,* the use of language to communicate. One principle underlies the relationship between the two: Comprehension precedes production. An 18-month-old may be able to understand a complex series of directions ("Pick up your coat from the floor and put it on the chair by the fireplace") but may not yet have strung more than two words together when speaking for herself. Throughout infancy, comprehension also outpaces production. For example, during infancy, comprehension of words expands at a rate of 22 new words a month, while production of words increases at a rate of about 9 new words a month, once talking begins (Tincoff & Jusczyk, 1999; Rescorla, Alley, & Christine, 2001; Cattani, 2010) (see Figure 3-13).

***Early Sounds and Communication.*** Spend 24 hours with even a very young infant and you will hear a variety of sounds: cooing, crying, gurgling, murmuring, and assorted types of other noises. These sounds, although not meaningful in themselves, play an important role in linguistic development, paving the way for true language (Bloom, 1993; O'Grady & Aitchison, 2005).

Although we tend to think of language in terms of the production of words and then groups of words, infants can begin to communicate linguistically well before they say their first word.

**language** the systematic, meaningful arrangement of symbols, which provides the basis for communication

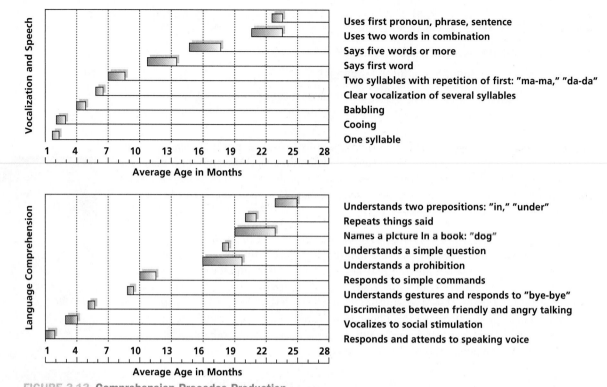

**FIGURE 3-13 Comprehension Precedes Production**
Throughout infancy, the comprehension of speech precedes the production of speech.
Source: Adapted from Bornstein & Lamb, 1992a.

*Prelinguistic communication* is communication through sounds, facial expressions, gestures, imitation, and other nonlinguistic means. When a father responds to his daughter's "ah" with an "ah" of his own, and then the daughter repeats the sound, and the father responds once again, they are engaged in prelinguistic communication. Clearly, the "ah" sound has no particular meaning. However, its repetition, which mimics the give-and-take of conversation, teaches the infant something about turn-taking and the back-and-forth of communication (Reddy, 1999).

The most obvious manifestation of prelinguistic communication is babbling. **Babbling**, making speechlike but meaningless sounds, starts at the age of 2 or 3 months and continues until around the age of 1 year. When they babble, infants repeat the same vowel sound over and over, changing the pitch from high to low (as in "ee-ee-ee," repeated at different pitches). After the age of 5 months, the sounds of babbling begin to expand, reflecting the addition of consonants (such as "bee-bee-bee-bee").

Babbling is a universal phenomenon, accomplished in the same way throughout all cultures. While they are babbling, infants spontaneously produce all of the sounds found in every language, not just the language they hear people around them speaking.

Babbling typically follows a progression from simple to more complex sounds. Although exposure to the sounds of a particular language does not seem to influence babbling initially, eventually experience does make a difference. By the age of 6 months, babbling reflects the sounds of the language to which infants are exposed. The difference is so noticeable that even untrained listeners can distinguish between babbling infants who have been raised in cultures in which French, Arabic, or Cantonese languages are spoken. Furthermore, the speed at which infants begin homing in on their own language is related to the speed of later language development (Blake & Boysson-Bardies, 1992; Whalen, Levitt, & Goldstein, 2007; Lee, Davis, & MacNeilage, 2010).

**First Words.** When a mother and father first hear their child say "Mama" or "Dada," or even "baba," as in the case of Maura, the baby described earlier in this section, it is hard to be

**babbling** making speechlike but meaningless sounds

anything but delighted. But their initial enthusiasm may be dampened a bit when they find that the same sound is used to ask for a cookie, a doll, and a ratty old blanket.

First words generally are spoken somewhere around the age of 10 to 14 months, but may occur as early as 9 months. Once an infant starts to produce words, vocabulary increases at a rapid rate. By the age of 15 months, the average child has a vocabulary of ten words and methodically expands until the one-word stage of language development ends at around 18 months. Once that happens, a sudden spurt in vocabulary occurs. In just a short period—a few weeks somewhere between 16 and 24 months of age—there is an explosion of language, in which a child's vocabulary typically increases from 50 to 400 words (Gleitman & Landau, 1994; Fernald et al., 1998; Nazzi & Bertoncini, 2003; McMurray, Aslin, & Toscano, 2009).

The first words in children's early vocabularies typically regard objects and things, both animate and inanimate. Most often they refer to people or objects who constantly appear and disappear ("Mama"), to animals ("kitty"), or to temporary states ("wet"). These first words are often **holophrases,** one-word utterances that stand for a whole phrase, whose meaning depends on the particular context in which they are used. For instance, a youngster may use the phrase "ma" to mean, depending on the context, "I want to be picked up by Mom" or "I want something to eat, Mom" or "Where's Mom?" (Dromi, 1987; O'Grady & Aitchison, 2005).

Culture has an effect on the type of first words spoken. For example, unlike North American English-speaking infants, who are more apt to use nouns initially, Chinese Mandarin-speaking infants use more verbs than nouns. On the other hand, by the age of 20 months, there are remarkable cross-cultural similarities in the types of words spoken. For example, a comparison of 20-month-olds in Argentina, Belgium, France, Israel, Italy, and the Republic of Korea found that children's vocabularies in every culture contained greater proportions of nouns than other classes of words (Tardif, 1996; Bornstein et al., 2004).

***First Sentences.***   When Aaron was 19 months old, he heard his mother coming up the back steps, as she did every day just before dinner. Aaron turned to his father and distinctly said, "Ma come." In stringing those two words together, Aaron took a giant step in his language development.

The explosive increase in vocabulary that comes at around 18 months is accompanied by another accomplishment: the linking together of individual words into sentences that convey a single thought. Although there is a good deal of variability in the time at which children first create two-word phrases, it is generally around 8 to 12 months after they say their first word.

The linguistic advance represented by two-word combinations is important because the linkage not only provides labels for things in the world but also indicates the relations between them. For instance, the combination may declare something about possession ("Mama key") or recurrent events ("Dog bark"). Interestingly, most early sentences don't represent demands or even necessarily require a response. Instead, they are often merely comments and observations about events occurring in the child's world (Halliday, 1975; O'Grady & Aitchison, 2005).

Two-year-olds using two-word combinations tend to employ particular sequences that are similar to the ways in which adult sentences are constructed. For instance, sentences in English typically follow a pattern in which the subject of the sentence comes first, followed by the verb, and then the object ("Josh threw the ball"). Children's speech most often uses a similar order, although not all the words are initially included. Consequently, a child might say "Josh threw" or "Josh ball" to indicate the same thought. What is significant is that the order is typically not "threw Josh" or "ball Josh," but rather the usual order of English, which makes the utterance much easier for an English speaker to comprehend (Brown, 1973; Hirsh-Pasek & Michnick-Golinkoff, 1995; Masataka, 2003).

Although the creation of two-word sentences represents an advance, the language used by children still is by no means adultlike. As we've just seen, 2-year-olds tend to leave out words that aren't critical to the message, similar to the way we might write a telegram for which we were paying by the word. For that reason, their talk is often called **telegraphic speech**. Rather than saying, "I showed you the book," a child using telegraphic speech might say, "I show book." "I am drawing a dog" might become "Drawing dog" (see Table 3-8).

By the age of 2, most children use two-word phrases, such as "ball play."

**holophrases** one-word utterances that stand for a whole phrase, the meaning of which depends on the particular context in which they are used

**telegraphic speech** speech in which words not critical to the message are left out

**TABLE 3-8** CHILDREN'S IMITATION OF SENTENCES SHOWING DECLINE OF TELEGRAPHIC SPEECH

| | Eve, 25.5 Months | Adam, 28.5 Months | Helen, 30 Months | Ian, 31.5 Months | Jimmy, 32 Months | June, 35.5 Months |
|---|---|---|---|---|---|---|
| I showed you the book. | I show book. | (I show) book. | C | I show you the book. | C | Show you the book. |
| I am very tall. | (My) tall. | I (very) tall. | I very tall. | I'm very tall. | Very tall. | I very tall. |
| It goes in a big box. | Big box. | Big box. | In big box. | It goes in the box. | C | C |
| I am drawing a dog. | Drawing dog. | I draw dog. | I drawing dog. | Dog. | C | C |
| I will read the book. | Read book. | I will read book. | I read the book. | I read the book. | C | C |
| I can see a cow. | See cow. | I want see cow. | C | Cow. | C | C |
| I will do that again. | Do-again. | I will that again. | I do that. | I again. | C | C |

C = correct imitation.

Source: Adapted from R. Brown & C. Fraser, 1963.

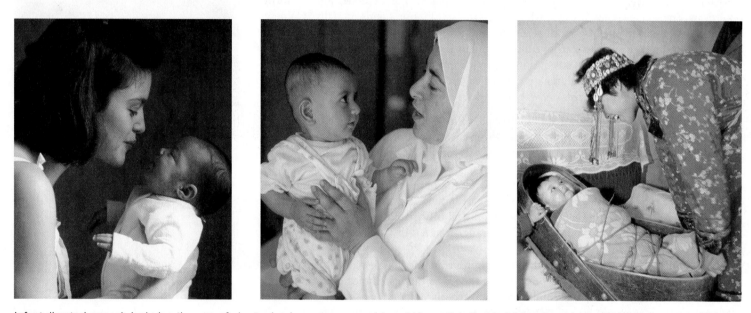

Infant-directed speech includes the use of short, simple sentences and is said in a pitch that is higher than that used with older children and adults.

**underextension** the overly restrictive use of words, common among children just mastering spoken language

**overextension** the overly broad use of words, overgeneralizing their meaning

Early language has other characteristics that differentiate it from the language used by adults. For instance, consider Sarah, who refers to the blanket she sleeps with as "blankie." When her Aunt Ethel gives her a new blanket, Sarah refuses to call the new one a "blankie," restricting the word to her original blanket.

Sarah's inability to generalize the label of "blankie" to blankets in general is an example of **underextension,** using words too restrictively, which is common among children just mastering spoken language. Underextension occurs when language novices think that a word refers to a specific instance of a concept, instead of to all examples of the concept (Caplan & Barr, 1989; Masataka, 2003).

As infants like Sarah grow more adept with language, the opposite phenomenon sometimes occurs. In **overextension,** words are used too broadly, overgeneralizing their meaning. For example, when Sarah refers to buses, trucks, and tractors as "cars," she is guilty of overextension, making the assumption that any object with wheels must be a car. Although overextension reflects speech errors, it also shows that advances are occurring in the child's thought processes: The child is beginning to develop general mental categories and concepts (Johnson & Eilers, 1998; McDonough, 2002).

Infants also show individual differences in the style of language they use. For example, some use a **referential style,** in which language is used primarily to label objects. Others tend to use an **expressive style,** in which language is used primarily to express feelings and needs about oneself and others (Bates et al., 1994; Nelson, 1996). Language styles reflect, in part, cultural factors. For example, mothers in the United States label objects more frequently than do Japanese mothers, encouraging a more referential style of speech. In contrast, mothers in Japan are more apt to speak about social interactions, encouraging a more expressive style of speech (Fernald & Morikawa, 1993).

## The Origins of Language Development

The immense strides in language development during the preschool years raise a fundamental question: How does proficiency in language come about? Linguists are deeply divided on how to answer this question.

*Learning Theory Approaches: Language as a Learned Skill.* One view of language development emphasizes the basic principles of learning. According to the **learning theory approach,** language acquisition follows the basic laws of reinforcement and conditioning discussed in Module 1.2 (Skinner, 1957). For instance, a child who articulates the word "da" may be hugged and praised by her father, who jumps to the conclusion that she is referring to him. This reaction reinforces the child, who is more likely to repeat the word. In sum, the learning theory perspective on language acquisition suggests that children learn to speak by being rewarded for making sounds that approximate speech. Through the process of *shaping,* language becomes more and more similar to adult speech.

There's a problem, though, with the learning theory approach. It doesn't seem to adequately explain how children acquire the rules of language as readily as they do. For instance, young children are reinforced when they make errors. Parents are apt to be just as responsive if their child says, "Why the dog won't eat?" as they are if the child phrases the question more correctly ("Why won't the dog eat?"). Both forms of the question are understood correctly, and both elicit the same response; reinforcement is provided for both correct and incorrect language usage. Under such circumstances, learning theory is hard-put to explain how children learn to speak properly.

Children are also able to move beyond specific utterances they have heard, and produce novel phrases, sentences, and constructions, an ability that also cannot be explained by learning theory. Furthermore, children can apply linguistic rules to nonsense words. In one study, 4-year-old children heard the nonsense verb "to pilk" in the sentence "the bear is pilking the horse." Later, when asked what was happening to the horse, they responded by placing the nonsense verb in the correct tense and voice: "He's getting pilked by the bear."

*Nativist Approaches: Language as an Innate Skill.* Such conceptual difficulties with the learning theory approach have led to the development of an alternative, championed by the linguist Noam Chomsky and known as the nativist approach (1968, 1978, 1991, 1999, 2005). The **nativist approach** argues that there is a genetically determined, innate mechanism that directs the development of language. According to Chomsky, people are born with an innate capacity to use language, which emerges, more or less automatically, due to maturation.

Chomsky's analysis of different languages suggests that all the world's languages share a similar underlying structure, which he calls **universal grammar.** In this view, the human brain is wired with a neural system called the **language-acquisition device (LAD),** that both permits the understanding of language structure and provides a set of strategies and techniques for learning the particular characteristics of the language to which a child is exposed. In this view, language is uniquely human, made possible by a genetic predisposition to both comprehend and produce words and sentences (Lidz & Gleitman, 2004; Stromswold, 2006; Boeckx, 2010; Lieven & Stoll, 2010).

**referential style** a style of language use in which language is used primarily to label objects

**expressive style** a style of language use in which language is used primarily to express feelings and needs about oneself and others

**learning theory approach** the theory that language acquisition follows the basic laws of reinforcement and conditioning

**nativist approach** the theory that a genetically determined, innate mechanism directs language development

**universal grammar** Noam Chomsky's theory that all the world's languages share a similar underlying structure

**language-acquisition device (LAD)** a neural system of the brain hypothesized to permit understanding of language

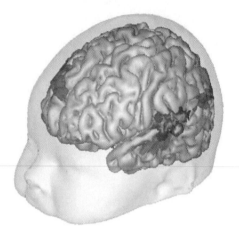

**FIGURE 3-14 Infant's Speech Processing**
This fMRI scan of a 3-month-old infant shows speech processing activity similar to that of an adult, suggesting there may be an evolutionary basis to language.
Source: Dehaene-Lambertz, Hertz-Pannier, & Dubois, 2006.

Support for Chomsky's nativist approach comes from recent findings identifying a specific gene related to speech production. Further support comes from research showing that language processing in infants involves brain structures similar to those in adult speech processing, suggesting an evolutionary basis to language (Wade, 2001; Monaco, 2005; Dehaene-Lambertz, Hertz-Pannier, & Dubois, 2006) (see Figure 3-14).

The view that language is an innate ability unique to humans also has its critics. For instance, some researchers argue that certain primates are able to learn at least the basics of language, an ability that calls into question the uniqueness of the human linguistic capacity. Others point out that although humans may be genetically primed to use language, its use still requires significant social experience in order for it to be used effectively (MacWhinney, 1991; Savage-Rumbaugh et al., 1993; Goldberg, 2004).

***The Interactionist Approaches.*** Neither the learning theory nor the nativist perspective fully explains language acquisition. As a result, some theorists have turned to a theory that combines both schools of thought. The *interactionist perspective* suggests that language development is produced through a combination of genetically determined predispositions and environmental circumstances that help teach language.

The interactionist perspective accepts that innate factors shape the broad outlines of language development. However, interactionists also argue that the specific course of language development is determined by the language to which children are exposed and the reinforcement they receive for using language in particular ways. Social factors are considered to be key to development, since the motivation provided by one's membership in a society and culture and one's interactions with others leads to the use of language and the growth of language skills (Dixon, 2004; Yang, 2006).

Just as there is support for some aspects of learning theory and nativist positions, the interactionist perspective has also received some support. We don't know, at the moment, which of these positions will ultimately provide the best explanation. More likely, different factors play different roles at different times during childhood.

## Speaking to Children: The Language of Infant-Directed Speech

Say the following sentence aloud: Do you like the applesauce?

Now pretend that you are going to ask the same question of an infant, and speak it as you would for a young child's ears.

Chances are several things happened when you translated the phrase for the infant. First of all, the wording probably changed, and you may have said something like, "Does baby like the applesauce?" At the same time, the pitch of your voice probably rose, your general intonation most likely had a singsong quality, and you probably separated your words carefully.

***Infant-Directed Speech.*** The shift in your language was due to your use of **infant-directed speech,** a style of speech that characterizes much of the verbal communication directed toward infants. This type of speech pattern used to be called *motherese*, because it was assumed that it applied only to mothers. However, that assumption was wrong, and the gender-neutral term *infant-directed speech* is now used more frequently.

Infant-directed speech is characterized by short, simple sentences. Pitch becomes higher, the range of frequencies increases, and intonation is more varied. There is also repetition of words, and topics are restricted to items that are assumed to be comprehensible to infants, such as concrete objects in the baby's environment (Soderstrom, 2007; Matsuda, 2010).

Sometimes infant-directed speech includes amusing sounds that are not even words, imitating the prelinguistic speech of infants. In other cases, it has little formal structure, but is similar to the kind of telegraphic speech that infants use as they develop their own language skills.

Infant-directed speech changes as children become older. Around the end of the first year, infant-directed speech takes on more adultlike qualities. Sentences become longer and more complex, although individual words are still spoken slowly and deliberately. Pitch is also used to focus attention on particularly important words (Soderstrom et al., 2008; Kitamura & Lam, 2009).

**infant-directed speech** a type of speech directed toward infants, characterized by short, simple sentences

Infant-directed speech plays an important role in infants' acquisition of language. As discussed next, infant-directed speech occurs all over the world, though there are cultural variations. Newborns prefer such speech to regular language, a fact that suggests that they may be particularly receptive to it. Furthermore, some research suggests that babies who are exposed to a great deal of infant-directed speech early in life seem to begin to use words and exhibit other forms of linguistic competence earlier (Englund & Behne, 2006; Soderstrom, 2007; Werker et al., 2007).

## Cultural Dimensions

### Is Infant-Directed Speech Similar Across All Cultures?

Do mothers in the United States, Sweden, and Russia speak the same way to their infants?

In some respects, they clearly do. Although the words themselves differ across languages, the way the words are spoken to infants is quite similar. According to a growing body of research, there are basic similarities across cultures in the nature of infant-directed speech (Rabain-Jamin & Sabeau-Jouannet, 1997; Werker et al., 2007; Fais et al., 2010).

For example, 6 of the 10 most frequent major characteristics of speech directed at infants used by native speakers of English and Spanish are common to both languages: exaggerated intonation, high pitch, lengthened vowels, repetition, lower volume, and heavy stress on certain key words (such as emphasizing the word "ball" in the sentence, "No, that's a *ball*") (Blount, 1982). Similarly, mothers in the United States, Sweden, and Russia all exaggerate and elongate the pronunciation of the three vowel sounds of "ee," "ah," and "oh" when speaking to infants in similar ways, despite differences in the languages in which the sounds are used (Kuhl et al., 1997).

Even deaf mothers use a form of infant-directed speech: When communicating with their infants, deaf mothers use sign language at a significantly slower tempo than when communicating with adults, and they frequently repeat the signs (Swanson, Leonard, & Gandour, 1992; Masataka, 1996, 1998, 2000).

**From an educator's perspective:** What are some implications of differences in the ways adults speak to boys and girls? How might such speech differences contribute to later differences not only in speech, but also in attitudes?

## What Can You Do to Promote Infants' Cognitive Development?

### Becoming an Informed Consumer of Development

All parents want their children to reach their full cognitive potential, but sometimes efforts to reach this goal take a bizarre path. For instance, some parents spend hundreds of dollars enrolling in workshops with titles such as "How to Multiply Your Baby's Intelligence" and buying books with titles such as *How to Teach Your Baby to Read* (Doman & Doman, 2002).

Do such efforts ever succeed? Although some parents swear they do, there is no scientific support for the effectiveness of such programs. For example, despite the many cognitive skills of infants, no infant can actually read. Furthermore, "multiplying" a baby's intelligence is impossible, and such organizations as the American Academy of Pediatrics and the American Academy of Neurology have denounced programs that claim to do so.

On the other hand, certain things can be done to promote cognitive development in infants. The following suggestions, based upon findings of developmental researchers, offer a starting point (Gopnik, Meltzoff, & Kuhl, 2000; Cabrera, Shannon, & Tamis-LeMonda, 2007):

- **Provide infants the opportunity to explore the world.** As Piaget suggests, children learn by doing, and they need the opportunity to explore and probe their environment.

- **Be responsive to infants on both a verbal and a nonverbal level.** Try to speak *with* babies, as opposed to *at* them. Ask questions, listen to their responses, and provide further communication (Merlo, Bowman, & Barnett, 2007).

- **Read to your infants.** Although they may not understand the meaning of your words, they will respond to your tone of voice and the intimacy provided by the activity. Reading together also is associated with later literacy skills and begins to create a lifelong reading habit. In fact, the American Academy of Pediatrics recommends daily reading to children starting at the age of 6 months (American Academy of Pediatrics, 1997; Holland, 2008; Robb, Richert, & Wartella, 2009).

- **Keep in mind that you don't have to be with an infant 24 hours a day.** Just as infants need time to explore their world on their own, parents and other caregivers need time off from child-care activities.

- **Don't push infants and don't expect too much too soon.** Your goal should not be to create a genius; it should be to provide a warm, nurturing environment that will allow an infant to reach his or her potential.

## REVIEW, CHECK, AND APPLY

### REVIEW

**L013** How do children learn to use language?

- Before they speak, infants understand many adult utterances and engage in several forms of prelinguistic communication.

- Children typically produce their first words between 10 and 14 months, and rapidly increase their vocabularies from that point on, especially during a spurt at about 18 months.

- Learning theorists believe that basic learning processes account for language development, whereas nativists like Noam Chomsky and his followers argue that humans have an innate language capacity. The interactionists suggest that language is a consequence of both environmental and innate factors.

**L014** How do infants influence adults' language?

- In using infant-directed speech, adults shift their use of language to a higher pitch and a style of speech using short, simple sentences.

### CHECK YOURSELF

1. Like other 2-year-olds, Mason can say "Doggie bye, bye" and "Milk gone." These two-word phrases are examples of _____ speech.

   a. holophrastic

   b. telegraphic

   c. interpretive

   d. active

2. One theory, the _____ approach, suggests that a genetically determined, innate mechanism directs language development.

3. Whenever 9-month-old Ana's mother talks to her, she uses short, simple sentences, repetitive words, and higher pitches. This shift in language is consistent with the use of _____ speech.

   a. infant-directed

   b. telegraphic

   c. nativist

   d. interactionist

### APPLYING LIFESPAN DEVELOPMENT

- What are some ways in which children's linguistic development reflects their acquisition of new ways of interpreting and dealing with their world?

✓●─[**Study** and **Review** on
**MyDevelopmentLab.com**

*Will you ace your test?* To find out, log onto
MyDevelopmentLab.com.

Answers: 1) b; 2) nativist; 3) a

---

## MODULE 3.3 Social and Personality Development in Infancy

# The Velcro Chronicles

*It was during the windy days of March that the problem in the child-care center first arose. Its source: 10-month-old Russell Ruud. Otherwise a model of decorum, Russell had somehow learned how to unzip the Velcro chin strap to his winter hat. He would remove the hat whenever he got the urge, seemingly oblivious to the potential health problems that might follow.*

*But that was just the start of the real difficulty. To the chagrin of the teachers in the child-care center, not to speak of the children's parents, soon other children were following his lead, removing their own caps at will.*

*Russell's mother, made aware of the anarchy at the child-care center—and the other parents' distress over Russell's behavior—pleaded innocent. "I never showed Russell how to unzip the*

*Velcro," claimed his mother, Judith Ruud, an economist with the Congressional Budget Office in Washington, D.C. "He learned by trial and error, and the other kids saw him do it one day when they were getting dressed for an outing."* (Goleman, 1993, C10)

*By then, though, it was too late for excuses: Russell, it seems, was an excellent teacher. Keeping the children's hats on their heads proved to be no easy task. Even more ominous was the thought that if the infants could master the Velcro straps on their hats, would they soon be unfastening the Velcro straps on their shoes and removing them?*

As babies like Russell show us, children are sociable from a very early age. This anecdote also demonstrates one of the side benefits of infants' participation in child care, and something research has begun to suggest: through their social interactions, babies acquire new skills and abilities from more "expert" peers. Infants, as we will see, have an amazing capacity to learn from other children, and their interactions with others can play a central role in their developing social and emotional worlds.

In this module we consider social and personality development in infancy. We begin by examining the emotional lives of infants, considering which emotions they feel and how well they can read others' emotions. We look at how babies view their own and others' mental lives.

We then turn to infants' social relationships. We look at how they forge bonds of attachment and the ways they interact with family members and peers. Finally, we cover the characteristics that differentiate one infant from another and discuss differences in the way children are treated depending on their gender. We'll consider the nature of family life and look at the advantages and disadvantages of infant child care outside the home, a child-care option that today's families increasingly employ.

# Developing the Roots of Sociability

LO15 Do infants experience emotions?

LO16 What sort of mental lives do infants have?

LEARNING OBJECTIVES

*Germaine smiles when he catches a glimpse of his mother. Tawanda looks angry when her mother takes away the spoon that she is playing with. Sydney scowls when a loud plane flies overhead.*

A smile. A look of anger. A scowl. The emotions of infancy are written all over a baby's face. Yet do infants experience emotions in the same way that adults do? When do they become capable of understanding what others are experiencing emotionally? And how do they use others' emotional states to make sense of their environment? We consider some of these questions as we seek to understand how infants develop emotionally and socially.

## Emotions in Infancy: Do Infants Experience Emotional Highs and Lows?

Anyone who spends any time at all around infants knows they display facial expressions that seem indicative of their emotional states. In situations in which we expect them to be happy, they seem to smile; when we might assume they are frustrated, they show anger; and when we might expect them to be unhappy, they look sad.

In fact, these basic facial expressions are remarkably similar across the most diverse cultures. Whether we look at babies in India, the United States, or the jungles of New Guinea, the expression of basic emotions is the same (see Figure 3-15). Furthermore, the nonverbal expression of emotion, called *nonverbal encoding,* is fairly consistent among people of all ages. These consistencies have led researchers to conclude that we are born with the capacity to display basic emotions (Scharfe, 2000; Sullivan & Lewis, 2003; Ackerman & Izard, 2004).

Infants display a fairly wide range of emotional expressions. Almost all mothers report that by the age of 1 month their babies nonverbally have expressed interest and joy. Careful coding of infants' nonverbal expressions shows that interest, distress, and disgust are present at birth, and that other emotions emerge over the next few months. Such findings are consistent with the work of the famous naturalist Charles Darwin, whose 1872 book *The Expression of the Emotions in Man and Animals* argued that humans and primates have an inborn, universal set of emotional expressions—a view consistent with today's evolutionary approach to development (Izard, 1982; Sroufe, 1996; Benson, 2003).

Although infants display similar *kinds* of emotions, the *degree* of emotional expressivity varies among infants. Children in different cultures show reliable differences in emotional expressiveness, even during infancy. For example, by the age of 11 months, Chinese infants are generally less expressive than European, American, and Japanese infants (Camras, Meng, & Ujiie, 2002; Camras et al., 2007; Izard, Woodburn, & Finlon, 2010).

**stranger anxiety** the caution and wariness displayed by infants when encountering an unfamiliar person

**separation anxiety** the distress displayed by infants when a customary care provider departs

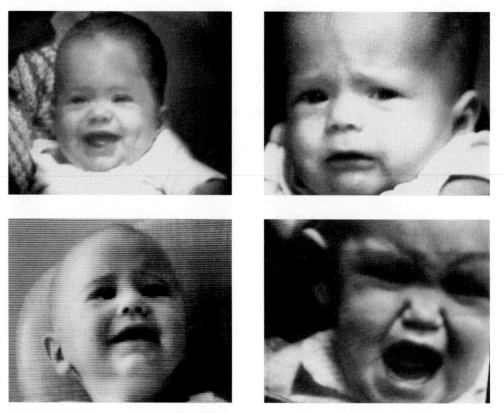

**FIGURE 3-15 Universals in Facial Expressions**
Across every culture, infants show similar facial expressions relating to basic emotions. Do you think such expressions are similar in nonhuman animals?

◉ Watch on **mydevelopmentlab.com**

*Has your virtual child shown any stranger anxiety? How are you addressing it?*
To see a child display stranger anxiety, watch the video in MyDevelopmentLab.com.

When infants smile at a person, rather than a nonhuman stimulus, they are displaying a social smile.

***Stranger Anxiety and Separation Anxiety.*** "She used to be such a friendly baby," thought Erika's mother. "No matter whom she encountered, she had a big smile. But almost the day she turned 7 months old, she began to react to strangers as if she were seeing a ghost. Her face crinkles up with a frown, and she either turns away or stares at them with suspicion. It's as if she has undergone a personality transplant." ◉ Watch on **mydevelopmentlab.com**

What happened to Erika is, in fact, quite typical. By the end of the first year, infants often develop both stranger anxiety and separation anxiety. **Stranger anxiety** is the caution and wariness displayed by infants when encountering an unfamiliar person. Such anxiety typically appears in the second half of the first year.

What brings on stranger anxiety? Brain development and the increased cognitive abilities of infants play a role. As infants' memory develops, they are able to separate the people they know from the people they don't. The same cognitive advances that allow them to respond so positively to those people with whom they are familiar also give them the ability to recognize people who are unfamiliar. Furthermore, between 6 and 9 months, infants begin trying to make sense of their world, trying to anticipate and predict events. When something happens that they don't expect—such as the appearance of an unknown person—they experience fear. It's as if an infant has a question but is unable to answer it (Volker, 2007).

**Separation anxiety** is the distress displayed by infants when a customary care provider departs. Separation anxiety, which is also universal across cultures, usually begins at about 7 or 8 months (see Figure 3-16). It peaks around 14 months, and then decreases. Separation anxiety is largely attributable to the same reasons as stranger anxiety. Infants' growing cognitive skills allow them to ask reasonable questions, but they may be questions that they are too young to understand the answer to: "Why is my mother leaving?" "Where is she going?" and "Will she come back?"

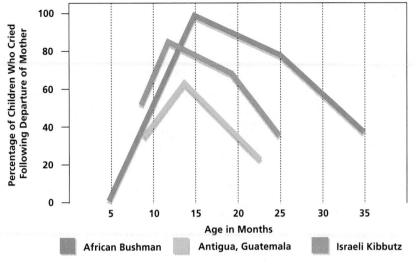

**FIGURE 3-16 Separation Anxiety**

Separation anxiety, the distress displayed by infants when their usual care provider leaves their presence, is a universal phenomenon beginning at around the age of 7 or 8 months. It peaks at around the age of 14 months and then begins to decline. Does separation anxiety have survival value for humans?

Source: From INFANCY: ITS PLACE IN HUMAN DEVELOPMENT by Jerome Kagan, Richard P. Kearsley, and Phillip R. Zelazo, p. 107, Cambridge, Mass.: Harvard University Press, Copyright © 1978 by the President and Fellows of Harvard University College.

Stranger anxiety and separation anxiety represent important social progress. They reflect both cognitive advances and the growing emotional and social bonds between infants and their caregivers—bonds that we'll consider later in the module when we discuss infants' social relationships.Has your virtual child experienced separation anxiety? How will you handle outside child care?  Watch on **mydevelopmentlab.com**

***Smiling.*** As Luz lay sleeping in her crib, her mother and father caught a glimpse of the most beautiful smile crossing her face. Her parents were sure that Luz was having a pleasant dream. Were they right?

Probably not. The earliest smiles expressed during sleep probably have little meaning, although no one can be absolutely sure. By 6 to 9 weeks babies begin to smile reliably at the sight of stimuli that please them, including toys, mobiles, and—to the delight of parents—people. The first smiles tend to be relatively indiscriminate, as infants first begin to smile at the sight of almost anything they find amusing. However, as they get older, they become more selective in their smiles.

A baby's smile in response to another person, rather than to nonhuman stimuli, is considered a *social smile*. As babies get older, their social smiles become directed toward particular individuals, not just anyone. By the age of 18 months, social smiling, directed more toward mothers and other caregivers, becomes more frequent than smiling directed toward nonhuman objects. Moreover, if an adult is unresponsive to a child, the amount of smiling decreases. In short, by the end of the second year children are quite purposefully using smiling to communicate their positive emotions, and they are sensitive to the emotional expressions of others (Bigelow & Rochat, 2006; Fogel et al., 2006; Gosselin, Perron, & Maassarani, 2010).

***Decoding Others' Facial Expressions.*** In Module 2.3, we discussed the possibility that neonates can imitate adults' facial expressions even minutes after birth. Although their imitative abilities certainly do not imply that they can understand the meaning of others' facial expressions, such imitation does pave the way for *nonverbal decoding* abilities, which begin to emerge fairly soon. Using these abilities, infants can interpret others' facial and vocal expressions that carry emotional meaning. For example, they can tell when a caregiver is happy to see them and pick up on worry or fear in the faces of others (Bornstein & Arterberry, 2003; Hernandez-Reif et al., 2006; Striano & Vaish, 2006).

In the first 6 to 8 weeks, infants' visual precision is sufficiently limited that they cannot pay much attention to others' facial expressions. But they soon begin to discriminate among different facial expressions of emotion and even seem to be able to respond to differences in

Research suggests that this 18-month-old is exhibiting a clearly developing sense of self.

**social referencing** the intentional search for information about others' feelings to help explain the meaning of uncertain circumstances and events

**self-awareness** knowledge of oneself

**theory of mind** knowledge and beliefs about how the mind works and how it affects behavior

emotional intensity conveyed by facial expressions. By the time they reach the age of 4 months, infants already have begun to understand the emotions that lie behind the facial and vocal expressions of others (Adamson & Frick, 2003; Bertin & Striano, 2006; Farroni et al., 2007).

## Social Referencing: Feeling What Others Feel

*Twenty-three-month-old Stephania watches as her older brother Eric and his friend Chen argue loudly with each other and begin to wrestle. Uncertain of what is happening, Stephania glances at her mother. Her mother, though, wears a smile, knowing that Eric and Chen are just playing. On seeing her mother's reaction, Stephania smiles too, mimicking her mother's facial expression.*

Like Stephania, most of us have been in situations in which we feel uncertain. In such cases, we sometimes turn to others to see how they are reacting. This reliance on others, known as social referencing, helps us decide what an appropriate response ought to be.

**Social referencing** is the intentional search for information about others' feelings to help explain the meaning of uncertain circumstances and events. Like Stephania, we use social referencing to clarify the meaning of a situation and so to reduce our uncertainty about what is occurring.

Social referencing first occurs around the age of 8 or 9 months. It is a fairly sophisticated social ability: Infants need it not only to understand the significance of others' behavior, by using such cues as their facial expressions, but also understand the meaning of those behaviors within the context of a specific situation (de Rosnay et al., 2006; Carver & Vaccaro, 2007; Stenberg, 2009).

**From a social worker's perspective:** In what situations do adults rely on social referencing to work out appropriate responses? How might social referencing be used to influence parents' behavior toward their children?

## The Development of Self: Do Infants Know Who They Are?

*Elysa, 8 months old, crawls past the full-length mirror that hangs on a door in her parents' bedroom. She barely pays any attention to her reflection as she moves by. On the other hand, her cousin Brianna, who is almost 2 years old, stares at herself in the mirror as she passes and laughs as she notices, and then rubs off, a smear of jelly on her forehead.*

Perhaps you have had the experience of catching a glimpse of yourself in a mirror and noticing a hair out of place. You probably reacted by attempting to push the unruly hair back into place. Your reaction shows more than that you care about how you look. It implies that you have a sense of yourself, the awareness and knowledge that you are an independent social entity to which others react, and which you attempt to present to the world in ways that reflect favorably upon you. **Watch** on **mydevelopmentlab.com**

However, we are not born with the knowledge that we exist independently from others and the larger world. Very young infants do not have a sense of themselves as individuals; they do not recognize themselves in photos or mirrors. However, the roots of **self-awareness,** knowledge of oneself, begin to grow after the age of 12 months.

We know this from a simple but ingenious experimental technique in which an infant's nose is secretly colored with a dab of red powder. Then the infant is seated in front of a mirror. If infants touch their noses or attempt to wipe off the rouge, we have evidence that they have at least some knowledge of their physical characteristics. Although some infants as young as 12 months seem startled on seeing the rouge spot, for most a reaction does not occur until between 17 and 24 months of age. This awareness is one step in infants' understanding of themselves as independent objects (Asendorpf, Warkentin, & Baudonniere, 1996; Rochat, 2004; Brownell et al., 2010).

## Theory of Mind: Infants' Perspectives on the Mental Lives of Others—and Themselves

What are infants' thoughts about thinking? Infants begin to understand certain things about their own and others' mental processes at quite an early age, developing a **theory of mind,** their knowledge and beliefs about how the mind works and how it influences behavior. Theories of mind are the explanations that children use to explain how others think.

**Watch** on **mydevelopmentlab.com**

*By the time your virtual child turns 1 year, he or she will begin to exhibit self-awareness.* To observe a child demonstrate self-awareness, watch the video in MyDevelopmentLab.com.

For instance, cognitive advances during infancy that we discussed in Module 3.2 permit older infants to see people in a very different way from other objects. They learn to see other people as *compliant agents,* beings similar to themselves who behave under their own power and who have the capacity to respond to infants' requests (Poulin-Dubois, 1999; Rochat, 1999, 2004).  👁 Watch on mydevelopmentlab.com

In addition, children's capacity to understand intentionality and causality grows during infancy. They begin to understand that others' behaviors have some meaning and that the behaviors they see people enacting are designed to accomplish particular goals, in contrast to the "behaviors" of inanimate objects. For example, a child comes to understand that his father has a specific goal when he is in the kitchen making sandwiches. In contrast, his father's car is simply parked in the driveway, having no mental life or goal (Ahn, Gelman, & Amsterlaw, 2000; Zimmer, 2003; Wellman et al., 2008).

Another piece of evidence for infants' growing sense of mental activity is that by the age of 2, infants begin to demonstrate the rudiments of empathy. **Empathy** is an emotional response that corresponds to the feelings of another person. At 24 months of age, infants sometimes comfort others or show concern for them. In order to do this, they need to be aware of the emotional states of others. For example, 1-year-olds are able to pick up emotional cues by observing the behavior of an actress on television (Gauthier, 2003; Mumm & Fernald, 2003).

Furthermore, during their second year, infants begin to use deception, both in games of "pretend" and in outright attempts to fool others. A child who plays "pretend" and who uses falsehoods must be aware that others hold beliefs about the world—beliefs that can be manipulated. In short, by the end of infancy children have developed the rudiments of their own personal theory of mind. It helps them understand the actions of others and it affects their own behavior (van der Mark et al., 2002; Caron, 2009).

> **empathy** an emotional response that corresponds to the feelings of another person

👁 Watch on mydevelopmentlab.com

To see the theory of mind at work, watch the video in MyDevelopmentLab.com.

## REVIEW, CHECK, AND APPLY

### REVIEW

**LO15  Do infants experience emotions?**

- Infants appear to express and to experience emotions, and their emotions broaden in range to reflect increasingly complex emotional states.
- The ability to decode the nonverbal facial and vocal expressions of others develops early in infants.

**LO16  What sort of mental lives do infants have?**

- Infants develop self-awareness, the knowledge that they exist separately from the rest of the world, after about 12 months of age, and by the age of 2, children have developed the rudiments of a theory of mind.

### CHECK YOURSELF

1. _____ is the caution and wariness expressed by infants when encountering an unfamiliar person.

2. Marcel has been attending day care without incident since he was 6 weeks old. Now at around 14 months he starts to express difficulty when his mother leaves. He cries, shouts "No!" and then grabs her leg as she attempts to leave for work. Which of the following concepts best explains Marcel's change in behavior?

   a. stranger anxiety
   b. intuition
   c. egocentrism
   d. separation anxiety

3. When Darius bumped his knee on the table, he gazed at his mother to look at her reaction. When he saw that she was alarmed, he began crying. This is an example of _____.

### APPLYING LIFESPAN DEVELOPMENT

- Why would the sad or flat emotional expressiveness of a depressed parent be hard on an infant? How might it be counteracted?

✔ Study and Review on
MyDevelopmentLab.com

Answers: 1) Stranger anxiety; 2) d; 3) social referencing

# Forming Relationships

**LO17 What roles do other people play in infants' social development?**

**LO18 How sociable are infants?**

LEARNING OBJECTIVES

*Louis Moore became the center of attention on the way home [from the hospital]. His father brought Martha, aged 5, and Tom, aged 3, to the hospital with him when Louis and his mother were discharged.*

**attachment** the positive emotional bond that develops between a child and a particular individual

**Ainsworth Strange Situation** a sequence of staged episodes that illustrate the strength of attachment between a child and (typically) his or her mother

**secure attachment pattern** a style of attachment in which children use the mother as a kind of home base and are at ease when she is present; when she leaves, they become upset and go to her as soon as she returns

*Martha rushed to see "her" new baby and ignored her mother. Tom clung to his mother's knees in the reception hall of the hospital.*

*A hospital nurse carried Louis to the car. . . . The two older children immediately climbed over the seat and swamped mother and baby with their attention. Both children stuck their faces into his, smacked at him, and talked to him. They soon began to fight over him with loud voices. The loud argument and the jostling of his mother upset Louis, and he started to cry. He let out a wail that came like a shotgun blast into the noisy car. The children quieted immediately and looked with awe at this new infant. His insistent wails drowned out their bickering. He had already asserted himself in their eyes.* (Brazelton, 1983, p. 48)

The arrival of a newborn brings a dramatic change to a family's dynamics. No matter how welcome a baby's birth, it causes a fundamental shift in the roles that people play within the family. Mothers and fathers must start to build a relationship with their infant, and older children must adjust to the presence of a new member of the family and build their own alliance with their infant brother or sister.

Although the process of social development during infancy is neither simple nor automatic, it is crucial: The bonds that grow between infants and their parents, siblings, family, and others provide the foundation for a lifetime's worth of social relationships.

## Attachment: Forming Social Bonds

The most important aspect of social development that takes place during infancy is the formation of attachment. **Attachment** is the positive emotional bond that develops between a child and a particular, special individual. When children experience attachment to a given person, they feel pleasure when they are with them and feel comforted by their presence at times of distress—like the infant Alex, described in the Chapter 3 opener, who cried in his crib until his mother or father came to comfort him. The nature of our attachment during infancy affects how we relate to others throughout the rest of our lives (Grossmann & Waters, 2005; Hofer, 2006; Johnson et al., 2010).

To understand attachment, the earliest researchers turned to the bonds that form between parents and children in the nonhuman animal kingdom. For instance, ethologist Konrad Lorenz (1965) observed newborn goslings, who have an innate tendency to follow their mother, the first moving object to which they typically are exposed after birth. Lorenz found that goslings hatched from an incubator, who viewed him just after hatching, would follow his every movement, as if he were their mother. As we discussed in Module 1.3, he labeled this process *imprinting*: behavior that takes place during a critical period and involves attachment to the first moving object that is observed.

Lorenz's findings suggested that attachment was based on biologically determined factors, and other theorists agreed. For instance, Freud suggested that attachment grew out of a mother's ability to satisfy a child's oral needs. Similarly, British psychiatrist John Bowlby (1951) argued that attachment is based primarily on infants' needs for safety and security. As they develop, infants come to learn that their safety is best provided by a particular individual, typically the mother, and they develop a relationship with the primary caregiver that is qualitatively different from the bonds formed with others. In his view, attachment provides a type of home base. As children become more independent, they can progressively roam further away from their secure base.

***The Ainsworth Strange Situation and Patterns of Attachment.*** Developmental psychologist Mary Ainsworth built on Bowlby's theorizing to develop a widely used experimental technique to measure attachment (Ainsworth et al., 1978). The **Ainsworth Strange Situation** consists of a sequence of staged episodes that illustrate the strength of attachment between a child and (typically) his or her mother. The "strange situation" follows this general eight-step pattern: (1) The mother and baby enter an unfamiliar room; (2) the mother sits down, leaving the baby free to explore; (3) an adult stranger enters the room and converses first with the mother and then with the baby; (4) the mother exits the room, leaving the baby alone with the stranger; (5) the mother returns, greeting and comforting the baby, and the stranger leaves; (6) the mother departs again, leaving the baby alone; (7) the stranger returns; and (8) the mother returns and the stranger leaves (Ainsworth et al., 1978).

## TABLE 3-9  CLASSIFICATIONS OF INFANT ATTACHMENT

**Classification Criteria**

| Label | Seeking Proximity with Caregiver | Maintaining Contact with Caregiver | Avoiding Proximity with Caregiver | Resisting Contact with Caregiver |
|---|---|---|---|---|
| Avoidant | Low | Low | High | Low |
| Secure | High | High (if distressed) | Low | Low |
| Ambivalent | High | High (often preseparation) | Low | High |
| Disorganized-disoriented | Inconsistent | Inconsistent | Inconsistent | Inconsistent |

Infants' reactions to the various aspects of the Strange Situation vary considerably, depending on the nature of their attachment to their mothers. One-year-olds typically show one of four major patterns—secure, avoidant, ambivalent, and disorganized-disoriented (summarized in Table 3-9). Children who have a **secure attachment pattern** use the mother as the type of home base that Bowlby described. These children seem at ease in the Strange Situation as long as their mothers are present. They explore independently, returning to her occasionally. Although they may or may not appear upset when she leaves, securely attached children immediately go to her when she returns and seek contact. Most North American children—about two-thirds—fall into the securely attached category.

In contrast, children with an **avoidant attachment pattern** do not seek proximity to the mother, and after she has left, they typically do not seem distressed. Furthermore, they seem to avoid her when she returns. It is as if they are indifferent to her behavior. Some 20 percent of 1-year-old children are in the avoidant category.

Children with an **ambivalent attachment pattern** display a combination of positive and negative reactions to their mothers. Initially, ambivalent children are in such close contact with the mother that they hardly explore their environment. They appear anxious even before the mother leaves, and when she does leave, they show great distress. But upon her return, they show ambivalent reactions, seeking to be close to her but also hitting and kicking, apparently in anger. About 10 to 15 percent of 1-year-olds fall into the ambivalent classification (Cassidy & Berlin, 1994).

Although Ainsworth identified only three categories, a more recent expansion of her work finds that there is a fourth category: disorganized-disoriented. Children who have a **disorganized–disoriented attachment pattern** show inconsistent, contradictory, and confused behavior. They may run to the mother when she returns but not look at her, or seem initially calm and then suddenly break into angry weeping. Their confusion suggests that they may be the least securely attached children of all. About 5 to 10 percent of all children fall into this category (Mayseless, 1996; Cole, 2005; Bernier & Meins, 2008).

The quality of attachment between infants and their mothers has significant consequences for relationships at later stages of life. For example, boys who are securely attached at the age of 1 year show fewer psychological difficulties at older ages than do avoidant or ambivalent children. Similarly, children who are securely attached as infants tend to be more socially and emotionally competent later, and others view them more positively (Mikulincer & Shaver, 2005; Simpson et al., 2007; MacDonald et al., 2008).

In cases in which the development of attachment has been severely disrupted, children may suffer from *reactive attachment disorder,* a psychological problem characterized by extreme problems in forming attachments to others. In young children, it results in feeding difficulties, unresponsiveness to social overtures from others, and a general failure to thrive. Reactive attachment disorder is rare and typically the result of abuse or neglect (Corbin, 2007; Hardy, 2007; Hornor, 2008; Schechter & Willheim, 2009).

**avoidant attachment pattern** a style of attachment in which children do not seek proximity to the mother; after the mother has left, they seem to avoid her when she returns as if they are angered by her behavior

**ambivalent attachment pattern** a style of attachment in which children display a combination of positive and negative reactions to their mothers; they show great distress when the mother leaves, but upon her return they may simultaneously seek close contact but also hit and kick her

**disorganized–disoriented attachment pattern** a style of attachment in which children show inconsistent, often contradictory behavior, such as approaching the mother when she returns but not looking at her; they may be the least securely attached children of all

## Producing Attachment: The Roles of the Mother and Father

*As 5-month-old Annie cries passionately, her mother comes into the room and gently lifts her from her crib. After just a few moments, as her mother rocks Annie and speaks softly, Annie's cries cease, and she cuddles in her mother's arms. But the moment her mother places her back in the crib, Annie begins to wail again, leading her mother to pick her up once again.*

The pattern is familiar to most parents. The infant cries, the parent reacts, and the child responds in turn. Such seemingly insignificant sequences as these, repeatedly occurring in the lives of infants and parents, help pave the way for the development of relationships between children, their parents, and the rest of the social world. We'll consider how each of the major caregivers and the infant play a role in the development of attachment.

**From a social worker's perspective:** What might a social worker seeking to find a good home for a foster child look for when evaluating potential foster parents?

*Mothers and Attachment.* Sensitivity to their infants' needs and desires is the hallmark of mothers of securely attached infants. Such a mother tends to be aware of her child's moods, and she takes into account her child's feelings as they interact. She is also responsive during face-to-face interactions, provides feeding "on demand," and is warm and affectionate to her infant (Thompson, Easterbrooks, & Padilla-Walker, 2003; McElwain & Booth-LaForce, 2006; Priddis & Howieson, 2009).

It is not only a matter of responding in *any* fashion to their infants' signals that separates mothers of securely attached and insecurely attached children. Mothers of secure infants tend to provide the appropriate level of response. In fact, overly responsive mothers are just as likely to have insecurely attached children as underresponsive mothers. In contrast, mothers whose communication involves *interactional synchrony*—in which caregivers respond to infants appropriately and both caregiver and child match emotional states—are more likely to produce secure attachment (Kochanska, 1998; Hane, Feldstein, & Dernetz, 2003).

*Fathers and Attachment.* Up to now, we've barely touched upon one of the key players involved in the upbringing of a child: the father. In fact, if you looked at the early theorizing and research on attachment, you'd find little mention of the father and his potential contributions to the life of the infant (Tamis-LeMonda & Cabrera, 1999; Freeman, Newland, & Coyl, 2010).

However, it has become increasingly clear that—despite societal norms that sometimes relegate fathers to secondary childrearing roles—infants can form their primary initial relationship with their fathers. Indeed, much of what we have said about mothers' attachment also applies to fathers. For example, fathers' expressions of nurturance, warmth, affection, support, and concern are extremely important to their children's emotional and social well-being. Furthermore, some psychological disorders, such as substance abuse and depression, have been found to be related more to fathers' than mothers' behavior (Veneziano, 2003; Parke, 2004; Roelofs et al., 2006).

Infants' social bonds extend beyond their parents, especially as they grow older. For example, one study found that although most infants formed their first primary relationship with one person, around one-third had multiple relationships, and it was often difficult to determine which attachment was primary. Furthermore, by the time the infants were 18 months old, most had formed multiple relationships. In sum, infants may develop attachments not only to their mothers, but to a variety of others as well (Silverstein & Auerbach, 1999; Booth, Kelly, & Spieker, 2003; Seibert & Kerns, 2009).

A growing body of research highlights the importance of a father's demonstration of love for his children. In fact, certain disorders such as depression and substance abuse have been found to be more related to fathers' than to mothers' behavior.

## Infants' Sociability with Their Peers: Infant–Infant Interaction

Although it is clear that they do not form "friendships" in the traditional sense, babies do react positively to the presence of peers from early in life, and they engage in rudimentary forms of social interaction.

## *Cultural Dimensions*

### Does Attachment Differ Across Cultures?

John Bowlby's observations of the biologically motivated efforts of the young of other species to seek safety and security were the basis for his views on attachment and his reason for suggesting that seeking attachment was biologically universal, an effort that we should find not only in other species, but among humans of all cultures as well.

Research has shown that human attachment is not as culturally universal as Bowlby predicted. Certain attachment patterns seem more likely among infants of particular cultures. For example, one study of German infants showed that most fell into the avoidant category. Other studies, conducted in Israel and Japan, have found a smaller proportion of infants who were securely attached than in the United States. Finally, comparisons of Chinese and Canadian children show that Chinese children are more inhibited than Canadians in the Strange Situation (Grossmann et al., 1982; Takahashi, 1986; Rothbaum et al., 2000; Tomlinson, Murray, & Cooper, 2010).

Do such findings suggest that we should abandon the notion that attachment is a universal biological tendency? Not necessarily. Most of the data on attachment have been obtained by using the Ainsworth Strange Situation, which may not be the most appropriate measure in non-Western cultures. For example, Japanese parents seek to avoid separation and stress during infancy, and they don't strive to foster independence to the same degree as parents in many Western societies. Because of their relative lack of prior experience in separation, infants placed in the Strange Situation may experience unusual stress—producing the appearance of less secure attachment in Japanese children. If a different measure of attachment were used, one that might be administered later in infancy, more Japanese infants could likely be classified as secure. In short, attachment is affected by cultural norms and expectations (Nakagawa, Lamb, & Miyaki, 1992; Vereijken et al., 1997; Dennis, Cole, & Zahn-Waxler, 2002).

Infants' sociability is expressed in several ways. From the earliest months of life, they smile, laugh, and vocalize while looking at their peers. They show more interest in peers than in inanimate objects and pay greater attention to other infants than they do to a mirror image of themselves. They also begin to show preferences for peers with whom they are familiar compared with those they do not know. For example, studies of identical twins show that twins exhibit a higher level of social behavior toward each other than toward an unfamiliar infant (Eid et al., 2003).

Infants' level of sociability rises with age. Nine- to 12-month-olds mutually present and accept toys, particularly if they know each other. They also play social games, such as peek-a-boo or crawl-and-chase. Such behavior is important, as it serves as a foundation for future social exchanges in which children will try to elicit responses from others and then offer reactions to those responses. These kinds of exchanges are important to learn, since they continue even into adulthood. For example, someone who says, "Hi, what's up?" may be trying to elicit a response to which he or she can then reply (Endo, 1992; Eckerman & Peterman, 2001).

Finally, as infants age, they begin to imitate each other (Russon & Waite, 1991). For instance, 14-month-old infants who are familiar with one another sometimes reproduce each other's behavior (Mueller & Vandell, 1979). Such imitation serves a social function and can also be a powerful teaching tool.

To some developmentalists, the capacity of young children to engage in imitation suggests that imitation may be inborn. In support of this view, research has identified a class of neurons in the brain that seems related to an innate ability to imitate. *Mirror neurons* are neurons that fire not only when an individual enacts a particular behavior, but also when the individual simply observes *another* organism carrying out the same behavior (Falck-Ytter, 2006).

For example, research on brain functioning shows activation of the inferior frontal gyrus both when an individual carries out a particular task and also when observing another individual carrying out the same task. Mirror neurons may help infants understand others' actions and develop a theory of mind. Dysfunction of mirror neurons may be related to the development of disorders involving children's theory of mind as well as autism, a psychological disorder involving significant emotional and linguistic problems (Kilner, Friston, & Frith, 2007; Martineau et al., 2008; Welsh et al., 2009).

Japanese parents seek to avoid separation and stress during infancy and do not foster independence. As a result, Japanese children often have the appearance of being less securely attached according to the Strange Situation, but using other measurement techniques they may well score higher in attachment.

## REVIEW, CHECK, AND APPLY

### REVIEW

**LO17** What roles do other people play in infants' social development?

- Attachment, the positive emotional bond between an infant and a significant individual, affects a person's later social competence as an adult.

- Infants and the persons with whom they interact engage in reciprocal socialization as they mutually adjust to one another's interactions.

**LO18** How sociable are infants?

- Infants react differently to other children than to inanimate objects. Babies react positively to the presence of peers from early in life, and they engage in rudimentary forms of social interactions.

### CHECK YOURSELF

1. _____ is the positive emotional bond that develops between a child and a particular individual.

2. Children who are attached to their primary caregivers feel _____ when they are with them and feel _____ during times of distress.

   a. concern; sad
   b. pleasure; comforted
   c. overwhelmed; distraught
   d. confused; comfort

3. One way mothers can improve the likelihood of secure attachment in their children is to respond to their needs appropriately. Another name for this communication in which mothers and children match emotional states is:

   a. emotion matching.
   b. goodness of fit.
   c. interactional synchrony.
   d. environmental assessment.

### APPLYING LIFESPAN DEVELOPMENT

- In what sort of society might an avoidant attachment style be encouraged by cultural attitudes toward childrearing? In such a society, would characterizing the infant's consistent avoidance of its mother as anger be an accurate interpretation?

✔•⎯ **Study** and **Review** on **MyDevelopmentLab.com**

Answers: 1) Attachment; 2) b; 3) c

---

# Differences among Infants

**LO19** What individual differences distinguish one infant from another?
**LO20** How does nonparental child care impact infants?

**LEARNING OBJECTIVES**

*Lincoln was a difficult baby, his parents both agreed. For one thing, it seemed like they could never get him to sleep at night. He cried at the slightest noise, a problem since his crib was near the windows facing a busy street. Worse yet, once he started crying, it seemed to take forever to calm him down again. One day his mother, Aisha, was telling her mother-in-law, Mary, about the challenges of being Lincoln's mom. Mary recalled that her own son, Lincoln's father Malcom, had been much the same way. "He was my first child, and I thought this was how all babies acted. So, we just kept trying different ways until we found out how he worked. I remember, we put his crib all over the apartment until we finally found out where he could sleep, and it ended up being in the hallway for a long time. Then his sister, Maleah, came along, and she was so quiet and easy, I didn't know what to do with my extra time!"*

As the story of Lincoln's family shows, babies are not all alike, and neither are their families. In fact, as we'll see, some of the differences among people seem to be present from the moment we are born. The differences among infants include overall personality and temperament, and differences in the lives they lead—differences based on their gender, the nature of their families, and the ways in which they are cared for.

## Personality Development: The Characteristics That Make Infants Unique

The origins of **personality,** the sum total of the enduring characteristics that differentiate one individual from another, stem from infancy. From birth onward, infants begin to show unique, stable traits and behaviors that ultimately lead to their development as distinct, special individuals (Caspi, 2000; Kagan, 2000; Shiner, Masten, & Roberts, 2003).

**personality** the sum total of the enduring characteristics that differentiate one individual from another

According to psychologist Erik Erikson, whose approach to personality development we first discussed in Module 1.2, infants' early experiences are responsible for shaping one of the key aspects of their personalities: whether they will be basically trusting or mistrustful.

**Erikson's theory of psychosocial development** considers how individuals come to understand themselves and the meaning of others'—and their own—behavior (Erikson, 1963). The theory suggests that developmental change occurs throughout people's lives in eight distinct stages, the first of which occurs in infancy.

According to Erikson, during the first 18 months of life, we pass through the **trust-versus-mistrust stage**. During this period, infants develop a sense of trust or mistrust, largely depending on how well their needs are met by their caregivers. Mary's attention to Malcom's needs, in the previous example, probably helped him develop a basic sense of trust in the world. Erikson suggests that if infants are able to develop trust, they experience a sense of hope, which permits them to feel as if they can fulfill their needs successfully. On the other hand, feelings of mistrust lead infants to see the world as harsh and unfriendly, and they may have later difficulties in forming close bonds with others.

During the end of infancy, children enter the **autonomy-versus-shame-and-doubt stage,** which lasts from around 18 months to 3 years. During this period, children develop independence and autonomy if parents encourage exploration and freedom within safe boundaries. However, if children are restricted and overly protected, they feel shame, self-doubt, and unhappiness.

Erikson argues that personality is primarily shaped by infants' experiences. However, as we discuss next, other developmentalists concentrate on consistencies of behavior that are present at birth, even before the experiences of infancy. These consistencies are viewed as largely genetically determined and as providing the raw material of personality.

## Temperament: Stabilities in Infant Behavior

Sarah's parents thought there must be something wrong. Unlike her older brother Josh, who had been so active as an infant that he seemed never to be still, Sarah was much more placid. She took long naps and was easily soothed on those relatively rare occasions when she became agitated. What could be producing her extreme calmness?

The most likely answer: The difference between Sarah and Josh reflected differences in temperament. As we first discussed in Module 2.1, **temperament** encompasses patterns of arousal and emotionality that are consistent and enduring characteristics of an individual (Kochanska & Aksan, 2004; Rothbart, 2007).

Temperament refers to *how* children behave, as opposed to *what* they do or *why* they do it. Infants show temperamental differences in general disposition from the time of birth, largely due initially to genetic factors, and temperament tends to be fairly stable well into adolescence. On the other hand, temperament is not fixed and unchangeable: Childrearing practices can modify temperament significantly. In fact, some children show little consistency in temperament from one age to another (McCrae et al., 2000; Rothbart & Derryberry, 2002; Wener et al., 2007).

Temperament is reflected in several dimensions of behavior. One central dimension is *activity level*, which reflects the degree of overall movement. Some babies (like Sarah and Maleah, in the earlier examples) are relatively placid, and their movements are slow and almost leisurely. In contrast, the activity level of other infants (like Josh) is quite high, with strong, restless movements of the arms and legs.

Another important dimension of temperament is the nature and quality of an infant's mood, and in particular a child's *irritability*. Some infants are relatively easygoing, while others are less so. For example, irritable infants fuss a great deal, and they are easily upset. They are also difficult to soothe when they do begin to cry. (Other aspects of temperament are listed in Table 3-10.)

*Categorizing Temperament: Easy, Difficult, and Slow-to-Warm Babies.* Because temperament can be viewed along so many dimensions, some researchers have asked whether there are broader categories that can be used to describe children's overall behavior. According to Alexander Thomas and Stella Chess, who carried out a large-scale study of a group of

**Erikson's theory of psychosocial development** the theory that considers how individuals come to understand themselves and the meaning of others'—and their own—behavior

**trust-versus-mistrust stage** according to Erikson, the period during which infants develop a sense of trust or mistrust, largely depending on how well their needs are met by their caregivers

**autonomy-versus-shame-and-doubt stage** the period during which, according to Erikson, toddlers (aged 18 months to 3 years) develop independence and autonomy if they are allowed the freedom to explore, or shame and self-doubt if they are restricted and overprotected

**temperament** patterns of arousal and emotionality that are consistent and enduring characteristics of an individual

## TABLE 3-10 DIMENSIONS OF TEMPERAMENT

| Dimension | Definition |
| --- | --- |
| Activity level | Proportion of active time periods to inactive time periods |
| Approach/withdrawal | The response to a new person or object, based on whether the child accepts the new situation or withdraws from it |
| Adaptability | How easily the child is able to adapt to changes in his or her environment |
| Quality of mood | The contrast of the amount of friendly, joyful, and pleasant behavior with unpleasant, unfriendly behavior |
| Attention span and persistence | The amount of time the child devotes to an activity and the effect of distraction on that activity |
| Distractibility | The degree to which stimuli in the environment alter behavior |
| Rhythmicity (regularity) | The regularity of basic functions such as hunger, excretion, sleep, and wakefulness |
| Intensity of reaction | The energy level or reaction of the child's response |
| Threshold of responsiveness | The intensity of stimulation needed to elicit a response |

infants that has come to be known as the *New York Longitudinal Study* (Thomas & Chess, 1980), babies can be described according to one of several profiles:

- Easy babies. **Easy babies** have a positive disposition. Their body functions operate regularly, and they are adaptable. They are generally positive, showing curiosity about new situations, and their emotions are moderate or low in intensity. This category applies to about 40 percent (the largest number) of infants.
- Difficult babies. **Difficult babies** have more negative moods and are slow to adapt to new situations. When confronted with a new situation, they tend to withdraw. About 10 percent of infants belong in this category.
- Slow-to-warm babies. **Slow-to-warm babies** are inactive, showing relatively calm reactions to their environment. Their moods are generally negative, and they withdraw from new situations, adapting slowly. Approximately 15 percent of infants are slow-to-warm.

As for the remaining 35 percent, they cannot be consistently categorized. These children show a variety of combinations of characteristics. For instance, one infant may have relatively sunny moods, but react negatively to new situations, or another may show little stability of any sort in terms of general temperament.

***The Consequences of Temperament: Does Temperament Matter?*** One obvious question to emerge from the findings of the relative stability of temperament is whether a particular kind of temperament is beneficial. The answer seems to be that no single type of temperament is invariably good or bad. Instead, children's long-term adjustment depends on the **goodness-of-fit** of their particular temperament to the nature and demands of the environment in which they find themselves. For instance, children with a low activity level and low irritability may do particularly well in an environment in which they are left to explore on their own and are allowed largely to direct their own behavior. In contrast, high-activity-level, highly irritable children may do best with greater direction, which permits them to channel their energy in particular directions (Thomas & Chess, 1980; Strelau, 1998; Schoppe-Sullivan et al., 2007). Mary, the grandmother in the earlier example, found ways to adjust the environment for her son, Malcom. Malcom and Aisha may need to do the same for their own son, Lincoln.

Some research does suggest that certain temperaments are, in general, more adaptive than others. For instance, difficult children, in general, are more likely to show behavior problems by school age than those classified in infancy as easy children. But not all difficult children experience problems. The key determinant seems to be the way parents react to their infants' difficult behavior. If they react by showing anger and inconsistency—responses that their child's difficult, demanding behavior readily evokes—then the child is ultimately

**easy babies** babies who have a positive disposition; their body functions operate regularly, and they are adaptable

**difficult babies** babies who have negative moods and are slow to adapt to new situations; when confronted with a new situation, they tend to withdraw

**slow-to-warm babies** babies who are inactive, showing relatively calm reactions to their environment; their moods are generally negative, and they withdraw from new situations, adapting slowly

**goodness-of-fit** the notion that development is dependent on the degree of match between children's temperament and the nature and demands of the environment in which they are being raised

more likely to experience behavior problems. On the other hand, parents who display more warmth and consistency in their responses are more likely to have children who avoid later problems (Thomas, Chess, & Birch, 1968; Teerikangas et al., 1998; Pauli-Pott, Mertesacker, & Bade, 2003).

**gender** the sense of being male or female

## Gender: Boys in Blue, Girls in Pink

"It's a boy." "It's a girl." One of these two statements, or some variant, is probably the first announcement made after the birth of a child. From the moment of birth, girls and boys are treated differently. Their parents send out different kinds of birth announcements. They are dressed in different clothes and wrapped in different-colored blankets. They are given different toys (Bridges, 1993; Coltrane & Adams, 1997; Serbin, Poulin-Dubois, & Colburne, 2001).

Parents play with boy and girl babies differently: From birth on, fathers tend to interact more with sons than daughters, while mothers interact more with daughters. Because, as we noted earlier in the module, mothers and fathers play in different ways (with fathers typically engaging in more physical, rough-and-tumble activities and mothers in traditional games such as peek-a-boo), male and female infants are clearly exposed to different styles of activity and interaction from their parents (Laflamme, Pomerleau, & Malcuit, 2002; Clearfield & Nelson, 2006; Parke, 2007).

The behavior exhibited by girls and boys is interpreted in very different ways by adults. For instance, when researchers showed adults a video of an infant whose name was given as either "John" or "Mary," adults perceived "John" as adventurous and inquisitive, while "Mary" was fearful and anxious, although it was the same baby performing a single set of behaviors (Condry & Condry, 1976). Clearly, adults view the behavior of children through the lens of gender. **Gender** refers to the sense of being male or female. The term "gender" is often used to mean the same thing as "sex," but they are not actually the same. *Sex* typically refers to sexual anatomy and sexual behavior, while gender refers to the social perceptions of maleness or femaleness.

***Gender Differences.*** There is a considerable amount of disagreement over both the extent and causes of such gender differences, even though most agree that boys and girls do experience at least partially different worlds based on gender. Some gender differences are fairly clear from the time of birth. For example, male infants tend to be more active and fussier than female infants. Boys' sleep tends to be more disturbed than that of girls. Boys grimace more, although no gender difference exists in the overall amount of crying. There is also some evidence that male newborns are more irritable than female newborns, although the findings are inconsistent. Differences between male and female infants, however, are generally minor (Crawford & Unger, 2004; Losonczy-Marshall, 2008).

Gender differences emerge more clearly as children age—and become increasingly influenced by the gender roles that society sets out for them. For instance, by the age of 1 year, infants are able to distinguish between males and females. Girls at this age prefer to play with dolls or stuffed animals, while boys seek out blocks and trucks. Often, of course, these are the only options available to them, due to the choices their parents and other adults have made in the toys they provide (Cherney, Kelly-Vance, & Glover, 2003; Alexander, Wilcox, & Woods, 2009).

By the time they reach the age of 2, boys behave more independently and less compliantly than girls. Much of this behavior can be traced to parental reactions to earlier behavior. For instance, when a child takes his or her first steps, parents tend to react differently, depending on the child's gender: Boys are encouraged more to go off and explore the world, while girls are hugged and kept close. It is hardly surprising, then, that by the age of 2, girls tend to show less independence and greater compliance (Kuczynski & Kochanska, 1990; Poulin-Dubois, Serbin, & Eichstedt, 2002).

Societal encouragement and reinforcement do not, however, completely explain differences in behavior between boys and girls. For example, one study examined girls who were exposed before birth to abnormally high levels of *androgen,* a male hormone, because their mothers unwittingly took a drug containing the hormone while pregnant. Later, these girls

The number of single-parent families has increased dramatically over the past 20 years. If the current trend continues, 60 percent of all children will live at some time with a single parent

were more likely to play with toys stereotypically preferred by boys (such as cars) and less likely to play with toys stereotypically associated with girls (such as dolls). Although there are many alternative explanations for these results—you can probably think of several yourself—one possibility is that exposure to male hormones affected the brain development of the girls, leading them to favor toys that involve certain kinds of preferred skills (Levine et al., 1999; Mealey, 2000; Servin et al., 2003; Kahlenberg & Hein, 2010).

In sum, differences in behavior between boys and girls begin in infancy, and—as we will see in future modules—continue throughout childhood (and beyond). Although gender differences have complex causes, representing some combination of innate, biologically related factors and environmental factors, they play a profound role in the social and emotional development of infants.

## Family Life in the Twenty-first Century

Family life today is very different from the way it was even a few decades ago. A quick review tells the story:

- The number of single-parent families has increased dramatically in the last two decades, as the number of two-parent households has declined. One-third of all families with children are headed by single parents. Nearly a quarter of children live with only their mothers, 4 percent live with only their fathers, and 4 percent live with neither of their parents (U.S. Bureau of the Census, 2000; ChildStats.gov, 2009).

- The average size of families is shrinking. Today, on average, there are 2.6 persons per household, compared to 2.8 in 1980. The number of people living in nonfamily households (without any relatives) is close to 30 million.

- Although the number of adolescents giving birth has declined substantially over the last five years, there are still half a million births to teenage women, the vast majority of whom are unmarried.

- More than half of mothers of infants work outside the home.

- One in three children lives in low-income households in the United States. The rates are even higher for African American and Hispanic families, and for single-parent families of young children. More children under 3 live in poverty than do older children, adults, or the elderly. Furthermore, the proportion of children living in low-income families began rising in 2000, reversing a decade of decline (Federal Interagency Forum on Child and Family Statistics, 2003; National Center for Children in Poverty, 2005).

At the very least, these statistics suggest that many infants are being raised in environments in which substantial stressors are present. Such stress makes it an unusually difficult task to raise children—never easy even under the best circumstances.

**From a social worker's perspective:** Imagine you are a social worker visiting a foster home. It is 11 AM. You find the breakfast dishes in the sink and books and toys all over the floor. The infant you have placed in the home is happily pounding on pots and pans as his foster mother claps time. The kitchen floor is gooey under the baby's high chair. What is your professional assessment?

On the other hand, society is adapting to the new realities of family life in the twenty-first century. Several kinds of social support exist for the parents of infants, and society is evolving new institutions to help in their care. One example is the growing array of child-care arrangements available to help working parents, as we discuss next.

## How Does Infant Child Care Affect Later Development?

*For most of the years my two kids were in child care, I worried about it. Did that weird day-care home where my daughter stayed briefly as a toddler do irreparable harm? Was my son irretrievably damaged by that child-care center he disliked? (Shellenbarger, 2003, p. D1)*

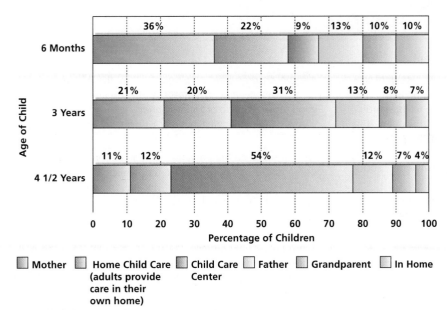

FIGURE 3-17 **Where Are Children Cared For?**
According to a major study by the National Institute of Child Health and Human Development, children spend more time in some kind of child care outside the home or family as they get older.
Source: NICHD, 2006.

Every day, parents ask themselves questions like these. The issue of how infant child care affects later development is a pressing one for many parents, who, because of economic, family, or career demands, leave their children to the care of others for a portion of the day. In fact, almost two-thirds of all children between 4 months and 3 years of age spend time in nonparental child care. Overall, more than 80 percent of infants are cared for by people other than their mothers at some point during their first year of life. The majority of these infants begin child care outside the home before the age of 4 months and are enrolled for almost 30 hours per week (Federal Interagency Forum on Child and Family Statistics, 2003; NICHD, 2006) (also see Figure 3-17). What effects do such arrangements have on later development?

Although the answer is largely reassuring, the newest research to come from the massive, long-term Study of Early Child Care and Youth Development, the longest-running examination of child care ever conducted, suggests that long-term participation in day care may have unanticipated consequences.

First the good news. According to most of the evidence, high-quality child care outside the home produces only minor differences from home care in most respects, and may even enhance certain aspects of development. For example, research finds little or no difference in the strength or nature of parental attachment bonds of infants who have been in high-quality child care compared with infants raised solely by their parents (NICHD Early Child Care Research Network, 1999, 2001; Vandell et al., 2005; Morrissey, 2010).

In addition to the direct benefits from involvement in child care outside the home, there are indirect benefits. For example, children in lower-income households and those whose mothers are single may benefit from the educational and social experiences in child care, as well as from the higher income produced by parental employment (Love et al., 2003; NICHD Early Child Care Research Network, 2003a; Dearing, McCartney, & Taylor, 2009).

Furthermore, children who participate in Early Head Start—a program that serves at-risk infants and toddlers in high-quality child-care centers—can solve problems better, pay greater attention to others, and use language more effectively than poor children who do not participate in the program. In

High-quality infant child care seems to produce only minor differences from home care in most respects, and some aspects of development may even be enhanced. What aspects of development might be enhanced by participation in infant child care outside the home?

# Choosing the Right Infant Care Provider

## Becoming an Informed Consumer of Development

One finding that emerges with absolute clarity from research conducted on the consequences of infant child-care programs is that the benefits of child care—peer learning, greater social skills, greater independence—occur only when child care is of high quality. But what distinguishes high-quality child care from low-caliber programs? Parents should consider these questions in choosing a program (Committee on Children, Youth and Families, 1994; Love et al., 2003; de Schipper et al., 2006):

- Are there enough providers? A desirable ratio is one adult for every three infants, although one to four can be adequate.

- Are group sizes manageable? Even with several providers, a group of infants should not be larger than eight.

- Has the center complied with all governmental regulations, and is it licensed?

- Do the people providing the care seem to like what they are doing? What is their motivation? Is child care just a temporary job, or is it a career? Are they experienced? Do they seem happy in the job, or is offering child care just a way to earn money?

- What do the caregivers do during the day? Do they spend their time playing with, listening and talking to, and paying attention to the children? Do they seem genuinely interested in the children? Is there a television constantly on?

- Are the children safe and clean? Does the environment allow infants to move around safely? Is the equipment and furniture in good repair? Do the providers adhere to the highest levels of cleanliness? After changing a baby's diaper, do providers wash their hands?

- What training do the providers have in caring for children? Do they demonstrate a knowledge of the basics of infant development and an understanding of how normal children develop? Do they seem alert to signs that development may depart from normal patterns?

- Finally, is the environment happy and cheerful? Child care is not just a babysitting service: For the time an infant is there, it is the child's whole world. You should feel fully comfortable and confident that the child-care center is a place where your infant will be treated as an individual.

In addition to following these guidelines, contact the National Association for the Education of Young Children (NAEYC), from which you can get the name of a resource and referral agency in your area. Go to the NAEYC website at www.naeyc.org or call (800) 424-2460.

---

addition, their parents (who are also involved in the program) benefit from their participation. Participating parents talk and read more to their children, and they are less likely to spank them. Likewise, children who receive good, responsive child care are more likely to play well with other children (NICHD Early Child Care Research Network, 2001a; Maccoby & Lewis, 2003; Loeb et al., 2004).

On the other hand, some of the findings on participation in child care outside the home are less positive. Infants may be somewhat less secure when they are placed in low-quality child care or if they are placed in multiple child-care arrangements. In addition, children who spend long hours in outside-the-home child-care situations have a lower ability to work independently and have less effective time management skills (Vandell et al., 2005).

The newest research, which focuses on preschoolers, finds that children who spend 10 or more hours a week in group child care for a year or more have an increased probability of being disruptive in class, and that the effect continues through the sixth grade. Although the increase in the likelihood of acting disruptive is not substantial—every year spent in a child-care center resulted in a 1 percent higher score on a standardized measure of problem behavior completed by teachers—the results were quite reliable (Belsky et al., 2007).

In sum, the ballooning body of research finds that the effects of participation in group child care are neither unambiguously positive nor unambiguously negative. What is clear, though, is that the *quality* of child care is critical. Ultimately, more research is needed on just who makes use of child care and how it is used by members of different segments of society to fully understand its consequences (Marshall, 2004; NICHD Early Child Care Research Network, 2005; Belsky, 2006, 2009; de Schipper et al., 2006).

# REVIEW, CHECK, AND APPLY

## REVIEW

**LO19**   What individual differences distinguish one infant from another?

- According to Erikson, during infancy individuals move from the trust-versus-mistrust stage of psychosocial development to the autonomy-versus-shame-and-guilt stage.

- Temperament encompasses enduring levels of arousal and emotionality that are characteristic of an individual.

- Gender differences become more pronounced as infants age.

**LO20**   How does nonparental child care impact infants?

- Child care outside of the home can have neutral, positive, or negative effects on the social development of children, depending largely on its quality.

## CHECK YOURSELF

1. Patterns of arousal and emotionality that are consistent and enduring in an individual are known as an individual's _____.

2. _____ are prescribed by societies as activities or positions appropriate for males and females.

   a. Gender expectations

   b. Sex roles

   c. Gender roles

   d. Sex expectations

3. Research finds significant differences in the strength and nature of the parental bond for infants raised in the home compared to infants exposed to high-quality day care.

   - True

   - False

## APPLYING LIFESPAN DEVELOPMENT

- If you were introducing a bill in Congress regarding the minimum licensing requirements for child-care centers, what would you emphasize?

✓•⊣ **Study** and **Review** on
**MyDevelopmentLab.com**

Answers: 1) temperament; 2) c; 3) False

# Putting It All Together
## Infancy

**FOUR-MONTH-OLD ALEX** (whom we met in this chapter's opener) was a model infant in almost every respect. However, there was one aspect of her behavior that posed a dilemma: how to respond when he woke up in the middle of the night and cried despondently. It usually was not a matter of being hungry, because typically he had been fed recently. And it was not caused by his diaper being soiled, because usually that had been changed recently. Instead, it seemed that Alex just wanted to be held and entertained, and when he wasn't, he cried and shrieked dramatically until someone came to him.

### MODULE 3.1 Physical Development in Infancy

- Alex's body is developing various rhythms (repetitive, cyclical patterns of behavior) that are responsible for the change from sleep to wakefulness. **(pp. 99–101)**

- Alex will sleep in spurts of around 2 hours, followed by periods of wakefulness until about 16 weeks, when he will begin to sleep as much as 6 continuous hours. **(p. 100)**

- Since Alex's sense of touch is one of his most highly developed senses (and one of the earliest developed), Alex will respond to gentle touches, such as a soothing caress, which can calm a crying, fussy infant. **(p. 112)**

### MODULE 3.2 Cognitive Development in Infancy

- Alex has learned that his behavior (crying) can produce a desired effect (someone holding and entertaining her). **(pp. 117–118)**

- As Alex's brain develops, he is able to separate people he knows from people he doesn't; this is why he responds so positively when someone he knows comes to comfort him during the night. **(pp. 122–123)**

## What would a PARENT do?

■ What strategies would you use in dealing with Alex? Would you go to him every time he cried? Or, would you try to wait him out, perhaps setting a time limit before going to him?

**HINT** Review pages 144–147.

*What's your response?*

■ Alex has developed attachment (the positive emotional bond between him and particular individuals) to those who care for him. **(p. 140)**

■ In order to feel secure, Alex needs to know that his caregivers will provide an appropriate response to the signals he is sending. **(p. 145)**

■ Part of Alex's temperament is that he is irritable. Irritable infants can be fussy and are difficult to soothe when they do begin to cry. **(pp. 145–147)**

■ Since irritability is relatively stable, Alex will continue to display this temperament at age 1 and even age 2. **(pp. 145–147)**

## What would a HEALTH CARE PROVIDER do?

■ How would you recommend that Alex's caregivers deal with the situation? Are there any dangers that the caregivers should be aware of?

**HINT** Review pages 144–147.

*What's your response?*

## What would an EDUCATOR do?

■ Suppose Alex spends a few hours every weekday afternoon in day care. If you were a child-care provider, how would you deal with Alex if he wakes up from naps soon after falling asleep?

**HINT** Review pages 148–150.

*What's your response?*

✳━[Explore on **mydevelopmentlab.com**

To read how real-life parents, health care providers, and educators responded to these questions, log onto MyDevelopmentLab.com. Do you agree or disagree with their responses? Why? What concepts that you've read about back up their opinion?

## What would YOU do?

■ How would you deal with Alex? What factors would affect your decision? Based on your reading, how do you think Alex will respond?

**HINT** Review pages 135–146.

*What's your response?*

# CHAPTER 4

# The Preschool Years

At his preschool, William had a reputation for mischief. A 3-year-old with red hair, a winning smile, and a twinkle in his eye, William always seemed to find new ways to keep himself, and often his classmates, laughing. He earned the secret nickname "Wild William" among his preschool teachers.

One afternoon in May, Wild William outdid himself. During naptime, he woke early and decided to take a stroll among his sleeping classmates to find something entertaining to do. Escaping the notice of the preschool teachers for a few minutes, William casually made his way to the back of the room and pulled open a drawer in the closet where he knew the teachers stored the class's snacks. To his delight, he found the Tupperware container and it was full of cookies. After a few attempts, William managed to pull off the Tupperware lid and help himself to several cookies.

Deciding he liked what could be found in these drawers, William quietly pulled open another one. This time he found a shoebox. When he opened it, he discovered a trove of markers and crayons, which he used enthusiastically. He was doggedly climbing onto a chair to reach the second shelf of the closet when a teacher finally

## MODULE **4.1** Physical Development in the Preschool Years

### When—and how—should children be toilet trained? see page 156.

## MODULE **4.2** Cognitive Development in the Preschool Years

### How accurate is a preschooler's memory? see page 164.

spotted him. His face was covered with cookie crumbs, and his clothes and the closet drawers were lavishly decorated with marker ink and crayon marks!

William smiled—but sheepishly rather than with the broad, toothy smile that was his trademark. He knew he was busted.

"I woke up," he said to his frowning teacher. "And I wanted cookies."

Three years ago, William could not even lift his head. Now he can move with confidence—walking across rooms, opening drawers and figuring out Tupperware, climbing chairs, drawing with markers. These advances in physicality are challenging to parents, who must rise to a whole new level of vigilance to prevent injuries, the greatest threat to preschoolers' physical well-being. (Think what would have happened if William had found a shoebox full of scissors.)

The preschool period is an exciting time in children's lives. In one sense, the preschool years mark a time of preparation: a period spent anticipating and getting ready for the start of a child's formal education, through which society will begin the process of passing on its intellectual tools to a new generation.

But it is a mistake to take the label "preschool" too literally. The years between 3 and 6 are hardly a mere way station in life, an interval spent waiting for the next, more important period to start. Instead, the preschool years are a time of tremendous change and growth, where physical, intellectual, and social development proceeds at a rapid pace.

## MODULE **4.3** Social and Personality Development in the Preschool Years

# Viewing violence on TV: Does it matter? see page 178.

## My Virtual Child

Experience the challenges and delights of the preschool years by helping your own virtual child through these years.

Log onto *My Virtual Child* through MyDevelopmentLab.com to get started.

In this chapter, we focus on the physical, cognitive, and social and personality growth that occurs during the preschool years. We begin by considering the physical changes children undergo during those years. We discuss weight and height, nutrition, and health and wellness. The brain and its neural pathways change too, and we will touch on some intriguing findings relating to gender differences in the way the brain functions. We also look at how both gross and fine motor skills change over the preschool years.

Intellectual development is the focus of the next section of the chapter. We examine the major approaches to cognitive development, including Piaget's stage theory, information processing approaches, and an emerging view of cognitive development that gives great weight to the influence of culture. We also consider the important advances in language development that occur during the preschool years, and we discuss several factors that influence cognitive development, including exposure to television and participation in child-care and preschool programs.

Finally, we look at social and personality development in these years, focusing first on how children figure out who they are and develop a sense of racial and gender identity. We discuss the nature of their friendships and the significance of the ways they play together. We next look at parents, considering the different styles of parenting that are common today as well as their implications for their children's future development and personalities. We conclude with a look at the ways in which preschool-age children begin to develop a moral sense and learn how to control aggression.

# MODULE 4.1 Physical Development in the Preschool Years

## Lisa

*Lisa Turing is 3 years old and, her father jokes, probably holds the world record for land speed achieved by a biped. He and Lisa's mother have been dazzled since Lisa's birth by her quickness. She crawled early, and at great speed. When she decided to stand, she soon mastered that skill and immediately moved on to walking. She walked at 10 months, walked quickly at about 11 months, and achieved a near-run by 1 year.*

*Now, at age 3, Lisa is a whirlwind, chasing Alley, the family dog, around the yard, tumbling gleefully every once in a while, laughing when Alley licks her face, and popping up and starting to run again. She follows the same pattern indoors, darting from room to room for the sheer joy of movement, flopping onto armchairs and sofas, and moving kitchen chairs to climb onto tables and countertops. If someone should ever forget to close the safety gate, Lisa would climb the stairs before anyone could stop her.*

*Lisa's mother needs two hands to count how many times in the last three years she and her husband have had to expand the definition of "child-proofing" to accommodate Lisa's rapidly developing physical abilities.* ◉ Watch on **mydevelopmentlab.com**

◉ Watch on **mydevelopmentlab.com**

To better understand the changes that the preschool period brings—and to get a sense of how parents and caregivers have to adjust to those changes—log onto *My Virtual Child* through MyDevelopmentLab.com.

*In just three years,* Lisa Turing has grown from a nearly immobile newborn to a whirlwind of activity. She moves with confidence—perhaps too much confidence. She runs at breakneck speed, chases her dog everywhere, fearlessly falls to the ground and rolls around, and then jumps up and starts all over again. Indoors she darts from room to room, pulls on handles and knobs, and climbs chairs to reach tables and countertops. These advances in mobility are challenging to her parents, who must rise to a whole new level of vigilance to prevent injuries, the greatest threat to preschoolers' physical well-being. (Think what might happen if someone left a rake or hoe in the yard or if any countertop corner were left unprotected.)

Parents and caregivers also must worry about colds and other illnesses, and, especially in recent years, about making sure their child gets enough of the right kinds of food to eat. As they watch their child grow active, they must insist on quiet time and a bedtime that will afford their child adequate sleep. If this seems like a long list of worries, remember that the list of delights that the preschool years bring is far longer.

# The Growing Body

**L01** What is the state of children's bodies and overall health during the preschool years?

During the preschool years, children experience rapid advances in their physical abilities that are nothing short of astounding. Just how far they develop is apparent when we look at the changes they undergo in their size, shape, and physical abilities.

By age 2, the average child in the United States weighs around 25 to 30 pounds and is close to 36 inches tall. By the time they are 6 years old, they weigh about 46 pounds and stand 46 inches tall (see Figure 4-1).

These averages mask significant individual differences. For instance, 10 percent of 6-year-olds weigh 55 pounds or more, and 10 percent weigh 36 pounds or less. Furthermore, average differences between boys and girls increase during the preschool years. Although at age 2 the differences are relatively small, during the preschool years boys start becoming taller and heavier, on average, than girls.

Economics also affects these averages. The better nutrition and health care typically received by children in developed countries translates into differences in growth. For instance, the average Swedish 4-year-old is as tall as the average 6-year-old in Bangladesh. Even within the United States, children in families with incomes below the poverty level are more likely to be short than children raised in more affluent homes (United Nations, 1991; Leathers & Foster, 2004; Petrou & Kupek, 2010).

## Changes in Body Shape and Structure

The bodies of a 2-year-old and a 6-year-old vary not only in height and weight, but also in shape. During the preschool years, boys and girls become less round and more slender. Moreover, their arms and legs lengthen, and the size relationship between the head and the rest of the body becomes more adultlike. In fact, by the time children reach age 6, their proportions are similar to those of adults.

Other physical changes occur internally. Muscle size increases, and children grow stronger. Bones become sturdier, and the sense organs continue to develop. For instance, the *eustachian tube* in the ear changes its orientation so radically that it may cause the earaches that are so typical of the preschool years.

## Nutrition: Eating the Right Foods

Because the rate of growth is slower than during infancy, preschoolers need less food, which may cause parents to worry. However, children tend to be adept at eating enough if they are provided with nutritious meals. In fact, anxiously encouraging children to eat more than they want may lead to **obesity,** which is defined as a body weight more than 20 percent higher than the average weight for a person of a given age and height. The prevalence of obesity among older preschoolers has increased significantly over the last 20 years.

The best strategy for parents is to make sure that they make a variety of low-fat, high-nutrition foods available. Foods that have a relatively high iron content are particularly important: Iron-deficiency anemia, which causes constant fatigue, is one of the prevalent

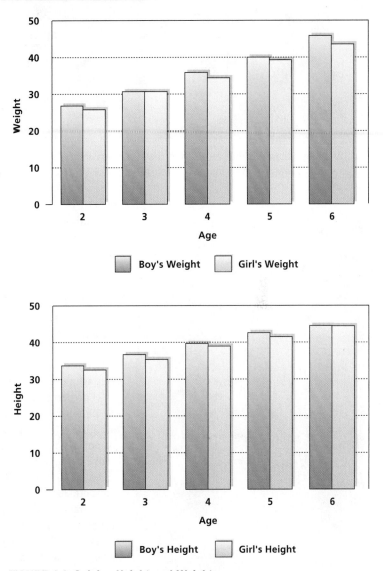

**FIGURE 4-1 Gaining Height and Weight**
The preschool years are marked by steady increases in height and weight. The figures show the median point for boys and girls at each age, in which 50 percent of children in each category are above this height or weight level and 50 percent are below.
Source: National Center for Health Statistics in collaboration with the National Center for Chronic Disease Prevention and Health Promotion, 2000.

**obesity** body weight more than 20 percent higher than the average weight for a person of a given age and height

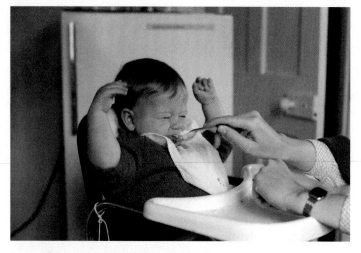

Encouraging children to eat more than they seem to want naturally may lead them to increase their food intake beyond an appropriate level.

The danger of injuries during the preschool years is in part a result of children's high levels of physical activity. It is important to take protective measures to reduce the hazards.

nutritional problems in developed countries (Ranade, 1993; Brotanek et al., 2007; Grant et al., 2007).

Within these bounds, children should be given the opportunity to develop their own preferences. Exposing children to new foods by encouraging them to take just one bite is a relatively low-stress way of expanding children's diets (Shapiro, 1997; Busick, 2008).

**From a health care worker's perspective:** How might biology and environment combine to affect the physical growth of a child adopted as an infant from a developing country and reared in a more industrialized one?

## Health and Illness

The average preschooler has 7 to 10 colds and other minor respiratory illnesses in each of the years from age 3 to 5. In the United States, a runny nose due to the common cold is the most frequent—and happily, the least severe—kind of health problem during the preschool years. In fact, the majority of children in the United States are reasonably healthy during this period (Kalb, 1997).

Although the sniffles and coughs that are the symptoms of such illnesses are certainly distressing to children, the unpleasantness is usually not too severe and the illnesses usually last only a few days.

The greatest risk that preschoolers face comes from neither illness nor nutritional problems but from accidents: Before the age of 10, children are twice as likely to die from an injury as from an illness. In fact, U.S. children have a one in three chance every year of receiving an injury that requires medical attention (National Safety Council, 1989; Field & Behrman, 2003; Granié, 2010).

The danger of injuries during the preschool years is in part a result of high levels of physical activity. Combine the physical activity, curiosity, and lack of judgment that characterize this age group, and it is no wonder that preschoolers are accident-prone.

Furthermore, some children are more apt than others to take risks and consequently to be injured. Boys, who typically are more active than girls and tend to take more risks, have a higher rate of injuries. Economic factors also play a role. Children raised under conditions of poverty in urban areas, whose inner-city neighborhoods may contain more hazards than more affluent areas, are two times more likely to die of injuries than children living in affluence (Morrongiello & Hogg, 2004; Morrongiello et al., 2006; Morrongiello, Klemencic, & Corbett, 2008).

Parents and caregivers can take precautions to prevent injuries, starting by "child-proofing" homes and classrooms with electrical outlet covers and child locks on cabinets. Car seats and bike helmets can help prevent injuries from accidents. Parents and teachers also need to be aware of the dangers from long-term hazards (Bull & Durbin, 2008; Morrongiello, Corbett, & Bellissimo, 2008; Morrongiello et al., 2009).

For example, lead poisoning is a significant danger for many children. Some 14 million children are at risk for lead poisoning due to exposure to lead, according to the Centers for Disease Control. Despite stringent legal restrictions on the amount of lead in paint and gasoline, lead is still found on painted walls and window frames—particularly in older homes—and in gasoline, ceramics, lead-soldered pipes, automobile and truck exhaust, and even dust and water. The U.S. Department of Health and Human Services has called lead poisoning the most severe health threat to children under age 6 (Duncan & Brooks-Gunn, 2000; Ripple & Zigler, 2003; Hubbs-Tait et al., 2005).

Even tiny amounts of lead can permanently harm children. Exposure to lead has been linked to lower intelligence, problems in verbal and auditory processing, and hyperactivity and distractibility. High lead levels have also been linked to higher levels of antisocial behavior, including aggression and delinquency in school-age children. At yet higher levels of exposure, lead poisoning results in illness and death (Kincl, Dietrich, & Bhattacharya, 2006; Nigg et al., 2008; Marcus, Fulton, & Clarke, 2010).

## REVIEW, CHECK, AND APPLY

### REVIEW

**LO1** What is the state of children's bodies and overall health during the preschool years?

- The preschool period is marked by steady physical growth and rapid advances in physical ability.

- Preschoolers tend to eat less than they did as babies, but generally regulate their food intake appropriately, given nutritious options and the freedom to develop their own choices and controls.

- The preschool period is generally the healthiest time of life, with only minor illnesses threatening children. Accidents and environmental hazards are the greatest threats.

### CHECK YOURSELF

1. During the preschool years, boys on the average start becoming taller and heavier than girls.
   - True
   - False

2. Which of the following suggestions is NOT recommended for preventing obesity in children?
   a. Provide food that is high in nutritional value.
   b. Make sure meals are low in fat.
   c. Ensure a consistent diet with little variety.
   d. Allow children to develop their own food preferences.

3. Which of the following benefits was NOT included in the discussion of minor illnesses in preschoolers?
   a. Prevents the development of empathy
   b. Builds up immunities
   c. Permits children to understand their bodies
   d. Helps children develop coping skills

### APPLYING LIFESPAN DEVELOPMENT

- What are some ways that increased understanding of issues relating to the physical development of preschoolers might help parents and caregivers in their care of children?

- Do you think the fact that preschool boys are more risk-prone than girls is genetic, environmental, or both? Why?

**Study** and **Review** on
**MyDevelopmentLab.com**

Answers: 1) True; 2) c; 3) a

# The Growing Brain

**LO2   How do preschool children's brains and physical skills develop?**

LEARNING OBJECTIVES

The brain grows at a faster rate than any other part of the body. Two-year-olds have brains that are about three-quarters the size and weight of an adult brain. By age 5, children's brains weigh 90 percent of average adult brain weight. In comparison, the average 5-year-old's total body weight is just 30 percent of average adult body weight (Lowrey, 1986; Nihart, 1993; House, 2007).

Why does the brain grow so rapidly? One reason is an increase in the number of interconnections among cells, which supports more complex communication between neurons and permits the rapid growth of cognitive skills. In addition, the amount of **myelin**—protective insulation that surrounds parts of neurons—increases, which speeds the transmission of electrical impulses along brain cells (Dalton & Bergenn, 2007).

## Brain Lateralization

By the end of the preschool period, the *corpus callosum,* a bundle of nerve fibers that connects the two hemispheres of the brain, becomes considerably thicker, developing as many as 800 million individual fibers that help coordinate brain functioning between the two hemispheres. At the same time, the two halves of the brain become increasingly differentiated and specialized. **Lateralization,** the process in which certain functions are located more in one hemisphere than the other, becomes more pronounced during the preschool years.

**myelin** protective insulation that surrounds parts of neurons—which speeds the transmission of electrical impulses along brain cells but also adds to brain weight

**lateralization** the process in which certain cognitive functions are located more in one hemisphere of the brain than in the other

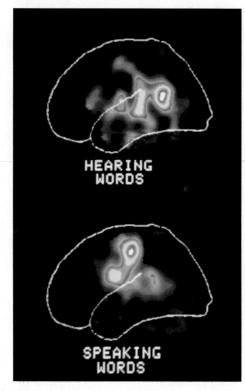

**FIGURE 4-2 Looking into the Brain**
This series of PET brain scans illustrates that activity in the right or left hemisphere of the brain differs according to the task in which a person is engaged. How might educators use this finding in their approach to teaching?

For most people, the left hemisphere is primarily involved with tasks that necessitate verbal competence, such as speaking, reading, thinking, and reasoning. The right hemisphere develops its own strengths, especially in nonverbal areas such as comprehension of spatial relationships, recognition of patterns and drawings, music, and emotional expression (Koivisto & Revonsuo, 2003; Pollak, Holt, & Wismer Fries, 2004; Watling & Bourne, 2007) (see Figure 4-2).

Each hemisphere also begins to process information in a slightly different manner. The left hemisphere processes data sequentially, one piece at a time. The right hemisphere processes information in a more global manner, reflecting on it as a whole (Ansaldo, Arguin, & Roch-Locours, 2002; Holowka & Petitto, 2002).

While there is some specialization, in most respects the two hemispheres act in tandem and are interdependent. In fact, each hemisphere can perform most of the tasks of the other. For example, the right hemisphere does some language processing and plays an important role in language comprehension (Corballis, 2003; Hutchinson, Whitman, & Abeare, 2003; Hall, Neal, & Dean, 2008).

There are also individual differences in lateralization. For example, many of the 10 percent of people who are left-handed or ambidextrous (able to use both hands interchangeably) have language centered in the right hemisphere or have no specific language center (Compton & Weissman, 2002; Isaacs et al., 2006).

Even more intriguing are differences in lateralization related to gender. For instance, starting during the first year and continuing in the preschool years, boys and girls show some hemispheric differences associated with lower-body reflexes and the processing of auditory information. Boys also clearly tend to show greater lateralization of language in the left hemisphere; among females, language is more evenly divided between the hemispheres. Such differences may help explain why girls' language development proceeds more rapidly during the preschool years than boys' (Grattan et al., 1992; Bourne & Todd, 2004; Castro-Schilo & Kee, 2010).

## The Links Between Brain Growth and Cognitive Development

Neuroscientists are beginning to understand the ways in which brain growth is related to cognitive development. While we do not yet know the direction of causality (does brain development produce cognitive advances, or vice versa?), we can clearly see the relationship.

For example, there are periods during childhood when the brain shows unusual growth spurts, and these periods are linked to advances in cognitive abilities. One study that measured electrical activity in the brain found unusual spurts at between 1½ and 2 years, a time when language abilities increase rapidly. Other spurts occurred around other ages when cognitive advances are particularly intense (Fischer & Rose, 1995; Mabbott et al., 2006; Westemann et al., 2007) (see Figure 4-3).

Other research has suggested that the increases in myelin in the brain (discussed earlier) may be related to preschoolers' growing cognitive capabilities. For example, myelination of the *reticular formation,* an area of the brain associated with attention and concentration, is completed by the time children are about 5 years old. This may be associated with children's growing attention spans as they approach school age. The improvement in memory that occurs during the preschool years may also be associated with myelination: During the preschool years, myelination is completed in the hippocampus, an area associated with memory (Rolls, 2000).

In addition, there is significant growth in the nerves connecting the *cerebellum,* a part of the brain that controls balance and movement, to the *cerebral cortex,* the structure responsible for sophisticated information processing. The growth in these nerve fibers is related to the significant advances in motor skills and cognitive processing during the preschool years (Carson, 2006; Gordon, 2007).

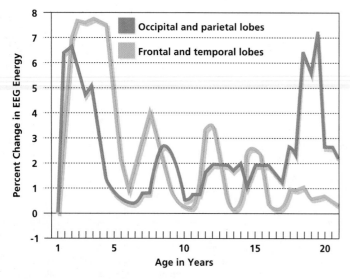

**FIGURE 4-3 Brain Growth Spurt**
According to one study, electrical activity in the brain has been linked to advances in cognitive abilities at various stages across the life span. In this graph, activity increases dramatically between 1½ and 2 years, a period during which language rapidly develops.
Source: Fischer & Rose, 1995.

## REVIEW, CHECK, AND APPLY

### REVIEW

**LO2**  How do preschool children's brains and physical skills develop?

- In addition to physical growth, the preschool period is marked by rapid brain growth. The increase in myelin in the brain is particularly important for intellectual development.

- Among other changes, the brain develops lateralization, a tendency of the two hemispheres to adopt specialized tasks.

### CHECK YOURSELF

1. During the preschool years, the two halves of the brain become more specialized in a process called _____.

2. Language differences between male and female brains may not be just the product of genetics, but also the environment. For example, females may have better language skills because:

   a. their brains are different in size.

   b. males are not equipped to learn language at the same pace as are females.

   c. they listen to language more intently when in the womb.

   d. they receive more encouragement for verbal skills than do boys.

### APPLYING LIFESPAN DEVELOPMENT

- Does brain growth cause cognitive development, or does cognitive development cause the brain to grow? Pick a side in this endless argument and defend it.

- What do you imagine thinking, planning, and reflection might be like if the two hemispheres of the brain could not communicate with each other (as is the case in some individuals with severe head injuries)?

✓•⎯⎤ **Study** and **Review** on
**MyDevelopmentLab.com**

Answers: 1) lateralization; 2) d

# Motor Development

**LO3  How does motor development evolve in preschool children?**

**LEARNING OBJECTIVES**

*Anya sat in the sandbox at the park, chatting with the other parents and playing with her two children, 5-year-old Nicholai and 13-month-old Smetna. While she chatted, she kept a close eye on Smetna, who would still put sand in her mouth sometimes if she wasn't stopped. Today, however, Smetna seemed content to run the sand through her hands and try to put it into a bucket. Nicholai, meanwhile, was busy with two other boys, rapidly filling and emptying the other sand buckets to build an elaborate sand city, which they would then destroy with toy trucks.*

When children of different ages gather at a playground, it's easy to see that preschool children have come a long way in their motor development. Both their gross and fine motor skills have become increasingly fine-tuned. Smetna, for example, is still mastering putting sand into a bucket, while her older brother Nicholai uses that skill easily as part of his larger goal of building a sand city.

## Gross Motor Skills

By the time they are 3 years old, children have mastered a variety of skills: jumping, hopping on one foot, skipping, and running. By 4 and 5, their skills have become more refined as they have gained increasing control over their muscles. For instance, at 4 they can throw a ball with enough accuracy that a friend can catch it, and by age 5 they can toss a ring and have it land on a peg 5 feet away. Five-year-olds can learn to ride bikes, climb ladders, and ski downhill—activities that all require considerable coordination (Clark & Humphrey, 1985). (Table 4-1 summarizes major gross motor skills that emerge during the preschool years.)

These achievements may be related to brain development and myelination of neurons in areas of the brain related to balance and coordination. Another likely reason is that children spend a great deal of time practicing these skills. During this period, the general level of activity is extraordinarily high. In fact, the activity level is higher at age 3 than at any other point in the entire life span (Eaton & Yu, 1989; Poest et al., 1990).

Girls and boys differ in certain aspects of gross motor coordination, in part because of differences in muscle strength, which is usually somewhat greater in boys than in girls. For

## TABLE 4-1 MAJOR GROSS MOTOR SKILLS IN EARLY CHILDHOOD

| 3-Year-Olds | 4-Year-Olds | 5-Year-Olds |
|---|---|---|
| Cannot turn or stop suddenly or quickly | Have more effective control of stopping, starting, and turning | Start, turn, and stop effectively in games |
| Jump a distance of 15 to 24 inches | Jump a distance of 24 to 33 inches | Can make a running jump of 28 to 36 inches |
| Ascend a stairway unaided, alternating the feet | Descend a long stairway alternating the feet, if supported | Descend a long stairway alternating the feet |
| Can hop, using largely an irregular series of jumps with some variations added | Hop 4 to 6 steps on one foot | Easily hop a distance of 16 feet |

Source: From Corbin, *A Textbook of Motor Development*, 1e. Copyright © 1973 The McGraw-Hill Companies. Reprinted with permission.

During the preschool years, children grow in both fine and gross motor skills.

instance, boys can typically throw a ball better and jump higher, and a boy's overall activity level tends to be greater than a girl's (Eaton & Yu, 1989). On the other hand, girls generally surpass boys in tasks that involve limb coordination. For instance, at age 5, girls are better than boys at jumping jacks and balancing on one foot (Cratty, 1979).

Another aspect of muscular skills—one that parents often find most problematic—is bowel and bladder control.

## The Potty Question: When—and How—Should Children Be Toilet Trained?

Few child-care issues raise so much concern among parents as toilet training. Current guidelines of the American Academy of Pediatrics suggest that there is no single time to begin toilet training and that training should begin only when children are ready (American Academy of Pediatrics, 2009; Lundblad, Hellström, & Berg, 2010).

When are children "ready"? The signs of readiness include staying dry at least 2 hours at a time during the day or waking up dry after naps; regular and predictable bowel movements; an indication, through facial expressions or words, that urination or a bowel movement is about to occur; the ability to follow simple directions; the ability to get to the bathroom and undress alone; discomfort with soiled diapers; asking to use the toilet or potty chair; and the desire to wear underwear.

Furthermore, children must be ready not only physically, but emotionally, and if they show strong signs of resistance to toilet training, toilet training should be put off. Similarly, it may be reasonable to delay toilet training if there is a major change in the home environment, such as the birth of a new baby or a major illness. Although some children show signs of readiness for toilet training between 18 and 24 months, some are not ready until 30 months or older (American Academy of Pediatrics, 2003; Fritz & Rockney, 2004; Connell-Carrick, 2006).

Partially in response to the American Academy of Pediatrics guidelines, toilet training has begun later over the last few decades. For example, in 1957, 92 percent of children were toilet trained by 18 months. In 1999, only 25 percent were toilet trained at that age, and just 60 percent of 36-month-olds were toilet trained. Some 2 percent were still not toilet trained at the age of 4 (Goode, 1999).

## Fine Motor Skills

At the same time, children are progressing in their ability to use fine motor skills, which involve more delicate, smaller body movements such as using a fork and spoon, cutting with scissors, tying shoelaces, and playing the piano.

The skills involved in fine motor movements require practice. The emergence of fine motor skills shows clear developmental patterns. At age 3, children can draw a circle and square with a crayon, and they can undo their clothes when they go to the bathroom. They can put a simple jigsaw puzzle together, and they can fit blocks of different shapes into matching holes. However, they do not show much precision and polish in these tasks, often, for example, forcing puzzle pieces into place.

By age 4, their fine motor skills are better. They can draw a person that looks like a person, and they can fold paper into triangular designs. And by the time they are 5, they can hold and manipulate a thin pencil properly.

> **handedness** the preference of using one hand over another

*Handedness.* How do preschoolers decide which hand to hold the pencil in as they work on their fine motor skills? For many, their choice was made soon after birth.

Beginning in early infancy, many children show signs of a preference for the use of one hand over the other—the development of **handedness.** By 7 months, some infants seem to favor one hand by grabbing more with it (Saudino & McManus, 1998; Segalowitz & Rapin, 2003; Marschik et al., 2008). Most children display a clear tendency by the end of the preschool years. Some 90 percent are right-handed and 10 percent are left-handed, and more boys than girls are left-handed.

## Keeping Preschoolers Healthy

### Becoming an Informed Consumer of Development

There is no way around it: Even the healthiest preschooler occasionally gets sick. Social interaction with others ensures that illnesses will be passed from one child to another. However, some diseases are preventable, and others can be minimized if simple precautions are taken:

- Preschoolers should eat a well-balanced diet containing the proper nutrients, particularly foods containing sufficient protein. Keep offering healthy foods; even if children initially reject them, they may grow to like them.

- Encourage preschoolers to exercise.

- Children should get as much sleep as they wish. Being fatigued makes children more susceptible to illness.

- Children should avoid contact with others who are ill. If they play with kids who are sick, parents should make sure they wash their hands thoroughly.

- Be sure that children follow an appropriate schedule of immunizations.

- Finally, if a child does get ill, remember this: Minor illnesses during childhood sometimes provide immunity to more serious illnesses later on.

## REVIEW, CHECK, AND APPLY

### REVIEW

**LO3** How does motor development evolve in preschool children?

- Gross and fine motor development advance rapidly during the preschool years.

- Boys' and girls' gross motor skills begin to diverge, with boys typically doing better at tasks requiring strength and girls doing better at tasks requiring coordination.

- Also during this period, children develop handedness—a decided preference for one hand over the other.

### CHECK YOURSELF

1. During the preschool years, there is significant pruning in the nerves connecting the cerebellum, the part of the brain that controls balance and movement to the cerebral cortex, the structure responsible for sophisticated information processing.

- True
- False

2. In addition to changes in myelination, another reason that motor skills develop so rapidly during the preschool years is because children spend a great deal of time:

a. using mental imagery.

b. practicing them.

c. observing adults performing the same behaviors.

d. sleeping.

### APPLYING LIFESPAN DEVELOPMENT

- To what extent do you think that gender differences in the development of gross motor skills are genetic versus environmental?

- If it could be shown that left-handers had a greater likelihood to be gifted than right-handers, would it make sense to train children to use their left hands for everyday tasks? Why?

✓•–⎡Study and Review on
**MyDevelopmentLab.com**

Answers: 1) False; 2) b

## MODULE 4.2 Cognitive Development in the Preschool Years

# Sam and Gill

*Three-year-old Sam was talking to himself in two very different voices. "Find your shoes," he said in a low voice. "Not today. I'm not going. I hate the shoes," he said in a higher-pitched voice. The lower voice answered, "You are a bad boy. Find the shoes, bad boy." The higher-voiced response was "No, no, no." Sam's parents realized that he was playing a game with his imaginary friend, Gill—a bad boy who often disobeyed his mother. In fact, according to Sam's musings, Gill often was guilty of the very same misdeeds for which his parents blamed Sam.*

In some ways, the intellectual sophistication of 3-year-olds is astounding. Their creativity and imagination leap to new heights, their language is increasingly sophisticated, and they reason and think about the world in ways that would have been impossible even a few months earlier. But what underlies the dramatic advances in intellectual development of the preschool years? In this module we will consider a number of approaches to understanding children's thinking and the development of cognitive abilities in the preschool years.

# Piaget's Approach to Cognitive Development

**LEARNING OBJECTIVES**

**L04** How does Piaget interpret cognitive development during the preschool years?

**L05** How does Piaget's approach stand up to the test of time?

## Piaget's Stage of Preoperational Thinking

Jean Piaget, whose stage approach to cognitive development we discussed in Module 3.2, saw the preschool years as a time of both stability and change. He placed the preschool years into a single stage of cognitive development—the preoperational stage—which lasts from age 2 until around age 7.

During the **preoperational stage,** children's use of symbolic thinking grows, mental reasoning emerges, and the use of concepts increases. Seeing Mom's car keys may prompt a question, "Go to store?" as the child comes to see the keys as a symbol of a car ride. In this way, children become better at representing events internally and less dependent on sensorimotor activity to understand the world around them. Yet they are still not capable of **operations**: organized, formal, logical mental processes.

According to Piaget, a key aspect of preoperational thought is *symbolic function,* the ability to use a mental symbol, a word, or an object to stand for or represent something that is not physically present. For example, preschoolers can use a mental symbol for a car (the word "car"), and they understand that a small toy car is representative of the real thing. They have no need to get behind the wheel of an actual car to understand its basic purpose and use.

***The Relation Between Language and Thought.*** Symbolic function is at the heart of one of the major advances of the preoperational period: the increasingly sophisticated use of language. Piaget suggests that the advances in language during the preschool years reflect improvements over the type of thinking that is possible during the earlier sensorimotor period. Instead of slow, sensorimotor-based thinking, symbolic thought, which relies on improved linguistic ability, allows preschoolers to represent actions virtually, at much greater speed.

Even more important, language allows children to think beyond the present to the future. Rather than being grounded in the here-and-now, preschoolers can imagine future possibilities through language in the form of fantasies and daydreams.

***Centration: What You See Is What You Think.*** Place a dog mask on a cat and what do you get? According to 3- and 4-year-old preschoolers, a dog. To them, a cat with a dog mask ought to bark like a dog, wag its tail like a dog, and eat dog food. In every respect, the cat has been transformed into a dog (deVries, 1969).

To Piaget, the root of this belief is centration, a key element, and limitation, of thinking in the preoperational period. **Centration** is the process of concentrating on one limited aspect of

**preoperational stage** according to Piaget, the stage from approximately age 2 to age 7 in which children's use of symbolic thinking grows, mental reasoning emerges, and the use of concepts increases

**operations** organized, formal, logical mental processes

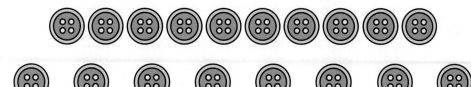

**FIGURE 4-4  Which Row Contains More Buttons?**
When preschoolers are shown these two rows and asked which row has more buttons, they usually respond that the lower row of buttons contains more, because it looks longer. They answer in this way even though they know quite well that 10 is greater than 8. Do you think preschoolers can be *taught* to answer correctly?

a stimulus—typically its superficial elements—and ignoring others. These elements come to dominate preschoolers' thinking, leading to inaccuracy.

Centration is the cause of the error illustrated in Figure 4-4. Asked which row contains more buttons, children who are 4 or 5 usually choose the row that looks longer, rather than the one that actually contains more buttons. This occurs even though children this age know quite well that 10 is more than 8. Rather than taking into account their understanding of quantity, they focus on appearance.

Preschoolers' focus on appearances might be related to another aspect of preoperational thought, the lack of conservation.

***Conservation: Learning That Appearances Are Deceiving.*** Consider the following scenario:

*Four-year-old Jaime is shown two drinking glasses. One is short and broad; the other, tall and thin. A teacher half-fills the short, broad glass with apple juice. The teacher then pours the juice into the tall, thin glass. The juice fills the tall glass almost to the brim. The teacher asks Jaime a question: Is there more juice in the second glass than there was in the first?*

If you view this as an easy task, so do children like Jaime. The problem is that they almost always get it wrong.

Most 4-year-olds say that there is more apple juice in the tall, thin glass than there was in the short, broad one. In fact, if the juice is poured back into the shorter glass, they are quick to say that there is now less juice than there was in the taller glass.

The reason is that children of this age have not mastered conservation. **Conservation** is the knowledge that quantity is unrelated to the arrangement and physical appearance of objects. Some other conservation tasks are shown in Figure 4-5 on page 166.

Why do children in the preoperational stage make conservation errors? Piaget suggests that the main reason is that their tendency toward centration prevents them from focusing on the relevant features of the situation. Furthermore, they cannot follow the sequence of transformations that accompanies changes in the appearance of a situation. ◉⬕Watch on mydevelopmentlab.com

***Incomplete Understanding of Transformation.*** A preoperational, preschool child who sees several worms during a walk in the woods may believe that they are all the same worm. The reason: She views each sighting in isolation, unable to understand that a transformation would be necessary for a worm to move quickly from one location to the next.

As Piaget used the term, **transformation** is the process in which one state is changed into another. For instance, adults know that if a pencil that is held upright is allowed to fall down, it passes through a series of successive stages until it reaches its final, horizontal resting spot. In contrast, children in the preoperational period are unable to envision or recall the successive transformations that the pencil followed in moving from the upright to the horizontal position.

***Egocentrism: The Inability to Take Others' Perspectives.*** Another hallmark of the preoperational period is egocentric thinking. **Egocentric thought** is thinking that does not take into account the viewpoints of others. Preschoolers do not understand that others have different

◉⬕Watch on **mydevelopmentlab.com**

To see a reenactment of the scenario you've just read about, log onto MyDevelopmentLab .com and check out the video clip "Conservation."

**centration** the process of concentrating on one limited aspect of a stimulus and ignoring other aspects

**conservation** the knowledge that quantity is unrelated to the arrangement and physical appearance of objects

**transformation** the process in which one state is changed into another

**egocentric thought** thinking that does not take into account the viewpoints of others

| Type of Conservation | Modality | Change in Physical Appearance | Average Age Invariance Is Grasped |
|---|---|---|---|
| Number | Number of elements in a collection | Rearranging or dislocating elements | 6–7 years |
| Substance (mass) | Amount of a malleable substance (e.g., clay or liquid) | Altering shape | 7–8 years |
| Length | Length of a line or object | Altering shape or configuration | 7–8 years |
| Area | Amount of surface covered by a set of plane figures | Rearranging the figures | 8–9 years |
| Weight | Weight of an object | Altering shape | 9–10 years |
| Volume | Volume of an object (in terms of water displacement) | Altering shape | 14–15 years |

FIGURE 4-5 **Common Tests of Children's Understanding of the Principle of Conservation**
Why is a sense of conservation important?

**Watch** on **mydevelopmentlab.com**

To watch an experiment that demonstrates egocentrism in preschoolers, check out the video clip "Egocentrism" on MyDevelopmentLab.com.

perspectives. Egocentric thought takes two forms: lack of awareness that others see things from a different physical perspective and failure to realize that others may hold thoughts, feelings, and points of view that differ from theirs. (Note that egocentric thought does *not* imply intentional selfishness or a lack of consideration.) **Watch** on **mydevelopmentlab.com**

Egocentric thinking lies behind children's lack of concern over their nonverbal behavior and the impact it has on others. For instance, a 4-year-old who receives a gift of socks may frown as he opens the package, unaware that his face can be seen by others and reveals his true feelings (Feldman, 1992).

Egocentrism largely explains why many preschoolers talk to themselves, even in the presence of others, and often ignore what others are telling them. This behavior illustrates the egocentric nature of preoperational children's thinking: the lack of awareness that their behavior acts as a trigger to others' reactions and responses. Consequently, much of preschoolers' verbal behavior has no social motivation but is meant purely for their own consumption.

Similarly, egocentrism can also be seen in hiding games. In hide-and-seek, 3-year-olds may "hide" by covering their faces with a pillow—even though they remain in plain view.

Their reasoning: If they cannot see others, others cannot see them. They assume that everyone else shares their view.

***The Emergence of Intuitive Thought.*** Because Piaget labeled this the "*pre*operational period" and focused on cognitive deficiencies, it is easy to assume that preschoolers are marking time, but the period is far from idle. Cognitive development proceeds steadily, and new abilities emerge, including intuitive thought.

**Intuitive thought** refers to preschoolers' use of primitive reasoning and their avid acquisition of world knowledge. From about age 4 through 7, curiosity blossoms. Children ask "Why?" questions about nearly everything. At the same time, they may act as if they are authorities on particular topics, certain that they have the final word on an issue. Their intuitive thought leads them to believe that they know answers to all kinds of questions, with little or no logical basis for this confidence.

In the late stages of the preoperational period, children's intuitive thinking prepares them for more sophisticated reasoning. For instance, preschoolers come to understand that pushing harder on the pedals makes a bicycle move faster, or that pressing a button on a remote control makes the television change channels. By the end of the preoperational stage, preschoolers begin to grasp *functionality*, the idea that actions, events, and outcomes are related to one another in fixed patterns. They also become aware of *identity*, the understanding that certain things stay the same, regardless of changes in shape, size, and appearance—for instance, that a lump of clay contains the same amount of clay whether it is clumped into a ball or stretched out like a snake. Comprehension of identity is necessary for children to develop an understanding of conservation (the understanding, as we discussed earlier, that quantity is not related to physical appearances). Piaget regarded the development of conservation as the transition from the preoperational period to the next stage, concrete operations, which we will discuss in the next chapter.

***Evaluating Piaget's Approach to Cognitive Development.*** Piaget, a masterly observer of children's behavior, provided a detailed portrait of preschoolers' cognitive abilities. The broad outlines of his approach have given us a useful way of thinking about the progressive advances in cognitive ability during the preschool years (Siegal, 1997).

However, it is important to consider Piaget's approach to cognitive development within the appropriate historical context and in light of more recent research findings. As we discussed earlier, his theory is based on extensive observations of relatively few children. Despite his insightful and groundbreaking observations, recent experimental investigations suggest that in certain regards, Piaget underestimated children's capabilities.

Take, for instance, Piaget's views of how children in the preoperational period understand numbers. He contended that preschoolers' thinking is seriously handicapped, as evidenced by their performance on tasks involving conservation and reversibility, the understanding that a transformation can be reversed to return something to its original state. Yet more recent experimental work suggests otherwise. For instance, children as young as 3 can easily tell the difference between rows of two and three toy animals, regardless of the animals' spacing. Older children are able to note differences in number, performing tasks such as identifying which of two numbers is larger and indicating that they understand some rudiments of addition and subtraction problems (McCrink & Wynn, 2007; Cordes & Brannon, 2009; Izard et al., 2009).

Gelman concludes that children have an innate ability to count, akin to the ability to use language that some theorists see as universal and genetically determined. This is clearly at odds with Piagetian notions, which suggest that children's numerical abilities do not blossom until after the preoperational period.

Some developmentalists (particularly those who favor the information processing approach) also believe that cognitive skills develop in a more continuous manner than Piaget's theory implies. They believe that rather than thought changing in quality, as Piaget argues, the changes in thinking ability are more quantitative, improving gradually (Gelman & Baillargeon, 1983; Case, 1991).

There are further difficulties with Piaget's view. His contention that conservation does not emerge until the end of the preoperational period has not stood up to experimental scrutiny. Children can learn to answer correctly on conservation tasks if they are given certain training and experiences. The fact that one can improve children's performance argues against the Piagetian view that children in the preoperational period have not reached a level of cognitive maturity to understand conservation (Ping & Goldin-Meadow, 2008).

In sum, Piaget tended to concentrate on preschoolers' *deficiencies* in logical thought. By focusing more on children's competence, recent theorists have found evidence for a surprising degree of capability in preschoolers.

---

## REVIEW, CHECK, AND APPLY

### REVIEW

**LO4** How does Piaget interpret cognitive development during the preschool years?

- According to Piaget, children in the preoperational stage develop symbolic function, a change in their thinking that is the foundation of further cognitive advances.

- Preoperational children are hampered by a tendency toward egocentric thought.

**LO5** How does Piaget's approach stand up to the test of time?

- Recent developmentalists, while acknowledging Piaget's gifts and contributions, take issue with his underestimation of preschoolers' capabilities.

### CHECK YOURSELF

1. Children in Piaget's _____ stage begin using symbolic thinking; however, they are not capable of _____, or organized, logical mental processes that characterize schoolchildren.

2. Egocentric thought can involve (a) the lack of awareness that others see things from a different physical perspective and (b) _____.

   a. the inability to present their own perspectives to others

   b. their unwillingness to consider how their perspectives have been consistent over time

   c. failure to realize that others may hold thoughts, feelings, and points of view that differ from theirs

   d. that preoperational children are intentionally selfish and inconsiderate

3. Piaget's perspective has been criticized by others because he overestimated children's abilities.

   - True
   - False

### APPLYING LIFESPAN DEVELOPMENT

- Do you think it is possible to break a preschooler's habit of egocentric thought by directly teaching him to take another person's point of view? Would showing him a picture of himself "hidden" behind a chair change his thinking? Why?

✔•⌐**Study** and **Review** on
**MyDevelopmentLab.com**

Answers: 1) preoperational/operations; 2) c; 3) False

---

# Information Processing and Vygotsky's Approach to Cognitive Development

**LEARNING OBJECTIVES**

**LO6** How do other views of cognitive development differ from Piaget's?

**LO7** What separates Vygotsky's approach from Piaget's?

*Even as an adult, Paco has clear recollections of his first trip to a farm, which he took when he was 3 years old. He was visiting his godfather, who lived in Puerto Rico, and the two of them went to a nearby farm. Paco recounts seeing what seemed like hundreds of chickens, and he clearly recalls his fear of the pigs, who seemed huge, smelly, and frightening. Most of all, he recalls the thrill of riding on a horse with his godfather.*

The fact that Paco has a clear memory of his farm trip is not surprising: Most people have unambiguous, and seemingly accurate, memories dating as far back as age 3. But are the processes used to form memories at that age similar to those that operate later in life? More broadly, what general changes in the processing of information occur during the preschool years?

Information processing approaches focus on changes in the kinds of "mental programs" that children use when approaching problems. They compare the changes in children's cognitive abilities during the preschool years to the way a computer program becomes more sophisticated as a programmer modifies it based on experience. For many child developmentalists, information processing approaches represent the dominant, most comprehensive, and most accurate explanation of how children develop cognitively (Siegler, 1994; Lacerda, von Hofsten, & Heimann, 2001).

We'll focus on two areas that highlight the approach taken by information processing theorists: understanding of numbers and memory development.

*Preschoolers' Understanding of Numbers.* As we saw earlier, preschoolers have a greater understanding of numbers than Piaget thought. Researchers using information processing approaches have found increasing evidence for the sophistication of preschoolers' numerical understanding. The average preschooler is not only able to count, but to do so in a fairly systematic, consistent manner (Siegler, 1998).

For instance, developmental psychologist Rochel Gelman suggests that preschoolers follow set principles in their counting. Shown a group of items, they know they should assign just one number to each item and count each item only once. Moreover, even when they get the *names* of numbers wrong, they are consistent in their usage. For instance, a 4-year-old who counts three items as "1, 3, 7" will say "1, 3, 7" when counting another group of different items. And if asked, she will probably say that there are seven items in the group (Gelman, 2006; Gallistel, 2007; Le Corre & Carey, 2007).

By the age of 4, most are able to carry out simple addition and subtraction problems by counting, and they are able to compare different quantities quite successfully (Donlan, 1998; Gilmore & Spelke, 2008).

*Memory: Recalling the Past.* Think back to your own earliest memory. If you are like Paco, described earlier, and most other people too, it probably is of an event that occurred after age 3. **Autobiographical memory,** memory of particular events from one's own life, achieves little accuracy until then and

This preschooler may recall this ride in six months, but by the time he is 12, it will probably be forgotten. Can you explain why?

increases gradually throughout the preschool years. The accuracy of preschoolers' memories is partly determined by when the memories are assessed. Not all autobiographical memories last into later life. For instance, a child may remember the first day of kindergarten 6 months or a year later, but later in life might not remember it at all. Further, unless an event is particularly vivid or meaningful, it is not likely to be remembered at all (Nelson & Fivush, 2004; Wang, 2008; Morris, Baker-Ward, & Bauer, 2010).

Preschoolers' autobiographical memories not only fade, but may not be wholly accurate. For example, if an event happens often, it may be hard to remember one specific time it happened. Preschoolers' memories of familiar events are often organized into **scripts,** broad representations in memory of events and the order in which they occur. For example, a young preschooler might represent eating in a restaurant in terms of a few steps: talking to a server, getting the food, and eating. With age, the scripts become more elaborate: getting in the car, being seated at the restaurant, choosing food, ordering, waiting for the meal to come, eating, ordering dessert, and paying for the food. Particular instances of such scripted events are recalled with less accuracy than events that are unscripted (Fivush, Kuebli, & Clubb, 1992; Sutherland, Pipe, & Schick, 2003).

Preschoolers' memories are also susceptible to suggestion. This is a special concern when children testify in legal situations, such as when abuse is suspected.

## Children's Eyewitness Testimony: Memory on Trial

*I was looking and then I didn't see what I was doing and it got in there somehow.... The mousetrap was in our house because there's a mouse in our house.... The mousetrap is down in the basement, next to the firewood.... I was playing a game called "Operation" and then I went downstairs and said to Dad, "I want to eat lunch," and then it got stuck in the mousetrap.... My daddy was down in the basement collecting firewood.... [My brother] pushed me [into the mousetrap].... It happened yesterday. The mouse was in my house yesterday. I caught my finger in it yesterday. I went to the hospital yesterday.* (Ceci & Bruck, 1993, p. A23)

Forensic developmental psychologists focus on the reliability of children's memories in a legal context.

Despite the detailed account by this 4-year-old boy of his encounter with a mousetrap and subsequent trip to the hospital, there's a problem: The incident never happened, and the memory is entirely false.

The 4-year-old's explicit memory of an imaginary incident was the product of a study on children's memory. Each week for 11 weeks, the boy was told, "You went to the hospital because your finger got caught in a mousetrap. Did this ever happen to you?"

**autobiographical memory** memory of particular events from one's own life

**scripts** broad representations in memory of events and the order in which they occur

The first week, the child accurately said, "No. I've never been to the hospital." But by the second week, the answer changed to, "Yes, I cried." In the third week, the boy said, "Yes. My mom went to the hospital with me." By the 11th week, the answer had expanded to the quote above (Ceci & Bruck, 1993; Bruck & Ceci, 2004).

The research study that elicited the child's false memories is part of a new and rapidly growing field: forensic developmental psychology. *Forensic developmental psychology* focuses on the reliability of children's autobiographical memories in the context of the legal system, when they may be witnesses or victims (Bruck & Ceci, 2004; Goodman, 2006).

Children's memories are susceptible to the suggestions of adults asking them questions. This is particularly true of preschoolers, who are considerably more vulnerable to suggestion than either adults or school-age children. The error rate is heightened when the same question is asked repeatedly. False memories—of the "mousetrap" type just reported—in fact may be more persistent than actual memories. In addition, when questions are highly suggestive (that is, when questioners attempt to lead a person to particular conclusions), children are more apt to make mistakes (Loftus & Bernstein, 2005; Goodman & Quas, 2008; Lowenstein, Blank, & Sauer, 2010).

***Information Processing in Perspective.*** According to information processing approaches, cognitive development consists of gradual improvements in the ways people perceive, understand, and remember information. With age and practice, preschoolers process information more efficiently and with greater sophistication, and they are able to handle increasingly complex problems. In this view, it is these quantitative advances in information processing—and not the qualitative changes suggested by Piaget—that constitute cognitive development (Goswami, 1998; Zhe & Siegler, 2000; Rose, Feldman, & Jankowski, 2009).

For supporters of information processing, the reliance on well-defined processes that can be tested by research is one of the perspective's most important features. Rather than relying on somewhat vague concepts, such as Piaget's notions of assimilation and accommodation, information processing approaches provide a comprehensive, logical set of concepts.

For instance, as preschoolers grow older, they have longer attention spans, can monitor and plan what they are attending to more effectively, and become increasingly aware of their cognitive limitations. This places some of Piaget's findings in a different light. For instance, increased attention allows older children—as distinct from preschoolers—to attend to both the height *and* width of tall and short glasses and to understand that the amount of liquid in the glasses stays the same when it is poured back and forth—that is, to grasp conservation (Miller & Seier, 1994; Hudson, Sosa, & Shapiro, 1997).

Yet information processing approaches have their detractors. One important criticism is that information processing approaches "lose the forest for the trees" by paying so much attention to the detailed, individual sequence of mental processes that they never adequately paint a comprehensive picture of cognitive development—which Piaget clearly did quite well.

Information processing approaches have been highly influential over the past several decades. They have inspired a tremendous amount of research that has helped us gain some insights into how children develop cognitively.

## Vygotsky's View of Cognitive Development: Taking Culture into Account

*As her daughter watches, a member of the Chilcotin Indian tribe prepares a salmon for dinner. When the daughter asks a question about a small detail of the process, the mother takes out another salmon and repeats the entire process. According to the tribal view of learning, understanding and comprehension can come only from grasping the total procedure, and not from learning about the individual subcomponents of the task.* (Tharp, 1989)

The Chilcotin view of how children learn about the world contrasts with the prevalent view of Western society, which assumes that only by mastering the separate parts of a problem can one fully comprehend it. Do differences in the ways particular cultures and societies approach problems influence cognitive development? According to Russian developmental psychologist Lev Vygotsky, who lived from 1896 to 1934, the answer is a clear yes.

Russian developmental psychologist Lev Vygotsky proposed that the focus of cognitive development should be on a child's social and cultural world, as opposed to the Piagetian approach concentrating on individual performance.

Vygotsky viewed cognitive development as the product of social interactions. Instead of concentrating on individual performance, Vygotsky's increasingly influential view focuses on the social aspects of development and learning.

Vygotsky saw children as apprentices, learning cognitive strategies and other skills from adult and peer mentors who not only present new ways of doing things, but also provide assistance, instruction, and motivation. Consequently, he focused on the child's social and cultural world as the source of cognitive development. According to Vygotsky, children gradually grow intellectually and begin to function on their own because of the assistance that adult and peer partners provide (Vygotsky, 1979, 1926/1997; Tudge & Scrimsher, 2003).

Vygotsky contends that culture and society establish the institutions, such as preschools and play groups, that promote development by providing opportunities for cognitive growth. Furthermore, by emphasizing particular tasks, culture and society shape the nature of specific cognitive advances. Unless we look at what is important and meaningful to members of a given society, we may seriously underestimate the nature and level of cognitive abilities that ultimately will be attained (Tappan, 1997, Schaller & Crandall, 2004). For example, children's toys reflect what is important and meaningful in a particular society. In Western societies, preschoolers commonly play with toy wagons, automobiles, and other vehicles, in part reflecting the mobile nature of the culture.

Vygotsky's approach is therefore quite different from Piaget's. Where Piaget looked at children and saw junior scientists, working by themselves to develop an independent understanding of the world, Vygotsky saw cognitive apprentices, learning from master teachers the skills valued in the child's culture (Kitchener, 1996; Fernyhough, 1997).

### The Zone of Proximal Development and Scaffolding: Foundations of Cognitive Development.

Vygotsky proposed that children's cognitive abilities increase through exposure to information that is new enough to be intriguing, but not too difficult to contend with. He called this the **zone of proximal development (ZPD),** the level at which a child can *almost,* but not fully, perform a task independently, but can do so with the assistance of someone more competent. For cognitive development to occur, new information must be presented—by parents, teachers, or more skilled peers—within the zone of proximal development. For example, a preschooler might not be able to figure out by herself how to stick a handle on the clay pot she's making, but she can do it with advice from her child-care teacher (Zuckerman & Shenfield, 2007; Norton & D'Ambrosio, 2008; Zhang, 2010). ◉ Watch on **mydevelopmentlab.com**

The concept of the zone of proximal development suggests that even though two children might be able to achieve the same amount without help, if one child receives aid, he or she may improve substantially more than the other. The greater the improvement that comes with help, the larger the zone of proximal development.

The assistance or structuring provided by others has been termed *scaffolding* after the temporary scaffolds that aid in building construction. **Scaffolding** is the support for learning and problem solving that encourages independence and growth (Puntambekar & Hübscher, 2005; Blewitt et al., 2009). As in construction, the scaffolding that older people provide, which facilitates the completion of identified tasks, is removed once children can solve a problem on their own (Warwick & Maloch, 2003; Taumoepeau & Ruffman, 2008). ◉ Watch on **mydevelopmentlab.com**

To Vygotsky, scaffolding not only helps children solve specific problems, it also aids in the development of their overall cognitive abilities. In education, scaffolding involves, first of all, helping children think about and frame a task appropriately. In addition, a parent or teacher is likely to provide clues to task completion that fit the child's level of development and to model behavior that can lead to task completion.

⊙ **From an educator's perspective:** If children's cognitive development is dependent on interactions with others, what obligations does society have regarding such social settings as preschools and neighborhoods?

One key aspect of the aid that more accomplished individuals provide to learners comes in the form of cultural tools. *Cultural tools* are actual, physical items (e.g., pencils, paper, calculators, computers, and so forth), as well as an intellectual and conceptual framework for solving problems. The framework includes the language that is used within a culture, its alphabetical and numbering schemes, its mathematical and scientific systems, and even its religious systems. These cultural tools provide a structure that can be used to help children

◉ Watch on **mydevelopmentlab.com**

Log onto MyDevelopmentLab.com and watch several videos of the zone of proximal development principle displayed in preschoolers.

◉ Watch on **mydevelopmentlab.com**

To watch a teacher using the scaffolding technique with preschoolers, log onto MyDevelopmentLab.com and watch the video clip "Scaffolding."

**zone of proximal development (ZPD)** according to Vygotsky, the level at which a child can *almost,* but not fully, perform a task independently, but can do so with the assistance of someone more competent

**scaffolding** the support for learning and problem solving that encourages independence and growth

define and solve specific problems, as well as an intellectual point of view that encourages cognitive development.

For example, consider the cultural differences in how people talk about distance. In cities, distance is usually measured in blocks ("the store is about 15 blocks away"). To a child from a rural background, more culturally meaningful terms are needed, such as yards, miles, such practical rules of thumb as "a stone's throw," or references to known distances and landmarks ("about half the distance to town"). To make matters more complicated, "how far" questions are sometimes answered in terms not of distance, but of time ("it's about 15 minutes to the store"), which will be understood variously to refer to walking or riding time, depending on context—and, if riding time, to different forms of riding—by ox cart, bicycle, bus, canoe, or automobile, again depending on cultural context. The nature of the tools available to children to solve problems and perform tasks is highly dependent on the culture in which they live.

***Evaluating Vygotsky's Contributions.*** Vygotsky's view has become increasingly influential, which is surprising given that he died more than 75 years ago at the age of 37 (Winsler, 2003; Gredler & Shields, 2008). His influence has grown because his ideas help explain a growing body of research on the importance of social interaction in promoting cognitive development. The idea that children's comprehension of the world flows from their interactions with their parents, peers, and other members of society is increasingly well supported. It is also consistent with a growing body of multicultural and cross-cultural research, which finds evidence that cognitive development is shaped, in part, by cultural factors (Daniels, 1996; Scrimsher & Tudge, 2003).

Of course, not every aspect of Vygotsky's theorizing has been supported, and he can be criticized for a lack of precision in his conceptualization of cognitive growth. For instance, such broad concepts as the zone of proximal development are not terribly precise, and they do not always lend themselves to experimental tests (Wertsch, 1999).

Furthermore, Vygotsky was largely silent on how basic cognitive processes such as attention and memory develop and how children's natural cognitive capabilities unfold. Because of his emphasis on broad cultural influences, he did not focus on how individual bits of information are processed and synthesized. These processes, essential to a complete understanding of cognitive development, are more directly addressed by information processing theories. Still, Vygotsky's melding of the cognitive and social worlds of children has been an important advance in our understanding of cognitive development.

## REVIEW, CHECK, AND APPLY

### REVIEW

**LO6** How do other views of cognitive development differ from Piaget's?

- Proponents of information processing approaches argue that quantitative changes in children's processing skills largely account for their cognitive development.

- Instead of focusing on children's cognitive limitations, developmentalists using an information processing approach focus on the cognitive advances that enable children to develop considerable abilities.

**LO7** What separates Vygotsky's approach from Piaget's?

- Vygotsky believed that children develop cognitively within a context of culture and society. His theory includes the concepts of the zone of proximal development and scaffolding.

- Piaget viewed children as working by themselves to develop an independent view of the world, whereas Vygotsky proposed that children learned the skills of their culture from master teachers.

### CHECK YOURSELF

1. According to the information processing approach of cognitive development, memories of particular events occurring in one's own life are also known as:

   a. autobiographical memory.

   b. explicit memory.

   c. personal memory.

   d. cultural memory.

2. _____ believed that children learn about their world through their interactions with others.

   a. Vygotsky

   b. Piaget

   c. Siegler

   d. Gelman

3. One reason Vygotsky has only begun to have an influence in psychology is because he was largely unknown to developmentalists.

   - True

   - False

### APPLYING LIFESPAN DEVELOPMENT

- Do you agree with the view that information processing approaches see too many trees and lose sight of the forest? Or do you think that Piaget saw too much forest without accounting for enough trees? Explain.

- In what ways have educators and others begun to apply Vygotsky's ideas in schools and communities? Should governments take an active role in this?

✓—[Study and Review on **MyDevelopmentLab.com**

Answers: 1) a; 2) a; 3) True

# The Growth of Language and Learning

**LO8**   How does language develop in the preschool years?

**LO9**   What effects does television have on preschoolers?

**LO10**   What kinds of preschool educational programs are available?

*I tried it out and it was very great!*
*This is a picture of when I was running through the water with Mommy.*
*Where are you going when I go to the fireworks with Mommy and Daddy?*
*I didn't know creatures went on floats in pools.*
*We can always pretend we have another one.*
*And the teacher put it up on the counter so no one could reach it.*
*I really want to keep it while we're at the park.*
*You need to get your own ball if you want to play "hit the tree."*
*When I grow up and I'm a baseball player, I'll have my baseball hat, and I'll put it on, and I'll play baseball.* (Schatz, 1994, p. 179)

Listen to Ricky, at age 3. In addition to recognizing most letters of the alphabet, printing the first letter of his name, and writing the word "HI," he is capable of producing these complex sentences.

During the preschool years, children's language skills reach new heights of sophistication. They begin the period with reasonable linguistic capabilities, but with significant gaps in both comprehension and production. In fact, no one would mistake a 3-year-old's language for an adult's. However, by the end of the preschool years, they can hold their own with adults, comprehending and producing language with many of the qualities of adults' language. How does this transformation occur?

## Language Development

Language blooms so rapidly between the late 2s and the mid-3s that researchers have yet to understand the exact pattern. What is clear is that sentence length increases steadily, and the number of ways children combine words and phrases to form sentences—known as **syntax**—doubles each month. By the time a preschooler is 3, the various combinations reach into the thousands (see Table 4-2 on page 174 for an example of one child's growth in the use of language; Wheeldon, 1999, Pinker, 2005).

There are also enormous leaps in the number of words children use. By age 6, the average child has a vocabulary of around 14,000 words—acquired at a rate of nearly one new word every 2 hours, 24 hours a day. They manage this feat through a process known as **fast mapping,** in which new words are associated with their meaning after only a brief encounter (Gershkoff-Stowe & Hahn, 2007; Krcmar, Grela, & Lin, 2007; Kan & Kohnert, 2009).

By the age of 3, preschoolers routinely use plurals and possessive forms of nouns (such as "boys" and "boy's"), the past tense (adding "-ed" at the end of words), and articles ("the" and "a"). They can ask, and answer, complex questions ("Where did you say my book is?" and "Those are trucks, aren't they?").

Preschoolers' skills extend to the appropriate formation of words that they have never before encountered. For example, in one classic experiment (Berko, 1958), the experimenter told the children that a figure was a "wug," and then showed them a card with two of the cartoon figures. "Now there are two of them," the children were told, and they were then asked to supply the missing word in the sentence, "There are two _____" (the answer to which, of course, is "wugs"). (See Figure 4-6.)

Not only did children show that they knew rules about the plural forms of nouns, but they understood possessive forms of nouns and the third-person singular and past-tense forms of verbs—all for words that they had never encountered, since they were nonsense words with no real meaning (O'Grady & Aitchison, 2005).

This is a wug.

Now there is another one.
There are two of them.
There are two _____ .

**FIGURE 4-6 Appropriate Formation of Words**
Even though no preschooler—like the rest of us—is likely to have ever before encountered a wug, they are able to produce the appropriate word to fill in the blank (which, for the record, is *wugs*).
Source: Reprinted by permission of Jean Berko Gleason.

**syntax**  the way in which an individual combines words and phrases to form sentences

**fast mapping**  instances in which new words are associated with their meaning after only a brief encounter

## TABLE 4-2 GROWING SPEECH CAPABILITIES

Over the course of just a year, the sophistication of the language of a boy named Adam increases amazingly, as these speech samples show:

| | |
|---|---|
| 2 years, 3 months: | Play checkers. Big drum I got horn. A bunny-rabbit walk. |
| 2 years, 4 months: | See marching bear go? Screw part machine. That busy bulldozer truck. |
| 2 years, 5 months: | Now put boots on. Where wrench go? Mommy talking about lady. What that paper clip doing? |
| 2 years, 6 months: | Write a piece of paper. What that egg doing? I lost a shoe. No, I don't want to sit seat. |
| 2 years, 7 months: | Where piece a paper go? Ursula has a boot on. Going to see kitten. Put the cigarette down. Dropped a rubber band. Shadow has hat just like that. Rintintin don't fly, Mommy. |
| 2 years, 8 months: | Let me get down with the boots on. Don't be afraid a horses. How tiger be so healthy and fly like kite? Joshua throw like a penguin. |
| 2 years, 9 months: | Where Mommy keep her pocket book? Show you something funny. Just like turtle make mud pie. |
| 2 years, 10 months: | Look at that train Ursula brought I simply don't want put in chair. You don't have paper. Do you want little bit, Cromer? I can't wear it tomorrow. |
| 2 years, 11 months: | That birdie hopping by Missouri in bag. Do want some pie on your face? Why you mixing baby chocolate? I finish drinking all up down my throat. I said why not you coming in? Look at that piece of paper and tell it. Do you want me tie that round? We going turn light on so you can't see. |
| 3 years, 0 months: | I going come in fourteen minutes. I going wear that to wedding. I see what happens. I have to save them now. Those are not strong mens. They are going sleep in wintertime. You dress me up like a baby elephant. |
| 3 years, 1 month: | I like to play with something else. You know how to put it back together. I gon' make it like a rocket to blast off with. I put another one on the floor. You went to Boston University? You want to give me some carrots and some beans? Press the button and catch it sir. I want some other peanuts. Why you put the pacifier in his mouth? Doggies like to climb up. |
| 3 years, 2 months: | So it can't be cleaned? I broke my racing car. Do you know the light wents off? What happened to the bridge? When it's got a flat tire it's need a go to the station. I dream sometimes. I'm going to mail this so the letter can't come off. I want to have some espresso. The sun is not too bright. Can I have some sugar? Can I put my head in the mailbox so the mailman can know where I are and put me in the mailbox? Can I keep the screwdriver just like a carpenter keep the screwdriver? |

Preschoolers also learn what *cannot* be said as they acquire the principles of grammar. **Grammar** is the system of rules that determine how our thoughts can be expressed. For instance, preschoolers come to learn that "I am sitting" is correct, while the similarly structured "I am knowing [that]" is incorrect. Although they still make frequent mistakes of one sort or another, 3-year-olds follow the principles of grammar most of the time. Some errors are very noticeable—such as the use of "mens" and "catched"—but these errors are actually quite rare. In fact, young preschoolers are correct in their grammatical constructions more than 90 percent of the time (deVilliers & deVilliers, 1992; Guasti, 2002; Abbot-Smith & Tomasello, 2010).

*Private Speech and Social Speech.* In even a short visit to a preschool, you're likely to notice some children talking to themselves during play periods. A child might be reminding a doll about a trip to the grocery store later, or, while playing with a toy racing car, might speak of an upcoming race. In some cases, the talk is sustained, as when a child, working on a puzzle, says things like, "This piece goes here. . . . Uh-oh, this one doesn't fit. . . . Where can I put this piece? . . . This can't be right."

Some developmentalists suggest that **private speech,** speech by children that is spoken and directed to themselves, performs an important function. For instance, Vygotsky suggested that it is used as a guide to behavior and thought. By communicating with themselves through private speech, children are able to try out ideas, acting as their own sounding boards. In this way, private speech facilitates children's thinking and helps them control their behavior—much as you might say "Take it easy" or "Calm down" when trying to control your anger over some situation. In Vygotsky's view, then, private speech serves an important social function and is also a forerunner to the internal dialogues that we use when we reason with ourselves during thinking (Winsler, De Leon, & Wallace, 2003; Winsler et al., 2006).

**grammar** the system of rules that determine how our thoughts can be expressed

**private speech** speech by children that is spoken and directed to themselves

In addition, private speech may be a way for children to practice the practical skills required in conversation, known as *pragmatics*. **Pragmatics** is the aspect of language relating to communicating effectively and appropriately with others. The development of pragmatic abilities permits children to understand the basics of conversations—turn-taking, sticking to a topic, and what should and should not be said, according to the conventions of society. When children are taught that the appropriate response to receiving a gift is "thank you," or that they should use different language in various settings (on the playground versus in the classroom), they are learning the pragmatics of language.

The preschool years also mark the growth of social speech. **Social speech** is speech directed toward another person and meant to be understood by that person. Before age 3, children seem to be speaking only for their own entertainment, apparently uncaring whether anyone else can understand. However, during the preschool years, children begin to direct their speech to others, wanting others to listen and becoming frustrated when they cannot make themselves understood. As a result, they begin to adapt their speech to others through pragmatics, as discussed earlier.

## Learning from the Media: Television and the Internet

Ask almost any preschooler, and she or he will be able to identify Snuffleupagus, as well as Big Bird, Bert, Ernie, and a host of other characters: the members of the cast of *Sesame Street*. *Sesame Street* is the most successful television show in history targeted at preschoolers; its audience is in the millions.

But *Sesame Street* is not all that preschoolers are watching or doing, for television, and more recently the Internet and computers, play a central role in many U.S. households. Television is a particularly potent stimulus, with the average preschooler watching more than 21 hours of TV a week. In more than a third of households with children 2 to 7 years of age, the television is on "most of the time," and in one study a fifth of children under the age of two had a television in their bedroom. In comparison, preschoolers spend three-quarters of an hour reading on the average day (Roberts et al., 1999; Bryant & Bryant, 2001, 2003; Center for Disease Control and Prevention, 2010).

Computers are also becoming influential in the lives of preschoolers. Seventy percent of preschoolers between the ages of 4 and 6 have used a computer, and a quarter of them use one every day. Those who use a computer spend an average of an hour a day, and the majority use it by themselves. With help from their parents, almost one-fifth have sent an e-mail (Rideout, Vandewater, & Wartella, 2003).

It's too early to know the effects of computer usage—and of other media such as video games—on preschoolers. However, there is a wealth of research on the consequences of viewing television, as we consider next (Rideout, Vandewater, & Wartella, 2003; Courage & Howe, 2010).

***Television: Controlling Exposure.***  Despite the introduction of a number of high-quality educational programs in recent decades, many children's programs are not of high quality or are not appropriate for a preschool audience. Accordingly, the American Academy of Pediatrics (AAP) recommends that exposure to television should be limited. The AAP suggests that until the age of 2, children watch *no* television, and after that age, no more than 1 to 2 hours of quality programming each day (AAP, 2009).

In fact, preschoolers are not particularly "television literate." They often do not fully understand the plots of the stories they are viewing, are unable to recall significant story details after viewing a program, and make limited and often erroneous inferences about the motivations of characters. Moreover, preschool children may have difficulty separating fantasy from reality, with some believing, for example, that there is a real Big Bird living on *Sesame Street* (Wright et al., 1994; Kimura & Kato, 2006).

Similarly, preschoolers exposed to TV advertising are not able to critically understand and evaluate the messages they see. Consequently, they are likely to fully accept advertisers' claims about their product. The likelihood of children believing advertising messages is so high that the American Psychological Association has recommended placing restrictions on advertising targeting children under age 8 (Kunkel et al., 2004; Pine, Wilson, & Nash, 2007; Nash, Pine, & Messer, 2009).

As they get older and their information processing capabilities improve, preschoolers' understanding of the material they see on television improves. They remember things more accurately,

**pragmatics** the aspect of language that relates to communicating effectively and appropriately with others

**social speech** speech directed toward another person and meant to be understood by that person

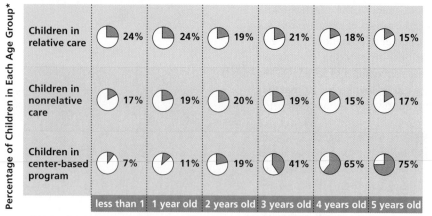

*Columns do not add up to 100 because some children participated in more than one type of day care.*

**FIGURE 4-7 Care Outside the Home**
Approximately 75 percent of children in the United States are enrolled in some form of care outside the home—a trend that is the result of more parents employed full time. Evidence suggests that children can benefit from early childhood education.
Source: U.S. Department of Education, National Center.

and they are better able to focus on the central message of a show. This improvement suggests that the powers of the medium of television may be harnessed to bring about cognitive gains—exactly what the producers of *Sesame Street* set out to do (Singer & Singer, 2000; Crawley, Anderson, & Santomero, 2002; Berry, 2003; Uchikoshi, 2006).

## Early Childhood Education: Taking the "Pre" Out of the Preschool Period

The term "preschool period" is something of a misnomer: Almost three-quarters of children in the United States are enrolled in some form of care outside the home, much of it designed either explicitly or implicitly to teach skills that will enhance intellectual and social abilities (see Figure 4-7). There are several reasons for this, but one major factor is the rise in the number of families in which both parents work outside the home. For instance, a high proportion of fathers work outside the home, and close to 60 percent of women with children under 6 are employed, most of them full-time (Gilbert, 1994; Borden, 1998; Tamis-LeMonda & Cabrera, 2002).

However, there is another reason that preschools are popular: Developmental psychologists have found evidence that children can benefit substantially from involvement in some form of educational activity before they enroll in formal schooling, which typically takes place at age 5 or 6 in the United States. When compared to children who stay at home and have no formal educational involvement, most children enrolled in good preschools experience clear cognitive and social benefits (National Institute of Child Health and Human Development [NICHHD], 1999, 2000; Campbell, Ramey, & Pungello, 2002).

*The Varieties of Early Education.* The variety of early education alternatives is vast. Some outside-the-home care for children is little more than babysitting, while other options are designed to promote intellectual and social advances. Among the major choices are the following:

- *Child-care centers* typically provide care for children outside the home, while their parents are at work. Although many child-care centers aim to provide some form of intellectual stimulation, their primary purpose tends to be more social and emotional than cognitive.

- Some child care is provided in *family child-care centers,* small operations run in private homes. Because centers in some areas are unlicensed, the quality of care can be uneven. Because teachers in licensed child-care programs are more often trained professionals than those who provide family child care, the quality of care is often higher.

- *Preschools* are explicitly designed to provide intellectual and social experiences for children. They tend to be more limited in their schedules than family care centers, typically providing care for only 3 to 5 hours per day. Because of this limitation, preschools serve children mainly from middle and higher socioeconomic levels, in cases where parents don't need to work full time.

  Like child-care centers, preschools vary enormously in the activities they provide. Some emphasize social skills, while others focus on intellectual development. Some do both.

- *School child care* is provided by some local school systems in the United States. Almost half the states fund prekindergarten programs for 4-year-olds, often aimed at disadvantaged children. Because they typically are staffed by better-trained teachers than less-regulated child-care centers, school child-care programs are often of higher quality than other early education alternatives.

*The Effectiveness of Child Care.* How effective are such programs? Most research suggests that preschoolers enrolled in child-care centers show intellectual development that at least matches that of children at home, and often is better. For instance, some studies find that preschoolers in child care are more verbally fluent, show memory and comprehension advantages, and even achieve higher IQ scores than at-home children. Other studies find that early and long-term participation in child care is particularly helpful for children from lower-income homes or those who are at risk (Clarke-Stewart & Allhusen, 2002; Vandell, 2004; Dowset et al., 2008).

Similar advantages are found for social development. Children in high-quality programs tend to be more self-confident, independent, and knowledgeable about the social world in which they live than those who do not participate. On the other hand, not all the outcomes of outside-the-home care are positive: Children in child care have been found to be less polite, less compliant, less respectful of adults, and sometimes more competitive and aggressive than their peers. Furthermore, children who spend more than 10 hours a week in preschools have a slightly higher likelihood of being disruptive in class (Clarke-Stewart & Allhusen, 2002; NICHD Early Child Care Research Network, 2003; Belsky et al., 2007).

It is important to keep in mind that not all early childhood care programs are equally effective. High-quality care provides intellectual and social benefits, while low-quality care not only is unlikely to furnish benefits, but actually may harm children (Votruba-Drzal, Coley, & Chase-Lansdale, 2004; NICHD Early Child Care Research Network, 2006; Dearing, McCartney, & Taylor, 2009).

***The Quality of Child Care.***  How can we define "high quality"? The major characteristics of high-quality care include the following (Love et al., 2003; Vandell, Shumow, & Posner, 2005; Layzer & Goodson, 2006; Leach et al., 2008; Rudd, Cain, & Saxon, 2008):

- The care providers are well trained.
- The child-care center has an appropriate overall size and ratio of care providers to children. Single groups should not have many more than 14 to 20 children, and there should be no more than five to ten 3-year-olds per caregiver, or seven to ten 4- or 5-year-olds per caregiver.
- The curriculum of a child-care facility is not left to chance, but is carefully planned out and coordinated among the teachers.
- The language environment is rich, with a great deal of conversation.
- The caregivers are sensitive to children's emotional and social needs, and they know when and when not to intervene.
- Materials and activities are age appropriate.
- Basic health and safety standards are followed.

No one knows how many programs in the United States can be considered "high quality," but there are many fewer than desirable. In fact, the United States lags behind almost

## *Cultural Dimensions*

### Preschools Around the World: Why Does the United States Lag Behind?

In France and Belgium, access to preschool is a legal right. Sweden and Finland provide child care for preschoolers whose parents want it. Russia has an extensive system of state-run *yasli-sads,* nursery schools and kindergartens, attended by 75 percent of children age 3 to 7 in urban areas.

In contrast, the United States has no coordinated national policy on preschool education—or on the care of children in general. There are several reasons for this. For one, decisions about education have traditionally been left to the states and local school districts. For another, the United States, unlike many other countries, has no tradition of teaching preschoolers. Finally, the status of preschools in the United States has been traditionally low. Consider, for instance, that preschool and nursery school teachers are the lowest paid of all teachers. (Teacher salaries increase as the age of students rises.

Thus, college and high school teachers are paid most, while preschool and elementary school teachers are paid least.)

Different societies view the purpose of early childhood education differently (Lamb et al., 1992). For instance, in a cross-country comparison of China, Japan, and the United States, researchers found that parents in the three countries view the purpose of preschools very differently. Whereas parents in China tend to see preschools primarily as a way of giving children a good start academically, Japanese parents view them mostly as a way of giving children the opportunity to be members of a group. In the United States, in comparison, parents regard the primary purpose of preschools as making children more independent and self-reliant, although obtaining a good academic start and having group experiences are also important (Tobin, Wu, & Davidson, 1989; Huntsinger et al., 1997; Johnson et al., 2003).

every other industrialized country in the quality of its child care as well as in its quantity and affordability (Zigler & Finn-Stevenson, 1995; Scarr, 1998; Muenchow & Marsland, 2007).

**From an educator's perspective:** What do you think might be some implications for a preschool teacher who has children from China, Japan, and the United States in the classroom?

## REVIEW, CHECK, AND APPLY

### REVIEW

**L08**  How does language develop in the preschool years?

- In the preschool years, children rapidly increase in linguistic ability, developing an improved sense of grammar and shifting gradually from private to social speech.

**L09**  What effects does television have on preschoolers?

- Preschoolers watch television at high levels, with mixed consequences.

**L10**  What kinds of preschool educational programs are available?

- Preschool educational programs are beneficial if they are of high quality, with trained staff, good curriculum, proper group sizes, and small staff–student ratios.

### CHECK YOURSELF

1. Being able to combine words and phrases in order to form sentences is also known as _____.

2. Preschoolers are able to learn the meaning of words after only a brief encounter. This is also known as:
   a. synaptic explosion.
   b. word unification.
   c. social speech.
   d. fast mapping.

3. When it comes to child care and its effectiveness, the key factor is _____.
   a. size
   b. program type (i.e., Montessori or Reggio Emilia)
   c. age of the child
   d. quality

### APPLYING LIFESPAN DEVELOPMENT

- Is private speech egocentric or useful? Do adults ever use private speech? What functions does it serve?

- In your view, how do thought and language interact in preschoolers' development? Is it possible to think without language? How do children who have been deaf from birth think?

✔●─Study and Review on **MyDevelopmentLab.com**

Answers: 1) syntax; 2) d; 3) d

---

## MODULE 4.3 Social and Personality Development in the Preschool Years

*Usman Rabbani was a graduate of Yale and Harvard. Clearly, he had experience writing application essays. But this time, he didn't know where to start. Of course, this application essay was unlike any he'd ever written before. It was an application essay for a preschool, written on behalf of his two twin toddlers, Humza and Raza.*

*In New York City, competition to get into elite preschools can be as intense as it is to get into any college. Parents hire consultants to advise them and spend hours putting together applications, hoping to get their children into the cream of the preschool crop. But as Usman Rabbani made his way through the application process, he was confronted with a compelling question: How do you describe a very young child in an essay? "What do you say about someone who just popped out?" he asked. "You're just getting to know them yourself."*

*Eventually, he decided to be creative. He described Humza as "a soft-hearted jock." Raza he called "a thinker and a mischievous lover." These might seem unconventional ways to characterize preschoolers, but clearly Usman did something right: both his sons got into their parents' first choice preschools.*

Like most preschool-age children, Usman Rabbani's sons were only just beginning to show the personalities that would develop during the rest of their lives. The task of writing an essay about them was probably only made harder by the fact that not only were their personalities new, they were also in flux.

In this module, we address social and personality development during the preschool period. We begin by examining how children continue to form a sense of self, focusing on how they develop their self-concepts, including their concept of gender. Next we focus on preschoolers' social lives, especially how they play with one another, and we consider how parents and other authority figures use discipline to shape children's behavior.

Finally, we examine two key aspects of social behavior: moral development and aggression. We consider how children develop a notion of right and wrong and we look at factors that lead preschool-age children to behave aggressively.

# Forming a Sense of Self

LO11 How do preschool-age children develop a concept of themselves?

LO12 How do children develop their sense of racial identity and gender?

Although the question "Who am I?" is not explicitly posed by most preschool-age children, it underlies much of their development during the preschool years, and the answer may affect them for the rest of their lives.

## Psychosocial Development: Resolving the Conflicts

*Mary-Alice's preschool teacher raised her eyebrows slightly when the 4-year-old took off her coat. Mary-Alice, usually dressed in well-matched play suits, was a medley of prints. She had on a pair of flowered pants, along with a completely clashing plaid top. The outfit was accessorized with a striped headband, socks in an animal print, and Mary-Alice's polka-dotted rain boots. Mary-Alice's mom gave a slightly embarrassed shrug. "Mary-Alice got dressed all by herself this morning," she explained as she handed over a bag containing spare shoes, just in case the rain boots became uncomfortable during the day.*

Psychoanalyst Erik Erikson may well have praised Mary-Alice's mother for helping Mary-Alice develop a sense of initiative (if not of fashion), and thereby promoting her psychosocial development. **Psychosocial development** encompasses changes in individuals' understanding of themselves and of others' behavior. According to Erikson, society and culture present a series of challenges, which shift as people age. Erikson believed that people pass through eight distinct stages, each characterized by a crisis or conflict that the person must resolve. Our experiences as we try to resolve these conflicts lead us to develop ideas about ourselves that can last for the rest of our lives.

In the early part of the preschool period, children are ending the autonomy-versus-shame-and-doubt stage and entering what Erikson called the **initiative-versus-guilt stage,** which lasts from around age 3 to age 6. During this period, children face conflicts between the desire to act independently of their parents and the guilt that comes if they don't succeed. They come to see themselves as persons in their own right, and they begin to make decisions on their own.

Parents (like Mary-Alice's mother) who react positively can help their children resolve these opposing feelings. By providing their children with opportunities to act self-reliantly, while still giving them direction and guidance, parents can support their children's initiative. On the other hand, parents who discourage their children's independence may contribute to a sense of guilt that persists throughout their lives and affects their self-concept, which begins to develop during this period.

## Self-Concept in the Preschool Years: Thinking About the Self

If you ask preschool-age children to specify what makes them different from other kids, they readily respond with answers like, "I'm a good runner" or "I'm a big girl." Such answers relate to **self-concept**—their identity, or their set of beliefs about what they are like as individuals (Brown, 1998; Tessor, Felson, & Suls, 2000; Marsh, Ellis, & Craven, 2002).

Psychosocial development relates to changes in an understanding of oneself and others behavior.

**psychosocial development** according to Erikson, development that encompasses changes both in the understandings individuals have of themselves as members of society and in their comprehension of the meaning of others' behavior

**initiative-versus-guilt stage** according to Erikson, the period during which children aged 3 to 6 years experience conflict between independence of action and the sometimes negative results of that action

**self-concept** a person's identity, or set of beliefs about what one is like as an individual

## *Cultural Dimensions*

### Developing Racial and Ethnic Awareness

The preschool years mark an important turning point for children. Their answer to the question of who they are begins to take into account their racial and ethnic identity.

For most preschool-age children, racial awareness comes relatively early. Certainly, even infants are able to distinguish different skin colors, but it is only later that children begin to attribute meaning to different racial characteristics.

By the time they are 3 or 4 years of age, preschool-age children notice differences among people based on skin color, and they begin to identify themselves as a member of a particular group, such as "Hispanic" or "Black." Although at first they do not realize that ethnicity and race are enduring features of who they are, later they begin to understand the significance that society places on ethnic and racial

membership (Cross & Cross, 2008; Quintana & McKown, 2008; Guerrero et al., 2010).

Some preschoolers have mixed feelings about their racial and ethnic identity. Some experience **race dissonance,** the phenomenon in which minority children indicate preferences for majority values or people. For instance, some studies find that as many as 90 percent of African American children, when asked about their reactions to drawings of Black and White children, react more negatively to those depicting Black children than White children. However, this reaction does not translate into lower self-esteem; rather, the White preference appears to be a result of the powerful influence of the dominant culture, rather than a disparagement of their own race (Holland, 1994; Quintana, 2007).

Children's self-concepts are not necessarily accurate. In fact, preschool children typically overestimate their skills and knowledge across all domains of expertise. Consequently, their view of the future is quite rosy: They expect to win the next game they play, to beat all opponents in an upcoming race, to write great stories when they grow up. Even when they have just experienced failure at a task, they are likely to expect to do well in the future. This optimistic view arises because they do not yet compare themselves and their performance against others, thereby gaining the freedom to take chances and try new activities (Dweck, 2002; Wang, 2004).

Preschool-age children's view of themselves reflects their culture. For example, many Asian societies tend to have a **collectivistic orientation,** in which individuals tend to regard themselves as parts of a larger social network in which they are interconnected with and responsible to others. In contrast, children in Western cultures are more likely to develop an **individualistic orientation** that emphasizes personal identity and the uniqueness of the individual, seeing themselves as self-contained and autonomous, in competition with others for scarce resources (Markus & Kitayama, 1991; Dennis et al., 2002; Lehman, Chiu, & Schaller, 2004; Wang, 2004, 2006).

Preschoolers' developing self-concepts can also be affected by their culture's attitudes toward various racial and ethnic groups. Preschoolers' awareness of their ethnic or racial identity is subtly influenced by the attitudes of the people, schools, and other cultural institutions with which they come into contact.

## Gender Identity: Developing Femaleness and Maleness

*Boys' awards: Very Best Thinker, Most Eager Learner, Most Imaginative, Most Enthusiastic, Most Scientific, Best Friend, Mr. Personality, Hardest Worker, Best Sense of Humor.*

*Girls' awards: All-Around Sweetheart, Sweetest Personality, Cutest Personality, Best Sharer, Best Artist, Biggest Heart, Best Manners, Best Helper, Most Creative.*

What's wrong with this picture? To one parent, whose daughter received one of the girls' awards during a kindergarten graduation ceremony, quite a bit. While the girls were getting pats on the back for their pleasing personalities, the boys were receiving awards for their intellectual and analytic skills (Deveny, 1994).

This situation is not rare: Girls and boys often live in very different worlds beginning at birth and continuing into the preschool years and beyond (Martin & Ruble, 2004; Bornstein et al., 2008).

**race dissonance** the phenomenon in which minority children indicate preferences for majority values or people

**collectivistic orientation** a philosophy that promotes the notion of interdependence

**individualistic orientation** a philosophy that emphasizes personal identity and the uniqueness of the individual

Gender, the sense of being male or female, is well established by the time children reach the preschool years. By age 2, children consistently label people as male or female (Raag, 2003; Campbell, Shirley, & Candy, 2004; Fivush, 2010).

One way gender shows up is in play. Preschool boys spend more time than girls in rough-and-tumble play, while preschool girls spend more time in organized games and role-playing. During this time boys begin to play more with boys, and girls with girls, a trend that increases during middle childhood. Girls begin to prefer same-sex playmates a little earlier than boys. They first have a clear preference for interacting with other girls at age 2, while boys don't show much preference for same-sex playmates until age 3 (Boyatzis, Mallis, & Leon, 1999; Martin & Fabes, 2001; Raag, 2003).

Preschool-age children often have very strict ideas about how boys and girls are supposed to act. In fact, their expectations about gender-appropriate behavior are even more gender-stereotyped than those of adults. Beliefs in gender stereotypes become increasingly pronounced up to age 5, and although they become somewhat less rigid by age 7, they do not disappear. In fact, the gender stereotypes held by preschoolers resemble those held by traditional adults in society (Lam & Leman, 2003; Ruble et al., 2007; Martin & Ruble, 2010).

Like adults, preschoolers expect that males are more apt to have traits involving competence, independence, forcefulness, and competitiveness. In contrast, females are viewed as more likely to have traits such as warmth, expressiveness, nurturance, and submissiveness. Although these are *expectations,* and say nothing about the way that men and women actually behave, such expectations provide the lens through which preschool-age children view the world and affect their behavior as well as the way they interact with peers and adults (Blakemore, 2003; Gelman, Taylor, & Nguyen, 2004).

**From a child-care provider's perspective:** If a girl in a preschool child-care setting loudly tells a boy that he can't play with the dolls in the play area because he's a boy, what is the best way to handle the situation?

Why should gender play such a powerful role during the preschool years (as well as during the rest of the life span)? Developmentalists have proposed several explanations.

During the preschool period, differences in play according to gender become more pronounced. In addition, boys tend to play with boys, and girls with girls.

***Biological Perspectives.*** It is hardly surprising that the biological characteristics associated with sex lead to gender differences. Hormones, for example, have been found to affect gender-based behaviors. Girls exposed to unusually high levels of *androgens* (male hormones) prenatally are more likely to display "typically male" behaviors than their sisters who were not exposed to androgens (Knickmeyer & Baron-Cohen, 2006; Burton et al., 2009; Mathews et al., 2009).

Androgen-exposed girls preferred boys as playmates and spent more time than other girls playing with toys associated with the male role, such as cars and trucks. Similarly, boys exposed prenatally to atypically high levels of female hormones are apt to display more behaviors that are stereotypically female than is usual (Servin et al., 2003; Knickmeyer & Baron-Cohen, 2006).

Some developmentalists see gender differences as serving the biological goal of survival of the species. Using an evolutionary approach, these theorists suggest that males with stereotypically masculine qualities, such as forcefulness and competitiveness, may have been able to attract females who could give them hardy offspring. Females who excelled at stereotypically feminine tasks, such as nurturing, may have been valued because they could help their children survive the dangers of childhood (Browne, 2006; Ellis, 2006).

Of course, it is difficult to attribute behavioral characteristics unambiguously to biological factors. Because of this, we must consider other explanations for gender differences.

***Social Learning Approaches.*** According to social learning approaches, children learn gender-related behavior and expectations by observing others, including parents, teachers, siblings, and even peers. A boy might admire a major league baseball player and become

**gender identity** the perception of oneself as male or female

**gender schema** a cognitive framework that organizes information relevant to gender

**gender constancy** the awareness that people are permanently males or females, depending on fixed, unchangeable biological factors

**androgynous** a state in which gender roles encompass characteristics thought typical of both sexes

interested in sports. A girl might watch her babysitter practicing cheerleading moves and begin to try them herself. Observing the praise and honor that gender-appropriate behavior earns leads the child to emulate that behavior (Rust et al., 2000).

Books and the media, and in particular television and video games, also play a role in perpetuating traditional views of gender-related behavior. Analyses of the most popular television shows find that male characters outnumber female characters by two to one. Furthermore, females are more apt to appear with males, whereas female–female relationships are relatively uncommon (Calvert, Kotler, & Zehnder, 2003).

Television also presents men and women in traditional gender roles. Television shows typically define female characters in terms of their relationships with males. Females are more likely to appear as victims than males (Wright et al., 1995; Turner-Bowker, 1996). They are less likely to be presented as productive or as decision makers, and more likely to be portrayed as characters interested in romance, their homes, and their families. Such models, according to social learning theory, have a powerful influence on preschoolers' definitions of appropriate behavior (Scharrer et al., 2006; Hust, Brown, & L'Engle, 2008; Nassif & Gunter, 2008).

In some cases, preschoolers learn social roles directly, not through models. For example, preschool-age children may be told by their parents to act like a "little girl" or "little man." What this generally means is that girls should behave politely and boys should be tough. Such direct training sends a clear message about expected behavior for the different genders (Leaper, 2002).

*Cognitive Approaches.* In the view of some theorists, one aspect of forming a clear sense of identity is the desire to establish a **gender identity,** a perception of oneself as male or female. To do this, children develop a **gender schema,** a cognitive framework that organizes information relevant to gender (Barbera, 2003; Martin & Ruble, 2004; Signorella & Frieze, 2008).

Gender schemas are developed early in life and serve as a lens through which preschoolers view the world, encompassing "rules" about what is appropriate and inappropriate for males and females. Some girls may decide that wearing pants is what boys do and apply the rule so rigidly that they refuse to wear anything but dresses. Or a preschool boy may reason that it is inappropriate for him to wear makeup for a school play because makeup is worn by girls—even though all the other boys and girls are wearing it (Frawley, 2008).

According to *cognitive-developmental theory,* proposed by Lawrence Kohlberg, this rigidity is in part a reflection of preschoolers' understanding of gender (Kohlberg, 1966). Specifically, young preschoolers erroneously believe that sex differences are based not on biological factors but on differences in appearance or behavior. Employing this view of the world, a boy may think he could turn into a girl if he put on a dress and tied his hair in a ponytail. However, by age 4 or 5, children develop an understanding of **gender constancy,** the awareness that people are permanently males or females, depending on fixed, unchangeable biological factors.

Interestingly, gender schemas appear well before children understand gender constancy. Even young preschool-age children assume that certain behaviors are appropriate—and others are not—on the basis of stereotypic views of gender (Martin & Ruble, 2004; Ruble et al., 2007; Karniol, 2009). ●─Watch on **mydevelopmentlab.com**

Is it possible to avoid viewing the world in terms of gender schemas? According to Sandra Bem (1987), one way is to encourage children to be **androgynous,** a state in which gender roles encompass characteristics thought typical of both sexes. For instance, parents and caregivers can encourage preschool children to see males as assertive but at the same time warm and tender. Similarly, girls might be encouraged to see the female role as both empathetic and tender and competitive, assertive, and independent.

Like the other approaches to gender development, the cognitive perspective does not imply that differences between the two sexes are in any way improper or inappropriate. Instead, it suggests that preschoolers should be taught to treat others as individuals. Furthermore, preschoolers need to learn the importance of fulfilling their own talents, acting as individuals and not as representatives of a gender.

●─Watch on **mydevelopmentlab.com**

Watch the video clip "Understanding Self and Others" on MyDevelopmentLab.com to see how preschoolers develop a self-concept and gender identity.

## REVIEW, CHECK, AND APPLY

### REVIEW

**LO11** How do preschool-age children develop a concept of themselves?

- According to Erikson's psychosocial development theory, preschool-age children move from the autonomy-versus-shame-and-doubt stage to the initiative-versus-guilt stage.
- During the preschool years, children develop their self-concepts, beliefs about themselves that they derive from their own perceptions, their parents' behaviors, and society.

**LO12** How do children develop their sense of racial identity and gender?

- Racial, ethnic, and gender awareness begin to form in the preschool years.

### CHECK YOURSELF

**1.** According to Erikson (1963), during the preschool years children face a key conflict relating to psychosocial development that involves the development of _____.

a. repression
b. identity
c. initiative
d. trust

**2.** Five-year-old Kayla has been practicing her jump-roping skills for the past 6 weeks so she can enter a contest at her school. After one afternoon of practice she told her mother, "I am a terrific jump roper." This statement is an example of Kayla's increasing understanding of her identity or _____.

**3.** Biological characteristics associated with a person's sex do not appear to be related to gender differences.

- True
- False

### APPLYING LIFESPAN DEVELOPMENT

- What sorts of activities might you encourage a preschool boy to undertake to help him adopt a less stereotypical gender schema?

✓• Study and Review on
**MyDevelopmentLab.com**

Answers: 1) c; 2) self-concept; 3) False

# Friends and Family: Preschoolers' Social Lives

**LEARNING OBJECTIVES**

**LO13** In what sorts of social relationships and play do preschool-age children engage?

**LO14** What sorts of disciplinary styles do parents employ, and what effects do they have?

**LO15** What factors contribute to child abuse and neglect?

*When Juan was 3, he had his first best friend, Emilio. Juan and Emilio, who lived in the same apartment building in San Jose, were inseparable. They played incessantly with toy cars, racing them up and down the apartment hallways until some of the neighbors began to complain about the noise. They pretended to read to one another, and sometimes they slept over at each other's home—a big step for a 3-year-old. Neither boy seemed more joyful than when he was with his "best friend"—the term each used for the other.*

As preschoolers get older, their conception of friendship evolves and the quality of their interactions changes.

An infant's family can provide nearly all the social contact he or she needs. As preschoolers, however, many children, like Juan and Emilio, begin to discover the joys of peer friendships. Let's take a look at both sides of preschoolers' social development, friends and family.

## The Development of Friendships

Before age 3, most social activity involves simply being in the same place at the same time, without real social interaction. However, at around the age of 3, children begin to develop real friendships as peers are seen as individuals who hold special qualities and rewards. While preschoolers'

According to developmentalist Lev Vygotshy, children are able, through make-believe play, to practice activities that are part of their particular culture and broaden their understanding of the way the world functions.

 Watch on **mydevelopmentlab.com**

To see all the types of play you've been reading about displayed in preschoolers, watch the clip "Play Styles" on MyDevelopmentLab.com.

**functional play** play that involves simple, repetitive activities typical of 3-year-olds

**constructive play** play in which children manipulate objects to produce or build something

**parallel play** action in which children play with similar toys, in a similar manner, but do not interact with each other

**onlooker play** action in which children simply watch others at play, but do not actually participate themselves

**associative play** play in which two or more children actually interact with one another by sharing or borrowing toys or materials, although they do not do the same thing

**cooperative play** play in which children genuinely interact with one another, taking turns, playing games, or devising contests

relations with adults reflect children's needs for care, protection, and direction, their relations with peers are based more on the desire for companionship, play, and fun. Gradually they come to view friendship as a continuing state that offers not just immediate pleasure, but the promise of future activity (Hay, Payne, & Chadwick, 2004; Sebanc et al., 2007; Dwyer et al., 2010).

Interactions with friends change during the preschool period. For 3-year-olds, the focus of friendship is the enjoyment of doing things together and playing jointly. Older preschoolers pay more attention to trust, support, and shared interests (Park, Lay, & Ramsay, 1993). Throughout the entire period, however, play remains an important part of all friendships.

***Playing by the Rules: The Work of Play.*** In Rosie Graiff's class of 3-year-olds, Minnie bounces her doll's feet on the table as she sings softly to herself. Ben pushes his toy car across the floor, making motor noises. Sarah chases Abdul around and around the perimeter of the room.

Play is more than what children of preschool age do to pass the time. Instead, play helps preschoolers develop socially, cognitively, and physically (Samuelsson & Johansson, 2006; Ginsburg et al., 2007; Whitebread et al., 2009).

**Categorizing Play.** At the beginning of the preschool years, children engage in **functional play**—simple, repetitive activities typical of 3-year-olds, such as pushing cars on the floor, skipping, and jumping. Functional play involves doing something to be active rather than to create something (Bober, Humphry, & Carswell, 2001; Kantrowitz & Evans, 2004).  Watch on **mydevelopmentlab.com**

By age 4, children become involved in a more sophisticated form of play. In **constructive play** children manipulate objects to produce or build something. A child who builds a house out of Legos or puts a puzzle together is involved in constructive play: He or she has an ultimate goal—to produce something. The creation need not be novel, since children may repeatedly build a house of blocks, let it fall, and then rebuild it.

Constructive play gives children a chance to practice their physical and cognitive skills and fine muscle movements. They gain experience in solving problems about the ways and the sequences in which things fit together. They also learn to cooperate with others as the social nature of play becomes more important to them (Edwards, 2000; Shi, 2003; Love & Burns, 2006).

**The Social Aspects of Play.** If two preschoolers sit side by side at a table, each assembling a different puzzle, are they engaged jointly in play?

According to pioneering work done by Mildred Parten (1932), the answer is yes. She suggests that these preschoolers are engaged in **parallel play,** in which children play with similar toys, in a similar manner, but do not interact with each other. Preschoolers also engage in another form of play, a highly passive one: onlooker play. In **onlooker play,** children simply watch others at play, but do not actually participate themselves.

As they get older, however, preschool-age children engage in more sophisticated forms of social play that involve greater interaction. In **associative play,** two or more children interact with one another by sharing or borrowing toys or materials, although they do not do the same thing. In **cooperative play,** children genuinely play with one another, taking turns, playing games, or devising contests.

Solitary and onlooker play continue in the later stages of the preschool period. There are simply times when children prefer to play by themselves. And when newcomers join a group, one strategy for becoming part of the group—often successful—is to engage in onlooker play, waiting for an opportunity to join the play more actively (Lindsey & Colwell, 2003).

The nature of pretend, or make-believe, play also changes during the period, becoming in some ways more *un*realistic—and imaginative—as preschoolers shift from using only realistic objects to using less concrete ones. Thus, at the start of the preschool period, children may pretend to listen to a radio only if they have a plastic radio on hand. Later, they may use an entirely different object, such as a large cardboard box, as a pretend radio (Bornstein et al., 1996).

Russian developmentalist Lev Vygotsky (1930/1978), discussed in Module 4.2, argued that pretend play, particularly if it involves social play, is an important means for

## *From Research to Practice*

### Does Play Promote Brain Development?

*As Janet took a lump of soft clay and pounded it into the shape of a long, curly snake, Franklin moved a toy truck across a tabletop so quickly that it flew off the side. He laughed, quickly picked it up off the floor, and repeatedly made it fly off the table while his friend Jason watched and giggled himself. At another table, Helena pretended to read a book, quietly talking to herself as she flipped from one page to another.*

A growing amount of research suggests that play like this, found in preschool classrooms around the world, goes well beyond simply fun and games. In fact, play not only leads to increases in self-control and the ability to plan ahead, but may even promote the development of the brain.

According to Adele Diamond, a developmental researcher at the University of British Columbia, play may help children learn self-regulation skills by teaching them the importance of controlling their impulses. By playing games in which they must plan out strategies, they learn the importance of planning ahead and regulating their emotions (Diamond & Amso, 2008).

Even more intriguing, some researchers believe that play helps the brain to develop and become more sophisticated. Based on experiments with nonhumans, neuroscientist Sergio Pellis has found not only that certain sorts of damage to the brain leads to abnormal sorts of play, but that depriving animals of the ability to play affects the course of brain development (Pellis & Pellis, 2007).

For instance, in one experiment, Pellis and his colleagues observed rats under two different conditions. In the control condition, a juvenile target rat was housed with three other young females, allowing them the opportunity to engage in the equivalent of rat play. In the experimental condition, the young target rats were housed with three adult females. Although young rats caged with adults don't have the opportunity to play, they do encounter social experiences with the adults, who will groom and touch them. When Pellis examined the brains of the rats, he found that the play-deprived rats showed deficiencies in the development of their prefrontal cortex (Pellis & Pellis, 2007; Henig, 2008; Bell, Pellis, & Kolb, 2009).

Although it's a big leap from rat play to toddler play, the results of the study do suggest the significance of play in promoting brain and cognitive development. Ultimately, play may be one of the engines that fuels the intellectual development of preschoolers (Bell, Pellis, & Kolb, 2010).

- What are the best ways to incorporate play in preschoolers' lives?
- Based on these new research findings, what would you say to educators who would reduce the amount of recess for budgetary reasons or to include more time for academic subjects?

expanding preschool-age children's cognitive skills. Through make-believe play, children are able to "practice" activities (such as pretending to use a computer or read a book) that are a part of their particular culture and broaden their understanding of the way the world functions. ◉ Watch on **mydevelopmentlab.com**

◉ Watch on **mydevelopmentlab.com**

Log onto MyDevelopmentLab.com and watch the video clip "Play in Early Childhood" to see preschoolers engaging in different types of play.

➔ **From an educator's perspective:** How might a nursery school teacher encourage a shy child to join a group of preschoolers who are playing?

## Preschoolers' Theory of Mind: Understanding What Others Are Thinking

One reason that children's play changes is the continuing development of preschoolers' theory of mind—their knowledge and beliefs about how the mind operates. Using their theory of mind, preschool children increasingly see the world from others' perspectives. Even children as young as 2 are able to understand that others have emotions. By age 3 or 4, preschoolers know that they can imagine something that is not physically present, such as a zebra, and that others can do the same. They can also pretend that something has happened and react as if it really had occurred, a skill that becomes part of their imaginative play (Cadinu & Kiesner, 2000; Mauritzson & Saeljoe, 2001; Andrews, Halford, & Bunch, 2003).

Preschool-age children also become more insightful regarding the motives and reasons behind people's behavior. They begin to understand that their mother is angry because she was late for an appointment, even if they themselves haven't seen her be late. Furthermore, by age 4, children's understanding that people can be fooled by physical reality (such as magic tricks involving sleight-of-hand) becomes surprisingly sophisticated. This increase in understanding helps children become more socially skilled as they gain insight into what others are thinking (Fitzgerald & White, 2002; Eisbach, 2004).

There are limits, however, to 3-year-olds' theory of mind. For instance, their understanding of "belief" is incomplete, as illustrated by their performance on the *false belief* task. In the false belief task, preschoolers are shown a doll named Maxi who places chocolate in a cabinet and then leaves. After Maxi is gone, his mother moves the chocolate somewhere else.

*"We've done a lot of important playing here today."*

Preschoolers are then asked where Maxi will look for the chocolate when he returns. Three-year-olds answer (erroneously) that Maxi will look for it in the new location. In contrast, 4-year-olds correctly realize that Maxi has the false belief that the chocolate is still in the cabinet, and that's where he will look for it (Flynn, O'Malley, & Wood, 2004; Amsterlaw & Wellman, 2006; Brown & Bull, 2007).

By the end of the preschool years, most children easily solve false belief problems. But one group has difficulty with it throughout their lifetimes: children with autism. *Autism* is a disorder that affects about 4 in 10,000 people—most of them males—and produces significant language and emotional difficulties. Persons with autism have trouble relating to others, in part because they find it difficult to understand what others are thinking. It is characterized by a difficulty in connecting to other people, even parents, and an avoidance of interpersonal situations (Heerey, Keltner, & Capps, 2003; Ropar, Mitchell, & Ackroyd, 2003; Pellicano, 2007).

## Preschoolers' Family Lives

*Four-year-old Benjamin was watching TV while his mom cleaned up after dinner. After a while, he wandered in and grabbed a towel, saying, "Mommy, let me help you do the dishes." Surprised by this unprecedented behavior, she asked him, "Where did you learn to do dishes?"*

*"I saw it on* Leave It to Beaver," *he replied, "Only it was the dad helping. Since we don't have a dad, I figured I'd do it."*

For many preschool-age children, life does not mirror old TV sitcoms. Many face the realities of an increasingly complicated world. For instance, in 1960, less than 10 percent of children under 18 lived with one parent. In 2000, a single parent headed 21 percent of White families, 35 percent of Hispanic families, and 55 percent of African American families.

Still, for most children the preschool years are not a time of turmoil. Instead, the period is characterized by growing interactions with the world at large. Preschoolers form genuine friendships and develop close ties with other children—a circumstance facilitated by a warm, supportive home environment. Research finds that strong, positive relationships between parents and children encourage children's relationships with others (Sroufe, 1994; Howes, Galinsky, & Kontos, 1998).

## Effective Parenting: Teaching Desired Behavior

*While she thinks no one is looking, Maria goes into her brother Alejandro's bedroom, where he has been saving the last of his Halloween candy. Just as she takes his last Reese's Peanut Butter Cup, the children's mother walks into the room and immediately takes in the situation.*

If you were Maria's mother, which of the following reactions seems most reasonable?

1. Tell Maria to go to her room and stay there for the rest of the day, and take away access to her favorite blanket, the one she sleeps with every night and during naps.

2. Mildly tell Maria that what she did was not such a good idea, and she shouldn't do it in the future.

3. Explain why her action would upset her brother, and tell her to go to her room for an hour as punishment.

4. Forget about it, and let the children sort it out themselves.

Each of these responses represents one of the major parenting styles identified by Diana Baumrind (1971, 1980) and updated by Eleanor Maccoby and colleagues (Baumrind, 1971, 1980; Maccoby & Martin, 1983).

Children with authoritative parents tend to be well adjusted, in part because the parents are supportive and take the time to explain things. What are the consequences of parents who are too permissive? Too authoritarian? Too uninvolved?

1. **Authoritarian parents** are controlling, punitive, rigid, and cold. Their word is law, and they value strict, unquestioning obedience. They do not tolerate expressions of disagreement.

2. **Permissive parents** provide lax and inconsistent feedback. They require little of their children and don't see themselves as holding much responsibility for how their children turn out. They place little or no limits or control on their children's behavior.

3. **Authoritative parents** are firm, setting clear and consistent limits. Although they tend to be relatively strict, like authoritarian parents, they are loving and emotionally supportive. They also try to reason with their children, explaining why they should behave in a particular way ("Alejandro is going to be upset"), and communicating the rationale for any punishment they may impose. Authoritative parents encourage their children to be independent.

4. **Uninvolved parents** show virtually no interest in their children, displaying indifferent, rejecting behavior. They are detached emotionally and see their role as no more than feeding, clothing, and providing shelter. In its most extreme form, uninvolved parenting results in *neglect*, a form of child abuse. (The four patterns are summarized in Table 4-3.)

Parents' disciplinary styles usually produce differences in children's behavior—although there are many exceptions (Simons & Conger, 2007; Hoeve et al., 2008; Cheah et al., 2009):

- Children of authoritarian parents tend to be withdrawn, show little sociability, are not very friendly, and often behave uneasily around their peers. Girls are especially dependent on their parents, whereas boys are unusually hostile.

- Children of permissive parents tend to be dependent and moody, and are low in social skills and self-control. They share many characteristics of children of authoritarian parents.

- Children of authoritative parents fare best. They generally are independent, friendly, self-assertive, and cooperative. They have strong motivation to achieve, and are typically successful and likable. They regulate their own behavior effectively, both in terms of their relationships with others and emotional self-regulation.

- Children of uninvolved parents are the worst off, showing disrupted emotional development. They feel unloved and emotionally detached, and their physical and cognitive development may be impeded as well.

---

**authoritarian parents** parents who are controlling, punitive, rigid, and cold, and whose word is law. They value strict, unquestioning obedience from their children and do not tolerate expressions of disagreement

**permissive parents** parents who provide lax and inconsistent feedback and require little of their children

**authoritative parents** parents who are firm, setting clear and consistent limits, but who try to reason with their children, giving explanations for why they should behave in a particular way

**uninvolved parents** parents who show almost no interest in their children and indifferent, rejecting behavior

---

## TABLE 4-3  Parenting Styles

| How Responsive Parents Are to a Child | How Demanding Parents Are of Children | |
| --- | --- | --- |
| | **Demanding** | **Undemanding** |
| **Highly Responsive** | **Authoritative**<br>Characteristics: firm, setting clear and consistent limits<br><br>Relationship with Children: Although they tend to be relatively strict, like authoritarian parents they are loving and emotionally supportive and encourage their children to be independent. They also try to reason with their children, giving explanations for why they should behave in a particular way, and communicate the rationale for any punishment they may impose. | **Permissive**<br>Characteristics: lax and inconsistent feedback<br><br>Relationship with Children: They require little of their children, and they don't see themselves as holding much responsibility for how their children turn out. They place little or no limits or control on their children's behavior. |
| **Low Responsive** | **Authoritarian**<br>Characteristics: controlling, punitive, rigid, cold<br><br>Relationship with Children: Their word is law, and they value strict, unquestioning obedience from their children. They also do not tolerate expressions of disagreement. | **Uninvolved**<br>Characteristics: displaying indifferent, rejecting behavior<br><br>Relationship with Children: They are detached emotionally and see their role as only providing food, clothing, and shelter. In its extreme form, this parenting style results in neglect, a form of child abuse. |

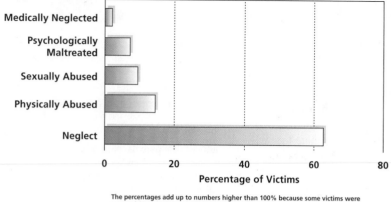

The percentages add up to numbers higher than 100% because some victims were exposed to multiple types of maltreatment. 62.8 percent of victims experienced neglect.

**FIGURE 4-8 Types of Child Abuse**
Neglect is the most frequent form of abuse. How can educators and health care providers help identify cases of child abuse?
Source: U.S. Department of Health and Human Services, Administration on Children, Youth and Families, 2007.

Of course, no classification system is an infallible predictor of how children will fare. In a significant number of cases the children of authoritarian and permissive parents develop successfully.

Furthermore, most parents are inconsistent, switching from their dominant mode to one of the others. For instance, when a child darts into the street, an authoritarian style is generally the most effective (Holden & Miller, 1999; Eisenberg & Valiente, 2002; Gershoff, 2002).

***Cultural Differences in Childrearing Practices.*** It's important to keep in mind that the findings regarding childrearing styles we have been discussing are chiefly applicable to Western societies. The style of parenting that is most successful may depend quite heavily on the norms of a particular culture—and what parents in a particular culture are taught regarding appropriate childrearing practices (Keller et al., 2008; Yagmurlu & Sanson, 2009; Yaman et al., 2010).

For example, the Chinese concept of *chiao shun* suggests that parents should learn to be strict, firm, and in tight control of their children's behavior. They accept that they have a duty to train their children to adhere to socially and culturally desirable standards of behavior, particularly in their school performance. Children's acceptance of this style is seen as a sign of parental respect (Chao, 1994; Wu, Robinson, & Yang, 2002; Ng, Pomerantz, & Lam, 2007).

In short, childrearing practices reflect cultural perspectives on the nature of children as well as on the appropriate role of parents. No single parenting pattern or style is universally appropriate (Wang & Tamis-LeMonda, 2003; Chang Pettit, & Katsurada, 2006; Wang, Pomerantz, & Chen, 2007). Similarly, it is important to keep in mind that parents are not the sole influence on children's development. Sibling and peer influences play a significant role, as does the child's unique genetic endowment (Boivin et al., 2005; Loehlin, Neiderhiser, & Reiss, 2005).

## Child Abuse and Psychological Maltreatment: The Grim Side of Family Life

The figures are disheartening: At least five children are killed by their parents or caretakers every day, and 140,000 others are physically injured every year. Around three million children are abused or neglected in the United States each year. The abuse takes several forms, ranging from actual physical abuse to psychological mistreatment (Briere et al., 1997; Parnell & Day, 1998; National Clearinghouse on Child Abuse and Neglect Information, 2004; U.S. Department of Health and Human Services, 2007) (see Figure 4-8).

***Physical Abuse.*** Child abuse can occur in any household, regardless of economic well-being or social status. It is most prevalent in families living in stressful environments. Poverty, single-parenthood, and higher-than-average levels of marital conflict help create such environments. Stepfathers are more likely to abuse stepchildren than genetic fathers to abuse their own offspring. Child abuse is also more likely when there is a history of violence between spouses (Kitzmann, Gaylord, & Holt, 2003; Litrownik, Newton, & Hunter, 2003; Osofsky, 2003; Evans, 2004). (Table 4-4 lists some of the warning signs of abuse.)

Abused children are more likely to be fussy, resistant to control, and not readily adaptable to new situations. They have more headaches and stomachaches, experience more bedwetting, are generally more anxious, and may show developmental delays. Children in certain age groups are also more likely to be the targets of abuse: Three- and 4-year-olds and 15- to 17-year-olds are somewhat more likely to be abused than children of other ages (Straus & Gelles, 1990; Ammerman & Patz, 1996; Haugaard, 2000).

***Reasons for Physical Abuse.*** Why does physical abuse occur? Most parents do not intend to hurt their children. In fact, most parents who abuse their children later express bewilderment and regret about their behavior.

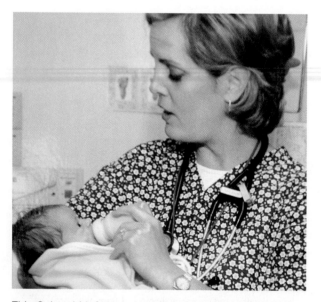

This 9-day-old infant, named Baby Vinnie, was found after being abandoned on the steps behind a church. He later was adopted by a foster family.

## TABLE 4-4  WHAT ARE THE WARNING SIGNS OF CHILD ABUSE?

Because child abuse is typically a secret crime, identifying the victims of abuse is particularly difficult. Still, there are several signs in a child that indicate that he or she is the victim of violence (Robbins, 1990):

- visible, serious injuries that have no reasonable explanation
- bite or choke marks
- burns from cigarettes or immersion in hot water
- feelings of pain for no apparent reason
- fear of adults or care providers
- inappropriate attire in warm weather (long sleeves, long pants, high-necked garments)—possibly to conceal injuries to the neck, arms, and legs
- extreme behavior—highly aggressive, extremely passive, extremely withdrawn
- fear of physical contact

If you suspect a child is a victim of aggression, it is your responsibility to act. Call your local police or the department of social services in your city or state, or call Childhelp U.S.A. at 1-800-422-4453.

Talk to a teacher or a member of the clergy. Remember, by acting decisively you can literally save someone's life.

One reason for child abuse is the vague demarcation between permissible and impermissible forms of physical violence. U.S. folklore says that spanking is not merely acceptable, but often necessary. Almost half of mothers with children under 4 have spanked their child in the previous week, and close to 20 percent believe it is appropriate to spank a child less than 1 year of age. In some other cultures, physical discipline is even more common (Straus, Gelles, & Steinmetz, 2003; Lansford et al., 2005; Deb & Adak, 2006; Shor, 2006).

Unfortunately, the line between "spanking" and "beating" is fuzzy, and spankings begun in anger can escalate into abuse. In fact, increasing scientific evidence suggests that spanking should be avoided entirely. Although physical punishment may produce immediate compliance, there are serious long-term side effects. For example, spanking is associated with inferior parent–child relationships, poorer mental health for both child and parent, higher levels of delinquency, and more antisocial behavior. Spanking also teaches children that violence is an acceptable solution to problems. Consequently, the American Academy of Pediatrics strongly recommends *against* the use of physical punishment of any sort (Kazdin & Benjet, 2003; Afifi et al., 2006; Zolotor et al., 2008).

Another factor that leads to high rates of abuse in Western countries is privacy. In most Western cultures children are raised in private, isolated households. In many other cultures, child-rearing is the joint responsibility of several people and even society as a whole, and other people are available to help out when a parent's patience is tested (Chaffin, 2006; Elliott & Urquiza, 2006).

***The Cycle of Violence Hypothesis.*** Many people who abuse children were themselves abused as children. According to the **cycle of violence hypothesis,** the abuse and neglect that children suffer predispose them as adults to abuse and neglect their own children (Miller-Perrin & Perrin, 1999; Widom, 2000; Heyman & Slep, 2002).

According to this hypothesis, victims of abuse have learned from their childhood experiences that violence is an appropriate and acceptable form of discipline, and they have failed to learn the skills needed to solve problems and instill discipline without violence (Straus, Sugarman, & Giles-Sims, 1997; Blumenthal, 2000; Ethier, Couture, & Lacharite, 2004).

Of course, being abused as a child does not inevitably lead to abuse of one's own children. In fact, statistics show that only about one-third of people who were abused or neglected as children abuse their own children (Cicchetti, 1996; Straus & McCord, 1998).

***Psychological Maltreatment.*** Children may also be the victims of more subtle forms of mistreatment. **Psychological maltreatment** occurs when parents or other caregivers harm children's behavioral, cognitive, emotional, or physical functioning. It may be the result of overt behavior or neglect (Hart, Brassard, & Karlson, 1996; Higgins & McCabe, 2003).

**cycle of violence hypothesis** the theory that the abuse and neglect that children suffer predispose them as adults to abuse and neglect their own children

**psychological maltreatment** abuse that occurs when parents or other caregivers harm children's behavioral, cognitive, emotional, or physical functioning

Two of the children in this large family alleg-edly were singled out for abuse by their par-ents and were severely malnourished, while the other children were seemingly well cared for. What might account for this unusual situation?

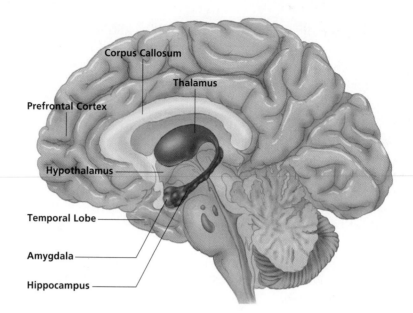

**FIGURE 4-9 Abuse Alters the Brain**
The limbic system, comprised of the hippocampus and amygdala, can be permanently altered as a result of childhood abuse.
Source: *Scientific American*, 2002.

👁 Watch on **mydevelopmentlab.com**

What type of temperament does your virtual child seem to have? To watch children displaying all the different temperaments, log onto MyDevelopmentLab.com and watch the video clip "Temperament."

For example, abusive parents may frighten, belittle, or humiliate their children, who may be made to feel like disappointments or failures. Parents may say that they wish that their children had never been born. Children may be threatened with abandonment or even death. In other instances, older children may be exploited. They may be forced to seek employment and then to give their earnings to their parents. 👁 Watch on **mydevelopmentlab.com**

In other cases of psychological maltreatment, the abuse takes the form of neglect. Parents may ignore their children or act emotionally unresponsive. The children may be given unre-alistic responsibilities or may be left to fend for themselves.

While some children are sufficiently resilient to survive psychological maltreatment, lasting damage often results. Psychological maltreatment has been associated with low self-esteem, lying, misbehavior, and underachievement in school. In extreme cases, it can produce criminal behavior, aggression, and murder. In other instances, children who have been psy-chologically maltreated become depressed and even commit suicide (Eigsti & Cicchetti, 2004; Koenig, Cicchetti, & Rogosch, 2004; Allen, 2008).

One reason that psychological maltreatment—as well as physical abuse—produces so many negative consequences is that the brains of victims undergo permanent changes due to the abuse (see Figure 4-9). For example, childhood maltreatment can lead to reductions in the size of the amygdala and hippocampus in adulthood. The stress, fear, and terror ac-companying abuse may also produce permanent changes in the brain due to overstimulation of the limbic system. Because the limbic system is involved in the regulation of memory and emotion, the result can be antisocial behavior during adulthood (Watts-English et al., 2006; Rick & Douglas, 2007; Twardosz & Lutzker, 2009).

## Resilience: Overcoming the Odds

Given the seriousness of child abuse and the damage it can cause, it's remarkable that not all chil-dren who have been abused are permanently scarred. In fact, some do surprisingly well. What enables some children to overcome stress and trauma that in most cases haunts others for life?

The answer appears to be resilience. **Resilience** is the ability to overcome high-risk circumstances, that place a child at high risk for psychological or physical damage, such as extremes of poverty, prenatal stress, or violence in the home. Several factors seem to reduce and, in certain cases, eliminate some children's reactions to difficult circumstances (Trickett, Kurtz, & Pizzigati, 2004; Collishaw et al., 2007).

**resilience** the ability to overcome circumstances that place a child at high risk for psychological or physical damage

# Disciplining Children

## Becoming an Informed Consumer of Development

The question of how to discipline children has been raised for generations. Answers from developmentalists today include the following (O'Leary, 1995; Brazelton & Sparrow, 2003; Flouri, 2005):

- **For most children in Western cultures, authoritative parenting works best.** Parents should be firm and consistent, providing clear direction and rules, but explaining why the rules make sense, using language that children can understand.

- **Spanking is never an appropriate discipline technique** according to the American Academy of Pediatrics. Not only is spanking ineffective, but it leads to additional unwanted outcomes, such as the potential for more aggressive behavior (American Academy of Pediatrics, 1998).

- **Use *time-out* for punishment.** It is best to remove children from a situation in which they have misbehaved and take away enjoyable activities for a set period.

- **Tailor parental discipline to the characteristics of the child and the situation.** Try to keep the child's personality in mind, and adapt discipline to it.

- **Use routines (such as a bath routine or a bedtime routine) to avoid conflict.** To avoid a nightly struggle, make the potential conflict situation predictably enjoyable. For instance, routinely reading a bedtime story or engaging in a nightly "wrestling" match with the child can defuse potential battles.

According to developmental psychologist Emmy Werner, resilient children tend to have temperaments that evoke positive responses. They tend to be affectionate, easy-going, and good-natured. They are easily soothed as infants, and elicit care from the most nurturant people in any given environment. In a sense, resilient children make their own environments by drawing out behavior in others that they need for their own development. As they grow to school age, they are socially pleasant, outgoing, and have good communication skills. They tend to be intelligent and independent, feeling that they can shape their own fate without depending on others or luck (Werner & Smith, 2002; Martinez-Torteya et al., 2009; Naglieri, Goldstein, & LeBuffe, 2010).

These characteristics suggest ways to help children who are at risk. Programs that have been successful in helping especially vulnerable children provide competent and caring adult models who teach the children problem-solving skills and help them to communicate their needs to those who are in a position to help (Davey et al., 2003; Maton, Schellenbach, & Leadbeater, 2004; Condly, 2006).

---

## REVIEW, CHECK, AND APPLY

### REVIEW

**L013**  In what sorts of social relationships and play do preschool-age children engage?

- In the preschool years, children develop friendships on the basis of personal characteristics, trust, and shared interests.

- The character of preschoolers' play changes over time, growing more sophisticated, interactive, and cooperative, and relying increasingly on social skills.

**L014**  What sorts of disciplinary styles do parents employ, and what effects do they have?

- There are several distinct childrearing styles, including authoritarian, permissive, authoritative, and uninvolved.

- Differences in parenting style are associated with different effects on children. In general, children of authoritative parents fare best, especially when the parents are flexible enough to use elements of different styles when circumstances call for it.

**L015**  What factors contribute to child abuse and neglect?

- Child abuse can occur in any household regardless of economic well-being or social status. It is most prevalent in families living in stressful environments, created in some cases by poverty, single parenthood, and high levels of marital conflict.

### CHECK YOURSELF

1. When it comes to play, younger preschoolers focus on _____ and older preschoolers focus on _____.

   a. sharing activities; trust and shared interests

   b. trust and shared interests; sharing activities

   c. parallel play; solitary play

   d. communicative play; nonverbal play

2. As preschoolers get older, their play shifts from more social to more functional.

   - True

   - False

3. Which of the following characteristics is NOT typical of a child who has authoritative parents?

   a. independent

   b. achievement-oriented

   c. dependent

   d. likeable

### APPLYING LIFESPAN DEVELOPMENT

- What cultural and environmental factors in the United States may have contributed to the shift from an authoritarian "spare the rod" parenting style to an authoritative one since World War II? Is another shift under way?

 **Study** and **Review** on **MyDevelopmentLab.com**

# Moral Development and Aggression

**LO16** How do children develop a sense of morality?

**LO17** How does aggression develop in preschool-age children?

Preschoolers believe in immanent justice. This child may worry that she will be punished even if no one sees her carrying out the misdeed.

*During snack time at preschool, playmates Jan and Meg inspected the goodies in their lunch boxes. Jan found two appetizing cream-filled cookies. Meg's snack offered less tempting carrot and celery sticks. As Jan began to munch on one of her cookies, Meg looked at the cut-up vegetables and burst into tears. Jan responded to Meg's distress by offering her companion one of her cookies, which Meg gladly accepted. Jan was able to put herself in Meg's place, understand Meg's thoughts and feelings, and act compassionately.* (Katz, 1989, p. 213)

In this short scenario we see many of the key elements of morality, preschool style. Changes in children's views of the right way to behave are an important element of growth during the preschool years.

At the same time, the kind of aggression displayed by preschoolers is also changing. We can consider the development of morality and aggression as two sides of the coin of human conduct, and both involve a growing awareness of others.

## Developing Morality: Following Society's Rights and Wrongs

**Moral development** refers to changes in people's sense of justice and of what is right and wrong, and in their behavior related to moral issues. Developmentalists have considered moral development in terms of children's reasoning about morality, attitudes toward moral lapses, and behavior when faced with moral issues. In the process of studying moral development, several approaches have evolved.

***Piaget's View of Moral Development.*** Child psychologist Jean Piaget was one of the first to study moral development. He suggested that moral development, like cognitive development, proceeds in stages (Piaget, 1932). He called the earliest stage *heteronomous morality,* in which rules are seen as invariant and unchangeable. During this stage, which lasts from about age 4 through age 7, children play games rigidly, assuming that there is one, and only one, way to play. At the same time, though, they may not even fully grasp game rules. Consequently, a group of children may be playing together, with each child playing according to a slightly different set of rules. Nevertheless, they enjoy playing with each other. Piaget suggests that every child may "win" such a game, because winning means having a good time, as opposed to competing.

Heteronomous morality is ultimately replaced by two later stages of morality: incipient cooperation and autonomous cooperation. In the *incipient cooperation stage,* which lasts from around age 7 to age 10, children's games become more clearly social. Children learn the actual rules and play according to this shared knowledge. Rules are still seen as largely unchangeable, and there is a "right" way to play the game.

It is not until the *autonomous cooperation stage,* which begins at about age 10, that children become fully aware that formal game rules can be modified if the players agree. This is the beginning of the understanding that rules of law are created by people and are subject to change according to the will of people.

***Social Learning Approaches to Morality.*** Whereas Piaget emphasizes how limitations in preschoolers' cognitive development lead to particular forms of moral *reasoning,* social learning approaches focus more on how the environment in which preschoolers operate produces **prosocial behavior,** helping behavior that benefits others (Eisenberg, 2004; Eisenberg & Bernt, 2007).

Social learning approaches acknowledge that some instances of children's prosocial behavior stem from situations in which they have received positive reinforcement for acting in a moral way. For instance, when Claire's mother tells her she has been a "good girl" for sharing a box of candy with her brother, Claire's behavior has been reinforced. As a consequence, she is more likely to engage in sharing behavior in the future (Ramaswamy & Bergin, 2009).

**moral development** the changes in people's sense of justice and of what is right and wrong, and in their behavior related to moral issues

**prosocial behavior** helping behavior that benefits others

However, not all prosocial behavior has to be directly reinforced. According to social learning theorists, children also learn moral behavior indirectly by observing the behavior of others, called *models* (Bandura, 1977). Children imitate models who receive reinforcement for their behavior and ultimately learn to perform the behavior themselves. For example, when Claire's friend Jake watches Claire share her candy with her brother, and Claire is praised for her behavior, Jake is more likely to engage in sharing behavior himself at some later point. Unfortunately, the opposite also holds true: If a model behaves selfishly, children who observe such behavior tend to behave more selfishly themselves (Hastings et al., 2007).

Children do more than simply mimic behavior that they see rewarded in others. When they observe moral conduct, they are reminded of society's norms about the importance of moral behavior as conveyed by parents, teachers, and other authority figures. They notice the connections between particular situations and certain kinds of behavior. This increases the likelihood that similar situations will elicit similar behavior in the observer.

Consequently, modeling paves the way for the development of more general rules and principles in a process called **abstract modeling**. Rather than always modeling the particular behavior of others, older preschoolers begin to develop generalized principles that underlie the behavior they observe. After observing repeated instances in which a model is rewarded for acting in a morally desirable way, children begin the process of inferring and learning the general principles of moral conduct (Bandura, 1991).

***Empathy and Moral Behavior.*** According to some developmentalists, **empathy**—the understanding of what another individual feels—lies at the heart of some kinds of moral behavior.

The roots of empathy grow early. One-year-old infants cry when they hear other infants crying. By ages 2 and 3, toddlers will offer gifts and spontaneously share toys with other children and adults, even strangers (Zahn-Wexler & Radke-Yarrow, 1990).

During the preschool years, empathy continues to grow as children's ability to monitor and regulate their emotional and cognitive responses increases. Some theorists believe that increasing empathy (along with other positive emotions, such as sympathy and admiration) leads children to behave morally. In addition, some negative emotions—such as anger at an unfair situation or shame over previous transgressions—also may promote moral behavior (Valiente, Eisenberg, & Fabes, 2004; Decety & Jackson, 2006; Rieffe, Ketelaar, & Wiefferink, 2010).

## Aggression and Violence in Preschoolers: Sources and Consequences

*Four-year-old Duane could not contain his anger and frustration any more. Although he usually was mild-mannered, when Eshu began to tease him about the split in his pants and kept it up for several minutes, Duane finally snapped. Rushing over to Eshu, Duane pushed him to the ground and began to hit him with his small, closed fists. Because he was so distraught, Duane's punches were not terribly effective, but they were severe enough to hurt Eshu and bring him to tears before the preschool teachers could intervene.*

Aggression among preschoolers is common, though attacks such as this are not. Verbal hostility, shoving matches, kicking, and other forms of aggression may occur throughout the preschool period, although the degree to which aggression is acted out changes as children become older.

Eshu's taunting is also a form of aggression. **Aggression** is intentional injury or harm to another person. Infants don't act aggressively; it is hard to contend that their behavior is *intended* to hurt others, even if they inadvertently manage to do so. In contrast, by the time they reach preschool age, children demonstrate true aggression.

During the early preschool years, some of the aggression is addressed at attaining a desired goal, such as getting a toy away from another person or using a particular space occupied by another person. Consequently, in some ways the aggression is inadvertent, and minor scuffles may in fact be a typical part of early preschool life. It is the rare child who does not demonstrate at least an occasional act of aggression.

On the other hand, extreme and sustained aggression is a cause of concern. In most children, the amount of aggression declines as they move through the preschool years, as

**abstract modeling** the process in which modeling paves the way for the development of more general rules and principles

**empathy** the understanding of what another individual feels

**aggression** intentional injury or harm to another person

Aggression, both physical and verbal, is present throughout the preschool period.

Social learning explanations of aggression suggest that children's observation of aggression on television can result in actual aggression.

**emotional self-regulation** the capability to adjust emotions to a desired state and level of intensity

**instrumental aggression** aggression motivated by the desire to obtain a concrete goal

**relational aggression** nonphysical aggression that is intended to hurt another person's psychological well-being

does the frequency and average length of episodes of aggressive behavior (Persson, 2005).

The child's personality and social development contribute to this decline in aggression. Throughout the preschool years, children become better at controlling the emotions that they are experiencing. **Emotional self-regulation** is the capability to adjust emotions to a desired state and level of intensity. Starting at age 2, children are able to talk about their feelings, and they engage in strategies to regulate them. As they get older, they develop more effective strategies, learning to better cope with negative emotions. In addition to their increasing self-control, children are also developing sophisticated social skills. Most learn to use language to express their wishes and to negotiate with others (Philippot & Feldman, 2005; Zeman et al., 2006; Cole et al., 2009).

Despite these typical declines in aggression, some children remain aggressive throughout the preschool period. Furthermore, aggression is a relatively stable characteristic: The most aggressive preschoolers tend to be the most aggressive children during the school-age years (Tremblay, 2001; Schaeffer, Petras, & Ialongo, 2003; Davenport & Bourgeois, 2008).

Boys typically show higher levels of physical, instrumental aggression than girls. **Instrumental aggression** is aggression motivated by the desire to obtain a concrete goal, such as playing with a desirable toy that another child is playing with.

On the other hand, although girls show lower levels of instrumental aggression, they may be just as aggressive, but in different ways from boys. Girls are more likely to practice **relational aggression,** which is nonphysical aggression that is intended to hurt another person's feelings. Such aggression may manifest as name-calling, withholding friendship, or simply saying mean, hurtful things that make the recipient feel bad (Werner & Crick, 2004; Murray-Close, Ostrov, & Crick, 2007; Valles & Knutson, 2008).

***The Roots of Aggression.*** How can we explain the aggression of preschoolers? Some theoreticians suggest that aggression is an instinct, part and parcel of the human condition. For instance, Freud's psychoanalytic theory suggests that we all are motivated by sexual and aggressive instincts (Freud, 1920). And ethologist Konrad Lorenz, an expert in animal behavior, argues that animals—including humans—share a fighting instinct that stems from primitive urges to preserve territory, maintain a steady supply of food, and weed out weaker animals (Lorenz, 1966, 1974).

Similar arguments are made by evolutionary theorists and *sociobiologists,* scientists who consider the biological roots of social behavior. They argue that aggression leads to increased opportunities to mate, improving the likelihood that one's genes will be passed on to future generations. In addition, aggression may help to strengthen the species and its gene pool as a whole, because the strongest survive. Ultimately, then, aggressive instincts promote the survival of one's genes to pass on to future generations (Archer, 2009).

Although instinctual explanations are logical, they have relatively little experimental support. They also fail to take into account the increasingly sophisticated cognitive abilities that humans develop as they get older. Moreover, they provide little guidance in determining when and how children, as well as adults, will behave aggressively, other than noting that aggression is an inevitable part of the human condition. Consequently, developmentalists have turned to other approaches.

***Social Learning Approaches to Aggression.*** The day after Duane lashed out at Eshu, Lynn, who had watched the entire scene, got into an argument with Ilya. They verbally bickered for a while, and suddenly Lynn balled her hand into a fist and tried to punch Ilya. The preschool teachers were stunned: It was rare for Lynn to get upset, and she had never displayed aggression before.

Is there a connection between the two events? Social learning theorists would answer yes, because to them aggression is largely a learned behavior based on children's observation and prior learning. To understand the causes of aggressive behavior, then, we should look at the system of rewards and punishments in a child's environment.

**FIGURE 4-10 Modeling Aggression**
This series of photos is from Albert Bandura's classic Bobo doll experiment, designed to illustrate social learning of aggression. The photos clearly show how the adult model's aggressive behavior (in the first row) is imitated by children who had viewed the aggressive behavior (second and third rows).

Social learning approaches emphasize how social and environmental conditions teach individuals to be aggressive. Using a behavioral perspective, they argue that aggressive behavior is learned through direct reinforcement. For instance, preschool-age children may learn that they can continue to play with the most desirable toys by aggressively refusing their classmates' requests for sharing. In the parlance of traditional learning theory, they have been reinforced for acting aggressively, and they are more likely to behave aggressively in the future.

But as we saw when discussing morality, social learning approaches suggest that reinforcement also comes indirectly. Research suggests that exposure to aggressive models leads to increased aggression, particularly if the observers are themselves angered, insulted, or frustrated. For example, Albert Bandura and his colleagues illustrated the power of models in a classic study of preschool-age children (Bandura, Ross, & Ross, 1963). One group of children watched a film of an adult playing aggressively and violently with a Bobo doll (a large, inflated plastic clown designed as a punching bag for children that always returns to an upright position after being knocked over). In comparison, children in another condition watched a film of an adult playing sedately with a set of Tinkertoys (see Figure 4-10). Later, the preschool-age children were allowed to play with a number of toys, which included both the Bobo doll and the Tinkertoys. But first, the children were led to feel frustration by being refused the opportunity to play with a favorite toy.

As predicted by social learning approaches, the preschool-age children modeled the behavior of the adult. Those who had seen the aggressive model playing with the Bobo doll were considerably more aggressive than those who had watched the calm, unaggressive model playing with the Tinkertoys.

***Viewing Violence on TV: Does It Matter?*** The majority of preschool-age children are exposed to aggression via television. Children's television programs contain higher levels of violence (69 percent) than other types of programs (57 percent). In an average hour, children's programs contain more than twice as many violent incidents as other types of programs (Wilson, 2002).

This high level of televised violence, viewed in light of research findings on modeling aggression, raises a significant question: Does viewing aggression increase the likelihood that children (and later adults) will perform aggressive acts?

The overwhelming weight of evidence suggests that observation of televised aggression does lead to subsequent aggression. Longitudinal studies have found that children's preferences for violent television shows at age 8 are correlated with the seriousness of criminal convictions by age 30. Other evidence supports the notion that observation of media violence can lead to bullying, a greater readiness to act aggressively, and insensitivity to the suffering of victims of violence (Slater, Henry, & Swaim, 2003; Ostrov, Gentile, & Crick, 2006; Christakis & Zimmerman, 2007).

**From an educator's perspective:** How might a preschool teacher or parent help children notice the violence in the programs they watch and protect them from its effects?

Television is not the only source of media violence. Many video games contain highly aggressive behavior, and many children play such games. For example, 14 percent of children age 3 and younger and around 50 percent of those 4 to 6 play video games. Because research conducted with adults shows that playing violent video games is associated with behaving aggressively, children who play video games containing violence may likewise be at risk for behaving aggressively (Barlett, Harris, & Baldassaro, 2007; Polman, de Castro, & van Aken, 2008; Fischer, Kastenmüller, & Greitemeyer, 2010).

Fortunately, social learning principles suggest not only the problem but the solution. Children can be explicitly taught to view violence with a critical eye. If they learn that violence is not representative of the real world, that viewing violence can affect them negatively, and that they should avoid imitating the behavior they see on television, they may interpret the programs differently and be less influenced by them (Persson & Musher-Eizenman, 2003; Donnerstein, 2005).

Furthermore, just as exposure to aggressive models leads to aggression, observation of *non*aggressive models can *reduce* aggression. Preschoolers can actually learn how to avoid confrontation and to control their aggression, as we'll discuss later.

***Cognitive Approaches to Aggression: The Thoughts Behind Violence.*** Two children, waiting for their turn in a game of kickball, inadvertently knock into one another. One child's reaction is to apologize; the other's is to shove, saying angrily, "Cut it out."

Despite the fact that each child bears the same responsibility for the minor event, they have different reactions. What the first child sees as an accident, the second child sees as a provocation.

The cognitive approach to aggression suggests that to understand preschoolers' moral development it is necessary to examine their interpretations of others' behavior and of the environmental context of the behavior. According to developmental psychologist Kenneth Dodge and his colleagues, some children are more prone than others to assume that actions are aggressively motivated. They are unable to pay attention to the appropriate cues in a situation and interpret the behaviors in the situation erroneously, assuming that what is happening is hostile. Subsequently, in deciding how to respond, they base their behavior on their inaccurate interpretation, behaving aggressively in response to a situation that never in fact existed (Petit & Dodge, 2003).

Although the cognitive approach describes the process that leads some children to behave aggressively, it fails to explain why they perceive situations inaccurately and why they so readily respond with aggression. On the other hand, the cognitive approach is useful in pointing out a means to reduce aggression: By teaching preschool-age children to interpret situations more accurately, we can induce them to be less prone to view others' behavior as motivated by hostility and less likely to respond with aggression themselves.

# Increasing Moral Behavior and Reducing Aggression in Preschool-Age Children

## Becoming an Informed Consumer of Development

Here are some practical and readily accomplished strategies for encouraging moral conduct and reducing aggression, based on ideas from the many approaches we have discussed (Goldstein, 1999; Bor & Bor, 2004):

- **Provide opportunities for preschool-age children to observe others acting in a cooperative, helpful, prosocial manner.** Encourage them to interact with peers in joint activities in which they share a common goal. Such cooperative activities can teach the importance and desirability of working with—and helping—others.

- **Do not ignore aggressive behavior.** Parents and teachers should intervene when they see aggression in preschoolers, sending a clear message that aggression is an unacceptable way to resolve conflicts.

- **Help preschoolers devise alternative explanations for others' behavior.** With children who are prone to aggression and apt to view others' conduct as more hostile than it actually is, parents and teachers should help them see that the behavior of their peers has several possible interpretations.

- **Monitor preschoolers' television viewing, particularly the violence that they view.** Discourage preschoolers from watching shows depicting aggression and encourage them to watch particular shows that are designed, in part, to foster moral conduct, such as *Sesame Street* and *Dora the Explorer*.

- **Help preschoolers understand their feelings.** When children become angry—and all children do—they must learn to deal with their feelings constructively. Tell them *specific* things they can do to improve the situation. ("I see you're really angry with Jake for not giving you a turn. Don't hit him, but tell him you want a chance to play with the game.")

- **Explicitly teach reasoning and self-control.** Preschoolers can understand the rudiments of moral reasoning, and they should be reminded why certain behaviors are desirable. For instance, explicitly saying "If you take all the cookies, others will have no dessert" is preferable to saying, "Good children don't eat all the cookies."

---

## REVIEW, CHECK, AND APPLY

### REVIEW

**LO16** How do children develop a sense of morality?

- Piaget believed that preschoolers are in the heteronomous morality stage of moral development, in which rules are seen as invariant and unchangeable.

- Social learning approaches to moral development emphasize the importance of reinforcement for moral actions and the observation of models of moral conduct.

- Psychoanalytic and other theories focus on children's empathy with others and their wish to help others so they can avoid unpleasant feelings of guilt themselves.

**LO17** How does aggression develop in preschool-age children?

- Research suggests that exposure to aggressive models leads to increased aggression, particularly if the observers are themselves angered, insulted, or frustrated.

- Aggression typically declines in frequency and duration as children become more able to regulate their emotions and use language to negotiate disputes.

### CHECK YOURSELF

1. The term _____ refers to changes in our sense of justice and our understanding of behaviors related to what is right and wrong.
   a. behavioral concern
   b. moral development
   c. perspective taking
   d. self-reflection

2. According to the _____ theory, the factor that increases the likelihood that a preschooler will engage in prosocial behavior is his or her environment.
   a. cognitive-behavioral
   b. social learning
   c. psychoanalytic
   d. humanistic

3. Aggression is an unstable characteristic in that aggressive preschoolers rarely grow up to be aggressive adults.
   - True
   - False

### APPLYING LIFESPAN DEVELOPMENT

- If high-prestige models of behavior are particularly effective in influencing moral attitudes and actions, are there implications for individuals in such industries as sports, advertising, and entertainment?

✔ **Study** and **Review** on
**MyDevelopmentLab.com**

Answers: 1) b; 2) b; 3) False

# *Putting It All Together*
## The Preschool Years

**WILLIAM,** whom we met in the chapter opener as "Wild William," a 3-year-old in his first days of preschool, was probably born curious and prone to explore. In the comparatively free environment of the preschool, William was testing the limits of his physical abilities and pushing against the barriers that confined him. William took advantage of opportunities to explore new objects and places, and used his developing skills to open sealed containers and closed drawers. He was able not only to work out the secrets of Tupperware lids, but to plan a multilevel attack on the closet as well. His outgoing personality seemingly enabled him to induce laughter from his preschool peers and ready forgiveness from his teachers. He showed an understanding of the limits that his classroom society imposed on its members, and when he bent those limits, he did so stealthily and felt embarrassed when caught. William was putting together all of his emerging developmental tools to exercise control over his world.

### MODULE 4.1 Physical Development in the Preschool Years

- William grew physically in preschool, learning to exercise with ease such abilities as walking, balancing, and climbing. **(pp. 161–163)**
- William also learned to use and control his gross and fine motor skills, showing considerable manual dexterity. **(pp. 161–163)**
- William's brain grew, and with it his cognitive abilities, such as the ability to plan. **(pp. 159–160)**

### MODULE 4.2 Cognitive Development in the Preschool Years

- William's memory capacity increased, enabling him to recall where the classroom snacks were stored. **(pp. 168–170)**
- William observed others and learned how to perform challenging tasks, such as opening tight container lids. **(pp. 170–172)**
- William's language skills continued to develop, permitting him to express himself effectively in most situations. **(pp. 173–175)**
- William developed the cognitive skills to anticipate what would amuse his classmates and to plan multistep exploits. **(pp. 164–167)**

## What would a PARENT do?

- How would you help William to consider the consequences of his adventures? How would you assess his readiness to consider consequences?
- What would you say to William about considering the effects of his actions on his peers?

  **HINT** Review pages 169–175.

  *What's your response?*

## What would a HEALTH CARE WORKER do?

- What would you tell William's caregivers about risks to which he is especially prone as he develops physically and cognitively?
- How would you advise William's parents to focus their child-proofing efforts in their home as William grows?

  **HINT** Review pages 156–159.

  *What's your response?*

---

**MODULE 4.3** Social and Personality Development in the Preschool Years

- William's entertaining personality has helped him ease his interactions with peers. **(p. 179)**
- William has developed a theory of mind that has enabled him to understand others' reactions to his expressiveness and charming smile. **(pp. 185–186)**
- William's sheepishness at being discovered by his teacher indicates that he has been developing a sense of morality. **(pp. 192–193)**
- William's level of moral understanding may not yet enable him to grasp that there might be anything wrong with eating snacks intended for his classmates. **(p. 192)**

## What would YOU do?

- What would you do to promote William's development? How would you advise William's caregivers in helping William to channel his expressiveness and curiosity in appropriate directions?
- How would you advise William's caregivers to deal with William's apparent fearlessness? Should it be discouraged?

  **HINT** Review pages 183–188.

  *What's your response?*

## What would an EDUCATOR do?

- What strategies would you use to promote William's social development? How would you help William understand the effects of his actions on his peers?
- How would you deal with William's potential leadership qualities? What would you do to help him avoid becoming a negative role model?
- What would you say to William's teachers about steps to take in monitoring the actions of children like William?

  **HINT** Review pages 179–186.

  *What's your response?*

---

**✳ Explore on mydevelopmentlab.com**

To read how real parents, social workers, and educators responded to these questions, log onto MyDevelopmentLab.com.

*Do you agree or disagree with their responses? Why? What concepts that you've read about back up their opinion?*

# CHAPTER 5

# Middle Childhood

Ryan was thrilled to *finally* reach first grade. On the "Wishing Star" he made for Parents' Night, he had his teacher write his wish for the year: "My #1 wish: I want to read and write."

But reading and writing were proving difficult for Ryan. It was hard for him to de-code even simple words, and hand–eye coordination made writing a chore, often resulting in a heavily smudged page.

In most ways, Ryan's physical and cognitive development was right on target for his 7 years. He was an enthusiastic hiker, and he was able to memorize complex stories. Testing showed that Ryan's intelligence was above average, but vision and motor problems were frustrating his attempts to achieve normal develop-mental goals.

These frustrations affected Ryan's social development, too. As a child who spent several hours each day in the special needs room, who could neither track the path of a soccer ball during a game nor ride a two-wheel bike, his social status was low. Several peers made fun of him, and he responded by withdrawing fur-ther into himself.

**MODULE 5.1** Physical Development in Middle Childhood

## How do visual, auditory, and speech impairments affect a child's social and personality development? see page 202.

**MODULE 5.2** Cognitive Development in Middle Childhood

## Schooling around the world and across genders: Who gets educated?

see page 213.

Ryan's parents and teachers kept in constant contact to discuss how best to support him both academically and socially. He worked with a reading specialist, and the school provided physical therapy services to help Ryan develop his motor skills.

The early intervention worked. It boosted Ryan's grades and his self-esteem. By the end of second grade, he was riding his bike all over the neighborhood, reading at a sixth-grade level, and writing rather than dictating stories about his favorite subject—pirates. In the regular classroom all day now, he made three close friends with whom he played "Star Wars" at recess, a happy, laughing, confident child.

**In middle childhood,** children enter school eager to learn all they can about the world. Often the regular classroom setting serves them well and contributes to their physical, intellectual, and social development; sometimes, however, children display needs or deficits that require special interventions—such as the reading specialist and physical therapist provided for Ryan—to make the most of their abilities and keep their self-esteem intact.

In this chapter, we follow children taking the crucial step into formal schooling. We look at the physical changes that prepare them for new challenges. We discuss the patterns of growth—and excess—that are typical of this period and the new levels of motor skills that enable them to perform actions as diverse as throwing a ball and playing the

**MODULE 5.3** Social and Personality Development in Middle Childhood

How does divorce affect a child's development? see page 235.

**My Virtual Child**

How would you approach raising a child during middle childhood? What decisions would you make, and what would the consequences of those decisions be?

Find out by logging onto *My Virtual Child* through MyDevelopmentLab.com.

violin. We also discuss threats to their well-being, and consider the special needs that can impinge on children's school lives.

Next we consider the growing intellectual and conceptual skills and the increasingly sophisticated use of language that are hallmarks of this period. We visit the place where they spend most of their time: school. We consider reading and the policy dispute over the best way to teach it. We also address the surprisingly controversial topic of intelligence.

Finally, we consider school-age children as members of society, including their membership in school and family. We look at the ways school-age children understand themselves and develop self-esteem. We consider how they relate to one another, including members of the opposite sex. We then examine the many shapes and configurations that families take, finishing with a further discussion of schooling.

## MODULE 5.1 Physical Development in Middle Childhood

*It is a hot summer day in Atlanta. Adults move slowly through the humid air, but not 8-year-old Suzanne McGuire. A look of triumph crosses her face as she rounds the corner from third base to home plate.*

*Moments before, she was waiting for the pitcher to throw the ball. Her first two turns at bat, Suzanne had struck out, leaving her unhappy and a bit humiliated.*

*On her third turn at bat, though, the pitch looked perfect. She swung at it with confidence and high hope. When the bat connected with the ball, lobbing it well beyond the left fielder for a home run, it created a moment she would never forget.*

Suzanne McGuire has come a long way since the preschool years, when quick, coordinated running and batting to the mark were not possible.

Such moments characterize middle childhood, as children's physical, cognitive, and social skills reach new heights. Beginning at age 6 and continuing to about age 12, this period is often called the "school years." Physical growth is remarkable. Motor skills soar.

We begin by examining physical and motor development in middle childhood. We discuss how children's bodies change, and the twin problems of malnutrition and obesity. We examine the development of gross motor skills—like swinging a bat—and fine motor skills—like playing scales on a piano. We discuss the health of children during this period, including their psychological health.

We finish the module by considering the sensory and learning difficulties of children with special needs. We also discuss a disorder that has grown in importance in recent decades, attention deficit hyperactivity disorder.

## The Growing Body

**LEARNING OBJECTIVES**

**L01** In what ways do children grow during the school years, and what factors influence their growth?

*Cinderella, dressed in yella,*
*Went upstairs to kiss her fellah.*
*But she made a mistake and she kissed a snake.*
*How many doctors did it take?*
*One, two,...*

*While the other girls chanted this jump-rope rhyme, Kat proudly displayed her new ability to jump backwards. In second grade, Kat was becoming quite good at jumping rope. In first grade, she simply had not been able to master it. But over the summer, she had spent many hours practicing, and now that practice was paying off.*

As Kat is gleefully experiencing, children make great physical strides in middle childhood, mastering many new skills. How does this progress occur? We'll first consider typical physical growth during this period, then turn our attention to exceptional children.

Slow but steady. These words characterize the nature of growth during middle childhood. In contrast to the swift growth from birth to age 5 and the remarkable growth spurt of adolescence, middle childhood is relatively tranquil. The body has not shifted into neutral; physical growth continues, but at a more stately pace than in the preschool years.

## Height and Weight Changes

In elementary school, children in the United States grow, on average, 2 to 3 inches a year. By age 11, the average height for girls is 4 feet, 10 inches while boys average 4 feet, 9½ inches. This is the only period in life when girls tend to be taller than boys. This reflects the slightly more rapid physical development of girls, who start their adolescent growth spurt around age 10.

Variations of 6 inches in height between children of the same age are not unusual and well within normal ranges.

Weight gain in middle childhood follows a similar pattern; boys and girls both gain around 5 to 7 pounds a year. Weight is also redistributed. As "baby fat" disappears, children's bodies become more muscular and their strength increases.

These average height and weight increases disguise significant individual differences. Children of the same age can be 6 or 7 inches apart in height.

## Cultural Patterns of Growth

Most children in North America receive sufficient nutrients to grow to their full potential. In other parts of the world, however, inadequate nutrition and disease take their toll, producing children who are shorter and weigh less. The discrepancies can be dramatic: Poor children in cities such as Calcutta, Hong Kong, and Rio de Janeiro are smaller than affluent children in the same cities.

In the United States, most variations in height and weight are the result of people's unique genetic inheritance, including genetic factors relating to racial and ethnic background. Asian and Oceanic Pacific children tend to be shorter than those of northern and central European ancestry. In addition, the rate of growth is generally more rapid for Black children than for White (Deurenberg, Deurenberg-Yap, & Guricci, 2002; Deurenberg et al., 2003).

Even within racial and ethnic groups, individuals vary significantly. We cannot attribute racial and ethnic differences solely to genetic factors because dietary customs as well as variations in levels of affluence also may contribute to differences. In addition, severe stress—brought on by factors such as parental conflict or alcoholism—can affect the pituitary gland, thereby affecting growth (Koska et al., 2002).

## Nutrition

There is a relationship between size and nutrition. But size isn't the only area affected by diet. For instance, nutrition is related to social and emotional functioning at school age. Children who receive more nutrients are more involved with their peers, show more positive emotion, and have less anxiety than children with less adequate nutrition. Nutrition is also linked to cognitive performance. For example, in one study, children in Kenya who were well nourished performed better on a test of verbal abilities and on other cognitive measures than those who had mild to moderate undernutrition. Malnutrition may influence cognitive development by dampening children's curiosity, responsiveness, and motivation to learn (Grigorenko, 2003; Ordovas, 2010).

Although undernutrition and malnutrition clearly lead to physical, social, and cognitive difficulties, in some cases *over*nutrition—the intake of too many calories—leads to problems of its own, in particular childhood obesity.

Inadequate nutrition and disease affect growth significantly. Children in poorer areas of cities such as Calcutta, Hong Kong, and Rio de Janeiro are smaller than their counterparts in affluent areas of the same cities.

## Childhood Obesity

When her mother asks if she would like bread with her meal, Ruthellen replies she better not—she thinks she may be getting fat. Ruthellen, who is of normal weight and height, is 6 years old.

Although height can be of concern to both children and parents, weight is an even greater worry for some. Weight concerns can border on obsession, particularly in girls. Many 6-year-old girls worry about becoming "fat," and some 40 percent of girls ages 9 to 10 are trying to lose weight. Their concern with weight often reflects the U.S. preoccupation with slimness, which permeates the entire society (Schreiber et al., 1996; Greenwood & Pietromonaco, 2004; Liechty, 2010).

Despite the prevalent view that thinness is a virtue, childhood obesity is rising. *Obesity* is defined as body weight that is more than 20 percent above the average for a given age and height. Fifteen percent of U.S. children are obese—a figure that has tripled since the 1960s (Brownlee, 2002; Dietz, 2004; Mann, 2005) (see Figure 5-1).

The costs of childhood obesity last a lifetime. Obese children are more likely to be overweight as adults, and have a greater risk of heart disease, diabetes, and other diseases. Some scientists believe an epidemic of obesity may be leading to a decline in life span in the United States (Krishnamoorthy, Hart, & Jelalian, 2006; Park, 2008; Keel et al., 2010).

Genetic and social characteristics as well as diet influence obesity. Particular inherited genes predispose certain children to be overweight. For example, adopted children's weights tend to reflect those of their birth parents rather than their adoptive parents (Whitaker et al., 1997; Bray, 2008).

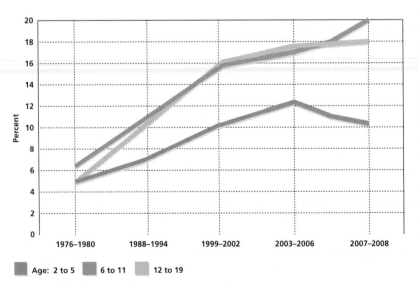

Age: 2 to 5  6 to 11  12 to 19

**FIGURE 5-1 Fat of the Land**
The percent of children and adolescents who are overweight has increased dramatically in the last 4 decades.
Source: CDC, 2009.

## *From Research to Practice*

### Do Media Images Affect Preadolescent Children's Body Image?

*Dissatisfaction with body image is on the rise. In one study of children ages 8–10, more than half of the girls and more than a third of the boys were already dissatisfied with their size, even at their young age. What's worse is that body image dissatisfaction is related to unhealthy behaviors such as eating disorders, smoking, depression, and low self-esteem (Wood, Becker, & Thompson, 1996; Jung & Peterson, 2007).*

Why are children acquiring dissatisfaction with their bodies? One answer relates to the media. Television, magazines, and other media present models of idealized beauty and fitness as if they are the norm in the real world. Not only are certain body types overrepresented, but people with such idealized body types are portrayed as admirable because of their looks. Children compare themselves to these idealized same-sex media images and often conclude that they just don't measure up (Fouts & Burggraf, 1999; Hargreaves & Tiggemann, 2003).

In reality, no one can measure up to some kinds of body representations. For example, the body dimensions of male action figures marketed to young boys are so exaggerated that they are actually physically unattainable in real life. Furthermore, male characters in video games that are popular with young boys are also exceedingly big and muscular (Pope, Olivardia, Gruber, & Borowiecki, 1999; Scharrer, 2004; Harrison & Bond, 2007; Downs & Smith, 2010).

Research also shows that boys and girls view media differently and reach different conclusions about their own body image as a result. One study of children aged 8–11 showed that boys' ideal body image is to be bigger and more muscular than they actually are, while girls' ideal image is to be considerably thinner. Interestingly, when girls' and boys' perceptions of their actual body image are assessed, girls see themselves more accurately as being heavier than their ideal. In contrast, boys have a distorted self-perception: they see themselves as bigger and more muscular than they actually are (Jung & Peterson, 2007).

Not only are children exposed to unrealistic body image portrayals in the media, but also they are apt to admire these characters and try to be like them. One suggestion for how parents and teachers can try to inoculate children against these influences is to teach them that media representations are often exaggerated and unattainable. Furthermore, children should be exposed to a healthier, broader range of body types—ones with which they can identify (Jung & Peterson, 2007).

- Do you think it is significant that big and strong male media characters are also often portrayed as being dominant and successful, or that slender and beautiful female media characters are also often portrayed as being popular with boys?
- What can parents and teachers do to reduce the influence of media images on children's body image?

Social factors also affect children's weight problems. Children need to control their own eating. Parents who are controlling and directive about their children's eating may produce children who lack internal controls to regulate their own food intake (Johnson & Birch, 1994; Faith, Johnson, & Allison, 1997; Wardle, Guthrie, & Sanderson, 2001).

Poor diets also contribute to obesity. Despite their knowledge that certain foods are necessary for a balanced, nutritious diet, many parents provide their children with too few fruits and vegetables and more fats and sweets than recommended. School lunch programs have sometimes contributed to the problem by failing to provide nutritious options (Johnston, Delva, & O'Malley, 2007; Story, Nanney, & Schwartz, 2009).

Given how energetic children this age can be, it is surprising that a major factor in childhood obesity is a lack of exercise. School-age children tend to engage in relatively little exercise and are not particularly fit. Around 40 percent of boys aged 6 to 12 are unable to do more than one pull-up, and a quarter can't do any. Furthermore, children have shown little or no improvement in the amount of exercise they get, despite national efforts to increase the fitness of school-age children, in part because many schools have reduced the time available for recess and gym classes. From ages 6 to 18, boys decrease their physical activity by 24 percent and girls by 36 percent (Moore, Gao, & Bradlee, 2003; Sallis & Glanz, 2006; Weiss & Raz, 2006).

Why is the level of exercise relatively low? One answer is that many kids are watching television and playing computer or video games. Such sedentary activities not only prevent exercise, but children often snack while viewing TV or surfing the Web (Anderson & Butcher, 2006; Pardee et al., 2007; Landhuis et al., 2008).

*"Remember when we used to have to fatten the kids up first?"*

**REVIEW**

**LO1** In what ways do children grow during the school years, and what factors influence their growth?

- In middle childhood, height and weight increase gradually.
- Differences in height and weight are influenced by both genetic and social factors.
- Adequate nutrition promotes physical, social, and cognitive development, while overnutrition and a sedentary lifestyle may lead to obesity.

**CHECK YOURSELF**

**1.** Due to the sudden changes taking place during this stage, it is not uncommon in middle school to see children of the same age who are 6 to 7 inches apart in height.

- True
- False

**2.** Which of the following is NOT a long-term outcome associated with childhood obesity?

a. cognitive deficits

b. being overweight as adults

c. greater risk of heart disease

d. higher prevalence of diabetes

**APPLYING LIFESPAN DEVELOPMENT**

- What are some aspects of U.S. culture that may contribute to obesity among school-age children?

✓—⌐**Study** and **Review** on **MyDevelopmentLab.com**

Answers: 1) True; 2) a

# Motor Development and Safety

**LEARNING OBJECTIVES**

**LO2** In what ways do motor skills develop over middle childhood?

**LO3** What are the main health concerns at this age?

The fact that the fitness level of school-age children is not as high as we would desire does not mean that such children are physically incapable. In fact, even without regular exercise, children's gross and fine motor skills develop substantially over the course of the school years.

## Gross Motor Skills

One important improvement in gross motor skills is in muscle coordination. Watching a softball player pitch a ball past a batter to her catcher, or Kat, the jump-roper described earlier in the module, we are struck by the many skills children have mastered since their awkward preschool days. Most can readily learn to ride a bike, ice skate, swim, and skip rope (Cratty, 1986) (see Figure 5-2).

Years ago developmentalists concluded that gender differences in gross motor skills became increasingly pronounced during these years, with boys outperforming girls (Espenschade, 1960). However, when comparing boys and girls who regularly take part in similar activities—such as softball—gender variations are minimal (Hall & Lee, 1984; Jurimae & Saar, 2003).

Why the change? Expectations probably played a role. Society did not expect girls to be highly active and told girls they would do worse than boys in sports. The girls' performance reflected that message.

Today, society's message has changed, at least officially. For instance, the American Academy of Pediatrics suggests that boys and girls should engage in the same sports and games, and that they can do so in mixed-gender groups. There is no reason to separate the sexes in physical exercise and sports until puberty, when the smaller size of females makes them more susceptible to injury in contact sports (Raudsepp & Liblik, 2002; Vilhjalmsson & Kristjansdottir, 2003; American Academy of Pediatrics, 1999, 2004).

During middle childhood, children master many types of skills that earlier they could not perform well, such as riding a bike, ice skating, swimming, and skipping rope. Is this the same for children of other cultures?

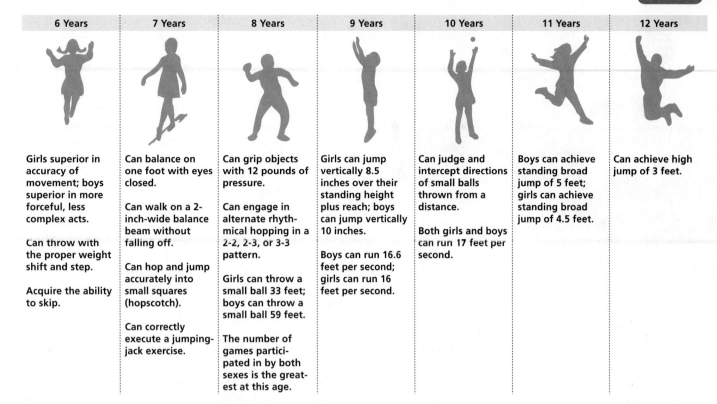

| 6 Years | 7 Years | 8 Years | 9 Years | 10 Years | 11 Years | 12 Years |
|---------|---------|---------|---------|----------|----------|----------|
| Girls superior in accuracy of movement; boys superior in more forceful, less complex acts.<br><br>Can throw with the proper weight shift and step.<br><br>Acquire the ability to skip. | Can balance on one foot with eyes closed.<br><br>Can walk on a 2-inch-wide balance beam without falling off.<br><br>Can hop and jump accurately into small squares (hopscotch).<br><br>Can correctly execute a jumping-jack exercise. | Can grip objects with 12 pounds of pressure.<br><br>Can engage in alternate rhythmical hopping in a 2-2, 2-3, or 3-3 pattern.<br><br>Girls can throw a small ball 33 feet; boys can throw a small ball 59 feet.<br><br>The number of games participated in by both sexes is the greatest at this age. | Girls can jump vertically 8.5 inches over their standing height plus reach; boys can jump vertically 10 inches.<br><br>Boys can run 16.6 feet per second; girls can run 16 feet per second. | Can judge and intercept directions of small balls thrown from a distance.<br><br>Both girls and boys can run 17 feet per second. | Boys can achieve standing broad jump of 5 feet; girls can achieve standing broad jump of 4.5 feet. | Can achieve high jump of 3 feet. |

**FIGURE 5-2 Gross Motor Skills Developed From 6 and 12 Years**
Source: Adapted from Cratty, B. J., PERCEPTUAL AND MOTOR DEVELOPMENT IN INFANTS AND CHILDREN, 3rd ed. Copyright © Pearson Education, Inc. Reprinted with permission from Pearson Education, Inc.

## Fine Motor Skills

Typing at a computer keyboard. Writing in cursive with pen and pencil. Drawing detailed pictures. These are some of the accomplishments that depend on the improved fine motor coordination of early and middle childhood. Six- and 7-year-olds are able to tie their shoes and fasten buttons; by age 8, they can use each hand independently; and by 11 and 12, they can manipulate objects with almost as much capability as they will show in adulthood.

One reason fine motor skills improve is that the amount of myelin in the brain increases significantly between the ages of 6 and 8 (Lecours, 1982), raising the speed at which electrical impulses travel between neurons. Messages reach muscles more rapidly and control them better. Myelin also provides protective insulation that surrounds parts of nerve cells.

## Health During Middle Childhood

*Imani was miserable. Her nose was running, her lips were chapped, and her throat was sore. Although she had stayed home from school and watched old reruns on TV, she still felt that she was suffering mightily.*

Despite her misery, Imani's situation is not so bad. She'll get over the cold in a few days and be none the worse for it. In fact, she may be a little *better* off, for she is now immune to the specific cold germs that made her ill.

Imani's cold may end up being the most serious illness she gets during middle childhood. This is generally a period of robust health, and most ailments children do contract tend to be mild and brief. Routine immunizations have produced a considerably lower incidence of the life-threatening illnesses that 50 years ago claimed a significant number of children.

However, illness is not uncommon. More than 90 percent of children are likely to have at least one serious medical condition over the 6-year period of middle childhood, according to one large survey. And though most children have short-term illnesses, about one in nine

Children's access to computers and the Internet needs to be monitored.

has a chronic, persistent condition, such as repeated migraine headaches (Dey & Bloom, 2005; Siniatchkin et al., 2010).

***Accidents.*** The increasing independence of school-age children leads to new safety issues. Between the ages of 5 and 14, the rate of injury for children increases. Boys are more apt to be injured than girls, probably because their overall level of physical activity is greater. Some ethnic and racial groups are at greater risk than others: Injury death rates are highest for American Indian and Alaska Natives, and lowest for Asian and Pacific Islanders. Whites and African-Americans have approximately the same death rates from injuries (Noonan, 2003; Borse et al., 2008).

The increased mobility of this age is a source of several kinds of accidents. Children who regularly walk to school, many traveling such a distance alone for the first time, face being hit by cars and trucks. Due to lack of experience, they may misjudge how far they are from an oncoming vehicle. Bicycle accidents pose an increasing risk, particularly as children venture out onto busier roads (Schnitzer, 2006).

The most frequent injury to children is automobile accidents. Auto crashes annually kill five out of every 100,000 children between the ages of 5 and 9. Fires and burns, drowning, and gun-related deaths follow in frequency (Field & Behrman, 2002; Schiller & Bernadel, 2004).

Two ways to reduce auto and bicycle injuries are to use seat belts consistently and to wear appropriate protective cycling gear. Bicycle helmets have significantly reduced head injuries, and in many localities their use is mandatory. Knee and elbow pads have proven to reduce injuries for roller-blading and skateboarding (American Academy of Pediatrics Committee on Accident and Poison Prevention, 1990; Lee, Schofer, & Koppelman, 2005; Blake et al., 2008).

***Safety on the Web.*** The newest threat to children's safety comes from a source that was unheard of a generation ago: the Internet. Although claims that cyberspace is overrun with pornography and child molesters are exaggerated, it is true that the Web makes available material many parents find objectionable. Furthermore, social-networking sites such as Facebook and video sites allow children to virtually interact with others about whom parents have little or no knowledge. Finally—as we'll consider later in the chapter when we discuss bullying—the Internet provides a place where children can be bullied (Brant, 2003; OSTWG, 2010).

Computer software developers have devised programs that will block particular computer sites, but most experts feel the most reliable safeguard is parental supervision. Parents should warn their children never to provide personal information, such as home addresses or telephone numbers, in chat rooms or on social-network sites such as Facebook. In addition, children should not hold face-to-face meetings with people they meet via computer, at least not without a parent present (National Center for Missing and Exploited Children, 2002; OSTWG, 2010).

**From an educator's perspective:** Do you think using blocking software or computer chips to screen offensive Internet content is a practical idea? Are such controls the best way to keep children safe in cyberspace?

## Psychological Disorders

*Tyler Whitley, 7, is 4 feet 4 inches and weighs 74 pounds. He has blond hair, blue eyes, a generous spirit—and bipolar disorder, a serious mental illness. Highly irritable and angry one minute, he'll be laughing hysterically the next. Grand illusions kick in: he can leap to the ground from the top of a tall tree or jump from a grocery cart and fly. And then there are the heart-wrenching bouts of depression when Tyler tells his parents, "I should never have been born. I need to go to heaven so people can be happy." (Kalb, 2003, p. 68)*

Bipolar disorder such as Tyler's is diagnosed when a person cycles back and forth between two extreme emotional states: unrealistically high spirits and energy, and depression. For years most people neglected the symptoms of such psychological disorders in children, and even today they may be overlooked. Yet it is a common problem: One in five children and adolescents has a psychological disorder that produces at least some impairment. For example, about 5 percent of preteens suffer from childhood depression, and 13 percent of children between ages 9 and 17 experience an anxiety disorder (Kalb, 2003; Beardslee & Goldman, 2003; Tolan & Dodge, 2005; Cicchetti & Cohen, 2006; Hirshfeld-Becker et al., 2010).

Psychological disorders may be neglected because children and adults express symptoms differently. Even when such disorders are diagnosed accurately, the correct treatment may be elusive. For example, in 2002 more than 10 million prescriptions for antidepressant drugs were written for children under 18 even though such drugs have never been approved for children's use. But because the drugs have been approved for adults, physicians who prescribe them for children are acting legally (Goode, 2004).

Advocates for the use of antidepressants such as Prozac, Zoloft, Paxil, and Wellbutrin for children suggest that drug therapies can successfully treat their depression and other psychological disorders. Drugs may provide the only relief in cases where traditional therapies that use verbal methods are ineffective. At least one clinical test shows that the drugs are effective with children (Ebmeier, Donaghey, & Steele, 2006; Barton, 2007; Lovrin, 2009).

Critics, however, question the long-term effectiveness of antidepressants for children. No one knows the consequences of their use on the developing brain, nor the overall long-term effects. Little is known about the correct dosage for age or size, and some observers suggest that children's versions of the drugs, in orange- or mint-flavored syrups, might lead to overdoses or eventually encourage the use of illegal drugs (Andersen & Navalta, 2004; Couzin, 2004; Cheung, Emslie, & Mayes, 2006).

Finally, some evidence links antidepressants with an increased risk of suicide. The possible link prompted the U.S. Federal Drug Administration to issue a warning about a class of antidepressants known as SSRIs in 2004. Some experts have urged their use with children and adolescents be banned completely (Bostwick, 2006; Gören, 2008; Sammons, 2009).

Although the use of antidepressants to treat children is controversial, it is clear that childhood depression and other psychological disorders remain a significant problem. These disorders must not be ignored. Not only are they disruptive during childhood, but they put children at risk for future disorders (Vedantam, 2004; Bostwick, 2006; Gören, 2008; Franić et al., 2010).

As we'll see next, adults also need to pay attention to other special needs that affect many school-age children.

## REVIEW, CHECK, AND APPLY

### REVIEW

**LO2** In what ways do motor skills develop over middle childhood?

- Gross motor skills continue to improve during the school years.
- Muscular coordination and manipulative skills advance to near-adult levels.

**LO3** What are the main health concerns at this age?

- Threats to safety include accidents, a result of increased independence and mobility, and unsupervised access to cyberspace.

### CHECK YOURSELF

1. One explanation for the advances in fine motor skills during middle school involves the increase in the amount of_____ in the brain.

2. When it comes to school-age children and injuries associated with accidents, which of the following statements is true?

   a. The number of accidents occurring in the school-age years is significantly fewer than in earlier years.

   b. Girls are significantly more likely to be injured in accidents than are boys.

   c. There is no relationship between gender and the prevalence of injuries associated with accidents.

   d. Boys are significantly more likely than girls to be injured.

### APPLYING LIFESPAN DEVELOPMENT

- How would you design an experiment to examine the roots of gender differences in gross motor skills? What impediments would you encounter in doing so?

✔•⫿**Study** and **Review** on
**MyDevelopmentLab.com**

Answers: 1) myelin; 2) d

# Children with Special Needs

**LO4** What special needs may become apparent during these years, and how can they be met?

Auditory impairments can produce both academic and social difficulties, and they may lead to speech difficulties.

*Andrew Mertz was a very unhappy little boy.... Third grade was a disaster, the culmination of a crisis that had been building since he entered kindergarten in suburban Maryland. He couldn't learn to read, and he hated school. "He would throw temper tantrums in the morning because he didn't want to go," recalls his mother, Suzanne. The year before, with much prodding from Suzanne, the school had authorized diagnostic tests for Andrew. The results revealed a host of brain processing problems that explained why he kept mixing up letters and sounds. Andrew's problem now had a label—he was officially classified as learning disabled—and he was legally entitled to help. (Wingert & Kantrowitz, 1997)*

Andrew joined millions of children who are classified as learning disabled, one of several special needs children can have. Although every child has different capabilities, children with *special needs* differ significantly in physical attributes or learning abilities. Their needs present major challenges for care providers and teachers.

We turn now to the most prevalent disorders affecting children of normal intelligence: sensory difficulties, learning disabilities, and attention deficit disorders. (We will consider the special needs of children who are significantly below and above average in intelligence later in the module.)

## Sensory Difficulties: Visual, Auditory, and Speech Problems

Anyone who has lost his or her eyeglasses or a contact lens knows how difficult even basic, everyday tasks must be for the sensory impaired. To function without adequate vision, hearing, or speech poses a tremendous challenge.

**Visual impairment** has both a legal and an educational meaning. Legal impairment is defined precisely: *Blindness* is visual acuity below 20/200 after correction (meaning the inability to see at 20 feet what is typically seen at 200 feet), while *partial sightedness* is visual acuity of less than 20/70 after correction.

Even if a child is not legally blind, visual problems may seriously affect schoolwork. For one thing, the legal criterion pertains solely to distance vision, while most school tasks require close-up vision. The legal definition does not consider abilities in the perception of color, depth, and light, either—all of which might influence a student's success. About one student in a thousand requires special education services due to visual impairment.

Most severe visual problems are identified fairly early, but an impairment can go undetected. Visual problems can also emerge gradually as development brings changes in the apparatus of the eye. Parents and teachers need to look out for frequent eye irritation (redness, sties, or infection), continual blinking and facial contortions when reading, holding reading material unusually close to the face, difficulty in writing, and frequent headaches, dizziness, or burning eyes. All are signs of visual problems.

**Auditory impairments** can cause social as well as academic problems since much peer interaction involves informal conversation. Hearing loss, affecting 1 to 2 percent of the school-age population, goes beyond not hearing enough, varying on a number of dimensions (Yoshinaga-Itano, 2003; Smith, Bale, & White, 2005).

In some cases, hearing is impaired at only certain frequencies, or pitches. For example, the loss may be great at pitches in the normal speech range yet minimal in other frequencies, such as those of very high or low sounds. Different levels of amplification at different frequencies may be required; a hearing aid that amplifies all frequencies equally may be ineffective, amplifying sounds the child can hear to an uncomfortable degree.

How a child adapts depends on when the hearing loss begins. The effects will likely be more severe in a child with little or no exposure to the sound of language, producing an inability to understand or produce speech. For a child who has learned language, hearing loss will not seriously affect subsequent linguistic development.

Severe and early loss of hearing can impair abstract thinking. Concrete concepts can be visually illustrated but abstract concepts depend on language for meaning. For example, it

**visual impairment** a difficulty in seeing that may include blindness or partial sightedness

**auditory impairment** a special need that involves the loss of hearing or some aspect of hearing

is difficult to explain the concept of "freedom" or "soul" without use of language (Butler & Silliman, 2002; Marschark, Spencer, & Newsom, 2003).

Auditory difficulties may be accompanied by **speech impairments,** one of the most public types of exceptionality: Speech that deviates from the norm is obvious whenever the child speaks. It also interferes with communication, and may produce maladjustment in the speaker. Speech impairments occur in around 3 to 5 percent of the school-age population (Bishop & Leonard, 2001).

**Stuttering,** the most common speech impairment, produces substantial disruption in the rhythm and fluency of speech. Despite much research, no specific cause has been identified. Occasional stuttering is not unusual in young children—or even normal adults—but chronic stuttering can be a severe problem. Stuttering hinders communication, and can be embarrassing or stressful for children, who may come to fear conversation and speaking aloud in class (Whaley & Parker, 2000; Altholz & Golensky, 2004).

Parents and teachers can help children who stutter by not drawing attention to the issue and giving them sufficient time to finish what they are saying, no matter how protracted the statement becomes. It does not help stutterers to finish their sentences for them or otherwise correct their speech (Ryan, 2001; Howell, Bailey, & Kothari, 2010).

## Learning Disabilities: Discrepancies Between Achievement and Capacity to Learn

Like Andrew Mertz, described earlier, 1 in 10 children is labeled learning disabled. **Learning disabilities** interfere with children's ability to listen, speak, read, write, reason, or do math. An ill-defined category, learning disabilities are diagnosed when children's academic performance differs from their potential to learn (Lerner, 2002; Bos & Vaughn, 2005).

Such a broad definition includes a wide and varied range of difficulties. For instance, *dyslexia,* a reading disability, can result in the visual misperception of letters, unusual difficulty in spelling or sounding out letters, and left-right confusion. Dyslexia is not fully understood, but the problem may lie in the part of the brain that breaks words into the sound elements that make up language (Paulesu et al., 2001; McGough, 2003; Lachmann et al., 2005).

Although learning disabilities are generally attributed to some form of brain dysfunction, probably due to genetic factors, their causes are not well understood and some experts suggest that environmental causes such as poor early nutrition or allergies are culprits (Shaywitz, 2004).

## Attention Deficit Hyperactivity Disorder

*Dusty Nash, an angelic-looking blond child of 7, awoke at five one recent morning in his Chicago home and proceeded to throw a fit. He wailed. He kicked. Every muscle in his 50-pound body flew in furious motion. Finally, after about 30 minutes, Dusty pulled himself together sufficiently to head downstairs for breakfast. While his mother bustled about the kitchen, the hyperkinetic child pulled a box of Kix cereal from the cupboard and sat on a chair.*

*But sitting still was not in the cards this morning. After grabbing some cereal with his hands, he began kicking the box, scattering little round corn puffs across the room. Next he turned his attention to the TV set, or rather, the table supporting it. The table was covered with checkerboard Con-Tact paper, and Dusty began peeling it off. Then he became intrigued with the spilled cereal and started stomping it to bits. At this point his mother interceded. In a firm but calm voice she told her son to get the stand-up dust pan and broom and clean up the mess. Dusty got out the dust pan but forgot the rest of the order. Within seconds he was dismantling the plastic dust pan, piece by piece....*

*It was only 7:30 a.m. (Wallis, 1994, p. 43)*

Dusty suffers from a disorder unheard of just a few decades ago—**attention deficit hyperactivity disorder (ADHD).** This disorder is marked by inattention, impulsiveness, low tolerance for frustration, and a great deal of inappropriate activity. All children show such traits at times, but for ADHD children such behavior is common, interfering with their home and school functioning (American Academy of Pediatrics, 2000a; Nigg, 2001; Whalen et al., 2002).

**speech impairment** speech that deviates so much from the speech of others that it calls attention to itself, interferes with communication, or produces maladjustment in the speaker

**stuttering** substantial disruption in the rhythm and fluency of speech; the most common speech impairment

**learning disabilities** difficulties in the acquisition and use of listening, speaking, reading, writing, reasoning, or mathematical abilities

**attention deficit hyperactivity disorder (ADHD)** a learning disorder marked by inattention, impulsiveness, a low tolerance for frustration, and generally a great deal of inappropriate activity

ADHD

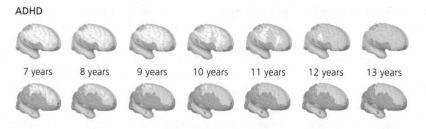

7 years    8 years    9 years    10 years    11 years    12 years    13 years

Typically developing controls

**FIGURE 5-3 The Brains of Children with ADHD**
The brains of children with ADHD (in the top row) show less thickening of the cortex compared to the brains of typical children at the same age.
Source: Shaw et al., 2007.

It is often difficult to distinguish between children who are highly active and those with ADHD. Common symptoms include:

- persistent difficulty in finishing tasks, following instructions, and organizing work
- fidgeting, squirming, inability to watch an entire television program
- frequent interruption of others or excessive talking
- a tendency to jump into a task before hearing all the instructions
- difficulty in waiting or remaining seated

Lacking a simple test to identify ADHD, it is hard to know for sure how many children have the disorder. Most estimates suggest that ADHD affects 3 to 7 percent of those under the age of 18. Accurate diagnosis requires an extensive evaluation by a trained clinician and interviews with parents and teachers (Sax & Kautz, 2003).

The causes of ADHD are not clear, although some research finds that it is related to a delay in neural development. Specifically, it may be that the thickening of the brain's cortex in children with ADHD lags three years behind that of children without the disorder (see Figure 5-3).

Considerable controversy surrounds the treatment of ADHD. Many physicians routinely prescribe drugs such as Ritalin or Dexadrine (which, paradoxically, are stimulants) because they reduce activity in hyperactive children (HMHL, 2005; Schachar et al., 2008; Arnsten, Berridge, & McCracken, 2009).

Although in many cases such drugs are effective in increasing attention span and compliance, in some cases the side effects (such as irritability, reduced appetite, and depression) are considerable, and the long-term health consequences of this treatment are unclear. It is also true that though the drugs often help scholastic performance in the short run, the long-term evidence for continuing improvement is mixed. In fact, some studies suggest that after a few years, children treated with drugs do not perform academically any better than untreated children with ADHD. Nonetheless the drugs are being prescribed with increasing frequency (Marshall, 2000; Zernike & Petersen, 2001; Mayes & Rafalovich, 2007; Rose, 2008).

In addition to drugs, behavior therapy is often used to treat ADHD. Parents and teachers learn techniques that primarily use rewards (such as verbal praise) to improve behavior. Teachers can increase the structure of classroom activities, among other management techniques, as ADHD children find unstructured tasks difficult (Chronis, Jones, & Raggi, 2006; DuPaul & Weyandt, 2006).

Finally, because some research has shown links between ADHD and children's diet, particularly in terms of fatty acids or food additives, dietary treatments have sometimes been prescribed. However, dietary treatments are usually insufficient by themselves (Cruz & Bahna, 2006; Stevenson, 2006). (Parents and teachers can receive support from the Children and Adults with Attention-Deficit/Hyperactivity Disorder organization at www.chadd.org.)

## Keeping Children Fit

### Becoming an Informed Consumer of Development

*Here is a brief portrait of a contemporary American: Sam works all week at a desk and gets no regular physical exercise. On weekends he spends many hours sitting in front of the TV, often snacking on sodas and sweets. Both at home and at restaurants, his meals feature high-calorie, fat-saturated foods.* (Segal & Segal, 1992, p. 235)

Although this sketch fits many adults, Sam is just 6. Many school-age children in the United States, like Sam, get little or no regular exercise and consequently are physically unfit and at risk for obesity and other health problems.

To encourage children to be more physically active (Tyre & Scelfo, 2003; Okie, 2005):

- **Make exercise fun.** Children repeat what they enjoy. Overly competitive activities or those that sideline children with inferior skills, though, may create a lifelong distaste for exercise.

- **Be an exercise role model.** Children who see their parents, teachers, or adult friends exercising regularly may view fitness as a regular part of their lives, too.

- **Gear activities to the child's physical level and motor skills.** Use child-size equipment to make children feel successful.

- **Encourage the child to find a partner.** Roller skating, hiking, and many other activities are more fun when shared with a friend, a sibling, or a parent.

- **Start slowly.** Ease sedentary children into regular physical activity. Try 5 minutes of exercise daily. Over 10 weeks, aim for 30 minutes three to five times a week.

- **Urge participation in organized sports activities, but do not push too hard.** Not every child is athletically inclined. Make participation and enjoyment—not winning—the goal.

- **Don't use physical activity as a punishment.** Encourage children to join organized activities they enjoy.

- **Provide a healthy diet.** Good nutrition gives children energy. Soda and sugary, fatty snack foods do not.

## REVIEW, CHECK, AND APPLY

### REVIEW

**LO4** What special needs may become apparent during these years, and how can they be met?

- Many children have special needs relating to vision, hearing, and speech that can impact their social relationships and school performance.

- Learning disabilities include difficulties in acquiring and using listening, speaking, reading, writing, reasoning, or mathematical abilities.

- Attention deficit hyperactivity disorder poses attention, organization, and activity problems for 3 to 5 percent of school-age children.

### CHECK YOURSELF

1. _____, the most common speech impairment, involves a substantial disruption in the rhythm and fluency of speech.

2. Attention deficit hyperactivity disorder (ADHD), according to the American Academy of Pediatrics, is marked by all of the following symptoms, EXCEPT _____.

   a. a tendency to lie

   b. a low tolerance for frustration

   c. inattention

   d. impulsiveness

### APPLYING LIFESPAN DEVELOPMENT

- If hearing is associated with abstract thinking, how do people who were born deaf think?

✓•⎯**Study** and **Review** on
**MyDevelopmentLab.com**

Answers: 1) Stuttering; 2) a

## MODULE 5.2 Cognitive Development in Middle Childhood

*There are few books in La-Toya Pankey's apartment on 102nd Street near Amsterdam Avenue in Manhattan, and even fewer places for an 8-year-old girl to steal away to read them.*

*There is no desk, no bookshelf, no reading lamp or even a bureau in La-Toya's small room, one of only two bedrooms in the apartment she shares with seven other people: her mother, her five sisters, and her infant brother.*

*At night, there is little light, save a couple of bare bulbs mounted on the peeling, beige walls. And there are few places to sit, except a lone, wooden chair at a battered kitchen table, which La-Toya must wait her turn to occupy.*

*Yet there was La-Toya, on a rainy evening earlier this month, leaning against that table and reading aloud, flawlessly, to her mother from the Roald Dahl classic* The Witches, *which she had borrowed from the makeshift library in her third-grade classroom.* (Steinberg, 1997, p. B1)

It was a significant moment for La-Toya. It marked a shift from the first-grade-level books that she had previously chosen to a far more challenging book, written at a grade level two years beyond her own.

Middle childhood is often referred to as the "school years" because it marks the beginning of formal education for most children. Sometimes the physical and cognitive growth that occurs during middle childhood is gradual; other times it is sudden; but always it is remarkable.

During middle childhood, children blossom with ideas and plans—and the language to express them orally and in writing. And it is during this period that much of their future development is charted.

We begin our discussion by examining several approaches to describe and explain cognitive development, including Piagetian and information processing theories and the important ideas of Vygotsky. We look at language development and the questions surrounding bilingualism— an increasingly pressing social policy issue in the United States.

Next we consider several issues involving schooling. After discussing the scope of education throughout the world, we examine the critical skill of reading and the nature of multicultural education. The chapter ends with a discussion of intelligence, a characteristic closely tied to school success. We look at the nature of IQ tests and at the education of children who are either significantly below or above the intellectual norm.

# Intellectual and Language Development

**LEARNING OBJECTIVES**

**LO5** In what ways do children develop cognitively during these years, according to major theoretical approaches?

**LO6** How do children in middle childhood develop memory?

**LO7** How does language develop during the middle childhood period?

*Jared's parents were delighted when he came home from kindergarten one day and announced he had learned why the sky was blue. He talked about the earth's atmosphere—although he mispronounced the word—and how tiny bits of moisture in the air reflected the sunlight. His explanation had rough edges (he couldn't quite grasp what "atmosphere" was), but he had the general idea. His parents felt it was quite an achievement for their 5-year-old.*

*Fast-forward six years. Jared, now 11, has already invested an hour in his homework. Having completed a two-page worksheet on multiplying and dividing fractions, he is working on his U.S. Constitution project. He is taking notes for his report, which explains what political factions were involved in creating the document and how the Constitution had been amended over time.*

Jared's vast intellectual advances are not uncommon. During middle childhood, cognitive abilities broaden, and children increasingly understand and master complex skills. But their thinking is not yet fully mature.

Several perspectives explain the cognitive advances and limitations of middle childhood.

## Piagetian Approaches to Cognitive Development

Let's return to Jean Piaget's view of the preschooler considered in Module 4.2. From Piaget's perspective, preschoolers think *preoperationally*. They are largely egocentric and lack the ability to use *operations*—organized, formal, logical mental processes.

***The Rise of Concrete Operational Thought.*** All this changes during the school years in what Piaget calls the **concrete operational stage.** Occurring between ages 7 and 12, this stage is characterized by the active, and appropriate, use of logic. Concrete operational thought applies *logical operations* to concrete problems. For instance, when children in this stage confront a conservation problem (such as determining whether the amount of liquid poured from one container to another of a different shape stays the same), they use cognitive and logical processes to answer, no longer judging solely by appearance. They are able to reason correctly that since

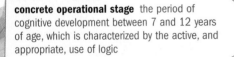

**concrete operational stage** the period of cognitive development between 7 and 12 years of age, which is characterized by the active, and appropriate, use of logic

none of the liquid has been lost, the amount stays the same. Being less ego-centric, they can consider multiple aspects of a situation, an ability known as **decentering.** Jared, the sixth-grader described earlier, used decentering to consider the views of the various factions behind the U.S. Constitution.

The shift from preoperational to concrete operational thought takes time. Children shift between these modes of thought before concrete operations take a firm hold—they are able to answer conservation problems but unable to explain why. When asked for their reasoning, they may simply respond, "Because."

However, once concrete operations take hold, children make several cognitive leaps, such as the concept of *reversibility*—the notion that transformations to a stimulus can be reversed. Grasping this, children realize that a ball of clay squeezed into a long, thin rope can become a ball again. More abstractly, this concept allows children to understand that if 3 + 5 equals 8, then 5 + 3 also equals 8—and, later, that 8 − 3 equals 5.

Concrete operational thinking also permits children to grasp such concepts as the relationship between time and speed. For instance, consider the problem in which two cars traveling different-length routes start and finish at the same points in the same amount of time. Children entering the concrete operational period reason that the cars' speed is the same. However, between ages 8 and 10, children begin to understand that for both cars to arrive simultaneously at the finish point, the car traveling the longer route must be moving faster.

Despite the advances that occur during the concrete operational stage, children still experience one critical limitation in their thinking. They remain tied to concrete, physical reality. Furthermore, they are unable to understand truly abstract or hypothetical questions, or ones that involve formal logic.

Cognitive development makes substantial advances in middle childhood.

***Piaget in Perspective: Right and Wrong.***    As we learned earlier, researchers who followed Piaget have found much to applaud—and much to criticize.

Piaget was a virtuoso observer of children. His many books contain brilliant, careful observations of children at work and play. His theories have had powerful educational implications, and many schools use his principles to guide instruction (Flavell, 1996; Siegler & Ellis, 1996; Brainerd, 2003).  Watch on mydevelopmentlab.com

In some ways, Piaget's approach succeeded in describing cognitive development (Lourenco & Machado, 1996). At the same time, critics have raised compelling and reasonable grievances. As noted earlier, many researchers argue that Piaget underestimated children's capabilities, in part due to the limitations of the mini-experiments he conducted. When a broader array of experimental tasks is used, children show less consistency within stages than Piaget predicted (Siegler, 1994; Bjorklund, 1997). Increasing evidence suggests that children's cognitive abilities emerge earlier than Piaget envisioned. Some children demonstrate concrete operational thinking before age 7, when Piaget suggested these abilities first appear.

Still, we cannot dismiss Piaget. Although some early cross-cultural research implied that children in certain cultures remain preoperational, failing to master conservation and develop concrete operations, more recent research suggests otherwise. For instance, with proper training in conservation, children in non-Western cultures who do not conserve learn to do so. In one study, urban Australian children—who develop concrete operations on Piaget's timetable—were compared to rural Aborigine children, who typically do not conserve at the age of 14 (Dasen, Ngini, & Lavallee, 1979). With training, the rural Aborigine children showed conservation skills similar to those of their urban counterparts, although about three years later (see Figure 5-4).

When children are interviewed by researchers from their own culture, who share their language and customs, and whose reasoning tasks relate to important cultural domains, the children are much more likely to display concrete operational thinking (Nyiti, 1982; Jahoda, 1983). Such research suggests that Piaget was right in arguing that concrete operations are universally achieved during middle childhood. Performance differences between Western and some non-Western children on Piagetian measures of conservation and concrete operations

⊙ Watch on **mydevelopmentlab.com**

To better understand Piaget's theories, log onto MyDevelopmentLab.com and watch children demonstrating what you'll be reading about in the video "Conservation."

**decentering** the ability to take multiple aspects of a situation into account

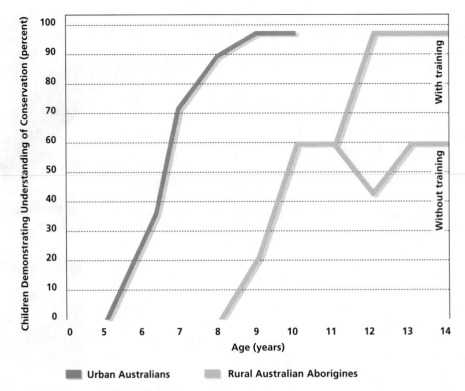

**FIGURE 5-4 Conservation Training**
Rural Australian Aborigine children trail their urban counterparts in the development of their understanding of conservation; with training, they later catch up. Without training, around half of 14-year-old Aborigines do not have an understanding of conservation. What can be concluded from the fact that training influences the understanding of conservation?
Source: Adapted from Dasen, Ngini, & Lavallee, 1979.

probably reflect a difference in experiences. The progress of cognitive development cannot be understood without considering a child's culture (Mishra, 1997; Lau, Lee, & Chiu, 2004; Maynard, 2008).

## Information Processing in Middle Childhood

It is a significant achievement for first-graders to learn basic math tasks, such as single-digit addition and subtraction, as well as the spelling of simple words like "dog." But by sixth grade, children are able to work with fractions and decimals, completing a worksheet like the one done by Jared, the boy cited earlier. They can spell words like "exhibit" and "residence."

According to *information processing approaches,* children handle information with increasing sophistication. Like computers, they process more data as the size of their memories increases and the "programs" they use to do this become more complex (Kuhn et al., 1995; Kail, 2003; Zelazo et al., 2003).

*Memory.* As noted, **memory** in the information processing model is the ability to record, store, and retrieve information. For a child to remember a piece of information, the three processes must all function properly. Through *encoding,* the child records the information in a form usable to memory. Children who never learned that 5 + 6 = 11, or who didn't heed this fact when it was taught, will never be able to recall it. They never encoded the information in the first place.

But exposure to a fact is not enough; the information also has to be *stored.* In our example, the information that 5 + 6 = 11 must be placed and maintained in the memory system. Finally, proper memory functioning requires that stored material must be *retrieved.* Through retrieval, material in storage is located, made conscious, and used.

**memory** the process by which information is initially recorded, stored, and retrieved

During middle childhood, short-term memory (also referred to as *working memory*) capacity greatly improves. Children are increasingly able to hear a string of digits ("1-5-6-3-4") and then repeat them in reverse order ("4-3-6-5-1"). At the start of the preschool period, they can remember and reverse only about two digits; by the beginning of adolescence, they can perform the task with as many as six digits. In addition, they use more sophisticated strategies for recalling information, which can be improved with training (Marshall, 2000; Zernike & Petersen, 2001; Mayes & Rafalovich, 2007; Rose, 2008).

Memory capacity may shed light on another issue in cognitive development. Some developmental psychologists suggest that preschool children may have difficulty solving conservation problems due to memory limitations (Siegler & Richards, 1982). They argue that young children simply may not be able to recall all the necessary information to solve such problems.

**Metamemory,** a grasp of the processes that underlie memory, also emerges and improves during middle childhood. By the start of first grade, when their theory of mind becomes more sophisticated, children have a general notion of what memory is. They understand that some people have better memories than others (Cherney, 2003; Ghetti et al., 2008; Jaswal & Dodson, 2009).

Students working in cooperative groups benefit from the insights of others.

School-age children understand memory in more sophisticated ways as they increasingly engage in *control strategies*—intentionally used tactics to improve cognitive processing. For instance, school-age children know that rehearsal, the repetition of information, improves memory, and they increasingly make use of this strategy. They also progress in organizing material into coherent patterns, a strategy that improves recall. For instance, faced with memorizing a list including cups, knives, forks, and plates, older school-age children are more likely than younger ones to group the items into coherent patterns—cups and plates, forks and knives (Sang, Miao, & Deng, 2002).

*Improving Memory.* Can children be trained to be more effective in the use of control strategies? Definitely. School-age children can be taught to use particular strategies, although such teaching is not a simple matter. For instance, children need to know not only how to use a memory strategy, but also when and where to use it most effectively.

For example, an innovative technique called the *keyword strategy* can help students learn a foreign language, the state capitals, or any information that pairs two sets of words or labels that sound alike (Wyra, Lawson, & Hungi, 2007). For instance, in learning foreign language vocabulary, a foreign word such as the Spanish word for duck (*pato*, pronounced *pot-o*) is paired with a common English word—in this case it might be "pot." The English word is the keyword. Once the keyword is chosen, children then form a mental image of the two words interacting with one another. For instance, a student might use an image of a duck taking a bath in a pot to remember the word *pato*.

## Vygotsky's Approach to Cognitive Development and Classroom Instruction

Learning environments can encourage children to adopt these strategies as well. Recall that Russian developmentalist Lev Vygotsky proposed that cognitive advances occur through exposure to information within a child's *zone of proximal development,* or ZPD. In the ZPD, a child can almost, but not quite, understand or perform a task.

Vygotsky's approach has particularly encouraged the development of classroom practices that promote children's active participation in their learning (e.g., Holzman, 1997). Consequently, classrooms are seen as places where children should experiment and try out new activities (Vygotsky, 1926/1997; Gredler & Shields, 2008).

According to Vygotsky, education should focus on activities that involve interaction with others. Both child–adult and child–child interactions can promote cognitive growth. The interactions must be carefully structured to fall within each child's zone of proximal development.

**metamemory**  an understanding about the processes that underlie memory, which emerges and improves during middle childhood

Vygotsky's work has influenced several current and noteworthy innovations. For example, *cooperative learning,* where children work in groups to achieve a common goal, uses several aspects of Vygotsky's theory. Students working in cooperative groups benefit from the insights of others. A wrong turn by one child may be corrected by others in the group. On the other hand, not every group member is equally helpful: As Vygotsky's approach would imply, individual children benefit most when some of the group members are more competent at the task and can act as experts (Gillies & Boyle, 2006; DeLisi, 2006; Law, 2008).

**From an educator's perspective:** Suggest how a teacher might use Vygotsky's approach to teach 10-year-olds about colonial America.

Reciprocal teaching is another educational practice that reflects Vygotsky's approach to cognitive development. *Reciprocal teaching* is a technique to teach reading comprehension strategies. Students are taught to skim the content of a passage, raise questions about its central point, summarize the passage, and finally predict what will happen next. A key to this technique is its reciprocal nature, its emphasis on giving students a chance to take on the role of teacher. In the beginning, teachers lead students through the comprehension strategies. Gradually, students progress through their zones of proximal development, taking more and more control over use of the strategies, until the students are able to take on a teaching role. The method has shown impressive success in raising reading comprehension levels, particularly for students experiencing reading difficulties (Greenway, 2002; Takala, 2006; Spörer, Brunstein, & Kieschke, 2009).

## Language Development: What Words Mean

If you listen to school-age children, their speech sounds similar to that of adults. However, the apparent similarity is deceiving. The linguistic sophistication of children—particularly early in the school-age period—still needs refining to reach adult levels.

*Mastering the Mechanics of Language.* Vocabulary continues to increase rapidly during the school years. The average 6-year-old has a vocabulary of from 8,000 to 14,000 words, whereas another 5,000 words appear from ages 9 to 11.

Children's mastery of grammar also improves. For instance, the passive voice is seldom used during the early school-age years (as in "The dog was walked by Jon," compared with the active-voice "Jon walked the dog"). Six- and 7-year-olds rarely use conditional sentences, such as "If Sarah will set the table, I will wash the dishes." During middle childhood, however, the use of passive voice and conditional sentences increases. In addition, children's understanding of *syntax,* the rules governing how words and phrases can be combined to form sentences, grows.

By first grade, most children pronounce words quite accurately. However, certain *phonemes,* units of sound, remain troublesome. For instance, the ability to pronounce *j, v, th,* and *zh* sounds develops later.

School-age children also may have difficulty decoding sentences when the meaning depends on *intonation,* or tone of voice. For example, consider the sentence, "George gave a book to David and he gave one to Bill." If the word "he" is emphasized, the meaning is "George gave a book to David and David gave a different book to Bill." But if the intonation emphasizes the word "and," then the meaning changes to "George gave a book to David and George also gave a book to Bill." School-age children cannot easily sort out subtleties such as these (Wells, Peppé, & Goulandris, 2004; Thornton, 2010).

Conversational skills also develop as children become more competent in using *pragmatics,* the rules governing the use of language to communicate in social settings.

For example, although children in early childhood are aware of the rules of conversational turn-taking, their use is sometimes primitive. Consider the following conversation between 6-year-olds Yonnie and Max:

**Yonnie:** My dad drives a FedEx truck.

**Max:** My sister's name is Molly.

**Yonnie:** He gets up really early in the morning.

**Max:** She wet her bed last night.

Later, however, conversations show more give-and-take, with children responding to each other's comments. For instance, this conversation between 11-year-olds Mia and Josh reflects a greater mastery of pragmatics:

**Mia:** I don't know what to get Claire for her birthday.

**Josh:** I'm getting her earrings.

**Mia:** She already has a lot of jewelry.

**Josh:** I don't think she has that much.

*Metalinguistic Awareness.* A significant development in middle childhood is children's increasing understanding of their own use of language, or **metalinguistic awareness.** By age 5 or 6, they understand that a set of rules governs language. In the early years they learn and comprehend these rules implicitly, but during middle childhood they understand them more explicitly (Benelli et al., 2006; Saiegh-Haddad, 2007).

Metalinguistic awareness helps children's comprehension when information is fuzzy or incomplete. For instance, when preschoolers receive ambiguous or unclear information, such as directions for a complicated game, they rarely ask for clarification, and tend to blame themselves for any confusion. By the age of 7 or 8, children realize that miscommunication may be due to the person communicating with them as well. Consequently, school-age children are more likely to ask for clarifications (Apperly & Robinson, 2002).

*How Language Promotes Self-Control.* Their growing sophistication with language helps children control and regulate their behavior. In one experiment, children were told they could have one marshmallow treat if they chose to eat it immediately, but two treats if they waited. Most of the children, who ranged in age from 4 to 8, chose to wait, but the strategies they used differed significantly.

The 4-year-olds often chose to look at the marshmallows while waiting, a strategy that was not terribly effective. In contrast, 6- and 8-year-olds used language to help overcome temptation, although in different ways. The 6-year-olds spoke and sang to themselves, reminding themselves they would get more treats if they waited. The 8-year-olds focused on aspects of the marshmallows unrelated to taste, such as appearance, which helped them to wait.

In short, children used "self-talk" to regulate their behavior. Their self-control grew as their linguistic capabilities increased.

## Bilingualism: Speaking in Many Tongues

*For picture day at New York's P.S. 217, a neighborhood elementary school in Brooklyn, the notice to parents was translated into five languages. That was a nice gesture, but insufficient: More than 40 percent of the children are immigrants whose families speak any one of twenty-six languages, ranging from Armenian to Urdu. (Leslie, 1991, p. 56)*

Across America, the voices with which children speak are changing. Nearly one in five people in the United States speaks a language other than English at home, a percentage that is growing. **Bilingualism**—the use of more than one language—is increasingly common (Shin & Bruno, 2003; Graddol, 2004) (see Figure 5-5).

Children with little or no English proficiency must learn both the standard school curriculum and the language in which it is taught. One approach to achieving this is *bilingual education,* in which children are initially taught in their native language, while they learn English. This enables students to develop a strong foundation in basic subject areas using their native language. The goal of most bilingual programs is to gradually shift instruction into English.

An alternative approach is to immerse students in English, teaching solely in that language. To proponents of this approach, initially teaching students in another language hinders their efforts to learn English and slows their integration into society.

**metalinguistic awareness** an understanding of one's own use of language

**bilingualism** the use of more than one language

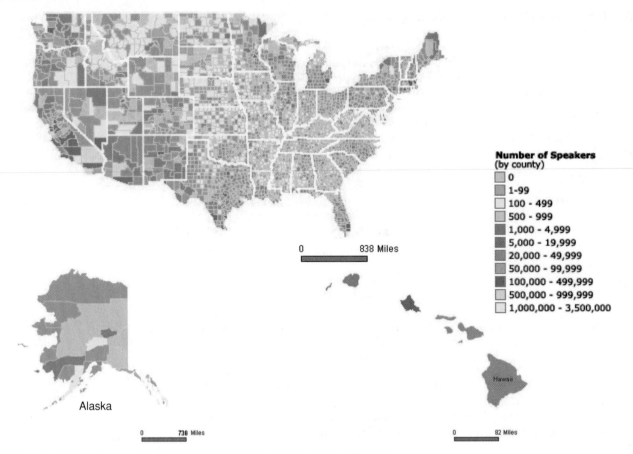

**FIGURE 5-5 The Top 10 Languages Other Than English Spoken in the United States**
These figures show the number of U.S. residents over the age of 5 who speak a language other than English at home. With increases in the number and variety of languages spoken in the United States, what types of approaches might an educator use to meet the needs of bilingual students?
Source: Modern Language Association, www.mla.org/census_map,2005. Based on data from U.S. Census Bureau, 2000.

These two quite different, highly politicized approaches have some politicians arguing for "English-only" laws, while others urge schools to respect the challenges nonnative speakers face by offering some instruction in their native language. Still, the psychological research is clear: Being bilingual offers cognitive advantages. With a wider range of linguistic possibilities to choose from in assessing a situation, speakers of two languages show greater cognitive flexibility. They solve problems with greater creativity and versatility. Learning in one's native tongue is also associated with higher self-esteem in minority students (Lesaux & Siegel, 2003; Chen & Bond, 2007; Bialystok & Viswanathan, 2009).

Bilingual students often have greater metalinguistic awareness, understand the rules of language more explicitly, and show great cognitive sophistication. They may even score higher on tests of intelligence, according to some research. Furthermore, brain scans comparing bilingual individuals with those who speak only one language find differences suggesting different types of brain activation (Swanson, Saez, & Gerber, 2004; Carlson & Meltzoff, 2008; Kovelman, Baker, & Petitto, 2008; Piller, 2010).

Finally, because many linguists contend that universal processes underlie language acquisition, as we noted in Chapter 3, instruction in a native language may enhance instruction in a second language. In fact, as we discuss next, many educators believe that second-language learning should be a regular part of elementary schooling for *all* children (Kecskes & Papp, 2000; McCardle & Hoff, 2006).

## REVIEW, CHECK, AND APPLY

### REVIEW

**LO5** In what ways do children develop cognitively during these years, according to major theoretical approaches?

- Piaget believed school-age children are in the concrete operational stage, while information processing approaches focus on quantitative improvements in memory and in the sophistication of the mental programs children use.
- Vygotsky suggests schoolchildren should have the opportunity to experiment and participate actively with their peers in their learning.

**LO6** How do children in middle childhood develop memory?

- Children gain increasing control over the memory processes—encoding, storage, and retrieval, and the development of metamemory improves cognitive processing and memorization.

**LO7** How does language develop during the middle childhood period?

- As language develops, vocabulary, syntax, and pragmatics improve; metalinguistic awareness grows; and language is used as a self-control device.

### CHECK YOURSELF

1. Which of the following best describes Piaget's approach to cognitive development in middle childhood?

   a. Piaget overestimated the degree to which young children could problem solve because of the types of tasks he used.

   b. Piaget considered the degree to which culture influences the kind of things we learn.

   c. Piaget's approach provided totally accurate descriptions of young children's cognitive development.

   d. Piaget's theory has had powerful implications for schools and educational materials.

2. Children who have the ability to focus on more than one aspect of a problem at a time are capable of _____.

   a. centering

   b. decentering

   c. irreversibility

   d. mental repression

3. As children reach middle childhood, they get better at understanding the processes that underlie their own memory, including strategies for doing better on tasks requiring memory.

   - True
   - False

### APPLYING LIFESPAN DEVELOPMENT

- Do adults use language (and self-talk) as a self-control device? How?

✓— **Study** and **Review** on
**MyDevelopmentLab.com**

# Schooling: The Three Rs (and More) of Middle Childhood

**LO8   What are some trends in schooling today?**

**LEARNING OBJECTIVES**

*As the six other children in his reading group turned to him, Glenn shifted uneasily in his chair. Reading was hard for him, and he always felt anxious when asked to read aloud. But with his teacher's encouraging nod, he plunged in, hesitant at first, then gaining momentum as he read the story of a mother's first day on a new job. He was happy and proud to find that he could read the passage quite nicely. He broke into a broad smile when his teacher said, "Well done, Glenn."*

Such moments, repeated over and over, make—or break—a child's educational experience. School is society's formal attempt to transfer its accumulated knowledge, beliefs, values, and wisdom to new generations. The success of this transfer determines, in a very real sense, the future fortunes of the world, as well as the success of each student.

## Schooling Around the World and Across Genders: Who Gets Educated?

In the United States, as in most developed countries, a primary school education is both a universal right and a legal requirement. Virtually all children enjoy a free education through the 12th grade.

Children in other parts of the world are not always so fortunate. More than 160 million of the world's children do not even receive a primary education. An additional 100 million

In almost all developing countries, more males than females receive formal education.

children are educated only to a level comparable to our elementary school, and close to a billion individuals (two-thirds of them women) are illiterate throughout their lives.

In almost all developing countries, fewer females than males receive formal education, a discrepancy found at every level of schooling. Even in developed countries, women lag behind men in their exposure to science and technological topics. These differences reflect widespread, deeply held cultural and parental biases that favor males over females. Educational levels in the United States are more nearly equal between men and women. Especially in the early years, boys and girls share equal access to opportunities.

## Reading: Learning to Decipher the Meaning Behind Words

The efforts of La-Toya Pankey (described in the prologue) to improve her reading are significant, for there is no task more fundamental to learning than reading. Reading involves a significant number of skills, from low-level cognitive skills (the identification of single letters and letter–sound association) to higher-level skills (matching written words with meanings stored in memory, and using context and prior knowledge to determine a sentence's meaning).

***Reading Stages.*** Learning to read usually occurs in several broad and frequently overlapping stages (Chall, 1979, 1992). In *Stage 0,* from birth to first grade, children learn the prerequisites for reading, including letter identification, recognition of familiar words (such as their name or *stop* on a stop sign), and perhaps writing their name.

*Stage 1* brings the first real type of reading, but it largely involves *phonological recoding* skills. At this stage, which usually encompasses the first and second grade, children can sound out words by blending the letters together. Children also complete the job of learning the names of letters and the sounds that go with them.

In *Stage 2,* typically around second and third grades, children learn to read aloud with fluency. However, they do not attach much meaning to the words, because the effort involved in simply sounding out words is usually so great that relatively few cognitive resources are left over to process the meaning of the words.

The next period, *Stage 3,* extends from fourth to eighth grade. Reading becomes a means to an end—in particular, a way to learn. Whereas earlier reading was an accomplishment in and of itself, by this point children use reading to learn about the world. However, even at this age, understanding gained from reading is not complete. For instance, one limitation children have at this stage is that they are able to comprehend information only when it is presented from a single perspective.

In the final period, *Stage 4,* children are able to read and process information that reflects multiple points of view. This ability, which begins during the transition into high school, permits children to develop a far more sophisticated understanding of material. This explains why great works of literature are not read at an earlier stage of education. It is not so much that younger children do not have the vocabulary to understand such works (although this is partially true); it is that they lack the ability to understand the multiple points of view that sophisticated literature invariably presents.

***How Should We Teach Reading?*** Educators have long been engaged in a debate over the most effective means of teaching reading. This debate centers on a disagreement about how information is processed during reading. According to proponents of *code-based approaches to reading*, teachers should focus on the basic skills that underlie reading. Code-based approaches emphasize the components of reading, such as letter sounds and combinations—phonics—and how letters and sounds combine to make words. They suggest that reading consists of processing the components of words, combining them into words, and using these to derive the meaning of sentences and passages (Vellutino, 1991; Jimenez & Guzman, 2003; Gray et al., 2007; Dickinson, Golinkoff, & Hirsh-Pasek, 2010).

In contrast, some educators argue that the most successful approach is *whole language,* which regards reading as a natural process, similar to the acquisition of oral language. According to this view, children learn to read through authentic writing, such as sentences, stories, poems, lists, and charts. Rather than sounding out words, children make guesses about the meaning of words based on the context. Children become proficient readers, learning whole words and phrases through such a trial-and-error approach (Shaw, 2003; Sousa, 2005; Donat, 2006).

A growing body of research suggests the code-based approach is superior to the whole-language approach. One study found that children tutored in phonics for a year improved their reading substantially, compared to a group of good readers, and that the neural pathways involved in reading became closer to those of good readers (Shaywitz et al., 2004; Shapiro & Solity, 2008).

Based on such research, the National Reading Panel and National Research Council support code-based instruction. Their position signals that the debate over the most effective approach may be nearing an end (Rayner et al., 2002).

> **cultural assimilation model** the model in which the goal was to assimilate individual cultural identities into a unique, unified American culture
>
> **pluralistic society model** the concept that American society is made up of diverse, coequal cultural groups that should preserve their individual cultural features

## Educational Trends: Beyond the Three Rs

Schooling in the twenty-first century has changed significantly in recent years, with U.S. schools returning to the traditional three Rs (reading, writing, and arithmetic). The focus on these fundamentals departs from prior trends that emphasized children's social well-being and allowing students to choose their own study topics instead of following a set curriculum (Schemo, 2003; Yinger, 2004).

Elementary schools today also stress individual accountability. Teachers may be held responsible for their students' learning, and both students and teachers may be required to take state or national tests to assess their competence (McDonnell, 2004).

As the U.S. population becomes more diverse, elementary schools are paying increased attention to student diversity issues and multiculturalism. And with good reason: Cultural, as well as language, differences affect students socially and educationally. The demographic makeup of students in the United States is undergoing an extraordinary shift. The proportion of Hispanics is likely to more than double in the next 50 years. By the year 2050, non-Hispanic Caucasians will likely be a minority of the United States' total population (U.S. Bureau of Census, 2001) (see Figure 5-6). Consequently, educators are increasingly serious about multicultural concerns. The accompanying Cultural Dimensions feature, on multicultural education, discusses how the goals for educating students from different cultures have changed significantly and are still being debated.

*Cultural Assimilation or Pluralistic Society?* Multicultural education, in part, is a response to a **cultural assimilation model** in which the goal was to assimilate individual cultural identities into a unique, unified American culture. In practice this meant that non-English speakers were discouraged from using their native language and totally immersed in English.

> **From an educator's perspective:** Should one goal of society be to foster cultural assimilation in children from other cultures? Why or why not?

In the early 1970s, however, educators and minority groups suggested that cultural assimilation should be replaced by a **pluralistic society model.** In this model, American society is made up of diverse, coequal cultural groups that preserve their unique cultural features.

The pluralistic model grew, in part, from the belief that teachers who emphasized the dominant culture and discouraged nonnative English speakers from

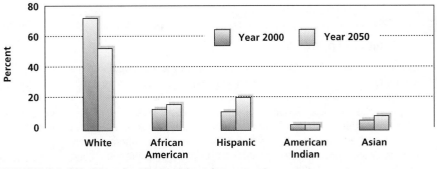

**FIGURE 5-6 The Changing Face of America**
Current projections of the population makeup of the United States show that by the year 2050, the proportion of non-Hispanic Whites will decline as the proportion of minority group members increases. What will be some of the impacts on social workers as the result of changing demographics?
Source: U.S. Census Bureau, 2000.

**bicultural identity** Maintaining one's original cultural identity while integrating oneself into the dominant culture

**multicultural education** a form of education in which the goal is to help minority students develop confidence in the culture of the majority group while maintaining positive group identities that build on their original cultures

using their native tongues in effect devalued subcultural heritages and lowered those students' self-esteem. Instructional materials inevitably feature culture-specific events and understandings. Thus, minority children might never be exposed to important aspects of their culture. For example, English-language texts rarely present the great themes in Spanish literature and history (such as the search for the Fountain of Youth and the Don Juan legend). Hispanic students risked missing important components of their heritage.

Ultimately, educators began to argue that the presence of students representing diverse cultures enriched and broadened the educational experience of all students. Pupils and teachers exposed to people from different backgrounds could better understand the world and gain greater sensitivity to the values and needs of others (Gurin, Nagda, & Lopez, 2004; Zirkel & Cantor, 2004).

Pupils and teachers exposed to a diverse group could better understand the world and gain a greater sensitivity to the values and needs of others. What are some ways of developing greater sensitivity in the classroom?

***Fostering a Bicultural Identity.*** Most educators now agree that minority children should develop a **bicultural identity,** where schools support children's original cultural identities while also integrating them into the dominant culture. In this view, an individual lives as a member of two cultures, with two cultural identities, without having to choose one over the other (Lu, 2001; Oyserman et al., 2003; Vyas, 2004).

The best way to achieve this goal is not clear. Consider children who enter school speaking only Spanish. The traditional "melting-pot" technique would immerse them in classes taught in English while providing a crash course in English language (and little else) until the children gain a reasonable proficiency. Unfortunately, this approach has a major drawback: Until they are proficient, students fall further and further behind their peers (First & Cardenas, 1986).

More contemporary bicultural approaches encourage children to maintain membership in more than one culture. For a Spanish-speaking child, instruction would begin in Spanish and shift rapidly to include English. The school would also conduct a multicultural program for all children, where material on the cultures of all students is presented. Such instruction is meant to enhance the self-image of every student (Bracey, Bamaca, & Umana-Taylor, 2004; Fowers & Davidov, 2006).

Although most educational experts favor bicultural approaches, the general public does not always agree. For instance, the "English-only" movement mentioned earlier seeks to prohibit school instruction in any non-English language. Which view will prevail remains to be seen.

## *Cultural Dimensions*

### Multicultural Education

Classrooms in the United States have always been populated by students with diverse backgrounds and experiences. Only recently, though, have variations in student backgrounds been viewed as a major challenge—and opportunity—that educators face.

In fact, this diversity in the classroom relates to a fundamental objective of education, which is to transmit the information a society deems important. As the famous anthropologist Margaret Mead (1942) once said, "In its broadest sense, education is the cultural process, the way in which each newborn human infant, born with a potentiality for learning greater than that of any other mammal, is transformed into a full member of a specific human society, sharing with the other members of a specific human culture" (p. 633).

*Culture,* then, can be seen as a set of behaviors, beliefs, values, and expectations shared by the members of a society. But culture is not simply "Western culture" or "Asian culture." It is also made up of *subcultural* groups. Membership in a cultural or subcultural group might be of minor concern to educators if it didn't substantially impact the way students experience school. In recent years, considerable thought has gone into providing **multicultural education,** with the goal of helping minority students develop competence in the majority culture while maintaining positive group identities built on their original cultures (Nieto, 2005; Ngo, 2010).

## REVIEW, CHECK, AND APPLY

### REVIEW

**LO8** What are some trends in schooling today?

- Schooling is considered a legal right in the United States and many other countries, but millions of the world's children do not receive even a primary education.

- Reading skills generally develop in several stages. There is growing evidence that code-based approaches to teaching reading are more successful than the whole language approach.

- U.S. schools have returned in recent decades to a focus on the traditional academic skills.

### CHECK YOURSELF

1. According to the _____ approach to reading, reading should be taught by presenting the basic skills underlying reading. Examples include phonics and how letters and words are combined to make words.

   a. whole-language

   b. linguistic

   c. code-based

   d. dynamic

2. The goal of multicultural education is to help minority students develop competence in the culture of the majority group while maintaining positive group identities that build on their original cultures.

   - True

   - False

### APPLYING LIFESPAN DEVELOPMENT

- Do you think that the emphasis on the traditional "three Rs" in middle school is appropriate? Do less "academic" subjects have a place in the regular curriculum, or should they be dealt with as "add-ons" and after-school activities. Why?

**Study** and **Review** on
**MyDevelopmentLab.com**

Answers: 1) c; 2) True

# Intelligence: Determining Individual Strengths

**LO9** How can intelligence be measured?

**LO10** How are exceptional children educated?

**LEARNING OBJECTIVES**

*"Why should you tell the truth?" "How far is Los Angeles from New York?" "A table is made of wood; a window of _____."*

*As 10-year-old Hyacinth sat hunched over her desk, faced with a series of questions like these, she tried to guess the point of the test she was taking. Clearly, the test covered material not discussed by her fifth-grade teacher, Ms. White-Johnston.*

*"What number comes next in this series: 1, 3, 7, 15, 31, _____?"*

*As she worked through the test, she gave up trying to guess its rationale. She'd leave that to her teacher and simply try to figure out the correct answers.*

Hyacinth was taking an intelligence test. It might surprise her to learn that others also questioned the meaning and importance of the test. Intelligence test items are painstakingly prepared, and the tests are designed to predict academic success (for reasons we'll soon discuss). Many developmentalists, however, harbor doubts that such tests are entirely appropriate for assessing intelligence.

Understanding just what intelligence means has proven a major challenge for researchers in defining what separates intelligent from unintelligent behavior. Although nonexperts have their own definitions (one survey found that laypersons view intelligence as three components: problem-solving ability, verbal ability, and social competence), it has been more difficult for experts to concur (Sternberg et al., 1981; Howe, 1997). Still, a general definition of intelligence is possible: **Intelligence** is the capacity to understand the world, think with rationality, and use resources effectively when faced with challenges (Wechsler, 1975).

**intelligence** the capacity to understand the world, think with rationality, and use resources effectively when faced with challenges

The Wechsler Intelligence Scale for Children–Fourth Edition (WISC-IV) is widely used as an intelligence test that measures verbal and performance (nonverbal) skills.

To understand how researchers have variously approached the task of defining intelligence and devising *intelligence tests,* we need to consider some of the historical milestones in this area.

## Intelligence Benchmarks: Differentiating the Intelligent from the Unintelligent

The Paris schools faced a problem as the twentieth century began: Regular instruction was failing many students. These children—many of whom were mentally retarded—were seldom identified early enough to shift them to special classes. The French minister of instruction asked psychologist Alfred Binet to devise a method for identifying students who might benefit from special instruction.

***Binet's Test.*** Binet took a practical approach. Years of observation suggested that prior tests for intelligence—some based on reaction time or eyesight—were ineffectual. Binet, using a trial-and-error approach, administered items and tasks to students identified as either "bright" or "dull." He retained the tasks that the bright students completed correctly and the dull students failed. Tasks that did not discriminate were discarded. The end result was a test that reliably distinguished fast and slow learners.

Binet's pioneering efforts left three important legacies. The first was his pragmatic approach to constructing intelligence tests. Binet did not have theoretical preconceptions about what intelligence was. Instead, he used a trial-and-error approach to psychological measurement that continues to be the predominant approach to test construction. His definition of intelligence as *that which his test measured* has been adopted by many modern researchers, and it is particularly popular among test developers who wish to avoid arguments about the underlying nature of intelligence.

Binet's legacy links intelligence and school success. His approach to constructing a test ensured that intelligence—defined as performance on the test—and school success would be virtually identical. Thus, Binet's intelligence test, and today's tests that use his methods, are reasonable predictors of school performance. They do not, however, provide useful information for other attributes, such as social skills or personality traits, that are largely unrelated to academic proficiency.

Finally, Binet developed a method to link each intelligence test score with a **mental age,** the age of the children who, on average, achieved that score. If a 6-year-old girl scored 30 on the test, and this was the average score for 10-year-olds, her mental age would be 10. Similarly, a 15-year-old boy who scored a 90—matching the mean score for 15-year-olds—would have a mental age of 15 (Wasserman & Tulsky, 2005).

Although mental age indicates how students are performing relative to their peers, it does not permit adequate comparisons between students of different **chronological (or physical) ages.** By using mental age alone, for example, it would be assumed that a 15-year-old whose mental age is 17 would be as bright as a 6-year-old whose mental age is 8, when actually the 6-year-old shows a much greater *relative* intelligence.

The **intelligence quotient,** or **IQ,** a score that accounts for a student's mental *and* chronological age, provides a solution. The traditional method of calculating an IQ score uses the following formula, in which MA equals mental age and CA equals chronological age:

$$\text{IQ score} = \frac{\text{MA}}{\text{CA}} \times 100$$

As this formula demonstrates, people whose mental age (MA) is equal to their chronological age (CA) will always have an IQ of 100. If the chronological age exceeds the mental age—implying below-average intelligence—the score will be below 100; and if the chronological age is lower than the mental age—suggesting above-average intelligence—the score will be above 100.

**mental age** the typical intelligence level found for people at a given chronological age

**chronological (or physical) age** the actual age of the child taking the intelligence test

**intelligence quotient (or IQ score)** a score that accounts for a student's mental *and* chronological age

Using this formula, consider our example of a 15-year-old who scores a mental age of 17. This student's IQ is $\frac{17}{15} \times 100$, or 113. In comparison, the IQ of a 6-year-old scoring a mental age of 8 is $\frac{8}{6} \times 100$, or 133—a higher IQ score.

IQ scores today are calculated in a more sophisticated manner and known as *deviation IQ scores*. The average deviation IQ score remains at 100, but now, by the degree of deviation from this score, the proportion of people with similar scores can be calculated. For instance, about two-thirds of all people fall within 15 points of 100, scoring between 85 and 115. Beyond this range, the percentage of people in the same score category drops significantly.

***Measuring IQ: Present-Day Approaches to Intelligence.*** Since Binet, intelligence tests have become increasingly accurate measures of IQ, though most remain rooted in his original work. For example, one of the most widely used tests—the **Stanford-Binet Intelligence Scales, Fifth Edition (SB5)**—began as an American revision of Binet's original test. The test consists of age-appropriate items—for example, young children are asked about everyday activities or given complex figures to copy. Older people are asked to explain proverbs, solve analogies, and describe similarities between word groups. Test-takers are given progressively more difficult problems until they are unable to proceed.

The **Wechsler Intelligence Scale for Children, Fourth Edition (WISC-IV)** is another widely used test. The test (an offshoot of the *Wechsler Adult Intelligence Scale*) breaks the total score into measures of verbal and performance (or nonverbal) skills. As you can see from Figure 5-7, word problems are used to test skills such as comprehension, while typical nonverbal tasks are copying a complex design, sequencing pictures, and assembling objects. The test's separate portions make it easier to identify specific problems a test-taker may have. For example, significantly higher scores on the performance part than on the verbal part may indicate linguistic development difficulties (Zhu & Weiss, 2005).

The **Kaufman Assessment Battery for Children, Second Edition (KABC-II)** takes a different approach. It tests children's ability to integrate different kinds of stimuli simultaneously and to use sequential thinking. The KABC-II's special virtue is its flexibility. It allows the test-giver to use alternative wording or gestures, or even to pose questions in a different language, in order to maximize performance. This makes testing more valid and equitable for children to whom English is a second language (Kaufman et al., 2005).

What do the IQ scores mean? For most children, they are reasonable predictors of school performance. That's not surprising, given that intelligence tests were developed to identify students who were having difficulties (Sternberg & Grigorenko, 2002).

But the story differs for performance outside of school; for example, although people with higher scores tend to finish more years of schooling, once this is statistically controlled for, IQ scores do not closely relate to income and later success in life. Two people with different scores may both earn bachelor's degrees at the same college, but the person with a lower IQ might have a higher income and a more successful career. These difficulties with traditional IQ scores have led researchers to consider alternative approaches (McClelland, 1993).

***What IQ Tests Don't Tell: Alternative Conceptions of Intelligence.*** The intelligence tests schools use most today regard intelligence as a single factor, a unitary mental ability. This attribute is commonly called *g* (Spearman, 1927; Lubinski, 2004). Assumed to underlie performance on every aspect of intelligence, the *g* factor is what IQ tests presumably measure.

However, many theorists disagree that intelligence is unidimensional. Some developmentalists suggest that two kinds of intelligence exist: fluid and crystallized (Catell, 1967, 1987). **Fluid intelligence** reflects information processing capabilities, reasoning, and memory; for example, a student asked to group a series of letters according to some criterion or to remember a set of numbers would be using fluid intelligence (Salthouse, Pink, & Tucker-Drob, 2008; Shangguan & Shi, 2009). In contrast, **crystallized intelligence** is the cumulative information, skills, and strategies people have learned and can apply in solving problems. A student would likely use crystallized intelligence to solve a puzzle or find the solution to a mystery (McGrew, 2005; Alfonso, Flanagan, & Radwan, 2005; MacCann, 2010).

**Stanford-Binet Intelligence Scales, Fifth Edition (SB5)** a test that consists of a series of items that vary according to the age of the person being tested

**Wechsler Intelligence Scale for Children, Fourth Edition (WISC-IV)** a test for children that provides separate measures of verbal and performance (or nonverbal) skills, as well as a total score

**Kaufman Assessment Battery for Children, Second Edition (KABC-II)** an intelligence test that measures children's ability to integrate different stimuli simultaneously and to use sequential thinking

**fluid intelligence** intelligence that reflects information processing capabilities, reasoning, and memory

**crystallized intelligence** the accumulation of information, skills, and strategies that people have learned through experience and that they can apply in problem-solving situations

| Name | Goal of Item | Example |
|---|---|---|
| **Verbal Scale** | | |
| Information | Assess general information | How many nickels make a dime? |
| Comprehension | Assess understanding and evaluation of social norms and past experience | What is the advantage of keeping money in the bank? |
| Arithmetic | Assess math reasoning through verbal problems | If two buttons cost 15 cents, what will be the cost of a dozen buttons? |
| Similarities | Test understanding of how objects or concepts are alike, tapping abstract reasoning | In what way are an hour and a week alike? |
| **Performance Scale** | | |
| Digit symbol | Assess speed of learning | Match symbols to numbers using key. |
| Picture completion | Visual memory and attention | Identify what is missing. |
| Object assembly | Test understanding of relationship of parts to wholes | Put pieces together to form a whole. |

**FIGURE 5-7 Measuring Intelligence**
The Wechsler Intelligence Scale for Children (WISC-IV) includes items such as these. What do such items cover? What do they miss?

Other theorists divide intelligence into even more parts. Psychologist Howard Gardner suggests that we have at least eight distinct intelligences, each relatively independent (see Figure 5-8). Gardner suggests that these intelligences operate together, depending on the activity we engage in (Gardner, 2000, 2003; Chen & Gardner, 2005; Gardner & Moran, 2006).

 **From an educator's perspective:** Does Howard Gardner's theory of multiple intelligences suggest that classroom instruction should be modified from an emphasis on the traditional three Rs of reading, writing, and arithmetic?

1. *Musical intelligence* (skills in tasks involving music). Case example:
When he was 3, Yehudi Menuhin was smuggled into the San Francisco Orchestra concerts by his parents. The sound of Louis Persinger's violin so entranced the youngster that he insisted on a violin for his birthday and Louis Persinger as his teacher. He got both. By the time he was 10 years old, Menuhin was an international performer.

2. *Bodily kinesthetic intelligence* (skills in using the whole body or various portions of it in the solution of problems or in the construction of products or displays, exemplified by dancers, athletes, actors, and surgeons). Case example:
Fifteen-year-old Babe Ruth played third base. During one game, his team's pitcher was doing poorly and Babe loudly criticized him from third base. Brother Mathias, the coach, called out, "Ruth, if you know so much about it, *you* pitch!" Babe was surprised and embarrassed because he had never pitched before, but Brother Mathias insisted. Ruth said later that at the very moment he took the pitcher's mound, he *knew* he was supposed to be a pitcher.

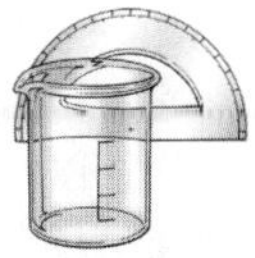

3. *Logical mathematical intelligence* (skills in problem solving and scientific thinking). Case example:
Barbara McClintock won the Nobel Prize in medicine for her work in microbiology. She describes one of her breakthroughs, which came after thinking about a problem for half an hour...: "Suddenly I jumped and ran back to the [corn] field. At the top of the field [the others were still at the bottom] I shouted, 'Eureka, I have it!'"

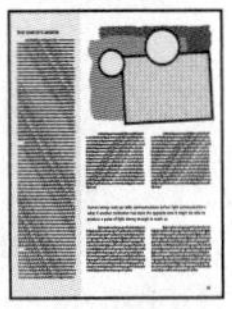

4. *Linguistic intelligence* (skills involved in the production and use of language). Case example:
At the age of 10, T. S. Eliot created a magazine called *Fireside*, to which he was the sole contributor. In a 3-day period during his winter vacation, he created eight complete issues.

5. *Spatial intelligence* (skills involving spatial configurations, such as those used by artists and architects). Case example:
Navigation around the Caroline Islands...is accomplished without instruments....During the actual trip, the navigator must envision mentally a reference island as it passes under a particular star and from that he computes the number of segments completed, the proportion of the trip remaining, and any corrections in heading.

6. *Interpersonal intelligence* (skills in interacting with others, such as sensitivity to the moods, temperaments, motivations, and intentions of others). Case example:
When Anne Sullivan began instructing the deaf and blind Helen Keller, her task was one that had eluded others for years. Yet, just 2 weeks after beginning her work with Keller, Sullivan achieved a great success. In her words, "My heart is singing with joy this morning. A miracle has happened! The wild little creature of 2 weeks ago has been transformed into a gentle child."

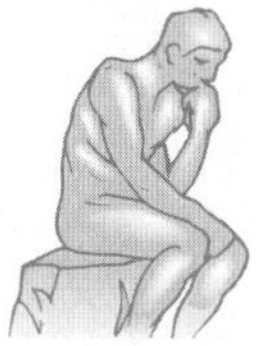

7. *Intrapersonal intelligence* (knowledge of the internal aspects of oneself; access to one's own feelings and emotions). Case example:
In her essay "A Sketch of the Past," Virginia Woolf displays deep insight into her own inner life through these lines, describing her reaction to several specific memories from her childhood that still, in adulthood, shock her: "Though I still have the peculiarity that I receive these sudden shocks, they are now always welcome; after the first surprise, I always feel instantly that they are particularly valuable. And so I go on to suppose that the shock-receiving capacity is what makes me a writer."

8. *Naturalist intelligence* (ability to identify and classify patterns in nature). Case example:
In prehistoric periods, hunter-gatherers required naturalist intelligence in order to identify what types of plants were edible.

**FIGURE 5-8 Gardner's Eight Intelligences**
Howard Gardner has theorized that there are eight distinct intelligences, each relatively independent.
Source: From "Gardners Eight Intelligences" from Walters, E., & Gardner, H. [1986]. *The theory of multiple intelligences: Some issues and answers.* In R. J. Sternberg & R. K. Wagner (Eds.) Practical Intelligence. Cambridge, England: Cambridge University Press.

Russian psychologist Lev Vygotsky, whose cognitive development approach we discussed earlier, took a very different approach to intelligence. He suggested we assess intelligence by looking not only at fully developed cognitive processes, but those in current development as well. To do this, he contended that assessment tasks should involve cooperative interaction between the assessed individual and the assessor—a process called *dynamic assessment*. In short, intelligence is reflected both in how children perform on their own and how they perform when helped by adults (Vygotsky, 1926/1976; Lohman, 2005).

Psychologist Robert Sternberg (1987, 1990, 2003a), taking another approach, suggests intelligence is best viewed as information processing. In this view, how people store material in memory and later use it to solve intellectual tasks provides the most precise concept of intelligence. Rather than focusing on the subcomponents that make up the *structure* of intelligence, information processing approaches examine the *processes* underlying intelligent behavior (Floyd, 2005).

Studies of the nature and speed of problem-solving processes show that people with higher intelligence levels differ from others in the number of problems they solve and the methods they use. People with high IQ scores spend more time on the initial stages of problem solving, retrieving relevant information from memory. In contrast, those who score lower tend to skip ahead and make less informed guesses. The processes used in solving problems may reflect important differences in intelligence (Sternberg, 2005).

Sternberg's work on information processing approaches led him to develop the **triarchic theory of intelligence.** In this model, three aspects of information processing denote intelligence: the componential, the experiential, and the contextual. The componential aspect reflects how efficiently people process and analyze information. Efficiency in these areas allows people to infer relationships among different parts of a problem, solve the problem, and then evaluate their solution. People with a strong componential element score highest on traditional tests of intelligence (Sternberg, 2005).

The *experiential* element is the insightful component of intelligence. People with a strong experiential element can easily compare new material with what they know, and can combine and relate known facts in novel and creative ways. Finally, the *contextual* element concerns practical intelligence, or ways of dealing with everyday demands.

In Sternberg's view, people vary in the degree to which they possess each of these elements. Our level of success at any task reflects the match between the task and our own pattern of strength on these three components (Sternberg, 2003b, 2008).

## Group Differences in IQ

A "jontry" is an example of a

    (a) rulpow

    (b) flink

    (c) spudge

    (d) bakwoe

If you found an item composed of nonsense words such as this on an intelligence test, you would likely complain. What sort of intelligence test uses items that incorporate meaningless terms?

Yet for some people, the items used on traditional intelligence tests might appear nonsensical. As a hypothetical example, suppose rural children were asked details about subways, while urban students were asked about the mating practices of sheep. In both cases, we would expect the test-takers' prior experiences to substantially affect their ability to answer the questions. On an IQ test, such questions could rightly be seen as a measure of prior experience rather than of intelligence. ◉ Watch on mydevelopmentlab.com

Although traditional IQ tests are not so obviously dependent upon test-takers' prior experiences, cultural background and experience can affect test scores. In fact, many educators feel that traditional measures of intelligence subtly favor White, upper- and middle-class students over other cultural groups (Ortiz & Dynda, 2005).

***Explaining Racial Differences in IQ.*** How cultural background and experience affect IQ test scores has led to much debate among researchers, fueled by the finding that certain racial

---

◉ Watch on **mydevelopmentlab.com**

How is your virtual child doing in school? Do you think that standardized testing should be used to assess his or her performance in school?

**triarchic theory of intelligence** a model that states that intelligence consists of three aspects of information processing: the componential element, the experiential element, and the contextual element

groups' IQ scores are consistently lower, on average, than those of other groups. For example, the mean score of African Americans tends to be about 15 points below the mean score of Whites—although the measured difference varies a great deal depending on the IQ test employed (Fish, 2001; Maller, 2003).

The question that emerges from such differences is whether they reflect differences in intelligence or biases in intelligence tests. For example, if Whites outperform African Americans on an IQ test because they are more familiar with the language of the test items, the test can hardly be judged a fair measure of African Americans' intelligence. Similarly, a test that solely used African American Vernacular English would not be an impartial measure of intelligence for Whites.

How to interpret differences between the IQ test scores of different cultural groups is a major controversy in child development: To what degree is intelligence determined by heredity, to what degree by environment? The social implications make this issue important. If intelligence is mostly hereditary and therefore largely fixed at birth, attempts to alter cognitive abilities, such as schooling, will have limited success. If intelligence is largely environmentally determined, modifying social and educational conditions is a more promising strategy to increase cognitive functioning (Weiss, 2003).

*The Bell Curve Controversy.* Although the relative contributions of heredity and environment to intelligence have been investigated for decades, the smoldering debate became a raging fire with the publication of a book by Richard J. Herrnstein and Charles Murray (1994), titled *The Bell Curve*. Herrnstein and Murray argue that the average 15-point IQ difference between Whites and African Americans is due primarily to heredity. They also argue that this difference accounts for the higher rates of poverty, lower employment, and higher use of welfare among minority groups.

Performance on traditional IQ tests is dependent in part on test-takers' prior experiences and cultural background.

These conclusions met with outrage, and many researchers who examined the data used in the book came to quite different conclusions. Most developmentalists and psychologists argued that racial differences in measured IQ can be explained by environmental differences. In fact, mean IQ scores of Black and White children are quite similar when various economic and social factors are statistically taken into account simultaneously. For instance, children from similar middle-class backgrounds, whether African American or White, tend to have similar IQ scores (Brooks-Gunn, Klebanov, & Duncan, 1996; Alderfer, 2003).

Critics also maintained there is little evidence that IQ causes poverty and other social ills. In fact, some critics suggested, as mentioned earlier, that IQ scores were unrelated to later success in life (e.g., Nisbett, 1994; Reifman, 2000; Sternberg, 2005).

Finally, members of cultural and social minority groups may score lower than those in the majority group due to the biases of the tests. Traditional IQ tests may discriminate against minority groups who lack exposure to the environment majority group members have experienced (Fagan & Holland, 2007; Razani et al., 2007).

Most traditional IQ tests are constructed using White, English-speaking, middle-class populations as their test subjects. Thus, children from different backgrounds may perform poorly on them—not because they are less intelligent, but because the questions are culturally biased in favor of the majority group. A classic study found that in one California school district, Mexican American students were 10 times more likely than Whites to be placed in special education classes (Mercer, 1973; Hatton, 2002). More recent findings show that nationally, twice as many African American students as White students are classified as mildly retarded, a difference attributed primarily to cultural bias and poverty (Reschly, 1996; Terman et al., 1996). Although certain IQ tests (such as the *System of Multicultural Pluralistic Assessment*, or *SOMPA*) are designed to be valid regardless of cultural background, no test can be completely unbiased (Reschly, 1996; Sandoval et al., 1998; Hatton, 2002).

In short, most experts were not convinced by *The Bell Curve* contention that genetic factors largely determine differences in group IQ scores. Still, we cannot put the issue to rest, because it is impossible to design a definitive experiment to determine the cause of these differences. (One cannot ethically assign children to different living conditions to find the effects of environment, nor genetically control or alter intelligence levels in unborn children.)

Today, IQ is seen as the product of *both* nature and nurture interacting in a complex manner. Genes are seen to affect experiences, and experiences are viewed as influencing the expression of genes. Psychologist Eric Turkheimer found evidence that while environmental factors

This boy with mental retardation is mainstreamed into this fifth-grade class.

play a larger role in the IQ of poor children, genes are more influential for affluent children (Turkheimer et al., 2003; Harden, Turkheimer, & Loehlin, 2007).

Ultimately, determining the absolute degree to which intelligence is influenced by genetic and environmental factors may be less important than improving children's living conditions and educational experiences. Enriching the quality of children's environments will better permit all children to reach their full potential and to maximize their contributions to society (Wachs, 1996; Wickelgren, 1999; Posthuma & de Geus, 2006; Nisbett, 2008).

## Below and Above Intelligence Norms: Intellectual Disabilities and Intellectual Giftedness

*Although Connie kept pace with her peers in kindergarten, by first grade, she was academically the slowest in almost every subject. She tried hard but it took her longer than the others to absorb new material, and she regularly required special attention to keep up with the class.*

*In some areas, though, she excelled: When asked to draw or produce something with her hands, her performance exceeded her classmates'. She produced beautiful work that was much admired. The other students in the class felt that there was something different about Connie, but they couldn't identify the source of the difference and spent little time pondering the issue.*

Connie's parents and teacher, though, knew what made her special. Extensive testing in kindergarten had shown that Connie's intelligence was well below normal, and she was officially classified as a special needs student.

If Connie had been attending school before 1975, she would most likely have been placed in a special needs classroom as soon as her low IQ was identified. Such classes, consisting of students with a range of afflictions, including emotional difficulties, severe reading problems, and physical disabilities such as multiple sclerosis, as well as those with lower IQs, were usually kept separate from the regular educational process.

All that changed in 1975 when Congress passed Public Law 94–142, the Education for All Handicapped Children Act. The intent of the law—an intent largely realized—was to ensure that special needs children were educated in the **least restrictive environment,** that is, the setting most similar to that of children without special needs (Yell, 1995; Rozalski, Stewart, & Miller, 2010).

In practice, the law has integrated children with special needs into regular classrooms and activities to the greatest extent possible, as long as doing so is educationally beneficial. Children are to be removed from the regular classroom only for those subjects specifically affected by their exceptionality; for all other subjects, they are to be taught in regular classrooms. Of course, some children with severe handicaps still need a mostly or entirely separate education. But the law integrates exceptional children and typical children to the fullest extent possible (Yell, 1995).

This approach to special education, designed to minimize the segregation of exceptional students, is called mainstreaming. In **mainstreaming,** exceptional children are integrated as much as possible into the regular education system and provided with a broad range of alternatives (Hocutt, 1996; Belkin, 2004).

The benefits of mainstreaming have led some professionals to promote an alternative educational model known as full inclusion. *Full inclusion* is the integration of all students, even those with the most severe disabilities, into regular classes. In such a system, separate special education programs would cease to operate. Full inclusion is controversial, and it remains to be seen how widespread such a practice will become (Brehm, 2003; Gersten & Dimino, 2006; Begeny & Martens, 2007; Lindsay, 2007).

Regardless of whether they are educated using mainstreaming or full inclusion, children whose intelligence is significantly beyond the typical range represent a challenge for educators. We will consider both those who are below and those who are above the norms.

**least restrictive environment** the setting that is most similar to that of children without special needs

**mainstreaming** an educational approach in which exceptional children are integrated to the extent possible into the traditional educational system and are provided with a broad range of educational alternatives

***Below the Norm: Mental Retardation (Intellectual Disability).*** Approximately 1 to 3 percent of the school-age population is considered to have mental retardation. **Mental retardation**—or **intellectual disability,** as it is increasingly being called—is characterized by significant limitations in intellectual functioning and in adaptive behavior involving conceptual, social, and practical skills (AAMR, 2002). (Although experts are increasingly using the term *intellectual disabilities* instead of *mental retardation,* our discussion will use the original term because it continues to be more widespread.)

Most cases of mental retardation are classified as *familial retardation,* in which no cause is apparent beyond a history of retardation in the family. In other cases, there is a clear biological cause. The most common such causes are *fetal alcohol syndrome,* resulting from the mother's use of alcohol while pregnant, and *Down syndrome,* caused by the presence of an extra chromosome. Birth complications, such as a temporary lack of oxygen, may also produce retardation (Plomin, 2005; West & Blake, 2005; Manning & Hoyme, 2007).

Although cognitive limitations can be measured using standard IQ tests, it is more difficult to gauge limitations in other areas. This leads to imprecision in the ways the label "mental retardation" is applied. It also means significant variation exists in the abilities of people categorized as mentally retarded, ranging from those who can be taught to work and function with little special attention to those who are virtually untrainable and who never develop speech or such basic motor skills as crawling or walking.

Some 90 percent of the mentally retarded have relatively low deficit levels. Classified with **mild retardation,** they score in the range of 50 or 55 to 70 on IQ tests. Their retardation may not be identified before they reach school, although their early development is often slower than average. Once they enter school, their retardation and need for special attention usually become apparent, as it did with Connie, the first-grader profiled earlier. With appropriate training, these students can reach a third- to sixth-grade level. Although they cannot do complex intellectual tasks, they can hold jobs and function independently and successfully.

Intellectual and adaptive limitations become more apparent at higher levels of mental retardation. People with IQ scores of 35 or 40 to 50 or 55 are classified with **moderate retardation.** The moderately retarded—5 to 10 percent of the mentally retarded population—behave distinctively early in their lives; that is, they are slow to develop language and motor skills. Regular schooling is seldom effective in teaching the moderately retarded academic skills because they generally cannot progress beyond a second-grade level. Still, they can learn occupational and social skills, and they can learn to travel independently to familiar places. Typically, they require moderate levels of supervision.

For those classified as **severely retarded** (IQs ranging from 20 or 25 to 35 or 40) and **profoundly retarded** (IQs below 20 or 25), functioning is severely limited. Usually, such people have little or no speech, poor motor control, and may need 24-hour nursing care. At the same time, some people with severe retardation are capable of learning basic self-care skills, such as dressing and eating, and they may become partially independent as adults. Still, relatively high levels of care are required throughout life, and most severely and profoundly retarded people are institutionalized for the majority of their lives.

***Above the Norm: The Gifted and Talented.*** *Before her second birthday, Audrey Walker recognized sequences of five colors. When she was 6, her father, Michael, overheard her telling a little boy: "No, no, no, Hunter, you don't understand. What you were seeing was a flashback."*

*At school, Audrey quickly grew bored as the teacher drilled letters and syllables until her classmates caught on. She flourished, instead, in a once-a-week class for gifted and talented children where she could learn as fast as her nimble brain could take her. (Schemo, 2004, p. A18)*

It sometimes surprises people that the gifted and talented are considered to have a form of exceptionality. Yet the 3 to 5 percent of such children present special challenges of their own.

There is no formal definition of **gifted and talented** students. However, the federal government considers the term *gifted* to include "children who give evidence of high performance capability in areas such as intellectual, creative, artistic, leadership capacity, or specific academic fields, and who require services or activities not ordinarily provided by the school in order to fully develop such capabilities" (Sec. 582, P.L. 97–35). In addition to intellectual exceptionality, unusual potential in nonacademic areas is also included in the concept. Gifted and talented

**mental retardation (intellectual disability)** a significantly subaverage level of intellectual functioning that occurs with related limitations in two or more skill areas

**mild retardation** retardation in which IQ scores fall in the range of 50 or 55 to 70

**moderate retardation** retardation in which IQ scores range from around 35 or 40 to 50 or 55

**severe retardation** retardation in which IQ scores range from around 20 or 25 to 35 or 40

**profound retardation** retardation in which IQ scores fall below 20 or 25

**gifted and talented** children who show evidence of high performance capability in areas such as intellectual, creative, artistic, leadership capacity, or specific academic fields

**acceleration** special programs that allow gifted students to move ahead at their own pace, even if this means skipping to higher grade levels

**enrichment** an approach through which students are kept at grade level but are enrolled in special programs and given individual activities to allow greater depth of study on a given topic

children, no less than students with low IQs, warrant special concern—although programs for them are often the first to be dropped when schools face budgetary problems (Robinson, Zigler, & Gallagher, 2000; Schemo, 2004; Mendoza, 2006).

Despite the stereotype that the gifted are "unsociable," "poorly adjusted," and "neurotic," research suggests that highly intelligent people tend to be outgoing, well adjusted, and popular (Bracken & Brown, 2006; Shaunessy et al., 2006; Cross et al., 2008).

For instance, one landmark, long-term study of 1,500 gifted students, which began in the 1920s, found that the gifted were healthier, better coordinated, and psychologically better adjusted than their less intelligent classmates. Furthermore, they received more awards and distinctions, earned more money, and made many more contributions in art and literature than the average person. By the time they had reached age 40, they had collectively produced more than 90 books, 375 plays and short stories, and 2,000 articles, and they had registered more than 200 patents. Perhaps not surprisingly, they reported greater satisfaction with their lives than the nongifted (Terman & Oden, 1959; Sears, 1977; Shurkin, 1992; Reis & Renzulli, 2004).

Yet being gifted and talented is no guarantee of school success. The verbal abilities that allow the expression of ideas and feelings can equally voice glib and persuasive statements that happen to be inaccurate. Furthermore, teachers sometimes misinterpret the humor, novelty, and creativity of unusually gifted children and regard their intellectual fervor as disruptive or inappropriate. And peers may be unsympathetic: Some very bright children try to hide their intelligence in an effort to fit in (Swiatek, 2002).

***Educating the Gifted and Talented.*** Educators have devised two approaches to teaching the gifted and talented: acceleration and enrichment. **Acceleration** allows gifted students to move ahead at their own pace, even if this means skipping grade levels. The materials in acceleration programs are not always different; they may simply be provided at a faster pace than for the average student (Smutny, Walker, & Meckstroth, 2007; Wells, Lohman, & Marron, 2009; Wood et al., 2010).

An alternative approach is **enrichment,** through which students are kept at grade level but are enrolled in special programs and given individual activities to allow greater depth of study. In enrichment, the material differs not only in the timing of its presentation, but in its sophistication as well. Thus, enrichment materials are designed to provide an intellectual challenge to the gifted student, encouraging higher-order thinking (Worrell, Szarko, & Gabelko, 2001; Rotigel, 2003).

## REVIEW, CHECK, AND APPLY

### REVIEW

**L09** How can intelligence be measured?

- Measuring intelligence has traditionally been a matter of testing skills that promote academic success. Among tests used to measure intelligence are the Wechsler Intelligence Scale for Children, Fourth Edition (WISC-IV), and the Kaufman Assessment Battery for Children, Second Edition (KABC-II).

- Recent theories of intelligence suggest there may be several distinct intelligences or several components of intelligence that reflect different ways of processing information.

**L010** How are exceptional children educated?

- U.S. educators are attempting to deal with large numbers of exceptional persons whose intellectual and other skills are significantly lower or higher than normal.

- By law, children with special needs must be educated in the least restrictive environment.

This has led to mainstreaming, which integrates such children into the regular education system as much as possible.

- The needs of gifted and talented children are sometimes addressed through acceleration and enrichment programs.

### CHECK YOURSELF

1. Intelligence is the capacity to understand the world, think with rationality, and use resources effectively when faced with challenges.
   - True
   - False

2. According to Howard Gardner, we have at least eight distinct intelligences, each relatively independent.
   - True
   - False

3. For children whose intelligence falls below the normal range, the recommendation from the

Education for All Handicapped Children Act is that they be educated in the _____ environment.

a. moderately restrictive

b. average educational

c. least restrictive

d. most restrictive

### APPLYING LIFESPAN DEVELOPMENT

- How do fluid and crystallized intelligence interact? Which of the two is likely to be more influenced by genetics and which by environment? Why?

✓—[**Study** and **Review** on **MyDevelopmentLab.com**

## MODULE 5.3 Social and Personality Development in Middle Childhood

*As a small child, Henry was popular and outgoing. He enjoyed his first day of preschool so much, with all the new playmates and activities, that he actually thanked his mother for taking him. It seemed he would never lack for friendship during his childhood years.*

*But as Henry advanced in grade school, things started to change. By the third grade, the boys in Henry's school had started to play football, a game Henry hated. He played with the girls for a while, but this brought teasing from the other boys. Plus, the girls began to form rival clubs, all of which had one thing in common: No boys allowed.*

*Eventually, Henry decided to give football a try. But in the end the game was just too rough for him. Henry's mother asked if there really weren't any other boys who didn't like football, either. "Some of them don't like football, either," Henry explained to her, "but they play because they don't want to be an outcast." Henry's mother understood the implications of her son's words all too well: the others didn't want to become "an outcast like me." (Renkl, 2009)*

Henry's experience is not uncommon. As children grow into middle childhood, the way they relate to others and the way they think of themselves undergo significant transformations. Sometimes, these transformations are fairly smooth. However, as Henry's story shows, they can also present children and parents with new and unexpected challenges.

In this module, we focus on social and personality development during middle childhood. It is a time when children's views of themselves change, they form new bonds with friends and family, and they become increasingly attached to social institutions outside the home.

We start our consideration of personality and social development during middle childhood by examining the changes that occur in the ways children see themselves. We discuss how they view their personal characteristics and examine the complex issue of self-esteem. Next, the module turns to relationships during middle childhood, discussing the stages of friendship and the ways gender and ethnicity affect how and with whom children interact. Finally, we explore the central societal institution in children's lives: the family. We consider the consequences of divorce, self-care children, and the phenomenon of group care.

# The Developing Self

LO11 **In what ways do children's views of themselves change during middle childhood?**

**LO12** Why is self-esteem important during middle childhood?

**LO13** How does children's sense of right and wrong change as they age?

**LEARNING OBJECTIVES**

*Nine-year-old Karl Haglund is perched in his eagle's nest, a treehouse built high in the willow that grows in his backyard. Sometimes he sits there alone among the tree's spreading branches, his face turned toward the sky, a boy clearly enjoying his solitude....*

*This morning Karl is busy sawing and hammering. "It's fun to build," he says. "I started the house when I was 4 years old. Then when I was about 7, my dad built me this platform. 'Cause all my places were falling apart and they were crawling with carpenter ants. So we destroyed them and then built me a deck. And I built on top of it. It's stronger now. You can have privacy here, but it's a bad place to go when it's windy 'cause you almost get blown off." (Kotre & Hall, 1990, p. 116)*

As children become older, they begin to characterize themselves in terms of their psychological attributes as well as their physical achievements.

Karl's growing sense of competence is reflected in his description of how he and his father built his treehouse. Conveying what psychologist Erik Erikson calls "industriousness," Karl's quiet pride in his accomplishment illustrates one way children's views of themselves evolve.

## Psychosocial Development in Middle Childhood: Industry versus Inferiority

According to Erik Erikson, middle childhood is largely about competence. Lasting from roughly ages 6 to 12, the **industry-versus-inferiority stage** is characterized by efforts to meet the challenges presented by parents, peers, school, and the complex modern world.

During this period, children direct their energies to mastering the enormous body of information presented in school and making a place for themselves in their social worlds. Success in this stage brings feelings of mastery and a growing sense of competence, like those expressed by Karl regarding his building experience. On the other hand, difficulties in this stage lead to feelings of failure and inadequacy. As a result, children may withdraw from academic pursuits, showing less interest and motivation to excel, and from interactions with peers.

The sense of industry that children such as Karl attain at this stage has lasting effects. One study examined how childhood industriousness and hard work were related to adult behavior by following a group of 450 men over a 35-year period, starting in early childhood (Vaillant & Vaillant, 1981). The men who were most industrious and hard-working as children were most successful as adults, both professionally and personally. In fact, childhood industriousness was more closely associated with adult success than was intelligence or family background.

## Understanding One's Self: A New Response to "Who Am I?"

During middle childhood, children seek to answer the question "Who am I?" Although the question will assume greater urgency in adolescence, elementary-age children still try to find their place in the world.

***The Shift in Self-Understanding from the Physical to the Psychological.*** The cognitive advances discussed in the previous module aid children in their quest for self-understanding. They begin to view themselves less in terms of external, physical attributes and more in terms of psychological traits (Marsh & Ayotte, 2003; Sotiriou & Zafiropoulou, 2003; Lerner, Theokas, & Jelicic, 2005; Thompson & Virmani, 2010).

For instance, 6-year-old Carey describes herself as "a fast runner and good at drawing"—characteristics dependent on motor skills in external activities. In contrast, 11-year-old Meiping characterizes herself as "pretty smart, friendly, and helpful to my friends." Because of her increasing cognitive skills, Meiping's view of herself is based on psychological characteristics, inner traits that are more abstract.

Children's views of who they are also become more complex. In Erikson's view, children are seeking endeavors where they can be successfully industrious. As they get older, children discover their strengths and weaknesses. Ten-year-old Ginny, for instance, comes to understand she is good at arithmetic but not very good at spelling; 11-year-old Alberto decides he is good at softball but lacks the stamina to play soccer well.

Children's self-concepts become divided into personal and academic spheres. They evaluate themselves in four major areas, each of which can be broken down further; for example, the nonacademic self-concept includes physical appearance, peer relations, and physical ability, while the academic self-concept is similarly divided. Research on students' self-concepts in English, mathematics, and nonacademic realms shows that the separate realms do not always correlate, although overlap exists. For example, a child who sees herself as a star math student will not necessarily feel she is great at English (Burnett & Proctor, 2002; Marsh & Ayotte, 2003; Marsh & Hau, 2004).

**industry-versus-inferiority stage** according to Erikson the period from age 6 to 12 characterized by a focus on efforts to attain competence in meeting the challenges presented by parents, peers, school, and the other complexities of the modern world

# Moral Development

*Your wife is near death from an unusual kind of cancer. One drug exists that the physicians think might save her—a form of radium that a scientist in a nearby city has recently developed. The drug, though, is expensive to manufacture, and the scientist is charging ten times what the drug costs him to make. He pays $1,000 for the radium and charges $10,000 for a small dose. You have gone to everyone you know to borrow money, but you can only get $2,500—one-quarter of what you need. You've told the scientist that your wife is dying and asked him to sell it more cheaply or let you pay later. But the scientist has said, "No, I discovered the drug and I'm going to make money from it." In desperation, you consider breaking into the scientist's laboratory to steal the drug for your wife. Should you do it?*

According to developmental psychologist Lawrence Kohlberg and his colleagues, the answer that children give to this question reveals central aspects of their sense of morality and justice. He suggests that people's responses to moral dilemmas such as this one reveal their stage of moral development—as well as information about their level of cognitive development (Kohlberg, 1984; Colby & Kohlberg, 1987).

Kohlberg contends that people pass through stages as their sense of justice evolves and the reasoning they use to make moral judgments changes. Younger school-age children tend to think in terms of either concrete, unvarying rules ("It is always wrong to steal" or "I'll be punished if I steal") or the rules of society ("Good people don't steal" or "What if everyone stole?").

By adolescence, however, individuals can reason on a higher plane, typically having reached Piaget's stage of formal operations. They are capable of comprehending abstract, formal principles of morality, and they consider broader issues of morality and of right and wrong in cases like the one just presented. ("Stealing may be acceptable if you are following your own conscience and doing the right thing.")

Kohlberg suggests that moral development emerges in a three-level sequence, further subdivided into six stages (see Table 5-1 on page 240). At the lowest level, *preconventional morality* (Stages 1 and 2), people follow rigid rules based on punishments or rewards (e.g., a student might evaluate the moral dilemma in the story by saying it was not worth stealing the drug because you could go to jail). 👁 Watch on **mydevelopmentlab.com**

In the next level, *conventional morality* (Stages 3 and 4), people approach moral problems as good, responsible members of society. Some would decide *against* stealing the drug because they would feel guilty or dishonest for violating social norms. Others would decide *in favor* of stealing the drug because they would be unable to face others if they did nothing. All of these people would be reasoning at the conventional level of morality.

Finally, individuals using *postconventional morality* (Stages 5 and 6) invoke universal moral principles that are considered broader than the rules of their particular society. People who would condemn themselves if they did not steal the drug because they would be violating their own moral principles are reasoning at the postconventional level.

Kohlberg's theory proposes that people move through the stages in a fixed order and are unable to reach the highest stage until adolescence, due to deficits in cognitive development before then (Kurtines & Gewirtz, 1987). However, not everyone is presumed to reach the highest stages: Kohlberg found that postconventional reasoning is relatively rare.

Although Kohlberg's theory provides a good account of the development of moral *judgments*, the links with moral *behavior* are less strong. Still, students at higher stages are less likely to engage in antisocial behavior at school and in the community. One experiment found that 15 percent of students who reasoned at the postconventional level cheated when given the opportunity, compared to more than half of students at lower levels. Though those at higher levels cheated less, they still cheated. Clearly, knowing what is right is not the same as acting that way (Snarey, 1995; Killen & Hart, 1995; Hart, Burock, & London, 2003; Semerci, 2006).

Kohlberg's theory has also been criticized because it is based solely on observations of Western cultures. In fact, cross-cultural research finds that those in more industrialized, technologically advanced cultures move through the stages more rapidly than members of nonindustrialized countries. One explanation is that Kohlberg's higher stages are based on moral reasoning involving governmental and societal institutions such as the police and court system. In less industrialized areas, morality may be based more on relationships between people. In short, the nature of morality may differ in diverse cultures, and Kohlberg's theory is more suited for Western cultures (Fu et al., 2007).

👁 Watch on **mydevelopmentlab.com**

Log onto MyDevelopmentLab.com and watch the video "Kohlberg and the Heinz Dilemma." In the interviews, children display Kohlberg's theories that you've just been reading about.

## TABLE 5-1 KOHLBERG'S SEQUENCE OF MORAL REASONING

| Level | Stage | Sample Moral Reasoning | |
|---|---|---|---|
| | | **In Favor of Stealing** | **Against Stealing** |
| **LEVEL 1** **Preconventional morality:** At this level, the concrete interests of the individual are considered in terms of rewards and punishments. | **STAGE 1** Obedience and punishment orientation: At this stage, people stick to rules in order to avoid punishment, and obedience occurs for its own sake. | "If you let your wife die, you will get in trouble. You'll be blamed for not spending the money to save her, and there'll be an investigation of you and the druggist for your wife's death." | "You shouldn't steal the drug because you'll get caught and sent to jail if you do. If you do get away, your conscience will bother you thinking how the police will catch up with you at any minute." |
| | **STAGE 2** Reward orientation: At this stage, rules are followed only for a person's own benefit. Obedience occurs because of rewards that are received. | "If you do happen to get caught, you could give the drug back and you wouldn't get much of a sentence. It wouldn't bother you much to serve a little jail term, if you have your wife when you get out." | "You may not get much of a jail term if you steal the drug, but your wife will probably die before you get out, so it won't do much good. If your wife dies, you shouldn't blame yourself; it isn't your fault she has cancer." |
| **LEVEL 2** **Conventional morality:** At this level, people approach moral problems as members of society. They are interested in pleasing others by acting as good members of society. | **STAGE 3** "Good boy" morality: Individuals at this stage show an interest in maintaining the respect of others and doing what is expected of them. | "No one will think you're bad if you steal the drug, but your family will think you're an inhuman husband if you don't. If you let your wife die, you'll never be able to look anybody in the face again." | "It isn't just the druggist who will think you're a criminal; everyone else will, too. After you steal the drug, you'll feel bad thinking how you've brought dishonor on your family and yourself; you won't be able to face anyone again." |
| | **STAGE 4** Authority and social-order-maintaining morality: People at this stage conform to society's rules and consider that "right" is what society defines as right. | "If you have any sense of honor, you won't let your wife die just because you're afraid to do the only thing that will save her. You'll always feel guilty that you caused her death if you don't do your duty to her." | "You're desperate and you may not know you're doing wrong when you steal the drug. But you'll know you did wrong after you're sent to jail. You'll always feel guilty for your dishonesty and law-breaking." |
| **LEVEL 3** **Postconventional morality:** At this level, people use moral principles, which are seen as broader than those of any particular society. | **STAGE 5** Morality of contract, individual rights, and democratically accepted law: People at this stage do what is right because of a sense of obligation to laws that are agreed upon within society. They perceive that laws can be modified as part of changes in an implicit social contract. | "You'll lose other people's respect, not gain it, if you don't steal. If you let your wife die, it will be out of fear, not out of reasoning. So you'll just lose self-respect and probably the respect of others, too." | "You'll lose your standing and respect in the community and violate the law. You'll lose respect for yourself if you're carried away by emotion and forget the long-range point of view." |
| | **STAGE 6** Morality of individual principles and conscience: At this final stage, a person follows laws because they are based on universal ethical principles. Laws that violate the principles are disobeyed. | "If you don't steal the drug, and if you let your wife die, you'll always condemn yourself for it afterward. You won't be blamed and you'll have lived up to the outside rule of the law, but you won't have lived up to your own standards of conscience." | "If you steal the drug, you won't be blamed by other people, but you'll condemn yourself because you won't have lived up to your own conscience and standards of honesty." |

Source: Adapted from Kohlberg, 1969.

In addition, developmental psychologist Elliot Turiel has argued that Kohlberg did not sufficiently distinguish moral reasoning from other sorts of reasoning. In Turiel's view, called *moral domain theory,* he argues that children distinguish between the domains of social conventional reasoning and moral reasoning. In social conventional reasoning, the focus is on rules that have been established by society such as eating mashed potatoes with a fork or asking to be excused after eating. Such rules are largely arbitrary (does it really matter if a child uses a spoon to eat mashed potatoes?). In contrast, moral reasoning focuses on issues of fairness, justice, the rights of others, and avoidance of harm to others. In comparison to social conventional rules, whose purpose is to ensure the smooth functioning of society, moral rules are based on more abstract concepts of justice (Turiel, 2006, 2008, 2010).

Finally, an additional problematic aspect of Kohlberg's theory is the difficulty it has explaining *girls'* moral judgments. Because Kohlberg's theory was based largely on data from males, some researchers have argued that it better describes boys' moral development than girls'. This would explain the surprising finding that women typically score at a lower level than men on tests of moral judgments using Kohlberg's stages. This result has led to an alternative account of moral development for girls.

***Moral Development in Girls.***  Psychologist Carol Gilligan (1982, 1987) has suggested that differences in the ways boys and girls are raised in our society lead to basic distinctions in how men and women view moral behavior. According to her, boys view morality primarily in terms of broad principles such as justice or fairness, while girls see it in terms of responsibility toward individuals and willingness to sacrifice themselves to help specific individuals within the context of particular relationships. Compassion for individuals, then, is a greater factor in moral behavior for women than it is for men (Gilligan, Ward, & Taylor, 1988; Gilligan, Lyons, & Hammer, 1990; Gump, Baker, & Roll, 2000; Fumagalli et al., 2010).

Gilligan views morality as developing among females in a three-stage process (summarized in Table 5-2). In the first stage, called "orientation toward individual survival," females first concentrate on what is practical and best for them, gradually making a transition from selfishness to responsibility, that is, thinking about what would be best for others. In the second stage, termed "goodness as self-sacrifice," females begin to think they must sacrifice their own wishes to those of others.

Ideally, women make a transition from "goodness" to "truth," in which they take into account their own needs, too. This transition leads to the third stage, "morality of nonviolence," in which women decide that hurting anyone is immoral—including themselves. This realization establishes a moral equivalence between themselves and others and represents, according to Gilligan, the most sophisticated level of moral reasoning.

## TABLE 5-2  GILLIGAN'S THREE STAGES OF MORAL DEVELOPMENT IN WOMEN

| Stage | Characteristics | Example |
|---|---|---|
| **Stage 1** | | |
| Orientation toward individual survival | Initial concentration is on what is practical and best for self. Gradual transition from selfishness to responsibility, which includes thinking about what would be best for others. | A first grader may insist on playing only games of her own choosing when playing with a friend. |
| **Stage 2** | | |
| Goodness as self-sacrifice | Initial view is that a woman must sacrifice her own wishes to what other people want. Gradual transition from "goodness" to "truth," which takes into account needs of both self and others. | Now older, the same girl may believe that to be a good friend, she must play the games her friend chooses, even if she herself doesn't like them. |
| **Stage 3** | | |
| Morality of nonviolence | A moral equivalence is established between self and others. Hurting anyone—including one's self—is seen as immoral. Most sophisticated form of reasoning, according to Gilligan. | The same girl may realize that both friends must enjoy their time together and look for activities that both she and her friend can enjoy. |

It is obvious that Gilligan's sequence of stages is quite different from Kohlberg's, and some developmentalists have suggested that her rejection of Kohlberg's work is too sweeping and that gender differences are not as pronounced as first thought (Colby & Damon, 1987). For instance, some researchers argue that both males and females use similar "justice" and "care" orientations in making moral judgments. Clearly, the question of how boys and girls differ in their moral orientations, as well as the nature of moral development in general, is far from settled (Weisz & Black, 2002; Jorgensen, 2006; Tappan, 2006; Donleavy, 2008).

## REVIEW, CHECK, AND APPLY

### REVIEW

**LO11** In what ways do children's views of themselves change during middle childhood?

- According to Erikson, children at this time are in the industry-versus-inferiority stage.

- In middle childhood, children begin to use social comparison, and self-concepts based on psychological rather than physical characteristics.

**LO12** Why is self-esteem important during middle childhood?

- In middle childhood children increasingly develop their own internal standards of success, and measure how well they compare to those standards.

**LO13** How does children's sense of right and wrong change as they age?

- According to Kohlberg, moral development proceeds from a concern with rewards and punishments, through a focus on social conventions and rules, toward a sense of universal moral principles. Gilligan has suggested, however, that girls may follow a different progression of moral development.

### CHECK YOURSELF

1. According to Erikson, children ages 6 to 12 focus on efforts to meet the challenges presented by parents, peers, and school. This stage is _____.
   a. autonomy versus shame and doubt
   b. trust versus mistrust
   c. self versus others
   d. industry versus inferiority

2. As children develop a better self-understanding in middle childhood, they begin to view themselves less in terms of physical attributes and more in terms of their _____.
   a. familial relationships
   b. psychological traits
   c. environmental characteristics
   d. motor skills

3. According to _____, people pass through a series of six stages as their sense of justice and their level of reasoning evolves with age and cognitive development.

### Applying Lifespan Development

- Kohlberg and Gilligan each suggest there are three major levels of moral development. Are any of their levels comparable? In which level of either theory do you think that the largest discrepancy between males and females would be observed?

✓●—[**Study** and **Review** on **MyDevelopmentLab.com**

Answers: 1) d; 2) b; 3) Kohlberg

# Relationships: Building Friendship in Middle Childhood

**LEARNING OBJECTIVES**

**LO14** What sorts of relationships and friendships are typical of middle childhood?

**LO15** How do relationships between boys and girls develop?

*In Lunch Room Number Two, Jamillah and her new classmates chew slowly on sandwiches and sip quietly on straws from cartons of milk.... Boys and girls look timidly at the strange faces across the table from them, looking for someone who might play with them in the schoolyard, someone who might become a friend.*

*For these children, what happens in the schoolyard will be just as important as what happens in the school. And when they're out on the playground, there will be no one to protect them. No child will hold back to keep from beating them at a game, humiliating them in a test of skill, or harming them in a fight. No one will run interference or guarantee membership in a group. Out on the playground, it's sink or swim. No one automatically becomes your friend. (Kotre & Hall, 1990, pp. 112–113)*

As Jamillah and her classmates demonstrate, friendship plays an increasingly important role in middle childhood. Building and maintaining friendships becomes a large part of social life.

Friends influence development in several ways. Friendships provide children with information about the world as well as themselves. Friends provide emotional support that allows children to respond more effectively to stress. Having friends makes a child a less likely target of aggression. It can teach them how to manage their emotions and help them interpret their own emotional experiences (Berndt, 2002). Friendships teach children how to communicate and interact with others. They also foster intellectual growth by increasing children's range of experiences (Harris, 1998; Nangle & Erdley, 2001; Gifford-Smith & Brownell, 2003).

Friends and other peers become increasingly influential at this stage but parents and other family members remain significant. Most developmentalists believe that children's psychological functioning and their general development is the product of multiple factors, including peers and parents (Vandell, 2000; Parke, Simpkins, & McDowell, 2002). (We'll talk more about the family's influence later in this module.)

Mutual trust is considered to be the centerpiece of friendship during middle childhood.

## Stages of Friendship: Changing Views of Friends

At this stage, a child's concept of friendship passes through three distinct stages, according to developmental psychologist William Damon (Damon & Hart, 1988).

***Stage 1: Basing Friendship on Others' Behavior.*** In this stage, from around ages 4 to 7, children see friends as others who like them and with whom they share toys and other activities. They view the children they spend the most time with as their friends. A kindergartner who was asked, "How do you know that someone is your best friend?" responded:

> *I sleep over at his house sometimes. When he's playing ball with his friends he'll let me play. When I slept over, he let me get in front of him in 4-squares. He likes me. (Damon, 1983, p. 140)*

What children in this stage seldom do, however, is consider others' personal qualities as the basis of friendships. Instead, they use a concrete approach, primarily choosing friends for their behavior. They like those who share, shunning those who don't share, who hit, or who don't play with them. In the first stage, friends are viewed largely as presenting opportunities for pleasant interactions.

***Stage 2: Basing Friendship on Trust.*** In the next stage, children's view of friendship becomes complicated. Lasting from around ages 8 to 10, this stage involves taking others' personal qualities and traits as well as the rewards they provide into consideration. But the centerpiece of friendship in this second stage is mutual trust. Friends are seen as those one can count on to help out when needed. Violations of trust are taken very seriously, and friends cannot make amends just by engaging in positive play, as they might at earlier ages. Instead, the expectation is that formal explanations and apologies must be provided before a friendship can be reestablished.

***Stage 3: Basing Friendship on Psychological Closeness.*** The third stage of friendship begins toward the end of middle childhood, from ages 11 to 15, when children develop the view of friendship they will hold in adolescence. Although we'll discuss this perspective in detail later, the main criteria for friendship shift toward intimacy and loyalty. Friendship becomes characterized by feelings of closeness, usually brought on by sharing personal thoughts and feelings. They are also somewhat exclusive. By the end of middle childhood, children seek friends who will be loyal, and view friendship less in terms of shared activities than in terms of the psychological benefits it brings.

Children also develop clear ideas about which behaviors they like and dislike in friends, preferring others who invite them to share in activities and who are helpful, both physically and psychologically. They dislike behaviors such as physical or verbal aggression.

A variety of factors lead some children to be unpopular and socially isolated from their peers.

## Individual Differences in Friendship: What Makes a Child Popular?

Why is it that some children are the schoolyard equivalent of the life of the party, while others are social isolates whose overtures toward peers are dismissed or disdained? Developmentalists have attempted to answer this question by examining individual differences in popularity.

***Status Among School-Age Children: Establishing One's Position.*** Children's friendships exhibit clear status hierarchies. **Status** is the evaluation of a role or person by other relevant members of a group. Children who have high status have greater access to resources such as games, toys, books, and information. Lower-status children are more likely to follow their lead. Status can be measured in several ways. Often, children are asked directly how much they like or dislike particular classmates. They also may be asked whom they would most (and least) like to play or work with.

Status is an important determinant of friendships. High-status children tend to befriend those of a higher status, while lower-status children are likely to have friends of lower status. Status is also related to the number of friends a child has: Higher-status children tend to have more friends than those of lower status.

But it is not only the quantity of social interactions that separates high-status children from low-status children; the nature of their interactions also differs. Higher-status children are more likely to be viewed as friends by other children. They are more likely to form cliques—groups viewed as exclusive and desirable—and to interact with a greater number of children. Lower-status children tend to play with younger or less popular children (Ladd, 1983). Popularity is a reflection of children's status. Mid- to high-status children are more likely to initiate and coordinate social interaction, making their general level of social activity higher than children of low status (Erwin, 1993).

***What Personal Characteristics Lead to Popularity?*** Popular children share several personality traits. They are usually helpful, cooperating with others on joint projects. They also tend to be funny and to appreciate others' attempts at humor. Compared with less popular children, they are better at reading nonverbal behavior and understanding the emotional experiences of others. They also control their nonverbal behavior more effectively, presenting themselves well. In short, popular children are high in **social competence**, the collection of social skills that permits individuals to perform successfully in social settings (Feldman, Tomasian, & Coats, 1999).

Although generally popular children are friendly, open, and cooperative, one subset of popular boys displays an array of negative behaviors, including being aggressive, disruptive, and causing trouble. Despite these behaviors, they are often remarkably popular, being viewed as cool and tough by their peers. This popularity may occur because they are seen as boldly breaking rules that others feel constrained to follow (Vaillancourt & Hymel, 2006; Meisinger et al., 2007; Woods, 2009).

***Social Problem-Solving Abilities.*** Another factor in popularity is children's skill at social problem-solving. **Social problem-solving** is the use of strategies for solving social conflicts in mutually satisfactory ways. Because social conflicts are frequent—even among best friends—successful strategies for dealing with them are an important element of social success (Rose & Asher, 1999; Murphy & Eisenberg, 2002; Siu & Shek, 2010).

According to developmental psychologist Kenneth Dodge, successful social problem-solving proceeds through a series of steps that correspond to children's information processing strategies (see Figure 5-9). Dodge argues that the ways children solve social problems are a result of the decisions they make at each point in the sequence (Dodge & Crick, 1990; Dodge & Price, 1994; Dodge et al., 2003).

By carefully delineating each of the stages, Dodge provides a means to target interventions toward a specific child's deficits. For instance, some children routinely misinterpret the meaning of others' behavior (Step 2), and then respond according to their misinterpretation.

**status** the evaluation of a role or person by other relevant members of a group

**social competence** the collection of social skills that permit individuals to perform successfully in social settings

**social problem-solving** the use of strategies for solving social conflicts in ways that are satisfactory both to oneself and to others

Generally, popular children are better at interpreting others' behavior. They also possess a wider inventory of techniques for dealing with social problems. In contrast, less popular children tend to show less understanding of others' behavior, and thus their reactions may be inappropriate. Their strategies for dealing with social problems are more limited; they sometimes simply don't know how to apologize or help someone who is unhappy feel better (Vitaro & Pelletier, 1991; Rose & Asher, 1999; Rinaldi, 2002).

Unpopular children may become victims of a phenomenon known as *learned helplessness*. Because they don't understand the root causes of their unpopularity, children may feel that they have little or no ability to improve their situation. As a result, they may simply give up and don't even try to become more involved with their peers. In turn, their learned helplessness becomes a self-fulfilling prophecy, reducing the chances that they will become more popular in the future (Seligman, 2007; Aujoulat, Luminet, & Deccache, 2007).

***Teaching Social Competence.*** Happily, unpopular children can learn social competence. Several programs aim to teach children the skills that seem to underlie general social competence. In one experimental program, a group of unpopular fifth- and sixth-graders were taught how to converse with friends. They were taught ways to disclose material about themselves, to learn about others by asking questions, and to offer help and suggestions in a nonthreatening way.

Compared with a group who did not receive training, the children in the experiment interacted more with their peers, held more conversations, developed higher self-esteem, and—most critically—were more accepted by their peers than before training (Asher & Rose, 1997; Bierman, 2004).

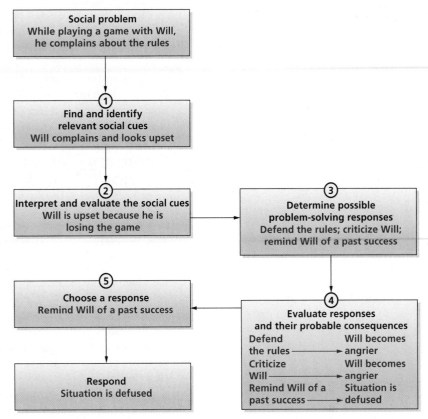

**FIGURE 5-9  Problem-Solving Steps**
Children's problem-solving proceeds through several steps involving different information processing strategies.
Source: EDUCATIONAL PSYCHOLOGY by K. A. Dodge. Copyright 1985 by Taylor & Francis Informa UK Ltd—Journals. Reproduced with permission of Taylor & Francis Informa UK Ltd—Journals in the format Textbook via Copyright Clearance Center.

## Bullying: Schoolyard and Online Victimization

*Phoebe Prince, who moved to South Hadley, MA, from Ireland just weeks before school started, became a target after she dated a senior, a football player. The coarse words and sneering insults that followed her around the school corridors were only part of the story: Cruel text messages inundated her cell phone. Internet postings followed her home. The torment was born in school but invaded her private space to the point that she had no respite.*

*Phoebe Prince, a 15-year-old freshman at South Hadley High School, hanged herself after being tormented by a group who just wouldn't leave her alone. (Cullen, 2010, p. 12)*

Phoebe is not alone in facing the torment of bullying, whether it comes at school or on the Internet. Almost 85 percent of girls and 80 percent of boys report experiencing some form of harassment in school at least once, and 160,000 U.S. schoolchildren stay home from school each day because they are afraid of being bullied. Others encounter bullying on the Internet, which may be even more painful because often the bullying is done anonymously or may involve public postings (Dehue, Bolman, & Völlink, 2008; Slonje & Smith, 2008; Smith et al., 2008; Mishna, Saini, & Solomon, 2009).

Those children who experience frequent bullying are most often loners who are fairly passive. They often cry easily, and they tend to lack the social skill that might otherwise defuse a bullying situation. For example, they are unable to think of humorous comebacks to bullies' taunts. But though children such as these are more likely to be bullied, even children without these characteristics occasionally are bullied during their school careers: Some 90 percent of middle-school students report being bullied at some point in their time at school, beginning as early as the preschool years (Ahmed & Braithwaite, 2004; Li, 2006, 2007; Katzer, Fetchenhauer, & Belschak, 2009). ⊙ Watch on mydevelopmentlab.com

⊙ Watch on **mydevelopmentlab.com**

Has your virtual child encountered issues with bullying? How have you handled it? Check MyDevelopmentLab.com for an Observations Video on bullying.

About 10 to 15 percent of students bully others at one time or another. About half of all bullies come from abusive homes—meaning, of course, that half don't. They tend to watch more television containing violence, and they misbehave more at home and at school than do nonbullies. When their bullying gets them into trouble, they may try to lie their way out of the situation, and they show little remorse for their victimization of others. Furthermore, bullies, compared with their peers, are more likely to break the law as adults. Although bullies are sometimes popular among their peers, some ironically become victims of bullies themselves (Haynie et al., 2001; Ireland & Archer, 2004; Barboza et al., 2009; Peeters, Cillessen & Scholte, 2010).

## Gender and Friendships: The Sex Segregation of Middle Childhood

*Girls rule; boys drool.*

*Boys are idiots. Girls have cooties.*

*Boys go to college to get more knowledge; girls go to Jupiter to get more stupider.*

Those are some of the views of elementary school boys and girls regarding members of the other sex. Avoidance of the other sex becomes quite pronounced at this age, with social networks often consisting almost entirely of same-sex groupings (McHale, Dariotis, & Kauh, 2003; Mehta & Strough, 2009).

Interestingly, this segregation of friendships occurs in almost all societies. In nonindustrialized societies, same-gender segregation may result from the types of activities children engage in. For instance, in many cultures, boys are assigned one type of chore and girls another (Whiting & Edwards, 1988). Participation in different activities may not wholly explain sex segregation, however: Children in more developed countries, who attend the same schools and participate in many of the same activities, still tend to avoid members of the other gender.

When boys and girls make occasional forays into the other gender's territory, the action often has romantic overtones. For instance, girls may threaten to kiss a boy, or boys might try to lure girls into chasing them. Such behavior, termed "border work," emphasizes the clear boundaries between the two sexes. In addition, it may pave the way for adolescent interactions that do involve romantic or sexual interests, when cross-sex interactions become socially endorsed (Thorne, 1986; Beal, 1994).

The lack of cross-gender interaction in middle childhood means that boys' and girls' friendships are restricted to their own sex. The nature of friendships within these two groups is quite different (Lansford & Parker, 1999; Rose, 2002).

Boys typically have larger networks of friends, and they tend to play in groups rather than pairing off. Differences in status within the group are usually pronounced, with an acknowledged leader and a hierarchy of members. Because of the fairly rigid rankings that represent the relative social power of those in the group, known as the **dominance hierarchy,** members of higher status can safely question and oppose those lower in the hierarchy (Beal, 1994; Pedersen et al., 2007).

Boys tend to be concerned with their place in the dominance hierarchy, and they attempt to maintain and improve their status. This makes for a style of play known as *restrictive*. In restrictive play, interactions are interrupted when a child feels his status is challenged. A boy who feels that he is unjustly challenged by a lower-status peer may attempt to end the interaction by scuffling over a toy or otherwise behaving assertively. Consequently, boys tend to play in bursts, rather than in more extended, tranquil episodes (Benenson & Apostoleris, 1993; Estell et al., 2008).

The language of friendship used among boys reflects their concern over status and challenge. Consider this conversation between two boys who were good friends:

Child 1: Why don't you get out of my yard?

Child 2: Why don't you *make* me get out of the yard?

Child 1: I *know* you don't want that.

Child 2: You're not gonna make me get out of the yard cuz you can't.

Child 1: Don't force me.

Child 2: You can't. Don't force me to hurt you (*snickers*). (Goodwin, 1990, p. 37)

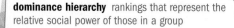

**dominance hierarchy** rankings that represent the relative social power of those in a group

Friendship patterns among girls are quite different. Rather than a wide network of friends, girls focus on one or two "best friends." In contrast to boys, who seek out status differences, girls avoid differences, preferring to maintain equal-status friendships.

Conflicts among girls are usually solved through compromise, by ignoring the situation, or by giving in, rather than by seeking to make one's point of view prevail. The goal is to smooth over disagreements, making social interaction easy and nonconfrontational (Goodwin, 1990; Noakes & Rinaldi, 2006).

According to developmental psychologist Carole Beal, the motivation of girls to solve social conflict indirectly does not stem from a lack of self-confidence or from apprehension over the use of more direct approaches. In fact, when school-age girls interact with other girls who are not friends or with boys, they can be quite confrontational. However, among friends their goal is to maintain equal-status relationships, with no dominance hierarchy (Beal, 1994; Zahn & Wexler, 2008).

The language used by girls tends to reflect their view of relationships. Rather than blatant demands ("Give me the pencil"), girls are more apt to use less confrontational and directive language. Girls tend to use indirect forms of verbs, such as "Let's go to the movies" or "Would you want to trade books with me?" rather than "I want to go to the movies" or "Let me have these books" (Goodwin, 1990; Besage, 2006).

As children age, there is a decline in the number of and depth of friendships outside their own racial group. What are some ways in which schools can foster mutual acceptance?

## Cross-Race Friendships: Integration In and Out of the Classroom

For the most part, friendships are not color-blind. Children's closest friendships tend to be with others of the same race. In fact, as children age there is a decline in the number and depth of friendships outside their own racial group. By age 11 or 12, it appears that African American children become particularly aware of and sensitive to the prejudice and discrimination directed toward members of their race. At that point, they are likely to make distinctions between members of ingroups (groups to which people feel they belong) and members of outgroups (groups to which they feel they do not belong) (Kao & Vaquera, 2006; Aboud & Sankar, 2007; Rowley et al., 2008).

When third-graders from one long-integrated school were asked to name a best friend, around one-quarter of White children and two-thirds of African American children chose a child of the other race. In contrast, by 10th grade, less than 10 percent of Whites and 5 percent of African Americans named a different-race best friend (Singleton & Taylor, 1982; McGlothlin & Killen, 2005).

## *Increasing Children's Social Competence*

### Becoming an Informed Consumer of Development

It is clear that building and maintaining friendships is critical in children's lives. Fortunately, there are strategies that parents and teachers can use to increase children's social competence.

- **Encourage social interaction.** Teachers can devise ways to get children to take part in group activities, and parents can encourage membership in such groups as Brownies and Cub Scouts or participation in team sports.

- **Teach listening skills to children.** Show them how to listen carefully and respond to the underlying meaning of a communication as well as its overt content.

- **Make children aware that people display emotions and moods nonverbally.** Consequently, they should pay attention to others' nonverbal behavior, not just to what they are saying.

- **Teach conversational skills, including the importance of asking questions and self-disclosure.** Encourage students to use "I" statements in which they clarify their own feelings or opinions, and avoid making generalizations about others.

- **Don't ask children to choose teams or groups publicly.** Instead, assign children randomly: It works just as well in ensuring a distribution of abilities across groups and avoids the public embarrassment of a situation in which some children are chosen last.

⊙ **From a social worker's perspective:** How might it be possible to decrease the segregation of friendships along racial lines? What factors would have to change in individuals or in society?

On the other hand, although they may not choose each other as best friends, Whites and African Americans—as well as members of other minority groups—can show a high degree of mutual acceptance. This pattern is particularly true in schools with ongoing integration efforts. This makes sense: A good deal of research supports the notion that contact between majority and minority group members can reduce prejudice and discrimination (Hewstone, 2003; Quintana, 2008).

## REVIEW, CHECK, AND APPLY

### REVIEW

**LO14** What sorts of relationships and friendships are typical of middle childhood?

- Children's understanding of friendship changes from the sharing of enjoyable activities, through the consideration of personal traits that can meet their needs, to a focus on intimacy and loyalty.

- Friendships in childhood display status hierarchies. Improvements in social problem-solving and social information processing can lead to better interpersonal skills and greater popularity.

**LO15** How do relationships between boys and girls develop?

- Boys and girls engage increasingly in same-sex friendships, with boys' friendships involving group relationships and girls' friendships characterized by pairings of girls with equal status.

### CHECK YOURSELF

1. Which of the following statements about friendship in middle childhood are true? Check all that apply.
   a. Friendships provide information about the world.
   b. Friends provide emotional support that is different from the support provided by parents.
   c. Children with friends are less likely to be the target of aggression.
   d. Friendships provide training in communication.
   e. Friendships protect children from interactions with others, which can enhance their intellectual growth.
   f. Children are only able to learn how to manage their emotions within the context of family.

2. _____ is the evaluation of the role or person by other relevant members of the group and is usually discussed in reference to children and their peer groups.

3. Which of the following descriptions best characterizes friendships in middle school?
   a. Boys and girls tend to remain in sex-segregated friendship networks.
   b. Boys and girls begin playing in larger groups including males and females.
   c. Boys are much more likely than girls to engage in activities considered more appropriate for the opposite sex.
   d. Girls typically have larger networks of friends than do boys.

### APPLYING LIFESPAN DEVELOPMENT

- Do you think the stages of friendship are a childhood phenomenon, or do adults' friendships display similar stages?

✔●—Study and Review on
**MyDevelopmentLab.com**

Answers: 1) a, b, c, d; 2) Status; 3) a

# Family Life in Middle Childhood

**LEARNING OBJECTIVES**

**LO16** How do today's diverse family and care arrangements affect children?

*The original plot goes like this: First comes love. Then comes marriage. Then comes Mary with a baby carriage. But now there's a sequel: John and Mary break up. John moves in with Sally and her two boys. Mary takes the baby Paul. A year later Mary meets Jack, who is divorced with three children. They get married. Paul, barely 2 years old, now has a mother, a father, a stepmother, a stepfather, and five step-brothers and stepsisters—as well as four sets of grandparents (biological and step) and countless aunts and uncles. And guess what? Mary's pregnant again. (Katrowitz & Wingert, 1990, p. 24)*

We've already noted in earlier chapters how the structure of the family has changed over the last few decades. With more parents who both work outside the home, a soaring divorce rate, and a rise in single-parent families, children passing through middle childhood in the twenty-first century face an environment different from the one faced by prior generations.

One of the biggest challenges of middle childhood is the increasing independence that characterizes children's behavior. Children move from being controlled to increasingly controlling their own destinies—or at least conduct. Middle childhood, then, is a period of **coregulation** in which children and parents jointly control behavior. Increasingly, parents provide broad guidelines for conduct, while children control their everyday behavior. For instance, parents may urge their daughter to buy a nutritious school lunch, but their daughter's decision to buy pizza and two desserts is her own.

## Family Life

During middle childhood, children spend less time with their parents. Still, parents remain their major influence, providing essential assistance, advice, and direction (Parke, 2004).

Siblings also have an important influence, for good and for bad. Although brothers and sisters can provide support, companionship, and security, they can also be a source of strife. *Sibling rivalry* can occur, especially when the siblings are the same sex and similar in age. Parents may intensify sibling rivalry by seeming to favor one child over another—a perception that may or may not be accurate. A decision as straightforward as granting older siblings more freedom may be interpreted as favoritism. In some cases, perceived favoritism may damage the self-esteem of the younger sibling. But sibling rivalry is not inevitable (Branje et al., 2004; McHale, Kim, & Whiteman, 2006).

What about children who have no siblings? Disproving the stereotype that only-children are spoiled and self-centered, they are as well adjusted as children with brothers and sisters. In fact, in some ways, only-children are better adjusted, with higher self-esteem and stronger motivation to achieve. In China, where a strict one-child policy is in effect, studies show that only-children often academically outperform children with siblings (Jiao, Ji, & Jing, 1996; Miao & Wang, 2003; Zheng, 2010).

Self-care children spend time after school alone while their parents are at work.

## Home and Alone: What Do Children Do?

*When 10-year-old Johnetta Colvin comes home after a day at Martin Luther King Elementary School, the first thing she does is grab a few cookies and turn on the computer. She takes a quick look at her email, and then typically spends an hour watching television. During commercials, she looks at her homework.*

*What she doesn't do is chat with her parents. She's home alone.*

Johnetta is a **self-care child,** the term for children who let themselves into their homes after school and wait alone until their parents return from work. Some 12 to 14 percent of children in the United States between the ages of 5 and 12 spend some time alone after school, without adult supervision (Lamorey et al., 1998; Berger, 2000).

In the past, such children were called *latchkey children,* a term connoting sadness, loneliness, and neglect. Today a new view is emerging. According to sociologist Sandra Hofferth, given the hectic schedule of many children's lives, a few hours alone may provide a helpful period of decompression. Furthermore, it may give children an opportunity to develop autonomy (Hofferth & Sandberg, 2001).

Research has identified few differences between self-care children and others. Although some children report negative experiences (such as loneliness), they do not seem emotionally damaged by the experience. In addition, if they stay by themselves rather than "hanging out" unsupervised with friends, they may avoid activities that can lead to difficulties (Belle, 1999; Goyette-Ewing, 2000).

The time alone also gives children a chance to focus on homework and school or personal projects. In fact, children with employed parents may have higher self-esteem because they feel they are contributing to the household (Goyette-Ewing, 2000).

## Divorce

Having divorced parents is no longer distinctive. Only around half the children in the United States spend their entire childhood in the same household with both parents. The rest will live

**coregulation**  a period in which parents and children jointly control children's behavior

**self-care children**  children who let themselves into their homes after school and wait alone until their caretakers return from work; previously known as *latchkey children*

in single-parent homes or with stepparents, grandparents, or other nonparental relatives; and some end up in foster care (Harvey & Fine, 2004).

How do children react to divorce? The answer is complex. For 6 months to 2 years following a divorce, children and parents may show signs of psychological maladjustment such as anxiety, depression, sleep disturbances, and phobias. Even though most children stay with their mothers, the quality of the mother–child relationship mostly declines, often because children feel caught in the middle between their mothers and fathers (Amato & Afifi, 2006; Juby et al., 2007; Lansford, 2009).

During the early stage of middle childhood, children often blame themselves for the breakup. By age 10, they feel pressure to choose sides and experience some degree of divided loyalty (Shaw, Winslow, & Flanagan, 1999).

The longer-term consequences of divorce are less clear. Some studies have found that 18 months to 2 years later, most children begin to return to their predivorce state of adjustment. For many children, long-term consequences are minimal (Hetherington & Kelly, 2002; Guttmann & Rosenberg, 2003; Harvey & Fine, 2004).

Other evidence suggests that the fallout from divorce lingers. For example, compared with children from intact families, twice as many children of divorced parents enter psychological counseling (although sometimes counseling is mandated by a judge as part of the divorce). In addition, people who have experienced parental divorce are more at risk for experiencing divorce themselves later in life (Wallerstein & Resnikoff, 2005; Huurre, Junkkari, & Aro, 2006).

How children react to divorce depends on several factors. One is the economic standing of the family the child is living with. In many cases, divorce brings a decline in both parents' standards of living. When this occurs, children may be thrown into poverty (Ozawa & Yoon, 2003; Fischer, 2007).

In other cases, the negative consequences of divorce are less severe because the divorce reduces the hostility and anger in the home. If the household before the divorce was overwhelmed by parental strife—as is the case in around 30 percent of divorces—the greater calm of a postdivorce household may be beneficial to children. This is particularly true for children who maintain a close, positive relationship with the parent with whom they do not live. Still, in the 70 percent of divorces where the predivorce level of conflict is not high, children may have a more difficult time adjusting (Faber & Wittenborn, 2010; Finley & Schwartz, 2010; Lansford, 2010).

**From the perspective of a health care provider:** How might the development of self-esteem in middle childhood be affected by a divorce? Can constant hostility and tension between parents lead to a child's health problems?

## Single-Parent Families

Almost one-quarter of all children under age 18 in the United States live with only one parent. If present trends continue, almost three-quarters will spend some portion of their lives in a single-parent family before they are 18. For minority children, the numbers are higher: Almost 60 percent of African American children and 35 percent of Hispanic children under 18 live in single-parent homes (U.S. Census Bureau, 2000).

In rare cases, death is the reason for single parenthood. More frequently, either no spouse was ever present, the spouses have divorced, or the spouse is absent. In the vast majority of cases, the single parent who is present is the mother.

What consequences are there for children in one-parent homes? Much depends on whether a second parent was present earlier and the nature of the parents' relationship at that time. Furthermore, the economic status of the single-parent family plays a role. Single-parent families are often less well-off financially than two-parent families, and living in relative poverty has a negative impact on children (Davis, 2003; Harvey & Fine, 2004).

## Multigenerational Families

In some households children, parents, and grandparents live together. Multigenerational families can make for a rich living experience for children, but there is also the potential for conflict if "layers" of adults act as disciplinarians without coordinating what they do.

The prevalence of three-generation families who live together is greater among African Americans than among Caucasians. In addition, African American families, which are more likely than White families to be headed by single parents, often rely substantially on the help of grandparents in everyday child care, and cultural norms tend to be highly supportive of grandparents taking an active role (Oberlander, Black, & Starr, 2007; Pittman & Boswell, 2007; Kelch-Oliver, 2008).

## Living in Blended Families

For many children, the aftermath of divorce includes a remarriage. In more than 10 million households in the United States, at least one spouse has remarried. More than 5 million remarried couples have at least one stepchild with them in what have come to be called **blended families.** Overall, 17 percent of all children in the United States live in blended families (U.S. Bureau of the Census, 2001; Bengtson et al., 2004).

Blended families occur when previously married husbands and wives with children remarry.

Children in a blended family face challenges. They often have to deal with *role ambiguity,* in which roles and expectations are unclear. They may be uncertain about their responsibilities, how to behave toward stepparents and stepsiblings, and how to make a host of tough everyday decisions. For instance, they may have to choose which parent to spend holidays and vacations with, or decide between conflicting advice from biological parent and stepparent. Some find the disruption of routine and of established family relationships difficult. For instance, a child used to her mother's complete attention may find it hard to see her mother showing interest and affection to a stepchild (Cath & Shopper, 2001; Belcher, 2003).

Still, school-age children in blended families often adjust relatively smoothly—especially compared with adolescents—for several reasons. For one thing, the family's financial situation is often improved after a parent remarries. In addition, there are usually more people to share the burden of household chores. Finally, the higher "population" of the family increases opportunities for social interaction (Greene, Anderson, & Hetherington, 2003; Hetherington & Elmore, 2003).

Families blend most successfully when the parents create an environment that supports self-esteem and a climate of family togetherness. Generally, the younger the children, the easier the transition (Kirby, 2006; Jeynes, 2007).

## Families with Gay and Lesbian Parents

An increasing number of children have two mothers or two fathers. Estimates suggest there are between 1 and 5 million families headed by two lesbian or two gay parents in the United States, and some 6 million children have lesbian or gay parents (Patterson & Friel, 2000; Patterson, 2007, 2009).

How do children in lesbian and gay households fare? A growing body of research on the effects of same-sex parenting on children shows that children develop similarly to the children of heterosexual families. Their sexual orientation is unrelated to that of their parents; their behavior is no more or less gender-typed; and they seem equally well adjusted (Parke, 2004; Fulcher, Sutfin, & Patterson, 2008; Patterson, 2002, 2003, 2009).

One recent large-scale analysis that examined 19 studies of children raised by gay and lesbian parents conducted over a 25-year period, encompassing well over a thousand gay, lesbian, and heterosexual families, confirmed these findings. The analysis found no significant differences between children raised by heterosexual parents and children raised by gay or lesbian parents on measures of children's gender role, gender identity, cognitive development, sexual orientation, and social and emotional development. The one significant difference that did emerge was the quality of the relationship between parent and child; interestingly, the gay and lesbian parents reported having *better* relationships with their children than did heterosexual parents (Crowl, Ahn, & Baker, 2008).

Other research shows that children of lesbian and gay parents have similar relationships with their peers as children of heterosexual parents. They also relate to adults—both those

**blended families** a remarried couple who has at least one stepchild living with them

Although the orphanages of the early 1900s were crowded and institutional (top), today the equivalent, called group homes or residential treatment centers (bottom), are much more pleasant.

who are gay and those who are straight—no differently from children whose parents are heterosexual. And when they reach adolescence, their romantic relationships and sexual behavior are no different from those of adolescents living with opposite-sex parents (Patterson, 1995, 2009; Golombok et al., 2003; Wainright, Russell, & Patterson, 2004; Goldberg, 2010a).

In short, research shows that there is little developmental difference between children whose parents are gay and lesbian and those who have heterosexual parents. What is clearly different for children with same-sex parents is the possibility of discrimination and prejudice due to their parents' homosexuality. As U.S. citizens engage in an ongoing and highly politicized debate regarding the legality of gay and lesbian marriage, children of such unions may feel singled out and victimized because of societal stereotypes and discrimination (Ryan & Martin, 2000; Davis, Saltzburg, & Locke, 2009).

## Race and Family Life

Although there are as many types of families as there are individuals, research finds some consistencies related to race (Parke, 2004). For example, African American families often have a particularly strong sense of family, offering welcome and support to extended family members in their homes. Because there is a relatively high level of female-headed households among African Americans, extended family often lend crucial social and economic support. In addition, there is a relatively high proportion of families headed by older adults, such as grandparents, and some studies find that children in grandmother-headed households are particularly well adjusted (McLoyd et al., 2000; Smith & Drew, 2002; Taylor, 2002).

Hispanic families tend to regard family life and community and religious organizations highly. Children are taught to value their family ties and to see themselves as a central part of an extended family. Ultimately, their sense of self stems from the family. Hispanic families also tend to be larger, with an average size of 3.71, compared to 2.97 for Caucasian families and 3.31 for African American families (Cauce & Domenech-Rodriguez, 2002; U.S. Census Bureau, 2003; Halgunseth, Ispa, & Rudy, 2006).

Although relatively little research has been conducted on Asian American families, emerging findings suggest that fathers are apt to be powerful figures who maintain discipline. In keeping with the collectivist orientation of Asian cultures, children tend to believe that family needs have a higher priority than personal needs, and males, in particular, are expected to care for their parents throughout their lifetimes (Ishi-Kuntz, 2000).

## Poverty and Family Life

Regardless of race, children in economically disadvantaged families face hardships. Poor families have fewer everyday resources, and there are more disruptions in children's lives. For example, parents may be forced to look for less expensive housing or a different job. As a result, parents may be less responsive to their children's needs and provide less social support (Evans, 2004).

The stress of difficult family environments, along with other stress in the lives of poor children—such as living in unsafe neighborhoods with high rates of violence and attending inferior schools—ultimately takes its toll. Economically disadvantaged children are at risk for poorer academic performance, higher rates of aggression, and conduct problems. In addition, declines in economic well-being are linked to physical and mental health problems. Specifically, the chronic stress associated with poverty makes children more susceptible to cardiovascular disease, depression, and diabetes (Sapolsky, 2005; Morales & Guerra, 2006; Tracy et al., 2008).

# Group Care: Orphanages in the Twenty-first Century

The term "orphanage" evokes stereotypical images of grim institutional life. The reality today is different. *Group homes* or *residential treatment centers* (the word "orphanage" is rarely used) typically house a relatively small number of children whose parents are no longer able to care for them adequately. They are typically funded by a combination of federal, state, and local aid.

Group care has grown significantly. In the period from 1995 to 2000, the number of children in foster care increased by more than 50 percent. Today, more than a half million children in the United States live in foster care (Roche, 2000; Jones-Harden, 2004; Bruskas, 2008).

About three-quarters of children in group care have suffered neglect and abuse. Each year, 300,000 are removed from their homes, most of whom can be returned to their homes after social service agencies intervene with their families. But the remaining one-quarter are so psychologically damaged that they are likely to remain in group care throughout childhood. Adoption (or even temporary foster care) is not an option for most of these children, who have developed severe emotional and behavior problems, such as high levels of aggression or anger (Bass, Shields, & Behrman, 2004; Chamberlain et al., 2006).

Group care is neither inherently good nor bad. The outcome depends on the staff of the group home and whether child- and youth-care workers know how to develop an effective, stable, and strong emotional bond with a child. If a child is unable to form a meaningful relationship with a worker in a group home, the setting may well be harmful (Hawkins-Rodgers, 2007; Knorth et al., 2008).

## REVIEW, CHECK, AND APPLY

### REVIEW

**LO16**  How do today's diverse family and care arrangements affect children?

- Self-care children may develop independence and enhanced self-esteem from their experience.

- How divorce affects children depends on such factors as financial circumstances and the comparative levels of tension in the family before and after the divorce.

- The effects of being raised in a single-parent household depend on financial circumstances, the amount of parent–child interaction, and the level of tension in the family.

### CHECK YOURSELF

1. According to sociologist Sandra Hofferth, self-care children may benefit from their situation by having more time to decompress from a hectic schedule and the opportunity to develop greater _____ or independence.

2. Which of the following characteristics have been associated with a child's response to divorce? Check all that apply.
   a. phobias
   b. increased anxiety
   c. schizophrenia
   d. sleep disturbances
   e. experiencing depression

3. The impact of living in a single-parent family is less about the number of parents and more about the economic status, stress level, and time spent together in the family.
   - True
   - False

### APPLYING LIFESPAN DEVELOPMENT

- Politicians often speak of "family values." How does this term relate to diverse family situations such as divorced parents, single parents, blended families, working parents, self-care children, and group care?

✓— **Study** and **Review** on
**MyDevelopmentLab.com**

Answers: 1) autonomy; 2) a, b, d, e; 3) True

# Putting It All Together
## Middle Childhood

**RYAN** (the student we met in the chapter prologue) entered first grade with boundless hope and a keen desire to read. Unfortunately, an undiagnosed vision problem interfered with his reading, and fine motor deficits made writing difficult. In most other ways, Ryan was at least the equal of his peers: physically active, imaginative, and highly intelligent. Socially, however, he was hampered by spending time in special education classes. Because he had been singled out and because he could not do some of the things his classmates could do, he was ignored, even bullied, by some of them. When he finally got the right treatment, though, most of his problems vanished. His physical and social skills advanced to match his cognitive abilities. He became more engaged in his schoolwork and more open to friendships. Ryan's story had a happy ending.

### MODULE 5.1 Physical Development in Middle Childhood

- Steady growth and increased abilities characterized Ryan's physical development in these years. **(pp. 202–203)**

- Ryan's gross and fine motor skills developed as muscle coordination improved and he practiced new skills. **(pp. 206–207)**

- Ryan's sensory problems interfered with his schoolwork. **(pp. 210–211)**

### MODULE 5.2 Cognitive Development in Middle Childhood

- Ryan's intellectual abilities such as language and memory became more skilled in middle childhood. **(pp. 214–217)**

- One of the key academic tasks for Ryan was to read fluently and with appropriate comprehension. **(pp. 222–223)**

- Ryan displayed many components and types of intelligence, and the development of his intellectual skills was aided by his social interactions. **(pp. 225–230)**

## What would a PARENT do?

- What strategies would you use to help Ryan overcome his difficulties and function effectively? How would you bolster his self-esteem?

**HINT** Review pages 236–238.

*What's your response?*

---

**MODULE 5.3** Social and Personality Development in Middle Childhood

- In this period, Ryan mastered many of the challenges presented by school and peers, which took on central importance in his life. **(pp. 244–245)**

- The development of Ryan's self-esteem was particularly crucial; when Ryan felt himself inadequate, his self-esteem suffered. **(pp. 237–238)**

- Ryan's friendships helped provide emotional support and fostered intellectual growth. **(pp. 244–245)**

## What would a HEALTH CARE PROVIDER do?

- How might you respond to Ryan's vision and motor problems? What if Ryan's parents had refused to believe that there was anything physically wrong with Ryan? How would you convince them to get treatment for Ryan?

**HINT** Review pages 210–212.

*What's your response?*

## What would YOU do?

- How would you deal with a situation in which your child had physical disabilities that would prevent him or her from progressing in school? How would you encourage your child? How would you deal with your child's frustration at falling behind in school?

**HINT** Review pages 202–211.

*What's your response?*

---

✳ Explore on **mydevelopmentlab.com**

To read how real-life parents, social workers, and educators responded to these questions, log onto MyDevelopmentLab.com.

*Do you agree or disagree with their responses? Why? What concepts that you've read about back up their opinions?*

## What would an EDUCATOR do?

- How would you deal with Ryan's difficulties in reading and writing? What would you do to help integrate him into his class and help him make friends with his classmates? What would you recommend in terms of educational specialists to deal with his problems?

**HINT** Review pages 210–212, 223, 236.

*What's your response?*

# Adolescence

During middle school, Andrea—or "Andi" as her friends and family call her—virtually lived on Facebook, checking the site numerous times each day. "How's Spacebook?" or "What's new on Faceplace?" her dad would ask. His "stupid" attempts at humor infuriated Andi, though silly wordplay had once been one of their shared loves. Her parents didn't understand how *everything* could change in her social world in one afternoon. It was vital to stay connected to her friends, which now included a number of boys. When she complained that her parents didn't take her seriously, they said, "We love you, honey, but after three teenagers, we just can't get too worked up anymore." Andi was secretly happy to be reminded of her parents' love, but their words still bugged her. She wasn't like her older siblings. She was sure no one had ever felt the way she felt.

The summer before high school, Andi developed the curves she'd been waiting for, but then things got out of control. Her curves were too curvy. She gained 10 pounds and became as obsessed with the bathroom scales as she was with Facebook. When several of her friends began dating, Andi blamed her lack of a

**MODULE 6.1** Physical Development in Adolescence

Teenage boys are affected by early maturation differently than girls. How? What about late maturation? see page 258.

**MODULE 6.2** Cognitive Development in Adolescence

How does socioeconomic status affect school performance? What about race and ethnicity?

see page 273.

"boyfriend" on her weight. "I'm too fat," she wailed. "You're not too fat," her brother said. "You're too smart. You scare guys off." Andi thought about this. Her best friend, Erica, was smart, too, but lately Erica had been quiet in class, volunteering few answers. Another friend, Jen, hadn't bothered much with homework since she'd landed her boyfriend. Andi felt confused, and a little scared. She wanted to keep her friends, and she wanted a boyfriend, but she liked being smart and independent. Those qualities were central to her identity.

In 10th grade, seeking something new, she signed up for a photography class. She'd always enjoyed taking photos of her friends for Facebook. Now she began photographing other subjects—landscapes, architecture, old people, little kids. Her instructor said she had an eye for composition. One of her photos won a prize in the local paper. But the best thing, to Andi, was the way she felt when she was on the hunt for subjects: free, independent, creative.

Her parents bought her a top-notch camera for her 16th birthday, and Andi began to think seriously of combining her love of photography with her gift for writing. "I've decided to become a photojournalist," she says. "It's so exactly me."

**In this chapter we study adolescence,** the transitional stage between childhood and adulthood. Adolescents face many challenges in all aspects of their life. Physically, their bodies are maturing quickly—sometimes distressingly quickly. Adolescents become sexually interested, and many of them face worries about their bodies as Andi did. We will look at some of the physical issues that sometimes plague adolescents,

## MODULE **6.3** Social and Personality Development in Adolescence

# What determines sexual orientation? see page 283.

## My Virtual Child

As your virtual child reaches adolescence, are you seeing any of the changes that Andi went through? How would you deal with Andi as her parent, educator, doctor, or friend?

Log onto *My Virtual Child* through MyDevelopmentLab.com to help your virtual child navigate the tumultuous adolescent stage.

including those relating to obesity and nutrition, harmful substances, and sexually transmitted infections.

Beyond the physical aspects of development, adolescents grow cognitively as well. The most notable change we will discuss is adolescents' growing awareness of their own thought processes. We also consider how adolescents deal with the institution that occupies a great deal of their waking time—school—and discuss the growing impact of the Internet on adolescents' lives, learning, and relationships.

Finally, we turn to the changes that adolescents undergo in their relationships with others. We begin with a consideration of the ways in which they create their concepts of themselves and how they form and protect their self-esteem and identity. We discuss their relationships with parents as adolescents redefine their place within the family. Finally, we discuss dating and sex, which achieve central importance during this period and which encompass issues of intimacy

## MODULE 6.1 Physical Development in Adolescence

# The Middle School Marathon

*Like most children, Luke Voss would sometimes complain about all the work he had to do. But it wasn't until he reached middle school that his mother, Gisela, realized he actually had something to complain about.*

*"He was at school from 8 to 3, and with soccer practice he wouldn't be done until 5," Gisela explained. "If we all ate dinner together—and it's important to me that we do—he wouldn't even start cracking the books until 7. He missed out on sleep, and his anxiety stressed everybody else out. We'd rush through the meal knowing that he had hours of work ahead of him, and he'd start begging for help even before he left the table."*

*Luke eventually grew more accustomed to the rigors of middle school. But this did not change the fundamentals of the situation, for Luke or for his mother: too much work, too many family and extracurricular responsibilites, and only so many hours in the day. "This is an insane way for families to live," Gisela admitted. (Mohler, 2009)*

Like Luke, many adolescents struggle to meet society's—and their own—demands as they traverse the challenges of the teenage years. These challenges extend far beyond managing an overstuffed schedule. With bodies that are conspicuously changing; temptations of sex, alcohol, and other drugs; cognitive advances that make the world seem increasingly complex; social networks that are in constant flux; and careening emotions, adolescents find themselves in a period of life that evokes excitement, anxiety, glee, and despair, sometimes in equal measure.

**Adolescence** is the developmental stage between childhood and adulthood. It is generally said to start just before the teenage years, and end just after them. Considered neither children nor adults, adolescents are in a transitional stage marked by considerable growth.

This module focuses on physical growth during adolescence. We first consider the extraordinary physical maturation that occurs during adolescence, triggered by the onset of puberty. We then discuss the consequences of early and late maturation and how they differ for males and females. We also consider nutrition. After examining the causes—and consequences—of obesity, we discuss eating disorders, which are surprisingly common at this stage.

The module concludes with a discussion of several major threats to adolescents' wellbeing—drugs, alcohol, tobacco, and sexually transmitted infections.

# Physical Maturation

**LO1**   What physical changes do adolescents experience?

**LO2**   What are the consequences of early and late maturation?

**LO3**   What are the nutritional needs and concerns of adolescents?

*For young males of the Awa tribe, adolescence begins with an elaborate and—to Western eyes—gruesome ceremony to mark the passage from childhood to adulthood. The boys are whipped for 2 or 3 days with sticks and prickly branches. Through the whipping, the boys atone for their previous infractions and honor tribesmen who were killed in warfare.*

We are no doubt grateful we were spared such physical trials when we entered adolescence. But members of Western cultures have their own rites of passage, admittedly less fearsome, such as bar mitzvahs and bat mitzvahs at age 13 for Jewish boys and girls, and confirmation ceremonies in many Christian denominations (Herdt, 1998; Eccles, Templeton, & Barber, 2003; Hoffman, 2003).

➤ **From an educator's perspective:** Why do you think many cultures regard the passage to adolescence as a significant transition that calls for unique ceremonies?

Regardless of their nature, the underlying purpose of these ceremonies tends to be the same across cultures: symbolically celebrating the physical changes that transform a child's body into an adult body capable of reproduction.

## Growth During Adolescence: The Rapid Pace of Physical and Sexual Maturation

In only a few months, adolescents can grow several inches as they are transformed, at least physically, from children to young adults. During such a growth spurt—a period of very rapid growth in height and weight—boys, on average, grow 4.1 inches a year and girls 3.5 inches. Some adolescents grow as much as 5 inches in a single year (Tanner, 1972; Caino et al., 2004).

Boys' and girls' growth spurts begin at different ages. As you can see in Figure 6-1, girls' spurts begin around age 10, while boys start around age 12. During the 2-year period from age 11, girls tend to be taller than boys. But by 13, boys, on average, are taller than girls—a state that persists for the remainder of the life span.

## Puberty: The Start of Sexual Maturation

**Puberty,** the period when the sexual organs mature, begins when the pituitary gland in the brain signals other glands to begin producing the sex hormones, *androgens* (male hormones) or *estrogens* (female hormones), at adult levels. (Males and females produce both types of sex hormones, but males have higher levels of androgens and females, of estrogens.) The pituitary gland also signals the body to produce more growth hormones. These interact with the sex hormones to cause the growth spurt and puberty. The hormone *leptin* also appears to play a role in the onset of puberty.

Like the growth spurt, puberty begins earlier for girls, starting at around age 11 or 12, whereas boys begin at about age 13 or 14. However, this varies widely. Some girls begin puberty as early as 7 or 8 or as late as age 16.

***Puberty in Girls.***   Although it is not clear why puberty begins when it does, environmental and cultural factors play a role. For example **menarche,** the onset of menstruation and probably the most obvious sign of puberty in girls, varies greatly around the world. In poorer, developing countries, menstruation begins later than in more economically advantaged

**adolescence**   the developmental stage that lies between childhood and adulthood

**puberty**   the period during which the sexual organs mature

**menarche**   the onset of menstruation

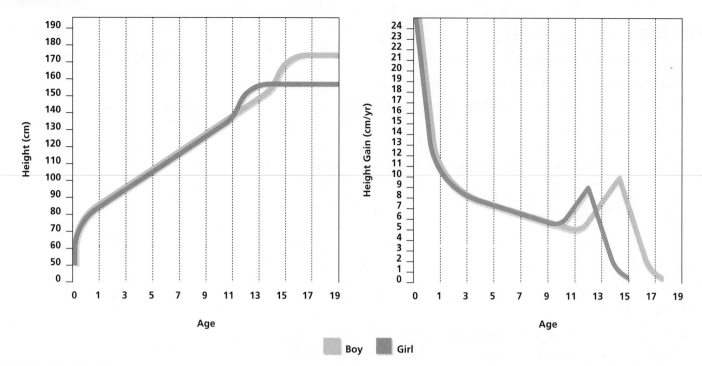

**FIGURE 6-1 Growth Patterns**

Patterns of growth are depicted in two ways. The first figure shows height at a given age, while the second shows the height increase that occurs from birth through the end of adolescence. Notice that girls begin their growth spurt around age 10, while boys begin their growth spurt at about age 12. However, by the age of 13, boys tend to be taller than girls. What are the social consequences of being taller or shorter than average for boys and girls?

Source: Adapted from Cratty, 1986.

countries. Even within wealthier countries, more affluent girls begin to menstruate earlier than less affluent girls.

It appears that girls who are better nourished and healthier tend to start menstruation earlier than those suffering from malnutrition or chronic disease. Some studies have suggested that weight or the proportion of fat to muscle in the body play a key role in the onset of menarche. For example, in the United States, athletes with a low percentage of body fat may start menstruating later than less active girls. Conversely, obesity—which increases the secretion of leptin, a hormone related to the onset of menstruation—leads to earlier puberty (Richards, 1996; Vizmanos & Marti-Henneberg, 2000; Woelfle, Harz, & Roth, 2007; Oswal & Yeo, 2010).

Other factors can affect the timing of menarche. For example, environmental stress from parental divorce or intense family conflict can effect an early onset (Kaltiala-Heino, Kosunen, & Rimpela, 2003; Ellis, 2004; Belsky et al., 2007).

Over the past century or so, girls in the United States and other cultures have been entering puberty at earlier ages. In the late nineteenth century, menstruation began, on average, around age 14 or 15, compared with today's 11 or 12. The average age for other indicators of puberty, such as the attaining of adult height and sexual maturity, has also dropped, probably due to reduced disease and improved nutrition (Hughes, 2007; McDowell, Brody, & Hughes, 2007; Harris, Prior, & Koehoorn, 2008).

The earlier start of puberty is an example of a significant **secular trend**. Secular trends occur when a physical characteristic changes over the course of several generations, such as earlier onset of menstruation or increased height resulting from better nutrition over the centuries.

Menstruation is one of several changes in puberty related to the development of primary and secondary sex characteristics. **Primary sex characteristics** are associated with the development of the organs and body structures related directly to reproduction. **Secondary sex characteristics** are the visible signs of sexual maturity that do not involve the sex organs directly.

**secular trend** a pattern of change occurring over several generations

**primary sex characteristics** characteristics associated with the development of the organs and structures of the body that directly relate to reproduction

**secondary sex characteristics** the visible signs of sexual maturity that do not directly involve the sex organs

Note the changes that have occurred in just a few years in these pre- and post-puberty photos of the same boy.

In girls, developing primary sex characteristics involves changes in the vagina and uterus. Secondary sex characteristics include the development of breasts and pubic hair. Breasts begin to grow around age 10, and pubic hair appears at about age 11. Underarm hair appears about 2 years later.

For some girls, signs of puberty start unusually early. One out of seven Caucasian girls develops breasts or pubic hair by age 8. For African American girls, the figure is one out of two. The reasons for this earlier onset are unclear, and what defines normal and abnormal onset is a controversy among specialists (Lemonick, 2000; The Endocrine Society, 2001; Ritzen, 2003).

***Puberty in Boys.*** Boys' sexual maturation follows a somewhat different course. Growth of the penis and scrotum accelerates around age 12, reaching adult size about 3 or 4 years later. As boys' penises enlarge, other primary sex characteristics develop. The prostate gland and seminal vesicles, which produce semen (the fluid that carries sperm), enlarge. A boy's first ejaculation, known as *spermarche,* usually occurs around age 13, more than a year after the body begins producing sperm. At first, the semen contains relatively few sperm, but the sperm count increases significantly with age. Secondary sex characteristics are also developing. Pubic hair begins to grow around age 12, followed by the growth of underarm and facial hair. Finally, boys' voices deepen as the vocal cords become longer and the larynx larger. (Figure 6-2 summarizes the changes that occur in sexual maturation during early adolescence.)

The surge in hormones that triggers puberty also may lead to rapid mood swings. Boys may have feelings of anger and annoyance associated with higher hormone levels. In girls, higher levels of hormones are associated with depression as well as anger (Buchanan, Eccles, & Becker, 1992).

***Body Image: Reactions to Physical Changes in Adolescence.*** Unlike infants, who also undergo rapid growth, adolescents are aware of what is happening to their bodies, and they may react with horror or joy. Few, though, are neutral about the changes they are witnessing.

Some of the changes of adolescence carry psychological weight. In the past, girls tended to view menarche with anxiety because Western society emphasized the negative aspects of menstruation, its cramps and messiness. Today, however, society views menstruation more positively, in part because more open discussion has demystified it; for example, television commercials for tampons are commonplace. As a result, menarche now typically increases

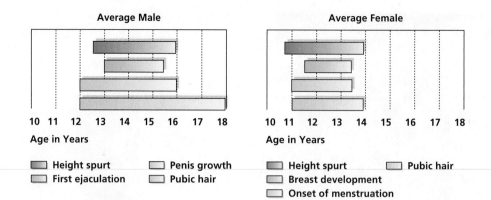

**FIGURE 6-2 Sexual Maturation**
The changes in sexual maturation that occur for males and females during early adolescence.
Source: Adapted from Tanner, 1978.

self-esteem, enhances status, and provides greater self-awareness, as girls see themselves as young adults (Johnson, Roberts, & Worell, 1999; Matlin, 2003).

A boy's first ejaculation is roughly equivalent to menarche. However, while girls generally tell their mothers about the onset of menstruation, boys rarely mention their first ejaculation to their parents or even their friends (Stein & Reiser, 1994). Why? One reason is that mothers provide the tampons or sanitary napkins girls need. For boys, the first ejaculation may be seen as a sign of their budding sexuality, an area they feel both uncertain about and reluctant to discuss with others.

Menstruation and ejaculations occur privately, but changes in body shape and size are quite public. Teenagers frequently are embarrassed by these changes. Girls, in particular, are often unhappy with their new bodies. Western ideals of beauty call for an extreme thinness at odds with the actual shape of most women. Puberty considerably increases the amount of fatty tissue, and enlarges the hips and buttocks—a far cry from the pencil-thin body society seems to demand (Unger & Crawford, 2004; McCabe & Ricciardelli, 2006; Cotrufo et al., 2007).

How children react to the onset of puberty depends in part on when it happens. Girls and boys who mature either much earlier or later than most of their peers are especially affected.

***The Timing of Puberty: The Consequences of Early and Late Maturation.*** There are social consequences for early or late maturation. And these social consequences are very important to adolescents.

**Early Maturation.** For boys, early maturation is largely a plus. Early-maturing boys tend to be more successful athletes, presumably because of their larger size. They also tend to be more popular and to have a more positive self-concept.

Early maturation in boys, though, does have a downside. Boys who mature early are more apt to have difficulties in school, and to become involved in delinquency and substance abuse. Being larger in size, they are more likely to seek the company of older boys and become involved in age-inappropriate activities. Early-maturers are also more conforming and lacking in humor although they are more responsible and cooperative in adulthood. Overall, though, early maturation is positive for boys (Taga, Markey, & Friedman, 2006; Costello et al., 2007; Lynne et al., 2007).

The story is a bit different for early-maturing girls. For them, the obvious changes in their bodies—such as the development of breasts—may lead them to feel uncomfortable and different from their peers. Moreover, because girls, in general, mature earlier than boys, early maturation tends to come at a very young age in the girl's life. Early-maturing girls may have to endure ridicule from their less mature classmates (Franko & Striegel-Moore, 2002; Olivardia & Pope, 2002; Mendle, Turkheimer, & Emery, 2007). ◉ Watch on **mydevelopmentlab.com**

Early maturation, though, is not a completely negative experience for girls. Those who mature earlier are more often sought as dates, and their popularity may enhance their

◉ Watch on **mydevelopmentlab.com**

Log onto MyDevelopmentLab.com to watch 12-year-old Kianna, her mother, and her best friend talk about how important body image is in adolescence.

self-concept. This can be psychologically challenging, however. Early-maturers may not be socially ready for the kind of one-on-one dating situations that most girls deal with at a later age. Moreover, their obvious deviance from their later-maturing peers may produce anxiety, unhappiness, and depression (Kaltiala-Heino et al., 2003).

Consequently, unless a young girl who has developed secondary sex characteristics early can handle the disapproval she may encounter when she conspicuously displays her growing sexuality, the outcome of early maturation may be negative. In countries in which attitudes about sexuality are more liberal, the results of early maturation may be more positive. For example, in Germany, which has a more open view of sex, early-maturing girls have higher self-esteem than such girls in the United States. Furthermore, the consequences of early maturation vary even within the United States, depending on the views of girls' peer groups and on prevailing community standards regarding sex (Petersen, 2000; Güre, Uçanok, & Sayil, 2006).

**Late Maturation.** As with early-maturers, the situation for late-maturers is mixed, although here boys fare worse than girls. Boys who are smaller and lighter tend to be considered less attractive. Being small, they are at a disadvantage in sports activities. They may also suffer socially as boys are expected to be taller than their dates. If these difficulties diminish a boy's self-concept, the disadvantages of late maturation could extend well into adulthood. Coping with the challenges of late maturation may actually help males, however. Late-maturing boys grow up to be assertive and insightful, and are more creatively playful than early maturers (Livson & Peskin, 1980; Kaltiala-Heino et al., 2003).

The picture for late-maturing girls is quite positive even though they may be overlooked in dating and other mixed-sex activities during junior high and middle school, and may have relatively low social status (Apter et al., 1981; Clarke-Stewart & Friedman, 1987). In fact, late-maturing girls may suffer fewer emotional problems. Before they reach 10th grade and have begun to mature visibly, they are more apt to fit the slender, "leggy" body type society idealizes than their early-maturing peers, who tend to look heavier in comparison (Petersen, 1988; Kaminaga, 2007; Leen-Feldner, Reardon, & Hayward, 2008).

The reactions to early and late maturation paint a complex picture. As we have seen, an individual's development is affected by a constellation of factors. Some developmentalists suggest that changes in peer groups, family dynamics, and particularly schools and other societal institutions may determine an adolescent's behavior more than age of maturation, and the effects of puberty in general (Dorn, Susman, & Ponirakis, 2003; Stice, 2003; Mendle, Turkheimer, & Emery, 2007; Spear, 2010).

## Nutrition, Food, and Eating Disorders: Fueling the Growth of Adolescence

*A rice cake in the afternoon, an apple for dinner. That was Heather Rhodes's typical diet her freshman year at St. Joseph's College in Rensselaer, Indiana, when she began to nurture a fear (exacerbated, she says, by the sudden death of a friend) that she was gaining weight. But when Heather, now 20, returned home to Joliet, Illinois, for summer vacation a year and a half ago, her family thought she was melting away.... Her 5'7" frame held a mere 85 pounds—down 22 pounds from her senior year in high school.... "[But] when I looked in the mirror," she says, "I thought my stomach was still huge and my face was fat." (Sandler, 1994, p. 56)*

Heather's problem: a severe eating disorder, anorexia nervosa. As we have seen, the cultural ideal of slim and fit favors late-developing girls. But when development does occur, how do girls, and increasingly, boys, cope with an image in the mirror that deviates from the popular media ideal?

The rapid physical growth of adolescence is fueled by an increase in food consumption. Particularly during the growth spurt, adolescents eat substantial quantities of food, increasing their intake of calories rather dramatically. During the teenage years, the average girl requires some 2,200 calories a day, and the average boy requires 2,800. Of course, not just any calories nourish this growth. Several nutrients are essential, particularly calcium and iron. Milk and certain vegetables provide calcium for bone growth, and calcium may prevent the

Obesity has become the most common nutritional concern during adolescence. In addition to issues of health, what are some psychological concerns about obesity in adolescence?

osteoporosis—the thinning of bones—that affects 25 percent of women in later life. Iron is also necessary, as iron-deficiency anemia is not uncommon among teenagers.

For most adolescents, the major issue is eating a sufficient balance of nutritious foods. Two extremes of nutrition concern a substantial minority and can create real threats to health: obesity and eating disorders like the one afflicting Heather Rhodes.

*Obesity.* The most common nutritional concern in adolescence is obesity. One in 5 adolescents is overweight, and 1 in 20 can be classified as obese (more than 20 percent above average body weight). The proportion of females who are classified as obese increases over the course of adolescence (Brook & Tepper, 1997; Critser, 2003; Kimm et al., 2003).

Adolescents are obese for the same reasons as younger children, but special concerns with body image may have severe psychological consequences at this age. The potential health consequences of obesity during adolescence are also problematic. Obesity taxes the circulatory system, increasing the risk of high blood pressure and diabetes. Obese adolescents also have an 80 percent chance of becoming obese adults (Blaine, Rodman, & Newman, 2007; Goble, 2008; Wang et al., 2008).

Lack of exercise is a major culprit. One survey found that by the end of the teenage years, few females get much exercise outside of school physical education classes. In fact, the older they get, the less they exercise. This is especially true for older Black female adolescents, more than half of whom report *no* physical exercise outside of school, compared with about a third of White adolescents (Deforche, De Bourdeaudhuij, & Tanghe, 2006; Delva, O'Malley, & Johnston, 2006; Reichert et al., 2009; Liou, Liou, & Chang, 2010).

Additional reasons for the high rate of obesity during adolescence include the easy availability of fast foods, which deliver large portions of high-calorie, high-fat cuisine at prices adolescents can afford. Furthermore, many adolescents spend a significant proportion of their leisure time inside their homes watching television, playing video games, and surfing the Web. Such sedentary activities not only keep adolescents from exercising, but they often are accompanied by snacks of junk foods (Rideout, Vandewater, & Wartella, 2003; Delmas et al., 2007; Krebs et al., 2007; Bray, 2008).

*Anorexia Nervosa and Bulimia.* Fear of fat and of growing obese can create its own problems—for example, Heather Rhodes suffered from **anorexia nervosa,** a severe eating disorder in which individuals refuse to eat. A troubled body image leads some adolescents to deny that their behavior and appearance, which may become skeletal, are out of the ordinary.

Anorexia is a dangerous psychological disorder; some 15 to 20 percent of its victims starve themselves to death. It primarily afflicts women between the ages of 12 and 40; intelligent, successful, and attractive White adolescent girls from affluent homes are the most susceptible. Anorexia is also becoming a problem for boys; about 10 percent of victims are male. This percentage is rising and is often associated with the use of steroids (Jacobi et al., 2004; Ricciardelli & McCabe, 2004; Crisp et al., 2006).

Though they eat little, anorexics tend to focus on food. They may shop often, collect cookbooks, talk about food, or cook huge meals for others. They may be incredibly thin but their body images are so distorted that they see themselves as disgustingly fat and try to lose more weight. Even when they grow skeletal, they cannot see what they have become.

**Bulimia,** another eating disorder, is characterized by *binge eating,* consuming large amounts of food, followed by *purging* through vomiting or the use of laxatives. Bulimics may eat an entire gallon of ice cream or a whole package of tortilla chips, but then feel such powerful guilt and depression that they intentionally rid themselves of the food. The disorder poses real risks. Though a bulimia sufferer's weight remains fairly normal, the constant vomiting and diarrhea of the binge-and-purge cycles may produce a chemical imbalance that triggers heart failure.

**anorexia nervosa** a severe eating disorder in which individuals refuse to eat, while denying that their behavior and appearance, which may become skeletal, are out of the ordinary

**bulimia** an eating disorder characterized by binges on large quantities of food, followed by purges of the food through vomiting or the use of laxatives

Why eating disorders occur is not clear, but several factors may be at work. Dieting often precedes the onset of eating disorders, as society exhorts even normal-weight individuals to be ever thinner. Losing weight may lead to feelings of control and success that encourage more dieting. Girls who mature early and have a higher level of body fat are more susceptible to eating disorders in later adolescence as they try to trim their mature bodies to fit the cultural ideal of a thin, boyish physique. Clinically depressed adolescents are also prone to develop eating disorders later (Giordana, 2005; Santos, Richards, & Bleckley, 2007; Courtney, Gamboz, & Johnson, 2008; Rodgers, Paxton, & Chabrol, 2010).

Some experts suggest that a biological cause may underlie both anorexia nervosa and bulimia. Twin studies suggest genetic components are involved. In addition, hormonal imbalances sometimes occur in sufferers (Kump et al., 2007; Kaye, 2008; Wade et al., 2008; Baker et al., 2009).

Other attempts to explain the eating disorders emphasize psychological and social factors. For instance, some experts suggest that the disorders are a result of perfectionistic, overdemanding parents or by-products of other family difficulties. Culture also plays a role. Anorexia nervosa, for instance, is found primarily in cultures that idealize slender female bodies. Because in most places such a standard does not hold, anorexia is not prevalent outside the United States (Haines & Neumark-Sztainer, 2006; Harrison & Hefner, 2006; Bennett, 2008).

For example, anorexia is relatively rare in Asia, with the exceptions of areas in which Western influence is greatest. Furthermore, anorexia nervosa is a fairly recent disorder. It was not seen in the seventeenth and eighteenth centuries, when the ideal of the female body was a plump corpulence. The increasing number of boys with anorexia in the United States may be related to a growing emphasis on a muscular male physique that features little body fat (Mangweth, Hausmann, & Walch, 2004; Makino et al., 2006; Greenberg, Cwikel, & Mirsky, 2007; Pearson, Combs, & Smith, 2010).

Because anorexia nervosa and bulimia have both biological and environmental causes, treatment typically requires a mix of approaches (e.g., both psychological therapy and dietary modifications). In more extreme cases, hospitalization may be necessary (Wilson, Grilo, & Vitousek, 2007; Keel & Haedt, 2008; Stein, Latzer, & Merick, 2009).

This young woman suffers from anorexia nervosa, a severe eating disorder in which people refuse to eat, while denying that their behavior and appearance are out of the ordinary.

## Brain Development and Thought: Paving the Way for Cognitive Growth

Teenagers tend to assert themselves more as they gain greater independence. This independence is, in part, the result of changes in the brain that bring significant advances in cognitive abilities. As the number of neurons (the cells of the nervous system) continues to grow, and their interconnections become richer and more complex, adolescent thinking becomes more sophisticated (Thompson & Nelson, 2001; Toga & Thompson, 2003; Petanjek et al., 2008).

The brain produces an oversupply of gray matter during adolescence, which is later pruned back by 1 to 2 percent each year (see Figure 6-3). Myelination—the process of insulating nerve cells with fat cells—increases, making the transmission of neural messages more efficient. Both pruning and increased myelination contribute to the growing cognitive abilities of adolescents (Sowell et al., 2001; Sowell et al., 2003).

The prefrontal cortex of the brain, which is not fully developed until the early 20s, undergoes considerable development during adolescence. The *prefrontal cortex* allows people to think, evaluate, and make complex judgments in a uniquely human way. It underlies the increasingly complex intellectual achievements that are possible during adolescence.

At this stage, the prefrontal cortex becomes increasingly efficient in communicating with other parts of the brain, creating a communication system that is more distributed and sophisticated, which permits the different areas of the brain to process information more effectively (Scherf, Sweeney, & Luna, 2006; Hare et al., 2008).

The prefrontal cortex also provides impulse control. An individual with a fully-developed prefrontal cortex is able to inhibit the desire to act on such emotions as anger or rage. In adolescence, however, the prefrontal cortex is biologically immature; the ability to inhibit impulses is not fully developed (Weinberger, 2001; Steinberg & Scott, 2003; Eshel et al., 2007).

The prefrontal cortex, the area of the brain responsible for impulse control, is biologically immature during adolescence, leading to some of the risky and impulsive behavior associated with the age group.

## The Immature Brain Argument: Too Young for the Death Penalty?

*Just after 2 a.m. on September 9, 1993, Christopher Simmons, 17, and Charles Benjamin, 15, broke into a trailer south of Fenton, Missouri, just outside of St. Louis. They woke Shirley Ann Crook, a 46-year-old truck driver who was inside, and proceeded to tie her up and cover her eyes and mouth with silver duct tape. They then put her in the back of her minivan, drove her to a railroad bridge and pushed her into the river below, where her body was found the next day. Simmons and Benjamin later confessed to the abduction and murder, which had netted them $6. (Raeburn, 2004, p. 26)*

This horrific case sent Benjamin to life in prison, but Simmons was given the death penalty. Simmons's lawyers appealed, and ultimately the U.S. Supreme Court ruled that no one under the age of 18 could be executed, citing their youth. Among the factors affecting the Court's decision was evidence from neuroscientists and child developmentalists that adolescents' brains were still developing in important ways and thus lacked judgment due to brain immaturity. This reasoning says adolescents are not fully capable of making sound decisions because their brains differ from those of adults.

The argument that adolescents may not be as responsible for their crimes stems from research showing continued brain growth and maturation during the teenage years, and beyond. For example, neurons that make up unnecessary gray matter begin to disappear. The volume of white matter begins to increase. This change permits more sophisticated, thoughtful cognitive processing (Beckman, 2004).

When the brain's frontal lobes contain more white matter, they are better at restraining impulsivity. Teenagers may act impulsively, responding with emotion rather than reason. Their ability to foresee consequences may also be hindered by their less mature brains.

Are adolescents' brains so immature that offenders should receive a lesser punishment for their crimes than adults? The answer to this difficult question may come from students of ethics rather than science.

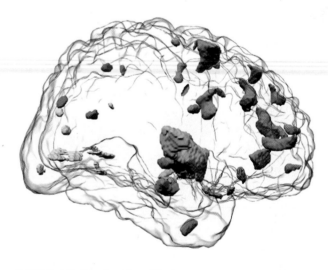

**FIGURE 6-3 Pruning Gray Matter**
This three-dimensional view of the brain shows areas of gray matter that are pruned from the brain between adolescence and adulthood.
Source: Sowell et al., 1999.

***Sleep Deprivation.*** With increasing academic and social demands, adolescents go to bed later and get up earlier, leaving them sleep-deprived. This deprivation coincides with a shift in their internal clocks. Older adolescents have a need to go to bed later and to sleep later in the morning, requiring 9 hours of sleep to feel rested. Yet half of adolescents sleep 7 hours or less each night, and almost one in five gets less than 6 hours. Because they typically have early morning classes but don't feel sleepy until late at night, they end up getting far less sleep than their bodies crave (National Sleep Foundation, 2002; Fuligni & Hardway, 2006; Epstein & Mardon, 2007; Loessl et al., 2008).

Sleep-deprived teens have lower grades, are more depressed, and have greater difficulty controlling their moods. They are also at great risk for auto accidents (Teixeira, Fischer, & Lowden, 2006; Dahl, 2008; Roberts, Roberts, & Duong, 2009).

---

## REVIEW, CHECK, AND APPLY

### REVIEW

**LO1** What physical changes do adolescents experience?

- Adolescence is a period of rapid physical growth, including the changes puberty brings.

**LO2** What are the consequences of early and late maturation?

- Adolescents' responses to puberty range widely—from confusion to increased self-esteem. Both boys and girls face positive as well as negative consequences regarding early and late maturation.

**LO3** What are the nutritional needs and concerns of adolescents?

- Adequate nutrition is essential to fuel adolescents' physical growth. Changing physical needs and environmental pressures can cause obesity or eating disorders.

### CHECK YOURSELF

1. The hormone _____ appears to play a role in the start of puberty for males and females.
   a. estrogen
   b. pituitary
   c. serotonin
   d. leptin

2. Which of the following is an example of a primary sex characteristic?
   a. growth of pubic hair
   b. development of breasts
   c. changes in the uterus
   d. sudden increase in height

3. The most common nutritional concern in adolescence is _____.
   a. anorexia
   b. bulimia
   c. sleep deprivation
   d. obesity

### APPLYING LIFESPAN DEVELOPMENT

- How can societal and environmental influences contribute to eating disorders?

 **Study** and **Review** on **MyDevelopmentLab.com**

Answers: 1) d; 2) c; 3) d

---

# Threats to Adolescents' Well-Being

**LO4**   **What are the major threats to the well-being of adolescents?**

**LO5**   **What dangers do adolescent sexual practices present, and how can these dangers be avoided?**

LEARNING OBJECTIVES

*Like most parents, I had thought of drug use as something you worried about when your kids got to high school. Now I know that, on the average, kids begin using drugs at 11 or 12, but at the time that never crossed our minds. Ryan had just begun attending mixed parties. He was playing Little League. In the eighth grade, Ryan started getting into a little trouble—one time he and another fellow stole a fire extinguisher, but we thought it was just a prank. Then his grades began to deteriorate. He began sneaking out at night. He would become belligerent at the drop of a hat, then sunny and nice again....*

*It wasn't until Ryan fell apart at 14 that we started thinking about drugs. He had just begun McLean High School, and to him, it was like going to drug camp every day. Back then, everything*

The use of marijuana among high school students has decreased since the late 1990s.

*was so available. He began cutting classes, a common tip-off, but we didn't hear from the school until he was flunking everything. It turned out that he was going to school for the first period, getting checked in, then leaving and smoking marijuana all day. (Shafer, 1990, p. 82)*

Ryan's parents learned that marijuana was not the only drug he was using. Ryan was what his friends called a "garbage head." He would try anything. Despite efforts to curb his drug use, he died at 16, hit by a car after wandering into the street while on drugs.

Though it rarely ends in such tragedy, drug use, as well as other kinds of substance use and abuse, is one of several health threats in adolescence, usually one of the healthiest periods of life. While the extent of risky behavior is unknown, drugs, alcohol, and tobacco pose serious threats to adolescents' health and well-being.

## Illegal Drugs

Illegal drug use in adolescence is very common. A recent survey of nearly 50,000 U.S. students showed that almost 50 percent of high school seniors and almost 20 percent of eighth graders had used marijuana within the past year. Although marijuana usage (and use of other drugs) has declined in recent years, the data on drug use still shows substantial use by adolescents (Nanda & Konnur, 2006; Johnston et al., 2009; Tang & Orwin, 2009) (see Figure 6-4).

Adolescents use drugs for many reasons. Some seek the pleasure they provide. Others hope to escape the pressures of everyday life, however temporarily. Some adolescents try drugs simply for the thrill of doing something illegal. The drug use of well-known role models, such as movie stars and athletes, may also be enticing. And peer pressure plays a role: Adolescents are especially influenced by their peer groups (Urberg, Luo, & Pilgrim, 2003; Nation & Heflinger, 2006; Young et al., 2006; Pandina, Johnson, & White, 2010).

The use of illegal drugs poses several dangers. Some drugs are addictive. **Addictive drugs** produce a biological or psychological dependence, leading users to increasingly crave them.

With a biological addiction, the drug's presence becomes so common that the body cannot function in its absence. Addiction causes actual physical—and potentially lingering—changes in the nervous system. The drug may no longer provide a "high," but may be necessary to maintain the perception of normalcy (Cami & Farré, 2003; Munzar, Cami, & Farré, 2003).

Drugs also can produce psychological addiction. People grow to depend on drugs to cope with everyday stress. If used as an escape, drugs may prevent adolescents from confronting—and

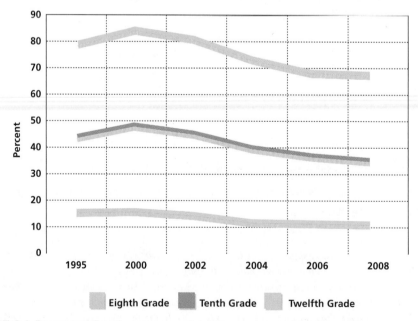

Legend: Eighth Grade   Tenth Grade   Twelfth Grade

**FIGURE 6-4 Downward Trend**
According to an annual survey, the proportion of students reporting marijuana use over the past 12 months has decreased since 1999. What might account for the decline in drug use?
Source: Johnston et al., 2009.

**addictive drugs** drugs that produce a biological or psychological dependence in users, leading to increasingly powerful cravings for them

solving—the problems that led to drug use in the first place. Even casual use of less hazardous drugs can escalate to dangerous forms of substance abuse.

Whatever the reason for using drugs in the first place, drug addiction is among the most difficult of all behaviors to modify. Even with extensive treatment, addictive cravings are hard to suppress (Thobaben, 2010).

## Alcohol: Use and Abuse

Three-fourths of college students have something in common: They've consumed at least one alcoholic drink during the last 30 days. More than 40 percent say they've had five or more drinks within the past 2 weeks, and some 16 percent drink 16 or more drinks per week. High school students, too, are drinkers: Nearly three-quarters of high school seniors report having consumed alcohol by the end of high school, and about two-fifths have done so by eighth grade. More than half of twelfth graders and nearly a fifth of eighth graders say that they have been drunk at least once in their lives (Ford, 2007; Johnston et al., 2009).

Binge drinking is a particular problem on college campuses. Binge drinking is defined for men as drinking five or more drinks in one sitting; for women, who tend to weigh less and whose bodies absorb alcohol less efficiently, binge drinking is defined as four drinks in one sitting. Surveys find that almost half of male college students and over 40 percent of female college students say they participated in binge drinking during the previous two weeks (Harrell & Karim, 2008; Beets et al., 2009) (see Figure 6-5).

Binge drinking affects even those who don't drink or drink very little. Two-thirds of lighter drinkers reported that they have been disturbed by drunken students while sleeping or studying. Around a third have been insulted or humiliated by a drunken student, and 25 percent of women said they have been the target of an unwanted sexual advance by a drunk classmate (Wechsler et al., 2000, 2002, 2003).

There are many reasons adolescents drink. For some—especially male athletes, who tend to drink more than their peers—drinking is a way to prove their prowess. As with drug use, others drink to release inhibitions and tension, and reduce stress. Many begin because they believe everyone else is drinking heavily, something known as the *false consensus effect* (Pavis, Cunningham-Burley, & Amos, 1997; Nelson & Wechsler, 2003; Weitzman, Nelson, & Wechsler, 2003).

Some adolescents cannot control their alcohol use. **Alcoholics** learn to depend on alcohol and are unable to stop drinking. They develop an increasing tolerance for it, and need to drink ever-larger amounts to get the positive effects they crave. Some drink throughout the day, while others go on binges.

Why some adolescents become alcoholics is not fully understood. Genetics plays a role: Alcoholism runs in families, though not all alcoholics have family members with alcohol problems. For adolescents with an alcoholic parent or family member, alcoholism may be triggered by efforts to deal with the stress (Berenson, 2005; Clarke et al., 2008).

Of course, the origins of an adolescent's alcohol or drug problems matter less than getting help. Parents, teachers, and friends can help a teen—if they realize there is a problem. Some of the telltale signs are described next.

## Tobacco: The Dangers of Smoking

Despite an awareness of the dangers of smoking, many adolescents indulge in it. Recent figures show that, overall, smoking is declining among adolescents, but the numbers remain substantial; and within certain groups the numbers are increasing. Smoking is on the rise among girls, and in several countries, including Austria, Norway, and Sweden, the proportion of girls who smoke is higher than for boys. There are racial differences, too: White children and those of lower socioeconomic status are more likely to experiment with cigarettes and to start smoking earlier than African American children and those of higher socioeconomic status. Also, significantly more White males of high school age smoke than do their African American male peers, although the difference is narrowing (Harrell et al., 1998; Stolberg, 1998; Baker, Brandon, & Chassin, 2004; Fergusson et al., 2007).

Smoking is becoming a habit that is harder to maintain because there are growing social sanctions against it. It's becoming more difficult to find a comfortable place to smoke: More places, including schools and places of business, have become "smoke-free." Even so, a good

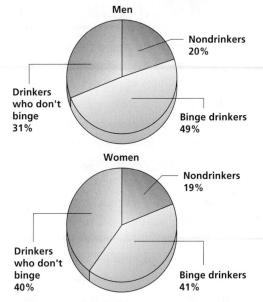

**FIGURE 6-5 Binge Drinking Among College Students**
For men, binge drinking is defined as consuming five or more drinks in one sitting; for women, the total is four or more. Why is binge drinking popular?
Source: Wechsler et al., 2003.

**alcoholics** persons with alcohol problems who have learned to depend on alcohol and are unable to control their drinking

## *Hooked on Drugs or Alcohol?*

### Becoming an Informed Consumer of Development

It is not always easy to know if an adolescent is abusing drugs or alcohol, but there are signals. Among them:

#### Identification with the drug culture

- Drug-related magazines or slogans on clothing
- Conversation and jokes that involve drugs
- Hostility discussing drugs
- Collection of beer cans

#### Signs of physical deterioration

- Memory lapses, short attention span, difficulty concentrating
- Poor physical coordination, slurred or incoherent speech
- Unhealthy appearance, indifference to hygiene and grooming
- Bloodshot eyes, dilated pupils

#### Dramatic changes in school performance

- Marked downturn in grades—not just from C's to F's, but from A's to B's and C's; assignments not completed
- Increased absenteeism or tardiness

#### Changes in behavior

- Chronic dishonesty (lying, stealing, cheating); trouble with the police
- Changes in friends; evasiveness in talking about new ones
- Possession of large amounts of money
- Increasing and inappropriate anger, hostility, irritability, secretiveness
- Reduced motivation, energy, self-discipline, self-esteem
- Diminished interest in extracurricular activities and hobbies (Adapted from Franck & Brownstone, 1991; National Institute on Drug Abuse, 2007)

If an adolescent—or anyone else—fits any of these descriptors, help is probably needed. Call the national hotline run by the National Institute on Drug Abuse at (800) 662-4357 or visit its website at www.nida.nih.gov. You can also find a local listing for Alcoholics Anonymous in the telephone book.

## *Cultural Dimensions*

### Selling Death: Pushing Smoking to the Less Advantaged

*In Dresden, Germany, three women in miniskirts offer passers-by a pack of Lucky Strikes and a leaflet that reads "You just got hold of a nice piece of America." Says a local doctor, "Adolescents time and again receive cigarettes at such promotions."*

*A Jeep decorated with the Camel logo pulls up to a high school in Buenos Aires. A woman begins handing out free cigarettes to 15- and 16-year-olds during their lunch recess.*

*At a video arcade in Taipei, free American cigarettes are strewn atop each game. At a disco filled with high school students, free packs of Salems are on each table. (Ecenbarger, 1993, p. 50)*

U.S. cigarette companies have sought new markets among the least advantaged people, both at home and abroad. In the early 1990s, the R.J. Reynolds tobacco company designed a brand of cigarettes it named "Uptown." The advertising made clear who the target was: African Americans living in urban areas (Quinn, 1990).

Subsequent protests caused the company to withdraw "Uptown" from the market (Quinn, 1990; Brown, 2009).

In addition to seeking new converts at home, tobacco companies aggressively recruit adolescent smokers abroad. In many developing countries the number of smokers is still low. Tobacco companies are using marketing strategies such as free samples to increase this number. In countries where American culture and products enjoy high esteem, advertising suggests cigarette smoking is an American—and consequently prestigious—habit (Sesser, 1993).

The strategy is effective. In some Latin American cities as many as 50 percent of teenagers smoke. According to the World Health Organization, smoking will prematurely kill some 200 million of the world's children and adolescents. Overall, 10 percent of the world's population will die from smoking (Ecenbarger, 1993; Picard, 2008).

number of adolescents still smoke, despite knowing the dangers of smoking and of second-hand smoke. Why, then, do adolescents begin to smoke and maintain the habit?

One reason is that for some adolescents, smoking is seen as an adolescent rite of passage, a sign of growing up. In addition, seeing influential models, such as film stars, parents, and peers smoking increases the chances that an adolescent will take up the habit. Cigarettes are also very addictive. Nicotine, the active chemical ingredient of cigarettes, can produce biological and psychological dependency very quickly. Although one or two cigarettes do not usually produce a lifetime smoker, it takes only a little more to start the habit. In fact, people who smoke as few as 10 cigarettes early in their lives stand an 80 percent chance of becoming habitual smokers (Kodl & Mermelstein, 2004; West, Romero, & Trinidad, 2007; Tucker et al., 2008; Wills et al., 2008).

## Sexually Transmitted Infections

One out of four adolescents contracts a **sexually transmitted infection (STI)** before graduating from high school. Overall, around 2.5 million teenagers contract an STI each year (Centers for Disease Control, 2009) (see Figure 6-6).

The most common STI is *human papilloma virus (HPV)*. HPV can be transmitted through genital contact without intercourse. Most infections do not have symptoms, but HPV can produce genital warts and in some cases lead to cervical cancer. A vaccine that protects against some kinds of HPV is now available. The U.S. Centers for Disease Control and Prevention recommends it be routinely administered to girls 11 to 12 years of age—a recommendation that has provoked considerable political reaction (Kahn, 2007; Casper & Carpenter, 2008; Caskey, Lindau, & Caleb, 2009).

Another common STI is *trichomoniasis,* an infection in the vagina or penis, which is caused by a parasite. Initially without symptoms, it can eventually cause a painful discharge. *Chlamydia*, a bacterial infection, starts with few symptoms, but later causes burning urination and a discharge from the penis or vagina. It can lead to pelvic inflammation and even to sterility. Chlamydia can be treated with antibiotics (Nockels & Oakshott, 1999; Fayers et al., 2003).

*Genital herpes* is a virus not unlike the cold sores that appear around the mouth. Its first symptoms are often small blisters or sores around the genitals, which may break open and become quite painful. Although the sores may heal after a few weeks, the infection often recurs and the cycle repeats itself. When the sores reappear, this incurable infection is contagious.

*Gonorrhea* and *syphilis* are the oldest known STIs, with cases recorded by ancient historians. Both infections were deadly before antibiotics, but can now be treated effectively.

*Acquired immunodeficiency syndrome,* or *AIDS,* is the deadliest of sexually transmitted diseases and a leading cause of death among young people. AIDS has no cure, but treatments have improved greatly in recent years and AIDS is no longer the sure death sentence that it used to be. Although it began as a problem that primarily affected homosexuals, it has spread to other populations, including heterosexuals and intravenous drug users. Minorities have been particularly hard hit: African Americans and Hispanics account for some 40 percent of AIDS cases, although they make up only 18 percent of the population. Already, 25 million people have died from AIDS, and people living with the disease number 33 million worldwide (Quinn & Overbaugh, 2005; UNAIDS, 2009).

**From a health care provider's perspective:** Why do adolescents' increased cognitive abilities, including the ability to reason and to think experimentally, fail to deter them from drug and alcohol abuse, tobacco use, and sexually transmitted infections? How might you use these abilities to design a program to prevent these problems?

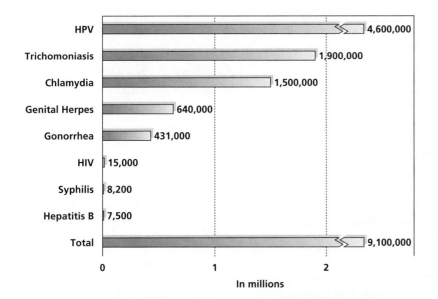

**FIGURE 6-6 Sexually Transmitted Infections (STIs) Among Adolescents**
Why are adolescents in particular in danger of contracting an STI?
Sources: Alan Guttmacher Institute, 2004; Weinstock, Berman, & Cates, 2006.

**sexually transmitted infection (STI)** a infection that is spread through sexual contact

## TABLE 6-1 SAFER SEX PRACTICES

The only foolproof method of avoiding a sexually transmitted infection (STI) is abstinence. However, by following the "safer sex" practices listed here, one can significantly reduce the risk of contracting an STI:

- *Know your sexual partner—well.* Before having sex with someone, learn about his or her sexual history.

- *Use condoms.* For those in sexual relationships, condoms are the most reliable means of preventing transmission of STIs. In addition, dental dams (also called vaginal dams) can provide a precautionary barrier during oral sex.

- *Avoid the exchange of bodily fluids, particularly semen.* In particular, avoid anal intercourse. The AIDS virus in particular can spread through small tears in the rectum, making anal intercourse without condoms particularly dangerous. Oral sex, once thought relatively safe, is now viewed as potentially dangerous for contracting the AIDS virus.

- *Stay sober.* Using alcohol and drugs impairs judgment and can lead to poor decisions—and it makes using a condom correctly more difficult.

- *Consider the benefits of monogamy.* People in long-term, monogamous relationships with partners who have been faithful are at a lower risk of contracting STIs.

## Avoiding STIs

Short of abstinence, there is no certain way to avoid STIs. However, there are ways to make sex safer; these are listed in Table 6-1.

Even with substantial sex education, the use of safer sex practices is far from universal. Teenagers believe their chances of contracting STIs are minimal. This is particularly true when they view their partner as "safe"—someone they know well and with whom they have had a relatively long-term relationship (Lefkowitz, Sigman, & Kit-fong Au, 2000; Tinsley, Lees, & Sumartojo, 2004).

Unfortunately, unless one knows a partner's complete sexual history and STI status, unprotected sex remains a risk. And that information is difficult to get. Not only is it embarrassing to ask, partners may not be accurate reporters, whether from ignorance of their own exposure, embarrassment, forgetfulness, or a sense of privacy. As a result, STIs remain a significant problem.

## REVIEW, CHECK, AND APPLY

### REVIEW

**LO4**  What are the major threats to the well-being of adolescents?

- The use of illegal drugs and alcohol is prevalent among adolescents as a way to find pleasure, avoid pressure, or gain the approval of peers.

- Despite the well-known dangers of smoking, adolescents often smoke to enhance their images or emulate adults.

**LO5**  What dangers do adolescent sexual practices present, and how can these dangers be avoided?

- One out of four adolescents contracts a sexually transmitted infection (STI) before graduating from high school.

- AIDS is the most serious of the sexually transmitted infections. Safe sex practices or abstinence can prevent AIDS, but adolescents often ignore these strategies.

### CHECK YOURSELF

1. Adolescents have a variety of reasons for using drugs. Circle all that apply.

   a. pleasurable feelings

   b. escape from everyday life

   c. thrill of doing something illegal

   d. parental pressure

   e. peer pressure

2. In response to declining markets in the United States, tobacco companies have increased their business by:

   a. selling cigarettes in countries where American culture and products are held in high esteem.

   b. diversifying into clothing promoting smoking.

   c. lowering their prices to sell more cigarettes.

   d. increasing their prices so they only have to sell half.

3. _____ is the most common sexually transmitted infection.

### APPLYING LIFESPAN DEVELOPMENT

- How might adolescents' concerns about self-image contribute to smoking and alcohol use?

✓●─Study and Review on
MyDevelopmentLab.com

Answers: 1) a, b, c, e; 2) a; 3) Human papilloma virus (HPV)

## MODULE 6.2 Cognitive Development in Adolescence

*It is no small feat to earn a 95 average at the Humanities Preparatory Academy in Greenwich Village and to graduate at the top of a class of 158. It is almost unheard of to pull it off in two years.*

*It certainly does not help if, like 18-year-old Elizabeth Murray, you did your homework in the littered Bronx hallways and stairwells where you usually slept because your mother had died of AIDS and your drug-addicted father was suffering from the same disease.*

*Across town, in Elmhurst, Queens, QiQi Cheng, 18, attained a 96 average, also squeezing four years of high school into two. When she graduates this June, it will be as valedictorian. Yet it was not even three years ago that she stepped off a plane from Shanghai, knowing only a few words of English.*

*And in Queens Village, LeTicia Williams will graduate with a 90 average, even though she virtually dropped out of school for more than two years, spending her days fighting with her drug-addicted mother for money to feed her younger brothers. (Kennedy, 1999, p. A18)*

The extraordinary success and perseverance of these students is but one example of the impressive intellectual growth that occurs during adolescence. In fact, by the end of this stage, adolescents match adults in cognitive abilities in major respects.

In this module, we examine adolescents' cognitive development. The module begins with a look at several theories. We first consider the Piagetian approach, discussing how adolescents use formal operations to solve problems. We then look at a different viewpoint: the increasingly influential information processing perspectives. We consider the growth of metacognitive abilities, through which adolescents gain awareness of their own thinking processes. We also look at the ways in which metacognition leads to egocentrism and the invention of personal fables.

The module then examines school performance. After discussing the profound impact that socioeconomic status has on school achievement, we consider school performance and ethnicity. We then look at the impact cyberspace has on education, the skills students must learn to use the Internet effectively, and the dangers the Internet poses. We close with a discussion of the role socioeconomic status plays in high school dropout rates.

# Cognitive Development

**LO6**   How does cognitive development proceed during adolescence?

**LO7**   What aspects of cognitive development cause difficulties for adolescents?

*Ms. Mejia smiled as she read a highly creative paper. As part of her eighth-grade American Government class, she asked students to write about what their lives would be like if America had not won its war for independence from Britain. She had tried a similar task with her sixth graders, but many of them were unable to imagine anything other than what they knew. Her eighth graders, however, were inventing some very interesting scenarios. One boy imagined himself as Lord Lucas; a girl imagined that she would serve a rich landowner; another that she would plot to overthrow the government.*

What is it that sets adolescents' thinking apart from that of younger children? One of the major changes is the ability to think beyond the concrete, current situation to what *might* or *could* be. Adolescents are able to keep in their heads a variety of abstract possibilities, and they can see issues in relative, as opposed to absolute, terms. Instead of viewing problems as having black-and-white solutions, they are capable of perceiving shades of gray.

Once again we can use several approaches to explain adolescents' cognitive development. We'll begin by returning to Piaget's theory, which has had a significant influence on how developmentalists think about thinking during adolescence.

## Piagetian Approaches to Cognitive Development: Using Formal Operations

Leigh, age 14, is asked to solve the problem: What determines the speed at which a pendulum moves back and forth? Leigh is given a weight hanging from a string and told that she can vary several things: the length of the string, the weight of the object, the amount of force used to push the string, and the height to which the weight is raised in an arc before it is released.

Leigh doesn't remember, but she was asked to solve the same problem at age 8 as part of a longitudinal research study. She was then in the concrete operational period, and her efforts were not very successful. Her haphazard approach showed no systematic plan of action. For instance, she simultaneously tried to push the pendulum harder *and* shorten the length of the string *and* increase the weight on the string. Because she varied so many factors at once, when the pendulum's speed changed, she had no way of knowing what had made the difference.

Now, Leigh is more systematic. Rather than immediately pushing and pulling at the pendulum, she stops to think about which factors to consider. She ponders how she might test which factor is important, forming a hypothesis. Then, as a scientist conducts an experiment, she varies only one factor at a time. By examining each variable separately and systematically, she comes to the correct solution: The length of the string determines the speed of the pendulum.

***Using Formal Operations to Solve Problems.*** Leigh's approach to the pendulum question, a problem devised by Piaget, shows she has moved into the formal operational period of cognitive development (Piaget & Inhelder, 1958). In the **formal operational stage** people develop the ability to think abstractly. Piaget suggested that people reach it at the start of adolescence, around age 12.

Adolescents can consider problems in abstract rather than concrete terms by using formal principles of logic. They can test their understanding by systematically conducting rudimentary experiments and observing the results. Thus, the adolescent Leigh could think about the pendulum problem abstractly, and she understood how to test her hypotheses.

Adolescents are able to use formal reasoning, starting with a general theory about what causes a certain outcome and then deducing explanations for the situations in which that outcome occurs. Like the scientists who form hypotheses, discussed in Chapter 1, they can test their theories. What distinguishes this kind of thinking from earlier stages is the ability to start with the abstract and move to the concrete; in previous stages, children are tied to the concrete present. At age 8, Leigh just moved things around to see what would happen in the pendulum problem, a concrete approach. At age 12, she began with the abstract idea that each variable should be tested separately.

Adolescents also can use propositional thought during this stage. *Propositional thought* is reasoning that uses abstract logic in the absence of concrete examples. Such thinking allows adolescents to understand that if certain premises are true, then a conclusion must also be true. For example:

| | |
|---|---|
| All men are mortal. | *[premise]* |
| Socrates is a man. | *[premise]* |
| Therefore, Socrates is mortal. | *[conclusion]* |

Adolescents understand that if both premises are true, then so is the conclusion. They are capable of using similar reasoning when premises and conclusions are stated more abstractly, as follows:

| | |
|---|---|
| All A's are B. | *[premise]* |
| C is an A. | *[premise]* |
| Therefore, C is a B. | *[conclusion]* |

Although Piaget proposed that the formal operational stage begins at the onset of adolescence, he also hypothesized that—as with all the stages—full cognitive capabilities emerge gradually through a combination of physical maturation and environmental experiences. It is not until around age 15, Piaget says, that adolescents fully settle into the formal operational stage.

In fact, evidence suggests that many people hone these skills at a later age, and some never fully employ them at all. Most studies show that only 40 to 60 percent of college students

**formal operational stage** the period at which people develop the ability to think abstractly

and adults achieve formal operational thinking completely, with some estimates as low as 25 percent. But many adults who do not use formal operational thought in every domain are fully competent in *some* aspects (Sugarman, 1988; Keating 1990, 2006).

The culture in which they are raised affects how adolescents use formal operations. People with little formal education, who live in isolated, technologically unsophisticated societies are less likely to use formal operations than formally educated persons in more sophisticated societies (Jahoda, 1980; Segall et al., 1990; Commons, Galaz-Fontes, & Morse, 2006).

It is not that adolescents (and adults) from cultures using few formal operations are incapable of attaining them. It is more likely that what characterizes formal operations—scientific reasoning—is not equally valued in all societies. If everyday life does not require or promote a certain type of reasoning, it is not likely that people will use such reasoning when confronting a problem (Gauvain, 1998).

Like scientists who form hypotheses, adolescents in the formal operational stage use systematic reasoning. They start with a general theory about what produces a particular outcome and then deduce explanations for specific situations in which they see that particular outcome.

### The Consequences of Adolescents' Use of Formal Operations.

The ability to reason abstractly, to use formal operations, changes adolescents' everyday behavior. Whereas earlier they may have blindly accepted rules and explanations, their increased abstract reasoning abilities may lead to strenuous questioning of their parents and other authority figures.

In general, adolescents become more argumentative. They enjoy using abstract reasoning to poke holes in others' explanations, and their increased critical thinking abilities zero in on parents' and teachers' perceived shortcomings. For instance, they may see their parents' arguments against using drugs as inconsistent if their parents used drugs in adolescence without consequence. But adolescents can be indecisive, too, as they are able to see the merits of multiple sides to issues (Elkind, 1996; Alberts, Elkind, & Ginsberg, 2007).

Coping with these new critical abilities can be challenging for parents, teachers, and other adults who deal with adolescents. But it makes adolescents more interesting, as they actively seek to understand the values and justifications they encounter.

### Evaluating Piaget's Approach.

Each time we've considered Piaget's theory, several concerns have arisen. Let's summarize some of them here:

- Piaget suggests that cognitive development proceeds in universal, step-like stages. Yet significant differences exist in cognitive abilities from one person to the next, especially when we compare individuals from different cultures. We also find inconsistencies within the same individual. People indicate they have reached a certain level of thinking in some tasks but not others. If Piaget were correct, a person ought to perform uniformly well upon reaching a given stage (Siegler, 2007).

- The Piagetian notion of stages suggests that cognitive growth occurs in relatively rapid shifts from one stage to the next. Many developmentalists, however, argue that cognitive development is more continuous—increasing in quantitative accumulations rather than qualitative leaps forward. They also contend that Piaget's theory better *describes* behavior at a given stage than *explains* why the shift to a new stage occurs (Case, 1999; Birney & Sternberg, 2006).

- Citing the nature of the tasks Piaget used to measure cognitive abilities, critics suggest that he underestimated the age at which certain abilities emerge. It is now widely accepted that infants and children are more sophisticated than Piaget asserted (Siegler, 2007; Siegler & Lin, 2010).

- Some developmentalists argue that formal operations are not the epitome of thinking and that more sophisticated forms do not emerge until early adulthood. Developmental psychologist Giesela Labouvie-Vief (2006) argues that a complex society requires thought not necessarily based on pure logic. Instead, thinking must be flexible, allow for interpretive processes, and reflect the subtlety of cause and effect in real world events—something that Labouvie-Vief calls *postformal thinking* (Labouvie-Vief, 2006).

These criticisms regarding Piaget's approach to cognitive development have genuine merit. Yet, Piaget's theory has inspired countless studies on the development of thinking capacities

**information processing perspective** the model that seeks to identify the way that individuals take in, use, and store information

**metacognition** the knowledge that people have about their own thinking processes, and their ability to monitor their cognition

and processes, and it also has spurred much classroom reform. His bold statements about the nature of cognitive development sparked opposition that brought forth new approaches, such as the information processing perspective we examine next (Taylor & Rosenbach, 2005; Kuhn, 2008).

## Information Processing Perspectives: Gradual Transformations in Abilities

From an information processing perspective, adolescents' cognitive abilities grow gradually and continuously. Unlike Piaget's view that increasing cognitive sophistication is a reflection of stage-like spurts, the **information processing perspective** sees changes in adolescents' cognitive abilities as gradual transformations in the capacity to take in, use, and store information. Multiple progressive changes occur in the ways people organize their thinking, develop strategies to deal with new situations, sort facts, and advance in memory capacity and perceptual abilities (Pressley & Schneider, 1997; Wyer, 2004).

Adolescents' general intelligence—as measured by traditional IQ tests—remains stable, but dramatic improvements occur in the specific abilities that underlie intelligence. Verbal, mathematical, and spatial abilities increase. Memory capacity grows, and adolescents become adept at handling more than one stimulus at a time—as when they study for a biology test while listening to a CD.

As Piaget noted, adolescents grow increasingly sophisticated in understanding problems, grasping abstract concepts and hypothetical thinking, and comprehending the possibilities inherent in situations. This permits them, for instance, to endlessly dissect the course their relationships might hypothetically take.

Adolescents know more about the world, too. Their store of knowledge increases as the amount of material they are exposed to grows and their memory capacity enlarges. In sum, mental abilities markedly improve during adolescence (Kail, 2003, 2004; Kail & Miller, 2006).

According to information processing theories of cognitive development, one of the main reasons for adolescents' advances in mental abilities is the growth of metacognition. **Metacognition** is the knowledge of one's own thinking processes, and the ability to monitor one's own cognition. Although younger children can use some metacognitive strategies, adolescents are much more adept at understanding their own mental processes.

For example, as their understanding of their memory capacity improves, adolescents can better gauge how long they need to memorize given material for a test. They also can judge when the material is fully memorized much more accurately than in younger days. Their improved metacognition permits adolescents to comprehend and master school material more effectively (Kuhn, 2000; Desoete, Roeyers, & De Clercq, 2003; Schneider, 2010).

These new abilities also can make adolescents deeply introspective and self-conscious—two characteristics which, as we see next, may produce a high degree of egocentrism.

## Egocentrism in Thinking: Adolescents' Self-Absorption

Carlos thinks his parents are "control freaks"; he cannot figure out why they insist he call and let them know where he is when he borrows the car. Jeri views Molly's purchase of earrings just like hers as the ultimate compliment, even though Molly may have been

Adolescents' personal fables may lead them to feel invulnerable and to engage in risky behavior, like these Brazilian boys (known as "surfistas") riding on the roof of a high-speed train.

unaware Jeri had a similar pair when she bought them. Lu is upset with his biology teacher for giving a long, difficult midterm exam on which he did poorly.

Adolescents' newly sophisticated metacognitive abilities make them readily imagine that others are focused on them, and they may create elaborate scenarios about others' thoughts. This is the source of the egocentrism that can dominate adolescents' thinking. **Adolescent egocentrism** is a state of self-absorption in which the world is seen as focused on oneself. This egocentrism makes adolescents highly critical of authority figures, hostile to criticism, and quick to find fault with others' behavior (Alberts, Elkind, & Ginsberg, 2007; Schwartz, Maynard, & Uzelac, 2008).  ⊙ Watch on **mydevelopmentlab.com**

Adolescents may develop an **imaginary audience,** fictitious observers who pay as much attention to their behavior as they do themselves. Unfortunately, these scenarios suffer from the same kind of egocentrism as the rest of their thinking. For instance, a student sitting in a class may be sure a teacher is focusing on her, and a teenager at a basketball game may be convinced that everyone is staring at the pimple on his chin.

Egocentrism leads to a second distortion in thinking: that one's experiences are unique. Adolescents develop **personal fables,** the view that what happens to them is unique, exceptional, and shared by no other. Teenagers whose romantic relationships have ended may feel that no one has ever hurt the way they do, that no one was ever treated so badly, and that no one can understand their pain (Alberts, Elkind, & Ginsberg, 2007).

> **adolescent egocentrism** a state of self-absorption in which the world is viewed from one's own point of view
>
> **imaginary audience** an adolescent's belief that his or her own behavior is a primary focus of others' attention and concerns
>
> **personal fables** the view held by some adolescents that what happens to them is unique, exceptional, and shared by no one else

⊙ Watch on **mydevelopmentlab.com**

> *Can you remember a time in your life when you developed an imaginary audience?* Watch the video on MyDevelopmentLab.com in which a teenager displays the concept of imaginary audience.

**From a social worker's perspective:** In what ways does egocentrism complicate adolescents' social and family relationships? Do adults entirely outgrow egocentrism and personal fables?

Personal fables may make adolescents feel invulnerable to the risks that threaten others. They may see no need to use condoms during sex because, in the personal fables they construct, pregnancy and sexually transmitted infections only happen to other kinds of people, not to them. They may drink and drive because in their personal fables they are careful drivers, always in control (Greene et al., 2000; Vartanian, 2000; Reyna & Farley, 2006). (Also see the "From Research to Practice" box.)

## From Research to Practice

### Telling All: Do Adolescents Reveal Too Much on Social Networking Sites?

The explosion in popularity of social networking websites such as Facebook has given rise to concerns about the safe use of these resources by adolescents. Fears surround the possibility of adolescents making themselves vulnerable to exploitation, online stalkers, or cyber-bullying by revealing too much personal information. Sensational media coverage of cases in which teenagers have been victimized online sometimes makes it seem that the problem of providing too much information on social networking sites is pervasive. Furthermore, the informality and immediacy of cyberspace can encourage adolescents to post information and videos impulsively, sometimes with disasterous consequences. For example, in one notorious case, a Rutgers University student commited suicide after his roommate posted a video on the Internet of him engaging in sex with another man (Kelley, 2009; Hu, 2010).

But do such headlines really reflect a widespread problem among adolescents, or are they merely isolated incidents? That was one of the questions investigated by researchers who recently undertook an ambitious study of the content of adolescents' social network sites. The researchers randomly selected over 9,000 profiles on MySpace to examine. (MySpace was, at the time the study was conducted, the most popular social networking site.) Of these, over 2,400 were valid profiles of adolescents (with slightly more than half of them female). Each of these profiles was carefully searched for a variety of specific types of personal information, including first and last name, age, contact information, references to drug and alcohol use, and photographs (Hinduja & Patchin, 2008).

The study concluded that some teenagers are indeed sharing excessive or inappropriate information, but that the problem is less widespread than it is often perceived to be. Of the adolescents whose profiles the researchers were able to view, about 80 percent listed their current city or town and over a quarter listed their specific school. More than half posted at least one photograph of themselves. This much information, taken together, could be enough for a stranger to find the teen. On the other hand, only 38 percent of adolescents revealed so much as their first name, and far fewer—less than 9 percent—revealed both first and last names. Only 1 percent indicated an email address and just a fraction of 1 percent posted a phone number.

There were some troublesome findings: For example, 18 percent of adolescents openly admitted to using alcohol, and over 5 percent posted photographs of themselves in swimwear or underwear. Such material could be used against these teenagers

Social network sites like Facebook are an increasingly large part of the lives of adolescents.

by cyberbullies or could catch the eye of sexual predators, and it could come back to haunt the teens when they apply for jobs or college admission.

A different study interviewed a small sample of adolescents to get a sense of how teenagers at different ages use social networking sites. This study found that younger adolescents use the sites to experiment with their identities by expressing aspects of themselves in creative ways using elaborate page designs. Older adolescents abandon such stylized and expressive social networking pages in favor of simple layouts that facilitate interconnections among friends. These teenagers seem more inclined to use social networking sites for limited self-expression, preferring to disclose more personal information in a more selective manner. Taken together, these studies give some indication that worries about adolescents' risk exposure during social networking, while a genuine concern, may be exaggerated in the media (Livingstone, 2008).

- What can parents and teachers do to minimize adolescents' risky behavior on social networking sites, short of restricting their access?
- Why do you think older adolescents tend to use social networking sites in more utilitarian ways than younger adolescents do?

## REVIEW, CHECK, AND APPLY

### REVIEW

**LO6** How does cognitive development proceed during adolescence?

- Adolescence corresponds to Piaget's formal operations period, a stage characterized by abstract reasoning and an experimental approach to problems.

- According to the information processing perspective, cognitive advances in adolescence are quantitative and gradual, as many aspects of thinking and memory improve. Growth in metacognition enables the monitoring of thought processes and mental capacities.

**LO7** What aspects of cognitive development cause difficulties for adolescents?

- Adolescents are susceptible to egocentrism and the perception that their behavior is constantly observed by an imaginary audience.

- Adolescents construct personal fables about their uniqueness and immunity to harm.

### CHECK YOURSELF

1. Fifteen-year-old Wyatt is able to solve the physics problem from class in abstract rather than in concrete terms. According to Piaget, Wyatt is now capable of _____.

   a. preoperational thought

   b. formal operational thought

   c. egocentrism

   d. sensorimotor thought

2. _____ is the knowledge that people have about their own thinking processes and their ability to monitor their cognition.

3. Rorie refuses to go to the eighth-grade dance because she is sure that the only thing everyone will see is the pimple on her face. Which of the following limitations in thinking associated with adolescence is at work here?

   a. imaginary audience

   b. personal fable

   c. invincibility fable

   d. hysteria

### APPLYING LIFESPAN DEVELOPMENT

- When facing complex problems, do you think most adults spontaneously apply formal operations like those used to solve the pendulum problem? Why or why not?

✓• **Study** and **Review** on
**MyDevelopmentLab.com**

Answers: 1) b; 2) Metacognition; 3) a

---

# School Performance

**LO8**  **What factors affect adolescent school performance?**

**LO9**  **How much of an influence does the Internet have on adolescent learning?**

LEARNING OBJECTIVES

*Jeri Camber is annoyed. His iPod has stopped working and now he has to pull out his earbuds, put his calculus textbook down, and pause the game he's playing on his Playstation 3. He fiddles with the iPod and finally gets it working. As he puts his earbuds back in and returns to his calculus book and video game, he shouts to his father to find out the score of the basketball game he hears playing in the next room. To his surprise, his father answers that he doesn't know because he's been reading a book instead of paying attention. Jeri rolls his eyes and silently judges his dad a bit dim-witted for being unable to do both things at the same time.*

Jeri's ability at age 17 to listen to music, do his homework, and play a videogame all at the same time may or may not signal some kind of advance over his father's limited focus on one thing at a time. In part, Jeri's talent for multitasking is surely due to the different eras in which he and his father were raised, but it may also be partly attributable to the cognitive changes that accompanied his advance into adolescence. Think of it this way: It is *possible* that Jeri actually can perform more mental tasks simultaneously than his father, but it is *certain* that he can do more tasks *well* than he could do just a few years earlier.

Do the advances in adolescents' metacognition, reasoning, and other cognitive abilities lead to improved school performance? If we use grades as the measure of performance, the answer is yes. High school students' grades have risen in the last decade. The mean grade point average for college-bound seniors was 3.3 (on a scale of 4), compared with 3.1 a decade ago. More than 40 percent of seniors reported average grades of A+, A, or A– (College Board, 2005).

At the same time, independent measures of achievement, such as SAT scores, have not risen. A more likely explanation for the higher grades is the phenomenon of grade inflation: Students have not changed; instead, instructors are awarding higher grades for the same performance (Cardman, 2004).

Further evidence for grade inflation comes from the relatively poor achievement of students in the United States when compared to students in other countries. For instance, students in the United States score lower on standardized math and science tests when compared to students in other industrialized countries (National Governors Association (2008) (see Figure 6-7).

There is no single reason for this achievement gap, but a combination of factors, such as less class time and less intensive instruction, are at work. The broad diversity of the U.S. school population also may affect performance relative to other countries in which the school population is more homogeneous and affluent (Stedman, 1997; Schemo, 2001).

High school graduation rates also reflect the lesser accomplishments of U.S. students. Once first in the number of high school graduates it produces—in terms of total population—the United States is now 24th among industrialized countries. Only 78 percent of U.S. high school students graduate (OECD, 1998; OECD, 2001).

As we discuss next, differences in socioeconomic status are also reflected in school performance within the United States (Stedman, 1997; Schemo, 2001).

Average is significantly higher than the U.S.

Average is significantly lower than the U.S.

| Mathematics (rank) | | Science (rank) | | Reading (rank) | | Problem Solving (rank) | |
|---|---|---|---|---|---|---|---|
| 1 | Finland | 1 | Finland | 1 | Finland | 1 | Korea |
| 2 | Korea | 2 | Canada | 2 | Korea | 2 | Finland |
| 3 | Netherlands | 3 | Japan | 3 | Canada | 3 | Japan |
| 4 | Switzerland | 4 | New Zealand | 4 | Australia | 4 | New Zealand |
| 5 | Canada | 5 | Australia | 5 | New Zealand | 5 | Australia |
| 6 | Japan | 6 | Netherlands | 6 | Ireland | 6 | Canada |
| 7 | New Zealand | 7 | Korea | 7 | Sweden | 7 | Belgium |
| 8 | Belgium | 8 | Germany | 8 | Netherlands | 8 | Switzerland |
| 9 | Australia | 9 | United Kingdom | 9 | Belgium | 9 | Netherlands |
| 10 | Denmark | 10 | Czech Republic | 10 | Norway | 10 | France |
| 11 | Czech Republic | 11 | Switzerland | 11 | Switzerland | 11 | Denmark |
| 12 | Iceland | 12 | Austria | 12 | Japan | 12 | Czech Republic |
| 13 | Austria | 13 | Belgium | 13 | Poland | 13 | Germany |
| 14 | Germany | 14 | Ireland | 14 | France | 14 | Sweden |
| 15 | Sweden | 15 | Hungary | 15 | United States | 15 | Austria |
| 16 | Ireland | 16 | Sweden | 16 | Denmark | 16 | Iceland |
| 17 | France | 17 | Poland | 17 | Iceland | 17 | Hungary |
| 18 | United Kingdom | 18 | Denmark | 18 | Germany | 18 | Ireland |
| 19 | Poland | 19 | France | 19 | Austria | 19 | Luxembourg |
| 20 | Slovak Republic | 20 | Iceland | 20 | Czech Republic | 20 | Slovak Republic |
| 21 | Hungary | 21 | United States | 21 | Hungary | 21 | Norway |
| 22 | Luxembourg | 22 | Slovak Republic | 22 | Spain | 22 | Poland |
| 23 | Norway | 23 | Spain | 23 | Luxembourg | 23 | Spain |
| 24 | Spain | 24 | Norway | 24 | Portugal | 24 | United States |
| 25 | United States | 25 | Luxembourg | 25 | Italy | 25 | Portugal |
| 26 | Portugal | 26 | Italy | 26 | Greece | 26 | Italy |
| 27 | Italy | 27 | Portugal | 27 | Slovak Republic | 27 | Greece |
| 28 | Greece | 28 | Greece | 28 | Turkey | 28 | Turkey |
| 29 | Turkey | 29 | Turkey | 29 | Mexico | 29 | Mexico |
| 30 | Mexico | 30 | Mexico | | | | |

FIGURE 6-7 U.S. 15-Year-Old Performance Compared with Other Countries

When compared to the math performance of students across the world, U.S. students perform at below-average levels.

Source: Adapted from National Governors Association, 2008.

*Socioeconomic Status and School Performance: Individual Differences in Achievement.* All students are entitled to an equal education, but some groups enjoy more advantages than others, as the relationship between educational achievement and socioeconomic status (SES) clearly indicates.

Middle- and high-SES students, on average, earn higher grades, score higher on standardized achievement tests, and complete more years of school than students from lower-SES homes. This disparity does not start in adolescence; the same findings hold for children in lower grades. However, by high school, the effects of socioeconomic status are more pronounced (Frederickson & Petrides, 2008; Shernoff & Schmidt, 2008).

Why do children from middle- and high-SES homes show greater academic success? Children living in poverty lack many of the advantages of their more affluent peers. Moreover, their nutrition and health may be poorer. If they live in crowded conditions or attend inadequate schools, they may have few places to study. Their homes may lack the books and computers common in more affluent households (Prater, 2002; Chiu & McBride-Chang, 2006; Wamba, 2010).

For these reasons, impoverished students may be disadvantaged from their first day of school. As they grow up, their school performance may continue to lag and, in fact, the difference may snowball. High school success builds heavily on basic skills presumably learned earlier. Children who experience early problems may find themselves falling ever further behind (Huston, 1991; Phillips et al., 1994; Biddle, 2001).

*Ethnic and Racial Differences in School Achievement.* Significant achievement differences between ethnic and racial groups paint a troubling picture of American education. School achievement data indicate that, on average, African American and Hispanic students perform at lower levels, receive lower grades, and score lower on standardized achievement tests than Caucasian students. In contrast, Asian American students tend to earn higher grades than Caucasian students (National Center for Educational Statistics, 2003; Frederickson & Petrides, 2008; Shernoff & Schmidt, 2008).

Socioeconomic factors create much of the ethnic and racial differences in academic achievement. More African American and Hispanic families live in poverty, and this fact may affect their children's school performance. In fact, when we compare different ethnic and racial groups at the same socioeconomic level, achievement differences diminish (but do not vanish) (Meece & Kurtz-Costes, 2001; Cokley, 2003; Guerrero et al., 2006).

Anthropologist John Ogbu (1988, 1992) argues that certain minority groups may perceive school success as relatively unimportant. They may believe societal prejudice in the workplace dictates they will not succeed, no matter how hard they try. They may conclude that effort in school will have no eventual payoff.

Ogbu suggests that minority group members who enter a new culture voluntarily are more likely to succeed in school than those brought into a new culture against their will. He notes that the sons and daughters of voluntary Korean immigrants to the United States tend to be quite successful in school. In contrast, Korean children in Japan, whose parents were forced to immigrate during World War II and work as forced laborers, tend to do poorly in school. Involuntary immigration apparently leaves lasting scars, reducing the motivation to succeed in subsequent generations. Ogbu suggests that in the United States, the involuntary immigration, as slaves, of the ancestors of many African American students might be related to their motivation to succeed (Ogbu, 1992; Gallagher, 1994).

⟶ **From an educator's perspective:** Why might descendants of people who were forced to immigrate to a country be less successful academically than those who came voluntarily? What approaches might be used to overcome this obstacle?

Another factor has to do with attributions for academic success. As we discussed previously, students from many Asian cultures tend to relate achievement to situational factors such as their effort. In contrast, African American students are apt to attribute success to external causes beyond their control, such as luck or societal biases. Students who believe effort leads to success, and expend that effort, are likely to do better in school than students who do not believe effort matters (Stevenson, Chen, & Lee, 1992; Fuligni, 1997; Saunders, Davis, & Williams, 2004).

**Adolescent Engagement in Online Activities**
Online Teens* (12–17)

| Go online | 93% |
|---|---|
| **Teens and Gen Y are more likely to engage in the following activities compared with older users:** | |
| Play games online | 78 |
| Watch videos online | 57 |
| Get info about a job | 30 |
| Send instant messages | 68 |
| Use social networking sites | 65 |
| Download music | 59 |
| Create an SNS profile | 55 |
| Read blogs | 49 |
| Create a blog | 28 |
| Visit a virtual world | 10 |
| **Activities where Gen X users or older generations dominate:** | |
| Get health info | 28 |
| Buy something online | 38 |
| Get religious info | 26 |
| **And for some activities, the youngest and oldest cohorts may differ, but there is less variation overall:** | |
| Use email | 73 |
| Get news | 63 |
| Download videos | 31 |
| Download podcasts | 19 |

* Source for Online Teens data: Pew Internet & American Life Project Surveys conducted Oct.–Nov. 2006 and Nov. 2007–Feb. 2008. Margin of error for online teens is ± 4% for Oct.–Nov. 2006 and ± 3% for Nov. 2007–Feb. 2008.

**FIGURE 6-8 Teenage Online Activity**
Today, the vast majority of teenagers use the Internet to communicate via email and instant messaging, and many also use the new technology for education-related material and research. How will this trend affect the way educators will teach in the future?
Source: Pew Internet & American Life Project Surveys, 2009.

Adolescents' beliefs about the consequences of poor school performance may also contribute to racial and ethnic differences. Specifically, African American and Hispanic students may believe they can succeed *despite* poor performance. This belief can cause them to expend less effort. In contrast, Asian American students may believe that they must do well in school to get a good job and be successful. Asian Americans, then, are motivated to work hard for fear of the consequences (Steinberg, Dornbusch, & Brown, 1992; Murphy et al., 2010).

## Achievement Testing in Schools: Will No Child Be Left Behind?

Concerns about the educational performance of students have led to considerable efforts to improve schooling. No educational reform has had a greater impact than the No Child Left Behind Act.

The No Child Left Behind Act, passed by Congress in 2002, requires that every U.S. state design and administer achievement tests that students must pass in order to graduate from high school. In addition, schools themselves are graded so that the public is aware of which schools have the best (and worst) test results. The basic idea behind the mandatory testing programs like the No Child Left Behind Act is to ensure that students graduate with a minimum level of proficiency. Proponents suggest that students—and teachers—will be motivated by the tests and that overall educational standards will be raised (Jehlen & Winans, 2005; Watkins, 2008; Opfer, Henry, & Mashburn, 2008).

Critics of the act (and other forms of mandatory standardized testing) argue that a number of unintended negative consequences will result from implementation of the law. To ensure that the maximum numbers of students pass the tests, they suggest that instructors "teach to the test," meaning that they focus on the content of the tests to the exclusion of material that is not tested. Moreover, because students from lower socioeconomic and ethnic and racial minority backgrounds and those with special needs fail tests disproportionately, critics have argued that mandatory testing programs may be inherently biased (Thurlow, Lazarus, & Thompson, 2005; Linn, 2008; Koretz, 2008).

## Adolescents' Media Use

An enormous variety of media and technologies are available to adolescents, ranging from more traditional sorts, such as radio and television, to newer forms, such as instant messaging, cell phones, and MP3 players. And adolescents make use of them—to a staggering degree.

According to a comprehensive survey using a sample of boys and girls 8 to 18 years old conducted by the Kaiser Family Foundation (a well-respected think tank), young people spend an average of 6.5 hours a day with media. Furthermore, because around a quarter of the time they are using more than one form of medium simultaneously, they are actually being exposed to the equivalent of eight-and-a-half hours per day (Rideout, Roberts, & Foehr, 2005; Boneva et al., 2006; Jordan et al., 2007) (see Figure 6-8).

The widespread availability of the Web has produced considerable changes in education, allowing adolescents to tap into a vast array of information. However, it is not yet obvious how Web access will change education or whether the impact will be uniformly positive. For instance, schools must change their curricula to include specific instruction in a key skill for deriving value from the Web: learning to sort through huge bodies of information to identify what is most useful and discard what is not. To obtain the full benefits of the Web, then, students must obtain the ability to search, choose, and integrate information in order to create new knowledge (Oblinger & Rush, 1997; Trotter, 2004).

Despite the substantial benefits of the Web, its use also has a downside. The Web makes material available that many parents and other adults find highly objectionable. In addition, there is a growing problem of Internet gambling. High school and college students can easily bet on sports events and participate in games such as poker on the Web using credit cards (Winters, Stinchfield, & Botzet, 2005; Fleming et al., 2006; Mitchell, Wolak, & Finkelhor, 2007; King, Delfabbro, & Griffiths, 2010; Derevensky, Shek, & Merrick, 2010).

The growing use of computers also presents a challenge involving socioeconomic status, race, and ethnicity. Poorer adolescents and members of minority groups have less access to computers than more affluent adolescents and members of socially advantaged groups—a phenomenon known as the *digital divide* (Sax et al., 2004; Fetterman, 2005; Olsen, 2009).

***Dropping Out of School.*** Most students complete high school, but, some half million students each year drop out prior to graduating. The consequences are severe. High school dropouts earn 42 percent less than graduates, and their unemployment rate is 50 percent.

Adolescents leave school for a variety of reasons. Some leave because of pregnancy or problems with the English language. Some must leave for economic reasons, needing to support themselves or their families.

Dropout rates differ according to gender and ethnicity. Males are more likely to drop out than females. Although the dropout rate for all ethnicities has been declining in recent decades, Hispanic and African American students still are less likely to finish high school than non-Hispanic White students. However, not all minority groups show higher dropout rates; for example, Asians drop out at a lower rate than Caucasians (National Center for Educational Statistics, 2003; Stearns & Glennie, 2006).

Poverty largely determines whether a student completes high school. Students from lower-income households are three times more likely to drop out than those from middle- and upper-income households. Because economic success is so dependent on education, dropping out often perpetuates a cycle of poverty (National Center for Education Statistics, 2002).

## REVIEW, CHECK, AND APPLY

### REVIEW

**LO8** What factors affect adolescent school performance?

- Academic performance is linked in complex ways to socioeconomic status and to race and ethnicity.

- Both gender and ethnicity affect the incidence of dropping out.

**LO9** How much of an influence does the Internet have on adolescent learning?

- The educational benefits of the Internet are many, but it also introduces adolescents to objectionable material and online gambling.

### CHECK YOURSELF

1. Due to the unfavorable comparison of U.S. standardized test scores to the scores of other countries, the gradual shift upward of adolescents' grades in the last decade has been attributed to _____.

   a. increased immigration

   b. grade inflation

   c. achievement deflation

   d. decreased motivation

2. Students who experience socioeconomic disadvantages, and consequently academic disadvantages, as young children usually overcome those disadvantages by adolescence.

   - True

   - False

3. Who is least likely to drop out of high school prior to graduation in the United States?

   a. males

   b. females

### APPLYING LIFESPAN DEVELOPMENT

- What sorts of *external* factors (i.e., not attributable to the students) might negatively affect the performance of U.S. students on international achievement tests?

✔●—[**Study** and **Review** on
**MyDevelopmentLab.com**

Answers: 1) b; 2) False; 3) b

---

## MODULE 6.3 Social and Personality Development in Adolescence

| | |
|---|---|
| **GIRL:** | *"hey ... hm. wut to say? iono lol/well I left you a comment ... u sud feel SPECIAL haha."* |
| **BOY:** | *"hello there ... umm I don't know what to say, but at least I wrote something ..."* |

> *It's not exactly Shakespeare. But in the brave new world of digital communication, these messages—posted on the respective Facebook pages of two teenagers—were the start of a romance. After these intital online flirtations, the two teens eventually began dating (Lewin, 2008, p. A20).*

Between Facebook, MySpace, blogs, Twitter, texting, and cell phones, the options for digital communication can often seem limitless. The new avenues for expression and interaction have added still another layer of complication at a stage of life—adolescence—when things were probably already complicated enough. Now teenagers must deal with the stigma of being dumped via text message, or parse the meaning of a potentially romantic posting on a social networking page.

Still, despite the reputation of adolescence as a time of confusion and rebellion, most teenagers pass through the period without much turmoil. Although they may "try on" different roles and flirt with activities that adults in their lives find objectionable, the majority of adolescents find adolescence an exciting time during which friendships grow, intimate relationships develop, and their sense of themselves deepens.

This is not to say that the transitions adolescents pass through are unchallenging. As we shall see in this module, where we discuss personality and social development, adolescence brings about major changes in the ways in which individuals must deal with the world.

We begin by considering how adolescents form their views of themselves. We look at self-concept, self-esteem, and identity development. We also examine two major psychological difficulties: depression and suicide.

Next, we discuss relationships. We consider how adolescents reposition themselves within the family and how the influence of family members declines in some spheres as peers take on new importance. We also examine the ways in which adolescents interact with their friends, and the ways in which popularity is determined.

Finally, the module considers dating and sexual behavior. We look at the role of dating and close relationships in adolescents' lives, and we consider sexual behavior and the standards that govern adolescents' sex lives. We conclude by looking at teenage pregnancy and at programs that seek to prevent unwanted pregnancy.

# Identity: Asking "Who Am I?"

**LEARNING OBJECTIVES**

**LO10** How does the development of self-concept, self-esteem, and identity proceed during adolescence?

**LO11** What role does religion and spirituality play during adolescence?

**LO12** What dangers do adolescents face as they deal with the stresses of adolescence?

*Thirteen is a hard age, very hard. A lot of people say you have it easy, you're a kid, but there's a lot of pressure being 13—to be respected by people in your school, to be liked, always feeling like you have to be good. There's pressure to do drugs, too, so you try not to succumb to that. But you don't want to be made fun of, so you have to look cool. You gotta wear the right shoes, the right clothes. (Carlos Quintana, 1998, p. 66)*

The thoughts of 13-year-old Carlos Quintana demonstrate a clear awareness—and self-consciousness—regarding his new place in society. During adolescence, questions like "Who am I?" and "Where do I belong in the world?" begin to take a front seat.

One reason issues of identity become so important is that adolescents' intellectual capacities become more adult-like. They see how they stack up to others and realize they are individuals, separate from everyone else. The dramatic physical changes of puberty make adolescents acutely aware of their own bodies and aware that others are reacting to them in new ways. Whatever the cause, adolescence brings major changes in teenagers' self-concepts and self-esteem—in sum, their views of their own identity.

## Self-Concept: What Am I Like?

Valerie describes herself this way: "Others look at me as laid-back, relaxed, and not worrying too much. But really, I'm often nervous and emotional."

The fact that Valerie distinguishes others' views from her own represents a developmental advance. In childhood, she would have characterized herself by traits that would not differentiate her view from others'. However, when adolescents describe who they are, they take into account both their own and others' views (Cole et al., 2001; Updegraff et al., 2004).

This broader view of themselves is one aspect of adolescents' increasing sense of identity. They can see various aspects of the self simultaneously, and this view becomes more organized and coherent. They look at the self from a psychological perspective, viewing traits not as concrete entities but as abstractions (Adams, Montemayor, & Gullotta, 1996). For example, teenagers are more likely than younger children to define themselves by their ideology (e.g., "I'm an environmentalist") than by physical characteristics (e.g.,"I'm the fastest runner in my class").

In some ways, this broader, multifaceted self-concept can be a mixed blessing, especially during early adolescence. At that time, they may be troubled by the complexity of their personalities. Younger adolescents may want to view themselves in a certain way ("I'm a sociable person and love to be with people"), and they may become concerned when their behavior contradicts that view ("Even though I want to be sociable, sometimes I can't stand being around my friends and just want to be alone"). By the end of adolescence, however, teenagers find it easier to accept that behaviors and feelings change with the situation (Trzesniewski, Donnellan, & Robins, 2003; Hitlin, Brown, & Elder, 2006).

## Self-Esteem: How Do I Like Myself?

Although adolescents increasingly perceive who they are (their self-concept), this does not mean they like themselves (their self-esteem). Their increasingly accurate self-concept permits them to see themselves fully—warts and all. It's what they do with these perceptions that determines their self-esteem.

The same cognitive sophistication that differentiates various aspects of the self also leads adolescents to evaluate those aspects in different ways (Chan, 1997; Cohen, 1999). An

adolescent may have high self-esteem regarding academic performance, but lower self-esteem in relationships. Or the opposite may apply, as this adolescent notes:

> *How much do I like the kind of person I am? Well, I like some things about me, but I don't like others. I'm glad that I'm popular since it's really important to me to have friends. But in school I don't do as well as the really smart kids. That's OK, because if you're too smart you'll lose your friends. So being smart is just not that important. Except to my parents. I feel like I'm letting them down when I don't do as well as they want. (Harter, 1990, p. 364)*

***Gender Differences in Self-Esteem.*** Several factors determine an adolescent's self-esteem, among them gender. Notably in early adolescence, girls' self-esteem tends to be lower and more vulnerable than boys' (Miyamoto et al., 2000; Ah-Kion, 2006; Heaven & Ciarrochi, 2008; McLean & Breen, 2009).

Compared to boys, girls tend to worry more about physical appearance and social success—as well as academic achievement. Although boys care about these things, their attitudes are often more casual. Stereotypical societal messages suggesting brains and popularity do not mix pose a difficult bind for girls: If girls do well academically, they jeopardize their social success. No wonder their self-esteem is more fragile than boys' (Unger, 2001; Ricciardelli & McCabe, 2003; Ata, Ludden, & Lally, 2007; van den Berg et al., 2010).

Although self-esteem tends to be higher in boys, they have their vulnerabilities too. Gender stereotypes may lead boys to believe they should always be confident, tough, and fearless. Boys facing difficulties (e.g., not making a sports team or being rejected for a date) may feel incompetent as males as well as miserable about their defeat (Pollack, 1999; Pollack, Shuster, & Trelease, 2001).

***Socioeconomic Status and Race Differences in Self-Esteem.*** Socioeconomic status (SES) and race also influence self-esteem. Adolescents of higher SES tend to have higher self-esteem than those of lower SES, especially in middle and later adolescence. Social status factors that enhance one's standing and self-esteem, such as having more expensive clothes or a car, may become more conspicuous at this time (Van Tassel-Baska et al., 1994).

Race and ethnicity also influence self-esteem, but less biased treatment of minorities has eased their impact. Early studies argued that minority status would lead to lower self-esteem, and this was initially supported by research. African Americans and Hispanics, researchers explained, had lower self-esteem than Caucasians because society's prejudice made them feel disliked and rejected, and this was incorporated into their self-concepts. Most recent research, however, suggests that African American adolescents differ little from Whites in their levels of self-esteem (Harter, 1990). One explanation is that social movements within the African American community to bolster racial pride have helped. Research finds that a stronger sense of racial identity is related to higher self-esteem in African Americans and Hispanics (Gray-Little & Hafdahl, 2000; Verkuyten, 2003; Phinney, 2008).

Another reason for a similarity in self-esteem between adolescents of different racial groups is that teenagers tend to focus their preferences and priorities on what they excel at. Consequently, African American youths may concentrate on what they most enjoy and gain self-esteem from their successes in that domain (Gray-Little & Hafdahl, 2000; Yang & Blodgett, 2000; Phinney, 2005).

Self-esteem may be influenced not by race alone, but by a complex combination of factors. Some developmentalists have considered race and gender simultaneously, coining the term *ethgender* to refer to their joint influence. One study that took both race and gender into account found that African American and Hispanic males had the highest levels of self-esteem, while Asian and Native American females had the lowest levels (Romero & Roberts, 2003; Saunders, Davis, & Williams, 2004; Biro et al., 2006; Adams, 2010).

## Identity Formation: Change or Crisis?

According to Erik Erikson, whose theory we discussed earlier, the search for identity inevitably leads some adolescents to an identity crisis involving substantial psychological turmoil (Erikson, 1963). Erikson's theory of this stage, which is summarized with his other stages in Table 6-2, suggests teenagers try to figure out what is unique and distinctive about themselves—a task they manage with increasing sophistication due to the cognitive gains of adolescence.

Erikson argues that adolescents strive to discover their strengths and weaknesses and the roles that best suit their future lives. This often involves "trying on" different roles or choices to see if they fit their capabilities and views about themselves. In this process, adolescents seek to understand who they are by narrowing and making choices about their personal, occupational, sexual, and political commitments. Erikson calls this the **identity-versus-identity-confusion stage.**

In Erikson's view, adolescents who do not find a suitable identity may go off course in several ways. They may adopt socially unacceptable roles to express what they do *not* want to be. Forming and maintaining lasting close relationships may elude them. In general, their sense of self becomes "diffuse," failing to organize around a unified core identity.

In contrast, those who forge an appropriate identity set a foundation for future psychosocial development. They learn their unique capabilities and believe in them, and they develop an accurate sense of self. They are prepared to take full advantage of their unique strengths (Archer & Waterman, 1994; Allison & Schultz, 2001).

*Societal Pressures and Reliance on Friends and Peers.* Societal pressures are also high during the identity-versus-identity-confusion stage. Adolescents feel pressure from parents and friends to decide whether their post-high-school plans include work or college and, if the former, which occupation to follow. Up to this point, their educational lives have followed a universal track, laid out by U.S. society. However, the track ends at high school, leaving adolescents with difficult choices about which path to follow.

During this period, friends and peers are increasingly sought as sources of information. Dependence on adults declines. As we discuss later, this increasing dependence on peers enables adolescents to forge close relationships. Comparing themselves to others helps to clarify their own identities.

This reliance on peers in defining their own identities and learning to form relationships links this stage of psychosocial development and the next stage Erikson proposed, known as intimacy versus isolation. It also relates to gender differences in identity formation. Erikson suggested that males and females move through the identity-versus-identity-confusion period differently. He argued that males are more likely to experience the social development stages in the order shown in Table 6-2, developing a stable identity before committing to an intimate relationship. In contrast, he suggested that females reverse the order, seeking intimate relationships and then defining their identities through these relationships. These ideas largely reflect the social conditions at the time he was writing, when women were less likely to go to

> **identity-versus-identity-confusion stage** the period during which teenagers seek to determine what is unique and distinctive about themselves

## TABLE 6-2  A SUMMARY OF ERIKSON'S STAGES

| Stage | Approximate Age | Positive Outcomes | Negative Outcomes |
|---|---|---|---|
| 1. Trust versus mistrust | Birth–1.5 years | Feelings of trust from others' support | Fear and concern regarding others |
| 2. Autonomy versus shame and doubt | 1.5–3 years | Self-sufficiency if exploration is encouraged | Doubts about self; lack of independence |
| 3. Initiative versus guilt | 3–6 years | Discovery of ways to initiate actions | Guilt from actions and thoughts |
| 4. Industry versus inferiority | 6–12 years | Development of sense of competence | Feelings of inferiority; little sense of mastery |
| 5. Identity versus identity confusion | Adolescence | Awareness of uniqueness of self; knowledge of roles | Inability to identify appropriate roles in life |
| 6. Intimacy versus isolation | Early adulthood | Development of loving, sexual relationships and close friendships | Fear of relationships with others |
| 7. Generativity versus stagnation | Middle adulthood | Sense of contribution to continuity of life | Trivialization of one's activities |
| 8. Ego-integrity versus despair | Late adulthood | Sense of unity in life's accomplishments | Regret over lost opportunities of life |

college or establish their own careers and instead often married early. Today, the experiences of boys and girls seem relatively similar during the identity-versus-identity-confusion period.

*Psychological Moratorium.* Because of the pressures of the identity-versus-identity-confusion period, Erikson suggested that many adolescents pursue a *psychological moratorium,* a period during which they take time off from the upcoming responsibilities of adulthood to explore various roles and possibilities. For example, many college students take a semester or year off to travel, work, or find another way to examine their priorities.

Many adolescents, for practical reasons, cannot pursue a psychological moratorium to leisurely explore various identities. For economic reasons, some must work part-time after school and then take jobs immediately after high school, leaving them little time to experiment. Such adolescents need by no means be psychologically damaged. Successfully holding a part-time job while attending school may offer a psychological reward that outweighs the lack of opportunity to try out various roles.

*Limitations of Erikson's Theory.* Erikson has been criticized for using male identity development as the standard against which to compare female identity. He saw males as developing intimacy only after achieving a stable identity, which is viewed as the norm. To critics, Erikson's view is based on male-oriented concepts of individuality and competitiveness. Alternatively, psychologist Carol Gilligan suggests that women develop identity while establishing relationships. In this view, the building of caring networks between herself and others is key to a woman's identity (Brown & Gilligan, 1990; Gilligan, 2004; Kroger, 2006).

## Marcia's Approach to Identity Development: Updating Erikson

Using Erikson's theory as a springboard, psychologist James Marcia suggests that identity can be seen in terms of which of two characteristics—crisis or commitment—is present or absent. *Crisis* is a period in which an adolescent consciously chooses between various alternatives and makes decisions. *Commitment* is psychological investment in a course of action or an ideology. One adolescent might career from one activity to another, with nothing lasting beyond a few weeks, while another becomes totally absorbed in volunteering at a homeless shelter (Marcia, 1980; Peterson, Marcia, & Carpendale, 2004).

After conducting lengthy interviews with adolescents, Marcia proposed four categories of identity (see Table 6-3).

1. **Identity achievement.** Teenagers in this category have successfully explored and thought through who they are and what they want to do. Following a period of crisis during which they considered various alternatives, these adolescents have committed to a particular identity. Teens who have reached this identity status tend to be psychologically healthier, higher in achievement motivation and moral reasoning, than adolescents of any other status.

2. **Identity foreclosure.** These are adolescents who have committed to an identity without passing through a period of crisis in which they explored alternatives. Instead, they

**identity achievement** the status of adolescents who commit to a particular identity following a period of crisis during which they consider various alternatives

**identity foreclosure** the status of adolescents who prematurely commit to an identity without adequately exploring alternatives

**TABLE 6-3** MARCIA'S FOUR CATEGORIES OF ADOLESCENT DEVELOPMENT

| | | COMMITMENT | |
|---|---|---|---|
| | | **Present** | **Absent** |
| **CRISIS/EXPLORATION** | **PRESENT** | Identity achievement<br>"I love animals; I'm going to become a vet." | Moratorium<br>"I'm going to work at the mall while I figure out what to do next." |
| | **ABSENT** | Identity foreclosure<br>"I am going into law, just like Mom." | Identity diffusion<br>"I don't have a clue." |

Source: From Marcia, J. E. (1980). "Identity in Adolescence" in J. Adelson (ed.), HANDBOOK OF ADOLESCENT PSYCHOLOGY. Reprinted with permission from John Wiley & Sons, Inc.

accepted others' decisions about what was best for them. Typical of this category is a son who enters the family business because it is expected, or a daughter who becomes a physician because her mother is one. Foreclosers are not necessarily unhappy but they tend to have something called "rigid strength": Happy and self-satisfied, they have a high need for social approval and tend to be authoritarian.

3. **Moratorium.** Adolescents in this category have explored some alternatives but made no commitments. As a result, Marcia suggests, they show relatively high anxiety and experience psychological conflict, though they are often lively and appealing, seeking intimacy with others. Such adolescents typically settle on an identity, but only after a struggle.

4. **Identity diffusion.** These adolescents neither explore nor commit to various alternatives. They tend to shift from one thing to the next. While appearing carefree, according to Marcia, their lack of commitment impairs their ability to form close relationships. They are often socially withdrawn.

According to Marcia's approach, psychologically healthy identity development can be seen in adolescents who choose to commit to a course of action of ideology.

Some adolescents shift among the four categories; for example, moving between moratorium and identity achievement in what is called a "MAMA" cycle (**m**oratorium—identity **a**chievement—**m**oratorium—identity **a**chievement). Or, a forecloser who selected a career path without much thought in early adolescence may reassess and make a more active choice later. For some individuals, identity formation takes place beyond adolescence. However, for most people, identity gels in the late teens and early 20s (Meeus, 2003; Kroger, 2007; Al-Owidha, Green, & Kroger, 2009).

> **From a social worker's perspective:** Do you believe that all four of Marcia's identity statuses can lead to reassessment and different choices later in life? Are there stages in Marcia's theory that may be difficult to achieve for adolescents who live in poverty? Why?

## Religion and Spirituality

*Ever wonder why God made mosquitoes? How about why God gave Adam and Eve the ability to rebel if He knew how much of a mess it would cause? Can someone be saved and later lose their salvation? Do pets go to Heaven?*

As exemplified in this blog post, questions of religion and spirituality begin to be asked during adolescence. Religion is important to many people because it offers a formal means of satisfying spirituality needs. *Spirituality* is a sense of attachment to some higher power such as God, nature, or something sacred. Although spirituality needs are typically tied to religious beliefs, they may be independent. Many people who consider themselves to be spiritual individuals do not participate in formal religious practices or are not tied to any particular religion.

Because their cognitive abilities increase during adolescence, teenagers are able to think more abstractly about religious matters. Furthermore, as they grapple with general questions of identity, religious identity may be questioned. After having accepted their religious identity in an unquestioning manner during childhood, adolescents may view religion more critically and seek to distance themselves from formal religion. In other cases, they may be drawn more closely to their religious affiliation because it offers answers to such abstract questions as "Why am I here on this earth?" and "What is the meaning of life?" (Good & Willoughby, 2008; Kiang, Yip, & Fuligni, 2008).

According to James Fowler, our understanding and practice of faith and spirituality proceeds through a series of stages that extend throughout the lifetime. During childhood, individuals hold a fairly literal view of God and Biblical figures. For example, children may think of God as living at the top of the earth and being able to see what everyone is doing (Fowler & Dell, 2006).

In adolescence, the view of spirituality becomes more abstract. As they build their identity, adolescents typically develop a core set of beliefs and values. On the other hand, in many cases, adolescents do not consider their views either in depth nor systematically, and it is not until later that they become more reflective.

**moratorium** the status of adolescents who may have explored various identity alternatives to some degree, but have not yet committed themselves

**identity diffusion** the status of adolescents who consider various identity alternatives, but never commit to one or never even consider identity options in any conscious way

As they leave adolescence, people typically move into the *individuative-reflective stage* of faith in which they reflect on their beliefs and values. They understand that their views are one of many, and that multiple views of God are possible. Ultimately, the final stage of faith development is the *conjunctive stage,* in which individuals develop a broad, inclusive view of religion and all humanity. They see humanity as a whole, and they may work to promote a common good. In this stage, they may move beyond formal religion and hold a unified view of people across the globe.

## Identity, Race, and Ethnicity

Forming an identity is often difficult for adolescents, but it is especially challenging for members of racial and ethnic groups that face discrimination. Society's contradictory values tell adolescents that society should be color blind, that race and ethnic background should not affect opportunities and achievement, and that if they do achieve, society will accept them. Based on a traditional *cultural assimilation model,* this view says individual cultural identities should be assimilated into a unified culture in the United States—the melting-pot model.

In contrast, the *pluralistic society model* suggests that U.S. society is made up of diverse, coequal cultural groups that should preserve their individual features. This model grew from the belief that cultural assimilation denigrates the heritage of minorities and lowers their self-esteem.

According to this view, then, racial and ethnic factors become a central part of adolescents' identity and are not submerged in an attempt to assimilate into the majority culture. From this perspective, identity development includes development of *racial and ethnic identity*—the sense of membership in a racial or ethnic group and the feelings that are associated with that membership. It includes a sense of commitment and ties with a particular racial or ethnic group (Phinney & Alipuria, 2006; Phinney, 2008).The middle ground says minority group members can form a *bicultural identity,* drawing from their own culture while integrating themselves into the dominant culture. This view suggests an individual can hold two cultural identities, without having to prefer one over the other (LaFromboise, Coleman, & Gerton, 1993; Shi & Lu, 2007). Choosing a bicultural identity is increasingly common. According to the 2000 U.S. census, a considerable number of individuals see themselves as belonging to more than one race (Schmitt, 2001).

The process of identity formation is always complex and may be doubly so for minority group members. Racial and ethnic identity takes time to form. For some, it may require a prolonged period, but the result can be a rich, multifaceted identity (Grantham & Ford, 2003; Nadal, 2004; Umana-Taylor & Fine, 2004; Quintana, 2007; Jensen, 2008).

## Depression and Suicide: Psychological Difficulties in Adolescence

*Brianne Camilleri had it all: Two involved parents, a caring older brother, and a comfortable home near Boston. But that didn't stop the overwhelming sense of hopelessness that enveloped her in ninth grade. "It was like a cloud that followed me everywhere," she says. "I couldn't get away from it."*

*Brianne started drinking and experimenting with drugs. One Sunday she was caught shoplifting at a local store and her mother, Linda, drove her home in what Brianne describes as a "piercing silence." With the clouds in her head so dark she believed she would never see light again, Brianne went straight for the bathroom and swallowed every Tylenol and Advil she could—a total of 74 pills. She was only 14, and she wanted to die. (Wingert & Kantrowitz, 2002, p. 54)*

Although the vast majority of teenagers weather the search for identity—as well as other challenges of the age—without major psychological difficulties, some find adolescence very stressful and some develop severe psychological problems. Two of the most serious are depression and suicide.

***Adolescent Depression.*** No one is immune to sadness and bad moods, including adolescents. The end of a relationship, failure at an important task, the death of a loved one—all may produce profound feelings of sadness, loss, and grief. In such situations, depression is a typical reaction.

Between 25 and 40 percent of girls, and 20 to 35 percent of boys, experience occasional episodes of depression during adolescence, although the incidence of major depression is far lower.

More than a quarter of adolescents report feeling so sad or hopeless for two or more weeks in a row that they stop doing their normal activities. Almost two-thirds of teenagers say they have experienced such feelings at some point. In contrast, only a small minority of adolescents—some 3 percent—experience *major depression*, a full-blown psychological disorder that is severe and lingers for long periods (Grunbaum, Lowry, & Kahn, 2001; Galambos, Leadbeater, & Barker, 2004).

Gender, ethnic, and racial differences also affect depression rates. As is true for adults, adolescent girls experience depression more often than boys. Some studies show African American adolescents having a higher rate of depression than White adolescents, though not all research supports this conclusion. Native Americans, too, have higher rates of depression (Hightower, 2005; Li, DiGiuseppe, & Froh, 2006; Zahn-Waxler, Shirtcliff, & Marceau, 2008).

In cases of severe, long-term depression, biological factors are often involved. Some adolescents do seem genetically predisposed to experience depression, but environmental and social factors related to the extraordinary changes in their social lives also have an impact. An adolescent who loses a loved one to death, for example, or who grows up with an alcoholic or depressed parent is at a higher risk of depression. Being unpopular, having few close friends, and rejection are also associated with adolescent depression (Goldsmith et al., 2002; Eley, Liang, & Plomin, 2004; Zalsman et al., 2006).

Why the depression rate is higher for girls than boys is puzzling. There is little evidence of a link to hormone differences or a particular gene. Some psychologists speculate that stress is greater for girls in adolescence due to the many, often conflicting, demands of the traditional female role. Recall the girl, quoted in our discussion of self-esteem, who feared academic achievement would endanger her popularity. Such conflict may make her feel helpless. Add to this the fact that traditional gender roles still give higher status to men than women (Gilbert, 2004; Hyde, Mezulis, & Abramson, 2008; Chaplin, Gillham, & Seligman, 2009).

Girls' higher levels of depression in adolescence may reflect gender differences in coping with stress, rather than differences in mood. Girls may be more likely to react to stress by turning inward, resulting in a sense of helplessness and hopelessness. In contrast, boys more often externalize the stress and act more impulsively or aggressively, or turn to drugs and alcohol (Hankin & Abramson, 2001; Winstead & Sanchez, 2005; Wisdom et al., 2007; Wu et al., 2007).

***Adolescent Suicide.*** Adolescent suicide in the United States has tripled in the last 30 years. One teenage suicide occurs every 90 minutes, for an annual rate of 12.2 suicides per 100,000 adolescents. The reported rate may actually understate the true number; parents and medical personnel often prefer to report a death as an accident rather than suicide. Even so, suicide is the third most common cause of death for 15- to 24-year-olds, after accidents and homicide. Despite this rise in suicide—more than for other age groups—the highest rate is still found in late adulthood (Grunbaum et al., 2002; Joe & Marcus, 2003; Conner & Goldston, 2007).

The rate of adolescent suicide is higher for boys, although girls *attempt* suicide more frequently. Attempts among males are more likely to be fatal because boys tend to use more violent means, such as guns, while girls tend to choose less violent means, such as drug overdose. Some estimates suggest there are as many as 200 attempted suicides by both sexes for every successful one (Joseph, Reznik, & Mester, 2003; Dervic et al., 2006; Pompili et al., 2009).

The reasons for the increase in adolescent suicide are unclear. The most obvious explanation is that adolescent stress has increased (Elkind, 1994). But why should stress have increased only for teenagers? The suicide rate for other age groups has remained fairly stable over the same period. Though we are not yet sure why adolescent suicide has increased, certain factors raise the risk. Depression is one. Depressed teenagers who feel profound hopelessness are at greater risk for suicide (although most depressed individuals do not commit suicide). Social inhibition, perfectionism, and high levels of stress and anxiety are also related to an increased risk. The easy availability of guns—more prevalent in the United States than in other industrialized nations—contributes to the suicide rate as well (Goldston, 2003; Zalsman, Levy, & Shoval, 2008; Wright, Wintemute, & Claire, 2008; Arnautovska & Grad, 2010).

Some suicide cases are associated with family conflicts and relationship or school difficulties. Some stem from a history of abuse and neglect. The rate of suicide among drug and alcohol abusers is also relatively high. As shown in Figure 6-9, teens who called a hotline because

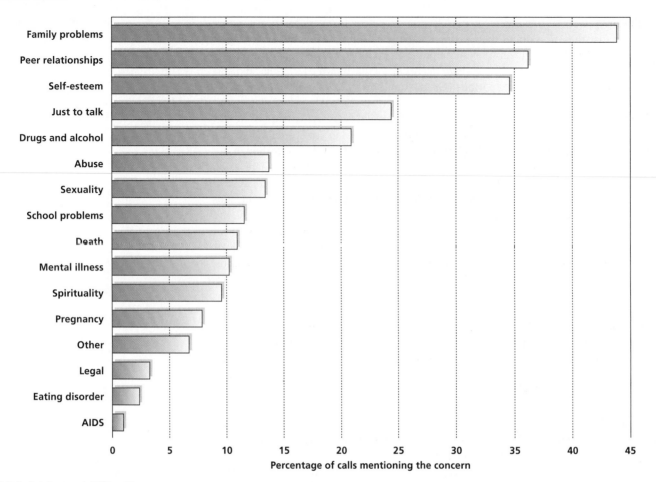

FIGURE 6-9 **Adolescent Difficulties**
Family, peer relationships, and self-esteem problems were most often mentioned by adolescents contemplating suicide, according to a review of phone calls to a telephone help line.
Source: Boehm & Campbell, 1995.

The rate of adolescent suicide has tripled in the last 30 years. These girls console one another following the suicide of a classmate.

they were considering suicide mentioned other factors as well (Lyon et al., 2000; Bergen, Martin, & Richardson, 2003; Wilcox, Conner, & Caine, 2004; Xing et al., 2010).

Some suicides appear to be caused by exposure to the suicide of others. In *cluster suicide,* one suicide leads to attempts by others to kill themselves. For instance, some high schools have experienced a series of suicides following a well-publicized case. As a result, many schools have established crisis intervention teams to counsel students when one student commits suicide (Arenson, 2004; Insel & Gould, 2008; Daniel & Goldston, 2009). There are several warning signs of potential suicide. Among them:

- Direct or indirect talk about suicide, such as "I wish I were dead" or "You won't have me to worry about any longer"
- School difficulties, such as missed classes or a decline in grades
- Making arrangements as if preparing for a long trip, such as giving away prized possessions or arranging for the care of a pet
- Writing a will
- Loss of appetite or excessive eating
- General depression, including a change in sleeping patterns, slowness and lethargy, and uncommunicativeness
- Dramatic changes in behavior, such as a shy person suddenly acting outgoing
- Preoccupation with death in music, art, or literature.

# Preventing Adolescent Suicide

## Becoming an Informed Consumer of Development

If you suspect an adolescent, or anyone else, is contemplating suicide, act! Here are several suggestions:

- Talk to the person. Listen with understanding and without judging.

- Talk specifically about suicidal thoughts; ask questions such as: Do you have a plan? Have you bought a gun? Where is it? Have you stockpiled pills? Where are they? The Public Health Service notes that, "contrary to popular belief, such candor will not give a person dangerous ideas or encourage a suicidal act."

- Try to distinguish between general upset and more serious danger, as when suicide plans *have* been made. If the crisis is acute, *do not leave the person alone.*

- Be supportive, let the person know you care, and try to break down his or her feelings of isolation.

- Take charge of finding help. Do not fear invading the person's privacy. Do not try to handle the problem alone. Get professional help immediately.

- Make the environment safe, removing (not just hiding) weapons such as guns, razors, scissors, medication, and other potentially dangerous items.

- Do not keep suicide talk or threats secret; these are calls for help and call for immediate action.

- Do not challenge, dare, or use verbal shock treatment on the person to correct his or her thinking.

- Make a contract with the person, getting a promise or commitment, preferably in writing, not to attempt suicide until you have talked further.

- Don't be overly reassured by a sudden improvement of mood. Such quick "recoveries" may be merely the relief of deciding to commit suicide or the temporary release of talking to someone; most likely, the underlying problems have not been resolved.

For immediate help with a suicide-related problem, call (800) 784-2433 or (800) 621-4000, national hotlines staffed with trained counselors.

## REVIEW, CHECK, AND APPLY

### REVIEW

**LO10**  How does the development of self-concept, self-esteem, and identity proceed during adolescence?

- Self-concept during adolescence grows more differentiated as the view of the self becomes more organized, broader, and more abstract, and takes account of the views of others.

- Both Erikson's identity-versus-identity-confusion stage and Marcia's four identity statuses focus on the adolescent's struggle to determine an identity and a role in society.

**LO11**  What role does religion and spirituality play during adolescence?

- Spirituality is a sense of attachment to some higher power such as God, nature, or something sacred.

- Because of an increase in their cognitive abilities, adolescents think more abstractly about religion and their religious identity.

**LO12**  What dangers do adolescents face as they deal with the stresses of adolescence?

- One of the dangers that adolescents face is depression, which affects girls more than boys. While reasons for increased suicide among adolescents are unclear, depression has been found to be one risk factor.

### CHECK YOURSELF

1. It is not uncommon for younger adolescents to be troubled by the multiple aspects of their personalities, especially when these aspects appear inconsistent with one another.
   - True
   - False

2. One of the reasons Erikson suggested that males and females moved through the identity-versus-identity-confusion period differently involved the:
   a. inherent genetic differences between men and women related to goals and needs.
   b. lack of apparent interest men had in raising children.
   c. social conditions at the time he was writing.
   d. lack of effort expended by women in reaching goals as compared to men.

3. Which of the following hypotheses may explain the higher incidence of depression in adolescent girls?
   a. Stress is more pronounced for girls due to the conflicting demands of the traditional female role.
   b. Females traditionally are less able to deal with stress than are males.

   c. Females are more likely to turn to drugs and alcohol than are males; therefore, their problems are more apparent.
   d. Parents are more concerned and protective of their daughters than their sons; therefore, they notice depression in girls earlier.

### APPLYING LIFESPAN DEVELOPMENT

- What are some consequences of the shift from reliance on adults to reliance on peers? Are there advantages? Dangers?

✓—**Study** and **Review** on
**MyDevelopmentLab.com**

Answers: 1) True; 2) c; 3) a

# Relationships: Family and Friends

**LO13** How do relationships between adolescents and their parents change?

**LO14** What does it mean to be popular and unpopular in adolescence, and how do adolescents respond to peer pressure?

**LO15** How do race and gender figure into adolescent relationships?

Compared with adolescents from more individualistic societies, adolescents from more collectivistic cultures tend to feel greater obligation to their families.

*When Paco Lizzagara entered junior high school, his good relationship with his parents changed drastically. Paco felt his parents were always "on his case." Instead of giving him the freedom he felt he deserved at age 13, they seemed to be more restrictive. Paco's parents saw things differently. They felt that they were not the source of tension in the house—he was. In their eyes, Paco, with whom they'd always enjoyed a stable, loving relationship, suddenly seemed transformed. They saw him shutting them out, and when he did speak with them, he criticized their politics, their dress, their preferences in TV shows. To his parents, Paco's behavior was upsetting and bewildering.*

## Family Ties: Changing Relations with Relations

The social world of adolescents is far wider than that of younger children. As relationships outside the home grow in significance, interactions with family evolve, taking on a new, and sometimes difficult, character (Collins & Andrew, 2004).

***The Quest for Autonomy.*** Parents are sometimes angered, and more frequently puzzled, by adolescents' conduct. Children who previously accepted their parents' judgments, declarations, and guidelines begin to question—and sometimes rebel against—their parents' views.

One cause of these clashes is the shifting roles children and parents confront during adolescence. Adolescents seek **autonomy,** independence and a sense of control over their lives. Most parents intellectually view this shift as a normal part of adolescence—a primary developmental task of the period—and in many ways they welcome it as a sign of growth. However, the day-to-day realities of adolescents' increasing autonomy may prove difficult for them to deal with (Smetana, 1995). Intellectually appreciating this growing independence and allowing a teen to attend an unsupervised party are two different things. To the adolescent, her parents' refusal indicates a lack of trust or confidence. To the parents, it's simply good sense: "I trust you," they may say. "It's the others who will be there that I worry about."

In most families, teenagers' autonomy grows gradually over the adolescent years. One study of adolescents' changing views of their parents found that as autonomy increases, parents are seen more realistically as persons in their own right. For example, rather than seeing their parents as authoritarian disciplinarians mindlessly reminding them to do their homework, they may come to see their parents' emphasis on excelling in school as evidence of parental regrets about their own lack of education and a wish to see their children have more options in life. At the same time, adolescents come to depend more on themselves and to feel more like separate individuals.

The increase in adolescent autonomy changes the parent–child relationship, which tends to be asymmetrical in early adolescence, when parents hold most of the power and influence. By the end of adolescence, power and influence are more balanced; the relationship is more egalitarian, although parents typically retain the upper hand (Goede, Branje, & Meeus, 2009).

***Culture and Autonomy.*** The degree of autonomy achieved varies from one family to the next. Cultural factors play a role. In Western societies, which value individualism, adolescents seek autonomy at a relatively early stage. In contrast, Asian societies are more collectivistic, believing the welfare of the group is above that of the individual. In such societies, adolescents' aspirations to autonomy are less pronounced (Kim et al., 1994; Raeff, 2004; Supple et al., 2009).

**From a social worker's perspective:** In what ways do you think parents with different styles—authoritarian, authoritative, permissive, and uninvolved—react to attempts to establish autonomy during adolescence? Are the styles of parenting different for a single parent? Are there cultural differences?

**autonomy** having independence and a sense of control over one's life

A sense of obligation to family also varies among cultures. In collectivistic cultures, adolescents tend to feel a greater obligation to fulfill their family's expectations—to provide assistance, show respect, and offer financial support. In such societies, the push for autonomy is weaker and its development is slower (Chao, 2001; Fuligni & Zhang, 2004; Leung, Pe-Pua, & Karnilowicz, 2006).

The extended timetable for autonomy in collectivistic cultures appears to have no negative consequences for adolescents. What matters is the match between cultural expectations and developmental patterns, not the specific timetable (Rothbaum et al., 2000; Zimmer-Gembeck & Collins, 2005; Updegraff et al., 2006).

Gender also plays a role. In general, male adolescents are permitted more autonomy at an earlier age than females. This is consistent with traditional gender stereotypes, in which males are seen as more independent and females as more dependent on others. In fact, parents who hold traditional views on gender are less likely to encourage their daughters' autonomy (Bumpus, Crouter, & McHale, 2001).

*The Myth of the Generation Gap.* Teen movies often depict adolescents and their parents in total opposition, victims of a **generation gap,** a deep divide in attitudes, values, aspirations, and world views. For example, the parent of an environmentalist might turn out to own a polluting factory. These exaggerations are funny because they contain a truth—parents and teenagers often see things differently.

The reality, however, is another matter. The generation gap, when it exists, is really quite narrow. Adolescents and their parents tend to agree on many things. Republican parents generally have Republican children; members of the Christian right have children with similar views; parents who advocate for abortion rights have children who are pro-choice. On social, political, and religious issues, parents and adolescents tend to be in synch, and children's worries mirror those of their parents. Adolescents' concerns about society's problems (see Figure 6-10) reflect those of many adults (Flor & Knap, 2001; Knafo & Schwartz, 2003; Smetana, 2005).

Most adolescents and their parents get along quite well. Despite their quest for autonomy and independence, most teenagers have deep love, affection, and respect for their parents—as their parents do for them. Although some parent–adolescent relationships are seriously troubled, the majority are positive and help adolescents avoid the kind of peer pressure discussed later in the module (Gavin & Furman, 1996; Resnick et al., 1997; Black, 2002; Riesch et al., 2010).

Even though teenagers spend less time with their families in general, the amount of time they spend alone with each parent remains remarkably stable across adolescence (see Figure 6-11).

There is no evidence that suggests family problems are worse in adolescence than at other stages of development (Steinberg, 1993; Larson et al., 1996; Granic, Hollenstein, & Dishion, 2003).

*Conflicts with Parents.* Of course, if most adolescents get along with their parents most of the time, that means sometimes they don't. No relationship is always smooth. Parents and teens may agree about social and political issues, but they often differ on matters of personal taste, such as music and clothing. Also, parents and children may disagree when children act on their autonomy and independence sooner than parents feel is right. Consequently, parent–child conflicts are more likely to occur during adolescence, particularly in the early stages, although not every family is affected to the same degree (Arnett, 2000; Smetana, Daddis, & Chuang, 2003).

**generation gap** a divide between parents and adolescents in attitudes, values, aspirations, and world views

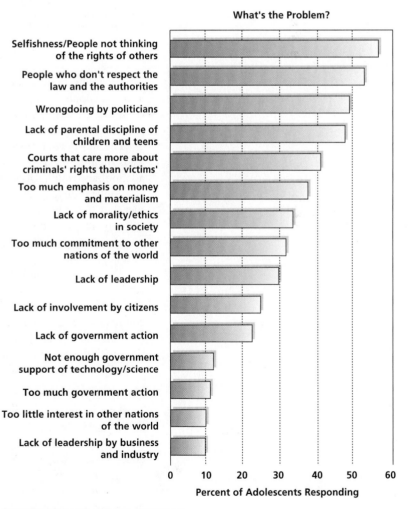

**What's the Problem?**

**FIGURE 6-10 What's the Problem?**
Adolescents' views of society's ills are ones with which their parents would be likely to agree.
Source: PRIMEDIA/Roper National Youth Survey, 1999.

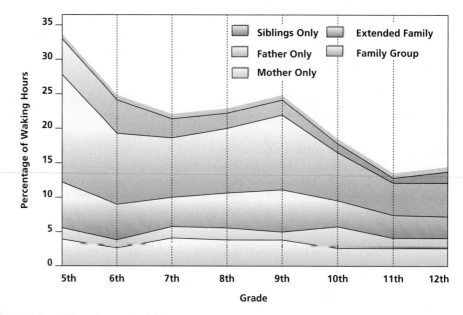

**FIGURE 6-11** Time Spent by Adolescents with Parents

Despite their quest for autonomy and independence, most adolescents have deep love, affection, and respect for their parents, and the amount of time they spend alone with each parent (the lower two segments) remains remarkably stable across adolescence.

Source: From Reed Larson et al., *Developmental Psychology*. Copyright © 1996 by the American Psychological Association. Reproduced with permission.

According to developmental psychologist Judith Smetana, conflict is greater in early adolescence because of differing definitions of, and rationales for, appropriate and inappropriate conduct. Parents may frown on multiple ear piercings because society traditionally deems it inappropriate, while adolescents may view the issue as one of personal choice (Smetana, 2005, 2006).

The newly sophisticated reasoning of adolescents (discussed in the previous module) leads them to regard parental rules in more complex ways. Arguments that might convince a school-age child ("Do it because I tell you to do it") are less compelling to an adolescent.

The argumentativeness and assertiveness of early adolescence may at first increase conflict, but they play a key role in the evolution of parent–child relationships. While parents may initially react defensively to their children's challenges and grow inflexible and rigid, in most cases they come to realize their children *are* growing up and they want to support them in that process.

As parents realize that their children's arguments are often compelling and fairly reasonable, and that they can be trusted with more freedom, they become more yielding, allowing and perhaps even encouraging independence. As this process occurs in mid-adolescence, the conflict of the early years declines.

This does not hold true for all adolescents. The majority of teenagers maintain stable relations with their parents, but as many as 20 percent pass through a fairly rough time (Dryfoos, 1990; Dmitrieva et al., 2004).

*Cultural Differences in Parent–Child Conflicts During Adolescence.* Parent–child conflicts are found in every culture, but there does seem to be less conflict between parents and teenagers in "traditional," preindustrial cultures. Teens in such cultures experience fewer mood swings and instances of risky behavior than teens in industrialized countries (Arnett, 2000; Nelson, Badger, & Wu, 2004; Kapadia, 2008; Eichelsheim et al., 2010).

The reason may be the degree of independence that adolescents expect and adults permit. In more industrialized societies, with an emphasis on individualism, independence is expected of adolescents. Consequently, adolescents and their parents must negotiate the amount and timing of that independence—a process that often leads to strife. In more traditional societies, individualism is less valued; therefore, adolescents are less inclined to seek independence. The result is less parent–child conflict (Dasen, 2000, 2002).

# Relationships with Peers: The Importance of Belonging

For many parents, the key symbols of adolescence are the cell phone and the computer. For their children, communicating with friends is an indispensable lifeline, a compulsive need that underscores their significance at this stage. Continuing the trend from middle childhood, adolescents spend increasing hours with their peers as these relationships grow in importance. In fact, there is probably no period of life in which peer relationships matter as much as in adolescence (Youniss & Haynie, 1992).

*Social Comparison.* Peers become more important for many reasons. They enable adolescents to compare and evaluate opinions, abilities, and even physical changes—a process called *social comparison.* Because the physical and cognitive changes of this age are so unique and so pronounced, especially in early puberty, adolescents turn to others who share and can shed light on their own experiences. Parents, being well beyond these changes, cannot provide social comparison. Adolescents' questioning of adult authority and their desire for autonomy also render parents—and adults in general—inadequate sources of knowledge (Schutz, Paxton, & Wertheim, 2002; Rankin, Lane, & Gibbons, 2004).

*Reference Groups.* As noted, adolescence is a time of trying out new identities, roles, and conduct. Peers provide information about what roles and behavior are most acceptable by serving as a reference group. **Reference groups** are people with whom one compares oneself. Just as a professional ballplayer compares his performance to that of other pro players, so do teenagers compare themselves to peers similar to them.

Reference groups offer a set of *norms,* or standards, by which abilities and social success can be judged. A teenager need not belong to a group for it to serve as a reference. Unpopular adolescents, belittled and rejected by members of a popular group, may yet use it as a reference group (Berndt, 1999).

*Cliques and Crowds: Belonging to a Group.* Increased cognitive sophistication allows adolescents to group others in more discriminating ways. Even if they do not belong to their reference group, they typically are part of some identifiable group. Rather than defining people in concrete terms by what they do ("football players" or "musicians") as a younger child might, adolescents use more abstract terms ("jocks" or "skaters" or "stoners") (Brown, 2004).

Adolescents form two types of groups: cliques and crowds. **Cliques** are groups of from 2 to 12 people whose members have frequent social interactions with one another. **Crowds** are larger, comprising individuals who share certain characteristics but do not necessarily interact. "Jocks" and "nerds" represent crowds found in many high schools.

Membership in a clique or a crowd is determined by the degree of similarity with other members. One key similarity is substance use; adolescents tend to choose friends whose alcohol and drug use matches their own. Their friends often mirror their academic success and general behavior patterns, although this is not always true. For instance, in early adolescence, peers who are aggressive may be more attractive than those who are well behaved (Kupersmidt & Dodge, 2004; Hutchinson & Rapee, 2007; Kiuru et al., 2009).

The emergence of distinct cliques and crowds at this stage reflects adolescents' increased cognitive capabilities. Group labels are abstractions, requiring teens to judge people they may seldom interact with and have little direct knowledge about. It is not until mid-adolescence that teenagers are cognitively able to make the subtle judgments that distinguish between different cliques and crowds (Burgess & Rubin, 2000; Brown & Klute, 2003; Witvliet et al., 2010).

*Gender Relations.* As children enter adolescence, their social groups are composed almost universally of same-sex friends. Boys hang out with boys; girls hang out with girls. This sex segregation is called the **sex cleavage.**

The situation changes with the onset of puberty. Boys and girls experience the hormonal surge that causes the sex organs to mature. At the same time, society suggests it is time for romantic involvement. These developments change the ways the opposite sex is viewed. Where a 10-year-old is likely to see every member of the other sex as "annoying" and "a pain," heterosexual teenage boys and girls regard each other's personality and sexuality with greater interest. (For gays and lesbians, pairing off holds other complexities, as we will see when we discuss adolescent dating.)

The sex segregation of childhood continues during the early stages of adolescence. However, by the time of middle adolescence, this segregation decreases, and boys' and girls' cliques begin to converge.

**reference groups** groups of people with whom one compares oneself

**cliques** groups of from 2 to 12 people whose members have frequent social interactions with one another

**crowds** larger groups than cliques, composed of individuals who share particular characteristics but who may not interact with one another

**sex cleavage** sex segregation in which boys interact primarily with boys and girls primarily with girls

In early puberty, boys' and girls' cliques, previously on parallel but separate tracks, begin to converge. Adolescents attend boy–girl dances or parties, although the boys still tend to socialize with boys, and the girls with girls (Richards et al., 1998). Soon, adolescents spend more time with the other sex. New cliques emerge, composed of both genders. Not everyone participates initially: Early on, the leaders of the same-sex cliques and those with the highest status lead the way. Eventually, however, most teenagers belong to mixed-gender cliques. At the end of adolescence, cliques and crowds become less influential. Many dissolve as pairing off occurs.

## Popularity and Rejection

Most adolescents are highly tuned in to who is popular and who is not. In fact, for some, popularity—or lack of it—is the central focus of their lives.

The social world of adolescents is more complex than who is popular or unpopular. Some adolescents are controversial. In contrast to *popular* adolescents, who are mostly liked,

## Cultural Dimensions

### Race Segregation: The Great Divide of Adolescence

*When Philip McAdoo, a [student] at the University of North Carolina, stopped one day to see a friend who worked on his college campus, a receptionist asked if he would autograph a basketball for her son. Because he was African American and tall, "she just assumed that I was on the basketball team," recounted McAdoo.*

*Jasme Kelly, an African American sophomore at the same college, had a similar story to tell. When she went to see a friend at a fraternity house, the student who answered the door asked if she was there to apply for the job of cook.*

*White students, too, find racial relations difficult and in some ways forbidding. For instance, Jenny Johnson, a white 20-year-old junior, finds even the most basic conversation with African American classmates difficult. She describes a conversation in which African American friends "jump at my throat because I used the word 'black' instead of African American. There is just such a huge barrier that it's really hard... to have a normal discussion."* (Sanoff & Minerbrook, 1993, p. 58)

The pattern of race segregation found at the University of North Carolina is repeated in schools and colleges throughout the United States: Even when they attend desegregated schools with significant diversity, people of different ethnicities and races interact very little. Even if they have a friend of a different ethnicity within the confines of a school, most adolescents don't interact with that friend outside of school (DuBois & Hirsch, 1990).

It doesn't start out this way. During elementary school and early adolescence, integration is common among students of differing ethnicities. However, by middle and late adolescence, students segregate (Spencer & Dornbusch, 1990; Ennett & Bauman, 1996).

Why is racial and ethnic segregation the rule, even in schools that have long been desegregated? One reason is that minority students may seek support from others who share their status (where "minority," used in its sociological sense, indicates a subordinate group lacking power compared to a dominant group). By associating with others of their own group, members of minority groups are able to affirm their own identity.

Members of different racial and ethnic groups may be segregated in the classroom as well. As discussed earlier, members of groups that have experienced discrimination tend to be less successful in school. Thus, ethnic and racial segregation in high school may be based on academic achievement rather than ethnicity.

By middle and late adolescence, racial and ethnic segregation is common.

Lower academic performance may place minority students in classes with fewer majority students, and vice versa. Such class assignment practices may maintain and promote racial and ethnic segregation, especially in schools where rigid academic tracking assigns students to "low," "medium," and "high" tracks depending on their prior achievement (Lucas & Berends, 2002).

Segregation in school may also reflect prejudice, both perceived and real, toward members of other groups. Students of color may feel that the White majority is discriminatory and hostile, and thus prefer to stick to same-race groups. White students may assume that minority students are antagonistic and unfriendly. Such mutually destructive attitudes make meaningful interaction difficult (Phinney, Ferguson, & Tate, 1997; Tropp, 2003).

Is this voluntary racial and ethnic segregation inevitable? No. Adolescents who have interacted regularly and extensively with other races in childhood are more likely to have friends of different races. Schools that actively promote integration in classes create an environment that fosters cross-race friendships (Hewstone, 2003).

Still, many societal pressures prevent social integration. Peer pressure, too, may discourage clique members from crossing racial and ethnic lines to form new friendships.

**controversial adolescents** are liked by some and disliked by others. A controversial adolescent may be highly popular within a particular group, such as the string orchestra, but less so among other classmates. There are also **rejected adolescents,** who are uniformly disliked, and **neglected adolescents,** who are neither liked nor disliked (see Figure 6-12)—whose status is so low everyone overlooks them.

In most cases, popular and controversial adolescents tend to enjoy a higher status, while rejected and neglected teenagers share a lower status. Popular and controversial adolescents have more close friends, engage in more activities with their peers, and disclose more about themselves than less popular students. They participate in more extracurricular school activities. Well aware of their own popularity, they are less lonely than their less popular classmates (Farmer et al., 2003; Zettergren, 2004; Becker & Luthar, 2007; Closson, 2009). ⊙–Watch on **mydevelopmentlab.com**

The social world of rejected and neglected adolescents is far less pleasant. They have fewer friends, engage in fewer social activities, and have less contact with the opposite sex. They see themselves—accurately   as less popular, and they are more likely to feel lonely (McElhaney, Antonishak, & Allen, 2008).

As illustrated in Table 6-4, men and women differ in their ideas of what determines status in high school. College men suggest that appearance is what most determines a girl's status, while college women believe it is her grades and intelligence (Suitor et al., 2001).

> **controversial adolescents** children who are liked by some peers and disliked by others.
>
> **rejected adolescents** children who are actively disliked, and whose peers may react to them in an obviously negative manner
>
> **neglected adolescents** children who receive relatively little attention from their peers in the form of either positive or negative interactions

⊙–Watch on **mydevelopmentlab.com**

> *As your virtual child reaches adolescence, what changes have you seen between your child and his or her friends? What about between you and your child?*
>
> Log onto MyDevelopmentLab.com and watch the video on adolescence to see teenagers aged 16 to 20 talk about making decisions, the transition to college, first relationships, and their relationships with their parents.

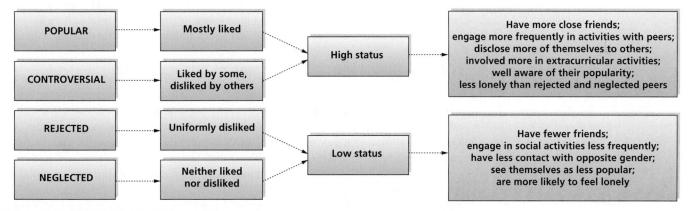

**FIGURE 6-12  The Social World of Adolescence**
An adolescent's popularity can fall into one of four categories, depending on the opinions of his or her peers. Popularity is related to differences in status, behavior, and adjustment.

## TABLE 6-4  HIGH SCHOOL STATUS

| What Makes High School Girls High in Status: | | What Makes High School Boys High in Status: | |
| --- | --- | --- | --- |
| **According to College Men:** | **According to College Women:** | **According to College Men:** | **According to College Women:** |
| 1. Physical attractiveness | 1. Grades/intelligence | 1. Participation in sports | 1. Participation in sports |
| 2. Grades/intelligence | 2. Participation in sports | 2. Grades/intelligence | 2. Grades/intelligence |
| 3. Participation in sports | 3. General sociability | 3. Popularity with girls | 3. General sociability |
| 4. General sociability | 4. Physical attractiveness | 4. General sociability | 4. Physical attractiveness |
| 5. Popularity with boys | 5. Clothes | 5. Car | 5. School clubs/government |

Note: Students at the following universities were asked in which ways adolescents in their high schools had gained prestige with their peers: Louisiana State University, Southeastern Louisiana University, State University of New York at Albany, State University of New York at Stony Brook, University of Georgia, and the University of New Hampshire.

Source: From Suitor, J. J., Minyard, S. A., & Carter, R. S. (2001), "'Did you see what I saw?' Gender differences in perceptions of avenues to prestige among adolescents," *Sociological Inquiry*, 71, 437–454. Copyright © 2001 Blackwell Publishing. Reprinted with permission.

**peer pressure** the influence of one's peers to conform to their behavior and attitudes

**undersocialized delinquents** adolescent delinquents who are raised with little discipline or with harsh, uncaring parental supervision

**socialized delinquents** adolescent delinquents who know and subscribe to the norms of society and who are fairly normal psychologically

👁 Watch on **mydevelopmentlab.com**

Log onto MyDevelopmentLab.com and watch a video of 18-year-old Tim and his mom talking about how peer pressure has affected Tim's life.

## Conformity: Peer Pressure in Adolescence

Whenever Aldos Henry said he wanted a particular brand of sneakers or a certain style of shirt, his parents blamed it on peer pressure and told him to think for himself.

In arguing with Aldos, his parents were taking a view prevalent in U.S. society: that teenagers are highly susceptible to **peer pressure,** the pressure to conform to the behavior and attitudes of one's peers. Were his parents correct? 👁 Watch on **mydevelopmentlab.com**

Adolescents *are* highly susceptible to the influence of their peers when considering what to wear, whom to date, and what movies to see. Wearing the right clothes, down to the right brand, can be a ticket to popularity. It shows you know what's what. But when it comes to nonsocial matters, such as choosing a career path or trying to solve a problem, they are more likely to consult an adult (Phelan, Yu, & Davidson, 1994).

Especially in middle and late adolescence, teenagers look to those they see as experts. For social concerns, they turn to the experts—their peers. For arenas where adults hold the knowledge, teenagers tend to ask their advice and accept their opinions (Young & Ferguson, 1979; Perrine & Aloise-Young, 2004).

Overall, susceptibility to peer pressure does not suddenly soar in adolescence. Instead, adolescence changes the source of influence. Whereas children conform fairly consistently to their parents, pressures to conform to peers increase in adolescence as teens establish an identity apart from their parents'.

Ultimately, adolescents conform less to both peers *and* adults as their autonomy increases. As their confidence grows and they are able to make their own decisions, adolescents are apt to act independently and to reject pressures from others. Before they learn to resist peer pressure, however, teenagers may get into trouble, often along with their friends (Steinberg & Monahan, 2007; Cook, Buehler, & Henson, 2009; Monahan, Steinberg, & Cauffman, 2009).

## Juvenile Delinquency: The Crimes of Adolescence

Adolescents, along with young adults, commit more crimes than any other age group. This is a somewhat misleading statistic: Because certain behaviors (such as drinking) are illegal for adolescents, it is easy for them to break the law. But even disregarding such crimes, adolescents are disproportionately responsible for violent crimes, such as murder, assaults, and rape, and property crimes involving theft, robbery, and arson.

What steers adolescents toward criminal activity? Some offenders, known as **undersocialized delinquents,** were raised with little discipline or by harsh, uncaring parents. Although they are influenced by peers, their parents did not teach them appropriate social behavior or how to regulate their own conduct. Undersocialized delinquents typically begin criminal activities well before the onset of adolescence (Hoeve et al., 2008; Thomas, 2010).

Undersocialized delinquents share several characteristics. They tend to be aggressive and violent early in life, leading to peer rejection and academic failure. They are more likely to have been diagnosed with attention deficit disorder as children, and they tend to be less intelligent than average (Silverthorn & Frick, 1999; Rutter, 2003).

Undersocialized delinquents often suffer from psychological problems, and as adults fit a pattern called antisocial personality disorder. They are unlikely to be successfully rehabilitated, and many undersocialized delinquents live on the margins of society their entire lives (Lynam, 1996; Frick et al., 2003).

A larger group of adolescent offenders are socialized delinquents. **Socialized delinquents** know and subscribe to the norms of society; they are fairly normal psychologically. For them, offenses committed in adolescence do not lead to a life of crime. Instead, most socialized delinquents engage in some petty crimes (such as shoplifting) during adolescence, but do not continue into adulthood.

Socialized delinquents are typically highly peer-influenced, their delinquency often occurring in groups. Some research also suggests that their parents supervise their behavior less than other parents. But these minor delinquencies are often a result of giving in to group pressure or seeking to establish one's identity as an adult (Fletcher et al., 1995; Thornberry & Krohn, 1997).

Undersocialized delinquents are raised with little discipline or by harsh, uncaring parents, and they begin antisocial activities at a relatively early age. In contrast, socialized delinquents know and usually follow the norms of society, and they are highly influenced by their peers.

## REVIEW, CHECK, AND APPLY

REVIEW

**REVIEW**

**LO13**  How do relationships between adolescents and their parents change?

- The search for autonomy may change relations between teenagers and their parents, temporarily creating conflict in some cases, but the generation gap is narrower than is generally thought.

**LO14**  What does it mean to be popular and unpopular in adolescence, and how do adolescents respond to peer pressure?

- Cliques and crowds serve as reference groups in adolescence, offering a means of social comparison. Sex cleavage gradually diminishes, until boys and girls begin to pair off.

- In early adolescence, adolescents may be highly susceptible to peer pressure, especially regarding what clothes to wear or movies to see, but as they mature and their confidence grows, adolescents look less to others and more to themselves in making decisions.

**LO15**  How do race and gender figure into adolescent relationships?

- Racial separation increases in adolescence, bolstered by socioeconomic status differences, different academic experiences, and mutually distrustful attitudes. Sex cleavage eventually dissolves as most teenagers join mixed gender cliques.

**CHECK YOURSELF**

**1.** Depending on one's cultural framework, some adolescents may expect less autonomy from their parents than will others.

- True
- False

**2.** _____ groups are groups of people with whom one compares oneself. For example, teens would compare themselves to other teens.

**3.** Cross-sex cliques begin forming:

   **a.** once parents and teachers begin rewarding students for cross-sex interactions.

   **b.** once the leaders in the same-sex cliques begin dating.

   **c.** after sixth grade.

   **d.** when same-sex peers become bored with one another.

**APPLYING LIFESPAN DEVELOPMENT**

- Thinking back to your own high school days, what was the dominant clique in your school, and what factors were related to group membership?

✓●—⌐**Study** and **Review** on
MyDevelopmentLab.com

Answers: 1) True; 2) Reference; 3) b

# Dating, Sexual Behavior, and Teenage Pregnancy

**LO16 What are the functions and characteristics of dating during adolescence?**

**LO17 How does sexuality develop in the adolescent years?**

LEARNING OBJECTIVES

*It took him almost a month, but Sylvester Chiu finally got up the courage to ask Jackie Durbin to the movies. It was hardly a surprise to Jackie, though. Sylvester had first told his friend Erik about his plans, and Erik had told Jackie's friend Cynthia, who had in turn told Jackie, who was primed to say "yes" when Sylvester finally called.*

Welcome to the complex world of adolescent dating, an important ritual in the liturgy of adolescent relationships.

## Dating: Close Relationships in the Twenty-first Century

Changing cultural factors largely determine when and how adolescents begin to date. Until recently, exclusive dating was a cultural ideal, viewed in the context of romance. Society encouraged dating as a way for adolescents to explore relationships that might lead to marriage. Today, some adolescents believe that dating is outmoded and limiting, and in some places "hooking up"—a vague term that covers everything from kissing to sexual intercourse—is regarded as more appropriate. Still, despite changing cultural norms, dating remains the dominant form of social interaction that leads to intimacy among adolescents (Denizet-Lewis, 2004; Manning, Giordano, & Longmore, 2006; Bogle, 2008).

***The Functions of Dating.***  Dating is a way to learn how to establish intimacy with another individual. It can provide entertainment and, depending on the status of the person one is dating, prestige. It even can be used to develop a sense of one's own identity (Zimmer-Gembeck & Gallaty, 2006; Friedlander, Connolly, & Pepler, 2007).

Unfortunately, dating, at least in early and middle adolescence, does not serve the function of developing intimacy very well. On the contrary, it is often a superficial activity in which the participants rarely let down their guards and never expose themselves emotionally. Psychological intimacy may be lacking even when sex is part of the relationship (Savin-Williams & Berndt, 1990; Collins, 2003; Furman & Shaffer, 2003).

True intimacy becomes more common during later adolescence. At that point, both participants may take dating more seriously as a way to select a possible mate for marriage.

For homosexual adolescents, dating presents special challenges. In some cases, blatant homophobic prejudice expressed by classmates may lead gays and lesbians to date members of the other sex in an effort to fit in. If they do seek relationships with other gays and lesbians, they may find it difficult to find partners, who may not openly express their sexual orientation. Homosexual couples who do openly date face possible harassment, making the development of a relationship all the more difficult (Savin-Williams, 2003, 2006).

*Dating, Race, and Ethnicity.* Culture influences dating patterns among adolescents of different racial and ethnic groups, particularly those whose parents have immigrated from other countries. Foreign-born parents may try to control dating behavior to preserve traditional values or confine dating to their own racial or ethnic group.

Asian parents may hold especially conservative attitudes because they themselves may be living in an arranged marriage and may never have experienced dating. They may insist that there will be no dating without chaperones, a position that will inevitably lead to conflict with their children (Hamon & Ingoldsby, 2003; Hoelter, Axinn, & Ghimire, 2004; Lau et al., 2009).

## Sexual Relationships

The hormonal changes of puberty trigger not only the maturation of the sexual organs, but also a new range of feelings. Sexual behavior and thoughts are among the central concerns of adolescents, occupying the minds of almost all adolescents a good deal of the time (Kelly, 2001; Ponton, 2001).

*Masturbation.* Often the first sex act in which adolescents engage is solitary sexual self-stimulation, or masturbation. By age 15, 80 percent of teenage boys and 20 percent of teenage girls report that they have masturbated. In males, frequency is high in the early teens and then begins to decline, while in females, frequency is lower initially and increases throughout adolescence. There are also racial differences. For example, African American men and women masturbate less than Whites (Schwartz, 1999; Hyde & DeLamater, 2004).

Although masturbation is widespread, it still may produce feelings of shame and guilt, a legacy from years of misguided views. In the nineteenth century, people were warned about the horrible effects of masturbation, including "dyspepsia, spinal disease, headache, epilepsy, various kinds of fits,… impaired eyesight, palpitation of the heart, pain in the side and bleeding at the lungs, spasm of the heart, and sometimes sudden death" (Gregory, 1856). Suggested remedies included bandaging the genitals, covering them with a cage, tying the hands, male circumcision without anesthesia (so that it might better be remembered), and for girls, the administration of carbolic acid to the clitoris. One physician, J. W. Kellogg, believed that certain grains would be less likely to provoke sexual excitation—leading to his invention of corn flakes (Hunt, 1974; Michael et al., 1994).

Today, experts on sexual behavior view masturbation as a normal, healthy, and harmless activity. In fact, some suggest that it provides a useful way to learn about one's own sexuality (Hyde & DeLamater, 2003; Levin, 2007).

*Sexual Intercourse.* Although it may be preceded by many different types of sexual intimacy, including deep kissing, massaging, petting, and oral sex, sexual intercourse remains a major milestone in the perceptions of most adolescents. Consequently, the main focus of researchers investigating sexual behavior has been on the act of heterosexual intercourse.

The average age at which adolescents first have sexual intercourse has been steadily declining over the last 50 years, and about one in five adolescents have had sex before the age of 15. Overall, the average age of first sexual intercourse is 17, and around three-quarters of adolescents have had sex before the age of 20 (see Figure 6-13). At the same time, though, many teenagers are postponing sex, and the number of adolescents who say they have never had sexual intercourse increased by 13 percent from 1991 to 2007 (Dailard, 2006; Guttmacher Institute, 2006; MMWR, 2008).

There also are racial and ethnic differences in timing of initial sexual intercourse: African Americans generally have sex for the first time earlier than do Puerto Ricans, who have sex earlier than Whites do. These racial and ethnic differences likely reflect differences in socioeconomic conditions, cultural values, and family structure (Singh et al., 2000; Hyde, 2008).

Strong societal norms govern sexual conduct. A few decades ago the prevailing norm was the *double standard:* Premarital sex was permissible for males but not females, but men should be sure to marry virgins. Today the double standard has begun to give way to *permissiveness with affection.* Under this standard, premarital intercourse is permissible for both men and women in the context of a long-term, committed, or loving relationship (Hyde & Delamater, 2004; Earle et al., 2007).

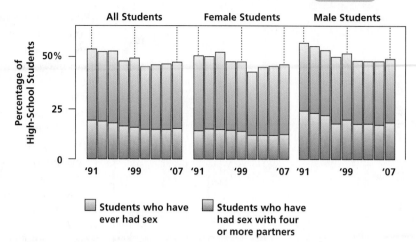

**FIGURE 6-13 Adolescents and Sexual Activity**
The age at which adolescents have sexual intercourse for the first time is declining, and about three-quarters have had sex before the age of 20.
Source: Morbidity and Mortality Weekly Report, 2008.

> **From the perspective of a health care provider:** A parent asks you how to prevent her 14-year-old son from engaging in sexual activity until he is older. What would you tell her?

The demise of the double standard is far from complete. Attitudes toward sexual conduct are still typically more lenient for males than for females, even in socially liberal cultures. And in some cultures, the standards for men and women are quite distinct. For example, in North Africa, the Middle East, and the majority of Asian countries, women are expected to abstain from sexual intercourse until they are married. In Mexico, males are considerably more likely than females to have premarital sex. In contrast, in Sub-Saharan Africa, women are more likely to have sexual intercourse before marriage, and intercourse is common among unmarried teenage women (Johnson et al., 1992; Peltzer & Pengpid, 2006; Wellings et al., 2006; Ghule, Balaiah, & Joshi, 2007).

## Sexual Orientation: Heterosexuality, Homosexuality, and Bisexuality

When we consider adolescents' sexual development, the most frequent pattern is *heterosexuality,* sexual attraction and behavior directed to the other sex. Yet some teenagers are *homosexual,* in which their sexual attraction and behavior is oriented to members of their own sex. (Many male homosexuals prefer the term *gay* and female homosexuals the label *lesbian,* because they refer to a broader array of attitudes and lifestyle than the term *homosexual,* which focuses on the sexual act.) Other people find they are *bisexual,* sexually attracted to people of both sexes.

Many teens experiment with homosexuality. Around 20 to 25 percent of adolescent boys and 10 percent of adolescent girls have at least one same-sex sexual encounter. In fact, homosexuality and heterosexuality are not completely distinct sexual orientations. Alfred Kinsey, a pioneer sex researcher, argued that sexual orientation should be viewed as a continuum in which "exclusively homosexual" is at one end and "exclusively heterosexual" is at the other. In between are people who show both homosexual and heterosexual behavior. Although accurate figures are difficult to obtain, most experts believe that between 4 percent and 10 percent of both men and women are exclusively homosexual during extended periods of their lives (Kinsey, Pomeroy, & Martin, 1948; McWhirter, Sanders, & Reinisch, 1990; Michael et al., 1994; Diamond, 2003a, 2003b; Russell & Consolacion, 2003).

Sexuality is further complicated by the distinction between sexual orientation, which refers to a person's sexual interests, and gender identity—the gender a person believes he or she is psychologically. Sexual orientation and gender identity are not necessarily related to one another: A man with a strong masculine gender identity may be attracted to other men, and traditional "masculine" or "feminine" behavior is not necessarily related to a person's sexual orientation or gender identity (Hunter & Mallon, 2000).

Some people feel they have been born the wrong physical sex (e.g., believing that they are a woman trapped in a man's body). These *transgendered* individuals may pursue sexual reassignment surgery, a prolonged course of treatment in which they receive hormones and reconstructive surgery to enable them to take on the physical characteristics of the other sex.

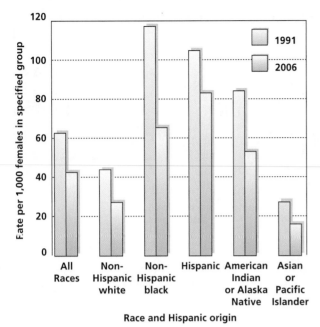

**FIGURE 6-14 Teenage Pregnancy Rates**
Although there has been a small increase in recent years, the rate of teenage pregnancies has dropped dramatically among all ethnic groups since 1991.
Source: National Vital Statistics Report, Vol. 57, 2009.

***What Determines Sexual Orientation?*** The factors that induce people to develop as heterosexual, homosexual, or bisexual are not well understood. Evidence suggests that genetic and biological factors play a central role. Identical twins are more likely to both be homosexual than pairs of siblings who don't share their genetic makeup. Other research finds that various structures of the brain are different in homosexuals and heterosexuals, and hormone production also seems to be linked to sexual orientation (Ellis et al., 2008; Fitzgerald, 2008; Santilla et al., 2008).

In the past, some theoreticians suggested that family or peer environmental factors play a role. For example, Freud argued that homosexuality was the result of inappropriate identification with the opposite-sex parent (Freud, 1922/1959). The difficulty with Freud's theoretical perspective and other, similar perspectives that followed is that there simply is no research evidence to suggest that any particular family dynamic or childrearing practice is consistently related to sexual orientation. Similarly, explanations based on learning theory, which suggest that homosexuality arises because of rewarding, pleasant homosexual experiences and unsatisfying heterosexual ones, are not supported by research (Bell & Weinberg, 1978; Isay, 1990; Golombok & Tasker, 1996).

In short, there is no accepted explanation of why some adolescents develop a heterosexual orientation and others a homosexual orientation. Most experts believe that sexual orientation develops out of a complex interplay of genetic, physiological, and environmental factors (LeVay & Valente, 2003).

***Challenges Facing Gay and Lesbian Adolescents.*** Adolescents who are attracted to members of the same sex face a more difficult time than other teens. U.S. society still harbors ignorance and prejudice about homosexuality, insisting that people have a choice in the matter—which they do not. Gay and lesbian teens may be rejected by their family or peers and harassed or even assaulted by others. As a result, adolescents who are homosexual are at greater risk for depression, with suicide rates significantly higher than for heterosexual adolescents (Eisenberg & Resnick, 2006; Silenzio et al., 2007; Bos et al., 2008; Doty et al., 2010).

Ultimately, though, most people become comfortable with their sexual orientation. And while lesbian, gay, and bisexual adolescents may experience mental health difficulties, homosexuality is not considered a psychological disorder by any of the major psychological or medical associations (van Wormer & McKinney, 2003; Davison, 2005; Russell & McGuire, 2006).

## Teenage Pregnancies

Feedings at 3:00 a.m., diaper changes, and visits to the pediatrician are not part of most people's vision of adolescence. Yet, every year, tens of thousands of adolescents in the United States give birth.

The good news, though, is that the number of teenage pregnancies has decreased significantly in the last decade, with the teenage birthrate dropping nearly a third in the last decade. Although there has been a small increase in recent years, the numbers are still at historic lows (see Figure 6-14). Births to African American teenagers have shown the steepest decline, with births down by more than 40 percent in a decade. Overall the pregnancy rate of teenagers is 43 births per 1,000 (Centers for Disease Control and Prevention, 2003; Colen, Geronimus, & Phipps, 2006; Hamilton et al., 2009).

Several factors explain the drop in teenage pregnancies:

- New initiatives have raised awareness of the risks of unprotected sex. For example, about two-thirds of U.S. high schools have comprehensive sex education programs (Villarosa, 2003; Corcoran & Pillai, 2007).

- The rate of sexual intercourse among teenagers has declined. The percent of teenage girls who have had sexual intercourse dropped from 51 percent to 43 percent from 1991 to 2001.

This 16-year-old mother and her child are representative of a major social problem: teenage pregnancy. Why is teenage pregnancy a greater problem in the United States than in other countries?

- The use of condoms and other forms of contraception has increased, with 57 percent of sexually active high school students reporting that they use condoms.
- Substitutes for sexual intercourse may be more prevalent. For example, data from the 1995 National Survey of Adolescent Males found that about half of 15- to 19-year-old boys reported having received oral sex, an increase of 44 percent since the late 1980s. It is possible that oral sex, which many teenagers do not even consider "sex," may increasingly be viewed as an alternative to sexual intercourse (Bernstein, 2004).

One thing that apparently hasn't led to a reduction in teenage pregnancies is asking adolescents to take a virginity pledge. These public pledges—a centerpiece of some forms of sex education—apparently are ineffective. In one study of 12,000 teenagers who had taken the pledge, 88 percent reported eventually having sexual intercourse. However, pledges did delay the start of sex an average of 18 months (Bearman & Bruckner, 2004).

An unintended pregnancy can be devastating to mother and child. Teenage mothers today are much less likely than in earlier years to be married. In many cases, mothers care for their children without the help of the father. Lacking financial and emotional support, the mother may have to abandon her own education and be relegated to unskilled, poorly paying jobs for the rest of her life. In some cases, she may develop long-term dependency on welfare. Furthermore, her physical and mental health may suffer as she faces unrelenting stress from the continual demands on her time (Manlove et al., 2004; Gillmore et al., 2006; Oxford et al., 2006).

## REVIEW, CHECK, AND APPLY

### REVIEW

**LO16** What are the functions and characteristics of dating during adolescence?

- Dating in adolescence serves a number of functions, including intimacy, entertainment, and prestige.
- Sexual intercourse is a major milestone that most people reach during adolescence. The age of first intercourse reflects cultural differences and has been declining over the last 50 years.

**LO17** How does sexuality develop in the adolescent years?

- Sexual orientation, which is most accurately viewed as a continuum rather than categorically, develops as the result of a complex combination of factors.

### CHECK YOURSELF

1. Dating has several functions in adolescence. Check all that apply.
   a. It usually leads to marriage.
   b. It provides entertainment.
   c. It can provide prestige depending on the status of the person one is dating.
   d. It assists in developing identity.
   e. It is a way to learn how to establish intimacy.

2. Overall, _____ of adolescents begin having intercourse between the ages of 15 and 18.
   a. 20 percent
   b. 10 percent
   c. 70 percent
   d. 50 percent

3. Which of the following factors are considered influential in reducing the teenage birth rate? Check all that apply.
   a. Awareness in teens has increased concerning the risks of unprotected sex.
   b. Teens are more likely to take the virginity pledge.
   c. Teens are using condoms and other forms of contraceptives at higher rates.
   d. Teens are so involved in school and sports activities that there is less time for sexual intercourse.
   e. Adolescents are engaging in sexual behaviors other than sexual intercourse.
   f. The rates of sexual intercourse among teens have declined.

### Applying Lifespan Development

- What aspects of the social world of adolescents work against the achievement of true intimacy in dating?

✔●—Study and Review on
MyDevelopmentLab.com

Answers: 1) b, c, d, e; 2) d; 3) a, c, e, f

# Putting It All Together
## Adolescence

**FROM AGE 13 TO AGE 18,** Andi, the young woman we met in the chapter opener, evolved from a young adolescent consumed with her friends and social status to a mature teenager capable of defining her own goals and confident of her choices. In mid-adolescence, she questioned whether she should play down her intelligence to get a boyfriend or remain true to what she valued. She did some exploring—taking a class in photography—and discovered both a talent and a passion all her own. She combined this new love with an old one, writing, and formulated a goal: to become a topnotch photojournalist. She'd come a long way from the middle-schooler who checked her Facebook page every few hours.

## MODULE 6.1 Physical Development in Adolescence

- Adolescents have many physical issues to deal with. **(pp. 259–263)**

- Andi's concern about the body changes and normal weight gain puberty brings is typical in adolescence, especially for girls. **(p. 260)**

- Adolescent brain development, including the growth of the prefrontal cortex of the brain, permitted Andi to think about and evaluate the behavior of her friends in comparison to her own identity and values. Such complex thinking, emerging in adolescence, can sometimes lead to confusion. **(p. 265)**

- Despite the pressures Andi felt to choose between popularity and remaining true to herself, she did not seek a solution or escape in drugs or alcohol—two major threats to the well-being of adolescents. **(pp. 268–270)**

## MODULE 6.2 Cognitive Development in Adolescence

- Adolescents' personal fables include a sense of uniqueness, which Andi expresses in her anger at being compared to her older siblings. **(pp. 277–278)**

- Andi's awareness of what she values in herself and her ability to reflect on what gives her the most joy exemplify adolescents' advanced mental abilities. **(p. 274–276)**

- Were Andi's parents insensitive to their daughter's need to belong to a social group? In what ways did they show their love for Andi? In what ways might they have been more supportive?

  **HINT** Review pages 282, 295–296.

  *What's your response?*

## MODULE **6.3** Social and Personality Development in Adolescence

- Andi's devotion to connecting with her friends on Facebook typifies the great importance of peer relationships in adolescence. **(pp. 297–300)**

- Though Andi knows her parents love her, she was annoyed that they didn't take the daily drama of her social world as seriously as she did. Such conflicts often occur in early adolescence when teens are struggling for autonomy and independence. **(pp. 295–296)**

- For Andi, being smart and making independent choices are positive, key aspects of her identity, answering the question, "Who am I?" **(pp. 284–288)**

- When Andi thinks she can't get a boyfriend because she's too fat, her self-esteem suffers, but her weight is not the only factor that affects her feelings about herself. **(pp. 285–286)**

- Andi's enrollment in a photography class and her subsequent decision to become a photojournalist is an example of Marcia's *identity achievement*. **(pp. 288–289)**

## What would a HEALTH CARE PROVIDER do?

- Andi's concern that the weight she gained during puberty makes her unattractive is typical of the way many adolescent girls feel about their new, mature bodies. How could a health care provider help Andi improve her body image? Should suggestions include advice about nutrition and exercise?

  **HINT** Review pages 259–263.

  *What's your response?*

## What would YOU do?

- If you were Andi's friend, how would you offer encouragement and support for the independent decisions she's making? Do you think your friendship would survive her choosing a path different from yours?

  **HINT** Review pages 274–276, 287.

  *What's your response?*

✳ **Explore** on **mydevelopmentlab.com**

To read how real-life parents, social workers, and educators responded to these questions, log onto MyDevelopmentLab.com. Do you agree or disagree with their responses? Why? What concepts that you've read about back up their opinions?

## What would an EDUCATOR do?

- If you were Andi's photography instructor, how would you help her prepare for a career in photojournalism? Would you advise her to develop other interests and experiment more before choosing a career path?

  **HINT** Review pages 273–278.

  *What's your response?*

# Early Adulthood

At 27, Bella Arnoff was feeling pressure to marry. She and Theodore Choi had been living together for more than four years, but suddenly the air around them was filled with what they called "The Urge to Wed."

The funny thing was that the pressure was not coming from their parents. Admittedly, his Korean family occasionally extolled the blessings of grandchildren and sometimes even reminded her that Theodore was an only child (and therefore the sole hope for the continuation of the Choi bloodline), but the Korean front had been surprisingly restrained, and her free-spirited Jewish parents even more so.

Less restrained was peer pressure. It seemed that everyone they knew was marrying. Bella had just accepted her sixth bridesmaid invitation, and Theodore was slated to be best man twice in the next three months and usher twice more in the next year. In their circle there was a sense of ticking clocks and a determination to raise children while still young.

---

**MODULE 7.1  Physical Development in Early Adulthood**

## How does stress affect the body? What are some strategies for coping with stress? see page 310.

---

**MODULE 7.2  Cognitive Development in Early Adulthood**

## What does gender bias in the classroom look like?

see page 322.

As Bella and Theodore discussed the tidal wave of marriages, they meandered through topics such as their present and future health, the nature of love and commitment, the "right" age for childrearing, their desired number of children, the need for one of them to become a stay-at-home parent, the temporary sacrifice of one of their incomes, the postponement of his return to graduate school, and many other things. Slowly they realized that somewhere during their conversation they had decided to marry.

**Early adulthood,** the period from approximately age 20 to 40, is a time of continued development. In fact, young adults like Bella and Theodore face some of the most pressing questions they will ever face and experience considerable stress as they answer them.

At their physical peak in their 20s, they are on the threshold of the worrisome 30s, when the body begins to send messages of decline and to exact a price for excess and inattention. Cognitively, most have stopped their formal learning, but some want to take it up again either in college or in some other setting. Socially, young adults are often settling into a career, and sometimes they have to consider whether the path they are on is right for them after all. And they still have to answer the really big questions about marriage and children. Staring so many weighty decisions in the face can cause young adults a great deal of stress.

In fact, some psychologists believe that the beginning of early adulthood can be characterized as a special stage of development known as emerging adulthood. *Emerging*

## MODULE **7.3** Social and Personality Development in Early Adulthood

# Is love the only thing that matters in seeking a spouse?

see page 336.

## MyDevelopmentLab

Log onto MyDevelopmentLab.com and watch two young people, just like Bella and Theodore, talk about all the issues and emotions that they've experienced as young adults.

*adulthood* is the period beginning in the late teenage years and extending into the mid-20s. Although they are no longer adolescents, people in their early 20s are not fully adults because they haven't fully taken on the responsibilities of adulthood. Instead, they are still seeking to identify who they are and what course their life will follow (Arnett, 2007; Tanner, Arnett, & Leis, 2009).

In this chapter, we'll look at the physical, cognitive, and social and personality changes that accompany young adulthood. This period of life, in which people are too often considered "developed" rather than "developing," in fact harbors many changes. Like Bella and Theodore, young adults continue to develop throughout the period.

## MODULE 7.1 Physical Development in Early Adulthood

*As Anton ate his lunch one sunny day in Bryant Park, he idly watched two young men playing a high-speed chess game at the next table. One of the players was sitting in a wheelchair. As the game proceeded, with first one player then the other announcing his moves and slamming his timer, Anton found himself hoping that the guy in the wheelchair would win the match.*

*No such luck. After only a few more moves, the opponent loudly and triumphantly called "Check," and the handicapped player, after surveying the board, tipped his king and conceded defeat. Anton was disappointed: He had hoped that the able-bodied player would go easy on his opponent.*

*But Anton almost choked on his sandwich when he saw the winner reach for his cane as he rose to shake the hand of the man in the wheelchair. The winner was blind. Both players had a disability, and the one who couldn't even see the board had won the match.*

As Anton learned, many people have disabilities, and focusing on what they lack instead of what they have is itself a kind of blindness. Offering sympathy for people with a disability may make them feel diminished, as if the rich, complex individuals they are is invisible.

Most people in early adulthood are at their physical peak. For them, the body acts as if it's on automatic pilot: Physical health and fitness are never better. Still, there are others who have mild or severe disabilities, and they too are developing during this period. And often, aside from the area of their disability, they too are at their peak.

Physical development proceeds throughout early adulthood, which starts at the end of adolescence (around age 20) and continues until roughly the start of middle age (around age 40). As we see throughout this chapter, significant changes occur as new opportunities arise and people choose to take on (or forgo) new roles in society.

This module focuses on physical development during this period. It begins with a look at the physical changes that extend into early adulthood. Though more subtle than the physical changes of adolescence, growth continues and various motor skills change as well. We look at diet and weight, examining the prevalence of obesity in this age group. We also consider what other health risks young adults face. Next, we look at physical disabilities and the ways that people deal with them. Finally, we discuss stress and coping during the early years of adulthood.

# Physical Development

**LEARNING OBJECTIVES**

**L01** How does the body develop during early adulthood?

**L02** What risks do young adults face?

*Grady McKinnon grinned as his mountain bike left the ground briefly. The 27-year-old financial auditor was delighted to be out for a camping and biking weekend with four of his college buddies. Grady had been worried that an upcoming deadline at work would make him miss this trip. When they were still in school, Grady and his friends used to go biking nearly every weekend. But jobs, marriage—and even a child for one of the guys—started taking up a lot of their attention. This was their only trip this summer. He was sure glad he hadn't missed it.*

Grady and his friends were probably in the best physical condition of their lives when they began mountain biking regularly in college. Even now, as Grady's life becomes more complicated and sports starts to take a back seat to work and other personal demands, he is still enjoying one of the healthiest periods of his life. Still, Grady has to cope with the stress produced by the challenges of adult life.

> **senescence** the natural physical decline brought about by aging

## Physical Development and the Senses

In most respects, physical development and maturation are complete at early adulthood. Most people have attained their full height, with limbs proportional to their size, rendering the gangliness of adolescence a memory. People in their early 20s tend to be healthy, vigorous, and energetic. Although **senescence,** the natural physical decline brought about by increasing age, has begun, age-related changes are not usually obvious until later in life. At the same time, some growth continues; for example, some people, particularly late maturers, continue to gain height in their early 20s.

Other parts of the body also reach full maturity. The brain grows in both size and weight, reaching its maximum during early adulthood (and then contracting later in life). The gray matter continues to be pruned back, and myelination (the process in which nerve cells are insulated by a covering of fat cells) continues to increase. These brain changes help support the cognitive advances of early adulthood (Sowell et al., 2001; Toga, Thompson, & Sowell, 2006).

The senses are as sharp as they will ever be. Although there are changes in the elasticity of the eye—a process that may begin as early as age 10—they are so minor that they produce no deterioration in vision. Hearing, too, is at its peak, although women can detect higher tones more readily than men (McGuinness, 1972). Under quiet conditions, the average young adult can hear the ticking of a watch 20 feet away. The other senses, including taste, smell, and sensitivity to touch and pain, are good and remain so throughout early adulthood.

## Motor Functioning, Fitness, and Health: Staying Well

If you are a professional athlete, you are generally considered over the hill by the end of your 20s. Although there are notable exceptions, even athletes who train constantly tend to lose their physical edge once they reach their 30s. In some sports, the peak passes even sooner. Swimmers are at their best in their late teens, and gymnasts even younger (Schultz & Curnow, 1988).

Our psychomotor abilities also peak during early adulthood. Reaction time is quicker, muscle strength greater, and eye–hand coordination better than at any other period (Sliwinski et al., 1994; Salthouse, 1993).

*Physical Fitness.* The fitness of early adulthood doesn't come naturally or to everyone. To reach their physical potential, people must exercise and maintain a proper diet.

Only a small time commitment is needed to yield significant health benefits. According to the American College of Sports Medicine and the Centers for Disease Control and Prevention, people should engage in at least 30 minutes of moderate physical activity at least 5 days a week. Exercise time can be continuous or in bouts of at least 10 minutes, as long as the daily total reaches 30 minutes. Moderate activity includes walking briskly at 3 to 4 mph, biking at speeds up to 10 mph, golfing while carrying or pulling clubs, fishing by casting from shore, playing ping-pong, or canoeing at 2 to 4 mph. Even common household chores, such as weeding, vacuuming, and mowing with a power mower, provide moderate exercise (American College of Sports Medicine, 1997).

⬇ **From an educator's perspective:** Can people be taught the lifelong advantages of regular exercise? Should school-based physical education programs be changed to foster a lifelong commitment to exercise?

People in their early 20s tend to be healthy, vigorous, and energetic, but they often experience quite a lot of stress.

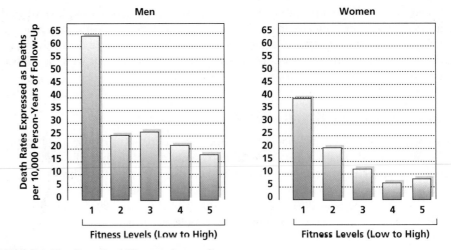

**Men** | **Women**

Death Rates Expressed as Deaths per 10,000 Person-Years of Follow-Up

Fitness Levels (Low to High) | Fitness Levels (Low to High)

FIGURE 7-1 **The Result of Fitness: Longevity**
The greater the fitness level, the lower the death rate tends to be for both men and women.
Source: From Blair et al., "Physical fitness and all-cause mortality: A prospective study of healthy men and women." *Journal of the American Medical Association,* 262 (1989), pp. 2395–2401. Copyright © 1989 American Medical Association. Reprinted with permission.

The advantages are many. Exercise increases cardiovascular fitness, meaning that the heart and circulatory system operate more efficiently. Furthermore, lung capacity increases, raising endurance. Muscles become stronger, and the body is more flexible. The range of movement is greater, and the muscles, tendons, and ligaments are more elastic. Moreover, exercise during this period helps reduce *osteoporosis,* the thinning of the bones, in later life.

Exercise also may optimize the immune response of the body, helping it fight off disease. It may even decrease stress and anxiety and reduce depression. It can provide a sense of control over the body and a feeling of accomplishment. Regular exercise offers the possibility of another, ultimately more important, reward: It is associated with increased longevity (Stevens et al., 2002; Rethorst, Wipfli, & Landers, 2009; Jung & Brawley, 2010) (see Figure 7-1).

**Health.** Health risks in general are slight during early adulthood. People are less susceptible to colds and other minor illnesses than they were as children, and they recover quickly from those that they do catch.

Adults in their 20s and 30s stand a higher risk of dying from accidents, primarily car accidents, than from most other causes. But there are other killers: Among the leading sources of death for people 25 to 34 are AIDS, cancer, heart disease, and suicide. Amid the grim statistics of mortality, the age 35 represents a significant milestone. It is at that point that illness and disease overtake accidents as the leading cause of death—the first time this is true since infancy.

Not all people fare equally well during early adulthood. Lifestyle decisions, such as the use—or abuse—of alcohol, tobacco, or drugs, or engaging in unprotected sex, can hasten *secondary aging,* physical declines brought about by environmental factors or behavioral choices. These substances can also increase the mortality risk from the causes just mentioned.

Cultural factors, including gender and race, are related to the risk of dying. For instance, men are more apt to die than women, primarily in automobile accidents. Furthermore, African Americans have twice the death rate of Caucasians, and minorities in general have a higher likelihood of dying than their Caucasian peers.

Another major cause of death for men in this age group is violence. The murder rate is significantly higher in the United States than in any other developed country (see Figure 7-2). Racial

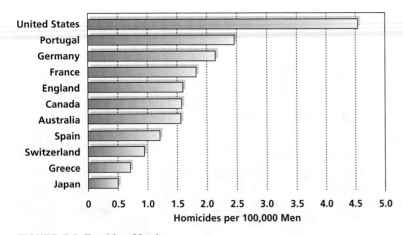

United States
Portugal
Germany
France
England
Canada
Australia
Spain
Switzerland
Greece
Japan

0   0.5   1.0   1.5   2.0   2.5   3.0   3.5   4.0   4.5   5.0
**Homicides per 100,000 Men**

FIGURE 7-2 **Tracking Murder**
The murder rate (per 100,000 men) is far higher in the United States than in any other developed country. What features of U.S. society contribute to this higher rate?
Source: United Nations Survey on Crime Trends, 2000.

The murder rate in the United States is significantly higher than in any other developed country.

factors also are related to the homicide rate in the United States. Although homicide is the third most frequent cause of death for White males between the ages of 20 to 34, it is *the* most frequent cause of death for Black males and the second most frequent cause of death for Hispanic males in the same age range.

Cultural factors also influence young adults' lifestyles and health-related behavior, as discussed in the "Cultural Dimensions" feature.

## *Cultural Dimensions*

### How Cultural Beliefs Influence Health and Health Care

*Manolita recently suffered a heart attack. She was advised by her doctor to change her eating and activity habits or face the risk of another life-threatening heart attack. During the period that followed, Manolita dramatically changed her eating and activity habits. She also began going to church and praying extensively. After a recent check-up, Manolita is in the best shape of her life. What are some of the reasons for Manolita's amazing recovery?* (Murguia, Peterson, & Zea, 1997, p. 16)

After reading the passage above, would you conclude that Manolita recovered her health because (a) she changed her eating and activity habits; (b) she became a better person; (c) God was testing her faith; or (d) her doctor prescribed the correct changes?

When asked this question in a survey, more than two-thirds of Latino immigrants from Central America, South America, or the Caribbean believed that "God was testing her faith" had a moderate or great effect on her recovery, although most also agreed that a change in eating and activity habits was important (Murguia, Peterson, & Zea, 1997; Gurung, 2010).

According to psychologists Alejandro Murguia, Rolf Peterson, and Maria Zea (1997), cultural health beliefs, along with demographic characteristics and psychological barriers, can affect the use of physicians and medical care. They suggest that Latinos are more likely than non-Hispanic Whites to believe in supernatural causes of illness, which may explain why Latinos are the least likely of any Western ethnic group to seek the help of a physician when they are ill.

Health care providers need to take cultural beliefs into account when treating members of different cultural groups. For example, if a patient believes that the source of his or her illness is a spell cast by a jealous romantic rival, the patient may not comply with medical regimens that ignore that perceived source. To provide effective health care, then, health care providers must be sensitive to such cultural health beliefs.

## REVIEW, CHECK, AND APPLY

### REVIEW

**LO1** How does the body develop during early adulthood?

- By young adulthood, the body and the senses are at their peak, but growth still proceeds, particularly in the brain.

**LO2** What risks do young adults face?

- Young adults are generally as fit and healthy as they will ever be. Accidents present the greatest risk of death.

- In the United States, violence is also a significant risk during young adulthood, particularly for non-White males.

### CHECK YOURSELF

1. _____ is the natural physical decline brought about by aging.

2. At the age of _____, illness and disease overtake accidents as the leading cause of death.
   a. 25
   b. 35
   c. 40
   d. 50

3. Compared to all other developed countries, one of the greatests risks for death in young adult men in the United States is murder.
   - True
   - False

### APPLYING LIFESPAN DEVELOPMENT

- What factors do you think contribute to the comparatively high risk of automobile accidents during young adulthood? How can this be changed?

✔ **Study** and **Review** on
**MyDevelopmentLab.com**

# Physical Limitations and Challenges

**LO3** What is the key to good health and proper weight?

**LO4** What types of challenges face people with disabilities?

*Aidan Tindell, accustomed to the shaving mirror in his own apartment, got a shock when he glimpsed his image in a friend's full-length mirror. It was not a pretty sight. Aidan had somehow developed a belly—and a pretty good-sized one. As if in a vision, he conjured up the long evenings he spent in a local sports bar with his friends. He saw the beers he downed without a second thought, the bar snacks he ate incessantly, and the burgers and fries and pizzas that were his basic food groups. Aidan knew something had to give, and he was afraid it was going to be his lifestyle.*

For many young adults, this period is the first time that they have to deal seriously with the negative consequences of developmental change. As they leave adolescence, they gradually learn that they can't simply extend their living habits indefinitely. One particularly painful area of change is diet.

## Good Nutrition: No Such Thing as a Free Lunch?

According to guidelines provided by the U.S. Department of Agriculture, people can achieve good nutrition by eating foods that are low in fat, including vegetables, fruits, whole-grain foods, fish, poultry, lean meats, and low-fat dairy products. In addition, whole-grain foods and cereal products, vegetables (including dried beans and peas), and fruit are beneficial in another way: They help people raise the amount of complex carbohydrates and fiber they ingest. Milk and other sources of calcium are also needed to prevent osteoporosis. Finally, people should reduce salt intake (USDA, 2006).

Adolescents don't suffer too much from a diet high in junk foods and fat because they are undergoing tremendous growth. The body is less forgiving to young adults, who must reduce their caloric intake to maintain their health (Insel & Roth, 1991).

## Obesity: A Weighty Concern

The adult population of the United States is growing—in more ways than one. Obesity, defined as body weight that is 20 percent or more above the average weight for a person of a given height, is on the rise in the United States. A third of adults are obese, a percentage that

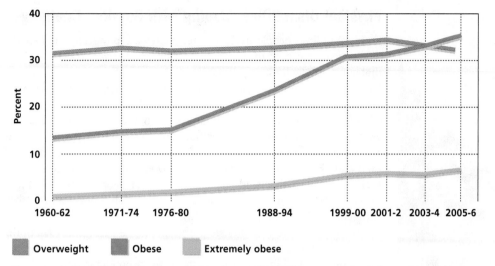

Overweight     Obese     Extremely obese

Note: Age-adjusted by the direct method to the year 2000 US Bureau of the Census using age groups 20-39, 40–59, and 60-74 years. Pregnant females excluded. Overweight defined as 25<=BMI<30; obesity defined as BMI>=30; Extreme obesity defined as BMI>40.

**FIGURE 7-3 Obesity on the Rise**
In spite of greater awareness of the importance of good nutrition, the percentage of adults with weight problems in the United States has risen dramatically over the past few decades. Why do you think this rise has occurred?
Source: Centers for Disease Control and Prevention, 2008.

has nearly tripled since the 1960s. Furthermore, as age increases, more and more people are classified as obese (Centers for Disease Control and Prevention, 2008) (see Figure 7-3).

Weight control is a difficult, and often losing, battle for many young adults. Most diets fail, producing nothing more than a seesaw cycle of gain and loss. Some obesity experts argue that the rate of dieting failure is so great that people should avoid dieting altogether. Instead, if people eat the foods they really want in moderation, they may be able to avoid the binge eating that often occurs when diets fail. Even though obese people may never reach their desired weight, they may, according to this reasoning, ultimately control their weight more effectively (Polivy & Herman, 2002; Lowe, 2004; Putterman & Linden, 2004; Quatromoni et al., 2006; Annunziato & Lowe, 2007; Roehrig et al., 2009).

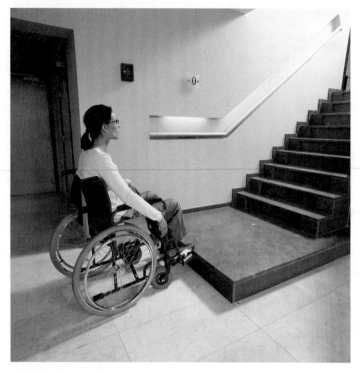

Despite the passage of the Americans with Disabilities Act (ADA), people with physical disabilities still cannot gain access to many older buildings.

## Physical Disabilities: Coping with Physical Challenge

Over 50 million people in the United States are physically or mentally challenged, according to the official definition of *disability*—a condition that substantially limits a major life activity such as walking or vision. In fact, we encountered people with both of these disabilities in the vignette about the chess players.

People with disabilities are in large part an undereducated and under-employed minority group. Fewer than 10 percent of people with major handicaps have finished high school, fewer than 25 percent of disabled men and 15 percent of disabled women work full-time, and unemployment rates are high. In addition, the jobs that people with disabilities find are often routine and low-paying positions (Schaefer & Lamm, 1992; Albrecht, 2005; Power & Green, 2010).

Some barriers to a full life are physical. Despite passage in 1990 of the landmark Americans with Disabilities Act (ADA), which mandates full access to public establishments such as stores, office buildings, hotels, and theaters, people in wheelchairs still cannot gain access to many older buildings.

➔ **From a social worker's perspective:** What sorts of inter-personal barriers do people with disabilities face? How can those barriers be removed?

Another barrier is prejudice. People with disabilities sometimes face pity or avoidance as nondisabled people focus so much on the disability that they overlook other characteristics. Others treat people with disabilities as if they were children. This can take its toll on the way people with disabilities think about themselves (French & Swain, 1997).

## REVIEW, CHECK, AND APPLY

### REVIEW

**LO3** What is the key to good health and proper weight?

- Even in young adulthood, health must be maintained by proper diet and exercise. Obesity is increasingly a problem for young adults.

**LO4** What types of challenges face people with disabilities?

- People with physical disabilities face not only physical barriers but also psychological barriers caused by prejudice.

### CHECK YOURSELF

1. As age increases, fewer individuals are classified as obese.
   - True
   - False

2. Over 50 million individuals in the United States are living with a _____, or a condition that substantially limits a major life activity such as walking or vision.

### APPLYING LIFESPAN DEVELOPMENT

- What developmental factors make it hard for young adults to understand that they may have to change their eating habits and personal choices?

✓ **Study** and **Review** on **MyDevelopmentLab.com**

Answers: 1) False; 2) disability

# Stress and Coping: Dealing With Life's Challenges

**LEARNING OBJECTIVES**

**LO5** What are the consequences of long-term stress?

**LO6** What are strategies for preventing or reducing stress?

*It's 5:00 p.m. Rosa Convoy, a 25-year-old single mother, has just finished her work as a receptionist at a dentist's office and is on her way home. She has exactly two hours to pick up her daughter Zoe from child care, get home, make and eat dinner, pick up and return with a babysitter from down the street, say goodbye to Zoe, and get to her 7 o'clock programming class at a local community college. It's a marathon she runs every Tuesday and Thursday night, and she knows she doesn't have a second to spare if she wants to reach the class on time.* ◉ Watch on **mydevelopmentlab.com**

◉ Watch on **mydevelopmentlab.com**

*Young adults experience many kinds of stress and cope in different ways.*
Log onto MyDevelopmentLab.com to hear two young adults, Amanda and Gary, talk about the stress in their lives.

Rosa Convoy is experiencing **stress,** the physical and emotional response to events that threaten or challenge us. Our lives are crowded with events and circumstances, known as stressors, that threaten our equilibrium. Stressors need not be unpleasant events: Even the happiest events—starting a long-sought job or planning a wedding—can produce stress (Crowley, Hayslip, & Hobdy, 2003; Shimizu & Pelham, 2004).

Researchers in the new field of **psychoneuroimmunology (PNI)**—the study of the relationship among the brain, the immune system, and psychological factors—have examined the outcomes of stress. The most immediate is a biological reaction, as hormones secreted by the adrenal glands cause a rise in heart rate, blood pressure, respiration rate, and sweating. In some situations, these immediate effects are beneficial because the "emergency reaction" they produce in the sympathetic nervous system enables people to defend themselves from a sudden, threatening situation (Ray, 2004; Kiecolt-Glaser, 2009).

On the other hand, long-term, continuous exposure to stressors may result in a reduction of the body's ability to deal with stress. As stress-related hormones are constantly secreted, the heart, blood vessels, and other body tissues may deteriorate. As a consequence, people become more susceptible to diseases as their ability to fight off germs declines. In short, both *acute stressors* (sudden, one-time events) and *chronic stressors* (long-term, continuing events) have the potential to produce significant physiological consequences (Lundberg, 2006; Graham, Christian, & Kiecolt-Glaser, 2006; Wheaton & Montazer, 2010).

## The Origins of Stress

Experienced job interviewers, college counselors, and owners of bridal shops all know that not everyone reacts the same way to a potentially stressful event. What makes the difference? According to psychologists Arnold Lazarus and Susan Folkman, people move through a series of stages that determine whether they will experience stress (Lazarus & Folkman, 1984; Lazarus, 1968, 1991).

**Primary appraisal** is the first step—the individual's assessment of an event to determine whether its implications are positive, negative, or neutral. If a person sees the event as primarily negative, he or she appraises it in terms of the harm that it has caused in the past, how threatening it is likely to be, and how likely it is that the challenge can be resisted successfully. For example, you are likely to feel differently about an upcoming French test if you passed the last one with flying colors than you would if you did poorly.

Secondary appraisal follows. **Secondary appraisal** is the person's answer to the question, "Can I handle it?," an assessment of whether the coping abilities and resources on hand are adequate. If resources are lacking and the threat is great, the person will feel stress. A traffic ticket is always upsetting, but if you can't afford the fine, the stress is greater.

Stress varies with the person's appraisal, and that appraisal varies with the person's temperament and circumstances. There are some general principles that help predict when an event will be appraised as stressful. Psychologist Shelley Taylor (1991) suggests the following characteristics of events that have a high likelihood of producing stress:

- Events and circumstances that produce negative emotions—for example, dealing with the illness of a loved one produces more stress than planning for the adoption of a new baby.

- Situations that are uncontrollable or unpredictable—for example, professors who give surprise quizzes produce more stress than those who schedule them in advance.

- Events and circumstances that are ambiguous and confusing—for example, a new job that does not have a clear job description is likely to produce more stress than a well-defined position.

- Having to simultaneously accomplish many tasks that strain a person's capabilities—for example, a graduate student who is expecting her first child the same month she is scheduled to submit her dissertation is likely to be feeling more stress than a student with less on her agenda.

**stress** the physical and emotional response to events that threaten or challenge us

**psychoneuroimmunology (PNI)** the study of the relationship among the brain, the immune system, and psychological factors

**primary appraisal** the assessment of an event to determine whether its implications are positive, negative, or neutral

**secondary appraisal** the assessment of whether one's coping abilities and resources are adequate to overcome the harm, threat, or challenge posed by the potential stressor

Although we commonly think of negative events, such as auto mishaps, as leading to stress, even welcome events, like getting married, can be stressful.

⊙ **From the perspective of a health care provider:** Are there periods of life that are relatively stress-free, or do people of all ages experience stress? Do stressors differ from age to age?

## The Consequences of Stress

Over the long run, the constant wear and tear of fighting off stress can have formidable costs. Headaches, backaches, skin rashes, indigestion, chronic fatigue, and even the common cold are stress-related illnesses (Cohen, Tyrrell, & Smith, 1997; Suinn, 2001; Kalynchuk, 2010).

In addition, *the immune system*—the organs, glands, and cells that are the body's line of defense against disease—may be damaged by stress. Stress can interfere with the immune system's ability to stop germs from reproducing or cancer cells from spreading. In addition, stress may overstimulate the immune system into attacking the body itself and damaging healthy tissue (Miller & Cohen, 2001; Cohen et al., 2002; Caserta et al., 2008).

Stress may also lead to **psychosomatic disorders,** medical problems caused by the interaction of psychological, emotional, and physical difficulties. For instance, ulcers, asthma, arthritis, and high blood pressure may sometimes be produced by stress (Davis et al., 2008; Marin et al., 2009).

To get a sense of how much stress you have in your own life, complete the questionnaire in Table 7-1.

## Coping with Stress

Stress is a normal part of every life. But some young adults are better than others at **coping,** the effort to control, reduce, or learn to tolerate the threats that lead to stress (Taylor & Stanton, 2007). What's the secret to coping? It turns out that people use a variety of strategies.

Some people use *problem-focused coping*—managing a threatening situation by directly changing it to make it less stressful. For example, a man having difficulties on the job may ask his boss to change his responsibilities, or he may look for another job.

**psychosomatic disorders** medical problems caused by the interaction of psychological, emotional, and physical difficulties

**coping** the effort to control, reduce, or learn to tolerate the threats that lead to stress

## TABLE 7-1  HOW STRESSED ARE YOU?

Test your level of stress by answering these questions, and adding the score from each box. Questions apply to the last month only. A key below will help you determine the extent of your stress.

1. How often have you been upset because of something that happened unexpectedly?

   ☐ 0 = never, 1 = almost never, 2 = sometimes, 3 = fairly often, 4 = very often

2. How often have you felt that you were unable to control the important things in your life?

   ☐ 0 = never, 1 = almost never, 2 = sometimes, 3 = fairly often, 4 = very often

3. How often have you felt nervous and "stressed"?

   ☐ 0 = never, 1 = almost never, 2 = sometimes, 3 = fairly often, 4 = very often

4. How often have you felt confident about your ability to handle your personal problems?

   ☐ 4 = never, 3 = almost never, 2 = sometimes, 1 = fairly often, 0 = very often

5. How often have you felt that things were going your way?

   ☐ 4 = never, 3 = almost never, 2 = sometimes, 1 = fairly often, 0 = very often

6. How often have you been able to control irritations in your life?

   ☐ 4 = never, 3 = almost never, 2 = sometimes, 1 = fairly often, 0 = very often

7. How often have you found that you could not cope with all the things that you had to do?

   ☐ 0 = never, 1 = almost never, 2 = sometimes, 3 = fairly often, 4 = very often

8. How often have you felt that you were on top of things?

   ☐ 4 = never, 3 = almost never, 2 = sometimes, 1 = fairly often, 0 = very often

9. How often have you been angered because of things that were outside your control?

   ☐ 0 = never, 1 = almost never, 2 = sometimes, 3 = fairly often, 4 = very often

10. How often have you felt difficulties were piling up so high that you could not overcome them?

   ☐ 0 = never, 1 = almost never, 2 = sometimes, 3 = fairly often, 4 = very often

**How You Measure Up**

Stress levels vary among individuals—compare your total score to the averages below:

| Age | | Gender | | Marital Status | |
|---|---|---|---|---|---|
| 18–29 | 14.2 | Men | 12.1 | Widowed | 12.6 |
| 30–44 | 13.0 | Women | 13.7 | Married or living with | 12.4 |
| 45–54 | 12.6 | | | Single or never wed | 14.1 |
| 55–64 | 11.9 | | | Divorced | 14.7 |
| 65 & over | 12.0 | | | Separated | 16.6 |

Source: From Cohen, S., Kamarck, T., & Mermelstein, R. (1983). "A global measure of perceived stress." *Journal of Health and Social Behavior*, 24, 385–396. Copyright © 1983 American Sociological Association. Reprinted with permission.

Other people employ *emotion-focused coping*—the conscious regulation of emotion. For instance, a mother having trouble finding appropriate care for her child while she is at work may tell herself that she should look at the bright side: At least she has a job in a difficult economy (Folkman & Lazarus, 1988; Master et al., 2009).

Sometimes people acknowledge that they are in a stressful situation that cannot be changed, but they cope by managing their reactions. For example, they may take up meditation or exercise to reduce their physical reactions.

Coping is also aided by the presence of *social support*, assistance and comfort supplied by others. Turning to others can provide both emotional support (in the form of a shoulder to cry on) and practical, tangible support (such as a temporary loan). In addition, others can provide information, offering specific advice on how to deal with stressful situations. The ability to learn from others' experiences is one of the reasons that people use the Web to connect with people who have similar experiences (Jackson, 2006; Coulson, Buchanan, & Aubeeluck, 2007; Kim, Sherman, & Taylor, 2008).

**defensive coping** coping that involves unconscious strategies that distort or deny the true nature of a situation

**hardiness** a personality characteristic associated with a lower rate of stress-related illness

Finally, even if people do not consciously cope with stress, some psychologists suggest that they may unconsciously use defensive coping mechanisms. **Defensive coping** involves unconscious strategies that distort or deny the true nature of a situation. For instance, people may trivialize a life-threatening illness or tell themselves that failing a major test is unimportant.

Another type of defensive coping is *emotional insulation,* through which people unconsciously try to block emotions and thereby avoid pain. But if defensive coping becomes a habitual response to stress, its reliance on avoidance can stand in the way of dealing with the reality of the situation (Ormont, 2001).

In some cases, people use drugs or alcohol to escape from stressful situations. Like defensive coping, drinking and drug use do not help address the situation causing the stress, and they can increase a person's difficulties. For example, people may become addicted to the substances that initially provided them with a pleasurable sense of escape.

***Hardiness, Resilience, and Coping.*** The success with which young adults deal with stress depends in part on their *coping style,* their general tendency to deal with stress in a particular way. For example, people with a "hardy" coping style are especially successful. **Hardiness** is a personality characteristic associated with a lower rate of stress-related illness.

Hardy individuals are take-charge people who revel in life's challenges. People who are high in hardiness are more resistant to stress-related illness than those with less hardiness. Hardy people react to stressors with optimism, convinced that they can respond effectively. By turning threats into challenges, they are less apt to experience high levels of stress (Maddi et al., 2006; Andrew et al., 2008; Delahaij, Gaillard, & van Dam, 2010).

For people who face the most profound difficulties—such as the unexpected death of a loved one—a key factor in their reactions is their level of resilience. As we discussed earlier, *resilience* is the ability to withstand, overcome, and even thrive after profound adversity (Bonanno, 2004; Werner, 2005; Norlander et al., 2005; Kim-Cohen, 2007).

Resilient young adults tend to be easy-going and good-natured, with good social and communication skills. They are independent, feeling that they can shape their own fate and are not dependent on others or luck. They work with what they have and make the best of any situation (Spencer et al., 2003; Deshields et al., 2005; Friborg et al., 2005; Clauss-Ehlers, 2008).

## Coping with Stress

### Becoming an Informed Consumer of Development

Some general guidelines can help people cope with stress, including the following (Sacks, 1993; Kaplan, Sallis, & Patterson, 1993; Bionna, 2006):

- Seek control over the situation. Taking charge of a situation that is producing stress can take you a long way toward coping with it. For example, if you are feeling stress about a test, do something about it—such as starting to study.

- Redefine "threat" as "challenge." Changing the definition can make a situation seem less threatening. "Look for the silver lining" is not bad advice. For example, if you're fired, look at it as an opportunity to get a new and better job.

- Find social support. Almost any difficulty can be faced more easily with the help of others. Friends, family members, and even telephone hotlines staffed by trained counselors can provide significant support. (For help in identifying appropriate hotlines, the

U.S. Public Health Service maintains a "master" toll-free number that can provide phone numbers and addresses of many national groups. Call 800-336-4794.)

- Use relaxation techniques. Reducing the physiological arousal brought about by stress can be effective in coping with stress. Techniques that produce relaxation, such as transcendental meditation, Zen and yoga, progressive muscle relaxation, and even hypnosis, have been shown to be effective. One that works particularly well was devised by physician Herbert Benson and is illustrated in Table 7-2 (Benson, 1993).

- Maintain a healthy lifestyle that will reinforce your body's natural coping mechanisms. Exercise, eat nutritiously, get enough sleep, and avoid or reduce use of alcohol, tobacco, or other drugs.

- If all else fails, keep in mind that a life without stress would be dull. Stress is natural, and successfully coping with it can be gratifying.

## TABLE 7-2  HOW TO ELICIT THE RELAXATION RESPONSE

Some general advice on regular practice of the relaxation response:

- Try to find 10 to 20 minutes in your daily routine; before breakfast is a good time.
- Sit comfortably.
- For the period you will practice, try to arrange your life so you won't have distractions. Put on the answering machine, and ask someone else to watch the kids.
- Time yourself by glancing periodically at a clock or watch (but don't set an alarm). Commit yourself to a specific length of practice, and try to stick to it.

There are several approaches to eliciting the relaxation response. Here is one standard set of instructions:

**Step 1.**   Pick a focus word or short phrase that's firmly rooted in your personal belief system. For example, a nonreligious individual might choose a neutral word like *one* or *peace* or *love*. A Christian person desiring to use a prayer could pick the opening words of Psalm 23, *The Lord is my shepherd;* a Jewish person could choose *Shalom*.

**Step 2.**   Sit quietly in a comfortable position.

**Step 3.**   Close your eyes.

**Step 4.**   Relax your muscles.

**Step 5.**   Breathe slowly and naturally, repeating your focus word or phrase silently as you exhale.

**Step 6.**   Throughout, assume a passive attitude. Don't worry about how well you're doing. When other thoughts come to mind, simply say to yourself, "Oh, well," and gently return to the repetition.

**Step 7.**   Continue for 10 to 20 minutes. You may open your eyes to check the time, but do not use an alarm. When you finish, sit quietly for a minute or so, at first with your eyes closed and later with your eyes open. Then do not stand for 1 or 2 minutes.

**Step 8.**   Practice the technique once or twice a day.

Source: Benson, 1993.

## REVIEW, CHECK, AND APPLY

### REVIEW

**LO5**   What are the consequences of long-term stress?

- Stress, which is healthy in small doses, can be harmful to body and mind if it is frequent or long-lasting.
- Long-term exposure to stressors may cause deterioration in the heart, blood vessels, and other body tissues. Stress is linked to many common ailments.

**LO6**   What are strategies for preventing or reducing stress?

- Strategies for coping with stress include problem-focused coping, emotion-focused coping, and the use of social support. Utilizing the relaxation technique can also be helpful. Another strategy, defensive coping, which relies on avoidance, can prevent a person from dealing with the reality of the situation.

### CHECK YOURSELF

1. Stressful events are limited to the negative events in our lives.
   - True
   - False

2. Researchers in the field of _____ study the relationship among the brain, the immune system, and psychological factors, and have found that stress can produce several outcomes.
   a. psychoanalysis
   b. disease management
   c. pilates
   d. psychoneuroimmunology

3. Avoiding thinking about a stressful situation by drinking, doing drugs, or just denying the true nature of a situation are all examples of _____ coping.
   a. defensive
   b. emotion-focused
   c. social support
   d. hardiness

### APPLYING LIFESPAN DEVELOPMENT

- In what circumstances can stress be an adaptive, helpful response? In what circumstances is it maladaptive?

✔●—[**Study** and **Review** on
**MyDevelopmentLab.com**

Answers: 1) False; 2) d; 3) a

# MODULE 7.2 Cognitive Development in Early Adulthood

*For Enrico Vasquez, there was never any doubt: He was headed for college. Enrico, the son of a wealthy Cuban immigrant who had made a fortune in the medical supply business after fleeing Cuba five years before Enrico's birth, had always had the importance of education drummed into him by his family. In fact, the question was never whether he would go to college, but what college he would be able to get into. As a consequence, Enrico found high school to be a pressure cooker: Every grade and extra-curricular activity was seen as helping—or hindering—his chances of admission to a "good" college.*

\*\*\*

*Armando Williams's letter of acceptance to Dallas County Community College is framed on the wall of his mother's apartment. To her, the letter represents nothing short of a miracle, an answer to her prayers. Growing up in a neighborhood saturated with drugs and drive-by shootings, Armando had always been a hard worker and a "good boy" in his mother's view. But when he was growing up, she never even entertained the possibility of his making it to college. To see him reach this stage in his education fills her with joy.*

Although Enrico and Armando followed two very different paths, they share the goal of a college education. They represent the increasing diversity in family background, socioeconomic status, race, and ethnicity that characterizes college populations today.

This module focuses on cognitive development during early adulthood. Although traditional approaches to cognitive development regarded adulthood as an inconsequential plateau, we will examine some new theories that suggest that significant cognitive growth occurs during the period. We also consider the nature of adult intelligence and the impact of life events on cognitive development.

The last part of the module considers college, an institution that shapes intellectual growth. We examine who goes to college, and how gender and race can influence achievement. We end by looking at the troubling issue of gambling among students, and examining some of the adjustment problems that college students face.

# Cognitive Development

**LEARNING OBJECTIVES**

**LO7** Does cognitive development continue in young adulthood?

**LO8** How does postformal thinking develop in early adulthood?

*Ben is known to be a heavy drinker, especially when he goes to parties. Tyra, Ben's wife, warns him that if he comes home drunk one more time, she will leave him and take the children. Tonight Ben is out late at an office party. He comes home drunk. Does Tyra leave Ben?*

The nature of thought changes qualitatively during early adulthood.

To the typical adolescent this case (drawn from research by Adams and Labouvie-Vief, 1986) is open-and-shut: Tyra leaves Ben. But in early adulthood, the answer is less clear. People become less concerned with sheer logic and instead take into account real-life concerns that may influence and temper behavior.

## Intellectual Growth in Early Adulthood

If we subscribed to the traditional view of cognitive development, we would expect to find little intellectual growth in early adulthood. Piaget argued that by the time people left adolescence, their thinking, at least qualitatively, had largely become what it would be for the rest of their lives. They might gather more information, but the ways in which they thought about it would not change.

Was Piaget's view correct? Increasing evidence suggests that he was mistaken.

# Postformal Thought

Developmental psychologist Giesela Labouvie-Vief suggests that the nature of thinking changes during early adulthood. She asserts that thinking based solely on formal operations (Piaget's final stage, reached during adolescence) is insufficient to meet the demands placed on young adults. The complexity of society, which requires specialization, and the challenge of finding one's way through that complexity require thought that transcends logic to include practical experience, moral judgments, and values (Labouvie-Vief, 1990, 2006).

For example, imagine a young, single woman in her first job. Her boss, a married man she respects greatly and who is in a position to help her career, invites her to go with him to make an important presentation to a client. When the presentation, which has gone very well, is over, he suggests they go out to dinner and celebrate. Later that evening, after sharing a bottle of wine, he attempts to accompany her to her hotel room. What should she do?

Logic alone doesn't answer such questions. Labouvie-Vief suggests that young adults' thinking must develop to handle ambiguous situations like these. She suggests that young adults learn to use analogies and metaphors to make comparisons, confront society's paradoxes, and become comfortable with a more subjective understanding. This requires weighing all aspects of a situation according to one's values and beliefs. It allows for interpretive processes and reflects the fact that reasons behind events in the real world are painted in shades of gray rather than black and white (Labouvie-Vief, 1990; Sinnott, 1998b; Thornton, 2004).

To demonstrate how this sort of thinking develops, Labouvie-Vief presented experimental subjects, ranging in age from 10 to 40, with scenarios similar to the Ben and Tyra scenario presented earlier. Each story had a clear, logical conclusion, but it could be interpreted differently if real-world demands and pressures were taken into account.

In responding to the scenarios, adolescents relied heavily on the logic of formal operations. They tended to predict that Tyra would immediately pack up her bags and leave with the children when Ben came home drunk. After all, that's what she said she would do. In contrast, young adults were more apt to consider various real-life possibilities: Would Ben be apologetic and beg Tyra not to leave? Did Tyra really mean it when she said she would leave? Does Tyra have someplace to go?

Young adults exhibited what Labouvie-Vief calls postformal thinking. **Postformal thought** is thinking that goes beyond Piaget's formal operations. Rather than being based on purely logical processes, with absolutely right and wrong answers to problems, postformal thought acknowledges that adult predicaments must sometimes be solved in relativistic terms.

Postformal thought also encompasses *dialectical thinking,* an interest in and appreciation for argument, counterargument, and debate (Basseches, 1984). Dialectical thinking accepts that issues are not always clear-cut, and that answers to questions must sometimes be negotiated. According to psychologist Jan Sinnott (1998b), postformal thinkers shift back and forth between an abstract, ideal solution and real-world constraints that might prevent implementation of that solution. Postformal thinkers understand that just as there can be multiple causes of a situation, there can be multiple solutions.

# Perry's Approach to Postformal Thinking

To psychologist William Perry (1970, 1981), the developmental growth of early adulthood involves mastering new ways of understanding the world. To examine intellectual and moral growth during college, Perry interviewed students at Harvard University. He found that students entering college tended to use *dualistic thinking* in their views of the world: something was either right or wrong; people were either good or bad; others were either for them or against them.

However, as these students encountered new ideas and points of view from other students and their professors, their dualistic thinking declined. Consistent with postformal thinking, students began to accept that issues can have more than one plausible side. Furthermore, they understood that it is possible to hold multiple perspectives on an issue. Their attitude toward authorities also changed: Instead of assuming that experts had all the answers, they began to realize that their own thinking had validity if their position was well thought-out and rational.

> **postformal thought** thinking that acknowledges that adult predicaments must sometimes be solved in relativistic terms

**acquisitive stage** according to Schaie, the first stage of cognitive development, encompassing all of childhood and adolescence

**achieving stage** the point reached by young adults in which intelligence is applied to specific situations involving the attainment of long-term goals regarding careers, family, and societal contributions

**responsible stage** the stage where the major concerns of middle-aged adults relate to their personal situations, including protecting and nourishing their spouses, families, and careers

**executive stage** the period in middle adulthood when people take a broader perspective than earlier, including concerns about the world

In fact, according to Perry, they had reached a stage in which knowledge and values were regarded as relativistic. Rather than seeing the world as having absolute standards and values, they argued that different societies, cultures, and individuals could have different standards and values, and all of them could be equally valid.

It's important to keep in mind that Perry's theory is based on a sample of interviews conducted with well-educated students attending an elite college. His findings may not apply as well to people who have never learned how to examine multiple points of view.

**From an educator's perspective:** Do you think it is possible for adolescent students to learn postformal thinking (e.g., by direct instruction on breaking the habit of dualistic thinking)? Why or why not?

## Schaie's Stages of Development

Developmental psychologist K. Warner Schaie offers another perspective on postformal thought. Taking up where Piaget left off, Schaie suggests that adults' thinking follows a set pattern of stages (illustrated in Figure 7-4). But Schaie focuses on the ways in which information is *used* during adulthood, rather than on changes in the acquisition and understanding of new information, as in Piaget's approach (Schaie & Willis, 1993; Schaie & Zanjani, 2006).

Schaie suggests that before adulthood, the main cognitive developmental task is acquisition of information. Consequently, he labels the first stage of cognitive development, which encompasses all of childhood and adolescence, the **acquisitive stage.** Information gathered before we grow up is largely squirreled away for future use. In fact, much of the rationale for education during childhood and adolescence is to prepare people for future activities.

The situation changes considerably in early adulthood when the focus shifts from the future to the here-and-now. According to Schaie, young adults are in the achieving stage, applying their intelligence to attain long-term goals regarding their careers, family, and contributions to society. During the **achieving stage,** young adults must confront and resolve several major issues, and the decisions they make—such as what job to take and whom to marry—have implications for the rest of their lives.

During the late stages of early adulthood and in middle adulthood, people move into the responsible and executive stages. In the **responsible stage,** middle-aged adults are mainly concerned with protecting and nourishing their spouses, families, and careers.

Sometime later, further into middle adulthood, many people (but not all) enter the **executive stage** in which they take a broader perspective, becoming more concerned about the larger world (Sinnott, 1997). People in the executive stage put energy into nourishing and sustaining societal institutions. They may become involved in town government, religious congregations, service clubs, charitable groups, factory unions—organizations that have a larger purpose in society.

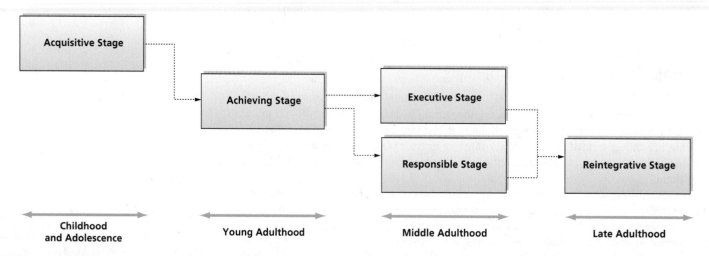

**FIGURE 7-4 Schaie's Stages of Adult Development**
Source: Schaie, 1977–1978.

Finally, the **reintegrative stage** is the period of late adulthood during which people focus on tasks that have personal meaning. They no longer focus on acquiring knowledge to solve potential problems that they may encounter. Instead, they acquire information about issues that specifically interest them. Furthermore, they have less interest in—and patience for—things that they do not see as having some immediate application to their lives.

> **reintegrative stage** the period of late adulthood during which the focus is on tasks that have personal meaning

## REVIEW, CHECK, AND APPLY

### REVIEW

**LO7** Does cognitive development continue in young adulthood?

- Cognitive development continues in young adulthood with the emergence of postformal thought, which goes beyond logic to encompass interpretive and subjective thinking.

**LO8** How does postformal thinking develop in early adulthood?

- Postformal thought acknowledges that adult predicaments must sometimes be solved in relativistic terms, rather than being based on purely logical processes with absolute right or wrong answers.

- Perry suggests that people move from dualistic thinking to relativistic thought during early adulthood.

- According to Schaie, people pass through five stages in the way they use information: acquisitive, achieving, responsible, executive, and reintegrative.

### CHECK YOURSELF

1. The idea that problem-solving in adulthood has to consider previous experiences, logical thinking, and the relative benefits and costs to a decision is also known as _____.

   a. formal operational thought

   b. concrete operational thought

   c. postformal thought

   d. dualistic thinking

2. Postformal thought and dialectical thinking acknowledge that the world sometimes lacks clearly right and wrong solutions to problems.

   - True

   - False

### APPLYING LIFESPAN DEVELOPMENT

- Can you think of situations that you would deal with differently as an adult than as an adolescent? Do the differences reflect postformal thinking?

✓—|Study and Review on
MyDevelopmentLab.com

Answers: 1) c; 2) True

# Intelligence: What Matters in Early Adulthood?

**LEARNING OBJECTIVES**

**LO9**   What are the major contemporary approaches to intelligence?

**LO10**  What causes cognitive growth in young adults?

*Your year on the job has been generally favorable. Performance ratings for your department are at least as good as they were before you took over, and perhaps even a little better. You have two assistants. One is quite capable. The other just seems to go through the motions and is of little real help. Even though you are well liked, you believe that there is little that would distinguish you in the eyes of your superiors from the nine other managers at a comparable level in the company. Your goal is rapid promotion to an executive position.* (Based on Wagner & Sternberg, 1985, p. 447)

How do you meet your goal?

The way adults answer this question may affect their future success. The question is one of a series designed to assess a particular type of intelligence that may have more of an impact on future success than the IQ measured by traditional tests.

## Smart Thinking: Alternative Views of Intelligence

Many researchers argue that the kind of intelligence measured by IQ tests is not the only valid kind. Depending on what one wants to know about individuals, other theories of intelligence—and other measures of it—may be more appropriate.

In his **triarchic theory of intelligence**, psychologist Robert Sternberg, who is responsible for the executive question just posed, suggests that intelligence is made up of three major components: componential, experiential, and contextual. The *componential* aspect involves the mental components used to solve problems (e.g., selecting and using formulas, choosing problem-solving strategies, and in general making use of what has been learned in the past). The *experiential* component refers to the relationship between intelligence, prior experience, and the ability to cope with new situations. This is the insightful aspect of intelligence, which allows people to relate what they already know to a new situation and facts never before encountered. Finally, the *contextual* component of intelligence takes account of the demands of everyday, real-world environments. For instance, the contextual component is involved in adapting to on-the-job professional demands (Sternberg, 2005).

Traditional IQ tests tend to focus on the componential aspect. Yet increasing evidence suggests that a more useful measure, particularly when comparing and predicting adult success, is the contextual component—the aspect of intelligence that has come to be called practical intelligence.

*Practical and Emotional Intelligence.*  According to Sternberg, traditional IQ scores relate quite well to academic success but not to other types of achievement, such as career success. Although it is clear that success in business requires some level of the IQ sort of intelligence, the rate of career advancement and the ultimate success of business executives is only marginally related to IQ scores (Cianciolo et al., 2006; Sternberg, 2006; Grigorenko et al., 2009).

Sternberg contends that success in a career necessitates practical intelligence (Sternberg et al., 1997). While academic success is based on knowledge obtained largely from reading and listening, **practical intelligence** is learned primarily by observing others and modeling their behavior. People with practical intelligence have good "social radar." They understand and handle even new situations effectively, reading people and circumstances insightfully based on their previous experiences. (See Figure 7-5 for sample items from a test of practical intelligence).

There is another, related type of intelligence. **Emotional intelligence** is the set of skills that underlies the accurate assessment, evaluation, expression, and regulation of emotions. Emotional intelligence is what enables people to get along well with others, to understand what they are feeling and experiencing, and to respond appropriately to their needs. Emotional intelligence is of obvious value to career and personal success as a young adult (Mayer, Salovey, & Caruso, 2008; Carmeli & Josman, 2006; Ferguson & Austin, 2010).

**From an educator's perspective:** Do you think educators can teach people to be more intelligent? Are there components or varieties of intelligence that might be more "teachable" than others? If so, which: componential, experiential, contextual, practical, or emotional?

## Creativity: Novel Thought

The hundreds of musical compositions of Wolfgang Amadeus Mozart, who died at the age of 35, were largely written during early adulthood. This pattern—major works produced during early adulthood—is true of many other creative individuals (Dennis, 1966a) (see Figure 7-6, on page 328).

One reason for the productivity of early adulthood may be that after this period creativity can be stifled by a phenomenon that psychologist Sarnoff Mednick (1963) called "familiarity breeds rigidity." By this he meant that the more people know about a subject, the less likely they are to be creative. Early adulthood may be the peak of creativity because many problems encountered professionally are novel.

On the other hand, many people do not reach their pinnacle of creativity until much later in life. For instance, Buckminster Fuller did not devise the geodesic dome until he was in his 50s. Frank Lloyd Wright designed the Guggenheim Museum in New York at age 70. Charles

**triarchic theory of intelligence**  Sternberg's theory that intelligence is made up of three major components: componential, experiential, and contextual

**practical intelligence**  according to Sternberg, intelligence that is learned primarily by observing others and modeling their behavior

**emotional intelligence**  the set of skills that underlie the accurate assessment, evaluation, expression, and regulation of emotions

### Management

You are responsible for selecting a contractor to renovate several large buildings. You have narrowed the choice to two contractors on the basis of their bids and after further investigation, you are considering awarding the contract to the Wilson & Sons Company. Rate the importance of the following pieces of information in making your decision to award the contract to Wilson & Sons.

_____ The company has provided letters from satisfied former customers.

_____ The Better Business Bureau reports no major complaints about the company.

_____ Wilson & Sons has done good work for your company in the past.

_____ Wilson & Sons' bid was $2000 less than the other contractor's (approximate total cost of the renovation is $325,000).

_____ Former customers whom you have contacted strongly recommended Wilson & Sons for the job.

### Sales

You sell a line of photocopy machines. One of your machines has relatively few features and is inexpensive, at $700, although it is not the least expensive model you carry. The $700 photocopy machine is not selling well and it is overstocked. There is a shortage of the more elaborate photocopy machines in your line, so you have been asked to do what you can to improve sales of the $700 machine. Rate the following strategies for maximizing your sales of the slow-moving photocopy machine.

_____ Stress to potential customers that although this model lacks some desirable features, the low price more than makes up for it.

_____ Stress that there are relatively few models left at this price.

_____ Arrange as many demonstrations as possible of the machine.

_____ Stress simplicity of use, since the machine lacks confusing controls that other machines may have.

### Academic Psychology

It is your second year as an assistant professor in a prestigious psychology department. This past year you published two unrelated empirical articles in established journals. You don't, however, believe there is yet a research area that can be identified as your own. You believe yourself to be about as productive as others. The feedback about your first year of teaching has been generally good. You have yet to serve on a university committee. There is one graduate student who has chosen to work with you. You have no external source of funding, nor have you applied for any.

Your goals are to become one of the top people in your field and to get tenure in your department. The following is a list of things you are considering doing in the next two months. You obviously cannot do them all. Rate the importance of each by its priority as a means of reaching your goals.

_____ Improve the quality of your teaching.

_____ Write a grant proposal.

_____ Begin a long-term research project that may lead to a major theoretical article.

_____ Concentrate on recruiting more students.

_____ Begin several related short-term research projects, each of which may lead to an empirical article.

_____ Participate in a series of panel discussions to be shown on the local public television station.

### College Student Life

You are enrolled in a large introductory lecture course. Requirements consist of three exams and a final. Please indicate how characteristic it would be of your behavior to spend time doing each of the following if your goal were to receive an A in the course.

_____ Attend class regularly.

_____ Attend optional weekly review sections with the teaching fellow.

_____ Read assigned text chapters thoroughly.

_____ Take comprehensive class notes.

_____ Speak with the professor after class and during office hours.

**FIGURE 7-5 Sample Items from a Test That Taps Four Domains of Practical Intelligence**
Source: Sternberg, 1993.

Darwin and Jean Piaget were still writing influential works well into their 70s, and Picasso was painting in his 90s. Furthermore, overall productivity, as opposed to the period of a person's most important output, remains fairly steady throughout adulthood, particularly in the humanities (Simonton, 2009).

Overall, the study of creativity reveals few consistent developmental patterns. One reason is the difficulty of determining just what constitutes **creativity,** which is defined as combining responses or ideas in novel ways. Because definitions of what is "novel" may vary from one person to the next, it is hard to identify a particular behavior unambiguously as creative.

This hasn't stopped psychologists from trying. One suggested component of creativity is a person's willingness to take risks that may yield high payoffs. Creative people are like successful stock market investors who follow the "buy low, sell high" rule. Creative people develop and endorse ideas that are unfashionable or regarded as wrong ("buying low"), assuming that

**creativity** the combination of responses or ideas in novel ways

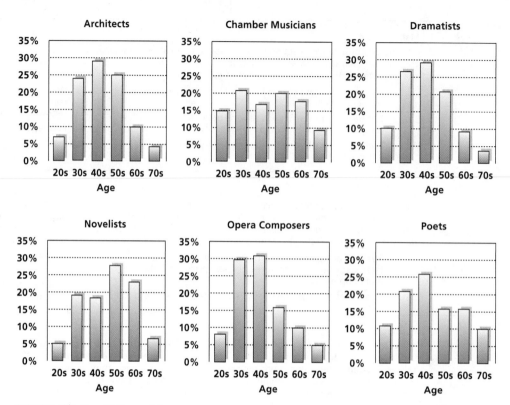

**FIGURE 7-6 Creativity and Age**
The period of maximum creativity differs depending on the particular field. The percentages refer to the percent of total lifetime major works produced during the particular age period. Why do poets peak earlier than novelists?
Source: JOURNAL OF GERONTOLOGY by W. Dennis. Copyright 1966 by The Gerontological Society of America. Reproduced with permission of The Gerontological Society of America in the format Textbook via Copyright Clearance Center.

eventually others will see their value and embrace them ("selling high"). According to this theory, creative adults take a fresh look at ideas that were initially discarded, particularly if the problem is a familiar one. They are flexible enough to move away from tried-and-true ways of doing things and to consider new approaches (Sternberg, Kaufman, & Peretz, 2002; Sternberg, 2009).

## Life Events and Cognitive Development

Marriage. The death of a parent. Starting a first job. The birth of a child. Buying a house. Milestones such as these, whether welcome or unwanted, can cause stress. But do they also cause cognitive growth?

Some research evidence—spotty and largely based on case studies—suggests that the answer may be yes. For instance, the birth of a child may trigger fresh insights into the nature of relationships, one's place in the world, and one's role in perpetuating humanity. Similarly, the death of a loved one may cause a reevaluation of what is important and a new look at the way life should be led (Aldwin, 1994; Woike & Matic, 2004).

Experiencing the ups and downs of life may lead young adults to think about the world in novel, more complex and sophisticated, less rigid ways. They are now capable of using postformal thought to see and grasp trends and patterns, personalities and choices. This allows them to deal effectively with the complex social worlds of which they are a part.

Profound events such as the birth of a child or the death of a loved one can stimulate cognitive development by offering an opportunity to reevaluate our place in the world. What are some other profound events that might stimulate cognitive development?

## REVIEW, CHECK, AND APPLY

### REVIEW

**LO9** What are the major contemporary approaches to intelligence?

- New views of intelligence encompass the triarchic theory, practical intelligence, and emotional intelligence.

- Creativity seems to peak during early adulthood, with young adults viewing even longstanding problems as novel situations.

**LO10** What causes cognitive growth in young adults?

- Major life events contribute to cognitive growth by providing opportunities and incentives to rethink one's self and one's world.

### CHECK YOURSELF

1. Sternberg's _____ theory of intelligence suggests that intelligence is made up of three major components.

2. According to psychologist Sarnoff Mednick (1963), creativity is at its highest in young adulthood because as we get older and more familiar with our areas of study (or occupations), creativity may be stunted.

 - True
 - False

3. Major life events can influence our cognitive development because positive and negative life circumstances lead us to think differently about our relationships with others, what's important to us, or our place in the world.

 - True
 - False

### APPLYING LIFESPAN DEVELOPMENT

- What does "familiarity breeds rigidity" mean? Can you think of examples of this phenomenon from your own experience?

✓—[**Study** and **Review** on
**MyDevelopmentLab.com**

Answers: 1) triarchic; 2) True; 3) True

# College: Pursuing Higher Education

**LO11** Who attends college today, and how is the college population changing?

**LO12** What difficulties do students face in college?

*It's 4:30 in the morning. Marion Mealey, a college student who has returned to school at age 27, looks in on her son, walks her dogs, and begins to study for a biology exam.*

*By 6:00 a.m., she leaves the house, taking the breakfast and lunch that she readied the night before. Her mother will soon wake up and get Mealey's son off to school.*

*Before she returns home at the end of the day, Mealey will have spent four hours in transit, fitting in some additional study time along the way, four hours in class, and three hours at a job that pays her family's living expenses. After a few hours with her family, she will do her reading for her classes tomorrow.* (Adapted from Dembner, 1995)

Marion Mealey, one of the one-third of college students who are above the age of 24, faces unusual challenges as she pursues her college degree. Older students like her are just one aspect of the increasing diversity—in family background, socioeconomic status, race, and ethnicity—that characterizes college campuses today.

For any student, though, attending college is a significant accomplishment. College attendance is not commonplace: Nationwide, high school graduates who enter college are in the minority.

## The Demographics of Higher Education

What types of students enter college? Mirroring the U.S. population, U.S. college students are primarily White and middle class. Nearly 69 percent of White high school graduates enter college, compared with 61 percent of African American graduates and 47 percent of Hispanic graduates. Even more striking, although the absolute number of minority students in college has increased, the overall *proportion* of the minority population that enters college has *decreased* over the past decade—probably because of the diminished availability of financial aid (U.S. Bureau of the Census, 1998, 2000).

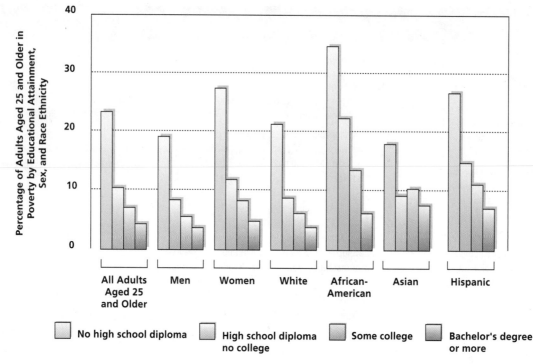

**FIGURE 7-7 College Enrollment by Racial Group**
The proportion of non-Whites who attend college has increased in the last few decades.
Source: The Condition of Education 2004, National Center for Education Statistics, 2004.

Furthermore, only around 40 percent of those who start college finish four years later with a degree. Although about half of those who drop out eventually finish college, the other half never obtain a college degree. For minorities, the picture is even worse: The national dropout rate for African American college students stands at 70 percent (American College Testing Program, 2001).

College attendance makes a difference in many aspects of life, including economic well-being. Just 3 percent of adults who have a college education live below the poverty line; high school dropouts, on the other hand, are 10 times more likely to be living in poverty (U.S. Census Bureau, 2003) (see Figure 7-7).

## The Gender Gap in College Attendance

More women than men attend college and the proportion of women, relative to men, is increasing. Women receive 133 bachelor's degrees for every 100 men receive. The gender gap is even more evident for minority students, with 166 African American women attending college for every 100 African American men (Sum, Fogg, & Harrington, 2003; Adebayo, 2008; Conger & Long, 2010).

Why the gender gap? It may be that men have more job opportunities when they graduate from high school. For instance, the military, trade unions, and jobs that require physical strength may be both more available and more attractive to men. Furthermore, women often have better high school academic records than men, and they may be admitted to college at greater rates (Dortch, 1997; Buchmann & DiPrete, 2006; England & Li, 2006).

## The Changing College Student: Never Too Late to Go to College?

The number of older students, starting or returning to college, continues to grow. More than a third of college students are 24 years old or older. Why are so many older, nontraditional students taking college courses?

If you picture the "average college student" as an 18- or 19-year-old, it's time to rethink. In fact, 26 percent of students taking college courses for credit in the United States are between 25 and 35, like Marion Mealey, the

27-year-old student profiled earlier. Thirty-six percent of community college students are over 30 (Dortch, 1997; U.S. Department of Education, 2005).

Why are so many older, nontraditional students taking college courses? One reason is economic. A college degree is becoming increasingly important for obtaining a job. Many employers encourage or require workers to undergo college-based training to learn new skills or update old ones.

In addition, as young adults age, they begin to feel the need to settle down with a family. This change in attitude can reduce their risk-taking behavior and make them focus more on acquiring the ability to support their family—a phenomenon that has been labeled *maturation reform*.

According to developmental psychologist Sherry Willis (1985), several broad goals underlie adults' participation in learning. First, adults sometimes seek to understand their own aging, trying to figure out what is happening to them and what to expect in the future. Second, some adults seek to understand more fully the rapid technological and cultural changes of modern life.

Third, some adult learners may be seeking a practical edge in combating obsolescence on the job by acquiring new vocational skills. Finally, education may be seen as helpful in preparing for future retirement. Concerned about shifting from a work orientation to a leisure orientation, they may see education as a means of broadening their possibilities.

⟶ **From an educator's perspective:** How is the presence of older students likely to affect the college classroom, given what you know about human development? Why?

## College Adjustment: Reacting to the Demands of College Life

When you began college, did you feel depressed, lonely, anxious, withdrawn? If so, you weren't alone. Many students, particularly recent high school graduates living away from home for the first time, have problems adjusting during their first year in college. The **first-year adjustment reaction** is a cluster of psychological symptoms, including loneliness, anxiety, and depression, relating to the college experience. Although any first-year student may experience this reaction, it is particularly prevalent among students who were unusually successful, either academically or socially, in high school. When they begin college, their sudden change in status may cause distress.

Students who have been successful and popular in high school are particularly vulnerable to first-year adjustment reaction in college. Counseling, as well as increasing familiarity with campus life, can help a student adjust.

**first-year adjustment reaction** a cluster of psychological symptoms, including loneliness, anxiety, withdrawal, and depression, relating to the college experience suffered by first-year college students

## When Do College Students Need Professional Help with Their Problems?

### Becoming an Informed Consumer of Development

How can you tell if a student who is feeling depressed and unhappy may need professional help? Although there are no hard-and-fast rules, there are signals that indicate that professional help is warranted (Engler & Goleman, 1992). Among them:

- psychological distress that lingers and interferes with a person's sense of well-being and ability to function
- feelings that one is unable to cope effectively with the stress
- hopeless or depressed feelings, with no apparent reason
- the inability to build close relationships
- physical symptoms—such as headaches, stomach cramps, or skin rashes—that have no apparent underlying cause

If some of these signals are present, it would be helpful to discuss them with a help-provider, such as a counseling psychologist, clinical psychologist, or other mental health worker. The best place to start is the campus medical center. A personal physician, neighborhood clinic, or local board of health can also provide a referral.

How prevalent are psychological problems? Surveys find that almost half of college students report having at least one significant psychological issue. Other research finds that more than 40 percent of students who visited a college counseling center reported being depressed (see Figure 7-8). Remember, though, that these figures include only the students who sought help. Consequently, they may not be representative of the entire college population (Benton et al., 2003).

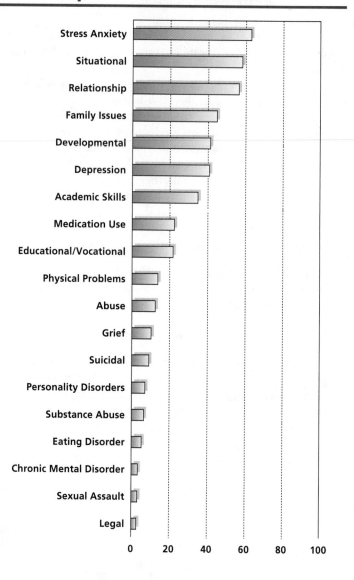

**FIGURE 7-8 College Problems**
The difficulties most frequently reported by college students visiting a campus counseling center.
Source: Benton et al., 2003.

First-generation college students, who are the first in their families to attend college, are particularly susceptible to difficulties during their first year of college. They may arrive at college without a clear understanding of how the demands of college differ from high school, and the social support they have from their families may be inadequate. In addition, they may be less well-prepared for college work (Barry et al., 2009).

Most often, first-year adjustment reaction passes as students make friends, experience academic success, and integrate themselves into campus life. In other cases, though, the problems remain and may fester, leading to more serious psychological difficulties. (Also see the "From Research to Practice" box.)

### Gender and College Performance

*I registered for a calculus course my first year at DePauw. Even twenty years ago I was not timid, so on the very first day I raised my hand and asked a question. I still have a vivid memory of the professor rolling his eyes, hitting his head with his hand in frustration, and announcing to everyone, "Why do they expect me to teach calculus to girls?" I never asked another question. Several weeks later I went to a football game, but I had forgotten to bring my ID. My calculus professor was at the gate checking IDs,*

## From Research to Practice

### Taking a Chance: Gambling Joins Drinking and Drug Use as Major Threat to College Student Well-Being

When you think of addictive behaviors that get many college students in trouble, you probably think of drinking and recreational drug use. But more and more college students are getting caught up in gambling and finding that it can be just as destructive to their lives and futures as substance abuse.

Some experts call gambling a "silent addiction" that is particularly dangerous to college students. Part of the problem is that it doesn't get the same attention as other addictive behaviors. Colleges are less likely to have explicit policies addressing gambling or to have intervention programs in place. Efforts to educate college students about the dangers of gambling fall short of educational efforts regarding other risky behaviors such as drinking or unsafe sex (Newbart, 2009).

The most recent data from an annual survey on college students' gambling habits conducted by the Annenberg Public Policy Center reveal just how widespread the problem is, particularly among male students. Nearly a third of male respondents indicated that they gamble on card games at least once a month, and nearly a quarter gamble on sporting events with the same frequency. More than half reported engaging monthly in some form of gambling—which includes lotteries, slot machines, and online gambling. College women are much less likely than the men to bet on sports, play cards for money, or engage in online gambling; nevertheless, nearly a third of them also engage in some form of gambling once a month (Annenberg Public Policy Center, 2008).

The problem with this high level of gambling is that gambling has significant addictive qualities. Addicted gamblers are unable to control the desire to gamble, even when they know their gambling is harming themselves or others. They are preoccupied with gambling, and they can't keep from gambling whether they are winning or losing. Some 5 to 7 percent of college students report behavior that is consistent with problem gambling (Holtgraves, 2009; Clark, 2010).

Gambling among college students has been on the rise for many years. Consequently, a task force made up of college leaders recently called for colleges to respond to student gambling with the same measures that they take to prevent underage drinking and drug use. According to the report of the task force, only 22 percent of colleges even have explicit policies on gambling and fewer still provide resources to help students with a gambling problem. Explicit prohibition is one of the task force's recommendations, but it importantly also emphasizes that problem gambling should be treated like a disorder rather than a disciplinary problem. This means that colleges should take active steps to identify students who gamble and to provide recovery resources as well as to offer reasonable accommodations to help these students get their lives back in order (Task Force on College Gambling Policies, 2009).

- Why do you think gambling has greater appeal for male college students than it does for female college students?
- Why do you think gambling is on the rise among college students overall?

*so I went up to him and said, "I forgot my ID but you know me, I'm in your class." He looked right at me and said, "I don't remember you in my class." I couldn't believe that someone who changed my life and whom I remember to this day didn't even recognize me.* (Sadker & Sadker, 1994, p. 162)

Although such blatant sexism is less likely today, prejudice and discrimination directed at women is still a fact of college life. For instance, the next time you are in class, consider the gender of your classmates—and the subject matter of the class. Although men and women attend college in roughly equal proportions, they tend to take different courses. Classes in education and the social sciences, for instance, typically have a larger proportion of women than men; and classes in engineering, the physical sciences, and mathematics tend to have more men than women.

Even women who start out in mathematics, engineering, and the physical sciences are more than twice as likely as men to drop out. And although the number of women seeking graduate degrees in science and engineering has been increasing, women still lag behind men (National Science Foundation, 2002; York, 2008).

These differences are no accident. They reflect the powerful influence of gender stereotypes. For instance, when women in their first year of college are asked to name a likely career choice, they are much less apt to choose careers that have traditionally been dominated by men, such as engineering or computer programming, and more likely to choose professions that have traditionally been populated by women, such as nursing and social work (Glick, Zion, & Nelson, 1988; CIRE, 1990; Conrad et al., 2010).

Women also expect to earn less than men, both when they start their careers and when they are at their peaks (Jackson, Gardner, & Sullivan, 1992; Desmarais & Curtis, 1997; Pelham & Hetts, 2001). These expectations jibe with reality: On average, women earn 77 cents for every dollar that men earn. Moreover, women who are members of minority groups do even worse: African American women earn 63 cents for every dollar men make, while for Hispanic women the figure is 52 cents (Institute for Women's Policy Research, 2006; Zhang, 2008).

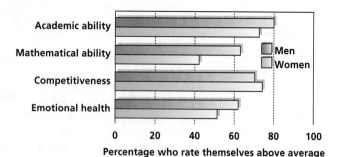

**Percentage who rate themselves above average**

**FIGURE 7-9 The Great Gender Divide**
During their first year of college, men, compared to women, are more apt to view themselves as above average on several spheres relevant to academic success. What is the root of this difference?
Source: CIRE, 1990; Astin, Korn, & Berz, Higher Education Research Institute, UCLA.

Male and female college students also have different expectations regarding their areas of competence. For instance, one survey asked first-year college students whether they were above or below average on a variety of traits and abilities. As shown in Figure 7-9, men were more likely than women to think of themselves as above average in overall academic and mathematical ability, and emotional health.

Both male and female college professors treat men and women differently, even though the different treatment is largely unintentional and the professors are unaware of their actions. Professors call on men more frequently than women and make more eye contact with men than with women. Furthermore, male students are more likely to receive extra help. Finally, the quality of the responses received by male and female students differs, with male students receiving more positive reinforcement for their comments than female students—exemplified by the startling illustration in Table 7-3 (Epperson, 1988; AAUW, 1992; Sadker & Sadker, 1994).

***Benevolent Sexism: When Being Nice Is Not So Nice.*** Although some cases of unequal treatment represent *hostile sexism* in which people treat women in a way that is overtly harmful, in other cases women are the victims of benevolent sexism. In *benevolent sexism,* women are placed in stereotyped and restrictive roles that appear, on the surface, to be positive.

## TABLE 7-3 GENDER BIAS IN THE CLASSROOM

The course on the U.S. Constitution is required for graduation, and more than 50 students, approximately half male and half female, file in. The professor begins by asking if there are questions on next week's midterm. Several hands go up.

**BERNIE:** Do you have to memorize names and dates in the book? Or will the test be more general?

**PROFESSOR:** You do have to know those critical dates and people. Not every one but the important ones. If I were you, Bernie, I would spend time learning them.

**ELLEN:** What kind of short-answer questions will there be?

**PROFESSOR:** All multiple choice.

**ELLEN:** Will we have the whole class time?

**PROFESSOR:** Yes, we'll have the whole class time. Anyone else?

**BEN** (calling out): Will there be an extra-credit question?

**PROFESSOR:** I hadn't planned on it. What do you think?

**BEN:** I really like them. They take some of the pressure off. You can also see who is doing extra work.

**PROFESSOR:** I'll take it under advisement. Charles?

**CHARLES:** How much of our final grade is this?

**PROFESSOR:** The midterm is 25%. But remember, class participation counts as well. Why don't we begin?

The professor lectures on the Constitution for 20 minutes before he asks a question about the electoral college. The electoral college is not as hot a topic as the midterm, so only four hands are raised. The professor calls on Ben.

**BEN:** The electoral college was created because there was a lack of faith in the people. Rather than have them vote for the president, they voted for the electors.

**PROFESSOR:** I like the way you think. (He smiles at Ben, and Ben smiles back.) Who could vote? (Five hands go up, five out of fifty.) Angie?

**ANGIE:** I don't know if this is right, but I thought only men could vote.

**BEN** (calling out): That was a great idea. We began going downhill when we let women vote. (Angie looks surprised but says nothing. Some of the students laugh, and so does the professor. He calls on Barbara.)

**BARBARA:** I think you had to be pretty wealthy, own property—JOSH (not waiting for Barbara to finish, calls out): That's right. There was a distrust of the poor, who could upset the democracy. But if you had property, if you had something at stake, you could be trusted not to do something wild. Only property owners could be trusted.

**PROFESSOR:** Nice job, Josh. But why do we still have electors today? Mike?

**MIKE:** Tradition, I guess.

**PROFESSOR:** Do you think it's tradition? If you walked down the street and asked people their views of the electoral college, what would they say?

**MIKE:** Probably they'd be clueless. Maybe they would think that it elects the Pope. People don't know how it works.

**PROFESSOR:** Good, Mike. Judy, do you want to say something? (Judy's hand is at "half-mast," raised but just barely. When the professor calls her name, she looks a bit startled.)

**JUDY** (speaking very softly): Maybe we would need a whole new constitutional convention to change it. And once they get together to change that, they could change anything. That frightens people, doesn't it? (As Judy speaks, a number of students fidget, pass notes, and leaf through their books; a few even begin to whisper.)

Source: Sadker & Sadker, 1994.

Both male and female college professors may unintentionally favor their male students over their female students, calling on their male students more and making more eye contact with them than with the female students. Why do you think unconscious sexism like this persists?

For instance, a male college professor may compliment a female student on her good looks or offer to give her an easier research project so she won't have to work so hard. While the professor may feel that he is merely being thoughtful, in fact he may be making the woman feel that she is not taken seriously and undermining her view of her competence. Benevolent sexism can be just as harmful as hostile sexism (Glick et al., 2000; Greenwood & Isbell, 2002; Dardenne, Dumont, & Bollier, 2007; Dumont, Sarlet, & Dardenne, 2010).

## Stereotype Threat and Disidentification with School

When African Americans start elementary school, their standardized test scores are only slightly lower than those of Caucasian students, and yet a two-year gap emerges by the sixth grade. And even though more African American high school graduates are enrolling in college, the increase has not been as large as for other groups (American Council on Education, 1995–1996).

Analogously, even though boys and girls perform virtually identically on standardized math tests in elementary and middle school, this changes when they reach high school. At that level, and even more so in college, males tend to do better in math than females. In fact, when women take college math, science, and engineering courses, they are more likely to do poorly than men who enter college with the same level of preparation and identical SAT scores. Strangely, though, this phenomenon does not hold true for other areas of the curriculum, where men and women perform at similar levels (Hyde, Fennema, & Lamon, 1990).

According to psychologist Claude Steele, the reason behind the declining levels of performance for both women and African Americans is the same: *academic disidentification,* a lack of personal identification with an academic domain. For women, disidentification is specific to math and science; for African Americans, it is more generalized across academic domains. In both cases, negative societal stereotypes produce a state of **stereotype threat** which are obstacles to performance that come from awareness of the stereotypes held by society about academic abilities (Steele, 1997; Carr & Steele).

For instance, women seeking to achieve in fields that rely on math and science may worry about the failure that society predicts for them. They may decide, paradoxically, that failure in a male-dominated field, because it would confirm societal stereotypes, presents such great

**stereotype threat** obstacles to performance that come from awareness of the stereotypes held by society about academic abilities

risks that the struggle to succeed is not worth the effort, and they may not try very hard (Inzlicht & Ben-Zeev, 2000).

Similarly, African Americans may work under the pressure of feeling that they must disconfirm the negative stereotype regarding their academic performance. The pressure can be anxiety-provoking and threatening, and can reduce their performance below their true ability level. Ironically, stereotype threat may be most severe for better, more confident students, who have not internalized the negative stereotype to the extent of questioning their own abilities (Carr & Steele, 2009).

In short, members of groups that are traditionally discriminated against are vulnerable to expectations regarding their future success. Happily, though, even relatively subtle changes in a situation—such as the way an assessment is described—can reduce vulnerability to stereotyping. Intervention programs designed to inform members of minority groups about the consequences of negative stereotypes may offer a means of reducing their impact (McGlone & Aronson, 2006, 2007; Rosenthal & Crisp, 2006; Crisp, Bache, & Maitner, 2009).

## REVIEW, CHECK, AND APPLY

### REVIEW

**LO11** Who attends college today, and how is the college population changing?

- Rates of college enrollment differ across gender, racial, and ethnic lines.
- The average age of college students is steadily increasing as more adults return to college.

**LO12** What difficulties do students face in college?

- The phenomena of academic disidentification and stereotype threat help explain the lower performance of women and African Americans in certain academic domains.
- First-year students may experience first-year adjustment reaction, characterized by a cluster of psychological symptoms including loneliness, anxiety, and depression.
- First-generation college students may lack a clear understanding of the demands of college and may be less well-prepared for the work.
- In addition to drinking and drug use, gambling—another addictive behavior—has become a threat to students' well-being.

### CHECK YOURSELF

1. Although attending college is an important event in one's life, the number of individuals who begin college _____.
   a. are in the majority
   b. has been decreasing
   c. are in the minority
   d. is the same as the number of people not entering college

2. More women than men attend and graduate from college, and the proportion of women, relative to men, is increasing.
   - True
   - False

3. Jared is having difficulty in his first year of college. Psychological symptoms include loneliness, anxiety, withdrawal, and depression. It appears Jared is suffering from a cluster of symptoms called _____.

4. Failing to identify oneself as successful in a certain academic domain such as math and science for women and academics in general for African Americans is known as _____.
   a. stereotype threat
   b. academic disidentification
   c. inadequate self-concept
   d. psychosomatic illness

### APPLYING LIFESPAN DEVELOPMENT

- How would you educate college professors who behave differently toward male and female students? What factors contribute to this phenomenon? Can this situation be changed?

✓•―[Study and Review on
**MyDevelopmentLab.com**

Answers: 1) c; 2) True; 3) first-year adjustment reaction; 4) b

## MODULE 7.3 Social and Personality Development in Early Adulthood

*Fate seemed to play a hand in the courtship between Anne Miller and Michael Davoli. They first met at a concert, but didn't see each other again for months, when Michael happened to be moving into Anne's apartment building. After Anne helped Michael get back into his apartment after he'd locked himself out, the two began to see one another casually.*

*But Michael realized that before he and Anne became serious, he had to tell her something about himself. Michael has Tourette's syndrome, a neurological condition that, in Michael, manifests itself mainly in minor physical tics such as rapid eye-blinking. Michael had dealt with the effects of Tourette's since childhood, and he understood that if he was to form a relationship with Anne, she would have to deal with it, too. "I wanted her to know I may never be*

*able to hold her hand in the way I would want to," he said. "I needed to know she'd be O.K. with that." (Segrè, 2009, p. ST13)*

*Happily, Anne was entirely understanding when Michael told her. In fact, his devotion to the band Phish, which he's seen close to 200 times, emerged as a much greater obstacle to their romance than Tourette's. Both avid followers of sports, Michael proposed to Anne after a baseball game they attended. The couple wed in August 2009. (Segrè, 2009)*

In early adulthood we face many developmental tasks (see Table 7-4). We come to grips with the notion that we are no longer other people's children, and we begin to perceive ourselves as adults, full members of society with significant responsibilities (Tanner, Arnett, & Leis, 2009; Arnett, 2010).

This module examines those challenges, concentrating on relationships with others. First, we consider the question of love in its many varieties, including gay and lesbian relationships. We look at how people choose partners, influenced by societal and cultural factors.

Then we examine marriage, including the choice of whether to marry and the factors that influence the success of marriage. We consider how children affect marital happiness and we look at the roles children play in a marriage for heterosexual, gay, and lesbian couples. Also,

## TABLE 7-4  THE DEVELOPMENTAL TASKS OF ADULTHOOD

| Early Adulthood (Ages 20–40) | Middle Adulthood (Ages 40–60) | Late Adulthood (Ages 60+) |
|---|---|---|
| 1. Psychological separation from parents. | 1. Dealing with body changes or illness and altered body image. | 1. Maintaining physical health. |
| 2. Accepting responsibility for one's own body. | 2. Adjusting to middle-life changes in sexuality. | 2. Adapting to physical infirmities or permanent impairment. |
| 3. Becoming aware of one's personal history and time limitation. | 3. Accepting the passage of time. | 3. Using time in gratifying ways. |
| 4. Integrating sexual experience (homosexual or heterosexual). | 4. Adjusting to aging. | 4. Adapting to losses of partner and friends. |
| 5. Developing a capacity for intimacy with a partner. | 5. Living through illness and death of parents and contemporaries. | 5. Remaining oriented to present and future, not preoccupied with the past. |
| 6. Deciding whether to have children. | 6. Dealing with realities of death. | 6. Forming new emotional ties. |
| 7. Having and relating to children. | 7. Redefining relationship to spouse or partner. | 7. Reversing roles of children and grandchildren (as caretakers). |
| 8. Establishing adult relationships with parents. | 8. Deepening relations with grown children or grandchildren. | 8. Seeking and maintaining social contacts: companionship vs. isolation and loneliness. |
| 9. Acquiring marketable skills. | 9. Maintaining longstanding friendships and creating new ones. | 9. Attending to sexual needs and (changing) expressions. |
| 10. Choosing a career. | 10. Consolidating work identity. | 10. Continuing meaningful work and play (satisfying use of time). |
| 11. Using money to further development. | 11. Transmitting skills and values to the young. | 11. Using financial resources wisely, for self and others. |
| 12. Assuming a social role. | 12. Allocating financial resources effectively. | 12. Integrating retirement into new lifestyle. |
| 13. Adapting ethical and spiritual values. | 13. Accepting social responsibility. | |
| | 14. Accepting social change. | |

Source: Colarusso & Nemiroff, 1981.

we discuss the factors that influence family size today, which reflect the complexity of issues young adults face in relationships.

Finally, we move to careers, another major preoccupation of young adults. We see how identity during early adulthood is often tied to one's job and how people decide on the kind of work they do. The module ends with a discussion of the reasons people work and ways to choose a career.

# Forging Relationships: Intimacy, Liking, and Loving During Early Adulthood

**LEARNING OBJECTIVES**

**LO13** How do young adults form loving relationships?

**LO14** How do people choose spouses?

**LO15** Are there differences between gay and lesbian relationships and heterosexual relationships?

*Asia Kaia Linn, whose parents chose her name while looking through a world atlas, met Chris Applebaum about six years ago at Hampshire College in Massachusetts and fell in love with him one Saturday night while they were dancing.*

*Although many women might swoon over a guy with perfect hair and fluid dance steps, it was his silly haircut and overall lack of coordination that delighted her. "He's definitely a funny dancer, and he spun me around and we were just being goofy," Ms. Linn recalled. "I realized how much fun we were having, and I thought this is ridiculous and fabulous and I love him." (Brady, 1995, p. 47)*

Asia followed her instincts and eventually she and Chris were married in an unconventional wedding ceremony at an art gallery. Guests were dressed in a psychedelic mix of fashion, and the ring-bearer delivered the wedding ring by steering a remote-control truck down the aisle of the gallery.

The road to love is not as smooth for everyone as it was for Asia. For some, it is tortuous, meandering through soured relationships and fallen dreams; for others, it is a road never taken. For some, love leads to marriage and the storybook picture of home, children, and long years together. For many, it leads to a less happy ending, to divorce and custody battles.

Intimacy and relationships are major considerations during early adulthood. Relationships are the core of young adults' happiness, and many worry whether they are developing serious relationships "on time." Even those who are not interested in forming long-term relationships typically are focused, to some extent, on connecting with others.

## Seeking Intimacy: Erikson's View of Young Adulthood

Erik Erikson regarded young adulthood as the time of the **intimacy-versus-isolation stage**, which spans the period of postadolescence into the early 30s. During this period, the focus is on developing close, intimate relationships with others.

Erikson's idea of intimacy comprises several aspects. One is selflessness, the sacrifice of one's own needs to those of another. Another is sexuality, the experience of joint pleasure from focusing not just on one's own gratification but also on that of one's partner. Finally, there is deep devotion, marked by efforts to fuse one's identity with the identity of a partner.

According to Erikson, those who experience difficulties during this stage are often lonely, isolated, and fearful of relationships. Their difficulties may stem from an earlier failure to develop a strong identity. In contrast, young adults who are able to form intimate relationships on a physical, intellectual, and emotional level successfully resolve the crisis of this stage of development.

**intimacy-versus-isolation stage** according to Erikson, the period of postadolescence into the early 30s that focuses on developing close, intimate relationships with others

Although Erikson's approach has been influential, it's troubling today because he limited healthy intimacy to heterosexuality. Same-sex partnerships, couples childless by choice, and other relationships different from Erikson's ideal were regarded as less than satisfactory. Furthermore, Erikson focused more on men than women, and did not consider racial and ethnic identity, greatly limiting the applicability of his theory (Yip, Sellers, & Seaton, 2006).

Still, Erikson's work has been influential historically because of its emphasis on examining the continued growth and development of personality throughout the life span. Furthermore, it inspired other developmentalists to consider psychosocial growth during young adulthood and the range of intimate relationships we develop, from friendship to mates for life (Whitbourne, Sneed, & Sayer, 2009).

> **emerging adulthood** according to Arnett the period from the end of teenage years through early 20's in which people are still sorting out their options for the future

## Emerging Adulthood

In contrast to Erikson's view, developmental psychologist Jeffery Arnett (2010) argues that the period from the end of the teenage years through the early 20s marks a unique developmental stage known as emerging adulthood. In his view, **emerging adulthood** is characterized as a period in which people are still sorting out their options for the future. They are exploring their identities, trying to figure out what they will become in the future, and focusing less on the present.

People in the emerging adulthood period may experience the feeling of being "in-between"—not quite adolescents and not quite adults. Although identity exploration is typical of the earlier stage of adolescence, during the 20s it takes on a new urgency as people feel the need to take on the tasks of adulthood such as getting a job and supporting themselves. The uncertainties of the future are particularly strongly felt in difficult economic times (Tanner, Arnett, & Leis, 2009).

Not everyone agrees that emerging adulthood is a unique period. According to critics, the concept of emerging adulthood does not apply very well to people in developing societies or to those in our own culture who marry early, or have children while teenagers, or who leave high school and immediately start working. For them, the period of emerging adulthood is something of a luxury (Hendy & Kloep, 2010; Henig, 2010; Diamond, Fagundes, & Butterworth, 2010).

Still, particularly for those who immediately enter college after graduation from high school, the concept of emerging adulthood seems an apt description of a time in which individuals in their early 20s are seeking to determine the future course of their lives. Emerging adulthood marks a significant transitional time before people fully enter adulthood (Arnett, 2010).

## Friendship

Most of our relationships are friendships, and maintaining them is an important part of adult life. Why? One reason is that people have a basic *need for belongingness* that leads them in early adulthood to establish and maintain at least a minimum number of relationships that foster a sense of belonging with others (Manstead, 1997; Rice, 1999).

But how do particular people end up becoming our friends? One of the most important factors is proximity—people form friendships with others who live nearby and with whom they have frequent contact. People who are nearby can obtain the rewards of friendship, such as companionship, social approval, and the occasional helping hand, at relatively little cost.

Similarity also plays an important role in friendship formation. Birds of a feather *do* flock together: People are more attracted to others who hold attitudes and values similar to their own (Simpkins et al., 2006; Morry, 2007; Selfhout et al., 2009).

The importance of similarity becomes evident when we consider cross-race friendships. As we noted in our discussion of adolescence, the number of cross-race close friendships dwindles throughout the life span. In fact, although most adults claim to have a close friend of a different race, when they are queried regarding the names of close friends, few include a person of a different race (see Figure 7-10).

We also choose friends for their personal qualities. What's most important? According to results of surveys, people are most attracted to others who keep confidences and are loyal, warm, and affectionate. In addition, people like those who are supportive, frank, and have a good sense of humor (Parlee, 1979; Hartup & Stevens, 1999).

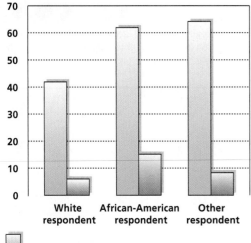

**Percent who say they have a close friend who is black or white**

**Percent who name a close friend who is of a different race**

**FIGURE 7-10 Rephrasing the Question**
Although a relatively high percentage of Whites and Blacks claim to have a close friend who is a member of a different race, only a small majority actually name a person of another race or ethnicity when asked to list the names of their close friends.
Source: Rephrasing the Question, from National Opinion Research Center [NORC]). (1998). Race and friends. Chicago, IL: General Social Survey. Reprinted with permission from NORC.

**stimulus-value-role (SVR) theory** the theory that relationships proceed in a fixed order of three stages: stimulus, value, and role

**passionate (or romantic) love** a state of powerful absorption in someone

**companionate love** the strong affection for those with whom our lives are deeply involved

## Falling in Love: When Liking Turns to Loving

*After a few chance encounters at the laundromat where they wash their clothes each week, Rebecca and Jerry begin talking. They find they have a lot in common and they begin to look forward to what are now semiplanned meetings. After several weeks, they go out on their first official date and discover that they are well suited to each other.*

If such a pattern seems predictable, it is: Most relationships develop by following a surprisingly regular progression (Burgess & Huston, 1979; Berscheid, 1985):

- Two people interact more often and for longer periods, and the range of settings increases.
- They increasingly seek each other's company.
- They open up more and more, disclosing more intimate information. They begin to share physical intimacies.
- They are more willing to share both positive and negative feelings, and they may offer criticism in addition to praise.
- They begin to agree on their goals for the relationship.
- Their reactions to situations become more similar.
- They begin to feel that their own psychological well-being is tied to the success of the relationship, viewing it as unique, irreplaceable, and cherished.
- Finally, their definition of themselves and their behavior changes: They begin to see themselves and act as a couple, rather than as two separate individuals.

Another view of the evolution of a relationship was put forward by psychologist Bernard Murstein (Murstein, 1976, 1986, 1987). According to **stimulus-value-role (SVR) theory,** relationships proceed in three stages.

In the first stage, the *stimulus stage,* relationships are built on surface, physical characteristics such as the way a person looks. Usually, this represents just the initial encounter. The second stage, the *value stage,* usually occurs between the second and the seventh encounter. In the value stage, the relationship is characterized by increasing similarity of values and beliefs. Finally, in the third stage, the *role stage,* the relationship is built on specific roles played by the participants. For instance, the couple may define themselves as boyfriend–girlfriend or husband–wife.

SVR theory has come under criticism because not every relationship follows a similar pattern (Gupta & Singh, 1982; Sternberg, 1986). For instance, there is no logical reason why value factors, rather than stimulus factors, could not predominate early in a relationship. Two people who meet at a political meeting could be attracted to each other's views of current issues.

## Passionate and Companionate Love: The Two Faces of Love

Is "love" just a lot of "liking"? Most developmental psychologists would say no; love not only differs quantitatively from liking, it represents a qualitatively different state. For example, love, at least in its early stages, involves relatively intense physiological arousal, all-encompassing interest, recurrent fantasies, and rapid swings of emotion. Furthermore, compared to liking, love includes closeness, passion, and exclusivity (Lamm & Wiesman, 1997; Hendrick & Hendrick, 2003; Ramsay, 2010).

Not all love is the same. We don't love our mothers the same way we love girlfriends or boyfriends, brothers or sisters, or lifelong friends. What distinguishes these different types of love? Some psychologists suggest that our love relationships can fall into two different categories: passionate or companionate.

**Passionate (or romantic) love** is a state of powerful absorption in someone. It includes intense physiological interest and arousal, and caring for another's needs. In comparison, **companionate love** is the strong affection that we have for those with whom our lives are deeply involved (Lamm & Wiesman, 1997; Hendrick & Hendrick, 2003).

What is it that fuels the fires of passionate love? According to one theory, strong emotions—even negative ones such as jealousy, anger, or fear of rejection—may be the source of deepening passionate love.

In psychologists Elaine Hatfield and Ellen Berscheid's **labeling theory of passionate love,** individuals experience romantic love when two events occur together: intense physiological arousal and situational cues that indicate that "love" is the appropriate label for the feelings being experienced (Berscheid & Walster, 1974). The physiological arousal can be produced by sexual arousal, excitement, or even negative emotions such as jealousy. If that arousal is subsequently labeled as "I must be falling in love" or "he really turns me on," the experience is attributed to passionate love.

The theory helps to explain why people may feel deepened love even in the face of rejection or hurt. If negative emotions produce strong physiological arousal and this arousal is interpreted as "love," then people may decide that they are even more in love than they were before they experienced the negative emotions.

But why should people label an emotional experience "love" when there are so many alternative explanations? One answer is that in Western cultures, romantic love is seen as possible, acceptable, and desirable. The virtues of passion are extolled in songs, commercials, TV shows, and films. Young adults are primed and ready to experience love in their lives (Dion & Dion, 1988; Hatfield & Rapson, 1993; Florsheim, 2003).

Always culturally determined, women's social clocks have changed over the years.

This is not universal across cultures; in many cultures, passionate, romantic love is a foreign concept. Marriages are arranged on the basis of economic and status considerations. Even in Western cultures, the concept of romantic love was not "invented" until the Middle Ages, when social philosophers first suggested that love ought to be a requirement for marriage. Their goal was to provide an alternative to the raw sexual desire that had served as the primary basis for marriage before (Xiaohe & Whyte, 1990; Haslett, 2004).

## Sternberg's Triangular Theory: The Three Faces of Love

Psychologist Robert Sternberg suggests that love is made up of three components: intimacy, passion, and decision/commitment. The **intimacy component** encompasses feelings of closeness, affection, and connectedness. The **passion component** comprises the motivational drives relating to sex, physical closeness, and romance. The **decision/commitment component** embodies both the initial cognition that one loves another person and the longer-term determination to maintain that love (Sternberg, 2006).

These components can be combined to form eight different types of love depending on which of the three components is either present or missing from a relationship (see Table 7-5). For instance, *nonlove* refers to people who have only the most casual of relationships; it consists of the absence of the three components of intimacy, passion, and decision/commitment. *Liking* develops when only intimacy is present; *infatuated love* exists when only passion is felt; and *empty love* exists when only decision/commitment is present.

Other types of love involve a mix of two or more components. For instance, *romantic love* occurs when intimacy and passion are present, and *companionate love* when intimacy and decision/commitment occur jointly. When two people experience romantic love, they are drawn together physically and emotionally, but they do not necessarily view the relationship as lasting. Companionate love, on the other hand, may occur in long-lasting relationships in which physical passion has taken a backseat.

*Fatuous love* exists when passion and decision/commitment, without intimacy, are present. Fatuous love is a kind of mindless loving in which there is no emotional bond between the partners.

Finally, the eighth kind of love is *consummate love*. In consummate love, all three components of love are present. But don't assume that consummate love is the "ideal" love. Many long-lasting and entirely satisfactory relationships are based on other types of love. Furthermore, the type of love that predominates in a relationship varies over time. In strong, loving relationships the level of decision/commitment peaks and remains fairly stable. By contrast, passion tends to peak early in a relationship, but then declines and levels off. Intimacy also increases fairly rapidly, but can continue to grow over time.

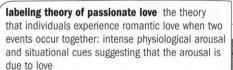

**labeling theory of passionate love** the theory that individuals experience romantic love when two events occur together: intense physiological arousal and situational cues suggesting that the arousal is due to love

**intimacy component** according to Sternberg the component of love that encompasses feelings of closeness, affection, and connectedness

**passion component** according to Sternberg the component of love that comprises the motivational drives relating to sex, physical closeness, and romance

**decision/commitment component** according to Sternberg the third aspect of love that embodies both the initial cognition that one loves another person and the longer-term determination to maintain that love

## TABLE 7-5 THE COMBINATIONS OF LOVE

| Type of Love | Intimacy | Passion | Decision/Commitment | Example |
|---|---|---|---|---|
| Nonlove | Absent | Absent | Absent | The way you might feel about the person who takes your ticket at the movies. |
| Liking | Present | Absent | Absent | Good friends who have lunch together at least once or twice a week. |
| Infatuated love | Absent | Present | Absent | A "fling" or short-term relationship based only on sexual attraction. |
| Empty love | Absent | Absent | Present | An arranged marriage or a couple who have decided to stay married "for the sake of the children." |
| Romantic love | Present | Present | Absent | A couple who have been happily dating a few months, but have not made any plans for a future together. |
| Companionate love | Present | Absent | Present | A couple who enjoy each other's company and their relationship, although they no longer feel much sexual interest in each other. |
| Fatuous love | Absent | Present | Present | A couple who decides to move in together after knowing each other for only 2 weeks. |
| Consummate love | Present | Present | Present | A loving, sexually vibrant, long-term relationship. |

Sternberg's triangular theory of love emphasizes both the complexity of love and its dynamic, evolving quality. As people and relationships develop, so does their love.

## Choosing a Partner: Recognizing Mr. or Ms. Right

For many young adults, the search for a partner is a major pursuit during early adulthood. Society offers a wealth of advice, as a glance at the magazines at supermarket check-out counters confirms. Still, the road to identifying a life partner is not always easy.

***Seeking a Spouse: Is Love the Only Thing That Matters?*** Most people have no hesitation in declaring that the major factor in choosing a spouse is love. Most people in the United States, that is: If we ask people in other societies, love becomes a secondary consideration. For instance, college students were asked in a survey if they would marry someone they did not love. Hardly anyone in the United States, Japan, or Brazil would consider it. On the other hand, a high proportion of college students in Pakistan and India would find it acceptable to marry without love (Levine, 1993). ⊙ Watch on **mydevelopmentlab.com**

What else matters? The characteristics differ considerably from one culture to another (see Table 7-6). For instance, a survey of nearly 10,000 people from around the world found that in China men ranked good health most important and women rated emotional stability and maturity most critical. In South Africa men from a Zulu background rated emotional stability first, and Zulu women rated dependable character the greatest concern (Buss et al., 1990; Buss, 2003b).

Yet, there are commonalities across cultures. For instance, love and mutual attraction, even if not at the top of a specific culture's list, were relatively highly desired across all cultures. Furthermore, traits such as dependability, emotional stability, pleasing disposition, and intelligence were highly valued almost universally.

Certain gender differences were similar across cultures—as confirmed by other surveys (e.g., Sprecher, Sullivan, & Hatfield, 1994). Men, more than women, prefer a potential marriage partner who is physically attractive. In contrast, women, more than men, prefer a potential spouse who is ambitious and industrious.

One explanation for cross-cultural similarities in gender differences rests on evolutionary theory. According to psychologist David Buss and colleagues (Buss, 2004), human beings, as a species, seek out certain characteristics in their mates that are likely to maximize the availability of beneficial genes. He argues that males in particular are genetically programmed to

⊙ Watch on **mydevelopmentlab.com**

Log onto MyDevelopmentLab.com to watch videos of Stephanie and Ralf, two young adults searching for love, but who approach it in different ways.

**TABLE 7-6  MOST DESIRED CHARACTERISTICS IN A MARRIAGE PARTNER**

| | China | | South African (Zulu) | | United States | |
|---|---|---|---|---|---|---|
| | **Males** | **Females** | **Males** | **Females** | **Males** | **Females** |
| Mutual Attraction—Love | 4 | 8 | 10 | 5 | 1 | 1 |
| Emotional Stability and Maturity | 5 | 1 | 1 | 2 | 2 | 2 |
| Dependable Character | 6 | 7 | 3 | 1 | 3 | 3 |
| Pleasing Disposition | 13 | 16 | 4 | 3 | 4 | 4 |
| Education and Intelligence | 8 | 4 | 6 | 6 | 5 | 5 |
| Good Health | 1 | 3 | 5 | 4 | 6 | 9 |
| Sociability | 12 | 9 | 11 | 8 | 8 | 8 |
| Desire for Home and Children | 2 | 2 | 9 | 9 | 9 | 7 |
| Refinement, Neatness | 7 | 10 | 7 | 10 | 10 | 12 |
| Ambition and Industriousness | 10 | 5 | 8 | 7 | 11 | 6 |
| Good Looks | 11 | 15 | 14 | 16 | 7 | 13 |
| Similar Education | 15 | 12 | 12 | 12 | 12 | 10 |
| Good Financial Prospects | 16 | 14 | 18 | 13 | 16 | 11 |
| Good Cook and Housekeeper | 9 | 11 | 2 | 15 | 13 | 16 |
| Favorable Social Status or Rating | 14 | 13 | 17 | 14 | 14 | 14 |
| Similar Religious Background | 18 | 18 | 16 | 11 | 15 | 15 |
| Chastity (no prior sexual intercourse) | 3 | 6 | 13 | 18 | 17 | 18 |
| Similar Political Background | 17 | 17 | 15 | 17 | 18 | 17 |

Note: Numbers indicate rank ordering of characteristics.

Source: Buss et al., 1990.

seek out mates with traits that indicate they have high reproductive capacity. Consequently, physically attractive, younger women might be more desirable since they are more capable of having children over a longer time period.

In contrast, women are genetically programmed to seek out men who have the potential to provide scarce resources in order to increase the likelihood that their offspring will survive. Consequently, they are attracted to mates who offer the highest potential of providing economic well-being (Li et al., 2002).

The evolutionary explanation for gender differences has come under heavy fire. Not only is the explanation untestable, but the similarities across cultures relating to different gender preferences may simply reflect similar patterns of gender stereotyping that have nothing to do with evolution. In addition, although some of the gender differences in what men and women prefer are consistent across cultures, there are numerous inconsistencies as well.

Finally, some critics of the evolutionary approach suggest that the finding that women prefer a partner who has good earning potential may have nothing to do with evolution and everything to do with the fact that men generally hold more power, status, and other resources fairly consistently across different cultures. Consequently, it is a rational choice for women to prefer a high-earning-potential spouse. On the other hand, because men don't need to take economic considerations into account, they can use more inconsequential criteria—like physical attractiveness—in choosing a spouse. In short, the consistencies that are found across cultures may be due to the realities of economic life that are similar throughout different cultures (Eagly & Wood, 2003; Wood & Eagly, 2010).

***Filtering Models: Sifting Out a Spouse.*** While surveys help to identify valued characteristics, they are less helpful in illuminating how individual partners are chosen. According to

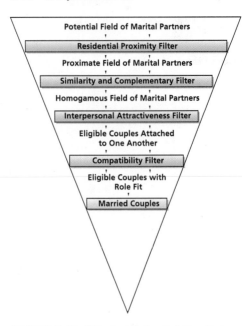

**FIGURE 7-11 Filtering Potential Marriage Partners**
According to one approach, we screen potential mates through successively finer-grained filters in order to settle on an appropriate spouse.
Source: From JANDA, HUMAN SEXUALITY, 1E. © 1980 Wadsworth, a part of Cengage Learning, Inc. Reproduced by permission, www.cengage.com/permissions.

Some psychologists believe that our attachment style as infants is repeated in the quality of our intimate relationships as adults.

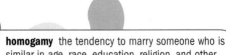

**homogamy** the tendency to marry someone who is similar in age, race, education, religion, and other basic demographic characteristics

**marriage gradient** the tendency for men to marry women who are slightly younger, smaller, and lower in status, and women to marry men who are slightly older, larger, and higher in status

the *filter explanation*, people seeking a mate screen potential candidates through successively finer-grained filters. The explanation assumes that people first filter for factors relating to broad determinants of attractiveness. Once these early screens have done their work, more sophisticated types of screening are used (see Figure 7-11). The end result is a choice based on compatibility between the two individuals (Janda & Klenke-Hamel, 1980).

What determines compatibility? People often marry according to the principle of homogamy. **Homogamy** is the tendency to marry someone who is similar in age, race, education, religion, and other basic demographic characteristics. Homogamy, long the dominant standard for U.S. marriages, has been declining recently, particularly among certain ethnic groups. For example, the rate of marriage between African American men and women of other races increased by three-quarters in the 1990s. Still, for other groups—such as Hispanic and Asian immigrants—the principle of homogamy still has considerable influence (Suro, 1999; Qian & Lichter, 2007; Fu & Heaton, 2008).

Another important societal standard is the **marriage gradient**, the tendency for men to marry women who are slightly younger, smaller, and lower in status, and women to marry men who are slightly older, larger, and higher in status (Bernard, 1982; Pyke & Adams, 2010).

**From a social worker's perspective:** How do the principles of homogamy and the marriage gradient work to limit options for high-status women? How do they affect men's options?

The marriage gradient has important, and unfortunate, effects on partner choice. For one thing, it limits the number of potential mates for women, especially as they age, while allowing men a wider choice of partners throughout life. But it is unfortunate for low-status men, who do not marry because they cannot find women of low enough status or cannot find women of the same or higher status who are willing to accept them as mates. Consequently, they are, in the words of sociologist Jessie Bernard (1982), "bottom of the barrel" men. On the other hand, some women will be unable to marry because they are higher in status or seek someone of higher status than anyone in the available pool of men—"cream of the crop" women, in Bernard's words.

The marriage gradient makes finding a spouse particularly difficult for well-educated African American women who would prefer to marry an African American man. Fewer African American men attend college than African American women, making the potential pool of men who are suitable—as defined by society and the marriage gradient—relatively small. The pool of men is further limited because of the relatively higher rate of incarceration of Black males (which is six times greater than that of Whites). Consequently, relative to women of other races, African American women are more apt to marry men who are less educated than they are—or not marry at all (Kiecolt & Fossett, 1997; Willie & Reddick, 2003; Johnson, 2010).

## Attachment Styles and Romantic Relationships: Do Adult Loving Styles Reflect Attachment in Infancy?

"I want a girl just like the girl that married dear old Dad." So go the lyrics of an old song, suggesting that the songwriter would like to find someone who loves him as much as his mother did. Is this just a corny tune, or is there a kernel of truth in this sentiment? Put more broadly, is the kind of attachment that people experience during infancy reflected in their adult romantic relationships?

Increasing evidence suggests that it very well may be. As we discussed earlier, attachment refers to the positive emotional bond that develops between a child and a particular individual. Most infants fall into one of three attachment categories: securely attached infants, who have healthy, positive, trusting relationships with their caregivers; avoidant infants, who are relatively indifferent to caregivers and avoid interactions with them; and ambivalent infants, who show great distress when separated from a caregiver but appear angry upon the caregiver's return.

Research finds that the quality of lesbian and gay relationships differs little from that of heterosexual relationships.

According to psychologist Phillip Shaver and his colleagues, attachment styles continue into adulthood and affect the nature of romantic relationships (Davis et al., 2006; Mikulincer & Shaver, 2007; Dinero et al., 2008). For instance, consider the following statements:

1. I find it relatively easy to get close to others and am comfortable depending on them and having them depend on me. I don't often worry about being abandoned or about someone getting too close to me.

2. I am somewhat uncomfortable being close to others; I find it difficult to trust them completely, difficult to allow myself to depend on them. I am nervous when anyone gets too close, and often love partners want me to be more intimate than I feel comfortable being.

3. I find that others are reluctant to get as close as I would like. I often worry that my partner doesn't really love me or won't want to stay with me. I want to merge completely with another person, and this desire sometimes scares people away (Shaver, Hazan, & Bradshaw, 1988).

According to Shaver, agreement with the first statement reflects a secure attachment style. Adults who agree with this statement readily enter into relationships and feel happy and confident about the future success of their relationships. Most young adults—just over half—display the secure style of attachment (Hazan & Shaver, 1987).

In contrast, adults who agree with the second statement typically display the avoidant attachment style. These individuals, who make up about a quarter of the population, tend to be less invested in relationships, have higher break-up rates, and often feel lonely.

Finally, agreement with the third category is reflective of an ambivalent style. Adults with an ambivalent style have a tendency to become overly invested in relationships, have repeated break-ups with the same partner, and have relatively low self-esteem. Around 20 percent of adults, gay and straight, fall into this category (Simpson, 1990).

Attachment style is also related to the care that adults give their romantic partners when they need assistance. Secure adults tend to provide more sensitive and supportive care, responding to their partner's psychological needs. In contrast, anxious adults are more likely to provide compulsive, intrusive (and ultimately less helpful) assistance (Feeney & Collins, 2003; Gleason, Iida, & Bolger, 2003; Mikulincer & Shaver, 2009).

In short, there are similarities between infants' attachment styles and their behavior as adults. People who are having difficulty in relationships might look back to their infancy as a root of their problems (Simpson et al., 2007; Berlin, Cassidy, & Appleyard, 2008; Draper et al., 2008).

## *Cultural Dimensions*

### Gay and Lesbian Relationships: Men with Men and Women with Women

Most developmental research has examined heterosexual relationships, but an increasing number of studies have looked at gay and lesbian relationships. The findings suggest that gay relationships are similar to straight relationships.

For example, gay men describe successful relationships in much the same way heterosexual couples do. They believe that successful relationships involve greater appreciation for the partner and the couple as a whole, less conflict, and more positive feelings toward the partner. Similarly, lesbian women in a relationship show high levels of attachment, caring, intimacy, affection, and respect (Brehm, 1992; Beals, Impett, & Peplau, 2002; Kurdek, 2006).

Furthermore, the age preferences expressed in the marriage gradient for heterosexuals also extend to homosexual men, who also prefer partners who are the same age or younger. On the other hand, lesbians' age preferences fall somewhere between those of heterosexual women and heterosexual men (Kenrick et al., 1995).

Finally, despite the stereotype that gay males, in particular, find it difficult to form relationships and are interested in only sexual alliances, the reality is different. Most gays and lesbians seek loving, long-term, and meaningful relationships that differ little qualitatively from those desired by heterosexuals. Although some research suggests that homosexual relationships are less long-lasting that heterosexual relationships, the factors that lead to relationship stability—partners' personality traits, support for the relationship from others, and dependence on the relationship—are similar for homosexual and heterosexual couples (Diamond, 2003; Diamond & Savin-Williams, 2003; Kurdek, 2005, 2008). There are virtually no scientific data regarding gay and lesbian marriage, which became a major social issue when the first legal homosexual marriages occurred in the United States in 2004. It is clear that the question produces strong reactions, but more so among older adults than younger ones. Although only 18 percent of those older than 65 support the legalization of gay marriage, a clear majority—61 percent—of people younger than 30 support the practice (Deakin, 2004).

## REVIEW, CHECK, AND APPLY

### REVIEW

**LO13** How do young adults form loving relationships?

- According to Erikson, young adults are in the intimacy-versus-isolation stage that focuses on developing close, intimate relationships with others.

**LO14** How do people choose spouses?

- Many factors go into choosing a spouse, including love and mutual attraction, which in some cultures are rated behind good health and maturity.
- Types of love include passionate and companionate love. Sternberg's triangular theory identifies three basic components (intimacy, passion, and decision/commitment).

**LO15** Are there differences between gay and lesbian relationships and heterosexual relationships?

- In general, the values applied to relationships by heterosexual, gay, and lesbian couples are more similar than different.

### CHECK YOURSELF

1. According to Erikson, adults spend their early adult years:
   a. consolidating careers.
   b. developing their identities.
   c. being industrious.
   d. focusing on developing relationships with others.

2. _____ love is the strong affection we have for those individuals with whom our lives are deeply involved.

3. According to Sternberg, to determine the type of love that best describes a relationship, one must look at the presence or absence of intimacy, passion, and commitment.
   - True
   - False

### APPLYING LIFESPAN DEVELOPMENT

- Consider a long-term marriage with which you are familiar. Do you think the relationship involves passionate love or companionate love (or both)? What changes when a relationship moves from passionate to companionate love? From companionate to passionate love? In which direction is it more difficult for a relationship to move? Why?

✔️—Study and Review on
MyDevelopmentLab.com

Answers: 1) d; 2) Companionate; 3) True

# The Course of Relationships

**LEARNING OBJECTIVES**

**LO16** What makes a successful marriage?

**LO17** Why do couples decide to have children?

*He wasn't being a chauvinist or anything, expecting me to do everything and him nothing. He just didn't volunteer to do things that obviously needed doing, so I had to put down some ground rules. Like if I'm in a bad mood, I may just yell: "I work eight hours just like you. This is half your house and half your child, too. You've got to do your share!" Jackson never changed the kitty litter box once in four years, but he changes it now, so we've made great progress. I just didn't expect it to take so much work. We planned this child together and we went through Lamaze together, and Jackson stayed home for the first two weeks. But then—wham—the partnership was over.* (Cowan & Cowan, 1992, p. 63)

Relationships are especially challenging in early adulthood. One of the primary questions young adults face is whether and when to marry.

## Marriage, POSSLQ, and Other Relationship Choices: Sorting Out the Options of Early Adulthood

For some people, the primary issue is not *whom* to marry, but *whether* to marry. Although surveys show that most heterosexuals (and a growing number of homosexuals) say they want to get married, a significant number choose some other route. For instance, the past three decades have seen both a decline in the number of married couples and a significant rise in couples living together without being married, a status known as **cohabitation** (see Figure 7-12). These people, whom the Census Bureau calls *POSSLQs* (for *Persons of the Opposite Sex Sharing Living Quarters*), now make up around 10 percent of all U.S. couples. In fact, married couples are now a minority: As of 2005, 49.7 percent of all U.S. households contained a married couple (Fields & Casper, 2001; Doyle, 2004b; Roberts, 2006).

POSSLQs tend to be young: Almost a quarter of cohabiting women and over 15 percent of cohabiting men are under 25. African Americans are more likely to cohabit than Whites. Other countries have even higher cohabitation rates, such as Sweden, where cohabitation is the norm. In Latin America, cohabitation has a long history and is widespread (Wiik, Bernhardt, & Noack, 2009).

Why cohabit? Some couples feel they are not ready for a lifelong commitment. Others feel that cohabitation provides "practice" for marriage. Some reject marriage altogether, maintaining that marriage is outmoded and that it is unrealistic to expect a couple to spend a lifetime together (Martin, Martin, & Martin, 2001; Guzzo, 2009).

Those who feel that cohabiting increases their chances of a happy marriage are incorrect. In fact, the chances of divorce are higher for those who have previously cohabited, according to data collected in both the United States and Western Europe (Doyle, 2004a; Hohmann-Marriott, 2006; Rhoades, Stanley, & Markman, 2006, 2009).

Despite the prevalence of cohabitation, marriage remains the preferred alternative for most people during early adulthood. Many see marriage as the appropriate culmination of a loving relationship, while others feel it is the "right" thing to do after reaching a particular age. Others seek marriage because spouses fill many roles, including economic, sexual, therapeutic, and recreational. Marriage is also the only fully accepted way to have children. Finally, marriage offers legal benefits and protections (Furstenberg, 1996).

Marriage is not a static institution. Fewer U.S. citizens are now married than at any time since the late 1890s. In part this is attributable to higher divorce rates, but the tendency of people to marry later in life is also a contributing factor. The median age of first marriage in the United States is now 27 for men and 25 for women—the oldest age for women since national statistics were first collected in the 1880s (Furstenberg, 1996; U.S. Bureau of the Census, 2001) (see Figure 7-13). ⊙ Watch on **mydevelopmentlab.com**

Many European countries offer legal alternatives to marriage. For instance, France offers "Civil Solidarity Pacts," in which couples receive many of the same legal rights as married couples. What differs is the lack of a legal lifetime commitment; Civil Solidarity Pacts can be dissolved more easily than marriages (Lyall, 2004).

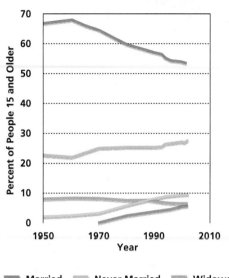

**FIGURE 7-12 POSSLQs**
The number of POSSLQs, or persons of the opposite sex sharing living quarters, has risen considerably in the last three decades. Why do you think this is the case?
Source: U.S. Bureau of the Census, 2001.

POSSLQs, or Persons of the Opposite Sex Sharing Living Quarters, now make up about 10 percent of all couples in the United States—almost 7.5 million people.

⊙ Watch on **mydevelopmentlab.com**

*There are different types of marriage.*
Log onto MyDevelopmentLab.com to watch videos of Rati and Subaz, who are in an arranged marriage, and Scherazade and Rod who are in a typical love marriage.

**cohabitation** couples living together without being married

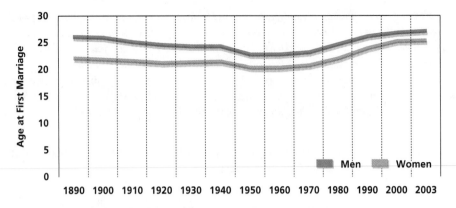

FIGURE 7-13 **Postponing Marriage**
The age at which women and men first marry is the highest since national statistics were first collected in the late 1800s. What factors account for this?
Source: U.S. Bureau of the Census, 2001.

Does this mean that marriage is losing its viability as a social institution? Probably not. Some 90 percent of people eventually marry, and on national polls almost everyone agrees that a good family life is important. In fact, almost nine out of ten 18- to 29-year-olds believe that a happy marriage is an ingredient of a good life (Roper Starch Worldwide, 1997).

Why are people getting married later in life? The delay reflects economic and career concerns. Choosing and starting a career presents a series of increasingly difficult decisions, and some young adults decide to put marriage on hold until they get a foothold on a career path and an adequate salary (Dreman, 1997).

**From a social worker's perspective:** Why do you think society has established such a powerful norm in favor of marriage? What effects might such a norm have on a person who prefers to remain single?

## What Makes Marriage Work?

Successful marriages share several characteristics. The partners visibly show affection and communicate relatively little negativity. They tend to perceive themselves as an interdependent couple rather than two independent individuals. They experience social homogamy, having similar interests and agreeing on role distribution—such as who takes out the garbage and who takes care of the children (Gottman, Fainsilber-Katz, & Hooven, 1996; Carrere et al., 2000; Huston et al., 2001; Stutzer & Frey, 2006).

The increasing understanding of the components of successful marriages has not prevented an epidemic of divorce. The statistics are grim: Only about half of U.S. marriages remain intact, and countries around the world have shown increases in divorce during the last several decades (see Figure 7-14). Over a million U.S. marriages end in divorce each year, and there are 5 divorces for every 1,000 individuals. This is a decline from the mid-1970s peak of 5.3 divorces per 1,000 people, and most experts think that the rate is leveling off (National Center for Health Statistics, 2001).

*Early Marital Conflict.* Conflict in marriage is not unusual. According to some statistics, nearly half of newly married couples experience a significant degree of conflict. One of the major reasons is that partners may initially idealize one another, but as reality sets in they become more aware of flaws. In fact, spousal perceptions of marital quality over the first 10 years of marriage decline in the early years, followed by a period of stabilization, and then additional decline (Kurdek, 1999, 2002, 2003b; Huston et al., 2001; Karney & Bradbury, 2005).

Common sources of marital conflict include difficulty making the transition from adolescence to adulthood; trouble developing a separate identity; and the challenge of allocating time across spouse, friends, and family members (Caughlin, 2002; Crawford, Houts, & Huston, 2002; Murray, Bellavia, & Rose, 2003).

Still, most married couples view the early years of marriage as deeply satisfying. In negotiating changes in their relationship and learning more about each other, many couples find themselves

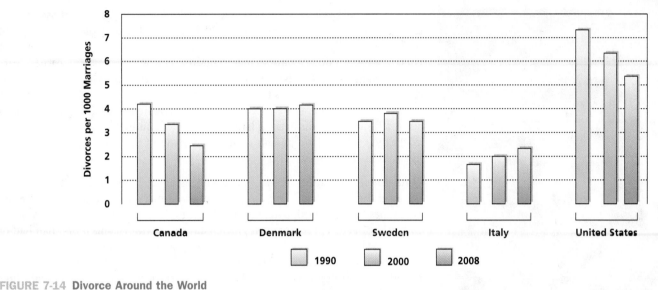

FIGURE 7-14 **Divorce Around the World**
Increases in divorce rates are not just a U.S. phenomenon: Data from other countries also show significant increases.
Source: Population Council Report, 1995.

more deeply in love than before. In fact, the newlywed period is for many couples one of the happiest of their married lives (Bird & Melville, 1994; Orbuch et al., 1996; McNulty & Karney, 2004).

## Parenthood: Choosing to Have Children

What makes a couple decide to have children? Certainly not economics: A middle-class family with two children spends around $233,000 for each child by age 18. Add the cost of college and the figure comes to over $300,000 per child (Lino & Carlson, 2009).

The most commonly cited reasons are psychological. Parents expect to derive pleasure from helping their children grow, fulfillment from their children's accomplishments, satisfaction from seeing them become successful, and enjoyment from forging a close bond with them. For some there may also be a self-serving element in the decision, focusing on the hope that their children will provide for them in their old age, maintain a family business or farm, or offer companionship. Others have children because of a strong societal norm: More than 90 percent of married couples have at least one child.

In some cases children are unplanned, the result of the failure or absence of birth control. If the couple had planned to have children in the future, the pregnancy may be welcome. But in families that had actively not wanted children, or already had "enough" children, the pregnancy can be problematic (Clinton & Kelber, 1993; Leathers & Kelley, 2000; Pajulo, Helenius, & MaYes, 2006).

The couples most likely to have unwanted pregnancies are often the most vulnerable—younger, poorer, and less educated couples. Fortunately, there has been a dramatic rise in the use and effectiveness of contraceptives, and the incidence of undesired pregnancies has declined in recent decades (Centers for Disease Control, 2003; Villarosa, 2003).

*Family Size.* The availability of effective contraceptives has also dramatically decreased the number of children in the average American family. Almost 70 percent of Americans polled in the 1930s agreed that the ideal number of children was three or more, but by the 1990s the percentage had shrunk to less than 40 percent. Today, most families seek to have no more than two children—although most say that three or more is ideal if money is no object (Kate, 1998; Gallup Poll, 2004).

These preferences have been translated into changes in the actual birth rate. In 1957, the *fertility rate* reached a post–World War II peak in the United States of 3.7 children per woman and then began to decline. Today, the rate is at 2.1 children per woman, which is less than the *replacement level,* the number of children that one generation must produce to replenish its numbers. In contrast, in some underdeveloped countries, the fertility rate is as high as 6.9 (World Bank, 2004).

What has produced this decline in the fertility rate? In addition to the availability of birth control, increasing numbers of women have joined the workforce. The pressures of simultaneously holding a job and raising a child have convinced many women to have fewer children.

As increasing numbers of women have joined the workforce, more are choosing to have fewer children and have them later.

Furthermore, many women who are developing their careers choose to have children later. In fact, women between 30 and 34 are the only ones whose rate of births has actually increased over earlier decades. Still, women who have their first child in their 30s do not have as many children as women who begin earlier. Also, research suggesting that there are health benefits for mothers who space their children apart may lead families to have fewer children (Marcus, 2004).

Financial considerations, particularly the increasing cost of college, may also act as a disincentive for bearing larger numbers of children. Finally, some couples doubt they will be good parents or simply don't want the work and responsibility involved in childrearing.

***Dual-Earner Couples.*** One of the major historical shifts affecting young adults began in the last half of the twentieth century: a marked increase in the number of families in which both parents work. Close to three-quarters of married women with school-aged children are employed outside the home, and more than half of mothers with children under age 6 are working. In the mid-1960s, only 17 percent of mothers of 1-year-olds worked full time; now, more than 50 percent do. In the majority of families, both husband and wife work (Darnton, 1990; Carnegie Task Force, 1994; Barnett & Hyde, 2001).

The availability of two incomes brings economic benefits, but it also takes a toll, particularly on women. Even when both spouses work similar hours, the wife generally spends more time caring for the children—even though the time men spend with their children has risen by 25 percent in the last 20 years (Kitterod & Pettersen, 2006).

Furthermore, what husbands and wives contribute to the household often differs. Men's chores (e.g., lawn mowing, home repairs) are more easily scheduled in advance, while women's chores tend to need immediate attention (e.g., child care, meal preparation), causing anxiety and stress (Haddock & Rattenborg, 2003; Lee, Vernon-Feagans, & Vazquez, 2003; Coltrane & Shih, 2010) (see Figure 7-15).

***The Transition to Parenthood: Two's a Couple, Three's a Crowd?*** Consider this quote from a spouse who just became a parent:

*We had no idea what we were getting into when our first child was born. We certainly prepared for the event, reading magazine articles and books and even attending a class on child care. But when Sheanna was actually born, the sheer enormity of the task of taking care of her, her presence at every moment of the day, and the awesome responsibility of raising another human being weighed on us like nothing we'd ever faced. Not that it was a burden. But it did make us look at the world with an entirely different perspective.*

The arrival of a child alters virtually every aspect of family life. Spouses are suddenly placed in new roles—"mother" and "father"—which may overwhelm their older, continuing roles of "wife" and "husband." In addition, new parents face significant physical and psychological demands, including near-constant fatigue, new financial responsibilities, and an increase in household chores (Meijer & van den Wittenboer, 2007).

Furthermore, in contrast with cultures in which childrearing is regarded as a communal task, Western culture's emphasis on individualism leaves parents to forge their own paths after the birth of a child, often without community support (Rubin & Chung, 2006; Lamm & Keller, 2007).

The consequence is that many couples experience the lowest level of marital satisfaction of any point in their marriage. This is particularly true for women, who tend to be more dissatisfied than men with their marriages after the arrival of children. The most likely reason is that women often bear the brunt of childrearing, even if both parents seek to share these responsibilities (Levy-Shiff, 1994; Laflamme, Pomerleau, & Malcuit, 2002; Lu, 2006).

Marital satisfaction does not decrease for all couples upon the birth of a child. According to work by John Gottman and colleagues (Shapiro, Gottman, & Carrère, 2000), satisfaction can stay steady or even rise. Three factors permit couples to successfully weather the stress that follows the birth of a child:

- Working to build fondness and affection toward each other
- Remaining aware of events in each other's life, and responding to those events
- Considering problems as controllable and solvable

In addition, couples who are well satisfied with their marriages as newlyweds are more likely to be satisfied as they raise their children. Couples who harbor realistic expectations regarding the effort involved in childrearing also tend to be more satisfied after they become parents. Furthermore, parents who work together as a *coparenting team,* thoughtfully adopting common childrearing goals and strategies, are more apt to be satisfied with their parenting roles (Schoppe-Sullivan et al., 2006; McHale & Rotman, 2007).

In short, having children can lead to greater marital satisfaction for couples already satisfied with their marriage. For dissatisfied couples, having children may make a bad situation worse (Shapiro et al., 2000; Driver, Tabares, & Shapiro, 2003; Lawrence et al., 2008).

## Gay and Lesbian Parents

In increasing numbers, children are being raised in families with two moms or two dads. Some 20 percent of gay men and lesbian women are parents.

How do lesbian and gay households compare to heterosexual households? Studies of couples before children arrive show that, compared to heterosexual households, homosexual partners tend to divide labor more evenly and the ideal of an egalitarian allocation of household work is more strongly held (Patterson, 1994; Parks, 1998; Kurdek, 1993, 2003a).

However, the arrival of a child (usually through adoption or artificial insemination) changes the dynamics of household life considerably. As in heterosexual unions, role specialization develops. For instance, childrearing tends to fall more to one member of the couple, while the other spends more time in paid employment. Although both partners usually say they share household tasks and decision-making equally, biological mothers are often more involved in child care (Patterson, 1995; Fulcher et al., 2006; Goldberg, 2010c).

The evolution of homosexual couples when children arrive appears to be more similar to that of heterosexual couples than dissimilar, particularly in the increased role specialization occasioned by the requirements of child care. The experience for children of being in a household with two parents of the same sex is also similar. Most research suggests that children raised in households in which the parents are homosexual show no differences in terms of eventual adjustment from those raised in heterosexual households. Although they may face greater challenges from a society in which the roots of prejudice against homosexuality are deep, children who have two moms or two dads ultimately seem to fare well (Crowl, Ahn, & Baker, 2008; Patterson, 2009; Goldberg, 2010c).

## Staying Single: I Want to Be Alone

For some people, living alone is the right path, consciously chosen, through life. In fact, *singlehood,* living alone without an intimate partner, has increased significantly in the last

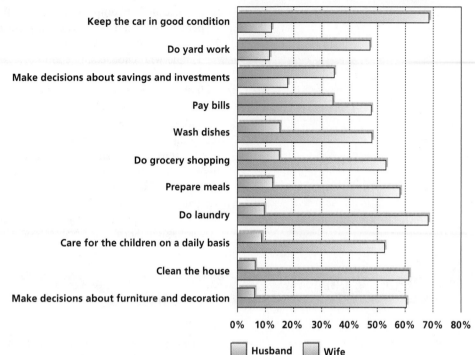

Keep the car in good condition
Do yard work
Make decisions about savings and investments
Pay bills
Wash dishes
Do grocery shopping
Prepare meals
Do laundry
Care for the children on a daily basis
Clean the house
Make decisions about furniture and decoration

0% 10% 20% 30% 40% 50% 60% 70% 80%

☐ Husband  ☐ Wife

**FIGURE 7-15 Division of Labor**
Although husbands and wives generally work at their paying jobs a similar number of hours each week, wives are apt to spend more time than their husbands doing home chores and in child-care activities. Why do you think this pattern exists?
Source: GPSS Lifestyle Poll, 2007.

*"If Heather has two mommies, and each of them has two brothers, and one of those brothers has another man for a 'roommate,' how many uncles does Heather have?"*

several decades, encompassing around 20 percent of women and 30 percent of men. Almost 10 percent will probably spend their entire lives in singlehood (U.S. Bureau of the Census, 2002; Gerber, 2002; DePaulo & Morris, 2006).

People who choose singlehood give several reasons for their decision. One is that they view marriage negatively. Rather than seeing marriage in idealized terms, they focus more on high divorce rates and marital strife. Ultimately, they conclude that the risks of forming a lifetime union are too high.

Others view marriage as too restrictive, valuing their personal change and growth, and reasoning that growth would be impeded by the stable, long-term commitment of marriage. Finally, some people simply do not meet anyone with whom they wish to spend their lives. Instead, they value their independence and autonomy (DePaulo & Morris, 2006). Despite the advantages of singlehood, there are also drawbacks. Society often stigmatizes single individuals, particularly women, holding up marriage as the idealized norm. Furthermore, there can be a lack of companionship and sexual outlets, and singles may feel that their futures are less secure financially (Byrne, 2000; Schachner, Shaver, & Gillath, 2008).

## REVIEW, CHECK, AND APPLY

### REVIEW

**LO16** What makes a successful marriage?

- Success in marriage includes partners who visibly show affection and communicate relatively little negativity, perceive themselves as an interdependent couple instead of two independent individuals, share similar interests, and agree on role distribution.

**LO17** Why do couples decide to have children?

- The most common reasons for having children are psychological. Parents derive pleasure from helping their children grow, fulfillment from their accomplishments, and enjoyment from forging a close bond with them.

### CHECK YOURSELF

1. During the past three decades there has been a decline in both the number of married couples and the number of individuals living together without being married.
   - True
   - False

2. Divorce is more likely to occur when couples marry without first cohabiting.
   - True
   - False

3. When asked why they want to have children, most young adults cite _____ reasons.
   a. personal
   b. physical
   c. psychological
   d. societal

### APPLYING LIFESPAN DEVELOPMENT

- In what ways do you think cognitive changes in early adulthood (e.g., the emergence of postformal thought and practical intelligence) affect how young adults deal with questions of marriage, divorce, and childrearing?

✓—⌐**Study** and **Review** on **MyDevelopmentLab.com**

Answers: 1) False; 2) False; 3) c

# Work: Choosing and Embarking on a Career

**LEARNING OBJECTIVES**

**LO18** What factors influence the choice of a career?

**LO19** How have women who pursue careers advanced in the workplace?

**LO20** Why do people work, and what elements of a job bring satisfaction?

*Why did I decide that I wanted to be a lawyer? The answer is embarrassing. When I got to my senior year of college, I began to worry about what I was going to do when I graduated. My parents kept asking what kind of work I was thinking about, and I felt the pressure rising with each call from home. At the time, the O. J. Simpson trial was in the news, and it got me thinking about what it might be like to be an attorney. I had always been fascinated by L.A. Law when it had been on television, and I could envision myself in one of those big corner offices with a view of the city. For these reasons, and just about none other, I decided to take the law boards and apply to law school.*

Early adulthood is a period of decisions with lifelong implications. One of the most critical is the choice of a career path. This decision influences financial prosperity, of course, but also status, the sense of self-worth, and the contribution that a person will make in life. Decisions about work go to the core of a young adult's identity.

## Identity During Young Adulthood: The Role of Work

According to psychiatrist George Vaillant, the stage of development that young adults reach is called career consolidation. During **career consolidation,** which begins between 20 and 40, young adults become centered on their careers. Vaillant based his conclusion on a comprehensive longitudinal study of male graduates of Harvard, begun when they were freshmen in the 1930s (Vaillant, 1977; Vaillant & Vaillant, 1990).

In their early 20s, the men tended to be influenced by their parents' authority. But in their late 20s and early 30s, they started to act with greater autonomy. They married, had children, and began to focus on their careers—the period of career consolidation.

Vaillant draws a relatively uninspiring portrait of people in this stage. His participants worked very hard as they climbed the corporate ladder. They tended to be rule-followers conforming to the norms of their professions. Rather than showing the independence and questioning that they had displayed in college, they threw themselves unquestioningly into their work.

Vaillant argues that work plays such an important role that the career consolidation stage should be seen as an addition to Erikson's intimacy-versus-isolation stage of psychosocial identity. In Vaillant's view, career concerns supplant the focus on intimacy, and the career consolidation stage marks a bridge between intimacy-versus-isolation and generativity-versus-stagnation. (Generativity refers to an individual's contribution to society, as we discuss later.)

The reaction to Vaillant's viewpoint has been mixed. Critics point out that Vaillant's sample, although relatively large, comprised a highly restricted, unusually bright group of men. Furthermore, societal norms have changed considerably since the 1930s, and people's views of the importance of work may have shifted. Finally, the lack of women in the sample and the fact that there have been major changes in the role of work in *women's* lives make Vaillant's conclusions even less generalizable.

Still, it is hard to dispute the importance of work in most people's lives, and research suggests that it makes up a significant part of both men's and women's identity—if for no other reason than that it occupies so much of their time (Deaux et al., 1995).

## Picking an Occupation: Choosing Life's Work

Some people know from childhood what they want to do for a living; for others, the choice of a career is a matter of chance. Many of us fall somewhere in the middle.

*Ginzberg's Career Choice Theory.* According to Eli Ginzberg (1972), people typically move through stages in choosing a career. The first stage is the **fantasy period,** which lasts until around age 11. During the fantasy period, people make and discard career choices without regard to skills, abilities, or available job opportunities. A child may decide she wants to be a rock star—despite being unable to carry a tune.

During the **tentative period,** which spans adolescence, people begin to think more practically about the requirements of various jobs and their own abilities and interests. They also consider how well a particular occupation might satisfy their personal values and goals.

Finally, in early adulthood, people enter the **realistic period,** in which they explore specific career options either through actual experience on the job or through training for a profession. After initially exploring what they might do, people begin to narrow their choices and eventually commit to a particular career.

Critics have charged that Ginzberg's theory oversimplifies the process of choosing a career. Because it was based on subjects from middle socioeconomic levels, his theory may overstate the choices available to people in lower socioeconomic levels. Furthermore, the ages associated with the various stages may be too rigid. For instance, a person who begins to work immediately after high school most likely makes serious career decisions earlier than a person

According to one theory, people move through a series of life stages in choosing a career. The first stage is the fantasy period, which lasts until a person is around 11 years old.

**career consolidation** according to Vaillant a stage that is entered between the ages of 20 and 40, when young adults become centered on their careers

**fantasy period** according to Ginzberg, the period, lasting until about age 11, when career choices are made, and discarded, without regard to skills, abilities, or available job opportunities

**tentative period** the second stage of Ginzberg's theory, which spans adolescence, when people begin to think more practically about the requirements of various jobs and how their own abilities might fit with them

**realistic period** the third stage of Ginzberg's theory, which occurs in early adulthood, when people begin to explore specific career options, either through actual experience on the job or through training for a profession, and then narrow their choices and make a commitment

who attends college. In addition, economic factors cause many people to change careers at different points in their adult lives.

***Holland's Personality Type Theory.*** Other theories of career choice emphasize how personality affects career decisions. According to John Holland, certain personality types match particularly well with certain careers. If the correspondence between personality and career is good, people will enjoy their careers more and be more likely to stay in them; but if the match is poor, they will be unhappy and more likely to shift to other careers (Holland, 1997).

According to Holland, six personality types are important in career choice:

- **Realistic.** These are down-to-earth, practical problem-solvers, physically strong but with mediocre social skills. They make good farmers, laborers, and truck drivers.
- **Intellectual.** Intellectual types are oriented toward the theoretical and abstract. Although not particularly good with people, they are well suited to careers in math and science.
- **Social.** People with this personality type have strong verbal skills and are good with people. They make good salespersons, teachers, and counselors.
- **Conventional.** Conventional types prefer highly structured tasks. They make good clerks, secretaries, and bank tellers.
- **Enterprising.** These are risk-takers and take-charge types. They are good leaders and may be particularly effective as managers or politicians.
- **Artistic.** These individuals use art to express themselves and often prefer the world of art to interactions with people. They are best suited to occupations involving the arts.

Holland's theory suffers from a central flaw: Not everyone fits neatly into personality types. Furthermore, there are clear exceptions, with people holding jobs that are "wrong" for their personality type. Still, the basics of the theory have been validated, and they form the foundation of several of the "job quizzes" that people take to see what occupations they might be right for (Deng, Armstrong, & Rounds, 2007; Armstrong, Rounds, & Hubert, 2008).

## Gender and Career Choices: Women's Work

*WANTED: Full-time employee for small family firm. DUTIES: Including but not limited to general cleaning, cooking, gardening, laundry, ironing and mending, purchasing, bookkeeping and money management. Child care may also be required. HOURS: Avg. 55/wk but standby duty required 24 hours/day, 7 days/wk. Extra workload on holidays. SALARY AND BENEFITS: No salary, but food, clothing, and shelter provided at employer's discretion; job security and benefits depend on continued goodwill of employer. No vacation. No retirement plan. No opportunities for advancement. REQUIREMENTS: No previous experience necessary, can learn on the job. Only women need apply.* (Unger & Crawford, 1992, p. 446)

A generation ago, many women entering early adulthood assumed that this admittedly exaggerated job description matched the position that they would occupy: housewife. Even women who sought work outside the home were relegated to certain professions. Until the 1960s, employment ads in U.S. newspapers were almost always divided into two sections: "Help Wanted: Male" and "Help Wanted: Female." The men's ads included such professions as police officer, construction worker, and legal counsel; the women's ads were for secretaries, teachers, cashiers, and librarians.

The breakdown of jobs reflected society's view of what the two genders were best suited for. Traditionally, women were considered most appropriate for **communal professions,** occupations associated with relationships, such as nursing. In contrast, men were perceived as best suited for agentic professions. **Agentic professions** are associated with getting things accomplished, such as carpentry. It is probably no coincidence that communal professions typically have lower status and pay than agentic professions (Eagly & Steffen, 1984, 1986; Hattery, 2000).

**From a social worker's perspective:** How does the division of jobs into communal and agentic relate to traditional views of male–female differences?

**communal professions** occupations that are associated with relationships, such as nursing

**agentic professions** occupations that are associated with getting things accomplished, such as carpentry

Although discrimination based on gender is far less blatant today than it was several decades ago—it is now illegal, for instance, to advertise a position specifically for one gender— remnants of gender prejudice persist. Women are less likely to be found in traditionally male-dominated professions such as engineering and computer programming. As shown in Figure 7-16, despite significant progress in the last 40 years, women's earnings still lag behind those of men. In fact, women in many professions earn significantly less than men in identical jobs (Frome et al., 2006; U.S. Bureau of the Census, 2006, 2009).

More women are working outside the home than ever. Between 1950 and 2003, the percentage of the female population (aged 16 and over) in the U.S. labor force increased from around 35 percent to over 60 percent, and women today make up around 55 percent of the labor force, a figure comparable to their presence in the general population. Almost all women expect to earn a living, and almost all do at some point in their lives. Furthermore, in about one-half of U.S. households, women earn about as much as their husbands (U.S. Bureau of Labor Statistics, 2003).

Opportunities for women have improved considerably. Women are more likely to be physicians, lawyers, insurance agents, and bus drivers than in the past. However, within job categories gender differences persist. For example, female bus drivers are more apt to have part-time school bus routes, while men hold better-paying full-time routes in cities. Female pharmacists are more likely to work in hospitals, while men work in higher-paying jobs in retail stores (Crawford & Unger, 2004).

Women and minorities in high-status, visible professional roles often hit what has come to be called the *glass ceiling*. The glass ceiling is an invisible barrier in an organization that prevents individuals from being promoted beyond a certain level. It operates subtly, and often the people responsible for it are unaware of how their actions perpetuate discrimination (Goodman, Fields, & Blum, 2003; Stockdale, Crosby, & Malden, 2004).

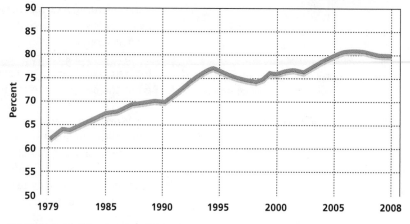

FIGURE 7-16 **The Gender–Wage Gap**
Women's weekly earnings as a percent of men's has increased since 1979, but still is only a bit more than 75 percent, and has remained steady over the past 3 years.
Source: U.S. Bureau of the Census, 2009.

## Why Do People Work? More Than Earning a Living

Young adults express many reasons—well beyond earning money—for seeking a job.

Extrinsic motivation drives people as a way of obtaining tangible rewards, such as money, prestige, or an expensive automobile. How might extrinsic motivation be illustrated in a less developed, nonwestern culture?

**extrinsic motivation** motivation that drives people to obtain tangible rewards, such as money and prestige

**intrinsic motivation** motivation that causes people to work for their own enjoyment, for personal rewards

**status** the evaluation of a role or person by other relevant members of a group or society

***Intrinsic and Extrinsic Motivation.*** Certainly, people work to obtain concrete rewards, or out of extrinsic motivation. **Extrinsic motivation** drives people to obtain tangible rewards, such as money and prestige (Singer, Stacey, & Lange, 1993).

But people also work for their own enjoyment, for personal rewards. This is known as **intrinsic motivation.** People in many Western societies tend to subscribe to the Puritan work ethic, the notion that work is important in and of itself. According to this view, working is a meaningful act that brings psychological well-being and satisfaction.

Work also contributes to personal identity. Consider what people say about themselves when they first meet someone. After their name and where they live, they typically tell what they do for a living. What they do is a large part of who they are.

Work may also be central to people's social lives as a source of friends and activities. Work relationships can easily become personal friendships. In addition, work brings social obligations, such as dinner with the boss or the annual year-end party.

Finally, the kind of work people do helps to determine **status,** the evaluation by society of the role a person plays. Many jobs are associated with a particular status. For instance, physicians and college teachers are near the top of the status hierarchy, while ushers and shoe shiners occupy the bottom.

***Satisfaction on the Job.*** Status affects job satisfaction: The higher the status of the job, the more satisfied people tend to be. Furthermore, the status of the job of the major wage-earner can affect the status of the other members of the family (Green, 1995; Schieman, McBrier, & van Gundy, 2003).

Of course, status isn't everything: Worker satisfaction depends on a number of factors, not the least of which is the nature of the job itself. For example, some people who work at computers are monitored on a minute-by-minute basis; supervisors can consistently see how many keystrokes they are entering. In some firms in which workers use the telephone for sales or to take customer orders, conversations are monitored by supervisors. Workers' Web use and email are also monitored or restricted by a large number of employers. Not surprisingly, such forms of job stress produce worker dissatisfaction (MacDonald, 2003).

Job satisfaction is higher when workers have input into the nature of their jobs and feel their ideas and opinions are valued. They also prefer jobs that offer variety over those that require only a few repeated skills. Finally, the more influence employees have over others, either directly as supervisors or more informally, the greater their job satisfaction (Peterson & Wilson, 2004; Thompson & Prottas, 2006; Carton & Aiello, 2009).

## *Choosing a Career*

### Becoming an Informed Consumer of Development

One of the greatest challenges of early adulthood is making a decision that will have lifelong implications: the choice of a career. Although most people can be happy in a variety of jobs, choosing among the options can be daunting. Here are some guidelines for facing the career question.

- Systematically evaluate your choices. Libraries contain a wealth of career information and most colleges and universities have helpful career centers.

- Know yourself. Evaluate your strengths and weaknesses, perhaps by completing a questionnaire on your interests, skills, and values at a college career center.

- Create a "balance sheet" listing the gains and losses from a particular profession. First list gains and losses for yourself and then for others, such as family members. Next, write down your projected self-approval or self-disapproval from the potential career—and the projected social approval or disapproval you are likely to receive from others.

- "Try out" different careers through paid or unpaid internships. By seeing a job first-hand, interns get a sense of what an occupation is truly like.

- Remember that there are no permanent mistakes. People today increasingly change careers in early adulthood and even beyond. No one should feel locked into a decision made earlier in life. As we have seen throughout this book, people develop substantially over the course of their lives.

- It is reasonable to expect that shifting values, interests, abilities, and life circumstances might make a different career more appropriate later in life than the one chosen during early adulthood.

## REVIEW, CHECK, AND APPLY

**LO18**  What factors influence the choice of a career?

- Choosing a career is an important step in early adulthood.

- According to Vaillant, young adults reach the stage of career consolidation where they focus on their careers.

- Ginzberg offers a three-stage period of career development.

- Holland describes how personality affects career decisions.

**LO19**  How have women who pursue careers advanced in the workplace?

- Gender stereotypes are changing, but women still experience subtle prejudice in career choices, roles, and wages.

**LO20**  Why do people work, and what elements of a job bring satisfaction?

- People work because of both extrinsic and intrinsic motivation factors.

- The nature of a job, the degree of status it confers, and the variety it offers all contribute to job satisfaction. It's also important to workers to feel their ideas and opinions are valued.

1. According to Vaillant, during young adulthood, individuals become centered on their careers. This stage is known as _____.

   a. career consolidation

   b. life comprehension

   c. personal attainment

   d. realism

2. Which of the following is NOT one of the six personality types Holland indicates is important when it comes to career choice?

   a. social

   b. realistic

   c. intellectual

   d. enterprising

3. Even though there are more job opportunities for women in many fields than there used to be, women are often not afforded the same opportunities as men for advancement within those fields. Specifically, many women are not promoted because they have hit what is known as the _____, or an invisible barrier to advancement.

- If Vaillant's study were performed today on women, in what ways do you think the results would be similar to or different from those of the original study?

✔—[Study and **Review** on
**MyDevelopmentLab.com**

Answers: 1) a; 2) b; 3) glass ceiling

# Putting It All Together
## Early Adulthood

**BELLA ARNOFF AND THEODORE CHOI** face many developmental issues typical of young adults. They have to consider the questions of health and aging, and the unspoken admission that they do not have all the time in the world. They have to look at their relationship and decide whether to take what society and nearly all their friends consider the next logical step: marriage. They have to face the question of children and career, and the possibility of giving up the luxury of being a two-earner family. They even have to reconsider Theodore's intention to continue his education. Fortunately they have each other to help deal with the stress of this weighty combination of questions and decisions—and a considerable developmental arsenal of useful skills and abilities.

## MODULE **7.1** Physical Development in Early Adulthood

- Bella and Theodore's bodies and senses are at their peak, with their physical development nearly complete. **(p. 311)**

- During this period, the couple will increasingly need to pay attention to diet and exercise. **(pp. 314–315)**

- Because they face so many important decisions, Bella and Theodore are prime candidates for stress. **(pp. 317–320)**

## MODULE **7.2** Cognitive Development in Early Adulthood

- Bella and Theodore are in Schaie's achieving stage, confronting major life issues, including career and marriage. **(p. 324)**

- They are able to apply postformal thought to the complex issues they face. **(pp. 323–324)**

- Dealing with major life events, while causing stress, may also foster cognitive growth in both of them. **(p. 328)**

- Theodore's desire to return to college is not unusual today, when colleges are serving a diversity of students, including many older students. **(pp. 329–331)**

## What would a HEALTH CARE PROVIDER do?

- Given that Bella and Theodore are young, in good health, and physically fit, what strategies would you advise them to pursue to stay that way?

  **HINT** Review pages 310–314.

  *What's your response?*

## What would a CAREER COUNSELOR do?

- Assuming Bella and Theodore decide to have children, what advice would you give them about handling the major expenses they face and the impact of children on their careers? Would you advise one of them to put his or her career on hold and pursue childrearing full-time? If so, how would you counsel them to decide which career should be put on hold?

  **HINT** Review pages 349–351.

  *What's your response?*

## What would YOU do?

- If you were a friend of Bella and Theodore, what factors would you advise them to consider as they contemplate moving from cohabitation to marriage? Would your advice be the same if only Bella or Theodore asked you?

  **HINT** Review pages 346–349.

  *What's your response?*

## What would an EDUCATOR do?

- A friend of Theodore's has told him that he would be "a fish out of water" if he went back to graduate school such a long time after getting his undergraduate degree. Do you agree? Would you advise Theodore to pursue his graduate school studies right away, before he gets too old, or to wait until his life settles down?

  **HINT** Review pages 329–332.

  *What's your response?*

---

MODULE **7.3** Social and Personality Development in Early Adulthood

- Bella and Theodore are at a time when love relationships and friendship are of major importance. **(p. 339)**
- The couple are likely to be experiencing a combination of intimacy, passion, and decision/commitment. **(pp. 341–342)**
- Bella and Theodore have been cohabiting and are now exploring marriage as a relationship option. **(p. 347)**
- Bella and Theodore are not unusual in deciding about marriage and children—decisions with major implications for the relationship. **(pp. 348–351)**
- The couple must also decide how to handle the shift from two careers to one, at least temporarily—a decision that is far more than financial. **(p. 350)**

**✳ Explore** on mydevelopmentlab.com

To read how a real health-care provider, career counselor, and educator responded to these questions, log onto MyDevelopmentLab.com

*Do you agree or disagree with their response? Why? What concepts that you've read about back up their opinion?*

# Middle Adulthood

W hen she packed off her youngest child to college last year, Jan Hughes divorced her husband, sold her house, and headed west to Berkeley, California. "There wasn't any emotional connection. We were just going through the motions," Jan, age 48, says of her relationship with her ex-husband.

Hughes left her job at a large architectural firm. "I've got my own business now. I'm growing it at a pace that's comfortable for me," she says. "At my old firm, I was expected to take whatever projects were handed to me. Now, I choose the jobs that interest me."

It was hard, she admits, to say good-bye to her East Coast friends, people with whom she'd shared the highs and lows of raising a family. "But my sister lives in San Francisco, and my best friend from college is in Monterey. I've got the seeds of a social network out here," she says.

The move to California has also enabled Jan to indulge year round in her favorite exercise—bicycling. She joined a cycling club where the median age is 45.

**MODULE 8.1** Physical Development in Middle Adulthood

## Do men experience the equivalent of menopause? see page 362

**MODULE 8.2** Cognitive Development in Middle Adulthood

## Does intelligence decline in adulthood? see page 377

"We're in training for a trip up the coast from Baja to Vancouver. Some days my thighs ache outrageously," she says, laughing, "but I'm healthy as an ox and the workouts feel great."

Cycling has brought other rewards. Three months ago, an attorney who, like Jan, was new to the area joined the club. "Mike and I hit it off right away," Jan says. "We began dating, and realized we have a lot in common. We both love opera, modern art, restoring old furniture, and French cooking." The sex, too, is amazing, she says. Without the distractions of family and the demands of a high-pressure firm, Jan is rediscovering what romance is all about.

Does she miss her old life? "I get nostalgic for New England Christmases, the kind we had when the kids were little, and I miss the women from my book club," Jan admits. "But it hit me in my mid-40s that once my kids left home, I probably had another half of my life ahead. In the first 40 years, I kind of figured out what I liked and didn't like, what I wanted and didn't want. Now, I've put all that together and created a life that allows me to do what I love."

**Middle adulthood is a time of significant transitions.** Grown children leave home. People change the way they view their career. Sometimes they change careers entirely. Marriages undergo reevaluation. Often, couples find this a period of strengthened ties as the "empty nest" leaves them free for uninterrupted intimacy. But sometimes they divorce, as Jan and her husband did. Middle age

## MODULE **8.3** Social and Personality Development in Middle Adulthood

# The midlife crisis: reality or myth? see page 384

## MyDevelopmentLab

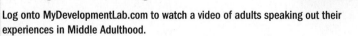

# Many adults in this stage of life are going through the same changes that Leigh is.

Log onto MyDevelopmentLab.com to watch a video of adults speaking out their experiences in Middle Adulthood.

is also a period of deepening roots. Family and friends ascend in importance as career ambitions begin to take a backseat. And there is more time for leisure activities.

In this chapter, we first look at the physical changes of middle adulthood and how people cope with them. Then we consider sexuality and menopause, and debate the use of hormone replacement drugs for women. We also look at health issues, especially heart disease and cancer, which become increasingly of concern in midlife.

Next we consider the changing intellectual abilities of middle-aged adults, and ask the question: Does intelligence decline over time? We investigate various types of intelligence and look at how each is affected by the aging process. We also look at memory. Does it decline in middle age, and what are some strategies for strengthening recall?

Finally, we look at social development and examine what changes and what remains stable over time in an adult's personality. We consider the evidence for the so-called midlife crisis and discuss how family relationships change in the face of changed circumstances. We end by considering work and leisure in middle age, examining how people are spending their increased leisure time.

## MODULE 8.1 Physical Development in Middle Adulthood

# Faster, Higher, Older

*Since 2005, Matt Carpenter has won 13 long-distance foot races, including one of 50 miles. His specialty is high-altitude running. He holds the course record at the Pikes Peak Marathon, a race that involves a 20-mile climb to a peak more than 14,000 feet above sea level. In 2005, he broke the course record at the Leadville Trail 100, a 100-mile race that ascends as high as 12,600 feet, by more than 93 minutes.*

*Matt is 44 years old.*

*Matt's running success comes at a price. He trains every day, alternating runs of more than three hours with ones of an hour and a half. Yet despite his age and the hard work required, Matt shows no signs of giving up competitive running. The motto he gives on his Web site: "Go out hard, when it hurts speed up!"* (Brick, 2009)

Matt Carpenter's success at high-altitude running is indicative of a revolution that is occurring in terms of the physical activity of people in middle adulthood. People reaching the midcentury mark are joining health clubs in record numbers, seeking to remain healthy and agile as they age.

It is in middle adulthood, roughly the period from age 40 to 65, that people often first notice and feel the effects of aging. Their bodies and, to some extent, their cognitive abilities begin to change in unwelcome ways. Looking at the physical, cognitive, and social changes of midlife, however, we see this is also a time when many people reach the height of their capabilities, when they are engaged in shaping their lives as never before.

We begin the module by considering physical development. We consider changes in height, weight, and strength, and discuss the subtle declines in various senses.

We also look at sexuality in middle adulthood. We examine the effects of change in hormone production for both men and women—particularly, menopause—and the various therapies available to ease this transition. We consider, too, the role attitude plays.

We then examine both health and illness in midlife. We consider the impact of stress, and pay special attention to two major health problems, heart disease and cancer.

# Physical Development

## L01 What physical changes affect people in middle adulthood?

*Soon after turning 40, Sharon Boker-Tov noticed that it took longer to bounce back from minor illnesses such as colds and the flu. Then she noticed changes in her eyesight: She needed more light to read fine print, and she had to adjust how far she held newspapers from her face in order to read them easily. Finally, she couldn't deny that the gray strands in her hair, which had first appeared in her late 20s, were becoming a virtual forest.*

## Physical Transitions: The Gradual Change in the Body's Capabilities

In middle adulthood, people become aware of the gradual changes in their bodies that aging brings. Some of these changes are the result of senescence, or naturally occurring declines. Other changes, however, are related to lifestyle choices, such as diet, exercise, smoking, and alcohol or drug use. As we'll see, lifestyle choices can have a major impact on people's physical, and even cognitive, fitness in midlife.

Although physical changes occur throughout life, these changes take on new significance in midlife, particularly in Western cultures that highly value a youthful appearance. The psychological significance of aging may far exceed the relatively minor and gradual changes a person experiences. Sharon Boker-Tov had gray hairs in her 20s, but in her 40s they multiplied to an extent she could not ignore. She was no longer young.

People's emotional reactions to midlife's physical changes depend in part on their self-concepts. When self-image is tied closely to one's physical attributes—as it often is for those who are very athletic or are physically quite attractive—middle adulthood can be particularly difficult. The changes the mirror reveals signal aging and mortality as well as a loss of physical attractiveness.

Physical appearance often plays an especially significant role in how women see themselves. This is particularly true in Western cultures, where women face strong societal pressures to retain a youthful look. Society applies a double standard to men and women regarding appearance: Older women tend to be viewed in unflattering terms, while older men are frequently seen as attractively "mature" (Andreoni & Petrie, 2008; Pruis & Janowsky, 2010).

## Height, Weight, and Strength: The Benchmarks of Change

Most people reach their maximum height in their 20s and remain close to that height until around age 55. People then begin a "settling" process in which the bones attached to the spinal column become less dense. Although the loss of height is very slow, women average a 2-inch decline and men a 1-inch decline over the rest of the life span (Rossman, 1977; Bennani et al., 2009).

Women are more prone to this decline because they are at greater risk of osteoporosis. **Osteoporosis,** a condition in which the bones become brittle, fragile, and thin, is often caused by a lack of calcium in the diet. Although it has a genetic component, osteoporosis is one aspect of aging that can be affected by lifestyle choices. Women—and men—can reduce the risk of osteoporosis by eating a calcium-rich diet (calcium is found in milk, yogurt, cheese, and other dairy products) and by exercising regularly (Alvarez-Leon, Roman-Vinas, & Serra-Majem, 2006; Prentice et al., 2006; Swaim, Barner, & Brown, 2008).

Body fat tends to increase in middle adulthood. Even those who have always been slim may begin to gain weight. Because height is not increasing, and actually may be declining, these gains increase the incidence of obesity. This weight gain can often be avoided. Lifestyle

**osteoporosis** a condition in which the bones become brittle, fragile, and thin, often brought about by a lack of calcium in the diet

choices play a major role. People who exercise regularly tend to avoid obesity, as do those who live in cultures where life is more active than it is in many Western cultures.

Declines in strength accompany height and weight changes. Strength gradually decreases, particularly in the back and leg muscles. By age 60, people average a 10 percent loss of their maximum strength. Still, such a loss is relatively minor, and most people are easily able to compensate for it (Spence, 1989). Again, lifestyle choices matter. Regular exercise tends to make people feel stronger and more able to compensate for any losses.

## The Senses: The Sights and Sounds of Middle Age

The vision changes Sharon Boker-Tov experienced are so common that reading glasses and bifocals have become a stereotypical emblem of middle age. Like Sharon, most people notice changes in the sensitivity, not only of their eyes, but also of other sense organs. All the organs seem to shift at about the same rate, but the changes are particularly marked in vision and hearing.

*Vision.* Starting at around age 40, *visual acuity*—the ability to discern fine spatial detail in both close and distant objects—begins to decline. The shape of the eye's lens changes and its elasticity deteriorates, which makes it harder to focus images sharply onto the retina. The lens becomes less transparent, so less light passes through the eye (DiGiovanna, 1994; Yan, Li, & Liao, 2010)

A nearly universal change in midlife is the loss of near vision, called **presbyopia.** Even people who have never needed glasses or contact lenses find themselves holding print at an increasing distance in order to bring it into focus. Eventually, they need reading glasses. For those who were already nearsighted, presbyopia may require bifocals or two sets of glasses (Kalsi, Heron, & Charman, 2001; Koopmans & Kooijman, 2006).

Midlife brings other vision changes. Depth perception, distance perception, and the ability to see in three dimensions all decline. The loss of elasticity in the lens also impairs people's ability to adapt to darkness, making it more difficult to navigate a dark room (Artal et al., 1993; Spear, 1993).

Although normal aging brings changes in vision, in some cases disease is involved. One of the most frequent eye problems is glaucoma, which may, if left untreated, lead to blindness. **Glaucoma** occurs when pressure in the fluid of the eye increases, either because the fluid cannot drain properly or because too much is produced. Around 1 to 2 percent of people over age 40 are afflicted, and African Americans are particularly susceptible (Wilson, 1989).

Initially, the increased pressure may constrict the neurons involved in peripheral vision and lead to tunnel vision. Ultimately, the pressure can become so high that all nerve cells are constricted, which causes complete blindness. Fortunately, with early detection, glaucoma can be treated. Medication can reduce the pressure, as can surgery to restore normal drainage of eye fluid (Plosker & Keam, 2006; Lambiase et al., 2009).

*Hearing.* Hearing declines in acuity in midlife, though the changes tend to be less evident than those affecting vision.

Environmental factors cause some of the hearing losses. People who work near loud noises—such as airplane mechanics and construction workers—are more apt to suffer debilitating and permanent hearing loss.

Many changes are simply related to aging. Age brings a loss of *cilia*, or *hair cells*, in the inner ear, which transmit neural messages to the brain when vibrations bend them. Like the lens of the eye, the eardrum becomes less elastic with age, reducing sensitivity to sound (Wiley et al., 2005).

The ability to hear high-pitched, high-frequency sounds usually degrades first, a problem called **presbycusis.** About 12 percent of people between 45 and 65 suffer from presbycusis. Men are more prone to hearing loss than women, starting at around age 55. People with hearing problems may also have trouble identifying the direction and origin of a sound, a process called *sound localization* (Willott, Chisolm, & Lister, 2001; Veras & Mattos, 2007).

**presbyopia** a nearly universal change in eyesight during middle adulthood that results in some loss of near vision

**glaucoma** a condition in which pressure in the fluid of the eye increases, either because the fluid cannot drain properly or because too much fluid is produced

**presbycusis** loss of the ability to hear sounds of high frequency

Declines in hearing do not markedly affect most people in middle age. Many compensate for any losses relatively easily—by asking people to speak up, turning up the volume of a television set, or paying closer attention to what others are saying.

## Reaction Time: Not-So-Slowing Down

One common concern is that people slow down once they reach middle adulthood. Such a worry is not valid in most cases. Reaction time does increase (i.e., it takes longer to react to a stimulus), but usually the increase is mild and hardly noticeable. For instance, reaction time in responding to a loud noise increases by about 20 percent from age 20 to 60. Tasks requiring the coordination of various skills—such as driving a car—show less of an increase. Still, it takes more time to move the foot from the gas pedal to the brake when a driver faces an emergency situation. Changes in the speed at which the nervous system processes nerve impulses increases reaction time (Nobuyuki, 1997; Roggeveen, Prime, & Ward, 2007; Godefroy et al., 2010).

Despite increased reaction time, middle-aged drivers have fewer accidents than younger ones, partly because they tend to be more careful and take fewer risks. Moreover, older drivers' greater experience benefits them. The minor slowing of reaction time is compensated by their expertise (Marczinski, Milliken, & Nelson, 2003; Makishita & Matsunaga, 2008; Cantin et al., 2009).

Lifestyle choices can retard the slowing down process. An active exercise program counteracts the effects of aging, improving health, muscle strength, and endurance (see Figure 8-1). Developmentalists would agree: "Use it or lose it" (Conn et al., 2003).

## The advantages of exercise include

### Muscle System

Slower decline in energy molecules, muscle cell thickness, number of muscle cells, muscle thickness, muscle mass, muscle strength, blood supply, speed of movement, stamina

Slower increase in fat and fibers, reaction time, recovery time, development of muscle soreness

### Nervous System

Slower decline in processing impulses by the central nervous system

Slower increase in variations in speed of motor neuron impulses

### Circulatory System

Maintenance of lower levels of LDLs and higher HDL/cholesterol and HDL/LDL ratios

Decreased risk of high blood pressure, atherosclerosis, heart attack, stroke

### Skeletal System

Slower decline in bone minerals

Decreased risk of fractures and osteoporosis

### Ψ Psychological Benefits

Enhanced mood

Feelings of well-being

Reduces stress

**FIGURE 8-1  The Benefits of Exercise**
There are many benefits from maintaining a high level of physical activity throughout life.
Source: From "The Benefits of Exercise," from A. G. DiGiovanna, Human Aging: Biological Perspectives.

## REVIEW, CHECK, AND APPLY

### REVIEW

**LO1** What physical changes affect people in middle adulthood?

- People in middle adulthood experience gradual changes in physical characteristics and appearance.
- The acuity of the senses, particularly vision and hearing, and speed of reaction declines slightly during middle age.
- Weight gain—commonly referred to as "middle-age spread"—can be controlled through regular exercise and a healthy diet.

### CHECK YOURSELF

1. Starting around age 40, visual acuity or the ability to discern fine spatial detail in both close and distant objects begins to decline.
   - True
   - False
2. ______________ occurs when pressure of the fluid in the eye increases, either because the fluid cannot drain properly or because too much is produced.
3. Although general reaction time increases in middle age, reaction time involving complex tasks such as driving a car shows less of an increase.
   - True
   - False

### APPLYING LIFESPAN DEVELOPMENT

- Would you rather fly on an airplane with a middle-aged pilot or a young one? Why?

**Study** and **Review** on **MyDevelopmentLab.com**

Answers: 1) True; 2) Glaucoma; 3) True

# Sexuality in Middle Adulthood

**LEARNING OBJECTIVES**

**LO2 What changes occur in sexuality for midlife men and women?**

**LO3 Why is there controversy over hormone therapy for women?**

*At age 51, Elaine was really looking forward to her postmenopausal life. Her youngest child had just left home to study art, and she had recently reduced her work schedule to a comfortable 30 hours a week. She envisioned the year to come as an opportunity for a "second honeymoon" with her husband, Greg, with no need for contraceptives or fears of becoming pregnant.*

*Her imagined honeymoon quickly evaporated in a heat wave of hot flashes and night sweats. Though Elaine recognized these as normal symptoms of menopause, she was having to change her clothing three or more times a day. And she was having more headaches. Her doctor prescribed hormone therapy to replace the estrogen she was losing through menopause. As she was not a likely candidate for any of the drug's negative side effects, she took her doctor's recommendation. The hormone therapy eased her symptoms and revitalized her spirits. Four months later, she and Greg booked a month's romantic getaway in Greece.*

Sexuality continues to be a vital part of most couples' lives in middle adulthood.

Although interest in sex remains fairly high for many people in middle adulthood, as Elaine's story illustrates, the physical changes associated with aging, such as menopause for women, can throw a curve ball at romance. We will look at some of the factors that affect men's and women's sexuality in midlife, and the roles both attitude and prescription drugs can play in alleviating some of the problems commonly associated with this life stage.

## The Ongoing Sexuality of Middle Age

The frequency of sexual intercourse declines with age (see Figure 8-2), but sexual pleasure remains a vital part of most middle-aged adults' lives. About half of men and women age 45 to 59 report having sexual intercourse once a week or more. Sex also remains an important activity for middle-aged gay and lesbian couples (Michael et al., 1994; Gabbay & Wahler, 2002; Cain, Johannes, & Avis, 2003; Kimmel & Sang, 2003; Duplassie & Daniluk, 2007).

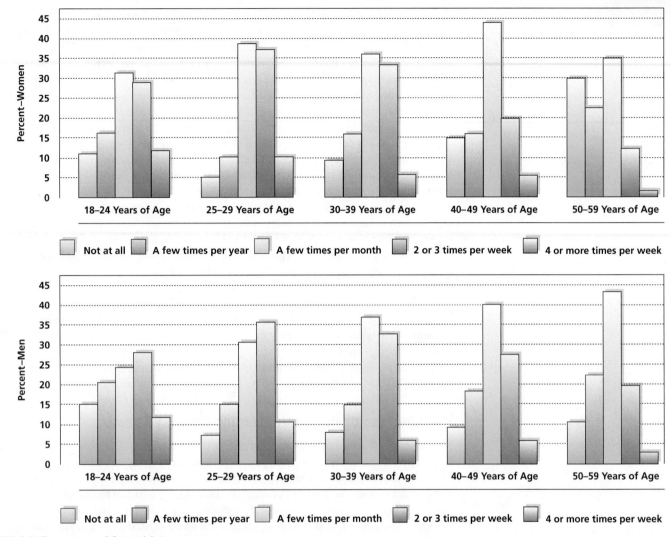

**FIGURE 8-2 Frequency of Sexual Intercourse**

As people age, the frequency of sexual intercourse declines.

Source: From SEX IN AMERICA by Robert T. Michael, John H. Gagnon, Edward O. Laumann, and Gina Kolata. Copyright © 1994 by CSG Enterprises, Inc., Edward O. Laumann, Robert T. Michael, and Gina Kolata. By permission of LITTLE, BROWN & COMPANY.

For many, midlife brings a sexual enjoyment and freedom that was missing earlier. With their children grown and away from home, married couples have more time for uninterrupted sex. Women who have gone through menopause no longer fear pregnancy or need to use birth control (Sherwin, 1991; Lamont, 1997).

Both men and women may face challenges to their sexuality in midlife. A man often needs more time to achieve an erection, and it takes longer after an orgasm to have another. The volume of fluid that is ejaculated declines, as does the production of *testosterone*, the male sex hormone (Hyde & Delameter, 2003).

For women, the vaginal walls thin and grow less elastic. The vagina begins to shrink and its entrance becomes compressed, which can make intercourse painful. For most women, though, the changes do not reduce sexual pleasure. Those women who do find intercourse less enjoyable can seek help from an increasing array of drugs, such as topical creams and testosterone patches, designed to increase sexual pleasure (Laumann, Paik, & Rosen, 1999; Freedman & Ellison, 2004; Nappi & Polatti, 2009).

***The Female Climacteric and Menopause.*** Women enter a period, around age 45, known as the climacteric that lasts for 15 to 20 years. The **female climacteric** marks the transition that ends the childbearing years.

**female climacteric** the period that marks the transition from being able to bear children to being unable to do so

**menopause** the cessation of menstruation

The most notable sign of this transition is menopause. **Menopause** is the cessation of menstruation. Menstrual periods begin to occur irregularly and less frequently during a 2-year period starting at around age 47 or 48, although this may begin as early as age 40 or as late as age 60. Menopause is completed when a woman passes a year without a menstrual period.

Menopause is important because it marks the end of a woman's natural fertility (although eggs implanted in a postmenopausal woman can produce a pregnancy). In addition, estrogen and progesterone levels—the female sex hormones—begin to drop (Schwenkhagen, 2007).

These changes in hormone production may produce a variety of symptoms, although this varies significantly for individuals. One of the most prevalent symptoms is "hot flashes," in which women experience a surge of heat above the waist. A woman may get red and begin to sweat when a hot flash occurs. Afterward, she may feel chilled. Some women have hot flashes several times a day; others, not at all.

During menopause, headaches, feelings of dizziness, heart palpitations, and aching joints are relatively common, though not universal. In one survey, only half of the women reported having hot flashes, and only about one-tenth of all women experience severe distress during menopause. Many women—perhaps as many as half—have no significant symptoms at all (Hyde & DeLamater, 2003; Grady, 2006; Ishizuka, Kudo, & Tango, 2008).

For many women, menopause symptoms may begin a decade before menopause actually occurs. *Perimenopause* describes this period prior to menopause when hormone production begins to change. It is marked by sometimes radical fluctuations in hormone levels, resulting in some of the same symptoms found in menopause (Winterich, 2003; Shea, 2006; Shuster et al., 2010).

For some women, the symptoms of perimenopause and menopause are considerable. Treating these problems, though, can be challenging, as we consider next.

## The Dilemma of Hormone Therapy: No Easy Answer

*Not long ago, a 40-something friend of ours stopped at a convenience store to pick up a sports drink for her 13-year-old son. As she was about to pay, she felt a sensation of intense heat throughout her body and became nauseated and dizzy. The alarmed cashier asked if she needed help. Our friend shook her head and quickly made her way outside. But when she and her son got back in the car, she panicked and told him to call 911 on her cell phone because she was sure she was having a heart attack. Within minutes, she heard sirens coming closer. It was only then, as the heat dissipated and she began to sweat, that our friend realized what all these symptoms meant. She'd had her first hot flash!* (Wingert & Kantrowitz, 2007, p. 38)

A decade ago, physicians would have had a straightforward remedy for hot flashes and other uncomfortable symptoms caused by the onset of menopause: They would have prescribed regular doses of a hormone replacement drug.

For millions of women who experienced similar difficulties, it was a solution that worked. In *hormone therapy (HT),* estrogen and progesterone are administered to alleviate the worst of the symptoms experienced by menopausal women. HT clearly reduces a variety of problems, such as hot flashes and loss of skin elasticity. In addition, HT may reduce coronary heart disease by changing the ratio of "good" cholesterol to "bad" cholesterol. HT also decreases the thinning of the bones related to osteoporosis, which, as we discussed, becomes a problem for many people in late adulthood (Palan et al., 2005; McCauley, 2007; Alexandersen, Karsdal, & Christiansen, 2009).

Furthermore, some studies show that HT is associated with reduced risks of stroke and colon cancer. Estrogen may improve memory and cognitive performance in healthy women, and reduce depression. Finally, increased estrogen may lead to a greater sex drive (Schwenkhagen, 2007; Cumming et al., 2009; Garcia-Portilla, 2009).

Although hormone therapy may sound like a cure-all, in fact since it became popular in the early 1990s, it has been well understood that there were risks involved. For instance, it seemed to increase the risk of breast cancer and blood clots. The thinking was, though, that the benefits of HT outweighed the risks. All that changed after 2002, when a large study conducted by the Women's Health Initiative determined that the long-term risks of HT outweighed the benefits. Women taking a combination of estrogen and progesterone were found to be at higher risk for breast cancer, stroke, pulmonary embolism, and heart disease. Increased risk of stroke and pulmonary embolism were later found to be associated with estrogen-alone therapy (Lobo, 2009).

The results of the Women's Health Initiative study led to a profound rethinking of the benefits of HT, calling into question the wisdom that HT could protect postmenopausal women against chronic disease. Many women stopped taking hormone replacement drugs, choosing instead to use alternative herbal and dietary therapies for menopausal symptoms; unfortunately, the most popular of these remedies have proven to be no more effective than a placebo (Ness, Aronow, & Beck, 2006; Newton et al., 2006; Chelebowski et al., 2009).

The sharp decline among menopausal women using HT is probably an overreaction, however. The most recent thinking among medical experts is that it's not a simple all-or-nothing proposition; some women are simply better candidates for HT than others. While HT seems to be less appropriate for older, postmenopausal women (such as those who participated in the Women's Health Initiative study) because of the increased risk of coronary heart disease and other health complications, younger women who are at the onset of menopause and experiencing severe symptoms might still benefit from the therapy, at least on a short-term basis (Plonczynski & Plonczynski, 2007; Rossouw et al., 2007; Lewis, 2009).

Ultimately, HT presents a risk, although one most physicians believe is worth taking. Women nearing menopause need to read literature on the topic, consult their physicians, and ultimately come to an informed decision about how to proceed.

### *The Psychological Consequences of Menopause.*

Traditionally, many people, including experts, believed that menopause was linked directly to depression, anxiety, crying spells, lack of concentration, and irritability. Some researchers estimated that as many as 10 percent of menopausal women suffered severe depression. It was assumed that the physiological changes of menopause caused such problems (Schmidt & Rubinow, 1991; Soares & Frey, 2010).

Today, most researchers take a different view, regarding menopause as a normal part of aging that does not, by itself, produce psychological symptoms. Some women do experience psychological difficulties, but they do so at other times in life as well (Dell & Stewart, 2000; Matthews et al., 2000; Freeman, Sammel, & Liu, 2004; Somerset et al., 2006; Wroolie & Holcomb, 2010).

Research shows that a woman's expectations can significantly affect her experience of menopause. Women who expect to have difficulties are more likely to attribute every physical symptom and emotional swing to menopause, while those with more positive attitudes are less apt to do so. A woman's attribution of physical symptoms, then, may affect her perception of menopause—and thus her actual experience of the period (Dell & Stewart, 2000; Breheny & Stephens, 2003; Bauld & Brown, 2009).

⊙ **From the perspective of a health care provider:** What cultural factors in the United States might contribute to a woman's negative experience of menopause? How?

### *The Male Climacteric.*

Do men experience the equivalent of menopause? Not really. Lacking anything akin to menstruation, they cannot experience its discontinuation. But men do experience changes in midlife that are referred to as the male climacteric. The **male climacteric** is the period of physical changes in the reproductive system (which may be accompanied by psychological changes) that occurs late in midlife, typically in a man's 50s.

Because the changes are gradual, it is hard to pinpoint the exact period of the male climacteric. For instance, despite declines in testosterone levels and sperm count, men are able to father children throughout middle age. And it is no easier in men than in women to attribute psychological symptoms to subtle physiological changes.

One physical change that occurs frequently is enlargement of the *prostate gland.* By age 40, about 10 percent of men have enlarged prostates, and the percentage increases to half of all men by the age of 80. Enlargement of the prostate produces problems with urination, including difficulty starting urination or a need to urinate frequently at night.

Sexual problems also increase as men age. In particular, *erectile dysfunction,* in which men are unable to achieve or maintain an erection, becomes more common. Drugs such as Viagra,

> **male climacteric** the period of physical and psychological change relating to the male reproductive system that occurs during late middle age

Levitra, and Cialis, as well as patches that deliver doses of testosterone, often prove an effective treatment (Kim & Park, 2006; Abdo et al., 2008).

Men, like women, undergo psychological development in middle adulthood, but the extent to which psychological changes—discussed in the next module—are related to reproductive or other physical changes remains an open question.

## REVIEW, CHECK, AND APPLY

### REVIEW

**LO2** What changes occur in sexuality for midlife men and women?

- Sexuality in middle adulthood changes slightly, but couples, freed from childbearing and parenting, can enjoy a new level of intimacy and pleasure.

- Physical changes affecting sexuality occur in both genders. Both the female climacteric, which includes menopause, and the male climacteric seem to have physical and perhaps psychological symptoms.

**LO3** Why is there controversy over hormone therapy for women?

- While some research has found that long-term risks of hormone therapy, including breast cancer, stroke, and heart disease, outweigh the benefits, current thinking among medical experts is that some women are better candidates for HT than others.

### CHECK YOURSELF

1. The period of time that marks a woman's transition from being able to bear children to not being able to do so is also known as the

   _____.

2. In hormone therapy, _____ and progesterone are administered to alleviate the worst of the symptoms experienced by menopausal women.

3. Roger is a middle-aged man who has started having difficulty with urinating. Sometimes he has difficulty starting to urinate. Other times he needs to urinate frequently at night. One of the first things his doctor will check is the functioning of his:

   **a.** liver.

   **b.** gall bladder.

   **c.** testicles.

   **d.** prostate.

### APPLYING LIFESPAN DEVELOPMENT

- How do you think society's view of women as losing their sexual allure in middle age affects women's physical and psychological experience of menopause?

✓●⌐**Study** and **Review** on
**MyDevelopmentLab.com**

Answers: 1) female climacteric; 2) estrogen; 3) d

# Health

**LEARNING OBJECTIVES**

**LO4** Is midlife a time of health or disease for men and women?

**LO5** Who is likely to get coronary disease?

**LO6** What causes cancer, and what tools are available to diagnose and treat it?

*It was a normal exercise session for Jerome Yanger. Up at 5:30 a.m., he climbed onto his exercise bike and began vigorously peddling, hoping to meet, and exceed, his average speed of 14 miles per hour. Stationed in front of the television, he used the remote control to tune to the morning business news. Occasionally glancing up at the television, he began reading a report he had begun the night before, silently cursing at some of the poor sales figures he was seeing. By the time his half-hour of exercise was over, he had finished the report, signed a few letters his administrative assistant had typed for him, and left two voice-mail messages for some colleagues.*

Most of us would be ready for a nap after such a packed half-hour. For Jerome Yanger, however, it was routine: He always tried to multitask, thinking it more efficient. Developmentalists might see it as symptomatic of a behavior style that puts Jerome at risk for coronary heart disease.

Although most people are healthy in middle adulthood, they also grow increasingly susceptible to many health problems. We will look at some typical midlife health issues, focusing on coronary heart disease and cancer.

# Wellness and Illness: The Ups and Downs of Middle Adulthood

Health concerns become increasingly important to people in middle age. Surveys asking what worries adults show health—as well as safety and money—to be an issue of concern. More than half of adults say they are either "afraid" or "very afraid" of having cancer (see Figure 8-3).

For most people, however, midlife is a period of health. According to census figures, the vast majority of middle-aged adults report no chronic health difficulties and face no limitations on their activities.

In fact, in some ways health is better in middle adulthood than in earlier periods of life. People ages 45 to 65 are less likely than younger adults to experience infections, allergies, respiratory diseases, and digestive problems. They may contract fewer of these diseases now because they have already experienced them and built up immunities (Sterns, Barrett, & Alexander, 1985).

Certain chronic diseases do begin to appear in middle adulthood. Arthritis typically begins after age 40, and diabetes is most likely to occur between ages 50 and 60, particularly in those who are overweight. Hypertension (high blood pressure) is one of the most frequent chronic disorders. Often called the "silent killer" because it is symptomless, hypertension, if left untreated, greatly increases the risk of strokes and heart disease. For such reasons, a variety of preventive and diagnostic medical tests are routinely recommended for adults during middle adulthood (Walters & Rye, 2009) (see Table 8-1).

The onset of chronic diseases in middle age boosts the death rate above that of earlier periods. Still, death remains rare: Only three out of every hundred 40-year-olds are expected to die before age 50, and eight out of every hundred 50-year-olds are expected to die before age 60. And the death rate for people between 40 and 60 has declined dramatically over the past 50 years. It now stands at just half of what it was in the 1940s. There also are cultural variations in health, as we consider next (Smedley & Syme, 2000).

Health becomes increasingly of concern during middle adulthood.

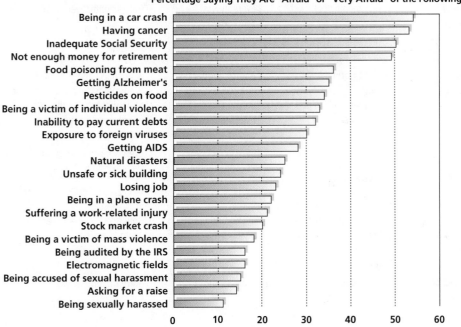

**Percentage Saying They Are "Afraid" or "Very Afraid" of the Following:**

- Being in a car crash
- Having cancer
- Inadequate Social Security
- Not enough money for retirement
- Food poisoning from meat
- Getting Alzheimer's
- Pesticides on food
- Being a victim of individual violence
- Inability to pay current debts
- Exposure to foreign viruses
- Getting AIDS
- Natural disasters
- Unsafe or sick building
- Losing job
- Being in a plane crash
- Suffering a work-related injury
- Stock market crash
- Being a victim of mass violence
- Being audited by the IRS
- Electromagnetic fields
- Being accused of sexual harassment
- Asking for a raise
- Being sexually harassed

0   10   20   30   40   50   60

**FIGURE 8-3 Worries of Adulthood**

As people enter middle adulthood, health and safety concerns become increasingly important, followed by financial worries.

Source: Originally appeared in the August 1997 issue of USA WEEKEND Magazine. Reprinted with permission.

## TABLE 8-1 ADULT PREVENTIVE HEALTH CARE SCREENING RECOMMENDATIONS

These are general guidelines for healthy adults who have no symptoms of disease.

| Screening | Description | Ages 40–49 | Ages 50–59 | Age 60+ |
|---|---|---|---|---|
| | | **ALL ADULTS** | | |
| Blood Pressure | Used to detect hypertension, which can lead to heart attack, stroke, or kidney disease. | Every 2 years. | Every 2 years. | Every 2 years, every year if family history of hypertension. |
| Cholestorol—Total/HDL | Used to detect high cholesterol levels, which increase risk of heart disease. | All adults should receive total cholesterol screening, HDL cholesterol, LDL cholesterol, and triglycerides AT LEAST ONCE. Cardiac risk factors and lipoprotein results will determine frequency of follow-up by your health care provider. | | |
| Eye Examination | Used to determine if glasses are required and to check for eye disease. | Every 2–4 years. Diabetics—Every year. | Every 2–4 years. Diabetics—Every year. | Every 2–4 years. At age 65 and over, every 1–2 years. Diabetics—Every year. |
| Flexible Sigmoidoscopy or Double Contrast Barium Enema or Colonoscopy | A procedure using a scope or x-ray to detect cancer of the colon and rectum. | – | Baseline at age 50. Every 3–5 years after initial test. | Every 3–5 years. Age to stop depends on health. Follow-up normal colonoscopy in 8–10 yrs. |
| Fecal Occult Blood Screening | Detects unseen blood in stool, which is early warning sign for colon cancer. | – | Every year. | Every year. |
| Rectal Exam (Digital) | Examination of prostate or ovaries to detect cancer. | – | Every year. | Every year. |
| Urinalysis Screening | Examination to detect presence of excess protein in urine. | Every 5 years. | Every 5 years. | Every 3–5 years. |
| Immunizations (Shots) Tetanus | Protection against infection after injury. | Every 10 years. | Every 10 years. | Every 10 years. |
| Influenza (Flu) | Protection against the influenza virus. | Any person with chronic medical conditions such as heart, lung, kidney disease, diabetes. | Annually, age 50 and over. | Annually, age 65 and over. |
| Pneumococcal | Protection against pneumonia. | | | At age 65, then every 6 years. |
| | | **ADDITIONAL GUIDELINES FOR WOMEN** | | |
| Breast Self-Exam/Breast Exam by Provider | Examination to detect changes in breast that may indicate cancer. | Every month/Every year. | Every month/ Every year. | Every month/Every year. |
| Mammogram | Low-dose x-ray used to locate tumors for early detection of breast cancer. | Every year. | Every year. | Every year. |
| Pap Smear | Test that takes small sample of cells to detect cervical cancer or precancer cells. | After 3 normal tests in a row, screen every 2–3 years unless at special risk. | After 3 normal tests in a row, screen every 2–3 years unless at special risk. | Women 70 and older with 3 normal tests in a row and no abnormal tests in the 10 years prior to age 70 may cease having Pap test. |
| Pelvic Exam | Examination to detect pelvic abnormality. | Every year (if ovaries remain after hysterectomy). | Every year (if ovaries remain after hysterectomy). | Every year (if ovaries remain after hysterectomy). |
| | | **ADDITIONAL GUIDELINES FOR MEN** | | |
| Prostate Specific Antigen | Blood test used to detect cancer of the prostate gland. | Positive family history of cancer—Every year (African Americans: Every year). | Every year upon doctor's advice. | Until age 75, every year upon doctor's advice. |
| Testicular Self-Exam | Examination to detect changes in testicles that may indicate cancer. | Every month. | Every month. | Every month. |

Source: Adapted from Ochsner Clinic Foundation, 2003. Reprinted with permission.

## *Cultural Dimensions*

### Individual Variation in Health: Ethnic and Gender Differences

Overall figures for the health of middle-aged adults mask vast individual differences. While most people are healthy, some are beset by a variety of ailments. Genetics play a role. For instance, hypertension often runs in families.

Social and environmental factors also affect health. For instance, the death rate for middle-aged African Americans in the United States is twice the rate for Caucasians. Why should this be true?

Socioeconomic status (SES) is a significant factor. For Whites and African Americans of the same SES level, the death rate for African Americans is actually lower than for Whites. Members of lower-income families, however, are more likely to experience a disabling illness. There are many reasons for this. People in lower-SES households are more apt to work in dangerous occupations, such as mining or construction work. Lower-income people also often have inferior health care coverage. The crime rates and environmental pollutants are generally higher in lower-income neighborhoods. A higher incidence of accidents and health hazards, and thus a higher death rate, are linked to lower levels of income (Fingerhut & Makuc, 1992; Dahl & Birkelund, 1997).

Gender also makes a difference. Women's overall mortality rate is lower than men's—a trend that holds true from birth—but the incidence of illness among midlife women is higher than for men.

Women are more susceptible to minor, short-term illness and chronic, but non-life-threatening diseases such as migraine headaches, while men are more susceptible to serious illnesses such as heart disease. Fewer women smoke than men, which reduces their risk for cancer and heart disease; women drink less alcohol than men, which lowers the incidence of cirrhosis of the liver and auto accidents; and they work at less dangerous jobs (McDonald, 1999).

Another reason for the higher rate of illness in women may be that more medical research targets men and the disorders they suffer. The vast majority of medical research money goes to preventing life-threatening diseases faced mostly by men, rather than to chronic conditions such as heart disease that may cause disability and suffering, but not necessarily death. Typically, research on diseases that strike both men and women focuses on men as subjects rather than women. This bias is now being addressed in initiatives by the U.S. National Institutes of Health, but the historical pattern has been one of gender discrimination by a male-dominated research community (Vidaver et al., 2000).

### Stress in Middle Adulthood

Stress continues to have a significant impact on health, as it did in young adulthood, although the stressors may have changed. For example, parents may worry about their adolescent child's potential drug use rather than whether their toddler is ready to give up his pacifier.

No matter what events trigger stress, the results are similar. *Psychoneuroimmunologists,* who study the relationship between the brain, the immune system, and psychological factors, report that stress has three main consequences, summarized in Figure 8-4. First, stress has direct physiological effects, ranging from increased blood pressure and hormonal activity to decreased immune system response. Second, stress leads people to engage in unhealthy behaviors, such as cutting back on sleep, smoking, drinking, or taking other drugs. Finally, stress has indirect effects on health-related behavior. People under a lot of stress may be less likely to seek out good medical care, exercise, or to comply with medical advice (Suls & Wallston, 2003; Zellner et al., 2006; Dagher et al., 2009). All of these can lead to or affect serious health conditions, including heart disease.

### The A's and B's of Coronary Heart Disease: Linking Health and Personality

More men die in middle age from diseases relating to the heart and circulatory system than from any other cause. Women are less vulnerable, as we'll see, but they are not immune. Each year such diseases kill around 151,000 people under the age of 65, and they are responsible for more loss of work and disability days due to hospitalization than any other cause (American Heart Association, 2010).

***Risk Factors for Heart Disease.*** Although heart and circulatory diseases are a major problem, some people have a much lower risk than others. The death rate in some countries, such as Japan, is only a quarter of the rate in the United States. A few other countries have a considerably higher death rate. Why?

**Type A behavior pattern** behavior characterized by competitiveness, impatience, and a tendency toward frustration and hostility

**Type B behavior pattern** behavior characterized by noncompetitiveness, patience, and a lack of aggression

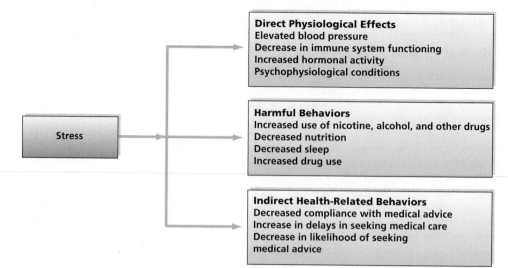

Stress

**Direct Physiological Effects**
Elevated blood pressure
Decrease in immune system functioning
Increased hormonal activity
Psychophysiological conditions

**Harmful Behaviors**
Increased use of nicotine, alcohol, and other drugs
Decreased nutrition
Decreased sleep
Increased drug use

**Indirect Health-Related Behaviors**
Decreased compliance with medical advice
Increase in delays in seeking medical care
Decrease in likelihood of seeking medical advice

**FIGURE 8-4 The Consequences of Stress**
Stress produces three major consequences: direct physiological effects, harmful behaviors, and indirect health-related behaviors.
Source: Adapted from Baum, 1994.

The answer is both genetics and environment. Some people seem genetically predisposed to heart disease. If a person's parents suffered from it, the likelihood is greater that she or he will too. Similarly, sex and age are risk factors: Men are more likely to suffer from heart disease, and the risk rises as people age.

Environment and lifestyle choices are also important. Cigarette smoking, a diet high in fats and cholesterol, and a lack of physical exercise all increase the risk of heart disease. Such factors may explain country-to-country variations in the rate of heart disease. For example, the death rate from heart disease in Japan is relatively low and may be due to differences in diet: The typical Japanese diet is much lower in fat than it is in the United States (Zhou et al., 2003; Wilcox, Castro, & King 2006; De Meersman & Stein, 2007).

Diet is not the only factor. Psychological factors—particularly how stress is perceived and experienced—appear to be related to heart disease. For instance, a set of personality characteristics, known as Type A behavior, appears to be a factor in the development of coronary heart disease.

The **Type A behavior pattern** is characterized by competitiveness, impatience, and a tendency toward frustration and hostility. Type A people are extremely ambitious and they engage in *polyphasic activities*—multiple activities carried out simultaneously. They are the true multitaskers whom you see talking on their phones while working on their laptop computers while riding the commuter train—and eating breakfast. Easily angered, they become both verbally and nonverbally hostile if prevented from reaching their goals.

In contrast, many people have virtually the opposite characteristics in what is known as the Type B behavior pattern. The **Type B behavior pattern** is characterized by noncompetitiveness, patience, and a lack of aggression. In contrast to Type A's, Type B's experience little sense of time urgency, and they are rarely hostile.

Most people are not purely Type A's or Type B's. In fact, these types represent the ends of a continuum. Most people fall somewhere in between. Still, the majority come close to one or the other of the two categories. These categories become important in midlife because research suggests the distinction is related to the risk of coronary heart disease. Type A men have twice the rate of coronary heart disease, a greater number of fatal heart attacks, and five times as many heart problems as Type B men (Strube, 1990; Wielgosz & Nolan, 2000).

It's important to note that not every component of the Type A behavior pattern is harmful. In fact, some evidence suggests that only certain components of Type A behavior are most involved in producing disease, and not the entire constellation of behaviors associated with the pattern. Specifically, it seems as if the hostility and anger components of Type A behavior are

In addition to being characterized as competitive, people with Type A personalities also tend to engage in polyphasic activities, or doing a number of things at once. Does a Type A personality deal with stress differently than a Type B personality?

the central link to coronary heart disease (Kahn, 2004; Eaker et al., 2004; Demaree & Everhart, 2004; Myrtek, 2007).

Although the relationship between at least some Type A behaviors and heart disease is clear, this does not mean that all middle-aged adults who can be characterized as Type A's are destined to suffer from coronary heart disease. For one thing, almost all the research conducted to date has focused on men, primarily because the incidence of coronary heart disease is much higher for males than for females. In addition, other types of negative emotions besides the hostility found in Type A behavior have been linked to heart disease. For example, psychologist Johan Denollet has identified behavior he calls *Type D*—for "distressed"—that is linked to coronary heart disease. He believes that insecurity, anxiety, and having a negative outlook put people at risk for heart attacks (Denollet, 2005; Schiffer et al., 2008; Pedersen et al., 2009; Mols & Denollet, 2010).

## The Threat of Cancer

Few diseases are as frightening as cancer, and many middle-aged adults view a cancer diagnosis as a death sentence. Although the reality is different—many forms of cancer respond well to medical treatment, and 40 percent of those diagnosed are still alive 5 years later—the disease raises many fears. And there is no denying that cancer is the second-leading cause of death in the United States (Smedley & Syme, 2000).

The precise trigger for cancer is still not known, but the process by which it spreads is clear. Certain cells in the body begin to multiply rapidly and uncontrollably. As they increase in number, these cells form tumors. Unimpeded, they draw nutrients from healthy cells and body tissue. Eventually, they destroy the body's ability to function.

Like heart disease, cancer is associated with a variety of genetic and environmental risk factors. Some cancers have clear genetic components. For example, a family history of breast cancer—the most common cause of cancer death among women—raises the risk for a woman.

Several environmental and behavioral factors are also related to the risk of cancer. Poor nutrition, smoking, alcohol use, exposure to sunlight, exposure to radiation, and particular occupational hazards (such as exposure to certain chemicals or asbestos) are all known to increase the chances of developing cancer.

After a diagnosis, several forms of treatment are possible, depending on the type of cancer. One treatment is *radiation therapy,* in which radiation targets the tumor in an attempt to destroy it. Patients undergoing *chemotherapy* ingest controlled doses of toxic substances meant to poison the tumor. Finally, surgery is used to remove the tumor (and often the surrounding tissue). The form of treatment is determined by how far the cancer has spread when it is first identified.

Because early detection improves a patient's chances, diagnostic techniques that help identify the first signs of cancer are of great importance. This is especially true in middle adulthood, when the risk of certain cancers increases.

Physicians urge that women do routine breast exams and men regularly check their testicles for signs of cancer. Cancer of the prostate gland, the most common type of cancer in men, can be detected by routine rectal exams and by a blood test that identifies prostate-specific antigen (PSA).

Mammograms provide internal scans of women's breasts to help identify early-stage cancer. However, at what age women should begin to routinely have the procedure has been controversial.

Women should routinely examine their breasts for signs of breast cancer.

## Routine Mammograms: At What Age Should Women Start?

*I eat right, exercise, breast fed my children, and buy organic when I can. I have never lived on a superfund site and I do not have cancer in my family line. The chance of me finding a lump in my breasts were—I thought—slim to none.*

*But 5 years ago, on a quiet Sunday morning at the start of spring in New England, everything I believed about my life changed forever. My husband and our two children, ages 4 and 1, were downstairs in the kitchen making breakfast. I was upstairs enjoying a much-needed hot shower. . . . As I let the water flow down my aching back, I started my usual self-breast exam. . . . I felt a lump.*

In some ways, this 38-year-old woman was lucky: she found her cancer early. Statistically, the earlier breast cancer is diagnosed, the better a woman's chances of survival. But just how to accomplish early identification has produced some degree of contention in the medical field. In particular, controversy surrounds the age at which *mammograms,* a kind of weak x-ray used to examine breast tissue, should be routinely administered to women.

Mammograms are among the best means of detecting breast cancer in its earliest stages. The technique allows physicians to identify tumors while they are still very small. Patients have time for treatment before the tumor grows and spreads to other parts of the body. Mammograms have the potential for saving many lives, and nearly all medical professionals suggest that at some point during middle adulthood women should routinely obtain them.

But at what age should women start having annual mammograms? The risk of breast cancer begins to grow at around the age of 30 and then becomes increasingly more likely. Ninety-five percent of new cases occur in women aged 40 and above (SEER, 2005).

Determining the age to begin routine screening mammograms is complicated by two considerations. First, there is the problem of *false positives,* instances in which the test suggests something is wrong when in fact there is no problem. Because the breast tissue of younger women is denser than that of older women, younger women are more likely to have false positives. In fact, some estimates suggest that as many as a third of all younger women who have repeated mammograms are likely to have a false positive that necessitates further testing or a biopsy. Furthermore, the opposite problem also may occur: *false negatives,* in which a mammogram does not detect indications of cancer (Wei et al., 2007; Destounis et al., 2009; Elmore et al., 2009).

In what proved to be a controversial proposal, the U.S. Preventive Services Task Force, a panel appointed by the government, recommended in 2009 that women in their 40s should *not* routinely have mammograms, and that women between the ages of 50 and 74 should have mammograms every two years, rather than annually. Their recommendation was based on a cost-benefit analysis showing that the risks of mammograms could be cut in half while still offering 80 percent of the benefits of annual mammograms (Nelson et al., 2009).

Their recommendation was immediately criticized by several major women's groups, along with the American Cancer Society and American College of Radiology. They argued that women aged 40 and above should receive annual screenings (Grady, 2009).

Ultimately, the determination of the timing of screenings is a highly personal one. Women should consult their health care providers and discuss the latest research regarding the frequency of mammograms. And for certain women, who have a history of breast cancer in their families or a mutation in a gene called BRCA, the evidence is clear that mammograms starting at age 40 are beneficial (Grady, 2009).

## REVIEW, CHECK, AND APPLY

### REVIEW

**LO4** Is midlife a time of health or disease for men and women?

- In general, middle adulthood is a period of good health, although susceptibility to chronic diseases, such as arthritis, diabetes, and hypertension, increases.

**LO5** Who is likely to get coronary disease?

- Heart disease is a risk for middle-aged adults. Both genetic and environmental factors contribute to heart disease, including the Type A behavior pattern.

**LO6** What causes cancer, and what tools are available to diagnose and treat it?

- The precise causes of cancer are still unknown, but the process by which it spreads is clear.

- Therapies such as radiation therapy, chemotherapy, and surgery can successfully treat cancer.

### CHECK YOURSELF

1. Insecurity, anxiety, and having a negative outlook put people at risk for heart attacks. This behavior is referred to as:

   a. Type D.

   b. Type B.

   c. Disassociative Identity Disorder.

   d. Type A.

2. Cancer is the _____ leading cause of death in the United States.

### APPLYING LIFESPAN DEVELOPMENT

- What social policies might be developed to lower the incidence of disabling illness among members of lower-socioeconomic groups?

✓●─[**Study** and **Review** on
**MyDevelopmentLab.com**

Answers: 1) a; 2) second

## MODULE 8.2 Cognitive Development in Middle Adulthood

# Playing Her Trump Card

*When Kate Dalton went back to school at the age of 46 to pursue a master's degree in education, she was the oldest student in her program by some 20 years—and the only one to carry the considerable responsibilities for a family, as well. Though Kate possessed a high level of energy and was in excellent health, she was long past the point in life where she could stay up all night writing lesson plans or researching a paper. And two decades had passed since she had sat in a lecture hall.*

*But Kate had three things in her favor. First, she had confidence. She knew exactly who she was and what she wanted from her advanced degree. Second, she knew her own strengths and weaknesses—how to play to the former and how to compensate for the latter. Third, and most significant, she had expertise in her field of study. Kate had been a parent for 15 years, and she had spent many hours in the classroom, helping teachers and taking on major school projects. She had also spent a year substitute teaching in schools to gain experience both in teaching and in classroom management. Her insights into children, their development and needs, not only earned her the highest rank in her program, she was hired on the spot in her second interview.*

Kate, like many people in midlife, took on the challenge of a new career. Not only did she have to learn and respond to a considerable amount of new material, but she had to compete against people half her age, both in the classroom and in the job search.

But Kate had something that younger people in her classes could not match: her experience and expertise. She also had the patience to allow herself extra time to learn new skills, many centered on the computer, which hadn't existed in student life the last time she was in college.

The second module of the chapter focuses on cognitive development in middle age. We look at the tricky question of whether intelligence declines during the period, and we consider the difficulty of answering the question fully. We also examine memory and how its capabilities change in middle adulthood.

# Cognitive Development

**LO7**  What happens to a person's intelligence in middle adulthood?

**LO8**  How does one attain expertise?

LEARNING OBJECTIVES

*It began innocently enough. Forty-five-year-old Bina Clingman couldn't remember whether she had mailed the letter that her husband had given her, and she wondered, briefly, whether this was a sign of aging. The next day, the question recurred when she spent 20 minutes looking for a phone number she knew she had written down on a piece of paper—somewhere. By the time she found it, she was surprised and even a little anxious. "Am I losing my memory?" she asked herself, feeling both annoyance and a degree of concern.*

Many people in their 40s feel more absentminded than they did 20 years earlier, and they have some concern about becoming less mentally able as they age. Common wisdom suggests that people lose some mental sharpness in midlife. But how accurate is this notion?

## Does Intelligence Decline in Adulthood?

For years, experts provided an unwavering response when asked whether intelligence declined in adulthood: Intelligence peaks at age 18, stays fairly steady until the mid-20s, and then gradually declines until the end of life.

Today, developmentalists view questions about changes in intelligence across the life span as more complicated—and they have come to different, and more complex, conclusions.

*The Difficulties in Answering the Question.* The conclusion that intelligence starts to diminish in the mid-20s was based on extensive research. *Cross-sectional studies*—which test people of different ages at the same point in time—clearly showed that older subjects were less likely to score well than younger subjects on traditional intelligence tests of the sort we discussed earlier.

But consider the drawbacks of cross-sectional research—in particular, the possibility that it may suffer from *cohort effects*. Recall that cohort effects are influences associated with growing up at a particular historical time that affect persons of a particular age. For instance, suppose that compared to younger subjects, the older people in a cross-sectional study had had less adequate educations, less stimulating jobs, or were less healthy. In that case, the lower IQ scores of the older group could not be attributed solely, or perhaps even partially, to differences in intelligence based on age. Because they do not control for cohort effects, cross-sectional studies may well *underestimate* intelligence in older subjects.

To overcome the cohort problems of cross-sectional studies, developmentalists began to use *longitudinal studies*, in which the same people are studied periodically over a span of time. These studies revealed a different developmental pattern for intelligence: Adults tended to show stable and even increasing intelligence test scores until their mid-30s, and in some cases up to their 50s. Then the scores began to decline (Bayley & Oden, 1955).

But let's consider the drawbacks of longitudinal studies, too. People taking an intelligence test repeatedly may perform better because they become familiar—and comfortable—with the testing situation. Similarly, through repeated exposure to the same test, they may begin to remember some of the test items. Consequently, practice effects may account for the superior performance of people on longitudinal measures of intelligence as opposed to cross-sectional measures (Salthouse, 2009).

It is also difficult for researchers using longitudinal studies to keep their samples intact. Participants may move away, decide they no longer want to participate, or become ill and die. Over time, the participants who remain may represent a healthier, more stable, and more psychologically positive group of people than those who are no longer part of the sample. If this is the case, longitudinal studies may *overestimate* intelligence in older subjects.

*Crystallized and Fluid Intelligence.* Drawing conclusions about age-related changes in intelligence is challenging. For instance, many IQ tests include sections based on physical performance, such as arranging a group of blocks. These sections are timed and scored on the

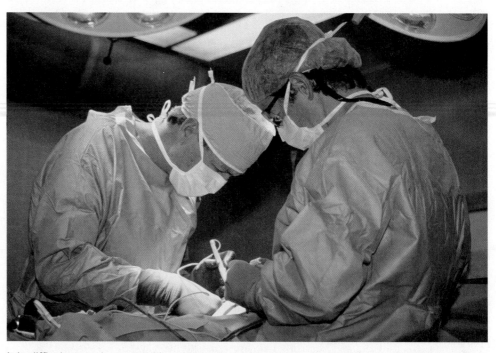

It is difficult to evaluate cognitive abilities in middle adulthood. While some types of mental abilities may begin to decline, crystallized intelligence holds steady and actually may increase.

basis of how quickly an item is completed. If older people take longer on physical tasks—recall that reaction time slows with age—then their poorer performance on IQ tests may result from physical rather than cognitive changes.

To complicate the issue further, many researchers believe there are two kinds of intelligence: fluid intelligence and crystallized intelligence. As we noted earlier, **fluid intelligence** reflects information processing capabilities, reasoning, and memory. To arrange a series of letters according to some rule or to memorize a set of numbers uses fluid intelligence. **Crystallized intelligence** is the information, skills, and strategies that people have accumulated through experience and that they can apply to solve problems. Someone who is solving a crossword puzzle or attempting to identify the murderer in a mystery story is using crystallized intelligence, relying on past experience as a resource.

Researchers once believed that fluid intelligence was largely determined by genetic factors, and crystallized intelligence by experiential, environmental factors. They later abandoned this distinction when they found that crystallized intelligence is determined in part by fluid intelligence. For instance, a person's ability to solve a crossword puzzle (which involves crystallized intelligence) relies on that person's proficiency with letters and patterns (a manifestation of fluid intelligence).

When developmentalists examined the two kinds of intelligence separately, they discovered there are two answers to the question of whether intelligence declines with age: yes and no. Yes, because fluid intelligence does decline with age; no, because crystallized intelligence holds steady and can actually improve (Salthouse, Atkinson, & Berish, 2003; Bugg et al., 2006; Salthouse, Pink, & Tucker-Drob, 2008; Deary, 2010; see Figure 8-5).

If we look at more specific types of intelligence, true age-related differences and developments begin to show up. According to developmental psychologist K. Warner Schaie, who has conducted extensive longitudinal research on adult intellectual development, we should consider many types of ability, such as spatial orientation, numeric ability, verbal ability, and so on, rather than the broad divisions of crystallized and fluid intelligence (Schaie, Willis, & Pennak, 2005).

Examined this way, the question of how intelligence changes in adulthood yields yet another, more specific, answer. Schaie has found that certain abilities, such as inductive reasoning, spatial orientation, perceptual speed, and verbal memory, begin to decline very gradually at around age 25 and continue to do so through old age. Numeric and verbal abilities show a different pattern. Numeric ability tends to increase until the mid-40s, is lower at age 60, and then remains steady. Verbal ability rises until the start of middle adulthood, around age 40, then stays fairly steady (Schaie et al., 2005).

> **fluid intelligence** reflects information processing capabilities, reasoning, and memory
>
> **crystallized intelligence** the accumulation of information, skills, and strategies that people have learned through experience and that they can apply in problem-solving situations

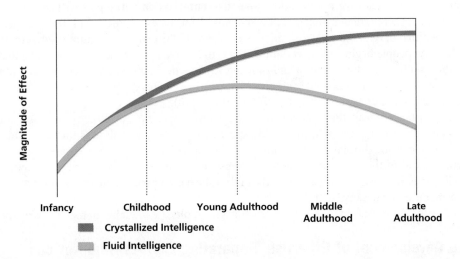

**FIGURE 8-5 Changes in Crystallized and Fluid Intelligence**
Although crystallized intelligence increases with age, fluid intelligence begins to decline in middle age. What are the implications for general competence in middle adulthood?
Source: From K. W. Schaie, "Longitudinal Studies of Adult Psychological Development," 1985. Copyright © Guilford Press. Reprinted with permission.

**selective optimization** the process by which people concentrate on particular skill areas to compensate for losses in other areas

**expertise** the acquisition of skill or knowledge in a particular area

One reason these changes occur is that brain functioning begins to change in middle adulthood. Researchers have found that 20 genes that are vital to learning, memory, and mental flexibility begin to function less efficiently as early as age 40 (Lu et al., 2004).

*Reframing the Issue: What Is the Source of Competence During Middle Adulthood?* It is during midlife that people come to hold some of the most important and powerful positions in society, despite gradual declines in certain cognitive abilities. How do we explain such continuing, even growing, competence?

Psychologist Timothy Salthouse (1990, 1994a; 2010) suggests there are four reasons why this discrepancy exists. First, it is possible that typical measures of cognitive skills tap a different type of cognition than what is required to be successful in certain occupations. Recall the earlier discussion of practical intelligence, in which we found that traditional IQ tests fail to measure cognitive abilities that are related to occupational success. Perhaps we would find no discrepancy between intelligence and cognitive abilities in midlife if we used measures of practical intelligence rather than traditional IQ tests to assess intelligence.

A second factor also relates to the measurement of IQ and occupational success. It is possible that the most successful middle-aged adults are not representative of midlife adults in general. It may be that only a small proportion of people are highly successful, and the rest, who experience only moderate or little success, have changed occupations, retired, or become sick and died. Highly successful people, then, may be an unrepresentative sample.

Also, the degree of cognitive ability required for professional success may simply not be that high. According to this argument, people can succeed professionally and still be on the decline in certain cognitive abilities. In other words, they have brains to spare.

Finally, it may be that older people are successful because they have developed specific kinds of expertise and particular competencies. Whereas IQ tests measure reactions to novel situations, occupational success may be influenced by very specific, well-practiced abilities. Consequently, middle-aged individuals may maintain and even expand the distinctive talents they need for professional accomplishment, despite a decline in overall intellectual skills. This explanation has generated research on expertise.

**From the perspective of an educator:** How do you think the apparent discrepancy between declining IQ scores and continuing cognitive competence in middle adulthood would affect the learning ability of middle adults who return to school?

For example, developmental psychologists Paul Baltes and Margaret Baltes have studied a strategy called selective optimization. **Selective optimization** is the process people use in concentrating on particular skill areas to compensate for losses in other areas. Baltes suggests that cognitive development during middle and later adulthood is a mixture of growth and decline. As people begin to lose certain abilities, they advance in other areas by strengthening their skills. In so doing, they avoid showing any practical deterioration. Overall cognitive competence, then, remains stable and may even improve (Baltes & Carstensen, 2003; Baltes & Freund, 2003; Ebner, Freund, & Baltes, 2006; Erber, 2010).

For instance, recall that reaction time lengthens as people age. Because reaction time is a component of typing skill, we would expect that typists would slow as they age. This is not the case. Though their reaction time is increasing, older typists compensate by looking further ahead in the material as they type. Similarly, a business executive may be slower to recall names, but he may have a mental file of deals he has completed and be able to forge new agreements easily because of it.

Selective optimization is one of several strategies adults use to maintain high performance.

## The Development of Expertise: Separating Experts from Novices

If you were ill and needed a diagnosis, would you rather visit a young physician fresh out of medical school, or a more experienced, middle-aged physician?

If you chose the older physician, you probably assumed that he or she would have more expertise. **Expertise** is the skill or knowledge acquired in a particular area. More focused than

People develop expertise as they devote attention and practice to a skill or subject area.

broad intelligence, expertise develops as people devote attention and practice to a subject or skill and, in so doing, gain experience. For example, physicians become better at diagnosing the symptoms of a medical problem as they gain experience. A person who does a lot of cooking comes to know how a recipe will taste if certain modifications are made.

What separates the experts from the less skilled? While beginners use formal procedures and rules, often following them very strictly, experts rely on experience and intuition, and they often bend the rules. Their experience allows them to process information automatically. Experts often have trouble articulating how they draw conclusions; their solutions just seem right to them—and *are* likely to be right. Brain imaging studies show that experts use different neural pathways than novices to solve problems (Grabner, Neubauer, & Stern, 2006).

Finally, experts develop better problem-solving strategies than nonexperts, and they're more flexible in their approach. Experience provides them with alternative solutions to the same problem, increasing the probability of success (Willis, 1996; Clark, 1998; Arts, Gijselaers, & Boshuizen, 2006; McGugin & Tanaka, 2010).

Not everyone develops an area of expertise in middle adulthood. Professional responsibilities, amount of leisure time, educational level, income, and marital status all affect the development of expertise.

## REVIEW, CHECK, AND APPLY

### REVIEW

**LO7** What happens to a person's intelligence in middle adulthood?

- The question of whether intelligence declines in middle adulthood is complicated by limitations in cross-sectional studies and longitudinal studies.

- Intelligence appears to be divided into components, some of which decline while others hold steady or even improve.

- In general, cognitive competence in middle adulthood holds fairly steady despite declines in some areas of intellectual functioning.

**LO8** How does one attain expertise?

- The skill or knowledge acquired in a particular area, expertise develops as people devote attention and practice to a subject or skill and, in so doing, gain experience.

### CHECK YOURSELF

1. According to_____ studies that test people of different ages at the same time, older subjects scored lower than younger subjects on traditional intelligence tests.

2. Because cross-sectional studies do not control for cohort effects, these research designs may underestimate intelligence in older subjects.

   - True
   - False

3. Over the years, one of the types of intelligence that increases with age is _____ intelligence, or the accumulation of information, skills, and strategies that people have learned through experience.

### APPLYING LIFESPAN DEVELOPMENT

- How might crystallized and fluid intelligence work together to help middle-aged people deal with novel situations and problems?

✓•—**Study** and **Review** on
**MyDevelopmentLab.com**

Answers: 1) d cross-sectional; 2) True; 3) crystallized

# Memory

**LO9** How does aging affect memory?

**LO10** How can memory be improved?

LEARNING OBJECTIVES

*Mary Donovan races around the kitchen and makes one last frantic search through her purse. "I must be losing my memory," she mutters. "I always leave my keys on the counter next to the toaster." It's not until her son David comes downstairs ready for hockey practice that Mary remembers she loaned him her car the day before. Sure enough, David produces the keys from the pocket of his varsity jacket. Relieved to have her keys in hand once more, Mary sighs. After all, she is 47. Such episodes are to be expected, she supposes.*

Like Bina Clingman, who was worried about forgetting letters and phone numbers, Mary probably believes that memory loss is common in middle age. However, if she is a typical midlife adult, her assessment may not be accurate. Research shows that most people exhibit minimal or no memory loss. Because of societal stereotypes, however, people may attribute their absentmindedness to aging, even though they have been that way all their lives. It is the *meaning* they give to their forgetfulness that changes, rather than their actual ability to remember (Chasteen et al., 2005; Hoessler & Chasteen, 2008; Hess, Hinson, & Hodges, 2009).

## Types of Memory

To understand the nature of memory changes, we must consider that memory is traditionally viewed as three sequential components: sensory memory, short-term memory (also called working memory), and long-term memory. *Sensory memory* is an initial, momentary storage of information. Information is recorded by the sensory system as a raw, meaningless stimulus. Next, information moves into *short-term memory*, which holds it for 15 to 25 seconds. If the information is rehearsed, it then moves into *long-term memory*, where it is stored on a relatively permanent basis.

Both sensory memory and short-term memory show virtually no weakening in middle age. Long-term memory, however, declines for some people. It appears this decline is not a fading or a complete loss of memory, but rather a less efficient registering and storing of information. Age also makes people less efficient at retrieving information. Even if the information was adequately stored in long-term memory, it may become more difficult to locate or isolate it (Salthouse, 2007; 2010).

Memory declines in middle age are relatively minor, and most can be compensated for by various cognitive strategies. Paying greater attention to material when it is first encountered can aid in its later recall. Your lost car keys may have more to do with your inattentiveness when you put them down than with a decline in memory.

Many middle adults find it hard to pay attention to certain things for some of the same reasons expertise develops. They are used to using memory shortcuts, *schemas*, to ease the burden of remembering the many things they experience each day.

***Memory Schemas.*** To recall information, people often use **schemas**, organized bodies of information stored in memory. Schemas represent the way the world is organized, allowing people to categorize and interpret new information. For example, if we have a schema for eating in a restaurant, we don't regard a meal in a new restaurant as a completely new experience. We know we will be seated at a table or counter and offered a menu from which to select food. Our schema for eating out tells us how to treat the server, what sorts of food to eat first, and that we should leave a tip.

People hold schemas for individuals (such as the particular behavior patterns of one's mother, wife, or child) as well as for categories of people (mail carriers, lawyers, or professors) and behaviors or events (dining in a restaurant or visiting the dentist). People's schemas organize their behavior and help them to interpret social events. A person who knows the schema for visiting the doctor will not be surprised when he is asked to undress.

Schemas also convey cultural information. Psychologists Susan Fiske and Shelley Taylor (1991) use an example of an old Native American folktale in which the hero participates with several companions in a battle and is shot by an arrow. He feels no pain. When he returns home and tells the story, something black emerges from his mouth, and he dies the next morning.

This tale puzzles most Westerners. They are unschooled in the particular Native American culture the story comes from. However, to someone familiar with that culture, the story makes

**schemas** organized bodies of information stored in memory

# *Effective Strategies for Remembering*

## Becoming an Informed Consumer of Development

We are all forgetful at times. However, there are techniques for more effective recall. **Mnemonics** (pronounced "nee-MON-iks") are formal strategies for organizing material in ways that make it easier to remember. Among the mnemonics that work are the following (Bloom & Lamkin, 2006; Morris & Fritz, 2006; Collins, 2007):

- **Get organized.** For people who have trouble recalling where they left their keys or remembering appointments, the simplest approach is to become more organized. Using a date book, hanging keys on a hook, or using Post-It notes can aid recall.

- **Pay attention.** You can improve your recall by paying close attention to new information, and purposefully thinking that you will need to recall it. For example, when you park your car at the mall, pay attention at the moment you park, and remind yourself that you really want to remember the location.

- **Use the encoding specificity phenomenon.** According to the encoding specificity phenomenon, people are most likely to recall information in environments that are similar to those in which they initially learned ("encoded") it (Tulving & Thompson, 1973). For instance, people are best able to recall information on a test if the test is held in the room in which they studied.

- **Visualize.** Making mental images of ideas can help you recall them later. For example, if you want to remember that global warming may lead to rising oceans, think of yourself on a beach on a hot day, with the waves coming closer and closer to where you're sitting.

- **Rehearse.** Practice makes memory perfect, or if not perfect, at least better. By practicing or rehearsing what you wish to recall, you can substantially improve your memory.

perfect sense: The hero feels no pain because his companions are ghosts, and the "black thing" coming from his mouth is his departing soul.

For a Native American, it may be easy to recall the story, because it makes sense in a way that it doesn't to members of other cultures. Material that fits into existing schemas is easier to recall than material that doesn't fit. For example, a person who usually puts her keys in her purse may lose them because she doesn't recall putting them on the counter. It's not the "usual place" (Tse et al., 2007).

> **mnemonics** formal strategies for organizing material in ways that make it more likely to be remembered

---

## REVIEW, CHECK, AND APPLY

### REVIEW

**LO9** How does aging affect memory?

- Memory may appear to decline in middle age, but, in fact, long-term memory deficits are probably due to ineffective strategies of storage and retrieval.

**LO10** How can memory be improved?

- People categorize and interpret new information according to the schemas they have developed about how the world is organized and operates.

- Mnemonics help people organize material in ways that improve recall. These formal strategies include getting organized, visualizing, rehearsing, paying attention, and using the encoding specificity phenomenon.

### CHECK YOURSELF

1. Both sensory memory and short-term memory show virtually no weakening during middle adulthood.
   - True
   - False

2. Middle-aged individuals find it hard to pay attention to everything that is going on around them and often rely on _____, or mental shortcuts, to reduce the stress of remembering so many things.

3. _____ are formal strategies for organizing material in ways that make it more likely to be remembered.
   - a. Mnemonics
   - b. Schemas
   - c. Perceptions
   - d. Heuristics

### APPLYING LIFESPAN DEVELOPMENT

- In what ways do schemas give midlife adults an edge over younger adults?

✓●—**Study** and **Review** on
**MyDevelopmentLab.com**

Answers: 1) True; 2) schemas; 3) a

## MODULE 8.3 Social and Personality Development in Middle Adulthood

# From Clothes to Rock to Talk

*To say that Mirandi Babitz's career path has taken a lot of twists would be an understatement. Her work has spanned from a fashionable Hollywood clothing boutique to a therapist's office, with a lot of rock'n' roll in between.*

*After getting married for the first time in the 1960s, Mirandi opened a clothing store in Los Angeles with her husband. The couple met with a lot of success. Mirandi helped design clothes for Jim Morrison of The Doors, Eric Clapton, and other prominent musicians of the era.*

*When Mirandi's marriage ended, though, she left the fashion industry. Through her connections in the music world, she eventually became a road manager. Again, Mirandi found success, and worked with major acts such as Bonnie Raitt and Crosby, Stills, and Nash. But increasingly Mirandi found that the rock'n'roll lifestyle was something she was not just managing, but living. After struggling with substance abuse, she entered rehab.*

*After getting sober, Mirandi eventually left the music business, but found as she approached 40 she didn't know the direction she wanted her career to take next. A psychologist friend suggested she consider therapy. Mirandi took to the idea, and earned her master's degree in clinical psychology.*

*Today, Mirandi has been a therapist for more than 14 years. She still often works with musicians, but in a very different capacity, of course, from her rock'n'roll days. Mirandi specializes in helping those coping with addiction, using her own unusual life story to benefit others.* (Nishi, 2008)

The twists and turns in Mirandi Babitz's life are not unusual: Few lives follow a set, predictable pattern through middle adulthood. In fact, one of the remarkable characteristics of middle age is its variety, as the paths that different people travel continue to diverge. In this module we focus on the personality and social development that occurs in midlife. We begin by examining the changes that typify this period. We also explore some of the controversies in developmental psychologists' understandings of midlife, including whether the midlife crisis, a phenomenon popularized in the media, is fact or fiction.

Next we consider the various familial ties that bind people together (or come unglued) in middle adulthood, including marriage, divorce, the empty nest, and grandparenting. We also look at a bleak, but prevalent, side of family relations: family violence.

Finally, the module examines work and leisure in midlife. We consider the changing role of work in people's lives and look at work-related problems, such as burnout and unemployment. The module concludes with a discussion of leisure time, which becomes more important during middle age.

# Personality Development

**LO11** In what ways does personality develop during middle adulthood?

**LO12** Is there continuity in personality development during adulthood?

*My 40th birthday was not an easy one. I did not wake up feeling different—that's never been the case. But during my 40th year, I did come to realize the finiteness of life. The die was cast. I understood that I probably wasn't going to be president of the United States—a secret ambition—or CEO of a major corporation. Time had become more of an adversary than an ally. But it was curious: My usual pattern of focusing on the future, planning each step, began to shift. I started appreciating what I had. I looked at my life and was pretty satisfied with some of my accomplishments. I began focusing on what was going right, not on what I was lacking. This didn't happen in a day; it took several years after turning 40 before I felt this way. Even now, it is hard to fully accept that I am middle-aged.*

As this 47-year-old man suggests, realizing that one has reached midlife can be difficult. In many Western societies, age 40 undeniably marks one as middle-aged—at least in the public eye—and suggests that one is on the threshold of a "midlife crisis." How true this view is, as we'll see, depends on your perspective.

## Perspectives on Adult Personality Development: Normative-Crisis versus Life Events

Traditional views of adult personality development have suggested that people move through a fixed series of stages, each tied closely to age. These stages are related to specific crises in which an individual undergoes an intense period of questioning and psychological turmoil. This perspective is a feature of the normative-crisis models of personality development. **Normative-crisis models** see personality development as universal stages of sequential, age-related crises. For example, Erik Erikson's psychosocial theory predicts that people move through a series of stages and crises throughout their life span.

Some critics suggest that normative-crisis approaches may be outmoded. They arose at a time when society had fairly rigid and uniform roles for people. Traditionally, men were expected to work and support a family; women were expected to stay at home and take care of the children. These roles played out at relatively uniform ages.

Today, there is considerable variety in both the roles and the timing. Some people marry and have children at 40. Others have children and marry later. Others never marry, and live with a partner of the same or opposite sex and perhaps adopt a child or forgo children altogether. In sum, social changes have called into question the normative-crisis models closely tied to age (Fugate & Mitchell, 1997; Barnett & Hyde, 2001; Fraenkel, 2003).

**From a social worker's perspective:** In what ways might normative-crisis models of personality development be specific to Western culture?

Because of this variation, some theorists, such as Ravenna Helson, focus on **life events models,** which suggest that particular events, rather than age per se, determine how personality develops. For instance, a woman who has her first child at age 21 may experience similar psychological forces as a woman who has her first child at age 39. These two women, despite their very different ages, share certain commonalities of personality development (Helson & Wink, 1992; Helson & Srivastava, 2001; Roberts, Helson, & Klohnen, 2002).

It is not clear whether the normative-crisis view or the life events perspective more accurately depicts personality development and change in adulthood. What is clear is that developmental theorists all agree that midlife is a time of continuing, significant psychological growth.

## Erikson's Stage of Generativity versus Stagnation

As we discussed earlier, psychoanalyst Erik Erikson characterized midlife as a period of **generativity versus stagnation.** One's middle adulthood, according to Erikson, is either spent in generativity—making a contribution to family, community, work, and society—or in stagnation. Generative people strive to guide and encourage future generations. Often, people find generativity through parenting, but other roles can fill this need, such as working directly with young people, acting as mentors. Or the need for generativity may be satisfied through creative and artistic output, seeking to leave a lasting contribution. The focus of generativity, then, is beyond the self, as one looks toward the continuation of one's own life through others (Peterson, 2006; Cheek & Piercy, 2008; Clark & Arnold, 2008).

A lack of psychological growth in this period results in stagnation. Focusing on their own trivial activities, people may feel they have contributed little to the world, that their presence has counted for little. Some people find themselves floundering, still seeking new, potentially more fulfilling careers. Others become frustrated and bored.

Erikson provides a broad overview, but some psychologists suggest that we need a more precise look at midlife changes in personality. We'll consider three alternative approaches.

**normative-crisis models** the approach to personality development that is based on fairly universal stages tied to a sequence of age-related crises

**life events models** the approach to personality development that is based on the timing of particular events in an adult's life rather than on age per se

**generativity-versus-stagnation** according to Erikson, the stage during middle adulthood in which people consider their contributions to family and society

## TABLE 8-2 GOULD'S TRANSFORMATIONS IN ADULT DEVELOPMENT

| Stage | Approximate Age | Development(s) |
|-------|-----------------|----------------|
| 1 | 16 to 18 | Desire to escape parental control |
| 2 | 18 to 22 | Leaving the family; peer-group orientation |
| 3 | 22 to 28 | Developing independence, commitment to a career and to children |
| 4 | 29 to 34 | Questioning self; role confusion; marriage and career vulnerable to dissatisfaction |
| 5 | 35 to 43 | Period of urgency to attain life's goals; awareness of time limitation, realignment of life's goals |
| 6 | 43 to 53 | Settling down; acceptance of one's life |
| 7 | 53 to 60 | More tolerance, acceptance of phase, less negativism, general mellowing |

Source: From *Transformations,* by R. L. Gould & M. D. Gould, 1978, New York: Simon & Schuster.

***Building on Erikson's Views: Vaillant, Gould, and Levinson.*** Developmentalist George Vaillant (1977) argues that an important period between ages 45 and 55 centers on "keeping the meaning" versus rigidity. Seeking to extract meaning from their lives, adults also seek to "keep the meaning" by accepting the strengths and weaknesses of others. Although they realize it is not perfect, they strive to safeguard their world, and they are relatively content. The man quoted at the beginning of this section, for example, appears content with the meaning he has found in his life. People who are unable to achieve this risk becoming rigid and increasingly isolated from others.

Psychiatrist Roger Gould (1978) offers an alternative to Erikson's and Vaillant's views. He agrees that people move through a series of stages and potential crises, but he suggests that adults pass through seven stages associated with specific age periods (see Table 8-2). According to Gould, people in their late 30s and early 40s begin to feel a sense of urgency about attaining life's goals as they realize that their life is finite. Coming to grips with this reality can propel people toward maturity.

Gould based his model of development on a small sample and relied heavily on his own clinical judgments. Little research has supported his description of the various stages, which was heavily influenced by the psychoanalytic perspective.

Another alternative to Erikson's work is psychologist Daniel Levinson's *seasons of life* theory. According to Levinson (1986, 1992), who intensively interviewed men, the early 40s are a period of transition and crisis. He suggests that adult men pass through a series of stages beginning with early adulthood, around age 20, and continuing into midlife. The beginning stages center on leaving one's family and entering the adult world.

However, at around age 40 or 45, people move to what Levinson calls the midlife transition. The *midlife transition* is a time of questioning, a focus on the finite nature of life. People begin to question some of their fundamental assumptions. They experience the first signs of aging, and they confront the fact that they will not accomplish all their aims before they die.

In Levinson's view, this assessment may lead to a **midlife crisis,** a stage of uncertainty and indecision. Facing signs of physical aging, men may also discover that even the accomplishments of which they are proudest have brought them less satisfaction than they expected. They may try to define what went wrong and seek ways to correct past mistakes. The midlife crisis is a painful and tumultuous period of questioning.

Levinson's view is that most people are susceptible to a fairly profound midlife crisis. Before accepting his perspective, we need to consider some critical drawbacks in his research.

**midlife crisis** a stage of uncertainty and indecision brought about by the realization that life is finite

First, his initial theory was based on 40 men, and his work with women was conducted years later and, again, on a small sample. Levinson also overstated the consistency and generality of the patterns he found. In fact, the notion of a universal midlife crisis has come under considerable criticism (McCrae & Costa, 1990; Stewart & Ostrove, 1998).

***The Midlife Crisis: Reality or Myth?***   Central to Levinson's model is the concept of midlife crisis, a period in the early 40s presumed to be marked by intense psychological turmoil. The notion has taken on a life of its own: There is a general expectation in U.S. society that age 40 is an important psychological juncture.

Such a view is problematic: The evidence is simply lacking. In fact, most research suggests that most people pass into middle age with relative ease. The majority regard midlife as a particularly rewarding time. If they are parents, the physically demanding period of child-rearing is usually over, and in some cases children have left the home, allowing parents the opportunity to rekindle their intimacy. Many people find that their careers have blossomed, and they feel quite content with their lives. Focusing on the present, they seek to maximize their involvement with family, friends, and other social groups. Those who regret the course of their lives may be motivated to change directions, and those who do change end up better off psychologically. Furthermore, most people feel younger entering midlife than they actually are (Wethington, Cooper, & Holmes, 1997; Stewart & Vandewater, 1999; Willis, Martin, & Rocke, 2010).

The evidence for the inevitability of midlife crisis is no more compelling than was the evidence for a stormy adolescence, discussed earlier. Yet, the notion of a universal midlife crisis seems well entrenched in "common wisdom." Why?

One reason may be that turmoil in middle age is both obvious and easily remembered by observers. A 40-year-old man who divorces his wife, trades his Ford Taurus station wagon for a red Saab convertible, and marries a much younger woman makes a greater impression than a happily married man who remains with his spouse (and Taurus) through middle adulthood. We are more likely to notice and recall marital difficulties than the lack of them. In this way the myth of a blustery and universal midlife crisis is perpetuated. For most people, though, a midlife crisis is more the stuff of fiction than of reality. In fact, for some people midlife brings few, if any, changes. As we consider in the "Cultural Dimensions" segment, in some cultures, middle age is not even considered a separate period of life.

In spite of there being no strong evidence that people universally experience "midlife crisis," the belief that it is commonplace remains. Why is this belief so prevalent?

## *Cultural Dimensions*

### Middle Age: In Some Cultures It Doesn't Exist

There's no such thing as middle age.

One could draw that conclusion by looking at the women living in the Oriya culture in Orissa, India. According to research by developmental anthropologist Richard Shweder, who studied how high-caste Hindu women view aging, a distinct period of middle age does not exist. These women view their life course not by chronological age, but by the nature of one's social responsibility, family management issues, and moral sense at a given time (Shweder, 1998, 2003).

The model of aging of the Oriyan women encompasses two phases of life: life in her father's house (*bapa gharo*), followed by life in her husband's mother's house (*sasu gharo*). These two segments fit the context of Oriyan family life, which consists of multigenerational households in which marriages are arranged. After they are married, husbands remain with their parents and wives are expected to move in with their in-laws. Upon marriage, a wife changes social status from a child (someone's daughter) to a sexually active female (a daughter-in-law).

The shift from child to daughter-in-law typically occurs around the ages of 18 or 20. However, chronological age, per se, does not mark significant boundaries in life for Oriyan women, nor do physical changes, such as the onset of menstruation nor its cessation at menopause. It is the change from daughter to daughter-in-law that significantly alters social responsibility. Women must shift their focus from their own parents to the parents of their husband, and they must become sexually active in order to perpetuate the husband's family line.

To a Western eye, the life course of these women might seem restricted, because they rarely have careers outside the home, but Oriyan women do not see themselves in this light. In fact, in the Oriya culture, domestic work is highly respected and valued. Oriyan women also view themselves as more cultured and civilized than men, who must work outside the home.

The notion of a separate middle age is clearly a cultural construction. The significance of a particular age range differs widely, depending on the culture in which one lives.

## Stability versus Change in Personality

Harry Hennesey, age 53 and a vice president of an investment banking firm, says he still feels like a kid. Many middle-aged adults would agree. Although most people say they have changed a good deal since adolescence—and mostly for the better—many also perceive important similarities in basic personality traits between their present and younger selves.

The degree to which personality is stable across the life span or changes as we age is a major issue of personality development in middle adulthood. Theorists such as Erikson and Levinson clearly suggest that substantial change occurs over time. Erikson's stages and Levinson's seasons describe set patterns of change. The change may be predictable and age-related, but it is substantial.

An impressive body of research, however, suggests that for individual traits, personality is quite stable and continuous over the life span. Developmental psychologists Paul Costa and Robert McCrae find remarkable stability in particular traits. Even-tempered 20-year-olds are even-tempered at age 75; affectionate 25-year-olds become affectionate 50-year-olds; and disorganized 26-year-olds are still disorganized at age 60. Similarly, self-concept at age 30 is a good indication of self-concept at age 80. In fact, traits may become more ingrained as people age (Srivastava, John, & Gosling, 2003; Terracciano, Costa, & McCrae, 2006; Terracciano, McCrae, & Costa, 2009) (also see Figure 8-6).

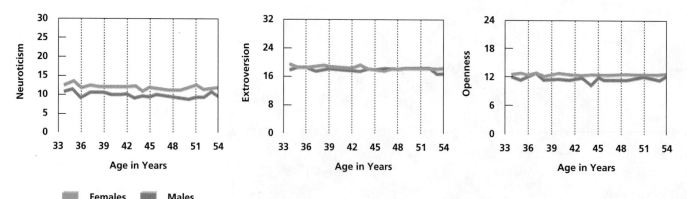

 Females  Males

**FIGURE 8-6 The Stability of Personality**
According to Paul Costa and Robert McCrae, basic personality traits such as neuroticism, extroversion, and openness are stable and consistent throughout adulthood.
Source: Adapted from Costa et al., 1989, p. 148.

***Stability and Change in the "Big Five" Personality Traits.*** Quite a bit of research has centered on the personality traits known as the "Big Five"—because they represent the five major clusters of personality characteristics. These are:

- Neuroticism, the degree to which a person is moody, anxious, and self-critical
- Extraversion, how outgoing or shy a person is
- Openness, a person's level of curiosity and interest in new experiences
- Agreeableness, how easygoing and helpful a person tends to be
- Conscientiousness, a person's tendencies to be organized and responsible

The majority of studies find that the Big Five traits are relatively stable past the age of 30, although variations exist for specific traits. In particular, neuroticism, extraversion, and openness to experience decline somewhat from early adulthood, while agreeableness and conscientiousness tend to increase—findings that are consistent across cultures. The basic pattern, however, is one of stability through adulthood (McCrae & Costa, 2003; Srivastava et al., 2003; Renner, 2010).

Does evidence for the stability of traits contradict the theories of personality change championed by Erikson, Gould, and Levinson? Not necessarily, for the contradictions may be more apparent than real.

People's basic traits do show continuity over the course of their adult lives. But, people are also susceptible to changes, and adulthood is packed with major changes in family status, career, and even the economy. The physical changes of aging, illness, the death of a loved one, and an increased awareness of life's finite span also can spur changes in how people view themselves and the world at large (Krueger & Heckhausen, 1993; Roberts, Walton, & Viechtbauer, 2006).

In support of this view, new research on a group of baby-boomers that stretches back to their college years traces changes in their personality that extend over the course of their adult lives, as we discuss in the "From Research to Practice" box.

## *From Research to Practice*

### Evolving Circumstances, Evolving Personality: How Our Personalities Change Through Adulthood

*I feel like I've grown and changed a lot over the last 20 years. After facing a bout of cancer in my mid-40s, and then being involved as one of my children struggled with a drug problem, and experiencing a merger at work in which my job changed radically, how could I not have become a different person in some important ways?*

As this 58-year-old's comment illustrates, personality change is often precipitated by life events over which we have no control. Our personalities change as a combination of our basic personality traits and the events that we encounter as part of everyday life.

This fluidity of personality is illustrated in a new study by researcher Susan Whitbourne and colleagues that followed two groups of baby-boomers from their college years until their mid-40s and mid-50s, respectively, on a measure of Erikson's stages. Changes over time in participants' responses on the measure showed personality development throughout adulthood. The childhood stages of trust, autonomy, and initiative continued to grow slowly through the mid-50s, suggesting that these qualities are not set in stone early in life but that they continue to be revisited throughout life as new challenges and life events emerge (Whitbourne, Sneed, & Sayer, 2009; Whitbourne, 2010).

Moreover, the study found that personality development does not progress the same way for everyone. For one thing, psychosocial growth occurs at different rates for different people, a finding that is consistent with Erikson's assertion that personality development is a personal process that depends in part on people's life experiences.

Other interesting variations of development emerged as well. The two different groups that were tracked represented early and late members of the baby-boomer generation, and because of this they tended to have different life experiences at different stages of development. The older group had a more traditional childhood, but they experienced considerable social rebellion when they entered college in the 1960s. The younger group did not experience the same social climate of rebelliousness when they came of age. Consequently, the two groups might be expected to show different patterns of psychosocial growth over the life span—and this is what happened. The older group showed lower industry than the younger group in college but showed greater subsequent increases. The older group also showed a greater increase in ego integrity in recent years (Whitbourne, 2010).

Taken together, the findings suggest that personality change occurs throughout adulthood, and in ways that are consistent with Erikson's theory. Furthermore, the changes progress at different rates for different people, and not necessarily in a fixed order. Finally, important life events that affect individual people's values and relationships have an influence on their subsequent psychosocial development (Whitbourne, Sneed, & Sayer, 2009).

- What kinds of life events might you expect to affect personality the most during adulthood? Why?
- What social forces might be influencing the psychosocial development of college students today, and in what ways?

While Erikson and Levinson suggest there is substantial personality change over time, other research has shown that personality in terms of individual traits remains stable over the life span. How many of these high school swimmers do you think are still physically active after 40 years? Why?

***Happiness Across the Life Span.*** Suppose you hit it big on *Jeopardy*. Would you be a happier person? For most people, the answer would be no. A growing body of research shows that adults' *subjective well-being* or general happiness remains stable over their lives. Even winning the lottery increases subjective well-being only temporarily; one year later, people's happiness tends to return to pre-lottery levels (Diener, 2000; Stone et al., 2010).

The steadiness of subjective well-being suggests that most people have a general "set point" for happiness, a level of happiness that is relatively consistent despite the day-to-day ups and downs of life. Although specific events may temporarily elevate or depress a person's mood (for example, a surprisingly high job evaluation or being laid off from work), people eventually return to their general level of happiness.

On the other hand, happiness set points are not completely fixed. Under some conditions, set points can change as a result of particular life events, such as divorce, death of a spouse, unemployment, and disability. Furthermore, people differ in the extent to which they can adapt to events (Lucas, 2007; Diener, Lucas, & Scollon, 2009).

Most people's happiness set points seem to be fairly high. Some 30 percent of people in the United States rate themselves as "very happy," while only 10 percent rate themselves as "not too happy." Most people say they are "pretty happy." These findings are similar across different social groups. Men and women rate themselves as equally happy, and African Americans rate themselves as "very happy" at only slightly lower rates than Whites. Regardless of their economic situation, residents of countries across the world have similar levels of happiness (Schkade & Kahneman, 1998; Diener, 2000; Diener, Oishi, & Lucas, 2003; Kahneman et al., 2006). The conclusion: Money doesn't buy happiness.

## REVIEW, CHECK, AND APPLY

### REVIEW

**LO11** In what ways does personality develop during middle adulthood?

- In normative-crisis models, people pass through age-related stages of development; life events models focus on how people change in response to various life events.

- Levinson argues that the transition to middle age can lead to a midlife crisis, but there is little evidence for this in the majority of people.

**LO12** Is there continuity in personality development during adulthood?

- Broad, basic personality characteristics are relatively stable. Specific aspects of personality do seem to change in response to life events.

### CHECK YOURSELF

1. According to _____ models, researchers understand personality development as the product of universal stages tied to age-related crises.

2. According to the _____ model, individuals at different ages can experience the same emotional and personality changes because they have shared common occurrences in their lives.

   a. normative-crisis

   b. psychosexual

   c. life events

   d. self-understanding

3. According to Roger Gould (1978, 1980) people in their late 30s and early 40s feel a sense of urgency in terms of reaching their life goals because they realize their lives are limited.

   - True

   - False

### APPLYING LIFESPAN DEVELOPMENT

- How do you think the midlife transition is different for a middle-aged person whose child has just entered adolescence versus a middle-aged person who has just become a parent for the first time?

✔●─ **Study** and **Review** on
**MyDevelopmentLab.com**

Answers: 1) normative-crisis; 2) c; 3) True

# Relationships: Family in Middle Age

**LO13** What are typical patterns of marriage and divorce in middle adulthood?

**LO14** What changing family situations do middle-aged adults face?

**LO15** What are the causes and characteristics of family violence in the United States?

LEARNING OBJECTIVES

*For Kathy and Bob, going to their son Jon's college orientation was a shockingly new experience in the life of their family. It hadn't really registered that he would be leaving home when he was accepted at a college on the other side of the country. It didn't hit them just how much this would change their family until they said good-bye and left him on his new campus. It was a wrenching experience. Kathy and Bob worried about their son in the ways that parents always do, but they also felt a profound loss—their job of raising their son, basically, was done. Now he was largely on his own. This thought filled them with pride and anticipation for his future, but with great sadness, too. They would miss him.*

For members of many non-Western cultures who live in extended families in which multiple generations spend their lives in the same household or village, middle adulthood is nothing special. But in Western cultures, family dynamics change significantly in midlife. For most parents, there are major shifts in their relationships with their children, and with other family members as well. It is a period of changing roles that, in 21st-century Western cultures, encompasses an increasing number of combinations and permutations. We'll start by looking at how marriage develops and changes over this period, and then consider some of the many alternative forms of family life today (Kaslow, 2001).

## Marriage

Fifty years ago, midlife was similar for most people. Men and women, married since early adulthood, were still married to each other. One hundred years ago, when life expectancy was much shorter, people in their 40s were usually married—but not necessarily to the persons they had first married. Spouses often died; people might be well into their second marriage by middle age.

Today, the story is different and more varied. More people are single at midlife, having never married. Single people may live alone or with a partner. Gay and lesbian adults may have committed relationships even though marriage is often not an option for them. Among heterosexuals, some have divorced, lived alone, and then remarried. Many people's marriages end in divorce, and many families "blend" together into new households, containing children and stepchildren from previous marriages. Some couples still spend 40 to 50 years together, the bulk of those years during middle adulthood. Many experience the peak of marital satisfaction during middle age.

***The Ups and Downs of Marriage.*** Even happily married couples have their ups and downs, with satisfaction rising and falling over the course of the marriage. In the past, most research has suggested that marital satisfaction follows the U-shaped configuration shown in Figure 8-7 (Figley, 1973). Specifically, marital satisfaction begins to decline just after the marriage, falling until it reaches its lowest point following the births of the couple's children. At that point, satisfaction begins to grow, eventually returning to the same level as before the marriage (Harvey & Weber, 2002; Gorchoff, John, & Helson, 2008; Medina, Lederhos, & Lillis, 2009).

On the other hand, newer research has called the U-shaped pattern into question. This research suggests that marital satisfaction actually continues to decline across the life span (Umberson et al., 2006; Liu, Elliott, & Umberson, 2010).

It is too early to reject the U-shaped view of marital satisfaction, and it may be that personality differences account for the discrepancy in findings. What is clear is that middle-aged couples cite several sources of marital satisfaction. For instance, both men and women typically state that their spouse is "their best friend" and that they like their spouses as people. They also view marriage as a long-term commitment and agree on their aims and goals. Finally, most also feel that their spouses have grown more interesting over the course of the marriage (Levenson, Carstensen, & Gottman, 1993; Schmitt, Kliegel, & Shapiro, 2007).

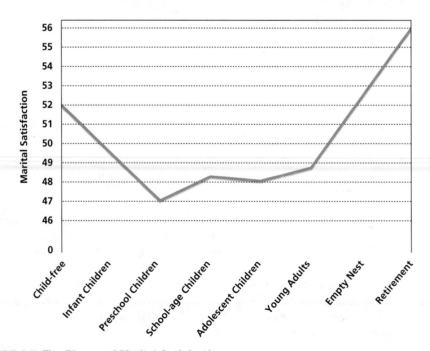

**FIGURE 8-7 The Phases of Marital Satisfaction**
For many couples, marital satisfaction falls and rises in a U-shaped configuration. It begins to decline after the birth of children but increases when the youngest child leaves home and eventually returns to a level of satisfaction similar to that at the start of marriage. Why do you think this pattern of satisfaction occurs?
Source: Adapted from Rollins & Cannon, 1974.

Sexual satisfaction is related to general marital satisfaction. What matters is not how often couples have sex. Instead, satisfaction is related to *agreeing* about their sex lives (Spence 1997; Litzinger & Gordon, 2005; Butzer & Campbell, 2008).

## Divorce

*Jane Burroughs knew 10 years into her marriage that it wasn't working. She and her husband argued constantly. He made all the decisions; she felt she had no say. But instead of divorcing, she stayed for 21 more years. It wasn't until she was 50, when her children were grown with kids of their own, that she finally got up the nerve to leave. Although she had wanted the divorce for years—and her husband eventually did, too—Burroughs, now 58, concedes it was the most difficult experience of her life and one that triggered conflicting emotions. "The hardest part was learning how to be alone," she says. "But I liked being independent." (Enright, 2004, p. 54)*

Divorce among midlife couples is actually rising, despite a decline in divorces overall in recent decades. One woman in eight who is in her first marriage will get divorced after the age of 40 (Uhlenberg, Cooney, & Boyd, 1990; Stewart et al., 1997; Enright, 2004).

There are many reasons why marriages unravel. One is that people spend less time together in middle adulthood than in earlier years. In individualistic Western cultures, people are concerned with their personal happiness. If their marriage is not satisfying, they feel that divorce may increase their happiness. Divorce is also more socially acceptable than in the past, and there are fewer legal impediments to it. In some cases—but certainly not all—the financial costs are not high. And, as the opportunities for women grow, wives may feel less dependent on their husbands, both emotionally and economically (Wallerstein, Lewis, & Blakeslee, 2000; Amato & Previti, 2003; Fincham, 2003).

Another reason for divorce is that romantic, passionate feelings may fade over time. Because Western culture emphasizes the importance of romance and passion, members of marriages in which passion has declined may feel that that is a sufficient reason to divorce. In some marriages, it is a lack of excitement and boredom that leads to marital dissatisfaction. Finally, there is a great deal of stress in households in which both parents work, and this stress puts a strain on marriages. Much of the energy directed toward families and maintaining relationships in the past is now directed toward work and other institutions outside the home (Macionis, 2001; Tsapelas, Aron, & Orbuch, 2009).

Finally, some marriages end because of *infidelity,* in which a spouse engages in sexual activity with a person outside of the marriage. Although statistics are highly suspect—if you lie to your spouse, why would you be honest to a pollster?—one survey found that 20 percent of men and 15 percent of women under the age of 35 say they have been unfaithful. In a given year, about 12 percent of men and 7 percent of women say they have had sex outside their marriage (Atkins & Furrow, 2008).

Whatever the causes, divorce can be especially difficult in midlife. It can be particularly hard for women who have played the traditional role of mother and never performed substantial work outside the home. They may face age discrimination, finding younger people are preferred, even in jobs with minimal requirements. Without a good deal of training and support, these divorced women, lacking recognized job skills, may remain virtually unemployable (McDaniel & Coleman, 2003; Williams & Dunne-Bryant, 2006; Hilton & Anderson, 2009).

Many people who divorce in midlife, though, end up happy. Women, in particular, are apt to find that developing a new, independent self-identity is a positive outcome. Both men and women who divorce in midlife are also likely to form new relationships, and they typically remarry (Enright, 2004).

***Remarriage.*** Many people who divorce—some 75 to 80 percent—end up marrying again, usually within 2 to 5 years. They are likely to marry people who are also divorced, partly because they tend to be available, but also because divorced people share a similar experience (McCarthy & Ginsberg, 2007).

Although the rate of remarriage is high, it is far higher in some groups than in others. For instance, it is harder for women to remarry than men, particularly older women. Whereas

90 percent of women under age 25 remarry after divorce, less than one-third of women over age 40 remarry (Bumpass, Sweet, & Martin, 1990; Besharov & West, 2002).

This age difference stems from the *marriage gradient* we discussed earlier: Societal norms push men to marry women who are younger, smaller, and lower in status than themselves. The older a woman is, the fewer socially acceptable men she has available to her since those men her age are likely to be looking for younger women. As we discussed earlier, women are also disadvantaged by double standards regarding physical attractiveness. Older women may be perceived as unattractive, while older men may be seen as "distinguished" and "mature" (Bernard, 1982; Buss, 2003b; Doyle, 2004b).

There are several reasons marrying again may be more appealing than remaining single. A person who remarries avoids the social consequences of divorce. Even in the twenty-first century, when divorce is common, it carries with it a certain stigma. In addition, divorced people overall report less satisfaction with life than married people (Lucas, 2005).

Divorced people miss the companionship that marriage provides. Men in particular report feeling lonely and experience more physical and mental health problems following divorce. Marriage also provides clear economic benefits, such as sharing the cost of a house and medical benefits reserved for spouses (Ross, Microwsky, & Goldsteen, 1991; Stewart et al., 1997).

Second marriages differ from first marriages. Older couples tend to be more mature and realistic in their expectations. They often view marriage in less romantic terms than younger couples, and they are more cautious. They are also likely to be more flexible about roles and duties; they share household chores and decision making more equitably (Hetherington, 1999).

Unfortunately, this doesn't guarantee second marriages will last. The divorce rate is slightly higher than for first marriages. One factor that explains this is that second marriages may include stresses not present in first marriages, such as the blending of different families. Another reason is that having experienced and survived one divorce, partners may be less committed and more ready to walk away from an unhappy second marriage. Finally, they may have personality and emotional characteristics that don't make them easy to live with (Cherlin, 1993; Warshak, 2000; Coleman, Ganong, & Weaver, 2001).

Despite the high divorce rate for second marriages, many people remarry quite successfully. In such cases, couples report as great a degree of satisfaction as those who are in successful first marriages (Bird & Melville, 1994; Michaels, 2006).

Most people who are divorced remarry, typically to someone who is also divorced.

# Family Evolutions: From Full House to Empty Nest

For many parents, a major midlife transition is the departure of children who are going to college, getting married, joining the military, or taking a job far from home. Even people who become parents at relatively late ages are likely to face this transition, since the middle adulthood spans nearly a quarter century. As we saw in Kathy and Bob's story, a child's departure can be wrenching—so much so, in fact, that it has been labeled the "empty nest syndrome." The **empty nest syndrome** refers to the unhappiness, worry, loneliness, and depression some parents feel when their children leave home (Lauer & Lauer, 1999; Erickson, Martinengo, & Hill, 2010).

Many parents report that major adjustments are required. For women who were stay-at-home mothers, the loss can be very difficult. Traditional homemakers, who focus significant time and energy on their children, face a challenging time.

While the loss can be difficult, parents also find that some aspects of this transition are quite positive. Even mothers who have stayed at home find they have time for other interests, such as community or recreational activities, when the children leave. They may also enjoy the opportunity to get a job or return to school. Finally, many women find that motherhood is not easy; surveys show that most people regard motherhood as harder than it used to be. Such women may now feel liberated from a difficult set of responsibilities (Heubusch, 1997; Morfei et al., 2004).

Though feelings of loss are common for most people, there is little, if any, evidence that the departure of children produces anything more than temporary feelings of sadness and distress. This is especially true for women who have worked outside the home (Antonucci, 2001; Crowley, Hayslip, & Hobdy, 2003).

In fact, there are discernible benefits when children leave home. Spouses have more time for one another. Married or unmarried people can attend to their own work without having to worry about helping the kids with homework, carpools, and the like. The house stays neater, and the telephone rings less often (Gorchoff, John, & Helson, 2008).

Most research on the so-called empty nest syndrome has focused on women. Men, traditionally not as involved in childrearing, were assumed to weather the transition more smoothly. However, some research suggests that men also experience feelings of loss when their children depart, although these feelings may differ from those felt by women.

One survey found that although most fathers felt either happy or neutral about the departure of their children, almost a quarter felt unhappy (Lewis, Freneau, & Roberts, 1979). Those fathers tended to mention lost opportunities, regretting things they had not done with their children. Some felt they had been too busy for their children or hadn't been sufficiently nurturing or caring.

The concept of the empty nest syndrome arose at a time when grown children tended to leave home for good. Today, as we discuss next, "boomerang children" frequently return to fill that empty nest.

# Boomerang Children: Refilling the Empty Nest

*Carole Olis doesn't know what to make of her 23-year-old son, Rob. He has been living at home since his graduation from college more than 2 years ago. Her six older children returned to the nest for just a few months and then bolted.*

*"I ask him, 'Why don't you move out with your friends?'" says Mrs. Olis. Rob has a ready answer: "They all live at home, too."*

Carole Olis is not alone in being surprised by the return of her son. In the United States, a significant number of young adults are coming back to live with their middle-aged parents.

Known as **boomerang children,** they typically cite money as the main reason for returning. In the current economy, many college graduates cannot find jobs, or the jobs they do find don't pay enough to make ends meet. Others return home after a divorce. About half of all 18- to-24-year-olds and about 14 percent of all young adults live with their parents in the United States. In some European countries, the proportion is even higher (Roberts, 2009).

> **empty nest syndrome** the experience that relates to parents' feelings of unhappiness, worry, loneliness, and depression resulting from their children's departure from home
>
> **boomerang children** young adults who return, after leaving home for some period, to live in the homes of their middle-aged parents

⊙ Watch on **mydevelopmentlab.com**

To better understand the sandwich generation,
log onto MyDevelopmentLab.com to watch a
video of Amy, a woman in her mid-40s who
cares for her 6-year-old son and her
82-year-old mother while balancing work and
other responsibilities.

Parents' reactions to the return of their children depend largely on the reasons for it. If their children are unemployed, their return may be a major irritant. Fathers in particular may not grasp what a difficult job market college graduates encounter, and may be decidedly unsympathetic. There may also be some subtle parent–child rivalry for the attention between the child and either spouse (Wilcox, 1992; Mitchell, 2006).

Mothers tend to sympathize more with children who are unemployed. Single mothers in particular may welcome the help and security returning children provide. Both mothers and fathers feel fairly positive about returning children who work and contribute to the household (Quinn, 1993; Veevers & Mitchell, 1998).

***The Sandwich Generation: Between Children and Parents.***   At the same time children are leaving the nest, or returning as boomerang children, many middle-aged adults face another challenge: the care of their own aging parents. The term **sandwich generation** refers to these middle adults who are squeezed between the needs of their children and their parents (Riley & Bowen, 2005; Grundy & Henretta, 2006; Chassin et al., 2009).

The sandwich generation is a relatively new phenomenon, produced by several converging trends. First, people are marrying later and having children at an older age. At the same time, people are living longer. Thus, it is not unlikely that midlife adults will have parents who are alive and require care while they still have children who need a significant amount of nurturing. ⊙ Watch on **mydevelopmentlab.com**

The care of aging parents can be psychologically tricky. There is a degree of role reversal, with children becoming more parental and parents becoming more dependent. As we'll discuss later, elderly people, used to being independent, may resent and resist their children's help. They do not want to be burdens. Almost all elderly people who live alone say they do not wish to live with their children (CFCEPLA, 1986; Merrill, 1997).

Middle-aged adults provide a range of care for their parents. They may provide financial support to supplement a parent's meager pension. They might also help manage a household, doing tasks such as removing storm windows in the spring or shoveling snow in the winter.

In some cases, elderly parents may be invited to live in their child's home. Census data reveal that multigenerational households—three or more generations—are the fastest-growing of all household arrangements. Increasing by more than a third between 1990 and 2000, they represent 4 percent of all households (Navarro, 2006).

Multigenerational families present a tricky situation, as roles are renegotiated. Typically, the adult children—who are no longer children—are in charge of the household. Both they and their parents must make adjustments and find some common ground in making decisions. Elderly parents may find their new dependence difficult, and this can be wrenching for their adult child as well. The youngest generation may resist including the oldest generation.

In many cases, the burden of care is not shared equally, with the larger share most often assumed by women. Even when both husband and wife are in the labor force, women tend to be more involved in the day-to-day care, even when the parent or parents are their in-laws (Soldo, 1996; Putney & Bengtson, 2001).

Culture also influences how caregivers view their roles. Members of Asian cultures, which are more collectivistic, are more likely to view caregiving as a traditional and ordinary duty. In contrast, members of more individualistic cultures may feel familial ties are less central, and caring for the older generation may be seen as a burden (Ho et al., 2003; Kim & Lee, 2003).

Despite the burden of being sandwiched in between two generations, which can stretch the caregiving child's resources, there are significant rewards. The psychological attachment between middle-aged children and their elderly parents can continue to grow. Both sides can see each other more realistically. They may grow closer, more accepting of each other's weaknesses and more appreciative of each other's strengths (Vincent, Phillipson, & Downs, 2006).

*"I'm in the sandwich generation—my parents don't approve of me and my kids hate me."*

## Becoming a Grandparent: Who, Me?

When her eldest son and daughter-in-law had their first child, Leah couldn't believe it. At age 54, she was a grandmother! She kept telling herself she felt far too young to be anybody's grandparent.

Middle adulthood often brings one of the unmistakable symbols of aging: becoming a grandparent. For some people, the new role has been eagerly awaited. They may miss the energy and excitement and even demands of young children, and they may see grandparenthood as the next stage in the natural progression of life. Others are less pleased with the prospect, seeing it as a clear signpost of aging.

Grandparenting tends to fall into different styles. *Involved* grandparents are actively engaged in and have influence over their grandchildren's lives. They hold clear expectations about the ways their grandchildren should behave. A retired grandparent who takes care of a grandchild while her parents work is an example of an involved grandparent (Cherlin & Furstenberg, 1986; Mueller, Wilhelm, & Elder, 2002; Fergusson, Maughan, & Golding, 2008).

In contrast, *companionate* grandparents are more relaxed. Rather than taking responsibility for their grandchildren, they act as supporters and buddies to them. Grandparents who visit and call frequently, and perhaps occasionally take their grandchildren on vacations or invite them to visit without their parents, are companionate grandparents.

Finally, the most aloof type of grandparents are *remote*. They are detached and distant, showing little interest in their grandchildren. Remote grandparents, for example, would rarely make visits to see their grandchildren and might complain about their childish behavior when they did see them.

There are marked gender differences in the extent to which people enjoy grandparenthood. Generally, grandmothers are more interested and experience greater satisfaction than grandfathers, particularly when they have a high level of interaction with younger grandchildren (Smith, 1995; Smith & Drew, 2002).

African American grandparents are more apt to be involved than White grandparents. The most reasonable explanation for this is the greater prevalence of multigenerational households among African Americans than among Caucasians. In addition, African American families are more likely to be headed by single parents. Thus, they often rely substantially on the help of grandparents in everyday child care, and cultural norms tend to be highly supportive of grandparents taking an active role (Baydar & Brooks-Gunn, 1998; Baird, John, & Hayslip, 2000; Crowther & Rodriguez, 2003; Stevenson, Henderson, & Baugh, 2007).

## Family Violence: The Hidden Epidemic

Domestic violence is epidemic in the United States, occurring in one-fourth of all marriages. More than half the women who were murdered in one recent 10-year period were murdered by a partner. Between 21 percent and 34 percent of women will be slapped, kicked, beaten, choked, or threatened or attacked with a weapon at least once by an intimate partner. In fact, continuing, severe violence characterizes close to 15 percent of all marriages in the United States. In addition, many women are victims of psychological abuse, such as verbal or emotional abuse. Domestic violence is also a worldwide problem. Estimates suggest that one in three women around the globe experience violent victimization during their lives (Walker, 1999; Garcia-Moreno et al., 2005).

In the United States, no segment of society is immune from spousal abuse. Violence occurs across social strata, races, ethnic groups, and religions. Both gay and straight partnerships can be abusive. It also occurs across genders: Although in most instances, the husband is the abuser, in about 8 percent of the cases wives physically abuse their husbands (Harway, 2000; Cameron, 2003; Dixon & Browne, 2003).

Certain factors increase the likelihood of abuse. Spousal abuse is more apt to occur in large families for whom both financial strain and verbal aggression are common. Those husbands and wives who grew up in families where violence was present are also more likely to be violent themselves (Straus & Yodanis, 1996; Ehrensaft, Cohen, & Brown, 2003; Lackey, 2003).

Parents who abuse their own spouses and children were often victims of abuse themselves as children, reflecting a cycle of violence.

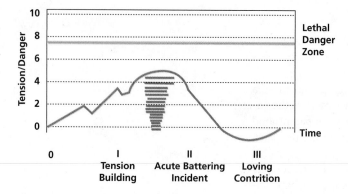

**FIGURE 8-8 Typical Cycle of Violence**
Source: From "The Battered Woman Syndrome," by Lenore Walker, 1984. Reprinted with permission from the author.

The factors that put a family at risk are similar to those associated with child abuse, another form of family violence. Child abuse occurs most frequently in stressful environments, at lower socioeconomic levels, in single-parent families, and in situations of intense marital conflict. Families with four or more children have higher abuse rates, and those with incomes under $15,000 a year have seven times the rate of families with higher incomes. But not all types of abuse are higher in poorer families: Incest is more likely to occur in affluent families (APA, 1996; Cox, Kotch, & Everson, 2003).

Marital aggression by a husband typically occurs in three stages (Walker, 1999) (see Figure 8-8). In the initial *tension-building* stage, a batterer becomes upset and shows dissatisfaction through verbal abuse. He may also use some physical aggression, such as shoving or grabbing. The wife may desperately try to avoid the impending violence, attempting to calm her spouse or withdraw from the situation. Such behavior may only enrage the husband, who senses his wife's vulnerability. Her efforts to escape may escalate his anger.

In the next stage—an *acute battering incident*—the physical abuse actually occurs, lasting from several minutes to hours. Wives may be shoved against walls, choked, slapped, punched, kicked, and stepped on. Their arms may be twisted or broken, they may be shaken severely, thrown down a flight of stairs, or burned with cigarettes or scalding liquids. About a quarter of wives are forced to engage in sexual activity, which takes the form of aggressive sexual acts and rape.

Finally, in some—but not all—cases, the episode ends with the *loving contrition* stage. At this point, the husband feels remorse and apologizes for his actions. He may provide first aid and sympathy, assuring his wife that he will never act violently again. Because wives may feel they were somehow partly at fault, they may accept the apology and forgive their husbands. They want to believe that the aggression will never occur again.

The loving contrition stage helps explain why many wives remain with abusive husbands and continue to be victims. Wishing desperately to keep their marriages intact, and believing that they have no good alternatives, some wives remain out of a vague sense that they are responsible for the abuse. In other cases, wives fear their husbands may come after them if they leave.

**The Cycle of Violence.** Still other wives stay with batterers because they, like their husbands, learned in childhood that violence is an acceptable means of settling disputes.

Individuals who abuse their spouses and children were often the victims of abuse themselves. According to the **cycle of violence hypothesis,** abuse and neglect of children predisposes them to abusiveness as adults. In line with social learning theory, the cycle of violence hypothesis suggests that family aggression is perpetuated from one generation to another. It is a fact that individuals who abuse their wives often witnessed spousal abuse at home as children, just as parents who abuse their children frequently were the victims of abuse as children (Serbin & Karp, 2004; Renner & Slack, 2006; Whiting et al., 2009).

**From the perspective of a health care provider:** What can be done to end the cycle of violence, in which people who were abused as children grow up to be abusers of others?

Growing up in an abusive home does not invariably lead to abusiveness as an adult. Only about one-third of people who were abused or neglected as children abuse their own children as adults, and two-thirds of abusers were not themselves abused as children. The cycle of violence, then, does not tell the full story of abuse (Jacobson & Gottman, 1998).

Whatever the causes of abuse, there are ways to deal with it, as we consider next.

**Spousal Abuse and Society: The Cultural Roots of Violence.** *After Dong Lu Chen beat his wife to death, he was sentenced to five years' probation. He had confessed to the act but*

**cycle of violence hypothesis** the theory that abuse and neglect of children leads them to be predisposed to abusiveness as adults

# *Dealing with Spousal Abuse*

## Becoming an Informed Consumer of Development

Spousal abuse occurs in some 25 percent of all marriages, but efforts to deal with victims of abuse are underfunded and inadequate to meet current needs. In fact, some psychologists argue that the same factors that led society to underestimate the magnitude of the problem for many years now hinder the development of effective interventions. Still, there are several measures to help the victims of spousal abuse (Browne, 1993; Koss et al., 1993):

- **Teach both wives and husbands a basic premise:** Violence is *never,* under *any* circumstances, an acceptable means of resolving disagreements.

- **Call the police.** Assault, including spousal assault, is against the law. It may be difficult to involve law enforcement officers, but this is a realistic way of handling the problem. Judges can also issue restraining orders requiring abusive husbands to stay away from their wives.

- **Understand that the remorse shown by a spouse, no matter how heartfelt, may have no bearing on possible future violence.** Even if a husband shows loving regret and vows that he will never be violent again, such a promise is no guarantee against future abuse.

- **If you are the victim of abuse, seek a safe haven.** Many communities have shelters for the victims of domestic violence that can house women and their children. Because addresses of shelters are kept confidential, an abusive spouse will not be able to find you. Telephone numbers are listed in the yellow or blue pages of phone books, and local police should also have the numbers.

- **If you feel in danger from an abusive partner, seek a restraining order** from a judge in court. A restraining order forbids a spouse to come near you, under penalty of law.

- **Call the National Domestic Violence Hotline at 1-800-799-7233** for immediate advice.

*claimed that his wife had been unfaithful to him. His lawyer (and an anthropologist) had argued in court that traditional Chinese values might have led to his violent reaction to his wife's purported infidelity.*

*After Lee Fong, a Laotian immigrant, had abducted a 16-year-old girl, he was acquitted of kidnapping, sexual assault, and menacing. During his trial, his lawyer argued that "bride stealing" is a traditional custom among the Hmong people of Laos.*

*Both cases were decided in courts in the United States. In both cases, lawyers based their arguments on the claim that in the Asian countries from which the defendants had emigrated, the use of violence against women was common and may even have received social approval. The juries obviously agreed with this "cultural defense" justification.* (Findlen, 1990)

Although marital violence and aggression is often seen as a particularly North American phenomenon, other cultures have traditions that regard violence as acceptable (Rao, 1997). Wife battering is especially prevalent in cultures that view women as inferior to men and treat them as property.

In Western societies, too, wife beating was once acceptable. According to English common law—the foundation of the legal system in the United States—husbands could beat their wives. In the 1800s, this law was modified to permit only certain kinds of beating. Specifically, a husband could not beat his wife with a stick or rod that was thicker than his thumb—the origin of the phrase "rule of thumb." It was not until the late nineteenth century that this law was removed from the books in the United States (Davidson, 1977).

Some experts on abuse suggest that its root cause is the traditional power structure in which women and men function. They argue that the more a society differentiates between men's and women's status, the more likely it is that abuse will occur.

They cite research examining the legal, political, educational, and economic roles of women and men. For example, some research has compared battering statistics across the various states in the United States. Abuse is more likely to occur in states where women are of particularly low or high status compared with women in other states. Apparently, relatively low status makes women easy targets of violence, while unusually high status may make husbands feel threatened and thus more likely to behave abusively (Dutton, 1994; Vandello & Cohen, 2003).

## REVIEW, CHECK, AND APPLY

### REVIEW

**LO13** What are typical patterns of marriage and divorce in middle adulthood?

- Marital satisfaction rises and falls over the course of marriage, generally following a U-shaped configuration over the years.

- Marital satisfaction tends to be highest when both partners feel that their spouse is "their best friend," when they like their spouses as people, when they agree on aims and goals, and when they view marriage as a long-term commitment. In happy marriages, most people also feel that their spouses have grown more interesting over the years.

- There are many reasons why marriages end in divorce, including lack of satisfaction, less time spent together, and infidelity. Divorce may increase happiness, and the process of divorce is more socially acceptable.

**LO14** What changing family situations do middle-aged adults face?

- Family changes in middle adulthood include the departure of children. In recent years, the phenomenon of "boomerang children" has emerged.

- Middle-aged adults often have increasing responsibilities for their aging parents.

**LO15** What are the causes and characteristics of family violence in the United States?

- Abuse is more likely to occur in large families who are experiencing financial strain and for whom verbal aggression is common. Adults who experienced family violence as children are also more likely to be violent themselves.

- Marital violence tends to pass through three stages: tension building, an acute battering incident, and loving contrition.

### CHECK YOURSELF

1. According to the U-shaped curve illustrating the changes in marital satisfaction, typically marriage satisfaction tends to decrease after marriage, reach its lowest point after the birth of children, and then:

   a. take a sharper dip that relates to more marriages ending in divorce.

   b. slowly begin to increase again, eventually returning to the same level it was before marriage.

   c. begin a drastic increase to levels surpassing premarriage levels of satisfaction.

   d. steadily decrease until children leave the house.

2. Both men and women who divorce during midlife are likely to enter new relationships, but typically do not remarry.

   - True

   - False

3. Couples who in middle adulthood need to take care of their aging parents and their children are often referred to by psychologists as the _____.

4. Match each of the following descriptions of spousal violence to its appropriate stage.

   a. Batterer expresses remorse and apologizes for actions.

   b. Batterer becomes upset and shows dissatisfaction through verbal abuse.

   c. Physical abuse actually occurs.

   1. Tension-building stage

   2. Acute battering incident

   3. Loving contrition stage

### APPLYING LIFESPAN DEVELOPMENT

- Are the phenomena of the empty nest, boomerang children, the sandwich generation, and grandparenting culturally dependent? Why might such phenomena be different in societies where multigenerational families are the norm?

✓•—**Study** and **Review** on

**MyDevelopmentLab.com**

Answers: 1) b; 2) False; 3) sandwich generation; 4) a-3, b-1, c-2

---

# Work and Leisure

**LEARNING OBJECTIVES**

**LO16** What are the characteristics of work in middle adulthood?

**LO17** How is leisure time different in middle adulthood?

*Enjoying a weekly game of golf…starting a neighborhood watch program…coaching a Little League baseball team…joining an investment club…traveling…taking a cooking class…attending a theater series…running for the local town council…going to the movies with friends…hearing lectures on Buddhism…fixing up a porch in the back of the house…chaperoning a high school class on an out-of-state trip…lying on a beach, reading a book during an annual vacation….*

Adults in their middle years actually enjoy a rich variety of activities. Although middle adulthood often represents the peak of career success and earning power, it is also a time when people throw themselves into leisure and recreational activities. In fact, midlife may be the period when work and leisure activities are balanced most easily. No longer feeling a need to prove themselves on the job, and increasingly valuing their contributions to family, community, and—more broadly—society, middle-aged adults may find that work and leisure complement one another in ways that enhance overall happiness.

## Work and Careers: Jobs at Midlife

For many, productivity, success, and earning power are greatest in middle age, but occupational success may become far less alluring than it once was. This is particularly true for those who have not achieved the career success they had hoped for. In such cases, family and other off-the-job interests become more important than work (Howard, 1992; Simonton, 1997).

The factors that make a job satisfying change during middle age. Younger adults focus on abstract and future-oriented concerns, such as the opportunity for advancement or the possibility of recognition and approval. Middle-aged employees care more about the here-and-now qualities of work. They are more concerned with pay, working conditions, and specific policies, such as how vacation time is calculated. As at earlier stages of life, changes in overall job quality are associated with changes in stress levels for both men and women (Hattery, 2000; Peterson & Wilson, 2004; Cohrs, Abele, & Dette, 2006).

In general, though, the relationship between age and work is positive: The older workers are, the more overall job satisfaction they experience. This is not altogether surprising, since younger adults who are dissatisfied with their jobs will quit them and find new positions that they like better. Also, because older workers have fewer opportunities to change jobs, they may learn to live with what they have, and accept that it is the best they are likely to get. Such acceptance may ultimately translate into satisfaction (Tangri, Thomas, & Mednick, 2003).

## Challenges of Work: On-the-Job Dissatisfaction

Job satisfaction is not universal in middle adulthood. For some people, dissatisfaction with working conditions or with the nature of the job increases their stress. Conditions may become so bad that the result is burnout or a decision to change jobs.

*Burnout.* For 44-year-old Peggy Augarten, her early-morning shifts in the intensive care unit of a suburban hospital were becoming increasingly difficult. It had always been hard to lose a patient, but recently she found herself crying over patients at the strangest moments: while she was doing the laundry, washing the dishes, or watching TV. When she began to dread going to work, she knew that her feelings about her job were undergoing a fundamental change.

Augarten's response probably reflects the phenomenon of burnout. **Burnout** occurs when workers experience dissatisfaction, disillusionment, frustration, and weariness from their jobs. It occurs most often in jobs that involve helping others, and it often strikes those who once were the most idealistic and driven. In some ways, such workers may be overcommitted to their jobs. Realizing that they can make only minor dents in huge social problems such as poverty and medical care can be disappointing and demoralizing (Demir, Ulusoy, & Ulusoy, 2003; Taris, van Horn, & Schaufeli, 2004; Bakker & Heuven, 2006).

A growing cynicism about one's work characterizes burnout. An employee might say to himself, "What am I working so hard for? No one is going to notice that I've come in on budget for the last two years." Workers also may feel indifferent about their job performance. The idealism a worker felt entering a profession may give way to pessimism and the attitude that no meaningful solution to a problem exists (Lock, 1992).

People can combat burnout, even in professions with high demands and seemingly insurmountable burdens. The nurse who despairs of not having enough time for every patient can adopt a more feasible, yet nurturing, goal—such as giving patients a quick back-rub. Jobs can also be structured so that workers (and their supervisors) note the small, daily victories, such

> **burnout** a situation that occurs when workers experience dissatisfaction, disillusionment, frustration, and weariness from their jobs

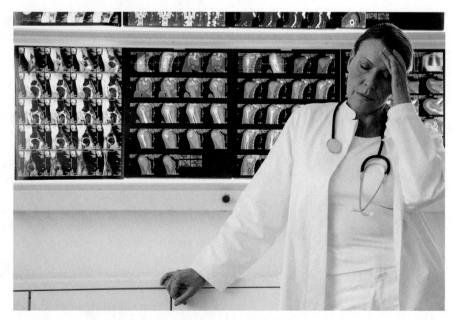

Burnout occurs most often in professions involving helping others.

Becoming unemployed in midlife can be a shattering experience that may taint your view of the world.

as a client's gratitude, even though disease, poverty, racism, and an inadequate educational system remain problems (Krasner et al., 2009; Peisah et al., 2009).

## Unemployment: The Dashing of the Dream

*The dream is gone—probably forever. And it seems like it tears you apart. It's just disintegrating away. You look alongside the river banks…there's all flat ground. There used to be a big scrap pile there where steel and iron used to be melted and used over again, processed. That's all leveled off. Many a time I pass through and just happen to see it. It's hard to visualize it's not there anymore. (Kotre & Hall, 1990, p. 290)*

It is hard not to view 52-year-old Matt Nort's description of an obsolete Pittsburgh steel mill as symbolic of his own life. Having been unemployed for several years, Matt's dreams for occupational success have died along with the mill in which he once worked.

For many workers, unemployment is a hard reality, affecting them psychologically and economically. For those who have been fired, laid-off by corporate downsizing, or forced out of jobs by technological advances, being out of work can be psychologically and even physically devastating (Sharf, 1992).

Unemployment can leave people feeling anxious, depressed, and irritable. Their self-confidence may plummet, and they may be unable to concentrate. According to one analysis, every time the unemployment rate goes up 1 percent, there is a 4 percent rise in suicide, and admissions to psychiatric facilities go up by some 4 percent for men and 2 percent for women (Connor, 1992; Inoue et al., 2006; Paul & Moser, 2009).

Even seemingly positive aspects of unemployment, such as having more time, can affect people negatively. Unemployed people may feel depressed and at loose ends, making them less apt to take part in community activities, use libraries, and read than employed people. They are more likely to be late for appointments and even for meals (Ball & Orford, 2002; Tyre & McGinn, 2003).

And these problems may linger. Middle-aged adults tend to stay unemployed longer than younger workers, and have fewer opportunities for gratifying work as they age. Employers may discriminate against older applicants, making it more difficult to find a new job. Such discrimination is both illegal and based on misguided assumptions: Research finds that older workers miss fewer work days, hold their jobs longer, are more reliable, and are more willing to learn new skills (Connor, 1992).

Midlife unemployment is a shattering experience. For some people, especially those who never find meaningful work again, it taints their view of life. Such involuntary—and premature—retirement can lead to pessimism, cynicism, and despondency. Accepting the new situation takes time and a good deal of psychological adjustment. And there are challenges for those who *do* find a new career, too (Waters & Moore, 2002).

## Switching—and Starting—Careers at Midlife

For some people, midlife brings a hunger for change. For those who are dissatisfied with their jobs, who switch careers after a period of unemployment, or who return to a job market they left years ago, development leads to new careers.

People change careers in middle adulthood for several reasons. Their job may offer little challenge, or they have achieved mastery, making the once difficult, routine. Other people switch because their jobs have changed in ways they do not like, or they may have lost their job. They may be asked to accomplish more with fewer resources, or technology may have drastically changed their daily activities and they no longer enjoy what they do.

Still others are unhappy with their status and wish to make a fresh start. Some are burned out or feel that they are on a treadmill. And some people simply want something new. They view middle age as the last chance to make a meaningful occupational change.

Finally, a significant number of people, most of them women, return to the job market after raising children. Some need to find paying work after a divorce. Since the mid-1980s, the number of women in the workforce who are in their 50s has grown significantly. Around half of women between the ages of 55 and 64—and an even larger percentage of those who graduated from college—are now in the workforce.

People may enter new professions with unrealistically high expectations and then be disappointed by the realities. Middle-aged people, starting new careers, may also be placed in entry-level positions. Thus, their peers on the job may be considerably younger than they are (Sharf, 1992; Barnett & Hyde, 2001). But in the long run, starting a new career in midlife can be invigorating. Those who switch or begin new careers may be especially valued employees (Connor, 1992; Adelmann, Antonucci, & Crohan, 1990; Bromberger & Matthews, 1994; Otto, Dette-Hagenmeyer, & Dalbert, 2010).

Some forecasters suggest that career changes will become the rule, not the exception. According to this view, technological advances will occur so rapidly that people will be forced periodically to change their profession, often dramatically. People will have not one, but several, careers during their lifetimes. As the "Cultural Dimensions" segment shows, this is especially true for those who make the major life and career change: immigrating to another country as adults.

**From the perspective of a social worker:** Why do you think immigrants' ambition and achievements are widely underestimated? Do conspicuous negative examples play a role (as they do in perceptions of the midlife crisis and stormy adolescence)?

## Leisure Time: Life Beyond Work

With the typical work week hovering between 35 and 40 hours—and becoming shorter for most people—most middle-aged adults have some 70 waking hours per week of leisure time (Kacapyr, 1997). What do they do with it? ☉─Watch on **mydevelopmentlab.com**

For one thing, they watch television. Middle-aged people average around 15 hours of television each week. But adults do much more with their leisure time. For many people, midlife offers a renewed opportunity to take up activities outside the home. As children leave, parents have substantial time to participate in leisure activities like sports or participate in town committees. Middle-aged adults in the United States spend about 6 hours each week socializing (Robinson & Godbey, 1997; Lindstrom et al., 2005).

☉─Watch on **mydevelopmentlab.com**

*What is it like when you go from working 40 to 50 hours a week to being retired?*
Log onto MyDevelopmentLab.com and listen to Mary and George talk about their experience with retirement and how their lives have changed.

## Cultural Dimensions

### Immigrants on the Job: Making It in America

*Seventeen years ago, Mankekolo Mahlangu-Ngcobo was placed in solitary confinement for 21 days in South Africa's Moletsane police station, falsely accused of terrorism. In 1980, once again in danger of imprisonment for her anti-apartheid protests, she fled to Botswana, leaving her 12-year-old son Ratijawe with her mother. She came to the U.S. in 1981, won political asylum in 1984 and now lives with her 13-year-old daughter Ntokozo in a $60,000 Baltimore row house. Her experiences left her with a deep appreciation of her adopted land. "If you have never lived somewhere else," she says, "you cannot know how much freedom you have here."*

*Ngcobo also found prosperity here. As with many of her fellow immigrants, the key was education. Since her arrival, she has earned a bachelor's degree, two master's, and a doctorate in theology—which she paid for largely with scholarships or with her own money. Her academic credentials and dedication to helping others have won her two soul-satisfying careers, as a lecturer in public health at Baltimore's Morgan State University and as assistant minister at the Metropolitan African Methodist Episcopal Church in Washington, D.C. (Kim, 1995, p. 133)*

Public opinion often portrays immigrants to the United States as straining the educational, health care, welfare, and prison systems while contributing little to society. But—as Mankekolo Mahlangu-Ngcobo's story shows—these assumptions are quite wrong.

With around 1.2 million immigrants entering the United States each year, foreign-born residents now represent 10 percent of the population, more than twice the percentage in 1970. First- and second-generation immigrants comprise almost a quarter of the population of the United States (Deaux, 2006).

Today's immigrants are somewhat different from those of the earlier waves at the beginning of the twentieth century. Only a third are White, compared with almost 90 percent of immigrants who arrived before 1960.

Critics argue that many new immigrants lack the skills that will allow them to make a contribution to the high-tech economy of the twenty-first century. However, the critics are wrong in many fundamental respects. For instance, consider the following data (Camarota, 2001; Flanigan, 2005; Gorman, 2010):

- **Most legal *and* illegal immigrants ultimately succeed financially.** Although they initially experienced higher rates of poverty, immigrants who arrived in the United States prior to 1980 and established themselves have a higher family income than native-born Americans. Immigrants match nonimmigrants in entrepreneurship, with one in nine owning their own business.

- **Only a few immigrants come to the United States to get on welfare.** Instead, most say they come for the opportunities to work and prosper. Nonrefugee immigrants of working age are less likely to be on welfare than native-born U.S. citizens.

- **Given time, immigrants contribute more to the economy than they take away.** Although initially costly to the government, often because they hold low-paying jobs and therefore pay no income taxes, immigrants become more productive as they get older.

Why are immigrants often ultimately financially successful? One explanation is that immigrants who voluntarily choose to leave their native countries are particularly motivated and driven to be successful.

---

A significant number of people find leisure so alluring that they take early retirement. For early retirees who have adequate financial resources to last the remainder of their years, life can be quite gratifying. Early retirees tend to be in good health, and they may take up a variety of new activities (Cliff, 1991; Jopp & Hertzog, 2010).

Although midlife offers the opportunity for more leisure, most people report that the pace of their lives does not seem slower. Much of their free time is scattered throughout the week in 15- and 30-minute chunks as they pursue a variety of activities. Thus, despite a documented increase of five hours of weekly leisure time since 1965, many people feel they have no more free time than they did earlier (Robinson & Godbey, 1997).

One reason why extra leisure time seems to evaporate is that the pace of life in the United States is considerably faster than in many countries. By measuring the length of time average pedestrians cover 60 feet, the time it takes to purchase a stamp, and the accuracy of public clocks, research has compared the tempo of living in a variety of countries. According to a composite of these measures, the United States has a quicker tempo than many other countries, particularly Latin American, Asian, Middle Eastern, and African countries. But, many countries outpace the United States. Western European countries and Japan move more quickly than the United States, with Switzerland ranking first (Levine, 1997a, 1997b).

## REVIEW, CHECK, AND APPLY

**REVIEW**

**LO16** What are the characteristics of work in middle adulthood?

- People in middle age view their jobs differently than before, placing more emphasis on specific job factors such as pay and working conditions, and less on career striving and ambition.

- Midlife career changes are becoming more prevalent, motivated usually by dissatisfaction, the need for more challenge or status, or the desire to return to the workforce after childrearing.

**LO17** How is leisure time different in middle adulthood?

- People in midlife usually have increased leisure time. Often they use it to become more involved outside the home in recreational and community activities.

**CHECK YOURSELF**

1. Burnout is more likely to strike individuals who are in helping professions.

   - True
   - False

2. Compared to younger adults, middle-aged adults who lose their jobs:

   a. tend to stay unemployed longer and have fewer opportunities for gratifying work as they age.

   b. tend to find jobs quickly because of their skills but find it difficult to stay employed.

   c. find it difficult to get new jobs, but once employed have a stable work history.

   d. are less likely to become depressed, which makes it easier for them to obtain employment.

**APPLYING LIFESPAN DEVELOPMENT**

- Why might striving for occupational success be less appealing in middle age than before? What cognitive and personality changes might contribute to this phenomenon?

✓●─[**Study** and **Review** on
**MyDevelopmentLab.com**

Answers: 1) True; 2) a

# Putting It All Together
## Middle Adulthood

**JAN HUGHES,** at 48, turned her entire life upside down. Chronologically and developmentally right in the middle of middle adulthood, she sent her youngest child to college, ended a lackluster marriage, quit her job at a large architectural firm, sold her house, and moved across the country to California. Though Jan was certainly in a midlife transition, she did not experience a "midlife crisis." This physically active and mentally alert woman started her own architectural business, joined a cycling club, and began a new romance. With her new partner, she shares many of her leisure time passions including cycling, opera, and French cooking. Nearing 50, she realized she still had half a life ahead of her if all went well, and she was determined to use the knowledge she'd gained about herself and the world in the first half to shape the second half to her liking.

## MODULE 8.1 Physical Development in Middle Adulthood

- Although certain chronic diseases, like arthritis and hypertension, do begin to appear in midlife, like most middle-aged adults, Jan is in good health.**(p. 371)**

- The cycling club she joined helps Jan stay healthy and agile as she ages, a goal shared by many of her same-age peers **(p. 365)**

- Jan's regular exercise compensates for the gradual loss of strength that occurs in middle adulthood. **(p. 365)**

- With an easing of work demands and obligations to her children, Jan has more time and energy to enjoy sex with her new partner. However, if she hasn't gone through menopause, she will still need to use contraception. **(pp. 367–369)**

## MODULE 8.2 Cognitive Development in Middle Adulthood

- Jan has developed expertise and a high competency in her work as an architect, which brings her continued success even though midlife brings an overall decline in intellectual skills. **(pp. 380–381)**

- Her understanding of what is involved in architectural design allows Jan to quickly evaluate a potential project, see what's involved, and decide if it interests her. **(p. 381)**

- It is likely that Jan has a great deal of practical intelligence in addition to the more traditional kind. **(pp. 377–380)**

- Though Jan is in midlife transition, the actions she takes to find more connected relationships, and to tailor her career in a way that's truly satisfying to her, result in growth rather than stagnation. **(pp. 385–387)**

- Jan's openness to new experiences, her extraversion, and her talent for organization are personality traits that have remained stable throughout her life. **(pp. 388–390)**

- Moving to a new place, starting her own business, and finding a new romance eased any sadness Jan might have experienced when her youngest child left for college. **(p. 395)**

### Explore on **mydevelopmentlab.com**

To read how real-life marriage counselors, health care providers, and career counselors responded to these questions, log onto MyDevelopmentLab.com.

*Do you agree or disagree with their responses? Why? What concepts that you've read about back up their opinion?*

## What would **YOU** do?

- Would you advise Jan to slow up on the transitions in her life, to consolidate her changes? Why or why not?

  **HINT** Review pages 384–389.

  *What's your response?*

## What would a **MARRIAGE COUNSELOR** do?

- Would you advise Jan to take her new romance with Mike slowly, since she's just come from a divorce? What advice would you give her if she decides to remarry?

  **HINT** Review pages 391–394.

  *What's your response?*

## What would a **HEALTH CARE PROVIDER** do?

- Considering her age and the physical changes her body is going through, what dietary and exercise guidelines would you recommend Jan observe to prevent fatigue and injury during her upcoming cycling trip up the West Coast?

  **HINT** Review pages 362–365.

  *What's your response?*

## What would a **CAREER COUNSELOR** do?

- Would you advise Jan to consider taking on an assistant in her business, perhaps a young architect who needs to learn the ropes and has the energy to do the legwork that will free up Jan to focus on the client and the project? Even if she can hold the business together by herself now, will she be able to do so in five years? In ten?

  **HINT** Review pages 377–381.

  *What's your response?*

# Late Adulthood

I t's 5 a.m., and Arthur Winston pulls into his parking space and clocks in, just as he has every workday for 70 years.

"They tell me I'm a workaholic," says Winston.

Winston, a cleaning supervisor at a Los Angeles bus yard, turned 98 this month. He's never been late, never called in sick, and never punched out early.

"I just love to come to work here," he says . . .

So what's his secret?

"I don't smoke, and I don't drink and I don't fool with these credit cards," he says . . .

Asked if he has any desire to retire, Winston says, "No, no, no, no."

Maybe when he's 100. Until then, he'll take it one day at a time.

"It's nice to walk out in the morning and say, 'Thank God. Let me see another day that I've never seen before. Just one,'" says Winston. (Whitaker, 2004)

\*\*\*

**MODULE 9.1** Physical Development in Late Adulthood

## Life expectancy: How long have I got? see page 410

**MODULE 9.2** Cognitive Development in Late Adulthood

## How can you exercise your brain to stay sharp? see page 426

Ben Tufty rolls over and checks his alarm clock, which has been silent for every one of the 27 years since he retired at age 63. It's 8:42.

Now 90, Tufty considers whether to have an active day: walking to town for a cup of decaf and a paper, then maybe stopping at the library—or a leisurely day: making his own decaf at home, listening to the news on the radio, and reading until it's time to plan his afternoon.

Asked if he misses working, the former aircraft engine technician laughs. "I retired as soon as I could. Not that I didn't like my job—I did. I just prefer doing my own thing with no particular schedule. I don't need constant companionship or the structure of the workday. I guess I'm a natural homebody. I don't even like to travel—maybe because I've seen jet engines up close," he says with a grin.

"My wife is long gone and there's been no one else I've been serious about," he adds. "I have grandkids and great-grandkids, but honestly, I'd rather hear from them long-distance. They know this and keep in touch by phone and the Internet."

Tufty's life may be quiet, but he manages to fill his days. "I'm not looking for things to do. My days are full enough. I exercise every day and keep up with the newest books and magazines. I occasionally call my friends, and we get together for a movie or a meal. Sometimes they come over and we play low-pressure *Scrabble* or checkers, and we always discuss politics and have a good laugh. All of us have seen just about everything, and we're always amazed when someone comes up with a 'new' idea that we know was tried a long, long time ago—to no effect.

"Am I happy? You bet I am. I wish I could have figured out how to do this 37 years ago instead of just 27. I was *made* for retirement."

## MODULE **9.3** Social and Personality Development in Late Adulthood

# How does culture affect how we treat people in late adulthood? see page 432

## MyDevelopmentLab

Arthur and Ben may lead different lives, but they both are going through many of the same changes in late adulthood.

Log onto MyDevelopmentLab.com and listen to several men and women in their 60s talk about changes in their health, their day-to-day lives, and losing loved ones.

The period of late adulthood, which starts around age 65, is characterized by great changes—and ongoing personal development. Older adults face profound physical, cognitive, and social changes, and by and large they figure out strategies for adjusting to them. No two strategies are exactly alike, as illustrated by the quite different paths chosen by Arthur Winston and Ben Tufty, but most older adults manage this stage successfully.

In late adulthood, people begin the decline that will be part of their lives until death. But we will see that all aspects of this period—physical, cognitive, and social—are largely misrepresented in popular stereotypes. Older people can maintain physical and mental strength virtually until the day they die, and their social worlds can also remain as vital and active as they want.

Physically, people over 65 certainly begin a gradual transition from full strength and health to an increasing concern about illness, pain, and disease. But this is not the only thing going on in their lives. They can stay healthy for quite a long time and can continue most if not all of the activities that they enjoyed when younger. Cognitively, we find that older people adjust quite well to the changes that seem designed to impede them by adopting new strategies for solving problems and compensating for lost abilities. And socially, many of them become adept at coping with the changes in their lives, such as the death of a spouse and retirement from work.

Arthur Winston and Ben Tufty are typical only in being atypical. Through their unique approaches to aging, they make the point that old age can be what people want it to be—not what society thinks it ought to be.

## MODULE 9.1 Physical Development in Late Adulthood

### A Better Way to Shell a Nut

*Jock Brandis had spent thirty years working in the film industry, solving tricky engineering problems as a lighting director. After a 2001 visit to Africa, though, Jock turned his career in a new direction. While visiting a friend in the Peace Corps in Malawi, Jock saw native women shelling peanuts, an important cash crop, with bloody fingers. Jock realized that the local economy would be helped immeasurably if they could use a machine that did the shelling for them.*

*When Jock returned to the United States, though, he found out that such a machine simply didn't exist. 'If you work in the movie business,' Josh says, 'if someone says can you make this, can you do this, the answer is always yes. And then you try to figure out how to do it. So I thought, well, I'll just invent the thing.'*

*Jock created the Universal Nut Sheller, a simple machine that shelled peanuts and that costs $28 to build. He also founded a nonprofit organization, The Full Belly Project, to help distribute the device. Today, the Universal Nut Sheller is used in seventeen countries, and the Full Belly Project continues its work to help those in the developing world get the tools they need to run successful and profitable farms. 'There are a lot of people who might think, 'Oh my God, you're in your sixties, you better hurry because you'll be on the front porch of the old folks home by the time you're seventy-five,' Jock says. 'I don't think so, I don't think along those lines...I'm starting off on an entirely other career that can take me as long as any of my previous ones.' (Essick, 2009; Brandis, 2010)*

Jock Brandis is not alone when it comes to showing extraordinary vitality in late adulthood. Increasingly, older people are pioneering new fields, achieving new athletic endeavors, and generally reshaping how we perceive the later stages of life. For a growing number of people in late adulthood, vigorous mental and physical activity remains an important part of daily life.

Old age used to be equated with loss: loss of brain cells, intellectual capabilities, energy, sex drive. That view is being displaced as **gerontologists,** specialists who study aging, paint a very different picture. Rather than a period of decline, late adulthood is seen as a stage in which people continue to change—to grow in some areas and, yes, to decline in others.

**gerontologists** specialists who study aging

Even the definition of "old" is changing. Many people in late adulthood, which begins around age 65 and continues to death, are as vigorous and involved with life as people several decades younger. We can no longer define old age by chronological years alone; we also must take into account people's physical and psychological well-being, their *functional ages*. Some researchers divide people into three groups according to functional ages: the *young old* are healthy and active; the *old old* have some health problems and difficulties with daily activities; and the *oldest old* are frail and need care. According to functional age, an active, healthy 100-year-old would be considered young old, while a 65-year-old in the late stages of emphysema would be among the oldest old.

We begin this module with a discussion of the myths and realities of aging, examining some stereotypes that color our understanding of late adulthood. We look at the outward and inward signs of aging and the ways the nervous system and senses change with age.

Next, we consider health and well-being. After examining some of the major disorders that affect older people, we look at what determines wellness and why old people are susceptible to disease. We then consider sexuality in late adulthood. We also focus on theories that seek to explain the aging process, as well as on gender, race, and ethnic differences in life expectancy.

# Physical Development in Late Adulthood

**LO1** What sorts of physical changes occur in old age?

**LO2** How are the senses affected by aging?

LEARNING OBJECTIVES

*The astronaut-turned-senator, John Glenn, was 77 years old when he returned to space on a 10-day mission to help NASA study how the elderly adjust to space travel. Although sheer altitude sets Glenn apart from others, many people lead active, vigorous lives during late adulthood, fully engaged with life.*

## Aging: Myth and Reality

Late adulthood holds a unique distinction among life's stages: Because people are living longer, late adulthood is getting longer. Whether we start counting at 65 or 70, there is today a greater proportion of people alive in late adulthood than at any time in world history. In fact, demographers have divided the period using the same terms—but with different meanings—as researchers of functional aging. For demographers, the terms are purely chronological. The *young old* are 65 to 74 years old. The *old old* are between 75 and 84, and the *oldest old* are 85 and older.

***The Demographics of Late Adulthood.*** One out of every eight Americans is 65 or older, and projections suggest that by 2050 nearly one-quarter of the population will be 65 and above. The number of people over 85 is projected to increase from 4 million to 18 million by 2050 (Schneider, 1999; Administration on Aging, 2003) (see Figure 9-1).

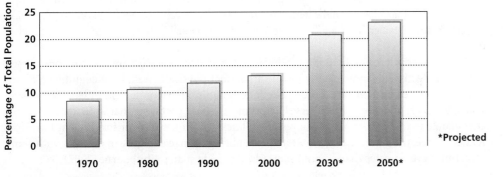

**FIGURE 9-1 The Flourishing Elderly**

The percentage of people over the age of 65 is projected to rise to almost 25 percent of the population by the year 2050. Can you name two factors that contribute to this?

Source: Adapted from U.S. Bureau of the Census, 2000.

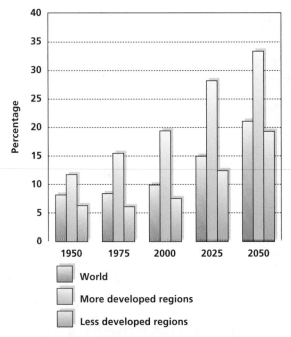

**FIGURE 9-2** **The Elderly Population Worldwide**
Longer life is transforming population profiles worldwide, with the proportion of those over the age of 60 predicted to increase substantially by the year 2050.
Source: United Nations Population Division, 2002.

What do you see when you look at this woman? Ageism is found in widespread negative attitudes toward older people, suggesting that they are in less than full command of their faculties.

**ageism** prejudice and discrimination directed at older people

The fastest growing segment of the population is the oldest old—people 85 or older. In the last two decades, the size of this group has nearly doubled. The population explosion among older people is not limited to the United States. As can be seen in Figure 9-2, the number of elderly is increasing substantially in countries around the globe. By 2050, the number of adults worldwide over 60 will exceed the number of people under 15 for the first time in history (Sandis, 2000; United Nations, 2002).

***Ageism: Confronting the Stereotypes of Late Adulthood.*** Crotchety. Old codger. Old coot. Senile. Geezer. Old hag.

Such are the labels of late adulthood. They don't draw a pretty picture: These words are demeaning and biased, representing both overt and subtle ageism. **Ageism** is prejudice and discrimination directed at older people.

Ageism suggests that older people are in less than full command of their mental faculties. Many attitude studies find that older adults are viewed more negatively than younger ones on a variety of traits, particularly those relating to general competence and attractiveness (Cuddy & Fiske, 2004; Angus & Reeve, 2006; Iverson, Larsen, & Solem, 2009; Helmes & Campbell, 2010).

Even when older and younger people perform exactly the same behavior, it is likely to be interpreted differently. Imagine you hear someone describing his search for his house keys. Would your perception of the person change if he was 80 rather than 20? Research says yes. Older adults are more likely to be viewed as chronically forgetful and perhaps suffering from some mental disorder. Young adults are judged more charitably, perhaps as temporarily forgetful because they have too much on their minds (Erber, Szuchman, & Rothberg, 1990; Nelson, 2004).

Many Western societies revere youth and admire a youthful appearance. It is the rare advertisement that includes an elderly person, unless it is for a product specifically designed for older adults. And in television programs, older persons are often presented as someone's parents or grandparents rather than as individuals in their own right (Vernon, 1990; McVittie, McKinlay, & Widdicombe, 2003; Ferguson & Brohaugh, 2010).

The ageism that produces such negative views of older people is reflected in the way they are treated. For instance, elderly individuals seeking jobs may face open prejudice, being told in job interviews that they lack the stamina for particular jobs. Or they sometimes are relegated to jobs for which they are overqualified. In addition, such stereotypes are accepted by people in late adulthood, becoming self-fulfilling prophecies that hinder performance (Hedge, Borman, & Lammlein, 2006; Rupp, Vodanovich, & Credé, 2006; Levy, 2009).

Today's ageism is, in some ways, a peculiarly modern and Western cultural phenomenon. In the American colonial period, a long life was an indication of a virtuous life, and older people were held in high esteem. Similarly, elders are venerated in most Asian societies because they have attained special wisdom by living so long, and many Native American societies have traditionally viewed older people as storehouses of information about the past (Cowgill & Holmes, 1972; Ng, 2002).

Today, however, negative views of older people prevail in U.S. society, and they are based on misinformation. Test your knowledge about aging by answering the questions in Table 9-1. Most people score no higher than chance on the items, getting about 50 percent correct (Palmore, 1988, 1992).

Given the prevalence of ageist stereotypes, it is reasonable to ask if there is a kernel of truth in them.

The answer is largely no. Aging produces consequences that vary greatly from one person to the next. Although some elderly people are in fact physically frail, have cognitive difficulties, and require constant care, others, like Jock Brandis, are vigorous and independent—and sharp, brilliant, and shrewd thinkers. Furthermore, some problems that at first glance seem attributable to old age are actually a result of illness, improper diet, or insufficient nutrition. As we will see, the autumn and winter of life can bring change and growth on a par with—and sometimes even greater than—earlier periods of the life span (Whitbourne, 2007).

**From a social worker's perspective:** When older people win praise and attention for being "vigorous," "active," and "youthful," is this a message that combats or supports ageism?

## TABLE 9-1  THE MYTHS OF AGING

1. The majority of old people (age 65 and older) have defective memory, are disoriented, or are demented. T or F?

2. The five senses (sight, hearing, taste, touch, and smell) all tend to weaken in old age. T or F?

3. The majority of old people have no interest in, nor capacity for, sexual relations. T or F?

4. Lung capacity tends to decline in old age. T or F?

5. The majority of old people are sick most of the time. T or F?

6. Physical strength tends to decline in old age. T or F?

7. At least one-tenth of the aged are living in long-stay institutions (such as nursing homes, mental hospitals, and homes for the aged). T or F?

8. Many older adults maintain large social networks of friends. T or F?

9. Older workers usually cannot work as effectively as younger workers. T or F?

10. Over three-fourths of the aged are healthy enough to carry out their normal activities. T or F?

11. The majority of old people are unable to adapt to change. T or F?

12. Old people usually take longer to learn something new. T or F?

13. It is almost impossible for the average old person to learn something new. T or F?

14. Older people tend to react slower than do younger people. T or F?

15. In general, old people tend to be pretty much alike. T or F?

16. The majority of old people say they are seldom bored. T or F?

17. The majority of old people are socially isolated. T or F?

18. Older workers have fewer accidents than do younger workers. T or F?

**Scoring**

All odd-numbered statements are false; all even-numbered statements are true. Most college students miss about six, and high school students miss about nine. Even college instructors miss an average of about three.

Source: From "The Myths of Aging" from Palmore, E. B. (1982). THE FACTS ON AGING QUIZ. New York: Springer. Reprinted with permission from the author.

## Physical Transitions in Older People

*"Feel the burn." That's what the exercise tape says, and many of the 14 women in the group are doing just that. As the tape continues through its drills, some of the women stretch and reach vigorously, while others mostly just sway to the music. It's not much different from thousands of exercise classes across the United States, and yet there is one surprise: The youngest woman in the group is 66 years old, and the oldest, dressed in a sleek Spandex leotard, is 81.*

The surprise registered by this observer reflects the stereotype that people over 65 are sedentary, incapable of vigorous exercise. The reality is different. Although their physical capabilities are likely to have changed, many older persons remain agile and fit long into old age (Fiatarone & Garnett, 1997; Riebe, Burbank, & Garber, 2002). Still, the outer and inner changes that began subtly during middle adulthood become unmistakable during old age.

As we discuss aging, we should take note of the distinction between primary and secondary aging. **Primary aging,** or *senescence,* involves universal and irreversible changes due to genetic programming. In contrast, **secondary aging** encompasses changes that are due to illness, health habits, and other individual factors, which are not inevitable. Although the physical and cognitive changes of secondary aging are common, they are potentially avoidable and can sometimes be reversed.  Watch on **mydevelopmentlab.com**

***Outward Signs of Aging.***  One of the most obvious indicators of aging is the hair, which usually becomes distinctly gray and eventually white, and may thin out. The face and other

Watch on **mydevelopmentlab.com**

Log onto MyDevelopmentLab.com to hear a 90-year-old man talk about the difference between what he used to enjoy doing and what he's physically capable of doing now.

**primary aging (or senescence)** aging that involves universal and irreversible changes that, due to genetic programming, occur as people get older

**secondary aging** changes in physical and cognitive functioning that are due to illness, health habits, and other individual differences, but are not due to increased age itself and are not inevitable

Although gray hair is often characterized as "distinguished" in men, the same trait in women is viewed more often as a sign of being "over the hill"—a clear double standard.

parts of the body become wrinkled as the skin loses elasticity and *collagen,* the protein that forms the basic fibers of body tissue (Bowers & Thomas, 1995; Medina, 1996).

People may become shorter by as much as 4 inches, partially due to changes in posture, but mostly because the cartilage in the disks of the backbone becomes thinner. This is particularly true for women, who are more susceptible than men to **osteoporosis,** or thinning of the bones, largely a result of reduced estrogen production.

Osteoporosis, which affects 25 percent of women over 60, is a primary cause of broken bones among older people. It is largely preventable if exercise is adequate and calcium and protein intake are sufficient earlier in life. Osteoporosis can be treated and even prevented with drugs such as Fosamax (alendronate) (Moyad, 2004; Picavet & Hoeymans, 2004; Swaim, Barner, & Brown, 2008).

Although negative stereotypes against appearing old affect both genders, they are particularly potent for women. In fact, in Western cultures there is a *double standard* for appearance, by which women are judged more harshly than men. For instance, gray hair in men is often viewed as "distinguished"; in women it is a sign of being "over the hill" (Sontag, 1979; Bell, 1989).

As a consequence, women feel considerably more pressure than men to hide the signs of aging by dyeing their hair, undergoing cosmetic surgery, and using age-concealing cosmetics (Unger & Crawford, 1992). The double standard is diminishing, however, as more men grow interested in looking younger and fall prey to a new wave of male-oriented cosmetic products, such as wrinkle creams. Ironically, as the double standard eases, ageism is becoming more of a concern for both sexes.

***Internal Aging.*** As the outward signs become more apparent, there are also changes in the internal functioning of the organ systems (Whitbourne, 2001; Aldwin & Gilmer, 2004).

The brain becomes smaller and lighter. As it shrinks, it pulls away from the skull; the space between the brain and skull doubles from age 20 to age 70. The brain uses less oxygen and glucose, and blood flow is reduced. The number of neurons, or brain cells, declines in some parts of the brain, although not as much as was once thought. Recent research suggests that the number of cells in the cortex may drop only minimally or not at all. In fact, some evidence suggests that certain types of neuronal growth may continue throughout the life span (Tisserand & Jolles, 2003; Lindsey & Tropepe, 2006; Raz et al., 2007; Ziegler et al., 2010).

The reduced flow of blood in the brain is due in part to the heart's reduced ability to pump blood through hardening and shrinking blood vessels. A 75-year-old man pumps less than three-quarters of the blood that he could pump during early adulthood (Kart, 1990; Yildiz, 2007).

**osteoporosis** a condition in which the bones become brittle, fragile, and thin, often brought about by a lack of calcium in the diet

Other bodily systems also work at lower capacity. The respiratory system is less efficient, and the digestive system produces less digestive juice and is less efficient in pushing food through the system—thereby increasing the incidence of constipation. Some hormones are produced at lower levels. Muscle fibers decrease both in size and in amount, and they become less efficient at using oxygen from the bloodstream and storing nutrients (Fiatarone & Garnett, 1997; Lamberts, van den Beld, & van der Lely, 1997; Deruelle et al., 2007; Suetta & Kjaer, 2010).

Although these changes are normal, they often occur earlier in people who have less healthy lifestyles. For example, smoking accelerates declines in cardiovascular capacity at any age.

Lifestyle factors can also slow the changes associated with aging. For instance, people whose exercise program includes weightlifting may lose muscle fiber at a slower rate than those who are sedentary. Similarly, physical fitness is related to better performance on mental tests, may prevent a loss of brain tissue, and may even aid in the development of new neurons. In fact, studies suggest that sedentary older adults who begin aerobic fitness training ultimately show cognitive benefits (Elder, DeGasperi, & GamaSosa, 2006; Colcombe et al., 2006; Kramer, Erickson, & Colcombe, 2006; Pereira et al., 2007).

## Slowing Reaction Time

*Karl winced as the "game over" message came up on his grandsons' video game system. He enjoyed trying out their games, but he just couldn't shoot down those bad guys as quickly as his grandkids could.*

As people get older, they take longer: longer to put on a tie, reach a ringing phone, press the buttons in a video game. One reason is a lengthening of reaction time, which begins to increase in middle age and by late adulthood may rise significantly (Fozard et al., 1994; Benjuya, Melzer, & Kaplanski, 2004; Der & Deary, 2006).

It is not clear why people slow down. One explanation, known as the **peripheral slowing hypothesis,** suggests that the peripheral nervous system, which encompasses the nerves that branch from the spinal cord and brain to the extremities of the body, becomes less efficient with age. Because of this, it takes longer for information from the environment to reach the brain and for commands from the brain to be transmitted to the muscles (Salthouse, 1989, 2006).

According to the **generalized slowing hypothesis,** on the other hand, processing in all parts of the nervous system, including the brain, is less efficient. As a consequence, slowing occurs throughout the body, including the processing of both simple and complex stimuli, and the transmission of commands to the muscles (Cerella, 1990).

Although we don't know which explanation is more accurate, it is clear that the slowing of reaction time and general processing results in a higher incidence of accidents for elderly persons. Slowed reaction and processing time means they can't efficiently receive information from the environment that may indicate a dangerous situation. Slowed decision-making processes impair their ability to remove themselves from harm's way. Drivers over 70 have as many fatal accidents per mile driven as teenagers (Whitbourne, Jacobo, & Munoz-Ruiz, 1996) (see Figure 9-3).

Although response time slows, the *perception* of time actually seems to speed up with age. The days and weeks seem to go by more quickly and time seems to rush by faster for older adults, perhaps because of changes in the way the brain coordinates its internal time clock (Mangan, 1997).

## The Senses: Sight, Sound, Taste, and Smell

Old age brings declines in the sense organs, which has major psychological consequences because the senses are people's link with the world.

*Vision.* Changes in the physical apparatus of the eye—the cornea, lens, retina, and optic nerve—diminish visual abilities. The lens becomes less transparent, allowing only a third as much light to reach the retina at 60 as at 20. The optic nerve also becomes less efficient in transmitting nerve impulses (Gawande, 2007). As a result, vision declines along several

**peripheral slowing hypothesis** the theory that suggests that overall processing speed declines in the peripheral nervous system with increasing age

**generalized slowing hypothesis** the theory that processing in all parts of the nervous system, including the brain, is less efficient as we age

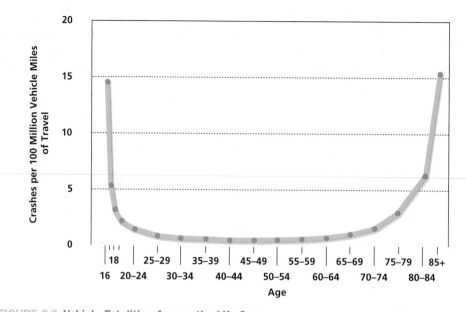

FIGURE 9-3 **Vehicle Fatalities Across the Life Span**
Drivers over age 70 have a fatal accident record comparable to that of teenagers when crashes are calculated per mile of driving. Why is this the case?
Source: National Highway Traffic Safety Administration, 1994.

dimensions. We see distant objects less well, need more light to see clearly, and take longer to adjust from dark to light and vice versa.

These changes cause everyday problems. Driving, particularly at night, becomes more challenging. Reading requires more light, and eye strain comes more easily. Of course, eyeglasses and contact lenses can correct many of these problems, and the majority of older people see reasonably well (Horowitz, 1994; Ball & Rebok, 1994; Owsley, Stalvey, & Phillips, 2003; Boerner et al., 2010).

Several eye diseases become more common during late adulthood. For instance, *cataracts*—cloudy or opaque areas on the lens of the eye that interfere with the passage of light—frequently develop. Cataracts bring blurred vision and glare in bright light. If cataracts are left untreated, the lens becomes milky white and blindness results. However, cataracts can be surgically removed, and eyesight can be restored with eyeglasses, contact lenses, or *intraocular lens implants,* in which a plastic lens is permanently placed in the eye (Walker, Anstey, & Lord, 2006).

Another serious problem among elderly individuals is glaucoma. As we noted earlier, *glaucoma* occurs when pressure in the fluid of the eye increases, either because the fluid cannot drain properly or because too much fluid is produced. Glaucoma can be treated by drugs or surgery if it is detected early enough.

The most common cause of blindness in people over 60 is *age-related macular degeneration* (AMD), which affects the *macula,* a yellowish area near the retina at which visual perception is most acute. When a portion of the macula thins and degenerates, the eyesight gradually deteriorates (see Figure 9-4). If diagnosed early, macular degeneration can sometimes be treated with medication or lasers. There is also some evidence that a diet rich in antioxidant vitamins (C, E, and A) can reduce the risk of AMD (Rattner & Nathans, 2006; Wiggins & Uwaydat, 2006; Coleman et al., 2008; Jager, Mieler, & Miller, 2008).

FIGURE 9-4 **The World Through Macular Degeneration**
Macular degeneration leads to a gradual deterioration of the center of the retina, leaving only peripheral vision. This is an example of what a person with macular degeneration might see.
Source: AARP, 2005, p. 34.

**Hearing.** Around 30 percent of adults between 65 and 74 have some hearing loss, and the figure rises to 50 percent among people over 75. Overall, more than 10 million elderly people in the United States have hearing impairments of one kind or another (*HHL,* 1997; Chisolm, Willott, & Lister, 2003).

Aging particularly affects the ability to hear higher frequencies. This makes it hard to hear conversations amid background noise or when several people are speaking simultaneously. Some elderly persons actually find loud noises painful.

Although hearing aids would probably be helpful around 75 percent of the time, only 20 percent of elderly people wear them. One reason is that hearing aids are far from perfect. They amplify background noises as much as conversations, making it difficult for wearers to separate what they want to hear from other sounds. Furthermore, many people feel that hearing aids make them appear even older and encourage others to treat them as if they were disabled (Lesner, 2003; Meister & von Wedel, 2003).

A hearing loss can be deadly to one's social life. Unable to hear conversations fully, some elderly people with hearing problems withdraw from others, unwilling to respond since they are unsure what was said to them. They can easily feel left out and lonely. Hearing loss can also lead to feelings of paranoia as conversational blanks are filled according to fear rather than reality. If someone hears "I hate going to Maude's" instead of "I hate going to the mall," a bland opinion about shopping can be interpreted as an expression of personal animosity (Myers, 2000; Goorabi, Hoseinabadi, & Share, 2008).

Hearing loss may hasten cognitive decline. The struggle to understand what is being said can shunt mental resources away from processing information, causing difficulties in remembering and understanding information (Wingfield, Tun, & McCoy, 2005).

***Taste and Smell.*** Elderly people who have always enjoyed eating may experience a real decline in the quality of life because of changes in sensitivity to taste and smell. Both senses become less discriminating, causing food to be less appetizing than it was earlier (Kaneda et al., 2000; Nordin, Razani, & Markison, 2003; Murphy, 2008). The decrease in taste and smell sensitivity has a physical cause. The tongue loses taste buds over time, making food less tasty. The problem is compounded as the olfactory bulbs in the brain begin to shrivel. Because taste depends on smell, this makes food taste even blander.

The loss of taste and smell sensitivity has an unfortunate side effect: Because food does not taste as good, people eat less and open the door to malnutrition. They may also oversalt their food, thereby increasing their risk of *hypertension,* or high blood pressure, one of the most common health problems of old age (Smith et al., 2006).

## REVIEW, CHECK, AND APPLY

### REVIEW

**L01**  What sorts of physical changes occur in old age?

- Older people are often subject to ageism—prejudice and discrimination against people based on their age.

- Old age brings many physical transitions, internal changes, and changes in sensory perception.

- Many of the physical changes associated with aging can cause social and psychological difficulties for older people.

**L02**  How are the senses affected by aging?

- Old age brings declines in vision, hearing, taste, and smell.

- The declines in the senses can have major psychological consequences.

### CHECK YOURSELF

1. The fastest growing segment of the elderly population is the oldest old, or people who are 85 and older.

   - True
   - False

2. _____ aging involves universal and irreversible changes that, due to genetic programming, occur as people get older.

3. According to the _____ slowing hypothesis, for elderly individuals processing in all parts of the nervous system, including the brain, is less efficient.

   **a.** automated

   **b.** global

   **c.** generalized

   **d.** peripheral

### APPLYING LIFESPAN DEVELOPMENT

- Should older people be subject to strict examinations to renew their drivers' licenses? Should such tests cover more than eyesight (e.g., response time, mental abilities)? What issues should be taken into consideration?

✓●─[**Study** and **Review** on **MyDevelopmentLab.com**

# Health and Wellness in Late Adulthood

**LEARNING OBJECTIVES**

**LO3** What is the general state of health of older people, and to what disorders are they susceptible?

**LO4** Can wellness and sexuality be maintained in late adulthood?

**LO5** How long can people expect to live, and what are the major causes of death?

Before his death at the age of 93, former President Ronald Reagan suffered from Alzheimer's disease for a decade.

*For an actor, there is no greater loss than the loss of his audience. I can part the Red Sea, but I can't part with you, which is why I won't exclude you from this stage in my life.*

*For now, I'm not changing anything. I'll insist on work when I can; the doctors will insist on rest when I must.*

*If you see a little less spring to my step, if your name fails to leap to my lips, you'll know why. And if I tell you a funny story for the second time, please laugh anyway.* (Heston, 2002)

With these words, the actor Charlton Heston, who died six years later at the age of 84, announced that he had joined the 4.5 million Americans with Alzheimer's disease, a debilitating condition that saps both physical and mental powers. In some ways, Alzheimer's—which led to the death of former president Ronald Reagan in 2004—feeds the stereotypical view of elderly people as more apt to be ill than healthy. In reality, as we have seen, most elderly people are in relatively good health for most of old age. Almost three-quarters of people 65 years old and above rate their health as good, very good, or excellent (USDHHS, 1990; Kahn & Rowe, 1999).

On the other hand, to be old is in fact to be susceptible to diseases. We now consider some of the major physical and psychological disorders of older people.

## Health Problems in Older People: Physical and Psychological Disorders

Most of the illnesses and diseases of late adulthood are not peculiar to old age; people of all ages suffer from cancer and heart disease, for instance. However, the incidence of these diseases rises with age, raising the odds that a person will be ill during old age. Moreover, older persons bounce back more slowly from illnesses than younger people, and a full recovery may be impossible.

***Common Physical Disorders.*** The leading causes of death in elderly people are heart disease, cancer, and stroke, which claim close to three-quarters of people in late adulthood. Because aging weakens the immune system, older adults are also more susceptible to infectious diseases (Feinberg, 2000). In addition, most older people have at least one chronic, long-term condition (AARP, 1990). For instance, *arthritis,* an inflammation of one or more joints, afflicts roughly half of older people. Arthritis can cause painful swelling, and it can be disabling, preventing people from performing the simplest of everyday tasks, such as unscrewing a jar of food or turning a key in a lock. Although aspirin and other drugs can relieve some of the swelling and reduce the pain, arthritis cannot be cured (Burt & Harris, 1994; Leverone & Epstein, 2010).

Around one-third of older people have *hypertension,* or high blood pressure. Many people who have high blood pressure are unaware of their condition because it has no symptoms, which makes it more dangerous. Left untreated, hypertension can weaken and damage blood vessels and the heart and may raise the risk of strokes (Wiggins & Uwaydat, 2006).

***Psychological and Mental Disorders.*** Some 15 to 25 percent of people over 65 are thought to show some symptoms of psychological disorder, a lower percentage than in younger adults. The behavioral symptoms related to these disorders are sometimes different in older and younger adults (Whitbourne, 2001).

One of the more prevalent problems is major depression, which is characterized by feelings of intense sadness, pessimism, and hopelessness. Among the reasons cited for depression are the experience of cumulative losses of their spouses and friends, and their own declining health and physical capabilities (Penninx et al., 1998; Kahn, Hessling, & Russell, 2003; Menzel, 2008; Vink et al., 2009).

Some elderly people suffer from psychological disorders induced by the combinations of drugs they may be taking for various medical conditions. They may also be taking inappropriate doses of some medications because the metabolism of a 75-year-old and that of a 25-year-old differ, and the doses appropriate for them may differ too. Because of these possibilities, older people who take medications must be careful to inform their physicians and pharmacists of every drug—with dosage information—that they take. They should also avoid medicating themselves with over-the-counter drugs, because a combination of nonprescription and prescription drugs may be dangerous.

The most common mental disorder of elderly people is **dementia,** a broad category of diseases encompassing serious memory loss accompanied by declines in other mental functioning. Although dementia has many causes, the symptoms are similar: declining memory, lessened intellectual abilities, and impaired judgment. The chances of experiencing dementia increase with age. Less than 2 percent of people between 60 and 65 are diagnosed with dementia, but the percentages double for every 5-year period past 65. Consequently, almost one-third of people over 85 suffer from some sort of dementia. There are some ethnic differences, too, with African Americans and Hispanics showing higher levels of dementia than Caucasians (National Research Council, 1997).

*Alzheimer's Disease.* **Alzheimer's disease,** a progressive brain disorder that produces loss of memory and confusion, leads to the deaths of 100,000 people in the United States each year. Nineteen percent of people age 75 to 84 have Alzheimer's, and nearly half of people over the age of 85 are affected by the disease. In fact, unless a cure is found, some 14 million people will be victims of Alzheimer's by 2050—more than triple the current number (Cowley, January 2000).

The first sign of Alzheimer's is usually forgetfulness. A person may have trouble recalling words during a conversation or may return to the grocery store several times after having already done the shopping. At first, recent memories are affected, and then older ones. Eventually, people with the disease are totally confused, unable to speak intelligibly or to recognize even their closest family and friends. In the final stages, they lose voluntary control of their muscles and are bedridden. Because victims of the disorder are initially aware of the future course of the disease, they may understandably suffer from anxiety, fear, and depression.

Biologically, Alzheimer's occurs when production of the protein *beta amyloid precursor protein*—which normally promotes the production and growth of neurons—goes awry, creating large clumps of cells that trigger inflammation and deterioration of nerve cells. The brain shrinks, and several areas of the hippocampus and frontal and temporal lobes show deterioration. Furthermore, certain neurons die, which leads to a shortage of various neurotransmitters, such as acetylcholine (Wolfe, 2006; Medeiros et al., 2007; Bredesen, 2009).

Although the physical changes that produce Alzheimer's are clear, what is not known is the trigger. Genetics clearly plays a role, with some families showing a much higher incidence of Alzheimer's than others. In fact, in certain families half the children appear to inherit the disease from their parents. Furthermore, years before Alzheimer's symptoms emerge, people who are genetically at high risk for the disease show differences in brain functioning when they are trying to recall information, as illustrated in the brain scans in Figure 9-5) (Coon et al., 2007; Thomas & Fenech, 2007; Baulac et al., 2009).

Most evidence suggests that Alzheimer's is an inherited disorder, but nongenetic factors such as high blood pressure or diet may increase susceptibility. In one cross-cultural study, poor Black residents in a Nigerian town were less likely to develop Alzheimer's than a comparable sample of African Americans living in the United States. The researchers speculate that variations in diet between the two groups—the residents of Nigeria ate mainly vegetables—might account for the differences in the Alzheimer's rates (Hendrie et al., 2001; Friedland, 2003; Wu, Zhou, & Chen, 2003; Lahiri et al., 2007; Chen et al., 2010).

Scientists are also studying certain viruses, dysfunctions of the immune system, and hormone imbalances that may produce the disease. Other studies have found that lower levels of linguistic ability in the early 20s are associated with declines in cognitive capabilities due to Alzheimer's much later in life (Snowdon et al., 1996; Alisky, 2007).

**dementia** the most common mental disorder of the elderly, it covers several diseases, each of which includes serious memory loss accompanied by declines in other mental functioning

**Alzheimer's disease** a progressive brain disorder that produces loss of memory and confusion

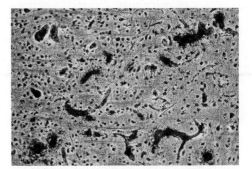

Brain scans of a patient with Alzheimer's disease show twisted clumps of nerve cells that are characteristic of the disease.

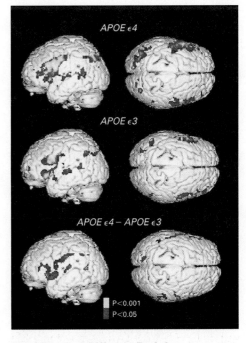

**FIGURE 9-5  A Different Brain?**
Brain scans during memory recall tasks show differences between the brains of people who have an inherited tendency toward Alzheimer's disease and those who do not. The brains at the top are a composite of those at risk; the brains in the middle are a composite of normal brains. The bottom row indicates areas of difference between the first two rows.
Source: Bookheimer et al., 2000.

# *Caring for People with Alzheimer's Disease*

## Becoming an Informed Consumer of Development

Alzheimer's disease is one of the most difficult illnesses to deal with, but several steps can be taken to help both patient and caregiver deal with Alzheimer's.

- Make patients feel secure in their home environments by keeping them occupied in everyday tasks of living as long as possible.

- Label everyday objects, furnish calendars and detailed but simple lists, and give oral reminders of time and place.

- Keep clothing simple: Provide clothes with few zippers and buttons, and lay them out in the order in which they should be put on.

- Put bathing on a schedule. People with Alzheimer's may be afraid of falling and of hot water, and may therefore avoid needed bathing.

- Prevent driving. Although patients often want to continue driving, their accident rate is high—some 20 times higher than average.

- Monitor telephone use. Alzheimer's patients who answer the phone may agree to offers from telephone salespeople and investment counselors.

- Provide opportunities for exercise, such as a daily walk. This prevents muscle deterioration and stiffness.

- Caregivers should remember to take time off and lead their own lives. Seek out support from community service organizations.

- Call or write the Alzheimer's Association, which can provide support and information. The Association can be reached at 225 N. Michigan Ave. Fl. 17, Chicago, IL 60601-7633; Tel. 1-800-272-3900; http://www.alz.org.

At present, there is no cure for Alzheimer's, only treatments for the symptoms. The most promising drugs are related to the loss of the neurotransmitter acetylcholine (Ach) that occurs in some forms of the disease. Donepezil (Aricept), galantamine (Razadyne), rivastigmine (Exelon), and tacrine (Cognex) are among the most common drugs prescribed, but they are effective in only half of Alzheimer's patients, and only temporarily (de Jesus Moreno, 2003; Miller, 2007; Gauthier & Scheltens, 2009).

Other drugs being studied include anti-inflammatory drugs, which may reduce the brain inflammation that occurs in Alzheimer's. In addition, the chemicals in vitamins C and E are being tested, since some evidence suggests that people who take such vitamins are at lower risk for developing the disorder (Alzheimer's Association, 2008; Mohajeri & Leuba, 2009; Sabbagh, 2009).

As victims lose the ability to feed and clothe themselves, or even to control bladder and bowel functions, they must be cared for 24 hours a day. Because of this, most people with Alzheimer's live out their lives in nursing homes, accounting for some two-thirds of the residents of nursing homes (Prigerson, 2003; Sparks, 2008).

Caregivers often become secondary victims of the disease. It is easy to become frustrated, angry, and exhausted by the demands of Alzheimer's patients, whose needs may be overpowering. In addition to the physical chore of providing total care, caregivers face the loss of a loved one, who not only is visibly deteriorating but can act emotionally unstable and even fly into rages (Thomas et al., 2006; Ott, Sanders, & Kelber, 2007; Sanders et al., 2008).

## Wellness in Late Adulthood: The Relationship Between Aging and Illness

Sickness is not inevitable in old age. Whether an older person is ill or well depends less on age than on a variety of factors, including genetic predisposition, past and present environmental factors, and psychological factors.

Certain diseases, such as cancer and heart disease, have a clear genetic component, but a genetic predisposition does not automatically mean that a person will get a particular illness. People's lifestyles—smoking, diet, exposure to cancer-causing agents such as sunlight or asbestos—may raise or lower their chances of coming down with such a disease.

Economic well-being also plays a role. Older individuals are less likely to have regular checkups, and when they finally go for treatment, their illnesses may be more advanced. Furthermore, poor people and even relatively well-off people may have difficulties finding affordable health care, the costs of which have increased significantly. For example, after adjusting for inflation, health care costs increased from $9,224 in 1992 to $15,081 in 2006 for older Americans. Out-of-pocket spending for health care services rose among those living in poverty from 12 percent to 28 percent for people age 65 and older (Federal Interagency Forum on Aging-Related Statistics, 2010).

Finally, psychological factors play an important role in determining susceptibility to illness. For example, a sense of control over one's environment, such as making choices involving everyday matters, leads to a better psychological state and superior health outcomes (Taylor et al., 1991; Levy et al., 2002).

***Promoting Good Health.***   People can enhance their physical well-being—and longevity—simply by doing what people of all ages should do: Eat wisely, exercise, and avoid obvious threats to health, such as smoking. The goal of medical and social service professionals is now to extend people's *active life spans,* the amount of time they remain healthy and able to enjoy their lives (Burns, 2000; Resnick, 2000; Sawatzky & Naimark, 2002; Gavin & Myers, 2003; Katz & Marshall, 2003).

Sometimes, older people have trouble following even these simple guidelines. For instance, estimates suggest that between 15 percent and 50 percent of elderly people do not have adequate nutrition, and several million experience hunger every day (Burt & Harris, 1994; deCastro, 2002; Donini, Savina, & Cannella, 2003).

The reasons are varied. Some elderly people have too little money to purchase adequate food, and some are too frail to shop or cook for themselves. Others feel little motivation to prepare and eat proper meals, particularly if they live alone or are depressed. For those with decreased taste and smell sensitivity, eating may no longer be enjoyable. And some older people may never have eaten well-balanced meals in earlier periods of their lives (Wolfe, Olson, & Kendall, 1998).

Obtaining sufficient exercise may also prove problematic for older persons. Illness may interfere with exercise, and inclement weather may confine an older person to the house. Furthermore, problems can combine: A poor person with insufficient money to eat properly may have little energy to put into physical activity (Traywick & Schoenberg, 2008; Logsdon et al., 2009; Hardy & Grogan, 2009; Kamijo et al., 2009; Kelley et al., 2009).

Economic well-being is an important factor in the relationship between aging and illness, in part because poverty restricts access to medical care.

## Sexuality in Old Age: Use It or Lose It

Do your grandparents have sex?

Quite possibly, yes. Increasing evidence suggests that people are sexually active well into their 80s and 90s, despite societal stereotypes prevalent in the United States suggesting that it is somehow improper for two 75-year-olds to have sexual intercourse, and even worse for a 75-year-old to masturbate. In many other cultures, elderly people are expected to remain sexually active, and in some societies, people are expected to become less inhibited as they age (Hyde, 1994; Hillman, 2000; Lindau et al., 2007). ◉⟦Watch on **mydevelopmentlab.com**

Two major factors determine whether an elderly person will engage in sexual activity (Masters, Johnson, & Kolodny, 1982). One is good physical and mental health. The other is previous regular sexual activity. "Use it or lose it" seems an accurate description of sexual functioning in older people. Sexual activity can and often does continue throughout the life span. Furthermore, there's some intriguing evidence that having sex may have some unexpected side benefits: One study found that having sex regularly is associated with an increased life span (Kellett, 2000; Henry & McNab, 2003; Huang et al., 2009)!

One survey found that 43 percent of men and 33 percent of women over the age of 70 masturbated. The average frequency for those who masturbated was once a week. Around two-thirds of married men and women had sex with their spouses, again averaging around once a week. In addition, the percentage of people who view their sexual partners as physically attractive actually increases with age (Brecher et al., 1984; Budd, 1999; Araujo, Mohr, & McKinlay, 2004).

Of course, there are some changes in sexual functioning. Testosterone declines during adulthood by approximately 30 to 40 percent from the late 40s to the early 70s. It takes a longer time, and more stimulation, for men to get a full erection. The refractory period—the time following an orgasm before a man can become aroused again—may last one or more days. Women's vaginas become thin and inelastic, and they produce less natural lubrication, making

◉⟦Watch on **mydevelopmentlab.com**

*What effect does lifestyle have on health?* Log onto MyDevelopmentLab.com and watch a video of Joan and Bill, a couple in their 70s; they both are avid hikers, rowers, play tennis, ski, and compete athletically.

**genetic programming theories of aging** theories that suggest that our body's DNA genetic code contains a built-in time limit for the reproduction of human cells

**wear-and-tear theories of aging** the theory that the mechanical functions of the body simply wear out with age

intercourse more difficult. It is important to realize that older adults—like younger ones—are susceptible to sexually transmitted diseases. In fact, 10 percent of people diagnosed with AIDS are over 50 (Seidman, 2003; National Institute of Aging, 2004).

## Approaches to Aging: Why Is Death Inevitable?

Hovering over late adulthood is the specter of death. At some point, no matter how healthy we have been throughout life, we know that we will experience physical declines and that life will end. But why?

There are two major approaches to explaining why we undergo physical deterioration and death: genetic programming theories and wear-and-tear theories.

**Genetic programming theories of aging** suggest that our body's DNA contains a built-in time limit for the reproduction of human cells. After a genetically determined period, the cells can no longer divide and the individual begins to deteriorate (Finch & Tanzi, 1997; Rattan, Kristensen, & Clark, 2006).

The theory comes in several variants. One is that the genetic material contains a "death gene" programmed to tell the body to deteriorate and die. Researchers who take an evolutionary viewpoint suggest that a long life span after the reproductive years is unnecessary for the survival of the species. According to this view, genetic diseases that strike later in life continue to exist because they allow people time to have children, thus passing along genes that are "programmed" to cause diseases and death.

Another variant is that the cells can duplicate only a certain number of times. Throughout our lives, new cells are produced through cell duplication to repair and replenish our various tissues and organs. According to this view, the genetic instructions for running the body can be read only a certain number of times before they become illegible and cells stop reproducing. Because the body is not being renewed at the same rate, bodily deterioration and death ensue (Hayflick, 1974; Thoms, Kuschal, & Emmert, 2007).

Evidence for the genetic programming theory comes from research showing that human cells permitted to divide in the laboratory can do so successfully only around 50 times. Each time they divide, *telomeres,* which are tiny, protective areas of DNA at the tip of chromosomes, grow shorter. When a cell's telomere has just about disappeared, the cell stops replicating, making it susceptible to damage and producing signs of aging (Chung et al., 2007; Epel, 2009).

On the other hand, **wear-and-tear theories of aging** argue that the mechanical functions of the body simply wear out—the way cars and washing machines do. In addition, some wear-and-tear theorists suggest that the body's constant manufacture of energy to fuel its activities creates by-products. These by-products, combined with the toxins and threats of everyday life (such as radiation, chemical exposure, accidents, and disease), eventually reach such high levels that they impair the body's normal functioning. The ultimate result is deterioration and death.

One specific category of by-products that has been related to aging includes free radicals, electrically charged molecules or atoms that are produced by the cells of the body. Because of their electrical charge, free radicals may cause negative effects on other cells of the body. A great deal of research suggests that oxygen-free radicals may be implicated in a number of age-related problems, including cancer, heart disease, and diabetes (Sierra, 2006; Hayflick, 2007; Sonnen et al., 2009).

*Reconciling the Theories of Aging.* Genetic programming theories and wear-and-tear theories make different suggestions about the inevitability of death. Genetic programming theories suggest that there is a built-in time limit to life—it's programmed in the genes, after all. On the other hand, wear-and-tear theories, particularly those that focus on the toxins that are built up during the course of life, paint a somewhat more optimistic view. They suggest that if a means can be found to eliminate the toxins produced by the body and by exposure to the environment, aging might well be slowed. For example, certain genes seem to slow aging and increase their ability to withstand age-related diseases (Ghazi, Henis-Korenblit, & Kenyon, 2009). We don't know which class of theories provides the more accurate account. Each is supported by some research, and each seems to explain certain aspects of aging. Ultimately, though, the mystery remains (Horiuchi, Finch, & Mesle, 2003; Friedman & Janssen, 2010).

According to genetic preprogramming theories of aging, our DNA genetic code contains a built-in limit on the length of life.

*Life Expectancy: How Long Have I Got?*   Although why we die is not fully understood, we do know how to calculate our average life expectancy: Most of us can expect to live into old age. The **life expectancy**—the average age of death for members of a population—of a person born in 2010, for instance, is 78 years of age.

Average life expectancy is on the rise. In 1776, average U.S. life expectancy was 35. By the early 1900s, it had risen to 47. And in only four decades, from 1950 to 1990, it increased from 68 to over 75. Predictions are that it will continue to rise steadily, possibly reaching 80 by the year 2050 (see Figure 9-6).

There are several reasons for this. Health and sanitation are generally better, with many diseases, such as smallpox, wiped out entirely. There are now vaccines and preventive measures for many diseases that used to kill young people, such as measles and mumps. Working conditions are better and products are safer. Many people are making healthful lifestyle choices such as keeping their weight down, eating fresh fruit and vegetables, and exercising—all of which can extend their active life spans, the years they spend in health and enjoyment of life.

Just how much can the life span be increased? The most common answer is around 120 years, the age reached by Jeanne Calment, the oldest person in the world until she died in 1997 at 122. Living longer would probably require major genetic alterations that are both technically and ethically improbable. Still, recent scientific and technological advances suggest that significantly extending the life span is not an impossibility.

> **life expectancy** the average age of death for members of a population

## Postponing Aging: Can Scientists Find the Fountain of Youth?

Are researchers close to finding the scientific equivalent of the fountain of youth?

Not yet, but they're getting closer, at least in nonhuman species. For instance, researchers have extended the lives of nematodes (microscopic, transparent worms that typically live for just 9 days) to 50 days—the equivalent of extending human life to 420 years. Researchers have also doubled fruit flies' lives (Whitbourne, 2001; Libert et al., 2007; Ocorr et al., 2007).

The most promising avenues for increasing the length of life are these:

- **Telomere therapy.** Telomeres are the tiny areas at the tip of chromosomes that grow shorter each time a cell divides and eventually disappear, ending cell replication. Some scientists believe that if telomeres could be lengthened, aging could be slowed. Researchers are now looking for genes that control the production of telomerase, an enzyme that seems to regulate the length of telomeres (Steinert, Shay, & Wright, 2000; Urquidi, Tarin, & Goodison, 2000; Chung et al., 2007).

- **Unlocking longevity genes.** Certain genes control the body's ability to cope with environmental challenges and physical adversity. If harnessed, those genes may provide a way to increase the life span. One particularly promising family of genes are *sirtuins*, which may regulate and promote longer life (Guarente, 2006; Sinclair & Guarente, 2006; Glatt et al., 2007).

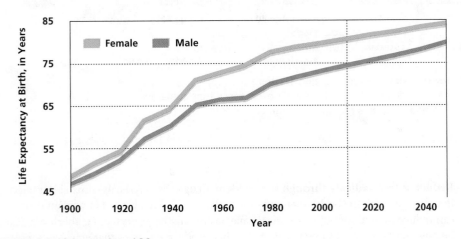

**FIGURE 9-6 Living to Age 100**

If increases in life expectancy continue, it may be a common occurrence for people to live to be 100 by the end of this century. What implications does this have for society?
Source: U.S. Bureau of the Census, 1997.

*Cultural Dimensions*

## Gender, Race, and Ethnic Differences in Average Life Expectancy: Separate Lives, Separate Deaths

- The average White child born in the United States is likely to live 78 years. The average African American child is likely to live 5 years less.

- A child born in Japan has a life expectancy of 79; for a child born in Gambia, life expectancy is less than 45.

- A male born in the United States today is expected to live to age 73; a female will probably live 7 years longer.

Let's consider the gender gap, which is particularly pronounced. Across the industrialized world, women live longer than men by 4 to 10 years (Holden, 1987). The female advantage begins just after conception: Although slightly more males are conceived, males are more likely to die during the prenatal period, infancy, and childhood. Consequently, by age 30 there are roughly equal numbers of men and women. But by age 65, 84 percent of females and only 70 percent of males are still alive. For those over 85, the gender gap gapes wider: For every male, 2.57 women are still alive (AARP, 2008).

One suggested explanation for this is that the naturally higher levels of hormones such as estrogen and progesterone in women provide some protection from diseases and conditions such as heart attacks. It is also possible that women engage in healthier behavior during their lives, such as eating well. However, there is no conclusive evidence for either explanation (Baerlocher, 2007; Emslie & Hunt, 2008; Lee, 2010).

Whatever its cause, the gender gap has continued to increase. During the early part of the twentieth century, there was only a 2-year difference in favor of women, but in the 1980s this gap grew to 7 years. The size of the gap now seems to have leveled off, largely due to the fact that men are more likely than previously to engage in positive health behaviors (such as smoking less, eating better, and exercising more).

Racial and ethnic differences are more troubling because they underline socioeconomic disparities in the United States. Life expectancy is almost 10 percent greater for Caucasians than for African Americans (see Figure 9-7). Furthermore, in contrast to Caucasians, whose life expectancy keeps edging up, African Americans have actually experienced slight declines in life expectancy in recent years.

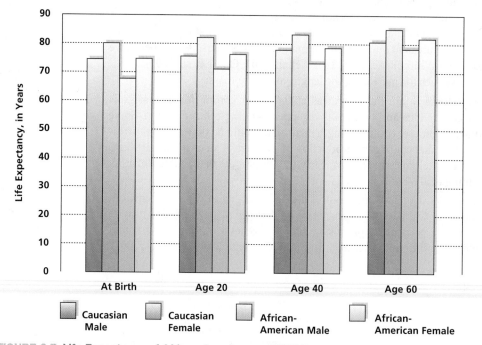

**FIGURE 9-7 Life Expectancy of African Americans and Whites**
Both male and female African Americans have a shorter life expectancy than male and female Caucasians. Are the reasons for this genetic, cultural, or both?
Source: Anderson, 2001.

- **Reducing free radicals through antioxidant drugs.** Free radicals—unstable molecules that drift through the body—damage other cells and lead to aging. Antioxidant drugs that can reduce the number of free radicals may eventually be perfected. Furthermore, it may be possible to insert in human cells genes that produce enzymes that act as antioxidants. In the meantime, nutritionists urge a diet rich in antioxidant vitamins, which are found in fruits and vegetables (Birlouez-Aragon & Tessier, 2003; Kedziora-Kornatowska et al., 2007; Haleem et al., 2008).

- **Restricting calories.** For at least the last decade, researchers have known that laboratory rats who are fed an extremely low-calorie diet, providing 30 to 50 percent of their normal intake, often live 30 percent longer than better-fed rats, providing they get all the vitamins and minerals they need. The reason appears to be that they produce fewer free radicals. Researchers hope to develop drugs that mimic the effects of calorie restriction without forcing people to feel hungry all the time (Mattson, 2003; Ingram, Young, & Mattison, 2007; Cuervo, 2008).

- **The bionic solution: replacing worn-out organs.** Heart transplants . . . liver transplants . . . lung transplants. We live in an age when replacing damaged or diseased organs seems nearly routine.

One major problem remains: Transplants often fail because the body rejects the foreign tissue. To overcome this problem, some researchers advocate growing replacement organs from the person's own cloned cells, which will not be rejected. Even more radically, genetically engineered cells from nonhumans that do not evoke rejection could be cloned, harvested, and transplanted into humans. Finally, it may be possible to create artificial organs that can completely replace diseased or damaged ones (Cascalho, Ogle, & Platt, 2006; Kwant et al., 2007; Li & Zhu, 2007).

Sci-fi ideas for extending human life are exciting, but society must work to solve a more immediate problem: the significant disparity in life expectancies between members of different racial and ethnic groups. We discuss this important issue in the accompanying "Cultural Dimensions" segment.

**From the perspective of a health care professional:** Given what you've learned about explanations of life expectancy, how might you try to extend your own life?

## REVIEW, CHECK, AND APPLY

### REVIEW

**LO3** What is the general state of health of older people, and to what disorders are they susceptible?

- Most illnesses and diseases of late adulthood are not peculiar to old age; however, incidents of cancer and heart disease rise with age. People in late adulthood are also more prone to develop arthritis, hypertension, dementia, and Alzheimer's disease.

**LO4** Can wellness and sexuality be maintained in late adulthood?

- Proper diet, exercise, and avoidance of health risks can lead to prolonged wellness during old age, and sexuality can continue throughout the life span in healthy adults.

**LO5** How long can people expect to live, and what are the major causes of death?

- Whether death is caused by genetic programming or by general physical wear and tear is an unresolved question. Life expectancy, which has risen for centuries, varies with gender, race, and ethnicity.

- New approaches to increasing life expectancy include telomere therapy, reducing free radicals through antioxidant drugs, restricting caloric intake, and replacing worn-out organs.

### CHECK YOURSELF

1. Although we may expect the elderly to be in poor health or sickly, approximately _____ of people 65 and older rate their health as good, very good, or excellent.
   a. one-half
   b. three-fourths
   c. two-thirds
   d. one-fourth

2. Which of the following is NOT a physical change in the brain associated with Alzheimer's?
   a. The hippocampus shows deterioration.
   b. The frontal and temporal lobes show deterioration.
   c. Specific neurons die, leading to a shortage of transmitters such as acetylcholine.
   d. The brain enlarges.

3. A strong relationship exists between economic well-being and illness in that those individuals who can afford to maintain good health care in their later years remain in better health.
   - True
   - False

### APPLYING LIFESPAN DEVELOPMENT

- In what ways is socioeconomic status related to wellness in old age and to life expectancy?

✓—**Study** and **Review** on
**MyDevelopmentLab.com**

## MODULE 9.2 Cognitive Development in Late Adulthood

# Don't Knock Old Age

*Three women were talking about the inconveniences of growing old.*

*"Sometimes," one of them confessed, "when I go to my refrigerator, I can't remember if I'm putting something in or taking something out."*

*"Oh, that's nothing," said the second woman. "There are times when I find myself at the foot of the stairs wondering if I'm going up or if I've just come down."*

*"Well, my goodness!" exclaimed the third woman. "I'm certainly glad I don't have any problems like that"—and she knocked on wood. "Oh," she said, starting up out of her chair, "there's someone at the door." (Dent, 1984, p. 38)*

The old joke at the start of this module sums up the stereotypic view of older people as befuddled and forgetful. Today the view is different. Researchers have come to discount the view that the cognitive abilities of older people inevitably decline. Overall intellectual ability and specific cognitive skills, such as memory and problem solving, are more likely to remain strong. In fact, with appropriate practice and environmental stimuli, cognitive skills can actually improve.

This module discusses intellectual development during late adulthood. We look at the nature of intelligence in older people and the various ways cognitive abilities change. We also assess how different types of memory fare during late adulthood, and we consider ways to reverse intellectual declines in older people.

# Intelligence

**LEARNING OBJECTIVES**

**LO6** How well do people in late adulthood function intellectually?

**LO7** What is the nature of intellectual change during late adulthood?

*When CNN didn't renew Daniel Schorr's reporting contract in 1985, he was 69 and no one was surprised to see him retiring.*

*Except Daniel Schorr.*

*Instead of hanging up his typewriter, Schorr quickly found work at National Public Radio (NPR). Until two weeks before his death at the age of 93, he continued to deliver regular analysis and commentary on NPR's* Weekend Edition, All Things Considered, *and other news programs.*

Daniel Schorr's story of durable intellectual activity is unusual but not unique. A growing number of people who depend on their wits for a livelihood, or just to keep going, have reached ages that would have been considered unthinkable when they started out—and have remained intellectually active. In the world of entertainment alone, comedians Bob Hope and George Burns and composer Irving Berlin all lived to see their hundredth birthdays.

## Intelligence in Older People

The notion that older people become less cognitively adept initially arose from misinterpretations of research evidence comparing younger and older people's performance on the same IQ test, using traditional cross-sectional experimental methods. For example, a group of 30-year-olds and 70-year-olds might have taken the same test and had their performance compared.

However, cross-sectional methods do not take into account *cohort effects*—influences attributable to growing up in a particular era. If the younger group—because of when they grew up—has more education, on average, they will probably do better on the test for that reason alone. Furthermore, older people might do worse on any intelligence test with a timed portion simply because of their slower reaction time.

Longitudinal studies, which follow the same individuals for many years, are not much better. As we discussed earlier, repeated exposure to the same test may cause overfamiliarity, and participants may become unavailable over time, leaving a smaller and possibly more cognitively skilled group of subjects.

**plasticity** the degree to which a developing structure or behavior is modifiable due to experience

## Recent Conclusions about the Nature of Intelligence in Late Adulthood

More recent research has attempted to address these drawbacks. In an ambitious—and ongoing—study of intelligence in older people, developmental psychologist K. Warner Schaie uses sequential methods, which combine cross-sectional and longitudinal methods by examining several different age groups at a number of points in time.

In Schaie's massive study, carried out in Seattle, Washington, 500 randomly chosen individuals took a battery of tests of cognitive ability. The people belonged to different age groups, starting at age 20 and extending at 5-year intervals to age 70. The participants were tested, and continue to be tested, every 7 years, and more people are recruited every year. At this point, more than 5,000 participants have been tested (Schaie, Willis, & Pennak, 2005).

The study, along with other research, supports several generalizations (Craik & Salthouse, 1999, 2008):

- Some abilities gradually decline starting at around age 25, while others stay relatively steady (see Figure 9-8). There is no uniform pattern of age-related intellectual changes. For example, fluid intelligence (the ability to deal with new problems and situations) declines with age, while crystallized intelligence (the store of information, skills, and strategies that people have acquired) remains steady and in some cases improves (Schaie, 1993).

- On average, some cognitive declines are found in all abilities by age 67, but they are minimal until the 80s. Even at age 81, less than half of the people tested showed consistent declines over the previous 7 years. ⊙ Watch on **mydevelopmentlab.com**

- There are also significant individual differences. Some people begin to show declines in their 30s, while others show no declines until their 70s. In fact, around a third of people in their 70s score higher than the average young adult.

- Environmental and cultural factors play a role. People with no chronic disease, higher socioeconomic status (SES), involvement in an intellectually stimulating environment, a flexible personality style, a bright spouse, good perceptual processing speed, and satisfaction with one's accomplishments in midlife or early old age showed less decline.

The relationship between environmental factors and intellectual skills suggests that with stimulation, practice, and motivation, older people can maintain their mental abilities. Such **plasticity** illustrates that the changes that occur in intellectual abilities during late adulthood are not fixed. In mental life, as in so many other areas of human development, the motto "use it or lose it" fits.

This suggests that there may be interventions to help older adults maintain their information processing skills, as we discuss in the "From Research to Practice" box.

However, not all developmentalists accept the "use it or lose it" hypothesis. Developmental psychologist Timothy Salthouse suggests that the rate of true, underlying cognitive decline in late adulthood is unaffected by mental exercise. Instead, he argues that some people—the kind who have consistently engaged in high levels of mental activity such as completing crossword puzzles—enter late adulthood

⊙ Watch on **mydevelopmentlab.com**

*81-year-old Thelma lives by the motto "use it or lose it." She attends the theatre, concerts, and takes college classes.*
Log onto MyDevelopmentLab.com and watch Thelma's witty discussion about her outlook on life.

| Inductive Reasoning | Spatial Orientation | Perceptual Speed | Numeric Ability | Verbal Ability | Verbal Memory |

**FIGURE 9-8 Changes in Intellectual Functioning**
Although some intellectual abilities decline across adulthood, others stay relatively steady.
Source: Changes in Intellectual Functioning from Schaie, K. W. (1994). "The course of adult intellectual development." p. 307. *American Psychologist, 49,* 304–313. Copyright © 1994 by the American Psychological Association. Reproduced with permission.

## *From Research to Practice*

### Big Body, Small Brain: The Link Between Brain Size and Cognitive Declines in Late Adulthood

Forget what you may have heard about "brain food"—too much feeding may actually cause your brain to shrink. At least that's the conclusion of researchers who studied brain images of cognitively healthy adults over 70 and found that the brains of the heavier elders were smaller on average than those of the thin elders.

The researchers used a brain imaging technique called *tensor-based morphometry,* which creates three-dimensional maps of the brain, to look more closely for evidence of brain shrinkage in a sample of elderly adults. The images showed that the elderly participants with higher body-mass indices tended to have smaller brains. Overweight elders showed a 6 percent decrease in brain size, while obese elders showed an 8 percent decrease as compared to their normal-weight peers. Put another way, relative to thin elders, the overweight elders' brains looked 8 years older and the obese elders' brains looked 16 years older. The differences were particularly pronounced in the frontal and temporal lobes, brain regions associated with planning and memory functions (Raji et al., in press).

Researchers have known for some time that obesity in middle age is associated with an increased risk of cognitive decline in late adulthood. Furthermore, certain health problems that are associated with

obesity, such as diabetes or high blood pressure, are also associated with brain shrinkage and cognitive decline. It may be that the artery-clogging effects of excess body mass may result in reduced blood flow to the brain and subsequent dying off of brain cells. Evidence of this link can be found in other research showing that the same brain areas that are shrunken in overweight elders remain normal in those who exercise (Schultz, 2009; Crivello et al., 2010).

What is unclear from these new findings is whether losing weight would reverse the trend. It is possible, for example, that it may be more important to maintain a healthy weight over the life span than to correct the problem later in life. Researchers also caution that any conclusion about obesity causing brain shrinkage is premature; the possibility that brain shrinkage precedes and leads to weight gain cannot yet be ruled out (Luchsinger & Gustafson, 2009; Ho et al., 2010).

- What reason is there to think that losing weight in older age may not reduce the increased risk of cognitive decline associated with obesity?

- How might researchers answer the question of whether obesity is a cause or a consequence of brain shrinkage?

with a "cognitive reserve." This allows them to continue to perform at relatively high mental levels, despite underlying declines. Still, most developmentalists accept the hypothesis that mental exercise is beneficial (Salthouse, 2006; Basak et al., 2008; Hertzog et al., 2008). (Also see the "From Research to Practice" box).

## REVIEW, CHECK, AND APPLY

### REVIEW

**LO6**  How well do people in late adulthood function intellectually?

- Although some intellectual abilities gradually decline throughout adulthood, starting at around age 25, others stay relatively steady. For example, research shows that while fluid intelligence declines with age, crystallized intelligence remains steady, and may even improve, in late adulthood.

**LO7**  What is the nature of intellectual change during late adulthood?

- The intellect retains considerable plasticity and can be maintained with stimulation, practice, and motivation.

### CHECK YOURSELF

1. One problem with conducting cross-sectional research on aging and cognition is that this method does not take into consideration _____, the influences attributable to growing up in a particular era.

2. Based on the sequential study of aging and cognition conducted by Schaie (1994), there is no uniform pattern in adulthood of age-related change across all intellectual abilities.

   - True
   - False

3. Not all developmentalists believe in the "use it or lose it" hypothesis. For example, Salthouse suggests that the rate of true, underlying cognitive decline in late adulthood is unaffected by mental exercise, and the lack of decline is a function of a larger cognitive reserve.

   - True
   - False

### APPLYING LIFESPAN DEVELOPMENT

- Do you think steady or increasing crystallized intelligence can partially or fully compensate for declines in fluid intelligence? Why or why not?

✔— **Study** and **Review** on
**MyDevelopmentLab.com**

# Memory

**LO8   How does memory capability change in late adulthood?**

*I have no trouble remembering everything that happened 40 or 50 years ago—dates, places, faces, music. But I'm going to be 90 my next birthday, November 14th, and I find I can't remember what happened yesterday.* (Time, 1980, p. 57)

This is the way composer Aaron Copland described his memory in old age. Our confidence in the accuracy of Copland's analysis is strengthened by an error in his statement: On his next birthday, he would be only 80 years old!

Is memory loss inevitable? Not necessarily. Cross-cultural research reveals that in societies that hold older people in relatively high esteem, such as in China, people are less likely to show memory losses. In such cultures, positive expectations may lead people to think more positively about their own capabilities (Levy & Langer, 1994; Hess, Auman, & Colcombe, 2003).

Even those memory declines that do occur are limited primarily to *episodic memories,* which relate to specific life experiences, such as when you first visited New York City. Other types of memory, such as *semantic memories* (general knowledge and facts, such as the capital of North Dakota) and *implicit memories* (memories about which people are not consciously aware, such as how to ride a bike), are largely unaffected by age (Nilsson et al., 1997; Dixon, 2003; Nilsson, 2003).

Memory capacity changes during old age. For instance, *short-term memory* slips gradually until age 70, when the decline becomes more pronounced. The largest drop is for information that is presented quickly and orally, such as when someone at a computer helpline rattles off a series of complicated steps for fixing a computer problem. In addition, older people find it harder to recall information about unfamiliar things, such as prose passages, names and faces of people, and the directions on a medicine label, possibly because new information is not registered and processed effectively when initially encountered. Still, these changes are minor and most elderly people automatically learn to compensate for them (Cherry & Park, 1993; Carroll, 2000; Light, 2000; Rentz, 2010).

Memory loss is not as common among Chinese elderly as it is in the West. What are some factors that contribute to cultural differences in memory loss of the elderly?

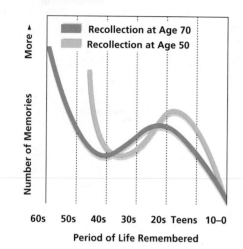

**FIGURE 9-9 Remembrances of Things Past**
Recall of autobiographical memories varies with age, with 70-year-olds recalling details from their 20s and 30s best, and 50-year-olds recalling memories from their teenage years and 20s. People of both ages also recall more recent memories best of all. Source: Rubin, 1986.

*Autobiographical Memory: Recalling the Days of Our Lives.* When it comes to **auto-biographical memory,** memories about one's own life, older people are as subject to lapses as younger individuals. For instance, recall frequently follows the *Pollyanna principle,* in which pleasant memories are more likely to be recalled than unpleasant memories. Similarly, people tend to forget information that is not congruent with the way they currently see themselves. Thus a strict parent who forgets that she got drunk at her high school prom is making her memories "fit" her current conception of herself (Rubin, 1996; Eacott, 1999; Rubin & Greenberg, 2003; Skowronski, Walker, & Betz, 2003; Loftus, 2003).

Everyone tends to recall particular periods of life better than others. As can be seen in Figure 9-9, 70-year-olds tend to recall autobiographical details from their 20s and 30s best, while 50-year-olds are likely to have more memories of their teenage years and their 20s. In both cases, recall is better for earlier years than for more recent decades, but not as complete as for very recent events (Fromholt & Larsen, 1991; Rubin, 2000).

People in late adulthood also use information that they recall in different ways from younger individuals when they make decisions. For example, they process information more slowly and may make poorer judgments when complex rules are involved, and they focus more on emotional content than younger people. On the other hand, the accumulated knowledge and experience of people in late adulthood can compensate for their deficits, particularly if they are highly motivated to make good decisions (Peters et al., 2007).

*Explaining Memory Changes in Old Age.* Explanations for memory changes in older people focus on three main categories: environmental factors, information processing deficits, and biological factors.

- **Environmental factors.** Certain environmental factors common to many older people may cause declines in memory. For example, older people often take prescription drugs that hinder memory, and this, rather than age *per se,* may account for their lower performance on memory tasks.

  In addition, retirees, no longer facing job challenges, may use memory less. Further, their motivation to recall information may be lower than before, and they may be less motivated than younger people to do their best in experimental testing situations.

- **Information processing deficits.** Memory declines may also be linked to changes in information processing capabilities. The ability to inhibit irrelevant information and thoughts that interfere with problem solving may decrease, and the speed of information processing may decline (Bashore, Ridderinkhof, & van der Molen, 1998; Palfai, Halperin, & Hoyer, 2003; Salthouse, Atkinson, & Berish, 2003).

  Another information processing view suggests that older adults lose the ability to concentrate on new material and have difficulty paying attention to appropriate stimuli and organizing material in memory. According to this information-processing-deficit approach, which has substantial research support, older people use less efficient processes to retrieve information from memory. This leads to declines in recall abilities (Castel & Craik, 2003; Luo & Craik, 2008, 2009).

- **Biological factors.** The last of the major approaches concentrates on biological factors. According to this view, memory changes are a result of brain and body deterioration. For instance, declines in episodic memory may be related to the deterioration of the frontal lobes of the brain or a reduction in estrogen. Some studies also show a loss of cells in the hippocampus, which is critical to memory. However, some memory deficits occur without any evidence of underlying biological deterioration (Eberling et al., 2004; Lye et al., 2004; Bird & Burgess, 2008; Stevens et al., 2008).

## Never Too Late to Learn

*The University of Arkansas campus is buzzing with talk of midterms and football. In a cafeteria, students are grousing about the food.*

*"Where are the dinner rolls?" says one. "I'm a vegetarian, and all they have is meat," complains another. Soon, though, everyone has moved on to complaining about classes.*

*A typical college scene—except for all the canes, hearing aids and white hair in evidence. This is Elderhostel, a program for people 60 and older run by a Boston nonprofit organization, formed*

**autobiographical memory** memories about one's own life

*in 1975, that recruits colleges to conduct weeklong educational sessions in everything from gene-*
*alogy to the archaeology of ancient Egypt.* (Stern, 1994, p. A1)

More than 250,000 people enroll annually in thousands of classes organized by Elderhostel, the largest educational program for people in late adulthood. Represented on campuses across the world, the Elderhostel movement is further evidence that intellectual growth and change continue throughout people's lives. As we saw earlier, exercising cognitive skills may help older adults maintain their intellectual functioning (Sack, 1999; Simson, Wilson, & Harlow-Rosentraub, 2006).

Although not everyone can afford Elderhostel tuitions, many public colleges encourage senior citizens to enroll in classes by offering free tuition. In addition, some retirement communities are located at or near college campuses, such as the University of Michigan and Penn State University (Powell, 2004).

Although some elderly people are doubtful about their intellectual capabilities and consequently hesitate to compete with younger students in regular classes, their concern is largely misplaced. Older adults often have no trouble maintaining their standing in rigorous college classes. Furthermore, professors and other students generally find the presence of older people, with their varied and substantial life experiences, a real educational benefit (Simson et al., 2006).

An increasing number of people in late adulthood are using technology.

## Technology and Learning in Late Adulthood

One of the biggest generational divides involves the use of technology. People 65 and older are far less likely to use technology than younger individuals (see Figure 9-10).

Why are older people less likely to use technology? One reason is that they are less interested and motivated, in part because they are less likely to be working and therefore less in need of learning new technology skills. But another barrier is cognitive. For example, because fluid intelligence (the ability to deal with new problems and situations) shows some declines with age, this may impact on the ability to learn technology (Ownby et al., 2008; Charness & Boot, 2009).

This hardly means that people in late adulthood are unable to learn to use technology. In fact, an increasing number of individuals are using email and social networking sites such as Facebook. It is likely that the lag in the adoption of technology between younger and older adults will decrease as technology use becomes even more widespread in the general society (Lee & Czaja, 2009).

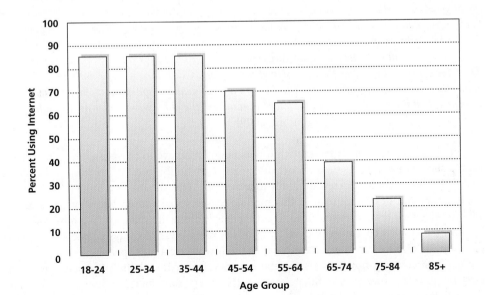

FIGURE 9-10 **Technology Use and Age**
Older individuals in the United States are far less likely to use the Internet than those who are younger.
Source: Charness & Boot, 2009, Figure 1A.

## REVIEW, CHECK, AND APPLY

### REVIEW

**LO8** How does memory capability change in late adulthood?

- Declines in memory affect mainly episodic memories and short-term memory.

- Explanations of memory changes in old age have focused on environmental factors, information processing declines, and biological factors.

### CHECK YOURSELF

**1.** When it comes to autobiographical memories, older individuals, like younger individuals, follow the _____, in that they are more likely to remember pleasant memories.

a. saliency effect

b. environmental effect

c. Pollyanna principle

d. positive effect

**2.** Explanations for changes in memory tend to focus on three main categories: environmental factors, biological factors, and _____.

a. social support

b. life changes

c. information processing deficits

d. personal influences

**3.** Despite concerns about memory and intellectual capabilities, older adults have no trouble maintaining their standing in rigorous college classes.

- True

- False

### APPLYING LIFESPAN DEVELOPMENT

- How might cultural factors, such as the esteem in which a society holds its older members, work to affect an older person's memory performance?

✓●─ **Study** and **Review** on **MyDevelopmentLab.com**

Answers: 1) c; 2) c; 3) True

## MODULE 9.3 Social and Personality Development in Late Adulthood

# Logging on Late in Life

*In 2007, Paula Rice, now 73, suffered a heart attack that left her housebound. Both her marriages had ended in divorce, and her four grown children lived far from her home in Island City, Kentucky. Paula was facing one of the persistent anxieties for older people: growing old alone.*

*Yet Paula is far from isolated. Despite being confined to her home, she remains an active participant in a vast social network: an online one. Paula is a member of Eons.com, a social networking site targeted to the elderly. She sometimes spends 14 hours a day online. "I was dying of boredom," Paula says. "Eons, all by its lonesome, gave me a reason to keep on going." (Clifford, 2009, p. D5)*

*Paula's embrace of online social networking is not exceptional, either. More and more elderly Americans are joining social networking sites such as Facebook and MySpace, as well as those like Eons that are specifically designed for seniors. Given how many elderly people live alone, the connections formed online can take on a great deal of importance. While we tend to associate digital friendships with a younger generation, the elderly are increasingly finding a place in the Internet community. (Clifford, 2009)*

The desire to connect and interact with others is not exclusive to any age group. For elderly people such as Paula Rice, the Internet offers an opportunity to establish relationships at a time of life when connections with family members and friends are often broken by distance, poor health, and death. We turn in this module to the social and emotional aspects of late adulthood, which remain as central as in earlier stages of the life span. We begin by considering how personality continues to develop, and we examine various ways people can age successfully. We also look at how culture governs the way we treat older people.

We then consider how various societal factors affect older adults. We discuss living arrangements and economic and financial issues. Next, we examine the influence of work and retirement on elderly individuals.

Finally, we consider relationships in late adulthood among married couples, relatives, and friends. We will see how social networks play an important—and sustaining—role in people's lives. We end with a discussion of elder abuse.

# Personality Development and Successful Aging

**LO9**  In what ways does personality develop during late adulthood?

**LO10**  How do people deal with aging?

*Greta Roach has a puckish manner, a habit of nudging you when she is about to say something funny. This happens often, because that is how she views the world. Even last year's knee injury, which forced her to drop out of her bowling league and halted the march of blue-and-chrome trophies across her living-room table, is not—in her mind—a frailty of age.*

*Roach, 93, takes the same spirited approach to life in her 90s as she did in her 20s, something not all elders can do. . . . "I enjoy life. I belong to all the clubs. I love to talk on the telephone. I write to my old friends." She pauses. "Those that are still alive."* (Pappano, 1994, pp. 19, 30)

In many ways, Roach, with her wit, high spirits, and enormous activity level, is the same person she was in earlier years. Yet for other older adults, time and circumstances bring changes in their outlook on life, their views of themselves, and perhaps even their basic personalities. In fact, one of the fundamental questions asked by lifespan developmentalists concerns the degree to which personality remains stable or changes in later adulthood.

## Continuity and Change in Personality During Late Adulthood

Is personality relatively stable throughout adulthood, or does it vary significantly? The answer depends on which facets of personality we consider. According to developmental psychologists Paul Costa and Robert McCrae, whose work we discussed earlier, the "Big Five" basic personality traits (neuroticism, extraversion, openness, agreeableness, and conscientiousness) are remarkably stable across adulthood. For instance, even-tempered people at 20 are still even-tempered at 75, and people who hold positive self-concepts early in adulthood still view themselves positively in late adulthood (Costa & McCrae, 1988, 1989, 1997; McCrae & Costa, 1990, 2003; Terracciano, McCrae, & Costa, 2010).

For example, at 93, Greta Roach is active and humorous, as she was in her 20s. There seems to be a fundamental continuity to personality (Field & Millsap, 1991).

Despite this continuity, change is still possible. Profound changes in people's social environments may produce personality changes. What is important to a person at 80 is not necessarily the same as what was important at 40.

To account for these changes, some theorists have focused on the discontinuities of development. As we'll see next, Erik Erikson, Robert Peck, Daniel Levinson, and Bernice Neugarten have examined personality changes that accompany new challenges in later adulthood.

***Ego Integrity versus Despair: Erikson's Final Stage.***  Psychoanalyst Erik Erikson characterizes late adulthood as the time when people move into the last of life's eight stages of psychosocial development. Labeled the **ego-integrity-versus-despair stage,** this period is characterized by a process of looking back over one's life, evaluating it, and coming to terms with it.

People who are successful in this stage of development experience satisfaction and accomplishment, which Erikson terms "integrity." When people achieve integrity, they feel they have fulfilled the possibilities that have come their way in life, and they have few regrets. Other people look back on their lives with dissatisfaction. They may feel that they have missed important opportunities and have not accomplished what they wished. Such individuals may be unhappy, depressed, angry, or despondent over what they have done, or failed to do, with their lives—in short, they despair.

***Peck's Developmental Tasks.***  Although Erikson's approach provides a picture of the broad possibilities of later adulthood, other theorists offer a more differentiated view of the final stage of life. Psychologist Robert Peck (1968) suggests that personality development in elderly people is occupied by three major developmental tasks or challenges.

**ego-integrity-versus-despair stage** Erikson's final stage of life, characterized by a process of looking back over one's life, evaluating it, and coming to terms with it

In Peck's view—part of a comprehensive description of change across adulthood—the first task in old age is to redefine oneself in ways that do not relate to work roles or occupations. He labels this stage **redefinition of self versus preoccupation with work role.** As we will see, the changes that occur when people stop working can trigger a difficult adjustment in the way people view themselves. Peck suggests that people must adjust their values to place less emphasis on themselves as workers or professionals and more on attributes that don't involve work, such as being a grandparent or a gardener.

The second major developmental task in late adulthood, according to Peck, is **body transcendence versus body preoccupation.** Elderly individuals can undergo significant changes in their physical abilities as a result of aging. In the body-transcendence-versus-body-preoccupation stage, people must learn to cope with and move beyond those physical changes (transcendence). If they don't, they become preoccupied with their physical deterioration, to the detriment of their personality development. Greta Roach, who gave up bowling only in her 90s, is an example of coping well with the physical changes of aging.

The third developmental task in old age is **ego transcendence versus ego preoccupation,** in which elderly people must come to grips with their coming death. They need to understand that although death is inevitable, and probably not too far off, they have made contributions to

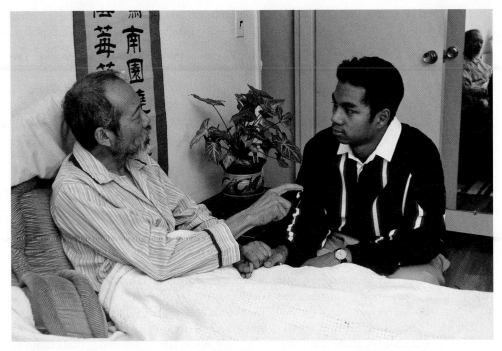

Older adults may become "venerated elders," whose advice is sought and relied upon.

society. If they see these contributions, which can take the form of children or work and civic activities, as lasting beyond their own lives, they will experience ego transcendence. If not, they may become preoccupied with asking whether their lives had value and worth to society.

***Levinson's Final Season: The Winter of Life.***   Daniel Levinson's theory of adult development does not focus as much on the challenges that aging adults must overcome. Instead, he looks at the processes that can lead to personality change as we grow old. According to Levinson, people enter late adulthood by passing through a transition stage that typically occurs around ages 60 to 65 (Levinson, 1986, 1992). During this stage, people come to view themselves as entering late adulthood—or, ultimately, as being "old." Knowing full well society's negative stereotypes about elderly individuals, they struggle with the notion that they are now in this category.

According to Levinson, people come to realize that they are no longer on the center stage, but are playing bit parts. This loss of power, respect, and authority may be difficult for individuals accustomed to having control in their lives.

On the other hand, people in late adulthood can serve as resources to younger individuals, and they may find that they are viewed as "venerated elders" whose advice is sought and relied upon. Furthermore, old age can bring a new freedom to do things simply for enjoyment and pleasure, rather than as obligations.

***Coping with Aging: Neugarten's Study.***   Bernice Neugarten (1972, 1977)—in what became a classic study—examined the different ways that people cope with aging. Neugarten found four different personality types in her research on people in their 70s:

- **Disintegrated and disorganized personalities.** Some people are unable to accept aging and experience despair as they get older. They are often found in nursing homes or hospitals.
- **Passive-dependent personalities.** Others become fearful—of falling ill, of the future, of their own inability to cope. They are so fearful that they may seek help from family and care providers, even when they don't need it.
- **Defended personalities.** Others respond to the fear of aging quite differently—by trying to stop it in its tracks. They may attempt to act young, exercising vigorously and engaging in youthful activities. Unfortunately, they may set unrealistic expectations and run the risk of disappointment as a result.
- **Integrated personalities.** The most successful individuals cope comfortably with aging. They accept it with a sense of self-dignity.

Neugarten found that the majority of the people she studied fell into the final category. They acknowledged aging, and could look back at their lives and gaze into the future with acceptance.

*Life Review and Reminiscence: The Common Theme of Personality Development.* **Life review,** in which people examine and evaluate their lives, is a major thread running through the work of Erikson, Peck, Neugarten, and Levinson, and a common theme among personality theorists who focus on late adulthood.

According to gerontologist Robert Butler (2002), life review is triggered by the increasingly obvious prospect of death. People look back on their lives, remembering and reconsidering what has happened to them. Far from being a harmful process of reliving the past, wallowing in past problems, and reviving old wounds, life review usually leads to a better understanding of the past. People may resolve lingering problems and conflicts with others, such as an estrangement from a child, and they may feel they can face their current lives with greater serenity (McKee et al., 2005; Bohlmeijer et al., 2007; Bohlmeijer, Westerhof, & de Jong, 2008).

Life review offers other benefits, including a sense of mutuality, a feeling of interconnectedness with others. Moreover, it can be a source of social interaction, as older adults share their experiences with others (Sherman, 1991; Parks, Sanna, & Posey, 2003).

Reminiscence may even have cognitive benefits, improving memory. By reflecting on the past, people activate a variety of memories, which may trigger other memories and bring back sights, sounds, and even smells of the past (Thorsheim & Roberts, 1990; Kartman, 1991).

On the other hand, life review can sometimes produce declines in psychological functioning. If people become obsessive about the past, reliving old insults and mistakes that cannot be rectified, they may end up feeling guilt, depression, and anger against acquaintances who may not even still be alive (DeGenova, 1993; Cappeliez, Guindon, & Robitaille, 2008).

Overall, though, the process of life review and reminiscence can play an important role by providing continuity between past and present, and increasing awareness of the contemporary world. It also can provide new insights into the past and into others, allowing people to continue personality growth and to function more effectively in the present (Webster & Haight, 2002; Coleman, 2005; Haber, 2006).

## Age Stratification Approaches to Late Adulthood

Age, like race and gender, provides a way of ranking people within a society. **Age stratification theories** suggest that economic resources, power, and privilege are distributed unequally among people at different stages of life. Such inequality is particularly pronounced during late adulthood.

Even as medical advances have lengthened the life span, power and prestige for the elderly have eroded, at least in highly industrialized societies. The peak earning years are the 50s; later, earnings tend to decline. Further, younger people are often physically removed from their elders, and their increased independence may make older adults feel less important. In addition, rapidly changing technology makes older adults seem out of date and lacking in important skills. Ultimately, they are seen as not particularly productive members of society and, in some cases, simply irrelevant (Cohn, 1982; Macionis, 2001). According to Levinson's theory, older people are keenly aware of their decline in status, and adjusting to it is the major transition of late adulthood.

Age stratification theories help explain why aging is viewed more positively in less industrialized societies. In predominantly agricultural societies, older people accumulate control over important resources such as animals and land. In such societies, the concept of retirement is unknown. Older individuals (especially males) are highly respected because they continue to be involved in daily activities central to the society. Furthermore, because the pace of change in agricultural societies is slower than in more technological societies, people in late adulthood have considerable relevant wisdom. Nor is respect for elders limited to agricultural countries; it is a characteristic of a variety of cultures.

## Does Age Bring Wisdom?

One of the benefits of age is supposed to be wisdom. But do people gain wisdom as they become older?

## Cultural Dimensions

### How Culture Shapes the Way We Treat People in Late Adulthood

Views of late adulthood are colored by culture. For example, compared to Western cultures, Asian societies generally hold elderly people, particularly family members, in higher esteem. Although this is changing in rapidly industrializing areas of Asia, the view of aging and the treatment of people in late adulthood still tend to be more positive than in Western cultures (Fry, 1985; Ikels, 1989; Cobbe, 2003; Degnen, 2007).

What is it about Asian cultures that leads to esteem for old age? In general, cultures that value the elderly are relatively homogeneous in socioeconomic terms. In addition, the roles that people play in those societies entail greater responsibility with increasing age, and elderly people control resources to a relatively large extent.

Moreover, the roles of people in Asian societies display more continuity throughout the life span than in Western cultures, and older adults continue to engage in activities that are valued by society. Finally, Asian cultures are more organized around extended families in which the older generations are well integrated into the family structure (Fry, 1985; Sangree, 1989). In such an arrangement, younger family members tend to rely on older members to share their considerable accumulated wisdom.

On the other hand, even societies that articulate strong ideals regarding older adults do not always live up to those standards. For instance, the attitudes of Chinese people, typified by admiration, respect, and even worship for individuals in late adulthood, are more positive than their actual behavior in all but the most elite segment of the society. Furthermore, sons and their wives—but not daughters—are typically expected to care for elderly parents; parents with only daughters may find themselves with no one to care for them. In short, broad, global statements about how older adults are treated in a given society almost always mask exceptions (Communian & Gielen, 2000; Browne, 2010).

Asian cultures are not alone in esteeming the elderly. In many Latino cultures, the elderly are thought to have a special inner strength, and in many African cultures, reaching an old age is seen as a sign of divine intervention (Diop, 1989; Holmes & Holmes, 1995; Lehr, Seiler, & Thomae, 2000).

What aspects of Asian cultures lead them to hold higher levels of esteem for old age?

---

In fact we don't know for sure, because the concept of **wisdom**—expert knowledge in the practical aspects of life—is only recently receiving attention from gerontologists and other researchers. This is partly due to the difficulty of defining and measuring the concept (Helmuth, 2003; Brugman, 2006). Wisdom can be seen as reflecting an accumulation of knowledge, experience, and contemplation, and by this definition, aging contributes to wisdom (Wink & Dillon, 2003; Kunzmann & Baltes, 2005; Staudinger, 2008).

Distinguishing wisdom from intelligence is tricky. Some researchers have made suggestions: While knowledge derived from intelligence is related to the here-and-now, wisdom is more timeless. While intelligence permits a person to think logically and systematically, wisdom provides an understanding of human behavior. According to psychologist Robert Sternberg, intelligence permits humans to invent the atom bomb, while wisdom prevents them from using it (Seppa, 1997).

Measuring wisdom is difficult. Ursula Staudinger and Paul Baltes (2000) designed a study showing that it is possible to assess people reliably on the concept. Pairs of people ranging in age from 20 to 70 discussed difficulties relating to life events. One problem involved someone

**wisdom** expert knowledge in the practical aspects of life

who gets a phone call from a friend who is planning to commit suicide. Another involved a 14-year-old girl who wanted to move out of her family home immediately. Participants were asked what they should do and consider.

Although there were no absolute right or wrong answers, the responses were evaluated against several criteria, including how much factual knowledge they brought to bear; their knowledge of decision-making strategies; how well the participants considered the context of the central character's life span and values; and their recognition that there might not be a single, absolute solution. Using these criteria, the older participants' responses were wiser than those of younger participants.

The study also found that the older participants benefited more from an experimental condition designed to promote wise thinking, and other research suggests that the very wisest individuals may be older adults.

Other research has looked at wisdom in terms of the development of a theory of mind: the ability to make inferences about others' thoughts, feelings, and intentions—their mental states. Older adults, drawing on their years of experience, appear to have a more sophisticated theory of mind (Happe, Winner, & Brownell, 1998).

## Successful Aging: What Is the Secret?

At age 77, Elinor Reynolds spends most of her time at home, leading a quiet, routine existence. Never married, Elinor receives visits from her two sisters every few weeks, and some of her nieces and nephews stop by on occasion. But for the most part, she keeps to herself. When asked, she says she is quite happy.

In contrast, Carrie Masterson, also 77, is involved in something different almost every day. If she is not visiting the senior center and participating in some activity, she is out shopping. Her daughter complains that Carrie is "never home" when she tries to reach her by phone, and Carrie replies that she has never been busier—or happier.

Clearly, there is no single way to age successfully. How people age depends on personality factors and people's circumstances. Some people become progressively less involved with the day-to-day, while others maintain active ties to people and their personal interests. Three major approaches provide explanations: disengagement theory, activity theory, and continuity theory.

***Disengagement Theory: Gradual Retreat.*** According to **disengagement theory,** late adulthood often involves a gradual withdrawal from the world on physical, psychological, and social levels (Cummings & Henry, 1961). On a physical level, elderly people have lower energy levels and slow down progressively. Psychologically, they begin to withdraw, showing less interest in the world around them and spending more time looking inward. Finally, on a social level, they engage in fewer interactions—both day-to-day, face-to-face encounters and participation in society as a whole. Older adults also become less involved and invested in the lives of others (Quinnan, 1997).

Disengagement theory suggests that withdrawal is a mutual process. Because of norms and expectations about aging, society begins to disengage from those in late adulthood. For example, mandatory retirement ages compel elderly people to withdraw from work, which accelerates disengagement.

While there is logic to disengagement theory, research support is limited. Furthermore, the theory has been criticized because it takes the failure of society to provide sufficient opportunities for meaningful engagement during late adulthood and then, in a sense, blames people in this age group for not being engaged.

Of course, some degree of disengagement is not necessarily all negative. For example, a gradual withdrawal in late adulthood may permit people to become more reflective about their own lives and less constrained by social roles. In addition, people can become more discerning in their social relationships, focusing on those who best meet their needs (Carstensen, 1995; Settersten, 2002; Wrosch, Bauer, & Scheier, 2005).

Today, most gerontologists reject disengagement theory, pointing out that disengagement is relatively uncommon. In most cases, people remain engaged, active, and busy throughout old age, and (especially in non-Western cultures) the expectation is that people will remain

**disengagement theory** the period in late adulthood that marks a gradual withdrawal from the world on physical, psychological, and social levels

actively involved in everyday life. Clearly, disengagement is not an automatic, universal process (Bergstrom & Holmes, 2000; Crosnoe & Elder, 2002).

***Activity Theory: Continued Involvement.*** Although early findings were consistent with disengagement theory, later research was not so supportive. For example, a follow-up study found that although some of the subjects were happily disengaged, others, who had remained involved and active, were as happy as—and sometimes happier than—those who disengaged. Furthermore, people in many non-Western cultures remain engaged, active, and busy throughout old age, and are expected to do so. Clearly, disengagement is not a universal process (Havighurst, 1973; Bergstrom & Holmes, 2000; Crosnoe & Elder, 2002).

The lack of support for disengagement theory led to an alternative. **Activity theory** suggests that successful aging occurs when people maintain the interests and activities of middle age and the amount and type of their social interactions. According to this perspective, happiness and satisfaction with life spring from involvement with the world (Charles, Reynolds, & Gatz, 2001; Consedine, Magai, & King, 2004; Hutchinson & Wexler, 2007).

Activity theory suggests that continuation of activities is important. Even when continuation is no longer possible—such as continuing work after retirement—activity theory argues that successful aging occurs when replacement activities are found.

But activity theory, like disengagement theory, is not the full story. For one thing, activity theory makes little distinction among activities. Not every activity will have an equal impact on a person's satisfaction with life; in fact, the nature and quality of the activities are likely to be more critical than mere quantity or frequency (Burrus-Bammel & Bammel, 1985; Adams, 2004).

A more significant concern is that for some people in late adulthood, the principle of "less is more" clearly holds: less activity brings greater enjoyment because they can slow down and do only the things that bring them the greatest satisfaction. In fact, some people view the ability to moderate their pace as one of the bounties of late adulthood. For them, a relatively inactive, and perhaps even solitary, existence is welcome (Ward, 1984; Hansson & Carpenter, 1994).

⬤ **From a social worker's perspective:** How might cultural factors affect an older person's likelihood of pursuing either the disengagement theory or the activity theory?

***Continuity Theory: A Compromise Position.*** Neither disengagement theory nor activity theory provides a complete picture of successful aging (Johnson & Barer, 1992; Rapkin & Fischer, 1992; Ouwehand, de Ridder, & Bensing, 2007). A compromise view is needed. **Continuity theory** suggests that people simply need to maintain their desired level of involvement in society in order to maximize their sense of well-being and self-esteem (Whitbourne, 2001; Atchley, 2003; Pushkar et al., 2010).

According to continuity theory, those who were highly active and social will be happiest if they largely remain so. Those who enjoy solitude and solitary interests, such as reading or walks in the woods, will be happiest pursuing that level of sociability (Holahan & Chapman, 2002).

It is also clear that most older adults experience positive emotions as frequently as younger individuals. Furthermore, they become more skilled at regulating their emotions.

Other factors enhance happiness during late adulthood. The importance of physical and mental health cannot be overestimated, and having enough financial security to provide for basic needs is critical. In addition, a sense of autonomy, independence, and personal control over one's life is a significant advantage (Morris, 2001; Charles, Mather, & Carstensen, 2003; Charles & Carstensen, 2010).

Finally, as we discussed earlier, people's perceptions can influence their happiness and satisfaction. Those who view late adulthood favorably are apt to perceive themselves more positively than those who view old age in a more pessimistic way (Levy, Slade, & Kasl, 2002; Levy, 2003).

Ultimately, surveys find that as a group, people in late adulthood report being happier than younger people. And it's not that those over 65 have always been happier. Instead, being older seems to bring a degree of contentment in the majority of people (Yang, 2008).

**activity theory** the theory suggesting that successful aging occurs when people maintain the interests, activities, and social interactions with which they were involved during middle age

**continuity theory** the theory suggesting that people need to maintain their desired level of involvement in society in order to maximize their sense of well-being and self-esteem

| **selective optimization** the process by which people concentrate on selected skill areas to compensate for losses in other areas |
| --- |

***Selective Optimization with Compensation: A General Model of Successful Aging.*** In considering the factors that lead to successful aging, developmental psychologists Paul Baltes and Margret Baltes focus on the "selective optimization with compensation" model. As we noted earlier, the assumption underlying the model is that late adulthood brings with it changes and losses in underlying capabilities, which vary from one person to another. However, it is possible to overcome such shifts in capabilities through selective optimization.

**Selective optimization** is the process by which people concentrate on particular skill areas to compensate for losses in other areas. They do this to fortify their general motivational, cognitive, and physical resources. A person who has run marathons all her life may have to cut back or give up entirely other activities in order to increase her training. By giving up other activities, she may be able to maintain her running skills through concentration on them (Baltes & Freund, 2003a, 2003b; Rapp, Krampe, & Baltes, 2006; Burnett-Wolle & Godbey, 2007).

Similarly, elderly individuals engage in compensation for age-related losses. For instance, a person may compensate for a hearing loss by using a hearing aid. Piano virtuoso Arthur Rubinstein provides another example of selective optimization with compensation. In his later years, he maintained his concert career by reducing the number of pieces he played at concerts—an example of being selective—and by practicing those pieces more often—optimization. Finally, in an example of compensation, he slowed down the tempo of musical passages immediately preceding faster passages, thereby fostering the illusion that he was playing as fast as ever (Baltes & Baltes, 1990).

In short, the model of selective optimization with compensation illustrates the fundamentals of successful aging. Although late adulthood may bring changes in capabilities, people who focus on making the most of particular areas may be able to compensate for limitations and losses. The outcome is a life that is reduced in some areas, but transformed and modified and, ultimately, successful.

## REVIEW, CHECK, AND APPLY

### REVIEW

**LO9**  In what ways does personality develop during late adulthood?

- Erikson calls older adulthood the ego-integrity-versus-despair stage, Peck focuses on three tasks that define the period, Levinson suggests that older people can experience liberation and self-regard, and Neugarten focuses on the ways people cope with aging.

**LO10**  How do people deal with aging?

- Societies in which elderly people are respected are generally characterized by social homogeneity, extended families, responsible roles for older people, and control of significant resources by older people.

- Disengagement theory suggests that older people gradually withdraw from the world, while activity theory suggests that the happiest people continue to be engaged with the world. A compromise theory—continuity theory—may be the most useful approach to successful aging, and the most successful model for aging may be selective optimization with compensation.

### CHECK YOURSELF

1. According to Erikson, individuals in late adulthood engage in looking back over their lives, evaluating their experiences, and coming to terms with decisions. This is also known as _____.
   a. ego transcendence versus ego preoccupation
   b. acceptance of growing old
   c. generativity versus stagnation
   d. ego integrity versus despair

2. According to Peck, the first major developmental task is to decide on your identity even though you are no longer employed. This is also known as _____.
   a. redefinition of self versus preoccupation with work role
   b. ego integrity versus despair
   c. body transcendence versus body preoccupation
   d. ego transcendence versus ego preoccupation

3. According to Levinson, as individuals enter late adulthood one of the hardest struggles they experience is the acceptance that they are "old."
   - True
   - False

### APPLYING LIFESPAN DEVELOPMENT

- How might personality traits account for success or failure in achieving satisfaction through the life review process?

✓•—☐**Study** and **Review** on **MyDevelopmentLab.com**

*Will you ace your test?* To find out, log onto MyDevelopmentLab.com.

# The Daily Life of Late Adulthood

**LO11** What is the quality of life in late adulthood?

**LO12** What is the nature of retirement?

*I hear all these retired folks complaining that they don't have this and they don't have that....I'm not pinched....My house is paid for. My car is paid for. Both my sons are grown up. I don't need many new clothes. Every time I go out and eat somewhere, I get a senior citizen's discount. This is the happiest period of my life. These are my golden years.* (Gottschalk, 1983, p. 1)

This positive view of life in late adulthood was expressed by a 74-year-old retired shipping clerk. Although not all retirees are so fortunate, many, if not most, find their post-work lives happy and involving. We will consider some of the ways in which people lead their lives in late adulthood, beginning with where they live.

Living in a multigenerational setting with children and their families can be rewarding and helpful for those in late adulthood. Are there any disadvantages to this type of situation? What are some solutions?

## Living Arrangements: The Places and Spaces of Their Lives

Think "old age," and your thoughts are likely to turn to nursing homes. But the reality is different. Only 5 percent of people finish their lives in nursing homes; most live out their entire lives in home environments, typically with at least one family member.

*Living at Home.*   Many older adults live alone. People over 65 represent a quarter of America's 9.6 million single-person households. Roughly two-thirds of people over 65 live with other members of the family, mostly spouses. Some older adults live with their siblings, and others live in multigenerational settings with their children, grandchildren, and even great-grandchildren.

The setting in which an older adult lives has varied effects. For married couples, living with a spouse represents continuity. On the other hand, moving in with children represents an adjustment to a multigenerational setting that can be jarring. Not only is there a potential loss of independence and privacy, but older adults may feel uncomfortable with the way their children are raising their grandchildren. Unless there are household ground rules about people's roles, conflicts can arise (Navarro, 2006).

For some groups, living in extended families is more typical than for other groups. For instance, African Americans are more likely than Whites to live in multigenerational families. Furthermore, the amount of influence that family members have over one another and the interdependence of extended families are generally greater in African American, Asian American, and Hispanic families than in Caucasian families (Becker, Beyene, & Newsom, 2003).

*Specialized Living Environments.*   For some 10 percent of those in late adulthood, home is an institution. In fact, there are many types of specialized environments in which elderly people live.

One of the more recent innovations is the **continuing-care community,** typically an environment in which all the residents are of retirement age or older. The community provides various levels of care, and residents sign contracts for the level they need. In many such communities, people start out in separate houses or apartments, living either independently or with occasional home care. As they age, they may move into *assisted living,* which involves independent housing supported by medical providers to the extent required. Continuing care ultimately extends all the way to full-time nursing care, which is often provided at an on-site nursing home.

Continuing-care communities tend to be fairly homogeneous in terms of religious, racial, and ethnic backgrounds, and they are often organized by private or religious organizations. Because joining may involve a substantial initial payment, members tend to be relatively well-off. Increasingly, though, continuing-care communities are making efforts to increase diversity and also to enhance intergenerational interaction by establishing day-care centers on the

**continuing-care community** a community that offers an environment in which all the residents are of retirement age or older

**adult day-care facilities** a facility in which elderly individuals receive care only during the day, but spend nights and weekends in their own homes

**skilled-nursing facilities** a facility that provides full-time nursing care for people who have chronic illnesses or are recovering from a temporary medical condition

**institutionalism** a psychological state in which people in nursing homes develop apathy, indifference, and a lack of caring about themselves

premises and developing programs that involve younger populations (Barton, 1997; Chaker, 2003; Berkman, 2006).

Several types of nursing institutions exist, ranging from those that provide part-time day care to homes that offer 24-hour-a-day, live-in care. In **adult day-care facilities,** elderly individuals receive care only during the day, but spend nights and weekends in their own homes. During the time that they are at the facility, people receive nursing care, take their meals, and participate in scheduled activities. Sometimes adult facilities are combined with infant and child day-care programs, an arrangement that allows for interaction between the old and the young (Ritchie, 2003; Tse & Howie, 2005; Gitlin et al., 2006; Dabelko & Zimmerman, 2008).

Other institutional settings offer more extensive care. The most intensive are **skilled-nursing facilities,** which provide full-time nursing care for people who have chronic illnesses or are recovering from a temporary medical condition. The number of people living in nursing homes increases dramatically with age. Specifically, 1.3 percent of 65- to 74-years-old, 4.4 percent of those 75 to 84, and 15.4 percent of persons 85 and older live in nursing homes and other institutions (Administration on Aging, 2010).

The more intensive the care, the greater the adjustment required of residents. Although some newcomers adjust relatively rapidly, the loss of independence may lead to difficulties. In addition, elderly people are as susceptible as other people to society's stereotypes about nursing homes, and their expectations may be negative. They may see themselves as just marking time until they die, forgotten and discarded by a society that venerates youth (Baltes, 1996; Natan, 2008; Kostka & Jachimowicz, 2010).

***Institutionalism and Learned Helplessness.*** Although the fears of those in nursing homes may be exaggerated, they can lead to **institutionalism,** a psychological state in which people develop apathy, indifference, and a lack of caring about themselves. Institutionalism is brought about, in part, by *learned helplessness,* a belief that one has no control over one's environment (Butler & Lewis, 1981; Peterson & Park, 2007).

The sense of helplessness brought about by institutionalism can be literally deadly. When people enter nursing homes in late adulthood, they lose control over their most basic activities. They may be told when and what to eat, when to sleep, and even when to go to the bathroom (Kane et al., 1997; Wolinsky, Wyrwich, & Babu, 2003).

During late adulthood, the range of socioeconomic well-being mirrors that of earlier years.

A classic experiment showed the consequences of such a loss of control. Psychologists Ellen Langer and Irving Janis (1979) divided elderly residents of a nursing home into two groups. One group was encouraged to make choices about their day-to-day activities. The other group was given no choices and was encouraged to let the nursing home staff care for them. The results were clear. The participants who had choices were not only happier, they were also healthier. In fact, 18 months after the experiment began, only 15 percent of the choice group had died—compared to 30 percent of the comparison group.

In short, loss of control can have a profound effect on well-being. The best nursing homes go out of their way to permit residents to make basic life decisions and maintain a sense of control over their lives.

**From the perspective of a health care provider:** What policies might a nursing home institute to minimize the chances that its residents will develop "institutionalism"? Why are such policies relatively uncommon?

## Financial Issues: The Economics of Late Adulthood

Like everyone, people in late adulthood range from one end of the socioeconomic spectrum to the other. Like the man quoted earlier, those who were relatively affluent during their working years tend to remain relatively affluent, while those who were poor tend to remain poor when they reach late adulthood.

However, social inequities affecting various groups earlier in life are magnified with increasing age. Even so, everyone who reaches late adulthood today may experience growing economic pressure because the increasing human life span means it is more likely they will run through their savings.

Overall, 10 percent of people age 65 and older live in poverty, a proportion about equal to that for people under 65, and around 6 percent of the elderly live in near poverty. However, there are significant gender and racial differences. Women are almost twice as likely as men to be living in poverty. About a quarter of elderly women living alone live on incomes below the poverty line. A married woman may also slip into poverty if she becomes widowed, for she may have used up savings to pay for her husband's final illness, and the husband's pension may cease with his death (Spraggins, 2003; Administration on Aging, 2010) (see Figure 9-11).

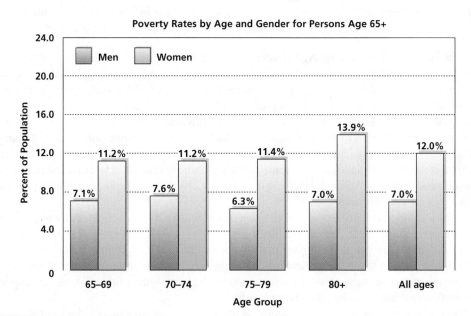

**FIGURE 9-11 Poverty and Elderly**
While 10 percent of those 65 years of age and older live in poverty, women are almost twice as likely as men to be living in poverty.
Source: U.S. Bureau of the Census, 2005.

Retirement is a different journey for each individual. Some are content with a more sedate lifestyle, while others continue to remain active and in some cases pursue new activities. Can you explain why many non-Western cultures do not follow the disengagement theory of retirement?
Source: Tomas del Amo/PacificStock.com.

**Watch on mydevelopmentlab.com**

Mary and George, a couple in their 70s, have recently retired and went through many of the same issues you've just read about.
Log onto MyDevelopmentLab.com to watch them talk about how they dealt with the changes that come with retirement.

As for racial differences, 8 percent of Whites in late adulthood live below the poverty line, contrasted with 19 percent of Hispanics and 24 percent of African Americans. Minority women fare the worst of any category. For example, 47 percent of divorced Black women aged 65 to 74 were below the poverty level (Rank & Hirschl, 1999; Federal Interagency Forum on Age-Related Statistics, 2000; U.S. Bureau of the Census, 2005).

One source of financial vulnerability is the reliance on a fixed income. The income of an elderly person, which typically comes from a combination of Social Security, pensions, and savings, rarely keeps up with inflation. What may have been a reasonable income at age 65 is worth much less 20 years later, as the elderly person gradually slips into poverty.

The rising cost of health care is another source of financial vulnerability in older adults. The average older person spends close to 20 percent of his or her income for health care costs. For those who require care in nursing home facilities, the financial costs can be staggering, running an average of close to $80,000 a year (MetLife Mature Market Institute, 2009).

Unless major changes are made in the way that Social Security and Medicare are financed, a larger proportion of younger people's pay will have to be taxed to fund benefits for the elderly. This is apt to lead to increasing friction and segregation between younger and older generations. Indeed, as we'll see, Social Security payments are one key factor in many people's decisions about how long to work.

## Work and Retirement in Late Adulthood

Deciding when to retire is a major decision faced by the majority of individuals in late adulthood. Some wish to work as long as they can. Others retire the moment their financial circumstances permit it.    **Watch on mydevelopmentlab.com**

When they do retire, many people have some difficulty with the identity shift from "worker" to "retiree." They lack a professional title, they may no longer have people asking them for advice, and they can't say "I work for the Diamond Company."

For others, though, retirement offers the chance to lead, perhaps for the first time in adulthood, a life of leisure. Because a significant number of people retire as early as age 55 or 60, and because life spans are expanding, many people spend far more time in retirement than in previous generations. Moreover, because the number of people in late adulthood continues to increase, retirees are an increasingly significant and influential segment of the U.S. population.

***Older Workers: Combating Age Discrimination.***    Many people continue to work, either full- or part-time, for some part of late adulthood. That they can do so is largely because of age discrimination legislation that was passed in the late 1970s, in which mandatory retirement ages were made illegal in almost every profession (Lindemann & Kadue, 2003).

Whether older adults continue to work for intellectual and social reasons or financial reasons, many encounter age discrimination, which is a reality despite laws against it. Some employers encourage older workers to leave their jobs so they can replace them with younger employees with lower salaries. And some employers believe that older workers are not up to the demands of the job or are less willing to adapt to a changing workplace—enduring stereotypes that laws can't change (Moss, 1997).

There is little evidence to support the idea that older workers lose their ability to perform their jobs. In many fields, such as art, literature, science, politics, and entertainment, it is easy to find examples of people who have made some of their greatest contributions during late adulthood. Even in those few professions that were specifically exempted from laws prohibiting mandatory retirement ages—those involving public safety—the evidence does not support the notion that workers should be retired early.

For instance, one large-scale, careful study of older police officers, firefighters, and prison guards concluded that age was not a good predictor of whether a worker was likely to be incapacitated on the job, or the level of his or her general work performance. Accurate prediction required a case-by-case analysis of the performance of individuals (Landy & Conte, 2004).

Although age discrimination remains a problem, market forces may help reduce its severity. As baby boomers retire and the workforce drastically shrinks, companies may begin to offer incentives to older adults to either remain in or return to the workforce. Still, for most older adults, retirement is the norm.

***Retirement: Filling a Life of Leisure.***   Why do people retire? Although the basic reason seems apparent—to stop working—there are actually many factors. For instance, sometimes workers burn out after a lifetime of work and seek to ease the tension and frustration of their jobs and the sense that they have not accomplished as much as they wished. Others retire because their health has declined, and still others because they receive incentives from their employers. Finally, some people have planned for years to retire and intend to use their increased leisure to travel, study, or spend more time with their children and grandchildren (Sener, Terzioglu, & Karabulut, 2007; Nordenmark & Stattin, 2009; Petkoska & Earl, 2009).

Whatever the reason they retire, people often pass through a series of retirement stages. Retirement may begin with a *honeymoon* period, in which people engage in a variety of activities, such as travel, that were previously hindered by work. The next phase may be *disenchantment,* in which they conclude that retirement is not all they thought it would be because they miss the stimulation and companionship of work or find it hard to keep busy (Atchley & Barusch, 2005).

The next phase is *reorientation,* in which retirees reconsider their options and become engaged in new, more fulfilling activities. If successful, this leads to the *retirement routine* stage, in which they come to grips with the realities of retirement and feel fulfilled. Not all people reach this stage; some may feel disenchanted for years.

The last phase is *termination.* Although for some people this occurs when they go back to work, for most it follows major physical deterioration. In this case, health becomes so bad that the person can no longer function independently.

Obviously, not everyone passes through all stages, and the sequence is not universal. In large measure, a person's reactions to retirement stem from the reasons he or she retired in the first place. For example, a person forced to retire for health reasons will have a different experience from a person who eagerly chose to retire at a particular age. Similarly, the retirement of people who loved their jobs may differ from that of people who despised their work.

In short, the psychological consequences of retirement vary from one individual to the next. For many people, retirement is a continuation of a life well-lived. Moreover, as we see next, there are ways to plan a good retirement.

## Planning for—and Living—a Good Retirement

### Becoming an Informed Consumer of Development

What makes for a good retirement? Gerontologists suggest several factors (Kreitlow & Kreitlow, 1997; Rowe & Kahn, 1998; Borchard, 2008; Noone, Stephens, & Alpass, 2009):

- **Plan ahead financially.** Because Social Security pensions are likely to be inadequate in the future, personal savings are critical, as is adequate health insurance.

- **Consider tapering off from work gradually.** Sometimes it is helpful to prepare for retirement by shifting from full-time to part-time work.

- **Explore your interests before you retire.** Assess what you like about your current job and think about how to translate those things into leisure activities.

- **If you are married or in a long-term partnership, spend some time discussing your views of the ideal retirement with your partner.** You may find that you need to negotiate a vision that will suit you both.

- **Consider where you want to live.** Try out, temporarily, a community to which you are thinking of moving.

- **Determine the advantages and disadvantages of downsizing your current home.**

- **Plan to volunteer your time.** People who retire have a wealth of skills that are often needed by nonprofit organizations and small businesses. Organizations such as the Retired Senior Volunteer Program or the Foster Grandparent Program can help match your skills with people who need them.

## REVIEW

**LO11** What is the quality of life in late adulthood?

- Elderly people live in a variety of settings, although most live at home with a family member. For others there are specialized living environments that range from continuing-care communities to skilled-nursing facilities.

- Financial issues can trouble older people, largely because their incomes are fixed, health care costs are increasing, and the life span is lengthening.

**LO12** What is the nature of retirement?

- After retirement, many people pass through stages, including a honeymoon period, disenchantment, reorientation, retirement routine, and termination.

- There are ways to plan a good retirement including tapering off from work gradually, exploring interests before retiring, and trying to plan ahead financially.

## CHECK YOURSELF

1. Older adults living in communities that offer an environment in which all the residents are of retirement age or older and need various levels of care reside in a _____ home.

   a. retirement

   b. single-family

   c. continuing-care

   d. multifamily

2. After age 65, women are twice as likely as men to be living in poverty.

   - True

   - False

3. Which of the following is NOT cited in your text as a reason older adults decide to retire?

   a. declining health

   b. job burnout

   c. incentives from their employers

   d. spouses have retired

## APPLYING LIFESPAN DEVELOPMENT

- Based on the research on successful aging, what advice would you give someone who is nearing retirement?

✓—[**Study** and **Review** on
**MyDevelopmentLab.com**

Answers: 1) c; 2) True; 3) d

---

# Relationships: Old and New

**LO13** How do marriages fare in late adulthood?

**LO14** What sorts of relationships are important to older adults?

*"Well, I tell you," says Eva Solymosi, and so she does, starting at the beginning when she first met Joseph. The youngest of 13, she was a poor cook in Hungary, befriended by an old woman who shared this advice: "When a kind face comes by, keep him."*

*Eva saw Joseph, an 18-year-old chimney sweep, getting a drink of cold water by the public well. "He had a kind face. So that's it," she says and shrugs. They married the next year, moved to the U.S., and have been together since. She is 97 and he is 93....*

*They are partners. When one is telling a story, the other quietly gets up and fetches a pertinent picture or letter. They share the chores and praise the other's efforts....*

*When Joseph is shopping or watching the news, Eva will spend hours going through her dozen photo albums. There is Joseph as a young man reading the newspaper, Eva eating an ear of corn in the 1920s, their first Christmas tree.... She comes across a picture of him when he was 18. "Ah ha, that is the kind face I fell in love with. In my eyes he is still as handsome." He says nothing, but gently taps her cane with his. (Ansberry, 1995, pp. A1, A17)*

The warmth and affection between Joseph and Eva are unmistakable. Their relationship, spanning eight decades, continues to bring them quiet joy, and their life is the sort to which many couples aspire. Yet it is also rare for the last stage of life. For every older person who is part of a couple, many more are alone.

What is the social world of late adulthood? To answer the question, we will first consider marriage.

# Marriage in the Later Years: Together, Then Alone

It's a man's world—at least when it comes to marriage after 65. The proportion of men who are married is far greater than that of women (see Figure 9-12). One reason is that 70 percent of women outlive their husbands by at least a few years. Because there are fewer men available (many have died), these women are unlikely to remarry (Barer, 1994).

Furthermore, the marriage gradient that we discussed earlier is still a powerful influence. Reflecting societal norms that women should marry older men, the marriage gradient keeps women single even in the later years of life. At the same time, it makes remarriage for men much easier, since the pool of eligible partners is much larger (AARP, 1990).

The vast majority of people who are still married in later life report that they are satisfied with their marriages. Their partners provide substantial companionship and emotional support. Because at this period in life they have typically been together for a long time, they have great insight into their partners (Brubaker, 1991; Levenson, Cerstensen, & Gottman, 1993; Jose & Alfons, 2007).

Still, not every aspect of marriage is satisfying, and marriages may undergo stress as spouses experience changes in their lives. For instance, the retirement of one or both spouses can shift the nature of a couple's relationship (Askham, 1994; Henry, Miller, & Giarrusso, 2005).

For some couples, the stress is so great that one spouse or the other seeks a divorce. Although the exact numbers are hard to come by, at least 2 percent of divorces in the United States involve women over 60 (Uhlenberg, Cooney, & Boyd, 1990).

The reasons for divorce so late in life are varied. Often, women divorce because their husbands are abusive or alcoholic. But in the more frequent case of a husband divorcing from his wife, the reason is often that he has found a younger woman. Often the divorce occurs soon after retirement, when men who have been highly involved in their careers are in psychological turmoil (Cain, 1982; Solomon et al., 1998).

Divorce so late in life is particularly difficult for women. Between the marriage gradient and the limited pool of eligible men, it is unlikely that an older divorced woman will remarry. For many women, marriage has been their primary role and the center of their identities, and they may view divorce as a major failure. As a consequence, happiness and the quality of life for divorced women often plummet (Goldscheider, 1994; Davies & Denton, 2002; Connidis, 2010).

Seeking a new relationship becomes a priority for many men and women who are divorced or whose spouses have died. People seeking to develop relationships use the same strategies to meet potential partners as younger people, such as joining singles organizations or even using the Internet to seek out companionship (Durbin, 2003).

Of course, some people enter late adulthood having never married. For this group—about 5 percent of the population—late adulthood may bring fewer transitions, since living status does not change. In fact, never-married individuals report feeling less lonely than do most people their age, and they have a greater sense of independence (Essex & Nam, 1987; Newston & Keith, 1997).

***Dealing with Retirement: Too Much Togetherness?*** When Morris Abercrombie finally stopped working full-time, his wife, Roxanne, found some aspects of his increased presence at home troubling. Although their marriage was strong, his intrusion into her daily routine and his constant questioning about whom she was on the phone with and where she was going were irksome. Finally, she began to wish he would spend less time around the house. This was ironic: She had passed much of Morris's preretirement years wishing that he would spend more time at home.

The situation in which Morris and Roxanne found themselves is not unique. For many couples, relationships need to be renegotiated since the couple will probably spend more time together than at any other point in their marriage. For others, retirement alters the longstanding distribution of household chores, with men taking on more responsibility than before for the everyday functioning of the household.

In fact, research suggests that an interesting role-reversal often takes place. In contrast to the early years of marriage, in late adulthood husbands' companionship needs tend to be

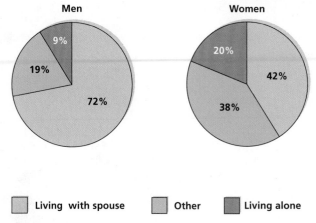

**FIGURE 9-12  Living Patterns of Older Americans**
What, if anything, do these patterns suggest about the relative health and adjustment of men and women?
Source: Administration on Aging, 2006.

One of the most difficult responsibilities of later adulthood can be caring for one's ill spouse.

greater than their wives'. The power structure of marriage also changes: Men become more affiliative and less competitive following retirement. At the same time, women become more assertive and autonomous (Blumstein & Schwartz, 1989; Bird & Melville, 1994).

***Caring for an Aging Spouse.*** The shifts in health that accompany late adulthood sometimes require women and men to care for their spouses in ways that they never envisioned. Consider, for example, one woman's comments of frustration:

> *I cry a lot because I never thought it would be this way. I didn't expect to be mopping up the bathroom, changing him, doing laundry all the time. I was taking care of babies at twenty; now I'm taking care of my husband.* (Doress et al., 1987, pp. 199–200)

At the same time, some people view caring for an ailing and dying spouse as a final opportunity to demonstrate love and devotion. In fact, some caregivers report feeling satisfied at fulfilling what they see as their responsibility to their spouse. And some of those who experience emotional distress initially find that the distress declines as they successfully adapt (Zarit & Reid, 1994).

Yet there is no getting around the fact that giving care is arduous, made more difficult by the fact that the spouses providing the care are probably not in the peak of health themselves. In fact, caregiving may be detrimental to the provider's own physical and psychological health. For instance, caregivers report lower levels of satisfaction with life than do noncaregivers (Vitaliano, Dougherty, & Siegler, 1994; Grant, Weaver, & Elliott, 2004; Choi & Marks, 2006; Percy, 2010).

In almost three-quarters of the cases, it should be noted, the spouse who provides the care is the wife. Part of the reason is demographic: Men tend to die earlier than women, and consequently to contract the diseases leading to death earlier than women. A second reason, though, relates to society's traditional gender roles, which view women as "natural" caregivers. As a consequence, health care providers may be more likely to suggest that a wife care for her husband than that a husband care for his wife (Polansky, 1976; Unger & Crawford, 1992).

***The Death of a Spouse: Becoming Widowed.*** Hardly any event is more painful and stressful than the death of one's spouse. Especially for those who married young, the death leads to profound feelings of loss and often brings drastic changes in economic and social circumstances. If the marriage was a good one, the death means the loss of a companion, a lover, a confidante, a helper.

Upon a partner's death, spouses suddenly assume a new and unfamiliar societal role: widowhood. At the same time, they lose the role with which they were most familiar: spouse. Suddenly, they are no longer part of a couple; instead, they are viewed by society, and themselves, as individuals. All this occurs as they are dealing with profound and sometimes overwhelming grief (which we discuss more in the next chapter).

Widowhood brings new demands and concerns. There is no longer a companion to share the day's events. If the deceased spouse primarily did the household chores, the surviving spouse must learn how to do these tasks every day. Although initially family and friends provide a great deal of support, this assistance quickly fades and newly widowed people are left to make the adjustment on their own (Wortman & Silver, 1990; Hanson & Hayslip, 2000).

People's social lives often change drastically. Married couples tend to socialize with other married couples; widowed people may feel like "fifth wheels" as they seek to maintain the friendships they enjoyed as part of a couple. Eventually, such friendships may cease, although they may be replaced by friendships with other single people (van den Hoonaard, 1994).

Economic issues are of major concern to many widowed people. Although many have insurance, savings, and pensions to provide economic security, some persons, most often women, experience a decline in their economic well-being as the result of a spouse's death. This can force wrenching decisions, such as selling the house in which the couple spent their married lives (Meyer, Wolf, & Himes, 2006).

The process of adjusting to widowhood encompasses three stages. In the first stage, *preparation,* spouses prepare, in some cases years and even decades ahead of time, for the eventual death of the partner. Consider, for instance, the purchase of life insurance, the preparation of a will, and the decision to have children who may eventually provide care in one's old age. Each of these actions helps prepare for the eventuality that one will be widowed and will require some degree of assistance (Heinemann & Evans, 1990; Roecke & Cherry, 2002).

The second stage of adjustment to widowhood, *grief and mourning,* is an immediate reaction to the death of a spouse. It starts with the shock and pain of loss, and continues as the survivor works through the emotions the loss brings up. The time a person spends in this period depends on the support received from others, as well as on personality factors. In some cases, grief and mourning may last for years, while in others it lasts a few months.

The last stage of adjustment to the death of a spouse is *adaptation.* In adaptation, the widowed individual starts a new life. The period begins with the acceptance of loss and continues with the reorganization of roles and the formation of new friendships. The adaptation stage also encompasses a period of reintegration in which a new identity—as an unmarried person—is developed. ◉ Watch on mydevelopmentlab.com

It is important to keep in mind that this three-stage model of loss and change does not apply to everyone, and the timing of the stages varies considerably. Moreover, some people experience *complicated grief,* a form of unrelenting mourning that continues sometimes for months and even years. In complicated grief, people find it difficult to let go of a loved one, and they have intrusive memories of the deceased that impede normal functioning (Holland et al., 2009; Piper et al., 2009; Zisook & Shear, 2009).

For most people, though, life returns to normal and becomes enjoyable once again after the death of a spouse. Still, the death of a spouse is a profound event in any period of life. During late adulthood, its implications are particularly powerful, since it can be seen as a forewarning of one's own mortality.

◉ **From a social worker's perspective:** What are some factors that can combine to make older adulthood a more difficult time for women than for men?

## The Social Networks of Late Adulthood

Elderly people enjoy friends as much as younger people do, and friendships play an important role in their lives. In fact, time spent with friends is often valued more highly during late adulthood than time spent with family, with friends often seen as more important providers of support. Furthermore, around a third of older persons report that they made a new friend within the past year, and many older adults engage in significant interaction (Hartshorne, 1994; Hansson & Carpenter, 1994; Ansberry, 1997) (see Figure 9-13).

◉ Watch on **mydevelopmentlab.com**

Log onto MyDevelopmentLab.com to watch a video of Bob, a man who recently lost his wife of 48 years. He talks about how her loss has affected him and how he still manages to keep a positive outlook on life.

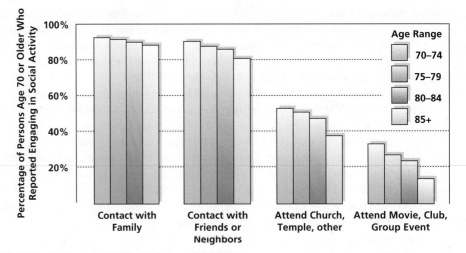

**FIGURE 9-13 Social Activity in Late Adulthood**
Friends and family play an important role in the social activity of the elderly.
Source: Federal Interagency Forum on Age Related Statistics, 2000.

***Friendship: Why Friends Matter in Late Adulthood.*** Friendships are characterized by a sense of control: In friendship relationships, unlike family relationships, we choose whom we like and whom we dislike. Because late adulthood often causes a gradual loss of control in other areas, such as in health, the ability to maintain friendships may take on more importance than in other stages of life (Pruchno & Rosenbaum, 2003; Stevens, Martina, & Westerhof, 2006).

In addition, friendships—especially recent ones—may be more flexible than family relationships, since they lack the long history of obligations and conflicts that often typify family ties and that can reduce the emotional sustenance they provide (Hartshorne, 1994; Magai & McFadden, 1996; McLaughlin, 2010).

Friendships in late adulthood are also important because of the increasing likelihood, over time, that one will be without a marital partner. When a spouse dies, people typically seek out friends to help deal with their loss and for some of the companionship that was provided by the deceased spouse.

Of course, it isn't only spouses who die during old age; friends die, too. The way adults view friendship in late adulthood determines how vulnerable they are to the death of a friend. If they have defined the friendship as irreplaceable, the loss of the friend may be quite difficult. On the other hand, if the friendship is defined as one of many, the death of a friend may be less traumatic (Hartshorne, 1994).

***Social Support: The Significance of Others.*** Friendships also provide one of the basic social needs: social support. **Social support** is assistance and comfort supplied by a network of caring, interested people. Such support plays a critical role in successful aging (Avlund, Lund, & Holstein, 2004; Gow et al., 2007; Evans, 2009).

Social support brings considerable benefits. A social support network can offer emotional support by lending a sympathetic ear and providing a sounding board for concerns. Furthermore, people who are experiencing similar problems—such as the loss of a spouse—can provide an unmatched degree of understanding and a pool of helpful suggestions for coping strategies that would be less credible coming from others.

Finally, people can furnish material support, such as helping with rides or picking up groceries. They can provide help in solving problems, such as dealing with a difficult landlord or fixing a broken appliance.

The benefits of social support extend to the provider as well as the recipient. People who offer support experience feelings of usefulness and heightened self-esteem, knowing that they are making a contribution to someone else's welfare.

What kinds of social support are most effective and appropriate? Certainly preparing food, accompanying someone to a movie, or inviting someone to dinner are helpful. But the

**social support** assistance and comfort supplied by another person or a network of caring, interested people

opportunity for reciprocity is important, too. Reciprocity is the expectation that if someone provides something positive to another person, eventually, the favor will be returned. In Western societies, older adults—like younger people—value relationships in which reciprocity is possible (Clark & Mills, 1993; Becker, Beyene, & Newsom, 2003).

With increasing age, it may be progressively more difficult to reciprocate the social support that one receives. As a consequence, relationships may become more asymmetrical, placing the recipient in a difficult psychological position (Selig, Tomlinson, & Hickey, 1991).

## Family Relationships: The Ties That Bind

Even after the death of a spouse, most older adults are part of a larger family unit. Connections with siblings, children, grandchildren, and even great-grandchildren continue and may be an important source of comfort to adults in the last years of their lives.

Siblings can provide unusually strong emotional support because they often share old, pleasant memories of childhood, and because they usually represent a person's oldest existing relationships. While not every memory of childhood may be pleasant, continuing interaction with brothers and sisters can enhance late adulthood (Moyer, 1992).

*Children.*  Even more important than siblings are children and grandchildren. Even in an age in which geographic mobility is high, most parents and children remain fairly close, both geographically and psychologically. Some 75 percent of children live within a 30-minute drive of their parents, and parents and children visit and talk with one another frequently. Daughters tend to be in more frequent contact with their parents than sons, and mothers tend to be the recipients of communication more often than fathers (Field & Minkler, 1988; Krout, 1988; Ji-liang, Li-qing, & Yan, 2003).

Because the great majority of older adults have at least one child who lives fairly close, family members still provide significant aid to one another. Moreover, parents and children tend to share similar views of how adult children should behave toward their parents (see Table 9-2). In particular, they expect that children should help their parents understand their resources, provide emotional support, and talk over such important matters as medical issues. Furthermore, it is most often children who end up caring for their aging parents when they require assistance (Dellmann-Jenkins & Brittain, 2003; Ron, 2006; Funk, 2010).

The bonds between parents and children are sometimes asymmetrical, with parents seeking a closer relationship and children a more distant one. Parents have a greater *developmental stake* in close ties, since they see their children as perpetuating their beliefs, values, and standards. On the other hand, children are motivated to maintain their autonomy and live independently from their parents. These divergent perspectives make parents more likely to minimize conflicts they experience with their children, and children more likely to maximize them (O'Connor, 1994).

For parents, their children remain a source of great interest and concern. Some surveys show, for instance, that even in late adulthood parents talk about their children nearly every day, particularly if the children are having some sort of problem. At the same time, children may turn to their elderly parents for advice, information, and sometimes tangible help, such as money (Greenberg & Becker, 1988).

*Grandchildren and Great-Grandchildren.*  As we discussed earlier, not all grandparents are equally involved with their grandchildren. Even those who take great pride in their grandchildren may be relatively detached, avoiding any direct care role (Cherlin & Furstenberg, 1986).

As we saw, grandmothers tend to be more involved than grandfathers, and most young adult grandchildren feel closer to their grandmothers. In addition, most express a preference for their maternal grandmothers over their paternal grandmothers (Hayslip, Shore, & Henderson, 2000; Lavers-Preston & Sonuga-Barke, 2003; Bishop et al., 2009).

African American grandparents tend to be more involved with their grandchildren than White grandparents, and African American grandchildren often feel closer to their grandparents. Moreover, grandfathers seem to play a more central role in the lives of African American children than in the lives of White children. These racial differences probably stem in large measure from the higher proportion of multigenerational families among African Americans than among Whites. In such families, grandparents usually play a central role in childrearing (Crowther & Rodriguez, 2003; Stevenson, Henderson, & Baugh, 2007).

## TABLE 9-2 PARENTS AND CHILDREN SHARE SIMILAR VIEWS OF HOW ADULT CHILDREN SHOULD BEHAVE TOWARD THEIR PARENTS

| Item | Children's Rank | Parent's Rank |
|---|---|---|
| Help understand resources | 1 | 2 |
| Give emotional support | 2 | 3 |
| Discuss matters of importance | 3 | 1 |
| Make room in home in emergency | 4 | 7 |
| Sacrifice personal freedom | 5 | 6 |
| Care when sick | 6 | 9 |
| Be together on special occasions | 7 | 5 |
| Provide financial help | 8 | 13 |
| Give parents advice | 9 | 4 |
| Adjust family schedule to help | 10 | 10 |
| Feel responsible for parent | 11 | 8 |
| Adjust work schedule to help | 12 | 12 |
| Believe that parent should live with child | 13 | 15 |
| Visit once a week | 14 | 11 |
| Live close to parent | 15 | 16 |
| Write once a week | 16 | 14 |

Source: JOURNAL OF GERONTOLOGY by Harmon & Blieszner. Copyright 1990 by The Gerontological Society of America. Reproduced with permission of The Gerontological Society of America in the format Textbook via Copyright Clearance Center.

**Watch** on **mydevelopmentlab.com**

*How involved were your grandparents in your life? What effects do you think that had on your grandparents' lives?*

To see one grandmother's perspective, log onto MyDevelopmentLab.com and watch a video of Maria, a 68-year-old woman who lives with her daughter and watches her grandchildren while their parents are at work.

Great-grandchildren play less of a role in the lives of both White and African American great-grandparents. Most great-grandparents do not have close relationships with their great-grandchildren. Close relationships tend to occur only when the great-grandparents and great-grandchildren live relatively near one another (Doka & Mertz, 1988).

There are several explanations for this relative lack of involvement. One is that by the time they reach great-grandparenthood, people are so old that they do not have much physical or psychological energy to expend on relationships with their great-grandchildren. Another is that there may be so many great-grandchildren that great-grandparents do not feel strong emotional ties to them and may not even be able to keep track of them. When President John Kennedy's mother, Rose Kennedy (who had given birth to a total of nine children), died at the age of 104, she had 30 grandchildren and 41 great-grandchildren!

Still, great-grandparents profit emotionally from the mere fact that they have great-grandchildren. They may see their great-grandchildren as representing both their own and their family's continuation, as well as providing a concrete sign of their longevity (Doka & Mertz, 1988). **Watch** on **mydevelopmentlab.com**

## Elder Abuse: Relationships Gone Wrong

*With good health and a sizable pension, 76-year-old Mary T. should have been enjoying a comfortable retirement. But in fact, her life was made miserable by a seemingly endless barrage of threats, insults, and indignities from her live-in adult son.*

*A habitual gambler and drug user, the son was merciless: he spat at Mary, brandished a knife in her face, stole her money, and sold her possessions. After several emergency room trips and two hospitalizations, social workers convinced Mary to move out and join a support group of other elderly people abused by their loved ones. With a new apartment and understanding friends, Mary finally had some peace. But her son found her, and feeling a mother's guilt and shame, Mary took him back—and opened another round of heartache. (Minaker & Frishman, 1995, p. 9)*

**elder abuse** the physical or psychological mistreatment or neglect of elderly individuals

Such cases are more common than we would like to believe. According to some estimates, **elder abuse,** the physical or psychological mistreatment or neglect of elderly individuals, may affect as many as two million people over age 60 each year. Even these estimates may be low, since people who are abused are often too embarrassed to report their plight. And as the number of elderly people increases, experts believe that elder abuse will also rise (Brubaker, 1991; Starr, 2010).

Elder abuse is most frequently directed at family members and particularly at parents. Those most at risk are likely to be less healthy and more isolated than average, and they are more likely to be living in a caregiver's home. Although there is no single cause for elder abuse, it often stems from economic, psychological, and social pressures on caregivers who must provide high levels of care 24 hours a day. Thus, people with Alzheimer's disease or other sorts of dementia are particularly likely to be targets of abuse (Tauriac & Scruggs, 2006; Baker, 2007; Lee, 2008).

The best way to deal with elder abuse is to prevent it. Family members caring for an older adult should take breaks and should contact social support agencies for advice and concrete support. For instance, the National Family Caregivers Association (800-896-3650) maintains a caregivers' network and publishes a newsletter.

Anyone suspecting that an elderly person is being abused should contact local authorities, such as their state's Adult Protective Services or Elder Protective Services.

## REVIEW, CHECK, AND APPLY

### REVIEW

**LO13**  How do marriages fare in late adulthood?

- While marriages in older adulthood are generally happy, the many changes of the period cause stresses that can bring divorce.

- The death of a spouse has major psychological, social, and material effects on the survivor and makes the formation and continuation of friendships highly important.

**LO14**  What sorts of relationships are important to older adults?

- Family relationships are a continuing part of most older people's lives, especially relationships with siblings and children.

- Friendships are highly valued in late adulthood and an important source of social support.

### CHECK YOURSELF

1. Individuals still married in later life report being significantly less satisfied with their marriages than they were in earlier years.

- True
- False

2. Elderly individuals often rely on _____, or the assistance and comfort supplied by another person or network of people, for successful aging.

3. Which of the following characteristics is associated with elder abuse?

   a. being healthy

   b. being a victim of Alzheimer's

   c. being less isolated

   d. having a caregiver who lives outside of the home

### APPLYING LIFESPAN DEVELOPMENT

- What are some ways the retirement of a spouse can bring stress to a marriage? Is retirement likely to be less stressful in households where both spouses work, or twice as stressful?

✓•—|**Study** and **Review** on
**MyDevelopmentLab.com**

Answers: 1) False; 2) social support; 3) b

# Putting It All Together
## Late Adulthood

**ARTHUR WINSTON AND BEN TUFTY** have chosen two distinct ways to live out their late adulthood. While Arthur loves his job and can't conceive of retiring, Ben couldn't wait to retire and now enjoys his leisure to the fullest. What the two retirees have in common is their commitment to maintaining their physical health, intellectual activity, and key relationships—even if they have chosen radically different ways to do these things. By paying attention to their needs in all three spheres, Arthur and Ben have remained optimistic and cheerful. Clearly, each looks forward to every day he spends in the world.

### MODULE 9.1 Physical Development in Late Adulthood

- Though both are chronologically among the "oldest old," Arthur and Ben are "young old" in their functional ages. **(p. 411)**

- Both defy ageist stereotypes in their health and attitudes. **(p. 412)**

- Both appear to have avoided Alzheimer's and most of the other physical and psychological disorders associated with old age. **(pp. 418-421)**

- Arthur and Ben have made healthy lifestyle choices—exercising, eating right, and avoiding bad habits. **(p. 423)**

### MODULE 9.2 Cognitive Development in Late Adulthood

- Both Arthur and Ben are apparently rich in crystallized intelligence—their store of information, skills, and strategies. **(p. 427)**

- They demonstrate plasticity by using stimulation, practice, and motivation to maintain their mental abilities. **(pp. 427-428)**

- Both men may have slight memory problems, such as a decline in episodic or autobiographical memory. **(p. 430)**

- Arthur and Ben are navigating Erikson's ego-integrity-versus-despair stage, but they seem to have chosen different answers to Peck's developmental task of redefinition of self versus preoccupation with work role. **(pp. 433-435)**

- The two appear to be coping with aging differently, according to Neugarten's personality categories. **(p. 435)**

- Both seem to have acquired wisdom with age, knowing who they are and how to deal with others. **(pp. 436-438)**

- In playing "low-pressure" games, Ben might be engaging in compensation for slowed reaction time or less-than-perfect recall. **(p. 440)**

- Both men have chosen to continue living at home. **(p. 441)**

- Neither man seems to have gone through the classic retirement stages. **(p. 445)**

**Explore on mydevelopmentlab.com**

To read how a real retirement counselor, health care provider, and educator responded to these questions, log onto MyDevelopmentLab.com.

*Do you agree or disagree with their responses? Why? What concepts that you've read about back up their opinions?*

## What would a RETIREMENT COUNSELOR do?

- What advice would you give a person who wants to stay on the job forever, the way Arthur has done? What advice would you give someone like Ben, who wants to retire early? What characteristics would you look for in these individuals that would help you give the right advice?

    **HINT** Review pages 444–445.

    *What's your response?*

## What would a HEALTH CARE PROVIDER do?

- Why do you think Arthur and Ben are in such good physical health? What strategies has Ben used that Arthur may not have? What strategies has Arthur used that Ben may not have? What strategies do they share?

    **HINT** Review pages 418–421.

    *What's your response?*

## What would YOU do?

- If you were asked to do an oral history project involving Arthur and Ben, how complete and accurate would you expect their recollections to be? Would they be more reliable about the 1950s or the 1990s? Which man do you think you would enjoy talking to more?

    **HINT** Review pages 429–431.

    *What's your response?*

## What would an EDUCATOR do?

- Would you recommend cognitive training for either Arthur or Ben? What about college courses via Elderhostel or online? Why or why not?

    **HINT** Review pages 426–428.

    *What's your response?*

# 10 Death and Dying

Archie Walker, 87, decided he did not want to spend his last days in a hospital. Faced with cancer his doctors were certain could not be treated successfully, Archie elected to leave his hospital bed and return home.

Archie's extended family and friends paid visits, while his wife, Judy, and his two children cared for him. In his last days, Archie did not seem frightened or despondent. Rather, he was cheerful, and made careful arrangements for his funeral. He joked with old friends and told stories about his childhood in Alabama.

Archie died in his own bed, his wife and children at his side. His end was peaceful, and was accompanied by one of his favorite jazz albums, which he had specifically requested be put on a few minutes before. And in accordance with Archie's wishes, his funeral was less a mournful goodbye than a celebration of the life he had lived.

## MODULE **10.1** Dying and Death Across the Life Span

### What are the moral and ethical issues surrounding defining death? see page 458

## MODULE **10.2** Confronting Death

### DNR, assisted suicide, euthanasia . . . Where do you stand? see page 465

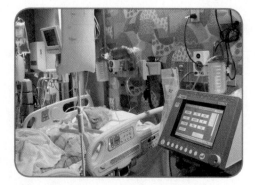

Appropriately enough, in this last chapter we discuss the final chapter of life. We begin by considering how the moment of death is defined, and we examine how people view and react to death at different points in the life span. Then we look at how people confront their own deaths, covering a theory that people pass through stages as they come to grips with their approaching death. We also look at how people endeavor to exert control over the circumstances that surround death, using living wills and assisted suicide. Finally, we consider bereavement and grief. We distinguish normal from unhealthy grief, and we discuss the consequences of a loss. Finally, we look at mourning and funerals, discussing how people acknowledge the passing of a loved one.

MODULE **10.3** Grief and Bereavement

# What's the difference between bereavement and grief? see page 472

## MyDevelopmentLab

You've just read about Archie Walker's end-of-life experience.

Now, log onto MyDevelopmentLab.com and watch a video in which Bob talks about the loss of both his daughter and his wife and the effects it had on him and his family.

# MODULE 10.1 Dying and Death Across the Life Span

## Choosing Death

*Ted Soulis knew he was about to die. He'd made his peace and said his goodbyes. His family was gathered around him, and he was not afraid. He closed his eyes and slumped over in his chair. His wife let out a gasp.*

*A hush fell over the room.*

*And then Mr. Soulis lifted his head, grinned like the devil and said, "Just a little joke."*

*The room erupted in laughter. It was exactly what everyone would expect of Ted Soulis, a man of great joie de vivre who lived life on his terms.*

*Mr. Soulis, 69, died a few hours later, with his wife and daughter at his side.*

*Mr. Soulis was diagnosed last month with an especially aggressive form of brain cancer.*

*Rather than endure the agony of chemotherapy to eke out a few more months of life, he chose to return home, surround himself with loved ones, and let the cancer run its course. The doctors gave him two weeks to live, so he bought a lot of food and a lot of wine and threw a party that drew 300 people and went on for hours.*

*"He went out in style," said his daughter, Shana Soulis. "I can't imagine it any differently. It was peaceful, it was beautiful, and it was on his terms." (Squatriglia, 2007, p. B7)*

If ever death can be said to be good, this was a good death. After 69 years, Ted Soulis slipped away in the company of those he loved.

Death is an experience that will happen to all of us, as universal to the human condition as birth. As such, it is central to an understanding of the life span.

Only recently have lifespan developmentalists given serious study to the developmental implications of dying. In this module we will discuss death and dying from several perspectives. We begin by considering how we define death—a determination that is more complex than it seems. We then examine how people view and react to death at different points in the life span. And we consider the very different views of death held by various societies.

## Defining Death: Determining the Point at Which Life Ends

**LEARNING OBJECTIVES**

**L01** What defines the moment of death?

*It took a major legal and political battle, but eventually Terri Schiavo's husband won the right to remove a feeding tube that had kept her alive for 15 years. Lying in a hospital bed all those years in what physicians called a "persistent vegetative state," Schiavo was never expected to regain consciousness after suffering brain damage due to respiratory and cardiac arrest. After a series of court battles, her husband—despite the wishes of her parents—was allowed to direct caretakers to remove the feeding tube; Schiavo died soon afterwards.*

Was Schiavo's husband right in seeking to remove her feeding tube? Was she already dead when it was removed? Were her constitutional rights ignored by her husband's action?

Such difficult questions illustrate the complexity of what are, literally, matters of life and death. Death is not only a biological event; it involves psychological aspects as well. We need to consider not only what defines death, but also how our conception of death changes across the life span.

What is death? The question seems clear, but defining the point at which life ceases is surprisingly complex. Medicine has advanced to the point where some people who would have been considered dead a few years ago would now be considered alive.

**Functional death** is defined by an absence of heartbeat and breathing. This definition, however, is more ambiguous than it seems. For example, a person whose heartbeat and breathing have ceased for as long as 5 minutes may be resuscitated and suffer little damage from the experience. Was the person who is now alive previously dead, as the functional definition would have it?

Because of this imprecision, brain functioning is now used to determine the moment of death rather than heartbeat or respiration. In **brain death,** all signs of brain activity, as measured by electrical brain waves, have ceased. When brain death occurs, it is impossible to restore functioning.

Some medical experts suggest that defining death only as a lack of brain waves is too restrictive. They argue that losing the ability to think, reason, feel, and experience the world may define death, as well. In this view, which considers the psychological ramifications, a person who suffers irreversible brain damage, who is in a coma, and who will never experience anything approaching a human life can be considered dead, even if some sort of primitive brain activity continues (Ressner, 2001; Young & Teitelbaum, 2010).

This argument, which moves us from strictly medical criteria to moral and philosophical considerations, is controversial. As a result, death is legally defined in most localities in the United States as the absence of brain functioning, although some laws still include the absence of respiration and heartbeat in their definition. In reality, no matter where a death occurs, brain waves are seldom measured. Usually, they are closely monitored only in special circumstances—when the time of death is significant, when organs may be transplanted, or when criminal or legal issues are involved.

The difficulty in establishing legal and medical definitions of death may reflect changes in understanding and attitudes that occur over the course of people's lives.

> **functional death**  the absence of a heartbeat and breathing
>
> **brain death**  a diagnosis of death based on the cessation of all signs of brain activity, as measured by electrical brain waves

## REVIEW, CHECK, AND APPLY

### REVIEW

**LO1  What defines the moment of death?**

- Functional death is defined as the cessation of heartbeat and respiration; brain death is defined by the absence of electrical brain waves.

- The definition of death has changed as medical advances allow us to resuscitate people who would once have been considered dead. Some medical experts believe that death occurs when a person can no longer think, reason, or feel, and can never again live anything resembling a human life.

### CHECK YOURSELF

1. Once an individual no longer has a heartbeat or breathing, he or she is said to have experienced a _____ death.

2. It is impossible to restore functioning or resuscitate a person after brain death occurs.
   - True
   - False

### APPLYING LIFESPAN DEVELOPMENT

- Do you think people who have lost the ability to think, feel, and experience the world, but still have detectable brain waves, should be declared dead? Why or why not? What criteria would you apply to the definition of death?

✔️—Study and **Review** on **MyDevelopmentLab.com**

Answers: 1) functional; 2) True

# Death Across the Life Span: Causes and Reactions

**LO2  How is death perceived at different stages of the life span?**

LEARNING OBJECTIVES

*Cheryl played flute in the school band. She had shoulder-length brown hair, brown eyes, and a smile that often gave way to a lopsided grin when her friends or older brother said something funny.*

*Cheryl's family owned a small farm, and it was her job to feed the chickens and gather any eggs every morning before the school bus arrived. After she completed her chores, she gathered up whatever sewing project she was working on in Family and Consumer Sciences—Cheryl loved designing and creating her own clothing—and waved good-bye to her parents. "Don't take any wooden nickels," her dad always called after her. Cheryl thought it was a really dumb joke, but she loved that her dad never forgot to say it.*

*One Friday night, Cheryl's dad suggested they hop in the truck and go get pizza. There were only two seat belts in the narrow cab, but Cheryl felt safe wedged in between her dad and her brother. They were riding down a two-lane highway, singing along with some silly song on the radio, when a car in the lane opposite lost control and crossed the center line, slamming into the truck. Without a seat belt, Cheryl's body flew through the windshield. Her father and brother survived, but for Cheryl, 13, life was over.*

Death is something we associate with old age, but for many individuals, death comes earlier. Because it seems "unnatural" for a young person like Cheryl to die, the reactions to such a death are particularly extreme. In the United States, in fact, some people believe that children should be sheltered from the reality of death. Yet people of every age can experience the death of friends and family members, as well as their own death. How do our reactions to death evolve as we age? We will consider several age groups.

***Death in Infancy and Childhood.*** Despite its wealth, the United States has a relatively high infant mortality rate. The rate has declined since the mid-1960s, but the United States still ranks behind 35 other countries in the proportion of infants who die in the first year of life (Centers for Disease Control, 2004).

As these statistics indicate, the number of parents who lose an infant is substantial. The death of a child arouses all the typical reactions one would have to a more timely death, but family members may suffer severe effects as they struggle to deal with death at such an early age. One common reaction is extreme depression (Murphy, Johnson, & Wu, 2003; Cacciatore, 2010).

One exceptionally difficult death to confront is prenatal death, or *miscarriage*. Parents often form psychological bonds with their unborn child, and may feel profound grief if it dies before birth. Moreover, friends and relatives often fail to understand the emotional impact of miscarriage, making parents feel their loss all the more keenly (Wheeler & Austin, 2001).

Another form of death that produces extreme stress, in part because it is so unanticipated, is sudden infant death syndrome. With **sudden infant death syndrome**, or **SIDS**, which usually occurs between the ages of 2 and 4 months, a seemingly healthy baby stops breathing and dies inexplicably.

In cases of SIDS, parents often feel intense guilt, and acquaintances may be suspicious of the "true" cause of death. However, there is no known cause for SIDS, which seems to strike randomly, and parents' guilt is unwarranted (Paterson et al., 2006; Kinney & Thach, 2009; Mitchell, 2009).

For children, accidents are the most frequent cause of death—motor vehicle crashes, fires, and drowning. However, a substantial number of children in the United States are homicide victims. By the early 1990s, homicides had nearly tripled since 1960 to become the fourth leading cause of death for children ages 1 to 9 (Finkelhor, 1997; Centers for Disease Control, 2004).

For parents, the death of a child produces a profound sense of loss and grief. There is no worse death for most parents, including the loss of a spouse or of one's own parents. They may feel their trust in the natural order of the world—where children "should" outlive their parents—has been violated. Believing it is their primary responsibility to protect their children from harm, they may feel they have failed when a child dies (Strength, 1999).

Parents are almost never prepared to deal with the death of a child, and they may obsessively ask themselves why the death occurred. Because the bond between children and parents is so strong, parents sometimes feel that a part of themselves has died as well. The stress is so profound that it significantly increases the risk of hospitalization for a mental disorder (Mahgoub & Lantz, 2006; Feigelman, Jordan, & Gorman, 2009).

***Childhood Conceptions of Death.*** Children do not really begin to develop a concept of death until around age 5. Although they are already well aware of death, they tend to view it as a temporary, reduced state of living, rather than a cessation. A preschool-age child might say, "Dead people don't get hungry—well, maybe a little" (Kastenbaum, 1985, p. 629).

Some preschool children think of death as a sleep people may wake from, just as Sleeping Beauty awoke in the fairy tale (Lonetto, 1980). For these children, death is not particularly fearsome; rather, it is a curiosity. If people merely tried hard enough—by administering medicine, providing food, or using magic—dead people might "return."

Children's misunderstanding of death can have devastating emotional consequences. Children may believe they are somehow responsible for a person's death. They may assume their bad behavior caused the death. They may also think that if the dead person really wanted to, she or he could return.

⊙ **From an educator's perspective:** Given their developmental level and understanding of death, how do you think preschool children react to the death of a parent?

Around age 5, children better grasp the finality and irreversibility of death. They may personify death as a ghostlike or devilish figure. They do not regard death as universal, however, but as something that happens only to certain people. It is not until about age 9 that they accept the universality and finality of death (Nagy, 1948). By middle childhood, there is an awareness of the customs around death, such as funerals, cremation, and cemeteries (Hunter & Smith, 2008; Corr, 2010).

*Death in Adolescence.* We might expect the significant cognitive development that occurs in adolescence to bring about a sophisticated, thoughtful, and reasoned view of death. However, in many ways, adolescents' views of death are as unrealistic as those of younger children, although along different lines.

Adolescents understand the finality and irreversibility of death, yet they tend to think it can't happen to them, which can lead to risky behavior. As we discussed earlier, adolescents develop a *personal fable,* a set of beliefs that makes them feel unique and special. Thus, they may believe they are invulnerable and that the bad things that happen to other people won't happen to them (Elkind, 1985).

This risky behavior causes many deaths in adolescence. For instance, accidents, often involving motor vehicles, are the most frequent cause of death at this age. Other frequent causes include homicide, suicide, cancer, and heart disease (ChildHealth, 2009).

When adolescent feelings of invulnerability confront a fatal illness, the results can be shattering. Adolescents who learn they are terminally ill often feel angry and cheated—that life has been unjust to them. Because they feel—and act—so negatively, it may be difficult for medical personnel to treat them effectively.

In contrast, some adolescents who are terminally ill react with total denial. Feeling indestructible, they may not accept the seriousness of their illness. If it does not cause them to reject medical treatment, some degree of denial may be useful, as it allows an adolescent to continue living a normal life as long as possible (Beale, Baile, & Aaron, 2005).

*Death in Young Adulthood.* Young adults feel primed to begin their lives. Past the preparatory time of childhood and adolescence, they are ready to make their mark on the world. Because death at such a point seems close to unthinkable, its occurrence is particularly difficult. In active pursuit of life goals, they are angry and impatient with any illness that threatens their future.

For young adults, the leading cause of death continues to be accidents, followed by suicide, homicide, and cancer. By the end of early adulthood, however, death from disease becomes more prevalent.

For young adults facing death, several concerns are acutely important. One is the desire to develop intimate relationships and express sexuality, each of which are inhibited, or completely prevented, by a terminal illness. For instance, people who test positive for the AIDS virus may find it quite difficult to start new relationships. Within evolving relationships, sexual activities present even more challenging issues (Rabkin, Remien, & Wilson, 1994).

Future planning is another concern of young adults. At a time when most people are mapping out careers and deciding when to start a family, young adults who are terminally ill face additional burdens. Should they marry, even though they may soon leave a partner widowed? Should a couple seek to conceive a child if it is likely to be raised by only one parent? How soon should one's employer be told about a terminal illness, when the revelation may cost the young adult his or her job? None of these questions is easily answered.

Adolescents' views of death may be highly romanticized and dramatic.

***Death in Middle Adulthood.*** For middle-aged people, the shock of a life-threatening disease—the most common cause of death in this period—is not so great. By this point, people are well aware that they will die someday, and they may be able to accept this possibility in a realistic manner.

Their sense of realism, though, doesn't make the possibility of dying any easier. Fears about death are often greater in midlife than at any time previously—or even in later life. These fears may lead people to switch their focus to the number of years they have remaining rather than the number of years they have already lived (Levinson, 1992; Akhtar, 2010).

The most frequent cause of death in midlife is heart attack or stroke. Dying so unexpectedly does not allow for preparation, but it may be easier than a slow and painful death from a disease such as cancer. It is the kind of death most people prefer: When asked, they say they would like an instant and painless death that does not involve loss of any body part (Taylor, 1991).

***Death in Late Adulthood.*** By late adulthood, people know that the end is approaching. They face an increasing number of deaths in their environment. Spouses, siblings, and friends may have already died, a constant reminder of their own mortality.

At this age, the most likely causes of death are cancer, stroke, and heart disease. What would happen if these were eliminated? According to demographers' estimates, the average 70-year-old's life expectancy would increase around 7 years (Hayward, Crimmins, & Saito, 1997).

## *Cultural Dimensions*

### Differing Conceptions of Death

*In the midst of a tribal celebration, an older man waits for his oldest son to place a cord around his neck. The older man has been sick, and he is ready to relinquish his ties to this earthly world. He asks that his son lift him to his death, and the son complies.*

\*\*\*

*To Hindus in India, death is not an ending, but rather part of a continual cycle. Because they believe in reincarnation, death is thought to be followed by rebirth into a new life. Death, then, is seen as a companion to life.*

People's responses to death take many forms, particularly in different cultures. But even in Western societies, reactions to death and dying are quite diverse. For instance, is it better for a man to die after a full life in which he has raised a family and been successful in his job, or for a courageous and valiant young soldier to die defending his country in wartime? Has one person died a better death than the other?

The answer depends on one's values, which reflect cultural and subcultural teachings, often shared through religious beliefs. Some societies view death as a punishment or as a judgment about one's contributions to the world. Others see death as redemption from an earthly life of travail. Some view death as the start of an eternal life, while others believe that an earthly life is all there is (Bryant, 2003).

For members of Native American tribes, death is seen as a continuation of life. Members of the Lakota tribe believe that in death, people move to a spirit land called "Wanagi Makoce," inhabited by all people and animals. Death, then, is not viewed with anger or seen as unfair. Similarly, some religions, such as Buddhism and Hinduism, believe in *reincarnation,* the conviction that the soul or spirit comes back to life in a newborn body, continuing the cycle of life (Huang, 2004).

The age at which people learn about death varies among cultures. In cultures with high levels of violence and death, an awareness of death may come earlier in life. Research shows that children in Northern Ireland and Israel understand the finality, irreversibility, and inevitability of death at an earlier age than children in the United States and Britain (Atchley, 2000; Braun, Pietsch, & Blanchette, 2000).

Differing conceptions of death lead to different rituals, as this ceremony in India illustrates.

The prevalence of death in the lives of the elderly makes them less anxious about dying. However, this does not mean that people in late adulthood welcome death. Rather, they are more realistic and reflective about it. They think about death, and they may begin to prepare for it. Some begin to pull away from the world as physical and psychological energy diminishes (Turner & Helms, 1994).

Impending death is sometimes accompanied by rapid declines in cognitive functioning. In what is known as the *terminal decline,* a significant drop in memory and reading ability may foreshadow death within the next few years (Wilson et al., 2007; Gerstorf et al., 2008; Thorvaldsson et al., 2008).

Some elderly people actively seek out death, turning to suicide. In fact, the suicide rate for men climbs steadily during late adulthood, and no age group has a higher suicide rate than White men over age 85. (Adolescents and young adults commit suicide in greater numbers, but their *rate* of suicide—the number of suicides as a proportion of the general adolescent population—is actually lower.) Suicide is often a consequence of severe depression or some form of dementia, or it may arise from the loss of a spouse (Chapple et al., 2006; Mezuk et al., 2008; Kjølseth, Ekeberg, & Steihaug, 2010).

A critical issue for older adults who are terminally ill is whether their lives still have value. More than younger adults, elderly people who are dying worry that they are burdens to their family or to society. They may even be given the message, sometimes inadvertently, that society no longer values them and that they are viewed as "dying" rather than being "very sick" (Kastenbaum, 2000).

In most cases, older people want to know if death is impending. Like younger patients, who usually prefer to know the truth about an illness, older people want the details. Ironically, caregivers usually wish to avoid telling patients that they are dying (Goold, Williams, & Arnold, 2000; Hagerty et al., 2004).

Not all people, however, wish to know about their condition or that they are dying. Individuals react to death in substantially different ways, in part due to personality factors. For example, people who are generally anxious worry more about death. There are also significant cultural differences in how people view and react to death, as we consider in the "Cultural Dimensions" box.

## REVIEW, CHECK, AND APPLY

### REVIEW

**LO2**  How is death perceived at different stages of the life span?

- The death of an infant or young child can be particularly difficult for parents, and for an adolescent death appears to be unthinkable.

- Cultural differences in attitudes and beliefs about death strongly influence people's reactions to it.

### CHECK YOURSELF

1. In spite of its economic wealth, the United States has a relatively high infant mortality rate.
   - True
   - False

2. Parents' extreme reaction to their child's death is partly based on the sense that the natural order of the world in which children "should" outlive their parents has now been violated.
   - True
   - False

### APPLYING LIFESPAN DEVELOPMENT

- Do you think people who are going to die should be told? Does your response depend on the person's age?

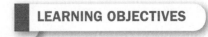 **Study** and **Review** on **MyDevelopmentLab.com**

Answers: 1) True; 2) True

# Death Education: Preparing for the Inevitable?

**LO3**  Why is it helpful to educate people about death and dying?

**LEARNING OBJECTIVES**

*"When will Mom come back from being dead?"*
  *"Why did Barry have to die?"*
  *"Did Grandpa die because I was bad?"*

**thanatologists** people who study death and dying

Children's questions such as these illustrate why many developmentalists, as well as **thanatologists,** people who study death and dying, have suggested that death education should be a component of everyone's schooling. Recently, such instruction has emerged. *Death education* encompasses programs designed to help people of all ages deal better with death, dying, and grief—both others' deaths and their own.

Death education arose as a response to the way we hide death, at least in most Western societies. We typically let hospitals deal with the dying, and we do not talk to children about death or allow them to go to funerals for fear of disturbing them. Even emergency workers and medical specialists are uncomfortable talking about it. Because it is seldom discussed and is so removed from everyday life, people may have little opportunity to confront their feelings about death or to gain a realistic sense of it (Wass, 2004; Kim & Lee, 2009; Waldrop & Kirkendall, 2009).

Several types of death education programs exist. Among them:

- **Crisis intervention education.** When the World Trade Center was attacked, children in the area were the subjects of several kinds of crisis intervention designed to deal with their anxieties. Younger children, whose conceptions of death were shaky at best, needed explanations of the loss of life that day geared to their levels of cognitive development. Crisis intervention education is used in less extreme times as well. For example, it is common for schools to make emergency counseling available if a student is killed or commits suicide (Sandoval, Scott, & Padilla, 2009; Markell, 2010).

- **Routine death education.** Although relatively little curricular material on death exists for elementary students, coursework in high schools is increasingly common. Colleges and universities increasingly include courses about death in such departments as psychology, human development, sociology, and education (Eckerd, 2009).

- **Death education for members of the helping professions.** Professionals who will deal with death, dying, and grief in their careers have a special need for death education. Almost all medical and nursing schools now offer some form of death education. The most successful programs not only offer providers ways to help patients deal with their own impending deaths or those of family members, but also allow students to explore their feelings about the topic (Kastenbaum, 1999; Haas-Thompson, Alston, & Holbert, 2008).

Although death education will not completely demystify death, the programs just described may help people come to grips with what is, along with birth, the most universal—and certain—of all human experiences.

## REVIEW, CHECK, AND APPLY

### REVIEW

**LO3** Why is it helpful to educate people about death and dying?

- Thanatologists recommend that death education become a normal part of learning to help people understand one of the most universal, and certain, of all human experiences.

### CHECK YOURSELF

1. _____ are people who study death and dying.

2. Emergency counseling provided within schools to help students deal with sudden events such as the 2001 attacks on the World Trade Center and the Pentagon is known as:

   a. routine death education.

   b. thanatology training.

   c. crisis intervention education.

   d. demystification training.

### APPLYING LIFESPAN DEVELOPMENT

- Do you think schools should teach preteens and adolescents about suicide? Are there disadvantages to teaching this age group about suicide, or is it best to deal with the topic early?

✓●─[**Study** and **Review** on
**MyDevelopmentLab.com**

Answers: 1) Thanatologists; 2) c

## MODULE 10.2 Confronting Death

## Deciding to Say Goodbye

*Helen Reynolds, 63, had undergone operations in January and April to repair and then replace a heart valve that was not permitting a smooth flow of blood. But by May her feet had turned the color of overripe eggplants, their mottled purple black an unmistakable sign of gangrene. In June she chose to have first her right leg, and then her left, amputated in hopes of stabilizing her condition. The doctors were skeptical about the surgery, but deferred to her wishes. . . .*

*But then Reynolds uncharacteristically began talking about her pain. On that Sunday afternoon in June, a nurse beckoned intern Dr. Randall Evans. Evans, a graduate of the University of New Mexico Medical School who planned a career in the critical-care field, was immensely popular with the nursing staff for his cordial and sympathetic manner. But, unlike the MICU nurses, he had difficulty reading Reynolds's lips (the ventilator made it impossible for her to speak aloud), and asked her to write down her request. Laboriously, she scrawled 16 words on the note pad: "I have decided to end my life as I do not want to live like this."* (Begley, 1991, p. 44–45)

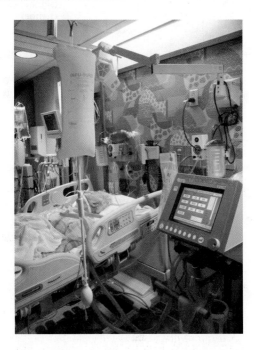

Less than a week later, after the ventilator that helped her to breathe had been removed at her request, Helen Reynolds died.

Reynolds's death raises difficult questions. Was her request equivalent to suicide? Should the medical staff have complied with it? Was she coping with her death effectively? How do people come to terms with death, and how do they react and adapt to it? Lifespan developmentalists and other specialists in death and dying have struggled to find answers.

In this module, we look at how people confront their own death. We discuss the theory that people move through stages as they come to grips with their approaching death. We also look at how people use living wills and assisted suicide.

## Understanding the Process of Dying: Taking Steps Toward Death

**L04**  In what ways do people face the prospect of their own death?

No individual has influenced our understanding of the way people confront death more than Elisabeth Kübler-Ross. A psychiatrist, Kübler-Ross developed a theory of death and dying based on interviews with dying people and those caring for them (Kübler-Ross, 1969, 1982).

Kübler-Ross initially suggested that people pass through five basic steps as they move toward death (summarized in Figure 10-1).

***Denial.***  "No, I can't be dying. There must be some mistake." It is typical for people to protest on learning that they have a terminal disease. This is the first stage of dying, *denial*. In denial, people resist the idea that they are going to die. They may argue that their test results have been mixed up, an x-ray has been misread, or their physician is just wrong. They may flatly reject the diagnosis, simply refusing to believe the news. In extreme cases, memories of weeks in the hospital are forgotten. In other forms of denial, patients fluctuate between refusing to accept the news and confiding that they know they are going to die (Teutsch, 2003).

Far from a sign of a lost sense of reality and deteriorating mental health, denial is a defense mechanism that helps people absorb the news on their own terms and pace. Then they can move on and come to grips with the reality of their death.

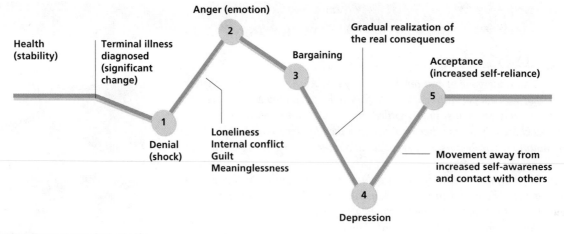

**FIGURE 10-1 Moving Toward the End of Life**
The steps toward death, according to Kübler-Ross (1975). Do you think there are cultural differences in the steps?

*Anger.* After denial, people may express *anger.* They may be angry at everyone: people in good health, spouses and family members, caregivers, children. They may lash out and wonder— sometimes aloud—why *they* are dying and not someone else. They may be furious at God, reasoning that they have led good lives and far worse people in the world should be dying.

It is not easy to be around people in the anger stage. They may say and do things that are painful and sometimes unfathomable. Eventually, though, most move beyond anger to another development—bargaining.

*Bargaining.* "If you're good, you'll be rewarded." Many people try to apply this pearl of childhood wisdom to their impending death, promising to be better people if they are rewarded by staying alive.

In *bargaining,* dying people try to negotiate their way out of death. They may swear to dedicate their lives to the poor if God saves them. They may promise that if they can just live long enough to see a son married, they will willingly accept death later.

However, these promises are rarely kept. If one request appears to be granted, people typically seek another, and yet another. Furthermore, they may be unable to fulfill their promises because their illnesses keep progressing and prevent them from achieving what they said they would do.

In some ways, bargaining may have positive consequences. Although death cannot be postponed indefinitely, having a goal of attending a particular event or living until a certain time may in fact delay death until then. For instance, death rates of Jewish people fall just before the Passover and rise just after. Similarly, the death rate among older Chinese women falls before and during important holidays and rises after (Philips, 1992).

In the end, of course, no one can bargain away death. When people eventually realize this, they often move into the depression stage.

*Depression.* Many dying people experience *depression.* Realizing that the issue is settled and can't be bargained away, they are overwhelmed with a deep sense of loss. They know that they are losing their loved ones and reaching the end of their lives.

Their depression may be reactive or preparatory. In *reactive depression,* the sadness is based on events that have already occurred: the loss of dignity with many medical procedures, the end of a job, or the knowledge that they will never return home. In *preparatory depression,* people feel sadness over future losses. They know that death will end their relationships and that they will never see future generations. The reality of death is inescapable in this stage, and it brings profound sadness over the unalterable conclusion of one's life.

*Acceptance.* Kübler-Ross suggested that the final step of dying is *acceptance.* People who have developed acceptance are fully aware that death is impending. Unemotional and uncommunicative, they have virtually no feelings—positive or negative—about the present or future. They have made peace with themselves, and they may wish to be left alone. For them, death holds no sting.

**From an educator's perspective:** Do you think Kübler-Ross's five steps of dying might be subject to cultural influences? Age differences? Why or why not?

*Evaluating Kübler-Ross's Theory.*   Kübler-Ross has had an enormous impact on the way we look at death. She is recognized as a pioneer in observing systematically how people approach their own deaths. She was almost single-handedly responsible for bringing death as a phenomenon into public awareness. Her contributions have been particularly influential among those who provide direct care to the dying.

On the other hand, there are some obvious limitations to her conception of dying. It is largely limited to those who are aware that they are dying and who die relatively slowly. It does not apply to people who suffer from diseases where the outcome and timing are uncertain.

The most important criticisms concern the "stages" in Kübler-Ross's theory. Not every person passes through every step, and some move through them in a different sequence. Some people even go through the same steps several times. Depressed patients may show bursts of anger, and an angry patient may bargain for more time (Kastenbaum, 1992). Furthermore, because Kübler-Ross's stages have become so familiar, well-meaning caregivers sometimes encourage patients to work through the steps in a prescribed order, without consideration of individual needs.

Finally, people's reactions to impending death differ. The cause of death; the duration of the dying process; the person's age, sex, and personality; and the social support available from family and friends all influence the course of dying and one's responses to it (Stroebe, Stroebe, & Hansson, 1993; Carver & Scheier, 2002).

In response to concerns about Kübler-Ross's account, other theorists have developed alternative ideas. Psychologist Edwin Shneidman, for example, suggests that "themes" in people's reactions to dying can occur—and recur—in any order. These include incredulity, a sense of unfairness, fear of pain or even general terror, and fantasies of being rescued (Leenaars & Shneidman, 1999).

Another theorist, Charles Corr, suggests that, as in other periods of life, people who are dying face a set of psychological tasks. These include minimizing physical stress, maintaining the richness of life, continuing or deepening their relationships with other people, and fostering hope, often through spiritual searching (Corr & Doka, 2001; Corr, Nabe, & Corr, 2000, 2006, 2010).

## REVIEW, CHECK, AND APPLY

### REVIEW

**LO4**   In what ways do people face the prospect of their own death?

- Elisabeth Kübler-Ross identified five steps toward dying: denial, anger, bargaining, depression, and acceptance.
- While Kübler-Ross has added to our understanding of the process of dying, the steps she identified are not universal. Recently, other theorists have developed alternative ideas.

### CHECK YOURSELF

1. Kübler-Ross initially suggested that individuals pass through basic steps or stages as they approach death. Match each of the following examples with its appropriate stage.

   a. "You can't mean me. I have never been sick a day in my life."

   b. "If I could just live a little longer so I can see my daughter get married, I will do anything."

   c. "I know I only have a little time left; can you help me accomplish a few things before that time comes?"

   d. "I don't know what to do. I can't eat, I can't sleep. I don't want to do anything or talk to anyone."

   e. "I hate you; I hate this disease. Leave me alone."

### APPLYING LIFESPAN DEVELOPMENT

- What response, if any, should a family member offer to a terminally ill relative in each of the stages that Kübler-Ross identified?

✓●—[**Study** and **Review** on **MyDevelopmentLab.com**

# Choosing the Nature of Death: Is DNR the Way to Go?

**LO5**  How do people exercise some control over the place and the manner in which they die?

*When Colin Rapasand was a first-year resident years ago, one of his first assignments was the geriatric ward. Cheerful and outgoing, Colin invariably addressed the patients as "Uncle" and "Auntie," reflecting his deep-South roots.*

*He recalls one patient in particular. "When my crazy schedule allowed, I loved spending time with Auntie Jessica. Auntie J was 93 years old, rapidly failing, but with the sharpest mind. When I had late rounds, I would sometimes sit on the foot of her bed and chat with her. Great stories, huge spirit, lively intelligence.*

*"Auntie J's chart had her listed as a DNR, and I knew that she didn't want 'any of that mechanical nonsense' done to her, as she put it. But one night I was all alone on rounds and stopped in to see her. Her respiration was just about zero and her heart was beating fitfully. I watched as her numbers got worse. Instead of 'letting nature take its course,' I went to her side and leaned over her, calling her name. At the same time I compressed her chest rapidly, 100 times a minute, performing CPR on her slight body. I got the respiration going fairly well, but her heart was still weak and fluttering.*

*"I grabbed the paddles and jolted her once, twice, then third time lucky. Her breathing became audible and her heartbeat returned to its usual level. Auntie J lived another four months.*

*"I claimed to the administrators that in the heat of the moment I had forgotten about the DNR. But I knew I hadn't. I had simply 'let nature take its course'—my nature, my human nature."*

The letters "DNR" on a patient's medical chart have a simple and clear meaning: "Do Not Resuscitate." DNR means that no extraordinary means are to be taken to keep a patient alive. For terminally ill patients, "DNR" may mean the difference between dying immediately or living additional days, months, or even years, kept alive only by the most extreme, invasive, and even painful medical procedures.

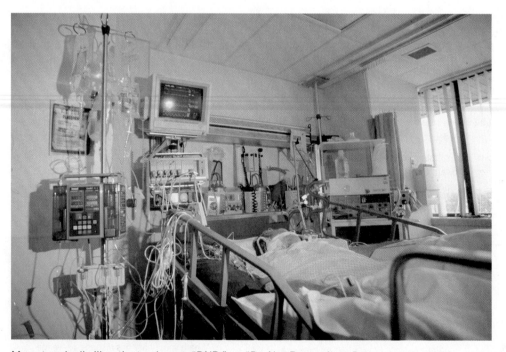

Many terminally ill patients choose "DNR," or "Do Not Resuscitate," as a way to avoid extraordinary medical interventions.

The DNR decision entails several issues. One is differentiating "extreme" and "extraordinary" measures from routine ones. There are no hard-and-fast rules; people making the decision must consider the needs of the patient, his or her prior medical history, and factors such as age and even religion. For instance, different standards might apply to a 12-year-old and an 85-year-old with the same medical condition. Other questions concern quality of life. How can we determine an individual's current quality of life and whether it will be improved or diminished by a medical intervention? Who makes these decisions—the patient, a family member, or medical personnel?

One thing is clear: Like Colin Rapasand in the prologue, medical personnel are reluctant to carry out the wishes of the terminally ill and their families to suspend aggressive treatment. Even when it is certain that a patient is going to die, and the patient does not wish further treatment, physicians often claim to be unaware of their patients' wishes. Although one-third of patients ask not to be resuscitated, less than half of these people's physicians say they know their patients' preferences. In addition, only 49 percent of patients have their wishes entered on their medical charts. Physicians and other providers may be reluctant to act on DNR requests in part because they are trained to save patients, not permit them to die, and in part to avoid legal liability (Knaus et al., 1995; Goold, Williams, & Arnold, 2000; McArdle, 2002).

*Living Wills.* To gain more control over death decisions, people are increasingly signing living wills. A **living will** is a legal document that designates the medical treatments a person does or does not want if the person cannot express his or her wishes (see Figure 10-2 on page 470).

Some people designate a specific person, called a *health care proxy,* to act as their representative for health care decisions. Health care proxies are authorized either in living wills or in a legal document known as a *durable power of attorney.* Health care proxies may be authorized to deal with all medical care problems (such as a coma) or only terminal illnesses.

As with DNR orders, living wills are ineffective unless people make sure their health care proxies and doctors know their wishes. Although they may be reluctant to do this, people should have frank conversations with their health care proxies.

*Euthanasia and Assisted Suicide.* Dr. Jack Kevorkian became well known in the 1990s for his invention and promotion of a "suicide machine," which allowed patients to push a button and release anesthesia and a drug that stops the heart. By supplying the machine and the drugs, which patients administered themselves, Kevorkian was participating in *assisted suicide,* providing the means for a terminally ill person to commit suicide. Kevorkian spent 8 years in prison for second-degree murder for his participation in an assisted suicide shown on the television show *60 Minutes.*

Assisted suicide is bitterly controversial in the United States and illegal in most states. The exception is Oregon, which passed a "right to die law" in 1998. Far from releasing a flood of assisted suicides, in its first decade fewer than 300 people took medication to end their lives (Ganzini, Beer, & Brouns, 2006; Davey, 2007).

In many countries, assisted suicide is accepted. For instance, in the Netherlands medical personnel may help end their patients' lives if they meet several conditions: At least two physicians must determine that the patient is terminally ill, there must be unbearable physical or mental suffering, the patient must give informed consent in writing, and relatives must be informed beforehand (Naik, 2002; Kleespies, 2004; Battin et al., 2007; Onwuteaka-Philipsen et al., 2010).

Assisted suicide is one form of **euthanasia,** the practice of assisting terminally ill people to die more quickly. Popularly known as "mercy killing," euthanasia has several forms. *Passive euthanasia* involves removing respirators or other medical equipment that may be sustaining a patient's life, to allow him or her to die naturally—such as when medical staff follow a DNR order. In *voluntary active euthanasia* caregivers or medical staff act to end a person's life before death would normally occur, perhaps by administering a lethal dose of pain medication. Assisted suicide, as we have seen, lies between passive and voluntary active euthanasia. For all the controversy surrounding the practice, euthanasia is surprisingly widespread. One survey of nurses in intensive care units found that 20 percent had deliberately hastened a patient's death at least once, and other experts assert that euthanasia is far from rare (Asch, 1996).

The controversy arises from the question of who should control life. Does the right to one's life belong to the individual, the person's physicians, his or her dependents, the government, or

**living wills** legal documents designating what medical treatments people want or do not want if they cannot express their wishes

**euthanasia** the practice of assisting people who are terminally ill to die more quickly

I,_____,
being of sound mind, make this statement as a directive to be followed if I become permanently unable to participate in decisions regarding my medical care. These instructions reflect my firm and settled commitment to decline medical treatment under the circumstances indicated below:

I direct my attending physician to withhold or withdraw treatment that merely prolongs my dying, if I should be in **an incurable or irreversible mental or physical condition** with no reasonable expectation of recovery, including but not limited to: (a) a **terminal condition**; (b) a **permanently unconscious condition**; or (c) a **minimally conscious condition in which I am permanently unable to make decisions or express my wishes.**

I direct that treatment be limited to measures to keep me comfortable and to relieve pain, including any pain that might occur by withholding or withdrawing treatment.
While I understand that I am not legally required to be specific about future treatments, **if I am in the condition(s) described above I feel especially strongly about the following treatments:**

I do not want cardiac resuscitation.
I do not want mechanical respiration.
I do not want tube feeding.
I do not want antibiotics.

However, I **do want** maximum pain relief, even if it may hasten my death.

Other directions (insert personal instructions):




These directions express my legal right to refuse treatment under federal and state law. I intend my instructions to be carried out, unless I have revoked them in a new writing or by clearly indicating that I have changed my mind.

Signed:_____ Date:_____

Address:_____

- - - - - - - - - - - - - - - - - - - - - - - - - - - - - - - - - -

**Statement by Witnesses**
I declare that the person who signed this document appears to be at least eighteen (18) years of age, of sound mind, and under no constraint or undue influence. The person who signed this document appeared to do so willingly and free from duress. He or she signed (or asked another to sign for him or her) this document in my presence.

Witness:_____

Address:_____


- - - - - - - - - - - - - - - - - - - - - - - - - - - - - - - - - -

Witness:_____

Address:_____


- - - - - - - - - - - - - - - - - - - - - - - - - - - - - - - - - -

FIGURE 10-2 **An Example of a Living Will**
What steps can people take to make sure the wishes they write into their living wills are carried out?

some deity? Because we claim to have the absolute right to create lives in the form of babies, some people argue that we should also have the absolute right to end our lives (Lester, 1996; Allen et al., 2006).

Many opponents argue that the practice is morally wrong. In their view, prematurely ending the life of a person, no matter how willing, is murder. Others point out that physicians are often inaccurate in predicting how long a person will live. For example, a large-scale study known as SUPPORT—the Study to Understand Prognoses and Preferences for Outcomes and Risks of Treatment—found that patients often outlive physicians' predictions of when they will die—in some cases living years after being given no more than a 50 percent chance of living 6 more months (Bishop, 2006).

Another argument against euthanasia focuses on the emotional state of the patient. Even if patients beg health care providers to help them die, they may be suffering from a form of depression that may be treated with antidepressant drugs. Once the depression lifts, patients may change their minds about wanting to die (Becvar, 2000; Gostin, 2006; McLachlan, 2008).

## REVIEW, CHECK, AND APPLY

### REVIEW

**LO5** How do people exercise some control over the place and the manner in which they die?

- Issues surrounding dying are highly controversial, including the measures that physicians should apply to keep dying patients alive and who should make the decisions about those measures.

- Assisted suicide and, more generally, euthanasia are highly controversial and are illegal in most of the United States, although many people believe they should be legalized if they are regulated.

### CHECK YOURSELF

1. In the medical community, DNR stands for
_____.

   a. Do Not Renew
   b. Daily Notice of Revision
   c. Do Not Revive
   d. Do Not Resuscitate

2. _____ is the practice of assisting people who are terminally ill to die more quickly.

### APPLYING LIFESPAN DEVELOPMENT

- Do you think assisted suicide should be permissible? Other forms of euthanasia? Why or why not?

✓● Study and Review on
MyDevelopmentLab.com

Answers: 1) d; 2) Euthanasia

# Caring for the Terminally Ill: The Place of Death

**LO6** What are some alternatives for providing end-of-life care for the terminally ill?

LEARNING OBJECTIVES

*Dina Bianga loves her work. Dina is a registered nurse with the Hospice of Michigan; her job is to meet the physical and psychological needs of the terminally ill.*

*"You need compassion and a good clinical background," she says. "You also have to be flexible. You go into the home, hospital, nursing home, adult foster care—wherever the patient is."*

*Dina likes the interdisciplinary approach that hospice work requires. "You form a team with others who provide social work, spiritual care, home health aid, grief support, and administrative support."*

*Surprisingly, the patients are not the most challenging part of the job. Families and friends are.*

*"Families are frightened, and everything seems out of control. They're not always ready to accept that death is coming soon, so you have to be careful and sensitive how you word things. If they are well informed on what to expect, the transition is smoother and a more comfortable atmosphere is created for the patient."*

**home care** an alternative to hospitalization in which dying people stay in their homes and receive treatment from their families and visiting medical staff

**hospice care** care provided for the dying in institutions devoted to those who are terminally ill

👁 Watch on **mydevelopmentlab.com**

You've just read about home care; now log onto MyDevelopmentLab.com to watch a video of a woman talking about the strain bringing her husband home to die had on her.

About half the people in the United States who die do so in hospitals. Yet, hospitals are among the least desirable places in which to face death. They are typically impersonal, with staff rotating through the day. Because visiting hours are limited, people frequently die alone, without the comfort of loved ones.

Hospitals are designed to make people better, not provide custodial care for the dying, which is extraordinarily expensive. Consequently, hospitals typically don't have the resources to deal adequately with the emotional requirements of terminally ill patients and their families.

Because of this, several alternatives to hospitalization have arisen. In **home care,** dying people stay in their homes and receive treatment from their families and visiting medical staff. Many dying patients prefer home care, because they can spend their final days in a familiar environment, with people they love and a lifetime accumulation of treasures around them.

But home care can be quite difficult for family members. True, giving something precious to people they love offers family members substantial emotional solace, but being on call 24 hours a day is extraordinarily draining, both physically and emotionally. Furthermore, because most relatives are not trained in nursing, they may provide less than optimal medical care (Perreault, Fothergill-Bourbonnais, & Fiset, 2004). 👁 Watch on **mydevelopmentlab.com**

Another alternative to hospitalization that is becoming increasingly prevalent is hospice care. **Hospice care** is care for the dying provided in institutions devoted to the terminally ill. They are designed to provide a warm, supportive environment for the dying. They do not focus on extending people's lives, but on making their final days pleasant and meaningful. Typically, people who go to hospices no longer face painful treatments or extraordinary or invasive means to extend their lives. The emphasis is on making patients' lives as full as possible, not on squeezing out every possible moment of life at any cost (Johnson, Kassner, & Kutner, 2004; Hanson et al., 2010).

Although the research is far from conclusive, hospice patients appear to be more satisfied with the care they receive than those who receive treatment in more traditional settings. Hospice care, then, provides a clear alternative to traditional hospitalization for the terminally ill (Tang, Aaronson, & Forbes, 2004; Seymour et al., 2007; Rhodes et al., 2008).

## REVIEW, CHECK, AND APPLY

### REVIEW

**LO6** What are some alternatives for providing end-of-life care for the terminally ill?

- Although most people in the United States die in hospitals, increasing numbers are choosing home care or hospice care for their final days.

### CHECK YOURSELF

1. In _____ care, terminally ill persons receive treatment from their families and visiting medical professionals, while _____ care offers terminal patients a supportive professional environment in which to spend their final days in comfort.

2. The focus in hospice care is on extending the last stage of life as long as possible.
   - True
   - False

### APPLYING LIFESPAN DEVELOPMENT

- Do you think it would be wise to suggest hospice care to a terminally ill family member who is in the bargaining stage of dying? Which of the stages identified by Kübler-Ross would be the most appropriate for making such a suggestion?

✔ **Study** and **Review** on **MyDevelopmentLab.com**

Answers: 1) home; hospice; 2) False

---

## MODULE 10.3 Grief and Bereavement

# Facing the Void

*No one ever told me that grief felt so like fear. I am not afraid, but the sensation is like being afraid. The same fluttering in the stomach, the same restlessness, the yawning. I keep on swallowing.*

*At other times it feels like being mildly drunk, or concussed. There is a sort of invisible blanket between the world and me. I find it hard to take in what anyone says. Or perhaps, hard to want to take it in. It is so uninteresting. (Lewis, 1985, p. 394)*

It is a universal experience, but most of us are surprisingly ill-prepared for the grief that follows the death of a loved one. Particularly in Western societies, where life expectancy is long and mortality rates are low, people view death as atypical rather than expected. This attitude makes grief all the more difficult to bear.

In this module, we consider bereavement and grief. We examine the difficulties in distinguishing normal from unhealthy grief and the consequences of loss. The module also looks at mourning and funerals, discussing how people can prepare themselves for the inevitability of death.

# Mourning and Funerals: Final Rites

LO7   **What are the basic components of a Western funeral rite, and how are other cultures' rites similar and different?**

*In our culture, only babies are buried; just about everyone else is cremated. When my father died, my elder brother took the lead and, with the other men observing, approached the pyre and lit it.*

*My father's body burned well. After the fire died down, my brother oversaw the gathering of the ashes and bone fragments, and we all took a bath to purify us. Despite this and subsequent baths, we in the close family were considered polluted for 13 days.*

*Finally, after the 13 days, we gathered for a big meal. The centerpiece was the preparation of rice balls (pinda), which we offered to the spirit of my father. At the end of the meal we dedicated gifts for distribution to the poor.*

*In Hindu culture, the idea behind these ceremonies is to honor the dead person's memory. More traditional people believe that it helps the soul pass to the realm of Yama, the god of death, rather than hanging on in this world as a ghost.*

This ritual is specifically Hindu, and yet, in its carefully prescribed roles for survivors and its focus on honoring the dead, it shares key elements with Western rituals. The first step in grieving, for most survivors in Western countries, is some sort of funeral. Death is a big business in the United States. The average funeral and burial costs $7,000, including an ornate, polished coffin, limousine transportation, and preservation and viewing of the body (Bryant, 2003; AARP, 2004).

Funerals are grandiose in part because of the vulnerability of the survivors who typically make the arrangements. Wishing to demonstrate love and affection, the survivors are susceptible to suggestions that they should "provide the best" for the deceased (Culver, 2003).

But in large measure, social norms and customs determine the nature of funerals just as they do for weddings. In a sense a funeral is not only a public acknowledgment that an individual has died, but recognition of everyone's mortality and an acceptance of the cycle of life.

In Western societies, funeral rituals follow a typical pattern. The body is prepared in some way and dressed in special clothing. There is usually a religious rite, a eulogy, a procession of some sort, and some formal period, such as the wake for Irish Catholics and shivah for Jews, in which relatives and friends visit the family and pay their respects. Military funerals typically include the firing of weapons and a flag draped over the coffin.

***Cultural Differences in Grieving.*** As we saw in the prologue, non-Western funerals are different. In some societies mourners shave their heads as a sign of grief, while in others they allow the hair to grow and stop shaving for a time. In other cultures, mourners may be hired to wail and grieve. Sometimes noisy celebrations take place, while in other cultures silence is the norm. Culture determines even the nature of emotional displays, such as the amount and timing of crying (Rosenblatt, 1988, 2001; Peters, 2010).

Mourners in Balinese funerals in Indonesia show little emotion, because they believe the gods will hear their prayers only if they are calm. In contrast, mourners at African American funerals show their grief, and funeral rituals allow attendees to display their feelings (Rosenblatt & Wallace, 2005; Collins & Doolittle, 2006).

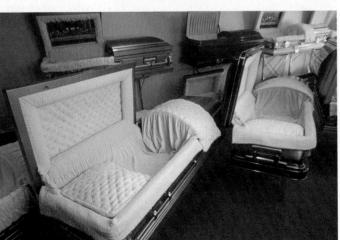

Because an individual's death represents an important transition, not only for loved ones but for an entire community, the rites associated with death take on an added importance. The emotional significance of death, combined with the pressure of enterprising salespersons, lead many to overspend on funerals.

Historically, some cultures developed rather extreme funeral rites. For example, in *suttee*, a traditional Hindu practice in India that is now illegal, a widow was expected to throw herself into the fire that consumed her husband's body. In ancient China, servants were sometimes buried (alive) with their masters' bodies.

Ultimately, no matter the ritual, all funerals basically serve the same function: They mark the endpoint of the life of the person who has died—and provide a formal forum for the feelings of the survivors, a place where they can come together, share their grief, and comfort one another.

## REVIEW, CHECK, AND APPLY

### REVIEW

**LO7** What are the basic components of a Western funeral rite, and how are other cultures' rites similar and different?

- After a death, most cultures prescribe some sort of funeral ritual to honor the passing of a community member.

- Funeral rites play a significant role in helping people acknowledge the death of a loved one, recognize their own mortality, and proceed with their lives.

### CHECK YOURSELF

1. Funeral rituals in modern times follow a universal pattern across cultures and societies.
   - True
   - False

2. Modern American funerals are grandiose and expensive largely because:
   a. American social norms essentially mandate that a funeral be complex and costly.
   b. the survivors are motivated to provide the best for their loved ones.
   c. the typical American funeral rite involves large numbers of mourners.
   d. the survivors wish to display their wealth and social standing.

### APPLYING LIFESPAN DEVELOPMENT

- What role do funeral planners play in tilting family members toward ostentatious funerals? How do they do this?

✓•—[Study and **Review** on
**MyDevelopmentLab.com**

Answers: 1) False; 2) b

# Bereavement and Grief: Adjusting to the Death of a Loved One

**LEARNING OBJECTIVES**

**LO8** How do survivors react to and cope with death?

*The news on June 25, 2009, hit the world like a tidal wave: Michael Jackson was dead at age 50. Jackson, a pop phenomenon who had earned hundreds of millions of dollars from his recordings and performances, seemed too young to die.*

*Jackson's death set off an explosion of public grief. The streets around the hospital where Jackson had died were blocked off. Offices around the world were shut down as workers left to watch the ceremony on television. Memorial services were conducted in many countries, and tributes poured in from politicians and celebrities. Musical tributes were held in many locales and sales of Michael Jackson and Jackson 5 records reached unprecedented levels. Amazon sold out its Michael Jackson CDs mere minutes after news of his death got out, and his songs topped the charts of the major online music retailers.*

After the death of a loved one, a painful period of adjustment follows, involving bereavement and grief. **Bereavement** is acknowledgment of the objective fact that one has experienced a death, while **grief** is the emotional response to one's loss.

The first stage of grief typically entails shock, numbness, disbelief, or outright denial. People try to avoid the reality of the situation and pursue their usual routines, although the pain may break through, causing anguish, fear, and deep sorrow and distress. In some ways, numbness may be beneficial, since it permits the survivor to make funeral arrangements and carry out other psychologically difficult tasks. Typically, people pass through this stage in a few days or weeks.

**bereavement** acknowledgment of the objective fact that one has experienced a death

**grief** the emotional response to one's loss

In the next phase, people begin to confront the death and realize the extent of their loss. They fully experience their grief and begin to acknowledge that the separation from the dead person will be permanent. They may suffer deep unhappiness or even depression, a normal feeling in this situation. They may yearn for the dead individual. Emotions can range from impatient to lethargic. However, they also begin to view their past relationship with the deceased realistically, good and bad. In so doing, they begin to free themselves from some of the bonds that tied them to the loved one (de Vries et al., 1997).

Finally, they reach the accommodation stage. They begin to pick up the pieces of their lives and to construct new identities. For instance, rather than seeing herself as a widowed spouse, a woman whose husband has died may come to regard herself as a single person. Still, there are moments when intense feelings of grief occur.

Ultimately, most people emerge from grieving and live new, independent lives. They form new relationships, and some even find that coping with the death has helped them to grow as individuals. They become more self-reliant and more appreciative of life.

It is important to keep in mind that not everyone passes through the stages of grief in the same manner and in the same order. People display vast individual differences, partly due to their personalities, the nature of the relationship with the deceased, and the opportunities that are available to them for continuing their lives after the loss. In fact, most bereaved people are quite resilient, experiencing strong positive emotions such as joy even soon after the death of a loved one. According to psychologist George Bonanno, who has studied bereavement extensively, humans are prepared in an evolutionary sense to move on after the death of someone close. He rejects the notion that there are fixed stages of mourning and argues that most people move on with their lives quite effectively (Bonanno, 2009).

After a death, people move through a painful period of bereavement and grief, even for those they may not have known well, as this tribute to Michael Jackson suggests.

## Differentiating Unhealthy Grief from Normal Grief

Although ideas abound about what separates normal grief from unhealthy grief, careful research has shown that many of the assumptions that both laypersons and clinicians hold are wrong. There is no particular timetable for grieving, particularly the common notion that grieving should be complete a year after a spouse has died. For some people (but not all), grieving may take considerably longer than a year. And some individuals experience *complicated grief* (or sometimes *prolonged grief disorder*), a type of mourning that continues unceasingly for months and years (as we discussed in the previous chapter). An estimated 15 percent of those who are bereaved suffer from complicated grief (Piper et al., 2009; Schumer, 2009; Zisook & Shear, 2009).

Research also contradicts the assumption that depression inevitably follows a death; only 15 to 30 percent of people show relatively deep depression following the loss of a loved one (Prigerson et al., 1995; Bonanno et al., 2002; Hensley, 2006).

Similarly, it is often assumed that people who show little initial distress are not facing up to reality, and that they are likely to have problems later. In fact, those who show the most intense distress immediately after a death are the most apt to have adjustment difficulties and health problems later (Boerner, Wortman, & Bonanno, 2005).

***The Consequences of Grief and Bereavement.*** In a sense, death is catching. Evidence suggests that widowed people are particularly at risk of death. Some studies find that the risk of death can be seven times higher than normal in the first year after the death of a spouse, particularly for men and younger women. Remarriage seems to lower the risk of death, especially for widowed men, although the reasons are not clear (Gluhoski et al., 1994; Martikainen & Valkonen, 1996; Aiken, 2000).

Bereavement is more likely to produce depression or other negative consequences if the person is already insecure, anxious, or fearful and therefore less able to cope effectively. Relationships marked by ambivalence before death are more apt to cause poor post-death outcomes than secure relationships. Highly dependent people are apt to suffer more after the death, as are those who spend a lot of time reflecting on the death and their own grief.

## From Research to Practice

### Living On Through Facebook

*I always wonder why it's so hard to write on here, and since it's hard, why do I do it? Why does anyone? . . . I want you to know that I still care about you. Maybe writing to you makes it feel a little more like you're just someplace else right now. Because, I feel like writing on here is somehow going to enable my messages to get to you better. I talk to you all the time out loud, or in my head. But—I feel like leaving you comments or writing you letters is more like actually \*talking\* to you. I think that's probably because writing letters to people is something that people normally do. It feels more real. I can see it, I send it, I know that it's going someplace. And I feel like somewhere, you will read it.* (Williams & Merten, 2009, p. 82)

Those words were written by an adolescent on the Facebook profile of a friend who had passed away. The explosion of social networking on sites such as Facebook and MySpace is giving rise to a new cultural phenomenon: the spontaneous conversion of profiles left behind by the deceased into a form of interactive memorial. For many people, as for the grieving teenager just quoted, social networking profiles have become an important means of interacting with the people in their lives. When one of those people dies, the profile lives on as a tangible representation of that person—a representation with which one can still interact as before.

Researchers interested in the grieving process studied the comments made by friends and relatives on the social networking profiles of twenty deceased adolescents, searching for common themes. Several major themes and commonalities among the nearly five thousand comments studied were noted (Williams & Merten, 2009).

Comments were almost entirely directed at the deceased rather than at living friends and relatives who were viewing the profile, underscoring the function of the profile as a channel for expressing sentiment to the lost loved one. Nearly half the comments included some indicator of emotional or cognitive coping strategies, such as expressions of anger, denial, or acceptance.

These kinds of comments showed an attempt to process, understand, and find perspective on the death. Following is an example of coping with anger:

*I hate the fact that u did this to yourself. I hate it that u didn't tell anyone. But there's nothing I can do. I can be mad all I want. But nothing will change, I wish u never would've made such a permanent decision. . . . No one or anything can bring u back now, I will NEVER see u again, ever. I will never talk to u again.* (Williams & Merten, 2009, p. 80)

Social networking sites like Facebook provide a means for public grieving.

A form of continuing interaction with the deceased by reminiscing about past shared experiences or discussing current events in one's life was another common theme. An example of this kind of comment follows.

*Just a couple weeks ago you sent me a message askin when we were gonna hang out again [though we can't now]. Just yesterday you made me laugh . . . in gym class. And in just a minute you were gone!!! I still remember the first time I met you. I will always remember what you told me though, about finding the right person cuz I deserve the best! I will never forget you, I wish you would have been able to realize just how many people really did love and care for you!* (Williams & Merten, 2009, p. 82)

Many comments pertained to the experience of attending the deceased's funeral service and seeing his or her body, particularly in reference to the realization prompted by that experience of the truth and the finality of the loved one's death. Many comments further referenced beliefs about the afterlife and where the deceased had gone. Finally, the researchers uncovered a theme that they weren't expecting: messages left by people who barely knew the deceased, or who did not know him or her at all. Given that the departed were all adolescents whose deaths were tragic occurrences that touched people throughout their communities, this observation makes sense.

- Why do you think grieving friends and relatives direct their comments to the deceased on his or her social networking profile, rather than to each other?

- How might "talking to the dead" in this manner help people through the grieving process?

# Helping a Child Cope with Grief

## Becoming an Informed Consumer of Development

Because of their limited understanding of death, younger children need special help in coping with grief. Among the strategies that can help are the following:

- **Be honest.** Don't say that the person is "sleeping" or "on a long trip." Use age-appropriate language to tell the truth. Gently but clearly point out that death is final and universal.

- **Encourage expressions of grief.** Don't tell children not to cry or show their feelings. Instead, tell them that it is understandable to feel terrible, and that they may always miss the deceased. Encourage them to draw a picture, write a letter, or express their feelings some other way.

- **Reassure children that they are not to blame.** Children sometimes attribute a loved one's death to their own behavior—if they had not misbehaved, they mistakenly reason, the person would not have died.

- **Understand that children's grief may surface in unanticipated ways.** Children may show little initial grief but later may become upset for no apparent reason or revert to behaviors like thumbsucking or wanting to sleep with their parents.

- **Children may respond to books for young persons about death.** One especially effective book is *When Dinosaurs Die,* by Laurie Krasny Brown and Marc Brown.

Bereaved people who lack social support from family, friends, or a connection to some other group, religious or otherwise, are more likely to experience feelings of loneliness, and therefore are more at risk. Finally, people who are unable to make sense of the death or find meaning in it (such as a new appreciation of life) show less overall adjustment (Davis & Nolen-Hoeksema, 2001; Nolen-Hoeksema, 2001; Nolen-Hoeksema & Davis, 2002; Torges, Stewart, & Nolen-Hoeksema, 2008; also see the "From Research to Practice" box).

The suddenness of the death also affects the course of grieving. People who unexpectedly lose their loved ones are less able to cope than those who could anticipate the death. In one study, people who experienced a sudden death had not fully recovered four years later. In part, this may be because sudden deaths are often the result of violence, which occurs more frequently among younger individuals (Rando, 1993; Burton, Haley, & Small, 2006).

**From a social worker's perspective:** Why do you think the risk of death is so high for people who have recently lost a spouse? Why might remarriage lower the risk?

As we noted earlier, children may need special help understanding and mourning the death of someone they love.

## REVIEW, CHECK, AND APPLY

### REVIEW

**LO8** How do survivors react to and cope with death?

- Bereavement refers to the loss of a loved one; grief refers to the emotional response to that loss.

- For many people, grief passes through denial, sorrow, and accommodation stages.

### CHECK YOURSELF

1. According to Rosenblatt (1998, 2001) the nature of emotional displays, such as the amount and timing of crying in response to someone's death, are determined culturally.

   - True
   - False

2. Bereaved people who lack _____ are more likely to experience feelings of loneliness and are therefore at greater risk for more negative post-death outcomes.

   a. ambivalence
   b. rituals
   c. independence
   d. social support

3. In the final stage of grief, people tend to:

   a. reach the accommodation stage, where they pick up the pieces of their lives and construct new identities.
   b. cycle back to numbness if the pain is too severe.
   c. avoid the reality of the situation through denial.
   d. suffer deep unhappiness and even depression.

### APPLYING LIFESPAN DEVELOPMENT

- Why do so many people in the United States feel reluctant to think and talk about death? Why do people in other cultures feel less reluctant?

✓—**Study** and **Review** on **MyDevelopmentLab.com**

Answers: 1) True; 2) d; 3) a

# *Putting It All Together*
## Death and Dying

**ARCHIE WALKER,** the 87-year-old man we met in the chapter opener, resigned to his impending death, decided not to spend the rest of his life in a hospital. He was determined to go out the way he wanted. Rather than the expensive and invasive procedures he would undergo in the hospital, or even the comfortable death that professional hospice providers offer, he opted for a peaceful end amid family and friends. He planned his funeral, relieving his family of that burden, and took the time to say proper good-byes to his loved ones. Then he sailed out onto his last voyage accompanied by the music he loved.

### MODULE **10.1** Dying and Death Across the Life Span

- Archie has confronted and provided a personal answer to the question of when life ends. **(pp. 458-459)**
- Archie, at age 87, clearly feels that he has had a full, satisfying life. **(pp. 462-463)**
- He has tried to anticipate and deal with in advance the feelings of his family members. **(p. 464)**

### MODULE **10.2** Confronting Death

- Archie appears to have passed successfully through the steps of dying. **(pp. 465-466)**
- He has decided to make his own life-or-death (e.g., DNR) decisions. **(pp. 468-469)**
- He does not seem to have even considered the idea of assisted suicide, preferring to die naturally at home with his wife and children at his side. **(p. 472)**
- Archie has clearly considered, and rejected, the hospital as a place to die. **(p. 472)**

## What would YOU do?

■ Given what you know about possible places to die, what would you recommend for your closest loved one, in the event it was needed: hospitalization, home care, or hospice care? Why? Would other choices be more appropriate for other loved ones you know?

   **HINT** Review page 471–472.

   *What's your response?*

## MODULE **10.3** Grief and Bereavement

■ Archie understands the importance of funeral ceremonies and has undertaken the planning of his own last rites. **(pp. 473-474)**

■ He has evidently anticipated the grief that his family will experience and has taken steps to minimize it or at least make it easier. **(pp. 474-477)**

■ Archie has clearly taken on the difficult task of speaking frankly to his wife and children about his own death. **(p. 475)**

## What would a POLICYMAKER do?

■ Should the government get involved in determining whether to permit individuals to make decisions about continuing their own lives in times of critical illness or extreme pain? Should this be a matter of law or of personal conscience?

   **HINT** Review page 468–471.

   *What's your response?*

## What would a HEALTH CARE PROVIDER do?

■ Which criteria are most important in deciding whether or not to discontinue life-support systems? Do you think the criteria differ in different cultures?

   **HINT** Review pages 468–471.

   *What's your response?*

**✴ Explore** on **mydevelopmentlab.com**

To read how a real policymaker, health care provider, and educator responded to these questions, log onto MyDevelopmentLab.com.

*Do you agree or disagree with their responses? Why? What concepts that you've read about back up their opinion?*

## What would an EDUCATOR do?

■ What sorts of topics should be covered in depth in death education courses for health providers? For laypeople?

   **HINT** Review page 463–464.

   *What's your response?*

# References

AARP (American Association of Retired Persons). (1990). *A profile of older Americans.* Washington, DC: Author.

AARP (American Association of Retired Persons). (2004, May 25). Funeral arrangements and memorial service. Available online at http://www.aarp.org/griefandloss/articles/73_a.html

AARP (American Association of Retired Persons). (2005). *A profile of older Americans.* Washington, DC: Author.

Abbot-Smith, K., & Tomasello, M. (2010). The influence of frequency and semantic similarity on how children learn grammar. *First Language, 30,* 79–101.

Abdo, C., Afif-Abdo, J., Otani, F., & Machado, A. (2008). Sexual satisfaction among patients with erectile dysfunction treated with counseling, sildenafil, or both. *Journal of Sexual Medicine, 5,* 1720–1726.

Aber, J. L., Bishop-Josef, S. J., Jones, S. M., McLearn, K. T., & Phillips, D. A. (Eds.). (2007). *Child development and social policy: Knowledge for action.* Washington, DC: American Psychological Association.

Aboud, F. E., & Sankar, J. (2007). Friendship and identity in a language-integrated school. *International Journal of Behavioral Development, 31,* 445–453.

Achenbach, T. A. (1992). Developmental psychopathology. In M. H. Bornstein & M. E. Lamb (Eds.), *Developmental psychology: An advanced textbook.* Hillsdale, NJ: Lawrence Erlbaum.

Ackerman, B. P., & Izard, C. E. (2004). Emotion cognition in children and adolescents: Introduction to the special issue. *Journal of Experimental Child Psychology, 89* [Special issue: Emotional cognition in children], 271–275.

Acocella, J. (August 18 & 25, 2003). Little people. *The New Yorker,* pp. 138–143.

ACOG. (2002). *Guidelines for perinatal care.* Elk Grove, IN: Author.

Adair, L. (2008). Child and adolescent obesity: Epidemiology and developmental perspectives. *Physiology & Behavior, 94,* 8–16.

Adams, K. B. (2004). Changing investment in activities and interests in elders' lives: Theory and measurement. *International Journal of Aging and Human Development, 58,* 87–108.

Adams, P. (2010). Understanding the different realities, experience, and use of self-esteem between Black and White adolescent girls. *Journal of Black Psychology, 36,* 255–276.

Adams Hillard, P. J. (2001). Gynecologic disorders and surgery. In N. L. Stotland & D. E. Stewart (Eds.), *Psychological aspects of women's health care: The interface between psychiatry and obstetrics and gynecology* (2nd ed.). Arlington, VA: American Psychiatric Publishing, Inc.

Adamson, L., & Frick, J. (2003). The still face: A history of a shared experimental paradigm. *Infancy, 4,* 451–473.

Adebayo, B. (2008). Gender gaps in college enrollment and degree attainment: An exploratory analysis. *College Student Journal, 42,* 232–237.

Administration on Aging. (2003). *A profile of older Americans: 2003.* Washington, DC: U.S. Department of Health and Human Services.

Administration on Aging. (2006). *Profiles of older Americans 2005: Research report.* Washington, DC: U.S. Department of Health and Human Resources.

Administration on Aging. (2010). A statistical profile of older Americans aged 65+. Washington, DC: Administration on Aging, U.S. Department of Health and Human Services.

Afifi, T., Brownridge, D., Cox, B., & Sareen, J. (2006, October). Physical punishment, childhood abuse and psychiatric disorders. *Child Abuse & Neglect, 30,* 1093–1103.

Agrawal, A., & Lynskey, M. (2008). Are there genetic influences on addiction: Evidence from family, adoption and twin studies. *Addiction, 103,* 1069–1081. Available online at http://search.ebscohost.com.

Ah-Kion, J. (2006, June). Body image and self-esteem: A study of gender differences among mid-adolescents. *Gender & Behaviour, 4,* 534–549.

Ahmed, E., & Braithwaite, V. (2004). Bullying and victimization: Cause for concern for both families and schools. *Social Psychology of Education, 7,* 35–54.

Ahn, W., Gelman, S., & Amsterlaw, J. (2000). Causal status effect in children's categorization. *Cognition, 76,* B35–B43.

Aiken, L. R. (2000). *Dying, death, and bereavement* (4th ed.). Mahwah, NJ: Lawrence Erlbaum.

Ainsworth, M. D. S., Blehar, M. C., Waters, E., & Wall, S. (1978). *Patterns of attachment: A psychological study of the strange situation.* Hillsdale, NJ: Lawrence Erlbaum.

Aitken, R. J. (1995, July 7). The complexities of conception. *Science, 269,* 39–40.

Akhtar, S. (2010). *The wound of mortality: Fear, denial, and acceptance of death.* Lanham, MD: Jason Aronson.

Akmajian, A., Demers, R. A., & Harnish, R. M. (1984). *Linguistics.* Cambridge, MA: MIT Press.

Akshoomoff, N. (2006). Autism spectrum disorders: Introduction. *Child Neuropsychology, 12,* 245–246.

Albers, L. L., & Krulewitch, C. J. (1993). Electronic fetal monitoring in the United States in the 1980s. *Obstetrics & Gynecology, 82,* 8–10.

Alberts, A., Elkind, D., & Ginsberg, S. (2007). The personal fable and risk-taking in early adolescence. *Journal of Youth and Adolescence, 36,* 71–76.

Albrecht, G. L. (2005). *Encyclopedia of disability* (General ed.). Thousand Oaks, CA: Sage Publications.

Alderfer, C. (2003). The science and nonscience of psychologists' responses to *The Bell Curve. Professional Psychology: Research & Practice, 34,* 287–293.

Aldwin, C. M. (1994). *Stress, coping, and development: An integrative perspective.* New York: Guilford Press.

Ales, K. L., Druzin, M. L., & Santini, D. L. (1990). Impact of advanced maternal age on the outcome of pregnancy. *Surgery, Gynecology & Obstetrics, 171,* 209–216.

Alexander, B., Turnbull, D., & Cyna, A. (2009). The effect of pregnancy on hypnotizability. *American Journal of Clinical Hypnosis, 52,* 13–22.

Alexander, G. M., & Hines, M. (2002). Sex differences in response to children's toys in nonhuman primates. *Evolution and Human Behavior, 23,* 467–479.

Alexandersen, P., Karsdal, M. A., & Christiansen, C. (2009). Long-term prevention with hormone-replacement therapy after the menopause: Which women should be targeted? *Womens Health (London, England), 5,* 637–647.

Alfonso, V. C., Flanagan, D. P., & Radwan, S. (2005). The impact of the Cattell-Horn-Carroll theory on test development and interpretation of cognitive and academic abilities. In D. P. Flanagan & P. L. Harrison (Eds.), *Contemporary intellectual assessment: Theories, tests, and issues.* New York: Guilford Press.

Alfred, M., & Chlup, D. (2010). Making the invisible, visible: Race matters in human resource development. *Advances in Developing Human Resources, 12,* 332–351.

Alibali, M., Phillips, K., & Fischer, A. (2009). Learning new problem-solving strategies leads to changes in problem representation. *Cognitive Development, 24,* 89–101. Available online at http://search.ebscohost.com

Alisky, J. M. (2007). The coming problem of HIV-associated Alzheimer's disease. *Medical Hypotheses, 12,* 47–55.

Allam, M. D., Marlier, L., & Schall, B. (2006). Learning at the breast: Preference formation for an artificial scent and its attraction against the odor of maternal milk. *Infant Behavior & Development, 29,* 308–321.

Allen, B. (2008). An analysis of the impact of diverse forms of childhood psychological maltreatment on emotional adjustment in early adulthood. *Child Maltreatment, 13,* 307–312.

Allen, J., Chavez, S., DeSimone, S., Howard, D., Johnson, K., LaPierre, L., et al. (2006, June). Americans' attitudes toward euthanasia and physician-assisted suicide, 1936–2002. *Journal of Sociology & Social Welfare, 33,* 5–23.

Allison, B., & Schultz, J. (2001). Interpersonal identity formation during early adolescence. *Adolescence, 36,* 509–523.

Al-Owidha, A., Green, K., & Kroger, J. (2009). On the question of an identity status category order: Rasch model step and scale statistics used to identify category order. *International Journal of Behavioral Development, 33,* 88–96.

Altholz, S., & Golensky, M. (2004). Counseling, support, and advocacy for clients who stutter. *Health & Social Work, 29,* 197–205.

Alvarez-Leon, E. E., Roman-Vinas, B., & Serra-Majem, L. (2006). Dairy products and health: A review of the epidemiological evidence. *British Journal of Nutrition, 96,* Supplement, S94–S99.

Alzheimer's Association. (2004, May 28). Standard prescriptions for Alzheimer's. Available online at http://www.alz.org/AboutAD/Treatment/Standard.asp

Amato, P., & Afifi, T. (2006, February). Feeling caught between parents: Adult children's relations with parents and subjective well-being. *Journal of Marriage and Family, 68,* 222–235.

American Academy of Pediatrics. (1997, April 16). Press release.

American Academy of Pediatrics. (1999, August). Media education. *Pediatrics, 104,* 341–343.

American Academy of Pediatrics. (2000). Clinical practice guideline: Diagnosis and evaluation of the child with attention-deficit/hyperactivity disorder. *Pediatrics.* Available online at http://www.pediatrics.org/cgi/content/full/105/5/1158

American Academy of Pediatrics. (2003). *Guide to toilet training.* Washington, DC: Author.

American Academy of Pediatrics. (2004, June 3). *Sports programs.* Available online at http://www.medem.com/medlb/article_detaillb_for_printer.cfm?article_

American Academy of Pediatrics. (2005). Breastfeeding and the use of human milk: Policy statement. *Pediatrics, 115,* 496–506.

American Academy of Pediatrics. (2009). *Toilet training.* Elk Grove Village, IL: Author.

American Academy of Pediatrics (Committee on Accident and Poison Prevention). (1990). Trampolines at home, school, and recreational centers. *Pediatrics, 103,* 1053–1056.

American Academy of Pediatrics (Committee on Psychosocial Aspects of Child and Family Health). (1998, April). Guidance for effective discipline. *Pediatrics, 101,* 723–728.

American Academy of Pediatrics, Dietz, W. H. (Ed.), & Stern, L. (Ed.). (1999). *American Academy of Pediatrics guide to your child's nutrition: Making peace at the table and building healthy eating habits for life.* New York: Villard.

American Academy of Pediatrics. (2009). *Caring for your baby and young child: Birth to age 5.* Washington, DC: Author.

American College of Medical Genetics. (2006). *Genetics in Medicine, 8* (5), Supplement.

American College of Sports Medicine. (1997, November 3). *Consensus development conference statement on physical activity and cardiovascular health.* Available online at http://www.acsm.org/nhlbi.htm

American College Testing Program. (2001). *National dropout rates.* Iowa City, IA: American College Testing Program.

American Council on Education. (1995–1996). *Minorities in higher education*. Washington, DC: Office of Minority Concerns.

American Heart Association. (1988). *Heart facts*. Dallas, TX: Author.

American Psychological Association. (2002). *Ethical principles of psychologists and code of conduct. Updated*. Washington, DC: Author.

Amitai, Y., Haringman, M., Meiraz, H., Baram, N., & Leventhal, A. (2004). Increased awareness, knowledge and utilization of preconceptional folic acid in Israel following a national campaign. *Preventive Medicine: An International Journal Devoted to Practice and Theory, 39*, 731–737.

Ammerman, R. T., & Patz, R. J. (1996). Determinants of child abuse potential: Contribution of parent and child factors. *Journal of Clinical Child Psychology, 25*, 300–307.

Amsterlaw, J., & Wellman, H. (2006). Theories of mind in transition: A microgenetic study of the development of false belief understanding. *Journal of Cognition and Development, 7*, 139–172.

Anand, K. J. S., & Hickey, P. R. (1992). Halothane-morphine compared with high-dose sufentanil for anesthesia and post-operative analgesia in neonatal cardiac surgery. *New England Journal of Medicine, 326*(1), 1–9.

Anders, T. F., & Taylor, T. (1994). Babies and their sleep environment. *Children's Environments, 11*, 123–134.

Anderson, P., & Butcher, K. (2006, March). Childhood obesity: Trends and potential causes. *The Future of Children, 16*, 19–45.

Anderson, R. N. (2001). *United States life tables, 1998. National vital statistics reports* (Vol. 48, No. 18). Hyattsville, MD: National Center for Health Statistics.

Andrews, G., Halford, G., & Bunch, K. (2003). Theory of mind and relational complexity. *Child Development, 74*, 1476–1499.

Angus, J., & Reeve, P. (2006, April). Ageism: A threat to "aging well" in the 21st century. *Journal of Applied Gerontology, 25*, 137–152.

Anisfeld, M. (1996). Only tongue protrusion modeling is matched by neonates. *Developmental Review, 16*, 149–161.

Annenberg Public Policy Center. (2008). *Internet gambling stays low among youth ages 14 to 22 but access to gambling sites continues*. Philadelphia: Annenberg Public Policy Center.

Annunziato, R., & Lowe, M. (2007, April). Taking action to lose weight: Toward an understanding of individual differences. *Eating Behaviors, 8*, 185–194.

Ansaldo, A. I., Arguin, M., & RochLocours, L. A. (2002). The contribution of the right cerebral hemisphere to the recovery from aphasia: A single longitudinal case study. *Brain Languages, 82*, 206–222.

Ansberry, C. (1997, November 14). Women of Troy: For ladies on a hill, friendships are a balm in the passages of life. *Wall Street Journal*, pp. A1, A6.

APA Reproductive Choice Working Group. (2000). *Reproductive choice and abortion: A resource packet*. Washington, DC: American Psychological Association.

Apperly, I., & Robinson, E. (2002). Five-year-olds' handling of reference and description in the domains of language and mental representation. *Journal of Experimental Child Psychology, 83*, 53–75.

Archer, J. (2009). The nature of human aggression. *International Journal of Law and Psychiatry, 32*, 202–208.

Archer, S. L., & Waterman, A. S. (1994). Adolescent identity development: Contextual perspectives. In C. B. Fisher & R. M. Lerner (Eds.), *Applied developmental psychology*. New York: McGraw-Hill.

Arenson, K. W. (2004, December 3). Worried colleges step up efforts over suicide. *New York Times*, p. A1.

Ariès, P. (1962). *Centuries of childhood*. New York: Knopf.

Armstrong, J., Hutchinson, I., Laing, D., & Jinks, A. (2007). Facial electromyography: Responses of children to odor and taste stimuli. *Chemical Senses, 32*, 611–621.

Armstrong, P., Rounds, J., & Hubert, L. (2008). Re-conceptualizing the past: Historical data in vocational interest research. *Journal of Vocational Behavior, 72*, 284–297.

Arnautovska, U., & Grad, O. (2010). Attitudes toward suicide in the adolescent population. *Crisis: The Journal of Crisis Intervention and Suicide Prevention, 31*, 22–29.

Arnett, J. (2007). Emerging adulthood: What is it, and what is it good for? *Child Development Perspectives, 1*, 68–73.

Arnett, J. (2010). Oh, grow up! Generational grumbling and the new life stage of emerging adulthood Commentary on Trzesniewski & Donnellan (2010). *Perspectives on Psychological Science, 5*, 89–92.

Arnett, J. J. (2000). Emerging adulthood: A theory of development from the late teens through the twenties. *American Psychologist, 55*, 469–480.

Arnsten, A., Berridge, C., & McCracken, J. (2009). The neurobiological basis of attention-deficit/hyperactivity disorder. *Primary Psychiatry, 16*, 47–54.

Arseneault, L., Moffitt, T. E., & Caspi, A. (2003). Strong genetic effects on cross-situational antisocial behavior among 5-year-old children according to mothers, teachers, examiner-observers, and twins' self-reports. *Journal of Child Psychology and Psychiatry and Allied Disciplines, 44*, 832–848.

Artal, P., Ferro, M., Miranda, I., & Navarro, R. (1993). Effects of aging in retinal image quality. *Journal of the Optical Society of America, 10*, 1656–1662.

Arts, J. A. R., Gijselaers, W. H., & Boshuizen, H. P. A. (2006). Understanding managerial problem-solving, knowledge use and information processing: Investigating stages from school to the workplace. *Contemporary Educational Psychology, 31*, 387–410.

Asch, D. A. (1996, May 23). The role of critical care nurses in euthanasia and assisted suicide. *New England Journal of Medicine, 334*, 1374–1379.

Asendorpf, J. B., Warkentin, V., & Baudonniere, P. (1996). Self-awareness and other-awareness II: Mirror self-recognition, social contingency awareness, and synchronic imitation. *Developmental Psychology, 32*, 313–321.

Asher, S. R., & Rose, A. J. (1997). Promoting chidren's social-emotional adjustment with peers. In P. Salovey & D. Sluyter (Eds.), *Emotional development and emotional intelligence: Educational implications*. New York: Basic Books.

Asher, S. R., Singleton, L. C., & Taylor, A. R. (1982). Acceptance vs. friendship. Paper presented at the meeting of the American Research Association, New York.

Ashton, R. (2010). Practitioner review: Beyond shaken baby syndrome: What influences the outcomes for infants following traumatic brain injury? *Journal of Child Psychology and Psychiatry, 51*, 967–980.

Askham, J. (1994). Marriage relationships of older people. *Reviews in Clinical Gerontology, 4*, 261–268.

Aslin, R. N. (1987). Visual and auditory development in infancy. In J. D. Osofsky (Ed.), *Handbook of infant development* (2nd ed.). New York: Wiley.

Astin, A., Korn, W., & Berg, E. (1989). *The American Freshman: National norms for Fall, 1989*. Los Angeles: University of California, Los Angeles, American Council on Education.

Ata, R. N., Ludden, A. B., & Lally, M. M. (2007). The effects of gender and family, friend, and media influences on eating behaviors and body image during adolescence. *Journal of Youth and Adolescence, 36*, 1024–1037.

Atchley, R. (2003). Why most people cope well with retirement. In J. Ronch & J. Goldfield (Eds.), *Mental wellness in aging: Strengths-based approaches*. Baltimore, MD: Health Professions Press.

Atchley, R. C. (2000). *Social forces and aging* (9th ed.). Belmont, CA: Wadsworth Thomson Learning.

Atchley, R. C., & Barusch, A. (2005). *Social forces and aging* (10th ed.). Belmont, CA: Wadsworth.

Auestad, N., Scott, D. T., Janowsky, J. S., Jacobsen, C., Carroll, R. E., Montalto, M. B., Halter, R., Qiu, W., Jacobs, J. R., Connor, W. E., Connor, S. L., Taylor, J. A., Neuringer, M., Fitzgerald, K. M., & Hall, R. T. (2003). Visual cognitive and language assessments at 39 months: A follow-up study of children fed formulas containing long-chain polyunsaturated fatty acids to 1 year of age. *Pediatrics, 112*, e177–e183.

Aujoulat, I., Luminet, O., & Deccache, A. (2007). The perspective of patients on their experience of powerlessness. *Qualitative Health Research, Vol. 17*, 772–785.

Avdiner, F., Yetkin, C. E., & Seli, E. (2010). Perspectives on emerging biomarkers for non-invasive assessment of embryo viability in assisted reproduction. *Current Molecular Medicine, 10*, 206–215.

Avlund, K., Lund, R., & Holstein, B. (2004). Social relations as determinant of onset of disability in aging. *Archives of Gerontology & Geriatrics, 38*, 85–99.

Axia, G., Bonichini, S., & Benini, F. (1995). Pain in infancy: Individual differences. *Perceptual and Motor Skills, 81*, 142.

Aylward, G. P., & Verhulst, S. J. (2000). Predictive utility of the Bayley Infant Neurodevelopmental Screener (BINS) risk status classifications: Clinical interpretation and application. *Developmental Medicine & Child Neurology, 42*, 25–31.

Ayoola, A., Nettleman, M., Stommel, M., & Canady, R. (2010). Time of pregnancy recognition and prenatal care use: A population-based study in the United States. *Birth: Issues in Perinatal Care, 37*, 37–43.

Ayoub, N. C. (2005, February 25). A pleasing birth: Midwives and maternity care in the Netherlands. *The Chronicle of Higher Education*, p. 9.

Bacchus, L., Mezey, G., & Bewley, S. (2006). A qualitative exploration of the nature of domestic violence in pregnancy. *Violence against Women, 12*, 588–604.

Badenhorst, W., Riches, S., Turton, P., & Hughes, P. (2006). The psychological effects of stillbirth and neonatal death on fathers: Systematic review. *Journal of Psychosomatic Obstetrics & Gynecology, 27*, 245–256.

Bader, A. P. (1995). Engrossment revisited: Fathers are still falling in love with their newborn babies. In J. L. Shapiro, M. J. Diamond, & M. Greenberg (Eds.), *Becoming a father*. New York: Springer.

Baer, J. S., Sampson, P. D., & Barr, H. M. (2003). A 21-year longitudinal analysis of the effects of prenatal alcohol exposure on young adult drinking. *Archives of General Psychiatry, 60*, 377–385.

Bailey, J. M., Kirk, K. M., Zhu, G., Dunne, M. P., & Martin, N. G. (2000). Do individual differences in sociosexuality represent genetic or environmentally contingent strategies? Evidence from the Australian twin registry. *Journal of Personality and Social Psychology, 78*, 537–545.

Baillargeon, R. (2004). Infants' physical world. *Current Directions in Psychological Science, 13*, 89–94.

Baillargeon, R. (2008). Innate ideas revisited: For a principle of persistence in infants' physical reasoning. *Perspectives on Psychological Science, 3*, 2–13.

Baker, J., Maes, H., Lissner, L., Aggen, S., Lichtenstein, P., & Kendler, K. (2009). Genetic risk factors for disordered eating in adolescent males and females. *Journal of Abnormal Psychology, 118*, 576–586.

Baker, J., Mazzeo, S., & Kendler, K. (2007). Association between broadly defined bulimia nervosa and drug use disorders: Common genetic and environmental influences. *International Journal of Eating Disorders, 40*, 673–678.

Baker, M. (2007, December). Elder mistreatment: Risk, vulnerability, and early mortality. *Journal of the American Psychiatric Nurses Association, 12*, 313–321.

Baker, T., Brandon, T., & Chassin, L. (2004). Motivational influences on cigarette smoking. *Annual Review of Psychology, 55*, 463–491.

Bal, E., Harden, E., Lamb, D., Van Hecke, A., Denver, J., & Porges, S. (2010). Emotion recognition in children with autism spectrum disorders: Relations to eye gaze and autonomic state. *Journal of Autism and Developmental Disorders, 40*, 358–370.

Ball, K., & Rebok, G. W. (1994). Evaluating the driving ability of older adults. *Journal of Applied Gerontology, 13* [Special issue: Research translation in gerontology: A behavioral and social perspective], 20–38.

Ballas, S. (2010). Neurocognitive complications of sickle cell anemia in adults. *JAMA: Journal of the American Medical Association, 303*, 1862–1863.

Ballen, L., & Fulcher, A. (2006). Nurses and doulas: Complementary roles to provide optimal maternity care. *Journal of Obstetric, Gynecologic, & Neonatal Nursing: Clinical Scholarship for the Care of Women, Childbearing Families, & Newborns, 35*, 304–311.

Baltes, M. M. (1996). *The many faces of dependency in old age*. New York: Cambridge University Press.

Baltes, M., & Carstensen, L. (2003). The process of successful aging: Selection, optimization and compensation. In U. Staudinger & U. Lindenberger (Eds.), *Understanding human development: Dialogues with lifespan psychology*. Netherlands: Kluwer Academic Publishers.

Baltes, P., & Freund, A. (2003a). Human strengths as the orchestration of wisdom and selective optimization with compensation. In L. Aspinwall & U. Staudinger (Eds.), *A psychology of human strengths: Fundamental questions and future directions for a positive psychology*. Washington, DC: American Psychological Association.

Baltes, P., & Freund, A. (2003b). The intermarriage of wisdom and selective optimization with compensation: Two meta-heuristics guiding the conduct of life. In C. Keyes & J. Haidt (Eds.), *Flourishing: Positive psychology and the life well-lived*. Washington, DC: American Psychological Association.

Baltes, P. B. (2003). On the incomplete architecture of human ontogeny: Selection, optimization and compensation as foundation of developmental theory. In U. M. Staudinger & U. Lindenberger (Eds.), *Understanding human development: Dialogues with lifespan psychology*. Dordrecht, Netherlands: Kluwer Academic Publishers.

Baltes, P. B., & Baltes, M. M. (1990). Psychological perspectives on successful aging: The model of selective optimization with compensation. In P. B. Baltes & M. M. Baltes (Eds.), *Successful aging: Perspectives from the behavioral sciences*. Cambridge, England: Cambridge University Press.

Baltes, P. B., Staudinger, U. M., & Lindenberger, U. (1999). Lifespan psychology: Theory and application to intellectual functioning. *Annual Review of Psychology, 50*, 471–507.

Bandura, A. (1977). *Social learning theory*. Englewood Cliffs, NJ: Prentice-Hall.

Bandura, A. (1991). Social cognitive theory of self-regulation. *Organizational Behavior and Human Decision Processes, Vol. 50*, [Special issue: Theories of cognitive self-regulation], 248–287.

Bandura, A. (1994). Social cognitive theory of mass communication. In J. Bryant & D. Zillmann (Eds.), *Media effects: Advances in theory and research. LEA's communication series*. Hillsdale, NJ: Lawrence Erlbaum.

Bandura, A. (2002). Social cognitive theory in cultural context. *Applied Psychology: An International Review, 51*, [Special Issue], 269–290.

Bandura, A., Grusec, J. E., & Menlove, F. L. (1967). Vicarious extinction of avoidance behavior. *Journal of Personality and Social Psychology, 5*, 16–23.

Bandura, A., Ross, D., & Ross, S. (1963). Vicarious extinction of avoidance behavior. *Journal of Personality and Social Psychology, 67*, 601–607.

Baptista, T., Aldana, E., Angeles, F., & Beaulieu, S. (2008). Evolution theory: An overview of its applications in psychiatry. *Psychopathology, 41*, 17–27.

Barberá, E. (2003). Gender schemas: Configuration and activation processes. *Canadian Journal of Behavioural Science, 35*, 176–180.

Barboza, G., Schiamberg, L., Oehmke, J., Korzeniewski, S., Post, L., & Heraux, C. (2009). Individual characteristics and the multiple contexts of adolescent bullying: An ecological perspective. *Journal of Youth and Adolescence, 38*, 101–121.

Barer, B. M. (1994). Men and women aging differently. *International Journal of Aging and Human Development, 38*, 29–40.

Barlett, C., Harris, R., & Baldassaro, R. (2007). Longer you play, the more hostile you feel: Examination of first person shooter video games and aggression during video game play. *Aggressive Behavior, 33*, 486–497.

Barnett, R. C., & Hyde, J. S. (2001). Women, men, work, and family. *American Psychologist, 56*, 781–796.

Barrett, T., & Needham, A. (2008). Developmental differences in infants' use of an object's shape to grasp it securely. *Developmental Psychobiology, 50*, 97–106.

Barry, L. M., Hudley, C., Kelly, M., & Cho, S. (2009). Differences in self-reported disclosure of college experiences by first-generation college student status. *Adolescence, 44*, 55–68.

Barton, J. (2007). The autobiographical self: Who we know and who we are. *Psychiatric Annals, 37*, 276–284.

Barton, L. J. (1997, July). A shoulder to lean on: Assisted living in the U.S. *American Demographics*, 45–51.

Basak, C., Boot, W., Voss, M., & Kramer, A. (2008). Can training in a real-time strategy video game attenuate cognitive decline in older adults? *Psychology and Aging, 23*, 765–777.

Bashore, T. R., Ridderinkhof, K. R., & van der Molen, M. W. (1998). The decline of cognitive processing speed in old age. *Current Directions in Psychological Science, 6*, 163–169.

Bass, S., Shields, M. K., & Behrman, R. E. (2004). Children, families, and foster care: Analysis and recommendations. *The Future of Children, 14*, 5–30.

Basseches, M. (1984). *Dialectical thinking and adult development*. Norwood, NJ: Ablex.

Bates, J. E., Marvinney, D., Kelly, T., Dodge, K. A., Bennett, D. S., & Pettit, G. S. (1994). Child-care history and kindergarten adjustment. *Developmental Psychology, 30*, 690–700.

Battin, M., van der Heide, A., Ganzini, L., van der Wal, G., & Onwuteaka-Philipsen, B. (2007). Legal physician-assisted dying in Oregon and the Netherlands: Evidence concerning the impact on patients in "vulnerable" groups. *Journal of Medical Ethics, 33*, 591–597.

Bauer, P. J. (2004). Getting explicit memory off the ground: Steps toward construction of a neuro-developmental account of changes in the first two years of life. *Developmental Review 24* [Special issue: Memory development in the new millennium], 347–373.

Bauer, P. J. (2007) Recall in infancy: A neurodevelopmental account. *Current Directions in Psychological Science, 16*, 142–146.

Baulac, S., Lu, H., Strahle, J., Yang, T., Goldberg, M., Shen, J., et al. (2009). Increased DJ-1 expression under oxidative stress and in Alzheimer's disease brains. *Molecular Neurodegeneration, 4*, 27–37.

Bauld, R., & Brown, R. (2009). Stress, psychological distress, psychosocial factors, menopause symptoms and physical health in women. *Maturitas, 62*, 160–165.

Baumrind, D. (1971). Current patterns of parental authority. *Developmental Psychology Monographs, 4* (1, pt. 2).

Baumrind, D. (1980). New directions in socialization research. *Psychological Bulletin, 35*, 639–652.

Bayley, N. (1969). *Manual for the Bayley Scales of Infant Development*. New York: Psychological Corporation.

Bayley, N., & Oden, M. (1955). The maintenance of intellectual ability in gifted adults. *Journal of Gerontology, 10*, 91–107.

Beach, B. A. (2003). Rural children's play in the natural environment. In D. E. Lytle (Ed.), *Play and educational theory and practice*. Westport, CT: Praeger Publishers/Greenwood Publishing Group.

Beal, C. R. (1994). *Boys and girls: The development of gender roles*. New York: McGraw-Hill.

Beale, E. A., Baile, W. F., & Aaron, J. (2003). Silence is not golden: Communicating with children dying from cancer. *Journal of Clinical Oncology, 23*, 3629–3631.

Beals, K., Impett, E., & Peplau, L. (2002). Lesbians in love: Why some relationships endure and others end. *Journal of Lesbian Studies, 6*, 53–63.

Bearce, K., & Rovee-Collier, C. (2006). Repeated priming increases memory accessibility in infants. *Journal of Experimental Child Psychology, 93*, 357–376.

Beardslee, W. R., & Goldman, S. (2003, September 22). Living beyond sadness. *Newsweek*, p. 70.

Bearman, P., & Bruckner, H. (2004). Study on teenage virginity pledge. Paper presented at meeting of the National STD Prevention Conference, Phildadelphia, PA.

Becker, B., & Luthar, S. (2007, March). Peer-perceived admiration and social preference: Contextual correlates of positive peer regard among suburban and urban adolescents. *Journal of Research on Adolescence, 17*, 117–144.

Becker, G., Beyene, Y., & Newsom, E. (2003). Creating continuity through mutual assistance: Intergenerational reciprocity in four ethnic groups. *Journals of Gerontology: Series B: Psychological Sciences & Social Sciences, 58B*, S151–S159.

Beckman, M. (2004, July 30). Neuroscience: Crime, culpability, and the adolescent brain. *Science*, pp. 305, 596–599.

Becvar, D. S. (2000). Euthanasia decisions. In F. W. Kaslow et al. (Eds.), *Handbook of couple and family forensics: A sourcebook for mental health and legal professionals*. New York: Wiley.

Beets, M., Flay, B., Vuchinich, S., Li, K., Acock, A., & Snyder, F. (2009). Longitudinal patterns of binge drinking among first year college students with a history of tobacco use. *Drug and Alcohol Dependence, 103*, 1–8.

Begeny, J., & Martens, B. (2007). Inclusionary education in Italy: A literature review and call for more empirical research. *Remedial and Special Education, 28*, 80–94.

Begley, S. (1991, August 26). Choosing death. *Newsweek*, pp. 43–46.

Begley, S. (1995, July 10). Deliver, then depart. *Newsweek*, p. 62.

Beilin, H. (1996). Mind and meaning: Piaget and Vygotsky on causal explanation. *Human Development, 39*, 277–286.

Belcher, J. R. (2003). Stepparenting: Creating and recreating families in America today. *Journal of Nervous & Mental Disease, 191*, 837–838.

Belkin, L. (1999, July 25). Getting the girl. *New York Times Magazine*, pp. 26–35.

Belkin, L. (2004, September 12). The lessons of Classroom 506: What happens when a boy with cerebral palsy goes to kindergarten like all the other kids. *New York Times Magazine*, pp. 41–49.

Bell, H., Pellis, S., & Kolb, B. (2010). Juvenile peer play experience and the development of the orbitofrontal and medial prefrontal cortices. *Behavioural Brain Research, 207*, 7–13.

Bell, A., & Weinberg, M. S. (1978). *Homosexuality: A study of diversities among men and women*. New York: Simon & Schuster.

Bell, I. P. (1989). The double standard: Age. In J. Freeman (Ed.), *Women: A feminist perspective* (4th ed.). Mountain View, CA: Mayfield.

Belle, D. (1999). *The after-school lives of children: Alone and with others while parents work*. Mahwah, NJ: Lawrence Erlbaum.

Belsky, J. (2006). Early child care and early child development: Major findings from the NICHD Study of Early Child Care. *European Journal of Developmental Psychology, 3*, 95–110.

Belsky, J. (2009). Classroom composition, childcare history and social development: Are childcare effects disappearing or spreading? *Social Development, 18*, 230–238.

Belsky, J., Vandell, D. L., Burchinal, M., Clarke-Stewart, A. K., McCartney, K., & Owen, M. T. (2007). Are there long-term effects of early child care? *Child Development, 78*, 188–193.

Bem, S. (1987). Gender schema theory and its implications for child development: Raising gender-aschematic children in a gender-schematic society. In M. R. Walsh (Ed.), *The psychology of women: Ongoing debates*. New Haven, CT: Yale University Press.

Bender, H., Allen, J., McElhaney, K., Antonishak, J., Moore, C., Kelly, H., et al. (2007, December). Use of harsh physical discipline and developmental outcomes in adolescence. *Development and Psychopathology, 19*, 227–242.

Benelli, B., Belacchi, C., Gini, G., & Lucangeli, D. (2006, February). "To define means to say what you know about things": The development of definitional skills as metalinguistic acquisition. *Journal of Child Language, 33*, 71–97.

Benenson, J. F., & Apostoleris, N. H. (1993, March). Gender differences in group interaction in early childhood. Paper presented at the biennial meeting of the Society for Research in Child Development, New Orleans, LA.

Bengtson, V. L., Acock, A. C., Allen, K. R., & Dilworth-Anderson, P. (Eds.). (2004). *Sourcebook of family theory and research*. Thousand Oaks, CA: Sage Publications.

Benjamin, J., Ebstein, R. P., & Belmaker, R. H. (2002). Personality genetics, 2002. *Israel Journal of Psychiatry and Related Sciences, 39* [Special issue], 271–279.

Benjuya, N., Melzer, I., & Kaplanski, J. (2004). Aging-induced shifts from a reliance on sensory input to muscle cocontraction during balanced standing. *Journal of Gerontology: Series A: Biological Sciences and Medical Sciences, 59*, 166–171.

Bennani, L., Allali, F., Rostom, S., Hmamouchi, I., Khazzani, H., El Mansouri, L., Ichchou, L., Abourazzak, F. Z., Abougal, R., & Hajjaj-Hassouni, N. (2009). Relationship between historical height loss and vertebral fractures in postmenopausal women. *Clinical Rheumatology, 28*, 1283–1289.

Bennett, A. (1992, October 14). Lori Schiller emerges from the torments of schizophrenia. *Wall Street Journal*, pp. A1, A10.

Bennett, J. (2008, September 15). It's not just white girls. *Newsweek*, p. 96.

Benson, E. (2003, March). "Goo, gaa, grr?" *Monitor on Psychology*, 50–51.

Benson, H. (1993). The relaxation response. In D. Goleman & J. Guerin (Eds.), *Mind–body medicine: How to use your mind for better health*. Yonkers, NY: Consumer Reports Publications.

Benton, S.A., Robertson, J. M., Tseng, W-C., Newton, F. B., & Benton, S. L. (2003). Changes in counseling center client problems across 13 years. *Professional Psychology: Research and Practice, 34*, 66–72.

Berenbaum, S. A., & Bailey, J. M. (2003). Effects on gender identity of prenatal androgens and genital appearance: Evidence from girls with congenital adrenal hyperplasia. *Journal of Clinical Endocrinology and Metabolism, 88*, 1102–1106.

Berenson, P. (2005). *Understand and treat alcoholism*. New York: Basic Books.

Bergen, H., Martin, G., & Richardson, A. (2003). Sexual abuse and suicidal behavior: A model constructed from a large community sample of adolescents. *Journal of the American Academy of Child & Adolescent Psychiatry, 42*, 1301–1309.

Berger, L. (2000, April 11). What children do when home and alone. *New York Times*, p. F8.

Bergmann, R. L., Bergman, K. E., & Dudenhausen, J. W. (2008). Undernutrition and growth restriction in pregnancy. *Nestle Nutritional Workshop Series; Pediatrics Program, 61*, 1030121.

Bergstrom, M. J., & Holmes, M. E. (2000). Lay theories of successful aging after the death of a spouse: A network text analysis of bereavement advice. *Health Communication, 12*, 377–406.

Berkman, R. (Ed.). (2006). *Handbook of social work in health and aging*. New York: Oxford University Press.

Berko, J. (1958). The child's learning of English morphology. *Word, 14*, 150–177.

Berlin, L., Cassidy, J., & Appleyard, K. (2008). The influence of early attachments on other relationships. *Handbook of attachment: Theory, research, and clinical applications* (2nd ed.) (pp. 333–347). New York: Guilford Press.

Bernard, J. (1982). *The future of marriage*. New Haven, CT: Yale University Press.

Berndt, T. J. (1999). Friends' influence on students' adjustment to school. *Educational Psychologist, 34*, 15–28.

Berndt, T. J. (2002). Friendship quality and social development. *Current Directions in Psychological Science, 11*, 7–10.

Bernier, A., & Meins, E. (2008). A threshold approach to understanding the origins of attachment disorganization. *Developmental Psychology, 44*, 969–982.

Bernstein, N. (2004, March 7). Behind fall in pregnancy, a new teenage culture of restraint. *New York Times*, pp. 1, 20.

Berry, G. L. (2003). Developing children and multicultural attitudes: The systemic psychosocial influences of television portrayals in a multimedia society. *Cultural Diversity and Ethnic Minority Psychology, 9*, 360–366.

Berscheid, E. (1985). Interpersonal attraction. In G. Lindzey & E. Aronson (Eds.), *Handbook of social psychology* (3rd ed.). New York: Random House.

Berscheid, E., & Walster, E. (1974). Physical attractiveness. In G. Lindzey & E. Aronson (Eds.), *Handbook of social psychology* (3rd ed.). New York: Random House.

Bertin, E., & Striano, T. (2006, April). The still-face response in newborn, 1.5-, and 3-month-old infants. *Infant Behavior & Development, 29*, 294–297.

Besage, V. E. (2006). *Understanding girls' friendships, fights and feuds: A practical approach to girls' bullying*; Maidenhead, Berkshire: Open University Press/McGraw-Hill Education.

Bialystok, E., & Viswanathan, M. (2009). Components of executive control with advantages for bilingual children in two cultures. *Cognition, 112*, 494–500.

Biddle, B. J. (2001). *Social class, poverty, and education*. London: Falmer Press.

Bierman, K. L. (2004). *Peer rejection: Developmental processes and intervention strategies*. New York: Guilford Press.

Bigelow, A., & Rochat, P. (2006). Two-month-old infants' sensitivity to social contingency in mother–infant and stranger–infant interaction. *Infancy, 9*, 313–325.

Bijeljac-Babic, R., Bertoncini, J., & Mehler, J. (1993). How do 4-day-old infants categorize multisyllabic utterances? *Developmental Psychology, 29*, 711–721.

Bionna, R. (2006). *Coping with stress in a changing world*. New York: McGraw-Hill.

Bird, G., & Melville, K. (1994). *Families and intimate relationships*. New York: McGraw-Hill.

Birlouez-Aragon, I., & Tessier, F. (2003). Antioxidant vitamins and degenerative pathologies: A review of vitamin C. *Journal of Nutrition, Health & Aging, 7*, 103–109.

Biro, F., Striegel-Moore, R., Franko, D., Padgett, J., & Bean, J. (2006, October). Self-esteem in adolescent females. *Journal of Adolescent Health, 39*, 501–507.

Bishop, D. V. M., & Leonard, L. B. (Eds.). (2001). *Speech and language impairments in children: Causes, characteristics, intervention and outcome*. Philadelphia: Psychology Press.

Bishop, D., Meyer, B., Schmidt, T., & Gray, B. (2009). Differential investment behavior between grandparents and grandchildren: The role of paternity uncertainty. *Evolutionary Psychology, 7*, 66–77.

Bishop, J. (2006, April). Euthanasia, efficiency, and the historical distinction between killing a patient and allowing a patient to die. *Journal of Medical Ethics, 32*, 220–224.

Bjorklund, D. (2006). Mother knows best: Epigenetic inheritance, maternal effects, and the evolution of human intelligence. *Developmental Review, 26*, 213–242.

Bjorklund, D. F. (1997a). In search of a metatheory of cognitive development (or Piaget is dead and I don't feel so good myself). *Child Development, 68*, 144–148.

Bjorklund, D. F. (1997b). The role of immaturity in human development. *Psychological Bulletin, 122*, 153–169.

Bjorklund, D. F., & Ellis, B. (2005). Evolutionary psychology and child development: An emerging synthesis. In B. J. Ellis (Ed.), *Origins of the social mind: Evolutionary psychology and child development*. New York: Guilford Press.

Black, K. (2002). Associations between adolescent–mother and adolescent–best friend interactions. *Adolescence, 37*, 235–253.

Black, M. M., & Matula, K. (1999). *Essentials of Bayley Scales of Infant Development II assessment*. New York: Wiley.

Blaine, B. E., Rodman, J., & Newman, J. M. (2007). Weight loss treatment and psychological well-being: A review and meta-analysis. *Journal of Health Psychology, 12*, 66–82.

Blair, P., Sidebotham, P., Berry, P., Evans, M., & Fleming, P. (2006). Major epidemiological changes in sudden infant death syndrome: A 20-year population-based study in the UK. *Lancet, 367*, 314–319.

Blake, G., Velikonja, D., Pepper, V., Jilderda, I., & Georgiou, G. (2008). Evaluating an in-school injury prevention programme's effect on children's helmet wearing habits. *Brain Injury, 22*, 501–507.

Blake, J., & de Boysson-Bardies, B. (1992). Patterns in babbling: A cross-linguistic study. *Journal of Child Language, 19*, 51–74.

Blakemore, J. (2003). Children's beliefs about violating gender norms: Boys shouldn't look like girls, and girls shouldn't act like boys. *Sex Roles, 48*, 411–419.

Blakeslee, S. (1995, August 29). In brain's early growth, timetable may be crucial. *New York Times*, pp. C1, C3.

Blass, E. M., Ganchrow, J. R., & Steiner, J. E. (1984). Classical conditioning in newborn humans 2–48 hours of age. *Infant Behavior and Development, 7*, 223–235.

Blewitt, P., Rump, K., Shealy, S., & Cook, S. (2009). Shared book reading: When and how questions affect young children's word learning. *Journal of Educational Psychology, 101*.

Bloom, L. (1993). *The transition from infancy to language: Acquiring the power of expression*. New York: Cambridge University Press.

Blount, B. G. (1982). Culture and the language of socialization: Parental speech. In D. A. Wagner & H. W. Stevenson (Eds.), *Cultural perspectives on child development*. San Francisco: Freeman.

Blumenthal, S. (2000). Developmental aspects of violence and the institutional response. *Criminal Behaviour & Mental Health, 10*, 185–198.

Blumstein, P., & Schwartz, P. (1989). *American couples: Money, work, sex*. New York: Morrow.

Bober, S., Humphry, R., & Carswell, H. (2001). Toddlers' persistence in the emerging occupations of functional play and self-feeding. *American Journal of Occupational Therapy, 55*, 369–376.

Boeckx, C. (2010). *Language in cognition: Uncovering mental structures and the rules behind them*. New York: Wiley-Blackwell.

Boehm, K. E., & Campbell, N. B. (1995). Suicide: A review of calls to an adolescent peer listening phone service. *Child Psychiatry & Human Development, 26*, 61–66.

Boerner, K., Brennan, M., Horowitz, A., & Reinhardt, J. (2010). Tackling vision-related disability in old age: An application of the life-span theory of control to narrative data. *Journals of Gerontology: Series B: Psychological Sciences and Social Sciences, 65B*, 22–31.

Boerner, K., Wortman, C. B., & Bonanno, G. A. (2005). Resilient or at risk? A 4-year study of older adults who initially showed high or low distress following conjugal loss. *Journals of Gerontology: Series B, Psychological Sciences and Social Sciences, 60*, P67–P73.

Bogle, K. A. (2008). 'Hooking Up': What educators need to know, *Chronicle of Higher Education*, p. A32.

Bohlmeijer, E., Roemer, M., Cuijpers, P., & Smit, F. (2007). The effects of reminiscence on psychological well-being in order adults: A meta-analysis. *Aging & Mental Health, 11*.

Bohlmeijer, E., Westerhof, G., & de Jong, M. (2008). The effects of integrative reminiscence on meaning in life: Results of a quasi-experimental study. *Aging & Mental Health, 12*, 639–646.

Boivin, M., Perusse, D., Dionne, G., Saysset, V., Zoccolilo, M., Tarabulsy, G. M., Tremblay, N., & Tremblay, R. E. (2005). The genetic-environmental etiology of parents' perceptions and self-assessed behaviours toward their 5-month-old infants in a large twin and singleton sample. *Journal of Child Psychology and Psychiatry, 46*, 612–630.

Boles, T., Le, H., & Nguyen, H. (2010). Persons, organizations, and societies: The effects of collectivism and individualism on cooperation. *Social decision making: Social dilemmas, social values, and ethical judgments.* New York: Routledge / Taylor & Francis Group.

Bonanno, G. A. (2004). Loss, trauma, and human resilience: Have we underestimated the human capacity to thrive after extremely aversive events? *American Psychologist, 59*, 20–28.

Bonanno, G. A. (2009). *The other side of sadness.* New York: Basic Books.

Bonanno, G. A., Wortman, C. B., Lehman, D. R., Tweed, R. G., Haring, M., Sonnega, J., et al. (2002). Resilience to loss and chronic grief: A prospective study from preloss to 18-months postloss. *Journal of Personality and Social Psychology, 83*, 1150–1164.

Bonanno, G., Galea, S., Bucciarelli, A., & Vlahov, D. (2006). Psychological resilience after disaster: New York City in the aftermath of the September 11th terrorist attack. *Psychological Science, 17*, 181–186.

Boneva, B., Quinn, A., Kraut, R., Kiesler, S., & Shklovski, I. (2006). Teenage communication in the instant messaging era. In R. Kraut & M. Brynin, *Computers, phones, and the Internet: Domesticating information technology.* New York: Oxford University Press.

Bonke, B., Tibben, A., Lindhout, D., Clarke, A. J., & Stijnen, T. (2005). Genetic risk estimation by healthcare professionals. *Medical Journal of Autism, 182*, 116–118.

Bookheimer, S. Y., Strojwas, M. H., Cophen, M. S., Saunders, A. M., Pericak-Vance, M. A., Mazziotta, J. C., & Small, G. W. (2000, August 17). Patterns of brain activation in people at risk for Alzheimer's disease. *New England Journal of Medicine, 343*, 450–456.

Bookstein, F. L., Sampson, P. D., Streissguth, A. P., & Barr, H. M. (1996). Exploiting redundant measurement of dose and developmental outcome: New methods from the behavioral teratology of alcohol. *Developmental Psychology, 32*, 404–415.

Booth, C., Kelly, J., & Spieker, S. (2003). Toddlers' attachment security to child-care providers: The Safe and Secure Scale. *Early Education & Development, 14*, 83–100.

Bor, W., & Bor, C. (2004). Prevention and treatment of childhood and adolescent aggression and antisocial behaviour: A selective review. *Australian & New Zealand Journal of Psychiatry, 38*, 373–380.

Borden, M. E. (1998). *Smart start: The parents' complete guide to preschool education.* New York: Facts on File.

Bornstein, M., & Arterberry, M. (2003). Recognition, discrimination and categorization of smiling by 5-month-old infants. *Developmental Science, 6*, 585–599.

Bornstein, M. H., Cote, L., & Maital, S. (2004). Cross-linguistic analysis of vocabulary in young children: Spanish, Dutch, French, Hebrew, Italian, Korean, and American English. *Child Development, 75*, 1115–1139.

Bornstein, M. H., Haynes, O. M., O'Reilly, A. W., & Painter, K. M. (1996). Solitary and collaborative pretense play in early childhood: Sources of individual variation in the development of representational competence. *Child Development, 67*, 2910–2929.

Bornstein, M. H., & Lamb, M. E. (1992). *Development in infancy: An introduction.* New York: McGraw-Hill.

Bornstein, M. H., Putnick, D. L., Suwalsky, T. D., & Gini, M. (2006). Maternal chronological age, prenatal and perinatal history, social support, and parenting of infants. *Child Development, 77*, 875–892.

Bornstein, M. H., Tamis-LeMonda, C. S., Hahn, C., & Haynes, O. M. (2008). Maternal responsiveness to young children at three ages: Longitudinal analysis of a multi-dimensional, modular, and specific parenting construct. *Developmental Psychology, 44*, 867–874.

Bos, C. S., & Vaughn, S. S. (2005). *Strategies for teaching students with learning and behavior problems* (6th ed.). Boston: Allyn & Bacon.

Bos, H., Sandfort, T., de Bruyn, E., & Hakvoort, E. (2008). Same-sex attraction, social relationships, psychosocial functioning, and school performance in early adolescence. *Developmental Psychology, 44*, 59–68.

Bostwick, J. M. (2006). Do SSRIs cause suicide in children? The evidence is underwhelming. *Journal of Clinical Psychology, 62*, 235–241.

Bouchard, T. J., & McGue, M. (1981). Familial studies of intelligence: A review. *Science, 212*, 1055–1059.

Bouchard, T. J., Jr. (1997, September/October). Whenever the twain shall meet. *The Sciences*, 52–57.

Bouchard, T. J., Jr. (2004). Genetic influence on human psychological traits: A survey. *Current Directions in Psychological Science, 13*, 148–153.

Bouchard, T. J., Jr., Lykken, D. T., McGue, M., Segal, N. L., & Tellegen, A. (1990, October 12). Sources of human psychological differences: The Minnesota study of twins reared apart. *Science, 250*, 223–228.

Boucher, N., Bairam, A., & Beaulac-Baillargeon, L. (2008). A new look at the neonate's clinical presentation after in utero exposure to antidepressants in late pregnancy. *Journal of Clinical Psychopharmacology, 28*, 334–339.

Bourne, V., & Todd, B. (2004). When left means right: An explanation of the left cradling bias in terms of right hemisphere specializations. *Developmental Science, 7*, 19–24.

Bower, T. G. R. (1977). *A primer of infant development.* San Francisco: Freeman.

Bowers, K. E., & Thomas, P. (1995, August). Handle with care. *Harvard Health Letter*, pp. 6–7.

Bowlby, J. (1951). Maternal care and mental health. *Bulletin of the World Health Organization, 3*, 355–534.

Bracey, J., Bamaca, M., & Umana-Taylor, A. (2004). Examining ethnic identity and self-esteem among biracial and monoracial adolescents. *Journal of Youth & Adolescence, 33*, 123–132.

Brown, E. (2006, June). Behavioral identification and assessment of gifted and talented students. *Journal of Psychoeducational Assessment, 24*, 112–122.

Bracken, B., & Lamprecht, M. (2003). Positive self-concept: An equal opportunity construct. *School Psychology Quarterly, 18*, 103–121.

Bradshaw, M., & Ellison, C. (2008). Do genetic factors influence religious life? Findings from a behavior genetic analysis of twin siblings. *Journal for the Scientific Study of Religion, 47*, 529–544. http://search.ebscohost.com,.

Brady, L. S. (1995, January 29). Asia Linn and Chris Applebaum. *New York Times*, p. 47.

Brainerd, C. (2003). Jean Piaget, learning research, and American education. In B. Zimmerman (Ed.), *Educational psychology: A century of contributions.* Mahwah, NJ: Lawrence Erlbaum.

Brandis, J. (2010). $100,000 Purpose Prize Winner. Video download at http://www.purposeprize.org/video/yt_video.cfm?candidateID=3779 on January 18, 2010

Branje, S. J. T., van Lieshout, C. F. M., van Aken, M. A. G., & Haselager, G. J. T. (2004). Perceived support in sibling relationships and adolescent adjustment. *Journal of Child Psychology and Psychiatry, 45*, 1385–1396.

Branum, A. (2006). Teen maternal age and very preterm birth of twins. *Maternal & Child Health Journal, 10*, 229–233.

Brant, M. (2003, September 8). Log on and learn. *Newsweek*, E14.

Braun, K. L., Pietsch, J. H., & Blanchette, P. L. (Eds.). (2000). *Cultural issues in end-of-life decision making.* Thousand Oaks, CA: Sage Publications.

Bray, G. A. (2008). Is new hope on the horizon for obesity? *The Lancet, 372*, 1859–1860.

Brazelton, T. B. (1969). *Infants and mothers: Differences in development* (Rev. ed.). New York: Dell.

Brazelton, T. B. (1973). *The Neonatal Behavioral Assessment Scale.* Philadelphia: Lippincott.

Brazelton, T. B. (1983). *Infants and mothers: Differences in development* (Rev. ed.). New York: Dell.

Brazelton, T. B. (1990). Saving the bathwater. *Child Development, 61*, 1661–1671.

Brazelton, T. B., & Sparrow, J. D. (2003). *Discipline: The Brazelton way.* New York: Perseus.

Brecher, E. M., & the Editors of Consumer Reports Books. (1984). *Love, sex, and aging.* Mount Vernon, NY: Consumers Union.

Bredesen, D. (2009). Neurodegeneration in Alzheimer's disease: Caspases and synaptic element interdependence. *Molecular Neurodegeneration, 4*, 52–59.

Breheny, M., & Stephens, C. (2003). Healthy living and keeping busy: A discourse analysis of mid-aged women's attributions for menopausal experience. *Journal of Language & Social Psychology, 22*, 169–189.

Brehm, K. (2003). Lessons to be learned at the end of the day. *School Psychology Quarterly, 18*, 88–95.

Brehm, S. S. (1992). *Intimate relationships* (2nd ed.). New York: McGraw-Hill.

Bremner, G., & Fogel, A. (Eds.). (2004). *Blackwell handbook of infant development.* Malden, MA: Blackwell Publishers.

Breslau, N., Bohnert, K., & Koenen, K. (2010). The 9/11 terrorist attack and posttraumatic stress disorder revisited. *Journal of Nervous and Mental Disease, 198*, 539–543.

Bridges, J. S. (1993). Pink or blue: Gender-stereotypic perceptions of infants as conveyed by birth congratulations cards. *Psychology of Women Quarterly, 17*, 193–205.

Brier, N. (2008). Grief following miscarriage: A comprehensive review of the literature. *Journal of Women's Health, 17*, 451–464.

Briere, J. N., Berliner, L., Bulkley, J., Jenny, C., & Reid, T. (Eds.). (1997). *The APSAC handbook on child maltreatment.* Thousand Oaks, CA: Sage Publications.

Brody, N. (1993). Intelligence and the behavioral genetics of personality. In R. Plomin & G. E. McClearn (Eds.), *Nature, nurture, and psychology.* Washington, DC: American Psychological Association.

Bronfenbrenner, U. (1989). Ecological systems theory. In R. Vasta (Ed.), *Six theories of child development.* Greenwich, CT: JAI Press.

Bronfenbrenner, U. (2000). Ecological theory. In A. Kazdin (Ed.), *Encyclopedia of psychology.* Washington, DC: American Psychological Association/Oxford University Press.

Brook, U., & Tepper, I. (1997). High school students' attitudes and knowledge of food consumption and body image: Implications for school-based education. *Patient Education & Counseling, 30*, 282–288.

Brooks-Gunn, J. (2003). Do you believe in magic? What we can expect from early childhood intervention programs. *Social Policy Report, 17*, 1–16.

Brooks-Gunn, J., Klebanov, P. K., & Duncan, G. J. (1996). Ethnic differences in children's intelligence test scores: Role of economic deprivation, home environment, and maternal characteristics. *Child Development, 67*, 396–408.

Brotanek, J., Gosz, J., Weitzman, M., & Flores, G. (2007). Iron deficiency in early childhood in the United States: Risk factors and racial/ethnic disparities. *Pediatrics, 120*, 568–575.

Brown, B. B., & Klute, C. (2003). Friendships, cliques, and crowds. In G. R. Adams & M. D. Berzonsky (Eds.)., *Blackwell handbook of adolescence.* Malden, MA: Blackwell Publishing, 330–348.

Brown, J. V., Bakeman, R., Coles, C. D., Platzman, K. A., & Lynch, M. E. (2004). Prenatal cocaine exposure: A comparison of 2-year-old children in prenatal and non-parental care. *Child Development, 75*, 1282–1295.

Brown, C. P. (2009). Pivoting a prekindergarten program off the child or the standard? A case study of integrating the practices of early childhood education into elementary school. *The Elementary School Journal, 110,* 202–227.

Brown, E. L., & Bull, R. (2007). Can task modifications influence children's performance on false belief tasks? *European Journal of Developmental Psychology, 4,* 273–292.

Brown, J. D. (1998). *The self.* New York, McGraw-Hill.

Brown, R. (1973). *A first language.* Cambridge, MA: Harvard University Press.

Brown, W. M., Hines, M., & Fane, B. A. (2002). Masculinized finger length patterns in human males and females with congenital adrenal hyperplasia. *Hormones and Behavior, 42,* 380–386.

Browne, C. (2010). Review of 'Asian American elders in the twenty-first century: Key indicators of well-being'. *Journal of Women & Aging, 22,* 151-153.

Browne, K. (2006, March). Evolved sex differences and occupational segregation. *Journal of Organizational Behavior, 27,* 143–162.

Brownell, C., Nichols, S., Svetlova, M., Zerwas, S., & Ramani, G. (2010). The head bone's connected to the neck bone: When do toddlers represent their own body topography? *Child Development, 81,* 797-810.

Brownlee, S. (2002, January 21). Too heavy, too young. *Time,* pp. 21–23.

Brubaker, T. (1991). Families in later life: A burgeoning research area. In A. Booth (Ed.), *Contemporary families.* Minneapolis, MN: National Council on Family Relations.

Bruck, M., & Ceci, S. (2004). Forensic developmental psychology: Unveiling four common misconceptions. *Current Directions in Psychological Science, 13,* 229–232.

Brueggeman, I. (1999). Failure to meet ICPD goals will affect global stability, health of environment, and well-being, rights and potential of people. *Asian Forum News, 8.*

Bruskas, D. (2008). Children in foster care: A vulnerable population at risk. *Journal of Child and Adolescent Psychiatric Nursing, 21,* 70–77.

Bryant, C. D. (Ed.). (2003). *Handbook of death and dying.* Thousand Oaks, CA: Sage Publications.

Bryant, J., & Bryant, J. (2003). Effects of entertainment televisual media on children. In E. Palmer & B. Young (Eds.), *The faces of televisual media: Teaching, violence, selling to children.* Mahwah, NJ: Lawrence Erlbaum.

Bryant, J., & Bryant, J. A. (Eds.). (2001). *Television and the American family* (2nd ed.). Mahwah, NJ: Lawrence Erlbaum.

Buchanan, C. M., Eccles, J. S., & Becker, J. B. (1992). Are adolescents the victims of raging hormones? Evidence for activational effects of hormones on moods and behavior at adolescence. *Psychological Bulletin, 111,* 62–107.

Budd, K. (1999). The facts of life: Everything you wanted to know about sex (after 50). *Modern Maturity, 42,* 78.

Bugg, J., Zook, N., DeLosh, E., Davalos, D., & Davis, H. (2006, October). Age differences in fluid intelligence: Contributions of general slowing and frontal decline. *Brain and Cognition, 62,* 9–16.

Bull, M., & Durbin, D. (2008). Rear-facing car safety seats: Getting the message right. *Pediatrics, 121,* 619–620.

Bullinger, A. (1997). Sensorimotor function and its evolution. In J. Guimon (Ed.), *The body in psychotherapy* (pp. 25–29). Basil, Switzerland: Karger.

Bumpus, M. F., Crouter, A. C., & McHale, S. M. (2001). Parental autonomy granting during adolescence: Exploring gender differences in context. *Developmental Psychology, 37,* 163–173.

Burbach, J., & van der Zwaag, B. (2009). Contact in the genetics of autism and schizophrenia. *Trends in Neurosciences, 32,* 69–72. Available online at http://search.ebscohost.com

Burd, L., Cotsonas-Hassler, T. M., Martsolf, J. T., & Kerbeshian, J. (2003). Recognition and management of fetal alcohol syndrome. *Neurotoxicological Teratology, 25,* 681–688.

Burgess, K. B., & Rubin, K. H. (2000). Middle childhood: Social and emotional development. In A. E. Kazdin (Ed.), *Encyclopedia of psychology (Vol. 5).* Washington, DC: American Psychological Association.

Burgess, R. L., & Huston, T. L. (Eds.). (1979). *Social exchanges in developing relationships.* New York: Academic Press.

Burnett, P., & Proctor, R. (2002). Elementary school students' learner self-concept, academic self-concepts and approaches to learning. *Educational Psychology in Practice, 18,* 325–333.

Burnett-Wolle, S., & Godbey, G. (2007). Refining research on older adults' leisure: Implications of selection, optimization, and compensation and socioemotional selectivity theories. *Journal of Leisure Research, 39,* 498–513.

Burnham, M., Goodlin-Jones, B., & Gaylor, E. (2002). Nighttime sleep–wake patterns and self-soothing from birth to one year of age: A longitudinal intervention study. *Journal of Child Psychology & Psychiatry & Allied Disciplines, 43,* 713–725.

Burns, D. M. (2000). Cigarette smoking among the elderly: Disease consequences and the benefits of cessation. *American Journal of Health Promotion, 14,* 357–361.

Burrus-Bammel, L. L., & Bammel, G. (1985). Leisure and recreation. In J. E. Birren & K. W. Schaie (Eds.), *Handbook of the psychology of aging.* New York: Van Nostrand Reinhold.

Burt, V. L., & Harris, T. (1994). The third National Health and Nutrition Examination Survey: Contributing data on aging and health. *Gerontologist, 34,* 486–490.

Burton, A., Haley, W., & Small, B. (2006, May). Bereavement after caregiving or unexpected death: Effects on elderly spouses. *Aging & Mental Health, 10,* 319–326.

Burton, L., Henninger, D., Hafetz, J., & Cofer, J. (2009). Aggression, gender-typical childhood play, and a prenatal hormonal index. *Social Behavior and Personality, 37,* 105–116.

Busick, D., Brooks, J., Pernecky, S., Dawson, R., & Petzoldt, J. (2008). Parent food purchases as a measure of exposure and preschool-aged children's willingness to identify and taste fruit and vegetables. *Appetite, 51,* 468–473.

Buss, D. (2009). The great struggles of life: Darwin and the emergence of evolutionary psychology. *American Psychologist, 64,* 140–148. Available online at http://search.ebscohost.com.

Buss, D. M. (2003). *The evolution of desire: Strategies of human mating* (Revised ed.). New York: Basic Books.

Buss, D. M. (2004). *Evolutionary psychology: The new science of the mind* (2nd ed.). Boston: Allyn & Bacon.

Buss, D. M., & Reeve, H. K. (2003). Evolutionary psychology and developmental dynamics: Comment on Lickliter and Honeycutt. *Psychological Bulletin, 129,* 848–853.

Buss, D. M., et al. (1990). International preferences in selecting mates: A study of 37 cultures. *Journal of Cross-Cultural Psychology, 21,* 5–47.

Butler, K. G., & Silliman, E. R. (2002). *Speaking, reading, and writing in children with language learning disabilities: New paradigms in research and practice.* Mahwah, NJ: Lawrence Erlbaum.

Butler, R. N. (2002). The life review. *Journal of Geriatric Psychiatry, 35,* 7–10.

Butler, R. N., & Lewis, M. I. (1981). *Aging and mental health.* St. Louis: Mosby.

Butterworth, G. (1994). Infant intelligence. In J. Khalfa (Ed.), *What is intelligence? The Darwin College lecture series* (pp. 49–71). Cambridge, England: Cambridge University Press.

Buysse, D. J. (2005). Diagnosis and assessment of sleep and circadian rhythm disorders. *Journal of Psychiatric Practice, 11,* 102–115.

Byrne, A. (2000). Singular identities: Managing stigma, resisting voices. *Women's Studies Review, 7,* 13–24.

Cabrera, N., Shannon, J., & Tamis-LeMonda, C. (2007). Fathers' influence on their children's cognitive and emotional development: From toddlers to pre-K. *Applied Developmental Science, 11,* 208–213.

Cacciatore, J. (2010). The unique experiences of women and their families after the death of a baby. *Social Work in Health Care, 49,* 134–148.

Cacciatore, J., & Bushfield, S. (2007). Stillbirth: The mother's experience and implications for improving care. *Journal of Social Work in End-of-Life & Palliative Care, 3,* 59–79.

Cadinu, M. R., & Kiesner, J. (2000). Children's development of a theory of mind. *European Journal of Psychology of Education, 15,* 93–111.

Cain, V., Johannes, C., & Avis, N. (2003). Sexual functioning and practices in a multi-ethnic study of midlife women: Baseline results from SWAN. *Journal of Sex Research, 40,* 266–276.

Caino, S., Kelmansky, D., Lejarraga, H., & Adamo, P. (2004). Short-term growth at adolescence in healthy girls. *Annals of Human Biology, 31,* 182–195.

Calhoun, F., & Warren, K. (2007). Fetal alcohol syndrome: Historical perspectives. *Neuroscience & Biobehavioral Reviews, 31,* 168–171.

Calvert, S. L., Kotler, J. A., Zehnder, S., & Shockey, E. (2003). Gender stereotyping in children's reports about educational and informational television programs. *Media Psychology, 5,* 139–162.

Cami, J., & Farré, M. (2003). Drug addiction. *New England Journal of Medicine, 349,* 975–986.

Campbell, A., Shirley, L., & Candy, J. (2004). A longitudinal study of gender-related cognition and behaviour. *Developmental Science, 7,* 1–9.

Campbell, D., Scott, K., Klaus, M., & Falk, M. (2007). Female relatives or friends trained as labor doulas: Outcomes at 6 to 8 weeks postpartum. *Birth: Issues in Perinatal Care, 34,* 220–227.

Campbell, F., Ramey, C., & Pungello, E. (2002). Early childhood education: Young adult outcomes from the Abecedarian Project. *Applied Developmental Science, 6,* 42–57.

Campos, J. J., Langer, A., & Krowitz, A. (1970). Cardiac responses on the visual cliff in prelocomotor human infants. *Science, 170,* 196–197.

Camras, L., Meng, Z., & Ujiie, T. (2002). Observing emotion in infants: Facial expression, body behavior, and rater judgments of responses to an expectancy-violating event. *Emotion, 2,* 179–193.

Camras, L., Oster, H., Bakeman, R., Meng, Z., Ujiie, T., & Campos, J. (2007). Do infants show distinct negative facial expressions for fear and anger? Emotional expression in 11-month-old European American, Chinese, and Japanese Infants. *Infancy, 11,* 131–155.

Canals, J., Fernandez-Ballart, J., & Esparo, G. (2003). Evolution of Neonatal Behavior Assessment Scale scores in the first month of life. *Infant Behavior & Development, 26,* 227–237.

Cantin, V., Lavallière, M., Simoneau, M., & Teasdale, N. (2009). Mental workload when driving in a simulator: Effects of age and driving complexity. *Accident Analysis and Prevention, 41,* 763–771.

Caplan, L. J., & Barr, R. A. (1989). On the relationship between category intensions and extensions in children. *Journal of Experimental Child Psychology, 47,* 413–429.

Cappeliez, P., Guindon, M., & Robitaille, A. (2008). Functions of reminiscence and emotional regulation among older adults. *Journal of Aging Studies, 22,* 266–272.

Carlson, S. M., & Meltzoff, A. N. (2008). Bilingual experience and executive functioning in young children. *Developmental Science, 11,* 282–298.

Carmeli, A., & Josman, Z. (2006). The relationship among emotional intelligence, task performance, and organizational citizenship behaviors. *Human Performance, 19,* 403–419.

Carnegie Task Force on Meeting the Needs of Young Children. (1994). *Starting points: Meeting the needs of our youngest children.* New York: Carnegie Corporation.

Caron, A. (2009). Comprehension of the representational mind in infancy. *Developmental*

Carr, P. B., & Steele, C. M. (2009). Stereotype threat and inflexible perseverance in problem solving. *Journal of Experimental Social Psychology, 45,* 853–859.

Carrere, S., Buehlman, K. T., Gottman, J. M., Coan, J. A., & Ruckstuhl, L. (2000). Predicting marital stability and divorce in newlywed couples. *Journal of Family Psychology, 14,* 42–58.

Carroll, L. (2000, February 1). Is memory loss inevitable? Maybe not. *New York Times,* pp. D1, D7.

Carson, R. G. (2006). Neural pathways mediating bilateral interactions between the upper limbs. *Brain Research Review, 49,* 641–662.

Carstensen, L. L. (1995). Evidence for a life-span theory of socioemotional selectivity. *Current Directions in Psychological Science, 4,* 151–156.

Carton, A., & Aiello, J. (2009). Control and anticipation of social interruptions: Reduced stress and improved task performance. *Journal of Applied Social Psychology, 39,* 169–185.

Carver, C., & Scheier, M. (2002). Coping processes and adjustment to chronic illness. In A. Christensen & M. Antoni (Eds.), *Chronic physical disorders: Behavioral medicine's perspective* (pp. 47–68). Malden, MA: Blackwell Publishers.

Carver, L., & Vaccaro, B. (2007, January). 12-month-old infants allocate increased neural resources to stimuli associated with negative adult emotion. *Developmental Psychology, 43,* 54–69.

Cascalho, M., Ogle, B. M., & Platt, J. L. (2006). The future of organ transplantation. *Annals of Transplantation, 11,* 44–47.

Case, R. (1991). Stages in the development of the young child's first sense of self. *Developmental Review, 11,* 210–230.

Case, R. (1999). Conceptual development. In M. Bennett, *Developmental psychology: Achievements and prospects.* Philadelphia: Psychology Press.

Case, R., Demetriou, A., & Platsidou, M. (2001). Integrating concepts and tests of intelligence from the differential and developmental traditions. *Intelligence, 29,* 307–336.

Caserta, M., O'Connor, T., Wyman, P., Wang, H., Moynihan, J., Cross, W., et al. (2008). The associations between psychosocial stress and the frequency of illness, and innate and adaptive immune function in children. *Brain, Behavior, and Immunity, 22,* 933–940.

Caskey, R., Lindau, S., & Caleb Alexander, G. (2009). Knowledge and early adoption of the HPV vaccine among girls and young women: Results of a national survey. *Journal of Adolescent Health, 45,* 453–462.

Casper, M., & Carpenter, L. (2008). Sex, drugs, and politics: The HPV vaccine for cervical cancer. *Sociology of Health & Illness, 30,* 886–899.

Caspi, A. (2000). The child is father of the man: Personality continuities from childhood to adulthood. *Journal of Personality and Social Psychology, 78,* 158–172.

Caspi, A., & Moffitt, T. E. (1993). *Continuity amidst change: A paradoxical theory of personality coherence.* Manuscript submitted for publication.

Cassidy, J., & Berlin, L. J. (1994). The insecure/ambivalent pattern of attachment: Theory and research. *Child Development, 65,* 971–991.

Castel, A., & Craik, F. (2003). The effects of aging and divided attention on memory for item and associative information. *Psychology & Aging, 18,* 873–885.

Castro, J., Jones, D., Lopez, M., Barradas, I., & Weiss, S. (2010). Making the case for circumcision as a public health strategy: Opening the dialogue. *AIDS Patient Care and STDs, 24,* 367–372.

Castro-Schilo, L., & Kee, D. (2010). Gender differences in the relationship between emotional intelligence and right hemisphere lateralization for facial processing. *Brain and Cognition, 73,* 62–67.

Catell, R. B. (1987). *Intelligence: Its structure, growth, and action.* Amsterdam: North-Holland.

Cath, S., & Shopper, M. (2001). *Stepparenting: Creating and recreating families in America today.* Hillsdale, NJ: Analytic Press.

Cattani, A., Bonifacio, S., Fertz, M., Iverson, J., Zocconi, E., & Caselli, M. (2010). Communicative and linguistic development in preterm children: A longitudinal study from 12 to 24 months. *International Journal of Language & Communication Disorders, 45,* 162–173.

Cauce, A., & Domenech-Rodriguez, M. (2002). Latino families: Myths and realities. In J. M. Contreras, J. K. A. Kerns, & A. M. Neal-Barnett (Eds.), *Latino children and families in the United States.* Westport, CT: Praeger.

Caughlin, J. (2002). The demand/withdraw pattern of communication as a predictor of marital satisfaction over time. *Human Communication Research, 28,* 49–85.

Cavallini, A., Fazzi, E., & Viviani, V. (2002). Visual acuity in the first two years of life in healthy term newborns: An experience with the Teller Acuity Cards. *Functional Neurology: New Trends in Adaptive & Behavioral Disorders, 17,* 87–92.

Ceci, S. J., & Bruck, M. (1993). The suggestibility of the child witness: A historical review and synthesis. *Psychological Bulletin, 113,* 403–439.

Center for Communication and Social Policy, University of California. (1998). *National television violence study, Vol. 2.* Thousand Oaks, CA: Sage Publications.

Centers for Disease Control. (2003). Incidence-surveillance, epidemiology, and end results program, 1973–2000. Atlanta, GA: Author.

Centers for Disease Control. (2004). Health behaviors of adults: United States, 1999–2001. *Vital and Health Statistics, Series 10, no. 219.* Washington, DC: U.S. Department of Health and Human Services.

Centers for Disease Control and Prevention (2008). Prevalance of oversight, obesity and extreme obesity among adults: United States, trends 1960–62 through 2005–2006. *Health & Stats.* Washington, DC: U.S. Department of Health and Human Services.

Centers for Disease Control, National Vital Statistics Reports. (2009). Births: Preliminary Data for 2007. Statistics available online at www.cdc.gov/nchs/data/nvsr/nvsr57/nvsr57_12.pdf

Centers for Disease Control and Prevention (CDC). (2010). *Sexually Transmitted Disease Surveillance, 2008.* Atlanta, GA: U.S. Department of Health and Human Services.

Cerella, J. (1990). Aging and information-processing rate. In J. E. Birren & K. W. Schaie (Eds.), *Handbook of the psychology of aging* (3rd ed.). San Diego: Academic Press.

Chaffin, M. (2006). The changing focus of child maltreatment research and practice within psychology. *Journal of Social Issues, 62,* 663–684.

Chaker, A. M. (2003, September 23). Putting toddlers in a nursing home. *Wall Street Journal,* D1.

Chall, J. S. (1979). The great debate: Ten years later, with a modest proposal for reading stages. In L. B. Resnick & P. A. Weaver (Eds.), *Theory and practice of early reading.* Hillsdale, NJ: Lawrence Erlbaum.

Chall, J. (1992). The new reading debates: Evidence from science, art, and ideology. *Teachers College Record, 94,* 315–328.

Chamberlain, P., Price, J., Reid, J., Landsverk, J., Fisher, P., & Stoolmiller, M. (2006, April). Who disrupts from placement in foster and kinship care? *Child Abuse & Neglect, 30,* 409–424.

Chamorro-Premuzic, T., Harlaar, N., Greven, C., & Plomin, R. (2010). More than just IQ: A longitudinal examination of self-perceived abilities as predictors of academic performance in a large sample of UK twins. *Intelligence, 38,* 385–392.

Chan, D. W. (1997). Self-concept and global self-worth among Chinese adolescents in Hong Kong. *Personality & Individual Differences, 22,* 511–520.

Chang, I. J., Pettit, R. W., & Katsurada, E. (2006). Where and when to spank: A comparison between U.S. and Japanese college students. *Journal of Family Violence, 21,* 281–286.

Chao, R. K. (1994). Beyond parental control and authoritarian parenting style: Understanding Chinese parenting through the cultural notion of training. *Child Development, 65,* 1111–1119.

Chao, R. K. (2001). Extending research on the consequences of parenting style for Chinese Americans and European Americans. *Child Development, 72,* 1832–1843.

Chaplin, T., Gillham, J., & Seligman, M. (2009). Gender, anxiety, and depressive symptoms: A longitudinal study of early adolescents. *Journal of Early Adolescence, 29,* 307–327.

Chapple, A., Ziebland, S., McPherson, A., & Herxheimer, A. (2006, December). What people close to death say about euthanasia and assisted suicide: A qualitative study. *Journal of Medical Ethics, 32,* 706–710.

Charles, S., & Carstensen, L. (2010). Social and emotional aging. *Annual Review of Psychology, 61,* 383–409.

Charles, S. T., Mather, M., & Carstensen, L. L. (2003). Aging and emotional memory: The forgettable nature of negative images for older adults. *Journal of Experimental Psychology: General, 132,* 237–244.

Charles, S. T., Reynolds, C. A., & Gatz, M. (2001). Age-related differences and change in positive and negative affect over 23 years. *Journal of Personality and Social Psychology, 80,* 136–151.

Charness, N., & Boot, W. R. (2009). Aging and information technology use: Potential and barriers. *Current Directions in Psychological Science, 18,* 253–258.

Cheah, C., Leung, C., Tahseen, M., & Schultz, D. (2009). Authoritative parenting among immigrant Chinese mothers of preschoolers. *Journal of Family Psychology, 23,* 311–320.

Chelebowski, R. T., Schwartz, A. G., Wakelee, H., Anderson, G. L., Stefanick, M. L., Manson, J. E., Rodabough, R. J., Chien, J. W., Wactawski-Wende, J., Gass, M., Kotchen, J. M., Johnson, K. C., O'Sullivan, M. J., Ockene, J. K., Chen, C., Hubbell, F. A., & Women's Health Initiative Investigators. (2009). Oestrogen plus progestin and lung cancer in postmenopausal women (Women's Health Initiative trial): a post-hoc analysis of a randomised controlled trial. *Lancet, 374,* 1243–1251.

Chen, C., Mizuno, T., Elston, R., Kariuki, M., Hall, K., Unverzagt, F., et al. (2010). A comparative study to screen dementia and APOE genotypes in an ageing East African population. *Neurobiology of Aging, 31,* 732–740.

Chen, J., & Gardner, H. (2005). Assessment based on multiple-intelligences theory. In D. P. Flanagan & P. L. Harrison (Eds.), *Contemporary intellectual assessment: Theories, tests, and issues.* New York: Guilford Press.

Chen, S. X., & Bond, M. H. (2007). Explaining language priming effects: Further evidence for ethnic affirmation among Chinese-English bilinguals., *Journal of Language and Social Psychology, 26,* 398–406.

Cherlin, A., & Furstenberg, F. (1986). *The new American grandparent.* New York: Basic Books.

Cherney, I. (2003). Young children's spontaneous utterances of mental terms and the accuracy of their memory behaviors: A different methodological approach. *Infant & Child Development, 12,* 89–105.

Cherney, I., Kelly-Vance, L., & Glover, K. (2003). The effects of stereotyped toys and gender on play assessment in children aged 18–47 months. *Educational Psychology, 23,* 95–105.

Cherry, K. E., & Park, D. C. (1993). Individual difference and contextual variables influence spatial memory in younger and older adults. *Psychology and Aging, 8,* 517–526.

Cheung, A. H., Emslie, G. J., & Mayes, T. L. (2006). The use of antidepressants to treat depression in children and adolescents. *Canadian Medical Association Journal, 174,* 193–200.

Chien, S., Bronson-Castain, K., Palmer, J., & Teller, D. (2006). Lightness constancy in 4-month-old infants. *Vision Research, 46*, 2139–2148.

Child Health USA. (2007). U.S. Department of Health and Human Services, Health Resources and Services Administration, Maternal and Child Health Bureau. *Child Health USA 2007*. Rockville, MD: U.S. Department of Health and Human Services.

Childers, J. (2009). Early verb learners: Creative or not? *Monographs of the Society for Research in Child Development, 74*, 133–139. Available online at http://search.ebscohost.com

ChildStats.gov. (2000). *America's children 2000*. Washington, DC: National Maternal and Child Health Clearinghouse.

ChildStats.gov. (2009). *America's children 2009*. Washington, DC: National Maternal and Child Health Clearinghouse.

Chisolm, T., Willott, J., & Lister, J. (2003). The aging auditory system: Anatomic and physiologic changes and implications for rehabilitation. *International Journal of Audiology, 12*, 2S3–2S10.

Chiu, M. M., & McBride-Chang, C. (2006). Gender, context, and reading: A comparison of students in 43 countries. *Scientific Studies of Reading, 10*, 331–362.

Choi, H., & Marks, N. (2006, December). Transition to caregiving, marital disagreement, and psychological well-being: A prospective U.S. National Study. *Journal of Family Issues, 27*, 1701–1722.

Chomsky, N. (1968). *Language and mind*. New York: Harcourt Brace Jovanovich.

Chomsky, N. (1978). On the biological basis of language capacities. In G. A. Miller & E. Lennenberg (Eds.), *Psychology and biology of language and thought* (pp. 199–220). New York: Academic Press.

Chomsky, N. (1991). Linguistics and cognitive science: Problems and mysteries. In A. Kasher (Ed.), *The Chomskyan turn*. Cambridge, MA: Blackwell.

Chomsky, N. (1999). On the nature, use, and acquisition of language. In W. C. Ritchie & T. J. Bhatia (Eds.), *Handbook of child language acquisition*. San Diego: Academic Press.

Chomsky, N. (2005). Editorial: Universals of human nature. *Psychotherapy and Psychosomatics [serial online], 74*, 263–268.

Choy, C. M., Yeung, Q. S., Briton-Jones, C. M., Cheung, C. K., Lam, C. W., & Haines, C. J. (2002). Relationship between semen parameters and mercury concentrations in blood and in seminal fluid from subfertile males in Hong Kong. *Fertility and Sterility, 78*, 426–428.

Christakis, D., & Zimmerman, F. (2007). Violent television viewing during preschool is associated with antisocial behavior during school age. *Pediatrics, 120*, 993–999.

Christophersen, E. R., & Mortweet, S. L. (2003). Disciplining your child effectively. In E. R. Christophersen & S. L. Mortweet, *Parenting that works: Building skills that last a lifetime*. Washington, DC: American Psychological Association.

Chronis, A., Jones, H., & Raggi, V. (2006, June). Evidence-based psychosocial treatments for children and adolescents with attention-deficit/hyperactivity disorder. *Clinical Psychology Review, 26*, 486–502.

Chung, S. A., Wei, A. Q., Connor, D. E., Webb, G. C., Molloy, T., Pajic, M., & Diwan, A. D. (2007). Nucleus pulposus cellular longevity by telomerase gene therapy. *Spine, 15*, 1188–1196.

Cianciolo, A. T., Matthew, C., & Sternberg, R. J. (2006). Tacit knowledge, practical intelligence, and expertise. In K. A. Ericsson, N. Charness, P. J. Feltovich, & R. R. Hoffman, *The Cambridge handbook of expertise and expert performance*. New York: Cambridge University Press.

Cicchetti, D. (1996). Child maltreatment: Implications for developmental theory and research. *Human Development, 39*, 18–39.

Cicchetti, D. (2003). Neuroendocrine functioning in maltreated children. In D. Cicchetti and E. Walker (Eds.), *Neurodevelopmental mechanisms in psychopathology*. New York: Cambridge University Press.

Cicchetti, D., & Cohen, D. J. (2006). *Developmental psychopathology, Vol. 1: Theory and method* (2nd ed.). Hoboken, NJ: Wiley.

CIRE (Cooperative Institutional Research Program of the American Council on Education). (1990). *The American freshman: National norms for fall 1990*. Los Angeles: American Council on Education.

Cirulli, F., Berry, A., & Alleva, E. (2003). Early disruption of the mother–infant relationship: Effects on brain plasticity and implications for psychopathology. *Neuroscience & Biobehavioral Reviews, 27*, 73–82.

Clark, J. E., & Humphrey, J. H. (Eds.). (1985). *Motor development: Current selected research*. Princeton, NJ: Princeton Book Company.

Clark, K. B., & Clark, M. P. (1947). Racial identification and preference in Negro children. In T. M. Newcomb & E. L. Hartley (Eds.), *Readings in social psychology*. New York: Holt, Rinehart & Winston.

Clark, L. (2010). Decision-making during gambling: An integration of cognitive and psychobiological approaches. *Philosophical Transactions of the Royal Society of London: B Biological Sciences, 365*, 319–330.

Clark, M. S., & Mills, J. (1993). The difference between communal and exchange relationships: What it is and is not. *Personality and Social Psychology Bulletin, 19*, 684–691.

Clark, R. (1998). *Expertise*. Silver Spring, MD: International Society for Performance Improvement.

Clark, R., Hyde, J. S., Essex, M. J., & Klein, M. H. (1997). Length of maternity leave and quality of mother–infant interactions. *Child Development, 68*, 364–383.

Clarke, A. R., Barry, R. J., McCarthy, R., Selikowitz, M., & Johnstone, S. J. (2008). Effects of imipramine hydrochloride on the EEG of children with Attention-Deficit/Hyperactivity Disorder who are non-responsive to stimulants. *International Journal of Psychophysiology, 68*, 186–192.

Clarke-Stewart, K., & Allhusen, V. (2002). Nonparental caregiving. In M. Bornstein (Ed.), *Handbook of parenting: Vol. 3: Being and becoming a parent* (2nd ed.). Mahwah, NJ: Lawrence Erlbaum.

Clauss-Ehlers, C. (2008). Sociocultural factors, resilience, and coping: Support for a culturally sensitive measure of resilience. *Journal of Applied Developmental Psychology, 29*, 197–212.

Claxton, L., McCarty, M., & Keen, R. (2009). Self-directed action affects planning in tool-use tasks with toddlers. *Infant Behavior & Development, 32*, 230–233.

Claxton, L. J., Keen R., & McCarty, M. E. (2003). Evidence of motor planning in infant reaching behavior. *Psychological Science, 14*, 354–356.

Clifford, S. (2009, June 2). Online, "a reason to keep on going." *New York Times*, p. D5.

Clinton, J. F., & Kelber, S. T. (1993). Stress and coping in fathers of newborns: Comparisons of planned versus unplanned pregnancy. *International Journal of Nursing Studies, 30*, 437–443.

Closson, L. (2009). Status and gender differences in early adolescents' descriptions of popularity. *Social Development, 18*, 412–426.

Cnattingius, S., Berendes, H., & Forman, M. (1993). Do delayed childbearers face increased risks of adverse pregnancy outcomes after the first birth? *Obstetrics and Gynecology, 81*, 512–516.

Cobbe, E. (2003, September 25). France ups heat toll. *CBS Evening News*.

Cohen, J. (1999, March 19). Nurture helps mold able minds. *Science, 283*, 1832–1833.

Cohen, L. B., & Cashon, C. H. (2003). Infant perception and cognition. In R. M. Lerner & M. A. Easterbrooks (Eds.), *Handbook of psychology: Developmental psychology, Vol. 6*. New York: Wiley.

Cohen, L., Wang, B., Nonacs, R., Viguera, A., Lemon, E., & Freeman, M. (2010). Treatment of mood disorders during pregnancy and postpartum. *Psychiatric Clinics of North America, 33*, 273–293.

Cohen, S., Hamrick, N., Rodriguez, M. S., Feldman, P. J., Rabin B. S., & Manuck, S. B. (2002). Reactivity and vulnerability to stress-associated risk for upper respiratory illness. *Psychosomatic Medicine, 64*, 302–310.

Cohen, S., Tyrell, D. A., & Smith, A. P. (1997). Psychological stress in humans and susceptibility to the common cold. In T. W. Miller (Ed.), *International Universities Press Stress and Health Series, Monograph 7. Clinical disorders and stressful life events* (pp. 217–235). Madison, CT: International Universities Press.

Cohn, R. M. (1982). Economic development and status change of the aged. *American Journal of Sociology, 87*, 1150–1161.

Cokley, K. (2003). What do we know about the motivation of African American students? Challenging the "anti-intellectual" myth. *Harvard Educational Review, 73*, 524–558.

Colby, A., & Kohlberg, L. (1987). *The measurement of moral adjudgment* (Vols. 1–2). New York: Cambridge University Press.

Colcombe, S. J., Erickson, K. I., Scalf, P. E., Kim, J. S., Prakash, R., McAuley, E., Elavsky, S., Marquez, D. X., Hu, L., & Kramer, A. F. (2006). Aerobic exercise training increases brain volume in aging humans. *Journals of Gerontology: Series A: Biological Sciences and Medical Sciences, 61*, 1166–1170.

Cole, D. A., Maxwell, S. E., Martin, J. M., Peeke, L. G., Seroczynski, A. D., Tram, J. M., Joffman, K. B., Ruiz, M. D., Jacquez, F., & Maschman, T. (2001). The development of multiple domains of child and adolescent self-concept: A cohort sequential longitudinal design. *Child Development, 72*, 1723–1746.

Cole, M. (1992). Culture in development. In M. H. Bornstein & M. E. Lamb (Eds.), *Developmental psychology: An advanced textbook* (3rd ed.). Hillsdale, NJ: Lawrence Erlbaum.

Cole, P., Dennis, T., Smith-Simon, K., & Cohen, L. (2009). Preschoolers' emotion regulation strategy understanding: Relations with emotion socialization and child self-regulation. *Social Development, 18*, 324–352.

Coleman, H., Chan, C., Ferris, F., & Chew, E. (2008). Age-related macular degeneration. *The Lancet, 372*, 1835–1845.

Coleman, P. (2005, July). Editorial: Uses of reminiscence: Functions and benefits. *Aging & Mental Health, 9*, 291–294.

Colen, C., Geronimus, A., & Phipps, M. (2006, September). Getting a piece of the pie? The economic boom of the 1990s and declining teen birth rates in the United States. *Social Science & Medicine, 63*, 1531–1545.

College Board. (2005). *2001 college bound seniors are the largest, most diverse group in history*. New York: College Board.

Collins, W., & Andrew, L. (2004). Changing relationships, changing youth: Interpersonal contexts of adolescent development. *Journal of Early Adolescence, 24*, 55–62.

Collins, W., & Doolittle, A. (2006, December). Personal reflections of funeral rituals and spirituality in a Kentucky African American family. *Death Studies, 30*, 957–969.

Collishaw, S., Pickles, A., Messer, J., Rutter, M., Shearer, C., & Maughan, B. (2007). Resilience to adult psychopathology following childhood maltreatment: Evidence from a community sample. *Child Abuse & Neglect, 31*, 211–229.

Colom, R., Lluis-Font, J. M., & Andrés-Pueyo, A. (2005). The generational intelligence gains are caused by decreasing variance in the lower half of the distribution: Supporting evidence for the nutrition hypothesis. *Intelligence, 33*, 83–91.

Colombo, J., & Mitchell, D. (2009). Infant visual habituation. *Neurobiology of Learning and Memory, 92*, 225–234.

Colpin, H., & Soenen, S. (2004). Bonding through an adoptive mother's eyes. *Midwifery Today Int Midwife, 70*, 30–31.

Coltrane, S., & Adams, M. (1997). Children and gender. In T. Arendell (Ed.), *Contemporary parenting: Challenges and* issues. *Understanding Families, Vol. 9* (pp. 219–253). Thousand Oaks, CA: Sage Publications.

Coltrane, S., & Shih, K. (2010). Gender and the division of labor. *Handbook of gender research in psychology, Vol. 2: Gender research in social and applied psychology.* New York: Springer Publishing Co.

Committee on Children, Youth and Families. (1994). *When you need child day care.* Washington, DC: American Psychological Association.

Compton, R., & Weissman, D. (2002). Hemispheric asymmetries in global-local perception: Effects of individual differences in neuroticism. *Laterality, 7,* 333–350.

Comunian, A. L., & Gielen, U. P. (2000). Sociomoral reflection and prosocial and antisocial behavior: Two Italian studies. *Psychological Reports, 87,* 161–175.

Condly, S. (2006, May). Resilience in children: A review of literature with implications for education. *Urban Education, 41,* 211–236.

Condry, J., & Condry, S. (1976). Sex differences: A study of the eye of the beholder. *Child Development, 47,* 812–819.

Conel, J. L. (1930/1963). *Postnatal development of the human cortex* (Vols. 1–6). Cambridge, MA: Harvard University Press.

Conger, D., & Long, M. (2010). Why are men falling behind? Gender gaps in college performance and persistence. *Annals of the American Academy of Political and Social Science, 627,* 184–214.

Conn, V. S. (2003). Integrative review of physical activity intervention research with aging adults. *Journal of the American Geriatrics Society, 51,* 1159–1168.

Connell-Carrick, K. (2006). Early child care and early child development: Major findings of the NICHD Study of Early Child Care. *Child Welfare Journal, 85,* 819–836.

Conner, K., & Goldston, D. (2007, March). Rates of suicide among males increase steadily from age 11 to 21: Developmental framework and outline for prevention. *Aggression and Violent Behavior, 12(2),* 193–207.

Connidis, I. (2010). *Family ties and aging* (2nd ed.). Thousand Oaks, CA: Pine Forge Press/Sage Publications.

Conrad, P., Carr, P., Knight, S., Renfrew, M., Dunn, M., & Pololi, L. (2010). Hierarchy as a barrier to advancement for women in academic medicine. *Journal of Women's Health, 19,* 799–805.

Consedine, N., Magai, C., & King, A. (2004). Deconstructing positive affect in later life: A differential functionalist analysis of joy and interest. *International Journal of Aging & Human Development, 58,* 49–68.

Cook, E., Buehler, C., & Henson, R. (2009). Parents and peers as social influences to deter antisocial behavior. *Journal of Youth and Adolescence, 38,* 1240–1252.

Coon, K. D., Myers, A. J., Craig, D. W., Webster, J. A., Pearson, J. V., Lince, D. H., Zismann, V. L., Beach, T. G., Leung, D., Bryden, L., Halperin, R. F., Marlowe, L., Kaleem, M., Walker, D. G., Ravid, R., Heward, C. B., Rogers, J., Papassotiropoulos, A., Reiman, E. M., Hardy, J., & Stephan, D. A. (2007). A high-density whole-genome association study reveals that APOE is the major susceptibility gene for sporadic late-onset Alzheimer's disease. *Journal of Clinical Psychiatry, 68,* 613–618.

Corballis, P. (2003). Visuospatial processing and the right-hemisphere interpreter. *Brain & Cognition, 53,* 171–176.

Corbin, J. (2007). Reactive attachment disorder: A biopsychosocial disturbance of attachment. *Child & Adolescent Social Work Journal, 24,* 539–552.

Corcoran, J., & Pillai, V. (2007, January). Effectiveness of secondary pregnancy prevention programs: A meta-analysis. *Research on Social Work Practice, 17,* 5–18.

Cordes, S., & Brannon, E. (2009). Crossing the divide: Infants discriminate small from large numerosities. *Developmental Psychology, 45,* 1583–1594.

Cornforth, S. (2010). Bridging the gap: Weaving humanism and poststructuralism. *British Journal of Guidance & Counselling, 38,* 167–178.

Cornish, K., Turk, J., & Hagerman, R. (2008). The fragile X continuum: New advances and perspectives. *Journal of Intellectual Disability Research, 52,* 469–482.

Corr, C. (2010a). Children, development, and encounters with death, bereavement, and coping. *Children's encounters with death, bereavement, and coping.* New York: Springer Publishing Co.

Corr, C. (2010b). Children's emerging awareness and understandings of loss and death. *Children's encounters with death, bereavement, and coping.* New York: Springer Publishing Co.

Corr, C. A., Nabe, C. M., & Corr, D. M. (2000). *Death and dying, life and living* (3rd ed.). Belmont, CA: Wadsworth/Thomson Learning.

Corr, C., Nabe, C., & Corr, D. (2006). *Death & dying, life & living* (6th ed.). Belmont, CA: Thomson Wadsworth.

Corr, C., Nabe, C., & Corr, D. (2010). *Death & dying, life & living* (8th ed.). Belmont, CA: Thomson Wadsworth.

Costa, P. T., & McCrae, R. R. (1997). Longitudinal stability of adult personality. In R. Hogan, J. A. Johnson, & S. R. Briggs (Eds.), *Handbook of personality psychology* (pp. 269–290). San Diego, CA: Academic Press.

Costa, P. T., Jr., & McCrae, R. R. (1988). Personality in adulthood: A six-year longitudinal study of self-report and spouse ratings on the NEO Personality Inventory. *Journal of Personality and Social Psychology, 54,* 853–863.

Costa, P. T., Jr., & McCrae, R. R. (1989). Personality continuity and the changes of adult life. In M. Storandt & G. R. VandenBos (Eds.), *The adult years: Continuity and change.* Washington, DC: American Psychological Association.

Costello, E., Compton, S., & Keeler, G. (2003). Relationships between poverty and psychopathology: A natural experiment. *JAMA: The Journal of the American Medical Association, 290,* 2023–2029.

Costello, E., Sung, M., Worthman, C., & Angold, A. (2007, April). Pubertal maturation and the development of alcohol use and abuse. *Drug and Alcohol Dependence, 88,* S50–S59.

Cotrufo, P., Monteleone, P., d'Istria, M., Fuschino, A., Serino, I., & Maj, M. (2000). Aggressive behavioral characteristics and endogenous hormones in women with bulimia nervosa. *Neuropsychobiology, 42,* 58–61.

Coulson, N. S., Buchanan, H., & Aubeeluck, A. (2007). Social support in cyberspace: A content analysis of communication within a Huntington's disease online support group. *Patient Education and Counseling, 68,* 173–178.

Couperus, J., & Nelson, C. (2006). Early brain development and plasticity. *Blackwell handbook of early childhood development.* New York: Blackwell Publishing.

Courage, M., & Howe, M. (2010). To watch or not to watch: Infants and toddlers in a brave new electronic world. *Developmental Review, 30,* 101–115.

Courtney, E., Gamboz, J., & Johnson, J. (2008). Problematic eating behaviors in adolescents with low self-esteem and elevated depressive symptoms. *Eating Behaviors, 9,* 408–414.

Couzin, J. (2002, June 21). Quirks of fetal environment felt decades later. *Science, 296,* 2167–2169.

Couzin, J. (2004, July 23). Volatile chemistry: Children and antidepressants. *Science, 305,* 468–470.

Cowan, C. P., & Cowan, P. A. (1992). *When partners become parents.* New York: Wiley.

Cowgill, D. O., & Holmes, L. D. (1972). *Aging and modernization.* New York: Appleton-Century-Crofts.

Cowley, G. (2000, January 31). Alzheimer's: Unlocking the mystery. *Newsweek,* pp. 46–51.

Craik, F., & Salthouse, T. A. (Eds.). (1999). *The handbook of aging and cognition* (2nd ed.). Mahwah, NJ: Erlbaum.

Crane, E., & Morris, J. (2006). Changes in maternal age in England and Wales—Implications for Down syndrome. *Down Syndrome: Research & Practice, 10,* 41–43.

Cratty, B. (1979). *Perceptual and motor development in infants and children* (2nd ed.). Englewood Cliffs, NJ: Prentice-Hall.

Cratty, B. (1986). *Perceptual and motor development in infants and children* (3rd ed.). Englewood Cliffs, NJ: Prentice-Hall.

Crawford, D., Houts, R., & Huston, T. (2002). Compatibility, leisure, and satisfaction in marital relationships. *Journal of Marriage & Family, 64,* 433–449.

Crawford, M., & Unger, R. (2004). *Women and gender: A feminist psychology* (4th ed.). New York: McGraw-Hill.

Crawley, A., Anderson, D., & Santomero, A. (2002). Do children learn how to watch television? The impact of extensive experience with *Blue's Clues* on preschool children's television viewing behavior. *Journal of Communication, 52,* 264–280.

Crisp, A., Gowers, S., Joughin, N., McClelland, L., Rooney, B., Nielsen, S., et al. (2006, May). Anorexia nervosa in males: Similarities and differences to anorexia nervosa in females. *European Eating Disorders Review, 14,* 163–167.

Crisp, R., Bache, L., & Maitner, A. (2009). Dynamics of social comparison in counter-stereotypic domains: Stereotype boost, not stereotype threat, for women engineering majors. *Social Influence, 4,* 171–184.

Critser, G. (2003). *Fat land: How Americans became the fattest people in the world.* Boston: Houghton Mifflin.

Crivello, F., Lemaître, H., Dufouil, C., Grassiot, B., Delcroix, N., Tzourio-Mazoyer, N., et al. (2010). Effects of ApoE-☒4 allele load and age on the rates of grey matter and hippocampal volumes loss in a longitudinal cohort of 1186 healthy elderly persons. *NeuroImage, 53,* 1064–1069.

Crosnoe, R., & Elder, G. H., Jr. (2002). Successful adaptation in the later years: A life course approach to aging. *Social Psychology Quarterly, 65,* 309–328.

Cross, T., Cassady, J., Dixon, F., & Adams, C. (2008). The psychology of gifted adolescents as measured by the MMPI-A. *Gifted Child Quarterly, 52,* 326–339.

Cross, W. E., & Cross, T. B. (2008). The big picture: Theorizing self-concept structure and construal. In P. B. Pedersen et al. (Eds.), *Counseling across cultures* (6th ed.). Thousand Oaks, CA: Sage Publications.

Crowl, A., Ahn, S., & Baker, J. (2008). A meta-analysis of developmental outcomes for children of same-sex and heterosexual parents. *Journal of GLBT Family Studies, 4,* 385–407.

Crowley, B., Hayslip, B., & Hobdy, J. (2003). Psychological hardiness and adjustment to life events in adulthood. *Journal of Adult Development, 10,* 237–248.

Crowther, M., & Rodriguez, R. (2003). A stress and coping model of custodial grandparenting among African Americans. In B. Hayslip & J. Patrick (Eds.), *Working with custodial grandparents.* New York: Springer Publishing Co.

Cruz, N., & Bahna, S. (2006, October). Do foods or additives cause behavior disorders? *Psychiatric Annals, 36,* 724–732.

Cuddy, A. J. C., & Fiske, S. T. (2004). Doddering but dear: Process, content, and function in stereotyping of older persons. In T. Nelson (Ed.), *Ageism: Stereotyping and prejudice against older persons.* Cambridge, MA: MIT Press.

Cuervo, A. (2008). Calorie restriction and aging: The ultimate "cleansing diet." *Journals of Gerontology: Series A: Biological Sciences and Medical Sciences, 63A,* 547–549.

Culbertson, J. L., & Gyurke, J. (1990). Assessment of cognitive and motor development in infancy and childhood. In J. H. Johnson & J. Goldman (Eds.), *Developmental assessment in clinical child psychology: A handbook* (pp. 100–131). New York: Pergamon Press.

Cullen, K. (2010, January 10). Too little too late against bully tactics. *Boston Globe,* p. 12.

Culver, V. (2003, August 26). Funeral expenses overwhelm survivors: $10,000-plus tab often requires aid. *Denver Post,* p. B2.

Cumming, G. P., Currie, H. D., Moncur, R., & Lee, A. J. (2009). Web-based survey on the effect of menopause on women's libido in a computer-literate population. *Menopause International, 15,* 8–12.

Cummings, E., & Henry, W. E. (1961). *Growing old*. New York: Basic Books.

Curlette, W., & Kern, R. (2010). Ethics, research, and applications. *The Journal of Individual Psychology, 66*, 133–134.

Dabelko, H., & Zimmerman, J. (2008). Outcomes of adult day services for participants: A conceptual model. *Journal of Applied Gerontology, 27*, 78–92.

Dagher, A., Tannenbaum, B., Hayashi, T., Pruessner, J., & McBride, D. (2009). An acute psychosocial stress enhances the neural response to smoking cues. *Brain Research, 129*, 340–348.

Dahl, E., & Birkelund, E. (1997). Health inequalities in later life in a social democratic welfare state. *Social Science & Medicine, 44*, 871–881.

Dahl, R. (2008). Biological, developmental, and neurobehavioral factors relevant to adolescent driving risks. *American Journal of Preventive Medicine, 35*, S278–SS284.

Dailard, C. (2006, Summer). Legislating against arousal: The growing divide between federal policy and teenage sexual behavior. *Guttmacher Policy Review, 9*, 12–16.

Daley, K. C. (2004). Update on sudden infant death syndrome. *Current Opinion in Pediatrics, 16*, 227–232.

Dalton, T. C., & Bergenn, V. W. (2007). *Early experience, the brain, and consciousness: An historical and interdisciplinary synthesis*. Mahwah, N: Lawrence Erlbaum.

Damon, W. (1983). *Social and personality development*. New York: Norton.

Damon, W., & Hart, D. (1988). *Self-understanding in childhood and adolescence*. New York: Cambridge University Press.

Daniel, S., & Goldston, D. (2009). Interventions for suicidal youth: A review of the literature and developmental considerations. *Suicide and Life-Threatening Behavior, 39*, 252–268.

Daniels, H. (Ed.). (1996). *An introduction to Vygotsky*. New York: Routledge.

Dardenne, B., Dumont, M., & Bollier, T. (2007). Insidious dangers of benevolent sexism: Consequences for women's performance. *Journal of Personality and Social Psychology, 93*, 764–779.

Dare, W. N., Noronha, C. C., Kusemiju, O. T., & Okanlawon, O. A. (2002). The effect of ethanol on spermatogenesis and fertility in male Sprague-Dawley rats pretreated with acetylsalicylic acid. *Nigeria Postgraduate Medical Journal, 9*, 194–198.

Darnton, N. (1990, June 4). Mommy vs. Mommy. *Newsweek*, pp. 64–67.

Dasen, P., Inhelder, B., Lavallee, M., & Retschitzki, J. (1978). *Naissance de l'intelligence chez l'enfant Baoule de Cote d'Ivoire*. Berne: Hans Huber.

Dasen, P., Ngini, L., & Lavallee, M. (1979). Cross-cultural training studies of concrete operations. In L. H. Eckenberger, W. J. Lonner, & Y. H. Poortinga (Eds.), *Cross-cultural contributions to psychology*. Amsterdam: Swets & Zeilinger.

Dasen, P. R., & Mishra, R. C. (2002). Cross-cultural views on human development in the third millennium. In W. W. Hartup & R. K. Silbereisen (Eds.), *Growing points in developmental science: An introduction*. Philadelphia: Psychology Press.

Davenport, B., & Bourgeois, N. (2008). Play, aggression, the preschool child, and the family: A review of literature to guide empirically informed play therapy with aggressive preschool children. *International Journal of Play Therapy, 17*, 2–23.

Davey, M. (2007, June 2). Kevorkian freed after years in prison for aiding suicide. *New York Times*, p. A1.

Davey, M., Eaker, D. G., & Walters, L. H. (2003). Resilience processes in adolescents: Personality profiles, self-worth, and coping. *Journal of Adolescent Research, 18*, 347–362.

Davies, S., & Denton, M. (2002). The economic well-being of older women who become divorced or separated in mid- or later life. *Canadian Journal on Aging, 21*, 477–493.

Davis, A. (2003). *Your divorce, your dollars: Financial planning before, during, and after divorce*. Bellingham, WA: Self-Counsel Press.

Davis, A. (2008). Children with Down syndrome: Implications for assessment and intervention in the school. *School Psychology Quarterly, 23*, 271–281. Available online at http://search.ebscohost.com

Davis, C., & Nolen-Hoeksema, S. (2001). Loss and meaning: How do people make sense of loss? *American Behavioral Scientist, 44*, 726–741.

Davis, D., Shaver, P., Widaman, K., Vernon, M., Follette, W., & Beitz, K. (2006, December). "I can't get no satisfaction": Insecure attachment, inhibited sexual communication, and sexual dissatisfaction. *Personal Relationships, 13*, 465–483.

Davis, M., & Emory, E. (1995). Sex differences in neonatal stress reactivity. *Child Development, 66*, 14–27.

Davis, M., Zautra, A., Younger, J., Motivala, S., Attrep, J., & Irwin, M. (2008). Chronic stress and regulation of cellular markers of inflammation in rheumatoid arthritis: Implications for fatigue. *Brain, Behavior, and Immunity, 22*, 24–32.

Davis, T. S., Saltzburg, S., & Locke, C. R. (2009). Supporting the emotional and psychological well being of sexual minority youth: Youth ideas for action. *Children and Youth Services Review, 31*, 1030–1041.

Davis-Kean, P. E., & Sandler, H. M. (2001). A meta-analysis of measures of self-esteem for young children: A framework for future measures. *Child Development, 72*, 887–906.

Davison, G. C. (2005). Issues and nonissues in the gay-affirmative treatment of patients who are gay, lesbian, or bisexual. *Clinical Psychology: Science & Practice, 12*, 25–28.

De Meersman, R., & Stein, P. (2007, February). Vagal modulation and aging. *Biological Psychology, 74*, 165–173.

de Onis, M., Garza, C., Onyango, A. W., & Borghi, E. (2007). Comparison of the WHO child growth standards and the CDC 2000 growth charts. *Journal of Nutrition, 137*, 144–148.

de Rosnay, M., Cooper, P., Tsigaras, N., & Murray, L. (2006, August). Transmission of social anxiety from mother to infant: An experimental study using a social referencing paradigm. *Behaviour Research and Therapy, 44*, 1165–1175.

de St. Aubin, E., & McAdams, D. P. (Eds.). (2004). *The generative society: Caring for future generations*. Washington, DC: American Psychological Association.

de St. Aubin, E., McAdams, D. P., & Kim, T. C. (Eds.). (2004). *The generative society: Caring for future generations*. Washington, DC: American Psychological Association.

de Vries, R. (2005). *A pleasing birth*. Philadelphia: Temple University Press.

Deakin, M. B. (2004, May 9). The (new) parent trap. *Boston Globe Magazine*, pp. 18–21, 28–33.

Dearing, E., McCartney, K., & Taylor, B. (2009). Does higher quality early child care promote low-income children's math and reading achievement in middle childhood? *Child Development, 80*, 1329–1349.

Deary, I. (2010). Cognitive epidemiology: Its rise, its current issues, and its challenges. *Personality and Individual Differences, 49*, 337–343.

Deater-Deckard, K., & Cahill, K. (2006). Nature and nurture in early childhood. *Blackwell handbook of early childhood development* (pp. 3–21). New York: Blackwell Publishing.

Deaux, K., Reind, A., Mizrahi, K., & Ethier, K. A. (1995). Parameters of social identity. *Journal of Personality and Social Psychology, 68*, 280–291.

Deb, S., & Adak, M. (2006, July). Corporal punishment of children: Attitude, practice and perception of parents. *Social Science International, 22*, 3–13.

Decarrie, T. G. (1969). A study of the mental and emotional development of the thalidomide child. In B. M. Foss (Ed.), *Determinants of infant behavior* (Vol. 4). London: Methuen.

DeCasper, A. J., & Fifer, W. P. (1980). Of human bonding: Newborns prefer their mothers' voices. *Science, 208*, 1174–1176.

DeCasper, A. J., & Spence, M. J. (1986). Prenatal material speech influences newborns' perception of speech sounds. *Infant Behavior and Development, 9*, 133–150.

deCastro, J. (2002). Age-related changes in the social, psychological, and temporal influences on food intake in free-living, healthy, adult humans. *Journals of Gerontology: Series A: Biological Sciences & Medical Sciences, 57A*, M368–M377.

Decety, J., & Jackson, P. L. (2006). A social-neuroscience perspective on empathy. *Current Directions in Psychological Science, 15*, 54–61.

Deforche, B., De Bourdeaudhuij, I., & Tanghe, A. (2006, May). Attitude toward physical activity in normal-weight, overweight and obese adolescents. *Journal of Adolescent Health, 38*, 560–568.

DeFrancisco, B., & Rovee-Collier, C. (2008). The specificity of priming effects over the first year of life. *Developmental Psychobiology, 50*, 486–501.

DeGenova, M. K. (1993). Reflections of the past: New variables affecting life satisfaction in later life. *Educational Gerontology, 19*, 191 201.

Degnen, C. (2007). Minding the gap: The construction of old age and oldness amongst peers. *Journal of Aging Studies, 21*, 69–80.

Dehaene-Lambertz, G., Hertz-Pannier, L., & Dubois, J. (2006). Nature and nurture in language acquisition: Anatomical and functional brain-imaging studies in infants. *Neurosciences 29*, [Special issue: Nature and nurture in brain development and neurological disorders], 367–373.

Dehue, F., Bolman, C., & Vollink, T. (2008). Cyberbullying: Youngsters' experiences and parental perception. *Cyber-Psychology & Behavior, 11*, 217–223.

Delahaij, R., Gaillard, A., & van Dam, K. (2010). Hardiness and the response to stressful situations: Investigating mediating processes. *Personality and Individual Differences, 49*, 386-390.

DeLisi, L., & Fleischhaker, W. (2007). Schizophrenia research in the era of the genome, 2007. *Current Opinion in Psychiatry, 20*, 109–110.

DeLisi, M. (2006). Zeroing in on early arrest onset: Results from a population of extreme career criminals. *Journal of Criminal Justice, 34*, 17–26.

Dell, D. L., & Stewart, D. E. (2000). Menopause and mood. Is depression linked with hormone changes? *Postgraduate Medicine, 108*, 34–36, 39–43.

Dellmann-Jenkins, M., & Brittain, L. (2003). Young adults' attitudes toward filial responsibility and actual assistance to elderly family members. *Journal of Applied Gerontology, 22*, 214–229.

Delmas, C., Platat, C., Schweitzer, B., Wagner, A., Oujaa, M., & Simon, C. (2007). Association between television in bedroom and adiposity throughout adolescence. *Obesity, 15*, 2495–2503.

Delva, J., O'Malley, P., & Johnston, L. (2006, October). Racial/ethnic and socioeconomic status differences in overweight and health-related behaviors among American students: National trends 1986–2003. *Journal of Adolescent Health, 39*, 536–545.

Demaree, H. A., & Everhart, D. E. (2004). Healthy high-hostiles: Reduced parasympathetic activity and decreased sympathovagal flexibility during negative emotional processing. *Personality and Individual Differences, 36*, 457–469.

Dembner, A. (1995, October 15). Marion Mealey: A determination to make it. *Boston Globe*, p. 22.

Deng, C., Armstrong, P., & Rounds, J. (2007). The fit of Holland's RIASEC model to US occupations. *Journal of Vocational Behavior, 71*, 1–22.

Denizet-Lewis, B. (2004, May 30). Friends, friends with benefits and the benefits of the local mall. *New York Times Magazine*, pp. 30–35, 54–58.

Dennis, T. A., Cole, P. M., Zahn-Wexler, C., & Mizuta, I. (2002). Self in context: Autonomy and relatedness in Japanese and U.S. mother–preschooler dyads. *Child Development, 73*, 1803–1817.

Dennis, W. (1966a). Age and creative productivity. *Journal of Gerontology, 21*, 1–8.

Dennison, B., Edmunds, L., Stratton, H., & Pruzek, R. (2006). Rapid infant weight gain predicts childhood overweight. *Obesity, 14,* 491–499.

Denollet, J. (2005). DS14: Standard assessment of negative affectivity, social inhibition, and Type D personality. *Psychosomatic Medicine, 67,* 89–97.

Dent, C. (1984). Development of discourse rules: Children's use of indexical reference and cohesion. *Developmental Psychology, 20,* 229–234.

DePaulo, B. M., & Morris W. L. (2006). The unrecognized stereotyping and discrimination against singles. *Current Directions in Psychological Science, 15,* 251–254.

Der, G., & Deary, I. (2006, March). Age sex differences in reaction time in adulthood: Results from the United Kingdom health and lifestyle survey. *Psychology and Aging, 21*(1), 62–73.

Derevensky, J., Shek, D., & Merrick, J. (2010). Adolescent gambling. *International Journal of Adolescent Medicine and Health, 22,* 1–2.

Deruelle, F., Nourry, C., Mucci, P., Bart, F., Grosbois, J. M., Lensel, G. H., & Fabre, C. (2008). Difference in breathing strategies during exercise between trained elderly men and women. *Scandinavian Journal of Medical Science in Sports, 18,* 213–220.

Dervic, K., Friedrich, E., Oquendo, M., Voracek, M., Friedrich, M., & Sonneck, G. (2006, October). Suicide in Austrian children and young adolescents aged 14 and younger. *European Child & Adolescent Psychiatry, 15,* 427–434.

de Schipper, E. J., Riksen-Walraven, J. M., & Geurts, S. A. E. (2006). Effects of child–caregiver ratio on the interactions between caregivers and children in child-care centers: An experimental study. *Child Development, 77,* 861–874.

Deshields, T., Tibbs, T., Fan, M. Y., & Taylor, M. (2005, August 12). Differences in patterns of depression after treatment for breast cancer. *Psycho-Oncology,* published online, John Wiley & Sons.

Desmarais, S., & Curtis, J. (1997). Gender and perceived pay entitlement: Testing for effects of experience with income. *Journal of Personality and Social Psychology, 72,* 141–150.

Desoete, A., Roeyers, H., & De Clercq, A. (2003). Can offline metacognition enhance mathematical problem solving? *Journal of Educational Psychology, 95,* 188–200.

Destounis, S., Hanson, S., Morgan, R., Murphy, P. Somerville, P., Seifert, P., Andolina, V., Aarieno, A., Skolny, M., & Logan-Young, W. (2009). Computer-aided detection of breast carcinoma in standard mammographic projections with digital mammography. *International Journal of Computer Assisted Radiological Surgery, 4,* 331–336.

Deurenberg, P., Deurenberg-Yap, M., Foo, L. F., Schmidt, G., & Wang, J. (2003). Differences in body composition between Singapore Chinese, Beijing Chinese and Dutch children. *European Journal of Clinical Nutrition, 57,* 405–409.

Deurenberg, P., Deurenberg-Yap, M., & Guricci, S. (2002). Asians are different from Caucasians and from each other in their body mass index/body fat percent relationship. *Obesity Review, 3,* 141–146.

DeVader, S. R., Neeley, N. L., Myles, T. D., & Leet, T. L. (2007). Evaluation of gestational weight gain guidelines for women with normal prepregnancy body mass index. *Obstetrics and Gynecology, 110,* 745–751.

Deveny, K. (1994, December 5). Chart of kindergarten awards. *Wall Street Journal,* p. B1.

deVilliers, P. A., & deVilliers, J. G. (1992). Language development. In M. H. Bornstein & M. E. Lamb (Eds.), *Developmental psychology: An advanced textbook.* Hillsdale, NJ: Lawrence Erlbaum.

Devlin, B., Daniels, M., & Roeder, K. (1997). The heritability of IQ. *Nature, 388,* 468–471.

deVries, R. (1969). Constancy of generic identity in the years 3 to 6. *Monographs of the Society for Research in Child Development, 34* (3, Serial No. 127).

Dey, A. N., & Bloom, B. (2005). Summary health statistics for U.S. children: National Health Interview Survey, 2003. *Vital Health Statistics 10, 223,* 1–78.

DeYoung, C., Quilty, L., & Peterson, J. (2007). Between facets and domains: 10 aspects of the Big Five. *Journal of Personality and Social Psychology, 93,* 880–896.

Diambra, L., & Menna-Barreto, L. (2004). Infradian rhythmicity in sleep/wake ratio in developing infants. *Chronobiology International, 21,* 217–227.

Diamond, A., & Amso, D. (2008). Contributions of neuroscience to our understanding of cognitive development. *Current Directions in Psychological Science, 17,* 136–141.

Diamond, L. (2003a). Love matters: Romantic relationships among sexual-minority adolescents. In P. Florsheim (Ed.), *Adolescent romantic relations and sexual behavior: Theory, research, and practical implications.* Mahwah, NJ: Lawrence Erlbaum.

Diamond, L. (2003b). Was it a phase? Young women's relinquishment of lesbian/bisexual identities over a 5-year period. *Journal of Personality & Social Psychology, 84,* 352–364.

Diamond, L., & Savin-Williams, R. (2003). The intimate relationships of sexual-minority youths. In G. Adams & M. Berzonsky (Eds.), *Blackwell handbook of adolescence.* Malden, MA: Blackwell Publishers.

Diamond, L. M., Fagundes, C. P., & Butterworth, M. R. (2010). Intimate relationships across the life span. In M. E. Lamb & A. M. Freund (Eds.), *The handbook of lifes-span development.* New York: Wiley.

Dick, D., Rose, R., & Kaprio, J. (2006). The next challenge for psychiatric genetics: Characterizing the risk associated with identified genes. *Annals of Clinical Psychiatry, 18,* 223–231.

Dickinson, D., Golinkoff, R., & Hirsh-Pasek, K. (2010). Speaking out for language: Why language is central to reading development. *Educational Researcher, 39,* 305–310.

Diego, M., Field, T., & Hernandez-Reif, M. (2008). Temperature increases in preterm infants during massage therapy. *Infant Behavior & Development, 31,* 149–152.

Diego, M., Field, T., & Hernandez-Reif, M. (2009). Procedural pain heart rate responses in massaged preterm infants. *Infant Behavior & Development, 32,* 226–229.

Diego, M., Field, T., Hernandez-Reif, M., Vera, Y., Gil, K., & Gonzalez-Garcia, A. (2007). Caffeine use affects pregnancy outcome. *Journal of Child & Adolescent Substance Abuse, 17,* 41–49.

Dietz, W. (2004). Overweight in childhood and adolescence. *New England Journal of Medicine, 350,* 855–857.

Dietz, W. H., & Stern, L. (Eds.). (1999). *American Academy of Pediatrics guide to your child's nutrition: Making peace at the table and building healthy eating habits for life.* New York: Villard.

DiGiovanna, A. G. (1994). *Human aging: Biological perspectives.* New York: McGraw-Hill.

Dildy, G. A., et al. (1996). Very advanced maternal age: Pregnancy after 45. *American Journal of Obstetrics and Gynecology, 175,* 668–674.

Dinero, R., Conger, R., Shaver, P., Widaman, K., & Larsen-Rife, D. (2008). Influence of family of origin and adult romantic partners on romantic attachment security. *Journal of Family Psychology, 22,* 622–632.

Dion, K. L., & Dion, K. K. (1988). Romantic love: Individual and cultural perspectives. In R. J. Sternberg & M. L. Barnes (Eds.), *The psychology of love.* New Haven, CT: Yale University Press.

Diop, A. M. (1989). The place of the elderly in African society. *Impact of Science on Society, 153,* 93–98.

DiPietro, J. A., Costigan, K. A., & Gurewitsch, E. D. (2003). Fetal response to induced maternal stress. *Early Human Development, 74,* 125–138.

DiPietro, J. A., Costigan, K. A., & Gurewitsch, E. D. (2005). Maternal psychophysiological change during the second half of gestation. *Biological Psychology, 69,* 23–39.

Dittman, M. (2005). Generational differences at work. *Monitor on Psychology, 36,* 54–55.

Dixon, W. E., Jr. (2003). There's a long, long way to go. *PsycCRITIQUES.*

Dmitrieva, J., Chen, C., & Greenberg, E. (2004). Family relationships and adolescent psychosocial outcomes: Converging findings from Eastern and Western cultures. *Journal of Research on Adolescence, 14,* 425–447.

Dobson, V. (2000). The developing visual brain. *Perception, 29,* 1501–1503.

Dodge, K. A. (1985). A social information processing model of social competence in children. In M. Perlmutter (Ed.), *Minnesota Symposia on Child Psychology, 18,* 77–126.

Dodge, K. A., Lansford, J. E., & Burks, V. S. (2003). Peer rejection and social information-processing factors in the development of aggressive behavior problems in children. *Child Development, 74,* 374–393.

Doka, K. J., & Mertz, M. E. (1988). The meaning and significance of great-grandparenthood. *Gerontologist, 28,* 192–197.

Doman, G., & Doman, J. (2002). *How to teach your baby to read.* Wyndmoor, PA: Gentle Revolution Press.

Dombrowski, S., Noonan, K., & Martin, R. (2007). Low birth weight and cognitive outcomes: Evidence for a gradient relationship in an urban, poor, African American birth cohort. *School Psychology Quarterly, 22,* 26–43.

Dominguez, H. D., Lopez, M. F., & Molina, J. C. (1999). Interactions between perinatal and neonatal associative learning defined by contiguous olfactory and tactile stimulation. *Neurobiology of Learning and Memory, 71,* 272–288.

Domsch, H., Lohaus, A., & Thomas, H. (2009). Prediction of childhood cognitive abilities from a set of early indicators of information processing capabilities. *Infant Behavior & Development, 32,* 91–102.

Domsch, H., Thomas, H., & Lohaus, A. (2010). Infant attention, heart rate, and looking time during habituation/dishabituation. *Infant Behavior & Development, 33,* 321–329.

Donat, D. (2006, October). Reading their way: A balanced approach that increases achievement. *Reading & Writing Quarterly: Overcoming Learning Difficulties, 22,* 305–323.

Dondi, M., Simion, F., & Caltran, G. (1999). Can newborns discriminate between their own cry and the cry of another newborn infant? *Developmental Psychology, 35,* 418–426.

Donini, L., Savina, C., & Cannella, C. (2003). Eating habits and appetite control in the elderly: The anorexia of aging. *International Psychogeriatrics, 15,* 73–87.

Donlan, C. (1998). *The development of mathematical skills.* Philadelphia: Psychology Press.

Donleavy, G. (2008). No man's land: Exploring the space between Gilligan and Kohlberg. *Journal of Business Ethics, 80,* 807–822.

Donnerstein, E. (2005, January). Media violence and children: What do we know, what do we do? Paper presented at the annual National Teaching of Psychology meeting, St. Petersburg Beach, FL.

Doress, P. B., Siegal, D. L., & The Midlife and Old Women Book Project. (1987). *Ourselves, growing older.* New York: Simon & Schuster.

Dorn, L., Susman, E., & Ponirakis, A. (2003). Pubertal timing and adolescent adjustment and behavior: Conclusions vary by rater. *Journal of Youth & Adolescence, 32,* 157–167.

Dortch, S. (1997, September). Hey guys: Hit the books. *American Demographics,* 4–12.

Doty, N., Willoughby, B., Lindahl, K., & Malik, N. (2010). Sexuality related social support among lesbian, gay, and bisexual youth. *Journal of Youth and Adolescence, 39*(10), 1134–1147.

Douglass, R., & McGadney-Douglass, B. (2008). The role of grandmothers and older women in the survival of children with kwashiorkor in urban Accra, Ghana. *Research in Human Development, 5,* 26–43.

Doussard-Roosevelt, J. A., Porges, S. W., Scanlon, J. W., Alemi, B., & Scanlon, K. B. (1997). Vagal regulation of heart rate in the prediction of developmental outcome for very low birth weight preterm infants. *Child Development, 68,* 173–186.

Downs, E., & Smith, S. (2010). Keeping abreast of hypersexuality: A video game character content analysis. *Sex Roles, 62,* 721–733.

Dowsett, C., Huston, A., Imes, A., & Gennetian, L. (2008). Structural and process features in three types of child care for children from high and low income families. *Early Childhood Research Quarterly, 23,* 69–93.

Doyle, R. (2004a, January). Living together. *Scientific American,* p. 28.

Doyle, R. (2004b, April). By the numbers: A surplus of women. *Scientific American, 290,* 33.

Draper, T., Holman, T., Grandy, S., & Blake, W. (2008). Individual, demographic, and family correlates of romantic attachments in a group of American young adults. *Psychological Reports, 103,* 857–872.

Dreman, S. (Ed.). (1997). *The family on the threshold of the 21st century.* Mahwah, NJ: Lawrence Erlbaum.

Driscoll, A. K., Russell, S. T., & Crockett, L. J. (2008). Parenting styles and youth well-being across immigrant generations. *Journal of Family Issues, 29,* 185–209.

Driver, J., Tabares, A., & Shapiro, A. (2003). Interactional patterns in marital success and failure: Gottman laboratory studies. In F. Walsh (Ed.), *Normal family processes: Growing diversity and complexity* (3rd ed.). New York: Guilford Press.

Dromi, E. (1987). *Early lexical development.* Cambridge, England: Cambridge University Press.

Dryfoos, J. G. (1990). *Adolescents at risk: Prevalence and prevention.* New York: Oxford University Press.

DuBois, D. L., & Hirsch, B. J. (1990). School and neighborhood friendship patterns of blacks and whites in early adolescence. *Child Development, 61,* 524–536.

Dudding, T. C., Vaizey, C. J., & Kamm, M. A. (2008). Obstetric anal sphincter injury: Incidence, risk factors, and management. *Annals of Surgery, 247,* 224–237.

Duenwald, M. (2003, July 15). After 25 years, new ideas in the prenatal test tube. *New York Times,* p. D5.

Dumont, M., Sarlet, M., & Dardenne, B. (2010). Be too kind to a woman, she'll feel incompetent: Benevolent sexism shifts self-construal and autobiographical memories toward incompetence. *Sex Roles, 62*(7-8), 545–553.

Duncan, G. J., & Brooks-Gunn, J. (2000). Family poverty, welfare reform, and child development. *Child Development, 71,* 188–196.

Duncan, J. R., Paterson, D. S., Hoffman, J. M., Mokler, D. J., Borenstein, N. S., Belliveau, R. A., Krous, H. F., Haas, E. A., Stanley, C., Nattie, E. E., Trachtenberg, F. L., & Kinney, H. C. (2010). Brainstem serotonergic deficiency in sudden infant death syndrome. *Journal of the American Medical Association, 303,* 430–437.

DuPaul, G., & Weyandt, L. (2006, June). School-based intervention for children with attention deficit hyperactivity disorder: Effects on academic, social, and behavioural functioning. *International Journal of Disability, Development and Education, 53,* 161–176.

Duplassie, D., & Daniluk, J. C. (2007). Sexuality: Young and middle adulthood. In A. Owens & M. Tupper (Eds.), *Sexual health: Vol. 1, Psychological foundations.* Westport, CT: Praeger.

Durbin, J. (2003, October 6). Internet sex unzipped. *McCleans,* p. 18.

Dweck, C. (2002). The development of ability conceptions. In A. Wigfield & J. Eccles (Eds.), *Development of achievement motivation.* San Diego: Academic Press.

Dwyer, K., Fredstrom, B., Rubin, K., Booth-LaForce, C., Rose-Krasnor, L., & Burgess, K. (2010). Attachment, social information processing, and friendship quality of early adolescent girls and boys. *Journal of Social and Personal Relationships, 27,* 91–116.

Eacott, M. J. (1999). Memory of the events of early childhood. *Current Directions in Psychological Science, 8,* 46–49.

Eagly, A. H., & Steffen, V. J. (1984). Gender stereotypes stem from the distribution of women and men into social roles. *Journal of Personality and Social Psychology, 46,* 735–754.

Eagly, A. H., & Steffen, V. J. (1986). Gender and aggressive behavior. A meta-analytic review of the social psychological literature. *Psychological Bulletin, 100,* 309–330.

Eagly, A. H., & Wood, W. (2003). In C. B. Travis (Ed.), *Evolution, gender, and rape.* Cambridge, MA: MIT Press.

Eaker, E. D., Sullivan, L. M., Kelly-Hayes, M., D'Agostino, R. B., Sr., & Benjamin, E. J. (2004). Anger and hostility predict the development of atrial fibrillation in men in the Framingham Offspring Study. *Circulation, 109,* 1267–1271.

Earle, J. R., Perricone, P. J., Davidson, J. K., Moore, N. B., Harris, C. T., & Cotton, S. R. (2007). Premarital sexual attitudes and behavior at a religiously-affiliated university: Two decades of change. *Sexuality & Culture: An Interdisciplinary Quarterly, 11,* 39–61.

Easton, J., Schipper, L., & Shackelford, T. (2007). Morbid jealousy from an evolutionary psychological perspective. *Evolution and Human Behavior, 28,* 399–402.

Eaton, W. O., & Yu, A. P. (1989). Are sex differences in child motor activity level a function of sex differences in maturational status? *Child Development, 60,* 1005–1011.

Eberling, J. L., Wu, C., Tong-Turnbeaugh, R., & Jagust, W. J. (2004). Estrogen- and tamoxifen-associated effects on brain structure and function. *Neuroimage, 21,* 364–371.

Ebmeier, K. P., Donaghey, C., & Steele, J. D. (2006). Recent developments and current controversies in depression. *The Lancet, 367,* 153–167.

Ebner, N., Freund, A., & Baltes, P. (2006, December). Developmental changes in personal goal orientation from young to late adulthood: From striving for gains to maintenance and prevention of losses. *Psychology and Aging, 21,* 664–678.

Eccles, J., Templeton, J., & Barber, B. (2003). Adolescence and emerging adulthood: The critical passage ways to adulthood. In M. Bornstein & L. Davidson (Eds.), *Well-being: Positive development across the life course.* Mahwah, NJ: Lawrence Erlbaum.

Ecenbarger, W. (1993, April 1). America's new merchants of death. *The Reader's Digest,* 50.

Eckerd, L. (2009). Death and dying course offerings in psychology: A survey of nine Midwestern states. *Death Studies, 33,* 762–770.

Eckerman, C. O., & Oehler, J. M. (1992). Very-low-birth-weight newborns and parents as early social partners. In S. L. Friedman & M. D. Sigman (Eds.), *The psychological development of low-birthweight children.* Norwood, NJ: Ablex.

Eckerman, C., & Peterman, K. (2001). Peers and infant social/communicative development. In G. Bremner & A. Fogel (Eds.), *Blackwell handbook of infant development* (pp. 326–350). Malden, MA: Blackwell Publishers.

Eddy, K., Keel, P., & Leon, G. (2010). Vulnerability to eating disorders in childhood and adolescence. *Vulnerability to psychopathology: Risk across the lifespan* (2nd ed.). New York: Guilford Press.

Edwards, C. P. (2000). Children's play in cross-cultural perspective: A new look at the Six Cultures study. *Cross-Cultural Research: The Journal of Comparative Social Science, 34,* 318–338.

Edwards, S. (2005). Constructivism does not only happen in the individual: Sociocultural theory and early childhood education. *Early Child Development & Care, 175,* 37–47.

Eichelsheim, V., Buist, K., Deković, M., Wissink, I., Frijns, T., van Lier, P., et al. (2010). Associations among the parent-adolescent relationship, aggression and delinquency in different ethnic groups: A replication across two Dutch samples. *Social Psychiatry and Psychiatric Epidemiology, 45,* 293–300.

Eid, M., Riemann, R., Angleitner, A., & Borkenau, P. (2003). Sociability and positive emotionality: Genetic and environmental contributions to the covariation between different facets of extraversion. *Journal of Personality, 71,* 319–346.

Eiden, R., Foote, A., & Schuetze, P. (2007). Maternal cocaine use and caregiving status: Group differences in caregiver and infant risk variables. *Addictive Behaviors, 32,* 465–476.

Eigsti, I., & Cicchetti, D. (2004). The impact of child maltreatment on expressive syntax at 60 months. *Developmental Science, 7,* 88–102.

Einarson, A., Choi, J., Einarson, T., & Koren, G. (2009). Incidence of major malformations in infants following antidepressant exposure in pregnancy: Results of a large prospective cohort study. *The Canadian Journal of Psychiatry / La Revue canadienne de psychiatrie, 54,* 242–246.

Eisenberg, M. E., & Resnick, M. D. (2006). Suicidality among gay, lesbian and bisexual youth: The role of protective factors. *Journal of Adolescent Health, 39,* 662–668.

Eisenberg, N. (2004). Another slant on moral judgment. *psycCRITIQUES, 12*–15.

Eisenberg, N., Fabes, R. A., Guthrie, I. K., & Reiser, M. (2000). Dispositional emotionality and regulation: Their role in predicting quality of social functioning. *Journal of Personality and Social Psychology, 78,* 136–157.

Elder, G. A., De Gasperi, R., & Gama Sosa, M. A. (2006). Research update: Neurogenesis in adult brain and neuropsychiatric disorders. *Mt. Sinai Journal of Medicine, 73,* 931–940.

Eley, T., Liang, H., & Plomin, R. (2004). Parental familial vulnerability, family environment, and their interactions as predictors of depressive symptoms in adolescents. *Child & Adolescent Social Work Journal, 21,* 298–306.

Eley, T. C., Lichtenstein, P., & Moffitt, T. E. (2003). A longitudinal behavioral genetic analysis of the etiology of aggressive and nonaggressive antisocial behavior. *Development and Psychopathology, 15,* 383–402.

Elkind, D. (1985). Egocentrism redux. *Developmental Review, 5,* 218–226.

Elkind, D. (1994). *Ties that stress: The new family imbalance.* Cambridge, MA: Harvard University Press.

Elkind, D. (1996). Inhelder and Piaget on adolescence and adulthood: A postmodern appraisal. *Psychological Science, 7,* 216–220.

Elkins, D. (2009). Why humanistic psychology lost its power and influence in American psychology: Implications for advancing humanistic psychology. *Journal of Humanistic Psychology, 49,* 267–291. Available online at http://search.ebscohost.com

Elliott, K., & Urquiza, A. (2006). Ethnicity, culture, and child maltreatment. *Journal of Social Issues, 62,* 787–809.

Ellis, B. H., MacDonald, H. Z., Lincoln, A. K., & Cabral, H. J. (2008). Mental health of Somali adolescent refugees: The role of trauma, stress, and perceived discrimination. *Journal of Consulting and Clinical Psychology, 76,* 184–193.

Ellis, L. (2006, July). Gender differences in smiling: An evolutionary neuroandrogenic theory. *Physiology & Behavior, 88,* 303–308.

Ellis, B. J. (2004). Timing of pubertal maturation in girls: An integrated life history approach. *Psychological Bulletin, 130,* 920–958.

Elmore, J. G., Jackson, S. L., Abraham, L., Miglioretti, D. L., Carney, P. A., Geller, B. M., Yankaskas, B. C., Kerlikowske, K., Onega, T., Rosenberg, R. D., Sickles, E. A., & Buist, D. S. (2009). Variability in interpretive performance at screening mammography and radiologists' characteristics associated with accuracy. *Radiology, 253,* 641–651.

Else-Quest, N. M., Hyde, J. S., & Clark, R. (2003). Breastfeeding, bonding, and the mother–infant relationship. *Merrill-Palmer Quarterly, 49,* 495–517.

Emslie, C., & Hunt, K. (2008). The weaker sex? Exploring lay understandings of gender differences in life expectancy: A qualitative study. *Social Science & Medicine, 67*, 808–816.

Endo, S. (1992). Infant–infant play from 7 to 12 months of age: An analysis of games in infant–peer triads. *Japanese Journal of Child and Adolescent Psychiatry, 33*, 145–162.

Engler, J., & Goleman, D. (1992). *The consumer's guide to psychotherapy.* New York: Simon & Schuster.

Englund, K., & Behne, D. (2006). Changes in infant directed speech in the first six months. *Infant and Child Development, 15*(2), 139–160.

Ennett, S. T., & Bauman, K. E. (1996). Adolescent social networks: School, demographic, and longitudinal considerations. *Journal of Adolescent Research, 11*, 194–215.

Epel, E. (2009). Telomeres in a life-span perspective: A new "psychobiomarker"? *Current Directions in Psychological Science, 18*, 6–10.

Epperson, S. E. (1988, September 16). Studies link subtle sex bias in schools with women's behavior in the workplace. *Wall Street Journal*, p. 19.

Epstein, L., & Mardon, S. (2007, September 17). Homeroom zombies. *Newsweek*, pp. 64–65.

Erber, J. (2010). *Aging and older adulthood* (2nd ed.). New York: Wiley-Blackwell.

Erber, J. T., Szuchman, L. T., & Rothberg, S. T. (1990). Everyday memory failure: Age differences in appraisal and attribution. *Psychology and Aging, 5*, 236–241.

Erikson, E. H. (1963). *Childhood and society.* New York: Norton.

Erlandsson, K., Dsilna, A., Fagerberg, I., & Christensson, K. (2007). Skin-to-skin care with the father after cesarean birth and its effect on newborn crying and prefeeding behavior. *Birth: Issues in Perinatal Care, 34*, 105–114.

Erwin, P. (1993). *Friendship and peer relations in children.* Chichester, England: Wiley.

Espenschade, A. (1960). Motor development. In W. R. Johnson (Ed.), *Science and medicine of exercise and sports.* New York: Harper & Row.

Essex, M. J., & Nam, S. (1987). Marital status and loneliness among older women: The differential importance of close family and friends. *Journal of Marriage and the Family, 49*, 92–106.

Essick, K. (2009, November 23). Profiles in later life. *Wall Street Journal*, p. R8.

Estell, D. B., Jones, M. H., Pearl, R., Van Acker, R., Farmer, T. W., & Rodkin, P. C. (2008). Peer groups, popularity, and social preference: Trajectories of social functioning among students with and without learning disabilities. *Journal of Learning Disabilities, 41*, 5–14.

Ethier, L., Couture, G., & Lacharite, C. (2004). Risk factors associated with the chronicity of high potential for child abuse and neglect. *Journal of Family Violence, 19*, 13–24.

Evans, G. W. (2004). The environment of childhood poverty. *American Psychologist, 59*, 77–92.

Evans, R. (2009). A comparison of rural and urban older adults in Iowa on specific markers of successful aging. *Journal of Gerontological Social Work, 52*, 423–438.

Faber, A., & Wittenborn, A. (2010). The role of attachment in children's adjustment to divorce and remarriage. *Journal of Family Psychotherapy, 21*, 89–104.

Fagan, J., & Holland, C. (2007). Racial equality in intelligence: Predictions from a theory of intelligence as processing. *Intelligence, 35*, 319–334.

Fagan, J., Holland, C., & Wheeler, K. (2007). The prediction, from infancy, of adult IQ and achievement. *Intelligence, 35*, 225–231.

Fagan, M. (2009). Mean length of utterance before words and grammar: Longitudinal trends and developmental implications of infant vocalizations. *Journal of Child Language, 36*, 495–527. Available online at http://search.ebscohost.com

Fais, L., Kajikawa, S., Amano, S., & Werker, J. (2010). Now you hear it, now you don't: Vowel devoicing in Japanese infant-directed speech. *Journal of Child Language, 37*, 319–340.

Faith, M. S., Johnson, S. L., & Allison, D. B. (1997). Putting the behavior into the behavior genetics of obesity. *Behavior Genetics, 27*, 423–439.

Falck-Ytter, T., Gredeback, G., & von Hofsten, C. (2006). Infants predict other people's action goals. *Nature Neuroscience, 9*, 878–879.

Fantz, R. (1963). Pattern vision in newborn infants. *Science, 140*, 296–297.

Fantz, R. L. (1961). The origin of form perception. *Scientific American, 72*.

Farmer, T. W., Estell, D. B., Bishop, J. L., O'Neal, K. K., & Cairns, B. D. (2003). Rejected bullies or popular leaders? The social relations of aggressive subtypes of rural African American early adolescents. *Developmental Psychology, 39*, 992–1004.

Farroni, T., Menon, E., Rigato, S., & Johnson, M. (2007). The perception of facial expressions in newborns. *European Journal of Developmental Psychology, 4*, 2–13.

Farzin, F., Charles, E., & Rivera, S. (2009). Development of multimodal processing in infancy. *Infancy, 14*, 563–578.

Fayers, T., Crowley, T., Jenkins, J. M., & Cahill, D. J. (2003). Medical student awareness of sexual health is poor. *International Journal STD/AIDS, 14*, 386–389.

Federal Interagency Forum on Age-Related Statistics. (2000). *Older Americans 2000: Key indicators of well-being.* Hyattsville, MD: Federal Interagency Forum on Age-Related Statistics.

Federal Interagency Forum on Aging-Related Statistics. (2010). *Older Americans 2010: Key indicators of well-being.* Washington, DC: Federal Interagency Forum on Aging-Related StatisticsAuthor.

Federal Interagency Forum on Child and Family Statistics. (2003). *America's children: Key national indicators of well-being, 2003.* Federal Interagency Forum on Child and Family Statistics. Washington, DC: U.S. Government Printing Office.

Feeney, B. C., & Collins, N. L. (2003). Motivations for caregiving in adult intimate relationships: Influences on caregiving behavior and relationship functioning. *Personality and Social Psychology Bulletin, 29*, 950–968.

Feigelman, W., Jordan, J., & Gorman, B. (2009). How they died, time since loss, and bereavement outcomes. *Omega: Journal of Death and Dying, 58*, 251–273.

Feldhusen, J. (2003). Precocity and acceleration. *Gifted Education International, 17*, 55–58.

Feldman, R., & Masalha, S. (2007). The role of culture in moderating the links between early ecological risk and young children's adaptation. *Development and Psychopathology, 19*, 1–21.

Feldman, R. S. (Ed.). (1992). *Applications of nonverbal behavioral theories and research.* Hillsdale, NJ: Lawrence Erlbaum.

Fell, J., & Williams, A. (2008). The effect of aging on skeletal-muscle recovery from exercise: Possible implications for aging athletes. *Journal of Aging and Physical Activity, 16*, 97–115. Available online at http://search.ebscohost.com

Fenwick, K., & Morrongiello, B. (1991). Development of frequency perception in infants and children. *Journal of Speech, Language Pathology, and Audiology, 15*, 7–22.

Ferguson, F., & Austin, E. (2010). Associations of trait and ability emotional intelligence with performance on Theory of Mind tasks in an adult sample. *Personality and Individual Differences, 49*, 414–418.

Ferguson, M., & Molfese, P. (2007). Breast-fed infants process speech differently from bottle-fed infants: Evidence from neuroelectrophysiology. *Developmental Neuropsychology, 31*, 337–347.

Ferguson, R., & Brohaugh, B. (2010). The aging of Aquarius. *Journal of Consumer Marketing, 27*, 76–81.

Fergusson, D. M., Horwood, L. J., & Ridder, E. M. (2006). Abortion in young women and subsequent mental health. *Journal of Child Psychology and Psychiatry, 47*, 16–24.

Ferholt, B., & Lecusay, R. (2010). Adult and child development in the zone of proximal development: Socratic dialogue in a playworld. *Mind, Culture, and Activity, 17*, 59–83.

Fernald, A. (2001). Hearing, listening, and understanding: Auditory development in infancy. In G. Bremner & A. Fogel (Eds.), *Blackwell handbook of infant development.* Malden, MA: Blackwell Publishers.

Fernald, A., & Morikawa, H. (1993). Common themes and cultural variations in Japanese and American mothers' speech to infants. *Child Development, 64*, 637–656.

Fernyhough, C. (1997). Vygotsky's sociocultural approach: Theoretical issues and implications for current research. In S. Hala (Ed.), *The development of social cognition* (pp. 65–92). Hove, England: Psychology Press/Lawrence Erlbaum, Taylor & Francis.

Feshbach, S., & Tangney, J. (2008). Television viewing and aggression: Some alternative perspectives. *Perspectives on Psychological Science, 3*, 387–389. http://search.ebscohost.com

Fetterman, D. M. (2005). Empowerment evaluation: From the digital divide to academic distress. In D. Fetterman & A. Wandersman (Eds.), *Empowerment evaluation principles in practice.* New York: Guilford Press.

Fiatarone, M. S. A., & Garnett, L. R. (1997, March). Keep on keeping on. *Harvard Health Letter*, pp. 4–5.

Field, D., & Minkler, M. (1988). Continuity and change in social support between young-old and old-old or very-old age. *Journal of Gerontology, 43* (4), 100–106.

Field, M. J., & Behrman, R. E. (Eds.). (2003). *When children die.* Washington, DC: National Academies Press.

Field, T., Diego, M., & Hernandez-Reif, M. (2006). Prenatal depression effects on the fetus and newborn: A review. *Infant Behavior & Development, 29*, 445–455.

Field, T., Diego, M., & Hernandez-Reif, M. (2008). Prematurity and potential predictors. *International Journal of Neuroscience, 118*, 277–289.

Field, T., Diego, M., & Hernandez-Reif, M. (2009). Depressed mothers' infants are less responsive to faces and voices. *Infant Behavior & Development, 32*, 239–244.

Field, T., Diego, M., & Hernandez-Reif, M. (2010). Preterm infant massage therapy research: A review. *Infant Behavior & Development, 33*, 115–124.

Field, T., Greenberg, R., Woodson, R., Cohen, D., & Garcia, R. (1984). Facial expression during Brazelton neonatal assessments. *Infant Mental Health Journal, 5*, 61–71.

Field, T., Hernandez-Reif, M., & Diego, M. (2006). Newborns of depressed mothers who received moderate versus light pressure massage during pregnancy. *Infant Behavior & Development, 29*(1), 54–58.

Field, T. M., & Millsap, R. E. (1991). Personality in advanced old age: Continuity or change? *Journals of Gerontology: Series B: Psychological Sciences and Social Sciences, 46*, P299–P308.

Finch, C. E., & Tanzi, R. E. (1997, October 17). Genetics of aging. *Science, 278*, 407–410.

Fingerhut, L. A., & MaKuc, D. M. (1992). Mortality among minority populations in the United States. *American Journal of Public Health, 82*, 1168–1170.

Finkelhor, D. (1997). The homicides of children and youth: A developmental perspective. In G. K. Kantor & J. L. Janinski (Ed.), *Out of the darkness: Contemporary perspectives on family violence* (pp. 17–34). Thousand Oaks, CA: Sage Publications.

Finkelstein, D. L., Harper, D. A., & Rosenthal, G. E. (1998). Does length of hospital stay during labor and delivery influence patient satisfaction? Results from a regional study. *American Journal of Managed Care, 4*, 1701–1708.

Finley, G., & Schwartz, S. (2010). The divided world of the child: Divorce and long-term psychosocial adjustment. *Family Court Review, 48*, 516–527.

First, J. M., & Cardenas, J. (1986). A minority view on testing. *Educational Measurement Issues and Practice, 5,* 6–11.

Fischer, K. W., & Hencke, R. W. (1996). Infants' construction of actions in context: Piaget's contributions to research on early development. *Psychological Science, 7,* 204–210.

Fischer, K. W., & Rose, S. P. (1995). Concurrent cycles in the dynamic development of brain and behavior. *Newsletter of the Society for Research in Child Development,* p. 16.

Fischer, P., Kastenmüller, A., & Greitemeyer, T. (2010). Media violence and the self: The impact of personalized gaming characters in aggressive video games on aggressive behavior. *Journal of Experimental Social Psychology, 46,* 192–195.

Fischer, T. (2007). Parental divorce and children's socioeconomic success: Conditional effects of parental resources prior to divorce, and gender of the child. *Sociology, 41,* 475–495.

Fish, J. M. (Ed.). (2001). *Race and intelligence: Separating science from myth.* Mahwah, NJ: Lawrence Erlbaum.

Fisher, C. (2005). Deception research involving children: Ethical practices and paradoxes. *Ethics & Behavior, 15,* 271–287.

Fisher, C., Hauck, Y., & Fenwick, J. (2006). How social context impacts on women's fears of childbirth: A Western Australian example. *Social Science & Medicine, 63,* 64–75.

Fisher, C. B. (2003). *Decoding the ethics code: A practical guide for psychologists.* Thousand Oaks, CA: Sage Publications.

Fisher, C. B. (2004). Informed consent and clinical research involving children and adolescents: Implications of the revised APA Ethics Code and HIPAA. *Journal of Clinical Child & Adolescent Psychology, 33,* 832–839.

Fitzgerald, D., & White, K. (2002). Linking children's social worlds: Perspective-taking in parent-child and peer contexts. *Social Behavior & Personality, 31,* 509–522.

Fitzgerald, P. (2008). A neurotransmitter system theory of sexual orientation. *Journal of Sexual Medicine, 5,* 746–748.

Fivush, R. (2010). Developing gender in a changing world. *Journal of Applied Developmental Psychology, 31,* 348–349.

Fivush, R., Kuebli, J., & Clubb, P. A. (1992). The structure of events and event representations: A developmental analysis. *Child Development, 63,* 188–201.

Flavell, J. H. (1994). Cognitive development: Past, present, and future. In R. D. Parke, P. A. Ornstein, J. J. Rieser, & C. Zahn-Waxler (Eds.), *A century of developmental psychology.* Washington, DC: American Psychological Association.

Flavell, J. H. (1996). Piaget's legacy. *Psychological Science, 7,* 200–203.

Fleming, M., Greentree, S., Cocotti-Muller, D., Elias, K., & Morrison, S. (2006, December). Safety in cyberspace: Adolescents' safety and exposure online. *Youth & Society, 38,* 135–154.

Fletcher, A. C., Darling, N. E., Steinberg, L., & Dornbusch, S. M. (1995). The company they keep: Relation of adolescents' adjustment and behavior to their friends' perceptions of authoritative parenting in the social network. *Developmental Psychology, 31,* 300–310.

Flom, R., & Bahrick, L. (2007). The development of infant discrimination of affect in multimodal and unimodal stimulation: The role of intersensory redundancy. *Developmental Psychology, 43,* 238–252.

Flor, D. L., & Knap, N. F. (2001). Transmission and transaction: Predicting adolescents' internalization of parental religious values. *Journal of Family Psychology, 15,* 627–645.

Florsheim, P. (2003). Adolescent romantic and sexual behavior: What we know and where we go from here. In P. Florsheim (Ed.), *Adolescent romantic relations and sexual behavior: Theory, research, and practical implications.* Mahwah, NJ: Lawrence Erlbaum.

Flouri, E. (2005). *Fathering and child outcomes.* New York: Wiley.

Floyd, R. G. (2005). Information-processing approaches to interpretation of contemporary intellectual assessment instruments. In D. P. Flanagan & P. L. Harrison (Eds.), *Contemporary intellectual assessment: Theories, tests, and issues.* New York: Guilford Press.

Flynn, E., O'Malley, C., & Wood, D. (2004). A longitudinal, microgenetic study of the emergence of false belief understanding and inhibition skills. *Developmental Science, 7,* 103–115.

Fogel, A., Hsu, H., Shapiro, A., Nelson-Goens, G., & Secrist, C. (2006, May). Effects of normal and perturbed social play on the duration and amplitude of different types of infant smiles. *Developmental Psychology, 42,* 459–473.

Fok, M. S. M., & Tsang, W.Y.W. (2006). 'Development of an instrument measuring Chinese adolescent beliefs and attitudes towards substance use': Response to commentary. *Journal of Clinical Nursing, 15,* 1062–1063.

Folkman, S., & Lazarus, R. S. (1988). Coping as a mediator of emotion. *Journal of Personality and Social Psychology, 54,* 466–475.

Ford, J. A. (2007). Alcohol use among college students: A comparison of athletes and nonathletes. *Substance Use & Misuse, 42,* 1367–1377.

Fouts, G., & Burggraf, K. (1999). Television situation comedies: Female body images and verbal reinforcements. *Sex Roles, 40,* 473–482.

Fowers, B. J., & Davidov, B. J. (2006). The virtue of multiculturalism: Personal transformation, character, and openness to the other. *American Psychologist, 61,* 581–594.

Fowler, J. W., & Dell, M. L. (2006). Stages of faith from infancy through adolescence: Reflections on three decades of faith development theory. In E. C. Roehlkepartain, P. E. King, L. Wagener, & P. L. Benson (Eds.), *The handbook of spiritual development in childhood and adolescence.* Thousand Oaks, CA: Sage Publications.

Fozard, J. L., Vercruyssen, M., Reynolds, S. L., Hancock, P. A., et al. (1994). Age differences and changes in reaction time: The Baltimore Longitudinal Study of Aging. *Journal of Gerontology, 49,* 179–189.

Franck, I., & Brownstone, D. (1991). *The parent's desk reference.* New York: Prentice-Hall.

Franić, S., Middeldorp, C., Dolan, C., Ligthart, L., & Boomsma, D. (2010). Childhood and adolescent anxiety and depression: Beyond heritability. *Journal of the American Academy of Child & Adolescent Psychiatry, 49,* 820–829.

Frankenburg, W. K., Dodds, J., Archer, P., Shapiro, H., & Bresnick, B. (1992). The Denver II: A major revision and restandardization of the Denver Developmental Screening Test. *Pediatrics, 89,* 91–97.

Franko, D., & Striegel-Moore, R. (2002). The role of body dissatisfaction as a risk factor for depression in adolescent girls: Are the differences Black and White? *Journal of Psychosomatic Research, 53,* 975–983.

Fransen, M., Meertens, R., & Schrander-Stumpel, C. (2006). Communication and risk presentation in genetic counseling: Development of a checklist. *Patient Education and Counseling, 61,* 126–133.

Frawley, T. (2008). Gender schema and prejudicial recall: How children misremember, fabricate, and distort gendered picture book information. *Journal of Research in Childhood Education, 22,* 291–303.

Frederickson, N., & Petrides, K. (2008). Ethnic, gender, and socio-economic group differences in academic performance and secondary school selection: A longitudinal analysis. *Learning and Individual Differences, 18,* 144–151.

Freedman, A. M., & Ellison, S. (2004, May 6). Testosterone patch for women shows promise. *Wall Street Journal,* pp. A1, B2.

Freedman, D. G. (1979, January). Ethnic differences in babies. *Human Nature,* 15–20.

Freeman, E., Sammel, M., & Liu, L. (2004). Hormones and menopausal status as predictors of depression in women in transition to menopause. *Archives of General Psychiatry, 61,* 62–70.

Freeman, H., Newland, L. A., & Coyl, D. D. (2010). New directions in father attachment. *Early Child Development and Care, 180,* 1–8.

Freeman, J. M. (2007). Beware: The misuse of technology and the law of unintended consequences. *Neurotherapeutics. 4,* 549–554.

French, S., & Swain, J. (1997). Young disabled people. In J. Roche & S. Tucker (Eds.), *Youth in society: Contemporary theory, policy and practice* (pp. 199–206). London, England: Sage Publications.

Freud, S. (1920). *A general introduction to psychoanalysis.* New York: Boni & Liveright.

Friborg, O., Barlaug, D., Martinussen, M., Rosenvinge, J. H., & Hjemdal, O. (2005). Resilience in relation to personality and intelligence. *International Journal of Methods in Psychiatric Research, 14,* 29–42.

Frick, P. J., Cornell, A. H., Bodin, S. D., Dane, H. A., Barry, C. T., & Loney, B. R. (2003). Callous-unemotional traits and developmental pathways to severe conduct problems. *Developmental Psychology, 39,* 246–260.

Friedland, R. (2003). Fish consumption and the risk of Alzheimer disease: Is it time to make dietary recommendations? *Archives of Neurology, 60,* 923–924.

Friedlander, L. J., Connolly, J. A., Pepler, D. J., & Craig, W. M. (2007). Biological, familial, and peer influences on dating in early adolescence. *Archives of Sexual Behavior, 36,* 821–830.

Friedman, W., & Janssen, S. (2010). Aging and the speed of time. *Acta Psychologica, 134,* 130–141.

Frisch, M., Friis, S., Kjear, S. K., & Melbye, M. (1995). Falling incidence of penis cancer in an uncircumcised population (Denmark 1943–90). *British Medical Journal, 311,* 1471.

Fritz, G., & Rockney, R. (2004). Summary of the practice parameter for the assessment and treatment of children and adolescents with enuresis. *Work Group on Quality Issues; Journal of the American Academy of Child & Adolescent Psychiatry, 43,* 123–125.

Frome, P., Alfeld, C., Eccles, J., & Barber, B. (2006, August). Why don't they want a male-dominated job? An investigation of young women who changed their occupational aspirations. *Educational Research and Evaluation, 12,* 359–372.

Fromholt, P., & Larsen, S. F. (1991). Autobiographical memory in normal, aging and primary degenerative dementia (dementia of the Alzheimer type). *Journal of Gerontology, 46,* 85–91.

Fry, C. L. (1985). Culture, behavior, and aging in the comparative perspective. In J. E. Birren & K. W. Schaie (Eds.), *Handbook of the psychology of aging.* New York: Van Nostrand Reinhold.

Fu, G., Xu, F., Cameron, C., Heyman, G., & Lee, K. (2007, March). Cross-cultural differences in children's choices, categorizations, and evaluations of truths and lies. *Developmental Psychology, 43*(2), 278–293.

Fu, X., & Heaton, T. (2008). Racial and educational homogamy: 1980 to 2000. *Sociological Perspectives, 51,* 735–758.

Fulcher, M., Sutfin, E., Chan, R., Scheib, J., & Patterson, C. (2006). Lesbian mothers and their children: Findings from the Contemporary Families Study. *Sexual orientation and mental health: Examining identity and development in lesbian, gay, and bisexual people.* Washington, DC: American Psychological Association.

Fuligni, A., & Hardway, C. (2006, September). Daily variation in adolescents' sleep, activities, and psychological well-being. *Journal of Research on Adolescence, 16,* 353–378.

Fuligni, A., & Yoshikawa, H. (2003). Socioeconomic resources, parenting, and child development among immigrant families. In M. Bornstein & R. Bradley (Eds.), *Socioeconomic status, parenting, and child development.* Mahwah, NJ: Lawrence Erlbaum.

Fuligni, A., & Zhang, W. (2004). Attitudes toward family obligation among adolescents in contemporary urban and rural China. *Child Development, 75,* 180–192.

Fuligni, A. J. (1997). The academic achievement of adolescents from immigrant families: The roles of family background, attitudes, and behavior. *Child Development, 68,* 351–368.

Fuligni, A. J., & Fuligni, A. S. (2007). Immigrant families and the educational development of their children. In J. E. Lansford et al (Eds.), *Immigrant families in contemporary society.* New York: Guilford Press.

Funk, L. (2010). Prioritizing parental autonomy: Adult children's accounts of feeling responsible and supporting aging parents. *Journal of Aging Studies, 24,* 57–64.

Furman, W., & Shaffer, L. (2003). The role of romantic relationships in adolescent development. In P. Florsheim (Ed.), *Adolescent romantic relations and sexual behavior: Theory, research, and practical implications.* Mahwah, NJ: Lawrence Erlbaum.

Furstenberg, F. F., Jr. (1996, June). The future of marriage. *American Demographics,* 34–40.

Gabbay, S., & Wahler, J. (2002). Lesbian aging: Review of a growing literature. *Journal of Gay & Lesbian Social Services: Issues in Practice, Policy & Research, 14,* 1–21.

Gabriele, A., & Schettino, F. (2008). Child malnutrition and mortality in developing countries: Evidence from a cross-country analysis. *Analyses of Social Issues and Public Policy (ASAP), 8,* 53–81.

Gagnon, S. G., & Nagle, R. J. (2000). Comparison of the revised and original versions of the Bayley Scales of Infant Development. *School Psychology International, 21,* 293–305.

Galambos, N., Leadbeater, B., & Barker, E. (2004). Gender differences in and risk factors for depression in adolescence: A 4-year longitudinal study. *International Journal of Behavioral Development, 28,* 16–25.

Gallagher, J. J. (1994). Teaching and learning: New models. *Annual Review of Psychology, 45,* 171–195.

Galler, J., Bryce, C., Waber, D., Hock, R., Exner, N., Eaglesfield, D., et al. (2010). Early childhood malnutrition predicts depressive symptoms at ages 11–17. *Journal of Child Psychology and Psychiatry, 51,* 789–798.

Gallistel, C. (2007). Commentary on Le Corre & Carey. *Cognition, 105,* 439–445.

Gallup Poll. (2004). How many children? *The Gallup Poll Monthly.*

Gangestad, S. (2010). Evolutionary biology looks at behavior genetics. *Personality and Individual Differences, 49,* 289–295.

Ganzini, L., Beer, T., & Brouns, M. (2006, September). Views on physician-assisted suicide among family members of Oregon cancer patients. *Journal of Pain and Symptom Management, 32,* 230–236.

Garcia, C., & Saewyc, E. (2007). Perceptions of mental health among recently immigrated Mexican adolescents. *Issues in Mental Health Nursing, 28,* 37–54.

Garcia, C., Bearer, E. L., & Lerner, R. M. (Eds.). (2004). *Nature and nurture: The complex interplay of genetic and environmental influences on human behavior and development.* Mahwah, NJ: Lawrence Erlbaum.

Garcia-Portilla, M. (2009). Depression and perimenopause: A review. *Actas Esp Psiquiatr, 37,* 231–321.

Gardner, H. (2000). *Intelligence reframed: Multiple intelligences for the 21st century.* New York: Basic Books.

Gardner, H. (2003). Three distinct meanings of intelligence. In R. Sternberg & J. Lautrey (Eds.), *Models of intelligence: International perspectives.* Washington, DC: American Psychological Association.

Gardner, H., & Moran, S. (2006). The science of multiple intelligences theory: A response to Lynn Waterhouse. *Educational Psychologist, 41,* 227–232.

Garlick, D. (2003). Integrating brain science research with intelligence research. *Current Directions in Psychological Science, 12,* 185–189.

Gartstein, M., Slobodskaya, H., & Kinsht, I. (2003). Cross-cultural differences in temperament in the first year of life:

United States of America (US) and Russia. *International Journal of Behavioral Development, 27,* 316–328.

Gaulden, M. E. (1992). Maternal age effect: The enigma of Down syndrome and other trisomic conditions. *Mutation Research, 296,* 69–88.

Gauthier, S., & Scheltens, P. (2009). Can we do better in developing new drugs for Alzheimer's disease? *Alzheimer's & Dementia, 5,* 489–491.

Gauvain, M. (1998). Cognitive development in social and cultural context. *Current Directions in Psychological Science, 7,* 188–194.

Gavin, L. A., & Furman, W. (1996). Adolescent girls' relationships with mothers and best friends. *Child Development, 67,* 375–386.

Gavin, T., & Myers, A. (2003). Characteristics, enrollment, attendance, and dropout patterns of older adults in beginner Tai-Chi and line-dancing programs. *Journal of Aging & Physical Activity, 11,* 123–141.

Gawande, A. (2007, April 30). The way we age now. *The New Yorker,* pp. 49–59.

Gazmararian, J. A., Petersen, R., Spitz, A. M., Goodwin, M. M., Saltzman, L. E., & Marks, J. S. (2000). Violence and reproductive health: Current knowledge and future research directions. *Mat Child Health, 4,* 79–84.

Gee, H. (2004). *Jacob's ladder: The history of the human genome.* New York: Norton.

Gelman, R. (2006, August). Young natural-number arithmeticians. *Current Directions in Psychological Science, 15,* 193–197.

Gelman, R., & Baillargeon, R. (1983). A review of some Piagetian concepts. In P. H. Mussen (Ed.), *Handbook of child psychology: Vol 3. Cognitive development* (4th ed., pp. 167–230). New York: Wiley.

Gelman, R., & Gallistel, C. R. (2004, October 15). Language and the origin of numerical concepts. *Science, 306,* 441–443.

Gelman, S. A., Taylor, M. G., & Nguyen, S. (2004). Mother–child conversations about gender. *Monographs of the Society for Research in Child Development, 69.*

Genovese, J. (2006). Piaget, pedagogy, and evolutionary psychology. *Evolutionary Psychology, 4,* 127–137.

Gerard, C. M., Harris, K. A., & Thach, B. T. (2002). Spontaneous arousals in supine infants while swaddled and unswaddled during rapid eye movement and quiet sleep. *Pediatrics, 110,* 70.

Gerber, M. S. (October 9, 2002). Eighty million strong—the singles lobby. *The Hill,* p. 45.

Gerken, L. (2010). Infants use rational decision criteria for choosing among models of their input. *Cognition, 115,* 362–366.

Gershkoff-Stowe, L., & Hahn, E. (2007). Fast mapping skills in the developing lexicon. *Journal of Speech, Language, and Hearing Research, 50,* 682–696.

Gershoff, E. T. (2002). Parental corporal punishment and associated child behaviors and experiences: A meta-analytic and theoretical review. *Pychological Bulletin, 128,* 539–579.

Gersten, R., & Dimino, J. (2006, January). RTI (response to intervention): Rethinking special education for students with reading difficulties (yet again). *Reading Research Quarterly, 41,* 99–108.

Gerstorf, D., Ram, N., Estabrook, R., Schupp, J., Wagner, G., & Lindenberger, U. (2008). Life satisfaction shows terminal decline in old age: Longitudinal evidence from the German Socio-Economic Panel Study (SOEP). *Developmental Psychology, 44,* 1148–1159.

Gesell, A. L. (1946). The ontogenesis of infant behavior. In L. Carmichael (Ed.), *Manual of child psychology.* New York: Harper.

Ghazi, A., Henis-Korenblit, S., & Kenyon, C. (2009). A transcription elongation factor that links signals from the reproductive system to lifespan extension in Caenorhabditis elegans. *PLoS Genetics, 5,* 71–77.

Ghetti, S., & Angelini, L. (2008). The development of recollection and familiarity in childhood and adolescence: Evidence from the dual-process signal detection model. *Child Development, 79,* 339–358.

Ghisletta, P., Kennedy, K., Rodrigue, K., Lindenberger, U., & Raz, N. (2010). Adult age differences and the role of cognitive resources in perceptual-motor skill acquisition: Application of a multilevel negative exponential model. *The Journals of Gerontology: Series B: Psychological Sciences and Social Sciences, 65B,* 163–173.

Ghule, M., Balaiah, D., & Joshi, B. (2007). Attitude towards premarital sex among rural college youth in Maharashtra, India. *Sexuality & Culture, 11,* 1–17.

Gibbs, N. (2002, April 15). Making time for a baby. *Time,* pp. 48–54.

Gifford-Smith, M., & Brownell, C. (2003). Childhood peer relationships: Social acceptance, friendships, and peer networks. *Journal of School Psychology, 41,* 235–284.

Gilbert, L. A. (1994). Current perspectives on dual-career families. *Current Directions in Psychological Science, 3,* 101–105.

Gilbert, S. (2004, March 16). New clues to women veiled in black. *New York Times,* p. D1.

Gilbert, W. M., Nesbitt, T. S., & Danielsen, B. (1999). Childbearing beyond age 40: Pregnancy outcome in 24,032 cases. *Obstetrics and Gynecology, 93,* 9–14.

Gillespie, N. A., Cloninger, C. R., & Heath, A. C. (2003). The genetic and environmental relationship between Cloninger's dimensions of temperament and character. *Personality and Individual Differences, 35,* 1931–1946.

Gillham, A., Law, A., & Hickey, L. (2010). A psychodynamic perspective. *Reaching out: The psychology of assertive outreach.* New York: Routledge/Taylor & Francis Group.

Gillies, R., & Boyle, M. (2006, May). Ten Australian elementary teachers' discourse and reported pedagogical practices during cooperative learning. *The Elementary School Journal, 106,* 429–451.

Gilligan, C. (1982). *In a different voice: Psychological theory and women's development.* Cambridge, MA: Harvard University Press.

Gilligan, C. (1987). Adolescent development reconsidered. In C. E. Irwin (Ed.), *Adolescent social behavior and health.* San Francisco: Jossey-Bass.

Gilligan, C., Lyons, N. P., & Hammer, T. J. (Eds.). (1990). *Making connections.* Cambridge, MA: Harvard University Press.

Gilligan, C., Ward, J. V., & Taylor, J. M. (Eds.). (1988). *Mapping the moral domain: A contribution of women's thinking to psychological theory and education.* Cambridge, MA: Harvard University Press.

Gilliland, A. L., & Verny, T. R. (1999). The effects of domestic abuse on the unborn child. *Journal of Prenatal and Perinatal Psychology and Health, 13* [Special issue], 235–246.

Gillmore, M., Gilchrist, L., Lee, J., & Oxford, M. (2006, August). Women who gave birth as unmarried adolescents: Trends in substance use from adolescence to adulthood. *Journal of Adolescent Health, 39,* 237–243.

Gilmore, C. K., & Spelke, E. S. (2008). Children's understanding of the relationship between addition and subtraction. *Cognition, 107,* 932–945.

Ginzberg, E. (1972). Toward a theory of occupational choice: A restatement. *Vocational Guidance Quarterly, 12,* 10–14.

Giordana, S. (2005). *Understanding eating disorders: Conceptual and ethical issues in the treatment of anorexia (Issues in Biomedical Ethics).* New York: Oxford University Press.

Gitlin, L., Reever, K., Dennis, M., Mathieu, E., & Hauck, W. (2006, October). Enhancing quality of life of families who use adult day services: Short- and long-term effects of the Adult Day Services Plus Program. *The Gerontologist, 46,* 630–639.

Glatt, S., Chayavichitsilp, P., Depp, C., Schork, N., & Jeste, D. (2007). Successful aging: From phenotype to genotype. *Biological Psychiatry, 62*, 282–293.

Gleason, M., Iida, M., & Bolger, N. (2003). Daily supportive equity in close relationships. *Personality & Social Psychology Bulletin, 29*, 1036–1045.

Gleitman, L., & Landau, B. (1994). *The acquisition of the lexicon.* Cambridge, MA: Bradford.

Glick, P., Fiske, S. T., Mladinic, A., Saiz, J. L., et al. (2000). Beyond prejudice as simple antipathy: Hostile and benevolent sexism across cultures. *Journal of Personality and Social Psychology, 79*, 763–775.

Glick, P., Zion, C., & Nelson, C. (1988). What mediates sex discrimination in hiring decisions? *Journal of Personality and Social Psychology, 55*, 178–186.

Gliga, T., Elsabbagh, M., Andravizou, A., & Johnson, M. (2009). Faces attract infants' attention in complex displays. *Infancy, 14*, 550–562.

Gluhoski, V., Leader, J., & Wortman, C. B. (1994). Grief and bereavement. In V. S. Ramachandran (Ed.), *Encyclopedia of human behavior.* San Diego: Academic Press.

Goble, M. M. (2008). Medical and psychological complications of obesity. In H. D. Davies et al. (Eds.), *Obesity in childhood and adolescence, Vol. 1: Medical, biological, and social issues.* Westport, CT: Praeger Publishers / Greenwood Publishing.

Godefroy, O., Roussel, M., Despretz, P., Quaglino, V., & Boucart, M. (2010). Age-related slowing: Perceptuomotor, decision, or attention decline? *Experimental Aging Research, 36*, 169–189.

Goede, I., Branje, S., & Meeus, W. (2009). Developmental changes in adolescents' perceptions of relationships with their parents. *Journal of Youth and Adolescence, 38*, 75–88.

Goetz, A., & Shackelford, T. (2006). Modern application of evolutionary theory to psychology: Key concepts and clarifications. *American Journal of Psychology, 119*, 567–584.

Goldberg, A. (2010a). Children of lesbian and gay parents: Adjustment and experiences. *Lesbian and gay parents and their children: Research on the family life cycle.* Washington, DC: American Psychological Association.

Goldberg, A. (2010b). Introduction: Lesbian and gay parents and their children—Research and contemporary issues. *Lesbian and gay parents and their children: Research on the family life cycle.* Washington, DC: American Psychological Association.

Goldberg, A. (2010c). *Lesbian and gay parents and their children: Research on the family life cycle.* Washington, DC: American Psychological Association.

Goldberg, A. E. (2004). But do we need universal grammar? Comment on Lidz et al. *Cognition, 94*, 77–84.

Goldberg, J., Pereira, L., & Berghella, V. (2002). Pregnancy after uterine artery embolization. *Obstetrics and Gynecology, 100*, 869–872.

Goldfarb, Z. (2005, July 12). Newborn medical screening expands. *Wall Street Journal,* p. D6.

Goldman, R. (2004). Circumcision policy: A psychosocial perspective. *Pediatrics and Child Health, 9*, 630–633.

Goldscheider, F. K. (1994). Divorce and remarriage: Effects on the elderly population. *Reviews in Clinical Gerontology, 4*, 253–259.

Goldschmidt, L., Richardson, G., Willford, J., & Day, N. (2008). Prenatal marijuana exposure and intelligence test performance at age 6. *Journal of the American Academy of Child & Adolescent Psychiatry, 47*, 254–263.

Goldsmith, L. T. (2000). Tracking trajectories of talent: Child prodigies growing up. In R. C. Friedman & B. M. Shore et al. (Eds.), *Talents unfolding: Cognition and development.* Washington, DC: American Psychological Association.

Goldsmith, S. K., Pellmar, T. C., Kleinman, A. M., & Bunney, W. E. (2002). *Reducing suicide: A national imperative.* Washington, DC: National Academies Press.

Goldstein, A. P. (1999). Aggression reduction strategies: Effective and ineffective. *Psychology Quarterly, 14*, 40–58.

Goldston, D. B. (2003). *Measuring suicidal behavior and risk in children and adolescents.* Washington, DC: American Psychological Association.

Goleman, D. (1993, July 21). Baby sees, baby does, and classmates follow. *New York Times,* p. C10.

Golombok, S., Golding, J., Perry, B., Burston, A., Murray, C., Mooney-Somers, J., & Stevens, M. (2003). Children with lesbian parents: A community study. *Developmental Psychology, 39*, 20–33.

Golombok, S., & Tasker, F. (1996). Do parents influence the sexual orientation of their children? Findings from a longitudinal study of lesbian families. *Developmental Psychology, 32*, 3–11.

Good, M., & Willoughby, T. (2008). Adolescence as a sensitive period for spiritual development. *Child Development Perspectives, 2*, 32–37.

Goode, E. (1999, January 12). Clash over when, and how, to toilet-train. *New York Times,* pp. A1, A17.

Goode, E. (2004, February 3). Stronger warning is urged on antidepressants for teenagers. *New York Times,* p. A12.

Goodman, G., & Quas, J. (2008). Repeated interviews and children's memory: It's more than just how many. *Current Directions in Psychological Science, 17*, 386–390.

Goodman, G. S. (2006). Children's eyewitness memory: A modern history and contemporary commentary. *Journal of Social Issues, 62*, 811–832.

Goodman, J. S., Fields, D. L., & Blum, T. C. (2003). Cracks in the glass ceiling: In what kinds of organizations do women make it to the top? *Group & Organization Management, 28*, 475–501.

Goodwin, M. H. (1990). Tactical uses of stories: Participation frameworks within girls' and boys' disputes. *Discourse Processes, 13*, 33–71.

Goold, S. D., Williams, B., & Arnold, R. M. (2000). Conflicts regarding decisions to limit treatment: A differential diagnosis. *JAMA: The Journal of the American Medical Association, 283*, 909–914.

Goorabi, K., Hoseinabadi, R., & Share, H. (2008). Hearing aid effect on elderly depression in nursing home patients. *Asia Pacific Journal of Speech, Language, and Hearing, 11*, 119–124.

Gopnik, A., Meltzoff, A. N., & Kuhl, P. K. (2000). *The scientist in the crib: What early learning tells us about the mind.* New York: HarperCollins.

Gordon, N. (2007). The cerebellum and cognition. *European Journal of Paediatric Neurology, 30*, 214–220.

Gosselin, P., Perron, M., & Maassarani, R. (2010). Children's ability to distinguish between enjoyment and non-enjoyment smiles. *Infant and Child Development, 19*, 297–312.

Gostin, L. (2006, April). Physician-assisted suicide a legitimate medical practice? *JAMA: The Journal of the American Medical Association, 295*, 1941–1943.

Goswami, U. (1998). *Cognition in children.* Philadelphia: Psychology Press.

Gottesman, I. I. (1991). *Schizophrenia genesis: The origins of madness.* New York: Freeman.

Gottlieb, G., & Blair, C. (2004). How early experience matters in intellectual development in the case of poverty. *Preventive Science, 5*, 245–252.

Gottman, J. M., Fainsilber-Katz, L., & Hooven, C. (1996). *Meta-emotion: How families communicate emotionally.* Mahwah, NJ: Lawrence Erlbaum.

Gould, S. J. (1977). *Ontogeny and phylogeny.* Cambridge, MA: Harvard University Press.

Gow, A., Pattie, A., Whiteman, M., Whalley, L., & Deary, I. (2007). Social support and successful aging: Investigating the relationships between lifetime cognitive change and life satisfaction. *Journal of Individual Differences, 28*, 103–115.

Goyette-Ewing, M. (2000). Children's after-school arrangements: A study of self-care and developmental outcomes. *Journal of Prevention & Intervention in the Community, 20*, 55–67.

Grabner, R. H., Neubauer, A., C., & Stern, E. (2006). Superior performance and neural efficiency: The impact of intelligence and expertise. *Brain Research Bulletin, 69*, 422–439.

Graddol, D. (2004, February 27). The future of language. *Science, 303*, 1329–1331.

Grady, D. (2006, November). Management of menopausal symptoms. *New England Journal of Medicine, 355*, 2338–2347.

Graham, I., Carroli, G., Davies, C., & Medves, J. (2005). Episiotomy rates around the world: An update. *Birth: Issues in Perinatal Care, 32*, 219–223.

Graham, J. E., Christian, L. M., & Kiecolt-Glaser, J. K. (2006). Stress, age, and immune function: Toward a lifespan approach. *Journal of Behavioral Medicine, 29*, 389–400.

Granic, I., Hollenstein, T., & Dishion, T. (2003). Longitudinal analysis of flexibility and reorganization in early adolescence: A dynamic systems study of family interactions. *Developmental Psychology, 39*, 606–617.

Granié, M. (2010). Gender stereotype conformity and age as determinants of preschoolers' injury-risk behaviors. *Accident Analysis and Prevention, Vol. 42*, 726–733.

Grant, C., Wall, C., Brewster, D., Nicholson, R., Whitehall, J., Super, L., et al. (2007). Policy statement on iron deficiency in pre-school-aged children. *Journal of Paediatrics and Child Health, 43*, 513–521.

Grant, J., Weaver, M., & Elliott, T. (2004). Family caregivers of stroke survivors: Characteristics of caregivers at risk for depression. *Rehabilitation Psychology, 49*, 172–179.

Grantham, T., & Ford, D. (2003). Beyond self-concept and self-esteem: Racial identity and gifted African American students. *High School Journal, 87*, 18–29.

Grantham-McGregor, S., Ani, C., & Fernald, L. (2001). The role of nutrition in intellectual development. In R. J. Sternberg & E. L. Grigorenko (Eds.), *Environmental effects on cognitive abilities.* Mahwah, NJ: Lawrence Erlbaum.

Grantham-McGregor, S., Powell, C., Walker, S., Chang, S., & Fletcher, P. (1994). The long-term follow-up of severely malnourished children who participated in an intervention program. *Child Development, 65*, 428–439.

Gratch, G., & Schatz, J. A. (1987). Cognitive development: The relevance of Piaget's infancy books. In J. D. Osofsky (Ed.), *Handbook of infant development* (2nd ed.). New York: Wiley.

Grattan, M. P., DeVos, E. S., Levy, J., & McClintock, M. K. (1992). Asymmetric action in the human newborn: Sex differences in patterns of organization. *Child Development, 63*, 273–289.

Gray, C., Ferguson, J., Behan, S., Dunbar, C., Dunn, J., & Mitchell, D. (2007, March). Developing young readers through the linguistic phonics approach. *International Journal of Early Years Education, 15*, 15–33.

Gray-Little, B., & Hafdahl, A. R. (2000). Factors influencing racial comparisons of self-esteem: A quantitative review. *Psychological Bulletin, 126*, 26–54.

Gredler, M. E., & Shields, C. C. (2008). *Vygotsky's legacy: A foundation for research and practice.* New York: Guilford Press.

Green, M. H. (1995). Influences of job type, job status, and gender on achievement motivation. *Current Psychology: Developmental, Learning, Personality, Social, 14*, 159–165.

Greenberg, J., & Becker, M. (1988). Aging parents as family resources. *Gerontologist, 28*, 786–790.

Greenberg, L., Cwikel, J., & Mirsky, J. (2007, January). Cultural correlates of eating attitudes: A comparison between native-born and immigrant university students in Israel. *International Journal of Eating Disorders, 40*, 51–58.

Greene, K., Krcmar, M., Walters, L. H., Rubin, D L., & Hale, J. L. (2000). Targeting adolescent risk-taking behaviors: The contribution of egocentrism and sensation-seeking. *Journal of Adolescence, 23*, 439–461.

Greene, S., Anderson, E., & Hetherington, E. (2003). Risk and resilience after divorce. In F. Walsh (Ed.), *Normal family processes: Growing diversity and complexity*. New York: Guilford Press.

Greenway, C. (2002). The process, pitfalls and benefits of implementing a reciprocal teaching intervention to improve the reading comprehension of a group of year 6 pupils. *Educational Psychology in Practice, 18*, 113–137.

Greenwood, D., & Isbell, L. (2002). Ambivalent sexism and the dumb blonde: Men's and women's reactions to sexist jokes. *Psychology of Women Quarterly, 26*, 341–350.

Greenwood, D. N., & Pietromonaco, P. R. (2004). The interplay among attachment orientation, idealized media images of women, and body dissatisfaction: A social psychological analysis. In L. J. Shrum (Ed.), *Psychology of entertainment media: Blurring the lines between entertainment and persuasion*. Mahwah, NJ: Lawrence Erlbaum.

Gregory, K. (2005). Update on nutrition for preterm and full-term infants. *Journal of Obstetrics and Gynecological Neonatal Nursing, 34*, 98–108.

Gregory, S. (1856). *Facts for young women*. Boston.

Griffith, D. R., Azuma, S. D., & Chasnoff, I. J. (1994). Three-year outcome of children exposed prenatally to drugs. *Journal of the American Academy of Child and Adolescent Psychiatry, 33*, 20–27.

Grigorenko, E. (2003). Intraindividual fluctuations in intellectual functioning: Selected links between nutrition and the mind. In R. Sternberg & J. Lautrey (Eds.), *Models of intelligence: International perspectives*. Washington, DC: American Psychological Association.

Grigorenko, E., Jarvin, L., Diffley, R., Goodyear, J., Shanahan, E., & Sternberg, R. (2009). Are SSATS and GPA enough? A theory-based approach to predicting academic success in secondary school. *Journal of Educational Psychology, 101*, 964–981.

Grissmer, D., Grimm, K., Aiyer, S., Murrah, W., & Steele, J. (2010). Fine motor skills and early comprehension of the world: Two new school readiness indicators. *Developmental Psychology, 46*, 1008–1017.

Groome, L. J., Swiber, M. J., Atterbury, J. L., Bentz, L. S., & Holland, S. B. (1997). Similarities and differences in behavioral state organization during sleep periods in the perinatal infant before and after birth. *Child Development, 68*, 1–11.

Groome, L. J., Swiber, M. J., Bentz, L. S., Holland, S. B., & Atterbury, J. L. (1995). Maternal anxiety during pregnancy: Effect on fetal behavior at 38 to 40 weeks of gestation. *Developmental and Behavioral Pediatrics, 16*, 391–396.

Groopman, J. (1998 February 8). Decoding destiny. *The New Yorker*, pp. 42–47.

Gross, R. T., Spiker, D., & Haynes, C. W. (Eds.). (1997). *Helping low-birthweight, premature babies: The Infant Health and Development Program*. Stanford, CA: Stanford University Press.

Grossman, K. E., Grossmann, K., & Waters, E. (Eds.). (2005). *Attachment from infancy to adulthood: The major longitudinal studies*. New York: Guilford Press.

Grossmann, K. E., Grossmann, K., Huber, F., & Wartner, U. (1982). German children's behavior towards their mothers at 12 months and their fathers at 18 months in Ainsworth's Strange Situation. *International Journal of Behavioral Development, 4*, 157–181.

Grunbaum, J. A., Kann, L., Kinchen, S. A., Williams, B., Ross, J. G., Lowry, R., & Kolbe, L. (2002). *Youth risk behavior surveillance—United States, 2001*. Atlanta, GA: Centers for Disease Control.

Grunbaum, J. A., Lowry, R., & Kann, L. (2001). Prevalence of health-related behaviors among alternative high school students as compared with students attending regular high schools. *Journal of Adolescent Health, 29*, 337–343.

Guarente, L. (2006, December 14). Sirtuins as potential targets for metabolic syndrome. *Nature, 14*, 868–874.

Guasti, M. T. (2002). *Language acquisition: The growth of grammar*. Cambridge, MA: MIT Press.

Guerrero, A., Hishinuma, E., Andrade, N., Nishimura, S., & Cunanan, V. (2006, July). Correlations among socioeconomic and family factors and academic, behavioral, and emotional difficulties in Filipino adolescents in Hawaii. *International Journal of Social Psychiatry, 52*, 343–359.

Guerrero, S., Enesco, I., Lago, O., & Rodríguez, P. (2010). Preschool children's understanding of racial cues in drawings and photographs. *Cognitive Development, 25*, 79–89.

Guerrini, I., Thomson, A., & Gurling, H. (2007). The importance of alcohol misuse, malnutrition and genetic susceptibility on brain growth and plasticity. *Neuroscience & Biobehavioral Reviews, 31*, 212–220.

Gump, L. S., Baker, R. C., & Roll, S. (2000). Cultural and gender differences in moral judgment: A study of Mexican Americans and Anglo-Americans. *Hispanic Journal of Behavioral Sciences, 22*, 78–93.

Gumz, A., Kästner, D., Geyer, M., Wutzler, U., Villmann, T., & Brähler, E. (2010). Instability and discontinuous change in the experience of therapeutic interaction: An extended single-case study of psychodynamic therapy processes. *Psychotherapy Research, 20*, 398–412.

Gupta, A., & State, M. (2007). Recent advances in the genetics of autism. *Biological Psychiatry, 61*, 429–437.

Gupta, U., & Singh, P. (1982). An exploratory study of love and liking and type of marriages. *Indian Journal of Applied Psychology, 19*, 92–97.

Gure, A., Ucanok, Z., & Sayil, M. (2006). The associations among perceived pubertal timing, parental relations and self-perception in Turkish adolescents. *Journal of Youth and Adolescence, 35*, 541–550.

Gurin, P., Nagda, B. R. A., & Lopez, G. E. (2004). The benefits of diversity in education for democratic citizenship. *Journal of Social Issues, 60*, 17–34.

Gurung, R. (2010). *Health psychology: A cultural approach* (2nd ed.). Belmont, CA: Wadsworth/Cengage Learning.

Guttmann, J., & Rosenberg, M. (2003). Emotional intimacy and children's adjustment: A comparison between single-parent divorced and intact families. *Educational Psychology, 23*, 457–472.

Guzzo, K. (2009). Marital intentions and the stability of first cohabitations. *Journal of Family Issues, 30*, 179–205.

Haas-Thompson, T., Alston, P., & Holbert, D. (2008). The impact of education and death-related experiences on rehabilitation counselor attitudes toward death and dying. *Journal of Applied Rehabilitation Counseling, 39*, 20–27.

Haber, D. (2006). Life review: Implementation, theory, research, and therapy. *International Journal of Aging & Human Development, 63*, 153–171.

Hack, M., Flannery, D. J., Schluchter, M., Cartar, L., Borawski, E., & Klein, N. (2002). Outcomes in young adulthood for very low birth weight infants. *New England Journal of Medicine, 346*, 149–157.

Haddock, S., & Rattenborg, K. (2003). Benefits and challenges of dual-earning: Perspectives of successful couples. *American Journal of Family Therapy, 31*, 325–344.

Haeffel, G., Getchell, M., Koposov, R., Yrigollen, C., DeYoung, C., af Klinteberg, B., et al. (2008). Association between polymorphisms in the dopamine transporter gene and depression: Evidence for a gene-environment interaction in a sample of juvenile detainees. *Psychological Science, 19*, 62–69.

Hagerty, R. G., Butow, P. N., Ellis, P. A., Lobb, E. A., Pendlebury, S., Leighl, N., Goldstein, D., Lo, S. K., & Tattersall, M. H. (2004). Cancer patient preferences for communication of prognosis in the metastatic setting. *Journal of Clinical Oncology, 22*, 1721–1730.

Haines, J., & Neumark-Sztainer, D. (2006, December). Prevention of obesity and eating disorders: A consideration of shared risk factors. *Health Education Research, 21*, 770–782.

Haith, M. H. (1986). Sensory and perceptual processes in early infancy. *Journal of Pediatrics, 109*(1), 158–171.

Haith, M. H. (1991, April). Setting a path for the 90s: Some goals and challenges in infant sensory and perceptual development. Paper presented at the biennial meeting of the Society for Research in Child Development, Seattle, WA.

Haley, D., Grunau, R., Weinberg, J., Keidar, A., & Oberlander, T. (2010). Physiological correlates of memory recall in infancy: Vagal tone, cortisol, and imitation in preterm and full-term infants at 6 months. *Infant Behavior & Development, 33*, 219–234.

Halgunseth, L. C., Ispa, J. M., & Rudy, D. (2006). Parental control in Latino families: An integrated review of the literature. *Child Development, 77*, 1282–1297.

Hall, E. G., & Lee, A. M. (1984). Sex differences in motor performance of young children: Fact or fiction? *Sex Roles, 10*, 217–230.

Hall, J. J., Neal, T., & Dean, R. S. (2008). Lateralization of cerebral functions. In A. M. McNeil & D. Wedding (Eds.), *The neuropsychology handbook* (3rd ed.). New York: Springer Publishing.

Hamilton, B. E., Martin, J. A., & Ventura, S. J. (2009). *National Vital Statistics Reports*. Washington, DC:

Hamilton, G. (1998). Positively testing. *Families in Society, 79*, 570–576.

Hamon, R. R., & Ingoldsby, B. B. (Eds.). (2003). *Mate selection across cultures*. Thousand Oaks, CA: Sage Publications.

Hane, A., Feldstein, S., & Dernetz, V. (2003). The relation between coordinated interpersonal timing and maternal sensitivity in four-month-old infants. *Journal of Psycholinguistic Research, 32*, 525–539.

Hankin, B. L., & Abramson, L. Y. (2001). Development of gender differences in depression: An elaborated cognitive vulnerability-transactional stress theory. *Psychological Bulletin, 127*, 773–796.

Hanson, D. R., & Gottesman, I. I. (2005). Theories of schizophrenia: A genetic-inflammatory-vascular synthesis. *BMC Medical Genetics, 6*, 7.

Hanson, R., & Hayslip, B. (2000). Widowhood in later life. In J. Harvey & E. Miller (Eds.), *Loss and trauma: General and close relationship perspectives*. New York: Brunner-Routledge.

Hanson, L., Schenck, A., Rokoske, F., Abernethy, A., Kutner, J., Spence, C., et al. (2010). Hospices' preparation and practices for quality measurement. *Journal of Pain and Symptom Management, 39*, 1–8.

Hansson, R. O., & Carpenter, B. N. (1994). *Relationship in old age: Coping with the challenge of transition*. New York: Guilford Press.

Happe, F. G. E., Winner, E., & Brownell, H. (1998). The getting of wisdom: Theory of mind in old age. *Developmental Psychology, 34*, 358–362.

Harden, K., Turkheimer, E., & Loehlin, J. (2007). Genotype by environment interaction in adolescents' cognitive aptitude. *Behavior Genetics, 37*, 273–283.

Hardy, L. T. (2007). Attachment theory and reactive attachment disorder: Theoretical perspectives and treatment implications. *Journal of Child and Adolescent Psychiatric Nursing, 20*, 27–39.

Hardy, S., & Grogan, S. (2009). Preventing disability through exercise: Investigating older adults' influences and motivations to engage in physical activity. *Journal of Health Psychology, 14*, 1036–1046.

Hare, T. A., Tottenham, N., Galvan, A., & Voss, H. U. (2008). Biological substrates of emotional reactivity and regulation in adolescence during an emotional go-nogo task. *Biological Psychiatry, 63*, 927–934.

Hargreaves, D., & Tiggemann, M. (2003). The effect of "thin ideal" television commercials on body dissatisfaction and schema activation during early adolescence. *Journal of Youth and Adolescence, 32*, 367–373.

Harrell, J. S., Bangdiwala, S. I., Deng, S., Webb, J. P., & Bradley, C. (1998). Smoking initiation in youth: The roles of gender, race, socioeconomics, and developmental status. *Journal of Adolescent Health, 23*, 271–279.

Harrell, Z. A., & Karim, N. M. (2008). Is gender relevant only for problem alcohol behaviors? An examination of correlates of alcohol use among college students. *Addictive Behaviors, 33,* 359–365.

Harris, J., Vernon, P., & Jang, K. (2007). Rated personality and measured intelligence in young twin children. *Personality and Individual Differences, 42,* 75–86.

Harris, J. R. (1998). *The nurture assumption: Why children turn out the way they do.* New York: Free Press.

Harris, J. R. (2000). Socialization, personality development, and the child's environments: Comment on Vandell. *Developmental Psychology, 36,* 711–723.

Harris, M., Prior, J., & Koehoorn, M. (2008). Age at menarche in the Canadian population: Secular trends and relationship to adulthood BMI. *Journal of Adolescent Health, 43,* 548–554.

Harrison, K., & Bond, B. (2007). Gaming magazines and the drive for muscularity in preadolescent boys: A longitudinal examination. *Body Image, 4,* 269–277.

Harrison, K., & Hefner, V. (2006, April). Media exposure, current and future body ideals, and disordered eating among preadolescent girls: A longitudinal panel study. *Journal of Youth and Adolescence, 35,* 153–163.

Hart, B. (2004). What toddlers talk about. *First Language, 24,* 91–106.

Hart, D., Burock, D., & London, B. (2003). Prosocial tendencies, antisocial behavior, and moral development. In A. Slater & G. Bremner (Eds.), *An introduction to developmental psychology.* Malden, MA: Blackwell Publishers.

Hart, S. N., Brassard, M. R., & Karlson, H. (1996). Psychological maltreatment. In J. N. Briere, L. Berliner, J. Bulkley, C. Jenny, & T. Reid (Eds.), *The APSAC handbook on child maltreatment.* Thousand Oaks, CA: Sage Publications.

Hart, S., & Carrington, H. (2002). Jealousy in six-month-old infants. *Infancy, 3,* 395–402.

Harter, S. (1990). Issues in the assessment of self-concept of children and adolescents. In A. LaGreca (Ed.), *Through the eyes of a child.* Boston: Allyn & Bacon.

Hartshorne, T. S. (1994). Friendship. In V. S. Ramachandran (Ed.), *Encyclopedia of human behavior.* San Diego: Academic Press.

Hartup, W. W., & Stevens, N. (1999). Friendships and adaptation across the life span. *Current Directions in Psychological Science, 8,* 76–79.

Harvey, J. H., & Fine, M. A. (2004). *Children of divorce: Stories of loss and growth.* Mahwah, NJ: Lawrence Erlbaum.

Hasher, L., & Zacks, R. T. (1984). Automatic processing of fundamental information: The case of frequency of occurrence. *American Psychologist, 39,* 1372–1388.

Haslam, C., & Lawrence, W. (2004). Health-related behavior and beliefs of pregnant smokers. *Health Psychology, 23,* 486–491.

Haslett, A. (2004, May 31). Love supreme. *The New Yorker,* pp. 76–80.

Hatfield, E., & Rapson, R. L. (1993). Historical and cross-cultural perspectives on passionate love and sexual desire. *Annual Review of Sex Research, 4,* 67–97.

Hattery, A. (2000). *Women, work, and family: Balancing and weaving.* Thousand Oaks, CA: Sage Publications.

Hatton, C. (2002). People with intellectual disabilities from ethnic minority communities in the United States and the United Kingdom. In L. M. Glidden (Ed.), *International review of research in mental retardation, Vol. 25.* San Diego: Academic Press.

Haugaard, J. J. (2000). The challenge of defining child sexual abuse. *American Psychologist, 55,* 1036–1039.

Havighurst, R. J. (1973). Social roles, work, leisure, and education. In C. Eisdorfer & M. P. Lawton (Eds.), *The psychology of adult development and aging.* Washington, DC: American Psychological Association.

Hawkins-Rodgers, Y. (2007). Adolescents adjusting to a group home environment: A residential care model of reorganizing attachment behavior and building resiliency. *Children and Youth Services Review, 29,*1131–1141.

Hay, D., Payne, A., & Chadwick, A. (2004). Peer relations in childhood. *Journal of Child Psychology & Psychiatry & Allied Disciplines, 45,* 84–108.

Hayden, T. (1998, September 21). The brave new world of sex selection. *Newsweek,* p. 93.

Hayflick, L. (1974). The strategy of senescence. *The Journal of Gerontology, 14,* 37–45.

Haynie, D. L., Nansel, T., Eitel, P., Crump, A. D., Saylor, K., Yu, K., & Simons-Morton, B. (2001). Bullies, victims, and bully/victims: Distinct groups of at-risk youth. *Journal of Early Adolescence, 21,* 29–49.

Hayslip, B., Jr., Shore, R. J., & Henderson, C. E. (2000). Perceptions of grandparents' influence in the lives of their grandchildren. In B. Hayslip, Jr., Goldberg, & G. Robin (Eds.), *Grandparents raising grandchildren: Theoretical, empirical, and clinical perspectives.* New York: Springer.

Hayward, M., Crimmins, E., & Saito, Y. (1997). Cause of death and active life expectancy in the older population of the United States. *Journal of Aging and Health,* 122–131.

Hazan, C., & Shaver, P. (1987). Romantic love conceptualized as an attachment process. *Journal of Personality and Social Psychology, 52,* 511–524.

Heaven, P., & Ciarrochi, J. (2008). Parental styles, gender and the development of hope and self-esteem. *European Journal of Personality, 22,* 707–724.

Hedge, J., Borman, W., & Lammlein, S. (2006). *Age stereotyping and age discrimination.* Washington, DC: American Psychological Association.

Heerey, E. A., Keltner, D., & Capps, L. M. (2003). Making sense of self-conscious emotion: Linking theory of mind and emotion in children with autism. *Emotion, 3,* 394–400.

Heimann, M. (2001). Neonatal imitation—a "fuzzy" phenomenon? In F. Lacerda & C. von Hofsten (Eds.), *Emerging cognitive abilities in early infancy.* Mahwah, NJ: Lawrence Erlbaum.

Heimann, M. (Ed.). (2003). *Regression periods in human infancy.* Mahwah, NJ: Lawrence Erlbaum.

Heinemann, G. D., & Evans, P. L. (1990). Widowhood: Loss, change, and adaptation. In T. H. Brubaker (Ed.), *Family relationships in later life.* Newbury Park, CA: Sage Publications.

Helmes, E., & Campbell, A. (2010). Differential sensitivity to administration format of measures of attitudes toward older adults. *The Gerontologist, 50,* 60–65.

Helms, J. E., Jernigan, M., & Mascher, J. (2005). The meaning of race in psychology and how to change it: A methodological perspective. *American Psychologist, 60,* 27–36.

Hendrick, C., & Hendrick, S. (2003). Romantic love: Measuring cupid's arrow. In S. Lopez & C. Snyder (Eds.), *Positive psychological assessment: A handbook of models and measures.* Washington, DC: American Psychological Association.

Hendrie, H. C., Ogunniyi, A., Hall, K. S., Baiyewu, O., Unverzagt, F. W., Gureje, O., Gao, S., Evans, R. M., Ogunseyinde, A. O., Adeyinka, A. O., Musick, B., & Hui, S. L. (2001). Incidence of dementia and Alzheimer disease in 2 communities: Yoruba residing in Ibadan, Nigeria, and African Americans residing in Indianapolis, Indiana. *JAMA: The Journal of the American Medical Association, 285,* 739–747.

Hendry, L., & Kloep, M. (2010). How universal is emerging adulthood? An empirical example. *Journal of Youth Studies, 13,* 169–179.

Henig, R. M. (2008). Taking play seriously. *New York Times Magazine,* 38–45, 60, 75.

Henig, R. W. (2010, August 18). What is it about 20-somethings? *New York Times Magazine.*

Henry, R., Miller, R., & Giarrusso, R. (2005). Difficulties, disagreements, and disappointments in late-life marriages. *International Journal of Aging & Human Development, 61,* 243–264.

Henry, J., & McNab, W. (2003). Forever young: A health promotion focus on sexuality and aging. *Gerontology & Geriatrics Education, 23,* 57–74.

Hensley, P. (2006, July). Treatment of bereavement-related depression and traumatic grief. *Journal of Affective Disorders, 92,* 117–124.

Herdt, G. H. (Ed.). (1998). *Rituals of manhood: Male initiation in Papua New Guinea.* Somerset, NJ: Transaction Books.

Hernandez, D. J., Denton, N. A., & McCartney, S. E. (2008). Children in immigrant families: Looking to America's Future. *Social Policy Report, 22,* 3–24.

Hernandez-Reif, M., Field, T., Diego, M., Vera, Y., & Pickens, J. (2006, January). Brief report: Happy faces are habituated more slowly by infants of depressed mothers. *Infant Behavior & Development, 29,* 131–135.

Herrnstein, R. J., & Murray, C. (1994). *The bell curve: Intelligence and class structure in American life.* New York: Free Press.

Hertelendy, F., & Zakar, T. (2004). Prostaglandins and the myometrium and cervix. *Prostaglandins, Leukotrienes and Essential Fatty Acids, 70,* 207–222.

Hertzog, C., Kramer, A., Wilson, R., & Lindenberger, U. (2008). Enrichment effects on adult cognitive development: Can the functional capacity of older adults be preserved and enhanced? *Psychological Science in the Public Interest, 9,* 1–65.

Hess, T., Auman, C., & Colcombe, S. (2003). The impact of stereotype threat on age differences in memory performance. *Journals of Gerontology: Series B: Psychological Sciences & Social Sciences, 58B,* P3–P11.

Hetherington, E., & Elmore, A. (2003). Risk and resilience in children coping with their parents' divorce and remarriage. In S. Luthar (Ed.), *Resilience and vulnerability: Adaptation in the context of childhood adversities.* New York: Cambridge University Press.

Hetherington, E. M., & Kelly, J. (2002). For better or worse: Divorce reconsidered. New York: Norton.

Hewstone, M. (2003). Intergroup contact: Panacea for prejudice? *Psychologist, 16,* 352–355.

Heyman, R., & Slep, A. M. (2002). Do child abuse and interparental violence lead to adulthood family violence? *Journal of Marriage & Family, 64,* 864–870.

HHL (Harvard Health Letter). (1997, May). Turning up the volume, *Harvard Mental Health Letter,* p. 4.

Hietala, J., Cannon, T. D., & van Erp, T. G. M. (2003). Regional brain morphology and duration of illness in never-medicated first-episode patients with schizophrenia. *Schizophrenia, 64,* 79–81.

Higgins, D., & McCabe, M. (2003). Maltreatment and family dysfunction in childhood and the subsequent adjustment of children and adults. *Journal of Family Violence, 18,* 107–120.

Hightower, J. R. R. (2005). Women and depression. In A. Barnes (Ed.), *Handbook of women, psychology, and the law.* New York: Wiley.

Hillman, J. (2000). *Clinical perspectives on elderly sexuality.* Dordrecht, Netherlands: Kluwer Academic Publishers.

Hinduja, S., & Patchin, J. (2008). Personal information of adolescents on the Internet: A quantitative content analysis of MySpace. *Journal of Adolescence, 31,* 125–146.

Hirshfeld-Becker, D., Masek, B., Henin, A., Blakely, L., Pollock-Wurman, R., McQuade, J., et al. (2010). Cognitive behavioral therapy for 4- to 7-year-old children with anxiety disorders: A randomized clinical trial. *Journal of Consulting and Clinical Psychology, 78,* 498–510.

Hirsh-Pasek, K., & Michnick-Golinkoff, R. (1995). *The origins of grammar: Evidence from early language comprehension.* Cambridge, MA: MIT Press.

Hitlin, S., Brown, J. S., & Elder, G. H., Jr. (2006). Racial self-categorization in adolescence: Multiracial development and social pathways. *Child Development, 77,* 1298–1308.

Hjelmstedt, A., Widström, A., & Collins, A. (2006). Psychological correlates of prenatal attachment in women who conceived after in vitro fertilization and women who conceived naturally. *Birth: Issues in Perinatal Care, 33,* 303–310.

HMHL (Harvard Mental Health Letter). (2005). The treatment of attention deficit disorder: New evidence. *Harvard Mental Health Letter, 21,* 6.

Ho, A., Stein, J., Hua, X., Lee, S., Hibar, D., Leow, A., et al. (2010). A commonly carried allele of the obesity-related FTO gene is associated with reduced brain volume in the healthy elderly. *PNAS Proceedings of the National Academy of Sciences of the United States of America, 107,* 8404–8409.

Hocutt, A. M. (1996). Effectiveness of special education: Is placement the critical factor? *The Future of Children, 6,* 77–102.

Hoek, J., & Gendall, P. (2006). Advertising and obesity: A behavioral perspective. *Journal of Health Communication, 11,* 409–423.

Hoelter L. F., Axinn, W. G., & Ghimire, D. J. (2004). Social change, premarital nonfamily experiences, and marital dynamics. *Journal of Marriage & Family, 66,* 1131–1151.

Hoeve, M., Blokland, A., Dubas, J., Loeber, R., Gerris, J., & van der Laan, P. (2008). Trajectories of delinquency and parenting styles. *Journal of Abnormal Child Psychology: An Official Publication of the International Society for Research in Child and Adolescent Psychopathology, 36,* 223–235.

Hofer, M. A. (2006). Psychobiological roots of early attachment. *Current Directions in Psychological Science, 15,* 84–88.

Hofferth, S., & Sandberg, J. F. (2001). How American children spend their time. *Journal of Marriage and the Family, 63,* 295–308.

Hoffman, L. (2003). Why high schools don't change: What students and their yearbooks tell us. *High School Journal, 86,* 22–37.

Hohmann-Marriott, B. (2006, November). Shared beliefs and the union stability of married and cohabiting couples. *Journal of Marriage and Family, 68,* 1015–1028.

Holahan, C., & Chapman, J. (2002). Longitudinal predictors of proactive goals and activity participation at age 80. *Journals of Gerontology: Series B: Psychological Sciences & Social Sciences, 57B,* P418–P425.

Holden, G. W., & Miller, P. C. (1999). Enduring and different: A meta-analysis of the similarity in parents' child rearing. *Psychological Bulletin, 125,* 223–254.

Holden, C. (1987, October 9). Why do women live longer than men? *Science, 233,* 158–160.

Holland, J. (2008). Reading aloud with infants: The controversy, the myth, and a case study. *Early Childhood Education Journal, 35,* 383–385.

Holland, J. L. (1997). *Making vocational choices: A theory of vocational personalities and environments* (3rd ed.). Odessa, FL: Psychological Assessment Resources.

Holland, J. M., Neimeyer, R. A., Boelen, P. A., & Prigerson, H. G. (2009). The underlying structure of grief: A taxometric investigation of prolonged and normal reactions to loss. *Journal of Psychopathology and Behavioral Assessment, 31,* 190–201.

Holland, N. (1994, August). Race dissonance—Implications for African American children. Paper presented at the annual meeting of the American Psychological Association, Los Angeles, CA.

Holmes, E. R., & Holmes, L. D. (1995). *Other cultures, elder years.* Thousand Oaks, CA: Sage Publications.

Holowaka, S., & Petitto, L. A. (2002). Left hemisphere cerebral specialization for babies while babbling. *Science, 287,* 1515.

Holtgraves, T. (2009). Gambling, gambling activities, and problem gambling. *Psychologically Addictive Behavior, 23,* 295–302.

Holzman, L. (1997). *Schools for growth: Radical alternatives to current educational models.* Mahwah, NJ: Lawrence Erlbaum.

Hooks, B., & Chen, C. (2008). Vision triggers an experience-dependent sensitive period at the retinogeniculate synapse. *The Journal of Neuroscience, 28,* 4807–4817. Available online at http://search.ebscohost.com

Hopkins, B., & Westra, T. (1989). Maternal expectations of their infants' development: Some cultural differences. *Developmental Medicine and Child Neurology, 31,* 384–390.

Hopkins, B., & Westra, T. (1990). Motor development, maternal expectation, and the role of handling. *Infant Behavior and Development, 13,* 117–122.

Hopkins-Golightly, T., Raz, S., & Sander, C. (2003). Influence of slight to moderate risk for birth hypoxia on acquisition of cognitive and language function in the preterm infant: A cross-sectional comparison with preterm-birth controls. *Neuropsychology, 17,* 3–13.

Horiuchi, S., Finch, C., & Mesle, F. (2003). Differential patterns of age-related mortality increase in middle age and old age. *Journals of Gerontology: Series A: Biological Sciences & Medical Sciences, 58A,* 495–507.

Hornor, G. (2008). Reactive attachment disorder. *Journal of Pediatric Health Care, 22,* 234–239.

Horowitz, A. (1994). Vision impairment and functional disability among nursing home residents. *Gerontologist, 34,* 316–323.

Horwitz, B. N., Luong, G., & Charles, G. T. (2008). Neuroticism and extraversion share genetic and environmental effects with negative and positive mood spillover in a nationally representative sample. *Personality and Individual Differences, 45,* 636–642.

Howe, M. J. (1997). *IQ in question: The truth about intelligence.* London, England: Sage Publications.

Howe, M. L. (2003). Memories from the cradle. *Current Directions in Psychological Science, 12,* 62–65.

Howe, M. L., Courage, M. L., & Edison, S. C. (2004). When autobiographical memory begins. In S. Algarabel, A. Pitarque, T. Bajo, S. E. Gathercole, & M. A. Conway (Eds.), *Theories of memory: Vol. 3.* New York: Psychology Press.

Howell, E., Mora, P., Chassin, M., & Leventhal, H. (2010). Lack of preparation, physical health after childbirth, and early postpartum depressive symptoms. *Journal of Women's Health, 19,* 703–708.

Howell, P., Bailey, E., & Kothari, N. (2010). Changes in the pattern of stuttering over development for children who recover or persist. *Clinical Linguistics & Phonetics, 24,* 556–575.

Howes, C., Galinsky, E., & Kontos, S. (1998). Child care caregiver sensitivity and attachment. *Social Development, 7,* 25–36.

Howes, O., & Kapur, S. (2009). The dopamine hypothesis of schizophrenia: Version III—The final common pathway. *Schizophrenia Bulletin, 35,* 549–562.

Hu, W. (2010, October 1). Legal debate swirls over charges in a student's suicide. *New York Times.*

Huang, A., Subak, L., Thom, D., Van Den Eeden, S., Ragins, A., Kuppermann, M., et al. (2009). Sexual function and aging in racially and ethnically diverse women. *Journal of the American Geriatrics Society, 57,* 1362–1368.

Huang, J. (2004). Death: Cultural traditions. From *On Our Own Terms: Moyers on Dying.* Available online at www.pbs.org

Hubbs-Tait, L., Nation, J. R., Krebs, N. F., & Bellinger, D. C. (2005). Neurotoxicants, micronutrients, and social environments: Individual and combined effects on children's development. *Journal of the American Psychological Society, 6,* 57–101.

Hubel, D. H., & Wiesel, T. N. (1979). Brain mechanisms of vision. *Scientific American, 241,* 150–162.

Hubel, D. H., & Wiesel, T. N. (2004). *Brain and visual perception: The story of a 25-year collaboration.* New York: Oxford University Press.

Hudson, J. A., Sosa, B. B., & Shapiro, L. R. (1997). Scripts and plans: The development of preschool children's event knowledge and event planning. In S. L. Friedman & E. K. Scholnick (Eds.), *The developmental psychology of planning: Why, how and when do we plan.* Mahwah, NJ: Lawrence Erlbaum.

Hugdahl, K., & Westerhausen, R. (2010). *The two halves of the brain: Information processing in the cerebral hemispheres.* Cambridge, MA: MIT Press.

Hughes, S. M., & Gore, A. C. (2007). How the brain controls puberty, and implications for sex and ethnic differences. *Family & Community Health, 30* (1, Suppl.), S112–S114.

Huijbregts, S., Tavecchio, L., Leseman, P., & Hoffenaar, P. (2009). Child rearing in a group setting: Beliefs of Dutch, Caribbean Dutch, and Mediterranean Dutch caregivers in center-based child care. *Journal of Cross-Cultural Psychology, 40,* 797–815. Available online at http://search.ebscohost.com

Huizink, A., Mulder, E., & Buitelaar, J. (2004). Prenatal stress and risk for psychopathology: Specific effects or induction of general susceptibility? *Psychological Bulletin, 130,* 115–142.

Human Genome Project. (2006). Available online at http://www.ornl.gov/sci/techresources/Human_Genome/medicine/genetest.shtml

Hunt, M. (1974). *Sexual behaviors in the 1970s.* New York: Dell.

Hunt, M. (1993). *The story of psychology.* New York: Doubleday.

Hunter, J., & Mallon, G. P. (2000). Lesbian, gay, and bisexual adolescent development: Dancing with your feet tied together. In B. Greene & G. L. Croom (Eds.), *Education, research, and practice in lesbian, gay, bisexual, and transgendered psychology: A resource manual, Vol. 5.* Thousand Oaks, CA: Sage Publications.

Hunter, S., & Smith, D. (2008). Predictors of children's understandings of death: Age, cognitive ability, death experience and maternal communicative competence. *Omega: Journal of Death and Dying, 57,* 143–162.

Huntsinger, C. S., Jose, P. E., Liaw, F., & Ching, W-D. (1997). Cultural differences in early mathematics learning: A comparison of Euro-American, Chinese-American, and Taiwan-Chinese families. *International Journal of Behavioral Development, 21,* 371–388.

Hust, S., & Brown, J. (2008). Gender, media use, and effects. *The handbook of children, media, and development* (pp. 98–120). Malden, MA: Blackwell Publishing.

Huston, A. (Ed.). (1991). *Children in poverty: Child development and public policy.* Cambridge, England: Cambridge University Press.

Huston, T. L., Caughlin, J. P., Houts, R. M., & Smith, S. E. (2001). The connubial crucible: Newlywed years as predictors of marital delight, distress, and divorce. *Journal of Personality and Social Psychology, 80,* 237–252.

Hutchinson, A., Whitman, R., & Abeare, C. (2003). The unification of mind: Integration of hemispheric semantic processing. *Brain & Language, 87,* 361–368.

Hutchinson, D., & Rapee, R. (2007). Do friends share similar body image and eating problems? The role of social networks and peer influences in early adolescence. *Behaviour Research and Therapy, 45,* 1557–1577.

Hutchinson, S., & Wexler, B. (2007, January). Is "raging" good for health? Older women's participation in the Raging Grannies. *Health Care for Women International, 28,* 88–118.

Hutton, P. H. (2004). *Phillippe Ariès and the politics of French cultural history.* Amherst: University of Massachusetts Press.

Huurre, T., Junkkari, H., & Aro, H. (2006, June). Long-term psychosocial effects of parental divorce: A follow-up study from adolescence to adulthood. *European Archives of Psychiatry and Clinical Neuroscience, 256,* 256–263.

Hyde, J., & Grabe, S. (2008). Meta-analysis in the psychology of women. In *Psychology of women: A handbook of issues and theories* (2nd ed.). Westport, CT: Praeger Publishers / Greenwood Publishing Group.

Hyde, J., Mezulis, A., & Abramson, L. (2008). The ABCs of depression: Integrating affective, biological, and cognitive models to explain the emergence of the gender difference in depression. *Psychological Review, 115,* 291–313.

Hyde, J. S. (1994). *Understanding human sexuality* (5th ed.). New York: McGraw-Hill.

Hyde, J. S., & DeLamater, J. D. (2003). *Understanding human sexuality* (8th ed.). New York: McGraw-Hill.

Hyde, J. S., & DeLamater, J. D. (2004). *Understanding human sexuality* (9th ed.). Boston: McGraw Hill.

Hyde, J. S., Fennema, E., & Lamon, S. J. (1990). Gender differences in mathematics performance: A meta-analysis. *Psychological Bulletin, 107*, 139–155.

Hyssaelae, L., Rautava, P., & Helenius, H. (1995). Fathers' smoking and use of alcohol: The viewpoint of maternity health care clinics and well-baby clinics. *Family Practice, 12*, 22–27.

Iglesias, J., Eriksson, J., Grize, F., Tomassini, M., & Villa, A. E. (2005). Dynamics of pruning in simulated large-scale spiking neural networks. *Biosystems, 79*, 11–20.

Ikels, C. (1989). Becoming a human being in theory and practice: Chinese views of human development. In D. I. Kertzer & K. W. Schaie (Eds.), *Age structuring in comparative perspective*. Hillsdale, NJ: Lawrence Erlbaum.

Ingersoll, E. W., & Thoman, E. B. (1999). Sleep/wake states of preterm infants: Stability, developmental change, diurnal variation, and relation with caregiving activity. *Child Development, 70*, 1–10.

Ingram, D. K., Young, J., & Mattison, J. A. (2007). Calorie restriction in nonhuman primates: Assessing effects on brain and behavioral aging. *Neuroscience, 14*, 1359–1364.

Insel, B. J., & Gould, M. S. (2008). Impact of modeling on adolescent suicidal behavior. *Psychiatric Clinics of North America, 31*, 293–316.

Institute for Women's Policy Research. (2006). The best and worst state economies for women. *Briefing Paper, No. R334*. Washington, DC: Institute for Women's Policy Research.

Interlandi, J. (2007). Chemo control. *Scientific American, 296*, 30–38.

International Cesarean Awareness Network. (2004). Available online at http://www.ican-online.org International Cesarean Awareness Network. (2007, April 10). Available online at http://www.birthchoiceuk.com

International Human Genome Sequencing Consortium. (2001). Initial sequencing and analysis of the human genome. *Nature, 409*, 860–921.

Inzlicht, M., & Ben-Zeev, T. (2000). A threatening intellectual environment: Why females are susceptible to experiencing problem-solving deficits in the presence of males. *Psychological Science, 11*, 365–371.

Ireland, J. L., & Archer, J. (2004). Association between measures of aggression and bullying among juvenile young offenders. *Aggressive Behavior, 30*, 29–42.

Irland, J. (2010). Childbirth. *Medical hypnosis primer: Clinical and research evidence*. New York: Routledge/Taylor & Francis Group.

Isaacs, K. L., Barr, W. B., Nelson, P. K., & Devinsky, O. (2006). Degree of handedness and cerebral dominance. *Neurology, 66*, 1855–1858.

Ishi-Kuntz, M. (2000). Diversity within Asian-American families. In D. H. Demo, K. R. Allen, & M. A. Fine (Eds.), *Handbook of family diversity*. New York: Oxford.

Ishizuka, B., Kudo, Y., & Tango, T. (2008). Cross-sectional community survey of menopause symptoms among Japanese women. *Maturitas, 61*, 260–267.

Iverson, T., Larsen, L., & Solem, P. (2009). A conceptual analysis of ageism. *Nordic Psychology, 61*, 4–22.

Izard, C. E. (1982). The psychology of emotion comes of age on the coattails of darwin. *PsycCRITIQUES, 27*, 426–429.

Izard, C., Woodburn, E., & Finlon, K. (2010). Extending emotion science to the study of discrete emotions in infants. *Emotion Review, 2*, 134–136.

Izard, V., Sann, C., Spelke, E., & Streri, A. (2009). Newborn infants perceive abstract numbers. *PNAS Proceedings of the National Academy of Sciences of the United States of America, 106*, 10382–10385.

Jackson, L. A., Gardner, P. D., & Sullivan, L. A. (1992). Explaining gender differences in self-pay expectations: Social comparison standards and perceptions of fair pay. *Journal of Applied Psychology, 77*, 651–663.

Jackson, T. (2006, May). Relationships between perceived close social support and health practices within community samples of American women and men. *Journal of Psychology: Interdisciplinary and Applied, 140*, 229–246.

Jacobi, C., Hayward, C., de Zwaan, M., Kraemer, H. C., & Agras, W. S. (2004). Coming to terms with risk factors for eating disorders: Application of risk terminology and suggestions for a general taxonomy. *Psychological Bulletin, 130*, 19–65.

Jager, R., Mieler, W., & Miller, J. (2008). Age-related macular degeneration. *The New England Journal of Medicine, 358*, 2606–2617.

Jahoda, G. (1980). Theoretical and systematic approaches in mass-cultural psychology. In H. C. Triandis & W. W. Lambert (Eds.), *Handbook of cross-cultural psychology* (Vol. 1). Boston: Allyn & Bacon.

Jahoda, G. (1983). European "lag" in the development of an economic concept: A study in Zimbabwe. *British Journal of Developmental Psychology, 1*, 113–120.

James, W. (1890/1950). *The principles of psychology*. New York: Holt.

Janda, L. H., & Klenke-Hamel, K. E. (1980). *Human sexuality*. New York: Van Nostrand.

Jaswal, V., & Dodson, C. (2009). Metamemory development: Understanding the role of similarity in false memories. *Child Development, 80*, 629–635.

Javawant, S., & Parr, J. (2007). Outcome following subdural hemorrhages in infancy. *Archives of the Disabled Child, 92*, 343–347.

Jaworski, M., & Accardo, P. (2010). Behavioral phenotypes: Nature versus nurture revisited. *Neurogenetic syndromes: Behavioral issues and their treatment*. Baltimore, MD: Paul H Brookes Publishing.

Jehlen, A., & Winans, D. (2005). No child left behind—myth or truth? *NEA Today, 23*, 32–34.

Jensen, A. (2003). Do age-group differences on mental tests imitate racial differences? *Intelligence, 31*, 107–121.

Jensen, L. A. (2008). Coming of age in a multicultural world: Globalization and adolescent cultural identity formation. In D. L Browning (Ed.) *Adolescent identities: A collection of readings*. New York: Analytic Press/Taylor & Francis Group.

Jiao, S., Ji, G., & Jing, Q. (1996). Cognitive development of Chinese urban only children and children with siblings. *Child Development, 67*, 387–395.

Ji-liang, S., Li-qing, Z., & Yan, T. (2003). The impact of intergenerational social support and filial expectation on the loneliness of elder parents. *Chinese Journal of Clinical Psychology, 11*, 167–169.

Jimenez, J., & Guzman, R. (2003). The influence of code-oriented versus meaning-oriented approaches to reading instruction on word recognition in the Spanish language. *International Journal of Psychology, 38*, 65–78.

Joe, S., & Marcus, S. (2003). Datapoints: Trends by race and gender in suicide attempts among U.S. adolescents, 1991–2001. *Psychiatric Services, 54*, 454.

Johnson, A. M., Wadsworth, J., Wellings, K., & Bradshaw, S. (1992). Sexual lifestyles and HIV risk. *Nature, 360*, 410–412.

Johnson, C. L., & Barer, B. M. (1992). Patterns of engagement and disengagement among the oldest old. *Journal of Aging Studies, 6*, 351–364.

Johnson, D. C., Kassner, C. T., & Kutner, J. S. (2004). Current use of guidelines, protocols, and care pathways for symptom management in hospice. *American Journal of Hospital Palliative Care, 21*, 51–57.

Johnson, D. J., Jaeger, E., Randolph, S. M., Cauce, A. M., Ward, J., & National Institute of Child Health and Human Development: Early Child Care Research Network. (2003). Studying the effects of early child care experiences on the development of children of color in the United States: Toward a more inclusive research agenda. *Child Development, 74*, 1227–1244.

Johnson, J. L., Primas, P. J., & Coe, M. K. (1994). Factors that prevent women of low socioeconomic status from seeking prenatal care. *Journal of the American Academy of Nurse Practitioners, 6*, 105–111.

Johnson, K., & Eilers, A. (1998). Effects of knowledge and development on subordinate level categorization. *Cognitive Development, 13*, 515–545.

Johnson, M. H. (1998). The neural basis of cognitive development. In D. Kuhn & R. S. Siegler (Eds.), *Handbook of child psychology: Vol. 2: Cognition, perception, and language* (5th ed.). New York: Wiley.

Johnson, N. G., Roberts, M. C., & Worell, J. (Eds.). (1999). *Beyond appearance: A new look at adolescent girls*. Washington, DC: American Psychological Association.

Johnson, S., Dweck, C., Chen, F., Stern, H., Ok, S., & Barth, M. (2010). At the intersection of social and cognitive development: Internal working models of attachment in infancy. *Cognitive Science: A Multidisciplinary Journal, 34*, 807–825.

Johnson, S. L., & Birch, L. L. (1994). Parents' and children's adiposity and eating style. *Pediatrics, 94*, 653–661.

Johnston, L. D., Bachman, J. G., & O'Malley, P. M. (2009). *Monitoring the future study*. Lansing: University of Michigan.

Johnston, L., Delva, J., & O'Malley, P. (2007). Soft drink availability, contracts, and revenues in American secondary schools. *American Journal of Preventive Medicine, 33*, S209–SS225.

Jones, A., & Crandall, R. (Eds.). (1991). Handbook of self-actualization. *Journal of Social Behavior and Personality, 6*, 1–362.

Jones, H. (2006). Drug addiction during pregnancy: Advances in maternal treatment and understanding child outcomes. *Current Directions in Psychological Science, 15*, 126–130.

Jones, S. (2006). Exploration or imitation? The effect of music on 4-week-old infants' tongue protrusions. *Infant Behavior & Development, 29*, 126–130.

Jones, S. (2007). Imitation in infancy: The development of mimicry. *Psychological Science, 18*, 593–599.

Jones-Harden, B. (2004). Safety and stability for foster children: A developmental perspective. *The Future of Children, 14*, 31–48.

Jordan, A., Trentacoste, N., Henderson, V., Manganello, J., & Fishbein, M. (2007). Measuring the time teens spend with media: Challenges and opportunities. *Media Psychology, 9*, 19–41.

Jorgensen, G. (2006, June). Kohlberg and Gilligan: Duet or duel? *Journal of Moral Education, 35*, 179–196.

Jose, O., & Alfons, V. (2007). Do demographics affect marital satisfaction? *Journal of Sex and Marital Therapy, 33*, 73–85.

Joseph, R. (1999). Environmental influences on neural plasticity, the limbic system, emotional development and attachment: A review. *Child Psychiatry & Human Development, 29*, 189–208.

Joseph, H., Reznik, I., & Mester, R. (2003). Suicidal behavior of adolescent girls: Profile and meaning. *Israel Journal of Psychiatry & Related Sciences, 40*, 209–219.

Juby, H., Billette, J., Laplante, B., & Le Bourdais, C. (2007). Nonresident fathers and children: Parents' new unions and frequency of contact. *Journal of Family Issues, 28*, 1220–1245.

Jung, J., & Peterson, M. (2007). Body dissatisfaction and patterns of media use among preadolescent children. *Family and Consumer Sciences Research Journal, 36*, 40–54.

Jung, M., & Brawley, L. (2010). Concurrent management of exercise with other valued life goals: Comparison of frequent and less frequent exercisers. *Psychology of Sport and Exercise, 11*, 372–377.

Jurimae, T., & Saar, M. (2003). Self-perceived and actual indicators of motor abilities in children and adolescents. *Perception and Motor Skills, 97*, 862–866.

Kagan, J. (2000, October). Adult personality and early experience. *Harvard Mental Health Letter*, pp. 4–5.

Kagan, J. (2003). An unwilling rebel. In R. J. Sternberg (Ed.), *Psychologists defying the crowd: Stories of those who battled the establishment and won*. Washington, DC: American Psychological Association.

Kagan, J. (2008). In defense of qualitative changes in development. *Child Development, 79*.

Kagan, J. (2010). *The temperamental thread: How genes, culture, time, and luck make us who we are*. Washington, DC: Dana Press.

Kagan, J., Arcus, D., & Snidman, N. (1993). The idea of temperament: Where do we go from here? In R. Plomin & G. E. McClearn (Eds.), *Nature, nurture, and psychology*. Washington, DC: American Psychological Association.

Kagan, J., Kearsley, R., & Zelazo, P. R. (1978). *Infancy: Its place in human development*. Cambridge, MA: Harvard University Press.

Kahn, J. (2007, February). Maximizing the potential public health impact of HPV vaccines: A focus on parents. *Journal of Adolescent Health, 40*, 101–103.

Kahn, J. P. (2004). Hostility, coronary risk, and alpha-adrenergic to beta-adrenergic receptor density ratio. *Psychosomatic Medicine, 66*, 289–297.

Kahn, J., Hessling, R., & Russell, D. (2003). Social support, health, and well-being among the elderly: What is the role of negative affectivity? *Personality & Individual Differences, 35*, 5–17.

Kahn, R. L., & Rowe, J. W. (1999). *Successful aging*. New York: Dell.

Kail, R. (2003). Information processing and memory. In M. Bornstein & L. Davidson (Eds.), *Well-being: Positive development across the life course*. Mahwah, NJ: Lawrence Erlbaum Associates.

Kail, R. V. (2004). Cognitive development includes global and domain-specific processes. *Merrill-Palmer Quarterly, 50* [Special issue: 50th anniversary issue: Part II, the maturing of the human development sciences: Appraising past, present, and prospective agendas], 445–455.

Kail, R. V., & Miller, C. A. (2006). Developmental change in processing speed: Domain specificity and stability during childhood and adolescence. *Journal of Cognition and Development, 7*, 119–137.

Kaiser, L. L., Allen, L., & American Dietetic Association. (2002). Position of the American Dietetic Association: Nutrition and lifestyle for a healthy pregnancy outcome. *Journal of the American Dietetic Association, 102*, 1479–1490.

Kalb, C. (1997, Spring/Summer). The top 10 health worries. *Newsweek Special Issue*, pp. 42–43.

Kalb, C. (2003, March 10). Preemies grow up. *Newsweek*, pp. 50–51.

Kalb, C. (2004, January 26). Brave new babies. *Newsweek*, pp. 45–53.

Kalsi, M., Heron, G., & Charman, W. (2001). Changes in the static accommodation response with age. *Ophthalmic & Physiological Optics, 21*, 77–84.

Kaltiala-Heino, R., Kosunen, E., & Rimpela, M. (2003). Pubertal timing, sexual behaviour and self-reported depression in middle adolescence. *Journal of Adolescence, 26*, 531–545.

Kaltiala-Heino, R., Rimpelae, M., Rantanen, P., & Rimpelae, A. (2000). Bullying at school—an indicator of adolescents at risk for mental disorders. *Journal of Adolescence, 23*, 661–674.

Kalynchuk, L. (2010). Behavioral and neurobiological consequences of stress. *Progress in Neuro-Psychopharmacology & Biological Psychiatry, 34*, 731–732.

Kamijo, K., Hayashi, Y., Sakai, T., Yahiro, T., Tanaka, K., & Nishihira, Y. (2009). Acute effects of aerobic exercise on cognitive function in older adults. *The Journals of Gerontology: Series B: Psychological Sciences and Social Sciences, 64B*, 356–363.

Kan, P., & Kohnert, K. (2009). Fast mapping by bilingual preschool children. *Journal of Child Language, 35*, 495–514.

Kane, R. A., Caplan, A. L., Urv-Wong, E. K., & Freeman, I. C. (1997). Everyday matters in the lives of nursing home residents: Wish for and perception of choice and control. *Journal of the American Geriatrics Society, 45*, 1086–1093.

Kaneda, H., Maeshima, K., Goto, N., Kobayakawa, T., Ayabe-Kanamura, S., & Saito, S. (2000). Decline in taste and odor discrimination abilities with age, and relationship between gustation and olfaction. *Chemical Senses, 25*, 331–337.

Kantrowitz, E. J., & Evans, G. W. (2004). The relation between the ratio of children per activity area and off-task behavior and type of play in day care centers. *Environment & Behavior, 36*, 541–557.

Kao, G. (2000). Psychological well-being and educational achievement among immigrant youth. In D. J. Hernandez (Ed.), *Children of immigrants: Health, adjustment, and public assistance*. Washington, DC: National Academy Press.

Kao, G., & Vaquera, E. (2006, February). The salience of racial and ethnic identification in friendship choices among Hispanic adolescents. *Hispanic Journal of Behavioral Sciences, 28*, 23–47.

Kapadia, S. (2008). Adolescent-parent relationships in Indian and Indian immigrant families in the US: Intersections and disparities. *Psychology and Developing Societies, 20*, 257–275.

Kaplan, H., & Dove, H. (1987). Infant development among the Ache of Eastern Paraguay. *Developmental Psychology, 23*, 190–198.

Kaplan, R. M., Sallis, J. F., Jr., & Patterson, T. L. (1993). *Health and human behavior: Age specific breast cancer annual incidence*. New York: McGraw-Hill.

Karagianni, P., Kyriakidou, M., Mitsiakos, G., Chatzioanidis, H., Koumbaras, E., Evangeliou, A., et al. (2010). Neurological outcome in preterm small for gestational age infants compared to appropriate for gestational age preterm at the age of 18 months: A prospective study. *Journal of Child Neurology, 25*, 165–170.

Karmiloff-Smith, A., Aschersleben, G., de Schonen, S., Elsabbagh, M., Hohenberger, A., & Serres, J. (2010). Constraints on the timing of infant cognitive change: Domain-specific or domain-general? *European Journal of Developmental Science, 4*, 31–45.

Karniol, R. (2009). Israeli kindergarten children's gender constancy for others' counter-stereotypic toy play and appearance: The role of sibling gender and relative age. *Infant and Child Development, 18*, 73–94.

Kart, C. S. (1990). *The realities of aging* (3rd ed.). Boston: Allyn & Bacon.

Kartman, L. L. (1991). Life review: One aspect of making meaningful music for the elderly. *Activities, Adaptations, and Aging, 15*, 42–45.

Kastenbaum, R. (1985). Dying and death: A life-span approach. In J. E. Birren & K. W. Schaie (Eds.), *Handbook of the psychology of aging*. New York: Van Nostrand Reinhold.

Kastenbaum, R. (1999). Dying and bereavement. In J. C. Cavanaugh & S. K. Whitbourne (Eds.), *Gerontology: An interdisciplinary perspective*. New York: Oxford University Press.

Kastenbaum, R. (2000). *The psychology of death* (3rd ed.). New York: Springer.

Kastenbaum, R. J. (1992). *The psychology of death*. New York: Springer-Verlag.

Kate, N. T. (1998, March). How many children? *American Demographics, 35*.

Kato, K., & Pedersen, N. L. (2005). Personality and coping: A study of twins reared apart and twins reared together. *Behavior Genetics, 35*, 147–158.

Katrowitz, B., & Wingert, P. (1990, Winter/Spring). Step by step. *Newsweek Special Edition*, pp. 24–34.

Katz, L. G. (1989, December). Beginners' ethics. *Parents*, p. 213.

Katz, S., & Marshall, B. (2003). New sex for old: Lifestyle, consumerism, and the ethics of aging well. *Journal of Aging Studies, 17*, 3–16.

Katzer, C., Fetchenhauer, D., & Belschak, F. (2009). Cyberbullying: Who are the victims? A comparison of victimization in Internet chatrooms and victimization in school. *Journal of Media Psychology: Theories, Methods, and Applications, 21*, 25–36.

Kaufman, J. C., Kaufman, A. S., Kaufman-Singer, J., & Kaufman, N. L. (2005). The Kaufman Assessment Battery for Children—Second Edition and the Kaufman Adolescent and Adult Intelligence Test. In D. P. Flanagan & P. L. Harrison (Eds.), *Contemporary intellectual assessment: Theories, tests, and issues*. New York: Guilford Press.

Kaye, W. (2008). Neurobiology of anorexia and bulimia nervosa. *Physiology & Behavior, 94*, 121–135.

Kayton, A. (2007). Newborn screening: A literature review. *Neonatal Network, 26*, 85–95.

Kazdin, A. E., & Benjet, C. (2003). Spanking children: Evidence and issues. *Current Directions in Psychological Science, 12*, 99–103.

Kecskes, I., & Papp, T. (2000). *Foreign language and mother tongue*. Mahwah, NJ: Lawrence Erlbaum.

Kedziora-Kornatowski, K., Szewczyk-Golec, K., Czuczejko, J., van Marke de Lumen, K., Pawluk, H., Motyl, J., Karasek, M., & Kedziora, J. (2007). Effect of melatonin on the oxidative stress in erythrocytes of healthy young and elderly subjects. *Journal of Pineal Research, 42*, 153–158.

Keefer, B. L., Kraus, R. F., Parker, B. L., Elliotst, R., et al. (1991). A state university collaboration program: Residents' perspectives. Annual Meeting of the American Psychiataric Association (1990, New York, New York). *Hospital and Community Psychiatry, 42*, 62–66.

Keel, P., & Haedt, A. (2008). Evidence-based psychosocial treatments for eating problems and eating disorders. *Journal of Clinical Child and Adolescent Psychology, 37*, 39–61.

Kelch-Oliver, K. (2008). African American grandparent caregivers: Stresses and implications for counselors. *The Family Journal, 16*, 43–50.

Keller, H., Otto, H., Lamm, B., Yovsi, R. D., & Kartner, J. (2008). The timing of verbal/vocal communications between mothers and their infants: A longitudinal cross-cultural comparison. *Infant Behavior & Development, 31*, 217–226.

Kellett, J. M. (2000). Older adult sexuality. In L. T. Szuchman & F. Muscarella et al. (Eds.), *Psychological perspectives on human sexuality*. New York: Wiley.

Kelley, G., Kelley, K., Hootman, J., & Jones, D. (2009). Exercise and health-related quality of life in older community-dwelling adults: A meta-analysis of randomized controlled trials. *Journal of Applied Gerontology, 28*, 369–394.

Kelly, G. (2001). *Sexuality today: A human perspective* (7th ed.) New York: McGraw-Hill.

Kelly-Weeder, S., & Cox, C. (2007). The impact of lifestyle risk factors on female infertility. *Women & Health, 44*, 1–23.

Kennell, J. H. (2002). On becoming a family: Bonding and the changing patterns in baby and family behavior. In J. Gomes-Pedro & J. K. Nugent (Eds.), *The infant and family in the twenty-first century*. New York: Brunner-Routledge.

Kenrick, D. T., Keefe, R. C., Bryna, A., Barr, A., & Brown, S. (1995). Age preferences and mate choice among homosexuals and heterosexuals: A case for modular psychological mechanisms. *Journal of Personality and Social Psychology, 69*, 1166–1172.

Kesselring, T., & Müller, U. (2010). The concept of egocentrism in the context of Piaget's theory. *New Ideas in Psychology, 10,* 56–63.

Kiang, L., Yip, T., & Fuligni, A. J. (2008). Multiple social identities and adjustment in young adults from ethnically diverse backgrounds. *Journal of Research on Adolescence, 18,* 643–670.

Kiecolt, K. J., & Fossett, M. A. (1997). The effects of mate availability on marriage among black Americans: A contextual analysis. In R. J. Taylor, J. S. Jackson, & L. M. Chatters (Eds.), *Family life in black America* (pp. 63–78). Thousand Oaks, CA: Sage Publications.

Kiecolt-Glaser, J. K. (2009). Psychoneuroimmunology: Psychology's gateway to biomedical future. *Perspectives on Psychological Science, 4* [Special issue: Next big questions in psychology], pp. 367–369.

Kilner, J. M., Friston, J. J., & Frith, C. D. (2007). Predictive coding: An account of the mirror neuron system. *Cognitive Processes, 33,* 88–997.

Kim, E. H., & Lee, E. (2009). Effects of a death education program on life satisfaction and attitude toward death in college students. *Journal of Korean Academic Nursing, 39,* 1–9.

Kim, H., Sherman, D., & Taylor, S. (2008). Culture and social support. *American Psychologist, 63,* 518–526.

Kim, S., & Park, H. (2006, January). Five years after the launch of Viagra in Korea: Changes in perceptions of erectile dysfunction treatment by physicians, patients, and the patients' spouses. *Journal of Sexual Medicine, 3,* 132–137.

Kim, U., Triandis, H. C., Kagitçibais, Ç., Choi, S., & Yoon, G. (Eds.). (1994). *Individualism and collectivism: Theory, method, and applications.* Thousand Oaks, CA: Sage Publications.

Kim-Cohen, J. (2007). Resilience and developmental psychopathology. *Child and Adolescent Psychiatric Clinics of North America, 16,* 271–283.

Kimm, S., Glynn, N. W., Kriska, A., Barton, B. A., Kronsberg, S. S., Daniels, S. R., Crawford, P. B., Sabry, Z., & Liu, K. (2003). Decline in physical activity in Black girls and white girls during adolescence, *New England Journal of Medicine, 347,* 709–715.

Kimmel, D., & Sang, B. (2003). Lesbians and gay men in midlife. In L. Garnets & D. Kimmel (Eds.), *Psychological perspectives on lesbian, gay, and bisexual experiences.* New York: Columbia University Press.

King, D., Delfabbro, P., & Griffiths, M. (2010). The convergence of gambling and digital media: Implications for gambling in young people. *Journal of Gambling Studies, 26,* 175–187.

Kinney, H. C., Randall, L. L., Sleeper, L. A., Willinger, M., Beliveau, R. A., Zec, N., Rava, L. A., Dominici, L., Iyasu, S., Randall, B., Habbe, D., Wilson, H., Mandell, F., McClain, M., & Welty, T. K. (2003). Serotonergic brainstem abnormalities in Northern Plains Indians with the sudden infant death syndrome. *Journal of Neuropathology and Experimental Neurology, 62,* 1178–1191.

Kinney, H., & Thach, B. (2009). Medical progress: The sudden infant death syndrome. *New England Journal of Medicine, 361,* 795–805.

Kinsey, A. C., Pomeroy, W. B., & Martin, C. E. (1948). *Sexual behavior in the human male.* Philadelphia: Saunders.

Kirby, J. (2006, May). From single-parent families to stepfamilies: Is the transition associated with adolescent alcohol initiation? *Journal of Family Issues, 27,* 685–711.

Kirchengast, S., & Hartmann, B. (2003). Impact of maternal age and maternal-somatic characteristics on newborn size. *American Journal of Human Biology, 15,* 220–228.

Kisilevsky, B., Hains, S., Brown, C., Lee, C., Cowperthwaite, B., Stutzman, S., et al. (2009). Fetal sensitivity to properties of maternal speech and language. *Infant Behavior & Development, 32,* 59–71.

Kitamura, C., & Lam, C. (2009). Age-specific preferences for infant-directed affective intent. *Infancy, 14,* 77–100.

Kitchener, R. F. (1996). The nature of the social for Piaget and Vygotsky. *Human Development, 39,* 243–249.

Kitterod, R., & Pettersen, S. (2006, September). Making up for mothers' employed working hours? Housework and childcare among Norwegian fathers. *Work, Employment and Society, 20,* 473–492.

Kitzmann, K., Gaylord, N., & Holt, A. (2003). Child witnesses to domestic violence: A meta-analytic review. *Journal of Consulting & Clinical Psychology, 71,* 339–352.

Kiuru, N., Nurmi, J., Aunola, K., & Salmela-Aro, K. (2009). Peer group homogeneity in adolescents' school adjustment varies according to peer group type and gender. *International Journal of Behavioral Development, 33,* 65–76.

Kjølseth, I., Ekeberg, Ø., & Steihaug, S. (2010). Why suicide? Elderly people who committed suicide and their experience of life in the period before their death. *International Psychogeriatrics, 22,* 209–218.

Kleespies, P. (2004). The wish to die: Assisted suicide and voluntary euthanasia. In P. Kleespies (Ed.), *Life and death decisions: Psychological and ethical considerations in end-of-life care.* Washington, DC: American Psychological Association.

Klier, C. M., Muzik, M., Dervic, K., Mossaheb, N., Benesch, T., Ulm, B., & Zeller, M. (2007). The role of estrogen and progesterone in depression after birth. *Journal of Psychiatric Research, 41,* 273–279.

Knafo, A., & Schwartz, S. H. (2003). Parenting and accuracy of perception of parental values by adolescents. *Child Development, 73,* 595–611.

Knaus, W. A., Conners, A. F., Dawson, N. V., Desbiens, N. A., Fulkerson, W. J., Jr., Goldman, L., Lynn, J., & Oye, R. K. (1995, November 22). A controlled trial to improve care for seriously ill hospitalized patients: The study to understand prognoses and preferences for outcomes and risks of treatments (SUPPORT). *JAMA: The Journal of the American Medical Association, 273,* 1591–1598.

Knickmeyer, R., & Baron-Cohen, S. (2006, December). Fetal testosterone and sex differences. *Early Human Development, 82,* 755–760.

Knight, K. (1994, March). Back to basics. *Essence,* pp. 122–138.

Knorth, E. J., Harder, A. T., Zandberg, T., & Kendrick, A. J. (2008). Under one roof: A review and selective meta-analysis on the outcomes of residential child and youth care. *Children and Youth Services Review, 30,* 123–140.

Kochanska, G. (1998). Mother–child relationship, child fearfulness, and emerging attachment: A short-term longitudinal study. *Developmental Psychology, 34,* 480–490.

Kochanska, G., & Aksan, N. (2004). Development of mutual responsiveness between parents and their young children. *Child Development, 75,* 1657–1676.

Kodl, M., & Mermelstein, R. (2004). Beyond modeling: Parenting practices, parental smoking history, and adolescent cigarette smoking. *Addictive Behaviors, 29,* 17–32.

Koenig, A., Cicchetti, D., & Rogosch, F. (2004). Moral development: The association between maltreatment and young children's prosocial behaviors and moral transgressions. *Social Development, 13,* 97–106.

Koenig, L. B., McGue, M., Krueger, R. F., & Bouchard, Jr., T. J. (2005). Genetic and environmental influences on religiousness: Findings for retrospective and current religiousness ratings. *Journal of Personality, 73,* 471–488.

Kohlberg, L. (1966). A cognitive-developmental anaylsis of children's sex-role concepts and attitudes. In E. E. Maccoby (Ed.), *The development of sex differences.* Stanford, CA: Stanford University Press.

Kohlberg, L. (1984). *The psychology of moral development: Essays on moral development* (Vol. 2). San Francisco: Harper & Row.

Kohut, S. A., & Riddell, R. P. (2009). Does the Neonatal Facial Coding System differentiate between infants experiencing pain-related and non-pain-related distress? *The Journal of Pain, 10,* 214–220.

Koivisto, M., & Revonsuo, A. (2003). Object recognition in the cerebral hemispheres as revealed by visual field experiments. *Laterality: Asymmetries of Body, Brain & Cognition, 8,* 135–153.

Kolata, G. (2004, May 11). The heart's desire. *New York Times,* p. D1.

König, R. (2005). Introduction: Plasticity, learning, and cognition. In R. König, P. Heil, E. Budinger, & H. Scheich (Eds.), *Auditory cortex: A synthesis of human and animal research.* Mahwah, NJ: Lawrence Erlbaum.

Koopmans, S., & Kooijman, A. (2006, November). Presbyopia correction and accommodative intraocular lenses. *Gerontechnology, 5,* 222–230.

Koretz, D. (2008). The pending reauthorization of NCLB: An opportunity to rethink the basic strategy. In Gail L. Sunderman (Ed.), *Holding NCLB accountable: Achieving, accountability, equity, & school reform.* Thousand Oaks, CA: Corwin Press.

Koroukian, S. M., Trisel, B., & Rimm, A. A. (1998). Estimating the proportion of unnecessary cesarean sections in Ohio using birth certificate data. *Journal of Clinical Epidemiology, 51,* 1327–1334.

Koshmanova, T. (2007). Vygotskian scholars: Visions and implementation of cultural-historical theory. *Journal of Russian & East European Psychology, 45,* 61–95.

Kotre, J., & Hall, E. (1990). *Seasons of life.* Boston: Little, Brown.

Kovelman, I., Baker, S. A., & Petitto, L. A. (2008). Bilingual and monolingual brains compared: A functional magnetic resonance imaging investigation of syntactic processing and a possible 'neural signature' of bilingualism. *Journal of Cognitive Neuroscience, 20,* 153–169.

Kramer, A. F., Erickson, K. I., & Colcombe, S. J. (2006). Exercise, cognition, and the aging brain. *Journal of Applied Physiology, 101,* 1237–1242.

Kramer, M., Aboud, F., Mironova, E., Vanilovich, I., Platt, R., Matush, L., et al. (2008). Breastfeeding and child cognitive development: New evidence from a large randomized trial. *Archives of General Psychiatry, 65,* 578–584.

Krcmar, M., Grela, B., & Lin, K. (2007). Can toddlers learn vocabulary from television? An experimental approach. *Media Psychology, 10,* 41–63.

Krebs, N. F., Himes, J. H., Jacobson, D., Nicklas, T. A., Guilday, P., & Styne, D. (2007). Assessment of child and adolescent overweight and obesity. *Pediatrics, 120* [Special issue: Assement of childhood and adolescent overweight and obesity], S193–S228.

Krishnamoorthy, J. S., Hart, C., & Jelalian, E, (2006). The epidemic of childhood obesity: Review of research and implications for public policy. *Social Policy Report, 19,* 3–19.

Kroger, J. (2006). *Identity development: Adolescence through adulthood.* Thousand Oaks, CA: Sage Publications.

Kroger, J. (2007). Why is identity achievement so elusive? *Identity: An International Journal of Theory and Research, 7,* 331–348.

Krojgaard, P. (2005). Infants' search for hidden persons. *International Journal of Behavioral Development, 29,* 70–79.

Krout, J. A. (1988). Rural versus urban differences in elderly parents' contact with their children. *Gerontologist, 28,* 198–203.

Kübler-Ross, E. (1969). *On death and dying.* New York: Macmillan.

Kübler-Ross, E. (Ed.). (1975). *Death: The final stage of growth.* Englewood Cliffs, NJ: Prentice-Hall.

Kuczynski, L., & Kochanska, G. (1990). Development of children's noncompliance strategies from toddlerhood to age 5. *Developmental Psychology, 26,* 398–408.

Kuhl, P. K., Andruski, J. E., Chistovich, I. A., Chistovich, L. A., Kozhevnikova, E. V., Ryskina, V. L., Stolyarova, E. I., Sundberg, U., & Lacerda, F. (1997, August 1). Cross-language analysis of phonetic units in language addressed to infants. *Science, 277,* 684–686.

Kuhn, D. (2000). Metacognitive devleopment. *Current Directions in Psychological Science, 9*, 178–181.

Kuhn, D. (2008). Formal operations from a twenty-first century perspective. *Human Development, 51*, 48–55.

Kuhn, D., Garcia-Mila, M., Zohar, A., & Andersen, C. (1995). Strategies of knowledge acquisition. With commentary by S. H. White, D. Klahr, & S. M. Carver, and a reply by D. Kuhn. *Monographs of the Society for Research in Child Development, 60*, 122–137.

Kump, S., & Krasovec, S. J. (2007). Education: A possibility for empowering adults. *International Journal of Lifelong Education, 26*, 635–649.

Kunkel, D., Wilcox, B. L., Cantor, J., Palmer, E., Linn, S., & Dowrick, P. (2004, February 20). *Report of the APA task force on advertising and children.* Washington, DC: American Psychological Association.

Kunzmann, U., & Baltes, P. (2005). *The psychology of wisdom: Theoretical and empirical challenges.* New York: Cambridge University Press.

Kupersmidt, J. B., & Dodge, K. A. (Eds.). (2004). *Children's peer relations: From development to intervention.* Washington, DC: American Psychological Association.

Kurdek, L. A. (1993). The allocation of household labor in gay, lesbian, and heterosexual married children. *Journal of Social Issues, 49*, 127–139.

Kurdek, L. A. (1999). The nature and predictors of the trajectory of change in marital quality for husbands and wives over the first 10 years of marriage. *Developmental Psychology, 35*, 1283–1296.

Kurdek, L. (2002). Predicting the timing of separation and marital satisfaction: An eight-year prospective longitudinal study. *Journal of Marriage & Family, 64*, 163–179.

Kurdek, L. (2003). Negative representations of the self/spouse and marital distress. *Personal Relationships, 10*, 511–534.

Kurdek, L. (2006, May). Differences between partners from heterosexual, gay, and lesbian cohabiting couples. *Journal of Marriage and Family, 68*, 509–528.

Kurdek, L. A. (2005). What do we know about gay and lesbian couples? *Current Directions in Psychological Science, 14*, 251–258.

Kurdek, L. (2008). Change in relationship quality for partners from lesbian, gay male, and heterosexual couples. *Journal of Family Psychology, 22*, 701–711.

Kurtines, W. M., & Gewirtz, J. L. (1987). *Moral development through social interaction.* New York: Wiley.

Kwant, P. B., Finocchiaro, T., Forster, F., Reul, H., Rau, G., Morshuis, M., El Banayosi, A., Korfer, R., Schmitz-Rode, T., & Steinseifer, U. (2007). The MiniACcor: Constructive redesign of an implantable total artificial heart, initial laboratory testing and further steps. *International Journal of Artificial Organs, 30*, 345–351.

Laas, I. (2006). Self-actualization and society: A new application for an old theory. *Journal of Humanistic Psychology, 46*, 77–91.

Labouvie-Vief, G. (1990). Modes of knowledge and the organization of development. In M. L. Commons, C. Armon, L. Kohlberg, F. A. Richards, T. A. Grotzer, & J. Sinnott (Eds.), *Adult development (Vol. 2). Models and methods in the study of adolescent thought.* New York: Praeger.

Labouvie-Vief, G. (2006). Emerging structures of adult thought. In J. J. Arnett & J. L. Tanner (Eds.), *Emerging adults in America: Coming of age in the 21st century.* Washington, DC: American Psychological Association.

Lacerda, F., von Hofsten, C., & Heimann, M. (2001). *Emerging cognitive abilities in early infancy.* Mahwah, NJ: Lawrence Erlbaum.

Lachmann, T., Berti, S., Kujala, T., & Schroger, E. (2005). Diagnostic subgroups of developmental dyslexia have different deficits in neural processing of tones and phonemes. *International Journal of Psychophysiology, 56*, 105–120.

Ladd, G. W. (1983). Social networks of popular, average and rejected children in social settings. *Merrill-Palmer Quarterly, 29*, 282–307.

Laditka, S., Laditka, J., & Probst, J. (2006). Racial and ethnic disparities in potentially avoidable delivery complications among pregnant Medicaid beneficiaries in South Carolina. *Maternal & Child Health Journal, 10*, 339–350.

Laflamme, D., Pomerleau, A., & Malcuit, G. (2002). A comparison of fathers' and mothers' involvement in childcare and stimulation behaviors during free-play with their infants at 9 and 15 months. *Sex Roles, 47*, 507–518.

LaFromboise, T., Coleman, H. L., & Gerton, J. (1993). Psychological impact of biculturalism: Evidence and theory. *Psychological Bulletin, 114*, 395–412.

Lafuente, M. J., Grifol, R., Segarra, J., & Soriano, J. (1997). Effects of the Firstart method of prenatal stimulation on psychomotor development: The first six months. *Pre- & PeriNatal Psychology, 11*, 151–162.

Lahiri, D. K., Maloney, B., Basha, M. R., Ge, Y. W., & Zawia, N. H. (2007). How and when environmental agents and dietary factors affect the course of Alzheimer's disease: The "LEARn" model (latent early-life associated regulation) may explain the triggering of AD. *Current Alzheimer Research, 4*, 219–228.

Lam, V., & Leman, P. (2003). The influence of gender and ethnicity on children's inferences about toy choice. *Social Development, 12*, 269–287.

Lamberts, S. W. J., van den Beld, A. W., & van der Lely, A-J. (1997, October 17). The endocrinology of aging. *Science, 278*, 419–424.

Lambiase, A., Aloe, L., Centofanti, M., Parisi, V., Mantelli, F., Colafrancesco, V., et al. (2009). Experimental and clinical evidence of neuroprotection by nerve growth factor eye drops: Implications for glaucoma. *PNAS Proceedings of the National Academy of Sciences of the United States of America, 106*, 13469–13474.

Lamm, B., & Keller, H. (2007). Understanding cultural models of parenting: The role of intracultural variation and response style. *Journal of Cross-Cultural Psychology, 38*, 50–57.

Lamm, H., & Wiesmann, U. (1997). Subjective attributes of attraction: How people characterize their liking, their love, and their being in love. *Personal Relationships, 4*, 271–284.

Lamont, J. A. (1997). Sexuality. In D. E. Stewart & G. E. Robinson (Eds.), *A clinician's guide to menopause. Clinical practice* (pp. 63–75). Washington, DC: Health Press International.

Lamorey, S., Robinson, B. E., & Rowland, B. H. (1998). *Latchkey kids: Unlocking doors for children and their families.* Newbury Park, CA: Sage Publications.

Landhuis, C., Poulton, R., Welch, D., & Hancox, R. (2008). Programming obesity and poor fitness: The long-term impact of childhood television. *Obesity, 16*, 1457–1459.

Landy, F., & Conte, J. M. (2004). *Work in the 21st century.* New York: McGraw-Hill.

Langer, E., & Janis, I. (1979). *The psychology of control.* Beverly Hills, CA: Sage Publications.

Langille, D. (2007). Teenage pregnancy: Trends, contributing factors and the physician's role. *Canadian Medical Association Journal, 176*, 1601–1602.

Lansford, J. (2010). Parental divorce and children's adjustment. *Perspectives on Psychological Science, 4*, 140–152.

Lansford, J. E., Chang, L, Dodge, K. A., Malone, P. S., Oburu, P., Palmérus, K., Bacchini, D., Pastorelli, C., Bombi, A. S., Zelli, A., Tapanya, S., Chaudhary, N., Deater-Deckard, K., Manke, B., & Quinn, N. (2005). Physical discipline and children's adjustment: Cultural normativeness as a moderator. *Child Development, 76*, 1234–1246.

Larsen, K. E., O'Hara, M. W., & Brewer, K. K. (2001). A prospective study of self-efficacy expectancies and labor pain. *Journal of Reproductive and Infant Psychology, 19*, 203–214.

Larson, R. W., Richards, M. H., Moneta, G., Holmbeck, G., & Duckett, E. (1996). Changes in adolescents' daily interactions with their families from ages 10 to 18: Disengagement and transformation. *Developmental Psychology, 32*, 744–754.

Lau, I., Lee, S., & Chiu, C. (2004). Language, cognition, and reality: Constructing shared meanings through communication. In M. Schaller & C. Crandall (Eds.), *The psychological foundations of culture.* Mahwah, NJ: Lawrence Erlbaum.

Lau, M., Markham, C., Lin, H., Flores, G., & Chacko, M. (2009). Dating and sexual attitudes in Asian-American adolescents. *Journal of Adolescent Research, 24*, 91–113.

Laugharne, J., Janca, A., & Widiger, T. (2007). Posttraumatic stress disorder and terrorism: 5 years after 9/11. *Current Opinion in Psychiatry, 20*, 36–41.

Laumann, E. O., Paik, A., & Rosen, R. C. (1999). Sexual dysfunction in the United States: Prevalence and predictors. *JAMA: The Journal of the American Medical Association, 281*, 537–544.

Lauter, J. L. (1998). Neuroimaging and the trimodal brain: Applications for developmental communication neuroscience. *Phoniatrica et Logopaedica, 50*, 118–145.

Lavers-Preston, C., & Sonuga-Barke, E. (2003). An intergenerational perspective on parent–child relationships: The reciprocal effects of tri-generational grandparent–parent–child relationships. In R. Gupta & D. Parry-Gupta (Eds.), *Children and parents: Clinical issues for psychologists and psychiatrists.* London: Whurr Publishers, Ltd.

Lavzer, J. I., & Goodson, B. D. (2006). The "quality" of early care and education settings: Definitional and measurement issues. *Evaluation Review, 30*, 556–576.

Lawrence, E., Rothman, A., Cobb, R., Rothman, M., & Bradbury, T. (2008). Marital satisfaction across the transition to parenthood. *Journal of Family Psychology, 22*, 41–50.

Lazarus, R. S. (1968). Emotions and adaptations: Conceptual and empirical relations. In W. Arnold (Ed.), *Nebraska symposium on motivation.* Lincoln: University of Nebraska.

Lazarus, R. S. (1991). *Emotion and adaptation.* New York: Oxford University Press.

Lazarus, R. S., & Folkman, S. (1984). *Stress, appraisal, and coping.* New York: Springer.

Le Corre, M., & Carey, S. (2007). One, two, three, four, nothing more: An investigation of the conceptual sources of the verbal counting principles. *Cognition, 105*, 395–438.

Le, H., Oh, I., Shaffer, J., & Schmidt, F. (2010). Implications of methodological advances for the practice of personnel selection: How practitioners benefit from meta-analysis. *Readings in organizational behavior.* New York: Routledge/Taylor & Francis.

Leach, P., Barnes, J., Malmberg, L., Sylva, K., & Stein, A. (2008). The quality of different types of child care at 10 and 18 months: A comparison between types and factors related to quality. *Early Child Development and Care, 178*, 177–209.

Leaper, C. (2002). Parenting girls and boys. In M. Bornstein (Ed.), *Handbook of parenting: Vol. 1: Children and parenting.* Mahwah, NJ: Lawrence Erlbaum.

Leathers, H. D., & Foster, P. (2004). *The world food problem: Tackling causes of undernutrition in the third world.* Boulder, CO: Lynne Rienner Publishers.

Leathers, S., & Kelley, M. (2000). Unintended pregnancy and depressive symptoms among first-time mothers and fathers. *American Journal of Orthopsychiatry, 70*, 523–531.

Leavitt, L. A., & Goldson, E. (1996). Introduction to special section: Biomedicine and developmental psychology: New areas of common ground. *Developmental Psychology, 32*, 387–389.

Lecours, A. R. (1982). Correlates of developmental behavior in brain maturation. In T. Bever (Ed.), *Regressions in mental development.* Hillsdale, NJ: Lawrence Erlbaum.

Lee, B. H., Schofer, J. L., & Koppelman, F. S. (2005). Bicycle safety helmet legislation and bicycle-related nonfatal injuries in California. *Accidental Analysis and Prevention, 37*, 93–102.

Lee, C. (2010). Gender, health, and health behaviors. *Handbook of gender research in psychology, Vol. 2: Gender research in social and applied psychology.* New York: Springer Publishing Co.

Lee, C. C., Czaja, S. J., & Sharit, J. (2009). Training older workers for technology-based employment. *Educational Gerontology, 35,* 15–31.

Lee, M. (2008). Caregiver stress and elder abuse among Korean family caregivers of older adults with disabilities. *Journal of Family Violence, 23,* 707–712.

Lee, M., Vernon-Feagans, L., & Vazquez, A. (2003). The influence of family environment and child temperament on work/family role strain for mothers and fathers. *Infant & Child Development, 12,* 421–439.

Lee, R. M. (2005). Resilience against discrimination: Ethnic identity and other-group orientation as protective factors for Korean Americans. *Journal of Counseling Psychology, 52,* 36–44.

Lee, S., Davis, B., & MacNeilage, P. (2010). Universal production patterns and ambient language influences in babbling: A cross-linguistic study of Korean- and English-learning infants. *Journal of Child Language, 37,* 293–318.

Leenaars, A. A., & Shneidman, E. S. (Eds.). (1999). *Lives and deaths: Selections from the works of Edwin S. Shneidman.* New York: Bruuner-Routledge.

Leen-Feldner, E. W., Reardon, L. E., Hayward, C., & Smith, R. C. (2008). The relation between puberty and adolescent anxiety: Theory and evidence. In M. J. Zvolensky & J. A. Smits (Eds.), *Anxiety in health behaviors and physical illness.* New York: Springer Science + Business Media.

Lefkowitz, E. S., Sigman, M., & Kit-fong Au, T. (2000). Helping mothers discuss sexuality and AIDS with adolescents. *Child Development, 71,* 1383–1394.

Legerstee, M., & Markova, G. (2008). Variations in 10-month-old infant imitation of people and things. *Infant Behavior & Development, 31,* 81–91.

Lehman, D., Chiu, C., & Schaller, M. (2004). Psychology and culture. *Annual Review of Psychology, 55,* 689–714.

Lehr, U., Seiler, E., & Thomae, H. (2000). Aging in a cross-cultural perspective. In A. L. Comunian & U. P. Gielen (Eds.), *International perspectives on human development.* Lengerich, Germany: Pabst Science Publishers.

Lemonick, M. D. (2000, October 30). Teens before their time. *Time,* pp. 68–74.

Lerner, J. W. (2002). *Learning disabilities: Theories, diagnosis, and teaching strategies.* Boston: Houghton Mifflin.

Lerner, R. M., Fisher, C. B., & Weinberg, R. A. (2000). Toward a science for and of the people: Promoting civil society through the application of developmental science. *Child Development, 71,* 11–20.

Lerner, R. M., Theokas, C., & Jelicic, H. (2005). Youth as active agents in their own positive development: A developmental systems perspective. In W. Greve, K. Rothermund, & D. Wentura, *Adaptive self: Personal continuity and intentional self-development.* Ashland, OH: Hogrefe & Huber.

Lesaux, N. K., & Siegel, L. S. (2003). The development of reading in children who speak English as a second language. *Developmental Psychology, 39,* 1005–1019.

Leslie, C. (1991, February 11). Classrooms of Babel. *Newsweek,* pp. 56–57.

Lesner, S. (2003). Candidacy and management of assistive listening devices: Special needs of the elderly. *International Journal of Audiology, 42,* 2S68–2S76.

Lester, D. (2006, December). Sexual orientation and suicidal behavior. *Psychological Reports, 99,* 923–924.

Leung, C., Pe-Pua, R., & Karnilowicz, W. (2006, January). Psychological adaptation and autonomy among adolescents in Australia: A comparison of Anglo-Celtic and three Asian groups. *International Journal of Intercultural Relations, 30,* 99–118.

LeVay, S., & Valente, S. M. (2003). *Human sexuality.* Sunderland, MA: Sinauer Associates.

Levenson, R. W., Carstensen, L. L., & Gottman, J. M. (1993). Long-term marriage: Age, gender, and satisfaction. *Psychology and Aging, 8,* 301–313.

Leverone, D., & Epstein, B. (2010). Nonpharmacological interventions for the treatment of rheumatoid arthritis: A focus on mind-body medicine. *Journal of Pharmacy Practice, 23,* 101–109.

Levin, R. J. (2007). Sexual activity, health and well-being—the beneficial roles of coitus and masturbation. *Sexual and Relationship Therapy, 22,* 135–148.

Levine, R. V. (1993, February). Is love a luxury? *American Demographics,* 29–37.

Levine, S. C., Huttenlocher, J., Taylor, A., & Langrock, A. (1999). Early sex differences in spatial skill. *Developmental Psychology, 35,* 940–949.

Levinson, D. (1992). *The seasons of a woman's life.* New York: Knopf.

Levinson, D. J. (1986). A conception of adult development. *American Psychologist, 41,* 3–13.

Levy, B. (2009). Stereotype embodiment: A psychosocial approach to aging. *Current Dirctions in Psychological Science, 18,* 332–336.

Levy, B. L., & Langer, E. (1994). Aging free from negative stereotypes: Successful memory in China and among the American deaf. *Journal of Personality and Social Psychology, 66,* 989–997.

Levy, B. R. (2003). Mind matters: Cognitive and physical effects of aging self-stereotypes. *Journal of Gerontology: Series B: Psychological Sciences and Social Sciences, 58B,* P203–P211.

Levy, B. R., Slade, M. D., & Kasl, S. V. (2002). Longitudinal benefit of positive self-perceptions of aging on functioning health. *Journal of Gerontology: Psychological Sciences, 57,* 166–195.

Levy, B. R., Slade, M. D., Kunkel, S. R., & Kasl, S. V. (2004). Longevity increased by positive self-perceptions of aging. *Journal of Personality and Social Psychology, 83,* 261–270.

Levy-Shiff, R. (1994). Individual and contextual correlates of marital change across the transition to parenthood. *Developmental Psychology, 30,* 591–601.

Lewin, T. (2008, November 19). Teenagers' Internet socializing not a bad thing. *The New York Times,* p. A20.

Lewin, T. (2005, December 15). See baby touch a screen: But does baby get it? *New York Times,* p. A1.

Lewin, V. (2009). Twinship: A unique sibling relationship. In V. Lewin & B. Sharp (Eds.), *Siblings in development: A psychoanalytic view.* London: Karnac Books.

Lewis, B., Legato, M., & Fisch, H. (2006). Medical implications of the male biological clock. *JAMA: The Journal of the American Medical Association, 296,* 2369–2371.

Lewis, C. S. (1985). A grief observed. In E. S. Shneidman (Ed.), *Death: Current perspectives* (3rd ed.). Palo Alto, CA: Mayfield.

Lewis, J., & Elman, J. (2008). Growth-related neural reorganization and the autism phenotype: A test of the hypothesis that altered brain growth leads to altered connectivity. *Developmental Science, 11,* 135–155.

Lewis, V. (2009). Undertreatment of menopausal symptoms and novel options for comprehensive management. *Current Medical Research Opinion, 25,* 2689–2698.

Lewkowicz, D. (2002). Heterogeneity and heterochrony in the development of intersensory perception. *Cognitive Brain Research, 14,* 41–63.

Li, C., DiGiuseppe, R., & Froh, J. (2006, September). The roles of sex, gender, and coping in adolescent depression. *Adolescence, 41,* 409–415.

Li, G. R., & Zhu, X. D. (2007). Development of the functionally total artificial heart using an artery pump. *ASAIO Journal, 53,* 288–291.

Li, N. P., Bailey, J. M., Kenrick, D. T., & Linsenmeier, J. A. W. (2002). The necessities and luxuries of mate preferences: Testing the tradeoffs. *Journal of Personality and Social Psychology, 82,* 947–955.

Li, Q. (2006). Cyberbullying in schools: A research of gender differences. *School Psychology International, 27,* 157–170.

Li, Q. (2007). New bottle but old wine: A research of cyberbullying in schools. *Computers in Human Behavior, 23,* 1777–1791.

Li, S. (2003). Biocultural orchestration of developmental plasticity across levels: The interplay of biology and culture in shaping the mind and behavior across the life span. *Psychological Bulletin, 129,* 171–194.

Libert, S., Zwiener, J., Chu, X., Vanvoorhies, W., Roman, G., & Pletcher, S. D. (2007, February 23). Regulation of Drosophila life span by olfaction and food-derived odors. *Science, 315,* 1133–1137.

Lickliter, R., & Bahrick, L. E. (2000). The development of infant intersensory perception: Advantages of a comparative convergent-operations approach. *Psychological Bulletin, 126,* 260–280.

Lidz, J., & Gleitman, L. R. (2004). Yes, we still need Universal Grammar: Reply. *Cognition, 94,* 85–93.

Liechty, J. (2010). Body image distortion and three types of weight loss behaviors among nonoverweight girls in the United States. *Journal of Adolescent Health,*

Lieven, E., & Stoll, S. (2010). Language. *Handbook of cultural developmental science.* New York: Psychology Press.

Light, L. L. (2000). Memory changes in adulthood. In S. H. Qualls & N. Abeles et al. (Eds.), *Psychology and the aging revolution: How we adapt to longer life* (pp. 73–97). Washington, DC: American Psychological Association.

Lindau, S., Schumm, L., Laumann, E., Levinson, W., O'Muircheartaigh, C., & Waite, L. (2007). A study of sexuality and health among older adults in the United States. *The New England Journal of Medicine, 357,* 762–775.

Lindemann, B. T., & Kadue, D. D. (2003). *Age discrimination in employment law.* Washington, DC: BNA Books.

Lindsay, G. (2007). Educational psychology and the effectiveness of inclusive education/mainstreaming. *British Journal of Educational Psychology, 77,* 1–24.

Lindsey, B. W., & Tropepe, V. (2006). A comparative framework for understanding the biological principles of adult neurogenesis. *Progressive Neurobiology, 80,* 281–307.

Lindsey, E., & Colwell, M. (2003). Preschoolers' emotional competence: Links to pretend and physical play. *Child Study Journal, 33,* 39–52.

Linn, R. L. (2008). Toward a more effective definition of adequate yearly progress. In

Lino, M. & Carlson (Eds.). (2009). *Expenditures on Children by Families, 2008.*

Liou, Y., Liou, T., & Chang, L. (2010). Obesity among adolescents: Sedentary leisure time and sleeping as determinants. *Journal of Advanced Nursing, 66,* 1246–1256.

Lipsitt, L. (2003). Crib death: A biobehavioral phenomenon? *Current Directions in Psychological Science, 12,* 164–170.

Lipsitt, L. P. (1986). Toward understanding the hedonic nature of infancy. In L. P. Lipsitt & J. H. Cantor (Eds.), *Experimental child psychologist: Essays and experiments in honor of Charles C. Spiker* (pp. 97–109). Hillsdale, NJ: Lawrence Erlbaum.

Litrownik, A., Newton, R., & Hunter, W. (2003). Exposure to family violence in young at-risk children: A longitudinal look at the effects of victimization and witnessed physical and psychological aggression. *Journal of Family Violence, 18,* 59–73.

Livingstone, S. (2008). Taking risky opportunities in youthful content creation: teenagers' use social networking sites for intimacy, privacy and self-expression. *New Media and Society, 10,* 393–411.

Livson, N., & Peskin, H. (1980). Perspectives on adolescence from longitudinal research. In J. Adelson (Ed.), *Handbook of adolescent psychology.* New York: Wiley.

Lobel, M., & DeLuca, R. (2007). Psychosocial sequelae of cesarean delivery: Review and analysis of their causes and implications. *Social Science & Medicine, 64,* 2272–2284.

Lobo, R. A. (2009). The risk of stroke in postmenopausal women receiving hormonal therapy. *Climacteric, 12,* Suppl 1:81-5.

Loeb, S., Fuller, B., Kagan, S. L., & Carrol, B. (2004). Child care in poor communities: Early learning effects of type, quality and stability. *Child Development, 75*, 47–65.

Loehlin, J. C., Neiderhiser, J. M., & Reiss, D. (2005). Genetic and environmental components of adolescent adjustment and parental behavior: A multivariate analysis. *Child Development, 76*, 1104–1115.

Loessl, B., Valerius, G., Kopasz, M., Hornyak, M., Riemann, D., & Voderholzer, U. (2008). Are adolescents chronically sleep-deprived? An investigation of sleep habits of adolescents in the southwest of Germany. *Child: Care, Health and Development, 34*, 549–556.

Loewen, S. (2006). Exceptional intellectual performance: A neo-Piagetian perspective. *High Ability Studies, 17*, 159–181.

Loftus, E. F. (2004). Memories of things unseen. *Current Directions in Psychological Science, 13*, 145–147.

Loftus, E. F., & Bernstein, D. M. (2005). Rich false memories: The royal road to success. In A. F. Healy, *Experimental cognitive psychology and its applications*. Washington, DC: American Psychological Association.

Logsdon, R., McCurry, S., Pike, K., & Teri, L. (2009). Making physical activity accessible to older adults with memory loss: A feasibility study. *The Gerontologist, 49* (Suppl. 1), S94–S99.

Lohman, D. (2005). Reasoning abilities. *Cognition and intelligence: Identifying the mechanisms of the mind*. New York: Cambridge University Press.

Lonetto, R. (1980). *Children's conception of death*. New York: Springer.

Lorenz, K. (1966). *On aggression*. New York: Harcourt Brace Jovanovich.

Lorenz, K. Z. (1965). *Evolution and the modification of behavior*. Chicago: University of Chicago Press.

Losonczy-Marshall, M. (2008). Gender differences in latency and duration of emotional expression in 7- through 13-month-old infants. *Social Behavior and Personality, 36*, 267–274.

Lourenco, O., & Machado, A. (1996). In defense of Piaget's theory: A reply to 10 common criticisms. *Psychological Review, 103*, 143–164.

Love, A., & Burns, M. S. (2006). 'It's a hurricane! It's a hurricane!': Can music facilitate social constructive and sociodramatic play in a preschool classroom? *Journal of Genetic Psychology, 167*, 383–391.

Love, J. M., Harrison, L., Sagi-Schwartz, A., van Ijzendoorn, M. H., Ross, C., Ungerer, J. A., Raikes, H., Brady-Smith, C., Boller, K., Brooks-Gunn, J., Constantine, J., Kisker, E. E., Paulsell, D., & Chazan-Cohen, R. (2003). Child care quality matters: How conclusions may vary with context. *Child Development, 74*, 1021–1033.

Lovrin, M. (2009). Treatment of major depression in adolescents: Weighing the evidence of risk and benefit in light of black box warnings. *Journal of Child and Adolescent Psychiatric Nursing, 22*, 63–68.

Lowe, M. R., & Timko, C. A. (2004). What a difference a diet makes: Towards an understanding of differences between restrained dieters and restrained nondieters. *Eating Behaviors, 5*, 199–208.

Lowenstein, J., Blank, H., & Sauer, J. (2010). Uniforms affect the accuracy of children's eyewitness identification decisions. *Journal of Investigative Psychology and Offender Profiling, 7*, 59–73.

Lowrey, G. H. (1986). *Growth and development of children* (8th ed.). Chicago: Year Book Medical Publishers.

Lu, L. (2006). The transition to parenthood: Stress, resources, and gender differences in a Chinese society. *Journal of Community Psychology, 34*, 471–488.

Lu, M. C., Prentice, J., Yu, S. M., Inkelas, M., Lange, L. O., & Halfon, N. (2003). Childbirth education classes: Sociodemographic disparities in attendance and the association of attendance with breastfeeding initiation. *Maternal Child Health, 7*, 87–93.

Lu, T., Pan, Y., Lap, S-Y., Li, C., Kohane, I., Chang, J., & Yankner, B. A. (2004, June 9). Gene regulation and DNA damage in the aging human brain. *Nature*, 1038.

Lu, X. (2001). Bicultural identity development and Chinese community formation: An ethnographic study of Chinese schools in Chicago. *Howard Journal of Communications, 12*, 203–220.

Lubinski, D. (2004). Introduction to the special section on cognitive abilities: 100 years after Spearman's (1904) "'General Intelligence,' objectively determined and measured." *Journal of Personality and Social Psychology, 86*, 96–111.

Lucas, S. R., & Berends, M. (2002). Sociodemographic diversity, correlated achievement, and de facto tracking. *Sociology of Education, 75*, 328–349.

Luchsinger, J., & Gustafson, D. (2009). Adiposity, type 2 diabetes, and Alzheimer's disease. *Journal of Alzheimer's Disease, 16*, 693–704.

Luke, B., & Brown, M. B. (2008). Maternal morbidity and infant death in twin vs triplet and quadruplet pregnancies. *American Journal of Obstetrics and Gynecology, 198*, 1–10.

Lundberg, U. (2006, July). Stress, subjective and objective health. *International Journal of Social Welfare, 15*, S41–S48.

Lundblad, B., Hellström, A., & Berg, M. (2010). Children's experiences of attitudes and rules for going to the toilet in school. *Scandinavian Journal of Caring Sciences, 24*, 219–223.

Luo, L., & Craik, F. (2008). Aging and memory: A cognitive approach. *The Canadian Journal of Psychiatry/La Revue canadienne de psychiatrie, 53*, 346–353.

Luo, L., & Craik, F. (2009). Age differences in recollection: Specificity effects at retrieval. *Journal of Memory and Language, 60*, 421–436.

Luo, Y., Kaufman, L., & Baillargeon R. (2009). Young infants' reasoning about physical events involving inert and self-propelled objects. *Cognitive Psychology, 58*, 441–486.

Lyall, S. (2004, February 15). In Europe, lovers now propose: Marry me, a little. *New York Times*, p. D2.

Lye, T. C., Piguet, O., Grayson, D. A., Creasey, H., Ridley, L. J., Bennett, H. P., & Broe, G. A. (2004). Hippocampal size and memory function in the ninth and tenth decades of life: The Sydney Older Persons Study. *Journal of Neurology, Neurosurgery, and Psychiatry, 75*, 548–554.

Lynam, D. R. (1996). Early identification of chronic offenders: Who is the fledgling psychopath? *Psychological Bulletin, 120*, 209–234.

Lynch, M. E., Coles, C. D., & Corely, T. (2003). Examining delinquency in adolescents: Risk factors. *Journal of Studies on Alcohol, 64*, 678–686.

Lynn, R. (2009). What has caused the Flynn effect? Secular increases in the Development Quotients of infants. *Intelligence, 37*, 16–24.

Lynne, S., Graber, J., Nichols, T., Brooks-Gunn, J., & Botvin, G. (2007, February). Links between pubertal timing, peer influences, and externalizing behaviors among urban students followed through middle school. *Journal of Adolescent Health, 40*, 35–44.

Lyon, M. E., Benoit, M., O'Donnell, R. M., Getson, P. R., Silber, T., & Walsh, T. (2000). Assessing African American adolescents' risk for suicide attempts: Attachment theory. *Adolescence, 35*, 121–134.

Lyons, M. J., Bar, J. L., & Kremen, W. S. (2002). Nicotine and familial vulnerability to schizophrenia: A discordant twin study. *Journal of Abnormal Psychology, 111*, 687–693.

Mabbott, D. J., Noseworthy, M., Bouffet, E., Laughlin, S., & Rockel, C. (2006). White matter growth as a mechanism of cognitive development in children. *Neuroimaging, 15*, 936–946.

MacCann, C. (2010). Further examination of emotional intelligence as a standard intelligence: A latent variable analysis of fluid intelligence, crystallized intelligence, and emotional intelligence. *Personality and Individual Differences, 49*, 490–496.

Maccoby, E. E., & Lewis, C. C. (2003). Less day care or different day care? *Child Development, 74*, 1069–1075.

Maccoby, E. E., & Martin, J. A. (1983). Socialization in the context of the family: Parent–child interaction. In P. H. Mussen (Ed.) & E. M. Hetherington (Vol. Ed.), *Handbook of child psychology: Vol. 4. Socialization, personality, and social development* (4th ed., pp. 1–101). New York: Wiley.

MacDonald, H., Beeghly, M., Grant-Knight, W., Augustyn, M., Woods, R., Cabral, H., et al. (2008). Longitudinal association between infant disorganized attachment and childhood posttraumatic stress symptoms. *Development and Psychopathology, 20*, 493–508.

MacDonald, W. (2003). The impact of job demands and workload stress and fatigue. *Australian Psychologist, 38*, 102–117.

MacDorman, M. F., Martin, J. A., Mathews, T. J., Hoyert, D. L., & Ventura, S. J. (2005). Explaining the 2001–02 infant mortality increase: Data from the linked birth/infant death data set. *National Vital Statistics Report, 53*, 1–22.

MacDorman, M., Declercq, E., Menacker, F., & Malloy, M. (2008). Neonatal mortality for primary cesarean and vaginal births to low-risk women: Application of an 'intention-to-treat' model. *Birth: Issues in Perinatal Care, 35*, 3–8.

Machaalani, R., & Waters, K. (2008). Neuronal cell death in the Sudden Infant Death Syndrome brainstem and associations with risk factors. *Brain: A Journal of Neurology, 131*, 218–228.

Macionis, J. J. (2001). *Sociology*. Upper Saddle River, NJ: Prentice Hall.

MacWhinney, B. (1991). Connectionism as a framework for language acquisition. In J. Miller (Ed.), *Research on child language disorders*. Austin, TX: Pro-ed.

Maddi, S. R., Harvey, R. H., Khoshaba, D. M., Lu, J. L., Persico, M., & Brow, M. (2006). The personality construct of hardiness, III: Relationships with repression, innovativeness, authoritarianism, and performance. *Journal of Personality, 74*, 575–598.

Magai, C., & McFadden, S. H. (Eds.). (1996). *Handbook of emotion, adult development, and aging*. New York: Academic Press.

Mahgoub, N., & Lantz, M. (2006, December). When older adults suffer the loss of a child. *Psychiatric Annals, 36*, 877–880.

Makino, M., Hashizume, M., Tsuboi, K., Yasushi, M., & Dennerstein, L. (2006, September). Comparative study of attitudes to eating between male and female students in the People's Republic of China. *Eating and Weight Disorders, 11*, 111–117.

Makishita, H., & Matsunaga, K. (2008). Differences of drivers' reaction times according to age and mental workload. *Accident Analysis & Prevention, 40*, 567–575.

Maller, S. (2003). Best practices in detecting bias in nonverbal tests. In R. McCallum (Ed.), *Handbook of nonverbal assessment*. New York: Kluwer Academic/Plenum Publishers.

Mangan, P. A. (1997, November). *Time perception*. Paper presented at the annual meeting of the Society for Neuroscience, New Orleans.

Mangweth, B., Hausmann, A., & Walch, T. (2004). Body fat perception in eating-disordered men. *International Journal of Eating Disorders, 35*, 102–108.

Manlove, J., Franzetta, K., McKinney, K., Romano-Papillo, A., & Terry-Humen, E. (2004). *No time to waste: Programs to reduce teen pregnancy among middle school-aged youth*. Washington, DC: National Campaign to Prevent Teen Pregnancy.

Mann, C. C. (2005, March 18). Provocative study says obesity may reduce U.S. life expectancy. *Science, 307*, 1716–1717.

Manning, M., & Hoyme, H. (2007). Fetal alcohol spectrum disorders: A practical clinical approach to diagnosis. *Neuroscience & Biobehavioral Reviews, 31*, 230–238.

Manning, W., Giordano, P., & Longmore, M. (2006, September). Hooking up: The relationship contexts of

## MIDDLE ADULTHOOD
(40 to 65 years)

## LATE ADULTHOOD
(65 years to death)

- Physical changes become evident. Vision declines noticeably, as does hearing, but less obviously.
- Height reaches a peak and declines slowly. Osteoporosis speeds this process in women. Weight increases, and strength decreases.
- Reaction time slows, but performance of complex tasks is mostly unchanged due to lifelong practice.
- Women experience menopause, with unpredictable effects. The male climacteric brings gradual changes in men's reproductive systems.

- Wrinkles and gray or thinning hair are marks of late adulthood. Height declines as backbone disk cartilage thins. Women are especially susceptible to osteoporosis.
- The brain shrinks, and the heart pumps less blood through the body. Reactions slow, and the senses become less acute. Cataracts and glaucoma may affect the eyes, and hearing loss is common.
- Chronic diseases, especially heart disease, grow more common. Mental disorders, such as depression and Alzheimer's disease, may occur.

- Some loss of cognitive functioning may begin in middle adulthood, but overall cognitive competence holds steady because adults use life experience and effective strategies to compensate.
- Slight declines occur in the efficiency of retrieval from long-term memory.

- Cognitive declines are minimal until the 80's. Cognitive abilities can be maintained with training and practice, and learning remains possible throughout the life span.

- Short-term memory and memory of specific life episodes may decline, but other types of memory are largely unaffected.

- People in middle adulthood take stock, appraising accomplishments against a "social clock" and developing a consciousness of mortality.
- Middle adulthood, despite the supposed "midlife crisis," usually is tranquil and satisfying. Individuals' personality traits are generally stable over time.
- While marital satisfaction is usually high, family relationships can present challenges.
- The view of one's career shifts from outward ambition to inner satisfaction or, in some cases, dissatisfaction. Career changes are increasingly common.

- Basic personality traits remain stable, but changes are possible. "Life review," a feature of this period, can bring either fulfillment or dissatisfaction.
- Retirement is a major event of late adulthood, causing adjustments to self-concept and self-esteem.
- A healthy lifestyle and continuing activity in areas of interest can bring satisfaction in late adulthood.
- Typical circumstances of late adulthood (reduced income, the aging or death of a spouse, a change in living arrangements) cause stress.

Generativity-versus-stagnation stage

Ego-integrity-versus-despair stage

# DISCOVERING THE LIFE SPAN

## SECOND EDITION

**ROBERT S. FELDMAN**
University of Massachusetts Amherst

**Pearson**

Boston   Columbus   Indianapolis   New York   San Francisco   Upper Saddle River   Amsterdam
Cape Town   Dubai   London   Madrid   Milan   Munich   Paris   Montreal   Toronto   Delhi
Mexico City   São Paulo   Sydney   Hong Kong   Seoul   Singapore   Taipei   Tokyo

**Editorial Director:** Craig Campanella
**Editor in Chief:** Jessica Mosher
**Executive Editor:** Jeff Marshall
**Editorial Project Manager:** LeeAnn Doherty
**Editorial Assistant:** Michael Rosen
**Director of Marketing:** Brandy Dawson
**Senior Marketing Manager:** Nicole Kunzmann
**Marketing Assistant:** Jessica Warren
**Managing Editor:** Maureen Richardson
**Project Manager:** Marianne Peters-Riordan
**Senior Operations Specialist:** Sherry Lewis
**Senior Art Director:** John Christiana
**Text and Cover Designer:** Mary Siener
**Cover Art:** Shutterstock
**Media Director:** Brian Hyland
**Senior Digital Media Editor:** Beth Stoner
**Supplements Editor:** LeeAnn Doherty
**Full-Service Project Management:** Priya Sundaram
**Composition:** S4Carlisle Publishing Services
**Printer/Binder:** Courier Kendallville
**Cover Printer:** Lehigh-Phoenix Color/Hagerstown
**Text Font:** Minion Pro 10/12

To Jon, Leigh, Josh, Julie, and Sarah

Credits and acknowledgments borrowed from other sources and reproduced, with permission, in this textbook appear on appropriate page within text, on pages xiii–xiv, or on page C-1.

**Library of Congress Cataloging-in-Publication Data**
Feldman, Robert S. (Robert Stephen), (date)
  Discovering the life span / Robert S. Feldman.—2nd ed.
      p. cm.
  Includes bibliographical references and index.
  ISBN-13: 978-0-205-23388-5
  ISBN-10: 0-205-23388-0
  1. Developmental psychology—Textbooks.   2. Life cycle, Human—Textbooks.
  3. Human growth—Textbooks. I. Title.
  BF713.F46 2011
  155—dc23

2011017327

10 9 8 7 6 5 4 3

student edition
ISBN 10: 0-205-23388-0
ISBN 13: 978-0-205-23388-5

instructor's review edition
ISBN 10: 0-205-06355-1
ISBN 13: 978-0-205-06355-0

à la carte edition
ISBN 10: 0-205-06352-7
ISBN 13: 978-0-205-06352-9

**PEARSON**

www.pearsonhighered.com

"nonrelationship" sex. *Journal of Adolescent Research, 21,* 459–483.

Manstead, A. S. R. (1997). Situations, belongingness, attitudes, and culture: Four lessons learned from social psychology. In C. McGarty & S. A. Haslam et al. (Eds.), *The message of social psychology: Perspectives on mind in society.* Oxford, England: Blackwell Publishers, Inc.

Mao, A., Burnham, M. M., Goodlin-Jones, B. L., Gaylor, E. E., & Anders, T. F. (2004). A comparison of the sleep-wake patterns of cosleeping and solitary-sleeping infants. *Child Psychiatry and Human Development, 35,* 95–105.

Marcia, J. E. (1980). Identity in adolescence. In J. Adelson (Ed.), *Handbook of adolescent psychology.* New York: Wiley.

Marcus, A. D. (2004, February 3). The new math on when to have kids. *Wall Street Journal,* pp. D1, D4.

Marcus, D., Fulton, J., & Clarke, E. (2010). Lead and conduct problems: A meta-analysis. *Journal of Clinical Child and Adolescent Psychology, 39,* 234–241.

Marczinski, C., Milliken, B., & Nelson, S. (2003). Aging and repetition effects: Separate specific and nonspecific influences. *Psychology & Aging, 18,* 780–790.

Marin, T., Chen, E., Munch, J., & Miller, G. (2009). Double-exposure to acute stress and chronic family stress is associated with immune changes in children with asthma. *Psychosomatic Medicine, 71,* 378–384.

Markell, K. (2010). Educating children about death-related issues. *Children's encounters with death, bereavement, and coping.* New York: Springer Publishing.

Markus, H. R., & Kitayama, S. (1991). Culture and the self: Implications for cognition, emotion, and motivation. *Psychological Review, 98,* 224–253.

Marschark, M., Spencer, P. E., & Newsom, C. A. (Eds.). (2003). *Oxford handbook of deaf students, language, and education.* London: Oxford University Press.

Marschik, P., Einspieler, C., Strohmeier, A., Plienegger, J., Garzarolli, B., & Prechtl, H. (2008). From the reaching behavior at 5 months of age to hand preference at preschool age. *Developmental Psychobiology, 50,* 512–518.

Marsh, H. W., & Ayotte, V. (2003). Do multiple dimensions of self-concept become more differentiated with age? The differential distinctiveness hypothesis. *International Review of Education, 49,* 463.

Marsh, H. W., & Hau, K. T. (2003). Big-fish-little-pond effect on academic self-concept. *American Psychologist, 58,* 364–376.

Marsh, H., Ellis, L., & Craven, R. (2002). How do preschool children feel about themselves? Unraveling measurement and multidimensional self-concept structure. *Developmental Psychology, 38,* 376–393.

Marshall, E. (2000, November 17). Planned Ritalin trial for tots heads into uncharted waters. *Science, 290,* 1280–1282.

Marshall, N. L. (2004). The quality of early child care and children's development. *Current Directions in Psychological Science, 13,* 165–168.

Martikainen, P., & Valkonen, T. (1996). Mortality after the death of a spouse: Rates and causes of death in a large Finnish cohort. *American Journal of Public Health, 86,* 1087–1093.

Martin, C., & Fabes, R. (2001). The stability and consequences of young children's same-sex peer interactions. *Developmental Psychology, 37,* 431–446.

Martin, C. L., & Ruble, D. (2004). Children's search for gender cues: Cognitive perspectives on gender development. *Current Directions in Psychological Science, 13,* 67–70.

Martin, C., & Ruble, D. (2010). Patterns of gender development. *Annual Review of Psychology, 61,* 353–381.

Martin, D., Greenwood, H., & Nisker, J. (2010). Public perceptions of ethical issues regarding adult predictive genetic testing. *Health Care Analysis, 18,* 103–112.

Martin, J. A., Hamilton, B. E., Sutton, P. D., Ventura, S. J., Menacker, F., & Munson, M. L. (2005). Births: Final data for 2003. *National Vital Statistics Reports, 54,* Table 1, p. 21.

Martin, P., Martin, D., & Martin, M. (2001). Adolescent premarital sexual activity, cohabitation, and attitudes toward marriage. *Adolescence, 36,* 601–609.

Martin, S., Li, Y., Casanueva, C., Harris-Britt, A., Kupper, L., & Cloutier, S. (2006). Intimate partner violence and women's depression before and during pregnancy. *Violence Against Women, 12,* 221–239.

Martineau, J., Cochin, S., Magne, R., & Barthelemy, C. (2008). Impaired cortical activation in autistic children: Is the mirror neuron system involved? *International Journal of Psychophysiology, 68,* 35–40.

Martinez-Torteya, C., Bogat, G., von Eye, A., & Levendosky, A. (2009). Resilience among children exposed to domestic violence: The role of risk and protective factors. *Child Development, 80,* 562–577.

Martini, J., Knappe, S., Beesdo-Baum, K., Lieb, R., & Wittchen, H. (2010). Anxiety disorders before birth and self-perceived distress during pregnancy: Associations with maternal depression and obstetric, neonatal and early childhood outcomes. *Early Human Development, 86,* 305–310.

Masataka, N. (1996). Perception of motherese in a signed language by 6-month-old deaf infants. *Developmental Psychology, 32,* 874–879.

Masataka, N. (1998). Perception of motherese in Japanese sign language by 6-month-old hearing infants. *Developmental Psychology, 34,* 241–246.

Masataka, N. (2000). The role of modality and input in the earliest stage of language acquisition: Studies of Japanese sign language. In C. Chamerlain & J. P. Morford (Eds.), *Language acquisition by eye.* Mahwah, NJ: Lawrence Erlbaum.

Masataka, N. (2003). *The onset of language.* Cambridge, England: Cambridge University Press.

Maslow, A. H. (1970). *Motivation and personality* (2nd ed.). New York: Harper & Row.

Massaro, A., Rothbaum, R., & Aly, H. (2006). Fetal brain development: The role of maternal nutrition, exposures and behaviors. *Journal of Pediatric Neurology, 4,* 1–9.

Master, S., Amodio, D., Stanton, A., Yee, C., Hilmert, C., & Taylor, S. (2009). Neurobiological correlates of coping through emotional approach. *Brain, Behavior, and Immunity, 23,* 27–35.

Masters, W. H., Johnson, V., & Kolodny, R. C. (1982). *Human sexuality.* Boston: Little, Brown.

Mathews, G., Fane, B., Conway, G., Brook, C., & Hines, M. (2009). Personality and congenital adrenal hyperplasia: Possible effects of prenatal androgen exposure. *Hormones and Behavior, 55,* 285–291.

Matlin, M. (2003). From menarche to menopause: Misconceptions about women's reproductive lives. *Psychology Science, 45,* 106–122.

Maton, K. I., Schellenbach, C. J., Leadbeater, B. J., & Solarz, A. L. (Eds.). (2004). *Investing in children, youth, families and communities.* Washington, DC: American Psychological Association.

Matson, J., & LoVullo, S. (2008). A review of behavioral treatments for self-injurious behaviors of persons with autism spectrum disorders. *Behavior Modification, 32,* 61–76.

Matsuda, Y., Ueno, K., Waggoner, R., Erickson, D., Shimura, Y., Tanaka, K., et al. (2010). Processing of infant-directed speech by adults. *NeuroImage, 54,* 122–131.

Matsumoto, D., & Yoo, S. H. (2006). Toward a new generation of cross-cultural research. *Perspectives on Psychological Science, 1,* 234–250.

Mattes, E., McCarthy, S., Gong, G., van Eekelen, J., Dunstan, J., Foster, J., et al. (2009). Maternal mood scores in mid-pregnancy are related to aspects of neonatal immune function. *Brain, Behavior, and Immunity, 23,* 380–388.

Matthews, K. A., Wing, R. R., Kuller, L. H., Meilahn, E. N., & Owens, J. F. (2000). Menopause as a turning point in midlife. In S. B. Manuck, R. Jennings, et al. (Eds.), *Behavior, health, and aging.* Mahwah, NJ: Lawrence Erlbaum.

Mattson, M. (2003). Will caloric restriction and folate protect against AD and PD? *Neurology, 60,* 690–695.

Mattson, S., Calarco, K., & Lang, A. (2006). Focused and shifting attention in children with heavy prenatal alcohol exposure. *Neuropsychology, 20,* 361–369.

Mauritzson, U., & Saeljoe, R. (2001). Adult questions and children's responses: Coordination of perspectives in studies of children's theories of other minds. *Scandinavian Journal of Educational Research, 45,* 213–231.

Mayer, J., Salovey, P., & Caruso, D. (2008). Emotional intelligence: New ability or eclectic traits? *American Psychologist, 63,* 503–517.

Mayes, L., Snyder, P., Langlois, E., & Hunter, N. (2007). Visuospatial working memory in school-aged children exposed in utero to cocaine. *Child Neuropsychology, 13,* 205–218.

Mayes, R., & Rafalovich, A. (2007). Suffer the restless children: The evolution of ADHD and paediatric stimulant use, 1900–80. *History of Psychiatry, 18,* 435–457.

Maynard, A. (2008). What we thought we knew and how we came to know it: Four decades of cross-cultural research from a Piagetian point of view. *Human Development, 51,* 56–65.

Mayseless, O. (1996). Attachment patterns and their outcomes. *Human Development, 39,* 206–223.

Mazoyer, B., Houdé, O., Joliot, M., Mellet, E., & Tzourio-Mazoyer, N. (2009). Regional cerebral blood flow increases during wakeful rest following cognitive training. *Brain Research Bulletin, 80,* 133–138. Available online at http://search.ebscohost.com.

McArdle, E. F. (2002). New York's Do-Not-Resuscitate law: Groundbreaking protection of patient autonomy or a physician's right to make medical futility determinations? *DePaul Journal of Health Care Law, 8,* 55–82.

McCabe, M. P., & Ricciardelli, L. A. (2006). A prospective study of extreme weight change behaviors among adolescent boys and girls. *Journal of Youth and Adolescence, 35,* 425–434.

McCabe, P., & Shaw, S. (2010). *Genetic and acquired disorders.* Thousand Oaks, CA. Washington, DC: Corwin Press.

McCall, R. B. (1979). *Infants.* Cambridge, MA: Harvard University Press.

McCardle, P., & Hoff, E. (Eds.). (2006). *Childhood bilingualism: Research on infancy through school age;* Clevedon, Avon, UK: Multilingual Matters.

McCauley, K. M. (2007). Modifying women's risk for cardiovascular disease. *Journal of Obstetric and Gynecological Neonatal Nursing, 36,* 116–124.

McClelland, D. C. (1993). Intelligence is not the best predictor of job performance. *Current Directions in Psychological Research, 2,* 5–8.

McCowan, L. M. E., Dekker, G. A., Chan, E., Stewart, A., Chappell, L. C., Hunger, M., Moss-Morris, R., & North, R. A. (2009). Spontaneous preterm birth and small for gestational age infants in women who stop smoking early in pregnancy: Prospective cohort study. *BMJ: British Medical Journal, 338*(7710), Jun 27, 2009.

McCrae, R. R., & Costa, P. T., Jr. (1990). *Personality in adulthood.* New York: Guilford Press.

McCrae, R. R., Costa, P. T., Jr., Ostendorf, F., Angleitner, A., Hebíková, M., Avia, M. D., Sanz, J., Sánchez-Bernardos, M. L., Kusdil, M. E., Woodfield, R., Saunders, P. R., & Smith, P. B. (2000). Nature over nurture: Temperament, personality, and life span development. *Journal of Personality and Social Psychology, 78,* 173–186.

McCrae, R., & Costa, P. (2003). *Personality in adulthood: A five-factor theory perspective* (2nd ed.). New York: Guilford Press.

McCrink, K., & Wynn, K. (2004). Large-number addition and subtraction by 9-month-old infants. *Psychological Science, 15,* 776–782.

McCrink, K., & Wynn, K. (2009). Operational momentum in large-number addition and subtraction by 9-month-olds. *Journal of Experimental Child Psychology, 103,* 400–408.

McCullough, M. E., Tsang, J., & Brion, S. (2003). Personality traits in adolescence as predictors of religiousness in early

maturity: Findings from the Terman longitudinal study. *Personality & Social Psychology Bulletin, 29,* 980–991.

McCutcheon-Rosegg, S., Ingraham, E., & Bradley, R. A. (1996). *Natural childbirth the Bradley way: Revised edition.* New York: Plume Books.

McDonald, K. A. (1999, June 25). Studies of women's health produce a wealth of knowledge on the biology of gender differences. *The Chronicle of Higher Education,* pp. A19, A22.

McDonald, L., & Stuart-Hamilton, I. (2003). Egocentrism in older adults: Piaget's three mountains task revisited. *Educational Gerontology, 29,* 417–425.

McDonnell, L. M. (2004). *Politics, persuasion, and educational testing.* Cambridge, MA: Harvard University Press.

McDonough, L. (2002). Basic-level nouns: First learned but misunderstood. *Journal of Child Language, 29,* 357–377.

McDowell, M., Brody, D., & Hughes, J. (2007). Has Age at Menarche Changed? Results from the National Health and Nutrition Examination Survey (NHANES) 1999–2004. *Journal of Adolescent Health, 40,* 227–231.

McElhaney, K., Antonishak, J., & Allen, J. (2008). "They like me, they like me not": Popularity and adolescents' perceptions of acceptance predicting social functioning over time. *Child Development, 79,* 720–731.

McElwain, N., & Booth-LaForce, C. (2006, June). Maternal sensitivity to infant distress and nondistress as predictors of infant–mother attachment security. *Journal of Family Psychology, 20,* 247–255.

McGlone, M., & Aronson, J. (2006, September). Stereotype threat, identity salience, and spatial reasoning. *Journal of Applied Developmental Psychology, 27,* 486–493.

McGlone, M., & Aronson, J. (2007). Forewarning and forearming stereotype-threatened students. *Communication Education, 56,* 119–133.

McGlothlin, H., & Killen, M. (2005). Children's perceptions of intergroup and intragroup similarity and the role of social experience. *Journal of Applied Developmental Psychology, 26,* 680–698.

McGough, R. (2003, May 20). MRIs take a look at reading minds. *The Wall Street Journal,* p. D8.

McGrew, K. S. (2005). The Cattell-Horn-Carroll theory of cognitive abilities: Past, present, and future. In D. P. Flanagan & P. L. Harrison (Eds.), *Contemporary intellectual assessment: Theories, tests, and issues.* New York: Guilford Press.

McGue, M. (2010). The end of behavioral genetics? *Behavior Genetics, 40,* 284–296.

McGue, M., Bouchard, T. J., Jr., Iacono, W., & Lykken, D. T. (1993). Behavioral genetics of cognitive ability: A lifespan perspective. In R. Plornin & G. E. McClearn (Eds.), *Nature, nurture, and psychology.* Washington, DC: American Psychological Association.

McGugin, R., & Tanaka, J. (2010). Transfer and interference in perceptual expertise: When expertise helps and when it hurts. *Generalization of knowledge: Multidisciplinary perspectives.* New York: Psychology Press.

McGuinness, D. (1972). Hearing: Individual differences in perceiving. *Perception, 1,* 465–473.

McHale, J. P., & Rotman, T. (2007). Is seeing believing? Expectant parents' outlooks on coparenting and later coparenting solidarity. *Infant Behavior & Development, 30,* 63–81.

McHale, S., Dariotis, J., & Kauh, T. (2003). Social development and social relationships in middle childhood. In R. Lerner & M. Easterbrooks (Eds.), *Handbook of psychology: Developmental psychology* (Vol. 6). New York: Wiley.

McHale, S. M., Kim, J-Y., & Whiteman, S. D. (2006). Sibling relationships in childhood and adolescence. In P. Noller & J. A. Feeney (Eds.), *Close relationships: Functions, forms and processes.* Hove, England: Psychology Press/Taylor & Francis.

McKee, K., Wilson, F., Chung, M., Hinchliff, S., Goudie, F., Elford, H., et al. (2005, November). Reminiscence, regrets and activity in older people in residential care: Associations with psychological health. *British Journal of Clinical Psychology, 44,* 543–561.

McLachlan, H. (2008). The ethics of killing and letting die: Active and passive euthanasia. *Journal of Medical Ethics, 34,* 636–638.

McLaughlin, D., Vagenas, D., Pachana, N., Begum, N., & Dobson, A. (2010). Gender differences in social network size and satisfaction in adults in their 70s. *Journal of Health Psychology, 15,* 671–679.

McLean, K., & Breen, A. (2009). Processes and content of narrative identity development in adolescence: Gender and well-being. *Developmental Psychology, 45,* 702–710.

McLoyd, V. C., Cauce, A. M., Takeuchi, D., & Wilson, L. (2000). Marital processes and parental socialization in families of color: A decade review of research. *Journal of Marriage and Family, 62,* 1070–1093.

McMurray, B., Aslin, R. N., & Toscano, J. C. (2009). Statistical learning of phonetic categories: Insights from a computational approach. *Developmental Science, 12,* 369–378.

McNulty, J. K., & Karney, B. R. (2004). Positive expectations in the early years of marriage: Should couples expect the best or brace for the worst? *Journal of Personality and Social Psychology, 86,* 729–743.

McVittie, C., McKinlay, A., & Widdicombe, S. (2003). Committed to (un)equal opportunities? "New ageism" and the older worker. *British Journal of Social Psychology, 42,* 595–612.

McWhirter, D. P., Sanders, S., & Reinisch, J. M. (1990). *Homosexuality, heterosexuality: Concepts of sexual orientation.* New York: Oxford University Press.

Mead, M. (1942). *Environment and education, a symposium held in connection with the fiftieth anniversary celebration of the University of Chicago.* Chicago: University of Chicago.

Meade, C., Kershaw, T., & Ickovics, J. (2008). The intergenerational cycle of teenage motherhood: An ecological approach. *Health Psychology, 27,* 419–429.

Mealey, L. (2000). *Sex differences: Developmental and evolutionary strategies.* Orlando, FL: Academic Press.

Medeiros, R., Prediger, R. D., Passos, G. F., Pandolfo, P., Duarte, F. S., Franco, J. L., Dafre, A. L., Di Giunta, G., Figueiredo, C. P., Takahashi, R. N., Campos, M. M., & Calixto, J. B. (2007). Connecting TNF-alpha signaling pathways to iNOS expression in a mouse model of Alzheimer's disease: Relevance for the behavioral and synaptic deficits induced by amyloid beta protein. *Journal of Neuroscience, 16,* 5394–5404.

Medina, J. J. (1996). *The clock of ages: Why we age—How we age—Winding back the clock.* New York: Cambridge University Press.

Mednick, S. A. (1963). Research creativity in psychology graduate students. *Journal of Consulting Psychology, 27,* 265–266.

Meece, J. L., & Kurtz-Costes, B. (2001). Introduction: The schooling of ethnic minority children and youth. *Educational Psychologist, 36,* 1–7.

Meeus, W. (2003). Parental and peer support, identity development and psychological well-being in adolescence. *Psychology: The Journal of the Hellenic Psychological Society, 10,* 192–201.

Mehta, C. M., & Strough, J. (2009). Sex segregation in friendships and normative contexts across the life span. *Developmental Review, 29,* 201–220.

Meijer, A. M., & van den Wittenboer, G. L. H. (2007). Contribution of infants' sleep and crying to marital relationship of first-time parent couples in the first year after childbirth. *Journal of Family Psychology, 21,* 49–57.

Meisinger, E., Blake, J., Lease, A., Palardy, G., & Olejnik, S. (2007). Variant and invariant predictors of perceived popularity across majority-Black and majority-White classrooms. *Journal of School Psychology, 45,* 21–44.

Meister, H., & von Wedel, H. (2003). Demands on hearing aid features—special signal processing for elderly users? *International Journal of Audiology, 42,* 2S58–2S62.

Melzer, D., Hurst, A., & Frayling, T. (2007). Genetic variation and human aging: Progress and prospects. *The Journals of Gerontology: Series A: Biological Sciences and Medical Sciences, 62,* 301–307. http://search.ebscohost.com

Meltzoff, A. (2002). Elements of a developmental theory of imitation. In A. Meltzoff & W. Prinz (Eds.), *The imitative mind: Development, evolution, and brain bases* (pp. 19–41). New York: Cambridge University Press.

Meltzoff, A. N. (1981). Imitation, intermodal coordination and representation in early infancy. In G. Butterworth (Ed.), *Infancy and epistemology.* Brighton, UK: Harvester Press.

Meltzoff, A. N., & Moore, M. K. (1977). Imitation of facial and manual gestures by human neonates. *Science, 198,* 75–78.

Meltzoff, A., & Moore, M. (2002). Imitation, memory, and the representation of persons. *Infant Behavior & Development, 25,* 39–61.

Mendle, J., Turkheimer, E., & Emery, R. E. (2007). Detrimental psychological outcomes associated with early pubertal timing in adolescent girls. *Developmental Review, 27,* 151–171.

Mendoza, C. (2006, September). Inside today's classrooms: Teacher voices on No Child Left Behind and the education of gifted children. *Roeper Review, 29,* 28–31.

Menzel, J. (2008). Depression in the elderly after traumatic brain injury: A systematic review. *Brain Injury, 22,* 375–380.

Mercado, E. (2009). Cognitive plasticity and cortical modules. *Current Directions in Psychological Science, 18,* 153–158.

Mercer, J. R. (1973). *Labeling the mentally retarded.* Berkeley: University of California Press.

Merlo, L., Bowman, M., & Barnett, D. (2007). Parental nurturance promotes reading acquisition in low socioeconomic status children. *Early Education and Development, 18,* 51–69.

Mervis, J. (2004, June 11). Meager evaluations make it hard to find out what works. *Science, 304,* 1583.

Messer, S. B., & McWilliams, N. (2003). The impact of Sigmund Freud and *The Interpretation of Dreams.* In R. J. Sternberg (Ed.), *The anatomy of impact: What makes the great works of psychology great* (pp. 71–88). Washington, DC: American Psychological Association.

MetLife Mature Market Institute. (2009). *The MetLife Market Survey of Nursing Home & Home Care Costs 2008.* Westport, CT: MetLife Mature Market Institute.

Meyer, M., Wolf, D., & Himes, C. (2006, March). Declining eligibility for social security spouse and widow benefits in the United States? *Research on Aging, 28,* 240–260.

Mezuk, B., Prescott, M., Tardiff, K., Vlahov, D., & Galea, S. (2008). Suicide in older adults in long-term care: 1990 to 2005. *Journal of the American Geriatrics Society, 56,* 2107–2111.

Miao, X., & Wang, W. (2003). A century of Chinese developmental psychology. *International Journal of Psychology, 38,* 258–273.

Michael, R. T., Gagnon, J. H., Laumann, E. O., & Kolata, G. (1994). *Sex in America: A definitive survey.* Boston: Little, Brown.

Miesnik, S., & Reale, B. (2007). A review of issues surrounding medically elective cesarean delivery. *Journal of Obstetric, Gynecologic, & Neonatal Nursing: Clinical Scholarship for the Care of Women, Childbearing Families, & Newborns, 36,* 605–615.

Mikhail, B. (2000). Prenatal care utilization among low-income African American women. *Journal of Community Health Nursing, 17,* 235–246.

Mikulincer, M., & Shaver, P. R. (2005). Attachment security, compassion, and altruism. *Current Directions in Psychological Science, 14,* 34–38.

Mikulincer, M., & Shaver, P. (2009). An attachment and behavioral systems perspective on social support. *Journal of Social and Personal Relationships, 26,* 7–19.

Miles, L., Keitel, M., Jackson, M., Harris, A., & Licciardi, F. (2009). Predictors of distress in women being treated for infertility. *Journal of Reproductive and Infant Psychology, 27*, 238–257.

Miles, R., Cowan, F., Glover, V., Stevenson, J., & Modi, N. (2006). A controlled trial of skin-to-skin contact in extremely preterm infants. *Early Human Development, 2* (7), 447–455.

Milevsky, A., Schlechter, M., Netter, S., & Keehn, D. (2007). Maternal and paternal parenting styles in adolescents: Associations with self-esteem, depression and life-satisfaction. *Journal of Child and Family Studies, 16*, 39–47.

Miller, E. M. (1998). Evidence from opposite-sex twins for the effects of prenatal sex hormones. In L. Ellis & L. Ebertz (Eds.), *Males, females, and behavior: Toward biological understanding.* Westport, CT: Praeger Publishers / Greenwood Publishing Group.

Miller, G., & Cohen, S. (2001). Psychological interventions and the immune system: A meta-analytic review and critique. *Health Psychology, 20*, 47–63.

Miller, L., Bishop, J., Fischer, J., Geller, S., & Macmillan, C. (2008). Balancing risks: Dosing strategies for antidepressants near the end of pregnancy. *Journal of Clinical Psychiatry, 69*, 323–324.

Miller, P. H., & Seier, W. L. (1994). *Strategy utilization deficiencies in children: When, where, and why.* San Diego: Academic Press.

Miller-Perrin, C. L., & Perrin, R. D. (1999). *Child maltreatment: An introduction.* Thousand Oaks, CA: Sage Publications.

Mills, E., & Siegfried, N. (2006). Cautious optimism for new HIV/AIDS prevention strategies. *The Lancet, 368*, 1236.

Mimura, K., Kimoto, T., & Okada, M. (2003). Synapse efficiency diverges due to synaptic pruning following overgrowth. *Physical Review E: Statistical, Nonlinear, and Soft Matter Physics, 68*, 124–131.

Minaker, K. L., & Frishman, R. (1995, October). Love gone wrong. *Harvard Health Letter*, pp. 9–12.

Mishna, F., Saini, M., & Solomon, S. (2009). Ongoing and online: Children and youth's perceptions of cyber bullying. *Children and Youth Services Review, 31*, 1222–1228.

Mishra, R. C. (1997). Cognition and cognitive development. In J. W. Berry, P. R. Dasen, & T. S. Saraswathi (Eds.), *Handbook of cross-cultural psychology, Vol. 2: Basic processes and human development* (2nd ed., pp. 143–175). Boston, MA: Allyn & Bacon.

Misri, S. (2007). Suffering in silence: The burden of perinatal depression. *The Canadian Journal of Psychiatry / La Revue canadienne de psychiatrie, 52*, 477–478.

Mitchell, B. A. (2006). *The boomerang age: Transitions to adulthood in families.* New Brunswick, NJ: AldineTransaction.

Mitchell, E. (2009). What is the mechanism of SIDS? Clues from epidemiology. *Developmental Psychobiology, 51*, 215–222.

Mitchell, K., Wolak, J., & Finkelhor, D. (2007, February). Trends in youth reports of sexual solicitations, harassment and unwanted exposure to pornography on the Internet. *Journal of Adolescent Health, 40*, 116–126.

Mitchell, S. (2002). *American generations: Who they are, how they live, what they think.* Ithaca, NY: New Strategists Publications.

Mittal, V., Ellman, L., & Cannon, T. (2008). Gene-environment interaction and covariation in schizophrenia: The role of obstetric complications. *Schizophrenia Bulletin, 34*, 1083–1094. Available online at http://search.ebscohost.com

Mittendorf, R., Williams, M. A., Berkey, C. S., & Cotter, R. F. (1990). The length of uncomplicated human gestation. *Obstetrics and Gynecology, 75*, 73–78.

Miyamoto, R. H., Hishinuma, E. S., Nishimura, S. T., Nahulu, L. B., Andrade, N. N., & Goebert, D. A. (2000). Variation in self-esteem among adolescents in an Asian/Pacific-Islander sample. *Personality & Individual Differences, 29*, 13–25.

Mizuno, K., & Ueda, A. (2004). Antenatal olfactory learning influences infant feeding. *Early Human Development, 76*, 83–90.

MMWR. (2008, August 1). Trends in HIV- and STD-related risk behaviors among high school students—United States, 1991–2007. *Morbidity and Mortality Weekly Report, 57*, 817–822.

Mohajeri, M., & Leuba, G. (2009). Prevention of age-associated dementia. *Brain Research Bulletin, 80*, 315–325.

Molfese, V. J., & Acheson, S. (1997). Infant and preschool mental and verbal abilities: How are infant scores related to preschool scores? *International Journal of Behavioral Development, 20*, 595–607.

Molina, J. C., Spear, N. E., Spear, L. P., Mennella, J. A., & Lewis, M. J. (2007). The International Society for Developmental Psychobiology 39th annual meeting symposium: Alcohol and development. Beyond fetal alcohol syndrome. *Developmental Psychobiology, 49*, 227–242.

Monahan, K., Steinberg, L., & Cauffman, E. (2009). Affiliation with antisocial peers, susceptibility to peer influence, and antisocial behavior during the transition to adulthood. *Developmental Psychology, 45*, 1520–1530.

Monastra, V. (2008). The etiology of ADHD: A neurological perspective. *Unlocking the potential of patients with ADHD: A model for clinical practice.* Washington, DC: American Psychological Association.

Montgomery-Downs, H., & Thomas, E. B. (1998). Biological and behavioral correlates of quiet sleep respiration rates in infants. *Physiology and Behavior, 64*, 637–643.

Moon, C. (2002). Learning in early infancy. *Advances in Neonatal Care, 2*, 81–83.

Moore, K. L. (1974). *Before we are born: Basic embryology and birth defects.* Philadelphia: Saunders.

Moore, K. L., & Persaud, T. V. N. (2003). *Before we were born* (6th ed.). Philadelphia: Saunders.

Moore, L., Gao, D., & Bradlee, M. (2003). Does early physical activity predict body fat change throughout childhood? *Preventive Medicine: An International Journal Devoted to Practice & Theory, 37*, 10–17.

Morales, J. R., & Guerra, N. F. (2006). Effects of multiple context and cumulative stress on urban children's adjustment in elementary school. *Child Development, 77*, 907–923.

Morbidity and Mortality Weekly Report. (2010). Television and video viewing time among children aged 2 years - Oregon, 2006-2007. *Morbidity and Mortality Weekly Report, 59*, 837–841.

Morelli, G. A., Rogoff, B., Oppenheim, D., & Goldsmith, D. (1992). Cultural variation in infants' sleeping arrangements: Questions of independence [Special section: Cross-cultural studies of development]. *Developmental Psychology, 28*, 604–613.

Moreton, C. (2007, January 13). World's first test-tube baby Louise Brown has a child of her own. *London: Independent.*

Morice, A. (1998, February 27-28). Future moms, please note: Benefits vary. *Wall Street Journal,* p. 15.

Morris, G., Baker-Ward, L., & Bauer, P. (2010). What remains of that day: The survival of children's autobiographical memories across time. *Applied Cognitive Psychology, 24*, 527–544.

Morris, L. B. (March 21, 2001). For elderly, relief for emotional ills can be elusive. *New York Times,* p. A6.

Morrissey, T. (2010). Sequence of child care type and child development: What role does peer exposure play? *Early Childhood Research Quarterly, 25*, 33–50.

Morrongiello, B., & Hogg, K. (2004). Mothers' reactions to children misbehaving in ways that can lead to injury: Implications for gender differences in children's risk taking and injuries. *Sex Roles, 50*, 103–118.

Morrongiello, B., Corbett, M., & Bellissimo, A. (2008). 'Do as I say, not as I do': Family influences on children's safety and risk behaviors. *Health Psychology, 27*, 498–503.

Morrongiello, B., Corbett, M., McCourt, M., & Johnston, N. (2006, July). Understanding unintentional injury-risk in young children I. The nature and scope of caregiver supervision of children at home. *Journal of Pediatric Psychology, 31*, 529–539.

Morrongiello, B., Klemencic, N., & Corbett, M. (2008). Interactions between child behavior patterns and parent supervision: Implications for children's risk of unintentional injury. *Child Development, 79*, 627–638.

Morrongiello, B., Zdzieborski, D., Sandomierski, M., & Lasenby-Lessard, J. (2009). Video messaging: What works to persuade mothers to supervise young children more closely in order to reduce injury risk? *Social Science & Medicine, 68*, 1030–1037.

Mortensen, C., & Cialdini, R. (2010). Full-cycle social psychology for theory and application. *Social and Personality Psychology Compass, 4*, 53–63.

Moss, M. (1997, March 31). Golden years? For one 73-year-old, punching time clock isn't a labor of love. *The Wall Street Journal,* pp. A1, A8.

Motschnig, R., & Nykl, L. (2003). Toward a cognitive-emotional model of Rogers's person-centered approach. *Journal of Humanistic Psychology, 43*, 8–45.

Mottl-Santiago, J., Walker, C., Ewan, J., Vragovic, O., Winder, S., & Stubblefield, P. (2008). A hospital-based doula program and childbirth outcomes in an urban, multicultural setting. *Maternal and Child Health Journal, 12*, 372–377.

Moyad, M. A. (2004). Preventing male osteoporosis: Prevalence, risks, diagnosis and imaging tests. *Urological Clinics of North America, 31*, 321–330.

Moyer, M. S. (1992). Sibling relationships among older adults. *Generations, 16*, 55–58.

Moyle, J., Fox, A., Arthur, M., Bynevelt, M., & Burnett, J. (2007). Meta-analysis of neuropsychological symptoms of adolescents and adults with PKU. *Neuropsychology Review, 17*, 91–101. Available online at http://search.ebscohost.com

Mueller, E., & Vandell, D. (1979). Infant–infant interactions. In J. Osofsky (Ed.), *Handbook of infant development.* New York: Wiley.

Mumme, D., & Fernald, A. (2003). The infant as onlooker: Learning from emotional reactions observed in a television scenario. *Child Development, 74*, 221–237.

Munzar, P., Cami, J., & Farré, M. (2003). Mechanisms of drug addiction. *New England Journal of Medicine, 349*, 2365–2365.

Murguia, A., Peterson, R. A., & Zea, M. C. (1997, August). Cultural health beliefs. Paper presented at the annual meeting of the American Psychological Association, Toronto, Canada.

Murphy, B., & Eisenberg, N. (2002). An integrative examination of peer conflict: Children's reported goals, emotions, and behaviors. *Social Development, 11*, 534–557.

Murphy, C. (2008). The chemical senses and nutrition in older adults. *Journal of Nutrition for the Elderly, 27*, 247–265.

Murphy, M. (2009). Language and literacy in individuals with Turner syndrome. *Topics in Language Disorders, 29*, 187–194. Available online at http://search.ebscohost.com

Murphy, M., & Mazzocco, M. (2008). Mathematics learning disabilities in girls with fragile X or Turner syndrome during late elementary school. *Journal of Learning Disabilities, 41*, 29–46. Available online at http://search.ebscohost.com

Murphy, P., Buehl, M., Zeruth, J., Edwards, M., Long, J., & Monoi, S. (2010). Examining the influence of epistemic beliefs and goal orientations on the academic performance of adolescent students enrolled in high-poverty, high-minority schools. *Personal epistemology in the classroom:*

*Theory, research, and implications for practice.* New York: Cambridge University Press.

Murphy, S., Johnson, L., & Wu, L. (2003). Bereaved parents' outcomes 4 to 60 months after their children's death by accident, suicide, or homicide: A comparative study demonstrating differences. *Death Studies, 27,* 39–61.

Murray, L., Cooper, P., Creswell, C., Schofield, E., & Sack, C. (2007, January). The effects of maternal social phobia on mother–infant interactions and infant social responsiveness. *Journal of Child Psychology and Psychiatry, 48,* 45–52.

Murray, S., Bellavia, G., & Rose, P. (2003). Once hurt, twice hurtful: How perceived regard regulates daily marital interactions. *Journal of Personality & Social Psychology, 84,* 126–147.

Murray-Close, D., Ostrov, J., & Crick, N. (2007, December). A short-term longitudinal study of growth of relational aggression during middle childhood: Associations with gender, friendship intimacy, and internalizing problems. *Development and Psychopathology, 19,* 187–203.

Murstein, B. I. (1976). *Who will marry whom? Theories and research in marital choice.* New York: Springer.

Murstein, B. I. (1986). *Paths to marriage.* Beverly Hills, CA: Sage Publications.

Murstein, B. I. (1987). A clarification and extension of the SVR theory of dyadic pairing. *Journal of Marriage and the Family, 49,* 929–933.

Myers, D. (2000). *A quiet world: Living with hearing loss.* New Haven, CT: Yale University Press.

Myers, R. H. (2004). Huntington's disease genetics. *NeuroRx, 1,* 255–262.

Myklebust, B. M., & Gottlieb, G. L. (1993). Development of the stretch reflex in the newborn: Reciprocal excitation and reflex irradation. *Child Development, 64,* 1036–1045.

Myrtek, M. (2007). *Type A behavior and hostility as independent risk factors for coronary heart disease.* Washington, DC: American Psychological Association.

Nadal, K. (2004). Filipino American identity development model. *Journal of Multicultural Counseling & Development, 32,* 45–62.

Nadel, S., & Poss, J. E. (2007). Early detection of autism spectrum disorders: Screening between 12 and 24 months of age. *Journal of the American Academy of Nurse Practitioners, 19,* 408–417.

Naglieri, J., Goldstein, S., & LeBuffe, P. (2010). Resilience and impairment: An exploratory study of resilience factors and situational impairment. *Journal of Psychoeducational Assessment, 28,* 349–356.

Nagy, E. (2006). From imitation to conversation: The first dialogues with human neonates. *Infant and Child Development, 15,* 223–232.

Nagy, M. (1948). The child's theories concerning death. *Journal of Genetic Psychology, 73,* 3–27.

Naik, G. (2002, November 22). The grim mission of a Swiss group: Visitor's suicides. *Wall Street Journal,* pp. A1, A6.

Naik, G. (2009, February 3). Parents agonize over treatment in the womb. *Wall Street Journal,* p. D1.

Nakagawa, M., Lamb, M. E., & Miyaki, K. (1992). Antecedents and correlates of the Strange Situation behavior of Japanese infants. *Journal of Cross-Cultural Psychology, 23,* 300–310.

Nanda, S., & Konnur, N. (2006, October). Adolescent drug & alcohol use in the 21st century. *Psychiatric Annals, 36,* 706–712.

Nangle, D. W., & Erdley, C. A. (Eds.). (2001). *The role of friendship in psychological adjustment.* San Francisco: Jossey-Bass.

Nappi, R., & Polatti, F. (2009). The use of estrogen therapy in women's sexual functioning. *Journal of Sexual Medicine, 6,* 603–616.

Nash, A., Pine, K., & Messer, D. (2009). Television alcohol advertising: Do children really mean what they say? *British Journal of Developmental Psychology, 27,* 85–104.

Nassif, A., & Gunter, B. (2008). Gender representation in television advertisements in Britain and Saudi Arabia. *Sex Roles, 58,* 752–760.

Nation, M., & Heflinger, C. (2006). Risk factors for serious alcohol and drug use: The role of psychosocial variables in predicting the frequency of substance use among adolescents. *American Journal of Drug and Alcohol Abuse, 32,* 415–433.

National Center for Children in Poverty. (2005). *Basic facts about low-income children in the United States.* New York: National Center for Children in Poverty.

National Center for Educational Statistics. (2003). *Public high school dropouts and completers from the common core of data: School year 2000–01 statistical analysis report.* Washington, DC: Author.

National Center for Health Statistics. (2001). *Division of vital statistics.* Washington, DC: Public Health Service.

National Center for Health Statistics. (2003). *Division of vital statistics.* Washington, DC: Public Health Service.

National Center for Health Statistics. (2007). *Division of vital statistics.* Washington, DC: Public Health Service.

National Clearinghouse on Child Abuse and Neglect Information. (2004). *Child maltreatment 2002: Summary of key findings/National Clearinghouse on Child Abuse and Neglect Information.* Washington, DC: Author.

National Highway Traffic Safety Administration. (1994). *Age-related incidence of traffic accidents.* Washington, DC: National Highway Traffic Safety Administration.

National Institute of Aging. (2004, May 31). Sexuality in later life. Available online at http://www.niapublications.org/engagepages/sexuality.asp

National Institutes of Health. (2006, December 13). Adult male circumcision significantly reduces risk of acquiring HIV. NIH news release. Retrieved January 7, 2006, from http://www.nih.gov/news/pr/dec2006/niaid-13.htm.

National Research Council. (1997). *Racial and ethnic differences in the health of older Americans.* New York: Author.

National Safety Council. (1989). *Accident facts: 1989 edition.* Chicago: National Safety Council.

National Science Foundation (NSF), Division of Science Resources Statistics. (2002). *Women, minorities, and persons with disabilities in science and engineering: 2002.* Arlington, VA: Author.

National Sleep Foundation. (2002). *Americans favor later high school start times, according to National Sleep Foundation Poll.* Washington, DC: Author.

Navarro, M. (2006, May 25). Families add 3rd generation to households. *New York Times,* pp. A1, A22.

Nazzi, T., & Bertoncini, J. (2003). Before and after the vocabulary spurt: Two modes of word acquisition? *Developmental Science, 6,* 136–142.

Needleman, H. L., & Bellinger, D. (Eds.). (1994). *Prenatal exposure to toxicants: Developmental consequences.* Baltimore: Johns Hopkins University Press.

Negy, C., Shreve, T., & Jensen, B. (2003). Ethnic identity, self-esteem, and ethnocentrism: A study of social identity versus multicultural theory of development. *Cultural Diversity & Ethnic Minority Psychology, 9,* 333–344.

Neisser, U. (2004). Memory development: New questions and old. *Developmental Review, 24,* 154–158.

Nelson, C. A., & Bosquet, M. (2000). Neurobiology of fetal and infant development: Implications for infant mental health. In C. H. Zeanah, Jr. (Ed.), *Handbook of infant mental health* (2nd ed.). New York: Guilford Press.

Nelson, H. D., Tyne, K., Naik, A., Bougatsos, C., Chan, B. K., & Humphrey, L. (2009). Screening for breast cancer: An update for the U.S. Preventive Services Task Force. *Annals of Internal Medicine, 151,* 727–737.

Nelson, K. (1996). *Language in cognitive development: Emergence of the mediated mind.* New York: Cambridge University Press.

Nelson, K., & Fivush, R. (2004). The emergence of autobiographical memory: A social cultural developmental theory. *Psychological Review, 111,* 486–511.

Nelson, L., Badger, S., & Wu, B. (2004). The influence of culture in emerging adulthood: Perspectives of Chinese college students. *International Journal of Behavioral Development, 28,* 26–36.

Nelson, T., & Wechsler, H. (2003). School spirits: Alcohol and collegiate sports fans. *Addictive Behaviors, 28,* 1–11.

Nesheim, S., Henderson, S., Lindsay, M., Zuberi, J., Grimes, V., Buehler, J., Lindegren, M. L., & Bulterys, M. (2004). *Prenatal HIV testing and antiretroviral prophylaxis at an urban hospital—Atlanta, Georgia, 1997–2000.* Atlanta, GA: Centers for Disease Control.

Ness, J., Aronow, W., & Beck, G. (2006). Menopausal symptoms after cessation of hormone replacement therapy. *Maturitas, 53,* 356–361.

Neugarten, B. L. (1972). Personality and the aging process. *The Gerontologist, 12,* 9–15.

Neugarten, B. L. (1977). Personality and aging. In J. E. Birren & K. W. Schaie (Eds.), *Handbook for the psychology of aging.* New York: Van Nostrand Reinhold.

Newbart, D. (2009, October 11). 'Silent addiction' on campus: gambling. *Chicago Sun Times,* p. A12.

Newman, R., & Hussain, I. (2006). Changes in preference for infant-directed speech in low and moderate noise by 4.5- to 13-month-olds. *Infancy, 10,* 61–76.

Newston, R. L., & Keith, P. M. (1997). Single women later in life. In J. M. Coyle (Ed.), *Handbook on women and aging* (pp. 385–399). Westport, CT: Greenwood Press.

Newton, K., Reed, S., LaCroix, A., Grothaus, L., Ehrlich, K., & Guiltinan, J. (2006). Treatment of vasomotor symptoms of menopause with black cohosh, multibotanicals, soy, hormone therapy, or placebo. *Annals of Internal Medicine, 145,* 869–879.

Ng, F. F., Pomerantz, E. M., & Lam, S. (2007). European American and Chinese parents' responses to children's success and failure: Implications for children's responses. *Developmental Psychology, 43,* 1239–1255.

Ng, S. (2002). Will families support their elders? Answers from across cultures. In T. Nelson (Ed.), *Ageism: Stereotyping and prejudice against older persons.* Cambridge, MA: MIT Press.

Ng, W., & Nicholas, H. (2010). A progressive pedagogy for online learning with high-ability secondary school students: A case study. *Gifted Child Quarterly, 54,* 239–251.

Ngo, B. (2010). Doing "diversity" at dynamic high: Problems and possibilities of multicultural education in practice. *Education and Urban Society, 42,* 473–495.

NICHD Early Child Care Research Network. (2001a). Child care and children's peer interaction at 24 and 36 months: The NICHD study of early child care. *Child Development, 72,* 1478–1500.

NICHD Early Child Care Research Network. (2001b). Child-care and family predictors of preschool attachment and stability from infancy. *Development Psychology, 37,* 847–862.

NICHD Early Child Care Research Network. (2003a). Does quality of child care affect child outcomes at age 4 1/2? *Developmental Psychology, 39,* 451–469.

NICHD Early Child Care Research Network. (2003b). Families matter—even for kids in child care. *Journal of Developmental and Behavioral Pediatrics, 24,* 58–62.

NICHD Early Child Care Research Network. (2005). *Child care and child development: Results from the NICHD study of early child care and youth development.* New York: Guilford Press.

NICHD Early Child Care Research Network. (2006). *The NICHD study of early child care and youth development: Findings for children up to age 4 1/2 years* (Figure 5, p. 20). Washington, DC: National Institute of Child Health and Human Development.

Niederhofer, H. (2004). A longitudinal study: Some preliminary results of association of prenatal maternal stress and fetal movements, temperament factors in early childhood and behavior at age 2 years. *Psychological Reports, 95,* 767–770.

Nieto, S. (2005). Public education in the twentieth century and beyond: high hopes, broken promises, and an uncertain future. *Harvard Educational Review, 75,* 43–65.

Nigg, J. T. (2001). Is ADHD a disinhibatory disorder? *Psychological Bulletin, 127,* 571–598.

Nigg, J., Knottnerus, G., Martel, M., Nikolas, M., Cavanagh, K., Karmaus, W., et al. (2008). Low blood lead levels associated with clinically diagnosed attention-deficit/hyperactivity disorder and mediated by weak cognitive control. *Biological Psychiatry, 63,* 325–331.

Nihart, M. A. (1993). Growth and development of the brain. *Journal of Child and Adolescent Psychiatric and Mental Health Nursing, 6,* 39–40.

Nilsson, L. (2003). Memory function in normal aging. *Acta Neurologica Scandinavica, 107,* 7–13.

Nilsson, L. G., Bäckman, L., Erngrund, K., Nyberg, L., et al. (1997). The Betula prospective cohort study: Memory, health, and aging. *Aging Neuropsychology & Cognition, 4,* 1–32.

Nisbett, R. (1994, October 31). Blue genes. *New Republic, 211,* 15.

Noakes, M. A., & Rinaldi, C. M. (2006). Age and gender differences in peer conflict, *Journal of Youth and Adolescence, 35,* 881–891.

Nobuyuki, I. (1997). Simple reaction times and timing of serial reactions of middle-aged and old men. *Perceptual & Motor Skills, 84,* 219–225.

Nockels, R., & Oakeshott, P. (1999). Awareness among young women of sexually transmitted chlamydia infection. *Family Practice, 16,* 94.

Nolen-Hoeksema, S. (2001). Ruminative coping and adjustment to bereavement. In M. Stroebe & R. Hansson (Eds.), *Handbook of bereavement research: Consequences, coping, and care.* Washington, DC: American Psychological Association.

Nolen-Hoeksema, S., & Davis, C. (2002). Positive responses to loss: Perceiving benefits and growth. In C. Snyder & S. Lopez (Eds.), *Handbook of positive psychology.* London: Oxford University Press.

Noonan, D. (2003, September 22). When safety is the name of the game. *Newsweek,* pp. 64–66.

Nordenmark, M., & Stattin, M. (2009). Psychosocial wellbeing and reasons for retirement in Sweden. *Ageing & Society, 29,* 413–430.

Nordin, S., Razani, L., & Markison, S. (2003). Age-associated increases in intensity discrimination for taste. *Experimental Aging Research, 29,* 371–381.

Norlander, T., Von Schedvin, H., & Archer, T. (2005). Thriving as a function of affective personality: Relation to personality factors, coping strategies and stress. *Anxiety, Stress & Coping: An International Journal, 18,* 105–116.

Norman, R. M. G., & Malla, A. K. (2001). Family history of schizophrenia and the relationship of stress to symptoms: Preliminary findings. *Australian & New Zealand Journal of Psychiatry, 35,* 217–223.

Nugent, J. K., Lester, B. M., & Brazelton, T. B. (Eds.). (1989). *The cultural context of infancy, Vol. 1: Biology, culture, and infant development.* Norwood, NJ: Ablex.

Nyiti, R. M. (1982). The validity of "culture differences explanations" for cross-cultural variation in the rate of Piagetian cognitive development. In D. Wagner & H. Stevenson (Eds.), *Cultural perspectives on child development.* New York: Freeman.

Nylen, K., Moran, T., Franklin, C., & O'Hara, M. (2006). Maternal depression: A review of relevant treatment approaches for mothers and infants. *Infant Mental Health Journal, 27,* 327–343.

O'Connor, M., & Whaley, S. (2006). Health care provider advice and risk factors associated with alcohol consumption following pregnancy recognition. *Journal of Studies on Alcohol, 67,* 22–31.

O'Connor, P. (1994). Very close parent/child relationships: The perspective of the elderly person. *Journal of Cross-Cultural Gerontology, 9,* 53–76.

O'Grady, W., & Aitchison, J. (2005). *How children learn language.* New York: Cambridge University Press.

O'Leary, S. G. (1995). Parental discipline mistakes. *Current Directions in Psychological Science, 4,* 11–13.

O'Toole, M. L., Sawicki, M. A., & Artal, R. (2003). Structured diet and physical activity prevent postpartum weight retention. *Journal of Women's Health, 12,* 991–998.

Oberlander, S. E., Black, M., & Starr, R. H. (2007). African American adolescent mothers and grandmothers: A multigenerational approach to parenting. *American Journal of Community Psychology, 39,* 37–46.

Oblinger, D. G., & Rush, S. C. (1997). *The learning revolution: The challenge of information technology in the academy.* Bolton, MA: Anker Publishing Co.

Ochsner Clinic Foundation. (2003). *Adult preventive health care screening recommendations.* New Orleans, LA: Ochsner Clinic Foundation.

Ocorr, K., Reeves, N. L., Wessells, R. J., Fink, M., Chen, H. S., Akasaka, T., Yasuda, S., Metzger, J. M., Giles, W., Posakony, J. W., & Bodmer, R. (2007). KCNQ potassium channel mutations cause cardiac arrhythmias in Drosophila that mimic the effects of aging. *Proceedings of the National Academy of Sciences, 104,* 3943–3948.

OECD (Organization for Economic Cooperation and Development). (1998). *Education at a glance: OECD indicators, 1998.* Paris: Author.

OECD (Organization for Economic Cooperation and Development). (2001). *Education at a glance: OECD indicators, 2001.* Paris: Author.

Ogbu, J. (1992). Understanding cultural diversity and learning. *Educational Researcher, 21,* 5–14.

Okie, S. (2005). *Winning the war against childhood obesity.* Washington, DC: Joseph Henry Publications.

Oksenberg, J., & Hauser, S. (2010). Mapping the human genome with newfound precision. *Annals of Neurology, 67,* A8–A10.

Olivardia, R., & Pope, H. (2002). Body image disturbance in childhood and adolescence. In D. Castle & K. Phillips (Eds.), *Disorders of body image.* Petersfield, England: Wrightson Biomedical Publishing.

Oliver, B., & Plomin, R. (2007). Twins' Early Development Study (TEDS): A multivariate, longitudinal genetic investigation of language, cognition and behavior problems from childhood through adolescence. *Twin Research and Human Genetics, 10,* 96–105.

Olness, K. (2003). Effects on brain development leading to cognitive impairment: A worldwide epidemic. *Journal of Developmental & Behavioral Pediatrics, 24,* 120–130.

Olsen, S. (2009, October 30). Will the digital divide close by itself? *New York Times.* Available online at http://bits.blogs.nytimes.com/2009/10/30/will-the-digital-divide-close-by-itself

Olson, E. (2006, April 27). You're in labor, and getting sleeeepy. *New York Times,* p. C2.

Onwuteaka-Philipsen, B., Rurup, M., Pasman, H., & van der Heide, A. (2010). The last phase of life: Who requests and who receives euthanasia or physician-assisted suicide? *Medical Care, 48,* 596–603.

Opfer, J. E., & Siegler, R. S. (2007). Representational change and children's numerical estimation. Citation. *Cognitive Psychology, 55,* 169–195.

Opfer, V. D., Henry, G. T., & Mashburn, A. J. (2008). The district effect: Systemic responses to high stakes accountability policies in six southern states. *American Journal of Education, 114,* 299–332.

Orbuch, T. L., House, J. S., Mero, R. P., & Webster, P. S. (1996). Marital quality over the life course. *Social Psychology Quarterly, 59,* 162–171.

Ordovas, J. (2010). Nutrition and cognitive health. *Mental capital and wellbeing.* Wiley-Blackwell.

Oretti, R. G., Harris, B., & Lazarus, J. H. (2003). Is there an association between life events, postnatal depression and thyroid dysfunction in thyroid antibody positive women? *International Journal of Social Psychiatry, 49,* 70–76.

Ormont, L. R. (2001). Developing emotional insulation (1994). In L. B. Fugeri, *The technique of group treatment: The collected papers of Louis R. Ormont.* Madison, CT: Psychosocial Press.

Ortiz, S. O., & Dynda, A. M. (2005). Use of intelligence tests with culturally and linguistically diverse populations. In D. P. Flanagan & P. L. Harrison (Eds.), *Contemporary intellectual assessment: Theories, tests, and issues.* New York: Guilford Press.

Osofsky, J. (2003). Prevalence of children's exposure to domestic violence and child maltreatment: Implications for prevention and intervention. *Clinical Child & Family Psychology Review, 6,* 161–170.

Ostrov, J., Gentile, D., & Crick, N. (2006, November). Media exposure, aggression and prosocial behavior during early childhood: A longitudinal study. *Social Development, 15,* 612–627.

OSTWG (Online Safety and Technology Working Group). (2010). *Youth safety on a living Internet: Report of the Online Safety and Technology Working Group.*

Oswal, A., & Yeo, G. (2010). Leptin and the control of body weight: A review of its diverse central targets, signaling mechanisms, and role in the pathogenesis of obesity. *Obesity, 18,* 221–229.

Ott, C., Sanders, S., & Kelber, S. (2007). Grief and personal growth experience of spouses and adult-child caregivers of individuals with Alzheimer's disease and related dementias. *The Gerontologist, 47,* 798–809.

Ouwehand, C., de Ridder, D. T., & Bensing, J. M. (2007). A review of successful aging models: Proposing proactive coping as an important additional strategy. *Clinical Psychology Review, 43,* 101–116.

Ownby, R. L., Czaja, S. J., Loewenstein, D., & Rubert, M. (2008). Cognitive abilities that predict success in a computer-based training program. *The Gerontologist, 48,* 170–180.

Owsley, C., Stalvey, B., & Phillips, J. (2003). The efficacy of an educational intervention in promoting self-regulation among high-risk older drivers. *Accident Analysis & Prevention, 35,* 393–400.

Oxford, M., Gilchrist, L., Gillmore, M., & Lohr, M. (2006, July). Predicting variation in the life course of adolescent mothers as they enter adulthood. *Journal of Adolescent Health, 39,* 20–26.

Oyserman, D., Kemmelmeier, M., Fryberg, S., Brosh, H., & Hart-Johnson, T. (2003). Racial ethnic self-schemas. *Social Psychology Quarterly, 66,* 333–347.

Ozawa, M., & Yoon, H. (2003). Economic impact of marital disruption on children. *Children & Youth Services Review, 25,* 611–632.

Paisley, T. S., Joy, E. A., & Price, R. J., Jr. (2003). Exercise during pregnancy: A practical approach. *Current Sports Medicine Reports, 2,* 325–330.

Pajkrt, E., Weisz, B., Firth, H. V., & Chitty, L. S. (2004). Fetal cardiac anomalies and genetic syndromes. *Prenatal Diagnosis, 24,* 1104–1115.

Pajulo, M., Helenius, H., & MaYes, L. (2006, May). Prenatal views of baby and parenthood: Association with sociodemographic and pregnancy factors. *Infant Mental Health Journal, 27,* 229–250.

Palan, P. R., Connell, K., Ramirez, E., Inegbenijie, C., Gavara, R. Y., Ouseph, J. A., & Mikhail, M. S. (2005). Effects of menopause and hormone replacement therapy on serum levels of coenzyme Q10 and other lipid-soluble antioxidants. *Biofactors, 25,* 61–66.

Palfai, T., Halperin, S., & Hoyer, W. (2003). Age inequalities in recognition memory: Effects of stimulus presentation time and list repetitions. *Aging, Neuropsychology, & Cognition, 10,* 134–140.

Palmore, E. B. (1988). *The facts on aging quiz.* New York: Springer Publishing Co.

Palmore, E. B. (1992). Knowledge about aging: What we know and need to know. *Gerontologist, 32,* 149–150.

Pandina, R., Johnson, V., & White, H. (2010). Peer influences on substance use during adolescence and emerging adulthood. *Handbook of drug use etiology: Theory, methods, and empirical findings* (pp. 383–401). Washington, DC: American Psychological Association.

Paneth, N. S. (1995). The problem of low birth weight. *The Future of Children, 5,* 19–34.

Pappano, L. (1994, November 27). The new old generation. *Boston Globe Magazine,* 18–38.

Pardee, P. E., Norman, G. J., Lustig, R. H., Preud'homme, D., & Schwimmer, J. B. (2007). Television viewing and hypertension in obese children. *American Journal of Preventive Medicine, 33, Dec.* [Special issue: Timing of repeat colonoscopy disparity between guidelines and endoscopists' recommendation], 439–443.

Paris, J. (1999). *Nature and nurture in psychiatry: A predisposition–stress model of mental disorders.* Washington, DC: American Psychiatric Press.

Park, A. (2008, June 23). Living large. *Time,* pp. 90–92.

Park, K. A., Lay, K., & Ramsay, L. (1993). Individual differences and developmental changes in preschoolers' friendships. *Developmental Psychology, 29,* 264–270.

Parke, R., Simpkins, S., & McDowell, D. (2002). Relative contributions of families and peers to children's social development. In P. Smith & C. Hart (Eds.), *Blackwell handbook of childhood social development.* Malden, MA: Blackwell Publishers.

Parke, R. D. (2004). Development in the family. *Annual Review of Psychology, 55,* 365–399.

Parker, S. T. (2005). Piaget's legacy in cognitive constructivism, niche construction, and phenotype development and evolution. In S. T. Parker & J. Langer (Eds.), *Biology and knowledge revisited: From neurogenesis to psychogenesis.* Mahwah, NJ: Lawrence Erlbaum.

Parks, C. A. (1998). Lesbian parenthood: A review of the literature. *American Journal of Orthopsychiatry, 68,* 376–389.

Parks, C., Sanna, L., & Posey, D. (2003). Retrospection in social dilemmas: How thinking about the past affects future cooperation. *Journal of Personality & Social Psychology, 84,* 988–996.

Parlee, M. B. (1979, October). The friendship bond. *Psychology Today, 13,* 43–45.

Parmalee, A. H., Jr., & Sigman, M. D. (1983). Prenatal brain development and behavior. In P. H. Mussen (Ed.), *Handbook of child psychology* (Vol. 2, 4th ed.). New York: Wiley.

Parnell, T. F., & Day, D. O. (Eds.). (1998). *Munchausen by proxy syndrome: Misunderstood child abuse.* Thousand Oaks, CA: Sage Publications.

Parten, M. B. (1932). Social participation among preschool children. *Journal of Abnormal and Social Psychology, 27,* 243–269.

Pasqualotto, F. F., Lucon, A. M., Sobreiro, B. P., Pasqualotto, E. B., & Arap, S. (2005). Effects of medical therapy, alcohol, smoking, and endocrine disruptors on male infertility. *Revista do Hospital das Clinicas, 59,* 375–382.

Patenaude, A. F., Guttmacher, A. E., & Collins, F. S. (2002). Genetic testing and psychology: New roles, new responsibilities. *American Psychologist, 57,* 271–282.

Paterson, D. S., Trachtenberg, F. L., Thompson, E. G., Belliveau, R. A., Beggs, A. H., Darnall, R., Chadwick, A. E., Krous, H. F., & Kinney, H. C. (2006). Multiple serotonergic brainstem abnormalities in sudden infant death syndrome. *JAMA: The Journal of the American Medical Association, 296,* 2124–2132.

Patterson, C. (2003). Children of lesbian and gay parents. In L. Garnets & D. Kimmel (Eds.), *Psychological perspectives on lesbian, gay, and bisexual experiences* (2nd ed.). New York: Columbia University Press.

Patterson, C. (2009). Children of lesbian and gay parents: Psychology, law, and policy. *American Psychologist* (64), 727–736.

Patterson, C. J. (1994). Lesbian and gay families. *Current Directions in Psychological Science, 3,* 62–64.

Patterson, C. J. (1995). Families of the baby boom: Parents' division of labor and children's adjustment. *Developmental Psychology, 31* [Special issue: Sexual orientation and human development], 115–123.

Patterson, C. J. (2002). Lesbian and gay parenthood. In M. Bornstein (Ed.), *Handbook of parenting.* Mahwah, NJ: Lawrence Erlbaum.

Patterson, C. J. (2007). *Handbook of counseling and psychotherapy with lesbian, gay, bisexual, and transgender clients* (2nd ed.), K. J. Bieschke, R. M. Perez, & K. A. DeBord (Eds); Washington, DC: American Psychological Association.

Patterson, C., & Friel, L. V. (2000). Sexual orientation and fertility. In G. R. Bentley & N. Mascie-Taylor (Eds.), *Infertility in the modern world: Biosocial perspectives.* Cambridge, UK: Cambridge University Press.

Paul, P. (2006, January 16). Want a brainier baby? *Time, 167* (3), p. 104.

Paulesu, E., Démonet, J. F., Fazio, F., McCrory, E., Chanoine, V., Brunswick, N., Cappa, S. F., Cossu, G., Habib, M., Frith, C. D., & Frith, U. (2001, March 16). Dyslexia: Cultural diversity and biological unity. *Science, 291,* 2165–2167.

Pauli-Pott, U., Mertesacker, B., & Bade, U. (2003). Parental perceptions and infant temperament development. *Infant Behavior & Development, 26,* 27–48.

Pavis, S., Cunningham-Burley, S., & Amos, A. (1997). Alcohol consumption and young people: Exploring meaning and social context. *Health Education Research, 12,* 311–322.

Pavlov, I. P. (1927). *Conditioned reflexes.* London: Oxford University Press.

Pearson, C., Combs, J., & Smith, G. (2010). A risk model for disordered eating in late elementary school boys. *Psychology of Addictive Behaviors, 22,* 88–97.

Peck, R. C. (1968). Psychological developments in the second half of life. In B. L. Neugarten (Ed.), *Middle age and aging.* Chicago: University of Chicago Press.

Pedersen, S., Vitaro, F., Barker, E. D., & Borge, A. I. H. (2007). The timing of middle-childhood peer rejection and friendship: Linking early behavior to early-adolescent adjustment. *Child Development, 78,* 1037–1051.

Pedersen, S., Yagensky, A., Smith, O., Yagenska, O., Shpak, V., & Denollet, J. (2009). Preliminary evidence for the cross-cultural utility of the type D personality construct in the Ukraine. *International Journal of Behavioral Medicine, 16,* 108–115.

Peeters, M., Cillessen, A., & Scholte, R. (2010). Clueless or powerful? Identifying subtypes of bullies in adolescence. *Journal of Youth and Adolescence, 39,* 1041–1052.

Peirano, P., Algarin, C., & Uauy, R. (2003). Sleep-wake states and their regulatory mechanisms throughout early human development. *Journal of Pediatrics, 143,* Supplement, S70–S79.

Pelham, B., & Hetts, J. (2001). Underworked and overpaid: Elevated entitlement in men's self-pay. *Journal of Experimental Social Psychology, 37,* 93–103.

Pellicano, E. (2007). Links between theory of mind and executive function in young children with autism: Clues to developmental primacy. *Developmental Psychology, 43,* 974–990.

Peltzer, K., & Pengpid, S. (2006). Sexuality of 16- to 17-year-old South Africans in the context of HIV/AIDS. *Social Behavior and Personality, 34,* 239–256.

Penninx, B., Guralnik, J. M., Ferrucci, L., Simonsick, E. M., Deeg, D., & Wallace, R. B. (1998). Depressive symptoms and physical decline in community-dwelling older persons. *JAMA: The Journal of the American Medical Association, 279,* 1720–1726.

Pennisi, E. (2000, May 19). And the gene number is . . .? *Science, 288,* 1146–1147.

Percy, K. (2010). *Working with aging families: Therapeutic solutions for caregivers, spouses, & adult children.* New York: Norton.

Pereira, A. C., Huddleston, D. E., Brickman, A. M., Sosunov, A. A., Hen, R., McKhann, G. M., Sloan, R., Gage, F. H., Brown, T. R., & Small, S. A. (2007). An in vivo correlate of exercise-induced neurogenesis in the adult dentate gyrus. *Proceedings of the National Academy of Sciences, 104,* 5638–5643.

Perreault, A., Fothergill-Bourbonnais, F., & Fiset, V. (2004). The experience of family members caring for a dying loved one. *International Journal of Palliative Nursing, 10,* 133–143.

Perrine, N. E., & Aloise-Young, P. A. (2004). The role of self-monitoring in adolescents' susceptibility to passive peer pressure. *Personality & Individual Differences, 37,* 1701–1716.

Persson, A., & Musher-Eizenman, D. R. (2003). The impact of a prejudice-prevention television program on young children's ideas about race. *Early Childhood Research Quarterly, 18,* 530–546.

Persson, G. E. B. (2005). Developmental perspectives on prosocial and aggressive motives in preschoolers' peer interactions. *International Journal of Behavioral Development, 29,* 80–91.

Petanjek, Z., Judas, M., Kostovic, I., & Uylings, H. B. M. (2008). Lifespan alterations of basal dendritic trees of pyramidal neurons in the human prefrontal cortex: A layer-specific pattern. *Cerebral Cortex, 18,* 915–929.

Peters, B. (2010). Under threat from HIV/AIDS: Burial societies in Limpopo Province, South Africa. *Mass trauma and emotional healing around the world: Rituals and practices for resilience and meaning-making, Vol. 2: Human-made disasters.* Santa Barbara, CA: Praeger/ABC-CLIO.

Peters, C., Claussen Bell, K. S., Zinn, A., Goerge, R. M., & Courtney, M. E. (2008). *Continuing in foster care beyond age 18: How courts can help.* Chicago: Chapin Hall at the University of Chicago.

Peters, E., Hess, T. M., Vastfjall, D., & Auman, C. (2007). Adult age differences in dual information processes: Implications for the role of affective and deliberative processes in older adults' decision making. *Perspectives on Psychological Science, 2,* 1–23.

Petersen, A. (2000). A longitudinal investigation of adolescents' changing perceptions of pubertal timing. *Developmental Psychology, 36,* 37–43.

Peterson, A. C. (1988, September). Those gangly years. *Psychology Today,* pp. 28–34.

Peterson, C., & Park, N. (2007). Explanatory style and emotion regulation. In J. J. Gross (Ed.), *Handbook of emotion regulation.* New York: Guilford Press.

Peterson, D. M., Marcia, J. E., & Carpendale, J. I. (2004). Identity: Does thinking make it so? In C. Lightfood, C. Lalonde, & M. Chandler, *Changing conceptions of psychological life.* Mahwah, NJ: Lawrence Erlbaum.

Peterson, M., & Wilson, J. F. (2004). Work stress in America. *International Journal of Stress Management, 11,* 91–113.

Peterson, R. A., & Brown, S. P. (2005). On the use of beta coefficients in meta-analysis. *Journal of Applied Psychology, 90,* 175–181.

Petit, G., & Dodge, K. A. (2003). Violent children: Bridging development, intervention, and public policy.

*Developmental Psychology, 39* [Special Issue: Violent Children], 187–188.

Petkoska, J., & Earl, J. (2009). Understanding the influence of demographic and psychological variables on retirement planning. *Psychology and Aging, 24,* 245-251.

Petrou, S. (2006). Preterm birth—What are the relevant economic issues? *Early Human Development, 82* (2), 75–76.

Petrou, S., & Kupek, E. (2010). Poverty and childhood undernutrition in developing countries: A multi-national cohort study. *Social Science & Medicine, 71,* 1366–1373.

Phelan, P., Yu, H. C., & Davidson, A. L. (1994). Navigating the psychosocial pressures of adolescence: The voices and experiences of high school youth. *American Educational Research Journal, 31,* 415–447.

Philippot, P., & Feldman, R. S. (Eds.). (2005). *The regulation of emotion.* Mahwah, NJ: Lawrence Erlbaum.

Phillips, D. (1992, September). Death postponement and birthday celebrations. *Psychosomatic Medicine, 26,* 12–18.

Phillips, D. A., Voran, M., Kisker, E., Howes, C., & Whitebook, M. (1994). Child care for children in poverty: Opportunity or inequity? *Child Development, 65,* 472–492.

Phinney, J. S. (2005). Ethnic identity in late modern times: A response to Rattansi and Phoenix. *Identity, 5,* 187–194.

Phinney, J. S. (2008). Ethnic identity exploration in emerging adulthood. In D. L. Browning (Ed.), *Adolescent identities: A collection of readings.* New York: Analytic Press/Taylor & Francis Group.

Phinney, J. S., & Alipuria, L. L. (2006). Multiple social categorization and identity among multiracial, multiethnic, and multicultural individuals: Processes and implications. In R. J. Crips & M. Hewstone (Eds.), *Multiple social categorization: Processes, models and applications.* New York: Psychology Press.

Phinney, J. S., Ferguson, D. L., & Tate, J. D. (1997). Intergroup attitudes among ethnic minority adolescents: A causal model. *Child Development, 68,* 955–969.

Piaget, J. (1952). *The origins of intelligence in children.* New York: International Universities Press.

Piaget, J. (1962). *Play, dreams and imitation in childhood.* New York: Norton.

Piaget, J. (1983). Piaget's theory. In W. Kessen (Ed.), P. H. Mussen (Series Ed.), *Handbook of child psychology: Vol. 1. History, theory, and methods* (pp. 103–128). New York: Wiley.

Picard, A. (2008, February 14). Health study: Tobacco will soon claim one million lives a year. *The Globe and Mail,* A15.

Picavet, H. S., & Hoeymans, N. (2004). Health related quality of life in multiple musculoskeletal diseases: SF-36 and EQ-5D in the DMC3 study. *Annals of the Rheumatic Diseases, 63,* 723–729.

Piller, I. (2010). Review of 'The bilingual edge: Why, when, and how to teach your child a second language'. *International Journal of Bilingual Education and Bilingualism, 13,* 115–118.

Pine, K. J., Wilson, P., & Nash, A. S. (2007). The relationship between television advertising, children's viewing and their requests to Father Christmas. *Journal of Developmental & Behavioral Pediatrics, 28,* 456–461.

Ping, R., & Goldin-Meadow, S. (2008). Hands in the air: Using ungrounded iconic gestures to teach children conservation of quantity. *Developmental Psychology, 44,* 1277–1287.

Pinker, S. (1994). *The language instinct.* New York: William Morrow.

Piper, W. E., Ogrodniczuk, J. S., Joyce, A. S., & Weidman, R. (2009). Follow-up outcome in short-term group therapy for complicated grief. *Group Dynamics: Theory, Research, and Practice, 13,* 46–58.

Pittman, L. D., & Boswell, M. K. (2007). The role of grandmothers in the lives of preschoolers growing up in urban poverty. *Applied Developmental Science, 11,* 20–42.

Plomin, R. (1994). *Genetics and experience: The interplay between nature and nurture.* Newbury Park, CA: Sage Publications.

Plomin, R. (2005). Finding genes in child psychology and psychiatry: When are we going to be there? *Journal of Child Psychology and Psychiatry, 46,* 1030–1038.

Plonczynski, D. J., & Plonczynski, K. J. (2007). Hormone therapy in perimenopausal and postmenopausal women: Examining the evidence on cardiovascular disease risks. *Journal of Gerontological Nursing, 33,* 48–55.

Plosker, G., & Keam, S. (2006). Bimatoprost: A pharmacoeconomic review of its use in open-angle glaucoma and ocular hypertension. *PharmacoEconomics, 24,* 297–314.

Poest, C. A., Williams, J. R., Witt, D. D., & Atwood, M. E. (1990). Challenge me to move: Large muscle development in young children. *Young Children, 45,* 4–10.

Polansky, E. (1976). Take him home, Mrs. Smith. *Healthright, 2*(2).

Polivy, J., & Herman, C. (2002). If at first you don't succeed: False hopes of self-change. *American Psychologist, 57,* 677–689.

Polkinghorne, D. E. (2005). Language and meaning: Data collection in qualitative research. *Journal of Counseling Psychology, 52* [Special issue: Knowledge in context: Qualitative methods in counseling psychology research], 137–145.

Pollack, W. (1999). *Real boys: Rescuing our sons from the myths of boyhood.* New York: Owl Books.

Pollack, W., Shuster, T., & Trelease, J. (2001). *Real boys' voices.* New York: Penguin.

Pollak, S., Holt, L., & Wismer Fries, A. (2004). Hemispheric asymmetries in children's perception of nonlinguistic human affective sounds. *Developmental Science, 7,* 10–18.

Polman, H., de Castro, B., & van Aken, M. (2008). Experimental study of the differential effects of playing versus watching violent video games on children's aggressive behavior. *Aggressive Behavior, 34,* 256–264.

Pomares, C. G., Schirrer, J., & Abadie, V. (2002). Analysis of the olfactory capacity of healthy children before language acquisition. *Journal of Developmental Behavior and Pediatrics, 23,* 203–207.

Pompili, M., Masocco, M., Vichi, M., Lester, D., Innamorati, M., Tatarelli, R., et al. (2009). Suicide among Italian adolescents: 1970–2002. *European Child & Adolescent Psychiatry, 18,* 525–533.

Ponton, L. E. (2001). *The sex lives of teenagers: Revealing the secret world of adolescent boys and girls.* New York: Penguin Putnam.

Pope, H., Olivardia, R., Gruber, A., & Borowiecki, J. (1999). Evolving ideals of male body image as seen through action toys. *International Journal of Eating Disorders, 26,* 65–72.

Population Council Report. (1995, May 30). The decay of families is global, studies says. *New York Times,* p. A5.

Porges, S. W., Lipsitt, & Lewis P. (1993). Neonatal responsivity to gustatory stimulation: The gustatory-vagal hypothesis. *Infant Behavior & Development, 16,* 487–494.

Porter, M., van Teijlingen, E., Yip, L., & Bhattacharya, S. (2007). Satisfaction with cesarean section: Qualitative analysis of open-ended questions in a large postal survey. *Birth: Issues in Perinatal Care, 34,* 148–154.

Porter, R. H., Bologh, R. D., & Malkin, J. W. (1988). Olfactory influences on mother–infant interactions. In C. Rovee-Collier & L. Lipsitt (Eds.), *Advances in infancy research* (Vol. 5). Norwood, NJ: Ablex.

Portes, A., & Rumbaut, R. (2001). *Legacies: The story of the immigrant second generation.* Los Angeles: University of California Press.

Posthuma, D., & de Geus, E. (2006, August). Progress in the molecular-genetic study of intelligence. *Current Directions in Psychological Science, 15,* 151–155.

Poulin-Dubois, D. (1999). Infants' distinction between animate and inanimate objects: The origins of naive psychology. In P. Rochat, *Early social cognition.* Hillsdale, NJ: Lawrence Erlbaum.

Poulin-Dubois, D., Serbin, L., & Eichstedt, J. (2002). Men don't put on make-up: Toddlers' knowledge of the gender stereotyping of household activities. *Social Development, 11,* 166–181.

Poulton, R., & Caspi, A. (2005). Commentary: How does socioeconomic disadvantage during childhood damage health in adulthood? Testing psychosocial pathways. *International Journal of Epidemiology, 23,* 51–55.

Powell, R. (2004, June 19). Colleges construct housing for elderly: Retiree students move to campus. *Washington Post,* p. F13.

Power, M., & Green, A. (2010). The attitudes to disability scale (ADS): Development and psychometric properties. *Journal of Intellectual Disability Research, 54,* 860–874.

Prater, L. (2002). African American families: Equal partners in general and special education. In F. Obiakor & A. Ford (Eds.), *Creating successful learning environments for African American learners with exceptionalities.* Thousand Oaks, CA: Corwin Press.

Prechtl, H. F. R. (1982). Regressions and transformations during neurological development. In T. G. Bever (Ed.), *Regressions in mental development.* Hillsdale, NJ: Lawrence Erlbaum.

Prentice, A., Schoenmakers, I., Laskey, M. A., de Bono, S., Ginty, F., & Goldberg, G. R. (2006). Nutrition and bone growth and development. *Proceedings of the Nutritional Society, 65,* 348–360.

Prescott, C., & Gottesman, I. (1993). Genetically mediated vulnerability to schizophrenia. *Psychiatric Clinics of North America, 16,* 245–267.

Pressley, M., & Schneider, W. (1997). *Introduction to memory development during childhood and adolescence.* Mahwah, NJ: Lawrence Erlbaum.

Prezbindowski, A. K., & Lederberg, A. R. (2003). Vocabulary assessment of deaf and hard-of-hearing children from infancy through the preschool years. *Journal of Deaf Studies and Deaf Education, 8,* 383–400.

Price, R., & Gottesman, I. (1991). Body fat in identical twins reared apart: Roles for genes and environment. *Behavior Genetics, 21,* 1–7.

Priddis, L., & Howieson, N. (2009). The vicissitudes of mother-infant relationships between birth and six years. *Early Child Development and Care, 179,* 43–53.

Prigerson, H. (2003). Costs to society of family caregiving for patients with end-stage Alzheimer's disease. *New England Journal of Medicine, 349,* 1891–1892.

Prigerson, H. G., Frank, E., Kasl, S. V., et al. (1995). Complicated grief and bereavement-related depression as distinct disorders: Preliminary empirical validation in elderly bereaved spouses. *American Journal of Psychiatry, 152,* 22–30.

PRIMEDIA/Roper. (1999). *Roper National Youth Survey.* Storrs, CT: Roper Center for Public Opinion Research.

Prince, M. (2000, November 13). How technology has changed the way we have babies. *The Wall Street Journal,* pp. R4, R13.

Propper, C., & Moore, G. (2006, December). The influence of parenting on infant emotionality: A multi-level psychobiological perspective. *Developmental Review, 26,* 427–460.

Pruis, T., & Janowsky, J. (2010). Assessment of body image in younger and older women. *Journal of General Psychology, 137,* 225–238.

Puchalski, M., & Hummel, P. (2002). The reality of neonatal pain. *Advances in Neonatal Care, 2,* 245–247.

Puntambekar, S., & Hübscher, R. (2005). Tools for scaffolding students in a complex learning environment: What have we gained and what have we missed? *Educational Psychologist, 40,* 1–12.

Pushkar, D., Chaikelson, J., Conway, M., Etezadi, J., Giannopoulus, C., Li, K., et al. (2010). Testing continuity and activity variables as predictors of positive and negative affect in retirement. *The Journals of Gerontology: Series B: Psychological Sciences and Social Sciences, 65B*, 42–49.

Putterman, E., & Linden, W. (2004). Appearance versus health: Does the reason for dieting affect dieting behavior? *Journal of Behavioral Medicine, 27*, 185–204.

Pyke, K., & Adams, M. (2010). What's age got to do with it? A case study analysis of power and gender in husband-older marriages. *Journal of Family Issues, 31*, 748–777.

Qian, Z-C, & Lichter, D. T. (2007). Social boundary and marital assimilation: Evaluating trends in racial and ethnic intermarriage. *American Sociological Review, 72*, 68–94.

Quatromoni, P., Pencina, M., Cobain, M., Jacques, P., & D'Agostino, R. (2006, August). Dietary quality predicts adult weight gain: Findings from the Framingham Offspring Study. *Obesity, 14*, 1383–1391.

Quinn, M. (1990, January 29). Don't aim that pack at us. *Time*, p. 60.

Quinn, P. (2008). In defense of core competencies, quantitative change, and continuity. *Child Development, 79*, 1633–1638.

Quinn, P., Uttley, L., Lee, K., Gibson, A., Smith, M., Slater, A., et al. (2008). Infant preference for female faces occurs for same- but not other-race faces. *Journal of Neuropsychology, 2*, 15–26.

Quinnan, E. J. (1997). Connection and autonomy in the lives of elderly male celibates: Degrees of disengagement. *Journal of Aging Studies, 11*, 115–130.

Quintana, C. (1998, May 17). Riding the rails. *New York Times Magazine*, pp. 22–24, 66.

Quintana, S. M., McKown, C., Cross, W. E., & Cross, T. B. (2008). In S. M. Quintana & C. McKown (Eds.), *Handbook of race, racism, and the developing child*. Hoboken, NJ: John Wiley.

Quintana, S. M., (2007). Racial and ethnic identity: Developmental perspectives and research. *Journal of Counseling Psychology. 54*, 259–270.

Raag, T. (2003). Racism, gender identities and young children: Social relations in a multi-ethnic, inner-city primary school. *Archives of Sexual Behavior, 32*, 392–393.

Rabain-Jamin, J., & Sabeau-Jouannet, E. (1997). Maternal speech to 4-month-old infants in two cultures: Wolof and French. *International Journal of Behavioral Development, 20*, 425–451.

Rabin, R. (2006, June 13). Breast-feed or else. *New York Times*, p. D1.

Rabkin, J., Remien, R., & Wilson, C. (1994). *Good doctors, good patients: Partners in HIV treatment*. New York: NCM Publishers.

Raeburn, P. (2004, October 1). Too immature for the death penalty? *New York Times Magazine*, 26–29.

Raeff, C. (2004). Within-culture complexities: Multifaceted and interrelated autonomy and connectedness characteristics in late adolescent selves. In M. E. Mascolo & J. Li (Eds.), *Culture and developing selves: Beyond dichotomization*. San Francisco, CA: Jossey-Bass.

Raji, C., Ho, A., Parikshak, N., Becker, J., Lopez, O., Kuller, L., Hua, X., Leow, A., Toga, A., & Thompson, P. (in press). Brain structure and obesity. *Human Brain Mapping*.

Rakison, D., & Oakes, L. (2003). *Early category and concept development: Making sense of the blooming, buzzing confusion*. London: Oxford University Press.

Ramaswamy, V., & Bergin, C. (2009). Do reinforcement and induction increase prosocial behavior? Results of a teacher-based intervention in preschools. *Journal of Research in Childhood Education, 23*, 527–538.

Ramos, É., St-André, M., Rey, É., Oraichi, D., & Bérard, A. (2008). Duration of antidepressant use during pregnancy and risk of major congenital malformations. *British Journal of Psychiatry, 192*, 344–350.

Ramsay, J. R. (2010). Relationships and social functioning. In *Nonmedication treatments for adult ADHD: Evaluating impact on daily functioning and well-being*. Washington, DC: American Psychological Association.

Ramsey-Rennels, J. L., & Langlois, J. H. (2006). Infants' differential processing of female and male faces. *Current Directions in Psychological Science, 15*, 59–62.

Ranade, V. (1993). Nutritional recommendations for children and adolescents. *International Journal of Clinical Pharmacology, Therapy, and Toxicology, 31*, 285–290.

Rando, T. A. (1993). *Treatment of complicated mourning*. Champaign, IL: Research Press.

Ranganath, C., Minzenberg, M., & Ragland, J. (2008). The cognitive neuroscience of memory function and dysfunction in schizophrenia. *Biological Psychiatry, 64*, 18–25. Available online at http://search.ebscohost.com

Rank, M. R., & Hirschl, T. A. (1999). Estimating the proportion of Americans ever experiencing poverty during their elderly years. *Journals of Gerontology Series B-Psychological Science and Social Sciences, 54*, S184–S193.

Rankin, J., Lane, D., & Gibbons, F. (2004). Adolescent self-consciousness: Longitudinal age changes and gender differences in two cohorts. *Journal of Research on Adolescence, 14*, 1–21.

Ransjö-Arvidson, A. B., Matthiesen, A. S., Lilja, G., Nissen, E., Widström, A. M., & Unväs-Moberg, K. (2001). Maternal analgesia during labor disturbs newborn behavior: Effects on breastfeeding, temperature, and crying. *Birth, 28*, 5–12.

Rapkin, B. D., & Fischer, K. (1992). Personal goals of older adults: Issues in assessment and prediction. *Psychology and Aging, 7*, 127–137.

Rapp, M., Krampe, R., & Baltes, P. (2006, January). Adaptive task prioritization in aging: Selective resource allocation to postural control is preserved in Alzheimer disease. *American Journal of Geriatric Psychiatry, 14*, 52–61.

Ratanachu-Ek, S. (2003). Effects of multivitamin and folic acid supplementation in malnourished children. *Journal of the Medical Association of Thailand, 4*, 86–91.

Rattan, S. I. S., Kristensen, P., & Clark, B. F. C. (Eds.). (2006). *Understanding and modulating aging*. Malden, MA: Blackwell Publishing on behalf of the New York Academy of Sciences, 2006.

Rattner, A., & Nathans, J. (2006, November). Macular degeneration: Recent advances and therapeutic opportunities. *Nature Reviews Neuroscience, 7*, 860–872.

Raudsepp, L., & Liblik, R. (2002). Relationship of perceived and actual motor competence in children. *Perception and Motor Skills, 94*, 1059–1070.

Ray, L., Bryan, A., MacKillop, J., McGeary, J., Hesterberg, K., & Hutchison, K. (2009). The dopamine D receptor (4) gene exon III polymorphism, problematic alcohol use and novelty seeking: Direct and mediated genetic effects. *Addiction Biology, 14*, 238–244. Available online at http://search.ebscohost.com

Ray, O. (2004). How the mind hurts and heals the body. *American Psychologist, 59*, 29–40.

Rayner, K., Foorman, B. R., Perfetti, C. A., Pesetsky, D., & Seidenberg, M. S. (2002, March). How should reading be taught? *Scientific American*, 85–91.

Raz, N., Rodrigue, K., Kennedy, K., & Acker, J. (2007, March). Vascular health and longitudinal changes in brain and cognition in middle-aged and older adults. *Neuropsychology, 21*, 149–157.

Razani, J., Murcia, G., Tabares, J., & Wong, J. (2007). The effects of culture on WASI test performance in ethnically diverse individuals. *The Clinical Neuropsy-chologist, 21*, 776–788.

Reddy, V. (1999). Prelinguistic communication. In M. Barrett (Ed.), *The development of language* (pp. 25–50). Philadelphia: Psychology Press.

Reed, R. K. (2005). *Birthing fathers: The transformation of men in American rites of birth*. New Brunswick, NJ: Rutgers University Press.

Reichert, F., Menezes, A., Wells, J., Dumith, C., & Hallal, P. (2009). Physical activity as a predictor of adolescent body fatness: A systematic review. *Sports Medicine, 39*, 279–294.

Reifman, A. (2000). Revisiting *The Bell Curve. Psycoloquy*, 11.

Reiner, W. G., & Gearhart, J. P. (2004). Discordant sexual identity in some genetic males with cloacal exstrophy assigned to female sex at birth. *The New England Journal of Medicine, 350*, 333–341.

Reis, S., & Renzulli, J. (2004). Current research on the social and emotional development of gifted and talented students: Good news and future possibilities. *Psychology in the Schools, 41*, 119–130.

Rembis, M. (2009). (Re)defining disability in the 'genetic age': Behavioral genetics, 'new' eugenics and the future of impairment. *Disability & Society, 24*, 585–597. Available online at http://search.ebscohost .com

Renkl, M. (2009). Five facts about kids' social lives. Available online at http://www.parenting.com/article/Child/Development/5-Facts-About-Kids-Social-Lives/1

Rentz, D., Locascio, J., Becker, J., Moran, E., Eng, E., Buckner, R., et al. (2010). Cognition, reserve, and amyloid deposition in normal aging. *Annals of Neurology, 67*, 353–364. Retrieved from PsycINFO database.

Reschly, D. J. (1996). Identification and assessment of students with disabilities. *The Future of Children, 6*, 40–53.

Rescorla, L., Alley, A., & Christine, J. (2001). Word frequencies in toddlers' lexicons. *Journal of Speech, Language, & Hearing Research, 44*, 598–609.

Resnick, B. (2000). A seven step approach to starting an exercise program for older adults. *Patient Education & Counseling, 39*, 243–252.

Resnick, M. D., Bearman, P. S., Blum, R. W., Bauman, K. E., Harris, M. R., Jones, L., Tabor, J., Beuhring, T., Sieving, R., Shew, M., Ireland, M., Bearinger, L. H., & Udry, J. R. (1997). Protecting adolescents from harm: Findings from the National Longitudinal Study on Adolescent Health. *JAMA: The Journal of the American Medical Association, 278*, 823–832.

Ressner, J. (2001, March 6). When a coma isn't one. *Time Magazine*, p. 62.

Resta, R., Biesecker, B. B., Bennett, R. L., Blum, S., Estabrooks. H. S., Strecker, M. N., & Williams J. L. (2006). A new definition of genetic counseling: National Society of Genetic Counselors' Task Force Report. *Journal of Genetic Counseling, 15*, 77–83.

Rethorst, C., Wipfli, B., & Landers, D. (2009). The antidepressive effects of exercise: A meta-analysis of randomized trials. *Sports Medicine, 39*, 491–511.

Reuters Health eLine. (2002, June 26). Baby's injuring points to danger of kids imitating television. *Reuters Health eLine*.

Reyna, V. F., & Farley, F. (2006). Risk and rationality in adolescent decision making. *Psychological Science in the Public Interest, 7*, 1–44.

Rhoades, G., Stanley, S., & Markman, H. (2006, December). Pre-engagement cohabitation and gender asymmetry in marital commitment. *Journal of Family Psychology, 20*, 553–560.

Rhoades, G., Stanley, S., & Markman, H. (2009). The pre-engagement cohabitation effect: A replication and extension of previous findings. *Journal of Family Psychology, 23*, 107–111.

Rhodes, R., Mitchell, S., Miller, S., Connor, S., & Teno, J. (2008). Bereaved family members' evaluation of hospice care: What factors influence overall satisfaction with services? *Journal of Pain and Symptom Management, 35*, 365–371.

Rhule, D. (2005). Take care to do no harm: Harmful interventions for youth problem behavior. *Professional Psychology: Research and Practice, 36*, 618–625.

Ricciardelli, L., & McCabe, M. (2003). Sociocultural and individual influences on muscle gain and weight loss strategies among adolescent boys and girls. *Psychology in the Schools, 40,* 209–224.

Ricciardelli, L. A., & McCabe, M. P. (2004). A biopsychosocial model of disordered eating and the pursuit of muscularity in adolescent boys. *Psychological Bulletin, 130,* 179–205.

Richards, M. H., Crowe, P. A., Larson, R., & Swarr, A. (1998). Developmental patterns and gender differences in the experience of peer companionship during adolescence. *Child Development, 69,* 154–163.

Richards, M. P. M. (1996). The childhood environment and the development of sexuality. In C. J. K. Henry & S. J. Ulijaszek (Eds.), *Long-term consequences of early environment: Growth, development and the lifespan developmental perspective.* Cambridge, England: Cambridge University Press.

Richardson, G., Goldschmidt, L., & Willford, J. (2009). Continued effects of prenatal cocaine use: Preschool development. *Neurotoxicology and Teratology, 31,* 325–333.

Richardson, K., & Norgate, S. (2007). A critical analysis of IQ studies of adopted children. *Human Development, 49,* 319–335.

Rick, S., & Douglas, D. (2007). Neurobiological effects of childhood abuse. *Journal of Psychosocial Nursing & Mental Health Services, 45,* 47–54.

Rideout V., Vandewater, E., & Wartella, E. (2003). *Zero to Six: Electronic media in the lives of infants, toddlers, and preschoolers.* Menlo Park, CA: Kaiser Family Foundation.

Riebe, D., Burbank, P., & Garber, C. (2002). Setting the stage for active older adults. In P. Burbank & D. Riebe (Eds.), *Promoting exercise and behavior change in older adults: Interventions with the transtheoretical mode.* New York: Springer Publishing Co.

Rieffe, C., Ketelaar, L., & Wiefferink, C. (2010). Assessing empathy in young children: Construction and validation of an Empathy Questionnaire (EmQue). *Personality and Individual Differences, 49,* 362–367.

Riesch, S., Anderson, L., Pridham, K., Lutz, K., & Becker, P. (2010). Furthering the understanding of parent-child relationships: A nursing scholarship review series. Part 5: Parent-adolescent and teen parent-child relationships. *Journal for Specialists in Pediatric Nursing, 15,* 182–201.

Rinaldi, C. (2002). Social conflict abilities of children identified as sociable, aggressive, and isolated: Developmental implications for children at-risk for impaired peer relations. *Developmental Disabilities Bulletin, 30,* 77–94.

Ripple, C., & Zigler, E. (2003). Research, policy, and the federal role in prevention initiatives for children. *American Psychologist, 58,* 482–490.

Ritchie, L. (2003). Adult day care: Northern perspectives. *Public Health Nursing, 20,* 120–131.

Ritzen, E. M. (2003). Early puberty: What is normal and when is treatment indicated? *Hormone Research, 60,* Supplement, 31–34.

Robb, M., Richert, R., & Wartella, E. (2009). Just a talking book? Word learning from watching baby videos. *British Journal of Developmental Psychology, 27,* 27–45. Available online at http://search.ebscohost.com.

Roberts, R. E., Phinney, J. S., Masse, L. C., Chen, Y. R., Roberts, C. R., & Romero, A. (1999). The structure of ethnic identity of young adolescents from diverse ethnocultural groups. *Journal of Early Adolescence, 19,* 301–322.

Roberts, R., Roberts, C., & Duong, H. (2009). Sleepless in adolescence: Prospective data on sleep deprivation, health and functioning. *Journal of Adolescence, 32,* 1045–1057.

Roberts, S. (2006, October 15). It's official: To be married means to be outnumbered. *New York Times,* p. 22.

Robins, R. W., & Trzesniewski, K. H. (2005). Self-esteem development across the lifespan. *Current Directions in Psychological Science, 14,* 158–162.

Robinson, A. J., & Pascalis, O. (2005). Development of flexible visual recognition memory in human infants. *Developmental Science, 7,* 527–533.

Robinson, A., & Stark, D. R. (2005). *Advocates in action.* Washington, DC: National Association for the Education of Young Children.

Robinson, G. E. (2004, April 16). Beyond nature and nurture. *Science, 304,* 397–399.

Robinson, N. M., Zigler, E., & Gallagher, J. J. (2000). Two tails of the normal curve: Similarities and differences in the study of mental retardation and giftedness. *American Psychologist, 55,* 1413–1421.

Rochat, P. (Ed.). (1999). *Early social cognition: Understanding others in the first months of life.* Mahwah, NJ: Erlbaum.

Rochat, P. (2004). Emerging co-awareness. In G. Bremner & A. Slater (Eds.), *Theories of infant development.* Malden, MA: Blackwell Publishers.

Roche, T. (2000, November 13). The crisis of foster care. *Time,* pp. 74–82.

Rodgers, R., Paxton, S., & Chabrol, H. (2010). Depression as a moderator of sociocultural influences on eating disorder symptoms in adolescent females and males. *Journal of Youth and Adolescence, 39,* 393–402.

Roecke, C., & Cherry, K. (2002). Death at the end of the 20th century: Individual processes and developmental tasks in old age. *International Journal of Aging & Human Development, 54,* 315–333.

Roehrig, M., Masheb, R., White, M., & Grilo, C. (2009). Dieting frequency in obese patients with binge eating disorder: Behavioral and metabolic correlates. *Obesity, 17,* 689–697.

Roelofs, J., Meesters, C., Ter Huurne, M., Bamelis, L., & Muris, P. (2006, June). On the links between attachment style, parental rearing behaviors, and internalizing and externalizing problems in non-clinical children. *Journal of Child and Family Studies, 15,* 331–344.

Roffwarg, H. P., Muzio, J. N., & Dement, W. C. (1966). Ontogenic development of the human sleep–dream cycle. *Science, 152,* 604–619.

Rogan, J. (2007). How much curriculum change is appropriate? Defining a zone of feasible innovation. *Science Education, 91,* 439–460.

Rogers, C. R. (1971). A theory of personality. In S. Maddi (Ed.), *Perspectives on personality.* Boston: Little, Brown.

Rogers, S., & Willams, J. (2006). *Imitation and the social mind: Autism and typical development.* New York: Guilford Press.

Roggeveen, A. B., Prime, D. J., & Ward, L. M. (2007). Lateralized readiness potentials reveal motor slowing in the aging brain. *Journals of Gerontology: Series B: Psychological Science and Social Science, 62,* P78–P84.

Rogoff, B., & Chavajay, P. (1995). What's become of research on the cultural basis of cognitive development? *American Psychologist, 50,* 859–877.

Rolls, E. (2000). Memory systems in the brain. *Annual Review of Psychology, 51,* 599–630.

Romero, A., & Roberts, R. (2003). The impact of multiple dimensions of ethnic identity on discrimination and adolescents' self-esteem. *Journal of Applied Social Psychology, 33,* 2288–2305.

Ron, P. (2006). Care giving offspring to aging parents: How it affects their marital relations, parenthood, and mental health. *Illness, Crisis, & Loss, 14,* 1–21.

Propar, D., Mitchell, P., & Ackroyd, K. (2003). Do children with autism find it difficult to offer alternative interpretations to ambiguous figures? *British Journal of Developmental Psychology, 21,* 387–395.

Roper Starch Worldwide. (1997, August). Romantic resurgence. *American Demographics, 35.*

Rose, A. J., & Asher, S. R. (1999). Children's goals and strategies in response to conflicts within a friendship. *Developmental Psychology, 35,* 69–79.

Rose, R. J., Viken, R. J., Dick, D. M., Bates, J. E., Pulkkinen, L., & Kaprio, J. (2003). It *does* take a village:

Nonfamilial environments and children's behavior. *Psychological Science, 14,* 273–278.

Rose, S. (2008, January 21). Drugging unruly children is a method of social control. *Nature, 451,* 521.

Rose, S. A., & Feldman, J. F. (1997). Memory and speed: Their role in the relation of infant information processing to later IQ. *Child Development, 68,* 630–641.

Rose, S. A., Feldman, J. F., & Jankowski, J. J. (2004). Dimensions of cognition in infancy. *Intelligence, 32,* 245–262.

Rosenblatt, P. C. (1988). Grief: The social context of private feelings. *Journal of Social Issues, 44,* 67–78.

Rosenblatt, P. C., & Wallace, B. R. (2005). *African American grief.* New York: Brunner-Routledge.

Rosenthal, H., & Crisp, R. (2006, April). Reducing stereotype threat by blurring intergroup boundaries. *Personality and Social Psychology Bulletin, 32,* 501–511.

Ross, J., Stefanatos, G., & Roeltgen, D. (2007). Klinefelter syndrome. *Neurogenetic developmental disorders: Variation of manifestation in childhood.* Cambridge, MA: MIT Press.

Rossman, I. (1977). Anatomic and body composition changes with aging. In C. E. Finch & L. Hayflick (Eds.), *Handbook of the biology of aging.* New York: Van Nostrand Reinhold.

Rossouw, J. E., Prentice, R. L., Manson, J. E., Wu, L., Barad, D., Barnabei, V. M., Ko, M., LaCroix, A. Z., Margolis, K. L., & Stefanick, M. L. (2007). Postmenopausal hormone therapy and risk of cardiovascular disease by age and years since menopause. *JAMA: The Journal of the American Medical Association, 297,* 1465–1477.

Roth, D., Slone, M., & Dar, R. (2000). Which way cognitive development? An evaluation of the Piagetian and the domain-specific research programs. *Theory & Psychology, 10,* 353–373.

Rothbart, M., & Derryberry, D. (2002). Temperament in children. In C. von Hofsten & L. Backman (Eds.), *Psychology at the turn of the millennium, Vol. 2: Social, developmental, and clinical perspectives.* Florence, KY: Taylor & Frances/Routledge.

Rothbaum, F., Weisz, J., Pott, M., Miyake, K., & Morelli, G. (2000). Attachment and culture: Security in the United States and Japan. *American Psychologist, 55,* 1093–1104.

Rotigel, J. V. (2003). Understanding the young gifted child: Guidelines for parents, families, and educators. *Early Childhood Education Journal, 30,* 209–214.

Rovee-Collier, C. (1993). The capacity for long-term memory in infancy. *Current Directions in Psychological Science, 2,* 130–135.

Rovee-Collier, C. (1999). The development of infant memory. *Current Directions in Psychological Science, 8,* 80–85.

Rowley, S., Burchinal, M., Roberts, J., & Zeisel, S. (2008). Racial identity, social context, and race-related social cognition in African Americans during middle childhood. *Developmental Psychology, 44,* 1537–1546.

Rozalski, M., Stewart, A., & Miller, J. (2010). How to determine the least restrictive environment for students with disabilities. *Exceptionality, 18,* 151–163.

Rubin, D. C. (1986). *Autobiographical memory.* Cambridge, England: Cambridge University Press.

Rubin, D. C. (Ed.). (1996). *Remembering our past: Studies in autobiographical memory.* New York: Cambridge University Press.

Rubin, D. C. (2000). Autobiographical memory and aging. In C. D. Park, N. Schwarz, et al. (Eds.), *Cognitive aging: A primer.* Philadelphia: Psychology Press/Taylor & Francis.

Rubin, D., & Greenberg, D. (2003). The role of narrative in recollection: A view from cognitive psychology and neuropsychology. In G. Fireman & T. McVay (Eds.), *Narrative and consciousness: Literature, psychology, and the brain.* London: Oxford University Press.

Rubin, K. H., & Chung, O. B. (Eds.). (2006). *Parenting beliefs, behaviors, and parent-child relations: A cross-cultural perspective.* New York: Psychology Press.

Ruble, D. N., Taylor, L. J., Cyphers, L., Greulich, F. K., Lurye, L. E., & Shrout, P. E. (2007). The role of gender constancy in early gender development. *Child Development, 78*, 1121–1136.

Rudd, L. C., Cain, D. W., & Saxon, T. F. (2008). Does improving joint attention in low-quality child-care enhance language development? *Early Child Development and Care, 178*, 315–338.

Rudy, D., & Grusec, J. (2006, March). Authoritarian parenting in individualist and collectivist groups: Associations with maternal emotion and cognition and children's self-esteem. *Journal of Family Psychology, 20*, 68–78.

Ruff, H. A. (1989). The infant's use of visual and haptic information in the perception and recognition of objects. *Canadian Journal of Psychology, 43*, 302–319.

Ruffman, T., Slade, L., & Redman, J. (2006). Young infants' expectations about hidden objects. *Cognition* [serial Online], *97*, B35–b43.

Runyan, D. (2008). The challenges of assessing the incidence of inflicted traumatic brain injury: A world perspective. *American Journal of Preventive Medicine, 34*, S112–SS115.

Rupp, D., Vodanovich, S., & Credé, M. (2006, June). Age bias in the workplace: The impact of ageism and causal attributions. *Journal of Applied Social Psychology, 36*, 1337–1364.

Russell, S. T., & McGuire, J. K. (2006). Critical mental health issues for sexual minority adolescents. citation. In F. A. Villarruel & T. Luster (Eds.), *The crisis in youth mental health: Critical issues and effective programs, Vol. 2: Disorders in adolescence.* Westport, CT: Praeger Publishers / Greenwood Publishing Group.

Russell, S., & Consolacion, T. (2003). Adolescent romance and emotional health in the United States: Beyond binaries. *Journal of Clinical Child & Adolescent Psychology, 32*, 499–508.

Russon, A. E., & Waite, B. E. (1991). Patterns of dominance and imitation in an infant peer group. *Ethology & Sociobiology, 12*, 55–73.

Rust, J., Golombok, S., Hines, M., Johnston, K., & Golding, J.; ALSPAC Study Team. (2000). The role of brothers and sisters in the gender development of preschool children. *Journal of Experimental Child Psychology, 77*, 292–303.

Rutter, M. (2003). Commentary: Causal processes leading to antisocial behavior. *Developmental Psychology, 39*, 372–378.

Rutter, M. (2006). *Genes and behavior: Nature-nurture interplay explained.* New York: Blackwell Publishing.

Ryan, B. P. (2001). *Programmed therapy for stuttering in children and adults* (2nd ed.) Springfield, IL: Charles C. Thomas.

Ryan, D., & Martin, A. (2000). Lesbian, gay, bisexual, and transgender parents in the school systems. *The School Psychology Review, 29*, 207–216.

Sabbagh, M. (2009). Drug development for Alzheimer's disease: Where are we now and where are we headed? *American Journal of Geriatric Pharmacotherapy (AJGP), 7*, 167–185.

Sack, K. (1999, March 21). Older students bring new life to campuses. *New York Times*, p. WH8.

Sacks, M. H. (1993). Exercise for stress control. In D. Goleman & J. Gurin (Eds.), *Mind–body medicine.* Yonkers, NY: Consumer Reports Books.

Sadker, M., & Sadker, D. (1994). *Failing at fairness: How America's schools cheat girls.* New York: Scribner's.

Saiegh-Haddad, E. (2007). Linguistic constraints on children's ability to isolate phonemes in Arabic. *Applied Psycholinguistics, 28*, 607–625.

Sales, B. D., & Folkman, S. (Eds.). (2000). *Ethics in research with human participants.* Washington, DC: American Psychological Association.

Sallis, J., & Glanz, K. (2006, March). The role of built environments in physical activity, eating, and obesity in childhood. *The Future of Children, 16*, 89–108.

Salthouse, T. (2009). When does age-related cognitive decline begin? *Neurobiology of Aging, 30*, 507–514.

Salthouse, T. (2010). *Major issues in cognitive aging.* New York: Oxford University Press.

Salthouse, T. A. (1989). Age-related changes in basic cognitive processes. In APA Master Lectures, *The adult years: Continuity and change.* Washington, DC: American Psychological Association.

Salthouse, T. A. (1990). Cognitive competence and expertise in aging. In J. E. Birren, W. K. Schaie, et al. (Eds.), *Handbook of the psychology of aging* (3rd ed.). San Diego: Academic Press.

Salthouse, T. A. (1993). Speed mediation of adult age differences in cognition. *Developmental Psychology, 29*, 722–738.

Salthouse, T. A. (1994). Aging associations: Influence of speed on adult age differences in associative learning. *Journal of Experimental Psychology: Learning, Memory, and Cognition, 20*, 1486–1503.

Salthouse, T. A. (2006). Mental exercise and mental aging: Evaluating the validity of the "Use it or lose it" hypothesis. *Perspectives on Psychological Science, 1*, 68–87.

Salthouse, T. A., Atkinson, T. M., & Berish, D. E. (2003). Executive functioning as a potential mediator of age-related cognitive decline in normal adults. *Journal of Experimental Psychology: General, 132*, 566–594.

Salthouse, T., Pink, J., & Tucker-Drob, E. (2008). Contextual analysis of fluid intelligence. *Intelligence, 36*, 464–486.

Samet, J. H., De Marini, D. M., & Malling, H. V. (2004, May 14). Do airborne particles induce heritable mutations? *Science, 304*, 971.

Sammons, M. (2009). Writing a wrong: Factors influencing the overprescription of antidepressants to youth. *Professional Psychology: Research and Practice, 40*, 327–329.

Samuelsson, I., & Johansson, E. (2006, January). Play and learning—inseparable dimensions in preschool practice. *Early Child Development and Care, 176*, 47–65.

Sanders, S., Ott, C., Kelber, S., & Noonan, P. (2008). The experience of high levels of grief in caregivers of persons with Alzheimer's disease and related dementia. *Death Studies, 32*, 495–523.

Sandis, E. (2000). The aging and their families: A cross-national review. In A. L. Comunian & U. P. Gielen (Eds.), *International perspectives on human development.* Lengerich, Germany: Pabst Science Publishers.

Sandler, B. (1994, January 31). First denial, then a near-suicidal plea: "Mom, I need your help." *People Weekly*, pp. 56–58.

Sandoval, J., Frisby, C. L., Geisinger, K. F., Scheuneman, J. D., & Grenier, J. R. (Eds.). (1998). *Test interpretation and diversity: Achieving equity in assessment.* Washington, DC: APA Books.

Sandoval, J., Scott, A., & Padilla, I. (2009). Crisis counseling: An overview. *Psychology in the Schools, 46*, 246–256.

Sang, B., Miao, X., & Deng, C. (2002). The development of gifted and nongifted young children in metamemory knowledge. *Psychological Science (China), 25*, 406–409, 424.

Sangree, W. H. (1989). Age and power: Life-course trajectories and age structuring of power relations in East and West Africa. In D. I. Kertzer & K. W. Schaie (Eds.), *Age structuring in comparative perspective.* Hillsdale, NJ: Lawrence Erlbaum.

Sanoff, A. P., & Minerbrook, S. (1993, April 19). Race on campus. *U.S. News and World Report*, pp. 52–64.

Santesso, D., Schmidt, L., & Trainor, L. (2007). Frontal brain electrical activity (EEG) and heart rate in response to affective infant-directed (ID) speech in 9-month-old infants. *Brain and Cognition, 65*, 14–21. Available online at http://search.ebscohost.com.

Santos, M., Richards, C., & Bleckley, M. (2007). Comorbidity between depression and disordered eating in adolescents. *Eating Behaviors, 8*, 440–449.

Sapolsky, R. (2005, December). Sick of poverty. *Scientific American*, 93–99.

Saudino, K., & McManus, I. C. (1998). Handedness, footedness, eyedness and earedness in the Colorado Adoption Project. *British Journal of Developmental Psychology, 16*, 167–174.

Saunders, J., Davis, L., & Williams, T. (2004). Gender differences in self-perceptions and academic outcomes: A study of African American high school students. *Journal of Youth & Adolescence, 33*, 81–90.

Savage-Rumbaugh, E. S., Murphy, J., Sevcik, R. A., Brakke, K. E., Williams, S. L., & Rumbaugh, D. M. (1993). Language and comprehension in ape and child. *Monographs of the Society for Research in Child Development, 58* (3–4, Serial No. 233).

Savin-Williams, R. C., & Berndt, T. J. (1990). Friendship and peer relations. In S. Feldman & G. Elliott (Eds.), *At the threshold: The developing adolescent.* Cambridge, MA: Harvard University Press.

Savin-Williams, R. (2003). Lesbian, gay, and bisexual youths' relationships with their parents. In L. Garnets & D. Kimmel (Eds.), *Psychological perspectives on lesbian, gay, and bisexual experiences* (2nd ed) New York: Columbia University Press.

Savin-Williams, R. (2006). *The new gay teenager.* Cambridge, MA: Harvard University Press.

Sawatzky, J., & Naimark, B. (2002). Physical activity and cardiovascular health in aging women: A health-promotion perspective. *Journal of Aging & Physical Activity, 10*, 396–412.

Sax, L., & Kautz, K. J. (2003). Who first suggests the diagnosis of attention-deficit/hyperactivity disorder? *Annals of Family Medicine, 1*, 171–174.

Sax, L., et al. (2004). *The American freshman: National norms for fall 2004.* Los Angeles: Higher Education Research Institute, UCLA.

Scarr, S. (1993). Biological and cultural diversity: The legacy of Darwin for development. *Child Development, 64*, 1333–1353.

Scarr, S. (1998). American child care today. *American Psychologist, 53*, 95–108.

Scarr, S., & Carter-Saltzman, L. (1982). Genetics and intelligence. In R. J. Sternberg (Ed.), *Handbook of human intelligence* (pp. 792–896). Cambridge, England: Cambridge University Press.

Schachar, R., Ickowicz, A., Crosbie, J., Donnelly, G. A. E., Reiz, J. L., Miceli, P. C., Harsanyi, Z., & Drake, A. C. (2008). Cognitive and behavioral effects of multilayer-release methylphenidate in the treatment of children with attention-deficit/hyperactivity disorder. *Journal of Child and Adolescent Psychopharmacology, 18*, 11–24.

Schachner, D., Shaver, P., & Gillath, O. (2008). Attachment style and long-term singlehood. *Personal Relationships, 15*, 479–491.

Schachter, E. P. (2005). Erikson meets the postmodern: Can classic identity theory rise to the challenge? *Identity, 5*, 137–160.

Schaefer, R. T., & Lamm, R. P. (1992). *Sociology* (4th ed.). New York: McGraw-Hill.

Schaeffer, C., Petras, H., & Ialongo, N. (2003). Modeling growth in boys' aggressive behavior across elementary school: Links to later criminal involvement, conduct disorder, and antisocial personality disorder. *Developmental Psychology, 39*, 1020–1035.

Schaie, K. W. (1977–1978). Toward a stage of adult theory of adult cognitive development. *Journal of Aging and Human Development, 8*, 129–138.

Schaie, K. W. (1993). The Seattle longitudinal studies of adult intelligence. *Current Directions in Psychological Science, 2*, 171–175.

Schaie, K. W., & Willis, S. L. (1993). Age difference patterns of psychometric intelligence in adulthood: Generalizability within and across ability domains. *Psychology and Aging, 8*, 44–55.

Schaie, K. W., & Zanjani, F. A. K. (2006). Intellectual development across adulthood. In C. Hoare, *Handbook of adult development and learning*. New York: Oxford University Press.

Schaller, M., & Crandall, C. S. (Eds.). (2004). *The psychological foundations of culture*. Mahwah, NJ: Lawrence Erlbaum.

Scharfe, E. (2000). Development of emotional expression, understanding, and regulation in infants and young children. In R. Bar-On & J. Parker (Eds.), *The handbook of emotional intelligence: Theory, development, assessment, and application at home, school, and in the workplace*. San Francisco: Jossey-Bass/Pfeiffer.

Scharrer, E. (2004). Virtual violence: Gender and aggression in video game advertisements. *Mass Communication & Society, 7*, 393–412.

Scharrer, E., Kim, D., Lin, K., & Liu, Z. (2006). Working hard or hardly working? Gender, humor, and the performance of domestic chores in television commercials. *Mass Communication and Society, 9*, 215–238.

Schatz, M. (1994). *A toddler's life*. New York: Oxford University Press.

Schechter, D., & Willheim, E. (2009). Disturbances of attachment and parental psychopathology in early childhood. *Child and Adolescent Psychiatric Clinics of North America, 18*, 665–686.

Schecter, T., Finkelstein, Y., & Koren, G. (2005). Pregnant "DES daughters" and their offspring. *Canadian Family Physician, 51*, 493–494.

Schellenberg, E. G., & Trehub, S. E. (1996). Natural musical intervals: Evidence from infant listeners. *Psychological Science, 7*, 272–277.

Schemo, D. J. (2001, December 5). U.S. students prove middling on 32-nation test. *New York Times*, p. A21.

Schemo, D. J. (2003, November 13). Students' scores rise in math, not in reading. *New York Times*, p. A2.

Schemo, D. J. (2004, March 2). Schools, facing tight budgets, leave gifted programs behind. *New York Times*, pp. A1, A18.

Scherf, K. S., Sweeney, J. A., & Luna, B. (2006). Brain basis of developmental change in visuospatial working memory. *Journal of Cognitive Neuroscience, 18*, 1045–1058.

Schieman, S., McBrier, D. B., & van Gundy, K. (2003). Home-to-work conflict, work qualities, and emotional distress. *Sociological Forum, 18*, 137–164.

Schiffer, A., Pedersen, S., Broers, H., Widdershoven, J., & Denollet, J. (2008). Type-D personality but not depression predicts severity of anxiety in heart failure patients at 1-year follow-up. *Journal of Affective Disorders, 106*, 73–81.

Schiller, J. S., & Bernadel, L. (2004). Summary health statistics for the U.S. population: National Health Interview Survey, 2002. *Vital Health Statistics, 10*, 1–110.

Schmidt, M., Pekow, P., Freedson, P., Markenson, G., & Chasan-Taber, L. (2006). Physical activity patterns during pregnancy in a diverse population of women. *Journal of Women's Health, 15*, 909–918.

Schmidt, P. J., & Rubinow, D. R. (1991). Menopause- related affective disorders: A justification for further study. *American Journal of Psychiatry, 148*, 844–852.

Schmitt, E. (2001, March 13). For 7 million people in census, one race category isn't enough. *New York Times*, pp. A1, A14.

Schneider, E. L. (1999, February 5). Aging in the third millennium. *Science, 283*, 796–797.

Schneider, W. (2010). Metacognition and memory development in childhood and adolescence. *Metacognition, strategy use, and instruction* (pp. 54-81). New York: Guilford Press.

Schoppe-Sullivan, S., Diener, M., Mangelsdorf, S., Brown, G., McHale, J., & Frosch, C. (2006, July). Attachment and sensitivity in family context: The roles of parent and infant gender. *Infant and Child Development, 15*, 367–385.

Schoppe-Sullivan, S., Mangelsdorf, S., Brown, G., & Sokolowski, M. (2007, February). Goodness-of-fit in family context: Infant temperament, marital quality, and early coparenting behavior. *Infant Behavior & Development, 30*, 82–96.

Schreiber, G. B., Robins, M., Striegel-Moore, R., Obarzanek, M., Morrison, J. A., & Wright, D. J. (1996). Weight modification efforts reported by black and white preadolescent girls: National Heart, Lung, and Blood Institute Growth and Health Study. *Pediatrics, 98*, 63–70.

Schuetze, P., Eiden, R., & Coles, C. (2007). Prenatal cocaine and other substance exposure: Effects on infant autonomic regulation at 7 months of age. *Developmental Psychobiology, 49*, 276–289.

Schultz, A. H. (1969). *The life of primates*. New York: Universe.

Schulz, L. E., & Bonawitz, E. B. (2007). Serious fun: Preschoolers engage in more exploratory play when evidence is confounded. *Developmental Psychology, 43*, 1045–1050.

Schultz, N. (2009, August 22). Do expanding waistlines cause shrinking brains? *New Scientist*, p. 9.

Schultz, R., & Curnow, C. (1988). Peak performance and age among superathletes: Track and field, swimming, baseball, tennis, and golf. *Journal of Gerontology, 43*, P113–P120.

Schumer, F. (2009, September 29). After a death, the pain that doesn't go away. *New York Times*, p. D1.

Schutt, R. K. (2001). *Investigating the social world: The process and practice of research*. Thousand Oaks, CA: Sage Publications.

Schutz, H., Paxton, S., & Wertheim, E. (2002). Investigation of body comparison among adolescent girls. *Journal of Applied Social Psychology, 32*, 1906–1937.

Schwartz, I. M. (1999). Sexual activity prior to coital interaction: A comparison between males and females. *Archives of Sexual Behavior, 28*, 63–69.

Schwartz, P., Maynard, A., & Uzelac, S. (2008). Adolescent egocentrism: A contemporary view. *Adolescence, 43*, 441–448.

Schwenkhagen, A. (2007). Hormonal changes in menopause and implications on sexual health. *The Journal of Sexual Medicine, 4*, Supplement, 220–226.

Scrimsher, S., & Tudge, J. (2003). The teaching/learning relationship in the first years of school: Some revolutionary implications of Vygotsky's theory. *Early Education and Development, 14* [Special issue], 293–312.

Sebanc, A., Kearns, K., Hernandez, M., & Galvin, K. (2007). Predicting having a best friend in young children: Individual characteristics and friendship features. *Journal of Genetic Psychology, 168*, 81–95.

SEER. (2005). Surveillance, Epidemiology, and End Results (SEER) Program (www.seer.cancer.gov). SEER*Stat Database: Incidence—SEER 9 Regs Public-Use, Nov 2004 Sub (1973–2002), National Cancer Institute, DCCPS, Surveillance Research Program, Cancer Statistics Branch, released April 2005, based on the November 2004 submission.

Segal, J., & Segal, Z. (1992, September). No more couch potatoes. *Parents*, p. 235.

Segal, N. L. (1993). Twin, sibling, and adoption methods: Tests of evolutionary hypotheses. *American Psychologist, 48*, 943–956.

Segal, N. L. (2000). Virtual twins: New findings on within-family environmental influences on intelligence. *Journal of Educational Psychology, 92*, 188–194.

Segall, M. H., Dasen, P. R., Berry, J. W., & Poortinga, Y. H. (1990). *Human behavior in global perspective*. Boston: Allyn & Bacon.

Segalowitz, S. J., & Rapin I. (Eds.). (2003). *Child neuropsychology, Part I*. Amsterdam, The Netherlands: Elsevier Science.

Segrè, F. (2009, August 16). Anne Miller and Michael Davoli. *New York Times*, p. ST13.

Seibert, A., & Kerns, K. (2009). Attachment figures in middle childhood. *International Journal of Behavioral Development, 33*, 347–355.

Seidman, S. (2003). The aging male: Androgens, erectile dysfunction, and depression. *Journal of Clinical Psychiatry, 64*, 31–37.

Selfhout, M., Denissen, J., Branje, S., & Meeus, W. (2009). In the eye of the beholder: Perceived, actual, and peer-rated similarity in personality, communication, and friendship intensity during the acquaintanceship process. *Journal of Personality and Social Psychology, 96*, 1152–1165.

Selig, S., Tomlinson, T., & Hickey, T. (1991). Ethical dimensions of intergenerational reciprocity: Implications for practice. *Gerontologist, 31*, 624–630.

Seligman, M. E. P. (2007). Coaching and positive psychology. *Australian Psychologist, 42*, 266–267.

Semerci, Ç. (2006). The opinions of medicine faculty students regarding cheating in relation to Kohlberg's moral development concept. *Social Behavior and Personality, 34*, 41–50.

Sener, A., Terzioglu, R., & Karabulut, E. (2007, January). Life satisfaction and leisure activities during men's retirement: A Turkish sample. *Aging & Mental Health, 11*, 30–36.

Seppa, N. (1997, February). Wisdom: A quality that may defy age. *APA Monitor*, pp. 1, 9.

Serbin, L., & Karp, J. (2004). The intergenerational transfer of psychosocial risk: Mediators of vulnerability and resilience. *Annual Review of Psychology, 55*, 333–363.

Serbin, L., Poulin-Dubois, D., & Colburne, K. (2001). Gender stereotyping in infancy: Visual preferences for and knowledge of gender-stereotyped toys in the second year. *International Journal of Behavioral Development, 25*, 7–15.

Serretti, A., Calati, R., Ferrari, B., & De Ronchi, D. (2007). Personality and genetics. *Current Psychiatry Reviews, 3*, 147–159.

Servin, A., Nordenström, A., Larsson, A., & Bohlin, G. (2003). Prenatal adrogens and gender-typed behavior: A study of girls with mild and severe forms of congenital adrenal hyperplasia. *Developmental Psychology, 39*, 440–450.

Sesser, S. (1993, September 13). Opium war redux. *The New Yorker*, 78–89.

Settersten, R. (2002). Social sources of meaning in later life. In R. Weiss & S. Bass (Eds.), *Challenges of the third age: Meaning and purpose in later life*. London: Oxford University Press.

Sexton, M., Byrd, M., & von Kluge, S. (2010). Measuring resilience in women experiencing infertility using the CD-RISC: Examining infertility-related stress, general distress, and coping styles. *Journal of Psychiatric Research, 44*, 236–241.

Seymour, J., Payne, S., Chapman, A., & Holloway, M. (2007). Hospice or home? Expectations of end-of-life care among white and Chinese older people in the UK. *Sociology of Health & Illness, 29*, 872–890.

Shafer, R. G. (1990, March 12). An anguished father recounts the battle he lost—trying to rescue a teenage son from drugs. *People Weekly*, pp. 81–83.

Shapiro, A. F., Gottman, J. M., & Carrère, S. (2000). The baby and the marriage: Identifying factors that buffer against decline in marital satisfaction after the first baby arrives. *Journal of Family Psychology, 14*, 124–130.

Shapiro, L. (1997, Spring/Summer). Beyond an apple a day. *Newsweek* [Special Issue], pp. 52–56.

Shapiro, J., & Solity, J. (2008). Delivering phonological and phonics training within whole-class teaching. *British Journal of Educational Psychology, 78*, 597–620.

Shaunessy, E., Suldo, S., Hardesty, R., & Shaffer, E. (2006, December). School functioning and psychological well-being of international baccalaureate and general education students: A preliminary examination. *Journal of Secondary Gifted Education, 17*, 76–89.

Shaver, P. R., Hazan, C., & Bradshaw, D. (1988). Love as attachment: The integration of three behavioral systems.

In R. J. Sternberg & M. L. Barnes (Eds.), *The psychology of love* (pp. 68–99). New Haven, CT: Yale University Press.

Shaw, B., Liang, J., & Krause, N. (2010). Age and race differences in the trajectories of self-esteem. *Psychology and Aging, 25*, 84–94.

Shaw, D. S., Winslow, E. B., & Flanagan, C. (1999). A prospective study of the effects of marital status and family relations on young children's adjustment among African American and European American families. *Child Development, 70*, 742–755.

Shaw, M. L. (2003). Creativity and whole language. In J. Houtz, *The educational psychology of creativity.* Cresskill, NJ: Hampton Press.

Shaw, P., Eckstrand, K., Sharp, W., Blumenthal, J., Lerch, J. P., Greenstein, D., Classen, L., Evans, A., Giedd, J., & Rapoport, J. L. (2007). Attention-deficit/hyperactivity disorder is characterized by a delay in cortical maturation. *Proceedings of the National Academy of Sciences, 104*, 19649–19654.

Shaywitz, B. A., Shaywitz, S. E., Blachman, B. A., Pugh, K. R., Fulbright, R. K., Skudlarski, P., Mencl, W. E., Constable, R. T., Holahan, J. M., Marchione, K. E., Fletcher, J. M., Lyon, G. R., & Gore, J. C. (2004). Development of left occipitotemporal systems for skilled reading in children after a phonologically-based intervention. *Biological Psychiatry, 55*, 926–933.

Shea, J. (2006, September). Cross-cultural comparison of women's midlife symptom-reporting: A China study. *Culture, Medicine and Psychiatry, 30*, 331–362.

Shea, K. M., Wilcox, A. J., & Little, R. E. (1998). Postterm delivery: A challenge for epidemiologic research. *Epidemiology, 9*, 199–204.

Sheldon, K. M., Joiner, T. E., Jr., & Pettit, J. W. (2003). Reconciling humanistic ideals and scientific clinical practice. *Clinical Psychology, 10*, 302–315.

Shellenbarger, S. (2003, January 9). Yes, that weird day-care center could scar your child, researchers say. *Wall Street Journal*, p. D1.

Sherman, E. (1991). *Reminiscence and the self in old age.* New York: Springer.

Sherman, S., Allen, E., Bean, L., & Freeman, S. (2007). Epidemiology of Down syndrome. *Mental Retardation and Developmental Disabilities Research Reviews, 13*, 221–227. Available online at http://search.ebscohost.com

Shernoff, D., & Schmidt, J. (2008). Further evidence of an engagement-achievement paradox among U.S. high school students. *Journal of Youth and Adolescence, 37*, 564–580.

Sherwin, B. B. (1991). The psychoendocrinology of aging and female sexuality. *Annual Review of Sex Research, 2*, 181–198.

Shi, L. (2003). Facilitating constructive parent–child play: Family therapy with young children. *Journal of Family Psychotherapy, 14*, 19–31.

Shi, X., & Lu, X. (2007). Bilingual and bicultural development of Chinese American adolescents and young adults: A comparative study. *Howard Journal of Communications, 18*, 313–333.

Shimizu, M., & Pelham, B. (2004). The unconscious cost of good fortune: Implicit and explicit self-esteem, positive life events, and health. *Health Psychology, 23*, 101–105.

Shin, H. B., & Bruno. R. (2003). *Language use and English speaking ability: 2000.* Washington, DC: U.S. Census Bureau.

Shiner, R., Masten, A., & Roberts, J. (2003). Childhood personality foreshadows adult personality and life outcomes two decades later. *Journal of Personality, 71*, 1145–1170.

Shor, R. (2006, May). Physical punishment as perceived by parents in Russia: Implications for professionals involved in the care of children. *Early Child Development and Care, 176*, 429–439.

Shurkin, J. N. (1992). *Terman's kids: The groundbreaking study of how the gifted grow up.* Boston: Little, Brown.

Shuster, L., Rhodes, D., Gostout, B., Grossardt, B., & Rocca, W. (2010). Premature menopause or early menopause: Long-term health consequences. *Maturitas, 65*, 161–166.

Shute, N. (1997, November 10). No more hard labor. *U.S. News & World Report*, pp. 92–95.

Sieber, J. E. (2000). Planning research: Basic ethical decision-making. In B. D. Sales & S. Folkman (Eds.), *Ethics in research with human participants.* Washington, DC: American Psychological Association.

Siegal, M. (1997). *Knowing children: Experiments in conversation and cognition* (2nd ed.). Hove, England: Psychology Press/Lawrence Erlbaum (UK), Taylor & Francis.

Siegel, S., Dittrich, R., & Vollmann, J. (2008). Ethical opinions and personal attitudes of young adults conceived by in vitro fertilisation. *Journal of Medical Ethics, 34*, 236–240.

Siegler, R. (2003). Thinking and intelligence. In M. Bornstein & L. Davidson (Eds.), *Well-being: Positive development across the life course* (pp. 311–320). Mahwah, NJ: Lawrence Erlbaum.

Siegler, R. (2007). Cognitive variability. *Developmental Science, 10*, 104–109.

Siegler, R., & Lin, X. (2010). Self-explanations promote children's learning. *Metacognition, strategy use, and instruction.* New York: Guilford Press.

Siegler, R. S. (1994). Cognitive variability: A key to understanding cognitive development. *Current Directions in Psychological Science, 3*, 1–5.

Siegler, R. S. (1995). How does change occur: A microgenetic study of number conservation. *Cognitive Psychology, 28*, 225–273.

Siegler, R. S. (1998). *Children's thinking* (3rd ed.). Upper Saddle River, NJ: Prentice Hall.

Siegler, R. S., & Ellis, S. (1996). Piaget on childhood. *Psychological Science, 7*, 211–215.

Siegler, R. S., & Richards, D. (1982). The development of intelligence. In R. Sternberg (Ed.), *Handbook of human intelligence.* London: Cambridge University Press.

Sierra, F. (2006, June). Is (your cellular response to) stress killing you? *Journals of Gerontology: Series A: Biological Sciences and Medical Sciences, 61*, 557–561.

Sigman, M., Cohen, S. E., & Beckwith, L. (1997). Why does infant attention predict adolescent intelligence? *Infant Behavior & Development, 20*, 133–140.

Signorella, M., & Frieze, I. (2008). Interrelations of gender schemas in children and adolescents: Attitudes, preferences, and self-perceptions. *Social Behavior and Personality, 36*, 941–954.

Silverstein, L. B., & Auerbach, C. F. (1999). Deconstructing the essential father. *American Psychologist, 54*, 397–407.

Silverthorn, P., & Frick, P. J. (1999). Developmental pathways to antisocial behavior: The delayed-onset pathway in girls. *Developmental & Psychopathology, 11*, 101–126.

Simmons, S. W., Cyna, A. M., Dennis, A. T., & Hughes, D. (2007). Combined spinal-epidural versus epidural analgesia in labour. *Cochrane Database and Systematic Review, 18*, CD003401.

Simons, L., & Conger, R. (2007, February). Linking mother–father differences in parenting to a typology of family parenting styles and adolescent outcomes. *Journal of Family Issues, 28*, 212–241.

Simons, S. H., van Dijk, M., Anand, K. S., Roofthooft, D., van Lingen, R. A., & Tibboel, D. (2003). Do we still hurt newborn babies? A prospective study of procedural pain and analgesia in neonates. *Archives of Pediatrics and Adolescence, 157*, 1058–1064.

Simonton, D. K. (2009). Varieties of (scientific) creativity: A hierarchical model of domain-specific disposition, development, and achievement. *Perspectives on Psychological Science, 4*, 441–452.

Simpkins, S., Parke, R., Flyr, M., & Wild, M. (2006, November). Similarities in children's and early adolescents' perceptions of friendship qualities across development, gender, and friendship qualities. *Journal of Early Adolescence, 26*, 491–508.

Simpson, J. A. (1990). Influence of attachment styles on romantic relationships. *Journal of Personality & Social Psychology, 59*, 971–980.

Simpson, J., Collins, W., Tran, S., & Haydon, K. (2007, February). Attachment and the experience and expression of emotions in romantic relationships: A developmental perspective. *Journal of Personality and Social Psychology, 92*, 355–367.

Simson, S. P., Wilson, L. B., & Harlow-Rosentraub, K. (2006). Civic engagement and lifelong learning institutes: Current status and future directions. In L. Wilson & S. P. Simson (Eds.), *Civic engagement and the baby boomer generation: Research, policy, and practice perspectives.* New York: Haworth Press.

Sinclair, D. A., & Guarente, L. (2006). Unlocking the secrets of longevity genes. *Scientific American, 294*, 48–51, 54–57.

Singer, D. G., & Singer, J. L. (Eds.). (2000). *Handbook of children and the media.* Thousand Oaks, CA: Sage Publications.

Singer, L. T., Arendt, R., Minnes, S., Farkas, K., & Salvator, A. (2000). Neurobehavioral outcomes of cocaine-exposed infants. *Neurotoxicology & Teratology, 22*, 653–666.

Singer, M. S., Stacey, B. G., & Lange, C. (1993). The relative utility of expectancy-value theory and social cognitive theory in predicting psychology student course goals and career aspirations. *Journal of Social Behavior and Personality, 8*, 703–714.

Singh, S., & Darroch, J. E. (2000). Adolescent pregnancy and childbearing: Levels and trends in developed countries. *The Canadian Journal of Human Sexuality, 9*, 67–72.

Siniatchkin, M., Jonas, A., Baki, H., van Baalen, A., Gerber, W., & Stephani, U. (2010). Developmental changes of the contingent negative variation in migraine and healthy children. *The Journal of Headache and Pain, 11*, 105–113.

Sinnott, J. D. (1997). Developmental models of midlife and aging in women: Metaphors for transcendence and for individuality in community. In J. Coyle (Ed.), *Handbook on women and aging* (pp. 149–163). Westport, CT: Greenwood.

Sinnott, J. D. (1998). *The development of logic in adulthood: Postformal thought and its applications.* New York: Plenum.

Siu, A., & Shek, D. (2010). Social problem solving as a predictor of well-being in adolescents and young adults. *Social Indicators Research, 95*, 393–406.

Skinner, B. F. (1957). *Verbal behavior.* New York: Appleton-Century-Crofts.

Skinner, B. F. (1975). The steep and thorny road to a science of behavior. *American Psychologist, 30*, 42–49.

Skinner, J. D., Ziegler, P., Pac, S., & Devaney, B. (2004). Meal and snack patterns of infants and toddlers. *Journal of the American Dietary Association, 104*, S65–S70.

Skowronski, J., Walker, W., & Betz, A. (2003). Ordering our world: An examination of time in autobiographical memory. *Memory, 11*, 247–260.

Slater, A., & Johnson, S. P. (1998). Visual sensory and perceptual abilities of the newborn: Beyond the blooming, buzzing confusion. In F. Simion, G. Butterworth, et al. (Eds.), *The development of sensory, motor and cognitive capacities in early infancy: From perception to cognition.* Hove, England: Psychology Press / Lawrence Erlbaum (UK) Taylor & Francis.

Slater, A., Mattock, A., & Brown, E. (1990). Size constancy at birth: Newborn infants' responses to retinal and real size. *Journal of Experimental Child Psychology, 49*, 314–322.

Slater, M., Henry, K., & Swaim, R. (2003). Violent media content and aggressiveness in adolescents: A downward spiral model. *Communication Research, 30*, 713–736.

Sleeboom-Faulkner, M. (2010). Reproductive technologies and the quality of offspring in Asia: Reproductive pioneering and moral pragmatism? *Culture, Health & Sexuality, 12*, 139–152.

Sliwinski, M., Buschke, H., Kuslansky, G., & Senior, G. (1994). Proportional slowing and addition speed in old and young adults. *Psychology and Aging, 9*, 72–80.

Sloan, S., Gildea, A., Stewart, M., Sneddon, H., & Iwaniec, D. (2008). Early weaning is related to weight and rate of weight gain in infancy. *Child: Care, Health and Development, 34*, 59–64.

Sloan, S., Stewart, M., & Dunne, L. (2010). The effect of breastfeeding and stimulation in the home on cognitive development in one-year-old infants. *Child Care in Practice, 16*, 101–110.

Slonje, R., & Smith, P. K. (2008). Cyberbullying: Another main type of bullying? *Scandinavian Journal of Psychology, 49*, 147–154.

Smedley, A., & Smedley, B. D. (2005). Race as biology is fiction, racism as a social problem is real: Anthropological and historical perspectives on the social construction of race. *American Psychologist, 60*, 16–26.

Smedley, B. D., & Syme, S. L. (Eds.). (2000). *Promoting health: Intervention strategies from social and behavioral research.* Washington, DC: National Academy of Sciences.

Smetana, J. G. (1995). Parenting styles and conceptions of parental authority during adolescence. *Child Development, 66*, 299–316.

Smetana, J. G. (2005). Adolescent–parent conflict: Resistance and subversion as developmental process. In L. Nucci (Ed.), *Conflict, contradiction, and contrarian elements in moral development and education.* Mahwah, NJ: Lawrence Erlbaum.

Smetana, J. G. (2006). Social-cognitive domain theory: Consistencies and variations in children's moral and social judgments. In M. Killen, & J. G. Smetana (Eds.), *Handbook of moral development.* Mahwah, NJ: Lawrence Erlbaum.

Smetana, J., Daddis, C., & Chuang, S. (2003). "Clean your room!" A longitudinal investigation of adolescent–parent conflict and conflict resolution in middle-class African American families. *Journal of Adolescent Research, 18*, 631–650.

Smith, N. A., & Trainor, L. J. (2008). Infant-directed speech is modulated by infant feedback. *Infancy, 13*, 410–420.

Smith, P. K., & Drew, L. M. (2002). Grandparenthood. In M. Bornstein (Ed.), *Handbook of parenting.* Mahwah, NJ: Lawrence Erlbaum.

Smith, P. K., Mahdavi, J., Carvalho, M., Fisher, S., Russell, Sh., & Tippett, N. (2008). Cyberbullying: Its nature and impact in secondary school pupils. *Journal of Child Psychology and Psychiatry, 49*, 376–385.

Smith, R. J., Bale, J. F., Jr., & White, K. R. (2005, March 2). Sensorineural hearing loss in children. *Lancet, 365*, 879–890.

Smith, S., Quandt, S., Arcury, T., Wetmore, L., Bell, R., & Vitolins, M. (2006, January). Aging and eating in the rural, southern United States: Beliefs about salt and its effect on health. *Social Science & Medicine, 62*, 189–198.

Smutny, J. F., Walker, S. Y., & Macksroth, E. A. (2007). *Acceleration for gifted learners, k-5.* Thousand Oaks, CA: Corwin Press.

Snarey, J. R. (1995). In a communitarian voice: The sociological expansion of Kohlbergian theory, research, and practice. In W. M. Kurtines & J. L. Gerwirtz (Eds.), *Moral development: An introduction.* Boston: Allyn & Bacon.

Snowdon, D. A., Kemper, S. J., Mortimer, J. A., Greiner, L. H., Wekstein, D. R., & Markesbery, W. R. (1996, February 21). Linguistic ability in early life and cognitive function and Alzheimer's disease in late life: Findings from the nun study. *JAMA: The Journal of the American Medical Association, 275*, 528–532.

Soares, C., & Frey, B. (2010). Challenges and opportunities to manage depression during the menopausal transition and beyond. *Psychiatric Clinics of North America, 33*, 295–308.

Soderstrom, M. (2007). Beyond babytalk: Re-evaluating the nature and content of speech input to preverbal infants. *Developmental Review, 27*, 501–532.

Soderstrom, M., Blossom, M., Foygel, R., & Morgan, J. (2008). Acoustical cues and grammatical units in speech

to two preverbal infants. *Journal of Child Language, 35*, 869–902.

Solomon, W., Richards, M., Huppert, F. A., Brayne, C., & Morgan, K. (1998). Divorce, current marital status and well-being in an elderly population. *International Journal of Law, Policy and the Family, 12*, 323–344.

Somerset, W., Newport, D., Ragan, K., & Stowe, Z. (2006). Depressive disorders in women: From menarche to beyond the menopause. In L. M. Keyes & S. H. Goodman (Eds.), *Women and depression: A handbook for the social, behavioral, and biomedical sciences.* New York: Cambridge University Press.

Sonnen, J., Larson, E., Gray, S., Wilson, A., Kohama, S., Crane, P., et al. (2009). Free radical damage to cerebral cortex in Alzheimer's disease, microvascular brain injury, and smoking. *Annals of Neurology, 65*, 226–229.

Sontag, S. (1979). The double standard of aging. In J. H. Williams (Ed.), *Psychology of women: Selected readings.* New York: Norton.

Soska, K., Adolph, K., & Johnson, S. (2010). Systems in development: Motor skill acquisition facilitates three-dimensional object completion. *Developmental Psychology, 46*, 129–138.

Sotiriou, A., & Zafiropoulou, M. (2003). Changes of children's self-concept during transition from kindergarten to primary school. *Psychology: The Journal of the Hellenic Psychological Society, 10*, 96–118.

Sousa, D. L. (2005). *How the brain learns to read.* Thousand Oaks, CA: Corwin Press.

Sowell, E. R., Thompson, P. M., Holmes, C. J., Jerrigan, T. L., & Toga, A. W. (1999). In vivo evidence for post-adolescent brain maturation in frontal and striatal regions. *Nature Neuroscience, 10*, 859–861.

Sowell, E. R., Thompson, P. M., Tessner, K. D., & Toga, A. W. (2001). Mapping continued brain growth and gray matter density reduction in dorsal frontal cortex: Inverse relationships during postadolescent brain maturation. *Journal of Neuroscience, 21*, 8819–8829.

Sowell E. R., Peterson, B. S., Thompson, P. M., Welcome, S. E., Henkenius, A. L., & Toga, A.W. (2003). Mapping cortical change across the human life span. *Nature Neuroscience, 6*, 309–315.

Spear, L. (2010). *The behavioral neuroscience of adolescence.* New York: Norton.

Spear, P. D. (1993). Neural bases of visual deficits during aging. *Vision Research, 33*, 2589–2609.

Spearman, C. (1927). *The abilities of man.* London: Macmillan.

Spence, S. H. (1998). Sex and relationships. In W. K. Halford & H. J. Markman (Eds.), *Clinical handbook of marriage and couples interventions* (pp. 73–105). Chichester, England: Wiley.

Spencer, S. J., Fein, S., Zanna, M. P., & Olson, J. M. (Eds.). (2003). *Motivated social perception: The Ontario Symposium* (Vol. 9). Mahwah, NJ: Lawrence Erlbaum.

Spörer, N., Brunstein, J., & Kieschke, U. (2009). Improving students' reading comprehension skills: Effects of strategy instruction and reciprocal teaching. *Learning and Instruction, 19*, 272–286.

Spraggins, R. E. (2003). *Women and men in the United States: March 2002.* Washington, DC: U.S. Department of Commerce.

Sprecher, S., Sullivan, Q., & Hatfield, E. (1994). Mate selection preferences: Gender differences examined in a national sample. *Journal of Personality and Social Psychology, 66*, 1074–1080.

Sprenger, M. (2007). *Memory 101 for educators.* Thousand Oaks, CA: Corwin Press.

Squatriglia, C. (2007, February 16). Ted Soulis—charitable painter, businessman. *San Francisco Chronicle*, p. B7.

Squire, L. R., & Knowlton, B. J. (1995). Memory, hippocampus, and brain systems. In M. S. Gazzaniga, *Cognitive neurosciences.* Cambridge, MA: MIT Press.

Sroufe, L. A. (1994). Pathways to adaptation and maladaptation: Psychopathology as developmental deviation. In D. Cicchetti (Ed.), *Developmental psychopathology: Past, present, and future.* Hillsdale, NJ: Lawrence Erlbaum.

Starr, L. (2010). Preparing those caring for older adults to report elder abuse. *The Journal of Continuing Education in Nursing, 41*, 231–235.

Staudinger, U. (2008). A psychology of wisdom: History and recent developments. *Research in Human Development, 5*, 107–120.

Staudinger, U. M., & Baltes, P. B. (1996). Interactive minds: A facilitative setting for wisdom-related performance? *Journal of Personality and Social Psychology, 71*, 746–762.

Staunton, H. (2005). Mammalian sleep. *Naturwissenschaften, 35*, 15.

Stearns, E., & Glennie, E. (2006, September). When and why dropouts leave high school. *Youth & Society, 38*, 29–57.

Stedman, L. C. (1997). International achievement differences: An assessment of a new perspective. *Educational Researcher, 26*, 4–15.

Steele, C. M. (1997). A threat in the air: How stereotypes shape intellectual identity and performance. *American Psychologist, 52*, 613–629.

Stein, D., Latzer, Y., & Merick, J. (2009). Eating disorders: From etiology to treatment. *International Journal of Child and Adolescent Health, 2*, 139–151.

Stein, J. H., & Reiser, L. W. (1994). A study of white middle-class adolescent boys' responses to "semenarche" (the first ejaculation). *Journal of Youth and Adolescence, 23*, 373–384.

Stein, Z., Susser, M., Saenger, G., & Marolla, F. (1975). *Famine and human development: The Dutch hunger winter of 1944–1945.* New York: Oxford University Press.

Steinberg, J. (1997, January 2). Turning words into meaning. *The New York Times*, pp. B1–B2.

Steinberg, L. (1993). *Adolescence.* New York: McGraw-Hill.

Steinberg, L. D., & Scott, S. S. (2003). Less guilty by reason of adolescence: Developmental immaturity, diminished responsibility, and the juvenile death penalty. *American Psychologist, 58*, 1009–1018.

Steinberg, L., & Monahan, K. C. (2007). Age differences in resistance to peer influence. *Developmental Psychology, 43*, 1531–1543.

Steinberg, L., Dornbusch, S., & Brown, B. B. (1992). Ethnic differences in adolescent achievement: An ecological perspective. *American Psychologist, 47*, 723–729.

Steiner, J. E. (1979). Human facial expressions in response to taste and smell stimulation. *Advances in Child Development and Behavior, 13*, 257.

Steinert, S., Shay, J. W., & Wright, W. E. (2000). Transient expression of human telomerase extends the life span of normal human fibroblasts. *Biochemical & Biophysical Research Communications, 273*, 1095–1098.

Steinhausen, H. C., & Spohr, H. L. (1998). Long-term outcome of children with fetal alcohol syndrome: Psychopathology, behavior, and intelligence. *Alcoholism, Clinical & Experimental Research, 22*, 334–338.

Stenberg, G. (2009). Selectivity in infant social referencing. *Infancy, 14*, 457–473.

Steri, A. O., & Spelke, E. S. (1988). Haptic perception of objects in infancy. *Cognitive Psychology, 20*, 1–23.

Stern, G. (1994, November 30). Going back to college has special meaning for Mrs. McAlpin. *Wall Street Journal*, p. A1.

Sternberg, J. (2005). The triarchic theory of successful intelligence. In D. P. Flanagan & P. L. Harrison (Eds.), *Contemporary intellectual assessment: Theories, tests, and issues.* New York: Guilford Press.

Sternberg, R. (2003a). A broad view of intelligence: The theory of successful intelligence. *Consulting Psychology Journal: Practice & Research, 55*, 139–154.

Sternberg, R. (2003b). Our research program validating the triarchic theory of successful intelligence: Reply to Gottfredson. *Intelligence, 31,* 399–413.

Sternberg, R. (2006). A duplex theory of love. *The new psychology of love.* New Haven, CT: Yale University Press.

Sternberg, R. J. (1985). *Beyond IQ: A triarchic theory of human intelligence.* New York: Cambridge University Press.

Sternberg, R. J. (1986). Triangular theory of love. *Psychological Review, 93,* 119–135.

Sternberg, R. J. (1987). Liking versus loving: A comparative evaluation of theories. *Psychological Bulletin, 102,* 331–345.

Sternberg, R. J. (1990). *Metaphors of mind: Conceptions of the nature of intelligence.* Cambridge, England: Cambridge University Press.

Sternberg, R. J. (2008). Schools should nurture wisdom. In B. Z. Presseisen (Ed.), *Teaching for intelligence* (2nd ed.). Thousand Oaks, CA: Corwin Press.

Sternberg, R. J. (2009). The nature of creativity. In R. J. Sternberg, J. C. Kaufman, & E. L. Grigorenko (Eds.), *The essential Sternberg: Essays on intelligence, psychology, and education.* New York: Springer Publishing Co.

Sternberg, R. J., & Grigorenko, E. L. (Eds.). (2002). *The general factor of intelligence: How general is it?* Mahwah, NJ: Lawrence Erlbaum.

Sternberg, R. J., Conway, B. E., Ketron, J. L., & Bernstein, M. (1981). Peoples' conceptions of intelligence. *Journal of Personality and Social Psychology, 41,* 37–55.

Sternberg, R. J., Kaufman, J. C., & Pretez, J. E. (2002). *The creativity conundrum: A propulsion model of creative contributions.* Philadelphia: Psychology Press.

Stettler, N. (2007). Nature and strength of epidemiological evidence for origins of childhood and adulthood obesity in the first year of life. *International Journal of Obesity, 31,* 1035–1043.

Stevens, J., Cai, J., Evenson, K. R., & Thomas, R. (2002). Fitness and fatness as predictors of mortality from all causes and from cardiovascular disease in men and women in the lipid research clinics study. *American Journal of Epidemiology, 156,* 832–841.

Stevens, N., Martina, C., & Westerhof, G. (2006, August). Meeting the need to belong: Predicting effects of a friendship enrichment program for older women. *The Gerontologist, 46,* 495–502.

Stevens, W., Hasher, L., Chiew, K., & Grady, C. (2008). A neural mechanism underlying memory failure in older adults. *The Journal of Neuroscience, 28,* 12820–12824.

Stevenson, H. W., Chen, C., & Lee, S. Y. (1992). A comparison of the parent–child relationship in Japan and the United States. In L. L. Roopnarine & D. B. Carter (Eds.), *Parent-child socialization in diverse cultures.* Norwood, NJ: Ablex.

Stevenson, J. (2006). Dietary influences on cognitive development and behaviour in children. *Proceedings of the Nutrition Society, 65,* 361–365.

Stevenson, M., Henderson, T., & Baugh, E. (2007, February). Vital defenses: Social support appraisals of black grandmothers parenting grandchildren. *Journal of Family Issues, 28,* 182–211.

Stice, E. (2003). Puberty and body image. In C. Hayward (Ed.), *Gender differences at puberty.* New York: Cambridge University Press.

Stiles, J., Moses, P., & Paul, B. M. (2006). The longitudinal study of spatial cognitive development in children with pre- or perinatal focal brain injury: Evidence for cognitive compensation and for the emergence of alternative profiles of brain organization. In S. G. Lomber & J. J. Eggermont (Eds.), *Reprogramming the cerebral cortex: Plasticity following central and peripheral lesions.* New York: Oxford University Press.

Stockdale, M. S., & Crosby, F. J. (2004). *Psychology and management of workplace diversity.* Malden, MA: Blackwell Publishers.

Stolberg, S. G. (1998, April 3). Rise in smoking by young blacks erodes a success story in health. *New York Times,* p. A1.

Storfer, M. (1990). *Intelligence and giftedness: The contributions of heredity and early environment.* San Francisco: Jossey-Bass.

Story, M., Nanney, M., & Schwartz, M. (2009). Schools and obesity prevention: Creating school environments and policies to promote healthy eating and physical activity. *Milbank Quarterly, 87,* 71–100.

Straus, M. A., & Gelles, R. J. (Eds.). (1990). *Physical violence in American families.* New Brunswick, NJ: Transaction.

Straus, M. A., Gelles, R. J., & Steinmetz, S. K. (2003). The marriage license as a hitting license. In M. Silberman (Eds.), *Violence and society: A reader.* Upper Saddle River, NJ: Prentice Hall.

Straus, M. A., & McCord, J. (1998). Do physically punished children become violent adults? In S. Nolen-Hoeksema (Ed.), *Clashing views on abnormal psychology: A Taking Sides custom reader* (pp. 130–155). Guilford, CT: Dushkin/McGraw-Hill.

Straus, M. A., Sugarman, D. B., & Giles-Sims, J. (1997). Spanking by parents and subsequent antisocial behavior of children. *Archives of Pediatrics and Adolescent Medicine, 151,* 761–767.

Straus, M. A., Gelles, R. J., & Steinmetz, S. K. (2003). The marriage license as a hitting license. In M. Silberman (Eds.), *Violence and society: A reader.* Upper Saddle River, NJ: Prentice Hall.

Streissguth, A. (2007). Offspring effects of prenatal alcohol exposure from birth to 25 years: The Seattle Prospective Longitudinal Study. *Journal of Clinical Psychology in Medical Settings, 14,* 81–101.

Strelau, J. (1998). *Temperament: A psychological perspective.* New York: Plenum Publishers.

Strength, J. (1999). Grieving the loss of a child. *Journal of Psychology & Christianity, 18,* 338–353.

Striano, T., & Vaish, A. (2006, November). Seven- to 9-month-old infants use facial expressions to interpret others' actions. *British Journal of Developmental Psychology, 24,* 753–760.

Strobel, A., Dreisbach, G., Müller, J., Goschke, T., Brocke, B., & Lesch, K. (2007, December). Genetic variation of serotonin function and cognitive control. *Journal of Cognitive Neuroscience, 19,* 1923–1931.

Stroebe, M. S., Stroebe, W., & Hansson, R. O. (Eds.). (1993). *Handbook of bereavement: Theory, research, and intervention.* Cambridge, England: Cambridge University Press.

Stromswold, K. (2006). Why aren't identical twins linguistically identical? Genetic, prenatal and postnatal factors. *Cognition, 101,* 333–384.

Strube, M. (Ed.). (1990). Type A behavior. *Journal of Social Behavior and Personality, 5* [Special issue].

Stutzer, A., & Frey, B. (2006, April). Does marriage make people happy, or do happy people get married? *The Journal of Socio-Economics, 35,* 326–347.

Suarez-Orozco, C., Suarez-Orozco, M., & Todorova, I. (2008). *Learning a new land: Immigrant students in American society.* Cambridge, MA: Belknap Press/Harvard University Press.

Subotnik, R. (2006). Longitudinal studies: Answering our most important questions of prediction and effectiveness. *Journal for the Education of the Gifted, 29,* 379–383.

Suetta, C., & Kjaer, M. (2010). What are the mechanisms behind disuse and age-related skeletal muscle atrophy?. *Scandinavian Journal of Medicine & Science in Sports, 20,* 167–168.

Suinn, R. M. (2001). The terrible twos—Anger and anxiety: Hazardous to your health. *American Psychologist, 56,* 27–36.

Suitor, J. J., Minyard, S. A., & Carter, R. S. (2001). "Did you see what I saw?" Gender differences in perceptions of avenues to prestige among adolescents. *Sociological Inquiry, 71,* 437–454.

Sullivan, M., & Lewis, M. (2003). Contextual determinants of anger and other negative expressions in young infants. *Developmental Psychology, 39,* 693–705.

Sullivan, M. W., Rovee-Collier, C. K., & Tynes, D. M. (1979). A conditioning analysis of infant long-term memory. *Child Development, 50,* 152–162.

Suls, J., & Wallston, K. (2003). *Social psychological foundations of health and illness.* Malden, MA: Blackwell Publishers.

Sum, A., Fogg, N., Harrington, P., Khatiwada, I., Palma, S., Pond, N., & Tobar, P. (2003). *The growing gender gaps in college enrollment and degree attainment in the U.S. and their potential economic and social consequences.* Boston: Center for Labor Market Studies, Northeastern University.

Super, C. M. (1976). Environmental effects on motor development: A case of African infant precocity. *Developmental Medicine and Child Neurology, 18,* 561–576.

Super, C. M., & Harkness, S. (1982). The infant's niche in rural Kenya and metropolitan America. In L. Adler (Ed.), *Issues in cross-cultural research.* New York: Academic Press.

Supple, A., Ghazarian, S., Peterson, G., & Bush, K. (2009). Assessing the cross-cultural validity of a parental autonomy granting measure: Comparing adolescents in the United States, China, Mexico, and India. *Journal of Cross-Cultural Psychology, 40,* 816–833.

Suro, R. (1999, November). Mixed doubles. *American Demographics, 57–62.*

Sutherland, R., Pipe, M., & Schick, K. (2003). Knowing in advance: The impact of prior event information on memory and event knowledge. *Journal of Experimental Child Psychology, 84,* 244–263.

Swaim, R., Barner, J., & Brown, C. (2008). The relationship of calcium intake and exercise to osteoporosis health beliefs in postmenopausal women. *Research in Social & Administrative Pharmacy, 4,* 153–163.

Swanson, H., Saez, L., & Gerber, M. (2004). Literacy and cognitive functioning in bilingual and nonbilingual children at or not at risk for reading disabilities. *Journal of Educational Psychology, 96,* 3–18.

Swanson, K., Chen, H., Graham, J., Wojnar, D., & Petras, A. (2009). Resolution of depression and grief during the first year after miscarriage: A randomized controlled clinical trial of couples-focused interventions. *Journal of Women's Health, 18,* 1245–1257.

Swanson, L. A., Leonard, L. B., & Gandour, J. (1992). Vowel duration in mothers' speech to young children. *Journal of Speech and Hearing Research, 35,* 617–625.

Swiatek, M. (2002). Social coping among gifted elementary school students. *Journal for the Education of the Gifted, 26,* 65–86.

Taga, K., Markey, C., & Friedman, H. (2006, June). A longitudinal investigation of associations between boys' pubertal timing and adult behavioral health and well-being. *Journal of Youth and Adolescence, 35,* 401–411.

Tajfel, H., & Turner, J. C. (2004). The social identity theory of intergroup behavior. In J. T. Jost & J. Sidanius (Eds.). *Political psychology: Key readings.* New York: Psychology Press.

Takala, M. (2006, November). The effects of reciprocal teaching on reading comprehension in mainstream and special (SLI) education. *Scandinavian Journal of Educational Research, 50,* 559–576.

Tallandini, M., & Scalembra, C. (2006). Kangaroo mother care and mother–premature infant dyadic interaction. *Infant Mental Health Journal, 27,* 251–275.

Tamis-LeMonda, C. S., & Cabrera, N. (1999). Perspectives on father involvement: Research and policy. *Social Policy Report, 13,* 1–31.

Tamis-LeMonda, C. S., & Cabrera, N. (2002). *Handbook of father involvement: Multidisciplinary perspectives.* Mahwah, NJ: Lawrence Erlbaum.

Tan, H., Wen, S. W., Mark, W., Fung, K. F., Demissie, K., & Rhoads, G. G. (2004). The association between fetal sex and preterm birth in twin pregnancies. *Obstetrics and Gynecology, 103,* 327–332.

Tanaka, K., Kon, N., Ohkawa, N., Yoshikawa, N., & Shimizu, T. (2009). Does breastfeeding in the neonatal period influence the cognitive function of very-low-birth-weight infants at 5 years of age? *Brain & Development, 31,* 288–293.

Tang, C., Wu, M., Liu, J., Lin, H., & Hsu, C. (2006). Delayed parenthood and the risk of cesarean delivery—Is paternal age an independent risk factor? *Birth: Issues in Perinatal Care, 33,* 18–26.

Tang, W. R., Aaronson, L. S., & Forbes, S. A. (2004). Quality of life in hospice patients with terminal illness. *Western Journal of Nursing Research, 26,* 113–128.

Tang, Z., & Orwin, R. (2009). Marijuana initiation among American youth and its risks as dynamic processes: Prospective findings from a national longitudinal study. *Substance Use & Misuse, 44,* 195–211.

Tanner, E., & Finn-Stevenson, M. (2002). Nutrition and brain development: Social policy implications. *American Journal of Orthopsychiatry, 72,* 182–193.

Tanner, J. (1972). Sequence, tempo, and individual variation in growth and development of boys and girls aged twelve to sixteen. In J. Kagan & R. Coles (Eds.), *Twelve to sixteen: Early adolescence.* New York: Norton.

Tanner, J. M. (1978). *Education and physical growth* (2nd ed.). New York: International Universities Press.

Tanner, J., Arnett, J., & Leis, J. (2009). Emerging adulthood: Learning and development during the first stage of adulthood. *Handbook of research on adult learning and development.* New York: Routledge/Taylor & Francis Group.

Tappan, M. (2006, March). Moral functioning as mediated action. *Journal of Moral Education, 35,* 1–18.

Tappan, M. B. (1997). Language, culture and moral development: A Vygotskian perspective. *Developmental Review, 17,* 199–212.

Tardif, T. (1996). Nouns are not always learned before verbs: Evidence from Mandarin speakers' early vocabularies. *Developmental Psychology, 32,* 492–504.

Task Force on College Gambling Policies. (2009). *A call to action addressing college gambling: Recommendations for science-based policies and programs.* Cambridge, MA: Division on Addictions at the Cambridge Health Alliance.

Task Force on Sudden Infant Death Syndrome. (2005). The changing concept of sudden infant death syndrome: Diagnostic coding shifts, controversies regarding the sleeping environment, and new variables to consider in reducing risk. *Pediatrics, 105,* 650–656.

Tatum, B. (2007). *Can we talk about race? And other conversations in an era of school resegregation.* Boston: Beacon Press.

Tauriac, J., & Scruggs, N. (2006, January). Elder abuse among African Americans. *Educational Gerontology, 32,* 37–48.

Taylor, D. M. (2002). *The quest for identity: From minority groups to Generation Xers.* Westport, CT: Praeger Publishers / Greenwood Publishing.

Taylor, R. J., Chatters, L. M., Tucker, M. B., & Lewis, E. (1991). Developments in research on black families. In A. Booth (Ed.), *Contemporary families.* Minneapolis, MN: National Council on Family Relations.

Taylor, R. L., & Rosenbach, W. E. (Eds.). (2005). *Military leadership: In pursuit of excellence* (5th ed.). Boulder, CO: Westview Press.

Taylor, S. E. (1991). *Health psychology* (2nd ed.). New York: McGraw-Hill.

Teerikangas, O. M., Aronen, E. T., Martin, R. P., & Huttunen, M. O. (1998). Effects of infant temperament and early intervention on the psychiatric symptoms of adolescents. *Journal of the American Academy of Child & Adolescent Psychiatry, 37,* 1070–1076.

Teixeira, L. R., Fscher, F. M., & Lowden, A. (2006). Sleep deprivation of working adolescents—A hidden work hazard. *Scandinavian Journal of Work, Environment & Health, 32,* 328–330.

Tellegen, A., Lykken, D. T., Bouchard, T. J., Jr., Wilcox, K. J., Segal, N. L., & Rich, S. (1988). Personality similarity in twins reared apart and together. *Journal of Personality and Social Psychology, 54,* 1031–1039.

Terman, D. L., Larner, M. B., Stevenson, C. S., & Behrman, R. E. (1996). Special education for students with disabilities: Analysis and recommendations. *The Future of Children, 6,* 4–24.

Terman, L. M., & Oden, M. H. (1959). *The gifted group at mid-life: Thirty-five years follow-up of the superior child.* Standord, CA: Standord University Press.

Terracciano, A., McCrae, R., & Costa, P. (2010). Intra-individual change in personality stability and age. *Journal of Research in Personality, 44,* 31–37.

Terry, D. (2000, August, 11). U.S. child poverty rate fell as economy grew, but is above 1979 level. *New York Times,* p. A10.

Terzidou, V. (2007). Preterm labour. Biochemical and endocrinological preparation for parturition. *Best Practices of Research in Clinical Obstetrics and Gynecology, 21,* 729–756.

Tessor, A., Felson, R. B., & Suls, J. M. (Eds.). (2000). *Psychological perspectives on self and identity.* Washington, DC: American Psychological Association.

Teutsch, C. (2003). Patient–doctor communication. *Medical Clinics of North America, 87,* 1115–1147.

Tharp, R. G. (1989). Psychocultural variables and constants: Effects on teaching and learning in schools. *American Psychologist, 44* [Special issue: Children and their development: Knowledge base, research agenda, and social policy application], 349–359.

The Endocrine Society. (2001, March 1). *The Endocrine Society and Lawson Wilkins Pediatric Endocrine Society call for further research to define precocious puberty.* Bethesda, MD: Endocrine Society.

Thelen, E., & Bates, E. (2003). Connectionism and dynamic systems: Are they really different? *Developmental Science, 6,* 378–391.

Thobaben, M. (2010). A drug abuse treatment guide available for home health nurses: The National Institute on Drug Abuse's Principles of Drug Addiction Treatment: A Research-Based Guide. *Home Health Care Management & Practice, 22,* 376–377.

Thoman, E. B., & Whitney, M. P. (1990). Sleep states of infants monitored in the home: Individual differences, developmental trends, and origins of diurnal cyclicity. *Infant Behavior and Development, 12,* 59–75.

Thomas, A., & Chess, S. (1980). *The dynamics of psychological development.* New York: Brunner-Mazel.

Thomas, A., Chess, S., & Birch, H. G. (1968). *Temperament and behavior disorders in children.* New York: New York University Press.

Thomas, C. (2010). Oppositional defiant disorder and conduct disorder. *Dulcan's textbook of child and adolescent psychiatry* (pp. 223–239). Arlington, VA: American Psychiatric Publishing, Inc.

Thomas, P. (1994, September 6). Washington's infant mortality rate, more than twice the U.S. average, reflects urban woes. *Wall Street Journal,* p. A14.

Thomas, P., & Fenech, M. (2007). A review of genome mutation and Alzheimer's disease. *Mutagenesis, 22,* 15–33.

Thomas, P., Lalloué, F., Preux, P., Hazif-Thomas, C., Pariel, S., Inscale, R., et al. (2006, January). Dementia patients caregivers quality of life: The PIXEL study. *International Journal of Geriatric Psychiatry, 21,* 50–56.

Thomas, R. M. (2001). *Recent human development theories.* Thousand Oaks, CA: Sage Publications.

Thompson, C., & Prottas, D. (2006, January). Relationships among organizational family support, job autonomy, perceived control, and employee well-being. *Journal of Occupational Health Psychology, 11,* 100–118.

Thompson, R. A., & Nelson, C. A. (2001). Developmental science and the media. *American Psychologist, 56,* 5–15.

Thompson, R., Easterbrooks, M., & Padilla-Walker, L. (2003). Social and emotional development in infancy. In R. Lerner & M. Easterbrooks (Eds.), *Handbook of psychology: Developmental psychology, Vol. 6* (pp. 91–112). New York: Wiley.

Thompson, R., & Virmani, E. (2010). Self and personality. *Handbook of cultural developmental science.* New York: Psychology Press.

Thoms, K. M., Kuschal, C., & Emmert, S. (2007). Lessons learned from DNA repair defective syndromes. *Experimental Dermatology, 16,* 532–544.

Thornberry, T. P., & Krohn, M. D. (1997). Peers, drug use, and delinquency. In D. M. Stoff, J. Breiling, & J. D. Maser (Eds.), *Handbook of antisocial behavior* (pp. 218–233). New York: Wiley.

Thorne, B. (1986). Girls and boys together, but mostly apart. In W. W. Hartup & Z. Rubin (Eds.), *Relationships and development* (pp. 167–184). Hillsdale, NJ: Erlbaum.

Thornton, J. (2004). Life-span learning: A developmental perspective. *International Journal of Aging & Human Development, 57,* 55–76.

Thornton, R. (2010). Verb phrase ellipsis in children's answers to questions. *Language Learning and Development, 6,* 1–31.

Thorsheim, H. I., & Roberts, B. B. (1990). *Reminiscing together: Ways to help us keep mentally fit as we grow older.* Minneapolis: CompCare Publishers.

Thorvaldsson, V., Hofer, S., Berg, S., Skoog, I., Sacuiu, S., & Johansson, B. (2008). Onset of terminal decline in cognitive abilities in individuals without dementia. *Neurology, 71,* 882–887.

Thurlow, M. L., Lazarus, S. S., & Thompson, S. J. (2005). State policies on assessment participation and accommodations for students with disabilities. *Journal of Special Education, 38,* 232–240.

Tikotzky, L., & Sadeh, A. (2009). Maternal sleep-related cognitions and infant sleep: A longitudinal study from pregnancy through the 1st year. *Child Development, 80,* 860–874.

*Time.* (1980, September 8). People section.

Tincoff, R., & Jusczyk, P. W. (1999). Some beginnings of word comprehension in 6-month-olds. *Psychological Science, 10,* 172–175.

Tinsley, B., Lees, N., & Sumartojo, E. (2004). Child and adolescent HIV risk: Familial and cultural perspectives. *Journal of Family Psychology, 18,* 208–224.

Tissaw, M. (2007). Making sense of neonatal imitation. *Theory & Psychology, 17,* 217–242.

Tisserand, D., & Jolles, J. (2003). On the involvement of prefrontal networks in cognitive ageing. *Cortex, 39,* 1107–1128.

Tobin, J. J., Wu, D. Y. H., & Davidson, D. H. (1989). *Preschool in three cultures: Japan, China, and the United States.* New Haven, CT: Yale University Press.

Toga, A. W., & Thompson, P. M. (2003). Temporal dynamics of brain anatomy. *Annual Review of Biomedical Engineering, 5,* 119–145.

Toga, A. W., Thompson, P. M., & Sowell, E. R. (2006). Mapping brain maturation. *Trends in Neuroscience, 29,* 148–159.

Tolan, P. H., & Dodge, K. A. (2005). Children's mental health as a primary care and concern: A system for comprehensive support and service. *American Psychologist, 60,* 601–614.

Tolchinsky, L. (2003). *The cradle of culture and what children know about writing and numbers before being taught.* Mahwah, NJ: Lawrence Erlbaum.

Tomblin, J. B., Hammer, C. S., & Zhang, X. (1998). The association of prenatal tobacco use and SLI. *International Journal of Language and Communication Disorders, 33,* 357–368.

Tomlinson, M., Murray, L., & Cooper, P. (2010). Attachment theory, culture, and Africa: Past, present, and future. *Attachment: Expanding the cultural connections.* New York: Routledge / Taylor & Francis Group.

Tompson, M., Pierre, C., Boger, K., McKowen, J., Chan, P., & Freed, R. (2010). Maternal depression, maternal expressed emotion, and youth psychopathology. *Journal of Abnormal Child Psychology: An official publication of the International Society for Research in Child and Adolescent Psychopathology, 38,* 105–117.

Tongsong, T., Iamthongin, A., Wanapirak, C., Piyamongkol, W., Sirichotiyakul, S., Boonyanurak, P., Tatiyapornkul, T., & Neelasri, C. (2005). Accuracy of fetal heart-rate variability interpretation by obstetricians using the criteria of the National Institute of Child Health and Human Development compared with computer-aided interpretation. *Journal of Obstetric and Gynaecological Research, 31,* 68–71.

Torges, C., Stewart, A., & Nolen-Hoeksema, S. (2008). Regret resolution, aging, and adapting to loss. *Psychology and Aging, 23,* 169–180.

Torvaldsen, S., Roberts, C. L, Simpson, J. M., Thompson, J. F., & Ellwood, D. A. (2006). Intrapartum epidural analgesia and breastfeeding: A prospective cohort study. *International Breastfeeding Journal, 24,* 1–24.

Toschke, A. M., Grote, V., Koletzko, B., & von Kries, R. (2004). Identifying children at high risk for overweight at school entry by weight gain during the first 2 years. *Archives of Pediatric Adolescence, 158,* 449–452.

Tracy, M., Zimmerman, F., Galea, S., McCauley, E., & Vander Stoep, A. (2008). What explains the relation between family poverty and childhood depressive symptoms? *Journal of Psychiatric Research, 42,* 1163–1175.

Trainor, L. J., Austin, C. M., & Desjardins, R. N. (2000). Is infant-directed speech prosody a result of the vocal expression of emotion? *Psychological Science, 11,* 188–195.

Traywick, L., & Schoenberg, N. (2008). Determinants of exercise among older female heart attack survivors. *Journal of Applied Gerontology, 27,* 52–77.

Treas, J., & Bengston, V. L. (1987). The family in later years. In M. B. Sussman & S. K. Steinmetz (Eds.), *Handbook of marriage and the family.* New York: Plenum.

Trehub, S. E. (2003). The developmental origins of musicality. *Nature Neuroscience, 6,* 669–673.

Tremblay, R. E. (2001). The development of physical aggression during childhood and the prediction of later dangerousness. In G. F. Pinard & L. Pagani (Eds.), *Clinical assessment of dangerousness: Empirical contributions.* New York: Cambridge University Press.

Triche, E. W., & Hossain, N. (2007). Environmental factors implicated in the causation of adverse pregnancy outcome. *Seminars in Perinatology, 31,* 240–242.

Trickett, P. K., Kurtz, D. A., & Pizzigati, K. (2004). Resilient outcomes in abused and neglected children: Bases for strengths-based intervention and prevention policies. In K. I. Maton & C. J. Schellenbach (Eds.), *Investing in children, youth, families and communities: Strength-based research and policy.* Washington, DC: American Psychological Association.

Tronick, E. Z. (1995). Touch in mother–infant interactions. In T. M. Field (Ed.), *Touch in early development.* Hillsdale, NJ: Lawrence Erlbaum.

Tropp, L. (2003). The psychological impact of prejudice: Implications for intergroup contact. *Group Processes & Intergroup Relations, 6,* 131–149.

Tropp, L., & Wright, S. (2003). Evaluations and perceptions of self, ingroup, and outgroup: Comparisons between Mexican-American and European-American children. *Self & Identity, 2,* 203–221.

Trotter, A. (2004, December 1). Web searches often overwhelm young researchers. *Education Week, 24,* 8.

Trzesniewski, K. H., Donnellan, M. B., & Robins, R. W. (2003). Stability of self-esteem across the life span. *Journal of Personality and Social Psychology, 84,* 205–220.

Tse, T., & Howie, L. (2005, September). Adult day groups: Addressing older people's needs for activity and companionship. *Australasian Journal on Ageing, 24,* 134–140.

Tudge, J., & Scrimsher, S. (2003). Lev S. Vygotsky on education: A cultural-historical, interpersonal, and individual approach to development. In B. Zimmerman (Ed.), *Educational psychology: A century of contributions.* Mahwah, NJ: Lawrence Erlbaum.

Turiel, E. (2006). *The development of morality. Handbook of child psychology: Vol. 3, Social, emotional, and personality development* (6th ed.). Hoboken, NJ: Wiley.

Turiel, E. (2008). Social decisions, social interactions, and the coordination of diverse judgments. *Social life and social knowledge: Toward a process account of development.* New York: Taylor & Francis Group / Lawrence Erlbaum Associates.

Turiel, E. (2010). Domain specificity in social interactions, social thought, and social development. *Child Development, 81,* 720–726.

Turkheimer, E., Haley, A., Waldreon, M., D'Onofrio, B., & Gottesman, I. I. (2003). Socioeconomic status modifies heritability of IQ in young children. *Psychological Science, 14,* 623–628.

Turner, J. S., & Helms, D. B. (1994). *Contemporary adulthood* (5th ed.). Forth Worth, TX: Harcourt Brace.

Turner-Bowker, D. M. (1996). Gender stereotyped descriptors in children's picture books: Does "Curious Jane" exist in the literature? *Sex Roles, 35,* 461–488.

Turney, K., & Kao, G. (2009). Barriers to school involvement: Are immigrant parents disadvantaged? *Journal of Educational Research, 102,* 257–271.

Turton, P., Evans, C., & Hughes, P. (2009). Long-term psychosocial sequelae of stillbirth: Phase II of a nested case-control cohort study. *Archives of Women's Mental Health, 12,* 35–41.

Twardosz, S., & Lutzker, J. (2009). Child maltreatment and the developing brain: A review of neuroscience perspectives. *Aggression and Violent Behavior, 15,* 59–68.

Twenge, J. M., & Campbell, W. K. (2001). Age and birth cohort differences in self-esteem: A cross-temporal meta-analysis. *Personality and Social Psychology Review, 5,* 321–344.

Twenge, J. M., & Crocker, J. (2002). Race and self-esteem: Meta-analyses comparing whites, blacks, Hispanics, Asians, and American Indians and comment on Gray-Little and Hafdahl (2000). *Psychological Bulletin, 128,* 371–408.

Twomey, J. (2006). Issues in genetic testing of children. *MCN: The American Journal of Maternal/Child Nursing, 31,* 156–163.

Tyre, P., & Scelfo, J. (2003, September 22). Helping kids get fit. *Newsweek,* pp. 60–62.

U.S. Bureau of the Census. (1997). *Life expectancy statistics.* Washington, DC: Author.

U.S. Bureau of the Census. (1998). *Statistical abstract of the United States* (118th ed.). Washington, DC: U.S. Government Printing Office.

U.S. Bureau of the Census. (2000). The condition of education. *Current Population Surveys, October 2000.* Washington, DC: Author.

U.S. Bureau of the Census. (2001). *Living arrangements of children.* Washington, DC: Author.

U.S. Bureau of the Census. (2002). *Statistical abstract of the United States* (122nd ed.). Washington, DC: U.S. Government Printing Office.

U.S. Bureau of the Census. (2003). *Population reports.* Washington, DC: U.S. Government Printing Office.

U.S. Bureau of the Census. (2005). *Current population survey.* Washington, DC: Author. U.S. Department of Agriculture, Center for Nutrition Policy and Promotion.

U.S. Bureau of Labor Statistics. (2003). *Wages earned by women.* Washington, DC: Author.

U.S. Department of Agriculture. (2006). *Dietary Guidelines for Americans 2005.* Washington, DC: Author.

U.S. Department of Education. (2005). 2003–2004 National Postsecondary Student Aid Study (NPSAS:04), unpublished tabulations. Washington, DC: Author.

U.S. Department of Education, National Center for Education Statistics. (1997). *Children in various types of day care.* Washington, DC: Author.

U.S. Department of Health and Human Services. (1990). *Health United States 1989* (DHHS Publication No. PHS 90–1232). Washington, DC: U.S. Government Printing Office.

U.S. Department of Health and Human Services. (2009). Centers of Disease Control and Prevention (CDC), National Center for Health Statistics (NCHS), Office of Analysis and Epidemiology (OAE), Division of Vital Statistics (DVS), Linked Birth / Infant Death Records 2003–2005 on CDC WONDER On-line Database. Available online at http://wonder.cdc.gov/lbd-current.html

U.S. Department of Health and Human Services, Administration on Children Youth and Families. (2007). *Child Maltreatment 2005.* Washington, DC: U.S. Government Printing Office.

Uchikoshi, Y. (2006). Early reading in bilingual kindergartners: Can educational television help? *Scientific Studies of Reading, 10,* 89–120.

Uhlenberg, P., Cooney, T., & Boyd, R. (1990). Divorce for women after midlife. *Journal of Gerontology, 45*(1), S3–S11.

Umana-Taylor, A., Diveri, M., & Fine, M. (2002). Ethnic identity and self-esteem among Latino adolescents: Distinctions among Latino populations. *Journal of Adolescent Research, 17,* 303–327.

Umana-Taylor, A., & Fine, M. (2004). Examining ethnic identity among Mexican-origin adolescents living in the United States. *Hispanic Journal of Behavioral Sciences, 26,* 36–59.

UNAIDS. (2009). *09 AIDS epidemic update.* Geneva, Switzerland: Author.

Underwood, M. (2005). Introduction to the special section: Deception and observation. *Ethics & Behavior, 15,* 233–234.

Unger, R. K. (Ed.). (2001). *Handbook of the psychology of women and gender.* New York: Wiley.

Unger, R., & Crawford, M. (1992). *Women and gender: A feminist psychology* (2nd ed.). New York: McGraw-Hill.

United Nations. (1990). *Declaration of the world summit for children.* New York: Author.

United Nations. (1991). *Declaration of the world summit for children.* New York: Author.

United Nations. (2004). *Hunger and the world's children.* New York: Author.

United Nations Population Division. (2002). *World population ageing: 1950–2050.* New York: United Nations.

United Nations World Food Programme. (2004). Available online at http://www.wfp.org

University of Akron. (2006). *A longitudinal evaluation of the new curricula for the D.A.R.E. middle (7th grade) and high school (9th grade) programs: Take charge of your life.* Akron, OH: Author.

Updegraff, K. A., Helms, H. M., McHale, S. M., Crouter, A. C., Thayer, S. M., & Sales, L. H. (2004). Who's the boss? Patterns of perceived control in adolescents' friendship. *Journal of Youth & Adolescence, 33,* 403–420.

Updegraff, K. A., McHale, S. M., Whiteman, S. D., Thayer, S. M., & Crouter, A. C. (2006). The nature and correlates of Mexican-American adolescents' time with parents and peers. *Child Development, 77,* 1470–1486.

Urberg, K., Luo, Q., & Pilgrim, C. (2003). A two-stage model of peer influence in adolescent substance use: Individual and relationship-specific differences in susceptibility to influence. *Addictive Behaviors, 28,* 1243–1256.

Urquidi, V., Tarin, D., & Goodison, S. (2000). Role of telomerase in cell senescence and oncogenesis. *Annual Review of Medicine, 51,* 65–79.

Uylings, H. (2006). Development of the human cortex and the concept of "critical" or "sensitive" periods. *Language Learning, 56,* 59–90.

Vaillancourt, T., & Hymel, S. (2006, July). Aggression and social status: The moderating roles of sex and peer-valued characteristics. *Aggressive Behavior, 32,* 396–408.

Vaillant, G. E. (1977). *Adaptation to life.* Boston: Little, Brown.

Vaillant, G. E., & Vaillant, C. O. (1981). Natural history of male psychological health, X: Work as a predictor of positive mental health. *The American Journal of Psychiatry, 138,* 1433–1440.

Vaillant, G. E., & Vaillant, C. O. (1990). Natural history of male psychological health, XII: A 45-year study of predictors of successful aging. *American Journal of Psychiatry, 147(1),* 31–37.

Valenti, C. (2006). Infant vision guidance: Fundamental vision development in infancy. *Optometry and vision development, 37,* 147–155.

Valiente, C., Eisenberg, N., & Fabes, R. A. (2004). Prediction of children's empathy-related responding from their effortful control and parents' expressivity. *Developmental Psychology, 40,* 911–926.

Valles, N., & Knutson, J. (2008). Contingent responses of mothers and peers to indirect and direct aggression in preschool and school-aged children. *Aggressive Behavior, 34,* 497–510.

Van Balen, F. (2005). The choice for sons or daughters. *Journal of Psychosomatic Obstetrics & Gynecology, 26,* 229–320.

Van de Graaf, K. (2000). *Human anatomy* (5th ed., p. 339). Boston: McGraw-Hill.

Van de Graaf, K. (2008). *Human anatomy* (8th ed). Boston: McGraw-Hill.

van den Berg, P., Mond, J., Eisenberg, M., Ackard, D., & Neumark-Sztainer, D. (2010). The link between body dissatisfaction and self-esteem in adolescents: Similarities across gender, age, weight status, race/ethnicity, and socioeconomic status. *Journal of Adolescent Health, 47,* 290–296.

van den Hoonaard, D. K. (1994). Paradise lost: Widowhood in a Florida retirement community. *Journal of Aging Studies, 8,* 121–132.

van der Mark, I., van ijzendoorn, M., & Bakermans-Kranenburg, M. (2002). Development of empathy in girls during the second year of life: Associations with parenting, attachment, and temperament. *Social Development, 11,* 451–468.

van Heugten, M., & Johnson, E. (2010). Linking infants' distributional learning abilities to natural language acquisition. *Journal of Memory and Language, 63,* 197–209.

Van Marle, K., & Wynn, K. (2006). Six-month-old infants use analog magnitudes to represent duration. *Developmental Science, 9,* F41–F49.

van Marle, K., & Wynn, K. (2009). Infants' auditory enumeration: Evidence for analog magnitudes in the small number range. *Cognition, 111,* 302–316.

van't Spijker, A., & ten Kroode, H. F. (1997). Psychological aspects of genetic counseling: A review of the experience with Huntington's disease. *Patient Education and Counseling, 32,* 33–40.

Van Tassel-Baska, J., Olszewski-Kubilius, P., & Kulieke, M. (1994). A study of self-concept and social support in advantaged and disadvantaged seventh and eighth grade gifted students. *Roeper Review, 16,* 186–191.

van Wormer, K., & McKinney, R. (2003). What schools can do to help gay/lesbian/bisexual youth: A harm reduction approach. *Adolescence, 38,* 409–420.

Vandell, D. L. (2000). Parents, peer groups, and other socializing influences. *Developmental Psychology, 36,* 699–710.

Vandell, D. L. (2004). Early child care: The known and the unknown. *Merrill-Palmer Quarterly, 50* [Special issue: The maturing of human developmental sciences: Appraising past, present, and prospective agendas], 387–414.

Vandell, D. L., Burchinal, M. R., Belsky, J., Owen, M. T., Friedman, S. L., Clarke-Stewart, A., McCartney, K., & Weinraub, M. (2005). Early child care and children's development in the primary grades: Follow-up results from the NICHD Study of Early Child Care. Paper presented at the biennial meeting of the Society for Research in Child Development, Atlanta, GA.

Vandell, D. L., Shumow, L., & Posner, J. (2005). After-school programs for low-income children: Differences in program quality. In J. L. Mahoney, R. W. Larson, & J. S. Ecccles (Eds.), *Organized activities as contexts of development: Extracurricular activities, after-school and community programs.* Mahwah, NJ: Lawrence Erlbaum.

Vanlierde, A., Renier, L., & De Volder, A. G. (2008). Brain plasticity and multisensory experience in early blind individuals. In J. J. Rieser, D. H. Ashmead, F. F. Ebner, & A. L. Corn (Eds.), *Blindness and brain plasticity in navigation and object perception.* Mahwah, NJ: Lawrence Erlbaum.

Vartanian, L. R. (2000). Revisiting the imaginary audience and personal fable constructs of adolescent egocentrism: A conceptual review. *Adolescence, 35,* 639–646.

Vaughan, V., McKay, R. J., & Behrman, R. (1979). *Nelson textbook of pediatrics* (11th ed.). Philadelphia: Saunders.

Vedantam, S. (2004, April 23). Antidepressants called unsafe for children: Four medications singled out in analysis of many studies. *Washington Post,* p. A03.

Vellutino, F. R. (1991). Introduction to three studies on reading acquisition: Convergent findings on theoretical foundations of code-oriented versus whole-language approaches to reading instruction. *Journal of Educational Psychology, 83,* 437–443.

Veneziano, R. (2003). The importance of paternal warmth. *Cross-Cultural Research: The Journal of Comparative Social Science, 37,* 265–281.

Veras, R. P., & Mattos, L. C. (2007). Audiology and aging: Literature review and current horizons. *Revista Brasileira de Otorrinolaringologia (English Edition), 73,* 122–128.

Vereijken, C. M., Riksen-Walraven, J. M., & Kondo-Ikemura, K. (1997). Maternal sensitivity and infant attachment security in Japan: A longitudinal study. *International Journal of Behavioral Development, 21,* 35–49.

Verkerk, G., Pop, V., & Van Son, M, (2003). Prediction of depression in the postpartum period: A longitudinal follow-up study in high-risk and low-risk women. *Journal of Affective Disorders, 77,* 159–166.

Verkuyten, M. (2003). Positive and negative self-esteem among ethnic minority early adolescents: Social and cultural sources and threats. *Journal of Youth & Adolescence, 32,* 267–277.

Vernon, J. A. (1990). Media stereotyping: A comparison of the way elderly women and men are portrayed on prime-time television. *Journal of Women and Aging, 2,* 55–68.

Vidaver, R. M., et al. (2000). Women subjects in NIH-funded clinical research literature: Lack of progress in both representation and analysis by sex. *Journal of Women's Health, Gender-Based Medicine, 9,* 495–504.

Vilhjalmsson, R., & Kristjansdottir, G. (2003). Gender differences in physical activity in older children and adolescents: The central role of organized sport. *Social Science Medicine, 56,* 363–374.

Villarosa, L. (2003, December 23). More teenagers say no to sex, and experts are sure why. *New York Times,* p. D6.

Vink, D., Aartsen, M., Comijs, H., Heymans, M., Penninx, B., Stek, M., et al. (2009). Onset of anxiety and depression in the aging population: Comparison of risk factors in a 9-year prospective study. *The American Journal of Geriatric Psychiatry, 17,* 642–652.

Vitaliano, P. P., Dougherty, C. M., & Siegler, I. C. (1994). Biopsychosocial risks for cardiovascular disease in spouse caregivers of persons with Alzheimer's disease. In R. P. Abeles, H. C. Gift, & M. G. Ory (Eds.), *Aging and quality of life.* New York: Springer.

Vittaro, F., & Pelletier, D. (1991). Assessment of children's social problem-solving skills in hypothetical and actual conflict situations. *Journal of Abnormal Child Psychology, 19,* 505–518.

Vizmanos, B., & Marti-Henneberg, C. (2000). Puberty begins with a characteristic subcutaneous body fat mass in each sex. *European Journal of Clinical Nutrition, 54,* 203–206.

Volker, S. (2007). Infants' vocal engagement oriented towards mother versus stranger at 3 months and avoidant attachment behavior at 12 months. *International Journal of Behavioral Development, 31,* 88–95.

Votruba-Drzal, E., Coley, R. L., & Chase-Lansdale, L. (2004). Child care and low-income children's development: Direct and moderated effects. *Child Development, 75,* 396–312.

Vyas, S. (2004). Exploring bicultural identities of Asian high school students through the analytic window of a literature club. *Journal of Adolescent & Adult Literacy, 48,* 12–18.

Vygotsky, L. S. (1926/1997). *Educational psychology.* Delray Beach, FL: St. Lucie Press.

Vygotsky, L. S. (1979). *Mind in society: The development of higher mental processes.* Cambridge, MA: Harvard University Press. (Original works published 1930, 1933, and 1935.)

Wachs, T. D. (1992). *The nature of nurture.* Newbury Park, CA: Sage Publications.

Wachs, T. D. (1993). The nature–nurture gap: What we have here is a failure to collaborate. In R. Plomin & G. E. McClearn (Eds.), *Nature, nurture, and psychology.* Washington, DC: American Psychological Association.

Wachs, T. D. (1996). Known and potential processes underlying developmental trajectories in childhood and adolescence. *Developmental Psychology, 32,* 796–801.

Wade, N. (2001, October 4). Researchers say gene is linked to language. *New York Times,* p. A1.

Wade, T. D. (2008). Shared temperament risk factors for anorexia nervosa: A twin study. *Psychosomatic Medicine, 70,* 239–244.

Wagner, R. K., & Sternberg, R. J. (1985). Alternate conceptions of intelligence and their implications for education. *Review of Educational Research, 54,* 179–223.

Wahlin, T. (2007). To know or not to know: A review of behaviour and suicidal ideation in preclinical Huntington's disease. *Patient Education and Counseling, 65,* 279–287.

Wainwright, J. L., Russell, S. T., & Patterson, C. J. (2004). Psychosocial adjustment, school outcomes, and romantic relationships of adolescents with same-sex parents. *Child Development, 75,* 1886–1898.

Wakefield, A., Murch, S., Anthony, A., Linnell, J., Casson, D., et al. (1998). Illeal-lymphoid-nodular hyperplasia, non-specific colitis, and pervasive developmental disorder in children. *The Lancet, 351,* 637–641.

Wakschlag, L. S., Leventhal, B. L., Pine, D. S., Pickett, K. E., & Carter, A. S. (2006). Elucidating early mechanisms of developmental psychopathology: The case of prenatal smoking and disruptive behavior. *Child Development, 77,* 893–906.

Walden, T., Kim, G., McCoy, C., & Karrass, J. (2007). Do you believe in magic? Infants' social looking during violations of expectations. *Developmental Science, 10,* 654–663.

Waldfogel, J. (2001). International policies toward parental leave and child care. *Caring for Infants and Toddlers, 11,* 99–111.

Waldrop, D. P., & Kirkendall, A. M. (2009). Comfort measures: A qualitative study of nursing home-based end-of-life care. *Journal of Palliative Medicine, 12,* 718–724.

Walker, J., Anstey, K., & Lord, S. (2006, May). Psychological distress and visual functioning in relation to vision-related disability in older individuals with cataracts. *British Journal of Health Psychology, 11,* 303–317.

Walker, W. A., & Humphries, C. (2005). *The Harvard Medical School guide to healthy eating during pregnancy.* New York: McGraw-Hill.

Walker, W. A., & Humphries, C. (2007, September 17). Starting the good life in the womb. *Newsweek,* pp. 56–57.

Wallerstein, J., & Resnikoff, D. (2005). Parental divorce and developmental progression: An inquiry into their relationship. In L. Gunsberg & P. Hymowitz, *A handbook of divorce and custody: Forensic, developmental, and clinical perspectives.* Hillsdale, NJ: Analytic Press, Inc.

Wallis, C. (1994, July 18). Life in overdrive. *Time,* pp. 42–50.

Walters, A., & Rye, D. (2009). Review of the relationship of restless legs syndrome and periodic limb movements in sleep to hypertension, heart disease, and stroke. *Sleep: Journal of Sleep and Sleep Disorders Research, 32,* 589–597.

Walters, E., & Gardner, H. (1986). The theory of multiple intelligences: Some issues and answers. In R. J. Sternberg & R. K. Wagner (Eds.), *Practical intelligence.* New York: Cambridge University Press.

Wamba, N. G. (2010). Poverty and literacy: An introduction. *Reading & Writing Quarterly: Overcoming Difficulties, 26,* 109–114.

Wang, H. J., Zhang, H., Zhang, W. W., Pan, Y. P., & Ma, J. (2008). Association of the common genetic variant upstream of INSIG2 gene with obesity related phenotypes in Chinese children and adolescents. *Biomedical and Environmental Sciences, 21,* 528–536.

Wang, Q. (2004). The emergence of cultural self-constructs: Autobiographical memory and self-description in European American and Chinese children. *Developmental Psychology, 40,* 3–15.

Wang, Q. (2006). Culture and the development of self-knowledge. *Current Directions in Psychological Science, 15,* 182–187.

Wang, Q. (2008). Emotion knowledge and autobiographical memory across the preschool years: A cross-cultural longitudinal investigation. *Cognition, 108,* 117–135.

Wang, Q., Pomerantz, E., & Chen, H. (2007). The role of parents' control in early adolescents' psychological functioning: A longitudinal investigation in the United States and China. *Child Development, 78,* 1592–1610.

Wang, S., & Tamis-LeMonda, C. (2003). Do child-rearing values in Taiwan and the United States reflect cultural values of collectivism and individualism? *Journal of Cross-Cultural Psychology, 34,* 629–642.

Wang, S-H., Baillargeon, R., & Paterson, S. (2005). Detecting continuity violations in infancy: A new account and new evidence from covering and tube events. *Cognition, 95,* 129–173.

Ward, R. A. (1984). *The aging experience: An introduction to social gerontology* (2nd ed.). New York: Harper & Row.

Wardle, J., Guthrie, C., & Sanderson, S. (2001). Food and activity preferences in children of lean and obese parents. *International Journal of Obesity & Related Metabolic Disorders, 25,* 971–977.

Warnock, F., & Sandrin, D. (2004). Comprehensive description of newborn distress behavior in response to acute pain (newborn male circumcision). *Pain, 107,* 242–255.

Warren, M. (2009). On the moral and legal status of abortion. *Defining the beginning and ending of life: Readings on personal identity and bioethics.* Baltimore, MD: Johns Hopkins University Press.

Warwick, P., & Maloch, B. (2003). Scaffolding speech and writing in the primary classroom: A consideration of work with literature and science pupil groups in the USA and UK. *Reading: Literacy & Language, 37,* 54–63.

Wass, H. (2004). A perspective on the current state of death education. *Death Studies, 28,* 289–308.

Wasserman, J. D., & Tulsky, D. S. (2005). The history of intelligence assessment. In D. P. Flanagan & P. L. Harrison (Eds.), *Contemporary intellectual assessment: Theories, tests, and issues.* New York: Guilford Press.

Waterhouse, J. M., & DeCoursey, P. J. (2004). Human circadian organization. In J. C. Dunlap & J. J. Loros (Eds.), *Chronobiology: Biological timekeeping.* Sunderland, MA: Sinauer Associates.

Waterland, R. A., & Jirtle, R. L. (2004). Early nutrition, epigenetic changes at transposons and imprinted genes, and enhanced susceptibility to adult chronic diseases. *Nutrition,* 63–68.

Watling, D., & Bourne, V. J. (2007). Linking children's neuropsychological processing of emotion with their knowledge of emotion expression regulation. *Laterality: Asymmetries of Body, Brain and Cognition, 12,* 381–396.

Watson, J. B. (1925). *Behaviorism.* New York: Norton.

Watson, J. B., & Rayner, R. (1920). Conditioned, emotional reactions. *Journal of Experimental Psychology, 3,* 1–14.

Watts-English, T., Fortson, B. L., Gibler, N., Hooper, S. R., & De Bellis, M. D. (2006). The psychobiologic of maltreatment in childhood. *Journal of Social Issues, 62,* 717–736.

Webster, J., & Haight, B. (2002). *Critical advances in reminiscence work: From theory to application.* New York: Springer Publishing Co.

Wechsler, D. (1975). Intelligence defined and undefined. *American Psychologist, 30,* 135–139.

Wechsler, H., Issac, R., Grodstein, L., & Sellers, M. (2000). *College binge drinking in the 1990s: A continuing problem: Results of the Harvard School of Public Health 1999 College Health Alcohol Study.* Cambridge, MA: Harvard University.

Wechsler, H., Lee, J. E., Kuo, M., Seibring, M., Nelson, T. F., & Lee, H. (2002). Trends in college binge drinking during a period of increased prevention efforts: Findings from 4 Harvard School of Public Health college alcohol study surveys, 1993–2001.

Wechsler, H., Nelson, T. F., Lee, J. E., Seibring, M., Lewis, C., & Keeling, R. P. (2003). Perception and reality: A national evaluation of social norms marketing interventions to reduce college students' heavy alcohol use. *Journal of Studies on Alcohol, 64,* 484–494.

Wei, J., Hadjiiski, L. M., Sahiner, B., Chan, H. P., Ge, J., Roubidoux, M. A., Helvie, M. A., Zhour, C., Wu, Y. T., Paramagul, C., & Zhang, Y. (2007). Computer-aided detection systems for breast masses: Comparison of performances on full-field digital mammograms and digitized screen-film mammograms. *Academy of Radiology, 14,* 659–669.

Weinberg, R. A. (2004). The infant and the family in the twenty-first century. *Journal of the American Academy of Child & Adolescent Psychiatry, 43,* 115–116.

Weinberger, D. R. (2001, March 10). A brain too young for good judgment. *New York Times,* p. D1.

Weinstock, H., Berman, S., & Cates, W., Jr. (2004). Sexually transmitted diseases among American youth: Incidence and prevalence estimates, 2000. *Perspectives on Sexual and Reproductive Health, 36,* 182–191.

Weiss, R. (2003, September 2). Genes' sway over IQ may vary with class. *Washington Post,* p. A1.

Weiss, R., & Raz, I. (2006, July). Focus on childhood fitness, not just fatness. *Lancet, 368,* 261–262.

Weisz, A., & Black, B. (2002). Gender and moral reasoning: African American youth respond to dating dilemmas. *Journal of Human Behavior in the Social Environment, 5,* 35–52.

Weitzman, E., Nelson, T., & Wechsler, H. (2003). Taking up binge drinking in college: The influences of person, social group, and environment. *Journal of Adolescent Health, 32,* 26–35.

Wellings, K., Collumbien, M., Slaymaker, E., Singh, S., Hodges, Z., Patel, D., & Bajos, N. (2006). Sexual behaviour in context: A global perspective. *The Lancet, 368,* 1706–1738.

Wellman, H., Lopez-Duran, S., LaBounty, J., & Hamilton, B. (2008). Infant attention to intentional action predicts preschool theory of mind. *Developmental Psychology, 44,* 618–623.

Wells, B., Peppe, S., & Goulandris, N. (2004). Intonation development from five to thirteen. *Journal of Child Language, 31,* 749–778.

Wells, R., Lohman, D., & Marron, M. (2009). What factors are associated with grade acceleration? An analysis and comparison of two U.S. databases. *Journal of Advanced Academics, 20,* 248–273.

Welsh, T., Ray, M., Weeks, D., Dewey, D., & Elliott, D. (2009). Does Joe influence Fred's action? Not if Fred has autism spectrum disorder. *Brain Research, 1248,* 141–148.

Werker, J. F., Pons, F., Dietrich, C., Kajikawa, S., Fais, L., & Amano, S. (2007). Infant-directed speech supports phonetic category learning in English and Japanese. *Cognition, 103,* 147–162.

Werner, E. E. (1972). Infants around the world: Cross-cultural studies of psychomotor development from birth to two years. *Journal of Cross-Cultural Psychology, 3,* 111–134.

Werner, E. E. (2005). What can we learn about resilience from large-scale longitudinal studies? In S. Goldstein & R. B. Brooks, *Handbook of resilience in children.* New York: Kluwer Academic/Plenum Publishers.

Werner, E. E., & Smith, R. S. (2002). Journeys from childhood to midlife: Risk, resilience and recovery. *Journal of Developmental and Behavioral Pediatrics, 23,* 456.

Werner, L. A., & Marean, G. C. (1996). *Human auditory development.* Boulder, CO: Westview Press.

Werner, N. E., & Crick, N. R. (2004). Maladaptive peer relationships and the development of relational and physical aggression during middle childhood. *Social Development, 13,* 495–514.

Wertsch, J. V. (1999). The zone of proximal development: Some conceptual issues. In P. Lloyd & C. Fernyhough (Eds.), *Lev Vygotsky: Critical assessments, Vol. 3: The zone of proximal development.* New York: Routledge.

Wertsch, J. (2008). From social interaction to higher psychological processes: A clarification and application of Vygotsky's theory. *Human Development, 51,* 66–79.

West, J. H., Romero, R. A., & Trinidad, D. R. (2007). Adolescent receptivity to tobacco marketing by racial/ethnic groups in California. *American Journal of Preventive Medicine, 33,* 121–123.

West, J. R., & Blake, C. A. (2005). Fetal alcohol syndrome: An assessment of the field. *Experimental Biology and Medicine, 230,* 354–356.

Westermann, G., Mareschal, D., Johnson, M. H., Sirois, S., Spratling, M. W., & Thomas, M. S. (2007). Neuroconstructivism. *Developmental Science, 10,* 75–83.

Wexler, B. (2006). *Brain and culture: Neurobiology, ideology, and social change.* Cambridge, MA: MIT Press.

Whalen, C. K., Jamner, L. D., Henker, B., Delfino, R. J., & Lozano, J. M. (2002). The ADHD spectrum and everyday life: Experience sampling of adolescent moods, activities, smoking, and drinking. *Child Development, 73,* 209–227.

Whalen, D., Levitt, A., & Goldstein, L. (2007). VOT in the babbling of French- and English-learning infants. *Journal of Phonetics, 35,* 341–352.

Whaley, B. B., & Parker, R. G. (2000). Expressing the experience of communicative disability: Metaphors of persons who stutter. *Communication Reports, 13,* 115–125.

Wheaton, B., & Montazer, S. (2010). Stressors, stress, and distress. *A handbook for the study of mental health: Social contexts, theories, and systems* (2nd ed.) New York: Cambridge University Press.

Wheeldon, L. R. (1999). *Aspects of language production.* Philadelphia: Psychology Press.

Wheeler, S., & Austin, J. (2001). The impact of early pregnancy loss. *American Journal of Maternal/Child Nursing, 26,* 154–159.

Whitaker, B. (2004, March 29). Employee of the century. *CBS Evening News.*

Whitaker, R. C., Wright, J. A., Pepe, M. S., Seidel, K. D., & Dietz, W. H. (1997, September 25). Predicting obesity in young adulthood from childhood and parental obesity. *New England Journal of Medicine, 337,* 869–873.

Whitbourne, S. K. (2001). *Adult development and aging: Biopsychosocial perspectives.* New York: Wiley.

Whitbourne, S. K. (October, 2007). *Crossing over the bridges of adulthood: Multiple pathways through midlife.* Presidential keynote presented at the 4th Biannual Meeting of the Society for the Study of Human Development, Pennsylvania State University, University Park PA.

Whitbourne, S. K., Zuschlag, M. K., Elliot, L. B., & Waterman, A. S. (1992). Psychosocial development in adulthood: A 22-year sequential study. *Journal of Personality and Social Psychology, 63,* 260–271.

Whitbourne, S., Jacobo, M., & Munoz-Ruiz, M. (1996). Adversity in the elderly. In R. S. Feldman (Ed.), *The psychology of adversity.* Amherst: University of Massachusetts Press.

Whitbourne, S., Sneed, J., & Sayer, A. (2009). Psychosocial development from college through midlife: A 34-year sequential study. *Developmental Psychology, 45,* 1328–1340.

White, K. (2007). Hypnobirthing: The Mongan method. *Australian Journal of Clinical Hypnotherapy and Hypnosis, 28,* 12–24.

Whitebread, D., Coltman, P., Jameson, H., & Lander, R. (2009). Play, cognition and self-regulation: What exactly are children learning when they learn through play? *Educational and Child Psychology, 26,* 40–52.

Whiting, B. B., & Edwards, C. P. (1988). *Children of different worlds: The formation of social behavior.* Cambridge, MA: Harvard University Press.

Wickelgren, W. A. (1999). Webs, cell assemblies, and chunking in neural nets: Introduction. *Canadian Journal of Experimental Psychology, 53,* 118–131.

Widaman, K. (2009). Phenylketonuria in children and mothers: Genes, environments, behavior. *Current Directions in Psychological Science, 18,* 48–52. Available online at http://search.ebscohost.com

Widom, C. S. (2000). Motivation and mechanisms in the "cycle of violence" In D. J. Hansen (Ed.), *Nebraska Symposium on Motivation Vol. 46, 1998: Motivation and child maltreatment* (Current theory and research in motivation series). Lincoln: University of Nebraska Press.

Wielgosz, A. T., & Nolan, R. P. (2000). Biobehavioral factors in the context of ischemic cardiovascular disease. *Journal of Psychosomatic Research, 48,* 339–345.

Wiggins, M., & Uwaydat, S. (2006, January). Age-related macular degeneration: Options for earlier detection and improved treatment. *Journal of Family Practice, 55,* 22–27.

Wilk, K. A., Bernhardt, E., & Noack, T. (2009). A study of commitment and relationship quality in Sweden and Norway. *Journal of Marriage & the Family, 71,* 465–477.

Wilcox, H. C., Conner, K. R., & Caine, E. D. (2004). Association of alcohol and drug use disorders and completed suicide: An empirical review of cohort studies. *Drug & Alcohol Dependence, 76* [Special issue: Drug abuse and suicidal behavior], S11–S19.

Wilcox, S., Castro, C. M., & King, A. C. (2006). Outcome expectations and physical activity participation in two samples of older women. *Journal of Health Psychology, 11,* 65–77.

Wilcox, T., Woods, R., Chapa, C., & McCurry, S. (2007). Multisensory exploration and object individuation in infancy. *Developmental Psychology, 43,* 479–495.

Wildberger, S. (2003, August). So you're having a baby. *Washingtonian,* pp. 85–86, 88–90.

Wiley, T. L., Nondahl, D. M., Cruickshanks, K. J., & Tweed, T. S. (2005). Five-year changes in middle ear function for older adults. *Journal of the American Academy of Audiology, 16,* 129–139.

Wilfond, B., & Ross, L. (2009). From genetics to genomics: Ethics, policy, and parental decision-making. *Journal of Pediatric Psychology, 34,* 639–647. Available online at http://search.ebscohost.com.

Wilkes, S., Chinn, D., Murdoch, A., & Rubin, G. (2009). Epidemiology and management of infertility: A population-based study in UK primary care. *Family Practice, 26,* 269–274.

Williams, A., & Merten, M. (2009). Adolescents' online social networking following the death of a peer. *Journal of Adolescent Research, 24,* 67–90.

Williams, J., & Ross, L. (2007). Consequences of prenatal toxin exposure for mental health in children and adolescents: A systematic review. *European Child & Adolescent Psychiatry, 16,* 243–253.

Willie, C., & Reddick, R. (2003). *A new look at black families* (5th ed.). Walnut Creek, CA: AltaMira Press.

Willis, S. (1996). Everyday problem solving. In J. E. Birren, K. W. Schaie, R. P. Abeles, M. Gatz, & T. A. Salthouse (Eds.), *Handbook of the psychology of aging* (4th ed.). San Diego: Academic Press.

Willis, S. L. (1985). Educational psychology of the older adult learner. In J. E. Birren & K. W. Schaie (Eds.), *Handbook of the psychology of aging* (2nd ed.). New York: Van Nostrand Reinhold.

Willott, J., Chisolm, T., & Lister, J. (2001). Modulation of presbycusis: Current state and future directions. *Audiology & Neuro-Otology, 6,* 231–249.

Wills, T., Sargent, J., Stoolmiller, M., Gibbons, F., & Gerrard, M. (2008). Movie smoking exposure and smoking onset: A longitudinal study of mediation processes in a representative sample of U.S. adolescents. *Psychology of Addictive Behaviors, 22,* 269–277.

Wilson, G. T., Grilo, C. M., & Vitousek, K. M. (2007). Psychological treatment of eating disorders. *American Psychologist, 62* [Special Issue: Eating disorders], 199–216.

Wilson, M. N. (1989). Child development in the context of the black extended family. *American Psychologist, 44,* 380–385.

Wilson, R., Beck, T., Bienias, J., & Bennett, D. (2007, February). Terminal cognitive decline: Accelerated loss of cognition in the last years of life. *Psychosomatic Medicine, 69,* 131–137.

Wilson, S. L. (2003). Post-Institutionalization: The effects of early deprivation on development of Romanian adoptees. *Child & Adolescent Social Work Journal, 20,* 473–483.

Wines, M. (2006, August 24). Africa adds to miserable ranks for child workers. *New York Times,* p. D1.

Winger, G., & Woods, J. H. (2004). *A handbook on drug and alcohol abuse: The biomedical aspects.* Oxford, England: Oxford University Press.

Wingert, P., & Kantrowitz, B. (1997, October 27). Why Andy couldn't read (bright children who are also learning disabled). *Newsweek, 130,* p. 56.

Wingert, P., & Katrowitz, B. (2002, October 7). Young and depressed. *Newsweek,* pp. 53–61.

Wingfield, A., Tun, P. A., & McCoy, S. L. (2005). Hearing loss in older adulthood: What it is and how it interacts with cognitive performance. *Current Directions in Psychological Science, 14,* 144–147.

Wink, P., & Dillon, M. (2003). Religiousness, spirituality, and psychosocial functioning in late adulthood: Findings from a longitudinal study. *Psychology & Aging, 18,* 916–924.

Winsler, A. (2003). Introduction to special issue: Vygotskian perspectives in early childhood education. *Early Education and Development, 14* [Special Issue], pp. 253–269.

Winsler, A., Feder, M., Way, E., & Manfra, L. (2006, July). Maternal beliefs concerning young children's private speech. *Infant and Child Development, 15,* 403–420.

Winstead, B. A., & Sanchez, J. (2005). Gender and psychopathology. In J. Maddux (Ed.), *Psychopathology: Foundations for a contemporary understanding.* Mahwah, NJ: Lawrence Erlbaum.

Winterich, J. (2003). Sex, menopause, and culture: Sexual orientation and the meaning of menopause for women's sex lives. *Gender & Society, 17,* 627–642.

Winters, K. C., Stinchfield, R. D., & Botzet, A. (2005). Pathways fo youth gambling problem severity. *Psychology of Addictive Behaviors, 19,* 104–107.

Wisborg, K., Kesmodel, U., Bech, B. H., Hedegaard, M., & Henriksen, T. B. (2003). Maternal consumption of coffee during pregnancy and stillbirth and infant death in first year of life: Prospective study. *British Medical Journal, 326,* 420.

Wisdom, J. P., Agnor, C. (2007). Family heritage and depression guides: Family and peer views influence adolescent attitudes about depression. *Journal of Adolescence, 30,* 333–346.

Witvliet, M., van Lier, P., Cuijpers, P., & Koot, H. (2010). Change and stability in childhood clique membership, isolation from cliques, and associated child characteristics. *Journal of Clinical Child and Adolescent Psychology, 39,* 12–24.

Woelfle, J. F., Harz, K., & Roth, C. (2007). Modulation of circulating IGF-I and IGFBP-3 levels by hormonal regulators of energy homeostasis in obese children. *Experimental and Clinical Endocrinology Diabetes, 115,* 17–23.

Woike, B., & Matic, D. (2004). Cognitive complexity in response to traumatic experiences. *Journal of Personality, 72,* 633–657.

Wolfe, M. S. (2006, May). Shutting down Alzheimer's. *Scientific American,* 73–79.

Wolfe, W., Olson, C., & Kendall, A. (1998). Hunger and food insecurity in the elderly: Its nature and measurement. *Journal of Aging & Health, 10,* 327–350.

Wolinsky, F., Wyrwich, K., & Babu, A. (2003). Age, aging, and the sense of control among older adults: A longitudinal reconsideration. *Journals of Gerontology: Series B: Psychological Sciences & Social Sciences, 58B,* S212–S220.

Wood, K., Becker, J., & Thompson, J. (1996). Body image dissatisfaction in preadolescent children. *Journal of Applied Developmental Psychology, 17,* 85–100.

Wood, R. (1997). Trends in multiple births, 1938–1995. *Population Trends, 87,* 29–35.

Wood, S., Portman, T., Cigrand, D., & Colangelo, N. (2010). School counselors' perceptions and experience with acceleration as a program option for gifted and talented students. *Gifted Child Quarterly, 54,* 168–178.

Wood, W., & Eagly, A. (2010). Gender. *Handbook of social psychology, Vol. 1* (5th ed.). Hoboken, NJ: Wiley.

Woods, R. (2009). The use of aggression in primary school boys' decisions about inclusion in and exclusion from playground football games. *British Journal of Educational Psychology, 79,* 223–238.

World Bank. (2004). *World development indicators 2004 (WDI).* Washington, DC: Author.

World Factbook. (2009). *Estimates of infant mortality.* Available online at https://www.cia.gov/library/publications/the-world-factbook/rankorder/2091rank.html

World Health Organization. (2007). *Male circumcision: Global trends and determinants of prevalence, safety and acceptability.* Paris: Author.

Worrell, F., Szarko, J., & Gabelko, N. (2001). Multi-year persistence of nontraditional students in an academic talent development program. *Journal of Secondary Gifted Education, 12,* 80–89.

Wortman, C. B., & Silver, R. C. (1990). Successful mastery of bereavement and widowhood: A life-course perspective. In P. B. Baltes & M. M. Baltes (Eds.), *Successful aging:*

Perspectives from the behavioral sciences. Cambridge, England: Cambridge University Press.

Wright, J. C., Huston, A. C., Reitz, A. L., & Piemyat, S. (1994). Young children's perceptions of television reality: Determinants and developmental differences. *Developmental Psychology, 30,* 229–239.

Wright, J. C., Huston, A. C., Truglio, R., Fitch, M., Smith, E., & Piemyat, S. (1995). Occupational portrayals on television: Children's role schemata, career aspirations, and perceptions of reality. *Child Development, 66,* 1706–1718.

Wright, M., Wintemute, G., & Claire, B. (2008). Gun suicide by young people in California: Descriptive epidemiology and gun ownership. *Journal of Adolescent Health, 43,* 619–622.

Wright, R. (1995, March 13). The biology of violence. *New Yorker,* pp. 68–77.

Wroolie, T., & Holcomb, M. (2010). Menopause. *A public health perspective of women's mental health.* New York: Springer Science + Business Media.

Wrosch, C., Bauer, I., & Scheier, M. (2005, December). Regret and quality of life across the adult life span: The influence of disengagement and available future goals. *Psychology and Aging, 20,* 657–670.

Wu, C., Zhou, D., & Chen, W. (2003). A nested case-control study of Alzheimer's disease in Linxian, northern China. *Chinese Mental Health Journal, 17,* 84–88.

Wu, P., Hoven, C. W., Okezie, N., Fuller, C. J., & Cohen, P. (2007). Alcohol abuse and depression in children and adolescents. *Journal of Child & Adolescent Substance Abuse, 17,* 51–69.

Wu, P., Robinson, C., & Yang, C. (2002). Similarities and differences in mothers' parenting of preschoolers in China and the United States. *International Journal of Behavioral Development, 26,* 481–491.

Wyer, R. (2004). The cognitive organization and use of general knowledge. In J. Jost & M. Banaji (Eds.), *Perspectivism in social psychology: The yin and yang of scientific progress.* Washington, DC: American Psychological Association.

Wyra, M., Lawson, M. J., & Hungi, N. (2007). The mnemonic keyword method: The effects of bidirectional retrieval training and of ability to image on foreign language vocabulary recall. *Learning and Instruction, 17,* 360–371.

Xiaohe, X., & Whyte, M. K. (1990). Love matches and arranged marriages: A Chinese replication. *Journal of Marriage and the Family, 52,* 709–722.

Xing, X., Tao, F., Wan, Y., Xing, C., Qi, X., Hao, J., et al. (2010). Family factors associated with suicide attempts among Chinese adolescent students: A national cross-sectional survey. *Journal of Adolescent Health, 46,* 592–599.

Yagmurlu, B., & Sanson, A. (2009). Parenting and temperament as predictors of prosocial behaviour in Australian and Turkish Australian children. *Australian Journal of Psychology, 61,* 77–88.

Yaman, A., Mesman, J., van IJzendoorn, M., Bakermans-Kranenburg, M., & Linting, M. (2010). Parenting in an individualistic culture with a collectivistic cultural background: The case of Turkish immigrant families with toddlers in the Netherlands. *Journal of Child and Family Studies, 19,* 617–628.

Yan, J., Li, H., & Liao, Y. (2010). Developmental motor function plays a key role in visual search. *Developmental Psychobiology, 52,* 505–512.

Yan, Z., & Fischer, K. (2002). Always under construction: Dynamic variations in adult cognitive microdevelopment. *Human Development, 45,* 141–160.

Yang, R., & Blodgett, B. (2000). Effects of race and adolescent decision-making on status attainment and self-esteem. *Journal of Ethnic & Cultural Diversity in Social Work, 9,* 135–153.

Yang, Y. (2008). Social inequalities in happiness in the U.S. 1972–2004: An age-period-cohort analysis." *American Sociological Review, 73,* 204–226.

Yardley, J. (2001, July 2). Child-death case in Texas raises penalty questions. *New York Times,* p. A1.

Yell, M. L. (1995). The least restrictive environment mandate and the courts: Judicial activism or judicial restraint? *Exceptional Children, 61,* 578–581.

Yildiz, O. (2007). Vascular smooth muscle and endothelial functions in aging. *Annals of the New York Academy of Sciences, 1100,* 353–360.

Yim, I., Glynn, L., Schetter, C., Hobel, C., Chicz-DeMet, A., & Sandman, C. (2009). Risk of postpartum depressive symptoms with elevated corticotropin-releasing hormone in human pregnancy. *Archives of General Psychiatry, 66,* 162–169.

Yinger, J. (Ed.). (2004). *Helping children left behind: State aid and the pursuit of educational equity.* Cambridge, MA: MIT Press.

Yip, T., Sellers, R. M., & Seaton, E. K. (2006). African American racial identity across the lifespan: Identity status, identity content, and depressive symptoms. *Child Development, 77,* 1504–1517.

York, E. (2008). Gender differences in the college and career aspirations of high school valedictorians. *Journal of Advanced Academics, 19,* 578–600.

Yoshinaga-Itano, C. (2003). From screening to early identification and intervention: Discovering predictors to successful outcomes for children with significant hearing loss. *Journal of Deaf Studies & Deaf Education, 8,* 11–30.

Young, G., & Teitelbaum, J. (2010). Brain drain: Using the deep venous system to declare brain death. *The Canadian Journal of Neurological Sciences/ Le Journal Canadien Des Sciences Neurologiques, 37,* 429–430.

Young, H., & Ferguson, L. (1979). Developmental changes through adolescence in the spontaneous nomination of reference groups as a function of decision context. *Journal of Youth and Adolescence, 8,* 239–252.

Young, S., Rhee, S., Stallings, M., Corley, R., & Hewitt, J. (2006, July). Genetic and environmental vulnerabilities underlying adolescent substance use and problem use: General or specific? *Behavior Genetics, 36,* 603–615.

Youniss, J., & Haynie, D. L. (1992). Friendship in adolescence. *Journal of Developmental and Behavioral Pediatrics, 13,* 59–66.

Yu, M., & Stiffman, A. (2007). Culture and environment as predictors of alcohol abuse/dependence symptoms in American Indian youths. *Addictive Behaviors, 32,* 2253–2259.

Zafeiriou, D. I. (2004). Primitive reflexes and postural reactions in the neurodevelopmental examination. *Pediatric Neurology, 31,* 1–8.

Zahn-Wexler, C., & Radke-Yarrow, M. (1990). The origins of empathic concern. *Motivation and Emotion, 14,* 107–130.

Zahn-Waxler, C., Shirtcliff, E., & Marceau, K. (2008). Disorders of childhood and adolescence: Gender and psychopathology. *Annual Review of Clinical Psychology, 4,* 275–303.

Zalenski, R., & Raspa, R. (2006). Maslow's hierarchy of needs: A framework for achieving human potential in hospice. *Journal of Palliative Medicine, 9,* 1120–1127.

Zalsman, G., Levy, T., & Shoval, G. (2008). Interaction of child and family psychopathology leading to suicidal behavior. *Psychiatric Clinics of North America, 31,* 237–246.

Zalsman, G., Oquendo, M., Greenhill, L., Goldberg, P., Kamali, M., Martin, A., et al. (2006, October). Neurobiology of depression in children and adolescents. *Child and Adolescent Psychiatric Clinics of North America, 15,* 843–868.

Zampi, C., Fagioli, I., & Salzarulo, P. (2002). Time course of EEG background activity level before spontaneous awakening in infants. *Journal of Sleep Research, 11,* 283–287.

Zarit, S. H., & Reid, J. D. (1994). Family caregiving and the older family. In C. B. Fisher & R. M. Lerner (Eds.), *Applied developmental psychology.* New York: McGraw-Hill.

Zauszniewski, J. A., & Martin, M. H. (1999). Developmental task achievement and learned resourcefulness in healthy older adults. *Archives of Psychiatric Nursing, 13,* 41–47.

Zeanah, C. (2009). The importance of early experiences: Clinical, research and policy perspectives. *Journal of Loss and Trauma, 14,* 266–279.

Zeedyk, M., & Heimann, M. (2006). Imitation and socio-emotional processes: Implications for communicative development and interventions. *Infant and Child Development, 15,* 219–222.

Zelazo, P. D., Muller, U., Frye, D., & Marcovitch, S. (2003). The development of executive function in early childhood. *Monographs of the Society for Research in Child Development, 68,* 103–122.

Zelazo, P. R. (1998). McGraw and the development of unaided walking. *Developmental Review, 18,* 449–471.

Zellner, D., Loaiza, S., Gonzalez, Z., Pita, J., Morales, J., Pecora, D., et al. (2006, April). Food selection changes under stress. *Physiology & Behavior, 87,* 789–793.

Zemach, I., Chang, S., & Teller, D. (2007). Infant color vision: Prediction of infants' spontaneous color preferences. *Vision Research, 47,* 1368–1381.

Zeman, J., Cassano, M., Perry-Parrish, C., & Stegall, S. (2006, April). Emotion regulation in children and adolescents. *Journal of Developmental & Behavioral Pediatrics, 27,* 155–168.

Zernike, K., & Petersen, M. (2001, August 19). Schools' backing of behavior drugs comes under fire. *New York Times,* pp. 1, 28.

Zettergren, P. (2003). School adjustment in adolescence for previously rejected, average and popular children. *British Journal of Educational Psychology, 73,* 207–221.

Zhang, J. (2010). Vygotsky's thinking: Its relevance to learning and education. *Mind, Culture, and Activity, 17,* 188–190.

Zhang, L. (2008). Gender and racial gaps in earnings among recent college graduates. *Review of Higher Education: Journal of the Association for the Study of Higher Education, 32,* 51–72.

Zhe, C., & Siegler, R. S. (2000). Across the great divide: Bridging the gap between understanding of toddlers' and older children's thinking. *Monographs of the Society for Research in Child Development, 65* (2, Serial No. 261).

Zheng, Y. (2010). One-child policy and child mental health. *Increasing awareness of child and adolescent mental health.* Lanham, MD: Jason Aronson.

Zhou, B. F., Stamler, J., Dennis, B., Moag-Stahlberg, A., Okuda, N., Robertson, C., Zhao, L., Chan, Q., Elliot, P.: INTERMAP Research Group. (2003). Nutrient intakes of middle-aged men and women in China, Japan, United Kingdom, and United States in the late 1990s: The INTERMAP study. *Journal of Human Hypertension, 17,* 623–630.

Zhu, J., & Weiss, L. (2005). The Wechsler Scales. In D. P. Flanagan & P. L. Harrison (Eds.), *Contemporary intellectual assessment: Theories, tests, and issues.* New York: Guilford Press.

Ziegler, D., Piguet, O., Salat, D., Prince, K., Connally, E., & Corkin, S. (2010). Cognition in healthy aging is related to regional white matter integrity, but not cortical thickness. *Neurobiology of Aging, 31,* 1912–1926.

Zigler, E. F., & Finn-Stevenson, M. (1995). The child care crisis: Implications for the growth and development of the nation's children. *Journal of Social Issues, 51,* 215–231.

Zimmer, C. (2003, May 16). How the mind reads other minds. *Science, 300,* 1079–1080.

Zimmer-Gembeck, M. J., & Collins, W. A. (2003). Autonomy development during adolescence. In G. R. Adams & M. D. Berzonsky, *Blackwell handbook of adolescence.* Malden, MA: Blackwell Publishing.

Zimmer-Gembeck, M. J., & Gallaty, K. J. (2006). Hanging out or hanging in? Young females' socioemotional functioning and the changing motives for dating and romance. In A. Columbus (Ed.) *Advances in psychology research, Vol. 44.* Hauppauge, NY: Nova Science Publishers.

Zimmerman, F. J., Christakis, D. A., & Meltzoff, A. N. (2007). Associations between media viewing and language development in children under age 2 years. *The Journal of Pediatrics, 151,* 364–368.

Zimmerman, F., & Christakis, D. (2007). Associations between content types of early media exposure and subsequent attentional problems. *Pediatrics, 120,* 986–992.

Zirkel, S., & Cantor, N. (2004). 50 years after *Brown v. Board of Education*: The promise and challenge of multicultural education. *Journal of Social Issues, 60,* 1–15.

Zisook, S., & Shear, K. (2009). Grief and bereavement: What psychiatrists need to know. *World Psychiatry, 8,* 67–74.

Zolotor, A., Theodore, A., Chang, J., Berkoff, M., & Runyan, D. (2008). Speak softly—and forget the stick corporal punishment and child physical abuse. *American Journal of Preventive Medicine, 35,* 364–369.

Zuckerman, G., & Shenfield, S. D. (2007). Child-adult interaction that creates a zone of proximal development. *Journal of Russian & East European Psychology, 45,* 43–69.

Zuckerman, M. (2003). Biological bases of personality. In T. Millon & M. J. Lerner (Eds.), *Handbook of psychology: Personality and social psychology,* Vol. 5. New York: Wiley.

Zwelling, E. (2006). A challenging time in the history of Lamaze international: An interview with Francine Nichols. *Journal of Perinatal Education, 15,* 10–17.

# Glossary

**abstract modeling**   the process in which modeling paves the way for the development of more general rules and principles. (p. 193)

**acceleration**   special programs that allow gifted students to move ahead at their own pace, even if this means skipping to higher grade levels. (p. 234)

**accommodation**   changes in existing ways of thinking that occur in response to encounters with new stimuli or events. (p. 115)

**achieving stage**   the point reached by young adults in which intelligence is applied to specific situations involving the attainment of long-term goals regarding careers, family, and societal contributions. (p. 324)

**acquisitive stage**   according to Schaie, the first stage of cognitive development, encompassing all of childhood and adolescence, in which the main developmental task is to acquire information. (p. 324)

**activity theory**   the theory suggesting that successful aging occurs when people maintain the interests, activities, and social interactions with which they were involved during middle age. (p. 439)

**addictive drugs**   drugs that produce a biological or psychological dependence in users, leading to increasingly powerful cravings for them. (p. 268)

**adolescence**   the developmental stage that lies between childhood and adulthood. (p. 258)

**adolescent egocentrism**   a state of self-absorption in which the world is viewed from one's own point of view. (p. 277)

**adult day-care facilities**   a facility in which elderly individuals receive care only during the day, but spend nights and weekends in their own homes. (p. 442)

**affordances**   the action possibilities that a given situation or stimulus provides. (p. 113)

**age stratification theories**   the view that an unequal distribution of economic resources, power, and privilege exists among people at different stages of life. (p. 436)

**ageism**   prejudice and discrimination directed at older people. (p. 412)

**agentic professions**   occupations that are associated with getting things accomplished, such as carpentry. (p. 354)

**aggression**   intentional injury or harm to another person. (p. 193)

**Ainsworth Strange Situation**   a sequence of staged episodes that illustrate the strength of attachment between a child and (typically) his or her mother. (p. 140)

**alcoholics**   persons with alcohol problems who have learned to depend on alcohol and are unable to control their drinking. (p. 269)

**Alzheimer's disease**   a progressive brain disorder that produces loss of memory and confusion. (p. 419)

**ambivalent attachment pattern**   a style of attachment in which children display a combination of positive and negative reactions to their mothers; they show great distress when the mother leaves, but upon her return they may simultaneously seek close contact but also hit and kick her. (p. 141)

**amniocentesis**   the process of identifying genetic defects by examining a small sample of fetal cells drawn by a needle inserted into the amniotic fluid surrounding the unborn fetus. (p. 49)

**androgynous**   a state in which gender roles encompass characteristics thought typical of both sexes. (p. 182)

**anorexia nervosa**   a severe eating disorder in which individuals refuse to eat, while denying that their behavior and appearance, which may become skeletal, are out of the ordinary. (p. 264)

**anoxia**   a restriction of oxygen to the baby, lasting a few minutes during the birth process, which can produce cognitive defects. (p. 73)

**Apgar scale**   a standard measurement system that looks for a variety of indications of good health in newborns. (p. 73)

**applied research**   research meant to provide practical solutions to immediate problems. (p. 32)

**artificial insemination**   a process of fertilization in which a man's sperm is placed directly into a woman's reproductive tract by a physician. (p. 62)

**assimilation**   the process in which people understand an experience in terms of their current stage of cognitive development and way of thinking. (p. 115)

**associative play**   play in which two or more children actually interact with one another by sharing or borrowing toys or materials, although they do not do the same thing. (p. 184)

**attachment**   the positive emotional bond that develops between a child and a particular individual. (p. 140)

**attention deficit hyperactivity disorder (ADHD)**   a learning disorder marked by inattention, impulsiveness, a low tolerance for frustration, and generally a great deal of inappropriate activity. (p. 211)

**auditory impairment**   a special need that involves the loss of hearing or some aspect of hearing. (p. 210)

**authoritarian parents**   parents who are controlling, punitive, rigid, and cold, and whose word is law. They value strict, unquestioning obedience from their children and do not tolerate expressions of disagreement. (p. 187)

**authoritative parents**   parents who are firm, setting clear and consistent limits, but who try to reason with their children, giving explanations for why they should behave in a particular way. (p. 187)

**autobiographical memory**   memories about one's own life. (pp. 169, 430)

**autonomy**   having independence and a sense of control over one's life. (p. 294)

**autonomy-versus-shame-and-doubt stage**   the period during which, according to Erikson, toddlers (aged 18 months to 3 years) develop independence and autonomy if they are allowed the freedom to explore, or shame and self-doubt if they are restricted and overprotected. (p. 145)

**avoidant attachment pattern**   a style of attachment in which children do not seek proximity to the mother; after the mother has left, they seem to avoid her when she returns as if they are angered by her behavior. (p. 141)

**babbling**   making speechlike but meaningless sounds. (p. 128)

**Bayley Scales of Infant Development**   a measure that evaluates an infant's development from 2 to 42 months. (p. 123)

**behavior modification**   a formal technique for promoting the frequency of desirable behaviors and decreasing the incidence of unwanted ones. (p. 16)

**behavioral genetics**   the study of the effects of heredity on behavior. (p. 47)

**behavioral perspective**   the approach that suggests that the keys to understanding development are observable behavior and outside stimuli in the environment. (p. 15)

**bereavement**   acknowledgment of the objective fact that one has experienced a death. (p. 474)

**bicultural identity**   maintaining one's original cultural identity while integrating oneself into the dominant culture. (p. 224)

**bilingualism**   the use of more than one language. (p. 219)

**bioecological approach**   the perspective suggesting that levels of the environment simultaneously influence individuals. (p. 20)

**blended families**   a remarried couple who has at least one stepchild living with them. (p. 251)

**body transcendence versus body preoccupation**   a period in which people must learn to cope with and move beyond changes in physical capabilities as a result of aging. (p. 434)

**bonding**   close physical and emotional contact between parent and child during the period immediately following birth. (p. 73)

**boomerang children**   young adults who return, after leaving home for some period, to live in the homes of their middle-aged parents. (p. 395)

**brain death**   a diagnosis of death based on the cessation of all signs of brain activity, as measured by electrical brain waves. (p. 459)

**Brazelton Neonatal Behavioral Assessment Scale (NBAS)**   a measure designed to determine infants' neurological and behavioral responses to their environment. (p. 105)

**bulimia** an eating disorder characterized by binges on large quantities of food, followed by purges of the food through vomiting or the use of laxatives. (p. 264)

**burnout** a situation that occurs when workers experience dissatisfaction, disillusionment, frustration, and weariness from their jobs. (p. 401)

**career consolidation** according to Vaillant a stage that is entered between the ages of 20 and 40, when young adults become centered on their careers. (p. 353)

**case studies** studies that involve extensive, in-depth interviews with a particular individual or small group of individuals. (p. 28)

**centration** the process of concentrating on one limited aspect of a stimulus and ignoring other aspects. (p. 165)

**cephalocaudal principle** the principle that growth follows a pattern that begins with the head and upper body parts and then proceeds down to the rest of the body. (p. 95)

**cerebral cortex** the upper layer of the brain. (p. 98)

**cesarean delivery** a birth in which the baby is surgically removed from the uterus, rather than traveling through the birth canal. (p. 81)

**chorionic villus sampling (CVS)** a test used to find genetic defects that involves taking samples of hairlike material that surrounds the embryo. (p. 49)

**chromosomes** rod-shaped portions of DNA that are organized in 23 pairs. (p. 43)

**chronological (or physical) age** the actual age of the child taking the intelligence test. (p. 226)

**classical conditioning** a type of learning in which an organism responds in a particular way to a neutral stimulus that normally does not bring about that type of response. (pp. 16, 47)

**cliques** groups of from 2 to 12 people whose members have frequent social interactions with one another. (p. 297)

**cognitive development** development involving the ways that growth and change in intellectual capabilities influence a person's behavior. (p. 6)

**cognitive neuroscience approaches** the approach that examines cognitive development through the lens of brain processes. (p. 18)

**cognitive perspective** the approach that focuses on the processes that allow people to know, understand, and think about the world. (p. 17)

**cohabitation** couples living together without being married. (p. 347)

**cohort** a group of people born at around the same time in the same place. (p. 8)

**collectivistic orientation** a philosophy that promotes the notion of interdependence. (p. 180)

**communal professions** occupations that are associated with relationships, such as nursing. (p. 354)

**companionate love** the strong affection for those with whom our lives are deeply involved. (p. 340)

**concrete operational stage** the period of cognitive development between 7 and 12 years of age, which is characterized by the active, and appropriate, use of logic. (p. 214)

**conservation** the knowledge that quantity is unrelated to the arrangement and physical appearance of objects. (p. 165)

**constructive play** play in which children manipulate objects to produce or build something. (p. 184)

**contextual perspective** the theory that considers the relationship between individuals and their physical, cognitive, personality, and social worlds. (p. 20)

**continuing-care community** a community that offers an environment in which all the residents are of retirement age or older. (p. 441)

**continuity theory** the theory suggesting that people need to maintain their desired level of involvement in society in order to maximize their sense of well-being and self-esteem. (p. 439)

**continuous change** gradual development in which achievements at one level build on those of previous levels. (p. 10)

**controversial adolescents** adolescents who are liked by some and disliked by others. (p. 298)

**cooperative play** play in which children genuinely interact with one another, taking turns, playing games, or devising contests. (p. 184)

**coping** the effort to control, reduce, or learn to tolerate the threats that lead to stress. (p. 318)

**coregulation** a period in which parents and children jointly control children's behavior. (p. 249)

**correlational research** research that seeks to identify whether an association or relationship between two factors exists. (p. 26)

**creativity** the combination of responses or ideas in novel ways. (p. 327)

**critical period** a specific time during development when a particular event has its greatest consequences and the presence of certain kinds of environmental stimuli are necessary for development to proceed normally. (p. 10)

**cross-sectional research** research in which people of different ages are compared at the same point in time. (p. 34)

**crowds** larger groups than cliques, composed of individuals who share particular characteristics but who may not interact with one another. (p. 297)

**crystallized intelligence** the accumulation of information, skills, and strategies that people have learned through experience and that they can apply in problem-solving situations. (pp. 227, 379)

**cultural assimilation model** the model in which the goal was to assimilate individual cultural identities into a unique, unified American culture. (p. 223)

**cycle of violence hypothesis** the theory that abuse and neglect of children leads them to be predisposed to abusiveness as adults. (pp. 189, 398)

**decentering** the ability to take multiple aspects of a situation into account. (p. 215)

**decision/commitment component** according to Steinberg the third aspect of love that embodies both the initial cognition that one loves another person and the longer-term determination to maintain that love. (p. 341)

**defensive coping** coping that involves unconscious strategies that distort or deny the true nature of a situation. (p. 320)

**dementia** the most common mental disorder of the elderly, it covers several diseases, each of which includes serious memory loss accompanied by declines in other mental functioning. (p. 419)

**dependent variable** the variable that researchers measure to see if it changes as a result of the experimental manipulation. (p. 30)

**developmental quotient** an overall developmental score that relates to performance in four domains: motor skills, language use, adaptive behavior, and personal-social. (p. 122)

**difficult babies** infants who have negative moods and are slow to adapt to new situations; when confronted with a new situation, they tend to withdraw. (p. 146)

**discontinuous change** development that occurs in distinct steps or stages, with each stage bringing about behavior that is assumed to be qualitatively different from behavior at earlier stages. (p. 10)

**disengagement theory** the period in late adulthood that marks a gradual withdrawal from the world on physical, psychological, and social levels. (p. 438)

**disorganized-disoriented attachment pattern** a style of attachment in which children show inconsistent, often contradictory behavior, such as approaching the mother when she returns but not looking at her; they may be the least securely attached children of all. (p. 141)

**dizygotic twins** twins who are produced when two separate ova are fertilized by two separate sperm at roughly the same time. (p. 44)

**DNA (deoxyribonucleic acid) molecules** the substance that genes are composed of that determines the nature of every cell in the body and how it will function. (p. 43)

**dominance hierarchy** rankings that represent the relative social power of those in a group. (p. 246)

**dominant trait** the one trait that is expressed when two competing traits are present. (p. 45)

**Down syndrome** a disorder produced by the presence of an extra chromosome on the 21st pair; once referred to as mongolism. (p. 48)

**easy babies** babies who have a positive disposition; their body functions operate regularly, and they are adaptable. (p. 146)

**ego transcendence versus ego preoccupation** the period in which elderly people must come to grips with their coming death. (p. 434)

**egocentric thought** thinking that does not take into account the viewpoints of others. (p. 165)

**ego-integrity-versus-despair stage** Erikson's final stage of life, characterized by a process of looking back over one's life, evaluating it, and coming to terms with it. (p. 433)

**elder abuse** the physical or psychological mistreatment or neglect of elderly individuals. (p. 453)

**embryonic stage** the period from 2 to 8 weeks following fertilization during which significant growth occurs in the major organs and body systems. (p. 60)

**emotional intelligence** the set of skills that underlie the accurate assessment, evaluation, expression, and regulation of emotions. (p. 326)

**emotional self-regulation** the capability to adjust emotions to a desired state and level of intensity. (p. 194)

**empathy** an emotional response that corresponds to the feelings of another person; the understanding of what another individual feels. (pp. 139, 193)

**empty nest syndrome** the experience that relates to parents' feelings of unhappiness, worry, loneliness, and depression resulting from their children's departure from home. (p. 395)

**enrichment** an approach through which students are kept at grade level but are enrolled in special programs and given individual activities to allow greater depth of study on a given topic. (p. 234)

**episiotomy** an incision sometimes made to increase the size of the opening of the vagina to allow the baby to pass. (p. 72)

**Erikson's theory of psychosocial development** the theory that considers how individuals come to understand themselves and the meaning of others'—and their own—behavior. (p. 145)

**euthanasia** the practice of assisting people who are terminally ill to die more quickly. (p. 469)

**evolutionary perspective** the theory that seeks to identify behavior that is a result of our genetic inheritance from our ancestors. (p. 22)

**executive stage** the period in middle adulthood when people take a broader perspective than earlier, including concerns about the world. (p. 324)

**experiment** a process in which an investigator, called an experimenter, devises two different experiences for participants. (p. 30)

**experimental research** research designed to discover causal relationships between various factors. (p. 26)

**expertise** the acquisition of skill or knowledge in a particular area. (p. 380)

**expressive style** a style of language use in which language is used primarily to express feelings and needs about oneself and others. (p. 131)

**extrinsic motivation** motivation that drives people to obtain tangible rewards, such as money and prestige. (p. 356)

**fantasy period** according to Ginzberg, the period, lasting until about age 11, when career choices are made, and discarded, without regard to skills, abilities, or available job opportunities. (p. 353)

**fast mapping** instances in which new words are associated with their meaning after only a brief encounter. (p. 173)

**female climacteric** the period that marks the transition from being able to bear children to being unable to do so. (p. 367)

**fertilization** the process by which a sperm and an ovum—the male and female gametes, respectively—join to form a single new cell. (p. 59)

**fetal alcohol effects (FAE)** a condition in which children display some, although not all, of the problems of fetal alcohol syndrome due to the mother's consumption of alcohol during pregnancy. (p. 68)

**fetal alcohol syndrome (FAS)** a disorder caused by the pregnant mother consuming substantial quantities of alcohol during pregnancy, potentially resulting in mental retardation and delayed growth in the child. (p. 68)

**fetal monitor** a device that measures the baby's heartbeat during labor. (p. 81)

**fetal stage** the stage that begins at about 8 weeks after conception and continues until birth. (p. 60)

**fetus** a developing child, from 8 weeks after conception until birth. (p. 60)

**field study** a research investigation carried out in a naturally occurring setting. (p. 31)

**first-year adjustment reaction** a cluster of psychological symptoms, including loneliness, anxiety, withdrawal, and depression, relating to the college experience suffered by first-year college students. (p. 331)

**fluid intelligence** intelligence that reflects information processing capabilities, reasoning, and memory. (pp. 227, 379)

**formal operational stage** the stage at which people develop the ability to think abstractly. (p. 274)

**Fragile X syndrome** a disorder produced by injury to a gene on the X chromosome, producing mild to moderate mental retardation. (p. 48)

**functional death** the absence of a heartbeat and breathing. (p. 459)

**functional play** play that involves simple, repetitive activities typical of 3-year-olds. (p. 184)

**gender** the sense of being male or female. (p. 147)

**gender constancy** the belief that people are permanently males or females, depending on fixed, unchangeable biological factors. (p. 182)

**gender identity** the perception of oneself as male or female. (p. 182)

**gender schema** a cognitive framework that organizes information relevant to gender. (p. 182)

**generalized slowing hypothesis** the theory that processing in all parts of the nervous system, including the brain, is less efficient as we age. (p. 415)

**generation gap** a divide between parents and adolescents in attitudes, values, aspirations, and world views. (p. 295)

**generativity-versus-stagnation** according to Erikson, the stage during middle adulthood in which people consider their contributions to family and society. (p. 385)

**genes** the basic unit of genetic information. (p. 43)

**genetic counseling** the discipline that focuses on helping people deal with issues relating to inherited disorders. (p. 48)

**genetic programming theories of aging** theories that suggest that our body's DNA genetic code contains a built-in time limit for the reproduction of human cells. (p. 422)

**genotype** the underlying combination of genetic material present (but not outwardly visible) in an organism. (p. 45)

**germinal stage** the first—and shortest—stage of the prenatal period, which takes place during the first 2 weeks following conception. (p. 60)

**gerontologists** specialists who study aging. (p. 410)

**gifted and talented** children who show evidence of high performance capability in areas such as intellectual, creative, artistic, leadership capacity, or specific academic fields. (p. 233)

**glaucoma** a condition in which pressure in the fluid of the eye increases, either because the fluid cannot drain properly or because too much fluid is produced. (p. 364)

**goodness-of-fit** the notion that development is dependent on the degree of match between children's temperament and the nature and demands of the environment in which they are being raised. (p. 146)

**grammar** the system of rules that determine how our thoughts can be expressed. (p. 174)

**grief** the emotional response to one's loss. (p. 474)

**habituation** the decrease in the response to a stimulus that occurs after repeated presentations of the same stimulus. (p. 87)

**handedness** the preference of using one hand over another. (p. 163)

**hardiness** a personality characteristic associated with a lower rate of stress-related illness. (p. 320)

**heterozygous** inheriting from parents different forms of a gene for a given trait. (p. 45)

**holophrases** one-word utterances that stand for a whole phrase, the meaning of which depends on the particular context in which they are used. (p. 129)

**home care** an alternative to hospitalization in which dying people stay in their homes and receive treatment from their families and visiting medical staff. (p. 472)

**homogamy** the tendency to marry someone who is similar in age, race, education, religion, and other basic demographic characteristics. (p. 344)

**homozygous** inheriting from parents similar genes for a given trait. (p. 45)

**hospice care** care provided for the dying in institutions devoted to those who are terminally ill. (p. 472)

**humanistic perspective** the theory that contends that people have a natural capacity to make decisions about their lives and control their behavior. (p. 20)

**hypothesis** a prediction stated in a way that permits it to be tested. (p. 26)

**identity achievement** the status of adolescents who commit to a particular identity following a period of crisis during which they consider various alternatives. (p. 288)

**identity diffusion** the status of adolescents who consider various identity alternatives, but never commit to one or never even consider identity options in any conscious way. (p. 289)

**identity foreclosure** the status of adolescents who prematurely commit to an identity without adequately exploring alternatives. (p. 288)

**identity-versus-identity-confusion stage** the period during which teenagers seek to determine what is unique and distinctive about themselves. (p. 287)

**imaginary audience** an adolescent's belief that his or her own behavior is a primary focus of others' attention and concerns. (p. 277)

**in vitro fertilization (IVF)** a procedure in which a woman's ova are removed from her ovaries, and a man's sperm are used to fertilize the ova in a laboratory. (p. 62)

**independent variable** the variable that researchers manipulate in an experiment. (p. 30)

**individualistic orientation** a philosophy that emphasizes personal identity and the uniqueness of the individual. (p. 180)

**industry-versus-inferiority stage** according to Erikson the period from age 6 to 12 characterized by a focus on efforts to attain competence in meeting the challenges presented by parents, peers, school, and the other complexities of the modern world. (p. 236)

**infant mortality** death within the first year of life. (p. 82)

**infant-directed speech** a type of speech directed toward infants, characterized by short, simple sentences. (p. 132)

**infantile amnesia** the lack of memory for experiences that occurred prior to 3 years of age. (p. 123)

**infertility** the inability to conceive after 12 to 18 months of trying to become pregnant. (p. 62)

**information processing approaches** the model that seeks to identify the ways individuals take in, use, and store information. (p. 18)

**information processing perspective** the model that seeks to identify the way that individuals take in, use, and store information. (p. 276)

**initiative-versus-guilt stage** according to Erikson, the period during which children aged 3 to 6 years experience conflict between independence of action and the sometimes negative results of that action. (p. 179)

**institutionalism** a psychological state in which people in nursing homes develop apathy, indifference, and a lack of caring about themselves. (p. 442)

**instrumental aggression** aggression motivated by the desire to obtain a concrete goal. (p. 194)

**intelligence** the capacity to understand the world, think with rationality, and use resources effectively when faced with challenges. (p. 225)

**intelligence quotient (or IQ score)** a score that accounts for a student's mental *and* chronological age. (p. 226)

**intimacy component** according to Steinberg the component of love that encompasses feelings of closeness, affection, and connectedness. (p. 341)

**intimacy-versus-isolation stage** according to Erikson, the period of postadolescence into the early 30s that focuses on developing close, intimate relationships with others. (p. 338)

**intrinsic motivation** motivation that causes people to work for their own enjoyment. (p. 356)

**intuitive thought** thinking that reflects preschoolers' use of primitive reasoning and their avid acquisition of knowledge about the world. (p. 167)

**Kaufman Assessment Battery for Children, Second Edition (KABC-II)** an intelligence test that measures children's ability to integrate different stimuli simultaneously and to use sequential thinking. (p. 227)

**Klinefelter's syndrome** a disorder resulting from the presence of an extra X chromosome that produces underdeveloped genitals, extreme height, and enlarged breasts. (p. 48)

**labeling theory of passionate love** the theory that individuals experience romantic love when two events occur together: intense physiological arousal and situational cues suggesting that the arousal is due to love. (p. 341)

**laboratory study** a research investigation conducted in a controlled setting explicitly designed to hold events constant. (p. 32)

**language** the systematic, meaningful arrangement of symbols, which provides the basis for communication. (p. 127)

**language-acquisition device (LAD)** a neural system of the brain hypothesized to permit understanding of language. (p. 131)

**lateralization** the process in which certain cognitive functions are located more in one hemisphere of the brain than in the other. (p. 159)

**learning disabilities** difficulties in the acquisition and use of listening, speaking, reading, writing, reasoning, or mathematical abilities. (p. 211)

**learning theory approach** the theory that language acquisition follows the basic laws of reinforcement and conditioning. (p. 131)

**least restrictive environment** the setting that is most similar to that of children without special needs. (p. 232)

**life events models** the approach to personality development that is based on the timing of particular events in an adult's life rather than on age per se. (p. 385)

**life expectancy** the average age of death for members of a population. (p. 423)

**life review** the point in life in which people examine and evaluate their lives. (p. 436)

**lifespan development** the field of study that examines patterns of growth, change, and stability in behavior that occur throughout the entire life span. (p. 5)

**living wills** legal documents designating what medical treatments people want or do not want if they cannot express their wishes. (p. 469)

**longitudinal research** research in which the behavior of one or more participants in a study is measured as they age. (p. 32)

**low-birthweight infants** infants who weigh less than 2,500 grams (around 5½ pounds) at birth. (p. 78)

**mainstreaming** an educational approach in which exceptional children are integrated to the extent possible into the traditional educational system and are provided with a broad range of educational alternatives. (p. 232)

**male climacteric** the period of physical and psychological change relating to the male reproductive system that occurs during late middle age. (p. 369)

**marriage gradient** the tendency for men to marry women who are slightly younger, smaller, and lower in status, and women to marry men who are slightly older, larger, and higher in status. (p. 344)

**maturation** the predetermined unfolding of genetic information. (p. 11)

**memory** the process by which information is initially recorded, stored, and retrieved. (pp. 122, 216)

**menarche** the onset of menstruation. (p. 259)

**menopause** the cessation of menstruation. (p. 368)

**mental age** the typical intelligence level found for people at a given chronological age. (p. 226)

**mental retardation (intellectual disability)** a significantly subaverage level of intellectual functioning that occurs with related limitations in two or more skill areas. (p. 233)

**metacognition** the knowledge that people have about their own thinking processes, and their ability to monitor their cognition. (p. 276)

**metalinguistic awareness** an understanding of one's own use of language. (p. 219)

**metamemory** an understanding about the processes that underlie memory, which emerges and improves during middle childhood. (p. 217)

**midlife crisis** a stage of uncertainty and indecision brought about by the realization that life is finite. (p. 386)

**mild retardation** retardation in which IQ scores fall in the range of 50 or 55 to 70. (p. 233)

**mnemonics** formal strategies for organizing material in ways that make it more likely to be remembered. (p. 383)

**moderate retardation** retardation in which IQ scores range from around 35 or 40 to 50 or 55. (p. 233)

**monozygotic twins** twins who are genetically identical. (p. 44)

**moral development** the changes in people's sense of justice and of what is right and wrong, and in their behavior related to moral issues. (p. 192)

**moratorium** the status of adolescents who may have explored various identity alternatives to some degree, but have not yet committed themselves. (p. 289)

**multicultural education** a form of education in which the goal is to help minority students develop confidence in the culture of the majority group while maintaining positive group identities that build on their original cultures. (p. 224)

**multifactorial transmission** the determination of traits by a combination of both genetic and environmental factors in which a genotype provides a range within which a phenotype may be expressed. (p. 51)

**multimodal approach to perception** the approach that considers how information that is collected by various individual sensory systems is integrated and coordinated. (p. 112)

**myelin** covering which speeds the transmission of electrical impulses along brain cells but also adds to brain weight. (pp. 98, 159)

**nativist approach** the theory that a genetically determined, innate mechanism directs language development. (p. 131)

**naturalistic observation** a type of correlational study in which some naturally occurring behavior is observed without intervention in the situation. (p. 28)

**neglected adolescents** children who receive relatively little attention from their peers in the form of either positive or negative interactions. (p. 298)

**neonates** the term used for newborns. (p. 71)

**neuron** the basic nerve cell of the nervous system. (p. 96)

**nonorganic failure** a disorder in which infants stop growing due to a lack of stimulation and attention as the result of inadequate parenting. (p. 107)

**normative-crisis models** the approach to personality development that is based on fairly universal stages tied to a sequence of age-related crises. (p. 385)

**norms** the average performance of a large sample of children of a given age. (p. 105)

**obesity** body weight more than 20 percent higher than the average weight for a person of a given age and height. (p. 157)

**object permanence** the realization that people and objects exist even when they cannot be seen. (p. 117)

**onlooker play** action in which children simply watch others at play, but do not actually participate themselves. (p. 184)

**operant conditioning** a form of learning in which a voluntary response is strengthened or weakened by its association with positive or negative consequences. (pp. 16, 47)

**operations** organized, formal, logical mental processes. (p. 164)

**osteoporosis** a condition in which the bones become brittle, fragile, and thin, often brought about by a lack of calcium in the diet. (pp. 363, 414)

**overextension** the overly broad use of words, overgeneralizing their meaning. (p. 130)

**parallel play** action in which children play with similar toys, in a similar manner, but do not interact with each other. (p. 184)

**passion component** according to Steinberg the component of love that comprises the motivational drives relating to sex, physical closeness, and romance. (p. 341)

**passionate (or romantic) love** a state of powerful absorption in someone. (p. 340)

**peer pressure** the influence of one's peers to conform to their behavior and attitudes. (p. 298)

**perception** the sorting out, interpretation, analysis, and integration of stimuli involving the sense organs and brain. (p. 110)

**peripheral slowing hypothesis** the theory that suggests that overall processing speed declines in the peripheral nervous system with increasing age. (p. 415)

**permissive parents** parents who provide lax and inconsistent feedback and require little of their children. (p. 187)

**personal fables** the view held by some adolescents that what happens to them is unique, exceptional, and shared by no one else. (p. 277)

**personality** the sum total of the enduring characteristics that differentiate one individual from another. (p. 144)

**personality development** development involving the ways that the enduring characteristics that differentiate one person from another change over the life span. (p. 6)

**phenotype** an observable trait; the trait that actually is seen. (p. 45)

**physical development** development involving the body's physical makeup, including the brain, nervous system, muscles, and senses, and the need for food, drink, and sleep. (p. 6)

**placenta** a conduit between the mother and fetus, providing nourishment and oxygen via the umbilical cord. (p. 60)

**plasticity** the degree to which a developing structure or behavior is modifiable due to experience. (pp. 98, 427)

**pluralistic society model** the concept that American society is made up of diverse, coequal cultural groups that should preserve their individual cultural features. (p. 223)

**polygenic inheritance** inheritance in which a combination of multiple gene pairs is responsible for the production of a particular trait. (p. 46)

**postformal thought** thinking that acknowledges that adult predicaments must sometimes be solved in relativistic terms. (p. 323)

**postmature infants** infants still unborn 2 weeks after the mother's due date. (p. 80)

**practical intelligence** according to Sternberg, intelligence that is learned primarily by observing others and modeling their behavior. (p. 326)

**pragmatics** the aspect of language that relates to communicating effectively and appropriately with others. (p. 175)

**preoperational stage** according to Piaget, the stage from approximately age 2 to age 7 in which children's use of symbolic thinking grows, mental reasoning emerges, and the use of concepts increases. (p. 164)

**presbycusis** loss of the ability to hear sounds of high frequency. (p. 364)

**presbyopia** a nearly universal change in eyesight during middle adulthood that results in some loss of near vision. (p. 364)

**preterm infants** infants who are born prior to 38 weeks after conception (also known as premature infants). (p. 78)

**primary aging** aging that involves universal and irreversible changes that, due to genetic programming, occur as people get older. (p. 413)

**primary appraisal** the assessment of an event to determine whether its implications are positive, negative, or neutral. (p. 317)

**primary sex characteristics** characteristics associated with the development of the organs and structures of the body that directly relate to reproduction. (p. 260)

**principle of hierarchical integration** the principle that simple skills typically develop separately and independently but are later integrated into more complex skills. (p. 96)

**principle of the independence of systems** the principle that different body systems grow at different rates. (p. 96)

**private speech** speech by children that is spoken and directed to themselves. (p. 174)

**profound retardation** retardation in which IQ scores fall below 20 or 25. (p. 233)

**prosocial behavior** helping behavior that benefits others. (p. 192)

**proximodistal principle** the principle that development proceeds from the center of the body outward. (p. 95)

**psychoanalytic theory** the theory proposed by Freud that suggests that unconscious forces act to determine personality and behavior. (p. 13)

**psychodynamic perspective** the approach that states behavior is motivated by inner forces, memories, and conflicts that are generally beyond people's awareness and control. (p. 13)

**psychological maltreatment** abuse that occurs when parents or other caregivers harm children's behavioral, cognitive, emotional, or physical functioning. (p. 189)

**psychoneuroimmunology (PNI)** the study of the relationship among the brain, the immune system, and psychological factors. (p. 317)

**psychophysiological methods** research that focuses on the relationship between physiological processes and behavior. (p. 28)

**psychosexual development** according to Freud, a series of stages that children pass through in which pleasure, or gratification, is focused on a particular biological function and body part. (p. 13)

**psychosocial development** according to Erikson, development that encompasses changes both in the understandings individuals have of themselves as members of society and in their comprehension of the meaning of others' behavior. (pp. 14, 179)

**psychosomatic disorders** medical problems caused by the interaction of psychological, emotional, and physical difficulties. (p. 318)

**puberty** the period during which the sexual organs mature. (p. 259)

**race dissonance** the phenomenon in which minority children indicate preferences for majority values or people. (p. 180)

**rapid eye movement (REM) sleep** the period of sleep that is found in older children and adults and is associated with dreaming. (p. 100)

**realistic period** the third stage of Ginzberg's theory, which occurs in early adulthood, when people begin to explore specific career options, either through actual experience on the job or through training for a profession, and then narrow their choices and make a commitment. (p. 353)

**recessive trait** a trait within an organism that is present, but is not expressed. (p. 45)

**redefinition of self versus preoccupation with work role** the theory that those in old age must redefine themselves in ways that do not relate to their work roles or occupations. (p. 434)

**reference groups** groups of people with whom one compares oneself. (p. 297)

**referential style** a style of language use in which language is used primarily to label objects. (p. 131)

**reflexes** unlearned, organized involuntary responses that occur automatically in the presence of certain stimuli. (pp. 84, 103)

**reintegrative stage** the period of late adulthood during which the focus is on tasks that have personal meaning. (p. 325)

**rejected adolescents** children who are actively disliked, and whose peers may react to them in an obviously negative manner. (p. 298)

**relational aggression** nonphysical aggression that is intended to hurt another person's psychological well-being. (p. 194)

**resilience** the ability to overcome circumstances that place a child at high risk for psychological or physical damage. (p. 190)

**responsible stage** the stage where the major concerns of middle-aged adults relate to their personal situations, including protecting and nourishing their spouses, families, and careers. (p. 324)

**rhythms** repetitive, cyclical patterns of behavior. (p. 99)

**sample** the group of participants chosen for the experiment. (p. 31)

**sandwich generation** couples in middle adulthood who must fulfill the needs of both their children and their aging parents. (p. 396)

**scaffolding** the support for learning and problem solving that encourages independence and growth. (p. 171)

**schemas** organized bodies of information stored in memory. (p. 382)

**scheme** an organized pattern of sensorimotor functioning. (p. 115)

**scientific method** the process of posing and answering questions using careful, controlled techniques that include systematic, orderly observation and the collection of data. (p. 25)

**scripts** broad representations in memory of events and the order in which they occur. (p. 169)

**secondary aging** changes in physical and cognitive functioning that are due to illness, health habits, and other individual differences, but are not due to increased age itself and are not inevitable. (p. 413)

**secondary appraisal** the assessment of whether one's coping abilities and resources are adequate to overcome the harm, threat, or challenge posed by the potential stressor. (p. 317)

**secondary sex characteristics** the visible signs of sexual maturity that do not directly involve the sex organs. (p. 260)

**secular trend** a pattern of change occurring over several generations. (p. 260)

**secure attachment pattern** a style of attachment in which children use the mother as a kind of home base and are at ease when she is present; when she leaves, they become upset and go to her as soon as she returns. (p. 141)

**selective optimization** the process by which people concentrate on particular skill areas to compensate for losses in other areas. (pp. 380, 440)

**self-awareness** knowledge of oneself. (p. 138)

**self-care children** children who let themselves into their homes after school and wait alone until their caretakers return from work; previously known as *latchkey children*. (p. 249)

**self-concept** a person's identity, or set of beliefs about what one is like as an individual. (p. 179)

**self-esteem** an individual's overall and specific positive and negative self-evaluation. (p. 237)

**senescence** the natural physical decline brought about by aging. (p. 311)

**sensation** the physical stimulation of the sense organs. (p. 110)

**sensitive period** a specific, but limited, time, usually early in an organism's life, during which the organism is particularly susceptible to environmental influences relating to some particular facet of development. (pp. 10, 98)

**sensorimotor stage** Piaget's initial major stage of cognitive development, which can be broken down into six substages. (p. 116)

**separation anxiety** the distress displayed by infants when a customary care provider departs. (p. 136)

**sequential studies** research in which researchers examine a number of different age groups over several points in time. (p. 34)

**severe retardation** retardation in which IQ scores range from around 20 or 25 to 35 or 40. (p. 233)

**sex cleavage** sex segregation in which boys interact primarily with boys and girls primarily with girls. (p. 297)

**sexually transmitted infection (STI)** a infection that is spread through sexual contact. (p. 271)

**sickle-cell anemia** a blood disorder that gets its name from the shape of the red blood cells in those who have it. (p. 48)

**skilled-nursing facilities** a facility that provides full-time nursing care for people who have chronic illnesses or are recovering from a temporary medical condition. (p. 442)

**slow-to-warm babies** infants who are inactive, showing relatively calm reactions to their environment; their moods are generally negative, and they withdraw from new situations, adapting slowly. (p. 146)

**small-for-gestational-age infants** infants who, because of delayed fetal growth, weigh 90 percent (or less) of the average weight of infants of the same gestational age. (p. 78)

**social competence** the collection of social skills that permit individuals to perform successfully in social settings. (p. 244)

**social development** the way in which individuals' interactions with others and their social relationships grow, change, and remain stable over the course of life. (p. 6)

**social problem-solving** the use of strategies for solving social conflicts in ways that are satisfactory both to oneself and to others. (p. 244)

**social referencing** the intentional search for information about others' feelings to help explain the meaning of uncertain circumstances and events. (p. 138)

**social speech** speech directed toward another person and meant to be understood by that person. (p. 175)

**social support** assistance and comfort supplied by another person or a network of caring, interested people. (p. 450)

**social-cognitive learning theory** learning by observing the behavior of another person, called a model. (p. 16)

**socialized delinquents** adolescent delinquents who know and subscribe to the norms of society and who are fairly normal psychologically. (p. 300)

**sociocultural theory** the approach that emphasizes how cognitive development proceeds as a result of social interactions between members of a culture. (p. 22)

**speech impairment**   speech that deviates so much from the speech of others that it calls attention to itself, interferes with communication, or produces maladjustment in the speaker. (p. 211)

**Stanford-Binet Intelligence Scales, Fifth Edition (SB5)**   a test that consists of a series of items that vary according to the age of the person being tested. (p. 227)

**state**   the degree of awareness an infant displays to both internal and external stimulation. (p. 99)

**states of arousal**   different degrees of sleep and wakefulness through which newborns cycle, ranging from deep sleep to great agitation. (p. 88)

**status**   the evaluation of a role or person by other relevant members of a group. (pp. 244, 356)

**stereotype threat**   obstacles to performance that come from awareness of the stereotypes held by society about academic abilities. (p. 335)

**stillbirth**   the delivery of a child who is not alive, occurring in fewer than 1 delivery in 100. (p. 82)

**stimulus-value-role (SVR) theory**   the theory that relationships proceed in a fixed order of three stages: stimulus, value, and role. (p. 340)

**stranger anxiety**   the caution and wariness displayed by infants when encountering an unfamiliar person. (p. 136)

**stress**   the physical and emotional response to events that threaten or challenge us. (p. 317)

**stuttering**   substantial disruption in the rhythm and fluency of speech; the most common speech impairment. (p. 211)

**sudden infant death syndrome (SIDS)**   the unexplained death of a seemingly healthy baby. (pp. 100, 460)

**survey research**   a type of study where a group of people chosen to represent some larger population are asked questions about their attitudes, behavior, or thinking on a given topic. (p. 28)

**synapse**   the gap at the connection between neurons, through which neurons chemically communicate with one another. (p. 96)

**synaptic pruning**   the elimination of neurons as the result of nonuse or lack of stimulation. (p. 98)

**syntax**   the way in which an individual combines words and phrases to form sentences. (p. 173)

**Tay-Sachs disease**   a disorder that produces blindness and muscle degeneration prior to death; there is no treatment. (p. 48)

**telegraphic speech**   speech in which words not critical to the message are left out. (p. 129)

**temperament**   patterns of arousal and emotionality that represent consistent and enduring characteristics in an individual. (pp. 51, 145)

**tentative period**   the second stage of Ginzberg's theory, which spans adolescence, when people begin to think more practically about the requirements of various jobs and how their own abilities might fit with them. (p. 353)

**teratogen**   a factor that produces a birth defect. (p. 65)

**thanatologists**   people who study death and dying. (p. 464)

**theoretical research**   research designed specifically to test some developmental explanation and expand scientific knowledge. (p. 32)

**theories**   broad explanations and predictions concerning phenomena of interest, providing a framework for understanding the relationships among an organized set of facts or principles. (pp. 12, 25)

**theory of mind**   knowledge and beliefs about how the mind works and how it affects behavior. (p. 138)

**transformation**   the process in which one state is changed into another. (p. 165)

**triarchic theory of intelligence**   Sternberg's model which states that intelligence consists of three aspects of information processing: the componential element, the experiential element, and the contextual element. (pp. 230, 326)

**trust-versus-mistrust stage**   according to Erikson, the period during which infants develop a sense of trust or mistrust, largely depending on how well their needs are met by their caregivers. (p. 145)

**Type A behavior pattern**   behavior characterized by competitiveness, impatience, and a tendency toward frustration and hostility. (p. 374)

**Type B behavior pattern**   behavior characterized by noncompetitiveness, patience, and a lack of aggression. (p. 374)

**ultrasound sonography**   a process in which high-frequency sound waves scan the mother's womb to produce an image of the unborn baby, whose size and shape can then be assessed. (p. 49)

**underextension**   the overly restrictive use of words, common among children just mastering spoken language. (p. 130)

**undersocialized delinquents**   adolescent delinquents who are raised with little discipline or with harsh, uncaring parental supervision. (p. 300)

**uninvolved parents**   parents who show almost no interest in their children and indifferent, rejecting behavior. (p. 187)

**universal grammar**   Noam Chomsky's theory that all the world's languages share a similar underlying structure. (p. 131)

**very-low-birthweight infants**   infants who weigh less than 1,250 grams (around 2.25 pounds) or, regardless of weight, have been in the womb less than 30 weeks. (p. 78)

**visual impairment**   a difficulty in seeing that may include blindness or partial sightedness. (p. 210)

**wear-and-tear theories of aging**   the theory that the mechanical functions of the body simply wear out with age. (p. 422)

**Wechsler Intelligence Scale for Children, Fourth Edition (WISC-IV)**   a test for children that provides separate measures of verbal and performance (or nonverbal) skills, as well as a total score. (p. 227)

**wisdom**   expert knowledge in the practical aspects of life. (p. 437)

**X-linked genes**   genes that are considered recessive and located only on the X chromosome. (p. 46)

**zone of proximal development (ZPD)**   according to Vygotsky, the level at which a child can almost, but not fully, perform a task independently, but can do so with the assistance of someone more competent. (p. 171)

**zygote**   the new cell formed by the process of fertilization. (p. 43)

# Credits

## Photographs

**Front matter** Page i (centre, right) Michael Newman/PhotoEdit; (centre, left) Laura Dwight/Stock Connection Distribution / Alamy; p. ii (top, left) Peter Cade/Iconica/Getty Images; (bottom, right) Moment / Alamy; p. iii Woodfin Camp & Associates, Inc.; p. vii Monkey Business Images/Shutterstock; p. ix Exactostock / SuperStock; p. x iStockphoto/Thinkstock; p. xi Jupiterimages/Goodshoot/Thinkstock; p. xii Kablonk / Purestock / SuperStock; p. xvi Jstudio/Dreamstime.com.

**Chapter 1** Page 2 AP Photo/Alastair Grant; INTERFOTO/Alamy; p. 3 Exactostock/SuperStock; Loisjoy Thurstun/Bubbles Photolibrary/Alamy; p. 4 67photo/Alamy; p. 7 Ben Edwards/Imagestate Media Partners Limited - Impact Photos/Alamy; p. 12 Bettmann/CORBIS; p. 13 Photo Researchers/Alamy; p. 15 Library of Congress; p. 16 Hulton Archive/Archive Photos/Getty Images; p. 17 Photofest; p. 18 Dr. Eric Courchesne; p. 22 Eddie Lawrence/Dorling Kindersley; p. 23 Nina Leen/Time Life Pictures/Getty Images; p. 28 Volker Steger/Peter Arnold Images/PhotoLibrary ; p. 32 Photolibrary.com ; p. 38 Exactostock/SuperStock; p. 39 (bottom, right) Asia Images Group/Getty Images; (top, right) Jim Esposito Photography L.L.C./Photodisc/Getty Images; (centre, right) Photodisc/Getty Images; (bottom, left) Mel Yates/Cultura/Getty Images.

**Chapter 2** Page 40 (top, left) Chad Ehlers / Alamy; (bottom, right) age fotostock / SuperStock; p. 41 (top, right) Andersen Ross/Blend Images/Getty Images; (bottom, left) AP Photo/Al Goldis; p. 43 (top, right) Frank Geisler/DocCheck Medical Services GmbH / Alamy; (centre, right) Custom Medical Stock Photo/Newscom; (bottom, left) MartinShields / Alamy; (centre, left) Don W. Fawcett / Photo Researchers, Inc.; p. 48 Eye of Science / Photo Researchers, Inc.; p. 49 Sally and Richard Greenhill / Alamy; p. 55 (top, right) Comstock / Thinkstock; (centre, right) Mark Cator/Imagestate Media Partners Limited - Impact Photos / Alamy; p. 61 (top, left) Photo Researchers, Inc.; (top, centre) Science Pictures Ltd. / Photo Researchers, Inc.; (top, right) Photo Researchers, Inc.; p. 69 Chris Harvey/Stone/Getty Images; p. 70 AP Photo/Al Goldis; p. 73 (bottom, right) George Lamson/Shutterstock; (centre, right) Jennie Woodcock/Encyclopedia/CORBIS; p. 75 (top, right) Purestock / Alamy; (bottom, right) Molly Schlachter/Pearson Education/PH College; p. 79 John Cole / Photo Researchers, Inc.; p. 81 Brian Gordon Green/National Geographic Image Collection / Alamy; p. 85 (centre, right) Corbis Premium RF / Alamy; (top, right) Geri Engberg Photography; p. 90 Andersen Ross/Blend Images/Getty Images; p. 91 (bottom, right) Rob Lewine/Image Source; (top, right) Photodisc/Getty Images; (centre, right) Mark Andersen/Rubberball/Getty Images; (centre, right) Jose Luis Pelaez Inc/Blend Images/Getty Images.

**Chapter 3** Page 92 (bottom, right) Bob Ebbesen/Alamy; (Centre, left) Simon Ritter/Alamy; p. 93 (bottom, left) dbimages/Alamy; (top, right) Monkey Business Images/Shutterstock; p. 94 Purestock/Getty Images; p. 99 Justin Guariglia/National Geographic; p. 104 (top, left) Laura Elliott/Jupiter Images; (top, centre) Woodfin Camp & Associates, Inc.; (top, right) Petit Format/Photo Researchers, Inc.; p. 106 Simon Balson/Alamy; p. 110 (bottom, left) Mark Richards/PhotoEdit; (top, left) Tim Ridley/Dorling Kindersley; p. 111 Creative Eye/MIRA.com; p. 112 Jupiterimages/Thinkstock; p. 113 Monkey Business Images/Shutterstock; p. 114 Alain Schroeder/Getty Images; p. 115 Bettmann/CORBIS; p. 119 Brocreative/Shutterstock; thoron/Shutterstock; p. 123 Atlaspix/Alamy; p. 127 Geri Engberg Photography; p. 129 Jennie Hart/Alamy; p. 130 (centre, left) Angela Hampton/Angela Hampton Picture Library/Alamy; (centre, right) Earl & Nazima Kowall/Documentary Value/CORBIS; (centre) Panos Pictures; p. 134 Steve Nagy/Design Pics Inc./Alamy; p. 136 (top) Dr. Carroll Izard; (bottom, left) Michael Newman/PhotoEdit; p. 137 Laura Dwight Photography; p. 142 Ruth Jenkinson/Dorling Kindersley; p. 143 Larry Williams/Flirt/CORBIS; p. 148 Brand X Pictures/Thinkstock; p. 149 Bob Ebbesen/Alamy; p. 152 Monkey Business Images/Shutterstock; p. 153 (top, right) Photodisc/Getty Images; (centre, right) Mark Andersen/Rubberball/Getty Images; (centre, right) Jose Luis Pelaez Inc/Blend Images/Getty Images; (bottom, right) Asia Images Group/Getty Images.

**Chapter 4** Page 154 Vladimir Godnik/Beyond Fotomedia GmbH/Alamy; (center, left) Geostock/Photodisc/Getty Images; p. 155 (top, center) Jstudio/Dreamstime.com; (bottom, left) © Lawrence Migdale/Pix; p. 156 Ghislain & Marie David de Lossy/Cultura/Alamy; p. 158 (top, left) Pedro Luz Cunha/Alamy; (center, left) David McGlynn/Taxi/Getty Images; p. 162 (center, left) scully scully/Imagebroker.net/PhotoLibrary; (bottom, left) Gondwana Photo Art/Alamy; p. 164 Vladimir Godnik/Beyond Fotomedia GmbH/Alamy; p. 169 (top, right) Alex Melnick/Shutterstock; (center, right) Rob Crandall/SCPhotos/Alamy; p. 170 Sovfoto/Eastfoto; p. 179 David R. Frazier Photolibrary, Inc./Alamy; p. 181 (top, right) Laura Dwight Photography; (center, right) Photo Researchers, Inc.; p. 183 Richard Hutchings/PhotoEdit; p. 184 ©Lawrence Migdale/Pix; p. 186 (bottom, left) SW Productions/Design Pics Inc./Alamy; p. 188 AP Photo/Department of Social Services, Cindy Loo; p. 190 AP Photo/Come Alive New Testament Church; p. 192 Stanley Fellerman/Corbis; p. 194 (top, left) Richard Hutchings/PhotoEdit; (center, left) Bill Aron/PhotoEdit; p. 195 Albert Bandura, Stanford University; p. 198 Jstudio/Dreamstime.com; p. 199 (top, right) Jim Esposito Photography L.L.C./Photodisc/Getty Images; (center, right) Photodisc/Getty Images; (center, right) Asia Images Group/Getty Images; (bottom, right) Mel Yates/Cultura/Getty Images.

**Chapter 5** Page 200 (bottom, right) Con Tanasiuk/Design Pics Inc. / Alamy; (centre, left) George Doyle/Stockbyte/Getty Images; p. 201 (top, right) Mike Kemp/Rubberball/Getty Images; (bottom, left) Stephen Flint/ Alamy; p. 202 George Doyle/Stockbyte/Getty Images; p. 203 Jeff Greenberg / The Image Works; p. 204 Woodfin Camp & Associates, Inc.; p. 206 Myrleen Pearson / Alamy; p. 208 Leila Cutler / Alamy; p. 210 Michael Newman / PhotoEdit; p. 214 Con Tanasiuk/Design Pics Inc. / Alamy; p. 215 Ryan McVay/Digital Vision/Thinkstock; p. 217 Jonathan A. Meyers/Stock Connection Distribution / Alamy; p. 222 JORGEN SCHYTTE/Still Pictures/PhotoLibrary; p. 224 Sally Greenhill/Sally and Richard Greenhill / Alamy; p. 226 Laura Dwight Photography; p. 231 Kevin R. Morris/Documentary Value/CORBIS; p. 232 Photo Researchers, Inc.; p. 235 Peter Mason/Cultura / Alamy; p. 236 Corbis Super RF / Alamy; p. 237 Merritt Vincent / PhotoEdit; p. 238 Richard Lord / The Image Works; p. 243 Jupiterimages/Thinkstock; p. 244 Angela Hampton/Bubbles Photolibrary / Alamy; p. 247 jackhollingsworthcom/Shutterstock.com; p. 249 Ian West/Bubbles Photolibrary / Alamy; p. 251 Denise Hager/Catchlight Visual Services / Alamy; p. 252 (centre, left) Elly Godfroy / Alamy; (top, left) Photo Collection Alexander Alland, Sr./Historical/CORBIS; p. 254 Mike Kemp/Rubberball/Getty Images; p. 255 (top, right) Jim Esposito Photography L.L.C./Photodisc/Getty Images; (centre, right) Photodisc/Getty Images; (centre, right) Asia Images Group/Getty Images;(bottom, right) Mel Yates/Cultura/Getty Images.

**Chapter 6** Page 256 (bottom, right) Wesley Hitt/Alamy; (centre, left) David Young-Wolff/PhotoEdit; p. 257 (top, right) iStockphoto/Thinkstock; (bottom, left)Tony Freeman/PhotoEdit; p. 258 Sally and Richard Greenhill/Alamy; p. 261 (top, left) Mark Edward Atkinson/Tetra Images/Alamy; (top, centre) Radius Images/Alamy; p. 264 Dorling Kindersley Media Library; p. 265 Angela Hampton/Bubbles Photolibrary/Alamy; p. 266 Syracuse Newspapers/John Berry/The Image Works; p. 268 ACE STOCK LIMITED/Alamy; p. 273 Wesley Hitt/Alamy; p. 275 Denise Hager/Catchlight Visual Services/ Alamy; p. 276 John Maier Jr/Lonely Planet Images/Alamy; p. 278 Picture Partners/Alamy; p. 284 Tony Freeman/PhotoEdit; p. 285 Alex Gregory/The New Yorker/Cartoon Bank; p. 289 Picture Partners/Alamy; p. 290 Richard Hutchings/PhotoEdit; p. 292 CLEO PHOTOGRAPHY/PhotoEdit; p. 294 Peter Turnley/CORBIS; p. 297 Adrian Sherratt/Alamy; p. 298 Richard T. Nowitz/Photo Researchers, Inc.; p. 300 Bobby Deal/RealDealPhoto/Shutterstock; p. 304 Jacky Chapman/Janine Wiedel Photolibrary/Alamy; p. 306 iStockphoto/Thinkstock; p. 307 (center & top, right) Photodisc/Getty Images; (center, right) Rob Lewine/Image Source; (bottom, right) Jose Luis Pelaez Inc/Blend Images/Getty Images.

**Chapter 7** Page 308 (center, left) Nelson Hancock/Rough Guides/DK Images; (bottom, right) Bob Daemmrich/ The Image Works ; p. 309 (top, right) blue jean images/Getty Images; (center, right) PhotoEdit; p. 310 Nelson Hancock/Rough Guides/DK Images; p. 311 bikeriderlondon/Shutterstock; p. 313 Jack Dagley Photography/Shutterstock.com; p. 316 David De Lossy/Photodisc/Thinkstock; p. 318 (top, center) Mikael Karlsson/Alamy; (top, right) Spencer Grant/Alamy; p. 322 (bottom, left) Manfred Vollmer/Das Fotoarchiv/Peter Arnold, Inc./Photolibrary; (top, left) Bob Daemmrich/ The Image Works ; p. 328 Belinsky Yuri/ITAR-TASS /Landov ; p. 330 Mike Booth/Alamy; p. 331 Lisa F. Young/Alamy; p. 335 David Butow/Corbis News/CORBIS SABA; p. 337 Sue Thraves/Alamy; p. 341 Raffaele Meucci/MARKA/Alamy; p. 344 David Hughes/Robert Harding World Imagery; p. 345 Punchstock/Getty Images Inc.; p. 347 DAJ/amana images inc./Alamy; p. 350 Ariel Skelley/Blend Images/Alamy; p. 353 Annie Griffiths Belt/Encyclopedia/CORBIS; p. 355 Directphoto.org/Alamy; p. 358 blue jean images/Getty Images; p. 359 (center, right) Laurence Mouton/PhotoAlto/Jupiter Images; (bottom, right) Jose Luis Pelaez Inc/Blend Images/Getty Images; (center, right) Sheer Photo, Inc/Stockbyte/Getty Images; (top, right) Photodisc/Getty Images; (center, right) Laurence Mouton/PhotoAlto/Jupiter Images.

**Chapter 8** Page 360 (centre, left) Sergio Ballivian/Aurora Photos / Alamy; (bottom, right) Ableimages/Digital Vision/Getty Images; p. 361 (top, right) Jupiterimages/Goodshoot/Thinkstock; (bottom, left) John Foraste/Creative Eye/MIRA.com; p. 362 Paul Bradbury / Alamy; p. 363 Gretje Ferguson/Queerstock, Inc. / Alamy; p. 366 Ariel Skelley/Blend Images / Alamy; p. 371 Antonia Reeve / Photo Researchers, Inc.; p. 374 Adrian Weinbrecht/PhotoLibrary; p. 375 Ebby May/Stone/Getty Images; p. 377 Ableimages/Digital Vision/Getty Images; p. 378 Index Stock Imagery/PhotoLibrary; p. 380 Tom Grill/Corbis Premium RF / Alamy; p. 384 Ilan Rosen / PhotoStock-Israel/Alamy; p. 387 Corbis Flirt / Alamy; p. 390 Michael J. Doolittle / The Image Works; p. 394 Ariel Skelley/Blend Images / Alamy; p. 397 Angela Hampton/Bubbles Photolibrary / Alamy; p. 401 FancyVeerSet15/Fancy/Alamy; p. 402 David Young-Wolff / PhotoEdit; p. 406 Jupiterimages/Goodshoot/Thinkstock; p. 407 (top, right) Sheer Photo, Inc/Stockbyte/Getty Images; (centre, right) Mark Andersen/Rubberball/Getty Images; (centre, right) Asia Images Group/Getty Images; (bottom, right) Jose Luis Pelaez Inc/Blend Images/Getty Images.

**Chapter 9** Page 408 (top, center) PhotoEdit Inc.; (bottom, right) Yellow Dog Productions/Digital Vision/Getty Images; p. 409 (top, right) Roy McMahon/Digital Vision/Getty Images; (bottom, left) Steve Mason/Photodisc/Thinkstock; p. 410 PhotoEdit Inc.; p. 412 Jack Sparticus/Alamy; p. 414 (top, center) Kevin Dodge/Masterfile; (top, right) Caroline Wood/Stone/Getty Images; p. 418 AP Photo/Reagan Office, Mike Guastella; p. 419 Bookheimer, S. Y., Strojwas, M. H., Cophen, M. S. Saunders, A. M., Pericak-Vance, M. A., Mazziotta, J. C., & Small, G. W. (2000, August 17). Patterns of brain activation in people at risk for Alzheimer's disease. New England Journal of Medicine, 343, 450-456. Copyright 2003 Massachusetts Medical Society. All right reserved; p. 421 Jeff Greenberg/Photo Edit; p. 422 Deco Images II/Alamy; p. 426 Yellow Dog Productions/Digital Vision/Getty Images; p. 429 Jeremy Sutton-Hibbert/Alamy; p. 431 Stockbroker/MBI/Alamy; p. 432 Realimage/Alamy; p. 435 MR ©Rhoda Sidney/The Image Works; p. 437 Richard Hutchings/PhotoEdit; p. 441 © Lawrence Migdale/Pix; p. 442 (bottom, right) Comstock/Thinkstock; (bottom, left) Jupiter Images; p. 444 Horizon International Images Limited/Alamy; p. 448 David Young-Wolff/Alamy; p. 454 Roy McMahon/Digital Vision/Getty Images; p. 455 (top, right) IMAGEMORE Co.,Ltd./Getty Images; (center, right) Rob Lewine/Image Source; (center, right) Photodisc/Getty Images; (bottom, right) Jose Luis Pelaez Inc/Blend Images/Getty Images.

**Chapter 10** Page 456 (bottom, right) Mediscan/Medical-on-Line / Alamy; (centre, left) Tim Brown/Stone/Getty Images; p. 457 (top, right) Kablonk / Purestock / SuperStock; (bottom, left) Stockbyte/Getty Images; p. 458 Tim Brown/Stone/Getty Images; p. 461 Tracy Whiteside/Shutterstock.Com; p. 462 Fredrik Renander / Alamy; p. 465 Mediscan/Medical-on-Line / Alamy; p. 468 Mark Richards / PhotoEdit; p. 473 (bottom, right) Randy Duchaine / Alamy; (centre, left) Stockbyte/Getty Images; p. 475 David Pearson / Alamy; p. 476 Keith Morris / Alamy; p. 478 Kablonk / Purestock / SuperStock; p. 479 (top, right) Fuse/Jupiter Images; (bottom, right) Jose Luis Pelaez Inc/Blend Images/Getty Images; (centre, right) Laurence Mouton/PhotoAlto/Jupiter Images; (centre, right) Mark Andersen/Rubberball/Getty Images.

# Name Index

Note: *Italicized* page numbers indicate illustrations.

AAMR, 233
Aaronson, L. S., 472
AARP, *416*, 418, 424, 447, 473
AAUW, 334
Abadie, V., 111
Abbot-Smith, K., 174
Abdo, C., 370
Abeare, C., 160
Abele, A., 401
Aber, J. L., 33
Aboud, F., 247
Aboud, F. E., 247
Abramson, L., 291
Abramson, L. Y., 291
Accardo, P., 53
Achenbach, T. A., 115
Acheson, S., 124
Ackerman, B. P., 135
Ackroyd, K., 186
Acocella, J., 12
Adair, L., 107
Adak, M., 189
Adams, G. R., 285
Adams Hillard, P. J., 67
Adams, K. B., 439
Adams, M., 147, 344
Adams, P., 286
Adebayo, B., 330
Adelmann, P. K., 403
Administration on Aging, 411, 441, 443, *447*
Adolph, K., 110
Afifi, T., 189, 250
Agrawal, A., 53
Ah-Kion, J., 286
Ahn, S., 251, 351
Ahn, W., 139
Aiello, J., 356
Aiken, L. R., 475
Ainsworth. M. D. S., 140, 141
Aitchison, J., 127, 129, 173
Aitken, R. J., 59
Akhtar, 462
Akmajian, A., 127
Aksan, N., 145
Aksham, J., 447
Akshoomoff, N., 19
Al-Owidha, A., 289
Alan Guttmacher Institute, *271*
Albers, L. L., 76, 81
Alberts, A., 275, 277
Albrecht, G. L., 316
Alderfer, C., 231
Aldwin, C., 414
Aldwin, C. M., 328
Ales, K. L., 66
Alexander, B., 75
Alexander, G., 147
Alexander, G. M., 85
Alexander, R. A., 371
Alexandersen, P., 368
Alfons, V., 447
Alfonso, V. C., 227
Alfred, M., 8
Algarin, C., 99
Alibali, M., 6
Alipuria, L. L., 290
Alisky, J. M., 419
Allam, M. D., 111
Allen, B., 190
Allen, J., 299, 471
Allen, L., 65
Alleva, E., 98
Alley, A., 127
Allhusen, V., 177
Allison, B., 287
Allison, D. B., 51, 205
Aloise-Young, P. A., 300

Altholz, S., 211
Alvarez-Leon, E. E., 363
Aly, H., 69
Alzheimer's Association, 420
Amato, P., 250, 393
American Academy of Family Physicians, 85, 86, 109
American Academy of Pediatrics, 36, 76, 77, 85, 86, 108, 109, 133, 162, 175, 189, 191, 206, 208, 211
American College of Medical Genetics, 76
American College of Obstetricians and Gynecologists, 76
American College of Sports Medicine, 311
American College Testing Program, 330
American Council on Education, 335
American Heart Association, 373
American Medical Association, 36, 85
American Psychological Association, 35, 36
American SIDS Institute, *101*
Amitai, Y., 69
Ammerman, R. T., 188
Amos, A., 269
Amso, D., 185
Amsterlaw, J., 139, 186
Anand, K. J. S., 112
Anders, T. F., 101
Anderson, D., 176
Anderson, E., 251
Anderson, P., 205
Anderson, T., 393
Andrés-Pueyo, A., 27
Andrew, L., 294
Andrew, M., 320
Andrews, G., 185
Angus, J., 412
Ani, C., 66, 107
Anisfeld, M., 88
Annenberg Public Policy Center, 333
Annunziato, R., 315
Ansaldo, A. I., 160
Ansberry, C., 446, 449
Anstey, K., 416
Antonishak, J., 299
Antonucci, T. C., 395, 403
APA, 398
APA Reproductive Choice Working Group, 64
Apgar, Virginia, 73
Apostoleris, N. H., 246
Apperly, I., 219
Apter, A., 263
Archer, J., 194, 246
Archer, P., *104*
Archer, S. L., 287
Arcus, D., 51, 55
Arenson, K. W., 292
Arguin, M., 160
Aries, P., 12
Armstrong, J., 10
Armstrong, P., 354
Arnett, J., 310, 337, 339
Arnett, J. J., 295, 296, 339
Arnold, J., 385
Arnold, M. L., 385
Arnold, R. M., 463, 469
Arnsten, A., 212
Aro, H., 250
Aron, A., 393
Aronow, W., 369
Aronson, J., 336
Arseneault, L., 78
Artal, P., 364
Arterberry, M., 137
Arts, J. A. R., 381
Asch, D. A., 469
Asendorpf, J. B., 138

Asher, S. R., 244, 245
Ashton, R., 98
Aslin, R. N., 110, 129
Astin, A., *334*
Ata, R. N., 286
Atchley, R., 439, 445, 462
Atkins, D. C., 393
Atkinson, T. M., 379, 430
Aubeeluck, A., 319
Auerbach, C. F., 142
Auestad, N., 108
Aujoulat, I., 245
Auman, C., 429
Austin, C. M., 88
Austin, E., 326
Austin, J., 460
Avis, N., 366
Avlund, K., 450
Axia, G., 112
Axinn, W. G., 302
Aylward, G. P., 124
Ayoola, A., 82
Ayotte, V., 236
Ayoub, N. C., 75
Azuma, S. D., 67

Babu, A., 441
Bacchus, L., 70
Bache, L., 336
Bade, U., 147
Badenhorst, W., 82
Bader, A. P., 76
Badger, S., 296
Baer, J. S., 68
Bahna, S., 212
Bahrick, L., 111, 112
Bailey, E., 211
Bailey, J. M., 53, 61
Baillargeon, R., 119, 167
Bairam, A., 67
Baird, A., 397
Baker, J., 47, 251, 265, 351
Baker, M., 453
Baker, R. C., 241
Baker, S. A., 220
Baker, T., 269
Baker-Ward, L., 169
Bakker, A., 401
Bal, E., 19
Balaiah, D., 303
Baldassaro, R., 196
Bale, J. F., Jr., 210
Ball, K., 416
Ball, M., 402
Ballas, S., 48
Ballen, L., 75
Baltes, B., 380, 440
Baltes, M., 380, 440, 441
Baltes, P., 380, 437, 440
Bamaca, M., 224
Bammel, G., 439
Bandura, A., 16, *24*, 193, 195
Baptista, T., 23
Barber, B., 259
Barberá, E., 182
Barboza, G., 246
Barer, B. M., 439, 447
Barker, E., 291
Barlett, C., 196
Barner, J., 363, 414
Barnett, D., 133
Barnett, R. C., 350, 385, 403
Baron-Cohen, S., 61, 181
Barr, H. M., 68
Barrett, G. V., 371
Barrett, T., 105

Barry, L. M., 332
Barton, J., 209
Barton, L. J., 441
Barusch, A., 445
Basak, C., 428
Bashore, T. R., 430
Bass, S., 253
Basseches, M., 323
Bates, E., 99
Bates, J. E., 131
Battin, 469
Baudonniere, P., 138
Bauer, I., 438
Bauer, P., 169
Bauer, P. J., 122, 123
Baugh, E., 397, 451
Baulac, S., 419
Bauld, R., 369
Baum, A., *374*
Bauman, K. E., 298
Baumrind, Diana, 186
Baydar, N., 397
Bayley, N., 124, 378
Beach, B. A., 28
Beal, C. R., 246, 247
Beale, 461
Beals, K., 346
Beardslee, W. R., 209
Bearer, E. L., 11
Bearman, P., 305
Beaulac-Baillargeon, L., 67
Beck, G., 369
Becker, B., 299
Becker, G., 441, 451
Becker, J., 205
Becker, J. B., 261
Becker, M., 451
Beckman, M., 266
Beckwith, L., 125
Becvar, D. S., 471
Beer, T., 469
Beets, M., 262
Begeny, J., 232
Begley, S., 76, 465
Behne, D., 133
Behrman, R., 44
Behrman, R. E., 158, 208, 253
Beilin, H., 22
Belcher, J. R., 251
Belkin, L., 45, 232
Bell, A., 304
Bell, H., 185
Bell, I. P., 414
Bellavia, G., 348
Belle, D., 249
Bellinger, D., 65
Bellissimo, A., 158
Belmaker, R. H., 55
Belschak, F., 245
Belsky, J., 150, 177, 260
Bem, Sandra, 182
Ben-Zeev, T., 336
Bender, H., 237
Benelli, B., 219
Benenson, J. F., 246
Bengston, V. L., 251, 396
Benini, F., 112
Benjamin, J., 55
Benjet, C., 189
Benjuya, N., 415
Bennani, L., 363
Bennett, A., 57
Bensing, J. M., 439
Benson, E., 135
Benson, H., 320, *321*
Benton, S. A., 332
Berenbaum, S. A., 61, 181

Kelch-Oliver, K., 251
Keller, H., 188, 350
Kellett, J. M., 421
Kelley, G., 278, 421
Kelley, M., 349
Kellogg, J. W., 302
Kelly, G., 302
Kelly, J., 250
Kelly-Vance, L., 147
Kelly-Weeder, S., 62
Keltner, D., 186
Kendler, K., 47
Kennedy, Rose, 452
Kennedy, S. R., 273
Kennell, J. H., 76
Kenrick, D. T., 346
Kenyon, C., 422
Kern, R., 35
Kerns, K., 142
Kershaw, T., 66
Kesselring, T., 18
Ketelaar, L., 193
Kevorkian, Jack, 469
Kiang, L., 289
Kiecolt-Glaser, J. K., 317
Kiecolt, K. J., 344
Kieschke, U., 218
Kiesner, J., 185
Killen, M., 239, 247
Kilner, J. M., 143
Kim, 464
Kim-Cohen, J., 320
Kim, H., 319
Kim, J., 404
Kim, J-S., 396
Kim, J-Y., 249
Kim, S., 370
Kim, T. C., 15
Kim, U., 294
Kim, Y., 83
Kimm, S. Y., 264
Kimmel, D., 366
Kimoto, T., 98
Kimura, M., 175
Kincl, L., 158
King, A., 439
King, A. C., 374
King, D., 282
Kinney, 460
Kinney, H., 101
Kinney, H. C., 65
Kinsey, A. C., 303
Kinsht, I., 106
Kirby, J., 251
Kirchengast, S., 66
Kirkendall, 464
Kisilevsky, B. S., 88
Kit-fong Au, T., 272
Kitamura, C., 132
Kitayama, S., 180
Kitchener, R. E., 171
Kitterod, R., 350
Kitzmann, K., 188
Kiuru, N., 297
Kjaer, M., 415
Kjølseth, 463
Klaus, M., 75
Klebanov, P. K., 231
Kleespies, P., 469
Klenke-Hamel, K. E., 344
Klier, C. M., 83
Kloep, M., 8, 339
Klohnen, E., 385
Klute, C., 297
Knafo, A., 295
Knap, N. F., 295
Knaus, W. A., 469
Knickmeyer, R., 61, 181
Knight, K., 74
Knorth, E. J., 253
Knowlton, B. J., 123
Knutson, J., 194
Kochanska, G., 142, 145, 147
Kodl, M., 270
Koehoorn, M., 260

Koenen, K., 8
Koenig, A., 190
Koenig, L. B., 56
Kohlberg, L., 182, 239, *240*, 241
Kohnert, K., 173
Kohut, S. A., 112
Koivisto, M., 160
Kolata, G., 63, *367*
Kolb, B., 185
Kolodny, R. C., 421
Konnur, N., 268
Kontos, S., 186
Kooijman, A., 364
Koopmans, S., 364
Koppelman, F. S., 208
Koren, G., 67
Koretz, D., 282
Koroukian, S. M., 81
Koshmanova, T., 22
Koska, J., 203
Koss, M. P., 399
Kosunen, E., 260
Kotch, J., 398
Kothari, N., 211
Kotler, J. A., 182
Kotre, J., 84, 235, 242, 402
Kovelman, I., 220
Kramer, A. F., 415
Kramer, M., 108
Kramer, M. S., 66
Krampe, R., 440
Krasner, M., 402
Krasny Brown, Laurie, 477
Krasovec, S. J., 265
Krause, N., 238
Krcmar, M., 173
Krebs, N. F., 264
Kreitlow, B., 445
Kreitlow, D., 445
Krishnamoorthy, J. S., 204
Krisjansdottir, G., 206
Kristensen, P., 422
Kroger, J., 288, 289
Krohn, M. D., 300
Krojgaard, P., 119
Krout, J. A., 451
Krueger, J., 389
Krulewitch, C. J., 81
Kübler-Ross, Elisabeth, 465–467
Kuczynski, L., 147
Kudo, Y., 368
Kuebli, J., 169
Kuhl, P., 133
Kuhl, P. K., 133
Kuhn, D., 216, 276
Kump, S., 265
Kunkel, D., 175
Kunzmann, U., 437
Kupek, E., 157
Kupersmidt, J. B., 297
Kurdek, L., 346, 348, 350, 351
Kurtines, W. M., 239
Kurtz-Costes, B., 281
Kurtz, D. A., 190
Kuschal, C., 422
Kutner, J. S., 472
Kwant, P. B., 425

Laas, I., 20
Labouvie-Vief, G., 275, 322, 323
Lacerda, F., 168
Lacharite, C., 189
Lachmann, T., 211
Lackey, C., 397
Ladd, G. W., 244
Laditka, J., 82
Laditka, S., 82
Laflamme, D., 147, 350
LaFromboise, T., 290
Lafuente, M. J., 99
Lahiri, D. K., 419
Lally, M. M., 286
Lam, C., 132

Lam, V., 181
Lamaze, Fernand, 74
Lamb, M. E., *128*, 143, 177
Lamberts, S. W. J., 415
Lambiase, A., 264
Lamkin, D., 383
Lamm, B., 350
Lamm, H., 340
Lamm, R. P., 316
Lammlein, S., 412
Lamon, S. J., 335
Lamont, J. A., 367
Lamorey, S., 249
Lamprecht, M., 237
Land, F., 445
Landau, B., 129
Landers, D., 312
Landhuis, C., 205
Lane, D., 297
Lang, A., 68
Lange, C., 356
Langer, A., 110
Langer, E., 429
Langer, Ellen, 443
Langille, D., 66
Langlois, J. H., 111
Lansford, J., 250
Lansford, J. E., 189, 246
Lantz, M., 460
Larsen, K. E., 74
Larsen, L., 412
Larsen, S. F., 430
Larson, R. W., 295, *296*
Lau, I., 216
Lau, M., 302
Lauer, J. C., 395
Lauer, R. H., 395
Laugharne, J., 8
Laumann, E. O., 367
Lauter, J. L., 60
Lavallee, M., 215, *216*
Lavers-Preston, C., 451
Law, A., 15
Lawrence, E., 351
Lawrence, W., 69
Lay, K., 184
Lazarus, R. S., 317, 319
Lazarus, S. S., 282
Le Corre, M., 169
Le, H., 21, 31
Leach, P., 177
Leadbeater, B., 291
Leadbeater, B. J., 191
Leaper, C., 182
Leathers, H. D., 157, 349
Leavitt, L. A., 59
LeBuffe, P., 191
Lecours, A. R., 207
Lecusay, R., 22
Lederberg, A. R., 28
Lederhos, C., 392
Lee, 453, 464
Lee, A. M., 206
Lee, B. H., 208
Lee, C., 424
Lee, E-H., 396
Lee, M., 350
Lee, R. M., 238
Lee, S., 128, 216
Lee, S. Y., 281
Leen-Feldmer, E. W., 263
Leenaars, A. A., 467
Lees, N., 272
Lefkowitz, E. S., 272
Legato, M., 62
Legerstee, M., 88
Lehman, D., 180
Lehr, U., 437
Leis, J., 337, 339
Leman, P., 181
Lemonick M. D., 261
Leonard, L. B., 133, 211
Lerner, J. W., 211
Lerner, R. M., 11, 32, 236, 237
Lesaux, N. K., 220

Lesner, S., 417
Lester, B. M., 106
Lester, D., 471
Leuba, G., 420
Leung, C., 295
LeVay, S., 304
Levenson, R. W., 392, 447
Leverone, D., 418
Levin, R. J., 302
Levine, R. V., 342, 404
Levine, S. C., 148
Levinson, D., 386–387, 433, 435, 436, 462
Levitt, A., 128
Levy, 412
Levy, B. L., 429
Levy, B. R., 421, 439
Levy-Schiff, R., 350
Lewin, T., 125
Lewin, V., 125
Lewis, B., 62
Lewis, C. C., 150
Lewis, C. S., 472
Lewis, J., 19
Lewis, J. M., 393
Lewis, M., 135
Lewis, M. I., 441
Lewis, P., 112
Lewis, R., 395
Lewis, V., 369
Lewkowicz, D., 112
Leyens, Jacques-Philippe, 30, *31*
Li, C., 291
Li, G. R., 425
Li, H., 364
Li, N. P., 343
Li, Q., 245
Li-qing, Z., 451
Li, S., 23, 47, 330
Liang, H., 291
Liang, J., 238
Liao, Y., 364
Libert, S., 423
Liblik, R., 206
Lichtenstein, P., 47
Lichter, D. T., 344
Lickliter, R., 112
Lidz, J., 131
Liechty, J., 204
Liem, D. G., 111
Lieven, C., 184
Light, L. L., 429
Lillis, T., 392
Lin, K, 173
Lin, X., 119, 275
Lindau, S., 271, 421
Lindemann, B. T., 444
Linden, W., 315
Lindsay, G., 232
Lindsey, B. W., 414
Lindsey, E., 184
Lindstrom, H., 403
Linn, R. L., 282
Lino, M., 349
Liou, T., 264
Liou, Y., 264
Lipsett, L., 101
Lipsitt, L. P., 87, 111
Lister, J., 364, 416
Litrowink, A., 188
Little, R. E., 80
Litzinger, S., 393
Liu, H., 392
Liu, L., 369
Livingstone, S., 278
Livson, N., 263
Lluis-Font, J. M., 27
Lobel, M., 81
Lobo, R. A., 369
Lock, R. D., 401
Locke, C. R., 252
Loeb, S., 150
Loehlin, J. C., 188
Loessl, B., 267
Loewen, S., 18
Loftus, E. F., 170, 430

# Subject Index